INDEX TO MINORITIES & CRIMINAL JUSTICE

An Index to Periodicals and Books
Relating to Minorities and Criminal Justice
in the United States

Edited by
Scott Christianson, Ph.D.

Published By
THE CENTER ON MINORITIES AND CRIMINAL JUSTICE
SCHOOL OF CRIMINAL JUSTICE
STATE UNIVERSITY OF NEW YORK AT ALBANY
ALBANY, NEW YORK 12222

INDEX TO MINORITIES & CRIMINAL JUSTICE: AN INDEX TO PERIODICALS AND BOOKS
RELATING TO MINORITIES AND CRIMINAL JUSTICE IN THE UNITED STATES

ISBN 0-940826-00-3

Distributed outside the United States of America and Canada by
D. REIDEL PUBLISHING COMPANY
DORDRECHT, HOLLAND

Printed in the United States of America

INDEX TO MINORITIES & CRIMINAL JUSTICE

The *Index to Minorities & Criminal Justice* is a subject and author index with abstracts, focused on the multi-disciplinary literature relating to minorities and criminal justice in the United States. Entries refer to articles in more than 400 periodicals, as well as to books, government reports, monographs, unpublished dissertations and scholarly papers, and selected court cases. The fields covered include criminal justice, criminology, sociology, psychology, law, history, medicine, philosophy, political science, social work, Afro-studies, ethnic studies, and journalism, among others. The *Index* is designed to reflect the diverse and growing literature about American minorities and criminal justice, and intended to stimulate scholarship and action contributing to social justice.

Scott Christianson, *Editor*

Richard J. Dehais, *Associate Editor*   Alice Green, *Associate Editor*

Assistant Editors

Frankie Bailey, Kenneth Boxley, Barry DeFoe, Sampson Oli, William Oliver
David Parry, Barbara Rockell, Barry C. Sample, and Vroman Wright

Production Assistants

Joanne DeSilva, Judy Pisarski

Acknowledgements

Prof. Daniel E. Georges-Abeyie, Southern Illinois Univ.; Laurin Anderson, National Conference of Black Lawyers; Prof. Jeannette Allen, Fayettville State Univ.; Prof. Roy L. Austin, Pennsylvania State Univ.; Prof. William K. Barnett, Lincoln Univ.; Prof. Jimmy Bell, Jackson State Univ.; John Boger, NAACP Legal Defense and Education Fund, Inc.; Prof. W. Haywood Burns, City Univ. of New York; Hon. John R. Carro, New York State Supreme Court; Agenor L. Castro, New York State Dept. of Correctional Services; Chicano Pinto Research Project; Chicano Research Network; Coalition for Hispanic Rights in Criminal Justice; Ernest A. Costa; Prof. Joseph Curtis, Mississippi Valley State Univ.; Dr. Julius Debro, Atlanta Univ.; Prof. Scott Decker, Univ. of Missouri-St. Louis; Frank Dunbaugh; Prof. Carolyn Eaglin, Bowie State College; Dr. Price Foster, Law Enforcement Assistance Administration; Prof. Laurence French, Univ. of Nebraska; Ruth Fraley, Hawley Library, State Univ. of New York at Albany; Dr. James Garofalo, National Council on Crime & Delinquency; Prof. Quinten Gresham, Talladega College; Dr. Mary S. Harper, National Institute of Mental Health; Prof. Alex Hawkins, Univ. of Pittsburgh; Lennox Hinds, Rutgers Univ.; Frank Jasmine, New York Governor's Office; E. J. Josey, New York State Dept. of Education; Irving Joyner, American Civil Liberties Union; Fay Honey Knopp, Prison Research Education Action Project; Ed Koren, American Civil Liberties Union; Prof. Larry LaFlore, Univ. of Southern Mississippi; Dr. Richard H. Lineback, Philosophy Documentation Center; Prof. Jose Lopez, California State Univ. at Long Beach; Prof. Patrick D. McAnany, Univ. of Illinois at Chicago Circle; Prof. Gregory Mark, Chaminade Univ.; Dr. Gary Mendez, National Urban League; Jean Moore, Law Enforcement Assistance Administration; Prof. James Opolot, Univ. of Alabama at Birmingham; Prof. Arnold Parks, Lincoln Univ.; Prof. Frank Pogue, State Univ. of New York at Albany; Prof. Khayrallah Safar, Florida A & M Univ.; Prof. Luis Salas, Florida International Univ.; Prof. Elsie Scott, St. Augustine's College; Prof. Richard Singleton, Bethune-Cookman College; Gerald E. Slivka, Philosophy Documentation Center; Prof. Lindburgh Smith, Albany State College; Monica Herrera Smith, Mexican American Correction Officers Association; Prof. Paul Takagi, Education Dept.; Prof. Lorenzo Thompson, Shaw Univ.; Prof. S.N. Wailes, Jackson State Univ.; Prof. William Wilbanks, Florida International Univ.; Hallem Williams, Positive Futures, Inc.; S. Brian Willson, National Moratorium on Prison Construction; and Prof. Laurin A. Wollan, Florida State University.

Assistance was also provided by the following persons at the School of Criminal Justice, SUNYA: Dean Donald J. Newman, Assistant Dean John E. Morgan, Prof. William Brown, Prof. Fred Cohen, Prof. David Duffee, Prof. Michael J. Hindelang, Prof. Lawrence W. Sherman, Prof. Hans Toch, Prof. Marguerite Warren, and Dr. Beverly Smith.

Also helping were several graduate assistants: Maria Casapini, Barry DeFoe, Larry Haas, David Parry, Barbara Rockell, and Gerald Stowell.

Special thanks are due to the following Minority Fellows who contributed to a better understanding of many of the issues confronting American minorities and criminal justice: Frankie Bailey, Marge Ballard, Arthur Bedford, Kenneth Boxley, Patrice Bradley, Herman Brown, Lisa Delay, Lance Evans, Alice Green, Elizabeth Gray, Washington Holifield, Cynthia Jackson, Rene Medina, Ricardo Nunez, William Oliver,   Charles Robinson, Teresa Royal, Sampson Oli, Ashton Thomas, Carmen Thomas, Cheryl Thomas, Ralph Soto, Stanley Smallwood, Joeannah H. Stinson, and Vroman Wright.

TABLE OF CONTENTS

LIST OF PERIODICALS INDEXED

Abbott's Wkly..........................Abbott's Weekly and Illustrated News (Defunct).

Acad Pol Sci Pro.......................Academy of Political Science Proceedings. ISSN 0065-0684 (2 times a yr.) Academy of Political Science, 619 W. 114th St., Suite 500, New York, NY 10025.

Accident Annal Prev....................Accident Analysis & Prevention. ISSN 0001-4775 (Q) $105. Permagon Press, Inc., Journals Division, Maxwell House, Fairview Park, Elmsford, NY 10523.

Act Criminologica......................Acta Criminologica. Les Presses de l'Universite de Montreal, C.P. 6128, Succ. A, Montreal, Quebec, Canada H3C 3J7.

Act Paedops...........................Acta Paedopsychiatrica: European Journal of Child and Adolescent Psychiatry. (6 times a yr.), Basel, Switzerland.

Addict Dis............................Addictive Diseases: An International Journal. (Q) $77. Permagon Press, Inc., Journals Division, Maxwell House, Fairview Park, Elmsfort, NY 10523.

Adoles................................Adolescence. ISSN 0001-8449 (Q) $20 indiv., $25 instit. Libra Publishers, Inc., 391 Willets Rd., Roslyn Heights, LI, NY 11577.

AFL-CIO Am F..........................AFL-CIO American Federationist. ISSN 0149-2489 (M) $2. AFL-CIO, 815 16th St., N.W., Washington, DC 20006.

Agenda................................Agenda. ISSN 0146-010X (M) $10. National Council of La Raza, 1725 I Street, N.W. Suite 210, Washington DC 20006.

Albany L Rev..........................Albany Law Review. ISSN 0703-3117 (4 times a yr.) $8.50. Albany Law School, 80 New Scotland Ave., Albany NY 12208.

Albuq J...............................Albuquerque Journal. 7th and Silver S.W., Albuquerque, NM 87102.

Al-Qalam..............................Al-Qalam. 343 S. Dearborn Street, Room 1607, Chicago, IL 60604.

Am Anthrop............................American Anthropologist. ISSN 0002-7294 (Q) $50. American Anthropological Association, 1703 New Hampshire Ave., N.W., Washington, DC 20009.

Am Bar A J............................American Bar Association Journal. ISSN 0002-7596 (M) $15. American Bar Association, 1155 E 60th St. Chicago, IL 60637.

Am Behav Sci..........................American Behavioral Scientist. (Bi-M) Ind. $18. Inst. $33. Sage Publications, Inc., 275 S. Beverly Dr., Beverly Hills, CA 90212.

Am Cath Sociol R......................American Catholic Sociological Review. ISSN 0038-0210 (Q) $15. Association for the Sociology of Religion, c/o Exec. Secretary Robert McNamara, Loyola University of Chicago, 6525 N. Sheridan Rd., Chicago, IL 60626.

Am Crim L Q...........................American Criminal Law Quarterly. (Q) $20. American Bar Association, Section of Criminal Justice, 1155 E 60th Street, Chicago, IL 60637.

Am Crim L Rev.........................American Criminal Law Review. ISSN 0002-8118 (Q) $20. American Bar Association, Section of Criminal Justice, 1155 E 60th St., Chicago, IL 60637.

Am Demog..............................American Demographics. (10 times a yr.) $30. American Demographics, Inc., Box 68, Ithaca, NY 14850.

Am Ethnol.............................American Ethnologist. ISSN 0094-0496 (Q) $25. American Anthropological Association, 1703 New Hampshire Ave., N.W., Washington, DC 20009.

Am Herit..............................American Heritage. ISSN 0002-8738 (Bi-M) $24. American Heritage Publishing Co., Inc., 10 Rockefeller Plaza, New York, NY 10020.

Am Indian Q...........................American Indian Quarterly. ISSN 0095-182X (Q) Society for American Indian, Studies and Research, P.O. Box 443, Hurst, TX 76053.

Am J Comm Psy.........................American Journal of Community Psychology. ISSN 0091-0562 (6 times a yr.) $76. Plenum Press, 227 W. 17th St., New York, NY 10011.

Am J Comp L...........................American Journal of Comparative Law. ISSN 0002-919X (Q) $15. American Association for the Comparative Study of Law, School of Law (Boalt Hall) University of California, Berkeley, CA 94720.

Am J Correct..........................American Journal of Correction. (Defunct). See Correct Today

Am J Crim L...........................American Journal of Criminal Law. ISSN 0092-2315 (3 times a yr.) $9.50. University of Texas at Austin, Law School Foundation, 2500 Red River, Austin, TX 78705.

Am J Drug Al Ab.......................American Journal of Drug and Alcohol Abuse. ISSN 0095-2990 (4 times a yr.) $68. Marcel Dekker Journals, 270 Madison Ave., New York, NY 10016.

Am J Orthopsych.......................American Journal of Orthopsychiatry. ISSN 0002-9432 (Q) $20. American Orthopsychiatry Association, 1775 Broadway, New York, NY 10019.

Am J Legal Hist.......................*American Journal of Legal History.* ISSN 0002-9319 (Q) $12. American Society for Legal History, Temple Univ., School of Law, N. Broad St., and Montgomery Ave., Philadelphia, PA 19122.

Am J Psychiatry.......................*American Journal of Psychiatry.* ISSN 0002-953X (M) $27. American Psychiatric Association, 1700 18th St., Washington, DC 20009.

Am J Psychol.........................*American Journal of Psychology.* ISSN 0002-9556 (Q) $5. University of Illinois Press, 54 E. Gregory, Box 5081, Station A, Champaign, IL 61820.

Am J Psychother......................*American Journal of Psychotherapy.* ISSN 0002-9564 (Q) $20. Association for the Advancement of Psychotherapy, 114 E. 78th St., New York, NY 10021.

Am J Public Health....................*American Journal of Public Health.* ISSN 0090-0036 (M) $40. American Public Health Association, 1015 15th St., N.W., Washington, DC 20005.

Am J Soc............................*American Journal of Sociology.* ISSN 0002-9602 (Bi-M) $18 Indv., $24 Inst. University of Chicago Press, 5801 S. Ellis Ave., Chicago, IL 60637.

Am Lit.............................*American Literature.* ISSN 0002-9831 (Q) $10. Indv., $12. Inst. Duke University Press, 6697 College Station, Durham, NC 27708.

Am Mercury........................*The American Mercury.* (Defunct).

Am Q..............................*American Quarterly.* ISSN 0003-0678 (Q) $75. University of Pennsylvania, Van Pelt Library CH., Philadelphia, PA 19104.

Am Rev............................*American Review.* ISSN 0569-7344 (Q) $5. Pescara Enterprises, 300 W. 49th St., New York, NY 10019.

Am Scholar.........................*American Scholar.* ISSN 0003-0937 (Q) $8. United Chapters of Phi Beta Kappa, 1811 Q St., N.W., Washington DC 20009.

Am Sociologist......................*American Sociologist.* ISSN 0003-1232 (Q) $12. non-mem., $16. Inst. American Sociological Association, 1722 N St., N.W., Washington, DC 20036.

Am Sociol Rev......................*American Sociological Review.* ISSN 0003-1224 (M) $15. non-mem., $30. Inst. American Sociological Assn., 1722 N St., N.W., Washington DC 20036.

Am Speech.........................*American Speech.* ISSN 0003-1283 (Q) $10. Indv., $12. Inst. University of Alabama Press, Box 2877, University, AL 35486.

Am U L Rev........................*American University Law Review.* ISSN 0003-1453 (4 times a yr.) $12. American University Washington College of Law, Massachusetts and Nebraska Avenues, Washington, DC 20016.

Ann Am Geog.......................*Annals of the Association of American Geographers.* ISSN 0004-5608 (Q) $6. Association of American Geographers, 1706 16th St., N.W., Washington, DC 20009.

Ann Am Poli........................*Annals of the American Academy of Political and Social Science.* ISSN 0002-7162 (Bi-M) $16. mem. American Academy of Political and Social Sciences, 3937 Chestnut St., Philadelphia, PA 19104.

Ann Reg Sci........................*Annals of Regional Science.* (3 times a yr.) $16. c/o Western Washington University, Bellingham, WA 98225.

Anthrop Q..........................*Anthropological Quarterly.* ISSN 0003-5491 (Q) $10. Indv., $15. Inst. Catholic University of America Press, 620 Michigan Ave., N.E. Washington, DC 20064.

Ant Rev...........................*Antioch Review.* ISSN 0003-5769. $10. Antioch Review, Inc., Box 148, Yellow Springs, OH 45387.

Arch Gen Psychiatry..................*Archives of General Psychiatry.* ISSN 0003-990X (M) $18. American Medical Association, 535 N. Dearborn St., Chicago, IL 60610.

Arch Sex Beh.......................*Archives of Sexual Behavior.* ISSN 0004-0002 (6 times a yr.) $41. Indv., $82. Inst. Plenum Press, 227 W. 17th St., New York, NY 10011.

Arena.............................*Arena.* ISSN 0004-0932 (Q) $4. Arena Publication Association, Box 36, Greensborough, Victoria, 3088, Australia.

Ariz & West........................*Arizona and the West.* ISSN 0004-1408 (Q) $10. University of Arizona, Library, Room C 327, Tucson, AZ 85721.

Ariz L Rev.........................*Arizona Law Review.* ISSN 0004-153X (4 times a yr.) $10. University of Arizona, College of Law, Tucson, AZ 85721.

Ark Bar Assoc Rep...................*Arkansas Bar Association Report.*

Aztlan . . . . *Aztlan-International Journal of Chicano Studies Research.* (3 times a yr.) $15. Indv., $20. Inst. U.C.L.A. Chicano Studies Center, Campbell Hall, Room 3122, 405 Hilgard Ave., Los Angeles, CA 90024.

Bar Bull. . . . . *Bar Bulletin of the New York County Lawyers Association.*

Berkeley J Soc. . . . . *Berkeley Journal of Sociology.* ISSN 0067-5830 (ann) $2.50 Indv.; $5.50 Inst.; $6.00 Foreign. Graduate Student Union, Department of Sociology, 410 Barrows Hall, University of California, Berkeley, CA 94720.

Black L J. . . . . *Black Law Journal.* ISSN 0045-2181 (3 times a yr.) $12.50 Indv., $25. Inst. University of California, Los Angeles, School of Law, Los Angeles, CA 90024.

Black Scholar. . . . . *Black Scholar.* ISSN 0006-4246 (10 times a yr.) $12. Black World Foundation, Box 908, Sausalito, CA 94965.

Black World. . . . . *Black World.* (Defunct)

Boston U L Rev. . . . . *Boston University Law Review.* ISSN 0006-8047 (5 times a yr.) $9. Boston University School of Law, 765 Commonwealth Ave., Boston, MA 02215.

Br J Addict. . . . . *British Journal of Addiction.* ISSN 0007-0890 (Q) $18. Longman Group Ltd., Journals Division, 43-35 Annadale St., Edinburgh, EH7 4AT Scotland.

Br J Crimin. . . . . *British Journal of Criminology.* ISSN 0007-0955 (Q) $12. (U.S. & Can) Fred B. Rothman & Co., 10368 W. Centennial Rd., Littleton, CO 80123.

Br J Delinq. . . . . *British Journal of Delinquency.* (Defunct)

Br J L Soc. . . . . *British Journal of Law and Society.* ISSN 0306-3704 (semi-ann) $15. Indv. $22. Inst. University College Cardiff Press, Box 78, Cardiff, CF1 IXL, Wales.

Br J Soc Cl Psy. . . . . *British Journal of Social and Clinical Psychology.* ISSN 0007-1293 (Q) $72. British Psychological Society, St. Andrews House, 48 Prince Rd. E. Leicester LE1 7DR, England.

Br J Sociol. . . . . *British Journal of Sociology.* ISSN 0007-1315 (Q) $16. Routledge and Kegan Paul Ltd., Broadway House, Newton Rd., Henley on Thames RG9 1EN England. (U.S. orders to: Routledge Journals, 9 Park St., Boston, MA 02108).

Brooklyn L Rev. . . . . *Brooklyn Law Review.* ISSN 0007-2362 (Q) $12. Brooklyn Law School, 250 Joraleman St., Brooklyn, NY 11201.

Buffalo L Rev. . . . . *Buffalo Law Review.* ISSN 0023-9356 (4 times a yr.) $15. State University of New York at Buffalo, Faculty of Law and Jursiprudence, John Lord O'Brian Hall, Amherst Campus, Buffalo, NY 14260.

Bull Am Acad Med. . . . . *Bulletin of the American Academy of Medicine.*

Bus & Soc Rev. . . . . *Business and Society Review.* ISSN 0045-3609 (Q) $38. Warren, Gorham and Lamont, Inc., 210 South St., Boston, MA 02111.

Bus Lawyer. . . . . *Business Lawyer.* American Bar Association, 1155 West 60th Street, Chicago, IL 60637.

Cal L Rev. . . . . *California Law Review.* ISSN 0008-1221 (6 times a yr.) $20. University of California, Berkeley School of law, Boalt Hall, Berkeley, CA 94720.

Cal Youth Author Q. . . . . *California Youth Authority Quarterly.* ISSN 0008-1671 (Q) free, Department of Youth Authority, 4241 Williamsburgh Dr., Sacramento, CA 95823.

Can F. . . . . *Canadian Forum.* ISSN 0008-9631 (M) $13. Survival Foundation, 70 the Esplanade, Toronto, Ont. M5E 1A6, Canada.

Can J Corr. . . . . *Canadian Journal of Corrections.* (Defunct). See *Canadian Journal of Criminology.*

Can J Crimin. . . . . *Canadian Journal of Criminology.* ISSN 0704-9722. Canadian Association for the Prevention of Crime, 55 Parkdale, Ottawa K1Y 1E5, Canada.

Can J Crim & Corr. . . . . *Canadian Journal of Criminology and Corrections.* (Defunct). See *Canadian Journal of Criminology.*

Can Psychi Assoc J. . . . . *Canadian Psychiatric Association Journal.* ISSN 0706-7437 (8/yr) $25. Canadian Psychiatric Assoc., 225 Lisgar St., Suite 103, Ottawa, Ont. K2P 0C6 Canada.

Car Selden Soc Yearbk. . . . . *Carolina Selden Society Yearbook.* (Defunct).

Case & Comment. . . . . *Case & Counsel.* ISSN 0008-7246 (M) Free, Social Service Board, State Capital, Bismarck, ND 58501.

Catalyst . . . . *Catalyst.* Free, Royal Melbourne Institute of Technology, Directorate of Student Publications, Box 2476 G.P.O., Melbourne 3000, Vic. Australia.

Cath U L Rev. . . . . *Catholic University Law Review.* Leahy Hall, Catholic University, Washington, DC 20064.

Eccles Court Dig..........................	Ecclesiastical Court Digest. ISSN 0424-2068 (M) $20. Juridical Digests Inst., 1860 Broadway, New York, NY 10023.
Ed & Psychol M..........................	Educational and Psychological Measurement. ISSN 0013-1644 (Q) $25. Box 6907, College Station, Durham, NC 27708.
Edit Res Rep.............................	Editorial Research Reports. ISSN 0013-0958 (4/M) $168. Congressional Quarterly Inc., 1414 22nd St., N.W., Washington, DC 20037.
El Dario-La Prensa.......................	El Dario-La Prensa. 181 Hudson St., New York, NY 10013.
El Mundo................................	El Mundo. c/o El Mundo Newspaper de Puerto Rico, 41 E. 42nd St., New York, NY 10017.
Esquire..................................	Esquire. ISSN 0194-9535 (M) $15. Esquire Publishing, Inc., 2 Park Ave., New York, NY 10016.
Essence.................................	Essence. ISSN 0014-1880 (M) $9. Essence Communications, Inc., 1500 Broadway, New York, NY 10036.
Essex Inst Hist Coll......................	Essex Institute Historical Collections. ISSN 0014-0953 (Q) $12. Essex Institute, 132 Essex St., Salem, MA 01970.
Ethn & Min Stud.........................	Ethnic and Minorities Studies Review. (Defunct).
Ethn & Racial S..........................	Ethnic and Racial Studies. ISSN 0141-9870 (Q) $23. Routledge Journals, 9 Park St., Boston, MA 02108.
Ethics..................................	Ethics. ISSN 0014-1704 (Q) $15. Indv., $20. Inst. University of Chicago Press, 5801 Ellis Ave., Chicago, IL 60637.
Evaluation Rev..........................	Evaluation Review. ISSN 0193-841X (6 times a yr.) $30. Indv., $40. Inst. Sage Publications Inc., 275 S. Beverly Dr., Beverly Hills, CA 90212.
Exc Child..............................	Exceptional Children. ISSN 0014-4029 (8 times a yr.) $20. Council for Exceptional Children, 1920 Association Drive, Reston, VA 22091.
FBI L Enf Bull..........................	F.B.I. Law Enforcement Bulletin Monthly. ISSN 0014-5688 (M) free. U.S. Federal Bureau of Investigation, Ninth St. and Pennsylvania Ave., Washington, DC 20535.
FCI Res Rep.............................	FCI Research Reports.
Fed B J.................................	Federal Bar Journal Quarterly. ISSN 0014-9039 (Q) $12. Federal Bar Association, 1815 H St., N.W., Washington, DC 20006.
Fed Prob...............................	Federal Probation. ISSN 0014-9128 (Q) free. Administrative Office of the United States Courts, Supreme Court Building, Washington, DC 20544.
Fed Reg................................	Federal Register. ISSN 0097-6326 (daily) $50. U.S. Office of the Federal Register, National Archives & Record Service, Washington, DC 20402.
For Affairs.............................	Foreign Affairs. ISSN 0015-7120 (5/yr.) $15. Council on Foreign Affairs, Inc., 58 E 68th St., New York, NY 10021.
Forensic Sci............................	Forensic Science. ISSN 0379-0738 (Bi-M) n.p., 200 Fr. Elsevier Sequid, S.A., P.O. Box 851, CH-1001 Lousana, Switzerland.
Fortune News...........................	Fortune News. ISSN 0015-8275 (M) $5. Fortune Society, 221 Park Ave., So., New York, NY 10003.
Forum..................................	Forum. ISSN 0015-8305 (5 times a yr.) Federal Bar Association, District of Columbia Chapter, 1815 H Street, N.W., Washington, DC 20006.
Freedomways...........................	Freedomways. ISSN 0016-061X (Q) $4.50. Freedomways Associates, 799 Broadway, New York, NY 10003.
Friend J................................	Friends Journals. ISSN 0016-1233 (S.M.) $9. Friends Publishing Corp., 152-N 15th St., Philadelphia, PA 19102.
George Wash L Rev......................	George Washington Law Review. ISSN 0015-8076 (5 times a yr.) $12.50. George Washington University, Washington, DC 20052.
Growth Chan...........................	Growth and Change. ISSN 0017-4815 (Q) $10. University of Kentucky, College of Business and Economics, Lexington, KY 40506.
Guild Pract.............................	Guild Practitioner. Box 673, Berkeley, CA 94701.
Harper's Mag...........................	Harper's Magazine. ISSN 0017-789X (M) $11.98. Harper's Magazine Cp., 2 Park Ave., New York, NY 10016.
Harvard CR-CL Rev......................	Harvard Civil Rights-Civil Liberties Law Review. Langfre; Hall 114, Harvard Law School, Cambridge, MA 02138.
Harv Educ Rev..........................	Harvard Educational Review. ISSN 0017-8055 (Q) $23. Harvard University, Graduate School of Education, 13 Appian Way, Cambridge, MA 02138.
Harv L Rev.............................	Harvard Law Review. ISSN 0017-811X (8 times a yr.) $25. Harvard Law Review Association, Gannett House, Cambridge, MA 02138.

Israel Ann Psychi Rel Disc.................Israel Annals of Psychiatry and Related Disciplines. ISSN 0021-1958 (Q) $30. Jerusalem Academic Press, Box 3640, Jerusalem, Israel.

Issues Crim............................Issues in Criminology. (Defunct) c/o Crime & Social Justice, Box 4373, Berkeley, CA 94704.

Jericho................................Jericho ISSN 0362-5613, Don. National Moratorium on Prison Construction, 324 S. St., S.E., Washington, DC 20003.

J Abnor Ch Psychol....................Journal of Abnormal Child Psychology. ISSN 0091-0627 (Q) $31. Indv., $62. Inst. Plenum Press, 227 W. 17th St., New York, NY 10011.

J Abnor & Soc Psychol.................Journal of Abnormal and Social Psychology.

J Abnorm Psychol......................Journal of Abnormal Psychology. ISSN 0021-843X (Bi-M) $28. American Psychological Association, 1200 17th St., N.W., Washington, DC 20036.

J Afro-Am I...........................Journal of Afro-American Issues. (Defunct).

J Am Hist.............................Journal of American History. ISSN 0021-8723 (Q) 112 N. Byran St., Bloomington, IN 47401.

J Am Inst Cr L Crim...................Journal of the American Institute of Criminal Law and Criminology. (See Journal of Criminal Law and Criminology.)

J Am Med Assoc........................Journal of the American Medical Association. ISSN 0098-7484 (W) $30. American Medical Association, 535 N. Dearborn St., Chicago, IL 60610.

J App Beh Sci.........................Journal of Applied Behavioral Science. ISSN 0021-8863 (Q) $19. NTL Institute for Applied Behavioral Science, Box 9155, Rosslyn Sta., Arlington, VA 22209.

J Appl Psyc...........................Journal of Applied Psychology. ISSN 0021-9010 (Bi-M) $32. American Psychological Association, 1200 17th St., Washington, DC 20036.

J App Soc.............................Journal of Applied Sociology. (Defunct). See Sociol & Soc Res.

J App So P............................Journal of Applied Social Psychology. ISSN 0021-9029 (Bi-M) $74. V. H. Winston & Sons, Inc., 7961 Eastern Ave., Silver Springs, MD 20910.

J Behav Econ..........................Journal of Behavioral Economics. ISSN 0090-5720 (semi-ann) $6. Western Illinois University, Center for Business & Eco Research, Macomb, IL 61455.

J Black St............................Journal of Black Studies. ISSN 0021-9347 (Q) $15. Indv., $28. Inst. Sage Publications, Inc., 275 S. Beverly Dr., Beverly Hills, CA 90212.

J Blk Psych...........................Journal of Black Psychology. ISSN 0095-7984 (semi-ann) $5. National Association of Black Psychologists, 104 Administration Bldg. Univ. of Cincinnati, Cincinnati, OH 45221.

J Child Psyc & Psychi.................Journal of Child Psychology & Psychiatry. ISSN 0021-9630 (Q) $72. Pergamon Press, Inc., Journals Division, Maxwell House, Fairview Park, Elmsford, NY 10523.

J Clin Psyc...........................Journal of Clinical Psychology. ISSN 0021-9762 (Q) $35. Clinical Psychology Pub. Co., Inc., 4 Conant Square, Brandon, VT 05733.

J Conflic Res.........................Journal of Conflict Resolution. ISSN 0022-0027 $16.50 Indv., $33. Inst. Sage Publications, Inc., 275 S. Beverly Dr., Beverly Hills, CA 90212.

J Consult Clin Psyc...................Journal of Consulting & Clinical Psychology. ISSN 0022-006X (Bi-M) $40. American Psychological Association, 1200 17th St., N.W., Washington, DC 20036.

J Correct Psych.......................Journal of Correctional Psychology. (Defunct).

J Crim Jus............................Journal of Criminal Justice. ISSN 0047-2352 (Q) $98. Pergamon Press, Inc., Journals Division, Maxwell House, Fairview Park, Elmsford, NY 10523.

J Crim L..............................Journal of Criminal Law. ISSN 0022-0182 (Q) 8. Red House, Staines Green, Hertford, Herts SG 14 2LN England.

J Crim L & Crimin.....................Journal of Criminal Law and Criminology. ISSN 0091-4169 (Q) $15. Williams & Wilkins Co., 428 E. Preston St., Baltimore, MD 21202.

J Crim L Crimin & Pol Sci.............Journal of Criminal Law, Criminology and Police Science. (See Journal of Criminal Law and Criminology.)

J Crim Psychop........................Journal of Criminal Psychopathology.

J Drug Educ...........................Journal of Drug Education. ISSN 0047-2379 (Q) $27. Indv., $45. Inst. Baywood Publishing Co., Inc., 120 Marine St., Farmingdale, NY 11735.

J Drug Issues.........................Journal of Drug Issues. ISSN 0022-0426 (Q) $30. Box 4021, Tallhassee, FL 32303.

J Environ Syst........................Journal of Environmental Systems. ISSN 0022-0906 (Bi-M) $15. Institute of Environmental Sciences, 940 E. Northwest Hwy., Mt. Prospect, IL 60056.

J Exp Soc Psych.......................Journal of Experimental Social Psychology. ISSN 0022-1031 (Bi-M) $53. Academic Press, Inc., 111 Fifth Avenue, New York, NY 10003.

J Soc Ther.............................Journal of Social Therapy. (Now Corrective and Social Therapy and Journal of Behavioral Technology Methods.) ISSN 0093-1551 (Q) $27. Martin Psychiatric Research Foundation, Mid-Continent Hospital, 122 North Cooper, Glathe, KS 66061.

J Sociol & Soc Wel.....................Journal of Sociology and Social Welfare. (Bi-M) $10. Indv. $15. Inst. University of Connecticut, School of Social Work, 1800 Asylum Ave., West Hartford, CT 06117.

J Southern Hist........................Journal of Southern History. ISSN 0022-4642 (Q) $15. Southern Historical Association, B. H. Wall, Sec., Treas., Tulane University, New Orleans, LA 70118.

J Stud Tech Careers....................Journal of Studies in Technical Careers. ISSN 0016-3252 (Q) $15. Southern Illinois University, Carbondale, School of Technical Careers, 809 S. Forest, Carbondale, IL 62901.

J Urban L..............................Journal of Urban Law. ISSN 0041-955A (Now University of Detroit Journal of Urban Law.) (4 times a yr.) $12. University of Detroit School of Law, 651 E. Jefferson Ave., Detroit, MI 48226.

J Youth Ado............................Journal of Youth and Adolescence. ISSN 0047-2891 (Bi-M) $42. Indv., $84. Inst. Plenum Press, 227 West 117th St., New York, NY 10011.

Judicature.............................Judicature. ISSN 0022-5800 (M) $10. American Judicature Society, 200 W. Monroe St., Suite 1606, Chicago, IL 60606.

Just Assist News.......................Justice Assistance News. Public Information Office, Office of Justice Assistance Research and Statistics, U.S. Dept. of Justice, Washington, DC 20531.

Just Syst J............................Justice System Journal. ISSN 0089-261X (3 times a yr.) $7.50 Institute for Court Management, c/o Johnson Hall, College of Business, Colorado State University, Ft. Collins, CO 80521.

Juv & Fam Ct J.........................Juvenile and Family Court Journal. ISSN 0016-7109 (Q) $12. National Council of Juvenile and Family Court Judges, Box 8978, University of Nevada, Reno, NV 89507.

Ky L J.................................Kentucky Law Journal. ISSN 0023-026X (Q) $12. University of Kentucky School of Law, Lexington, KY 40506.

Labor Law J............................Labor Law Journal. Circulation Manager, Labor Law Journal, 4025 W. Peterson Avenue, Chicago, IL 60646.

Lancet.................................Lancet. ISSN 0023-5707 (ann) $30. Little, Brown and Co., 34 Beacon St., Boston, MA 02126.

Law & Order............................Law and Order. 37 W. 38th Street, New York, NY 10018.

Law & Contemp Prob.....................Law and Contemporary Problems. ISSN 0023-9286 (Q) $20. Duke University Press, Box 6697, College Station, Durham, NC 27706.

Law & Soc Rev..........................Law and Society Review. ISSN 0023-9216 (Q) $35. Law and Society Association, University of Denver College of Law, 200 W. 14th Ave., Denver, CO 80204.

Law Enf J..............................Law Enforcement Journal. P.O. Box 2039, Martinez, CA 94553.

Law Enf News...........................Law Enforcement News. ISSN 0364-1724 (S-M) $9.50 L.E.N. Inc., 444 W. 56th St., New York, NY 10019.

Law Hum Beh............................Law and Human Behavior. ISSN 0147-7307 (Q) $20. Indv., $35. Inst. Plenum Press, 227 W. 17th St., New York, NY 10011.

Law in Tran............................Law in Transition. (Now Guild Practitioner) ISSN 0017-5390 (Q) $6. National Lawyers Guild, Box 673, Berkeley, CA 94701.

Law Lib J..............................Law Library Journal. ISSN 0023-9283 (Q) $24. American Association of Law Libraries, 53 W. Jackson Blvd., Chicago, IL 60604.

Leg Aid Brief..........................Legal Aid Briefcase. (Now NLADA Briefcase) ISSN 0024-0338 (Q) $15. National Legal Aid & Defender Assn., 1155 E. 60th St., Chicago, IL 60637.

Life...................................Life. ISSN 0024-3019 (M) $18. Time, Inc., 1271 Avenue of the Americas, New York, NY 10020.

Lincoln L Rev..........................Lincoln Law Review. ISSN 0024-368X $7. Lincoln University College of Law, 281 Masonic Ave., San Francisco, CA 94118.

Look...................................Look. (Defunct).

Mag Am Hist............................Magazine of American History. With Notes and Queries, Illustrated. (Defunct).

Man Info Serv Rep......................Management Information Service Report. ISSN 0047-5262 (M) $80. International City Management Association, 1140 Connecticut Ave., N.W., Washington, DC 20036.

Mankind Q..............................Mankind Quarterly. ISSN 0025-2344 (Q) $30. Institute for the Study of Man, Inc., 1716 New Hampshire Ave., N.W., Washington, DC 20009.

Med Opin & Rev. . . . . *Medical Opinion and Review.* (M) $14. 575 Madison Avenue, New York, NY 10022.

Ment Health Court Digest. . . . . *Mental Health Court Digest.*

Mich L Rev. . . . . *Michigan Law Review.* ISSN 0026-2234 (8 times a yr.) $76. Research Group, Inc., Box 7178, Charlotteville, VA 22906.

Ment Hyg. . . . . *Mental Hygiene.* (Defunct).

Midw J Pol Sci. . . . . *Midwest Journal of Political Science.* (Now *Journal of Political Science*). ISSN 0092-5853 (Q)d $30. University of Texas Press, Box 7819, Austin, TX 78712.

Mil Pol J. . . . . *Military Police Law Enforcement Journal.* (Q) $3.50 U.S. Army Military Police School, Fort McClellan, AL 36205.

Minn Med. . . . . *Minnesota Medicine.* ISSN 0026-556X (M) $10. Minnesota Medical Association, 101 E. Fifth St., N., 900 St. Paul, MN 55101.

Miss L J. . . . . *Mississippi Law Journal.* ISSN 0026-6280 (Bi-M) $14. University of Mississippi Law School, Box 146, University, MS 38677,

Mod Age. . . . . *Modern Age.* ISSN 0026-7457 (Q) $10. Inter-collegiate Studies Institute, Inc., 14 S. Bryn Mawr Avenue, Bryn Mawr, PA 09010.

Monthly Lab Rev. . . . . *U.S. Bureau of Labor Statistics Monthly Labor Review.* ISSN 0027-004X (M) $20. U.S. Bureau of Labor Statistics, 441 G St., N.W., Washington, Dc 20212.

Ms. . . . . *Ms.* ISSN 0047-8318 (M) $10. Ms. Magazine Corporation, 310 Lexington Avenue, New York, NY 10017.

Museum N Ariz Note. . . . . *Museum of Northern Arizona, Museum Notes.* See Plateau.

Nation. . . . . *Nation.* ISSN 0027-8387 (W) $21. Nation Associates, Inc., 333 Sixth Avenue, New York, NY 10014.

Nat Bar J. . . . . *National Bar Journal.*

Nat Geogr. . . . . *National Geographic.* ISSN 0027-9358 (M) $10. National Geographic Society, 17th and M Sts., N.W., Washington, DC 20036.

Nat Med Assoc J. . . . . *National Medical Association Journal.* ISSN 0027-9684 (M) Appleton-Century-Crofts, 292 Madison Ave., New York, NY 10017.

Nat Prob Assn Yearbk. . . . . *National Probation Association Yearbook.* (Defunct).

Nat Taiwan U J Soc. . . . . *National Taiwan University Journal of Sociology.* ISSN 0077-5851 (ann) $2.50. National Taiwan University, Department of Sociology, 21 Hsu-Chow Road, Taipei, Taiwan 100 Republic of China.

Nat Cities. . . . . *Nation's Cities.* (Now *Nation's Cities Weekly*) ISSN 0028-9488 (W) $12. National League of Cities, 1620 Eye St., N.W., Washington, DC 20006.

N Car Cent L J. . . . . *North Carolina Central Law Journal.* North Carolina Central University, Durham, NC.

N Car L J. . . . . *North Carolina Law Journal.* (Defunct).

Negro Dig. . . . . *Negro Digest.* (Defunct).

Negro Ed Rev. . . . . *Negro Educational Review.* (Q) $10. Negro Educational Review, Inc., Box 2895 West Bay Annex, Jacksonville, FL 32216.

Negro Hist Bull. . . . . *Negro History Bulletin.* ISSN 0028-2529 (Bi-M) $8. Association for the Study of Afro-American Life and History, Inc., 1407 Fourteenth St., N.W., Washington, DC 20005.

N Eng J Med. . . . . *New England Journal of Medicine.* ISSN 0028-4793 (W) $25. Massachusetts Medical Society, 10 Shattuck St., Boston, MA 02115.

New Eng J Prison L. . . . . *New England Journal on Prison Law.* ISSN 0095-7364 $10. $6. prisoners and students. New England School of Law, 126 New Berry St., Boston, MA 02116.

New Eng Q. . . . . *New England Quarterly.* ISSN 0028-4866 (Q) $8. Colonial Society of Massachusetts, c/o Herbert Brown, Ed., Hubbard Hall, Bowdoin College, Brunswick, ME 04011.

New L. . . . . *New Leader.* ISSN 0028-6044 (Bi-W) $15. American Labor Conference on International Affairs, Inc., 212 Fifth Avenue, New York, NY 10010.

New Mex L Rev. . . . . *New Mexico Law Review.* ISSN 0028-6214 (semi-ann) $10. University of New Mexico, School of Law, 1117 Sanford, N.E., Albuquerque, NM 87131.

New Pol. . . . . *New Politics.* ISSN 0028-6494 (Q) New Politics Publishing Co., 507 Fifth Ave., New York, NY 10017.

New R. . . . . *New Republic.* ISSN 0028-6583 (48 times a yr.) New Republic Printing & Publishing Co., Ltd., 531 Main St., Vancouver, BC V6A 2V1, Canada.

New South. . . . . *New South.*

Newsweek . . . . *Newsweek.* ISSN 0023-9604 (W) $29.95. Newsweek, Inc., 444 Madison Avenue, New York, NY 10022.

NLADA Brief. . . . . *NLADA Briefcase.* Subscription Dept., National Legal Aid and Defender Assoc., 2100 M St., N.W., Suite 601, Washington, DC 20037.

No Car L Rev. . . . . *North Carolina Law Review.* ISSN 0029-0245 $15. University of North Carolina at Chapel Hill, School of Law, Chapel Hill, NC 27514.

Northwest Med. . . . . *Northwest Medicine.*

Northw Univ L Rev. . . . . *Northwestern University Law Review.* ISSN 0029-3571 (Bi-W) $15. Northwestern University, School of Law, 357 E. Chicago Ave., Chicago, IL 60611.

Notre Dame Law. . . . . *Notre Dame Lawyer.* ISSN 0029-4535 (5 times a yr.) $12. University of Notre Dame, School of Law, Box 486, Notre Dame, IN 46556.

Nuestro . . . . *Nuestro.* ISSN 0147-3247 (M) $12. Nuestro Publications, Inc., 1140 Avenue of the Americas, New York, NY 10036.

NY . . . . *New York Magazine.* ISSN 0028-7369 (W) $18. 755 Second Avenue, New York, NY 10017.

NYHSQ. . . . . *New York Historical Society Quarterly.* ISSN 0028-7253 (Q) $12. New York Historical Society, 710 Central Park West, New York, NY 10024.

NY J Crim Just. . . . . *New York Journal of Crime and Justice.* (Defunct).

NY L Forum. . . . . *New York Law Forum.* ISSN 0028-8318. (Now *New York Law School Law Review.*) (4 times a yr.) $15. 57 Worth St., New York, NY 10013.

NY L J. . . . . *New York Law Journal Daily.* $125. New York Law Publishing Co., 233 Broadway, New York, NY 10007.

NY Rev Bks. . . . . *New York Review of Books.* ISSN 0028-7504 (22 times a yr.) $14.50 NYREV, Inc., 250 W. 57th St., New York, NY 10019.

NYS Bar J. . . . . *New York State Bar Journal.* ISSN 0028-7547 (8 times a yr.) $2. New York State Bar Association, 1 Elk St., Albany, NY 12207.

NYT . . . . *New York Times.* The New York Times Co., 229 West 43rd St., New York, NY 10036.

NYT Mag. . . . . *New York Times Magazine.* (W) The New York Times Co., 229 W. 42nd St., New York, NY 10036.

NYU L Rev. . . . . *New York University Law Review.* ISSN 0028-7881 (6 times a yr.) $15. New York University, Law Review, 249 Sullivan St., New York, NY 10012.

NYU Rev L & S C. . . . . *New York University Review of Law and Social Change.* 249 Sullivan St., New York, NY 10012.

Ohio S L J. . . . . *Ohio State Law Journal.* ISSN 0048-1572 (Q) $10. Ohio State University, College of Law, 1659 North High St., Columbus, OH.

Opport. . . . . *Opportunity.* (Defunct).

Ore L Rev. . . . . *Oregon Law Review.* (4 times a yr.) $8. University of Oregon, School of Law, Eugene, OR 94703.

Pac Soc Rev. . . . . *Pacific Sociological Review.* ISSN 0030-8919 (Q)$15. Indv., $28. Inst. Sage Publications, Inc., 275 So. Beverly St., Beverly Hills, CA 90212.

Peacemaker. . . . . *The Peacemaker.* ISSN 0031-3602 (M) $4.-$6. Peacemaker Movement, Box 627, Garberville, CA 95440.

Pedagog Sem. . . . . *Pedagogical Seminary.* (Defunct).

Pediatric Ann. . . . . *Pediatric Annals.* ISSN 0090-448$ (M) $27.50. Insight Pub., Co., Inc., 501 Madison Avenue, New York, NY 10022.

Pa Geographer. . . . . *Pennsylvania Geographer.*

Penn Mag Hist Biog. *Pennsylvania Magazine of History & Biography.* (Q) $10. Historical Society of Pennsylvania, 1300 Locust St., Philadelphia, PA 19107.

Penthouse. . . . . *Penthouse.* ISSN 0031-4935 (M) $20. Penthouse International Ltd., R.C. Guccione, Ed. & Pub. 909 Third Ave., New York, NY 10022.

Perc Mot Sk. . . . . *Perceptual & Motor Skills.* ISSN 0031-5125 (Bi-M) $97.20. Box 9229, Missoula, MT 59807.

Pers & Guid J. . . . . *Personnel and Guidance Journal.* ISSN 0031-5737 (M) $20. American Personnel and Guidance Association, Two Skyline Pl., Ste. 400, 5203 Leeburg Pike, Falls Church, VA 22041.

Per Soc Psyc Bull. . . . . *Personality & Social Psychology Bulletin.* (Q) $18. Society for Personality & Social Psychology, 1200 17th St., N.W., Washington, DC 20036.

Phila Inquirer. . . . . *Philadelphia Inquirer.* 400 N. Broad St., Philadelphia, PA 19130.

Philos Pub Aff. . . . . *Philosophy & Public Affairs.* ISSN 0048-3915 $15. Inst., $6.50 students, $9.75 others. Princeton University Press, Princeton, NJ 08540.

S Car H M. . . . . *South Carolina History Magazine.* ISSN 0038-3082 (Q) $15. South Carolina Historical Society, Fireproof Building, Charleston, SC 29401.

Soc Casework. . . . . *Social Casework.* ISSN 0037-7678 (M) $16. Indv., $25 Inst. Family Service Association of America, 44 E. 23rd St., New York, NY 10010.

Soc Forces. . . . . *Social Forces.* ISSN 0037-7732 (4 times a yr.) $15. Indv., $17.60 Inst. University of North Carolina Press, Box 2288 Chapel Hill, NC 27514.

Social Policy. . . . . *Social Policy.* ISSN 0037-7783. 33 West 42nd St., New York, NY 10036.

Society. . . . . *Society.* ISSN 0147-2011 (Bi-M) $15. Indv., $21. Inst. Transaction Periodical Consortium, Rutgers University, New Brunswick, NJ 08903.

Social Psychi. . . . . *Social Psychiatry.* ISSN 0037-7813 (Q) $73.10. Springer-Verlag, 175 Fifth Ave., New York, NY 10010.

Social Prob. . . . . *Social Problems.* ISSN 0037-7791 (5 times a yr.) Society for the Study of Social Problems, 208 Rockwell Hall, State University College at Buffalo, 1300 Elmwood Ave., Buffalo, NY 14222.

Social Sci Q. . . . . *Social Science Quarterly.* ISSN 0038-4941 (Q) $16. Indv., $30. Inst. Southwestern Social Science Association, University of Texas Press, Box 7919, Austin, TX 78712.

Social Serv Rev. . . . . *Social Service Review.* ISSN 0037-7961 (Q) $16. Indv., $22. Inst. University of Chicago Press, 5801 S. Ellis Avenue, Chicago, IL 60637.

Social Wk. . . . . *Social Work.* (Q) $4. Philippine Association of Social Workers, 1680 Kansas Street, 2nd fl., National Social Work Training Labratory, Malate Metra Manila, Philippines.

Socio-Econ Plan Sci. . . . . *Socio-Economic Planning Sciences.* ISSN 0038-0121 (Bi-M) $99. Pergamon Press, Inc., Journals Division Maxwell House, Fairview Park, Elmsford, NY 10523.

Sociol Anal. . . . . *Sociological Analysis* ISSN 0038-0210 (Q) $15. Association for the Sociology of Religion, c/o Executive Secretary, Robert McNamara, Loyola University of Chicago, 6525 N. Sheridan Rd., Chicago, IL 60626.

Sociol Q. . . . . *Sociological Quarterly.* ISSN 0038-0253 (Q) $12. Indv., $15. Inst. Midwest Sociological Society, Department of Sociology, Southern Illinois University, Carbondale, IL 62901.

Sociol Soc Res. . . . . *Sociology and Social Research.* ISSN 0038-0393 (Q) $13. University of Southern California, Los Angeles, CA 90007.

S Car L Rev. . . . . *South Carolina Law Review.* University of South Carolina, School of Law, Columbia, SC 29208.

S Cal L Rev. . . . . *Southern California Law Review.* ISSN 0038-3910 (6 times a yr.) $17.50. University of Southern California Law Center, Room 314, University Park, Los Angeles, CA 90007.

S Exposure. . . . . *Southern Exposure.* ISSN 0038p-4070 (Q). Southeastern Professional Photo Graphers Association Inc., Box 355, Talladega, AL 35160.

Southern Workman. . . . . *Southern Workman.* (Defunct).

Sw J Anthrop. . . . . *Southwestern Journal of Anthropology.* (*Journal of Anthropological Research*) (Q) $10. Indv., $16. Inst. University of New Mexico, Department of Anthropology, Albuquerque, NM 87131.

S West Univ L Rev. . . . . *Southwestern University Law Review.* 675 S. Westmoreland Avenue, Los Angeles, CA 90005.

Stanford L Rev. . . . . *Stanford Law Review.* ISSN 0038-9765 (6 times a yr.) $15. Stanford University, Stanford Law School, Stanford, CA 94305.

State Peace Off J. . . . . *State Peace Officers Journal.*

Stat Bull. . . . . *Statistical Bulletin.* (*Irish Statistical Bulletin*) (Q) 50p. per. no. Central Statistics Office, Earls Fort Terrace, Dublin 2, Ireland.

Stat Reptr. . . . . *Statistical Reporter.* ISSN 0039-050X (M) $9.70. U.S. Department of Commerce, Office of Federal Statistical Policy and Standard, Washington, DC 20402.

Suffolk U L Rev. . . . . *Suffolk University Law Review.* ISSN 0039-4696 (5 times a yr.) $10. Suffolk University Law School, 41 Temple St., Boston, MA 02114.

Survey. . . . . *Survey.* (Defunct).

Survey Gr. . . . . *Survey Graphic.* (Defunct).

Survey Midm. . . . . *Survey Midmonthly.* (Defunct).

Temple L Q. . . . . *Temple Law Quarterly.* ISSN 0040-2974 (Q) $8. Temple University School of Law, 1715 N. Broad St., Philadelphia, PA 19122.

Texas Monthly. . . . . *Texas Monthly.* ISSN 0148-7736 (M) $15. Mediatex Communications Corp., Box 1569, Austin, TX 78767.

Tex Observ.............................Texas Observer. ISSN 0040-4519 $14. Texas Observer Publishing Co., 600 W. Seventh, Austin, TX 78701.

Tex L Rev.............................Texas Law Review. ISSN 0040-4411 (8 times a yr.) $18. Texas Law Review Publications, Inc., 2500 Red River, Austin, TX 78705.

Time.................................Time. ISSN 0040-871X (W) $31. Time, Inc., Time & Life Building, New York, NY 10020.

Trans-Act............................Trans-Action. ISSN 0147-2011 (Bi-M) $15. Transaction Periodicals Corporation, Rutgers University, New Brunswick, NJ 08903.

Trial................................Trial. Association of Trial Lawyers of American, 1050 31st St., N.W., Washington, DC 20007.

Trooper..............................Trooper. ISSN 0564-3287 (Bi-M) free. State Police Public Security Building, State Campus, Albany, NY 12226.

UCLA L Rev..........................UCLA Law Review. ISSN 0041-5650 (6 times a yr.) $20. University of California, Los Angeles, School of Law, 405 Hilgard Ave., Los Angeles, CA 90024.

U Chi L Rev..........................University of Chicago Law Review. ISSN 0041-9494 (Q) $10. University of Chicago Law School, 111 E. 60th St., Chicago, IL 60637.

U Cinc L Rev.........................University of Cincinnati Law Review. ISSN 0009-5881 (Q) $10. University of Cincinnati, College of Law, Cincinnati, OH 45221.

U Colo L Rev.........................University of Colorado Law Review. ISSN 0041-9561 (4 times a yr.) $10. University of Colorado, School of Law Bldg., Room 290, Boulder, CO 80309.

U Kan L Rev.........................University of Kansas Law Review. University of Kansas Law Review, Inc., Green Hall, Lawrence, KS 66044.

U Miami L Rev.......................University of Miami Law Review. ISSN 0041-9818 (5 times a yr.) $16. University of Miami, School of Law, Coral Gables, FL 33124.

Univ Penn L Rev.....................University of Pennsylvania law Review. ISSN 0041-9907 (6 times a yr.) $18. University of Pennsylvania Law School, 3400 Chestnut St., Philadelphia, PA 19174.

U San Fran L Rev....................University of San Francisco Law Review. ISSN 0042-0018 (4 times a yr.) $10. University of San Francisco School of Law, Kendrick Hall, 2130 Fulton St., San Francisco, CA 94117,

U Toledo L R........................University of Toledo Law Review. ISSN 0042-0190 (3 times a yr.) $8. University of Toledo, College of Law, Office of the Editor-in-Chief, Toledo, OH 43606.

Urb Aff Q...........................Urban Affairs Quarterly. ISSN 0042-0816 (Q) $15. Indv., $30. Inst., Sage Publications, Inc., 275 So. Beverly Dr., Beverly Hills, CA 90212.

Urb Data Serv.......................Urban Data Service Report. ISSN 0049-5654 (M) $125. International City Management Association, 1140 Connecticut Ave., N.W., Washington, DC 20036.

Urb Health..........................Urban Health. ISSN 0191-8257 (10 times a yr.) $12. Urban Publishing Co., Box 42409, Atlanta, GA 30311.

Urb Lawyer..........................Urban Lawyer. Hope M. Bulger, Managing Editor, American Bar Association, 1155 West 60th St., Chicago, IL 60637.

Urb League Rev......................Urban League Review. ISSN 0147-1740 $8. Indv., $10. Inst. National Urban League Research Department, Transaction Periodicals Consortium, Rutgers University, New Brunswick, NJ 08903.

Urb Life............................Urban Life. ISSN 0098-3039 (Q) $15. Indv., $28. Inst. Sage Publications, Inc., 275 So. Beverly Dr., Beverly Hills, CA 90212.

USA Today...........................USA Today. ISSN 0161-7389 (M) $18.95. Society for the Advancement of Education, 1860 Broadway, New York, NY 10023.

US News.............................U.S. News and World Report. ISSN 0041-5537 (W) $26. U.S. News and World Report, Inc., 2300 N. St., N.W., Washington, DC 20037.

Utah L Rev..........................Utah Law Review. ISSN 0042-1448 (Q) $15. Utah Law Review Society, University of Utah College of Law, Salt Lake City, UT 84112.

Vand J Trans L......................Vanderbilt Journal of Transnational Law. (Q) $12.50, $13.50 foreign. Vanderbilt University, School of Law, Nashville, TN 37240.

Vand L Rev..........................Vanderbilt Law Review. ISSN 0042-2533 (6 times a yr.) $15. Vanderbilt University, School of Law, Nashville, TN 37240.

Victimol............................Victimology. ISSN 0361-5170 (Q) $20. Indv., $35. Inst. Visage Press, Inc., 2333 N. Vernon St., Arlington, VA 22207.

Vill Voice..........................Village Voice. ISSN 0042-6180 (W) $8.50. University St., New York, NY 10003.

BOOK PUBLISHERS INDEXED

Atheneum............Atheneum
122 E. 42nd St.
New York, NY 10017

Atlanta Univ.........Atlanta University
223 Chestnut St., S.W.
Atlanta, GA 30314

Atlanta Univ Pr........Atlanta University Press
223 Chestnut St., S.W.
Atlanta, GA 30314

Avon................Avon
959 Eighth Avenue
New York, NY 10019

Ballantine............Ballantine
Div. of Random House
201 E. 50th St.
New York, NY 10022

Ballinger.............Ballinger Publishing Co.
17 Dunston St.
Harvard Square
Cambridge, MA 02138

Bantam..............Bantam
666 5th Ave.
New York, NY 10019

Basic Books...........Basic Books
10 E. 53rd St.
New York, NY 10022

Baylor Univ...........Baylor University
Waco, TX 76703

Bd Trust W Penit.......Board of Trustees of the Western Penitentiary of Pennsylvania (Defunct)

Beacon Pr............Beacon Press
25 Beacon St.
Boston, MA 02108

Bela Marsh...........Bela Marsh (Defunct)

Bio Med-For Crim......International Center for Biological and
Medico-Forensic Criminology
Sao Paulo, Brazil

BJS.................Bureau of Justice Statistics
633 Indiana Ave., N.W.
Washington, DC 20531

Bobbs-Merrill.........Bobbs-Merrill
4 West 58th St.
New York, NY 10019

Bookman Associates...Bookman Associates (Defunct)

Books Libraries Pr......Books for Libraries Press (Defunct)

Bowling Green St U....Bowling Green State University
Popular Culture Center
Bowling Green, OH 43403

Brandeis Univ.........Brandeis University
415 South St.
Waltham, MA 02154

Brandeis, Lemberg.....Brandeis University
Lemberg Center for the Study of Violence
(Defunct)

Braziller..............Braziller George Inc.
One Park Avenue
New York, NY 10016

Brigham Young Univ...Brigham Young University Press
218 University Press Building
Provo, UT 84602

Broadside Pr..........Broadside Press
74 Glendale Avenue
Highland Park, MI 48203

Brooklyn College......Brooklyn College
Brooklyn, NY 11210

Brooks/Cole..........Brooks/Cole
555 Obrego St.
Monterey, CA 93940

Brunner/Mazel........Brunner/Mazel
19 Union Square W.
New York, NY 10003

Bur App Soc Res.......Bureau of Applied Social Research
Columbia University
New York, NY 10027

C V Mosby............C. V. Mosby
Westline Industrial Drive
St. Louis, MO 63141

CSS.................Community Service Society
105 East 22nd St.
New York, NY 10010

Calif Atty Gen.........State of California
Office of the Attorney General
555 Capitol Mall
Sacramento, CA 95814

Calif Judic Coun.......State of California
Judicial Council
Administrative Office of the Courts
Library & Courts Bldg.
Sacramento, CA 95814

Calif St Univ LA........California State University at Los Angeles
Los Angeles, CA 90032

Cambridge Univ Pr.....Cambridge University Press
32 E. 57th Street
New York, NY 10022

Canfield Pr...........Canfield Press
c/o Harper & Row Pubs., Inc.
1700 Montgomery St.
San Francisco, CA 94111

Carnegie Corp NY.....Carnegie Corporation of New York
437 Madison Ave.
New York, NY 10022

Carnegie-M USI.......Carnegie-Mellon University
Urban Systems Institute
Baker Hall 233
Pittsburgh, PA 15213

Catholic Univ.........Catholic University of America Press
620 Michigan Avenue, N.W.
Washington, DC 20064

Cesar Cauce. . . . . Cesar Cauce

Chamb of Commerce. . . Chamber of Commerce of the U.S.
16 H St., N.W.
Washington, DC 20062

Chandler. . . . . Chandler & Sharp Pubs., Inc.
11A Commercial Blvd.
Novato, CA 94947

Chapman and Crimes. . Chapman and Crimes, Inc. (Defunct)

Charity Organ Soc. . . . . Charity Organization Society (Defunct)

Chas C Thomas. . . . . Charles C Thomas
301-327 E. Lawrence Ave.
Springfield, IL 62717

Chas L Evans. . . . . Charles L Evans

Chas Merrill. . . . . Charles E Merrill Pub. Co.
1300 Alum Creek Dr.
Columbus, OH 43216

Chatto & Windus. . . . . . . Chatto and Windus
40-42 William IV St.
London WC2N 4DF England

Chicago Park Dist. . . . . . Chicago Park District

Chicago State Univ. . . . . Chicago State University
Chicago, IL 60628

Chicano Pinto Proj. . . . . Chicano Pinto Project
2211 S. Atlantic Blvd.
Suite F
Monterey Park, CA 91754

Christopher Pub. . . . . . . Christopher Publishing House
53 Billings Rd.
N. Quincy, MA 02171

City Univ of NY. . . . . City University of New York

Collier Books. . . . . Collier Books
Division of Macmillan Publishing Co.
866 3rd Ave.
New York, NY 10022

Columbia Teach Col. . . . Columbia University Teachers College
Columbia University
1234 Amsterdam Ave.
New York, NY 10027

Columbia Univ Pr. . . . . . Columbia University Press
562 West 113th St.
New York, NY 10025

Comm Interrac Coop. . . Commission on Interracial Cooperation
(Defunct)

Comm Racial Just. . . . . . Commission for Racial Justice
United Church of Christ
297 Park Ave., South
New York, NY 10010

Commission. . . . . State of California
Commission on Peace Officer Standards
and Training
Dept. of Justice
7100 Bowling Drive
Sacramento, CA 95814

Consensus Pub. . . . . Consensus Publishers, Inc.
155 Franciscan Dr.
San Ramon, CA 94583

Cornell Univ Pr. . . . . Cornell University Press
124 Roberts Place
Ithaca, NY 14850

Corrections Dept. . . . . . . State of New York
Dept. of Correctional Services
Bldg. 2
State Office Bldg. Campus
Albany, NY 12226

Coun Plan Librar. . . . . . . Council of Planning Librarians
P.O. Box 229
Monticello, IL 61856

Council on CJ. . . . . State of Wisconsin
Council on Criminal Justice
Office of the Governor
122 W. Washington Ave.
Madison, WI 53702

Coward McCann. . . . . . . Coward, McCann & Geoghegan, Inc.
200 Madison Ave.
New York, NY 10016

Crime Info Bureau. . . . . Crime Information Bureau
Wisconsin Dept. of Justice
Division of Law Enforcement Services
State Capital
Madison, WI 53702

Criminal Just Pr. . . . . . . Criminal Justice Press
P.O. Box 159
Kennedale, TX 76060

D Appleton & Co. . . . . . . D. Appleton and Co. (Defunct)

Daniel Fanshaw. . . . . . . Daniel Fanshaw (Defunct)

David McKay. . . . . David McKay, Inc.
2 Park Avenue
New York, NY 10016

Davis Pub Co. . . . . Davis Publishing Co.
250 Potrero St.
Santa Cruz, CA 95060

Delacorte Pr. . . . . Delacorte Press
1 Dag Hammarskjold Plaza
245 E. 47th St.
New York, NY 10017

Dell. . . . . Dell Publishing
1 Dag Hammarskjold Plaza
245 E. 47th St.
New York, NY 10017

Delmar. . . . . Delmar
50 Wolf Road
Albany, NY 12205

Delta. . . . . Delta
1 Dag Hammarskjold Plaza
245 E. 47th St.
New York, NY 10017

Denver Juvenile Ct. . . . . Denver Juvenile Court
Denver, CO 80202

Dept Corrections. . . . . . . State of California
Dept. of Corrections
3001 E St.
Sacramento, CA 95816

Dept Corrections. . . . . . . State of Georgia
                     Dept. of Offender Rehabilitation
                     800 Peachtree St., NE
                     Suite 500
                     Atlanta, GA 30365

Dept Corrections. . . . . . . State of New Jersey
                     Dept. of Corrections
                     Whittlesey Rd.
                     P.O. Box 7387
                     Trenton, NJ 08628

Dept Corrections. . . . . . . Texas Dept. of Corrections
                     P.O. Box 99
                     Huntsville, TX 77340

Dept Corrections. . . . . . . Virginia Corrections Dept.
                     429 South Belvidere St.
                     Richmond, VA 23220

Dept Pub Safety. . . . . . . State of Iowa
                     Dept. of Public Safety
                     Wallace State Office Bldg.
                     520 E. 90th St.
                     Des Moines, IA 50319

Dial Pr. . . . . Dial Press
                     1 Dag Hammarskjold Plaza
                     245 E. 47th St.
                     New York, NY 10017

Dorrance and Co. . . . . . . Dorrance and Co.
                     35 Cricket Terrace
                     Ardmore, PA 19003

Dorsey Pr. . . . . Dorsey Press
                     Richard D. Irwin, Inc.
                     1818 Ridge Rd.
                     Homewood, IL 60430

Doubleday. . . . . Doubleday and Co.
                     Garden City, NY 11530

Doubleday-Anchor. . . . . Doubleday-Anchor
                     Garden City, NY 11530

Douglas Book Corp. . . . . Douglas Book Corp.
                     145 W. 55th St.
                     New York, NY 10019

Douglass Pub. . . . . Douglass Publishers
                     P.O. Box 3270
                     Alexandria, VA 22302

Dover. . . . . Dover
                     180 Varick St.
                     New York, NY 10014

Dryden Pr. . . . . Dryden Press
                     901 N. Elm
                     Hinsdale, IL 60521

Du Sable Museum. . . . . Du Sable Museum of African-American
                     History
                     740 East 56th Place
                     Chicago, IL 60637

Duke Univ Pr. . . . . Duke University Press
                     6697 College Station
                     Durham, NC 27708

Dunbaugh. . . . . Frank Dunbaugh
                     744 North Holly Drive
                     Annapolis, MD 21401

Dustbooks. . . . . Dustbooks
                     P.O. Box 1056
                     Paradise, CA 95969

E P Dutton. . . . . E. P. Dutton and Co.
                     2 Park Avenue
                     New York, NY 10016

Elsevier . . . . Elsevier Scientific Publishing
                     52 Vanderbilt Avenue
                     New York, NY 10017

Emerson Hall. . . . . Emerson Hall Publishers, Inc.
                     215 West 98th Street
                     New York, NY 10025

Emory & Henry. . . . . Emory and Henry College
                     Emory, VA 24327

Emory Univ. . . . . Emory University
                     Atlanta, GA 30322

Epic Publications. . . . . . . Epic Publications
                     4420 Westover Drive
                     Orchard Lake, MI 48033

Exposition Pr. . . . . Exposition Press
                     900 South Oyster Bay Road
                     Hicksville, NY 11801

Family Serv Assoc. . . . . Family Service Association of America
                     44 East 23rd Street
                     New York, NY 1003

Farrar Straus Gir. . . . . . . Farrar, Straus and Giroux
                     19 Union Square, West
                     New York, NY 10003

Fawcett Pub. . . . . Fawcett Publications (Defunct)

Fem Off Prog W Pa. . . . . Female Offenders Program of Western
                     Pennsylvania, Inc. (Defunct)

Florida State Univ. . . . . . Florida State University
                     Tallahassee, FL 32306

Fordham Hisp R Cen. . . . Fordham University Hispanic Research
                     Center
                     Bronx, NY 10458

Fordham Univ. . . . . Fordham University
                     Bronx, NY 10458

Free Pr. . . . . Free Press
                     866 Third Avenue
                     New York, NY 10022

Friendship Pr. . . . . Friendship Press
                     475 Riverside Drive
                     Room 722
                     New York, NY 10027

G H Ellis. . . . . G. H. Ellis (Defunct)

G K Hall Co. . . . . G. K. Hall Co.
                     70 Lincoln Street
                     Boston, MA 02111

G P Putnam's. . . . . G. P. Putnam's Sons
                     200 Madison Avenue
                     New York NY 10016

Gardner. . . . . Gardner Press, Inc.
      19 Union Square West
      New York, NY 10003

Garrett Park Pr. . . . . Garrett Park Press
      Garrett Park, MD 20766

Ginn & Co. . . . . Ginn and Co.
      191 Spring Street
      Lexington, MA 02173

Glencoe Pr. . . . . Glencoe Press
      17337 Ventura Blvd.
      Encino, CA 91316

Goodyear . . . . Goodyear Publishing
      1640 5th Street
      Santa Monica, CA 90401

Gorham Pr. . . . . Gorham Press (Defunct)

Governor's Comm. . . . . . State of Pennsylvania
      Governor's Study Commission on Capital
        Punishment
      c/o Governor's Office
      Harrisburg, PA 17120

Governor's Office. . . . . . Texas Office of the Governor
      State Capitol
      100 11th St., E.
      Austin, TX 78701

Greenhaven Prison. . . . Greenhaven State Correctional Facility
      Stormville, NY 12582

Greenwood Pr. . . . . Greenwood Press
      51 Riverside Ave.
      Westport, CT 06880

Grossman Pub. . . . . . Grossman Publishers
      7071 Convoy Court
      Suite 301
      San Diego, CA 92111

Grove Pr. . . . . Grove Press
      196 W. Houston St.
      New York, NY 10014

Gulf . . . . Gulf Publishing Co.
      P.O. Box 2608
      Houston, TX 77001

HS Crocker. . . . . H. S. Crocker (Defunct)

Harcourt. . . . . Harcourt (Defunct)

Harcourt Brace. . . . . Harcourt, Brace, Jovanovich, Inc.
      757 Third Ave.
      New York, NY 10017

Harlo . . . . Harlo
      50 Victor Avenue
      Detroit, MI 48203

Harper. . . . . Harper (Defunct)

Harper & Bros. . . . . Harper and Brothers (Defunct)

Harper & Row. . . . . Harper and Row
      10 E. 53rd St.
      New York, NY 10022

Harper Colophon. . . . . . Harper Colophon Books (See Harper and
      Row)

Harper Torchbook. . . . . Harper Torchbook (See Harper and Row)

Harpers Mag Pr. . . . . . . Harper's Magazine Press (See Harper and
      Row)

Harrington Pub. . . . . . . Harrington Publications (Defunct)

Harv L Sch Cen C J. . . . . Harvard Law School
      Center for Criminal Justice
      Cambridge, MA 02138

Harvard Univ Pr. . . . . . . Harvard University Press
      79 Garden St.
      Cambridge, MA 02173

Heath. . . . . D. C. Heath and Co.
      125 Spring St.
      Lexington, MA 02173

Hellcoal Pr. . . . . Hellcoal Press
      Brown University
      P.O. Box 4 S.A.O.
      Providence, RI 02912

Henry Holt. . . . . Henry Holt (Defunct)

Herman Graf. . . . . Herman Graf Associates
      c/o Dell Publishing
      1 Dag Hammarskjold Plaza
      245 E. 47th St.
      New York, NY 10017

Hill & Wang. . . . . Hill and Wang
      19 Union Square
      New York, NY 10003

Holt Rinehart Wins. . . . . Holt, Rinehart and Winston, Inc.
      383 Madison Ave.
      New York, NY 10017

Houghton Mifflin. . . . . . Houghton Mifflin Co.
      2 Park St.
      Boston, MA 02107

House of Rep. . . . . Texas House of Representatives
      State Capitol
      Austin, TX 78701

Howard U. . . . . Howard University
      2935 Upton St., N.W.
      Washington, DC 20008

Howard U Cen Y C S. . . . Howard University
      Center for Youth and Community Studies
      2935 Upton St., N.W.
      Washington, DC 10008

Howard U Ins U A R. . . . Howard University
      Institute for Urban Affairs and Research
      2935 Upton St., N.W.
      Washington, DC 20008

Hum Dev Plan Proj. . . . . Human Development Planning Project
      St. Louis, MO (Defunct)

ICD. . . . . State of Illinois
      Dept. of Corrections
      1301 Concordia Ct.
      Springfield, IL 62702

IACP. . . . . International Association of Chiefs of
      Police
      11 Firstfield Road
      Gaithersburg, MD 20760

Il Inst Techn. . . . . Illinois Institute of Technology
      Chicago, IL 60616

Indian Histor Bur. . . . . . Indian Historical Bureau (Defunct)

Long Island Univ. . . . . . . Long Island University
The Brooklyn Center
University Plaza
Brooklyn, NY 11201

Lousiana St Univ. . . . . . . Louisiana State University
Baton Rouge, LA 70803

MIT Pr. . . . . M. I. T. Press
28 Carleton St.
Cambridge, MA 02142

MSS Inform. . . . . MSS Information Corp.
P.O. Box 985
Edison, NJ 08817

Macmillan. . . . . Macmillan Co.
866 Third Avenue
New York, NY 10022

Major Books. . . . . Major Books
21335 Roscoe Blvd.
Phoenix, AZ 85016

Marine Res Society. . . . . Marine Research Society (Defunct)

Markham Pub. . . . . Markham Publishing Co.
P.O. Box 7600
Chicago, IL 60680

Marquette Univ. . . . . . . Marquette University
1131 W. Wisconsin Ave.
Milwaukee, WI 53233

Marzani & Munsell. . . . . Marzani & Munsell
New York, NY (Defunct)

McGraw-Hill. . . . . McGraw-Hill Book Co.
1221 Ave. of the Americas
New York, NY 10020

McNally & Loftin. . . . . . . McNally and Loftin Pub. Co. (Defunct)

Mentor Books. . . . . Mentor Books
c/o New American Library, Inc.
1301 Ave. of the Americas
New York, NY 10019

Meredith . . . . Meredith Books
New York, NY (Defunct)

Meridian Books. . . . . . . Meridian Books
c/o New American Library, Inc.
1301 Ave. of the Americas
New York, NY 10019

Merit. . . . . Merit (Defunct)

Metrop App Res Cen. . . Metropolitan Applied Research Center,
Inc. (Defunct)

Michigan St Univ. . . . . . Michigan State University
East Lansing, MI 48824

Mich St U I C D. . . . . Michigan State University
Institute for Community Development
Kellogg Center
East Lansing, MI 48824

Mitre Corp. . . . . Mitre Corporation
Rt. 62
Bedford, MA 01730

Moffat, Yard. . . . . Moffat, Yard (Defunct)

Monthly Rev Pr. . . . . . . Monthly Review Press
62 W. 14th St.
New York, NY 10011

Monument Bar Assn. . . . Monumental Bar Association

Morrow . . . . William Morrow and Co.
105 Madison Ave.
New York, NY 10016

N C B L. . . . . National Conference of Black Lawyers
126 W. 119th St.
New York, NY 10026

N I C. . . . . National Institute of Corrections
320 1st St., N.W.
Washington, DC 20534

N L Brown. . . . . N. L. Brown (Defunct)

N Texas St Univ. . . . . . . North Texas State University
Denton, TX 76203

NAACP. . . . . National Association for the Advancement
of Colored People
261 W. 125th St.
New York, NY 10027

NC Prison Project. . . . . . North Carolina Women's Prison Project
(Defunct)

NC Social Stud. . . . . National Council for the Social Studies
3615 Wisconsin Ave., N.W.
Washington, DC 20016

NCCD. . . . . National Council on Crime and Delinquency
Continental Plaza
411 Hackensack Avenue
Hackensack, NJ 07601

NCJISS. . . . . National Criminal Justice Information and
Statistics Service (see Bureau of Justice
Statistics)

NCJRS . . . . National Criminal Justice Reference Service
Box 6000
Rockville, MD 20350

NCLOE . . . . National Commission on Law Observance
and Enforcement (Wickersham Commission) (Defunct)

NE Univ Cent ASR. . . . . . Northeastern University
Center for Applied Social Research
423 UR
Boston, MA 02115

NIAAA . . . . National Institute on Alcohol Abuse &
Alcoholism
5600 Fishers Lane
Rockville, MD 20857

NIJ. . . . . National Institute of Justice
633 Indiana Ave., N.W.
Washington, DC 20531

NILECJ . . . . National Institute of Law Enforcement and
Criminal Justice (Defunct—See National
Institute of Justice)

NIMH. . . . . National Institute of Mental Health
Rockville, MD 20852

NY County L Assn. . . . . . New York County Lawyers' Association
14 Vesey St.
New York, NY 10007

NYC Bd Correct......... New York City Board of Corrections
51 Chambers St
New York, NY 10007

NYC Human Rights...... New York City Commission on
Human Rights
52 Duane St.
New York, NY 10007

NYC Police Dept........ New York City Police Department
1 Police Plaza
New York, NY 10038

Nat Cen Heal Stat...... National Center for Health Statistics
Federal Center Bldg. Rm 1-57
3700 East West Highway
Hyattsville, MD 20782

Nat Cen Juv Just....... National Center for Juvenile Justice
3900 Forbes Avenue
Pittsburgh, PA 15260

Nat Cent Prosec Man... National Center for Prosecution Management
National District Attorneys Association
666 N. Lake Shore Dr., Suite 1432
Chicago, IL 60611

Nat Cent State Cts...... National Center for State Courts
300 Newport Ave.
Williamsburg, Va 23185

Nat Clear Crim Jus..... National Clearinghouse for Criminal
Justice Planning and Architecture
University of Illinois at Urbana-
Champaign
505 East Green St., Suite 200
Champaign, IL 61820

Nat Coal Span Spea.... National Coalition of Spanish Speaking
Mental Health and Human Services
Organizations
1015 15th St., N.W.
Suite 402
Washington, DC 20005

Nat Comm Priso Lab.... National Committee on Prison Labor
(Defunct)

Nat Con Chr & Jews.... National Conference of Christians and
Jews
43 W. 57th St.
New York, Ny 10019

Nat Dist Attys A........ National District Attorneys Association
666 North Lake Shore Drive, Rm. 1432
Chicago, IL 60611

Nat Lawy Guild........ National Lawyers Guild
853 Broadway Rm. 1705
New York, NY 10003

Nat Urb League........ National Urban League, Inc.
500 E. 62 St.
New York, NY 10021

Negro Univ Pr......... Negro Universities Press
Riverside Avenue
Westport, CT 06880

Nelson-Hall........... Nelson-Hall
325 West Jackson Blvd.
Chicago, IL 60606

New Am Lib........... New America Library, Inc.
1301 Avenue of the Americas
New York, NY 10019

New Directions........ New Directions
80 Eighth Ave.
New York, NY 10011

New York Univ........ New York University
New York, NY 10003

New York Univ Pr...... New York University Press
21 W. 4th St.
New York, NY 10012

Northeastern U........ Northeastern University
Boston, MA 02115

Norton............... W. W. Norton and Co.
500 5th Ave.
New York, NY 10036

Oceana Pubs.......... Oceana Publications, Inc.
Dobbs Ferry, NY 10522

Octagon Bks.......... Octagon Books
19 Union Square W.
New York, NY 10003

Office Atty Gen........ State of New Mexico
Office of the Attorney General
P.O. Drawer 1508
Santa Fe, NM 87501

Ohio PO Tr Acad....... Ohio Peace Officers Training Academy
London, OH 43140

Ohio State Univ........ Ohio State University
220 W. 12th Ave.,
Columbus, OH 43210

Ohio State Univ Pr..... Ohio State University Press
Hitchcock Hall,Rm. 316
2070 Neil Avenue
Columbus, OH 43210

OJARS .... Office of Justice Assistance, Research &
Statistics
633 Indiana Ave., N.W.
Washington, DC 20531

Opport Systems........ Opportunity Systems, Inc.
1330 Massachusetts Ave., N.W.
Washington, DC 20005

Outerbridge Lazard.... Outerbridge and Lazard

Overbrook Pr.......... Overbrook Press (Defunct)

Oxford Univ Pr........ Oxford University Press
200 Madison Ave.
New York, NY 10016

Pantheon............. Pantheon Books
Random House, Inc.
201 East 50th St.
New York, NY 10022

Pathfinder Pr.......... Pathfinder Press
410 West St.
New York, NY 10014

Patterson Smith........ Patterson Smith
                        23 Prospect Terrace
                        Montclair, NJ 07042
Penguin Books........ Penguin Books
                      625 Madison Ave.
                      New York, NY 10022
People's Pub Co....... Peoples Publishing Co. (Defunct)
Pergamon Pr.......... Pergamon Press
                      Maxwell House
                      Fairview Park
                      Elmsford, NY 10523
Personnel Decision..... Personnel Decisions, Inc.
                        2515 Foshay Tower
                        Minneapolis, MN 55402
Perspective Pubs....... Perspective Publications
                        509 Madison Avenue
                        New York, NY 10022
Philosophical Lib....... Philosophical Library, Inc.
                         15 E. 40th St.
                         New York, NY 10016
Pocket Books.......... Pocket Books
                       Div. of Simon & Schuster, Inc.
                       1230 Avenue of the Americas
                       New York, NY 10020
Police Foundation...... Police Foundation
                        1909 K St., N.W.
                        Washington, DC 20006
Popular Lib.......... Popular Library
                      1515 Broadway
                      New York, NY 10036
Potomac Associates.... Potomac Associates
                       1707 L St., N.W.
                       Washington, DC 20036
Pr of Benson.......... Press of Benson (Defunct)
Practising L Ins........ Practising Law Institute
                        810 7th Ave.
                        New York, NY 10019
Praeger.............. Praeger Publishing
                      111 Fourth Avenue
                      New York, NY 10003
Prentice-Hall.......... Prentice-Hall, Inc.
                        Englewood Cliffs, NJ 07632
Princeton Univ Pr...... Princeton University Press
                        Princeton, NJ 08540
Public Aff Comm....... Public Affairs Committee
                       381 Park Ave., S.
                       New York, NY 10016
Public Aff Pr.......... Public Affairs Press
                       419 New Jersey Ave.
                       Washington, DC 20003
Putnam.............. Putnam
                     G.P. Putnam's Sons
                     200 Madison Ave.
                     New York, NY 10016
Pyramid.............. Pyramid Publications, Inc.
                      9 Garden St.
                      Moonachie, NJ 07074

Quadrangle Books..... Quadrangle Books
                      12 E Delaware Place
                      Chicago, Il 60611
Quinto Sol Pubs........ Quinto Sol Publications, Inc.
                        P.O. Box 9275
                        Berkeley, CA 94709
R & E Research......... R and E Research Associates, Inc.
                        936 Industrial Ave.
                        Palo Alto, CA 94303
R E Burdick............ R E Burdick, Inc.
                        12-01 12th St.
                        Fairlawn, NJ 07410
Rand Corp............ Rand Corporation
                      1700 Main St.
                      Santa Monica, CA 90406
Rand Instit............ Rand Institute
                       545 Madison Ave.
                       New York, NY 10022
Rand McNally......... Rand McNally
                      P.O. Box 7600
                      Chicago, IL 60680
Random House........ Random House, Inc.
                      201 East 50th St.
                      New York, NY 10022
Reader's Dig Pr........ Reader's Digest Press
                       200 Park Ave.
                       New York, NY 10017
Research Anal Corp.... Research Analysis Corp.
                       McLean, VA
Rice Univ............. Rice University
                      Rice Campus Store
                      P.O. Box 1892
                      Houston, TX 77001
Rinehart.............. Rinehart (Defunct)
Ronald Pr............ Ronald Press
                      605 Third Avenue
                      New York, NY 10016
Routledge & Kegan.... Routledge and Kegan Paul, Ltd.
                      Broadway House
                      68-74 Carter Lane
                      London, England
Royal Soc Medicine.... Royal Society of Medicine
                       Chandos House
                       2 Queen Anne St.
                       London, England W1M OBR
Russell & Russell....... Russell and Russell, Publications
                        597 Fifth Ave.
                        New York, NY 10017
Russell Sage Found.... Russell Sage Foundation
                       230 Park Avenue
                       New York, NY 10017
Rutgers Univ.......... Rutgers University
                       30 College Avenue
                       New Brunswick, NJ 08903

S C S Lynching. . . . . Southern Commission on the
Study of Lynching
Atlanta, GA (Defunct)

S Houston St Univ. . . . . . Sam Houston State University
Huntsville, TX 77340

S Il CSC & Del. . . . . Southern Illinois University
Center for the Study of Crime,
Delinquency and Corrections
Carbondale, IL 62901

S Illinois Univ. . . . . Southern Illinois University
Carbondale, IL 62901

S Illinois Univ Pr. . . . . . . Southern Illinois University Press
Carbondale, IL 62901

S Regional Council. . . . . Southern Regional Council
75 Marietta Street, N.W.
Atlanta, GA 30303

S Regional Ed Bd. . . . . . . Southern Regional Education Board
130 Sixth St., N.W.
Atlanta, GA 30313

SMU Pr. . . . . Southern Methodist University Press
Dallas, TX 75275

SMU Stud Soc. . . . . Southern Methodist University
Studies in Sociology
Dallas, TX 75275

SUNY Albany. . . . . State University of New York at Albany
1400 Washington Avenue
Albany, NY 12222

SUNYA C J. . . . . State University of New York at Albany
School of Criminal Justice
135 Western Avenue
Albany, NY 12222

Safer Society Pr. . . . . Safer Society Press
3049 East Genesee Street
Syracuse, NY 13224

Sage. . . . . Sage Publications Inc.
275 South Beverly Drive
Beverly Hills, CA 90212

Sam Houston CJC. . . . . . Sam Houston State University
Criminal Justice Center
Huntsville, TX 77340

Sam Houston ICC. . . . . . Sam Houston State University
Institute of Contemporary Corrections
and Behavioral Science
Huntsville, TX 77340

San Jose St Col. . . . . San Jose State College
San Jose, CA 95192

Scarecrow Pr. . . . . Scarecrow Press
52 Liberty Street
Box 656
Metuchen, NJ 08840

Schenkman Pub. . . . . . . Schenkman Publishing Co.
3 Mount Auburn Place
Cambridge, MA 02138

Schocken. . . . . Schocken Books
200 Madison Avenue
New York, NY 10016

Sci & Behav Bks. . . . . Science and Behavior Books
P.O. Box 11457
Palo Alto, CA 94306

Scott Foresman. . . . . Scott Foresman and Co.
1900 East Lake Avenue
Glenview, IL 60025

Scribner's. . . . . Charles Scribner's Sons
597 5th Avenue
New York, NY 10017

Seabury Pr. . . . . The Seabury Press
815 Second Avenue
New York, NY 10017

Second Coming Pr. . . . . . Second Coming Press
P. O. Box 31249
San Francisco, CA 94131

Seminar Pr. . . . . Seminar Press
111 Fifth Street
New York, NY 10003

Signet. . . . . Signet
c/o New American Library, Inc.
1301 Avenue of the Americas
New York, NY 10019

Simon & Schuster. . . . . . Simon and Schuster
1 West 39th Street
New York, NY 10018

Social Res Group. . . . . . Social Research Group
University of California
Berkeley, CA 94720

Social Sci Pr. . . . . The Social Science Press
P.O. Box 5188
Southern Station
Hattiesburg, MS 39401

Social Sci Res C. . . . . Social Science Research Council
605 Third Avenue
New York, NY 10016

Southern Univ. . . . . Texas Southern University
Houston, TX 77004

Spectrum Pub. . . . . Spectrum Publications
175-20 Wexford Terrace
Jamaica, NY 11432

St Louis Univ. . . . . St. Louis University
St. Louis, MO 63104

Stanford Univ. . . . . Stanford University
Stanford, CA 94305

Stanford Univ Pr. . . . . . . Stanford University Press
Stanford, CA 94305

Stanley Paul. . . . . Stanley Paul and Co.
London, England

Stein & Day. . . . . Stein and Day
Scarborough House
Briarcliff Manor, NY 10510

Stoeger . . . . Stoeger Publishing Co.
55 Ruta Court
Hackensack, NJ 07606

Swallow Pr. . . . . Swallow Press
811 West Junior Terrace
Chicago, IL 60613

Syracuse Univ. . . . . Syracuse University
Syracuse, NY 13210

Syracuse Univ Pr. . . . . . . Syracuse University Press
1011 East Water Street
Syracuse, NY 13210

Tavistock . . . . Tavistock Publications Ltd.
11 New Fetter Lane
London EC4P 4EE England

Temple Univ Pr. . . . . Temple University Press
Philadelphia, PA 19122

Tex Christian U Pr. . . . . . Texas Christian University Press
Box 30783
Fort Worth, TX 76129

Thos R Gray. . . . . Thomas R. Gray (Defunct)

Thos Y Crowell. . . . . Thomas Y Crowell, Co.
c/o Harper & Row, Pub.
Scranton, PA 18512

Transaction Books. . . . . . Transaction Books
Bldg. 4051, Rutger-State University
New Brunswick, NJ 08903

Tuskegee Institute. . . . . Tuskegee Institute
Tuskegee, AL 36088

Twayne . . . . Twayne Publishers, Inc.
G. K. Hall & Co.
70 Lincoln St.
Boston, MA 0211

U of Penn P & U P. . . . . . University of Pennsylvania
School of Public and Urban Policy
39th and Walnut Streets
Philadelphia, PA 19104

U CA Chicano Stud. . . . . University of California
Chicano Studies Center
3121 Campbell Hall
405 Hilgard Avenue
Los Angeles, CA 90024

U CA Inst G and PA. . . . . University of California
Institute of Governmental and Public
Affairs
Berkeley, CA 94720

U CA Inst G Stud. . . . . . . University of California—Berkeley
Institute of Governmental Studies
109 Moses Hall
Berkeley, CA 94720

U CA Inst Ind Rel. . . . . . . University of California
Institute of Industrial Relations
405 Hilgard Avenue
Los Angeles, CA 90024

U CA Mex Am S P. . . . . . University of California
Mexican American Studies Project
Los Angeles, CA 90024

U CA Pr. . . . . University of California Press
2223 Fulton Street
Berkeley, CA 94720

U CO TriEthn R P. . . . . . . University of Colorado
Tri-Ethnic Research Project
Boulder, CO 80309

U Calif Sant Barb. . . . . . University of California at Santa Barbara
Santa Barbara, CA 93106

U Chicago Ind R C. . . . . . University of Chicago
Industrial Relations Center
Chicago, IL 60637

U Notre Dame Pr. . . . . . . University of Notre Dame Press
Notre Dame, IN 46556

Univ Mich-Wayne S. . . . University of Michigan-Wayne State
Institute of Labor and Industrial Relations
401 Fourth Street
Ann Arbor, MI 48106

Univ Microfilms. . . . . . . University Microfilms
300 N. Zeeb Rd.
Ann Arbor, MI 48106

Univ Minn CU & RA. . . . . University of Minnesota
College of Urban and Regional Affairs
Minneapolis, MN 55455

UCLA . . . . University of California at Los Angeles
Los Angeles, CA 90024

US Bureau Prisons. . . . . . U.S. Bureau of Prisons
320 1st Street, N.W.
Washington, DC 20534

US Comp Gen. . . . . U.S. Comptroller General
441 G Street, N.W.
Washington, DC 20548

US Congress. . . . . U.S. Congress
The Capitol
Washington, DC 20510

US Dept HEW. . . . . U.S. Department of Health, Education
and Welfare
(now Dept. of Health & Human Services)
200 Independence Avenue, S.W.
Washington, DC 20201

US Dept Justice. . . . . U.S. Department of Justice
Constitution Avenue and 110th St., N.W.
Washington, DC 20530

US Dept Labor. . . . . U.S. Department of Labor
200 Constitution Avenue, N.W.
Washington, DC 20210

US GAO. . . . . U.S. General Accounting Office
441 G Street, N.W.
Washington, DC 20548

US Internat Univ. . . . . . . United States International University
10455 Pomerado Rd.
San Diego, CA 92131

US News Books. . . . . U.S. News Books
2300 N Street, N.W.
Washington, DC 20037

USCCR . . . . U.S. Commission on Civil Rights
1121 Vermont Avenue, N.W.
Washington, DC 20425

USCSC . . . . U.S. Civil Service Commission
Federal Plaza
New York, NY 10007

USGPO. . . . . Superintendent of Documents
U.S. Government Printing Office
North Capitol and H Streets, N.W.
Washington, DC 20401

Ummah . . . . Ummah Publications, Inc.
P.O. Box 1814
Hyattsville, MD 20781

Unitarian U S C. . . . . Unitarian Universalist Service Committee
1251 2nd Avenue
San Francisco, CA 94122

United Brethren. . . . . . . United Brethren Publishing Co. (Defunct)

Univ of Calif. . . . . University of California
Berkeley, CA 94720

Univ of Colorado. . . . . . University of Colorado
Denver, CO 80202

Univ of Denver. . . . . University of Denver
Denver, CO 80208

Univ of Illinois. . . . . University of Illinois
Chicago Circle
Chicago, IL 60680

Univ of Kansas. . . . . University of Kansas
Lawrence, KS 66045

Univ of Michigan. . . . . . University of Michigan
Ann Arbor, MI 48104

Univ of Missouri. . . . . . . University of Missouri
Kansas City, MO 64110

Univ of Montana. . . . . . . University of Montana
Missoula, MT 59812

Univ of N Car. . . . . University of North Carolina
Chapel Hill, NC 27514

Univ of Penn. . . . . University of Pennsylvania
Philadelphia, PA 19104

Univ of Penn Pr. . . . . University of Pennsylvania Press
3933 Walnut Street
Philadelphia, PA 19104

Univ of Pitts. . . . . University of Pittsburgh
Pittsburgh, PA 19104

Univ of S Calif. . . . . University of Southern California
University Park
Los Angeles, CA 90007

Univ of Stockholm. . . . . University of Stockholm
Stockholm, Sweden

Univ of Tenn Pr. . . . . University of Tennessee Press
293 Communications Bldg.
Knoxville, TN 37916

Univ of Tennessee. . . . . University of Tennessee
Knoxville, TN 37916

Univ of Utah. . . . . University of Utah
Salt Lake City, UT 84112

Univ of Virginia. . . . . . . University of Virginia
Charlottesville, VA 22903

Univ of Wisconsin. . . . . . University of Wisconsin
Madison, WI 53706

Univ AL Pr. . . . . University of Alabama Press
Box 2877
University, AL 35486

Univ Ariz Pr. . . . . University of Arizona Press
P.O. Box 3398
Tucson, AZ 85722

Univ Chicago Pr. . . . . . . University of Chicago Press
5801 South Ellis Ave.
Chicago, IL 60637

Univ Illinois Pr. . . . . University of Illinois Press
54 E. Gregory Dr., P.O. Box 5081
Station A
Champaign, IL 61820

Univ Iowa Soc Wk. . . . . . University of Iowa
School of Social Work
Iowa City, IA 52242

Univ MD ICJ & C. . . . . . . University of Maryland
Institute for Criminal Justice and
Criminology
1101 Undergraduate Library Bldg.
College Park, MD 20742

Univ Michigan Pr. . . . . . University of Michigan Press
P.O. Box 1104
Ann Arbor, MI 48106

Univ Minn Pr. . . . . University of Minnesota Press
2037 University Ave., W.E.
Minneapolis, MN 55455

Univ N Car Pr. . . . . University of North Carolina Press
P.O. Box 2288
Chapel Hill, NC 27514

Univ N Mex Pr. . . . . University of New Mexico Press
1812 Las Lomas, N.E.
Alburquerque, NM 87131

Univ Oklahoma Pr. . . . . University of Oklahoma Press
1005 Asp Ave.
Norman, OK 73019

Univ Pittsburgh Pr. . . . . . University of Pittsburgh Press
126 N. Bellefield Ave.
Pittsburgh, PA 15260

Univ Pr America. . . . . . . University Press of America
4710 Auth Place, S.E.
Washington, DC 20023

Univ Puerto Rico. . . . . . . University of Puerto Rico
P.O. Box X, U.P.R. St.
Rio Piedras, PR 00931

Univ Research Corp. . . . University Research Corporation
5530 Wisconsin Ave.
Washington, DC 20015

Univ S CA Pr. . . . . University of Southern California Press
Student Union 400
University of Southern California
Los Angeles, CA 90007

Univ Texas Austin. . . . . . University of Texas at Austin
Austin, TX 78712

Univ Tex Cen S H R. . . . . University of Texas
Center for the Study of Human Resources
Austin, TX 78712

Univ Texas Pr. . . . . University of Texas Press
P.O. Box 7819
University Station
Austin, TX 78712

Univ Toronto Pr. . . . . University of Toronto Press
St. George Campus
Toronto, Ontario M5S 1A6 Canada

Univ Washington Pr. . . . University of Washington Pr
Seattle, WA 98105

Univ Wisc Inst RP. . . . . . . University of Wisconsin
Institute for Research on Poverty
3412 Social Science Bldg.
1180 Observatory Drive
Madison, WI 53706

Univ Wisconsin Pr. . . . . . University of Wisconsin Press
114 North Murray St.
Madison, WI 53715

Urban Info Interpr. . . . . . Urban Information Interpreters, Inc.
P.O. Box AH
College Park, MD 20740

Utah C Cr J Admin. . . . . Utah Council on Criminal Justice
Administration
Dept. of Social Services
255 S. Third East
Salt Lake City, UT 84111

Van Nostrand. . . . . Van Nostrand Pub. Co.
135 W. 50th St.
New York, NY 10020

Vance Bibliog. . . . . Vance Bibliographies
P.O. Box 229
Monticello, IL 61856

Vanguard Pr. . . . . Vanguard Press
424 Madison Ave.
New York, NY 10017

Viking Pr. . . . . The Viking Press
625 Madison Avenue
New York, NY 10022

Vintage . . . . Vintage Books
c/o Random House, Inc.
201 E. 50th St.
New York, NY 10022

W B Saunders. . . . . W. B. Saunders and Co.
Columbia Broadcasting System, Inc.
West Washington Square
Philadelphia, PA 19105

W H Freeman. . . . . W. H. Freeman
1736 Stocton St.
San Francisco, CA 94133

W I C H E. . . . . Western Interstate Commission for
Higher Education
P.O. Drawer P
Boulder, CO 80302

Wadsworth Pub Co. . . . . Wadsworth Publishing Co.
10 Davis Dr.
Belmont, CA 94002

Walker & Co. . . . . Walker and Company
720 Fifth Avenue
New York, NY 10019

Wash Univ S S Inst. . . . . Washington University
Social Science Institute
St. Louis, MO 63130

Washington St Univ. . . . Washington State University
Pullman, WA 99163

Washington Univ. . . . . . Washington University
St. Louis, MO 63130

Wayne St Univ. . . . . Wayne State University
The Leonard N. Simons Bldg.
5959 Woodward Ave.
Detroit, MI 48202

Weidenfel & Nich. . . . . . Weidenfeld and Nicholson Ltd.
11 St. Johns Hill
London SW11 1XA England

Wesleyan U C Adv S. . . . Wesleyan University
Center for Advanced Studies
55 High St.
Middletown, CT 06457

Wetzel Pub Co. . . . . Wetzel Publishing Co. (Defunct)

Whitston Pub Co. . . . . . . Whitston Publishing Co
P.O. Box 958
Troy, NY 12181

Wider Opp Women. . . . Wider Opportunities for Women, Inc.
1511 K St., N.W.
Suite, 345
Washington, DC 20005

Wiley . . . . John Wiley and Sons
605 3rd Ave.
New York, NY 10016

William Frederick. . . . . . William-Frederick Press
308 E 79th St.
New York, NY 10021

Williams & Wilkins. . . . . The Williams and Wilkins Company
428 East Preston Street
Baltimore, MD 21201

Wm Alling. . . . . William Alling (Defunct)

Wm Harned. . . . . William Harned (Defunct)

World. . . . . World Publishing Co. (Defunct)

World Soc Cong. . . . . . . World Sociology Congress
International Sociological Association
P.O. Box 719, Station A
Montreal, PQ, Canada H3C ZV2

Yale Univ. . . . . Yale University
New Haven, CT 06520

Yale Univ Pr. . . . . Yale University Press
92 A Yale Station
New Haven, CT 06520

Youth Authority. . . . . . . State of California
Department of the Youth Authority
4241 Williamsborough Drive
Sacramento, CA 95823

Zebra/Scorpio . . . . Zebra/Scorpio
21 EAst 40th Street
New York, NY 10016

ABBREVIATIONS

abst . . . . abstract
Ag . . . . August
ann . . . . annual
annot . . . . annotated
anon . . . . anonymous
anthol . . . . anthology
Ap . . . . April
assoc . . . . association
Aut . . . . Autumn
bd . . . . board
bi-ann . . . . bi-annual
bibliog . . . . bibliography
bi-m . . . . bi-monthly
cen . . . . center
comp(s) . . . . compiler(s)
conf . . . . conference
cont . . . . continued, continuation
crim . . . . crime, criminal
crim just . . . . criminal justice
D . . . . December
diss . . . . dissertation
dist . . . . district
ed(s) . . . . editor(s)
F . . . . February
Fl . . . . Fall
glos . . . . glossary
govt . . . . government
il . . . . illustrated
intnl . . . . international
intro . . . . introduction, introduced
intvw . . . . interview
j . . . . justice
Ja . . . . January
Je . . . . June
Jl . . . . July
jr . . . . junior
jt auth . . . . joint author
jt ed . . . . joint editor
just . . . . justice
LEAA . . . . Law Enforcement Assistance Administration
M . . . . May
m . . . . monthly
mono . . . . monograph

Mr . . . . March
N . . . . November
NACCJSG . . . . National Advisory Commission on Criminal Justice Standards and Goals (1971-73)
NCCD . . . . National Council on Crime and Delinquency
NCJRS . . . . National Criminal Justice Reference Service
NCLOE . . . . National Commission on Law Observance and Enforcement (Wickersham Commission, 1929-31)
n.d. . . . . no date
no . . . . number
n.p. . . . . no place
O . . . . October
p . . . . page
pol . . . . police
poli . . . . political
Pres Crime Comm. . President's Commission on Law Enforcement and Administration of Justice (1965-67)
pseud . . . . pseudonym
pt(s) . . . . part(s)
pub . . . . publisher, published
q . . . . quarterly
res . . . . research
rev . . . . revised, review
S . . . . September
2d . . . . second
Spr . . . . Spring
sr . . . . senior
St . . . . State
stat . . . . statistics
Sum . . . . Summer
supp . . . . supplement
3d . . . . third
tr . . . . translated, translator
univ . . . . university
unpub . . . . unpublished
US . . . . United States
v . . . . volume(s)
Wint . . . . Winter

Guidance on the Use of the Subject Index

The Subject Index contains an alphabetical listing of significant keywords and proper names which describe the subject content of the materials indexed. Works are listed under numerous subject headings to increase their accessibility and to make the references under each subject descriptor as comprehensive as possible. Extensive cross referencing is also provided.

The following categories demonstrate the nature and scope of the subject headings:

1. Racial and ethnic groups (e.g., ASIAN— AMERICANS, BLACKS, HISPANICS, INDIANS, ITALIANS, WHITES, etc.);

2. Geographic locations, including regions, states, counties, and cities;

3. Substantive issues, such as AFFIRMATIVE ACTION, ALCOHOL, ATTITUDES TOWARD CRIMINAL JUSTICE, CIVIL RIGHTS, CRIME AND RACE, CRIMINOLOGY, DEATH PENALTY, HOMICIDE, POLICE - DEADLY FORCE, PRISON REFORM. etc.;

4. Noted individuals who are the subject of specific writings (e.g., J. EDGAR HOOVER, GEORGE JACKSON, REV. MARTIN LUTHER KING JR., MARVIN E. WOLFGANG, et al.);

5. Names of institutions, organizations, and agencies (e.g., ATTICA PRISON, NY: BLACK PANTHERS: PRESIDENT'S CRIME COMMISSION: LEAA, U S SUPREME COURT, etc.);

6. Specific topics, such as BLACK-ON-BLACK CRIME, EXECUTION SERMONS, OFFENDER-BASED STATISTICS, TONG WARS, etc.

Entries under each subject heading are listed chronologically, starting with the oldest publication indexed and ending with the most recent. This feature is intended to help the reader gain a better insight as to how the literature on a particular topic has developed over time. It is also consistent with the Editor's attempt to devote special attention to historical development and historical studies.

Following each of the more than 900 key words included in this subject listing, the reader will find the bibliography for each subject heading. The title and author's last name of each document is provided. For more detailed information on these works, simply consult the Author Index with Abstracts. Scan the alphabetical listing of subject descriptors for the topic or topics you are researching.

AFFIRMATIVE ACTION

Blacks Versus Women—When Victims Collide. Hogan, B.

Affirmative Discrimination: Ethnic Inequality And Public Policy. Glazer, Nathan.

California: Affirmative Action Statistics, Report No 3. California Dept Of The Youth Authority.

Marquette University—Center For Criminal Justice Agency Organization And Minority Employment Opportunities—Final Report. Marquette University, Center For Criminal Justice Agency Organization .

Minority Recruitment Handbook, Revd, (Commission On Peace Officer Stand & Training). Williams, F E.

Race Relations In Corrections—An Annotated Bibliography. American Bar Association.

Report Of The LEAA Task Force On Women. U S Dept Of Justice, LEAA.

Changing Status Of Women In Police Professions. Stuart, C G.

Discrimination In Selection And Promotion Of Minorities And Women In Municipal Employment. Ivie, S D.

Equal Employment Opportunity And Affirmative Action In Law Enforcement Agencies. Jefferson, A M.

Law Enforcement And Affirmative Action. Williams, Samuel L.

Minority Recruiting: The Tucson Police Experience. Grant, R and Milne, R and White, R.

Recruitment And Promotion Of A Minority Group Into An Established Institution—The Police. Regoli, R M and Jerome, D E.

Women In Corrections—A Process Of Change. Becker, A M.

Affirmative Action—The Answer To Discrimination? American Enterprise Institute For Public Policy Research.

Manual For The Recruitment Of Minority And Females. Avello, J A and Mendoza, M G.

Minority Recruitment Manual For Ohio Peace Officers Report, 1977. Snarr, R W and Mc Cauley, R P.

Study Of Problems And Methods Of Police Recruitment From Disadvantaged Minorities. Gazell, James A.

A View Of The Quota System In The San Francisco Police Department. Balzer, A.

Affirmative Action Position. Berman, S.

Affirmative Action And The Quest For Job Equality. Hill, H.

Equal Employment Opportunity—Affirmative Action Programs For Federal Government Contractors. Kelly, R S and Thorkelson, M M.

Evaluating The -impact Of Affirmative Action—A Look At The Federal Contract Compliance Program—A Symposium. Lipsky, D B (ed).

Minority Employment In Police Services—A Management Analysis For Police Departments. Moore, L M and Schwartz, J A.

Recruitment And Retention Of Minority Race Persons As Police Officers. Van Blaricon, D P.

Special Task Force—Positive Recruitment Of Qualified Minorities. Ronzan, J.

Ten Maxims: Minority Recruitment And Retention. Witt, James and Robinson, Eugene.

Women In Criminal Justice—A Policy Statement. National Council On Crime And Delinquency.

Women In Policing. Triplett, Peggy E.

Women In The Criminal Justice System. Robinson, L O.

Women Judges. Sassower, D L.

Affirmative Action Versus Seniority—Is Conflict Inevitable? Cebulski, B G.

Affirmative Action For Women—A Practical Guide For Women And Management. Jongeward, D and Scott, D.

Affirmative Action—A Guide For The Perplexed. Squires, G D.

Candidate Preparation And Retention. Reynolds, L H.

Development Of A Comprehensive Personnel Plan For Non–Judicial Employees Of The Kansas Appellate Courts. Lawson, H O and Kuban, G B.

Eliminators. Reynolds, L H.

How To Utilize Community Resources. Reynolds, L H.

Institutes On Affirmative Action Leadership Development In Correctional Institutions: Final Report. National Civil Service League.

Oral Interview Standards. Reynolds, L H.

Police Personnel Selection Process. Territo, L and Swanson Jr, C R and Chamelin, N C.

Potential Candidates And Using Community Resources For Recruiting. Reynolds, L H.

Recruitment And Retention Of Females In Law Enforcement Occupations. Dutton, A and Britt, B.

Wisconsin Council On Criminal Justice: Equal Opportunity/Affirmative Action Program For 1978. Robinson, N E.

Working For You—A Guide To Employing Women In Non–Traditional Jobs. Hart, L G.

Blacks And Women To Be Hired For Louisiana Police–Fire Jobs. Marro, Anthony.

Equal Employment Opportunity For Minorities In Municipal Government. Hall, G and Saltzstein, A.

Four Cities In Louisiana Defy US On Hiring More Blacks And Women. Anonymous.

Norwalk Police Battle In Court Over Racial Hiring Issues. Tomasson, Robert E.

Police Are Sued. Anonymous.

Police Recruit Minorities. Anonymous.

Reversing Discrimination—A Perspective. Pati, G and Reilly, C W.

The Bakke Debate: A Mexican–American Protests That Affirmative Action Is Unfair To Minorities. Rodriguez, R.

Law Enforcement Minority Manpower Project—Final Report. Reynolds, L H.

Leadership By Women In Criminal Justice—There Is Room At The Top. Strosnider, C S.

An Approach To Minority Recruitment. Goff, R W.

An Historical Perspective On The Constitutional Debate Over Affirmative Action Admissions. Kimball, Bruce A.

Commitment To The Disadvantaged Among Urban Administrators—The Case Of Minority Hiring. Thompson, F J and Brown, B.

Integrating The Keepers: A Comparison Of Black And White Prison Guards In Illinois. Jacobs, James B and Kraft, Larry J.

Minorities Employed In Law Libraries. Brecht, A and Mills, R.

Affirmative Action—A Comprehensive Recruitment Manual. Calvert, R J R.

Affirmative Action In Criminal Justice. U S Dept Of Justice, National Criminal Justice Reference Service.

Capable Cops—Women Behind The Shield—A Selected Bibliography On Women Police Officers. Martin, C A.

General Recruitment Strategies For Criminal Justice Agencies. National Criminal Justice Reference Service.

The Impact Of Affirmative Action And Civil Service On American Police Personnel Systems. Locke, Hubert G.

Critical Equal Employment Issues In Criminal Justice. Jones, Clinton B.

Enforcement Workshop—Minority Quotas For Police Promotions: A Comment On Detroit Police Officers Association Versus Young. Sherman, Lawrence W.

Minority Police Hiring—Is Cooperation Possible? Saudler, D.

Preferential Remedies And Affirmative Action In Employment In The Wake Of *Bakke.* Edwards, Harry T.

Race As An Employment Qualification To Meet Police Department Operational Needs. Comment.

Should There Be Affirmative Action For The Judiciary? Goldman, S.

The Thirteenth Amendment And Private Affirmative Action. Note.

Women Police: A Study Of Education, Attitudes, Problems. Martin, C A.

Affirmative Action Equal Employment Opportunity In The Criminal Justice System: A Selected Bibliography. U S Dept Of Justice, National Institute Of Justice.

Women As Probation Parole, And Correctional Officers In The Criminal Justice Field—A Selected Bibliography. Martin, C A.

Hispanics Underrepresented As Criminal Justice Professionals. Carro, John.

Hispanics In The System—Trying To Count The Numbers. Castro, Agenor L.

Sex Discrimination In Prison Employment: The Bona Fide Occupational Qualification And Prisoners' Privacy Rights. Tharnish, D M.

Tapping The Talents Of A New Generation. Mendoza, Ruben.

AFRICAN COLONIZATION MOVEMENT

The African Colonization Movement, 1816–1865. Staudenraus, P J.

The Black Image In The White Mind: The Debate On Afro–American Character And Destiny, 1817–1914. Frederickson, George M.

AFRO-AMERICANS *see* Blacks

AGE

Intelligence, Race, And Age As Selective Factors In Crime. Fox, Vernon.

Pilot Study: Age, Race And Recidivism As Factors In Prison Infractions. Johnson, Elmer H.

AGE

Age Composition And Patterns Of Change In Criminal Statistics. Sagi, P and Wellford, C.

Age, Occupation And Conviction Rates Of White And Negro Males: A Case Study. Forslund, Morris A.

Juvenile Delinquents: Relationships Between Wisc Scores, Offenses, Race, Chronological Age, And Residence. Mc Conochie, W A.

Standardization Of Negro Crime Rates For Negro–White Differences In Age And Status. Forslund, Morris A and Malry, L.

Mortality Trends For Homicide By Age, Color, And Sex: United States, 1960–1972. Klebba, A Joan.

Changing Patterns Of Delinquent Behavior Among Americans 13–16 Years Old, 1967-1972: Report # 1 Of The National Survey Of Youth, 1972. Gold, Martin and Reimer, David J.

Changing Patterns Of Delinquent Behavior Among Americans 13 Through 16 Years Old: 1967–1972. Gold, Martin and Reimer, David.

"Crimes Against The Elderly––Findings From Interviews With Blacks, Mex–Amer, And Whites" in *Justice And Older Americans*, Young, M (ed). Ragan, P K.

Justice And Older Americans. Young, Marlene A (ed).

The Drug Arrest: Empirical Observations On The Age, Sex And Race Of Drug Law Offenders In A Midwestern City. Petersen, D M and Schwirian, K P and Bleda, S E.

Violent Crime Perpetrated Against The Elderly In The City Of Dallas, October 1974–September 1975. Georges, Daniel E and Kirksey, Kirk.

"Minority Elderly" in *Police And The Elderly*, Goldstein, A P et al (eds). Wise, V L and Hoyer, W J.

Stress And Old Age. Watson, Wilbur.

AGENT PROVOCATEUR see Police, Investigation

AGGRESSION

"Overcrowding And Human Aggression" in *The History Of Violence In America*, Graham, Hugh D And T Gurr (eds), 751-761. Carstairs, George M.

Aggressive Behavior Of Delinquent, Dependent, And 'Normal' White And Black Boys In Social Conflicts. Berger, Stephen E and Tedeschi, James T.

Aggression And Ghetto–Reared American Negro Children. Meers, D R and Gordon, G .

Biracial Aggression: I, Effect Of Verbal Attack And Sex Of Victim. Gentry, W D.

Variables In Interracial Aggression Anonymity, Expected Retaliation, And A Riot. Donnerstein, Edward et al.

Physical Aggression As A Function Of Racial Prejudice And The Race Of The Target. Genthner, R W and Taylor, S P.

The Fire This Time: Effects Of Race Of Target, Insult, And Potential Retaliation On Black Aggression. Wilson, L and Rogers, R W.

Effects Of Class, Race, Sex And Educational Status On Patterns Of Aggression Of Lower Class Youth. Lucterhand, Elmer and Weller, Leonard.

Tests Of The Language–Aggression Hypothesis. Boone, S L and Moutare, A.

"Aggressive And Simple Sociopaths: Ten Years Later" in *Biology And Crime*, Jeffrey, C R (ed). Dynes, Patrick S and Carlson, Eric W and Allen, Harry E.

ALABAMA

see also Birmingham, Al, Montgomery, Al

Child Saving In Alabama. Washington, Josephine T.

Scottsboro Boy. Patterson, Haywood and Conrad, Earl.

The Youthful Male Offender In Alabama: A Study In Delinquency Causation. Caldwell, Morris G.

Report Of The Pennsylvania Joint Legislative Committee On Capital Punishment. Joint Legis Comm On Capital Punishment.

Hustler: The Autobiography Of A Thief, R Lincoln Keiser (ed). Williamson, Henry (pseudonym).

All God's Dangers: The Life Of Nate Shaw. Rosegarten, Theodore.

Alabama's State Police Leads In Black Percentage With 4:5%. Anonymous.

"Classifying Black Inmates: The Alabama Prison Classification Project" in *Blacks And Criminal Justice*, Owens And Bell (eds), 129–142. Owens, Charles E.

Alabama Bound: Forty–Five Years Inside A Prison System. March, Ray A.

Balancing Inmates' Rights To Privacy With Equal Employment For Prison Guards. Reisner, S L.

ALASKA

see also Fairbanks, Ak

Suicide And Culture In Fairbanks: A Comparison Of Three Cultural Groups In A Small City Of Interior Alaska. Parkin, M.

Alaska Felony Sentencing Patterns: A Multivariate Statistical Analysis (1974–1976), Preliminary Report. Alaska Judicial Council.

Judicial Council Findings Regarding Possible Racial Impact In Sentencing. Alaska Judicial Council.

Statistical Analysis Of Misdemeanor Sentences In Anchorage And Fairbanks: 1974–1976. Rubinstein, Michael L and Maroules, Nicholas and White, Teresa.

ALBANY, NY

The Big Blue Line: Police Power Versus Human Rights. Cray, Ed.

Varieties Of Police Behavior: The Management Of Law And Order In Eight Communities. Wilson, James Q.

The Cops Can't Find The Pusher. Christianson, K Scott.

In Prison: A Contagion Of Suicide. Christianson, Scott.

Black Arson In Albany, NY: November 1793. Gerlach, Don R.

Visible Man: A True Story Of Post–Racist America. Gilder, George.

The Regimentation Of Blacks On The Urban Frontier In Colonial Albany, New York City And Philadelphia. Williams, Oscar R.

ALBUQUERQUE, NM

The World Of The Burglar: Five Criminal Lives. David, Pedro R.

ALCOHOL

Negro Crime And Strong Drink. Washington, Booker T.

Indians, Alcohol And Homicide. Baker, J L.

A Study Of The Negro Alcoholic. Strayer, R.

The Negro Drinker And Assaulter As A Criminal Type. Roebuck, Julian B and Johnson, R.

Questions Regarding American Indian Criminality. Stewart, Omer.

Drinking Patterns And Alcoholism Among American Negroes. Sterne, M.

"Pauperism And Alcoholism" in *The Philadelphia Negro*, Orig Pub 1899, 269–286. Du Bois, W E B.

Task Force Report: Drunkenness. President's Comm On Law Enforcement & Adm Of Justice.

Navajo Drinking: Some Tentative Hypotheses. Ferguson, Francis N.

Alcohol Abuse: A Crucial Factor In The Social Problems Of Negro Men. King, Lucy J et al.

Gambling And Alcoholism: Symptom Substitution And Functional Equivalents. Adler, N and Goleman, D.

Navajo Criminal Homicide. Levy Jerrold E and Kunitz, Stephen J and Everett, Michael.

Alcoholism, Sex, Socioeconomic Status And Race In Two Hospitalized Samples. Rimmer, J et al.

Ascertaining Police Bias In Arrests For Drunken Driving. Hyman, Merton M and Helrich, Alice R and Benson, Gwen.

Hidden Deviance And The Labelling Approach: The Case For Drinking And Driving. Marshall, Harvey and Purdy, Ross.

Indian Drinking Patterns. Lurie, Nancy Oestreich.

Violent Death And Alcohol Use Among The Chippewa In Minnesota. Westermeyer, Joseph and Brantner, John.

"Indian Drinking: Problems Of Data Collection And Interpretation" in *Proceedings Of The 1st Annual Alcohol Conf, NIAAA*, 217–236. Levy, Jerrold E and Kunitz, Stephen J.

Suicide, Homicide, And Alcoholism Among American Indians—Guidelines For Help. Frederick, C J.

Cops And Drunks—Police Attitudes And Actions In Dealing With Drunks. Stratton, J.

Alcoholic Sensitivity And Ethnic Background. Ewing, J A and Rouse, B A and Pellizzari, E D.

Alcohol Abuse And Black America. Harper, Frederick D (ed).

Alcohol Legalization And Native Americans: A Sociological Inquiry. May, Phillip A.

Alcohol Use Among Native Americans: A Selective Annotated Bibliography. Street, P B and Wood, R C and Chowenhill, R C.

Alcohol Use Among The Spanish Speaking: A Selective Annotated Bibliography. Treiman, B R et al.

"The Impact Of Alcohol On Crime In The Black Community" in *Crime And Its Impact On The Black Community*, Gary, L P & L E Brown (eds), 77–84. Harper, Frederick D.

Alcohol Abuse In The Black Community. Harper, Frederick D and Dawkins, M P.

ARREST

Getting Busted: Personal Experiences Of Arrest, Trial And Prison. Firestone, Ross (ed).

Police And Minority Groups: Toward A Theory Of Negative Contacts. Kuykendall, Jack L.

Race, Social Status, And Criminal Arrest. Green, Edward.

Drug Usage And Arrest Charges: A Study Of Drug Usage And Arrest Charges Among Arrestees In Six Metropolitan Areas Of The United States. Eckerman, William et al.

"Patterns Of Behavior In Police And Citizen Transactions" in *Race, Crime, And Justice*, Reasons, C E And J L Kuykendall (eds), 176–205. Black, Donald J and Reiss Jr, Albert J.

Ascertaining Police Bias In Arrests For Drunken Driving. Hyman, Merton M and Helrich, Alice R and Benson, Gwen.

Patterns Of Arrest And The Dangers Of Public Visibility. Katz, Michael.

Analysis Of Arrest Rates For Trends In Criminality. Blumstein, Alfred and Nagin, Daniel S.

Arrests And Delinquency In Two Generations: A Study Of Black Urban Families And Their Children. Robins, Lee N and West, P A and Herjanic, B L.

Factors Affecting Post Arrest Dispositions: A Model For Analysis. Burke, P and Turk, A.

Policing In A Free Society. Goldstein, Herman.

Race And The Decision To Arrest: An Analysis Of Warrants Issued. Hepburn, John R.

The Blackout, in *1977 Annual Report Of The New York City Board Of Correction*, 17–24. New York City Board Of Correction.

A Report On The Blackout Looting: New York City, July 13, 1977. Curvin, Robert and Porter, Bruce.

Robbery And Burglary—A Study Of The Characteristics Of The Persons Arrested And The Handling Of Their Cases In Court. Williams, K M and Lucianovic, J.

The Rich Get Richer And The Poor Get Prison. Reiman, Jeffrey H.

Wisconsin Criminal Justice Information: Crime And Arrests 1979. Wisconsin Dept Justice, Div Law Enf Serv.

ARRESTS, MASS

Contingency Planning For The Administration Of Justice During Civil Disorder And Mass Arrest. Friedman, H G.

Civil Disturbances, Mass Processing And Misdemeanants: Rights, Remedies And Realities. Ginsberg, George and Starkman, Gary.

The Blackout, in *1977 Annual Report Of The New York City Board Of Correction*, 17–24. New York City Board Of Correction.

ARSON

see also Riots

The Ecology Of Urban Unrest: The Case Of Arson In Newark, New Jersey. Georges, Daniel E.

Black Arson In Albany, NY: November 1793. Gerlach, Don R.

ASIAN-AMERICANS

Pictures Of Old Chinatown. Irwin, Will.

"Race Prejudice And Japanese American Relations" in *Race And Culture*, Hughes, Everett C et al (eds). Park, Robert E.

New Style Highbinder Fights Tong Wars Today. Manion, Jack.

Tong War. Gong, Eng Ying and Grant, Bruce.

Oriental Crime In California: A Study Of Offenses Committed By Orientals In That State, 1900–1927. Beach, W G.

Orientals In American Life. Palmer, Albert.

The Japanese American Cases—A Disaster. Rostow, Eugene V.

Chinatown: Its History, Its People, Its Importance. Jue, George K.

Delinquent, Neglected And Dependent Chinese Boys And Girls Of The San Francisco Bay Region. Lee, R H.

A Study Of Teen-age Behavior Among Negroes, Mexicans, Puerto Ricans, Japanese, Chinese, Filipino And American Indians. Harris, Richard E.

The Chinese In The United States. Lee, Rose Hum.

A Note On Capital Executions In The United States. Sellin, Thorsten.

The Hatchet Men. Dillon, Richard H.

Ethnic Differentials In Delinquency In Honolulu. Voss, Harwin.

Success Story: Japanese-American Style. Peterson, William.

The Chinese Narcotic Addict In The United States. Ball, J C and Lau, M.

Minorities In A Changing World. Barron, Milton L (ed).

The Story Of The Chinese In America. Sung, Betty Lee.

Chinese-American Child-Rearing Practices And Juvenile Delinquency. Sollenberger, Richard T.

Juvenile Delinquency In San Francisco's Chinese-American Community: 1961–1966. Abbott, Kenneth A and Abbott, Elizabeth Lee.

On The Validity Of Official Statistics—A Comparative Study Of White, Black And Japanese High School Boys. Chambliss, William J and Nagasawa, Richard H.

"The Attack On Japanese Americans During World War II" in *Conspiracy*, Curry, Richard O And Thomas M Brown (eds). Tenbroek, Jacobus and Barnhart, Edward N and Matson, Floyd M.

Inter-Ethnic Conflict. Glazer, Nathan.

Characteristics Of The Population By Ethnic Origin: March 1972 And 1971. U S Dept Of Commerce, Bureau Of The Census.

Origins Of Narcotic Control. Musto, David F.

Dispute Settlement In Chinese American Communities. Doo, L W.

Socioeconomic Mobility Among Three Generations Of Japanese Americans. Levine, Gene N and Montero, Darrel M.

Chinese Americans. Lyman, Stanford M.

A Study Of Juvenile Delinquency Amongst Asians And Half-Asians: A Comparative Study In A Northern Town Based On Official Statistics. Batta, I D and Mc Culloch, J W and Smith, N J.

Social Class And Crime: The Case Of The Japanese-Americans. Fujimoto, Tetsuya.

Years Of Infamy. Weglyn, Michi.

Asian American Employment—From Outright Exclusion To Modern Discrimination. Lem, K.

Eskimos, Chicanos, Indians: Children Of Crisis, V4. Coles, Robert.

At The Threshold Of The Golden Gate: Special Problems Of A Neglected Minority. Huang, K and Pilisok, M.

The New Gangs Of Chinatown. Rice, Berkeley.

The Research Experience In A Chinese-American Community. Weiss, Melford S.

Bibliography On Racism: 1972–1975, V2. National Institute Of Mental Health.

"Crime And Criminal Justice: Their Impact Upon Asian American Communities" in *National Minority Advisory Council Report*. Takagi, Paul.

Behind The Gilded Ghetto: An Analysis Of Race, Class And Crime In Chinatown. Takagi, Paul and Platt, Tony.

Chinatown—No Longer A Cozy Assignment. Wilson, Rob.

The Inequality Of Justice: A Report On Crime And The Administration Of Justice In The Minority Coummunity. National Minority Advisory Council On Crim Just.

Race, Crime And Social Policy: The Chinese In Oregon, 1871–1885. Tracy, Charles A.

Lights And Shadows Of Chinatown. Bode, William.

ASPIRATION

Aspiration Levels Of Negro Delinquent, Dependent, And Public School Boys. Mitchell, Lonnie E.

Delinquency And Opportunity: A Theory Of Delinquent Gangs. Cloward, Richard A and Ohlin, Lloyd E.

Socioeconomic Status, Race, Level Of Aspiration And Juvenile Delinquency: A Limited Empirical Test Of Merton's Concept Of Deviation. Epps, Edgar G.

Relative Occupational Anticipations And Aspirations Of Delinquents And Nondelinquents. Frederick, M A and Molnar, M.

Level Of Aspiration And Locus Of Control In Disadvantaged Children. Milgram, N A et al.

Aspiration Vs Opportunity: "Careers" In The Inner City. Bullock, Paul.

Aspirations And Social Concerns—Crime, Blacks, Inequality And Women. Watts, W and Free, L A.

ASSASSINATION

The Last Year Of Malcolm X: The Evolution Of A Revolutionary. Breitman, George.

He Slew The Dreamer: My Search, With James Earl Ray, For The Truth About The Murder Of Martin Luther King. Huie, William Bradford.

An American Death: The True Story Of The Assassination Of Dr Martin Luther King, Jr, And The Greatest Manhunt Of Our Time. Frank, Gerold.

Malcolm X: An Untold Story? Anonymous.

ASSAULT

see also Crime, Violent; Rape; Violence, Criminal

Violent Crime: Homicide, Assault, Rape And Robbery. National Commission On The Causes And Prevention Of Violence.

ATTITUDES TOWARD CRIM JUSTICE

A Survey: Black Attitudes Toward Police And The Courts. Dillingham, Gerald.

Justification For No Obligation: Views Of Black Males Toward Crime And The Criminal Law. Davis, John A.

Evaluating The Police: A Comparison Of Black Street And Household Respondents. Boggs, Sara L and Galliher, John F.

"Black Attitudes Toward Crime And Crime Prevention" in *Crime And Its Impact On The Black Community*, Gary, L E And L P Brown (eds), 13–30. Scott, Elsie K.

Black Perspectives On Crime And The Criminal Justice System. Woodson, Robert L (ed).

State Of Black America, 1977. National Urban League, Inc.

"Perception Of Crime" in *Black Perspectives On Crime And The Criminal Justice System*, Woodson, Robert L (ed), 5–22. Napper, George.

Citizen Contact And Legal System Support. Walker, D.

Having Their Day In Court—Defendant Evaluations Of The Fairness Of Their Treatment. Casper, Jonathan D.

Public Saftey: Crime Is Up, But What About Punishment? Seidman, David.

The Figgie Report On Fear Of Crime: America Afraid, Part 1, The General Public. A–T–O, Inc.

ATTORNEYS

Crime: Its Causes And Treatment. Darrow, Clarence.

The South's Challenge To The Negro Lawyer. Anderson Jr, Charles W.

Negro Lawyers In Virginia: A Survey. Comment.

Bar Must Encourage More Negro Lawyers. Gossett, W T.

Minority Lawyer: Link To The Ghetto. Clark, L D.

The Black Lawyer. Carter, R L.

With Justice For Some: An Indictment Of The Law By Young Advocates. Wasserstein, Bruce (ed) and Green, Mark J (ed).

The National Bar Association—Not Just An Opinion. Ortique, Revius O.

Law Against The People. Letcourt, Robert (ed).

Radical Lawyers: Their Role In The Movement And In The Courts. Black, Jonathan (ed).

A New Role For The Black Law Graduate—A Reality Or An Illusion. Edwards, Harry T.

The Black American And The Legal Profession: A Study Of Commitment. Jackson, Maynard H.

The Black Lawyer, An American Hero. Bell, Edward F.

National Legal Network: Organizing For Change; Black Lawyers And The Criminal Justice System. Hinds, Lennox S.

Minority Opportunities In Law For Blacks, Puerto Ricans And Chicanos. Clark, C P (ed).

Step Toward Equal Justice—Programs To Increase Black Lawyers In The South, 1969–1973. Spearman, R W and Stevens, H.

Black Lawyers Responsibility To Poor Communities. Banks, Sharon P.

The Black Philadelphia Lawyer. Mitchell, Charles L.

From The Black Bar. Ware, Gilbert (ed).

Unequal Justice: Lawyers And Social Change In Modern America. Auerbach, Jerold S.

Counsel For The Poor: Criminal Defense In Urban America. Hermann, Robert and Single, Eric and Boston, John.

Justice And Reform: The Formative Years Of The American Legal Service Program. Johnson Jr, Earl.

Inadequate Defense Counsel—An Empirical Analysis Of Prisoners' Perceptions. Alpert, Geoffrey P.

Team Defense: The Holistic Approach: An Interview With Millard Farmer. Eisenberg, Howard.

ATTITUDES

Changing Attitudes Of Black Youths. Cizanckas, Victor I and Purviance, Carlton W.

AUBURN PRISON, NY

On The Penitentiary System In The United States And Its Application In France, Francis Lieber (trans), Orig Pub 1833. Beaumont, Gustave De and Tocqueville, Alexis De.

AUTHORITY

A Study Of Minority Group Authoritarianism. Adelson, J A.

The Negro Offender: An Urban Research Project. Kephart, William M.

Police Encounters With Juveniles. Piliavin, Irving and Briar, Scott.

Black Resistance Before The Civil War. Cheek, William F (ed).

Race, Maternal Authority And Adolescent Aspiration. Kandel, D B.

Interpersonal Dynamics In A Simulated Prison. Haney, Craig and Banks, Curtis and Zimbardo, Philip.

AUTO THEFT *see* Theft, Motor Vehicles

AWARENESS, RACE

Race Awareness In Young Children. Goodman, M E.

Racial Issues In Corrections: Cultural Awareness—How To Achieve It. Fox, Vernon.

AYUDA

Ayuda. Ahlgren, R D.

BAIL

A Study Of The Administration Of Bail In New York City. Foote, Caleb.

Ransom: A Critique Of The American Bail System. Goldfarb, Ronald L.

A Criminal Justice System And The Indigent. Oaks, Dallin H and Lehman, Warren.

Bail And Civil Disorder. Calista, F P and Domonkas, Michael.

Discrimination Against Negroes In The Adminstration Of Criminal Law In Missouri. Gerard, Jules B and Terry Jr, T Rankin.

New Perspectives On Urban Crime. American Bar Association.

Bail And Pre–Trial Detention In The District Of Columbia: An Empirical Analysis. Just, Bernice.

The Case For Double Jeopardy: Black And Poor. Dolan, Thomas J.

Women's Jail—Pretrial And Post–Conviction Alternatives—A Report On Women Arrested In San Francisco. Bresler, L and Leonard, D.

BAKKE

The Bakke Debate: A Mexican–American Protests That Affirmative Action Is Unfair To Minorities. Rodriguez, R.

Toward An Understanding Of Bakke. U S Commission On Civil Rights.

Preferential Remedies And Affirmative Action In Employment In The Wake Of *Bakke*. Edwards, Harry T.

The *Bakke* Problem—Allocation Of Scarce Resources In Education And Other Areas. Griswold, Erwin N.

BALTIMORE, MD

The Administration Of Rape Cases In The City Of Baltimore And The State Of Maryland. Howard, Joseph C.

Preliminary Report On Crime And Addiction Within A Community—Wide Population Of Narcotic Addicts. Nurco, D N and Du Pont, R L.

BARRIO

The View From The Barrio. Peattie, Lisa R.

El Barrio's Worst Block Is Not All Bad. Burnham, David.

"The Barrio As An Internal Colony," in *Urban Affairs Annual Review*, V6, Hahn, Harlan (ed), 465–498. Berrera, M and Munos, C and Ornelasin, C.

Community Organizing Of Gang Barrios. Pineda, Charles.

Heroin Use In The Barrio. Bullington, Bruce.

Homeboys: Gangs, Drugs, And Prison In The Barrios Of Los Angeles. Moore, Joan et al.

A Model For Chicano Drug Use And For Effective Utilization Of Employment And Training Resources By Barrio Addicts And Ex–Offenders. Chicano Pinto Research Project, Inc.

Chicanos In A Changing Society: From Mexican Pueblos To American Barrios In Santa Barbara And Southern California, 1848–1930. Camarillo, Alberto.

Joan W Moore, Et Al: Homeboys: Gangs, Drugs, And Prisons In The Barrios Of Los Angeles. Trujillo, Larry D.

BEDFORD STUYVESANT, NY

Visibility And Contact With Others: Mediating Factors In The Neighborhood Crime Complex. Kleinman, Paula H and David, Deborah S.

Victimization And Perception Of Crime In A Ghetto Community. Kleinman, Paula H and David, Deborah S.

BEHAVIOR, ANTISOCIAL

Father Absence And Antisocial Behavior In Negro And White Males. Mosher, L R.

BEHAVIOR, VERBAL

Verbal Performance IQ Differences Of White And Negro Delinquents On The WISC And WAIS. Henning, John J and Levy, Russell H.

Biracial Aggression: I, Effect Of Verbal Attack And Sex Of Victim. Gentry, W D.

Adolescent Verbal Behavior—Investigation Of Noncontent Styles As Related To Race And Delinquency Status. Wool, R and Clements, C B.

BEHAVIOR, VERBAL

Efficiency Of Peabody Picture Vocabulary In Estimating WISC Scores For Delinquents. Condit, J E and Lewandowski, D G and Saccuzzo, D P.

BEHAVIOR MODIFICATION

'Behavior Modification' In The Prison System. Cobb, Charles E.

From Phrenology To Psychosurgery And Back Again: Biological Studies In Criminality. Nassi, A J and Abramowitz, S I.

BELLEVUE, WA

Recruitment And Retention Of Minority Race Persons As Police Officers. Van Blaricon, D P.

BIAS

Cultural·Bias In The American Legal System. Swett, Daniel.

The Case Of The Racist Researcher. America, Richard F.

Ascertaining Police Bias In Arrests For Drunken Driving. Hyman, Merton M and Helrich, Alice R and Benson, Gwen.

Partial Justice: A Study Of Bias In Sentencing. Gaylin, Willard.

Racial Bias In The Decision To Grant Parole. Carroll, Leo and Mondrick, Margaret E.

BILINGUAL EDUCATION

Rights Of Spanish Speaking Minorities. Nuñez, Luis.

Development Of A Plan For Bilingual Interpreters In The Criminal Courts Of New Jersey. Hippchen, L J.

A Close Look At The Hispanic Inmates And Methods Of Meeting Their Needs. Castro, Agenor L.

The Importance Of Spanish Language Training For Law Enforcement Officers. Tatum, William M.

The Latino Prisoners In The US—Managing Effective Participation. Mc Collum, Sylvia.

"Bilingual Education And The Hispanic Challenge" in *1979 Annual Report Of The Carnegie Corporation Of New York.* Pifer, Alan.

Against Bilingual Education: Why Johnny Can't Speak English. Bethell, Tom.

Bilingualism In Corrections: National Hispanic Conference On Law Enforcement And Criminal Justice. Castro, Agenor L.

The Criminal Justice System: An Analysis Of Hispanic Issues. Baca, Salvador.

Less Spanish, Please. Molina, Mauricio.

BIOLOGICAL THEORIES

Medico—Legal Jurisprudence. Johnson, E A.

Criminal Man According To The Classifications Of Cesare Lombroso. Ferrers, Gina Lombroso.

Causes And Cures Of Crime. Mosby, Thomas Speed.

Physical Basis Of Crime As Observed By A Prison Physican. Sleyster, Rock.

The Criminal Physique: A Preliminary Report On The Physical Examination Of 1521 Prisoners At Wisconsin State Prison. Sleyster, Rock.

Causes Of Crime: Biological Theories In The United States, 1800–1915. Fink, Arthur E.

The Varieties Of Human Physique, With Collaboration Of S S Stevens And W B Tucker. Sheldon, W H.

Physique And Delinquency. Glueck, Sheldon and Glueck, Eleanor.

The Leopard's Spots: Scientific Attitudes Toward Race In America, 1815–1859. Stanton, William.

A *Try Simplest Cases* Approach To The Heredity—Poverty—Crime Problem. Shockley, W.

Genetics And Sociology: A Reconsideration. Eckland, Bruce K.

Race And Crime: A Revisit To An Old Concept. Sagarin, Edward.

YY Syndrome In An American Negro. Telfer, M A and Baker, D and Longtin, L.

The Myth Of The Criminal Type. Sarbin, Theodore R.

An XYZ Survey In A Negro Prison Population. Fattig, W Donald.

The XYY Offender: A Modern Myth? Fox, Richard G.

Delinquency And Crime: A Biopsychosocial Approach. Cortes, Juan B and Gatti, Florence M.

Perceived Opportunity, Delinquency, Race, And Body Build Among Delinquent Youth. Mc Candless, Boyd R and Person, Scott and Roberts, Albert.

Alcoholic Sensitivity And Ethnic Background. Ewing, J A and Rouse, B A and Pellizzari, E D.

IQ: Heritability And Inequality, Part I. Block, N J and Dworkin, G.

Notes On A Bit Of Psychological Nonsense: Race Differences In Intelligence. Schoenfeld, W N.

Race Differences In Intelligence. Loehlin, John C and Lindzey, Gardner and Spuhler, J N.

IQ: Heritability And Inequality, Part II. Block, N J and Dworkin, G.

From Phrenology To Psychosurgery And Back Again: Biological Studies In Criminality. Nassi, A J and Abramowitz, S I.

Biosocial Bases Of Criminal Behavior. Mednick, S and Christiansen, K O.

Biology And Crime. Jeffrey, C Ray (ed).

Ecologic—Biochemical Approaches To The Treatment Of Delinquents And Criminals. Hippchen, Leonard J (ed).

"Aggressive And Simple Sociopaths: Ten Years Later" in *Biology And Crime*, Jeffrey, C R (ed). Dynes, Patrick S and Carlson, Eric W and Allen, Harry E.

"Biology And Crime: The New Neo—Lombrosians" in *Biology And Crime*, Jeffrey, C Ray (ed). Jeffrey, C Ray.

"Biosociology And Crime" in *Biology And Crime*, Jeffrey, C R (ed). Kelly, Henry E.

"Learning Disabilities And Juvenile Delinquency: Biological And Sociological Theories" in *Biology And Crime*, Jeffrey, C R (ed). Holzman, Harold R.

"Politics In A Biobehavioral Perspective" in *Biology And Crime*, Jeffrey, C R (ed). Kort, Fred and Maxson, Stephen C.

"Punishment And Deterrence: A Psychobiological Statement" in *Biology And Crime*, Jeffrey, C Ray (ed). Jeffrey, C Ray.

"The Violent Brain: Is It Everyone's Brain" in *Biology And Crime*, Jeffrey, C R (ed). Ginsburg, Benson E.

"What Is The Potential For Biological Violence Control" in *Biology And Crime*, Jeffrey, C Ray (ed). Moyer, Kenneth.

The Brain Of A Negro Murderer. Mills, Charles K.

The Criminal Type. Noyes, William B.

Characteristics Of Criminals. Middleton, A B.

BIRMINGHAM, AL

Letter From Birmingham City Jail. King Jr, Martin Luther.

Crime, Police, And Race Relations: A Study In Birmingham. Lambert, J R and Jenkinson, R F.

BIRTH CONTROL

Genocide: Birth Control And The Black American. Weisbond, R G.

The Legacy Of Malthus: The Social Costs Of The New Racism. Chase, Allan.

BLACK-ON-BLACK CRIME see Crime, Black—on—black

BLACK ATTORNEYS

Racial Discrimination In The Legal Profession. Brown Jr, William H.

The South's Challenge To The Negro Lawyer. Anderson Jr, Charles W.

Negro Lawyers In Virginia: A Survey. Comment.

Bar Must Encourage More Negro Lawyers. Gossett, W T.

The Black Lawyer. Carter, R L.

The National Bar Association—Not Just An Opinion. Ortique, Revius O.

A New Role For The Black Law Graduate—A Reality Or An Illusion. Edwards, Harry T.

Blacks And The Law. Alexander, Raymond Pace.

The Black American And The Legal Profession: A Study Of Commitment. Jackson, Maynard H.

The Black Lawyer, An American Hero. Bell, Edward F.

National Legal Network: Organizing For Change; Black Lawyers And The Criminal Justice System. Hinds, Lennox S.

Minority Opportunities In Law For Blacks, Puerto Ricans And Chicanos. Clark, C P (ed).

Step Toward Equal Justice—Programs To Increase Black Lawyers In The South, 1969–1973. Spearman, R W and Stevens, H.

Black Lawyers Responsibility To Poor Communities. Banks, Sharon P.

The Black Philadelphia Lawyer. Mitchell, Charles L.

From The Black Bar. Ware, Gilbert (ed).

BLACK CODES

The North Carolina Black Code. Browning, James B.

The Black Codes Of The South. Wilson, T R.

"Racism And American Law" in *Law Against The People*, Lefcourt, Robert (ed), 38–54. Burns, Haywood.

BLACK COMMUNITY

The Black Community: Attitudes Toward Community Problems, Crime And The Police. Knowles, Lyle and Brewer, Jesse.

Crime In The Black Community—An Exploratory Bibliography. Davis, Lenwood G.

BLACK POWER

The Impossible Revolution: Black Power And The American Dream. Killian, Lewis.

Die Nigger Die. Brown, H Rap.

The Political Economy Of Black Power. Franklin, Raymond.

Black Awakening In Capitalist America. Allen, R L.

Black Power. Mac Donald Jr, A P.

BLACK PRISONERS

California Prisoners 1977 And 1978: Summary Of Statistics Of Felony Prisoers And Parolees. California Dept Of Corrections.

The Negro Offender. William, George C.

A Study Of 200 Negroes In The Western Penitentiary Of Pennsylvania. Reid, Ira De A.

A Psychological And Educational Survey Of 1916 Prisoners In The Western Penitentiary Of Pennsylvania. Root Jr, William T.

"Work And Law Observance In The Histories Of Men In Sing–Sing Prison" in *Report On The Causes Of Crime*, V1, 193–255,315–320. Kleeck, Mary V.

The Negro Goes To Sing Sing. Reid, Ira De A.

When Prisoners Run Amuck. Mitchell, Clifford C.

When Prisoners Run Amuck. Mitchell, Clifford C.

Let Me Live. Herndon, Angelo.

Scottsboro Boy. Patterson, Haywood and Conrad, Earl.

On The Penitentiary System In The United States And Its Application In France, Francis Lieber (trans), Orig Pub 1833. Beaumont, Gustave De and Tocqueville, Alexis De.

The Autobiography Of Malcolm X: With The Assistance Of Alex Haley. X, Malcolm.

The Performance Of Male Prisonsers On The Marlowe–Crowne Social Desirability Scale: II, Differences As A Function Of Race And Crime. Fisher, Gary.

Poems From Prison. Knight, Etheridge.

Soul On Ice. Cleaver, Eldridge.

The Detroit Riot: A Profile Of 500 Prisoners. U S Dept Of Labor, Manpower Administration.

The Life And Dying Speech Of Arthur, A Negro Man. Arthur.

The Negro Federal Offender. Debro, Julius.

The Historical Background And Present Status Of The County Chain Gang In South Carolina. Brailsford, Daniel T.

Black Voices From Prison. Knight, Etheridge (ed).

Soledad Brother: The Prison Letters Of George Jackson. Jackson, George.

The Crime Of Martin Sostre. Copeland, Vincent.

The Trial Of Bobby Seale. Seale, Bobby.

An XYZ Survey In A Negro Prison Population. Fattig, W Donald.

Using Racism At San Quentin. Minton Jr, Robert J and Rice, Stephen.

A Black View Of Prison. Aswadu, Ahmad Ali.

Black Prisoners, White Law. Chrisman, Robert.

Book Review On *Black Voices From Prison*, By Etheridge Knight. Wilcox, Preston.

Fascism At Soledad. Rollins, Clifford (Jabali).

Pages From The Life Of A Black Prisoner. Chapman, Frank E.

The Black Prisoner As Victim. Burns, Haywood.

Blood In My Eye. Jackson, George.

Maximum Security: Letters From California's Prisons. Pell, Eve (ed).

Poetry Of Prison: Poems By Black Prisoners. Anonymous.

Rel Bet Selected Personal Char Of Confined Narcotic Off And The Amn't Of Time Serv'd Prior To Their Official Referral Consideration. Green, Charles Bernard.

Who Took The Weight: Black Voices From Norfolk Prison. Norfolk Prison Brothers.

400 Miles From Harlem: Courts, Crime And Corrections. Wylie, Max.

Bender–Gestalt Protocols Of Adult Negro Male Offenders: Normative Data. Matranga, James T and Jensen, Diane E and Prandoni, Jaques R.

Counselor, Community And The Black Prisoner. Jones, Martin C and Jones, Martin H.

George Jackson Radicalized The Brothers In Soledad And San Quentin. Szulc, Tad.

The Prison As A Lawless Agency. Greenberg, David F and Stender, Fay.

"The Penal Population Of California" in *Voices: Readings From El Grito*, Octavio Ignacio Romano (ed). Del Pinal, Jorge H.

No Beast So Fierce. Bunker, Edward.

The Brothers Of Attica. Clark, Richard X.

My Days In Solitary. Newton, Huey.

Betcha Ain't: Poems From Attica. Tisdale, Celes (ed).

Hacks, Blacks And Cons: Race Relations In A Maximum Security Prison. Carroll, Leo.

DAPs Of Black And Whites Juvenile Incarcerates. Baugh, B Duncan and Prytula, Robert E.

Impact Of Incarceration On The Black Inmate. Adair, A V et al.

Notes On Blacks And The Penal System. Swan, L Alex.

Racism, Prisons, And Prisoners' Rights. Reasons, Charles E.

The Black Offender As Victim. Debro, Julius.

An Analysis Of Proxemics And Self–Disclosing Behavior Of Recidivist And Non–Recidivist Adult Social Offenders. Braithwaite, Ronald L.

Captive Voices: An Anthology From Folsom Prison. Anonymous.

Erroneous Zone. Rice, David L.

Soledad Prison: University Of The Poor. Faith, Karlene (ed).

The Analysis Of Self–Concept And Self Actualization Manifestations By Incarcerated And Free Black Youth. Davis, Charles.

The Sixteenth Round. Carter, Rubin "Hurricane".

Self–Defense Against Rape: The Joanne Little Case. Bond, Julian.

Baby Chocolate And Other Stories. Bullock, Clifton.

Bound And Free: The Poetry Of Warriors Behind Bars. Black Prisoners Of Florida State Prison, Starke.

Break De Chains Of Legalized Slavery. Anonymous.

My Life Of Absurdity. Himes, Chester.

My Rhythm Flows From A Different Beat. Lucas, Henry N.

The Development And Change Of The Peyote Ceremony Through Time And Space. Brito, Silvester John.

Uncle Yah Yah. Dickens, Al.

Who Killed George Jackson: Fantasies, Paranoia And The Revolution. Durden– Smith, Jo.

The Prison Inmate As Victim. Drapkin, Israel.

"Correctional Philosophy: A Special Issue: Race And Criminal Justice" in *New Jersey Correctional Master Plan*. New Jersey Dept Of Corrections.

Capital Punishment 1976. U S Dept Of Justice, LEAA, NCJISS.

Humanizing The System: Report Of Operations And Development For 1977. New York State, Dept Of Correctional Services.

Killing Time: Life In The Arkansas Penitentiary. Jackson, Bruce.

"Classifying Black Inmates: The Alabama Prison Classification Project" in *Blacks And Criminal Justice*, Owens And Bell (eds), 129–142. Owens, Charles E.

"Institutional Racism" in *Black Perspectives On Crime And The Criminal Justice System*, Woodson, Robert L (ed), 143–160. Debro, Julius.

Prisoners Of Race. Kroll, Michael A.

The Victim As Criminal And Artist: Literature From The American Prison. Franklin, H Bruce.

An Assessment Of The Black Female Prisoners In The South. French, Laurence.

Prison Plantation: The Story Of Angola. Vodicka, John.

The Incarcerated Black Female: The Case Of Social Double Jeopardy. French, Laurence.

"Race Relations And The Prisoner Subculture" in *Crime And Justice: An Annual Review Of Research*, Morris, N And M Tonry (eds). Jacobs, James B.

Capital Punishment, 1978. U S Dept Of Justice, LEAA, NCJIsS.

The Historical Development Of Imprisonment Of Blacks In The US. Christianson, Scott.

Mental Health And Black Offenders. Owens, Charles E.

Prisons In Turmoil. Irwin, John.

Profile Of Inmates Of Local Jails: Sociodemographic Findings From The 1978 Survey Of Inmates Of Local Jails. U S Dept Of Justice, Bureau Of Justice Statistics.

The Black Incarceration Rate In The United States: A Nationwide Problem. Christianson, Scott and Dehais, Richard.

"An Interview With Willie Tate" in *Punishment And Penal Discipline*, Platt, Tony And Paul Takagi (eds), 176–183. Begel, Debby.

"The San Quentin Six Case: Perspective And Analysis" in *Punishment And Penal Discipline*, Platt, Tony And Paul Takagi (eds), 165–175. Wald, Karen.

The Narrative & Confession Of Thomas Powers, A Negro, Who Was In The 10th Year Of His Age Was Executed For Committing A Rape. Powers, Thomas.

BLACK PRISONERS

The Address Of Abraham Johnstone, A Black Man, Who Was Hanged In New Jersey. Johnstone, Abraham.

BLACK STUDIES

Black Studies In Historical Perspective. Bailey, Ronald.

BLACKS

California Prisoners 1977 And 1978: Summary Of Statistics Of Felony Prisoers And Parolees. California Dept Of Corrections.

Negro Criminality. Baker, S C.

The Criminal Negro. Kellor, Frances A.

The Criminal Negro. Kellor, Frances A.

The Criminal Negro. Kellor, Frances A.

The Criminal Negro. Kellor, Frances A.

The Criminal Negro. Kellor, Frances A.

The Criminal Negro. Kellor, Frances A.

"Negro Crime" in *Notes On Negro Crime, Particularly In Georgia*, Du Bois, W E D (ed). Sanborn, Frank B.

The History Of Negro Servitude In Illinois And Of The Slavery Agitation In That State 1719–1864. Harris, N Dwight.

"Some Causes Of Criminality Among Colored Persons" in *The Negro In The Cities Of The North.* Waring, J H N.

The Negro Criminal Class—How Best Reached—Part I. Scarborough, W S.

The Negro Criminal Class—How Best Reached—Part II. Scarborough, W S.

Do Negroes Constitute A Race Of Criminals? Jackson, Ida Joyce.

Prohibition And The Negro. Washington, Booker T.

The Negro In Pennsylvania: Slavery–Servitude–Freedom, 1639–1861. Turner, Edward Raymond.

Negro Criminality. Smyth, J A.

Negro Crime And Strong Drink. Washington, Booker T.

Negro Criminality In The South. Work, Monroe N.

The American Negro As A Dependent, Defective And Delinquent. Mc Cord, Charles H.

Racial Assimilation In Secondary Groups With Particular Reference To The Negro. Park, Robert E.

Hidden Negro Criminality. Ramsey, D.

Education And Crime Among Negroes. Stephenson, G T.

Negro Population: 1790–1915. U S Dept Of Commerce, Bureau Of The Census.

Fifty Years Of Negro Citizenship As Qualified By The United States Supreme Court. Woodson, Carter G.

An Account Of The Late Intended Insurrection Among A Portion Of The Blacks Of This City. Hamilton Jr, James.

The Negro Offender. William, George C.

Negro Race Consciousness As Reflected In Race Literature. Park, Robert E.

A Study Of 200 Negroes In The Western Penitentiary Of Pennsylvania. Reid, Ira De A.

Types Of Crime And Intelligence Of Negro Criminals. Burfield, H.

A Survey Of Crime Among Negroes In Philadelphia. Thompson, Anna J–.

Negro Labor In The United States, 1850–1925. Wesley, C H.

An Analysis Of Negro Crime Statistics For Minneapolis For 1923, 1924, And 1925. Boie, Maurine.

The Negro Criminal: A Statistical Note. Sellin, Thorsten.

"The Negro And The Problem Of Law Observance And Administration" in *The Negro In American Civilization*, Johnson, C S (ed). Sellin, Thorsten.

The Negro In American Civilization: A Study Of Negro Life And Relations In The Light Of Social Research. Johnson, Charles S.

Racial Discrimination In The Legal Profession. Brown Jr, William H.

The Negro And Homicide. Brearley, H C.

The North Carolina Black Code. Browning, James B.

"Note On The Negroe's Relation To Work And Law Observation" in *Report On The Causes Of Crime*, V13. Reid, Ira De A.

"Work And Law Observance In The Histories Of Men In Sing–Sing Prison" in *Report On The Causes Of Crime*, V1, 193–255,315–320. Kleeck, Mary V.

Crime And The Negro. Cantor, Nathaniel.

Juvenile Delinquency And The Negro. Beckham, A S.

Thirty Delinquent Negro Children. Halliday, A P.

"Juvenile Delinquency" in *The Negro Family In Chicago.* Frazier, E Franklin.

Negro Homicides In The United States. Barnhart, Kenneth E.

Negroes Who Run Afoul Of The Law. Brinton, Hugh P.

Personality Differences Between Delinquent And Non–Delinquent Negro Boys. Daniel, Robert P.

The Negro Goes To Sing Sing. Reid, Ira De A.

Care Of The Negro Delinquent. Washington, Forrester B.

Delinquency In The Negro Community. Moses, Earl R.

Negro Crime In A Small Urban Community. Lightfoot Jr, R M.

Penal Slavery And Southern Reconstruction. Mc Kelvey, Blake.

The Negroes And Crime In Virginia. Chamberlain, B P.

Community Factors In Negro Delinquency. Moses, Earl R.

Negro And Crime. Hill, Joseph T.

"The Negro And Racial Conflict" in *Our Racial And National Minorities*, Brown, F J And J S Roucek (eds), 549–560. Johnson, James Weldon.

Caste And Class In A Southern Town. Dollard, John.

Negroes And The Law. Styles, Fitzhugh Lee.

American Slave Insurrections Before 1861. Wish, Harvey.

Every Opportunity. Himes, Chester.

Crime In Negro Columbus. Hines, Joseph S.

Negro Slave Revolts In The United States, 1526–1860. Aptheker, Herbert.

Notes On Negro Crime. Hines, Joseph S.

A History Of The Amistad Captives. Barber, John Warner.

Native Son. Wright, Richard.

Negro Crime. Spirer, Jess.

The Legal Status Of The Negro. Magnum, Charles S.

Criminality Of The Negro. Von Hentig, Hans.

The Problems And Needs Of Negro Youth As Revealed By Delinquency And Crime Statistics. Diggs, Mary H.

An Appraisal Of The Negro In Colonial South Carolina: A Study Of Americanization. Klingberg, Frank J.

The Myth Of The Negro Past. Herskovits, Melville J.

Slave Law And The Social Structure. Moore, Wilbert E.

The Negro And Crime. Johnson, Guy B.

Narrative Of The Barbarous Treatment Of Two Unfortunate Females, Natives Of Concordia LA By Joseph & Enoch, Runaway Slaves. Joseph and Enoch.

The Negro In Colonial New England. Greene, Lorenzo M.

A Nation Within A Nation, The Negro And The Supreme Court. Konvitz, Milton R.

Day To Day Resistance To Slavery. Bauer, Raymond A and Bauer, Alice H.

Negro Delinquent. Chivers, W R.

The Criminality Of The Colored Woman, Series C. Von Hentig, Hans.

Cultural And Racial Variations In Patterns Of Intellect, Peformance Of Negro And White Children On The Bellevue Adult Intelligence Scale. Machover, Solomon.

Racial Handicaps In The Negro Delinquent. Wyatt, D W.

The Zoot–Suit Riots. Mc Williams, Carey.

"Crime" in *An American Dilemma: The Negro Problem And Modern Democracy*, 966–979. Myrdal, Gunnar.

Characteristics Of The American Negro. Klineberg, Otto (ed).

Proceedings Of The Conspiracy Formed By Some White People For Burning The City Of NY In America And Murdering The Inhabitants. Horsmanden, Daniel.

The Negro At The Bar: The South. Shores, Arthur D.

Discriminative Value And Patterns Of The Wechsler–Bellevue Scales In The Examination Of Delinquent Negro Boys. Franklin, J C.

Race Relations In Puerto Rico And The Virgin Islands. Williams, Eric.

The South's Challenge To The Negro Lawyer. Anderson Jr, Charles W.

The Upgrading Of The Negro's Status By Supreme Court Decisions. Alexander, Raymond Pace.

American Slave Discontent In Records Of The High Courts. Russell, Marion J.

Differentials In Crime Rates Between Negroes And Whites, Based On Comparisons Of Four Socio–Economically Equated Areas. Moses, Earl R.

Negro Police In Southern Cities. Southern Regional Council.

Negroes On Juries. West, John S.

Negro Police In Southern Cities. Southern Regional Council.

"The Negro In Crime" in *Encyclopedia Of Criminology*, Branham, V C And S B Kutask (eds). Canady, Herman B.

Negroes In American Society. Davie, Maurice R.

The Delinquent Negro Child. Cochrane, Hortense S.

A Documentary History Of The Negro People In The United States. Aptheker, Herbert (ed).

BLACKS

Negro And White Male Institutionalized Delinquents. Axelrad, Sidney.

Slave Names In Colonial South Carolina. Cohen, Hennig.

A Study Of Teen–age Behavior Among Negroes, Mexicans, Puerto Ricans, Japanese, Chinese, Filipino And American Indians. Harris, Richard E.

Towards An Understanding Of Juvenile Delinquency. Lander, Bernard.

The Negro Offender: An Urban Research Project. Kephart, William M.

Group Belongingness Among Negroes. Grossack, M.

The Negro Offender In A Northern Industrial Area. Fox, Vernon and Volakalis, Joan.

The Negro In Indiana; A Study Of A Minority. Thornbrough, Emma Lou.

Aspiration Levels Of Negro Delinquent, Dependent, And Public School Boys. Mitchell, Lonnie E.

Cats, Kicks, And Color. Finestone, Harold.

Effects Of Unemployment On White And Negro Prison Admissions In Louisiana. Dobbins, D A and Bass, Bernard M.

The Negro Crime Rate: A Failure In Integration. Anonymous.

The Martyrs & The Fugitive, Or A Narrative Of The Captivity, Sufferings & Death Of An African Family & The Escape Of Their Son. Platt, Reverend S H.

The Newcomers: Negroes And Puerto Ricans In A Changing Metropolis. Handlin, Oscar.

Educational Level And Juvenile Delinquency Among Negroes. Miller, Carroll L.

Juvenile Delinquency Among Negroes: A Critical Summary. Lewis, H.

Juvenile Delinquency: As Social Dimension. Lohman, Joseph D.

Lawlessness And Violence In America And Their Special Manifestations In Changing Negro–White Relations. Grimshaw, Allen.

Negro Family Disorganization And Juvenile Delinquency. Cavan, Ruth S.

Slavery And The Genesis Of American Race Prejudice. Degler, Carl N.

The Extent And Characteristics Of Juvenile Delinquency Among Negroes In The United States. Douglas, Joseph H.

The Metropolis And Juvenile Delinquency Among Negroes. Hill, Mozell.

The Role Of The Negro Community In Delinquency Prevention Among Negro Youth. Mays, Benjamin E.

African Homicide And Suicide. Bohannon, P (ed).

Police Work And The Negro. Rudwick, Elliot M.

The Death Penalty And The Negroes. Williams, Franklin H.

A Study Of The Negro Alcoholic. Strayer, R.

Differential Study Of Recidivism Among Negro And White Boys. Henton, Comradge L and Washington, Charles.

Economic Deprivation And Extremism: A Study Of Unemployed Negroes. Street, D and Leggett, J C.

Negro Police Employment In The Urban South. Rudwick, Elliot M.

The Negro Armed Robber As A Criminal Type: The Construction And Application Of A Typology. Roebuck, Julian D and Cadwallader, Mervyn L.

The Southern Negro Policeman And The White Offender. Rudwick, Elliot M.

Black Bourgeoisie. Frazier, E Franklin.

Black Metropolis: A Study Of Negro Life In A Northern City, Rev'd Ed Orig Pub 1945. Cayton, Horace R and Drake, St Clair.

Black Nationalism: A Search For Identity In America. Essien– Udom, E U.

Negroes With Guns. Williams, Robert F.

Chattel Slavery And Concentration Camps. Thorpe, Earl E.

Comment: Black Muslims In Prison—Of Muslim Rites And Constitutional Rights. Anonymous.

Ecological Pattern Of Negro Homicide. Pettigrew, Thomas F and Spier, Rosalind B.

J Edgar Hoover—The Negro And The FBI. Booker, Simeon.

Patterns Of Segregation And Discrimination: Contributing Factors To Crime Among Negroes. Vontress, Clemmont E.

The Legal Status Of The Slave In South Carolina, 1670–1740. Sirmans, M Eugene.

The Negro Drug Addict As An Offender Type. Roebuck, Julian B.

The Negro Drinker And Assaulter As A Criminal Type. Roebuck, Julian B and Johnson, R.

Why The Negro Carries Weapons. Schultz, Leroy G.

Beyond The Melting Pot: The Negroes, Puerto Ricans, Jews, Italians, And Irish Of New York City. Glazer, Nathan and Moynihan, Daniel P.

Negro Thought In America, 1880–1915. Meier, August.

Male Young Adult Criminality Deviant Values, And Differential Opportunities In Two Lower Class Negro Neighborhoods. Spergel, Irving.

Negro Delinquents In Public Training. Baker, Gordon H and Adams, William T.

Negro In The Supreme Court, 1963. Gill, Robert L.

Negro In The Supreme Court. Gill, Robert L.

Occupational Benefits To Whites From The Subordination Of Negroes. Glenn, Norval.

Prejudice Toward Mexican And Negro Americans: A Comparison. Pinkney, Alphonso.

The Image Of The Negro In Colonial Literature. Cantor, Milton.

The Negro Numbers Man As A Criminal Type: The Construction And Application Of A Typology. Roebuck, Julian D.

"Negro American Crime" in *A Profile Of The Negro American*, 136–156. Pettigrew, Thomas F.

A Profile Of The Negro American. Pettigrew, Thomas.

The Fire Next Time. Baldwin, James.

A Memorandum On Identity And Negro Youth. Erikson, Eric H.

Predicting Juvenile Delinquency Among Negroes. Kramer, Samuel A.

Survey Of Negro Attitudes Toward Law. Zeitz, Leonard.

The 'Short Con' Man. Roebuck, Julian D and Johnson, R C.

The Negro, Prejudice And The Police. Cross, Granville J.

The Question Of Negro Crime. Coles, Robert.

Towards Freedom: An Analysis Of Slave Revolts In The United States. Kilson, Marion D De B.

"Crime And Delinquency" in *The Negro In The United States*, 638–653, Orig Pub 1949. Frazier, E Franklin.

"Negro And White Sex Crime Rates" in *Sexual Behavior And The Law*, Slovenko, Ralph (ed), 210–220. Savitz, Leonard D and Lief, H I.

A Minority Group In American Society. Yinger, J Milton.

Dark Ghetto. Clark, Kenneth B.

The Negro Family: The Case For National Action. Moynihan, Daniel Patrick.

The Souls Of Black Folk, Orig Pub 1904. Du Bois, W E B (ed).

Black Muslims And The Police. Brown, Lee P.

Civil Rights Activity And Reduction Of Crime Among Negroes. Salomon, Frederic et al.

Negro Subordination And White Gains. Cutright, Phillip.

The Social And Economic States Of The Negro In The United States. Drake, St Clair.

The Wonder Is There Have Been So Few Riots. Clark, Kenneth B.

"The Legal Status Of The Negro In The United States" in *The American Negro Reference Book*, Davis, John P (ed), 484–521. Motley, Constance Baker.

An Exploratory Study Of The Effects Of Incarceration On The Families Of Negro Inmates Of A Medium–Security Prison. Schneller, Donald P.

Drinking Patterns And Alcoholism Among American Negroes. Sterne, M.

Negro Social And Political Thought, 1850–1920. Brotz, H (ed).

The American Negro Reference Book. Davis, J P (ed).

The Negro Family In The United States, Orig Pub 1949. Frazier, E Franklin.

The Strange Career Of Jim Crow. Woodward, C Vann.

A Comparison Of The Scores Of White And Negro Male Juvenile Delinquients On Three Projective Tests. Megargee, Edwin I.

Negro And Indian: A Comparison Of Their Constitutional Rights. Kane, A.

Racial Perspectives And Attitudes Among Negro And White Delinquent Boys: An Empirical Examination. Segal, Bernard E.

Servant Into Slave: The Evolution Of The Legal Status Of The Negro Laborer In Colonial Virginia. Palmer, Paul C.

The Negro Crime Rate: Its Causes And Cure. Rice, Charles E.

The Truth About Negro Crime. Pogue Jr, Frank.

White Gains From Negro Subordination. Glenn, Norval.

"The Negro Criminal" in *The Philadelphia Negro*, Chapter 13, Orig Pub 1899. Du Bois, W E B.

Death At An Early Age: The Destruction Of The Hearts And Minds Of Negro Children In The Boston Schools. Kozol, Jonathan.

Minorities In A Changing World. Barron, Milton L (ed).

Tally's Corner: A Study Of The Negro Streetcorner Men. Liebow, Elliot.

The Crisis Of The Negro Intellectual: From Its Origins To The Present. Cruse, H.

The Moynihan Report And The Politics Of Controversy. Rainwater, Lee and Yancey, William L.

BLACKS

Personality Patterns Of White, Black, And Mexican American Patrolmen As Measured By The Sixteen Personality Factor Questionaire. Snibbe, H M and Fabricatore, Joseph and Azen, Stanley P.

Police Conduct And The Black Community——The Case Of Jackson, Mississippi. Mitchell, G T and Mc Lemore, L B.

Rape, Race And The Death Penalty In Georgia. Wolfgang, Marvin E and Riedel, Marc.

Reentry And The Black Parolee. Swan, L Alex.

Role Playing And Group Experience To Facilitate Attitude And Value Changes Among Black And White Police Officers. Teahan, John E.

Some Social And Psychological Effects Of Incarceration On The Families Of Negro Prisoners. Schneller, Donald P.

South Carolina Fugitives As Viewed Through Local Newspapers With Emphasis On Runaway Notices 1732–1800. Meaders, Daniel.

The Police And Black Separatism: A Problem For Public Policy. Lazin, F A.

The Sex Offenses Of Blacks And Whites. Kirk, Stuart A.

The Struggle Of Ben Chavis And The Wilmington 10. Davis, Angela Y.

To Be Young, Black And Oppressed. Staples, Robert.

Validity Of The MMPI Pd Scale Among Black Males. Elion, Victor H and Megargee, Edwin I.

White Racism, Black Crime And American Justice: An Application Of The Colonial Model To Explain Crime And Race. Staples, Robert.

"Black Crime And Delinquency" in *Introduction To Black Sociology*, 212–247. Staples, Robert.

"Towards A Sociology Of The Black Family" in *Afro–Americans: A Social Science Perspective*, Dennis, Rutledge M And Charles Jarmon (eds). Staples, Robert.

Alcohol Abuse And Black America. Harper, Frederick D (ed).

Aspirations And Social Concerns—Crime, Blacks, Inequality And Women. Watts, W and Free, L A.

Being Black Is Detrimental To One's Mental Health: Myth Or Reality? Cannon, Mildred S and Locke, Ben Z.

Drug Use And Abuse Among US Minorities: An Annotated Bibliography. Iiyama, P and Nishi, S M and Johnson, B B.

From Plantation To Ghetto. Meier, August and Rudwick, Elliot.

Introduction To Black Sociology. Staples, Robert.

The Development And Change Of The Peyote Ceremony Through Time And Space. Brito, Silvester John.

"Black Attitudes Toward Crime And Crime Prevention" in *Crime And Its Impact On The Black Community*, Gary, L E And L P Brown (eds), 13–30. Scott, Elsie K.

"Black Business And The Crime Of Uneconomic Communities" in *Crime And Its Impact On The Black Community*, Gary, L E & L P Brown (eds), 31–38. Burrell, Berkeley G.

"Black Self–Identity And Crime" in *Crime And Its Impact On The Black Community*, Gary, L E And L P Brown (eds), 109–120. Gullattee, Alyce C.

"Citizens Action As A Deterrent To Crime" in *Crime And Its Impact On The Black Community*, Gary, L E And L P Brown (eds), 122–126. Payne, Ethel L.

"Court Monitoring—A Necessity" in *Crime And Its Impact On The Black Community*, Gary, L E And L P Brown (eds), 165–175. Alexander, Harry T.

"Crime And The Public Schools" in *Crime And Its Impact On The Black Community*, Gary, L E And L P Brown (eds), 59–68. Banks, Samuel L.

"Employment And Discrimination" in *Crime And Its Impact On The Black Community*, Gary, L E And L P Brown (eds), 69–76. Padgett, Squire.

"Historical Overview Of Crime And Blacks Since 1876" in *Crime And Its Impact On The Black Community*, Gary, L E And L P Brown (eds), 3–11. Davis, Lenwood G.

"Media, Crime And The Black Reality" in *Crime And Its Impact On The Black Community*, Gary, L E And L P Brown (eds), 97–108. Goodlett, Carlton B.

"New Directions In Law Enforcement" in *Crime And Its Impact On The Black Community*, Gary, L E And L P Brown (eds), 143–154. Brown, Lee P.

"New Directions In Corrections" in *Crime And Its Impact On The Black Community*, Gary, L E And L P Brown (eds), 177–194. Owens, Charles E.

"Philosophical/Research Implications Of Definitions Of Crime" in *Crime And Its Impact On The Black Community*, Gary, L & Brown (eds), 51–55. Goodman, James A.

"Race And Family Violence" in *Crime And Its Impact On The Black Community*, Gary, L E And L P Brown (eds), 85–96. Staples, Robert.

"Successful Passage Of Black Parolees From Prison To Prison" in *Crime And Its Impact On The Black Community*, Gary And Brown (eds), 177–194. Swan, L Alex.

"The Criminal Justice System" in *Crime And Its Impact On The Black Community*, Gary, L E And L P Brown (eds), 48–61. Lyles, Barbara.

"The Impact Of Alcohol On Crime In The Black Community" in *Crime And Its Impact On The Black Community*, Gary, L P & L E Brown (eds), 77–84. Harper, Frederick D.

Black Justice Under White Law——Criminal Prosecutions Of Blacks In Antebellum South Carolina. Hindus, Michael Stephen.

Blackness Is My Mental Health: A Mind Set For Black Drug Abuse Prevention And Treatment Programs. Wheeler, William Henry III.

Blacks, Crime And American Culture. Davis, John A.

Book Review: Criminal Violence And The Poor Black Male. Pfohl, Stephen J.

Continuities In Delinquency And Riot Patterns, In Black Residential Areas. Kapsis, Robert E.

Differential Social Perception And Attribution Of Intergroup Violence: Testing The Lower Limits Of Stereotyping Of Blacks. Duncan, B L.

Dimensions Of Racial Ideology: A Study Of Urban Black Attitudes. Turner, C B and Wilson, W J.

Parolees' Perceptions Of The Justice System: Black–White Differences. Berman, John J.

Relative Deprivation, Rising Expectations And Black Militancy. Abeles, R P.

Role Of The Police And The Courts In The Survival Of Black Youth. Alexander, Gordon G.

Test Of An Arousal Theory Of Delinquency——Stimulation–Seeking In Delinquent And Nondelinquent Black Adolescents. Farley, Frank H and Sewell, Trevor.

The 'Black Shift' Phenomenon In Criminal Justice. Adams, Stuart.

The Black Addict: I Methodology, Chronology Of Addiction, And Overview Of The Population. Halikas, J A et al.

The Black Matriarchy Controversy And Black Male Delinquency. Perry, Robert L.

Voir Dire—The Due Process Clause Of The Fourteenth Amendment [And Jurors' Racial Prejudice]. Comment.

"Crimes Against The Elderly——Findings From Interviews With Blacks, Mex–Amer, And Whites" in *Justice And Older Americans*, Young, M (ed). Ragan, P K.

Black Crime: A Police View. Bryce, Harrington J (ed).

Black Perspectives On Crime And The Criminal Justice System. Woodson, Robert L (ed).

Black/Brown/White Relations: Race Relations In The 1970's. Willie, Charles V (ed).

Blacks And Criminal Justice. Owens, Charles E (ed) and Bell, Jimmy (ed).

Culture And Crisis In Confinement. Johnson, Robert.

Slave Testimony: Two Centuries Of Letters, Speeches, Interviews, And Autobiographies. Blassingame, John W (ed).

State Of Black America, 1977. National Urban League, Inc.

The Black Revolts: Racial Stratification In The USA. Scott, Joseph.

The Minority Presence In American Literature, 1600–1900, 2v. Butcher, P.

"Black Women: Income And Incarceration" in *Blacks And Criminal Justice*, Owens, Charles E And Jimmy Bell (eds), 85–92. Wyrick, Saunders and Owens, Holloway O.

"Bridges Over Troubled Waters" in *Black Perspectives On Crime And The Criminal Justice System*, Woodson, Robert L (ed), 79–106. Brown, Lee P.

"Causes Of Crime" in *Black Crime: A Police View*, Bryce, H J (ed), 37–66. Brown, Lee P.

"Challenge For The Judicial System: Economic And Racial Equality" in *Blacks And Criminal Justice*, Owens, Charles E And Jimmy Bell (eds). Crockett Jr, George W.

"Classifying Black Inmates: The Alabama Prison Classification Project" in *Blacks And Criminal Justice*, Owens And Bell (eds), 129–142. Owens, Charles E.

"Crime In The Black Community" in *Blacks And Criminal Justice*, Owens, Charles E And Jimmy Bell (eds), 69–74. Bell, Jimmy and Joyner, Irving.

"Discretionary Justice And The Black Offender" in *Blacks And Criminal Justice*, Owens, Charles E And Jimmy Bell (eds), 37–46. Banks, Taunya L.

"Higher Education: Roles In Criminal Justice" in *Blacks And Criminal Justice*, Owens, Charles E And Jimmy Bell (eds), 113–117. Bell, Jimmy.

"Improving Police Relations In The Black Community" in *Blacks And Criminal Justice*, Owens, Charles E And Jimmy Bell (eds), 114–127. Swan, L Alex.

BOSTON, MA

Absentee Ownership And Management In The Black Ghetto: Social And Economic Consequences. Reiss Jr, Albert J and Aldrich, Howard.

Correlates Of Civil Rights Activity And Negro Intra–Racial Violence. Mc Donald, Thomas D.

BRIDGEPORT, CT

Bridgeport Guardians, Inc V Members Of The Bridgeport Civil Service, 345 F Supp 779, US Dist Ct D Conn Jan 29, 1973. Anonymous.

Bridgeport Guardians, Inc V Members Of Civil Service Com'n, 497 F 2d 113 (Conn), US Court Of Appeals, Second Circuit, June 3, 1974. Anonymous.

BRIGHTON, NY

Varieties Of Police Behavior: The Management Of Law And Order In Eight Communities. Wilson, James Q.

BRONX, NY

The Mugging. Hunt, Morton.

Policing The Bronx. Bouza, Anthony.

Street Gangs—Profiles For Police. Collins, H C.

BROOKLYN, NY

Crimes Of Puerto Ricans In Brooklyn. Alter, Julius.

Police Power: A Study Of Provocation. Chevigny, Paul.

New Evidence Of Black Unrest In Colonial Brooklyn. Skemer, Don C.

Ducks Versus Hard Rocks. Hunter, Deairich.

BROWN, H RAP

Die Nigger Die. Brown, H Rap.

BROWN, WILLIAM

Commonwealth Versus William Brown. Houston, Charles M.

BUFFALO, NY

The Crime Of Martin Sostre. Copeland, Vincent.

BUREAU OF INDIAN AFFAIRS

Bureau Of Indian Affairs Law Enforcement Division—Indian Police. Dijoseph, J.

BUREAUCRACY

Law, Procedure And Punishment In Early Bureaucracies. Mac Leod, W C.

BURGLARY

The World Of The Burglar: Five Criminal Lives. David, Pedro R.

Recidivist Impacts Of Differential Sentencing Practices For Burglary Offenders. Bartell, Ted and Winfree Jr, L Thomas.

Study Of Sentencing In Hennepin County And Ramsey County District Courts. Rhodes, W M.

Post–Arrest Release Decisions: An Empirical Examination Of Social And Legal Criteria. Pope, Carl E.

Criminal's Image Of The City. Carter, R I and Hill, K Q.

Robbery And Burglary—A Study Of The Characteristics Of The Persons Arrested And The Handling Of Their Cases In Court. Williams, K M and Lucianovic, J.

BURT, CYRIL

The Cyril Burt Question: New Findings. Dorfman, D D.

CALIFORNIA

see also Folsom Prison, Ca, Los Angeles, Menlo Park, Ca; Oakland, Ca; Oxnard, Ca, Sacramento, Ca; San Diego, Ca; San Francisco, Ca, San Jose, Ca, San Quentin Prison, Ca, Santa Barbara, Ca, Santa Clara County, Ca; Soledad Prison, Ca; Watts, Ca

California Prisoners 1977 And 1978: Summary Of Statistics Of Felony Prisoers And Parolees. California Dept Of Corrections.

Summaries Of Studies On The Recruitment And Retention Of Minority Correctional Employees. Beard, Eugene.

Oriental Crime In California: A Study Of Offenses Committed By Orientals In That State, 1900–1927. Beach, W G.

Horace Mann's Letters On The Extension Of Slavery Into California And New Mexico. Mann, Horace.

North From Mexico, Orig Pub 1949. Mc Williams, Carey.

Report On Crime And The Foreign Born, Orig Pub 1931. Abbott, Edith.

Patterns Of Conflict Among Higher Maturity Urban Negro Delinquents (Community Treatment Project). Neto, Virginia and Palmer, Ted.

A Study Of The California Penalty Jury In First–Degree Murder Trials. Note.

Gambling And Alcoholism: Symptom Substitution And Functional Equivalents. Adler, N and Goleman, D.

The Death Penalty In California: A Statistical And Composite Portrait. Carter, Robert M and Smith, A La Mont.

Colonialism: The Case Of The Mexican–Americans. Moore, Joan W.

The Other Californians: Prejudice And Discrimination Under Spain, Mexico, And The United States To 1920. Heizer, Robert F and Almquist, Alan F.

Maximum Security: Letters From California's Prisons. Pell, Eve (ed).

"A Study Of Grand Jury Service" in *Race, Crime, And Justice*, Reasons, Charles E And Jack L Kuykendall (eds), 324–339. California Rural Legal Assistance.

"The Penal Population Of California" in *Voices: Readings From El Grito*, Octavio Ignacio Romano (ed). Del Pinal, Jorge H.

Political & Economic Aspects Of Mexican Immigration Into California And The US Since 1941. Williams, Dean L.

Politics Of Punishment—A Critical Analysis Of Prisons In America. Wright, Erik Olin.

The Melancholy History Of Soledad Prison. Yee, Ming S.

Voices: Readings From El Grito, A Journal Of Contemporary Mexican American Thought, 1967–1973. Romano, Octavio Ignacio (ed).

Inequalities Of The Parole System In California. Bailey, D'Army.

An Examination Of Institutional Racism: Black People In California's Criminal Justice And Mental Health Systems. Ogleton, Betty and Crittendon, Stephanie and Seda, Cozetta.

Chicanoizing Drug Abuse Programs. Aron, William S and Alger, Norman and Gonzales, Ricardo T.

Violent Crime Indices Among Community–Retained Delinquents. Andrew, J M.

California: Affirmative Action Statistics, Report No 3. California Dept Of The Youth Authority.

Sentencing Of California Felony Offenders. Pope, Carl E.

Soledad Prison: University Of The Poor. Faith, Karlene (ed).

Women In Corrections—A Process Of Change. Becker, A M.

California Prisoners 1976: Summary Statistics Of Felon Prisoners And Parolees. California Dept Of Corrections.

California: Report To The Judicial Council On The Language Needs Of Non–English–Speaking Persons, Interim Phase 2 Report. U S Dept Of Justice, LEAA.

Who Killed George Jackson: Fantasies, Paranoia And The Revolution. Durden– Smith, Jo.

Ethnic/Racial Misidentification In Death: A Problem Which May Distort Suicide Statistics. Andress, V R.

Post–Arrest Release Decisions: An Empirical Examination Of Social And Legal Criteria. Pope, Carl E.

Chicanos In A Changing Society: From Mexican Pueblos To American Barrios In Santa Barbara And Southern California, 1848–1930. Camarillo, Alberto.

"The San Quentin Six Case: Perspective And Analysis" in *Punishment And Penal Discipline*, Platt, Tony And Paul Takagi (eds), 165–175. Wald, Karen.

CAPITAL PUNISHMENT *see* Death Penalty

CAPITALISM

Punishment And Social Structure. Rusche, Georg and Kirchheimer, Otto.

Capitalism And Slavery. Williams, Eric.

Black Awakening In Capitalist America. Allen, R L.

The Myth Of Black Capitalism. Ofari, E.

Class And The Economics Of Crime. Gordon, David M.

Capitalism, Class And Crime In America. Gordon, David M.

Critique Of Legal Order: Crime Control In Capitalist Society. Quinney, Richard.

Problems In Political Economy: An Urban Perspective. Gordon, David M.

Rape, Racism And The Capitalist Setting. Davis, Angela Y.

CAPTIVITY NARRATIVES

The Significance Of The Captivity Narrative. Pearce, Roy H.

The Victim As Criminal And Artist: Literature From The American Prison. Franklin, H Bruce.

Memoirs Of American Prisoners: An Annotated Bibliography. Suvak, Daniel (comp).

CARR, JAMES

Bad: An Autobiography. Carr, James.

CARTER, RUBIN

The Sixteenth Round. Carter, Rubin "Hurricane".

CAUCASIANS *see* Whites

CENSUS, U S

Negro Population: 1790–1915. U S Dept Of Commerce, Bureau Of The Census.

CENSUS, U S

Crime Conditions In The United States As Reflected In Census Statistics Of Imprisoned Offenders. U S Dept Of Commerce, Bureau Of Census.

Growth Of The Black Population: A Study Of Demographic Trends. Farley, Reynolds.

Persons Of Spanish Origin In The United States, November 1969. U S Dept Of Commerce, Bureau Of The Census.

Characteristics Of The Population By Ethnic Origin: March 1972 And 1971. U S Dept Of Commerce, Bureau Of The Census.

Persons Of Spanish Origin In The United States: March 1972 And 1971. U S Dept Of Commerce, Bureau Of The Census.

Persons Of Spanish Origin In The United States: March 1974. U S Dept Of Commerce, Bureau Of The Census.

Persons Of Spanish Origin In The United States: March 1973. U S Dept Of Commerce, Bureau Of The Census.

American Language Loyalty And The Validity Of The 1970 Census. Thompson, Roger M.

Persons Of Spanish Origin In The United States: March 1975. U S Dept Of Commerce, Bureau Of The Census.

The Social And Economic Status Of The Black Population In The United States, 1974. U S Dept Of Commerce, Bureau Of The Census.

Population Redistribution In The US In The 1970's. Berry, Brian J and Dahmann, Donald C.

Persons Of Spanish Origin In The United States: March 1978. U S Dept Of Commerce, Bureau Of The Census.

The 1980 Census: Making Sure We Count. Martinez, Douglas.

Demographics Of The 1980's. Reynolds, Reid and Robey, Brayant and Russell, Cheryl.

Crime And The Census. Falkner, Rolland, P.

CHAIN GANG

see also Prison Labor

The North Carolina Chain Gang: A Study Of County Convict Road Work, Orig Pub 1927. Steiner, Jesse F and Brown, Roy M.

The Historical Background And Present Status Of The County Chain Gang In South Carolina. Brailsford, Daniel T.

CHANGE, INDIVIDUAL

Changing Criminals: The Application Of The Theory Of Differential Association. Cressey, Donald R.

The Response Of Adults To Delinquency Prevention Programs: The Race Factor. Hackler, J C and Linden, E.

Changing Attitudes Of Black Youths. Cizanckas, Victor I and Purviance, Carlton W.

Group Counseling For Offenders. Pew, Miriam L and Speer, David C and Williams, James.

Ethnic Self–Help Groups In Prison And On Parole. Burdman, Milton.

CHANGE, INSTITUTIONAL

Interrogations In New Haven: The Impact Of *Miranda.* Wald, Michael et al.

Minimizing Racism In Jury Trials. Ginger, Ann Fagan (ed).

Violent Men: An Inquiry Into The Psychology Of Violence. Toch, Hans.

White Institutions And Black Rage. Boesel, D et al.

Radical Lawyers: Their Role In The Movement And In The Courts. Black, Jonathan (ed).

Changing The Police: The Impossible Dream? Germann, A C.

Litigating Against The Death Penalty: The Strategy Behind *Furman.* Meltsner, Michael.

"The Black Judge As A Change Agent" in *The Administration Of Criminal Justice: A View From Black America*, Brown, Lee P (ed), 23–27. Alexander, Harry T.

Women In Corrections—A Process Of Change. Becker, A M.

Discrimination In The Imposition Of Death Penalty: A Comparison Of The Characteristics Of Offenders Sentenced Pre–Furman And Post–Furman. Riedel, Marc.

The Man Who Beat Clout City. Mc Clory, R.

Reform Without Change: The Future Of Prisoners' Rights. Bronstein, Alvin J.

Justice And Reform: The Formative Years Of The American Legal Service Program. Johnson Jr, Earl.

Mississippi Has Come A Long Way, But It Had A Long Way To Come. Gettinger, Steve.

Race And The Police: An Early Report On A Change Effort. Fyfe, James J.

CHANGE, ORGANIZATIONAL

Change In Crisis–Relevant Organizations: Police Departments And Civil Disturbances. Kreps, Gary A.

Policemen: Agents Of Change—A Crime Prevention Report. Ferguson, R F.

East LA's Gang Project: Prevention Or Bribery? Bernstein, Dan.

CHANGE, SOCIAL

Shaping Of Race Relations By The Federal Judiciary. Gill, Robert L.

Negro Social And Political Thought, 1850–1920. Brotz, H (ed).

Black Power, White Resistance: Notes On The New Civil War. Powledge, Fred.

Equality By Statute: The Revolution In Civil Rights. Berger, Monroe.

The Impossible Revolution: Black Power And The American Dream. Killian, Lewis.

Urban Riots: Violence And Social Change. Connery, Robert H (ed).

Change And Resistance: A Psychotherapeutic View Of Race Relations. Wachetel, Paul.

Looting In Civil Disorders: An Index Of Social Change. Dynes, R and Quarantelli, E.

Black Awakening In Capitalist America. Allen, R L.

Police–Ghetto Relations: Some Findings And A Proposal For Structural Change. Mast, Robert.

Black Policemen Denounce Racism. Fraser, C Gerald.

Race Relations, Models And Social Change. Tabb, W K.

Awakening Minorities: American Indians, Mexican Americans, Puerto Ricans. Howard, John R (ed).

Emergence Of Deviant Minorities—Social Problems And Social Change. Winslow, R W.

Migrant In The City: The Life Of A Puerto Rican Action Group. Rogler, Lloyd H.

Eradication Of Racism And Poverty As A Means Of Stopping Escalation Of Crime And Violence: A Dream Deferred. Higginbotham Jr, A Leon.

The Attitudes Of Black And White High School Seniors Toward Integration. Mastroianni, M and Khatena, J.

The Viability And Reliability Of The US Supreme Court As An Institution For Social Change And Progress Beneficial To Blacks. Tollett, Kenneth S.

Developing A Community And Computer Based Anti–Color–Code Strategy To Resist And Reduce Violent Crimes In Black Ghettoes. Haynes Jr, Andrew B.

Indian Powerlessness In Minnesota. Westermeyer, Joseph.

National Legal Network: Organizing For Change; Black Lawyers And The Criminal Justice System. Hinds, Lennox S.

Black Policemen Bring Reform. Stevens, William K.

Justice, The Courts, And Change. Crockett Jr, George W.

Violence As A Technique For Social Change For Black Americans. Wood, John Atkins.

The Effects Of The Findings Of The US National Advisory Commission On Civil Disorders: An Experimental Study Of Attitude Change. Davis, E E and Fine, M.

Unequal Justice: Lawyers And Social Change In Modern America. Auerbach, Jerold S.

Black Bolshevik: Autobiography Of An Afro–American Communist. Haywood, H.

A Model For Chicano Drug Use And For Effective Utilization Of Employment And Training Resources By Barrio Addicts And Ex–Offenders. Chicano Pinto Research Project, Inc.

CHARLESTON, SC

An Account Of The Late Intended Insurrection Among A Portion Of The Blacks Of This City. Hamilton Jr, James.

CHAVIS, BEN

Rev Ben Chavis And The Wilmington Ten—A Fact Sheet. Anonymous.

The Struggle Of Ben Chavis And The Wilmington 10. Davis, Angela Y.

CHEROKEE

Cherokee Tragedy. Wilkins, Thurman.

Fire And The Spirits—Cherokee Law From Clan To Court. Strickland, R.

CHEYENNE

The Cheyenne Way: Conflict And Case Law In Primitive Jurisprudence. Llewellyn, K and Hoebel, E Adamson.

CHICAGO, IL

The Chicago Race Riots. Sandburg, Carl.

Delinquency Areas. Shaw, Clifford et al.

The Delinquent Girl In Chicago: I—A Comprison Of Four National And Racial Groups. Davis, E R.

CIVIL RIGHTS

The Southwest Indian Report. U S Commission On Civil Rights.

The Federal Civil Rights Enforcement Effort—1974: Volume VI, To Extend Federal Financial Assistance. U S Commission On Civil Rights.

Negro Demonstrations And The Law: Danville As A Test Case. Ely Jr, James W.

American Minorities: The Justice Issue. Long, Elton et al.

The Navajo Nation: An American Colony. U S Commission On Civil Rights.

Violence As A Technique For Social Change For Black Americans. Wood, John Atkins.

Civil Rights And Corrections—The Impact Of LEAA Compliance Requirements. Rice, H C.

Police Homicide In A Democracy. Kobler, Arthur L.

Cointelpro: The FBI's Secret War On Political Freedom. Blackstone, Nelson.

Puerto Ricans In The Continental United States: An Uncertain Future. U S Commission On Civil Rights.

Analytic Report On The Civil Rights Compliance Survey, 3v. Opportunity Systems, Inc.

Justice In Flagstaff: Are These Rights Inalienable? Arizona Committee To The U S Commission On Civil Rights.

Policing In A Free Society. Goldstein, Herman.

Unfinished Business—Twenty Years Later—A Report Submitted To The USCCR By 51 State Advisory Committees. U S Commission On Civil Rights.

Civil Rights Movement—To The Courtroom. Bond, Julian.

Reform Without Change: The Future Of Prisoners' Rights. Bronstein, Alvin J.

Civil Rights Enforcement Under The Jordan Amendment: Progress, 1976–1978. L E A A, Office Of Civil Rights Compliance.

Constitutional Rights Of The Accused—Cases And Comments. Lewis, Peter W and Peoples, Kenneth D.

The National Civil Rights Directory: An Organized Directory. Bundy, Mary Lee (ed) and Gilchrist, Irvin (ed).

Toward An Understanding Of Bakke. U S Commission On Civil Rights.

Developments In The Law—Section 1981. Comment.

Did The FBI Kill Viola Liuzzo? Greene, Johnny.

CIVIL RIGHTS ACT, 1964

CORE And The Strategy Of Non–Violence. Bell, Inge Powell.

CIVIL SERVICE

Police Civil Service Selection Prodecures And New York City—Comparison Of Ethnic Groups. Chaiken, J M and Cohen, Bernard.

CLARK, RICHARD X

The Brothers Of Attica. Clark, Richard X.

CLARKE COUNTY, MS

Southern Justice. Friedman, Leon (ed).

CLARKSDALE, MS

Southern Justice. Friedman, Leon (ed).

CLASS

Justice And The Poor. Smith, Reginald H.

Crime: Its Causes And Treatment. Darrow, Clarence.

Caste And Class In A Southern Town. Dollard, John.

Caste, Class And Race. Cox, Oliver Cromwell.

Poverty, Race And Crime. Mc Keown, James Edward.

Lower Class Culture As A Generating Milieu Of Gang Delinquency. Miller, Walter B.

Social Class And Delinquent Etiology. Hines, Joseph S.

Socio–Economic Status And Delinquent Behavior. Nye, F Ivan and Short Jr, James F and Olson, Virgil J.

Class And Class Conflict In Industrial Society. Dahrendorf, Ralf.

Color, Class, Personality And Juvenile Delinquency. Clark, Kenneth B.

Black Bourgeoisie. Frazier, E Franklin.

Black Metropolis: A Study Of Negro Life In A Northern City, Rev'd Ed Orig Pub 1945. Cayton, Horace R and Drake, St Clair.

Caste, Class And Vandalism. Bates, William.

Race, Class, And Power. Mack, Raymond W (ed).

The Lower–Class Value Stretch. Rodman, Hyman.

Moral Indignation And Middle Class Psychology: A Sociological Study, Ranulf, Svend.

Defense Of The Poor: The National Report, 3v. Silverstein, Lee.

"Race, Poverty And The Law" in *The Law Of The Poor*, Tenbroek, Jacobus (ed), 62–82. Miller, Loren.

The Equal Protection Clause And Imprisonment Of The Indigent For Non–Payment Of Fines. Note.

"Pauperism And Alcoholism" in *The Philadelphia Negro*, Orig Pub 1899, 269–286. Du Bois, W E B.

A *Try Simplest Cases* Approach To The Heredity––Poverty––Crime Problem. Shockley, W.

Inequality: A Cross–Sectional Analysis. Cutright, Phillip.

A Criminal Justice System And The Indigent. Oaks, Dallin H and Lehman, Warren.

Deprivation, Mobility, And Orientation Toward Protest Of The Urban Poor. Bowen, Donald Et Al.

Detroit 1967: Racial Violence Or Class Warfare. Corsi, Jerome.

Law, Justice And The Poor. Berger, C J.

Socio–Economic Status And Delinquent Behavior: A Retest. Akers, Ronald L.

Three Views Of Urban Violence: Civil Disturbance, Racial Revolt, Class Assault. Grimshaw, Allen.

Criminality And Economic Conditions. Bonger, Willem Adriaen.

Ethnicity, Poverty And Selected Attitudes: A Test Of The Culture Of Poverty Hypothesis. Irelan, L M and Moles, O C and O' Shea, R M.

Interracial Social Contact And Middle Class White Reaction To The Watts Riot. Jeffries, Vincent and Ransford, H E.

Poverty, Race And Violence. Fishman, J R.

"Black Culture Or Lower Class Culture" in *Soul*, Rainwater, Lee (ed). Berger, B.

"Black Culture: Lower Class Result Or Ethnic Creation" in *Soul*, Rainwater, Lee (ed), 129–166. Blauner, Robert.

Class And The Economics Of Crime. Gordon, David M.

Inequality: A Reassessment Of The Effect Of Family And Schooling In America. Jencks, Christopher.

Double Standard Of American Justice. Nagel, Stuart and Weitzman, Leonard J.

Eradication Of Racism And Poverty As A Means Of Stopping Escalation Of Crime And Violence: A Dream Deferred. Higginbotham Jr, A Leon.

The Nonculture Of Poverty Among Black Youths. Gruber, Murray.

The Black Urban Condition. Lynch, Hollis R.

Bugs In The Driving Dream: The Technocratic War Against Poverty. Tollett, Kenneth.

Race, Socioeconomic Status And Sentencing In The Juvenile Justice System. Thornberry, Terence P.

The Case For Double Jeopardy: Black And Poor. Dolan, Thomas J.

Social Problems And Public Policy, V1: Inequality And Justice, A Survey Of Inequalities Of Class, Status, Sex And P. Rainwater Lee (ed).

Violence By Blacks And Low–Income Whites: Some New Evidence On The Subculture Of Violence Thesis. Erlanger, Howard S.

Discrimination In Supermarket, Prices And Location In Nashville. Steel, William F.

Historical Notes On Chicano Oppression: The Dialectics Of Racial And Class Domination In North America. Almaguer, Tomás.

Occupational Choice And Perception Of Attainment Blockage—Study Of Lower Class Delinquent And Nondelinquent Black Males. Picou, J S et al.

Success Values: Are They Universal Or Class Differentiated? Della Faxe, Richard L.

The Culture Of Poverty Revisited: A Strategy For Research. Della Faxe, Richard L.

Crime And Privilege: Toward A New Criminology. Krisberg, Barry.

Subordinating The Poor. Feagin, Joe R.

The Social And Economic Status Of The Black Population In The United States, 1974. U S Dept Of Commerce, Bureau Of The Census.

Unemployment And Prison Population Trends In Georgia: 1967–1974. Cox, George H and Carr, Timothy S.

Welfare In America: Controlling The "Dangerous Classes". Mandell, Betty R (ed).

Social Class As A Factor Affecting Judicial Disposition. Willick, Daniel H and Gehlker, Gretchen and Mc Farland, Anita.

Social Class And Crime: The Case Of The Japanese–Americans. Fujimoto, Tetsuya.

Socioeconomic Status And Criminal Sentencing. Chiricos, Theodore G and Waldo, Gordon P.

CLASS

An Assessment Of Legal And Cultural Stigma Regarding Unskilled Workers. Palys, T S.

Book Review: Criminal Violence And The Poor Black Male. Pfohl, Stephen J.

Effects Of Class, Race, Sex And Educational Status On Patterns Of Aggression Of Lower Class Youth. Lucterhand, Elmer and Weller, Leonard.

Inequality, Unemployment And Crime: A Cross–National Analysis. Krohn, M D.

Class, State And Crime. Quinney, Richard

Punishment And The Post–Industrial Society: A Study Of Unemployment, Crime And Imprisonment In The US. Jankovic, Ivan.

Labor Market And Imprisonment. Jankovic, Ivan.

Political Economy Of Criminal Oppression. Johnson, R C.

Poor Minority Juveniles Said More Likely To Be Locked Up. Anonymous.

Housing The Poor: A Case For Heroism. Polikoff, Alexander.

The Declining Significance Of Race. Wilson, William Julius.

'Street' Crime—A View From The Left. Platt, Anthony.

Behind The Gilded Ghetto: An Analysis Of Race, Class And Crime In Chinatown. Takagi, Paul and Platt, Tony.

Inequality And The Legal Order: An Ecological Test Of The Conflict Model. Jacobs, David.

Social Class And Criminal Sentencing. Jankovic, Ivan.

The Class Nature Of The Urban Police During The Period Of Black Municipal Power. Green, Edward.

The Death Penalty: Continuing Threat To America's Poor. Hinds, Lennox S.

The Economic Basis Of Indian Life. Sorkin, Allan.

Social Structure And Rates Of Imprisonment: A Research Note. Garofalo, James.

Race And Class In The Southwest: A Theory Of Racial Inequality. Barrera, Mario.

The Rich Get Richer And The Poor Get Prison. Reiman, Jeffrey H.

Theoretical Interpretations Of Social Class And Racial Differentials In Legal Decision Making For Juveniles. Liska, Allen E and Tausig, Mark.

A Matter Of Class. Gershman, Carl.

Double Marginality Of Black Policement: A Reassessment. Campbell, Valencia.

Reconciling Race And Class Differences In Self–Reported And Official Estimates Of Delinquency. Elliot, D S.

The Role Of Race. Clark, Kenneth B.

CLEAVER, ELDRIDGE

Soul On Ice. Cleaver, Eldridge.

Internal Colonialism And Ghetto Revolt. Blauner, Robert.

Where I'm Bound: Patterns Of Slavery And Freedom In Black American Autobiography. Smith, Sidonie.

CLEVELAND, OH

New Answer To Riots: Keep White Police Away? Gillece, James et al.

Shootout In Cleveland: Black Militants And The Police (Violence Commission Report, Volume 5). Masotti, Louis and Corsi, Jerome.

The Nonculture Of Poverty Among Black Youths. Gruber, Murray.

CLINTON, LA

Southern Justice. Friedman, Leon (ed).

CLUM, JOHN P

Apache Agent: The Story Of John P Clum. Clum, W.

COCAINE see Drugs

COHORT ANALYSIS

Delinquency In A Birth Cohort. Wolfgang, Marvin E and Figlio, Robert M and Sellin, Thorsten.

Race, Socioeconomic Status And Sentencing In The Juvenile Justice System. Thornberry, Terence P.

Delinquency Among Wind River Indian Reservation Youth. Forslund, Morris A and Meyers, Ralph E.

Changing Patterns Of Delinquent Behavior Among Americans 13 Through 16 Years Old: 1967–1972. Gold, Martin and Reimer, David.

Race, Achievement, And Delinquency—A Further Look At Delinquency In A Birth Cohort. Jensen, Gary F.

Childhood Deviance As A Developmental Process: A Study Of 223 Urban Black Men From Birth To 18. Robins, Lee N and Wish, Eric.

COLONIALISM

Capitalism And Slavery. Williams, Eric.

White Settlers And Native Peoples. Price, A G.

Black Mother: The Years Of The African Slave Trade. Davidson, Basil.

The Wretched Of The Earth. Fanon, Frantz.

The Colonizer And The Colonized. Memmi, A.

Internal Colonialism And Ghetto Revolt. Blauner, Robert.

Colonialism: The Case Of The Mexican–Americans. Moore, Joan W.

"The Barrio As An Internal Colony," in *Urban Affairs Annual Review*, V6, Hahn, Harlan (ed), 465–498. Berrera, M and Munos, C and Ornelasin, C.

Racial Oppression In America. Blauner, Robert.

A Definition Of Colonialism. Horvath, Ronald J.

The Invasion Of America: Indians, Colonialism, And The Cant Of Conquest. Jennings, Francis.

To Be Young, Black And Oppressed. Staples, Robert.

White Racism, Black Crime And American Justice: An Application Of The Colonial Model To Explain Crime And Race. Staples, Robert.

Introduction To Black Sociology. Staples, Robert.

"Race And Family Violence" in *Crime And Its Impact On The Black Community*, Gary, L E And L P Brown (eds), 85–96. Staples, Robert.

Colonialism And Ethnicity: A Theory And Comparative Case Study. Cross, Malcolm.

Internal Colonialism: White, Black And Chicano Self Conceptions. Hurstfield, Jennifer.

Savagism And Civility: Indians And Englishmen In Colonial Virginia. Sheehan, Bernard W.

COLUMBIA UNIVERSITY

Black Power And Student Unrest: Reflections On Columbia University And Harlem. Ginzberg, Eli.

COLUMBUS, OH

Crime In Negro Columbus. Hines, Joseph S.

COMANCHE

United States—Comanche Relations. Hagan, W T.

COMMITMENT

Race, Commitment To Deviance, And Spoiled Identity. Harris, Anthony R.

COMMUNISTS

Black Bolshevik: Autobiography Of An Afro–American Communist. Haywood, H.

The True Story Of The Greensboro Massacre. Bermanzohn, Paul C and Bermanzohn, Sally A.

COMMUNITY

The Metropolis And Juvenile Delinquency Among Negroes. Hill, Mozell.

Homicide In An Urban Community. Bensing, Robert C and Schroeder, Oliver.

Soul Side: Inquires Into Ghetto Culture And Community. Hannerz, Ulf.

The Response Of The Washington DC Community And Its Criminal Justice System To The April 1968 Riot. Cheminick, Paul W (ed).

The Integration Of Blacks In Suburban Neighborhoods: A Reexamination Of The Contact Hypothesis. Zeal, Carolyn and Humphrey, Craig.

Developing A Community And Computer Based Anti–Color–Code Strategy To Resist And Reduce Violent Crimes In Black Ghettoes. Haynes Jr, Andrew B.

"Criminal Justice And The Minority Community" in *Urban Minority Groups In Houston: Problems, Progress And Prospects*, 205–248. Lede, Naomi W and Dixon, Hortense W.

The Community And The Police: Conflict Or Cooperation. Sealy, Lloyd G and Fink, Joseph.

Crime In The Minority Community. Joyner, Irving and Scott, Elsie K.

Relating Academic Research To Community Concerns: A Case Study In Collaborative Effort. Bengston, Vern L et al.

The Law Enforcement Assistance Administration And Minority Communities. Salas, Luis P and Lewis, Ralph G.

COMMUNITY- CRIME'S IMPACT ON

The Geography Of Crime And Violence: A Spatial And Ecological Perspective. Georges, Daniel E.

COMMUNITY, DISORGANIZATION

Some Ecological Patterns Of Community Disorganization In Honolulu. Lind, Andrew W.

COMMUTATION

The Effect Of Mandatory And Discretionary Death Sentences On Commutations And Executions In Pennsylvania. Riedel, Marc.

COMPETENCY TO STAND TRIAL

A Comparison Of Blacks And Whites Committed For Evaluation Of Competency To Stand Trial On Criminal Charges. Cooke, Gerald and Pogany, Eric and Johnston, Norman G.

CON-ARTISTS

Cats, Kicks, And Color. Finestone, Harold.

The 'Short Con' Man. Roebuck, Julian D and Johnson, R C.

Hustler: The Autobiography Of A Thief, R Lincoln Keiser (ed). Williamson, Henry (pseudonym).

To Reach A Dream. Heard, Nathan C.

Swindling And Knavery, Inc. Hart, Philip A.

CONCENTRATION CAMPS

Human Behavior In A Concentration Camp. Cohen, Elie A.

Slavery: A Problem In American Institutional & Intellectual Life. Elkins, Stanley M.

Chattel Slavery And Concentration Camps. Thorpe, Earl E.

CONFLICT RESOLUTION

Dispute Settlement In Chinese American Communities. Doo, L W.

Evaluating The Dade County Citizen Dispute, Settlement Program. Salas, Luis P and Schneider, Ronald.

CONFLICT THEORY

Conflict And Criminality. Turk, Austin.

Criminality And Legal Order. Turk, Austin.

Socioeconomic Status And Criminal Sentencing. Chiricos, Theodore G and Waldo, Gordon P.

Stratification And Conflict Among Prison Inmates. Jacobs, James B.

An Empirical Examination Of Conflict Theory: Race And Sentence Length. Dison, Jack E.

Judicial Decision—Making In The Juvenile Court: An Empirical Test Of A Labelling/Conflict Proposition. Marshall, Ineke M.

Extra—Legal Factors In Chicago's Criminal Courts: Testing The Conflict Model Of Criminal Justice. Lizotte, Alan J.

Inequality And The Legal Order: An Ecological Test Of The Conflict Model. Jacobs, David.

Patterns Of Conflict Preceding The 1964 Riots: Harlem And Bedford—Stuyvesant. Monti, D J.

CONGRESS, U S

"Crime As A Concern Of Congress" in *Black Crime: A Police View*, Bryce, H J (ed), 21–28. Conyers, John R.

CONGRESS OF RACIAL EQUALITY

CORE And The Strategy Of Non—Violence. Bell, Inge Powell.

CONJUGAL VISITS

Mississippi Has Come A Long Way, But It Had A Long Way To Come. Gettinger, Steve.

CONNECTICUT *see* New Haven, Ct, Norwalk, Ct, Stamford, Ct

CONSPIRACY

An Account Of The Late Intended Insurrection Among A Portion Of The Blacks Of This City. Hamilton Jr, James.

Proceedings Of The Conspiracy Formed By Some White People For Burning The City Of NY In America And Murdering The Inhabitants. Horsmanden, Daniel.

The Slave Insurrection In New York In 1712. Scott, Kenneth.

He Slew The Dreamer: My Search, With James Earl Ray, For The Truth About The Murder Of Martin Luther King. Huie, William Bradford.

White Terror: The Ku Klux Klan Conspiracy In Southern Reconstruction. Trelease, Alan.

History Of The Rise And Fall Of The Slave Power In America, 3v. Wilson, Henry.

Who Killed George Jackson: Fantasies, Paranoia And The Revolution. Durden—Smith, Jo.

Mafia: The Prototypical Alien Conspiracy. Smith, Dwight C.

The Grand Jury—Its Use And Misuse. Cobden, Lynn.

Othello. Volkman, Ernest.

CONSTITUTION, U S

Penal Servitude. Whitin, E Stagg.

Race Relations And American Law. Greenberg, Jack.

Anti—Miscegenation Laws And The Fourteenth Amendment: The Original Intent. Avins, A.

Disparity And Inequality Of Criminal Sentences: Constitutional And Legislative Remedies. De Costa, Frank A.

Freedoms And The Politics Of Mass Participation: Perspective On The 1967 Detroit Riot. Smith, John and Smith, Lois.

Black Man, Red Man, And White American: The Constitutional Approach To Genocide. Willhelm, Sidney M.

Black Resistance/White Law: A History Of Constitutional Racism In America. Berry, Mary F.

El Chicano And The Constitution: The Legacy Of Hernandez Versus Texas. Comment.

The Prison As A Lawless Agency. Greenberg, David F and Stender, Fay.

Race, Racism And American Law. Bell Jr, Derrick A.

Citado A Comparecer—Language Barriers And Due Process—Is Mailed Notice In English Constitutionally Sufficient? Comment.

Enforcing The Constitutional Rights Of Prisoners. Singer, Linda R.

Voir Dire—The Due Process Clause Of The Fourteenth Amendment [And Jurors' Racial Prejudice]. Comment.

Voir Dire Of Jurors: Constitutional Limits To The Right Of Inquiry Into Prejudice. Gaba, J M.

An Historical Perspective On The Constitutional Debate Over Affirmative Action Admissions. Kimball, Bruce A.

Balancing Inmates' Rights To Privacy With Equal Employment For Prison Guards. Reisner, S L.

The Death Penalty And The Current State Of The Law. Davis, Peggy C.

Constitutional Rights Of The Accused—Cases And Comments. Lewis, Peter W and Peoples, Kenneth D.

Eighth Amendment Proportionality. Clapp, Randy.

The Thirteenth Amendment And Private Affirmative Action. Note.

Unconstitutional Detention Of Mexican And Canadian Prisoners By The United States Government. Paust, J J.

CONTRACT COMPLIANCE

Civil Rights And Corrections—The Impact Of LEAA Compliance Requirements. Rice, H C.

Evaluating The -impact Of Affirmative Action—A Look At The Federal Contract Compliance Program—A Symposium. Lipsky, D B (ed).

Equal Employment Opportunity Under Federal Contracts. Read, J C.

Meeting Compliance Review Standards—The Problem Of Federal Contractors. Levine, M J.

Conducting Civil Rights Compliance Reviews—A Manual Draft. Griggs, E A et al.

CONTROL THEORY

Causes Of Delinquency. Hirschi, Travis.

Control Theory Re—examined: Race And The Use Of Neutralizations Among Institutionalized Delinquents. Mannle, Henry W and Lewis, Peter W.

CONVICTION

Conviction: The Determination Of Guilt Or Innocence Without Trial. Newman, Donald J.

Whitmore. Shapiro, Fred C.

Age, Occupation And Conviction Rates Of White And Negro Males: A Case Study. Forslund, Morris A.

Empathy As A Factor In Determining Jury Verdicts. Adler, Freda.

The Sixteenth Round. Carter, Rubin "Hurricane".

Conviction And Sentencing In The Fourth Judicial District Of Nebraska. Kulig, F H and Hawkinson, T.

Conviction Records As Barriers To Employment—Racial Discrimination Under Title 7: Green Versus Missouri Pacific Railroad. Comment.

Plea Bargaining—An Annotated Bibliography. Markowtiz, J.

Conviction Of A Defendant As A Function Of Juror—Victim Racial Similarity. Miller, M and Hewitt, J.

Exclusion Of Blacks From Juries Voids Fifteen—Year—Old Conviction. Anonymous.

The Rich Get Richer And The Poor Get Prison. Reiman, Jeffrey H.

CONVICTS *see* Prisoners

COOK'S RAILROAD GAME

Personality And Situational Influences On Changes In Prejudice: A Replication Of Cook's Railroad Game In A Prison Setting. Foley, L A.

CORPORATIONS

The Corporation And The Ghetto. Sengstack, Mary.

CORRECTIONS

see also Alternatives To Incarceration, Imprisonment, Rates Of, Institutionalization, Adult, Institutionalization, Juvenile, Parole, Prison Headings, Probation, Rehabilitation, Specific Prisons, By Name

Differences That Make The Difference. Mc Nickle, Roma (ed).

COURTS, TRIBAL

Justice And The American Indian, V2. National American Indian Court Judges Assoc.

Justice And The American Indian, V4: Examination Of The Basis Of Tribal Law And Order Authority. White, J.

Criminal Jurisdiction In Indian Country: Tribal Sovereignty And Defendant's Rights In Conflict. Vollman, T.

Indian Justice—A Research Bibliography. University Of Nebraska.

Native American Justice—the Courts Of The Navajo Nation. Fahey, R P.

American Indian Tribal Courts—Separate: 'Yes' Equal: 'Probably Not'. Brakel, S J.

In Our Image: After Our Likeness—The Drive For The Assimilation Of Indian Court Systems. Kickingbird, K.

Tribal Courts, The Model Code And The Police Idea In American Indian Policy. Barsh, R L and Henderson, J Y.

American Indian Courts And Tribal Self–Government. Collins, R B and Johnson, R W.

American Indian Tribal Courts: The Costs Of Separate Justice. Brakel, Samuel J.

CRIME *see* Delinquency, Specific Offense, Eg, Rape

CRIME, BLACK-ON-BLACK

Inter– And Intra–Racial Crime Relative To Sentencing. Green, Edward.

Why Blacks Kill Blacks. Poussaint, A.

Crime In The Black Community—An Exploratory Bibliography. Davis, Lenwood G.

"Lessons In Crime From The All–Black Town" in *Crime And Its Impact On The Black Community*, Gary, L E And L P Brown (eds). Street, Lloyd.

"Crime In The Black Community" in *Blacks And Criminal Justice*, Owens, Charles E And Jimmy Bell (eds), 69–74. Bell, Jimmy and Joyner, Irving.

Homicide Among Blacks. Shin, Yongsock and Jedlicka, Davor and Lee, Everett.

Black Violence. Button, James W.

Black On Black Crime—The Cause, The Consequences, The Cures. Johnson, J H (ed).

CRIME, COST OF

Task Force Report: Crime And Its Impact—An Assessment. President's Comm On Law Enforcement & Adm Of Justice.

The Economics Of Crime And Punishment. Rottenberg, Simon (ed).

"Impact Of Crime/Criminal Justice System On The Black Community" in *Social Research And The Black Community*, Gary, Lawrence E (ed), 88–98. Brown, Lee P.

CRIME, DRUG RELATED

Manchild In The Promised Land. Brown, Claude.

The Addict And The Law. Lindesmith, Alfred R.

Task Force Report: Narcotics And Drugs. President's Comm On Law Enforcement & Adm Of Justice.

Dealer: Portrait Of A Cocaine Merchant. Woodley, Richard.

Drug Usage And Arrest Charges: A Study Of Drug Usage And Arrest Charges Among Arrestees In Six Metropolitan Areas Of The United States. Eckerman, William et al.

Rel Bet Selected Personal Char Of Confined Narcotic Off And The Amn't Of Time Serv'd Prior To Their Official Referral Consideration. Green, Charles Bernard.

Origins Of Narcotic Control. Musto, David F.

Pretreatment Criminality Of Male And Female Drug Abuse Patients In The United States. Ball, John C et al.

Manny—A Criminal–Addict's Story. Retting, R P and Torres, M J and Garrett, G R.

Preliminary Report On Crime And Addiction Within A Community—Wide Population Of Narcotic Addicts. Nurco, D N and Du Pont, R L.

Homeboys: Gangs, Drugs, And Prison In The Barrios Of Los Angeles. Moore, Joan et al.

The Drug Arrest: Empirical Observations On The Age, Sex And Race Of Drug Law Offenders In A Midwestern City. Petersen, D M and Schwirian, K P and Bleda, S E.

Multicultural Perspectives On Drug Abuse And Its Prevention: A Resource Book. Messolonghites, Louisa.

Racism In United States: Drug Legislation And The Trade–Off Behind It. Heiligman, A C.

War On Narcotics—The State Of Hostilities In New York. Macguire, R J.

CRIME, FEAR OF

The Fear Of Crime. Harris, Richard.

The Self–Inflicted Wound. Graham, Fred P.

Fear Of Crime And Fear Of The Police. Block, Richard L.

CRIME, ORGANIZED

Task Force Report: Organized Crime. President's Comm On Law Enforcement & Adm Of Justice.

Merchants Of Heroin. Moscow, Alvin.

The Politics Of Heroin In Southeast Asia. Mc Coy, Albert.

Vizzini. Vizzini, Sal.

Ethnic Succession In Organized Crime: A Summary Report. Ianni, Francis A J.

Black Mafia: Ethnic Succession In Organized Crime. Ianni, Francis A J.

New Mafia: Black, Hispanic And Italian Styles. Ianni, Francis A J.

The Truth About The Black Mafia. Stewart, Ted.

Drugs And Minority Oppression. Helmer, John.

The Crime Society: Organized Crime And Corruption In America. Ianni, Francis A J and Reuss, Elizabeth.

Mafia: The Prototypical Alien Conspiracy. Smith, Dwight C.

America's Newest Crime Syndicate: The Mexican Mafia. Adams, Nathan M.

The Ethnic Vice Industry. Light, I.

CRIME, POLITICAL

Political Justice: The Use Of Legal Procedure For Political Ends. Kirchheimer, Otto.

"Political Crime And The Negro Revolution" in *Criminal Behavior Systems*, Clinard, Marshall B And Richard Quinney (eds). Moudelos, Joseph C.

How The Government Breaks The Law. Lieberman, Jethro K.

The Politicizing Of Crime, The Criminal And The Criminologist. Reasons, Charles E.

Critique Of Legal Order: Crime Control In Capitalist Society. Quinney, Richard.

The Political Criminal: The Problem Of Morality And Crime. Schafer, Stephen.

Political Crime In The United States—Analyzing Crime By And Against Government. Roebuck, Julian B and Weeber, S C.

CRIME, PROFESSIONAL

Outside The Law: A Thief's Primer. Jackson, Bruce.

In The Life: Versions Of The Criminal Experience. Jackson, Bruce.

The World Of The Burglar: Five Criminal Lives. David, Pedro R.

CRIME, RURAL

Criminal Justice In Rural And Urban Communities: A Study Of The Bureaucratization Of Justice. Hagan, John.

CRIME, SEX

"Negro And White Sex Crime Rates" in *Sexual Behavior And The Law*, Slovenko, Ralph (ed), 210–220. Savitz, Leonard D and Lief, H I.

Sexual Assaults In The Philadelphia Prison System And Sheriff's Vans. Davis, A J.

Patterns In Forcible Rape. Amir, Menachem.

"A Comparison Of White–Black Offender Groups" in *Sexual Behaviors*, Resnick, H L And Marvin E Wolfgang (eds). Gebhard, Paul H.

Toward A Cultural Interpretation Of Forcible Rape By American Blacks. Curtis, Lynn A.

Race, Sex And Violence: A Laboratory Test Of The Sexual Threat Of The Black Male Hypothesis. Schulman, G I.

Self–Defense Against Rape: The Joanne Little Case. Bond, Julian.

The Sex Offenses Of Blacks And Whites. Kirk, Stuart A.

Sexual Assault: The Victim And The Rapist. Walker, Marcia J (ed) and Brodsky, Stanley L (ed).

Forcible Rape: The Crime, The Victim, And The Offender. Chappell, Duncan and Geis, Robley (ed) and Geis, Gilbert (ed).

Humanitarian Reform And Biracial Sexual Assault In A Maximum Security Prison. Carroll, Leo.

Rape, Racism And The Capitalist Setting. Davis, Angela Y.

Aftermath Of Rape. Mc Cahill, T W and Meyer, L C and Fischman, A M.

Prison Sexual Violence. Lockwood, Daniel.

CRIME, STREET

Caste, Class And Vandalism. Bates, William.

Crime In The City. Glaser, Daniel (ed).

The Urban Crisis And Crime. Krantz, Sheldon and Kramer, William D.

The Mugging. Hunt, Morton.

Thinking About Crime. Wilson, James Q.

Assault With A Deadly Weapon: The Autobiography Of A Street Criminal. Allen, John.

CRIME, STREET

"Urban Street Crime—Hustling" in *Black Perspectives On Crime And The Criminal Justice System*, Woodson, Robert L (ed), 23–36. Carmichael, Benjamin G.

'Street' Crime—A View From The Left. Platt, Anthony.

Race And Involvement In Common Law Personal Crimes. Hindelang, Michael J.

Race And Involvement In Common Law Personal Crime: A Response To Hindelang. Mc Neely, Roger and Pope, Carl.

CRIME, VIOLENT

Violent Crime: Homicide, Assault, Rape And Robbery. National Commission On The Causes And Prevention Of Violence.

The Negro And Homicide. Brearley, H C.

Homicide In The United States. Brearley, H C.

Research Note On Inter– And Intra–Racial Homicides. Garfinkel, Harold.

Racial Violence And Law Enforcement. Mc Millan, George.

The Negro Armed Robber As A Criminal Type: The Construction And Application Of A Typology. Roebuck, Julian D and Cadwallader, Mervyn L.

Negroes With Guns. Williams, Robert F.

Walk Along The Worst Block: East 100th Street. Samuels, Gertrude.

Why The Negro Carries Weapons. Schultz, Leroy G.

Changing Patterns Of Racial Violence In The United States. Grimshaw, Allen.

On Racial Violence. West, L J.

The Subculture Of Violence: Towards An Integrated Theory In Criminology. Wolfgang, Marvin E and Ferracuti, Franco.

The Changing Nature Of Racial Violence. Spear, Allan.

Violence And The American Character Structure. Holden Jr, Matthew.

Crimes Of Violence (Violence Commission Report, Volume 11). Mulvihill, D J et al.

Violence In The City. Justice, Blair.

"The Dynamics Of Black And White Violence" in *The History Of Violence In America*, Graham, Hugh D And T Gurr (eds), 444–464. Comer, James P.

Navajo Criminal Homicide. Levy Jerrold E and Kunitz, Stephen J and Everett, Michael.

On Theories Of Urban Violence. Lupsha, Peter.

Sniping—A New Pattern Of Violence? Knopf, Terry Ann.

Patterns Of Criminal Homicide: A Comparison Of Chicago And Philadelphia. Hepburn, John R and Voss, H L.

The Violent Black Minority. Hacker, Andrew.

Why Blacks Kill Blacks. Poussaint, A.

Criminal Violence: Patterns And Policy In Urban America. Wolfgang, Marvin E and Curtis, Lynn A.

Violence And Robbery: A Case Study. Normandeau, Andre.

Violence By Blacks And Low–Income Whites: Some New Evidence On The Subculture Of Violence Thesis. Erlanger, Howard S.

Violence And Black America: The Political Implications. Staples, Robert.

Violent Crime Indices Among Community–Retained Delinquents. Andrew, J M.

Homicide Trends In The United States, 1900–1974. Klebba, A Joan.

Pathologies Among Homicide Offenders: Some Cultural Profiles. Landau, S F.

Self–Defense Against Rape: The Joanne Little Case. Bond, Julian.

Violence Among The Eskimos. Jayewardene, C H S.

Violence By Youth Gangs And Youth Groups In Major American Cities—Final Report. Miller, Walter B.

Book Review: Criminal Violence And The Poor Black Male. Pfohl, Stephen J.

Some Social Characteristics Of Young Gunshot Fatalities. Klein, D et al.

The Black Minority Criminal And Violent Crime: The Role Of Self Control. Heilbrun Jr, Alfred B and Heilbun, Kirk S.

The Management Of Police Killings. Harring, Sid et al.

Violence And Victimization Within A State Prison System. Fuller, Dan A and Orsagh, Thomas.

Criminal Violence, Criminal Justice. Silberman, Charles E.

Firearm Use In Violent Crime: A Selected Bibliography. Ray, M W (comp) and Brenner, Robert N (comp) and Kravitz, Marjorie (comp).

The Geography Of Crime And Violence: A Spatial And Ecological Perspective. Georges, Daniel E.

An Analysis Of Indian Violence. French, Laurence and Hornbuckle, J.

Gunfights In The Cocaine Coral. Schorr, Mark.

Race, Criminal Violence, And Length Of Parole. Heilbrun Jr, Alfred B.

Subculture Of Violence: Youth Offender Value Systems. Poland, James M.

Violent Crime Perpetrated Against The Elderly In The City Of Dallas, October 1974–September 1975. Georges, Daniel E and Kirksey, Kirk.

Understanding Violence. Newman, Graeme R.

Books Of The Times. Wilkins, Roger.

Community, Environment And Violent Crime. Block, Richard L.

Criminal Violence: An Exchange. Anonymous.

Silberman—Back To Root Causes. Anonymous.

The Minority Perspective On Violence. French, Laurence.

The Politics Of Explaining Crime. Kelman, Mark G.

Trends In State Correction; Juveniles And The Violent Young Offender. Vinter, Robert D.

CRIME, WHITE-COLLAR

Principles Of Criminology, Orig Pub 1924. Sutherland, Edwin H and Cressey, Donald R.

Critique Of Legal Order: Crime Control In Capitalist Society. Quinney, Richard.

CRIME AND NATIONALITY

The Immigrant's Day In Court. Claghorn, Kate M.

"Crime And Criminal Justice Among The Mexicans Of Illinois" in *Report On Crime And The Foreign Born*, V11. Warnheis, Paul L.

"Recent Statistics On Crime And The Foreign Born" in *Report On Crime And The Foreign Born*, V10. Bowler, Alida C.

"The Mexican Immigrant And The Problem Of Crime And Criminal Justice" in *Report On Crime And The Foreign Born*. Taylor, Paul.

Nationality And Crime. Taft, Donald R.

Crime As An American Way Of Life. Bell, Daniel.

"Race And Nationality In The Gang" in *The Gang: A Study Of 1,313 Gangs In Chicago*, Orig Pub 1927, 130–154. Thrasher, Frederick M.

Strangers In The Lands: Patterns Of American Nativism, 1860–1925. Higham, John.

"Ethnicity, Crime And Delinquency" in *Readings In Criminology And Penology*, Dressler, D (ed), 261–266. Shulman, Harry Manuel.

"The Criminality Of The Foreign Born" in *Readings In Criminology And Penology*, Dressler, D (ed), 253–260. Van Vechten, C C.

Success Story: Japanese–American Style. Peterson, William.

Report On Crime And The Foreign Born, Orig Pub 1931. Abbott, Edith.

Race, Nationality And Crime. Weyl, Nathaniel.

CRIME AND RACE

Negro Criminality. Baker, S C.

The Criminal Negro. Kellor, Frances A.

The Criminal Negro. Kellor, Frances A.

The Criminal Negro. Kellor, Frances A.

The Criminal Negro. Kellor, Frances A.

The Criminal Negro. Kellor, Frances A.

The Criminal Negro. Kellor, Frances A.

"Negro Crime" in *Notes On Negro Crime, Particularly In Georgia*, Du Bois, W E D (ed). Sanborn, Frank B.

"Some Causes Of Criminality Among Colored Persons" in *The Negro In The Cities Of The North*. Waring, J H N.

The Negro Criminal Class—How Best Reached—Part I. Scarborough, W S.

Degeneration And Crime: The Twin Evils Of Discrimination And Oppression. Newsom, John T C.

Do Negroes Constitute A Race Of Criminals? Jackson, Ida Joyce.

Negro Criminality. Smyth, J A.

Negro Crime And Strong Drink Washington, Booker T.

Negro Criminality In The South. Work, Monroe N.

The American Negro As A Dependent, Defective And Delinquent. Mc Cord, Charles H.

Hidden Negro Criminality. Ramsey, D.

Race, Betterment And The Crime Doctors. Lyon, F Emory.

Education And Crime Among Negroes. Stephenson, G T.

The Negro Offender. William, George C.

Types Of Crime And Intelligence Of Negro Criminals. Burfield, H.

A Survey Of Crime Among Negroes In Philadelphia. Thompson, Anna J–.

An Analysis Of Negro Crime Statistics For Minneapolis For 1923, 1924, And 1925. Boie, Maurine.

The Negro Criminal: A Statistical Note. Sellin, Thorsten.

The Negro And Homicide. Brearley, H C.

"Note On The Negroe's Relation To Work And Law Observation" in *Report On The Causes Of Crime*, V13. Reid, Ira De A.

CRIME AND RACE

CRIME AND RACE

Crime In The Black Community—An Exploratory Bibliography. Davis, Lenwood G.

Violence, Race And Culture. Curtis, Lynn A.

Patterns Of Criminal Prosecution In Eighteenth–Century New York. Greenberg, Douglas S.

White Racism, Black Crime And American Justice: An Application Of The Colonial Model To Explain Crime And Race. Staples, Robert.

"Black Crime And Delinquency" in *Introduction To Black Sociology*, 212–247. Staples, Robert.

Antecedents Of Urban Indian Crime. Williams, L E.

Crime & Its Impact On The Black Community. Gary, Lawrence E (ed) and Brown, Lee P (ed).

Crime In The Minority Community. Joyner, Irving and Scott, Elsie K.

"Historical Overview Of Crime And Blacks Since 1876" in *Crime And Its Impact On The Black Community*, Gary, L E And L P Brown (eds), 3–11. Davis, Lenwood G.

"Lessons In Crime From The All–Black Town" in *Crime And Its Impact On The Black Community*, Gary, L E And L P Brown (eds). Street, Lloyd.

Blacks, Crime And American Culture. Davis, John A.

From Phrenology To Psychosurgery And Back Again: Biological Studies In Criminality. Nassi, A J and Abramowitz, S I.

The Hispanic Tide—Some Implications Of Its Continuing Growth. Holman, Ben.

Black Crime: A Police View. Bryce, Harrington J (ed).

Black Perspectives On Crime And The Criminal Justice System. Woodson, Robert L (ed).

Blacks And Criminal Justice. Owens, Charles E (ed) and Bell, Jimmy (ed).

Crime And Incarceration; A Reanalysis. Nagel, Jack H.

"Causes Of Crime" in *Black Crime: A Police View*, Bryce, H J (ed), 37–66. Brown, Lee P.

"Crime In The Black Community" in *Blacks And Criminal Justice*, Owens, Charles E And Jimmy Bell (eds), 69–74. Bell, Jimmy and Joyner, Irving.

Crime, Delinquency And The American Indian. Jensen, Gary and Stauss, Joseph and Harris, William.

Forced Conformity: Puritan Criminal Justice And Indians. Kawashima, Yasuhide.

Homicide Among Blacks. Shin, Yongsock and Jedlicka, Davor and Lee, Everett.

On Behalf Of A Moratorium On Prison Construction. Nagel, William G.

The Black Minority Criminal And Violent Crime: The Role Of Self Control. Heilbrun Jr, Alfred B and Heilbun, Kirk S.

Crime And The American Indian: A Survey Of The Literature. May, Phillip A.

Racial Issues In The Measurement Of Criminal Involvement. Mc Neely, Roger L and Pope, Carl E.

Criminal Violence, Criminal Justice. Silberman, Charles E.

Behind The Gilded Ghetto: An Analysis Of Race, Class And Crime In Chinatown. Takagi, Paul and Platt, Tony.

Blacks And Crime—Can America Break The Chain Of Failure. Renshaw, Benjamin et al.

Can You Photograph *Suspicious–Looking Blacks* Who Enter The Premises? Anonymous.

Crime And Justice: VI: Race And Crime. Pinkney, Alphonso.

Race And Involvement In Common Law Personal Crimes. Hindelang, Michael J.

Race And Involvement In Common Law Personal Crime: A Response To Hindelang. Mc Neely, Roger and Pope, Carl.

The Enforcers. Johnson, Thomas A.

The System. Williams, Hubert.

The Victimizers. Brown, Lee P.

The Victims. Renshaw, Benjamin H and Lehnen, Robert.

Black On Black Crime—The Cause, The Consequences, The Cures. Johnson, J H (ed).

Crime—Some Popular Beliefs. Doleschal, Eugene.

Criminal Violence: An Exchange. Anonymous.

Race And Crime Revisited. Pope, Carl E.

The Politics Of Explaining Crime. Kelman, Mark G.

Prison And Plantation: Crime, Justice, And Authority In Massachusetts And South Carolina, 1767–1878. Hindus, Michael Stephen.

The Criminal Justice System And Minority Crime. Georges– Abeyie, Daniel E.

The Inequality Of Justice: A Report On Crime And The Administration Of Justice In The Minority Coummunity. National Minority Advisory Council On Crim Just.

"Race, Inferiority, Crime, And Research Taboos" in *Taboos In Criminology*, Sagarin, Edward (ed). Karmen, Andrew.

Race, Crime And Social Policy: The Chinese In Oregon, 1871–1885. Tracy, Charles A.

The Crime Of Reform. Davis, David Brion.

Women, Race And Crime. Young, Vernetta D.

The Brain Of A Negro Murderer. Mills, Charles K.

Negro Criminality: An Address Delivered Before The American Social Sciences Association At Saratoga, September 6, 1899. Willcox, Walter F.

Negro Criminality: An Address Delivered Before The American Social Science Association At Saratoga, September 6, 1899. Wilcox, Walter F.

The Negro And Crime. Du Bois, W E B.

CRIME AND SEX

The Criminality Of The Colored Woman, Series C. Von Hentig, Hans.

Race, Sex And Violence: A Laboratory Test Of The Sexual Threat Of The Black Male Hypothesis. Schulman, G I.

Violent Crime Indices Among Community–Retained Delinquents. Andrew, J M.

Report Of The LEAA Task Force On Women. U S Dept Of Justice, LEAA.

CRIME PREVENTION

The Crime Classes—Causes And Cures. Miller, D R.

The Negro Criminal Class—How Best Reached—Part I. Scarborough, W S.

Civil Rights Activity And Reduction Of Crime Among Negroes. Salomon, Frederic et al.

The Negro Crime Rate: Its Causes And Cure. Rice, Charles E.

The Challenge Of Crime In A Free Society. President's Comm On Law Enforcement & Adm Of Justice.

Youth Patrols: An Experiment In Community Participation. Knopf, Terry Ann.

Crime In America: Causes And Cures. Newman, Joseph.

New Perspectives On Urban Crime. American Bar Association.

Developing A Community And Computer Based Anti–Color–Code Strategy To Resist And Reduce Violent Crimes In Black Ghettoes. Haynes Jr, Andrew B.

What The Negro Can Do About Crime. Parker, J A and Brownfield, Allan C.

Crime Prevention And The Protection Of Lives: A Mechanism To Change Police Behavior In The Community. Swan, L Alex.

Getting The Crime Rate Down: Political Pressure And Crime Reporting. Seidman, D and Couzens, M.

Policemen: Agents Of Change—A Crime Prevention Report. Ferguson, R F.

"Black Attitudes Toward Crime And Crime Prevention" in *Crime And Its Impact On The Black Community*, Gary, L E And L P Brown (eds), 13–30. Scott, Elsie K.

"Citizens Action As A Deterrent To Crime" in *Crime And Its Impact On The Black Community*, Gary, L E And L P Brown (eds), 122–126. Payne, Ethel L.

A Framework For Developing Drug Abuse Prevention Strategies For Young People In Ghetto Areas. Dembo, R et al.

Blackness Is My Mental Health: A Mind Set For Black Drug Abuse Prevention And Treatment Programs. Wheeler, William Henry III.

Crime Prevention For Older Americans: Multanomah County's Victimization Study. Brown, Lee P and Ritai, Marlene A Young.

"Prison Construction Moratorium" in *Black Perspectives On Crime And The Criminal Justice System*, Woodson, Robert L (ed), 123–142. Boone, John O.

"The Role Of Police In Reducing Crime" in *Black Crime: A Police View*, Bryce, H J (ed), 67–88. Peirson, Gwynne.

Strategies For Controlling Crime—A Position Paper. National Urban League, Inc.

Can You Photograph *Suspicious–Looking Blacks* Who Enter The Premises? Anonymous.

Multicultural Perspectives On Drug Abuse And Its Prevention: A Resource Book. Messolonghites, Louisa.

"What Is The Potential For Biological Violence Control" in *Biology And Crime*, Jeffrey, C Ray (ed). Moyer, Kenneth.

CRIME RATES

Uniform Crime Reports For The United States. U S Dept Of Justice, Federal Bureau Of Investigation.

An Analysis Of Negro Crime Statistics For Minneapolis For 1923, 1924, And 1925. Boie, Maurine.

"The Pattern Of Violence" in *Culture In The South*, Couch, W T (ed), 678–692. Brearly, H C.

Post—War Trends In Employment, Crime, Insanity, And Heart Disease. Simpson, Ray Mars.

Research Memorandum On Crime In The Depression. Sellin, Thorsten.

Crime And Punishment—1938. Ford, Nick and Hill, Mozell C.

Recent Increase In Homicide. Metropolitan Life Insurance Company.

Differentials In Crime Rates Between Negroes And Whites, Based On Comparisons Of Four Socio—Economically Equated Areas. Moses, Earl R.

The Criminality Of Women. Pollak, Otto.

The Negro Crime Rate: A Failure In Integration. Anonymous.

Uniform Crime Reports: A Critical Appraisal. Wolfgang, Marvin E.

Task Force Report: Crime And Its Impact—An Assessment. President's Comm On Law Enforcement & Adm Of Justice.

The Criminal Patterns Of Boston Since 1849. Ferdinand, Theodore.

Metropolitan Crime Rates And Relative Deprivation. Everts, P and Schwirian, K.

On Theories Of Urban Violence. Lupsha, Peter.

Crime, Police, And Race Relations: A Study In Birmingham. Lambert, J R and Jenkinson, R F.

"Negro And White Crime Rates," in *The Sociology Of Crime And Delinquency*, 2nd Ed, Wolfgang, M et al (ed), 430–439. Moses, Earl R.

A Comparison Of Negro And White Crime Rates. Forslund, Morris A.

Patterns Of Criminal Homicide: A Comparison Of Chicago And Philadelphia. Hepburn, John R and Voss, H L.

Standardization Of Negro Crime Rates For Negro White Differences In Age And Status. Forslund, Morris A and Malry, L.

The Urban Crisis And Crime. Krantz, Sheldon and Kramer, William D.

The Geography Of Urban Crime: The Spatial Pattern Of Serious Crime In The City Of Renuer. Lee, Yuk and Egan, Frank J.

Who Called The Cops: Decisions To Report Criminal Victimization. Hawkins, R O.

Getting The Crime Rate Down: Political Pressure And Crime Reporting. Seidman, D and Couzens, M.

Homicide Trends In The United States, 1900–1974. Klebba, A Joan.

Analysis Of Arrest Rates For Trends In Criminality. Blumstein, Alfred and Nagin, Daniel S.

Crime Trends In Southern And Non—Southern Cities: A Twenty—Year Perspective. Jacobsen, Alvin.

Criminal Victimization In Eight American Cities. Hindelang, Michael J.

Crime Change Patterns In American Cities. Jones, E Terrence.

Explaining Urban Crime Rates. Danziger, Sheldon.

Inequality, Unemployment And Crime: A Cross—National Analysis. Krohn, M D.

Violent Deaths In A Metropolitan County: Changing Patterns In Homicide, 1958–1974. Rushford, Norman B et al.

Crime Rates, Crime Myths And Official Smokescreens. Chambliss, William J.

Explaining Crime. Nettler, Gwynn.

Crime Rates, Sanction Levels, And Constraints On Prison Population. Nagin, Daniel.

Crime—Unemployment Cycle. Becnel, B.

Inequality And The Legal Order: An Ecological Test Of The Conflict Model. Jacobs, David.

Correlates Of Delinquency: The Illusion Of Discrepancy Between Self—Report And Offical Measures. Hindelang, Michael J and Hirschi, Travis and Weis, Joseph G.

Criminal Victimization In The U S: Summary Findings Of 1978–1979 Changes In Crime And Of Trends Since 1973. U S Dept Of Justice, Bureau Of Justice Statistics.

Wisconsin Criminal Justice Information: Crime And Arrests 1979. Wisconsin Dept Justice, Div Law Enf Serv.

Reconciling Race And Class Differences In Self—Reported And Official Estimates Of Delinquency. Elliot, D S.

Increase Of Crime And Positive Criminology. Lea, H C.

CRIMINAL AUTOBIOGRAPHY

The Confessions Of Nat Turner, The Leader Of The Late Insurrection In Southampton, Va. Turner, Nat.

Every Opportunity. Himes, Chester.

Letter From Birmingham City Jail. King Jr, Martin Luther.

Hustler: The Autobiography Of A Thief, R Lincoln Keiser (ed). Williamson, Henry (pseudonym).

Manchild In The Promised Land. Brown, Claude.

Solitudes Crowded With Loneliness. Kaufman, Bob.

Howard Street. Heard, Nathan C.

Poems From Prison. Knight, Etheridge.

Soul On Ice. Cleaver, Eldridge.

The Life And Dying Speech Of Arthur, A Negro Man. Arthur.

Outside The Law: A Thief's Primer. Jackson, Bruce.

Black Voices From Prison. Knight, Etheridge (ed).

Getting Busted: Personal Experiences Of Arrest, Trial And Prison. Firestone, Ross (ed).

Soledad Brother: The Prison Letters Of George Jackson. Jackson, George.

The Felon. Irwin, John.

Dealer: Portrait Of A Cocaine Merchant. Woodley, Richard.

If They Come In The Morning: Voices Of Resistance. Davis, Angela Y et al.

Book Review On *Black Voices From Prison*, By Etheridge Knight. Wilcox, Preston.

Pages From The Life Of A Black Prisoner. Chapman, Frank E.

Blood In My Eye. Jackson, George.

In The Life: Versions Of The Criminal Experience. Jackson, Bruce.

Maximum Security: Letters From California's Prisons. Pell, Eve (ed).

Poetry Of Prison: Poems By Black Prisoners. Anonymous.

The Prison: Voices From The Inside. Chang, Dae H (ed) and Armstrong, Warren B (ed).

To Reach A Dream. Heard, Nathan C.

Who Took The Weight: Black Voices From Norfolk Prison. Norfolk Prison Brothers.

Imprisoned In America: Prison Communications 1776 To Attica. Philip, Cynthia Owen (ed).

No Beast So Fierce. Bunker, Edward.

My Days In Solitary. Newton, Huey.

Betcha Ain't: Poems From Attica. Tisdale, Celes (ed).

Seven Long Times. Thomas, Piri.

Captive Voices: An Anthology From Folsom Prison. Anonymous.

Erroneous Zone. Rice, David L.

Soledad Prison: University Of The Poor. Faith, Karlene (ed).

Baby Chocolate And Other Stories. Bullock, Clifton.

Bound And Free: The Poetry Of Warriors Behind Bars. Black Prisoners Of Florida State Prison, Starke.

In Prison: Sometime Federal Prisoner 21669. O' Hare, Kate Richards.

My Life Of Absurdity. Himes, Chester.

My Rhythm Flows From A Different Beat. Lucas, Henry N.

Uncle Yah Yah. Dickens, Al.

Animal Factory. Bunker, Edward.

Assault With A Deadly Weapon: The Autobiography Of A Street Criminal. Allen, John.

Dark Smoke. Aguila, Pancho.

Greenhaven Diary. Conway, Edward.

The Victim As Criminal And Artist: Literature From The American Prison. Franklin, H Bruce.

Memoirs Of American Prisoners: An Annotated Bibliography. Suvak, Daniel (comp).

"An Interview With Willie Tate" in *Punishment And Penal Discipline*, Platt, Tony And Paul Takagi (eds), 176–183. Begel, Debby.

"The San Quentin Six Case: Perspective And Analysis" in *Punishment And Penal Discipline*, Platt, Tony And Paul Takagi (eds), 165–175. Wald, Karen.

The Narrative & Confession Of Thomas Powers, A Negro, Who Was In The 10th Year Of His Age Was Executed For Committing A Rape. Powers, Thomas.

The Address Of Abraham Johnstone, A Black Man, Who Was Hanged In New Jersey. Johnstone, Abraham.

CRIMINAL JUSTICE SYSTEM

American Indian In The Criminal Justice System: A Selected Bibliography. Gleason, J (ed).

The Hispanic Experience In Criminal Justice. Sissons, Peter L.

CRIMINAL JUSTICE SYSTEM

The Adminstration Of Justice To Minority Groups In Los Angeles County. Lemert, Edwin M and Rosberg, Judy.

The Modernization Of Urban Law And Order. Holden Jr, Matthew.

Crime In The Cities: Improving The Administration Of Criminal Justice. Kennedy, Robert F.

Disparities In Criminal Procedures. Nagel, Stuart.

Texas Sentencing Practices: A Statistical Study. Baab, George W and Ferguson, William R.

A Criminal Justice System And The Indigent. Oaks, Dallin H and Lehman, Warren.

The Limits Of The Criminal Sanction. Packer, Herbert.

Crime And The Legal Process. Chambliss, William J.

Institutional Racism In America. Knowles, Louis L (ed) and Prewitt, Kenneth (ed).

Discrimination Against Negroes In The Adminstration Of Criminal Law In Missouri. Gerard, Jules B and Terry Jr, T Rankin.

Crime And Justice: American Style. Schrag, Clarence.

More Than Murder: Administration Of Justice. Johnson, James Weldon.

American Criminal Justice: The Defendant's Perspective. Casper, Jonathan D.

Criminal Justice—Law And Politics. Cole, G F.

Criminal Injustice From The Chicano Point Of View. Morales, Armando.

New Perspectives On Urban Crime. American Bar Association.

Race, Crime And Justice. Reasons, Charles E and Kuykendall, Jack L (ed).

Robbery And The Criminal Justice System. Conklin, John E.

The Mugging. Hunt, Morton.

"Discrimination In The Administration Of Justice" in *Race, Crime, And Justice*, Reasons, Charles E And Jack L Kuykendall (eds), 264–276. Overby, Andrew.

Double Standard Of American Justice. Nagel, Stuart and Weitzman, Leonard J.

Native Americans And Discrimination In Kansas: Trials From Injustice. Bean, Jerry L.

The Administration Of Criminal Justice In The Minority Communities. Reid, Herbert O.

Politics Of Punishment—A Critical Analysis Of Prisons In America. Wright, Erik Olin.

'Law And Order' And The Criminal Justice System. Motley, Constance Baker.

Ideology And Criminal Justice Policy. Miller, Walter B.

The Case For Double Jeopardy: Black And Poor. Dolan, Thomas J.

An Examination Of Institutional Racism: Black People In California's Criminal Justice And Mental Health Systems. Ogleton, Betty and Crittendon, Stephanie and Seda, Cozetta.

Blacks And The Criminal Justice System: Proceedings Form The Conference Held February 24–27, 1974 At The University Of Alabama. Owens, Charles E.

Criminal Justice In America. Quinney, Richard (ed).

Partial Justice: A Study Of Bias In Sentencing. Gaylin, Willard.

Sourcebook Of Criminal Justice Statistics: 1973. U S Dept Of Justice, LEAA, NCJISS.

The Administration Of Criminal Justice: A View From Black America. Brown, Lee P (ed).

The Crime Establishment. Silver, Isidore (ed).

"Impact Of Crime/Criminal Justice System On The Black Community" in *Social Research And The Black Community*, Gary, Lawrence E (ed), 88–98. Brown, Lee P.

Blacks And The US Criminal Justice System. Anonymous.

Crime, Criminal Justice And The Black Community. Brown, Lee P.

Discretionary Justice In The United States. Reiss Jr, Albert J.

The War Model In Criminal Justice: No Substitute For Victory. Christianson, Scott.

Administration Of Injustice. Sikes, M P.

How The Criminal Justice System Fails The Spanish-Speaking Community Of New York City And What Should Be Done About It. Special Committee On Penal And Correctional Reform.

Sourcebook Of Criminal Justice Statistics: 1974. U S Dept Of Justice, LEAA, NCJISS.

The Administration Of Criminal Justice: An Exploratory Bibliography. Davis, Lenwood G.

Crime: A Common Concern. Joyner, Irving and Scott, Elsie K.

Factors Affecting Post Arrest Dispositions: A Model For Analysis. Burke, P and Turk, A.

Selectivity In The Criminal Justice System. Baker, Timothy and Mann, Fredrica and Friedman, C Jack.

"The Criminal Justice System" in *Crime And Its Impact On The Black Community*, Gary, L E And L P Brown (eds), 48–61. Lyles, Barbara.

Non-English-Speaking Persons In The Criminal Justice System: Current State Of The Law. Cronheim, A J and Schwartz, A H.

Blacks And Criminal Justice. Owens, Charles E (ed) and Bell, Jimmy (ed).

Sourcebook Of Criminal Justice: 1975. U S Dept Of Justice, LEAA, NCJISS.

Sourcebook Of Criminal Justice Statistics: 1976. U S Dept Of Justice, LEAA, NCJISS.

Citizen Contact And Legal System Support. Walker, D.

Criminal Justice In Rural And Urban Communities: A Study Of The Bureaucratization Of Justice. Hagan, John.

The Justice System And Sentencing: The Importance Of Race In The Military. Perry, Ronald W.

Introduction To Criminal Justice, 2nd Ed. Newman, Donald J.

Sourcebook Of Criminal Justice Statistics: 1977. U S Dept Of Justice, LEAA, NCJISS.

The Dysfunctional Alliance: Emotion And Reason In Justice Administration. Kennedy, D B.

The Invisible Justice System Discretion And The Law. Atkins, B and Pogrebin, M.

Women, Crime, And The Criminal Justice System. Bowker, Lee H and Chesney, Meda and Pollock, Joy.

"Crime And Criminal Justice: Their Impact Upon Asian American Communities" in *National Minority Advisory Council Report*. Takagi, Paul.

Blacks In The American Criminal Justice System: A Study Of Sanctioned Deviance. Jones, T.

Chivalry And Paternalism—Disparities Of Treatment In The Criminal Justice System. Moulds, E F.

Extra-Legal Factors In Chicago's Criminal Courts: Testing The Conflict Model Of Criminal Justice. Lizotte, Alan J.

Indians And The Criminal Justice System. Starr, F M.

The System. Williams, Hubert.

Racial Justice: Black Judges And Defendants In An Urban Trial Court. Uhlman, Thomas M.

Sourcebook Of Criminal Justice Statistics: 1978. U S Dept Of Justice, LEAA, NCJISS.

The Impact Of New Sentencing Laws On State Prison Populations In Pennsylvania; Final Report. Urban Systems Institute.

The Rich Get Richer And The Poor Get Prison. Reiman, Jeffrey H.

Theory And Research In Criminal Justice: Current Perspectives. Conley, John A (ed).

Hispanics In The Criminal Justice System: The 'Non-Existent Problem. Mandel, Jerry.

Race And Crime Revisited. Pope, Carl E.

"Implementing A Black Perspective In Criminal Justice" in *Improving Management In Criminal Justice*, Cohn, Alvin W And Benjamin Ward (eds). Caldwell, Loretta and Greene, Helen E Taylor.

American Indians And The Criminal Justice System. Benjamin, Roger and Choong Nam Kim.

Improving Management In Criminal Justice. Cohn, Alvin W (ed) and Ward, Benjamin (ed).

Sourcebook Of Criminal Justice Statistics: 1979. U S Dept Of Justice, LEAA, NCJISS.

The Criminal Justice System: An Analysis Of Hispanic Issues. Baca, Salvador.

Hispanics And The US Criminal Justice System. Breiter, Tony (ed).

CRIMINOLOGY

The Crime Classes—Causes And Cures. Miller, D R.

Criminal Man According To The Classifications Of Cesare Lombroso. Ferrers, Gina Lombroso.

Causes And Cures Of Crime. Mosby, Thomas Speed.

The Criminal Physique: A Preliminary Report On The Physical Examination Of 1521 Prisoners At Wisconsin State Prison. Sleyster, Rock.

Crime: Its Causes And Treatment. Darrow, Clarence.

Principles In Criminology. Sutherland, Edwin H.

Criminality And Immigration. Hacker, Ervin.

DEATH PENALTY

Statement In Opposition To Capital Punishment. Community Service Society.

"Race, Rape And The Death Penalty" in *Forcible Rape—The Crime, The Victim And The Offender*, Chappell, D; R Geis, And G Geis (eds). Wolfgang, Marvin E and Riedel, Marc.

Black Arson In Albany, NY: November 1793. Gerlach, Don R.

Capital Punishment Symposium. Symposium.

The Value Of Life: An Argument For The Death Penalty. Lehtinen, Marlene W.

The Value Of Life, Arguments Against The Death Penalty: A Reply To Professor Lehtinen. Smith, Gerald W.

Neither Cruel Nor Unusual. Carrington, Frank G.

In Defense Of The Death Penalty: A Legal—Practical—Moral Analysis. Van Den Haag, Ernest.

The Death Penalty: Social Philosophy And Social Science Research. Wolfgang, Marvin E.

The Death Penalty And The Current State Of The Law. Davis, Peggy C.

The Death Penalty: Continuing Threat To America's Poor. Hinds, Lennox S.

Capital Punishment As A Case Study In The Incremental Evaluation Of Guided Discretion. Bowers, William J and Pierce, Glenn L.

Capital Punishment Dilemma, 1950–1977: A Subject Bibliography. Triche, C W.

Capital Punishment, 1978. U S Dept Of Justice, LEAA, NCJIsS.

Preliminary Tabulations Reflecting Arbitrariness And Discrimination Under Post–'Furman' Capital Statutes. Bowers, William J and Pierce, Glenn L.

Changing Attitudes Toward Capital Punishment. Rankin, J H.

Killing The Killers: A Post–*Furman* Profile Of Florida's Condemned. Lewis, Peter W.

Team Defense: The Holistic Approach: An Interview With Millard Farmer. Eisenberg, Howard.

The Death Penalty: A Life And Death Issue. Lehtinen, Marlene W.

Will He Be The First? Range, Peter R.

Death Row. Jackson, Bruce and Christian, Diane.

The Penalty Of Death. Sellin, Thorsten.

Arbitrariness And Discrimination Under Post–'Furman' Capital Statutes. Bowers, William J and Pierce, Glenn L.

Capital Punishment In 1740. Belden, Bauman L.

The Narrative & Confession Of Thomas Powers, A Negro, Who Was In The 10th Year Of His Age Was Executed For Committing A Rape. Powers, Thomas.

The Address Of Abraham Johnstone, A Black Man, Who Was Hanged In New Jersey. Johnstone, Abraham.

DEATH ROW

Waiting On Death Row: North Carolina. Lopez, Luisita.

Death Row. Jackson, Bruce and Christian, Diane.

DELINQUENCY

The American Negro As A Dependent, Defective And Delinquent. Mc Cord, Charles H.

Crime, Delinquency, And Immigration. Orebaugh, David A.

Delinquency Areas. Shaw, Clifford et al.

Juvenile Delinquency And The Negro. Beckham, A S.

Thirty Delinquent Negro Children. Halliday, A P.

"Juvenile Delinquency" in *The Negro Family In Chicago.* Frazier, E Franklin.

Juvenile Delinquency. Reckless, Walter C and Smith, Mapheus.

Personality Differences Between Delinquent And Non–Delinquent Negro Boys. Daniel, Robert P.

Care Of The Negro Delinquent. Washington, Forrester B.

Delinquency In The Negro Community. Moses, Earl R.

The Delinquent Girl In Chicago: I—A Comprison Of Four National And Racial Groups. Davis, E R.

Community Factors In Negro Delinquency. Moses, Earl R.

Native Son. Wright, Richard.

The Problems And Needs Of Negro Youth As Revealed By Delinquency And Crime Statistics. Diggs, Mary H.

A Comparative Clinical Study Of Delinquent And Nondelinquent Boys. Watts, Frederick P.

Juvenile Delinquency And Urban Areas. Shaw, Clifford and Mc Kay, Henry.

Negro Delinquent. Chivers, W R.

Racial Handicaps In The Negro Delinquent. Wyatt, D W.

Discriminative Value And Patterns Of The Wechsler–Bellevue Scales In The Examination Of Delinquent Negro Boys. Franklin, J C.

The Delinquency Of The American Indian. Von Hentig, Hans.

The First Generation And A Half: Notes On The Delinquency Of Native Whites Of Mixed Parentage. Von Hentig, Hans.

The Relationship Of Juvenile Delinquency, Race And Economic Status. Blue Jr, John T.

Delinquent Behavior Of Peoples. Elliot, Mabel A.

The Delinquent Negro Child. Cochrane, Hortense S.

Juvenile Delinquency In A Period Of Tension. Lloyd, R G.

Delinquent, Neglected And Dependent Chinese Boys And Girls Of The San Francisco Bay Region. Lee, R H.

Negro And White Male Institutionalized Delinquents. Axelrad, Sidney.

The Youthful Male Offender In Alabama: A Study In Delinquency Causation. Caldwell, Morris G.

A Study Of Teen–age Behavior Among Negroes, Mexicans, Puerto Ricans, Japanese, Chinese, Filipino And American Indians. Harris, Richard E.

Juvenile Delinquency (Indians). U S Senate Committee On The Judiciary.

Towards An Understanding Of Juvenile Delinquency. Lander, Bernard.

Factors Linked To Race Among Boys In Trouble With Detroit Police 1948. Wattenberg, W W.

Juvenile Delinquency (Indians). U S Senate Committee On The Judiciary.

Juvenile Delinquency Among The Indians. U S Senate Committee On The Judiciary.

Juvenile Delinquency Among The Indians. U S Senate Committee On The Judiciary.

Physique And Delinquency. Glueck, Sheldon and Glueck, Eleanor.

A Self–Report Comparison Of Indian And Anglo Delinquency In Wyoming. Forslund, Morris A and Cranston, Virginia A.

Aspiration Levels Of Negro Delinquent, Dependent, And Public School Boys. Mitchell, Lonnie E.

Family Status And The Delinquent Child: A Reappraisal And Some New Findings. Monahan, Thomas P.

Lower Class Culture As A Generating Milieu Of Gang Delinquency. Miller, Walter B.

Rosenzweig Picture—Frustration Study Results With Minority Group Juvenile Delinquents. Norman, Ralph D and Kleinfeld, Gerald J.

Social Class And Delinquent Etiology. Hines, Joseph S.

Socio–Economic Status And Delinquent Behavior. Nye, F Ivan and Short Jr, James F and Olson, Virgil J.

Are Educational Norms And Goals Conforming, Truant And Delinquent Adolescent Influenced By Group Position In American Society? Reiss Jr, Albert J and Rhodes, Albert Louis.

Color, Class, Personality And Juvenile Delinquency. Clark, Kenneth B.

Concepts And Methodology In The Field Of Juvenile Delinquency. Blue Jr, John T.

Educational Level And Juvenile Delinquency Among Negroes. Miller, Carroll L.

Juvenile Delinquency Among Negroes: A Critical Summary. Lewis, H.

Juvenile Delinquency: As Social Dimension. Lohman, Joseph D.

Negro Family Disorganization And Juvenile Delinquency. Cavan, Ruth S.

The Extent And Characteristics Of Juvenile Delinquency Among Negroes In The United States. Douglas, Joseph H.

The Metropolis And Juvenile Delinquency Among Negroes. Hill, Mozell.

The Role Of The Negro Community In Delinquency Prevention Among Negro Youth. Mays, Benjamin E.

Delinquency And Opportunity: A Theory Of Delinquent Gangs. Cloward, Richard A and Ohlin, Lloyd E.

Measuring Delinquency: A Study Of Probation Department Referrals. Eaton, Joseph W.

Differential Study Of Recidivism Among Negro And White Boys. Henton, Comradge L and Washington, Charles.

On The Trend In Delinquency. Monahan, Thomas P.

Young Offenders: Psychopathology And Social Factors. London, N J and Myers, J K.

The Analysis Of Self–Descriptions By Members Of Delinquent Gangs. Strodtbeck, Fred L and Short Jr, James F and Kolegar, Ellen.

The Sources Of Delinquency: A Diagnostic Study. St Louis Human Development Planning Project.

Behavior Dimensions Of Gang Delinquency. Short Jr, James F and Tennyson, Ray A and Howard, Kenneth I.

Court Records, Undetected Delinquency And Decision–Making. Erickson, Maynard L and Empey La Mar, T.

DELINQUENCY

Ethnic Differentials In Delinquency In Honolulu. Voss, Harwin.

Male Young Adult Criminality Deviant Values, And Differential Opportunities In Two Lower Class Negro Neighborhoods. Spergel, Irving.

Negro Delinquents In Public Training. Baker, Gordon H and Adams, William T.

Street Corner Groups And Patterns Of Delinquency: A Progress Report. Short Jr, James F.

The Juvenile Gang: A Cultural Reflex. Bloch, Herbert A.

The Relationship Of The Social Structure Of An Indian Community To Adult And Juvenile Delinquency. Minnis, Mhyra S.

Values And Gang Delinquency: A Study Of Street–Corner Groups. Gordon, Robert A et al.

"Gang Delinquency And Anomie" in Anomie And Deviant Behavior: A Discussion And Critique, Clinard, Marshall B (ed), 98–127. Short Jr, James F.

Delinquency And Drift. Matza, David.

"Ethnicity, Crime And Delinquency" in Readings In Criminology And Penology, Dressler, D (ed), 261–266. Shulman, Harry Manuel.

Adult–Adolescent Relations And Gang Delinquency. Short Jr, James F and Rivera, Ramon and Marshall, Harvey.

Crime, Delinquency, And Social Areas. Quinney, Richard.

Gang Member Delinquency: Its Extent, Sequence And Typology. Robin, Gerald D.

Interacting Factors In Juvenile Delinquency. Palmore, E B and Hammond, Phillip.

Juvenile Delinquency In Racially Mixed Areas. Willie, Charles V and Gershenovitz, A.

Predicting Juvenile Delinquency Among Negroes. Kramer, Samuel A.

Racial Group Membership And Juvenile Delinquency. Segal, Bernard E.

"Crime And Delinquency" in The Negro In The United States, 638–653, Orig Pub 1949. Frazier, E Franklin.

Manchild In The Promised Land. Brown, Claude.

A Five–Year Encounter With A Mexican–American Conflict Gang: Its Implications For Delinquency Theory. Farris, Buford and Brymer, Richard.

Perceived Opportunities, Gang Membership, And Delinquency. Short Jr, James F and Rivera, Ramon and Tennyson, Ray.

Race And Delinquency. Willie, Charles V et al.

A Comparison Of The Scores Of White And Negro Male Juvenile Delinquents On Three Projective Tests. Megargee, Edwin I.

Analysis Of Selected Social And Cultural Characteristics Involving Juvenile Delinquency In Mexican–American Slums Of South El Paso. Knowlton, Clark S.

Differences In Smoking, Drinking, And Social Behavior By Race And Delinquency Status In Adolescent Males. Schonfeld, J.

Effect Of Parents In The Home On Juvenile Delinquency. Eisner, V.

Racial Perspectives And Attitudes Among Negro And White Delinquent Boys: An Empirical Examination. Segal, Bernard E.

Delinquency Research: An Appraisal Of Analytic Methods. Hirschi, Travis and Selvin, Hanan C.

Task Force Report: Juvenile Delinquency And Youth Crime. President's Comm On Law Enforcement & Adm Of Justice.

A Comparative Study Of Delinquents And Non–Delinquents: Family Affect, Religion, And Personal Income. Allen, Donald E and Sandhu, Harjit S.

Delinquency Amongst Immigrants. Bottoms, A E.

Discrimination In The Handling Of Juvenile Offenders By Social Control Agencies. Terry, Robert M.

Socioeconomic Status, Race, Level Of Aspiration And Juvenile Delinquency: A Limited Empirical Test Of Merton's Concept Of Deviation. Epps, Edgar G.

The Juvenile Delinquent's Home–Differentiated Attitudinal And Behavioral Patterns Among Three Ethnic Groups. Minnis, Mhyra S.

A Study Of Recidivism Among Female Juvenile Delinquents. Offord, D R and Aponte, J F and Frei, R J.

Chinese–American Child–Rearing Practices And Juvenile Delinquency. Sollenberger, Richard T.

Comment On Lerman's 'Gangs, Networks, And Subcultural Delinquency'. Short Jr, James F.

Delinquency Among Minorities: Afro–Americans. Bromberg, Walter.

Juvenile Delinquency In San Francisco's Chinese–American Community: 1961–1966. Abbott, Kenneth A and Abbott, Elizabeth Lee.

Juvenile Delinquency: Clique Interaction Among Three Ethnic Groups. Minnis, Mhyra S.

Negro–White Differentials And Delinquency. Stephenson, Richard M and Scarpitti, Frank R.

Socio–Economic Status And Delinquent Behavior: A Retest. Akers, Ronald L.

A Socio–Cultural And Socio–Legal Analysis Of Juvenile Delinquency In Puerto Rico. Kupperstein, Lenore R and Toro–Calder, Jaime.

A Study Of Delinquency Among Urban Mexican–American Youth. Rusk, Marian T.

Causes Of Delinquency. Hirschi, Travis.

Delinquency, Crime, And Social Process. Cressey, Donald R (ed) and Ward, David A (ed).

Delinquency In Three Cultures. Rosenquist, Carl M and Megargee, Edwin I.

Judging Delinquents: Context And Process In The Juvenile Court. Emerson, Robert M.

Patterns Of Conflict Among Higher Maturity Urban Negro Delinquents (Community Treatment Project). Neto, Virginia and Palmer, Ted.

Psychometric And Demographic Comparisons Of Negro And White Delinquents. Levine, B L.

Aggressive Behavior Of Delinquent, Dependent, And 'Normal' White And Black Boys In Social Conflicts. Berger, Stephen E and Tedeschi, James T.

Matriarchy And Lower Class Negro Male Delinquency. Rosen, Lawrence.

Racial Conflict And Delinquency: A Theoretical Approach. Schiller, Barry M.

Relative Occupational Anticipations And Aspirations Of Delinquents And Nondelinquents. Frederick, M A and Molnar, M.

Who Defines Delinquency: A Comparison Of Self–Reported And Officially–Reported Indices Of Delinquency For Three Racial Groups. Gould, Leroy C.

Delinquent Behavior In An American City. Gold, Martin.

The Sociology Of Crime And Delinquency. Wolfgang, Marvin E (ed) and Savitz, Leonard D (ed) and Johnston, Norman (ed).

"Diagnosing Delinquency" in Law And Order: Modern Criminals, Short Jr, James F (ed), 19–31. Hamblin, R L and Abrahamson, M J and Burgess, R L.

Deadline, Vengeance, And Tribute: A Prescription For Black Juvenile Delinquency. Echols, Alvin E.

Delinquency Potential And Attitudes Toward The Criminal Justice System. Waldo, Gordon P and Hall, N E.

Inner–City Youth, The Police, The Juvenile Court And Justice. Ferdinand, Theodore W and Luchterhand, Elmer G.

Juvenile Delinquents: Relationships Between Wisc Scores, Offenses, Race, Chronological Age, And Residence. Mc Conochie, W A.

Personality Characteristics Of White And Negro Adolescent Delinquents. Henning, John J.

Police Control Of Juveniles. Black, Donald and Reiss Jr, Albert.

The Image Of The Criminal: A Critique Of Crime And Delinquency Theories. Poveda, Tony G.

Helping Understand Delinquent Behavior In An Urban Setting. State Of Colorado.

Juvenile Delinquency: A Critical Annotated Bibliography. Cabot, Philippe Sidney DeQ.

The PAS Study Of Delinquency And Race. Malon J V.

Decisions By Juvenile Officers. Weiner, Normal L and Willie, Charles V.

Exploration In The Institutionalization Of Juvenile Delinquency. Vaz, Edmund W.

Imitation Of Self–Reward Standards By Black And White Female Delinquents. Thelan, Mark H and Fryrear, Jerry L.

Marital Instability And Juvenile Delinquency Among The Nez Perćes. Ackerman, L A.

Personality Factors In Delinquent Boys: Differences Between Blacks And Whites. Cross, Herbert J and Tracy, James J.

The Incarcerated Mexican–American Delinquent. Rudoff, Alvin.

"Identifying Juvenile Delinquents Among Negroes" in Identification Of Predelinquents, Glueck, S (ed), 22–35. Kramer, Samuel A.

Delinquency In A Birth Cohort. Wolfgang, Marvin E and Figlio, Robert M and Sellin, Thorsten.

Delinquency And Crime: A Biopsychosocial Approach. Cortes, Juan B and Gatti, Florence M.

Delinquency And City Life. Lalli, Michael and Savitz, Leonard D.

Schools And Delinquency. Polk, Kenneth and Schafer, Walter E.

DELINQUENCY

The Effect Of Father Absence On Delinquent Males: Dependency And Hypermasculinity. Moran, Patricia Anne.

Delinquency And Adolescent Self–Conceptions: A Study Of The Personal Relevance Of Infraction. Jensen, Gary F.

From Delinquent Behavior To Official Delinquency. Williams, Jay R and Gold, Martin.

Perceived Opportunity, Delinquency, Race, And Body Build Among Delinquent Youth. Mc Candless, Boyd R and Person, Scott and Roberts, Albert.

"Behavior Therapy And The Black Delinquent" in *Behavior Therapy With Delinquents*, Stumphauzer, J (ed), 49–53. Kimbles, Samuel L.

The Personality And Self Concept Characteristics Of Negro And White Delinquent And Non–Delinquent Boys. Zipper, Barry Oser.

Delinquent Acting–Out And Task Of Sexual Identification In Black Male Adolescents—Replication Study. Mc Nabb, D P.

Psychopathy, Race, And Delay Of Gratification By Adolescent Delinquents. Unikel, I P and Blanchard, E B.

Seriousness Of Delinquency, The Adjudicative Decision, And Recidivism—A Longitudinal Configuration Analysis. Meade, A.

Changing Patterns Of Delinquent Behavior Among Americans 13–16 Years Old, 1967-1972: Report # 1 Of The National Survey Of Youth, 1972. Gold, Martin and Reimer, David J.

Community Organizing Of Gang Barrios. Pineda, Charles.

Compulsive Masculinity And Delinquency: An Empirical Investigation. Silverman, I J and Dinitz, Simon.

Delinquency Among Wind River Indian Reservation Youth. Forslund, Morris A and Meyers, Ralph E.

Gang Youth And Hustling: The Psychology Of Survival. Krisberg, Barry.

Honor, Normative Ambiguity And Gang Violence. Horowitz, Ruth and Schwartz, Gary.

Occupational Choice And Perception Of Attainment Blockage—Study Of Lower Class Delinquent And Nondelinquent Black Males. Picou, J S et al.

Self–Concept In Negro And White Pre–Adolescent Delinquent Boys. Wax, Douglas E.

Violent Crime Indices Among Community–Retained Delinquents. Andrew, J M.

Delinquency Dispositions: Case Empirical Analysis Of Processing Decisions In Three Juvenile Courts. Cohen, Lawrence E.

Delinquents And Nondelinquents In The Puerto Rican Slum Culture. Ferracuti, Franco and Dinitz, Simon and De Brenes, E Acosta.

A Study Of Juvenile Delinquency Amongst Asians And Half–Asians: A Comparative Study In A Northern Town Based On Official Statistics. Batta, I D and Mc Culloch, J W and Smith, N J.

Adolescent Verbal Behavior—Investigation Of Noncontent Styles As Related To Race And Delinquency Status. Wool, R and Clements, C B.

Arrests And Delinquency In Two Generations: A Study Of Black Urban Families And Their Children. Robins, Lee N and West, P A and Herjanic, B L.

Attribution And Achievement Motivation Differences Between Delinquent And Non–Delinquent Black Adolescents. Farley, Frank H and Sewell, Trevor.

Changing Patterns Of Delinquent Behavior Among Americans 13 Through 16 Years Old: 1967–1972. Gold, Martin and Reimer, David.

Differential Effects Of Group Counseling With Black And White Female Delinquents One Year Later. Redferin, D L.

Factorial Dimensions Of Jesness Inventory With Black Delinquents. Woodbury, Roger and Shurling, James.

Psychological And Ethnic Correlates Of Interpersonal Maturity Among Delinquents. Werner, Eric.

Youth Crime In Urban Communities: A Descriptive Analysis Of Street Hustlers And Their Crimes. Carmichael, Benjamin G.

"Black Crime And Delinquency" in *Introduction To Black Sociology*, 212–247. Staples, Robert.

"Prevalence: The Rare Datum In Delinquency Measurement" in *The Juvenile Justice System*, Klein, Malcolm (ed), 201–284. Gordon, Robert A.

The Children Of Ham. Brown, Claude.

Continuities In Delinquency And Riot Patterns, In Black Residential Areas. Kapsis, Robert E.

Efficiency Of Peabody Picture Vocabulary In Estimating WISC Scores For Delinquents. Condit, J E and Lewandowski, D G and Saccuzzo, D P.

Ego Development And Female Delinquency: A Cognitive–Developmental Approach. Frank, Susan and Quinlan, Donald M.

Race, Achievement, And Delinquency—A Further Look At Delinquency In A Birth Cohort. Jensen, Gary F.

Role Of The Police And The Courts In The Survival Of Black Youth. Alexander, Gordon G.

Test Of An Arousal Theory Of Delinquency—Stimulation–Seeking In Delinquent And Nondelinquent Black Adolescents. Farley, Frank H and Sewell, Trevor.

The Black Matriarchy Controversy And Black Male Delinquency. Perry, Robert L.

"Juvenile Delinquency, Justice & Black Youth" in *Black Perspectives On Crime And The Criminal Justice System*, Woodson, Robert L (ed), 55–78. Swan, L Alex.

Black Female Gangs In Philadelphia. Brown, Waln K.

Crime, Delinquency And The American Indian. Jensen, Gary and Stauss, Joseph and Harris, William.

Delinquents And The Tapping Test. Andrew, J M.

Intelligence And Delinquency: A Revisionist Review. Hirschi, Travis and Hindelang, Michael J.

An Analysis Of The Evidence And Seriousness Of Self–Reported Delinquency And Crime. Tracy, Paul E.

Black Gangs As Family Extensions. Brown, Waln K.

Importance Of Police Contact In The Formulation Of Youths' Attitudes Toward Police. Rusinko, W T and Johnson, K W and Hornung, C A.

Profile Of Mood States: Racial Differences In A Delinquent Population. Fagan, T J and Lira, F T.

Race, Father–Absence And Female Delinquency. Austin, Roy L.

Residential Succession And Delinquency: A Test Of Shaw And McKay's Theory Of Cultural Transmission. Kapsis, Robert E.

Delinquency 1975—United States Estimates Of Cases Processed By Courts With Juvenile Jurisdiction. Smith, D D et al.

Ecologic—Biochemical Approaches To The Treatment Of Delinquents And Criminals. Hippchen, Leonard J (ed).

Psychological World Of The Juvenile Delinquent. Offer, D.

"Learning Disabilities And Juvenile Delinquency: Biological And Sociological Theories" in *Biology And Crime*, Jeffrey, C R (ed). Holzman, Harold R.

A Comparative Analysis Of Male And Female Delinquency. Cernkovich, Stephen A and Giordano, Peggy C.

Chicano Gangs In The East LA (Los Angeles, CA) Barrio. Torres, D M.

Control Theory Re–examined: Race And The Use Of Neutralizations Among Institutionalized Delinquents. Mannle, Henry W and Lewis, Peter W.

Correlates Of Delinquency: The Illusion Of Discrepancy Between Self–Report And Offical Measures. Hindelang, Michael J and Hirschi, Travis and Weis, Joseph G.

Some Evidence Of Race Bias In The Diagnosis And Treatment Of The Juvenile Offender. Lewis, Dorothy O and Balla, David A and Shanok, Shelley S.

"Research On IQ, Race, And Delinquency: Taboo Or Not Taboo" in *Taboos In Criminology*, Sagarin, Edward (ed). Gordon, Robert A.

Ducks Versus Hard Rocks. Hunter, Deairich.

Reconciling Race And Class Differences In Self–Reported And Official Estimates Of Delinquency. Elliot, D S.

DELINQUENCY PREVENTION

How Effective Are Current Delinquent Preventive Measures? Robinson, Sophia.

The Role Of Youth Character–Building Organizations In Juvenile Delinquency Prevention. Daniel, Walter G.

The Role Of School In Juvenile Delinquency Prevention. Hipps, Irene.

The Role Of The Negro Community In Delinquency Prevention Among Negro Youth. Mays, Benjamin E.

The Response Of Adults To Delinquency Prevention Programs: The Race Factor. Hackler, J C and Linden, E.

Street Gangs And Street Workers. Klein, Malcolm.

DEMOGRAPHICS

Population Density And Social Pathology. Calhoun, J B.

A Demographic Profile Of The Mexican Immigration To The United States. Álvarez, José Hernández.

Age Composition And Patterns Of Change In Criminal Statistics. Sagi, P and Wellford, C.

DEMOGRAPHICS

Psychometric And Demographic Comparisons Of Negro And White Delinquents. Levine, B L.

Growth Of The Black Population: A Study Of Demographic Trends. Farley, Reynolds.

Demographic Factors In Opiate Addiction Among Mexican Americans. Chambers, C D and Cuskey, W R and Moffett, A D.

The Geography Of Urban Crime: The Spatial Pattern Of Serious Crime In The City Of Renuer. Lee, Yuk and Egan, Frank J.

Population Breakdown Of Spanish–Speaking Residents. U S Dept Of Justice, Bureau Of Prisons, Education Branch.

For American Blacks: A New Identity—The Black Diaspora. Cannon, J Alfred.

Population Redistribution In The US In The 1970's. Berry, Brian J and Dahmann, Donald C.

Are Hispanics The 'minority For The 1980's'? Dreyfuss, Joel.

Demographics Of The 1980's. Reynolds, Reid and Robey, Brayant and Russell, Cheryl.

Hispanics In The United States: Yesterday, Today And Tomorrow. Anson, R.

DENVER, CO

Helping Understand Delinquent Behavior In An Urban Setting. State Of Colorado.

The Geography Of Urban Crime: The Spatial Pattern Of Serious Crime In The City Of Renuer. Lee, Yuk and Egan, Frank J.

"Minority Recruiting: Denver Colorado" in *Community Relations: Studies In Minority Programs*, V4, Platt, R (ed), 52–55. Herrera, Chris L.

"Minority Recruiting—Denver, Colorado" in *Police–Community Relations Series, V4: Case Studies In Minority Programs*. Platt, R (ed).

Who Gets Detained: An Empirical Analysis Of The Pre–Adjudicatory Detention Of Juveniles In Denver. Cohen, Lawrence E.

DEPRIVATION

Economic Deprivation And Extremism: A Study Of Unemployed Negroes. Street, D and Leggett, J C.

Deprivation, Mobility, And Orientation Toward Protest Of The Urban Poor. Bowen, Donald Et Al.

Metropolitan Crime Rates And Relative Deprivation. Everts, P and Schwirian, K.

"Race, Deprivation, And Drug Abuse In The USA" in *Proceedings Of The Anglo–American Conference On Drug Abuses*, 69–76. Holden Jr, Matthew.

Justice, Deprivation And The Chicano. Rivera, J.

Impact Of Incarceration On The Black Inmate. Adair, A V et al.

Race, Deprivation And Adolescent Self–Images. Hulbary, W E.

Relative Deprivation, Rising Expectations And Black Militancy. Abeles, R P.

DES MOINES, IA

Minority Recruitment And Retention In The Des Moines Police Department: A Survey Of Opinions. Boettcher, W D.

Minority Recruitment And Retention In The Des Moines Police Department—A Survey Of Opinions. Boettcher, W D.

DETERMINISM

The Compatibility Of Free Will And Determinism In Criminology: Comments On An Alleged Problem. Glaser, Daniel.

DETERRENCE

"Citizens Action As A Deterrent To Crime" in *Crime And Its Impact On The Black Community*, Gary, L E And L P Brown (eds), 122–126. Payne, Ethel L.

Capital Punishment Symposium. Symposium.

Mandatory Prison Sentences: Their Projected Effects On Crime And Prison Populations. Petersilia, Joan and Greenwood, Peter W.

Perceived Risk Of Punishment And Self–Reported Delinquency. Jensen, Gary F and Erickson, Maynard L and Gibbs, Jack P.

"Punishment And Deterrence: A Psychobiological Statement" in *Biology And Crime*, Jeffrey, C Ray (ed). Jeffrey, C Ray.

DETROIT, MI

Report Of The Mayor's Committee On Race Relations. Detroit Bureau Of Governmental Research, Inc.

Racial Conflict: Lessons Of The Detroit Riot. National Urban League, Inc.

What Caused The Detroit Riot? White, Walter and Marshall, Thurgood.

The Detroit Riots—And After. Norton, William J.

The Gestapo In Detroit. Marshall, Thurgood.

Why Race Riots: Lessons From Detroit. Brown, Earl.

The Relationship Of Juvenile Delinquency, Race And Economic Status. Blue Jr, John T.

Factors Linked To Race Among Boys In Trouble With Detroit Police 1948. Wattenberg, W W.

Breakdown Of Law And Order. Parmenter, Tom.

The Algiers Motel Incident. Hersey, John.

The Detroit Riot: A Profile Of 500 Prisoners. U S Dept Of Labor, Manpower Administration.

Children Of The Detroit Riots: A Study Of Their Participation And Their Mental Health. Komisaruk, R and Pearson, Carol.

Detroit 1967: Racial Violence Or Class Warfare. Corsi, Jerome.

Freedoms And The Politics Of Mass Participation: Perspective On The 1967 Detroit Riot. Smith, John and Smith, Lois.

The Detroit Riot Of 1967. Locke, Hubert G.

Neighborhood Structure And Riot Behavior In Detroit: Some Exploratory Findings. Warren, Donald.

Harlem And Detroit Riots Of 1943: A Comprehensive Analysis. Swan, L Alex.

Latitude And Severity Of Sentencing Options, Race Of The Victim And Decisions Of Simulated Jurors. Kaplan, J.

Mass Media And Racial Crisis: A Study Of The New Bethel Church Incident In Detroit. Warren, D I.

The Dialectics Of Legal Repression: Black Rebels Before The American Criminal Courts. Balbus, Isaac D.

Black Policemen: A Study Of Self–Images. Bannon, James D and Wilt, G Marie.

Justice, The Courts, And Change. Crockett Jr, George W.

Criminal Victimization Surveys In The Nation's Five Largest Cities. U S Dept Of Justice, LEAA, NCJISS.

Violence By Youth Gangs And Youth Groups In Major American Cities—Final Report. Miller, Walter B.

Minority Police: Tramping Through A Racial Minefield. Cory, Bruce.

DEVIANCE

Cultural Factors And Socialization Into Deviance. Jessor, Lee.

The Socio Cultural Context Of Deviance. Hasson, Robert C.

Theory And Method In The Study Of Deviance In A Tri–Ethnic Community. Jessor, Richard.

Wayward Puritans: A Study In The Sociology Of Deviance. Erikson, Kai T.

Patterns Of Deviant Reaction: Some Theoretical Issues. Duster, Troy.

Causes Of Delinquency. Hirschi, Travis.

Family Background And Peer Group Deviance In A Puerto Rican District. Doob, C B.

"Actuarial Evaluation Of The Causes/Consequences Of Deviant Behavior In Young Black Men" in *Life History Research*, Roff, M et al (eds). Robins, Lee N.

Emergence Of Deviant Minorities—Social Problems And Social Change. Winslow, R W.

Human Deviance, Social Problems, And Social Control. Lemert, Edwin M.

"The Labeling Approach To Deviance" in *Issues In The Classification Of Children*, Hobbs, Nicholas (ed), 88–100. Duster, Troy et al.

"The Normal And The Pathological" in *Social Deviance*, Farrell, Ronald And Victoria Swigert (eds). Durkheim, Emile.

A Study Of Drug Addiction And Conformity Behavior: A Biosocial Approach To The Understanding Of A Form Of Social Deviance. Chase, Stanley Harvey.

Race, Commitment To Deviance, And Spoiled Identity. Harris, Anthony R.

Childhood Deviance As A Developmental Process: A Study Of 223 Urban Black Men From Birth To 18. Robins, Lee N and Wish, Eric.

Blacks In The American Criminal Justice System: A Study Of Sanctioned Deviance. Jones, T.

DIAGNOSIS

"Diagnosing Delinquency" in *Law And Order: Modern Criminals*, Short Jr, James F (ed), 19–31. Hamblin, R L and Abrahamson, M J and Burgess, R L.

Some Evidence Of Race Bias In The Diagnosis And Treatment Of The Juvenile Offender. Lewis, Dorothy O and Balla, David A and Shanok, Shelley S.

DIFFERENTIAL ASSOCIATION

Principles In Criminology. Sutherland, Edwin H.

Changing Criminals: The Application Of The Theory Of Differential Association. Cressey, Donald R.

DIFFERENTIAL ASSOCIATION

Principles Of Criminology, Orig Pub 1924. Sutherland, Edwin H and Cressey, Donald R.

DISABILITY, LEARNING

"Learning Disabilities And Juvenile Delinquency: Biological And Sociological Theories" in *Biology And Crime*, Jeffrey, C R (ed). Holzman, Harold R.

DISCRETION

The Incidence Of The Death Penalty For Rape In Virginia. Partington, Donald H.

Disparities In Criminal Procedures. Nagel, Stuart.

Discretionary Justice: A Preliminary Inquiry. Davis, Kenneth Culp.

Sentencing As A Human Process. Hogarth, John.

Struggle For Justice. American Friends Service Committee.

Juvenile Court Dispositions: Factors In The Decision Making Process. Scarpitti, Frank R and Stephenson, Richard M.

Police Discretion And Discriminatory Enforcement. Tierger, Joseph H.

Criminal Sentences: Law Without Order. Frankel, Marvin E.

The Effect Of Mandatory And Discretionary Death Sentences On Commutations And Executions In Pennsylvania. Riedel, Marc.

Judicial Discretion And The Sentencing Process. Drew, James.

Race, Judicial Discretion And The Death Penalty. Wolfgang, Marvin E and Riedel, Marc.

Capital Punishment: The Inevitability Of Caprice And Mistake. Black, Charles L.

Discretionary Justice In The United States. Reiss Jr, Albert J.

The Use Of Discretion In Determining The Severity Of Punishment For Incarcerated Offenders. Scott, Joseph E.

Pre–Adjudicatory Detention In Three Juvenile Courts: An Empirical Analysis Of The Factors Related To Detention Decison Outcomes. Cohen, Lawrence E.

Discretionary Decision–Making In The Criminal Justice System And The Black Offender: Some Alternatives. Banks, Taunya L.

Factors Affecting Post Arrest Dispositions: A Model For Analysis. Burke, P and Turk, A.

Juvenile Court Intake: An Analysis Of Discretionary Decision–Making. Thomas, Charles W and Sieverdes, Christopher M.

Selectivity In The Criminal Justice System. Baker, Timothy and Mann, Fredrica and Friedman, C Jack.

Social Class As A Factor Affecting Judicial Disposition. Willick, Daniel H and Gehlker, Gretchen and Mc Farland, Anita.

The Discriminatory Application Of Penal Laws By State Judicial And Quasi–Judicial Officers. Weissman, Andrew B.

Discretionary Justice In Early Massachusetts. Lee, Carol F.

"Discretionary Justice And The Black Offender" in *Blacks And Criminal Justice*, Owens, Charles E And Jimmy Bell (eds), 37–46. Banks, Taunya L.

Judicial Decision–Making In The Juvenile Court: An Empirical Test Of A Labelling/Conflict Proposition. Marshall, Ineke M.

The Dysfunctional Alliance: Emotion And Reason In Justice Administration. Kennedy, D B.

The Invisible Justice System Discretion And The Law. Atkins, B and Pogrebin, M.

Capital Punishment As A Case Study In The Incremental Evaluation Of Guided Discretion. Bowers, William J and Pierce, Glenn L.

Dynamics Of Courthouse Justice: A Critical Review Of The Literature. Neubauer, D W.

DISCRIMINATION, INSTITUTIONAL

Racial Discrimination In The Legal Profession. Brown Jr, William H.

The Legal Status Of The Negro. Magnum, Charles S.

The Black Codes Of The South. Wilson, T R.

Institutional Racism In America. Knowles, Louis L (ed) and Prewitt, Kenneth (ed).

Race Distinctions In American Law, Org Pub 1910. Stephenson, Gilbert T.

"Legal Status Of The Slave In South Carolina, 1670–1740" in *Colonial American Essays In Political/Social Development*, Katz (ed), 404–415. Senese, Donald.

"Racism And American Law" in *Law Against The People*, Lefcourt, Robert (ed), 38–54. Burns, Haywood.

"Racism In The Law" in *Race, Crime, And Justice*, Reasons, Charles E And Jack L Kuykendall (eds), 13–27. Crockett Jr, George W.

Race, Racism And American Law. Bell Jr, Derrick A.

An Examination Of Institutional Racism: Black People In California's Criminal Justice And Mental Health Systems. Ogleton, Betty and Crittendon, Stephanie and Seda, Cozetta.

Institutional Racism: A Empirical Study Of Blacks And The Jury Selection Process In Ten Southern States. Benokraitic, Nijoye Vaicartis.

Institutional Racism In Federal Sentencing. Debro, Julius.

"Institutional Racism" in *Black Perspectives On Crime And The Criminal Justice System*, Woodson, Robert L (ed), 143–160. Debro, Julius.

"Institutional Racism And Crime Clearance" in *Black Perspectives On Crime And The Criminal Justice System*, Woodson, Robert L (ed), 107–122. Peirson, Gwynne.

Police Are Sued. Anonymous.

An Introductory Study Of Institutional Racism In Police Law Enforcement. Peirson, Gwynne W.

Institutional Racism In Mental Health And Criminal Justice. Morales, Armando.

DISCRIMINATION, OFFICIAL

Racial Exclusion In Jury Trials. Armistead, Henry M.

Race Prejudice In The Administration Of Justice. Sellin, Thorsten.

Racial Factors And Urban Law Enforcement. Kephart, William M.

The Negro Offender: An Urban Research Project. Kephart, William M.

The Death Penalty And The Negroes. Williams, Franklin H.

Police Encounters With Juveniles. Piliavin, Irving and Briar, Scott.

Race And Crime: A Revisit To An Old Concept. Sagarin, Edward.

Cops In The Ghetto: A Problem Of The Police System. Levy, Burton.

Institutional Racism In Social Welfare. Gibbs, I L.

Race And Ethnicity Relative To Other Factors In Juvenile Court Dispositions. Arnold, William R.

Administration Of Justice: Chicanos In Monterey County. Garza, H.

Mandatory Inclusion Of Racial Minorities On Jury Panels. Potash, D.

Racism And The Early American Legal Process, 1619–1896. Higginbotham Jr, A Leon.

Exploring Racial Prejudice On Voir Dire: Constitutional Requirements And Policy Considerations. Mormino, Susan C.

Discretionary Decision–Making In The Criminal Justice System And The Black Offender: Some Alternatives. Banks, Taunya L.

Personality Patterns Of White, Black, And Mexican American Patrolmen As Measured By The Sixteen Personality Factor Questionaire. Snibbe, H M and Fabricatore, Joseph and Azen, Stanley P.

Rape, Race And The Death Penalty In Georgia. Wolfgang, Marvin E and Riedel, Marc.

A Review Of The Law Enforcement Assistance Administration's Relationship To The Black Community. National Urban League, Inc.

Antecedents Of Urban Indian Crime. Williams, L E.

Non–English–Speaking Persons In The Criminal Justice System: Current State Of The Law. Cronheim, A J and Schwartz, A H.

Race Differences In Police Patrolmen: A Failure To Replicate The Chicago Study. Snibbe, H M et al.

Voir Dire—The Due Process Clause Of The Fourteenth Amendment [And Jurors' Racial Prejudice]. Comment.

Racial Discrimination In Jury Selection: *United States V Robinson*. Soja, Thomas.

Underrepresentation Of Economic Groups On Federal Juries. Handman, L R.

Race And Crime Revisited. Pope, Carl E.

Some Evidence Of Race Bias In The Diagnosis And Treatment Of The Juvenile Offender. Lewis, Dorothy O and Balla, David A and Shanok, Shelley S.

DISCRIMINATION, RACIAL

The Hispanic Experience In Criminal Justice. Sissons, Peter L.

The Causes Of Race Superiority. Ross, Edward A.

Degeneration And Crime: The Twin Evils Of Discrimination And Oppression. Newsom, John T C.

"Race Prejudice And Japanese American Relations" in *Race And Culture*, Hughes, Everett C et al (eds). Park, Robert E.

Negro Race Consciousness As Reflected In Race Literature. Park, Robert E.

The Bases Of Race Prejudice. Park, Robert E.

Racial Discrimination In The Legal Profession. Brown Jr, William H.

Racial Exclusion In Jury Trials. Armistead, Henry M.

Race Prejudice In The Administration Of Justice. Sellin, Thorsten.

The Negro At The Bar: The South. Shores, Arthur D.

Race Discrimination And The Law. Mc Williams, Carey.

Racial Discrimination And The Military Judgment. Dembitz, Nanette.

DISCRIMINATION, RACIAL

Native Americans And Discrimination In Kansas: Trials From Injustice. Bean, Jerry L.

Racial Issues In Corrections: Cultural Awareness—How To Achieve It. Fox, Vernon.

The Image Of The Indian In The Southern Colonial Mind. Nash, Gary B.

The New Racism: An Analysis Of The Use Of Racial And Ethnic Criteria In Decision-Making. Alexander, Elaine T and Alexander, Lawrence A.

Politics Of Punishment—A Critical Analysis Of Prisons In America. Wright, Erik Olin.

Racism And Mental Health. Willie, Charles V et al (eds).

The Dialectics Of Legal Repression: Black Rebels Before The American Criminal Courts. Balbus, Isaac D.

A Look At The Effect Of Racism On Clinical Work. Cooper, S.

Administration Of Justice: Chicanos In Monterey County. Garza, H.

Are Cops Prejudiced? Rafky, David M and Thibault, Edward and Lynch, Lawrence.

Bridgeport Guardians, Inc v Members Of The Bridgeport Civil Service, 345 F Supp 779, US Dist Ct D Conn Jan 29, 1973. Anonymous.

Civil Petitioner's Right To Representative Grand Juries And Statistical Method Of Showing Discrimination In Jury Selection Cases Generally. Comment.

Davis v Washington, 348 F Supp 15 (Dist Of Col) US Dist Ct DC July 21, 1972. Anonymous.

Does Justice Have A Color: Law: Is It A Skin Game. Moore Jr, Howard.

Hodnett v Slayton, 343 F Supp 1142 (Va) US Dist Ct WD Va, May 16, 1972. Anonymous.

Institutional Racism And The American Psychological Association. Sawyer, Jack and Senn, David J.

Litigating Against The Death Penalty: The Strategy Behind *Furman*. Meltsner, Michael.

Mandatory Inclusion Of Racial Minorities On Jury Panels. Potash, D.

Race, Socioeconomic Status And Sentencing In The Juvenile Justice System. Thornberry, Terence P.

Racism And The Early American Legal Process, 1619–1896. Higginbotham Jr, A Leon.

The American Dilemma In Uniform: Race In The Armed Forces. Moskos, Charles.

The Case For Double Jeopardy: Black And Poor. Dolan, Thomas J.

The Effect Of Client Race And Social Class On Clinical Judgements. Fischer, J and Miller, H.

Executions In America. Bowers, William J and Carr, Andrea and Pierce, Glenn L.

Partial Justice: A Study Of Bias In Sentencing. Gaylin, Willard.

The Federal Civil Rights Enforcement Effort—1974: Volume VI, To Extend Federal Financial Assistance. U S Commission On Civil Rights.

"Race And The Courts" in *The Administration Of Criminal Justice: A View From Black America*, Brown, Lee P (ed), 12–22. Crockett Jr, George W.

A Brief Review Of The Effects Of Race In Clinical Service Interactions. Siegel, J M.

Bridgeport Guardians, Inc v Members Of Civil Service Com'n, 497 F 2d 113 (Conn), US Court Of Appeals, Second Circuit, June 3, 1974. Anonymous.

Discrimination In Supermarket, Prices And Location In Nashville. Steel, William F.

Exploring Racial Prejudice On Voir Dire: Constitutional Requirements And Policy Considerations. Mormino, Susan C.

Extra-Legal Attributes And Criminal Sentences: An Assessment Of A Sociological Viewpoint. Hagan, John.

Minorities In Correction—Nondiscrimination, Equal Opportunity And Legal Issues. Skoler, Daniel and Lowenstein, Ralph.

Racism And Its Effects On Puerto Rican Continentals. Longers Jr, J F.

Scientific Racism And IQ: The Silent Mugging Of The Black Community. Williams, Robert L.

The Validity Of The MMPI As A Discriminator Of Social Deviance Among Black Males. Elion, Victor H.

American Minorities: The Justice Issue. Long, Elton et al.

Criminal Sentencing: An Empirical Analysis Of Variations On Sentences Imposed In Federal District Courts. Sutton, Lester P.

Indian Justice—A Research Bibliography. University Of Nebraska.

Institutional Racism: A Empirical Study Of Blacks And The Jury Selection Process In Ten Southern States. Benokraitic, Nijoye Vaicartis.

Race As A Factor In The Intra-Prison Outcomes Of Youthful First Offenders. Brown, Shirley Ann Vinsing.

Racial Discrimination In The United States. Pettigrew, Thomas F (ed).

Bangs And Whimpers: Black Youths In The Courts. Wright, Bruce Mc M.

Black Perspective On Pretrial Diversion. Smith, A R.

Constitutional Law—Juror Selection—Equal Protection Denied When Master Grand Jury Lists Significantly Underrepresents Defendant's Race. Note.

Discretionary Decision-Making In The Criminal Justice System And The Black Offender: Some Alternatives. Banks, Taunya L.

Inequality In The Types Of Sentences Received By Native Americans And Whites. Hall, Edwin L and Simkus, Albert A.

Personality Patterns Of White, Black, And Mexican American Patrolmen As Measured By The Sixteen Personality Factor Questionaire. Snibbe, H M and Fabricatore, Joseph and Azen, Stanley P.

Racial Discrimination In Sentencing. Howard, Joseph C.

Racial Discrimination In Urban Police Departments. Rafky, David M.

Rape, Race And The Death Penalty In Georgia. Wolfgang, Marvin E and Riedel, Marc.

The Discriminatory Application Of Penal Laws By State Judicial And Quasi-Judicial Officers. Weissman, Andrew B.

United States v McDaniels, 379 F Supp 1243, (Louisiana) US District Court E D Louisiana, May 22 1974. Anonymous.

A Review Of The Law Enforcement Assistance Administration's Relationship To The Black Community. National Urban League, Inc.

An Empirical Examination Of Conflict Theory: Race And Sentence Length. Dison, Jack E.

Antecedents Of Urban Indian Crime. Williams, L E.

From Plantation To Ghetto. Meier, August and Rudwick, Elliot.

Institutional Racism In Federal Sentencing. Debro, Julius.

Judicial Administration And Racial Discrimination: Fifteen Years Of Literature. Martin, George.

"Employment And Discrimination" in *Crime And Its Impact On The Black Community*, Gary, L E And L P Brown (eds), 69–76. Padgett, Squire.

A Comparison Of Defense Strategy And Race As Influences In Differential Sentencing. Kelly, Henry E.

Asian American Employment—From Outright Exclusion To Modern Discrimination. Lem, K.

City Liable Under Human Rights Act For Policeman's Racial Abuses. Anonymous.

Conviction Records As Barriers To Employment—Racial Discrimination Under Title 7: Green Versus Missouri Pacific Railroad. Comment.

Criminal Procedure—Voir Dire—The Right To Question Jurors On Racial Prejudice. Bryson, C B.

Differential Social Perception And Attribution Of Intergroup Violence: Testing The Lower Limits Of Stereotyping Of Blacks. Duncan, B L.

Discrimination In The Imposition Of Death Penalty: A Comparison Of The Characteristics Of Offenders Sentenced Pre-Furman And Post-Furman. Riedel, Marc.

Jury Selection As A Biased Social Process. Alker, Howard L and Hoslicka, Carl and Mitchell, Michael.

Race Differences In Police Patrolmen: A Failure To Replicate The Chicago Study. Snibbe, H M et al.

Race Of Inmate, Race Of Officer, And Disciplinary Proceedings At A Federal Correctional Institution. Boyd, Jeffrey L.

Racial Bias In The Decision To Grant Parole. Carroll, Leo and Mondrick, Margaret E.

Racial Discrimination And White Gain. Szymanski, Albert.

Voir Dire—The Due Process Clause Of The Fourteenth Amendment [And Jurors' Racial Prejudice]. Comment.

Alaska Felony Sentencing Patterns: A Multivariate Statistical Analysis (1974–1976), Preliminary Report. Alaska Judicial Council.

Blacks And Criminal Justice. Owens, Charles E (ed) and Bell, Jimmy (ed).

Crime And Incarceration; A Reanalysis. Nagel, Jack H.

"Challenge For The Judicial System: Economic And Racial Equality" in *Blacks And Criminal Justice*, Owens, Charles E And Jimmy Bell (eds). Crockett Jr, George W.

"Discretionary Justice And The Black Offender" in *Blacks And Criminal Justice*, Owens, Charles E And Jimmy Bell (eds), 37–46. Banks, Taunya L.

"Institutional Racism" in *Black Perspectives On Crime And The Criminal Justice System*, Woodson, Robert L (ed), 143–160. Debro, Julius.

DISCRIMINATION, RACIAL

"Race, Rape And The Death Penalty" in *Forcible Rape—The Crime, The Victim And The Offender*, Chappell, D; R Geis, And G Geis (eds). Wolfgang, Marvin E and Riedel, Marc.

"Rape, Race, And Research" in *Blacks And Criminal Justice*, Owens, Charles E And Jimmy Bell (eds). Evans, P.

Minorities' Constitutional Rights To Police Department Employment. Rothenberg, S and Barnes, M.

Poor Minority Juveniles Said More Likely To Be Locked Up. Anonymous.

Racial Discrimination In Jury Selection: *United States* v *Robinson*. Soja, Thomas.

The Subtlety Of White Racism, Arousal, And Helping Behavior. Gaertner, S L and Dovidio, J F.

US Charges Los Angeles With Police Hiring Bias. Anonymous.

Underrepresentation Of Economic Groups On Federal Juries. Handman, L R.

An Introductory Study Of Institutional Racism In Police Law Enforcement. Peirson, Gwynne W.

Bibliography On Racism: 1972–1975, V2. National Institute Of Mental Health.

In The Matter Of Color. Higginbotham Jr, A Leon.

Judicial Council Findings Regarding Possible Racial Impact In Sentencing. Alaska Judicial Council.

Report Of The Task Force Investigation Allegations Of Discriminatory Practices At The Joliet And Stateville Correctional Centers. Illinois Corrections Department.

Visible Man: A True Story Of Post–Racist America. Gilder, George.

"Crime And Criminal Justice: Their Impact Upon Asian American Communities" in *National Minority Advisory Council Report*. Takagi, Paul.

Can You Photograph *Suspicious–Looking Blacks* Who Enter The Premises? Anonymous.

Criminal Justice And The American Indian. Randall, Archie and Randall, Betty.

Do 'They All Look Alike' The Effects Of Race, Sex, Experience, And Attitudes On The Ability To Recognize Faces. Brigham, J C and Barkowitz, P.

Exclusion Of Blacks From Juries Voids Fifteen–Year–Old Conviction. Anonymous.

Police Discrimination: An Elusive Question. Griswold, David B.

Race And Involvement In Common Law Personal Crime: A Response To Hindelang. Mc Neely, Roger and Pope, Carl.

Race And The Decision To Arrest: An Analysis Of Warrants Issued. Hepburn, John R.

Race As A Determinant Of Criminal Sentences: A Methodological Critique And A Case Study. Gibson, James L.

Race–Discrimination Picture Is Confusing. Anonymous.

The Causes And Cost Of Racial Exclusion From Job Authority. Kluegel, James R.

The Numbers Game. Miller, Marc.

"Criminal Justice/Racial Justice Nexus" in *Critical Issues In Criminal Justice*, Iacovetta, R G And D H Chang (eds). Jones, Clinton B.

"The Effect Of Race On Sentence" in *Theory And Research In Criminal Justice*, Conley, J A (ed). Foley, Linda and Rasch, Christine E.

Racial Differences In Criminal Sentencing. Unnever, James D and Frangier, Charles and Henretta, Juan C.

Preliminary Tabulations Reflecting Arbitrariness And Discrimination Under Post–'Furman' Capital Statutes. Bowers, William J and Pierce, Glenn L.

Sentencing Guidelines Project: Report To The Administrative Director Of The Courts On The Relationship Between Race And Sentencing. Sheflin, N.

Statistical Analysis Of Misdemeanor Sentences In Anchorage And Fairbanks: 1974–1976. Rubinstein, Michael L and Maroules, Nicholas and White, Teresa.

The Rich Get Richer And The Poor Get Prison. Reiman, Jeffrey H.

Differential Treatment Between Runaway Boys And Girls In Juvenile Court. Mann, Coramae R.

Racial Identity, Length Of Incarceration And Parole Decision Making. Elion, Victor H and Megargee, Edwin I.

Some Evidence Of Race Bias In The Diagnosis And Treatment Of The Juvenile Offender. Lewis, Dorothy O and Balla, David A and Shanok, Shelley S.

The Effects Of Ethnicity, Age And Sex Upon Processing Through And Emergency Alcohol Health Care Delivery System. Westie, K S and Mc Bride, D C.

Theoretical Interpretations Of Social Class And Racial Differentials In Legal Decision Making For Juveniles. Liska, Allen E and Tausig, Mark.

Effects Of Race On Plea Bargaining Decisions. Horney, Julie.

The Black Incarceration Rate In The United States: A Nationwide Problem. Christianson, Scott and Dehais, Richard.

The Inequality Of Justice: A Report On Crime And The Administration Of Justice In The Minority Coummunity. National Minority Advisory Council On Crim Just.

The Police, The Courts, And The Minority Community. Witt, James W.

Arbitrariness And Discrimination Under Post–'Furman' Capital Statutes. Bowers, William J and Pierce, Glenn L.

Corrections Law Developments: Legal Implications Of Racially Disproportionate Incarceration Rates. Christianson, Scott.

Corrections Law Developments: Racial Discrimination And Prison Confinement—A Follow–Up. Christianson, Scott.

Hispanics Underrepresented As Criminal Justice Professionals. Carro, John.

Justice For Hispanics Often Falls Short. U S Dept Of Justice.

Race, Crime And Social Policy: The Chinese In Oregon, 1871–1885. Tracy, Charles A.

DISCRIMINATION, REVERSE

DeFunis Versus Odegaard And The University Of Washington, 3v. Ginger, Ann Fagan (ed).

Affirmative Discrimination: Ethnic Inequality And Public Policy. Glazer, Nathan.

Affirmative Action—The Answer To Discrimination? American Enterprise Institute For Public Policy Research.

Reverse Discrimination. Stencel, S.

Reversing Discrimination—A Perspective. Pati, G and Reilly, C W.

Discrimination In Reverse—Is Turnabout Fair Play? Gross, B R.

DISCRIMINATION, SEX

Sex And Racism In America. Hernton, C C.

Aspirations And Social Concerns—Crime, Blacks, Inequality And Women. Watts, W and Free, L A.

Exclusion Of Women From The Judicial Process. Tolchin, S.

Women, Crime, And The Criminal Justice System. Bowker, Lee H and Chesney, Meda and Pollock, Joy.

Women In The Criminal Justice System. Feinman, C.

Women, Crime, And Justice. Datesman, Susan K (ed) and Scarpitti, Frank R (ed).

Developing An Equal Protection Standard For Gender Discrimination Cases—Where's The Rub? Note.

DISEASE

The Significance Of Disease In Extinction Of The New England Indians. Cook, Sherburne F.

DISPUTE SETTLEMENT

Dispute Settlement In Chinese American Communities. Doo, L W.

Evaluating The Dade County Citizen Dispute, Settlement Program. Salas, Luis P and Schneider, Ronald.

DISTRICT ATTORNEY *see* Prosecutor

DISTRICT OF COLUMBIA

The Response Of The Washington DC Community And Its Criminal Justice System To The April 1968 Riot. Cheminick, Paul W (ed).

The Woman Participant In Washington's Riots. Miller, Eugene.

Absentee Ownership And Management In The Black Ghetto: Social And Economic Consequences. Reiss Jr, Albert J and Aldrich, Howard.

Absentee Ownership And Management In The Black Ghetto: Social And Economic Consequences. Reiss Jr, Albert J and Aldrich, Howard.

Bail And Pre–Trial Detention In The District Of Columbia: An Empirical Analysis. Just, Bernice.

Davis v Washington, 348 F Supp 15 (Dist Of Col) US Dist Ct DC July 21, 1972. Anonymous.

Identifying Responsive Inner–City Policemen. Kelly, Rita Mae and Farber, Martin G.

Attitudes And Perceptions Of Black Police Officers Of The District Of Columbia Metropolitan Police Department. Beard, Eugene and Brown, Lee P and Gary, Lawrence E.

Assault With A Deadly Weapon: The Autobiography Of A Street Criminal. Allen, John.

DISTRICT OF COLUMBIA

The Black Police In Washington DC. Beard, Eugene.

DIVERSION

Pretrial Diversion From The Criminal Process. Note.

Black Perspective On Pretrial Diversion. Smith, A R.

DOCILITY

Rebelliousness And Docility In The Negro Slave: A Critique Of The Elkins Thesis. Genovese, Eugene D.

DOGMATISM

An Assessment Of Dogmatism Among Adult Inmates In A State Correctional Institution In New Jersey. Carden, Francis Xavier.

DOUGLAS COUNTY, NE

Conviction And Sentencing In The Fourth Judicial District Of Nebraska. Kulig, F H and Hawkinson, T.

DOUGLASS, FREDERICK

My Bondage And My Freedom. Douglass, Frederick.

DRUGS

The Negro Drug Addict As An Offender Type. Roebuck, Julian B.

The Addict And The Law. Lindesmith, Alfred R.

Differences In Smoking, Drinking, And Social Behavior By Race And Delinquency Status In Adolescent Males. Schonfield, J.

The Chinese Narcotic Addict In The United States. Ball, J C and Lau, M.

Task Force Report: Narcotics And Drugs. President's Comm On Law Enforcement & Adm Of Justice.

Merchants Of Heroin. Moscow, Alvin.

The Epidemiology Of Opiate Addiction In The United States. Ball, J C (ed) and Chambers, C D (ed).

Demographic Factors In Opiate Addiction Among Mexican Americans. Chambers, C D and Cuskey, W R and Moffett, A D.

"Drugs And Drug Control" in *Crime And Justice In American Society,* Douglas, J (ed). Duster, Troy.

Dealer: Portrait Of A Cocaine Merchant. Woodley, Richard.

Drug Usage And Arrest Charges: A Study Of Drug Usage And Arrest Charges Among Arrestees In Six Metropolitan Areas Of The United States. Eckerman, William et al.

Heroin And The Black Community. Taylor, Victor E.

The Cops Can't Find The Pusher. Christianson, K Scott.

New Perspectives On Urban Crime. American Bar Association.

Rel Bet Selected Personal Char Of Confined Narcotic Off And The Amn't Of Time Serv'd Prior To Their Official Referral Consideration. Green, Charles Bernard.

The Chicano Addict: An Analysis Of Factors Influencing Rehabilitation In A Treatment Program. Auman, Jon et al.

The Politics Of Heroin In Southeast Asia. Mc Coy, Albert.

Vizzini. Vizzini, Sal.

Multiple Drug Use In A Sample Of Experienced Marijuana Smokers. Grupp, Stanley E.

Patterns Of Drug Abuse Epidemiology In Prisoners. Edmundson, Walter F et al.

"Race, Deprivation, And Drug Abuse In The USA" in *Proceedings Of The Anglo–American Conference On Drug Abuses,* 69–76. Holden Jr, Matthew.

Origins Of Narcotic Control. Musto, David F.

The Needle And The Boot: Heroin Maintenance. Cuskey, Walter R and Krasner, William.

Kind And Usual Punishment: The Prison Business. Mitford, Jessica.

Black–White Differences In Social Background And Military Drug Abuse Patterns. Nail, R L and Gunderson, E K E and Arthur, R J.

Chicanoizing Drug Abuse Programs. Aron, William S and Alger, Norman and Gonzales, Ricardo T.

Methadone: The Forlorn Hope. Epstein, Edward Jay.

The Politics Of Drugs: An Inquiry In The Sociology Of Social Problems. Reasons, Charles E.

A Study Of Drug Addiction And Conformity Behavior: A Biosocial Approach To The Understanding Of A Form Of Social Deviance. Chase, Stanley Harvey.

Drugs And Minority Oppression. Helmer, John.

Pretreatment Criminality Of Male And Female Drug Abuse Patients In The United States. Ball, John C et al.

Racial, Economic And Political Factors In The Development Of America's First Drug Laws. Mark, Greg Yee.

The Dynamics And Treatment Of The Young Drug Abuser In An Hispanic Therapeutic Community. Freudenberger, Herbert J.

Drug Use And Abuse Among US Minorities: An Annotated Bibliography. Iiyama, P and Nishi, S M and Johnson, B B.

El Tecato: Cultural And Sociologic Factors Affecting Drug Use Among Chicanos. Casvantes, Edward J.

The Development And Change Of The Peyote Ceremony Through Time And Space. Brito, Silvester John.

A Framework For Developing Drug Abuse Prevention Strategies For Young People In Ghetto Areas. Dembo, R et al.

Blackness Is My Mental Health: A Mind Set For Black Drug Abuse Prevention And Treatment Programs. Wheeler, William Henry III.

The Black Addict: I Methodology, Chronology Of Addiction, And Overview Of The Population. Halikas, J A et al.

Heroin Use In The Barrio. Bullington, Bruce.

Manny—A Criminal–Addict's Story. Retting, R P and Torres, M J and Garrett, G R.

Preliminary Report On Crime And Addiction Within A Community—Wide Population Of Narcotic Addicts. Nurco, D N and Du Pont, R L.

Homeboys: Gangs, Drugs, And Prison In The Barrios Of Los Angeles. Moore, Joan et al.

Wildcat Experiment—An Early Test Of Supported Work In Drug Abuse Rehabilitation. Friedman, L N.

Gunfights In The Cocaine Coral. Schorr, Mark.

The Drug Arrest: Empirical Observations On The Age, Sex And Race Of Drug Law Offenders In A Midwestern City. Petersen, D M and Schwirian, K P and Bleda, S E.

A Model For Chicano Drug Use And For Effective Utilization Of Employment And Training Resources By Barrio Addicts And Ex–Offenders. Chicano Pinto Research Project, Inc.

Ecologic—Biochemical Approaches To The Treatment Of Delinquents And Criminals. Hippchen, Leonard J (ed).

Multicultural Perspectives On Drug Abuse And Its Prevention: A Resource Book. Messolonghites, Louisa.

National Directory Of Drug Abuse And Alcoholism Treatment Programs. National Institute On Alcohol Abuse And Alcoholism.

Racism In United States: Drug Legislation And The Trade–Off Behind It. Heiligman, A C.

War On Narcotics—The State Of Hostilities In New York. Macguire, R J.

What Happened In Harlem: Analysis Of A Decline In Heroin Use Among A Generation Unit Of Urban Black Youth. Boyle, John M and Brunswick, Ann F.

DUE PROCESS

Due Process Of Law In Race Cases. Moore, Loring B.

The Limits Of The Criminal Sanction. Packer, Herbert.

Blacks, Due Process And Efficiency In The Clash Of Values As The Supreme Court Moves To The Right. Mc Gee Jr, Henry W.

Citado A Comparecer—Language Barriers And Due Process—Is Mailed Notice In English Constitutionally Sufficient? Comment.

Interpreters For The Defense: Due Process For The Non–English–Speaking Defendant. Chang, W B C and Araujo, M U.

DURKHEIM, EMILE

Punishment And Social Organization: A Study Of Durkheim's Theory Of Penal Evolution. Spitzer, Steven.

ECONOMETRIC ANALYSIS

The Economics Of Slavery And Other Studies In Econometric History. Conrad, Alfred H and Meyer, John R.

The Economics Of Crime And Punishment. Rottenberg, Simon (ed).

ECONOMIC FACTORS

see also Class, Unemployment

American Negro Slavery: A Survey Of The Supply, Employment And Control Of Negro Labor As Determined By The Plantation Régime. Phillips, Ulrich Bonnell.

Crime: Its Causes And Treatment. Darrow, Clarence.

Social Aspects Of The Business Cycle. Davies, George R.

Unemployment And Prison Commitments. Simpson, Ray Mars.

Research Memorandum On Crime In The Depression. Sellin, Thorsten.

The Effect Of The Depression On Prison Commitments And Sentences. Stern, Leon Thomas.

Differentials In Crime Rates Between Negroes And Whites, Based On Comparisons Of Four Socio–Economically Equated Areas. Moses, Earl R.

ECONOMIC FACTORS

Poverty, Race And Crime. Mc Keown, James Edward.

The Relationship Of Juvenile Delinquency, Race And Economic Status. Blue Jr, John T.

Effects Of Unemployment On White And Negro Prison Admissions In Louisiana. Dobbins, D A and Bass, Bernard M.

Socio–Economic Status And Delinquent Behavior. Nye, F Ivan and Short Jr, James F and Olson, Virgil J.

Economic Deprivation And Extremism: A Study Of Unemployed Negroes. Street, D and Leggett, J C.

Walk Along The Worst Block: East 100th Street. Samuels, Gertrude.

Ransom: A Critique Of The American Bail System. Goldfarb, Ronald L.

The Social And Economic States Of The Negro In The United States. Drake, St Clair.

Socioeconomic Status, Race, Level Of Aspiration And Juvenile Delinquency: A Limited Empirical Test Of Merton's Concept Of Deviation. Epps, Edgar G.

A Criminal Justice System And The Indigent. Oaks, Dallin H and Lehman, Warren.

Socio–Economic Status And Delinquent Behavior: A Retest. Akers, Ronald L.

Criminality And Economic Conditions. Bonger, Willem Adriaen.

Poverty, Race And Violence. Fishman, J R.

"The Tipped Scales Of American Justice" in *Law And Order: The Scales Of Justice*, Blumberg, Abraham S (ed), 47–66. Nagel, Stuart.

Class And The Economics Of Crime. Gordon, David M.

The Integration Of Blacks In Suburban Neighborhoods: A Reexamination Of The Contact Hypothesis. Zeal, Carolyn and Humphrey, Craig.

Sowing The Wind, . Welford, Harrison.

The Prison Of Unemployment. Taggart, R.

Theories Of Poverty And Unemployment. Gordon, David M.

The Nonculture Of Poverty Among Black Youths. Gruber, Murray.

Bugs In The Driving Dream: The Technocratic War Against Poverty. Tollett, Kenneth.

Capitalism, Class And Crime In America. Gordon, David M.

The Case For Double Jeopardy: Black And Poor. Dolan, Thomas J.

The Correctional System. Takagi, Paul.

The System Propagates Crime. Jordan Jr, Vernon E.

Race And Economics. Sowell, Thomas.

Social Class As A Factor Affecting Judicial Disposition. Willick, Daniel H and Gehlker, Gretchen and Mc Farland, Anita.

Social Class And Crime: The Case Of The Japanese–Americans. Fujimoto, Tetsuya.

"Black Business And The Crime Of Uneconomic Communities" in *Crime And Its Impact On The Black Community*, Gary, L E & L P Brown (eds), 31–38. Burrell, Berkeley G.

An Assessment Of Legal And Cultural Stigma Regarding Unskilled Workers. Palys, T S.

Homicide And Robbery In New York City: An Economic Model. Mathieson, Donald and Passell, Peter.

The Influence Of Income And Other Factors On Whether Criminal Defendants Go To Prison. Clarke, Stevens H and Koch, Gary.

The Legacy Of Malthus: The Social Costs Of The New Racism. Chase, Allan.

Labor Market And Imprisonment. Jankovic, Ivan.

Political Economy Of Criminal Oppression. Johnson, R C.

Crime And Employment Issues: A Collection Of Policy Relevant Monographs. American University Law School.

Strategies For Controlling Crime—A Position Paper. National Urban League, Inc.

The Declining Significance Of Race. Wilson, William Julius.

Crime—Unemployment Cycle. Becnel, B.

The Economic Basis Of Indian Life. Sorkin, Allan.

A Matter Of Class. Gershman, Carl.

The Role Of Race. Clark, Kenneth B.

EDUCATION LEVEL

Education And Crime Among Negroes. Stephenson, G T.

Educational Level And Juvenile Delinquency Among Negroes. Miller, Carroll L.

Death At An Early Age: The Destruction Of The Hearts And Minds Of Negro Children In The Boston Schools. Kozol, Jonathan.

Inequality: A Reassessment Of The Effect Of Family And Schooling In America. Jencks, Christopher.

EGO

Ego Development And Female Delinquency: A Cognitive–Developmental Approach. Frank, Susan and Quinlan, Donald M.

EL PASO, TX

Analysis Of Selected Social And Cultural Characteristics Involving Juvenile Delinquency In Mexican–American Slums Of South El Paso. Knowlton, Clark S.

ELDERLY

Violent Crime Perpetrated Against The Elderly In The City Of Dallas, October 1974–September 1975. Georges, Daniel E and Kirksey, Kirk.

ELKINS, STANLEY M

Rebelliousness And Docility In The Negro Slave: A Critique Of The Elkins Thesis. Genovese, Eugene D.

EMPATHY

Empathy As A Factor In Determining Jury Verdicts. Adler, Freda.

Second Thoughts On Crime And Sympathy. Malinovich, M M.

EMPLOYMENT, PUBLIC

First Come, First Served, And Some Other Problems Of Manpower Policy–Making. Ludlow, H T.

A Review Of The Law Enforcement Assistance Administration's Relationship To The Black Community. National Urban League, Inc.

Preferences In Public Employment. Vaughn, R G.

ENVIRONMENTAL APPROACHES

The City. Park, Robert E and Burgess, Ernest W and Mc Kenzie, Roderick D.

Delinquency Areas. Shaw, Clifford et al.

Juvenile Delinquency And Urban Areas. Shaw, Clifford and Mc Kay, Henry.

The Criminal Area. Morris, Terrence.

"Overcrowding And Human Aggression" in *The History Of Violence In America*, Graham, Hugh D And T Gurr (eds), 751–764. Carstairs, George M.

The Social Order Of The Slum. Suttles, Gerald.

Eradication Of Racism And Poverty As A Means Of Stopping Escalation Of Crime And Violence: A Dream Deferred. Higginbotham Jr, A Leon.

The Geography Of Crime And Justice. Harries, Keith D.

Residential Succession And Delinquency: A Test Of Shaw And McKay's Theory Of Cultural Transmission. Kapsis, Robert E.

Criminal's Image Of The City. Carter, R l and Hill, K Q.

Community, Environment And Violent Crime. Block, Richard L.

Crime And Environment. Harries, Keith D.

EQUAL EMPLOYMENT OPPORTUNITY

Minority Recruitment In Corrections—New Federal Aid Requirements. American Bar Association.

Non Discrimination, Equal Opportunity And Legal Issues On Minorities In Corrections. Skoler, Daniel L and Lowenstein, Ralph.

Guidelines For Agency Internal Evaluation Of Equal Employment Opportunity Programs. U S Civil Service Commission.

Blacks Versus Women—When Victims Collide. Hogan, B.

Minorities In Correction—Nondiscrimination, Equal Opportunity And Legal Issues. Skoler, Daniel and Lowenstein, Ralph.

Equal Employment And The Texas Criminal Justice System. Texas Office Of The Governor.

How To Eliminate Discriminatory Practices—A Guide To EEO (Equal Employment Opportunity). American Management Association.

Discrimination In Selection And Promotion Of Minorities And Women In Municipal Employment. Ivie, S D.

Equal Employment Opportunity And Affirmative Action In Law Enforcement Agencies. Jefferson, A M.

Equal Opportunity And Seniority—Trends And Manpower Implications. Craft, J A.

Racial Discrimination In Urban Police Departments. Rafky, David M.

Testing And Equal Opportunity—Getting A Fair Chance. White, W P.

Equal Employment Opportunity Plan Development Participant's Reference Handbook. Griggs, E and Sayer, K.

Iowa - Department Of Public Safety - Equal Employment Opportunity Coordinator - Preliminary Evaluation. Cohan, M.

Practitioner's View Of EEOC Requirements With Special Reference To Job Analysis. Baher, M E.

Affirmative Action And The Quest For Job Equality. Hill, H.

Asian American Employment—From Outright Exclusion To Modern Discrimination. Lem, K.

ETHNICITY

Ethnicity: Theory And Experience. Glazer, Nathan (ed) and Moynihan, Daniel Patrick (ed).

Determining Ethnic Origin In An Interview Survey: Problems And Recommendations. U S Dept Of H E W.

Race And Ethnic Standards For Federal Statistics And Administrative Reporting. Wallman, K K and Hodgdon, J.

Colonialism And Ethnicity: A Theory And Comparative Case Study. Cross, Malcolm.

Harvard Encyclopedia Of American Ethnic Groups. Cortés, C E.

ETHNOCENTRICITY

Apparent Minority Ethnocentricity And Majority Antipathy. Catton, Chick Hong.

EUGENICS

The Eugenics Movement: Some Insight Into The Institutionalization Of Racism. Fong, Melanie and Johnson, Larry D.

EVANS, AHMAD

The Framing Of Ahmad Evans. Mallory, Mae.

EVIDENCE

Voir Dire Of Jurors: Constitutional Limits To The Right Of Inquiry Into Prejudice. Gaba, J M.

The Psychology Of Eyewitness Testimony. Yarmey, A Daniel.

Social Science Evidence In The Courts: Reaching Beyond The Adversary Process. Sperlich, Peter W.

EX-CONVICTS

The Los Angeles Pinto: Background Papers And Advance Report Of The Chicano Pinto Project. Chicano Pinto Research Project, Inc.

"The Ex–Offender As Paraprofessional" in *Corrections*, Sagarin, E (ed), 145–152. Callanan, Thomas J.

Ethnic Self Help Groups In Prison And On Parole. Burdman, Milton.

Conviction Records As Barriers To Employment—Racial Discrimination Under Title 7: Green Versus Missouri Pacific Railroad. Comment.

A Case Study Of Collaboration: The Chicano Pinto Research Project. Moore, Joan W.

Hispanic Women Offenders And Ex–Offenders. Daldio, Maria Gomez.

A Model For Chicano Drug Use And For Effective Utilization Of Employment And Training Resources By Barrio Addicts And Ex–Offenders. Chicano Pinto Research Project, Inc.

Today: Ron LeFlore Only Steals Bases. Mitchell, Greg.

EXCLUSIONARY RULE

The Erosion Of The Fourth Amendment Exclusionary Rule. Quintana, Marsha A.

EXECUTION SERMONS

The Life And Dying Speech Of Arthur, A Negro Man. Arthur.

The Victim As Criminal And Artist: Literature From The American Prison. Franklin, H Bruce.

The Narrative & Confession Of Thomas Powers, A Negro, Who Was In The 10th Year Of His Age Was Executed For Committing A Rape. Powers, Thomas.

The Address Of Abraham Johnstone, A Black Man, Who Was Hanged In New Jersey. Johnstone, Abraham.

EXECUTIONS see Death Penalty

EXILES

Cubans In Exile: Disaffection And The Revolution. Fagen, R and Brody, R and O' Leary, T.

EXTRA-LEGAL FACTORS see Discrimination

EXTRADITION

Justice And The American Indian, V3: The Effect Of Having No Extradition Procedures For Indian Reservations. Steisel, M D.

EXTREMISM

The Challenge Of The Klan. Frost, Stanley.

Economic Deprivation And Extremism: A Study Of Unemployed Negroes. Street, D and Leggett, J C.

War Behind Walls. Bunker, Edward.

The Violent Rebirth Of The Klan. King, Wayne.

FAIR TRIAL

Equal Protection Of The Law And Fair Trials In Maryland. Mc Guinn, Henry J.

Note, Riot Control: The Constitutional Limits Of Search, Arrest And Fair Trial Procedure. Anonymous.

Can A Black Man Get A Fair Trial In This Country? Burns, Haywood.

Trying Non–English Conversant Defendants: The Use Of An Interpreter. Bergenfield, G.

FAIRBANKS, AK

Suicide And Culture In Fairbanks: A Comparison Of Three Cultural Groups In A Small City Of Interior Alaska. Parkin, M.

FAIRNESS, PERCEPTION OF

A Comparative Study Of Puerto Rican Attitudes Toward The Legal System Dealing With Crime. Toro– Calder, Jaime and Cedeno, C and Reckless, Walter.

Right On With The Young Lords. Yglesias, Jose.

Black And White Perceptions Of Justice In The City. Jacob, Herbert.

The Ghetto Resident's View Of Police Procedures And Their Constitutionality. Mathias, William J.

Criminal Justice: The Consumer Perspective. Casper, Jonathan D.

Justification For No Obligation: Views Of Black Males Toward Crime And The Criminal Law. Davis, John A.

Parolees' Perceptions Of The Justice System: Black–White Differences. Berman, John J.

Prisoners' Attitudes Toward Components Of The Legal And Judicial System. Hicks, Donald A and Alpert, Geoffrey P.

Having Their Day In Court—Defendant Evaluations Of The Fairness Of Their Treatment. Casper, Jonathan D.

FAMILY

"Juvenile Delinquency" in *The Negro Family In Chicago.* Frazier, E Franklin.

The Martyrs & The Fugitive, Or A Narrative Of The Captivity, Sufferings & Death Of An African Family & The Escape Of Their Son. Platt, Reverend S H.

The Negro Family: The Case For National Action. Moynihan, Daniel Patrick.

An Exploratory Study Of The Effects Of Incarceration On The Families Of Negro Inmates Of A Medium–Security Prison. Schneller, Donald P.

The Negro Family In The United States, Orig Pub 1949. Frazier, E Franklin.

Black Families In White America. Billingsley, Andrew.

"The Moynihan Report: The Negro Family And Crime" in *The Sociology Of Crime And Delinquency*, Wolfgang, M et al (ed), 440–450. U S Dept Of Labor, Office Of Planning And Research.

The Consequences Of Familial Separation For Chicano Inmates (School Of Ed). Gonzales, Josephine.

Explorations In Inmate–Family Relationships, Research Report No 46. Holt, Norman and Miller, Donald.

"Rebellious Youth" in *The Negro Family In The United States*, 268–280, Orig Pub 1949. Frazier, E Franklin.

The Relative Function Of Kin: A Comparative Study Of Middle And Lower Class Black Families. Yost, James Alvin.

The Effects Of Racial Milieu And Parental Racial Attitudes And Rearing Practices On Black Children's Racial Identity/Self–Esteem/Behavior. Smith, Willie D.

"Mexican–American Family" in *Chicanos: Social And Psychological Perspectives.* Murillo, Nathan.

"Towards A Sociology Of The Black Family" in *Afro–Americans: A Social Science Perspective*, Dennis, Rutledge M And Charles Jarmon (eds). Staples, Robert.

"The Mexican American Family" in *Ethnic Families In America*, Mindel, C And R Habenstein (eds). Alvirez, D and Bean, F.

"The Puerto Rican Family" in *Ethnic Families In America*, Mindel, C And R Habenstein (eds). Fitzpatrick, Joseph.

"Urban Families And Assault: A Framework For Research Focused On Black Families" in *Colloquium On The Correlates Of Crime*, Otten, L (ed). Perry, L and Crowley, J E.

FAMILY, EXTENDED

Black Gangs As Family Extensions. Brown, Waln K.

FAMILY - ABUSE AND NEGLECT

see also Child Abuse

Child Abuse As Psychopathology: A Sociological Critique And Reformulation. Gelles, R J.

FAMILY - FATHER ABSENCE

An Exploratory Study Of The Effects Of Incarceration On The Families Of Negro Inmates Of A Medium–Security Prison. Schneller, Donald P.

Father Absence And Antisocial Behavior In Negro And White Males. Mosher, L R.

The Effect Of Father Absence On Delinquent Males: Dependency And Hypermasculinity. Moran, Patricia Anne.

FAMILY - FATHER ABSENCE

The Black Family And The Prisons. Spain, Johnny.

Race And The Father–Son Connection: The Conditional Relevance Of Father Absence For The Orientations And Identities Of Adolescent Boys. Hunt, Larry L and Hunt, Janet G.

Some Social And Psychological Effects Of Incarceration On The Families Of Negro Prisoners. Schneller, Donald P.

Children Of Imprisoned Fathers. Sack, W H.

Race, Father–Absence And Female Delinquency. Austin, Roy L.

FAMILY - MATRIARCHY

The Negro Family: The Case For National Action. Moynihan, Daniel Patrick.

The Moynihan Report And The Politics Of Controversy. Rainwater, Lee and Yancey, William L.

Matriarchy And Lower Class Negro Male Delinquency. Rosen, Lawrence.

The Myth Of The Black Matriarchy. Staples, Robert.

Race, Maternal Authority And Adolescent Aspiration. Kandel, D B.

Black Families And The Moynihan Report: A Research Evaluation. Berger, Alan S and Simon, William.

"Race And Family Violence" in *Crime And Its Impact On The Black Community*, Gary, L E And L P Brown (eds), 85–96. Staples, Robert.

The Black Matriarchy Controversy And Black Male Delinquency. Perry, Robert L.

Why Punish The Children: A Study Of Children Of Women Prisoners. Mc Gowan, Brenda G and Blumenthal, Karen L.

FAMILY - RESEARCHING THE

Delinquency And City Life. Lalli, Michael and Savitz, Leonard D.

Ethnic Minority Family Research In An Urban Setting: A Process Of Exchange. Cromwell, R E and Vaughn, E C and Mindel, C H.

FAMILY - SOCIALIZATION

Effect Of Parents In The Home On Juvenile Delinquency. Eisner, V.

FAMILY CRIMINALITY

"Race And Family Violence" in *Crime And Its Impact On The Black Community*, Gary, L E And L P Brown (eds), 85–96. Staples, Robert.

Spouse Abuse In Texas—A Special Report. Stachura, S and Teske Jr, R H C.

FAMILY DISORGANIZATION

Family Status And The Delinquent Child: A Reappraisal And Some New Findings. Monahan, Thomas P.

The Differential Impact Of Family Disorganization. Toby, Jackson.

Negro Family Disorganization And Juvenile Delinquency. Cavan, Ruth S.

Women Prisoners And Their Families. Zalba, S.

"Crime And Delinquency" in *The Negro In The United States*, 638–653, Orig Pub 1949. Frazier, E Franklin.

The Negro Family: The Case For National Action. Moynihan, Daniel Patrick.

The Moynihan Report And The Politics Of Controversy. Rainwater, Lee and Yancey, William L.

Marital Instability And Juvenile Delinquency Among The Nez Perćes. Ackerman, L A.

"Rebellious Youth" in *The Negro Family In The United States*, 268–280, Orig Pub 1949. Frazier, E Franklin.

Families And Friends Of Men In Prison: The Uncertain Relationship. Brodsky, Stanley L.

A Methodological Critique Of The Moynihan Report. Swan, L Alex.

Some Social And Psychological Effects Of Incarceration On The Families Of Negro Prisoners. Schneller, Donald P.

FARMER, MILLARD

Team Defense: The Holistic Approach: An Interview With Millard Farmer. Eisenberg, Howard.

FASCISM

Race And Crime, Margaret Mathews Hordyk (trans). Bonger, Willem Adriaen.

The Gestapo In Detroit. Marshall, Thurgood.

Fascism At Soledad. Rollins, Clifford (Jabali).

The War Against The Jews, 1933–1945. Dawidowicz, Lucy S.

FBI

Uniform Crime Reports For The United States. U S Dept Of Justice, Federal Bureau Of Investigation.

J Edgar Hoover—The Negro And The FBI. Booker, Simeon.

Uniform Crime Reports: A Critical Appraisal. Wolfgang, Marvin E.

Investigating The FBI. Watters, Pat (ed) and Gillers, Stephen (ed).

Cointelpro: The FBI's Secret War On Political Freedom. Blackstone, Nelson.

Did The FBI Kill Viola Liuzzo? Greene, Johnny.

Othello. Volkman, Ernest.

FEDERAL BUREAU OF INVESTIGATION *see* FBI

FEMALE OFFENDERS

The Delinquent Girl In Chicago: I—A Comprison Of Four National And Racial Groups. Davis, E R.

The Criminality Of The Colored Woman, Series C. Von Hentig, Hans.

The Criminality Of Women. Pollak, Otto.

A Self–Report Comparison Of Indian And Anglo Delinquency In Wyoming. Forslund, Morris A and Cranston, Virginia A.

The Woman Participant In Washington's Riots. Miller, Eugene.

The Female Offender In Philadelphia. Adler, F S.

Women In Prison. Burkhart, Kathryn Watterson.

Self–Defense Against Rape: The Joanne Little Case. Bond, Julian.

The 'Black Shift' Phenomenon In Criminal Justice. Adams, Stuart.

Female Offender Workshop Guide, Female Offender Resource Center. American Bar Association.

The Social System Of A Medium Security Women's Prison. Spencer, Elousie J.

The Incarcerated Black Female: The Case Of Social Double Jeopardy. French, Laurence.

Hispanic Women Offenders And Ex–Offenders. Daldio, Maria Gomez.

Female Offenders: Who Are They And What Are The Problems Confronting Them? U S General Accounting Office.

Program For Women Offenders—How To Start, Fund, Maintain. Female Offenders Program Of Western Pennsylvania, Inc.

The Innocence Of Joan Little. Reston Jr, James.

Women, Race And Crime. Young, Vernetta D.

FEMALES

The Chicana: A Comprehensive Bibliographic Study. Duran, P H.

The Juvenile Female In The Judicial Process. Mann, Coramae R.

The Delinquent Girl In Chicago: I—A Comprison Of Four National And Racial Groups. Davis, E R.

The Criminality Of The Colored Woman, Series C. Von Hentig, Hans.

The Criminality Of Women. Pollak, Otto.

Lady Sings The Blues, By Billie Holiday. Fagan, Eleanora and Dufty, William F.

Case For The Promotion Of Police Women In The City Of New York. Shpritzer, Felicia.

Women's Prison: Sex And Social Structure. Ward, David A and Kassenbasum, Gene G.

Society Of Women: A Study Of A Women's Prison. Giallombardo, R.

A Study Of Recidivism Among Female Juvenile Delinquents. Offord, D R and Aponte, J F and Frei, R J.

Suicide, And White Reformatory Girl's Preference For Negro Men. Hammer, M.

The Woman Participant In Washington's Riots. Miller, Eugene.

Sisterhood Is Powerful: An Anthology Of Writings From The Women's Liberation Movement. Morgan, Robin (ed).

Attribution Of Blame, Anger, & Aggression In [Poor] Female Negro Adults. Forbes, Gordon B and Mitchell, Shirley.

Constance Baker Motley: Black Woman, Black Judge. Washington, Michelle.

Imitation Of Self–Reward Standards By Black And White Female Delinquents. Thelan, Mark H and Fryrear, Jerry L.

La Causa Chicana: The Movement For Justice. Mangold, Margaret M.

The Female Offender In Philadelphia. Adler, F S.

Mortality Trends For Homicide By Age, Color, And Sex: United States, 1960–1972. Klebba, A Joan.

Women In Prison. Burkhart, Kathryn Watterson.

Patterns In Forcible Rape: A Review Essay. Mintz, Betty.

Women In Policing—A Manual. Abramowitz, A et al.

Blacks Versus Women—When Victims Collide. Hogan, B.

Report Of The LEAA Task Force On Women. U S Dept Of Justice, LEAA.

Differential Effects Of Group Counseling With Black And White Female Delinquents One Year Later. Redferin, D L.

Discrimination In Selection And Promotion Of Minorities And Women In Municipal Employment. Ivie, S D.

FEMALES

Pretreatment Criminality Of Male And Female Drug Abuse Patients In The United States. Ball, John C et al.

Women In Corrections—A Process Of Change. Becker, A M.

Norm Neutralization, Anomia And Self–Concept Among Institutionalized Female Delinquents. Lilly, J R and Ball, R A.

Aspirations And Social Concerns—Crime, Blacks, Inequality And Women. Watts, W and Free, L A.

City Layoffs—The Effect On Minorities And Women. New York City Commission On Human Rights.

Manual For The Recruitment Of Minority And Females. Avello, J A and Mendoza, M G.

Ego Development And Female Delinquency: A Cognitive–Developmental Approach. Frank, Susan and Quinlan, Donald M.

Liberation And Crime: The Invention Of The New Female Criminal. Weis, Joseph G.

Women In Criminal Justice—A Policy Statement. National Council On Crime And Delinquency.

Women In The Criminal Justice System. Robinson, L O.

Women Judges. Sassower, D L.

"Unequal Protection For Males And Females In The Juvenile Courts" in *Juvenile Delinquency*, Ferdinand, Theodore N (ed), 59–77. Datesman, Susan K and Scarpitti, Frank R.

Affirmative Action For Women—A Practical Guide For Women And Management. Jongeward, D and Scott, D.

Breaking And Entering—Policewomen In The Police World. Martin, S E.

Female Offender Workshop Guide, Female Offender Resource Center. American Bar Association.

Recruitment And Retention Of Females In Law Enforcement Occupations. Dutton, A and Britt, B.

Working For You—A Guide To Employing Women In Non–Traditional Jobs. Hart, L G.

"Black Women: Income And Incarceration" in *Blacks And Criminal Justice*, Owens, Charles E And Jimmy Bell (eds), 85–92. Wyrick, Saunders and Owens, Holloway O.

"Women In Policing—Changing Perspectives On The Role" in *Criminal Justice Planning*, Scott, J E And S Dinitz (eds). Breece, C M and Garrett, G R.

Black Female Gangs In Philadelphia. Brown, Waln K.

Exclusion Of Women From The Judicial Process. Tolchin, S.

"From Matron To Commanding Officer—Women's Changing Role In Law Enforcement" in *Law Enforcement Bible*, Scanlon, Robert A (ed). Acerra, L.

Expectations Which Have Shaped Women's Role In Policing New York City. Sichel, J L.

Leadership By Women In Criminal Justice—There Is Room At The Top. Strosnider, C S.

The Social System Of A Medium Security Women's Prison. Spencer, Elousie J.

Women In The Courts. Hepperle, W L (ed) and Crites, L (ed).

Women, Crime, And The Criminal Justice System. Bowker, Lee H and Chesney, Meda and Pollock, Joy.

Women's Jail—Pretrial And Post–Conviction Alternatives—A Report On Women Arrested In San Francisco. Bresler, L and Leonard, D.

An Assessment Of The Black Female Prisoners In The South. French, Laurence.

Race, Father–Absence And Female Delinquency. Austin, Roy L.

The Incarcerated Black Female: The Case Of Social Double Jeopardy. French, Laurence.

"Black Women And Homicide" in *Lethal Aspects Of Urban Violence*, Rose, Harold M (ed), 83–90. Letcher, Maxine.

"Century Of Women In Policing" in *Modern Police Administration*, Schultz, Donald O (ed). Price, B and Gavin, S.

"Children Of Incarcerated Mothers" in *Child Development*, Green, R And T Yawkey (eds). La Point, Velma.

"The Effect Of Race On Sentence" in *Theory And Research In Criminal Justice*, Conley, J A (ed). Foley, Linda and Rasch, Christine E.

Hispanic Women Offenders And Ex–Offenders. Daldio, Maria Gomez.

Capable Cops—Women Behind The Shield—A Selected Bibliography On Women Police Officers. Martin, C A.

Female Offenders: Who Are They And What Are The Problems Confronting Them? U S General Accounting Office.

La Chicana: The Mexican American Woman. Mirandé, Alfredo and Enriques, Evangelina.

Program For Women Offenders—How To Start, Fund, Maintain. Female Offenders Program Of Western Pennsylvania, Inc.

Revolt Against Chivalry: Jessie Daniel Ames And The Women's Campaign Against Lynching. Hall, Jacqueline Dowd.

The Innocence Of Joan Little. Reston Jr, James.

A Comparative Analysis Of Male And Female Delinquency. Cernkovich, Stephen A and Giordano, Peggy C.

Equal Employment Opportunity Legislation And The Income Of Women And Nonwhites. Burstein, P.

Mexican Women In The United States: Struggles Past And Present. Mora, Magdalena and Del Castillo, Adelaida (ed).

Women As Probation Parole, And Correctional Officers In The Criminal Justice Field—A Selected Bibliography. Martin, C A.

Women In The Criminal Justice System. Feinman, C.

Women, Crime, And Justice. Datesman, Susan K (ed) and Scarpitti, Frank R (ed).

Developing An Equal Protection Standard For Gender Discrimination Cases—Where's The Rub? Note.

Sex Discrimination In Prison Employment: The Bona Fide Occupational Qualification And Prisoners' Privacy Rights. Tharnish, D M.

Should Women Guards Work In Prisons For Men? Potter, Joan.

Women, Race And Crime. Young, Vernetta D.

FINES

The Equal Protection Clause And Imprisonment Of The Indigent For Non–Payment Of Fines. Note.

FLAGSTAFF, AZ

Justice In Flagstaff: Are These Rights Inalienable? Arizona Committee To The U S Commission On Civil Rights.

FLORIDA

see also Dade County, Fl, Miami, Fl

The Legal Status Of The Negro. Magnum, Charles S.

Trial And Imprisonment Of Jonathan Walker, At Pensacola, For Aiding Slaves To Escape From Bondage. Walker, Jonathan.

Report Of The Pennsylvania Joint Legislative Committee On Capital Punishment. Joint Legis Comm On Capital Punishment.

Rape: Selective Electrocution Based On Race. American Civil Liberties Union Of Florida.

The Convict–Lease System In Florida, 1866–1923. Carper, Noel Gordon.

Race And Ethnicity Relative To Other Factors In Juvenile Court Dispositions. Arnold, William R.

My Rhythm Flows From A Different Beat. Lucas, Henry N.

Race Relations Training With Correctional Officers. Wittmer, J and Lanier, J E and Parker, M.

Capital Punishment 1976. U S Dept Of Justice, LEAA, NCJISS.

Killing The Killers: A Post–*Furman* Profile Of Florida's Condemned. Lewis, Peter W.

Will He Be The First? Range, Peter R.

FLORIDA STATE PRISON

Bound And Free: The Poetry Of Warriors Behind Bars. Black Prisoners Of Florida State Prison, Starke.

FOLSOM PRISON, CA

If They Come In The Morning: Voices Of Resistance. Davis, Angela Y et al.

No Beast So Fierce. Bunker, Edward.

Captive Voices: An Anthology From Folsom Prison. Anonymous.

Dark Smoke. Aguila, Pancho.

FRANKLIN COUNTY, OH

Ascertaining Police Bias In Arrests For Drunken Driving. Hyman, Merton M and Helrich, Alice R and Benson, Gwen.

FRAUD

Fraud And Abuse In Government Benefit Programs. Lange, A G (ed) and Bowers, R A (ed).

FREE WILL

The Compatibility Of Free Will And Determinism In Criminology: Comments On An Alleged Problem. Glaser, Daniel.

FRUSTRATION - AGGRESSION

Rosenzweig Picture—Frustration Study Results With Minority Group Juvenile Delinquents. Norman, Ralph D and Kleinfeld, Gerald J.

The Study Of Urban Violence: Some Implications Of Laboratory Studies Of Frustration And Aggression. Berkowitz, Leonard.

FRUSTRATION - AGGRESSION

The Hunters Point Riot: Politics Of The Frustrated. Carmichael, Benjamin G.

Attribution Of Blame, Anger, & Aggression In [Poor] Female Negro Adults. Forbes, Gordon B and Mitchell, Shirley.

FUGITIVES

Twenty–Two Years A Slave And Forty Years A Freeman. Stewart, Austin.

Narrative Of The Barbarous Treatment Of Two Unfortunate Females, Natives Of Concordia LA By Joseph & Enoch, Runaway Slaves. Joseph and Enoch.

Trial And Imprisonment Of Jonathan Walker, At Pensacola, For Aiding Slaves To Escape From Bondage. Walker, Jonathan.

Horace Mann's Letters On The Extension Of Slavery Into California And New Mexico. Mann, Horace.

The Fugitive Slave Bill: Its History And Unconstitutionality. American Anti–Slavery Society.

The Autobiography Of A Fugitive Negro. Ward, Samuel Ringgold.

The Martyrs & The Fugitive, Or A Narrative Of The Captivity, Sufferings & Death Of An African Family & The Escape Of Their Son. Platt, Reverend S H.

Many Thousand Gone: The Ex–Slaves' Account Of Their Bondage And Freedom. Nichols, Charles H.

The Slave Catchers. Campbell, S W.

Black Men In Chains: Narrative By Escaped Slaves. Nichols, Charles H.

Flight And Rebellion: Slave Resistance In Eighteenth Century Virginia. Mullin, Gerald W.

South Carolina Fugitives As Viewed Through Local Newspapers With Emphasis On Runaway Notices 1732–1800. Meaders, Daniel.

Underground Rail Road Record. Still, William.

Fugitive Slaves 1619–1865. Mc Dougall, Marion Gleason.

FULTON COUNTY, GA

Race As A Determinant Of Criminal Sentences: A Methodological Critique And A Case Study. Gibson, James L.

GALLUP, NM

Sleeping It Off In Gallup, NM. Katel, Peter.

GAMBLING

The Negro Numbers Man As A Criminal Type: The Construction And Application Of A Typology. Roebuck, Julian D.

Gambling And Alcoholism: Symptom Substitution And Functional Equivalents. Adler, N and Goleman, D.

GANGS

New Style Highbinder Fights Tong Wars Today. Manion, Jack.

Delinquency Areas. Shaw, Clifford et al.

Street Corner Society. Whyte, William Foote.

Gangs Of Mexican–American Youth. Bogardus, Emory S.

Lower Class Culture As A Generating Milieu Of Gang Delinquency. Miller, Walter B.

Delinquency And Opportunity: A Theory Of Delinquent Gangs. Cloward, Richard A and Ohlin, Lloyd E.

Real West Side Story, Life Of Jose Rivera. Morgan, T B.

The Hatchet Men. Dillon, Richard H.

The Analysis Of Self–Descriptions By Members Of Delinquent Gangs. Strodtbeck, Fred L and Short Jr, James F and Kolegar, Ellen.

"Race And Nationality In The Gang" in *The Gang: A Study Of 1,313 Gangs In Chicago*, Orig Pub 1927, 130–154. Thrasher, Frederick M.

Behavior Dimensions Of Gang Delinquency. Short Jr, James F and Tennyson, Ray A and Howard, Kenneth I.

Street Corner Groups And Patterns Of Delinquency: A Progress Report. Short Jr, James F.

The Juvenile Gang: A Cultural Reflex. Bloch, Herbert A.

Values And Gang Delinquency: A Study Of Street–Corner Groups. Gordon, Robert A et al.

"Gang Delinquency And Anomie" in *Anomie And Deviant Behavior: A Discussion And Critique*, Clinard, Marshall B (ed), 98–127. Short Jr, James F.

Adult–Adolescent Relations And Gang Delinquency. Short Jr, James F and Rivera, Ramon and Marshall, Harvey.

Gang Member Delinquency: Its Extent, Sequence And Typology. Robin, Gerald D.

Group Process And Gang Delinquency. Gordon, Robert A et al.

A Five–Year Encounter With A Mexican–American Conflict Gang: Its Implications For Delinquency Theory. Farris, Buford and Brymer, Richard.

Perceived Opportunities, Gang Membership, And Delinquency. Short Jr, James F and Rivera, Ramon and Tennyson, Ray.

Analysis Of Selected Social And Cultural Characteristics Involving Juvenile Delinquency In Mexican–American Slums Of South El Paso. Knowlton, Clark S.

"Gang Members And The Police" in *The Police: Six Sociological Essays*, Bordua, David J (ed), 58–98. Werthman, Carl and Piliavin, Irving.

Comment On Lerman's 'Gangs, Networks, And Subcultural Delinquency'. Short Jr, James F.

Fire And Blackstone. Fry, John.

The Vice Lords: Warriors Of The Streets. Keiser, R Lincoln.

Delinquent Behavior In An American City. Gold, Martin.

The Violent Gang. Yablonsky, Lewis.

House Of Lords. Anonymous.

Police Control Of Juveniles. Black, Donald and Reiss Jr, Albert.

Right On With The Young Lords. Yglesias, Jose.

The Young Lords And The Spanish Congregation. Kelley, Dean M.

Palante: Young Lords Party. Young Lords and Abramson, Michael.

Street Gangs And Street Workers. Klein, Malcolm.

LUCHA In Agencyland: A Chicano Self–Help Organization Meets The Establishment. Moore, Joan W.

Racial Violence At San Quentin Prison/War Behind Walls. Bunker, Edward.

"The Legitimation Of Violence: Political Socialization And New Gangs" in *Poltics And Crime*, Sylvester Jr, Sawyer F And Edward Sagarin (eds). Johnson, Audrey L.

Community Organizing Of Gang Barrios. Pineda, Charles.

Gang Youth And Hustling: The Psychology Of Survival. Krisberg, Barry.

Honor, Normative Ambiguity And Gang Violence. Horowitz, Ruth and Schwartz, Gary.

Race, Sex And Gangs: The Saints And The Roughnecks. Chambliss, William J.

Race, Sex And Gangs: The Molls. Miller, Walter B.

Race, Sex, And Gangs: Black Crusaders, The Rise And Fall Of Political Gangs. Helmreich, William B.

Street Gangs Behind Bars. Jacobs, James B.

The 'Low–Riders': Portrait Of An Urban Youth Subculture. Holtz, Janice Marie Allard.

Violence By Youth Gangs And Youth Groups In Major American Cities—Final Report. Miller, Walter B.

"Youth Gangs In The Urban Crisis Era" in *Delinquency, Crime And Society*, Short Jr, James F (ed), 91–128. Miller, Walter B.

Stateville: The Penitentiary In Mass Society. Jacobs, James B.

America's Newest Crime Syndicate: The Mexican Mafia. Adams, Nathan M.

Black Female Gangs In Philadelphia. Brown, Waln K.

Inside The Mexican Mafia. Hammarley, John.

The New Gangs Of Chinatown. Rice, Berkeley.

Homeboys: Gangs, Drugs, And Prison In The Barrios Of Los Angeles. Moore, Joan et al.

A Year With The Gangs Of East Los Angeles. Murphy, Suzanne.

Black Gangs As Family Extensions. Brown, Waln K.

Street Gangs—Profiles For Police. Collins, H C.

Chicano Gangs In The East LA (Los Angeles, CA) Barrio. Torres, D M.

Estrangement, Machismo And Gang Violence. Erlanger, Howard S.

Joan W Moore, Et Al: Homeboys: Gangs, Drugs, And Prisons In The Barrios Of Los Angeles. Trujillo, Larry D.

At Stateville, The Calm Is Tense. Krajick, Kevin.

Ducks Versus Hard Rocks. Hunter, Deairich.

East LA's Gang Project: Prevention Or Bribery? Bernstein, Dan.

GARVEY, MARCUS

Garveyism And African Nationalism. Langley, J A.

Philosophy And Opinions Of Marcus Garvey, Amy Jacques–Garvey (ed). Garvey, Marcus.

GENETICS

Genetics And Sociology: A Reconsideration. Eckland, Bruce K.

YY Syndrome In An American Negro. Telfer, M A and Baker, D and Longtin, L.

An XYZ Survey In A Negro Prison Population. Fattig, W Donald.

The XYY Offender: A Modern Myth? Fox, Richard G.

GENOCIDE

Human Behavior In A Concentration Camp. Cohen, Elie A.

GENOCIDE

Black Man, Red Man, And White American: The Constitutional Approach To Genocide. Willhelm, Sidney M.

Fears Of Genocide Among Black Americans As Related To Age, Sex, And Region. Turner, Castellano and Darity, William A.

The Significance Of Disease In Extinction Of The New England Indians. Cook, Sherburne F.

Genocide: Birth Control And The Black American. Weisbond, R G.

The Invasion Of America: Indians, Colonialism, And The Cant Of Conquest. Jennings, Francis.

The War Against The Jews, 1933–1945. Dawidowicz, Lucy S.

Genocide And State Power, 3rd Edition. Horowitz, Irving Louis.

Savagism And Civility: Indians And Englishmen In Colonial Virginia. Sheehan, Bernard W.

GEOGRAPHY

The City. Park, Robert E and Burgess, Ernest W and Mc Kenzie, Roderick D.

Delinquency Areas. Shaw, Clifford et al.

Juvenile Delinquency And Urban Areas. Shaw, Clifford and Mc Kay, Henry.

The Criminal Area. Morris, Terrence.

The Metropolis And Juvenile Delinquency Among Negroes. Hill, Mozell.

Walk Along The Worst Block: East 100th Street. Samuels, Gertrude.

Crime, Delinquency, And Social Areas. Quinney, Richard.

The Social Order Of The Slum. Suttles, Gerald.

The Geography Of Urban Crime: The Spatial Pattern Of Serious Crime In The City Of Renuer. Lee, Yuk and Egan, Frank J.

Black Neighbors: Negroes In A Northern Rural Community. Hesslink, G K.

The Geography Of Crime And Justice. Harries, Keith D.

City Characteristics And Racial Violence. Jiobu, R M.

The Geography Of Stupidity In The USA. Weyl, Nathaniel.

The Black Community: Diversity And Unity. Blackwell, James E.

A Rejoinder To 'The Geography Of Crime: A Political Critique'. Lee, Yuk.

Radical Theory, Relevance, And The Geography Of Crime. Phillips, Phillip D.

Recent Literature On The Geography Of Crime: Review And Comment. Harries, Keith D.

Rejoinder To Richard Peet 'The Geography Of Crime; A Political Critique'. Harries, Keith D.

The Ecology Of Urban Unrest: The Case Of Arson In Newark, New Jersey. Georges, Daniel E.

The Geography Of Crime: A Political Critique. Peet, Richard.

Federal Sentencing Patterns: A Study Of Geographical Variations. U S Dept Of Justice, LEAA, NCJISS.

The Geography Of Crime And Violence: A Spatial And Ecological Perspective. Georges, Daniel E.

Residential Succession And Delinquency: A Test Of Shaw And McKay's Theory Of Cultural Transmission. Kapsis, Robert E.

The Geography Of Despair. Rose, Harold M.

Community Safety And Criminal Activity In Black Suburbs. Nichols Jr, Woodrow W.

Crime And Environment. Harries, Keith D.

Geographic Correlates Of Police Shooting: A Microanalysis. Fyfe, James J.

GEORGIA

see also Atlanta, Ga, Fulton County, Ga

"Negro Crime" in *Notes On Negro Crime, Particularly In Georgia*, Du Bois, W E D (ed). Sanborn, Frank B.

Let Me Live. Herndon, Angelo.

Some Notes On Negro Crime, Particularly In Georgia, Orig Pub 1904. Du Bois, W E B (ed).

Negro Boys In The Youth Development Centers Of Georgia. Smith, W C.

Unemployment And Prison Population Trends In Georgia: 1967–1974. Cox, George H and Carr, Timothy S.

Rape, Race And The Death Penalty In Georgia. Wolfgang, Marvin E and Riedel, Marc.

The Black Minority Criminal And Violent Crime: The Role Of Self Control. Heilbrun Jr, Alfred B and Heilbun, Kirk S.

Impulsive And Premeditated Homicide: An Analysis Of Subsequent Parole Risk Of The Murderer. Heilbrun Jr, Alfred B and Heilbrun, Lynn C and Heilbrun, Kim L.

Race As A Determinant Of Criminal Sentences: A Methodological Critique And A Case Study. Gibson, James L.

Race, Criminal Violence, And Length Of Parole. Heilbrun Jr, Alfred B.

GHETTO

The Ghetto And The Slum. Lind, Andrew W.

Island In The City. Wakefield, Dan.

Black Metropolis: A Study Of Negro Life In A Northern City, Rev'd Ed Orig Pub 1945. Cayton, Horace R and Drake, St Clair.

The Urban Villagers. Gans, Herbert J.

Dark Ghetto. Clark, Kenneth B.

The Wonder Is There Have Been So Few Riots. Clark, Kenneth B.

Black Chicago: The Making Of A Negro Ghetto, 1890–1920. Spear, Allan.

Tally's Corner: A Study Of The Negro Streetcorner Men. Liebow, Elliot.

The Poor Pay More. Caplovitz, David.

Notes On Instant Urban Renewal. Montgomery, Roger.

Violence In Ghetto Children. Coles, R.

The Unheavenly City: The Nature And The Future Of Our Urban Crisis. Banfield, Edward C.

"Between White And Blacks: The Faces Of American Institutions In The Ghetto" in *Riot Commission, Supplemental Studies*, 69–215. Rossi, Peter et al.

"Police In The Ghetto" in *Riot Commission, Supplemental Studies*, 103–114. Rossi, Peter et al.

Cops In The Ghetto: A Problem Of The Police System. Levy, Burton.

Social Sources Of Support For Violence And Non–Violence In A Negro Ghetto. Feagin, Joe R.

The Corporation And The Ghetto. Sengstack, Mary.

The Dynamics Of Recent Ghetto Riots. Hundly, James.

The Landlord–Tenant Relation In Low Income Areas. Vaugh, Ted.

Coming Up Black: Patterns Of Ghetto Socialization. Schultz, D.

Soul Side: Inquires Into Ghetto Culture And Community. Hannerz, Ulf.

The Vertical Ghetto: Everyday Life In An Urban Project. Moore Jr, William.

El Barrio's Worst Block Is Not All Bad. Burnham, David.

Minority Lawyer: Link To The Ghetto. Clark, L D.

Urban Law Enforcement: A Plea From The Ghetto. Byrn, Robert M.

Behind Ghetto Walls: Black Families In A Federal Slum. Rainwater, Lee.

The Political Economy Of The Black Ghetto. Tabb, William.

Police Perceptions Of A Hostile Ghetto: Realism Or Projection. Groves, Eugene and Rossi, Peter.

The Social Order Of The Slum. Suttles, Gerald.

Absentee Ownership And Management In The Black Ghetto: Social And Economic Consequences. Reiss Jr, Albert J and Aldrich, Howard.

Anomie, In The Ghetto: A Study Of Neighborhood Type, Race And Anomie. Wilson, R A.

Ghetto Assessments Of Police Protection And Authority. Hahn, Harlan.

The Integration Of Blacks In Suburban Neighborhoods: A Reexamination Of The Contact Hypothesis. Zeal, Carolyn and Humphrey, Craig.

Sowing The Wind, . Welford, Harrison.

The Prison Of Unemployment. Taggert, R.

"The Ghetto, The Ghettoized And Crime" in *Police–Community Relationships*, Bopp, W (ed), 144–155. Tucker, Sterling.

Developing A Community And Computer Based Anti–Color–Code Strategy To Resist And Reduce Violent Crimes In Black Ghettoes. Haynes Jr, Andrew B.

Police Overperception Of Ghetto Hostility. Crawford, T J.

Victimization And Perception Of Crime In A Ghetto Community. Kleinman, Paula H and David, Deborah S.

The Unheavenly City Revisited: A Revision Of The Unheavenly City. Banfield, Edward C.

Delinquents And Nondelinquents In The Puerto Rican Slum Culture. Ferracuti, Franco and Dinitz, Simon and De Brenes, E Acosta.

Ghetto Cops. Henderson, Bruce.

From Plantation To Ghetto. Meier, August and Rudwick, Elliot.

Patterns Of Alienation In Inner City Ghettos. Philliber, W W.

Black Ghetto Diversity And Anomie: A Sociopolitical View. Kapsis, Robert E.

The Police And The Ghetto. Cooper, John L.

Ducks Versus Hard Rocks. Hunter, Deairich.

GRAFFITI

Graffiti In The 1970's. Wales, E and Brewer, B.

Graffiti And Crime: A Transcultural Study Of Narcissistic Rage. Lomas, H D and Singer, R D.

GRAND JURIES see Juries

GRATIFICATION

Psychopathy, Race, And Delay Of Gratification By Adolescent Delinquents. Unikel, I P and Blanchard, E B.

Ethnic Differences In Delay Of Gratification. Price– Williams, D R and Ramirez, M.

GREAT MEADOW PRISON, NY

Seven Long Times. Thomas, Piri.

GREENHAVEN PRISON, NY

Greenhaven Diary. Conway, Edward.

A Prison And A Prisoner. Sheehan, Susan.

GREENSBORO, NC

The True Story Of The Greensboro Massacre. Bermanzohn, Paul C and Bermanzohn, Sally A.

GREGORY, DICK

Nigger: An Autobiography. Gregory, Dick and Lipsyte, Robert.

GUIDELINES, SENTENCING

Sentencing Guidelines Project: Report To The Administrative Director Of The Courts On The Relationship Between Race And Sentencing. Sheflin, N.

GYPSIES

Gypsy Lifestyles. Mc Laughlin, John B.

HABITUAL OFFENDER see Recidivism, Sentencing

HABITUAL OFFENDERS

Recidivist Impacts Of Differential Sentencing Practices For Burglary Offenders. Bartell, Ted and Winfree Jr, L Thomas.

HAMPTON, FRED

The Death Of Fred Hampton. Calhoun, Lillian S.

HARLEM, NYC

Crime In Harlem. Carter, Michael.

Native Son. Wright, Richard.

Manchild In The Promised Land. Brown, Claude.

"The Zoot Effect On Personality: A Race Riot Participant" in Racial Violence In The United States, Grimshaw, A (ed), 413–420. Clark, Kenneth and Barker, James.

The Harlem Riot Of 1935. Hill, Robert B.

Black Power And Student Unrest: Reflections On Columbia University And Harlem. Ginzberg, Eli.

400 Miles From Harlem: Courts, Crime And Corrections. Wylie, Max.

Harlem And Detroit Riots Of 1943: A Comprehensive Analysis. Swan, L Alex.

Black Mafia: Ethnic Succession In Organized Crime. Ianni, Francis A J.

What Happened In Harlem: Analysis Of A Decline In Heroin Use Among A Generation Unit Of Urban Black Youth. Boyle, John M and Brunswick, Ann F.

HARM

"Victims, Harm And Justice" in Victimology: A New Focus, V1, Drapkin, Israel And Emilio Viano (eds), 77–87. Reiman, Jeffrey.

HELPING BEHAVIOR

Victim Characteristics And Helping Behavior In A Rural Southern Setting. Franklin, Billy J.

Helping A Motorist In Distress: The Effects Of Sex, Race And Neighborhood. West, S G and Whitney, G and Schnedler, R.

The Role Of Racial Attitudes In Helping Behavior. Gaertner, S L.

The Subtlety Of White Racism, Arousal, And Helping Behavior. Gaertner, S L and Dovidio, J F.

HENNEPIN COUNTY, MN

Study Of Sentencing In Hennepin County And Ramsey County District Courts. Rhodes, W M.

HEREDITY

Causes Of Crime: Biological Theories In The United States, 1800–1915. Fink, Arthur E.

YY Syndrome In An American Negro. Telfer, M A and Baker, D and Longtin, L.

An XYZ Survey In A Negro Prison Population. Fattig, W Donald.

The XYY Offender: A Modern Myth? Fox, Richard G.

Biosocial Bases Of Criminal Behavior. Mednick, S and Christiansen, K O.

HEROIN see Drugs

HEROIN MAINTENANCE

The Needle And The Boot: Heroin Maintenance. Cuskey, Walter R and Krasner, William.

HIGHER EDUCATION

Teaching Corrections Law To Corrections Personnel. Statsky, William P.

DeFunis Versus Odegaard And The University Of Washington, 3v. Ginger, Ann Fagan (ed).

Police And The Behavioral Sciences. Steinberg, J L and Mc Evoy, D W.

The Police And Higher Education: The Challenge Of The Times. Brown, Lee P.

"Higher Education: Roles In Criminal Justice" in Blacks And Criminal Justice, Owens, Charles E And Jimmy Bell (eds), 113–117. Bell, Jimmy.

Importance Given Selected Job Characteristics By Individuals Who Possess A Criminal Justice Degree. Sullivan, T T.

Study On The Status Of Black Criminology In The United States. Debro, Julius and Taylor, Helen.

An Historical Perspective On The Constitutional Debate Over Affirmative Action Admissions. Kimball, Bruce A.

Comment: Involving The Humanities In Doctoral Education In Criminology And Criminal Justice. Czajkoski, Eugene H.

The Bakke Problem—Allocation Of Scarce Resources In Education And Other Areas. Griswold, Erwin N.

Black And Hispanic Enrollment In Higher Education, 1978: Trends In The Nation And The South. Mingle, James R.

Less Spanish, Please. Molina, Mauricio.

HIGHLAND PARK, IL

Varieties Of Police Behavior: The Management Of Law And Order In Eight Communities. Wilson, James Q.

HIMES, CHESTER

Lonely Crusade. Himes, Chester.

The Quality Of Hurt. Himes, Chester.

My Life Of Absurdity. Himes, Chester.

HINDELANG, MICHAEL J

Race And Involvement In Common Law Personal Crime: A Response To Hindelang. Mc Neely, Roger and Pope, Carl.

HISPANIC CULTURE

Ethos Components In Modern Latin American Culture. Gillin, John.

The Children Of Sanchez. Lewis, Oscar.

La Vida: A Puerto Rican Family In The Culture Of Poverty—San Juan And New York. Lewis, Oscar.

Mexican Americans: Problems And Prospects. Moore, Joan W.

A Socio–Cultural And Socio–Legal Analysis Of Juvenile Delinquency In Puerto Rico. Kupperstein, Lenore R and Toro– Calder, Jaime.

"Mexican American Opiate Addicts" in The Epidemiology Of Opiate Addiction In The United States, Ball, John C (ed). Chambers, Carl D and Cuskey, Walter R and Moffett, Arthur D.

Social Character In A Mexican Village: A Sociopsychoanalytic Study. Fromm, Erich and Maccoby, Michael.

Stranger In One's Land. Salazar, Ruben.

The Consequences Of Familial Separation For Chicano Inmates (School Of Ed). Gonzales, Josephine.

Puerto Rican Americans: The Meaning Of Migration To The Mainland. Fitzpatrick, Joseph P.

The Chicano: From Caricature To Self–Portrait. Simmen, Edward (ed).

The Other Californians: Prejudice And Discrimination Under Spain, Mexico, And The United States To 1920. Heizer, Robert F and Almquist, Alan F.

The Puerto Ricans In Newark, New Jersey. Hidalgo, Hilda.

The Social Order Of The Slum. Suttles, Gerald.

Levels Of Acculturation And Of Attitudes Toward Deviance, Criminal Behavior And Police Law Enforcement Practices Among Puerto Ricans In NYC. Cotton, W L.

Savior, Savior, Hold My Hand. Thomas, Piri.

"Freedom In A Cage" in Reinterpretation Of American History And Culture, Cartwright, William H And Robert L Watson, Jr (eds). Acuña, Rodolfo.

Growing Up Puerto Rican. Cooper, Paulette.

Voices: Readings From El Grito, A Journal Of Contemporary Mexican American Thought, 1967–1973. Romano, Octavio Ignacio (ed).

The Chicano Family: A Review Of Research. Monteil, Miguel.

Chicano. Rosaldo, R et al.

Carlito's Way. Torres, Edwin.

Delinquents And Nondelinquents In The Puerto Rican Slum Culture. Ferracuti, Franco and Dinitz, Simon and De Brenes, E Acosta.

HISPANIC CULTURE

Limitations For The Prevention Of Violence: The Latin American Reality And Its Criminological Theory. Del Olmo, Rosa.

"Mexican–American Family" in *Chicanos: Social And Psychological Perspectives*. Murillo, Nathan.

El Tecato: Cultural And Sociologic Factors Affecting Drug Use Among Chicanos. Casavantes, Edward J.

Puerto Ricans In The Continental United States: An Uncertain Future. U S Commission On Civil Rights.

"The Mexican American Family" in *Ethnic Families In America*, Mindel, C And R Habenstein (eds). Alvirez, D and Bean, F.

"The Puerto Rican Family" in *Ethnic Families In America*, Mindel, C And R Habenstein (eds). Fitzpatrick, Joseph.

A History Of The Mexican American People. Samora, Julian and Simon, Patricia Vandel.

Culture And Crisis In Confinement. Johnson, Robert.

Culture Sensitivity And The Puerto Rican Client. Ghali, Sonia.

Graffiti And Crime: A Transcultural Study Of Narcissistic Rage. Lomas, H D and Singer, R D.

Joan W Moore, Et Al: Homeboys: Gangs, Drugs, And Prisons In The Barrios Of Los Angeles. Trujillo, Larry D.

From Indians To Chicanos: A Sociocultural History. Vigil, J D.

Mexican Women In The United States: Struggles Past And Present. Mora, Magdalena and Del Castillo, Adelaida (ed).

The Mexican Americans: A People On The Move. Smith Jr, Griffin.

HISPANIC POPULATION GROWTH

Persons Of Spanish Origin In The United States, November 1969. U S Dept Of Commerce, Bureau Of The Census.

Persons Of Spanish Origin In The United States: March 1972 And 1971. U S Dept Of Commerce, Bureau Of The Census.

Persons Of Spanish Origin In The United States: March 1974. U S Dept Of Commerce, Bureau Of The Census.

Persons Of Spanish Origin In The United States: March 1973. U S Dept Of Commerce, Bureau Of The Census.

Persons Of Spanish Origin In The United States: March 1975. U S Dept Of Commerce, Bureau Of The Census.

The Hispanic Tide—Some Implications Of Its Continuing Growth. Holman, Ben.

Persons Of Spanish Origin In The United States: March 1978. U S Dept Of Commerce, Bureau Of The Census.

Are Hispanics The 'minority For The 1980's'? Dreyfuss, Joel.

Hispanics In The Criminal Justice System: The 'Non–Existent Problem. Mandel, Jerry.

The 1980 Census: Making Sure We Count. Martinez, Douglas.

Hispanics In The US: Ethnic 'Sleeping Giant' Awakens, Part 4. Godsell, Geoffrey.

Hispanics In The US: Ethnic 'Sleeping Giant' Awakens, Part 3. Godsell, Geoffrey.

Hispanics In Local Government: A Growing Force. Pachon, Harry P.

Hispanics In The US: Ethnic 'Sleeping Giant' Awakens, Part 5. Godsell, Geoffrey.

Hispanics In The US: Ethnic 'Sleeping Giant' Awakens, Part 2. Godsell, Geoffrey.

Hispanics In The United States: Yesterday, Today And Tomorrow. Anson, R.

Hispanics In The System—Trying To Count The Numbers. Castro, Agenor L.

Hispanics In The US: Ethnic 'Sleeping Giant' Awakens, Part 1. Godsell, Geoffrey.

Tapping The Talents Of A New Generation. Mendoza, Ruben.

The Undocumented Immigrant: The Limits Of Cost–Benefit Analysis. Gutierrez, G G.

HISPANIC PRISONERS

"The Hispanic Inmate In Our Nation's Prisons Today". Castro, Agenor L.

California Prisoners 1977 And 1978: Summary Of Statistics Of Felony Prisoers And Parolees. California Dept Of Corrections.

The Hispanic Experience In Criminal Justice. Sissons, Peter L.

Mexico's Tres Marias Penal Colony. Jewell, Donald P.

Down These Mean Streets. Thomas, Piri.

Mexican Americans And The Administration Of Justice In The Southwest. U S Commission On Civil Rights.

The Crime Of Martin Sostre. Copeland, Vincent.

The Consequences Of Familial Separation For Chicano Inmates (School Of Ed). Gonzales, Josephine.

The Incarcerated Mexican–American Delinquent. Rudoff, Alvin.

Savior, Savior, Hold My Hand. Thomas, Piri.

Rights Of Spanish Speaking Minorities. Nuñez, Luis.

"The Penal Population Of California" in *Voices: Readings From El Grito*, Octavio Ignacio Romano (ed). Del Pinal, Jorge H.

Through The Veil Of Partial Comprehension: NY City's Hispanic Defendant And The Criminal Justice System. New York City Board Of Correction.

Canto Y Grito Mi Liberación. Sánchez, Ricardo.

Jail House Blues: Studies Of Suicidal Behavior In Jail And Prison. Danto, Bruce L (ed).

Population Breakdown Of Spanish–Speaking Residents. U S Dept Of Justice, Bureau Of Prisons, Education Branch.

Viaje/Trip. Salinas, Raul R.

Voices: Readings From El Grito, A Journal Of Contemporary Mexican American Thought, 1967–1973. Romano, Octavio Ignacio (ed).

Chicano Prisoners: The Key To San Quentin. Davidson, R Theodore.

Seven Long Times. Thomas, Piri.

An Analysis Of Proxemics And Self–Disclosing Behavior Of Recidivist And Non–Recidivist Adult Social Offenders. Braithwaite, Ronald L.

Short Eyes. Piñero, Miguel.

Profiling The Hispanic Inmate: A Correctional Dilemma. Castro, Agenor L.

"Hispanics: The Anonymous Prisoners" in *New Jersey Correctional Master Plan*, V4. Lee, Robert Joe.

Hispanic English Language Development In Prison. Bruno, N J and Orris Jr, J V and Gatje, C T.

"Correctional Philosophy: A Special Issue: Race And Criminal Justice" in *New Jersey Correctional Master Plan*. New Jersey Dept Of Corrections.

A Profile Of Puerto Rican Prisoners In New Jersey And Its Implications For The Administration Of Justice. Lee, Robert Joe.

Dark Smoke. Aguila, Pancho.

Profile Of Puerto Rican Inmates Under Departmental Custody. Morgenbesser, Leonard.

Meeting The Special Needs Of Hispanic Inmates. Castro, Agenor L.

Homeboys: Gangs, Drugs, And Prison In The Barrios Of Los Angeles. Moore, Joan et al.

A Close Look At The Hispanic Inmates And Methods Of Meeting Their Needs. Castro, Agenor L.

Hispano En Presidios Eu Buscan Logar Mejor Trato: Barrera Del Idioma Es Obstáculo. Anonymous.

The Latino Prisoners In The US—Managing Effective Participation. Mc Collum, Sylvia.

Hispanics In Corrections: The Statistical Dilemma In Finding Relevant Employee/Inmate Data. Castro, Agenor L.

Hispanic Women Offenders And Ex–Offenders. Daldio, Maria Gomez.

Assignment In Mexico: The Experience Of United States Magistrates In The Mexican Prisoner Transfer Program. Peterson, R W.

Comunidades Latinas Deben Cooperar Con Prisones. Hernandez, Conrado.

Joan W Moore, Et Al: Homeboys: Gangs, Drugs, And Prisons In The Barrios Of Los Angeles. Trujillo, Larry D.

Mexican Aliens Aren't A Problem: They're A Solution. Ehrlichman, John.

Unconstitutional Detention Of Mexican And Canadian Prisoners By The United States Government. Paust, J J.

Exploring The Re–Entry And Support Services For Hispanic Offenders, Natnl Hispanic Con L Enf, & CJ. Smith, Monica Herrera.

Psychological Testing Of Incarcerated Hispanics, Natl Hispanic Con L Enf & CJ. Torre, Marcella De La.

Report Of The Attorney General On The February 2 And 3, 1980 Riot At The Penitentiary Of New Mexico: Part 2. New Mexico Attorney General.

Report Of The Attorney General On The February 2 And 3, 1980 Riot At The Penitentiary Of New Mexico: Part 1. New Mexico Attorney General.

Hispanics In The System—Trying To Count The Numbers. Castro, Agenor L.

Mexican Nationals In US Prisons. Belsky, Michael.

New Mexico: The Anatomy Of A Riot. Serrill, Michael S and Katel, Peter.

The Santa Fe Prison Riots: 'The Flower Of The Dragon'. Mandel, Jerry.

HISPANICS

California Prisoners 1977 And 1978: Summary Of Statistics Of Felony Prisoers And Parolees. California Dept Of Corrections.

Public Information Materials For Language Minorities. National Criminal Justice Reference Service.

The Chicana: A Comprehensive Bibliographic Study. Duran, P H.

The Hispanic Experience In Criminal Justice. Sissons, Peter L.

The Los Angeles Pinto: Background Papers And Advance Report Of The Chicano Pinto Project. Chicano Pinto Research Project, Inc.

More Bars Against Mexicans. Taylor, Paul.

"Crime And Criminal Justice Among The Mexicans Of Illinois" in *Report On Crime And The Foreign Born,* V11. Warnheis, Paul L.

"The Mexican Immigrant And The Problem Of Crime And Criminal Justice" in *Report On Crime And The Foreign Born.* Taylor, Paul.

The Mexican In The United States. Bogardus, Emory S.

Gangs Of Mexican–American Youth. Bogardus, Emory S.

The Zoot–Suit Riots. Mc Williams, Carey.

Race Relations In Puerto Rico And The Virgin Islands. Williams, Eric.

The Morality Of Race Mixing In Puerto Rico. Rogler, C C.

Personal Crimes In Puerto Rico. Toro– Calder, Jaime.

Puerto Ricans In New York. Mills, C Wright.

Growing Up And Its Price In Three Puerto Rican Subcultures. Wolf, K L.

The Rising Puerto Rican Problem. Probst, Nathan and Olmsted, Sophia A.

A Study Of Teen–age Behavior Among Negroes, Mexicans, Puerto Ricans, Japanese, Chinese, Filipino And American Indians. Harris, Richard E.

Ethos Components In Modern Latin American Culture. Gillin, John.

Crimes Of Puerto Ricans In Brooklyn. Alter, Julius.

Up From Puerto Rico. Padilla, Elena.

With His Pistol In His Hand: A Border Ballad And Its Hero. Paredes, Américo.

Rosonzweig Picture––Frustration Study Results With Minority Group Juvenile Delinquents. Norman, Ralph D and Kleinfeld, Gerald J.

The Newcomers: Negroes And Puerto Ricans In A Changing Metropolis. Handlin, Oscar.

Identification Of Teen–Age Girls With Mexican–American Minority. Livermore, Jean.

Real West Side Story, Life Of Jose Rivera. Morgan, T B.

The Children Of Sanchez. Lewis, Oscar.

Report From A Spanish Harlem 'fortress'. Hammer, Richard.

Beyond The Melting Pot: The Negroes, Puerto Ricans, Jews, Italians, And Irish Of New York City. Glazer, Nathan and Moynihan, Daniel P.

Prejudice Toward Mexican And Negro Americans: A Comparison. Pinkney, Alphonso.

La Vida: A Puerto Rican Family In The Culture Of Poverty—San Juan And New York. Lewis, Oscar.

Spanish Harlem. Sexton, Patricia Coyo.

The Texas Rangers. Webb, Walter Prescott.

A Five–Year Encounter With A Mexican–American Conflict Gang: Its Implications For Delinquency Theory. Farris, Buford and Brymer, Richard.

Mexican Americans: Problems And Prospects. Moore, Joan W.

Mexican–American Youth: Forgotten Youth At The Crossroads. Heller, Celia S.

Personal Characteristics And Parole Outcome. Glaser, Daniel and O' Leary, Vincent.

A Demographic Profile Of The Mexican Immigration To The United States. Álvarez, José Hernández.

Analysis Of Selected Social And Cultural Characteristics Involving Juvenile Delinquency In Mexican–American Slums Of South El Paso. Knowlton, Clark S.

Down These Mean Streets. Thomas, Piri.

Minorities In A Changing World. Barron, Milton L (ed).

The Spanish Americans Of New Mexico: A Distinctive Heritage. González, Nancie L.

Cubans In Exile: Disaffection And The Revolution. Fagen, R and Brody, R and O' Leary, T.

North From Mexico, Orig Pub 1949. Mc Williams, Carey.

The View From The Barrio. Peattie, Lisa R.

A Comparative Study Of Puerto Rican Attitudes Toward The Legal System Dealing With Crime. Toro– Calder, Jaime and Cedeno, C and Reckless, Walter.

A Socio–Cultural And Socio–Legal Analysis Of Juvenile Delinquency In Puerto Rico. Kupperstein, Lenore R and Toro– Calder, Jaime.

A Study Of Delinquency Among Urban Mexican–American Youth. Rusk, Marian T.

Delinquency In Three Cultures. Rosenquist, Carl M and Megargee, Edwin I.

Mexican Americans In The Southwest. Galarza, Ernest0 and Gallegos, Herman and Samora, Julian.

El Barrio's Worst Block Is Not All Bad. Burnham, David.

The Puerto Ricans: Protest Or Submission. Maldonado– Denis, Manuel.

"Mexican American Opiate Addicts" in *The Epidemiology Of Opiate Addiction In The United States,* Ball, John C (ed). Chambers, Carl D and Cuskey, Walter R and Moffett, Arthur D.

Mexican Americans, With Alfredo Cuellar. Moore, Joan W.

Mexican Americans And The Administration Of Justice In The Southwest. U S Commission On Civil Rights.

Social Character In A Mexican Village: A Sociopsychoanalytic Study. Fromm, Erich and Maccoby, Michael.

Stranger In One's Land. Salazar, Ruben.

The Mexican–American People: The Nation's Second Largest Minority. Grebler, Leo and Moore, Joan W and Guzman, Ralph C.

Colonialism: The Case Of The Mexican–Americans. Moore, Joan W.

Demographic Factors In Opiate Addiction Among Mexican Americans. Chambers, C D and Cuskey, W R and Moffett, A D.

Family Background And Peer Group Deviance In A Puerto Rican District. Doob, C B.

House Of Lords. Anonymous.

Recent Changes Among Chicanos. Penalosa, F.

Right On With The Young Lords. Yglesias, Jose.

The Young Lords And The Spanish Congregation. Kelley, Dean M.

The Consequences Of Familial Separation For Chicano Inmates (School Of Ed). Gonzales, Josephine.

A Documentary History Of The Mexican Americans. Moquin, W E and Van Doren, C and Rivera, F

American Attitudes Toward Mexican Immigration. Lipshultz, Robert J.

Chicano Manifesto. Rendon, Armando.

Los Mojados: The Wetback Story. Samora, Julian.

Mexican Immigration To The United States. Gamio, Manuel.

Palante: Young Lords Party. Young Lords and Abramson, Michael.

Persons Of Spanish Origin In The United States, November 1969. U S Dept Of Commerce, Bureau Of The Census.

Puerto Rican Americans: The Meaning Of Migration To The Mainland. Fitzpatrick, Joseph P.

The Chicano: From Caricature To Self–Portrait. Simmen, Edward (ed).

The Other Californians: Prejudice And Discrimination Under Spain, Mexico, And The United States To 1920. Heizer, Robert F and Almquist, Alan F.

The Puerto Ricans In Newark, New Jersey. Hidalgo, Hilda.

Tree Of Hate: Propaganda And Prejudices Affecting United States Relations With The Hispanic World. Powell, Philip W.

El Chicano And The Constitution: The Legacy Of Hernandez Versus Texas. Comment.

La Opinion Serves Notice To The Spanish Speaking Community? Note.

Life In The Neighborhood: A Factor Analytic Study Of Puerto Rican Males In The New York City Area. Hoffman, Gerard and Fishman, Joshua A.

The Incarcerated Mexican–American Delinquent. Rudoff, Alvin.

Toward A Perspective On Chicano History. Gómez– Quiñones, Juan.

"The Barrio As An Internal Colony," in *Urban Affairs Annual Review,* V6, Hahn, Harlan (ed), 465–498. Berrera, M and Munos, C and Ornelasin, C.

A Study Of Mexican–American Perceptions Of Law Enforcement Policies And Practices In East Los Angeles. Morales, Armando.

Ando Sangrando (I Am Bleeding): A Study Of Mexican American - Police Conflict. Morales, Armando.

Awakening Minorities: American Indians, Mexican Americans, Puerto Ricans. Howard, John R (ed).

Criminal Injustice From The Chicano Point Of View. Morales, Armando.

La Causa Chicana: The Movement For Justice. Mangold, Margaret M.

Levels Of Acculturation And Of Attitudes Toward Deviance, Criminal Behavior And Police Law Enforcement Practices Among Puerto Ricans In NYC. Cotton, W L.

Migrant In The City: The Life Of A Puerto Rican Action Group. Rogler, Lloyd H.

Occupied America: The Chicano's Struggle Toward Liberation. Acuña, Rodolfo.

Savior, Savior, Hold My Hand. Thomas, Piri.

HISPANICS

The Chicano Addict: An Analysis Of Factors Influencing Rehabilitation In A Treatment Program. Auman, Jon et al.

The Chicanos: A History Of Mexican Americans. Meier, Matt S and Rivera, Feliciano.

Vizzini. Vizzini, Sal.

"Eliminating The Language Barrier" in *Police–Community Relationships,* Bopp, W (ed), 442–444. Ross, Donald J and Cobarruviaz, Louis.

Castro V Beecher, 459 F 2d 725 (Mass), US Court Of Appeals, First Circuit, May 24, 1972. Anonymous.

LUCHA In Agencyland: A Chicano Self–Help Organization Meets The Establishment. Moore, Joan W.

Rights Of Spanish Speaking Minorities. Nuñez, Luis.

The 'Wetback' As Deviant: An Application Of Labeling Theory. Bustamante, Jorge A.

"Freedom In A Cage" in *Reinterpretation Of American History And Culture,* Cartwright, William H And Robert L Watson, Jr (eds). Acuña, Rodolfo.

"The Penal Population Of California" in *Voices: Readings From El Grito,* Octavio Ignacio Romano (ed). Del Pinal, Jorge H.

"The So–Called Crime Of Being A Wetback" in *Chicanos, Life/Struggles Of The Mexican Minority In The US,* Lopez Y Rivas, G (ed). Bustamante, Jorge A.

Through The Veil Of Partial Comprehension: NY City's Hispanic Defendant And The Criminal Justice System. New York City Board Of Correction.

Canto Y Grito Mi Liberación. Sánchez, Ricardo.

Characteristics Of The Population By Ethnic Origin: March 1972 And 1971. U S Dept Of Commerce, Bureau Of The Census.

Ethnic Succession In Organized Crime: A Summary Report. Ianni, Francis A J.

Growing Up Puerto Rican. Cooper, Paulette.

Persons Of Spanish Origin In The United States: March 1972 And 1971. U S Dept Of Commerce, Bureau Of The Census.

Political & Economic Aspects Of Mexican Immigration Into California And The US Since 1941. Williams, Dean L.

Population Breakdown Of Spanish–Speaking Residents. U S Dept Of Justice, Bureau Of Prisons, Education Branch.

Viaje/Trip. Salinas, Raul R.

Voices: Readings From El Grito, A Journal Of Contemporary Mexican American Thought, 1967–1973. Romano, Octavio Ignacio (ed).

"Police Deployment Theories And The Mexican–American Community" in *The Urban Policeman In Transition,* Snibbe, J (ed), 341–353. Morales, Armando.

Administration Of Justice: Chicanos In Monterey County. Garza, H.

Alienation Of A New Generation Of Chicanos. Rodriquez, J.

Citado A Comparecer—Language Barriers And Due Process—Is Mailed Notice In English Constitutionally Sufficient? Comment.

Justice, Deprivation And The Chicano. Rivera, J.

The Angry Chicano. Sunseri, Alvin R.

The Chicano Family: A Review Of Research. Monteil, Miguel.

"Criminal Justice And The Minority Community" in *Urban Minority Groups In Houston: Problems, Progress And Prospects,* 205–248. Lede, Naomi W and Dixon, Hortense W.

A Comparison Of Mexican–American And Caucasian Male Juvenile Detainees. Hunter, Michael Nathan.

An Awakening Minority: The Mexican Americans, 2nd Ed. Servín, Manuel.

Chicano Revolt In A Texas Town. Shockley, John Staples.

Chicano. Rosaldo, R et al.

La Causa Politica: A Chicano Politics Reader. Garcia, F Chris.

Minority Opportunities In Law For Blacks, Puerto Ricans And Chicanos. Clark, C P (ed).

Persons Of Spanish Origin In The United States: March 1973. U S Dept Of Commerce, Bureau Of The Census.

Persons Of Spanish Origin In The United States: March 1974. U S Dept Of Commerce, Bureau Of The Census.

Puerto Rico And The Puerto Ricans: A Study Of Puerto Rican History And Immigration To The United States. Hauberg, Clifford A.

Seven Long Times. Thomas, Piri.

The Decision To Parole: A Study Of The Parole Decision Process With Juveniles. Hussey, Frederick Alan.

The Mexico–United States Border: Public Policy And Chicano Economic Welfare. Briggs Jr, Vernon M.

Unwanted Mexican Americans In The Great Depression––Tucson. Hoffman, Abraham.

A Comparison Of Negro, Anglo And Spanish–American Adolescents' Self–Concepts. Healey, G W and Deblassie, R R.

American Language Loyalty And The Validity Of The 1970 Census. Thompson, Roger M.

Chicanoizing Drug Abuse Programs. Aron, William S and Alger, Norman and Gonzales, Ricardo T.

Community Organizing Of Gang Barrios. Pineda, Charles.

Historical Notes On Chicano Oppression: The Dialectics Of Racial And Class Domination In North America. Almaguer, Tomás.

La Evolucion Del 'Bandido' Al 'Pachuco': A Critical Examination And Evaluation Of Criminological Literature On Chicanos. Trujillo, Larry D.

New Mafia: Black, Hispanic And Italian Styles. Ianni, Francis A J.

Puertoriquens In US—Impact Of Double–Discrimination. King, L M.

Racism And Its Effects On Puerto Rican Continentals. Longers Jr, J F.

An Analysis Of Proxemics And Self–Disclosing Behavior Of Recidivist And Non–Recidivist Adult Social Offenders. Braithwaite, Ronald L.

Carlito's Way. Torres, Edwin.

Delinquents And Nondelinquents In The Puerto Rican Slum Culture. Ferracuti, Franco and Dinitz, Simon and De Brenes, E Acosta.

How The Criminal Justice System Fails The Spanish–Speaking Community Of New York City And What Should Be Done About It. Special Committee On Penal And Correctional Reform.

Persons Of Spanish Origin In The United States: March 1975. U S Dept Of Commerce, Bureau Of The Census.

Puerto Ricans In New York City, Welfare Council Of New York City. Committee On Puerto Ricans.

Handling The Needs Of Non–English–Speaking Persons. Blake, Frank.

Interpreters For The Defense: Due Process For The Non–English–Speaking Defendant. Chang, W B C and Araujo, M U.

Legal Education Of Chicano Students: A Study In Mutual Accomodation And Cultural Conflict. Delgado, R and Romero, L M.

Limitations For The Prevention Of Violence: The Latin American Reality And Its Criminological Theory. Del Olmo, Rosa.

Profiling The Hispanic Inmate: A Correctional Dilemma. Castro, Agenor L.

The Dynamics And Treatment Of The Young Drug Abuser In An Hispanic Therapeutic Community. Freudenberger, Herbert J.

"Hispanics: The Anonymous Prisoners" in *New Jersey Correctional Master Plan,* V4. Lee, Robert Joe.

"Mexican–American Family" in *Chicanos: Social And Psychological Perspectives.* Murillo, Nathan.

Hispanic English Language Development In Prison. Bruno, N J and Orris Jr, J V and Gatje, C T.

Alcohol Use Among The Spanish Speaking: A Selective Annotated Bibliography. Treiman, B R et al.

California: Report To The Judicial Council On The Language Needs Of Non–English–Speaking Persons, Interim Phase 2 Report. U S Dept Of Justice, LEAA.

Drug Use And Abuse Among US Minorities: An Annotated Bibliography. Iiyama, P and Nishi, S M and Johnson, B B.

El Tecato: Cultural And Sociologic Factors Affecting Drug Use Among Chicanos. Casavantes, Edward J.

Puerto Ricans In The Continental United States: An Uncertain Future. U S Commission On Civil Rights.

"The Mexican American Family" in *Ethnic Families In America,* Mindel, C And R Habenstein (eds). Alvirez, D and Bean, F.

"The Puerto Rican Family" in *Ethnic Families In America,* Mindel, C And R Habenstein (eds). Fitzpatrick, Joseph.

Careers In Law For Minorities: A Puerto Rican's Perspective On Recent Developments In Legal Education. Cabranes, C A.

Counseling Offenders Of Spanish Heritage. Chaves, F J.

Non–English–Speaking Persons In The Criminal Justice System: Current State Of The Law. Cronheim, A J and Schwartz, A H.

The Hispanic Tide—Some Implications Of Its Continuing Growth. Holman, Ben.

"Crimes Against The Elderly––Findings From Interviews With Blacks, Mex–Amer, And Whites" in *Justice And Older Americans,* Young, M (ed). Ragan, P K.

A Descriptive Study Of The Control Of Illegal Mexican Migration In The Southwestern US. Toney, William T.

A History Of The Mexican American People. Samora, Julian and Simon, Patricia Vandel.

A Profile Of Puerto Rican Prisoners In New Jersey And Its Implications For The Administration Of Justice. Lee, Robert Joe.

HISPANICS

Anglo Over Bracero: A History Of The Mexican Worker In The United States From Roosevelt To Nixon. Kirstein, Peter N.

Black/Brown/White Relations: Race Relations In The 1970's. Willie, Charles V (ed).

Eskimos, Chicanos, Indians: Children Of Crisis, V4. Coles, Robert.

Heroin Use In The Barrio. Bullington, Bruce.

A Case Study Of Collaboration: The Chicano Pinto Research Project. Moore, Joan W.

America's Newest Crime Syndicate: The Mexican Mafia. Adams, Nathan M.

Culture Sensitivity And The Puerto Rican Client. Ghali, Sonia.

Desperate Mexican Children Swarm Over Border To Commit Crimes—Situation Seems Without Solution. Anonymous.

Development Of A Plan For Bilingual Interpreters In The Criminal Courts Of New Jersey. Hippchen, L J.

Gathering Complete Response From Mexican–Americans By Personal Interview. Zusman, Marty E and Olson, Arnold O.

Inside The Mexican Mafia. Hammarley, John.

MMPI Differences Among Black Mexican–American And White Male Offenders. Mc Creary, C and Padilla, E.

Meeting The Special Needs Of Hispanic Inmates. Castro, Agenor L.

No Comprendo: The Non–English–Speaking Defendant And The Criminal Process. Safford, Joan Bainbridge.

The Bakke Debate: A Mexican–American Protests That Affirmative Action Is Unfair To Minorities. Rodriguez, R.

The Role Of Informal Policy Making In US–Mexico Border Cities. Sloan, J and West, J.

Bibliography On Racism: 1972–1975, V2. National Institute Of Mental Health.

Homeboys: Gangs, Drugs, And Prison In The Barrios Of Los Angeles. Moore, Joan et al.

Mexican Migration To The United States: Causes, Consequences, And US Responses. Cornelius, Wayne A.

Puerto Ricans And Health: Findings From New York City. Alers, Jose Oscar.

The Illegals. Halsell, Grace.

Views Across The Border: The United States And Mexico. Ross, Stanley R (ed).

Wildcat Experiment—An Early Test Of Supported Work In Drug Abuse Rehabilitation. Friedman, L N.

A Close Look At The Hispanic Inmates And Methods Of Meeting Their Needs. Castro, Agenor L.

A Profile Of Hispanics In The US Work Force. Newman, Morris.

A Year With The Gangs Of East Los Angeles. Murphy, Suzanne.

Citizenship And The American Empire: Notes On The Legislative History Of The United States Citizenship Of Puerto Ricans. Cabranes, Jose A.

Going Home: The Puerto Ricans' New Migration. Stockton, William.

Hispano En Presidios Eu Buscan Logar Mejor Trato: Barrera Del Idioma Es Obstáculo. Anonymous.

Internal Colonialism: White, Black And Chicano Self Conceptions. Hurstfield, Jennifer.

Spanish Harlem. Shorris, Earl.

The Importance Of Spanish Language Training For Law Enforcement Officers. Tatum, William M.

The Latino Prisoners In The US—Managing Effective Participation. Mc Collum, Sylvia.

To What Extent Was Enrique Soto The Creation Of Pedro Juan Soto? Kennedy, William.

Trying Non–English Conversant Defendants: The Use Of An Interpreter. Bergenfield, G.

"Bilingual Education And The Hispanic Challenge" in *1979 Annual Report Of The Carnegie Corporation Of New York.* Pifer, Alan.

Hispanics In Corrections: The Statistical Dilemma In Finding Relevant Employee/Inmate Data. Castro, Agenor L.

Hispanic Women Offenders And Ex–Offenders. Daldio, Maria Gomez.

The Employment Of Hispanics In Corrections. Campos, Leonel.

A Model For Chicano Drug Use And For Effective Utilization Of Employment And Training Resources By Barrio Addicts And Ex–Offenders. Chicano Pinto Research Project, Inc.

Chicanos In A Changing Society: From Mexican Pueblos To American Barrios In Santa Barbara And Southern California, 1848–1930. Camarillo, Alberto.

Gunpowder Justice: A Reassessment Of The Texas Rangers. Samora, Julian and Bernal, Joe and Pena, Albert.

La Chicana: The Mexican American Woman. Mirandé, Alfredo and Enriques, Evangelina.

Persons Of Spanish Origin In The United States: March 1978. U S Dept Of Commerce, Bureau Of The Census.

Race And Class In The Southwest: A Theory Of Racial Inequality. Barrera, Mario.

Slave Trade Today: American Exploitation Of Illegal Aliens. Lewis, Sasha G.

Against Bilingual Education: Why Johnny Can't Speak English. Bethell, Tom.

Are Hispanics The 'minority For The 1980's'? Dreyfuss, Joel.

Assignment In Mexico: The Experience Of United States Magistrates In The Mexican Prisoner Transfer Program. Peterson, R W.

Chicano Gangs In The East LA (Los Angeles, CA) Barrio. Torres, D M.

Comunidades Latinas Deben Cooperar Con Prisones. Hernandez, Conrado.

Dishonor In The Sun: The Violation Of Human Rights, Texas–Style. Lyon, Matthew.

Estrangement, Machismo And Gang Violence. Erlanger, Howard S.

Evaluating The Dade County Citizen Dispute, Settlement Program. Salas, Luis P and Schneider, Ronald.

Hispanics In The Criminal Justice System: The 'Non–Existent Problem. Mandel, Jerry.

Joan W Moore, Et Al: Homeboys: Gangs, Drugs, And Prisons In The Barrios Of Los Angeles. Trujillo, Larry D.

Mexican Aliens Aren't A Problem: They're A Solution. Ehrlichman, John.

Silberman—Back To Root Causes. Anonymous.

Unconstitutional Detention Of Mexican And Canadian Prisoners By The United States Government. Paust, J J.

Bilingualism In Corrections. National Hispanic Conference On Law Enforcement And Criminal Justice. Castro, Agenor L.

Psychological Testing Of Incarcerated Hispanics, Natl Hispanic Con L Enf & CJ. Torre, Marcella De La.

From Indians To Chicanos: A Sociocultural History. Vigil, J D.

Mexican Women In The United States: Struggles Past And Present. Mora, Magdalena and Del Castillo, Adelaida (ed).

The Criminal Justice System: An Analysis Of Hispanic Issues. Baca, Salvador.

The Hispanic Victim: National Crime Survey Report SD–NCS–N–16A, NCJ–67706. U S Dept Of Justice, Bureau Of Justice Statistics.

The Inequality Of Justice: A Report On Crime And The Administration Of Justice In The Minority Coummunity. National Minority Advisory Council On Crim Just.

The Mexican American: A Critical Guide To Research Aids. Robinson, Barbara J (comp) and Robinson, J Cordell (comp).

Gunpowder Justice: A Reassessment Of The Texas Rangers (Book Review). Trujillo, Larry D.

Hispanics In The US: Ethnic 'Sleeping Giant' Awakens, Part 2. Godsell, Geoffrey.

Hispanics In The US: Ethnic 'Sleeping Giant' Awakens, Part 4. Godsell, Geoffrey.

Hispanics In The US: Ethnic 'Sleeping Giant' Awakens, Part 3. Godsell, Geoffrey.

Hispanics In The US: Ethnic 'Sleeping Giant' Awakens, Part 5. Godsell, Geoffrey.

Hispanics In The United States: Yesterday, Today And Tomorrow. Anson, R.

Hispanics And The US Criminal Justice System. Breiter, Tony (ed).

Hispanics Underrepresented As Criminal Justice Professionals. Carro, John.

Hispanics In The System—Trying To Count The Numbers. Castro, Agenor L.

Hispanics Have To Work Closely With Blacks. Garcia, Robert.

Hispanics In The US: Ethnic 'Sleeping Giant' Awakens, Part 1. Godsell, Geoffrey.

Justice For Hispanics Often Falls Short. U S Dept Of Justice.

Less Spanish, Please. Molina, Mauricio.

Mexican Nationals In US Prisons. Belsky, Michael.

New Mexico: The Anatomy Of A Riot. Serrill, Michael S and Katel, Peter.

Prison Perspective (Santa Fe Prison Riot). Anonymous.

The Mexican Americans: A People On The Move. Smith Jr, Griffin.

HISTORICAL STUDIES

The History Of Negro Servitude In Illinois And Of The Slavery Agitation In That State 1719–1864. Harris, N Dwight.

The Negro In Pennsylvania: Slavery–Servitude–Freedom, 1639–1861. Turner, Edward Raymond.

A History Of Penal Methods. Ives, George.

The Police Control Of The Slave In South Carolina. Henry, Howell M.

The County Court In North Carolina Before 1750. Mc Cain, Paul M.

American Negro Slavery: A Survey Of The Supply, Employment And Control Of Negro Labor As Determined By The Plantation Régime. Phillips, Ulrich Bonnell.

Fifty Years Of Negro Citizenship As Qualified By The United States Supreme Court. Woodson, Carter G.

The Southern Planatation Overseer: As Revealed In His Letters. Bassett, John Spencer.

Negro Labor In The United States, 1850–1925. Wesley, C H.

Slave Ships And Slaving. Dow, George Francis (ed).

Criminal Law In Colonial Virginia. Scott, Arthur P.

The North Carolina Black Code. Browning, James B.

Crime And The Negro. Cantor, Nathaniel.

The Jails Of Virginia: A Study Of The Local Penal System. Hoffer, Frank William and Mann, Delbert Martin and House, Floyd Nelson.

Law, Procedure And Punishment In Early Bureaucracies. Mac Leod, W C.

Pro–Slavery Thought In The Old South. Jenkins, William S.

Penal Slavery And Southern Reconstruction. Mc Kelvey, Blake.

American Prisons: A Study In American Social History. Mc Kelvey, Blake.

American Slave Insurrections Before 1861. Wish, Harvey.

Causes Of Crime: Biological Theories In The United States, 1800–1915. Fink, Arthur E.

Slave Insurrections In The United States, 1800–1865. Carroll, Joseph Cephas.

Negro Slave Revolts In The United States, 1526–1860. Aptheker, Herbert.

Punishment And Social Structure. Rusche, Georg and Kirchheimer, Otto.

Equal Protection Of The Law And Fair Trials In Maryland. Mc Guinn, Henry J.

An Appraisal Of The Negro In Colonial South Carolina: A Study Of Americanization. Klingberg, Frank J.

The Myth Of The Negro Past. Herskovits, Melville J.

Slave Law And The Social Structure. Moore, Wilbert E.

The Negro In Colonial New England. Greene, Lorenzo M.

Day To Day Resistance To Slavery. Bauer, Raymond A and Bauer, Alice H.

Capitalism And Slavery. Williams, Eric.

The Upgrading Of The Negro's Status By Supreme Court Decisions. Alexander, Raymond Pace.

American Slave Discontent In Records Of The High Courts. Russell, Marion J.

The Significance Of The Captivity Narrative. Pearce, Roy H.

White Settlers And Native Peoples. Price, A G.

A Documentary History Of The Negro People In The United States. Aptheker, Herbert (ed).

Slave Names In Colonial South Carolina. Cohen, Hennig.

The Legal Status Of The Indian In Colonial Virginia. Robinson Jr, W Stitt.

Catching The Criminal In Nineteenth–Century South Carolina. Williams, Jack Kenny.

Mr Seward For The Defense. Conrad, Earl.

The Peculiar Institution: Slavery In The Ante–Bellum South. Stampp, Kenneth M.

Slavery: A Problem In American Institutional & Intellectual Life. Elkins, Stanley M.

Lawlessness And Violence In America And Their Special Manifestations In Changing Negro–White Relations. Grimshaw, Allen.

Slavery And The Genesis Of American Race Prejudice. Degler, Carl N.

Black Mother: The Years Of The African Slave Trade. Davidson, Basil.

North Of Slavery. Litwack, Leon F.

The African Colonization Movement, 1816–1865. Staudenraus, P J.

The Slave Insurrection In New York In 1712. Scott, Kenneth.

Black Metropolis: A Study Of Negro Life In A Northern City, Rev'd Ed Orig Pub 1945. Cayton, Horace R and Drake, St Clair.

Chattel Slavery And Concentration Camps. Thorpe, Earl E.

The Legal Status Of The Slave In South Carolina, 1670–1740. Sirmans, M Eugene.

The Vesey Plot: A Reconsideration. Wade, Richard.

Negro Thought In America, 1880–1915. Meier, August.

Race: The History Of An Idea In America. Gossett, Thomas F.

Strangers In The Lands: Patterns Of American Nativism, 1860–1925. Higham, John.

The Freedmen Of South Carolina. Nordhoff, Charles.

The Image Of The Negro In Colonial Literature. Cantor, Milton.

A Political History Of The Texas Penal System, 1829–1951. Crow, H.

Race Riot At East St Louis: July 2, 1917. Rudwick, Elliot M.

Slavery In The Cities: The South, 1820–1860. Wade, Richard.

The Convict Lease System In Florida, 1866–1923. Carper, Noel Gordon.

The Economics Of Slavery And Other Studies In Econometric History. Conrad, Alfred H and Meyer, John R.

Death Sentences In New Jersey, 1907–1964. Bedau, Hugo Adam.

Towards Freedom: An Analysis Of Slave Revolts In The United States. Kilson, Marion D De B.

Suppression Of The African Slave Trade To The United States, 1638–1870. Du Bois, W E B (ed).

The Addict And The Law. Lindesmith, Alfred R.

The Black Codes Of The South. Wilson, T R.

The Texas Rangers. Webb, Walter Prescott.

Capital Punishment In Oregon 1903–1964. Bedau, Hugo Adam.

Negro Social And Political Thought, 1850–1920. Brotz, H (ed).

The Problem Of Slavery In Western Culture. Davis, David Brion.

The Strange Career Of Jim Crow. Woodward, C Vann.

Wayward Puritans: A Study In The Sociology Of Deviance. Erikson, Kai T.

A Demographic Profile Of The Mexican Immigration To The United States. Álvarez, José Hernández.

Servant Into Slave: The Evolution Of The Legal Status Of The Negro Laborer In Colonial Virginia. Palmer, Paul C.

The Origins Of The Navajo Indian Police, 1872–1873. Jones Jr, Oakah L.

Black Chicago: The Making Of A Negro Ghetto, 1890–1920. Spear, Allan.

Policing The City: Boston, 1822–1885. Lane, Roger.

The Crisis Of The Negro Intellectual: From Its Origins To The Present. Cruse, H.

The Negro American: A Documentary History. Fishel Jr, Leslie and Quarles, Benjamin.

The Spanish Americans Of New Mexico: A Distinctive Heritage. González, Nancie L.

The Story Of The Chinese In America. Sung, Betty Lee.

Rebelliousness And Docility In The Negro Slave: A Critique Of The Elkins Thesis. Genovese, Eugene D.

Resistance To Slavery. Frederickson, George M and Lasch, Christopher.

The Criminal Patterns Of Boston Since 1849. Ferdinand, Theodore.

From Slavery To Freedom. Franklin, John Hope.

Judicial Cases Concerning American Slavery And The Negro, 5v. Catterall, Helen H (ed).

Report On Crime And The Foreign Born, Orig Pub 1931. Abbott, Edith.

Sins Of The Fathers: A Study Of The Atlantic Slave Traders, 1441–1807. Pope–Hennessy, James.

The Burden Of Race: A Documentary History Of Negro–White Relations In America. Osofsky, Gilbert (ed).

Bibliography Of Crime And Criminal Justice, 1927–1931, Orig Pub 1934. Culver, Dorothy Campbell (comp).

Black Rage. Grier, William H and Cobbs, Price M.

Custer Died For Your Sins. Deloria, Vine.

Many Thousand Gone: The Ex–Slaves' Account Of Their Bondage And Freedom. Nichols, Charles H.

On Lynching. Barnett, Ida B Wells.

Report On The Penitentiaries Of The United States, Orig Pub 1835. Crawford, William.

The Negro In Maryland, Orig Pub 1889. Brackett, Jeffrey R.

The North Carolina Chain Gang: A Study Of County Convict Road Work, Orig Pub 1927. Steiner, Jesse F and Brown, Roy M.

"Historical Patterns Of Violence In America" in *Violence In America*, Graham, Hugh D And T Gurr (eds), 45–83. Brown, Richard Maxwell.

Capital Punishment In Texas, 1924–1968. Koeninger, R C.

Italians And Crime In Chicago: The Formative Years, 1890–1920. Nelli, Humbert S.

Our Racist History. Van Woodward, C Vann.

Red, White And Gray: Equal Protection And The American Indian. Mc Meekin, Daniel.

HISTORICAL STUDIES

The Historical Background And Present Status Of The County Chain Gang In South Carolina. Brailsford, Daniel T.

The Image Of The Negro In The Maryland Gazette, 1745–1774. Wax, Darold D.

The Origins Of Racism. Pinderhughes, C A.

Indian Policy After The Civil War: The Reservation Experience. Hagan, W T.

The Image Of The Indian In Pre–Civil War America. Prucha, Francis P.

Black Resistance Before The Civil War. Cheek, William F (ed).

The American Race Problem, Revd Ed By Jitsuichi Masuoka. Reuter, Edward Byron.

The Slave Catchers. Campbell, S W.

White Racism: Its History, Pathology And Practice. Schwartz, Barry N and Disch, Robert and Disch, Barry N.

A More Equitable Past: Southern Supreme Courts And The Protection Of The Ante–Bellum Negro. Nash, A E Keir.

Colonialism: The Case Of The Mexican–Americans. Moore, Joan W.

Fairness And Formalism In The Trials Of Blacks In The State Supreme Courts Of The Old South. Nash, A E Keir.

Judicial Administration And Racial Discrimination: Fifteen Years Of Literature. Martin, George.

Popular Uprisings And Civil Authority In Eighteenth–Century America. Maier, Pauline.

"Legal Status Of The Slave In South Carolina, 1670–1740" in *Colonial American Essays In Political/Social Development*, Katz (ed), 404–415. Senese, Donald.

"Slave Resistance In The US" in *Key Issues In The Afro–American Experience*, Huggins, N; M Kilson And D M Fox (eds). Aptheker, Herbert.

A Documentary History Of The Mexican Americans. Moquin, W E and Van Doren, C and Rivera, F.

Black Resistance/White Law: A History Of Constitutional Racism In America. Berry, Mary F.

Cherokee Tragedy. Wilkins, Thurman.

Key Issues In The Afro–American Experience. Huggins, Nathan and Kilson, Martin and Fox, Daniel M.

Once A Slave: The Slaves' View Of Slavery. Feldstein, Stanley.

Politics And Punishment: The History Of The Louisiana State Penal System. Carleton, Mark T.

The Black Image In The White Mind: The Debate On Afro–American Character And Destiny, 1817–1914. Frederickson, George M.

The Other Californians: Prejudice And Discrimination Under Spain, Mexico, And The United States To 1920. Heizer, Robert F and Almquist, Alan F.

White Terror: The Ku Klux Klan Conspiracy In Southern Reconstruction. Trelease, Alan.

The Texas Supreme Court And The Trial Rights Of Blacks. Nash, A E Keir.

Toward A Perspective On Chicano History. Gómez– Quiñones, Juan.

Black Men In Chains: Narrative By Escaped Slaves. Nichols, Charles H.

Denmark Vesey: The Slave Conspiracy Of 1822. Starobin, Robert (ed).

Flight And Rebellion: Slave Resistance In Eighteenth Century Virginia. Mullin, Gerald W.

History Of The Rise And Fall Of The Slave Power In America, 3v. Wilson, Henry.

Neither Slave Nor Free: The Freedman Of African Descent In The Slave Societies Of The New World. Cohen, David M (ed) and Greene, Jack P (ed).

Occupied America: The Chicano's Struggle Toward Liberation. Acuña, Rodolfo.

Servitude And Slavery In Colonial South Carolina, 1670–1776. Duncan, John Donald.

The Chicanos: A History Of Mexican Americans. Meier, Matt S and Rivera, Feliciano.

Wake Up Dead Man: Afro–American Worksongs From Texas Prisons. Jackson, Bruce (ed).

A Definition Of Colonialism. Horvath, Ronald J.

Black Faith In A Racist Land: Summary Review Of Racism In American Law. Bell Jr, Derrick A.

Harlem And Detroit Riots Of 1943: A Comprehensive Analysis. Swan, L Alex.

The Image Of The Indian In The Southern Colonial Mind. Nash, Gary B.

Imprisoned In America: Prison Communications 1776 To Attica. Philip, Cynthia Owen (ed).

Origins Of Narcotic Control. Musto, David F.

Race, Racism And American Law. Bell Jr, Derrick A.

The American Indian And The United States: A Documentary History. Washburn, W E.

They Came In Chains: Americans From Africa. Redding, J Saunders.

Historians And The Origins Of British North American Slavery. Starr, Raymond.

Narratives Of Negro Crime In New England, 1775–1880. Slotkin, Richard.

Preferences For Slaves In Colonial America. Wax, Darold D.

Racism And The Early American Legal Process, 1619–1896. Higginbotham Jr, A Leon.

The Significance Of Disease In Extinction Of The New England Indians. Cook, Sherburne F.

When Whites Riot—The East St Louis Massacre. Swan, L Alex.

All God's Dangers: The Life Of Nate Shaw. Rosengarten, Theodore.

Behind The Trail Of Broken Treaties. De Loria Jr, Vine.

Black Majority: Negroes In Colonial South Carolina From 1670 Through The Stone Rebellion. Wood, Peter H.

Crime And Law Enforcement In The Colony Of New York, 1691–1776. Greenberg, Douglas S.

Get Your Ass In The Water And Swim Like Me: Narrative Poetry From Black Oral Tradition. Jackson, Bruce.

Puerto Rico And The Puerto Ricans: A Study Of Puerto Rican History And Immigration To The United States. Hauberg, Clifford A.

Roll, Jordan, Roll: The World The Slaves Made. Genovese, Eugene D.

The Law Of Primitive Man. Hoebel, E Adamson.

Unwanted Mexican Americans In The Great Depression––Tucson. Hoffman, Abraham.

Where I'm Bound: Patterns Of Slavery And Freedom In Black American Autobiography. Smith, Sidonie.

Criminal Procedure In Slave Trials In The Antebellum South. Flanigan, Daniel J.

Historical Notes On Chicano Oppression: The Dialectics Of Racial And Class Domination In North America. Almaguer, Tomás.

Legacy Of Violence: The Opera House Lynching. Elliot, Jeffrey M.

Philanthropy Of Bargain Prices: Notes On The Economics Of Gradual Emancipation. Fogel, Robert William and Engerman, Stanley L.

American Minorities: The Justice Issue. Long, Elton et al.

Indian Law Enforcement History. U S Dept Of Interior, Bureau Of Indian Affairs.

The Invasion Of America: Indians, Colonialism, And The Cant Of Conquest. Jennings, Francis.

The Problem Of Slavery In The Age Of Revolution, 1770–1823. Davis, David Brion.

Crime Trends In Southern And Non–Southern Cities: A Twenty–Year Perspective. Jacobsen, Alvin.

Crosby Smith: Forgotten Witness To A Mississippi Nightmare. Shostak, David.

Development Of Criminal Jurisdiction Over Indian Lands—The Historical Perspective. Clinton, R N.

History And Role Of Black Law Schools. Washington, H R.

New Evidence Of Black Unrest In Colonial Brooklyn. Skemer, Don C.

Patterns Of Criminal Prosecution In Eighteenth–Century New York. Greenberg, Douglas S.

Prison And Native People. Blackhorse, F D.

Racial, Economic And Political Factors In The Development Of America's First Drug Laws. Mark, Greg Yee.

South Carolina Fugitives As Viewed Through Local Newspapers With Emphasis On Runaway Notices 1732–1800. Meaders, Daniel.

The Philadelphia Race Riot Of 1918. Franklin, Vincent P.

American Indian Policy In Crisis: Christian Reformers And The Indian: 1865–1900. Prucha, Francis P.

From Plantation To Ghetto. Meier, August and Rudwick, Elliot.

Jefferson's Nephews: A Frontier Tragedy. Merrill Jr, Boynton.

Rescued From Evil: Origins Of The Juvenile Justice System In Memphis, Tennessee, 1900–1917. Shelden, Randall G.

Roots. Haley, Alex.

Slavery And The Penal System. Sellin, Thorsten.

"Historical Overview Of Crime And Blacks Since 1876" in *Crime And Its Impact On The Black Community*, Gary, L E And L P Brown (eds), 3–11. Davis, Lenwood G.

HISTORICAL STUDIES

Black Justice Under White Law—Criminal Prosecutions Of Blacks In Antebellum South Carolina. Hindus, Michael Stephen.

Discretionary Justice In Early Massachusetts. Lee, Carol F.

Prison Reform And Indians. Keller, C.

Racial Remediation: An Historical Perspective On Current Conditions. Bell Jr, Derrick A.

The Great American Search: Causes Of Crime, 1876–1976. Hirschi, Travis and Rudisill, David.

A History Of The Mexican American People. Samora, Julian and Simon, Patricia Vandel.

Night Riders In Black Folk History. Fry, Gladys–Marie.

Slave Testimony: Two Centuries Of Letters, Speeches, Interviews, And Autobiographies. Blassingame, John W (ed).

Stateville: The Penitentiary In Mass Society. Jacobs, James B.

White Over Black: American Attitudes Toward The Negro, 1550–1812, Orig Pub 1968. Jordan, Winthrop D.

Black Arson In Albany, NY: November 1793. Gerlach, Don R.

Book Review—Slavery And The Penal System. Christianson, Scott.

Criminal Justice And Politics In America From The Sedition Act To Watergate And Beyond. Beckman, Eric.

Forced Conformity: Puritan Criminal Justice And Indians. Kawashima, Yasuhide.

Alabama Bound: Forty–Five Years Inside A Prison System. March, Ray A.

Blue Coats—Black Skin—The Black Experience In The New York City Police Department Since 1891. Alexander, J I.

In The Matter Of Color. Higginbotham Jr, A Leon.

Indian Treaties: Two Centuries Of Dishonor. Costo, Rupert and Henry, Jeanette.

The Victim As Criminal And Artist: Literature From The American Prison. Franklin, H Bruce.

Criminal Justice And The American Indian. Randall, Archie and Randall, Betty.

Prison Plantation: The Story Of Angola. Vodicka, John.

The Origins Of Afro–American Society In Tidewater Maryland And Virginia, 1700 To 1790. Kulikoff, Allan.

The Regimentation Of Blacks On The Urban Frontier In Colonial Albany, New York City And Philadelphia. Williams, Oscar R.

Chicanos In A Changing Society: From Mexican Pueblos To American Barrios In Santa Barbara And Southern California, 1848–1930. Camarillo, Alberto.

Gunpowder Justice: A Reassessment Of The Texas Rangers. Samora, Julian and Bernal, Joe and Pena, Albert.

Race And Class In The Southwest: A Theory Of Racial Inequality. Barrera, Mario.

Revolt Against Chivalry: Jessie Daniel Ames And The Women's Campaign Against Lynching. Hall, Jacqueline Dowd.

Theory And Research In Criminal Justice: Current Perspectives. Conley, John A (ed).

Violent Death In The City: Suicide, Accident, And Murder In Nineteenth–Century Philadelphia. Lane, Roger.

American Terror. Hughes, Graham.

Dynamics Of Courthouse Justice: A Critical Review Of The Literature. Neubauer, D W.

Southern Violence—Regional Problem Or National Nemesis—Legal Attitudes Toward Southern Homicide In Historical Perspective. Brown, Richard Maxwell.

The Man In The Middle, The Black Slave Driver. Miller, Randall M.

Trends In Incarceration In The United States Since 1880: A Summary Of Reported Rates And Distribution Of Offenses. Cahalan, Margaret.

The Historical Development Of Imprisonment Of Blacks In The US. Christianson, Scott.

Been In The Storm So Long: The Aftermath Of Slavery. Litwack, Leon F.

From Indians To Chicanos: A Sociocultural History. Vigil, J D.

From Rebellion To Revolution: Afro–American Slave Revolts In The Making Of The Modern World. Genovese, Eugene D.

Mexican Women In The United States: Struggles Past And Present. Mora, Magdalena and Del Castillo, Adelaida (ed).

Prison And Plantation: Crime, Justice, And Authority In Massachusetts And South Carolina, 1767–1878. Hindus, Michael Stephen.

Savagism And Civility: Indians And Englishmen In Colonial Virginia. Sheehan, Bernard W.

Women In The Criminal Justice System. Feinman, C.

Gunpowder Justice: A Reassessment Of The Texas Rangers (Book Review). Trujillo, Larry D.

Race, Crime And Social Policy: The Chinese In Oregon, 1871–1885. Tracy, Charles A.

The Crime Of Reform. Davis, David Brion.

The American Ideal Of Equality And Constitutional Change. Redenius, Charles M.

Fugitive Slaves 1619–1865. Mc Dougall, Marion Gleason.

Capital Punishment In 1740. Belden, Bauman L.

Slavery And Servitude In The Colony Of North Carolina. Bassett, John Spencer.

HOLIDAY, BILLIE

Lady Sings The Blues, By Billie Holiday. Fagan, Eleanora and Dufty, William F.

HOMICIDE

Violent Crime: Homicide, Assault, Rape And Robbery. National Commission On The Causes And Prevention Of Violence.

The Negro And Homicide. Brearley, H C.

Homicide In The United States. Brearley, H C.

Negro Homicides In The United States. Barnhart, Kenneth E.

Recent Increase In Homicide. Metropolitan Life Insurance Company.

Research Note On Inter– And Intra–Racial Homicides. Garfinkel, Harold.

Mr Seward For The Defense. Conrad, Earl.

Patterns In Criminal Homicide. Wolfgang, Marvin E.

Indians, Alcohol And Homicide. Baker, J L.

African Homicide And Suicide. Bohannon, P (ed).

Homicide In An Urban Community. Bensing, Robert C and Schroeder, Oliver.

The Psychology Of Murder. Palmer, S.

Ecological Pattern Of Negro Homicide. Pettigrew, Thomas F and Spier, Rosalind B.

Justifiable Homicide By Police Officers. Robin, Gerald D.

Suicide And Homicide: A Comparative Analysis By Race And Occupational Levels. Lalli, Michael and Turner, Stanley.

Navajo Criminal Homicide. Levy Jerrold E and Kunitz, Stephen J and Everett, Michael.

Patterns Of Criminal Homicide: A Comparison Of Chicago And Philadelphia. Hepburn, John R and Voss, H L.

Suicides And Homicides Among Indians. Ogden, Michael and Spector, M I and Hill Jr, C A.

More Than Murder: Administration Of Justice. Johnson, James Weldon.

Why Blacks Kill Blacks. Poussaint, A.

"Sociological Factors In Homicide" in *Rebellion And Retreat*, Palmer, S (ed), 95–108. Wolfgang, Marvin E.

Mortality Trends For Homicide By Age, Color, And Sex: United States, 1960–1972. Klebba, A Joan.

Suicide, Homicide, And Alcoholism Among American Indians—Guidelines For Help. Frederick, C J.

"Victim Precipitated Criminal Homicide" in *Crime And Criminal Justice*, Patterson, D (ed), 80–90. Wolfgang, Marvin E.

An Analysis Of 248 Persons Killed By New York City Policemen. Jenkins, Betty and Faison, Adrienne.

Racial Differences In The Personality Of Murderers. Perdue, William C and Lester, David.

Homicide Trends In The United States, 1900–1974. Klebba, A Joan.

Fatal Indian Violence In North Carolina. Kupferer, H J and Humphrey, J A.

Homicide In Chicago: A Nine–Year Study (1965–1973). Block, Richard.

On Urban Homicide. Barnett, A.

Pathologies Among Homicide Offenders: Some Cultural Profiles. Landau, S F.

Police Homicide In A Democracy. Kobler, Arthur L.

Jefferson's Nephews: A Frontier Tragedy. Merrill Jr, Boynton.

Murder, Inequality, And The Law. Swigert, Victoria Lynn and Farrell, Ronald A.

Felony Murder Rape, And The Mandatory Death Penalty. Bedau, Hugo Adam.

Homicide And Robbery In New York City: An Economic Model. Mathieson, Donald and Passell, Peter.

Minorities As Victims Of Police Shootings: Interpretation Of Racial Disproportionality And Police Use Of Deadly Force. Goldkamp, John S.

Prison Homicide. Sylvester, Sawyer F and Reed, John P and Nelson, David P.

IMPRISONMENT, RATES OF

The Effect Of The Depression On Prison Commitments And Sentences. Stern, Leon Thomas.

Effects Of Unemployment On White And Negro Prison Admissions In Louisiana. Dobbins, D A and Bass, Bernard M.

On The Penitentiary System In The United States And Its Application In France, Francis Lieber (trans), Orig Pub 1833. Beaumont, Gustave De and Tocqueville, Alexis De.

A Theory Of The Stability Of Punishment. Blumstein, Alfred and Cohen, Jacqueline.

Prison Use: A Canadian And International Comparison. Waller, Irvin and Chan, Janet.

Unemployment And Prison Population Trends In Georgia: 1967–1974. Cox, George H and Carr, Timothy S.

Prison Reform In Social Perspective. Vogel, Richard.

Survey Of Inmates Of State Correctional Facilities, 1974. U S Dept Of Justice, LEAA, NCJISS.

Iowa Prison Crisis: Economic Problem. Bruner, Charles.

Census Of Prisoners In State Correctional Facilities 1973. U S Dept Of Justice, LEAA.

Crime And Incarceration; A Reanalysis. Nagel, Jack H.

Federal Prison Construction: Alternative Approaches. Congressional Budget Office.

Mandatory Prison Sentences: Their Projected Effects On Crime And Prison Populations. Petersilia, Joan and Greenwood, Peter W.

Prison Population And Policy Choices: V1 & 3. Rutherford, Andrew et al.

Punishment And The Post–Industrial Society: A Study Of Unemployment, Crime And Imprisonment In The US. Jankovic, Ivan.

Labor Market And Imprisonment. Jankovic, Ivan.

On Behalf Of A Moratorium On Prison Construction. Nagel, William G.

Rate And Length Of Imprisonment. Doleschal, Eugene.

Prisoners Of Race. Kroll, Michael A.

Annual Statistical Report Of Felons & Misdemeanants Committed To The VA State Correctional System During The Year Ended June 30, 1977. Virginia Corrections Department.

Demographically Disaggregated Projections Of Prison Populations. Blumstein, Alfred and Cohen, Jacqueline and Miller, Harold D.

Prisoners In State And Federal Institutions On December 31, 1976. U S Dept Of Justice, LEAA, NCJISS.

Crime Rates, Sanction Levels, And Constraints On Prison Population. Nagin, Daniel.

Inequality And The Legal Order: An Ecological Test Of The Conflict Model. Jacobs, David.

Mandatory Prison Sentences: Their Projected Effects On Crime And Prison Populations. Petersilia, Joan and Greenwood, Peter W.

The Numbers Game. Miller, Marc.

Social Structure And Rates Of Imprisonment: A Research Note. Garofalo, James.

Overcrowding In Texas Prisons, Special Legislative Report No 43. Texas House Of Representatives.

Prisoners In State And Federal Institutions On December 31, 1977. U S Dept Of Justice, LEAA, NCJISS.

Racially Disproportionate Rates Of Incarceration In The United States. Dunbaugh, Frank M.

Trends In Incarceration In The United States Since 1880: A Summary Of Reported Rates And Distribution Of Offenses. Cahalan, Margaret.

The Historical Development Of Imprisonment Of Blacks In The US. Christianson, Scott.

Prisoners In State And Federal Institutions On December 31, 1978: National Prisoner Statistics Bulletin SD–NPS–PSF–6. U S Dept Of Justice, Bureau Of Justice Statistics.

Profile Of Inmates Of Local Jails: Sociodemographic Findings From The 1978 Survey Of Inmates Of Local Jails. U S Dept Of Justice, Bureau Of Justice Statistics.

The Black Incarceration Rate In The United States: A Nationwide Problem. Christianson, Scott and Dehais, Richard.

Corrections Law Developments: Racial Discrimination And Prison Confinement—A Follow–Up. Christianson, Scott.

Corrections Law Developments: Legal Implications Of Racially Disproportionate Incarceration Rates. Christianson, Scott.

INCAPACITATION

see also Preventive Detention

INCOME

A Comparative Study Of Delinquents And Non–Delinquents: Family Affect, Religion, And Personal Income. Allen, Donald E and Sandhu, Harjit S.

Inequality: A Cross–Sectional Analysis. Cutright, Phillip.

Racial Discrimination And White Gain. Szymanski, Albert.

The Influence Of Income And Other Factors On Whether Criminal Defendants Go To Prison. Clarke, Stevens H and Koch, Gary.

"Black Women: Income And Incarceration" in *Blacks And Criminal Justice*, Owens, Charles E And Jimmy Bell (eds), 85–92. Wyrick, Saunders and Owens, Holloway O.

INDIAN POLICE

Apache Agent: The Story Of John P Clum. Clum, W.

Police And Punishment Among Native Americans On The Plains. Mac Leod, W C.

Indian Police And Judges. Hagan, W T.

The Origins Of The Navajo Indian Police, 1872–1873. Jones Jr, Oakah L.

Indian Career Officer. Tedwell, D.

Lawmen For The Reservation. Metareltis, G S.

Law And Order On The Reservation—A Look At The Indian Police. State Peace Officers Journal.

Indian Law Enforcement History. U S Dept Of Interior, Bureau Of Indian Affairs.

Tribal Courts, The Model Code And The Police Idea In American Indian Policy. Barsh, R L and Henderson, J Y.

Problem Areas In The Operation Of Tribal Police Programs. National Congress Of American Indians.

INDIAN PRISONERS

Prison And Native People. Blackhorse, F D.

Prison Reform And Indians. Keller, C.

Incarcerated Native. Lane, E B and Daniels, H W.

INDIANA

The Negro In Indiana; A Study Of A Minority. Thornbrough, Emma Lou.

Black Voices From Prison. Knight, Etheridge (ed).

An Approach To Minority Recruitment. Goff, R W.

INDIANS

American Indian In The Criminal Justice System: A Selected Bibliography. Gleason, J (ed).

Criminal Court Procedures Manual: A Guide For American Indian Court Judges. National American Indian Court Judges Assoc.

Apache Agent: The Story Of John P Clum. Clum, W.

Navajo Common Law II: Navajo Law And Justice. Van Valkenburgh, R.

Police And Punishment Among Native Americans On The Plains. Mac Leod, W C.

Redman Reservations. Wissler, C.

The Cheyenne Way: Conflict And Case Law In Primitive Jurisprudence. Llewellyn, K and Hoebel, E Adamson.

Police And Tribal Welfare In Plains Indian Cultures. Humphrey, Norman D.

Variability In The Criminal Behavior Of American Indians. Hayner, Norman S.

Some Notes On Apache Criminality. De Vereaux, G and Loeb, E M.

Notes On Navajo Suicide. Wyman, L and Thorne, B.

The Delinquency Of The American Indian. Von Hentig, Hans.

The Significance Of The Captivity Narrative. Pearce, Roy H.

White Settlers And Native Peoples. Price, A G.

A Case Of A 'Psychotic' Navaho Indian Male. Jewell, Donald P.

The Legal Status Of The Indian In Colonial Virginia. Robinson Jr, W Stitt.

A Study Of Teen–age Behavior Among Negroes, Mexicans, Puerto Ricans, Japanese, Chinese, Filipino And American Indians. Harris, Richard E.

Juvenile Delinquency (Indians). U S Senate Committee On The Judiciary.

Juvenile Delinquency (Indians). U S Senate Committee On The Judiciary.

Juvenile Delinquency Among The Indians. U S Senate Committee On The Judiciary.

Juvenile Delinquency Among The Indians. U S Senate Committee On The Judiciary.

A Self–Report Comparison Of Indian And Anglo Delinquency In Wyoming. Forslund, Morris A and Cranston, Virginia A.

Extent Of Washington Criminal Jurisdiction Over Indians. Carr, A L and Johanson, S M.

Indians And Other Americans. Fey, H E and Mc Nickle, D.

Indians, Alcohol And Homicide. Baker, J L.

The American Indian. Flickinger, S J.

Selected Social Problems Of Fort Hall Reservation. Minnis, Mhyra S.

INDIANS

INDIANS

Indian Reservation Criminal Justice: Task Force Analysis, 1974–1975. U S Dept Of Interior, Bureau Of Indian Affairs.

United States—Comanche Relations. Hagan, W T.

American Indian Tribal Courts—Separate: 'Yes' Equal: 'Probably Not'. Brakel, S J.

Confrontation With The Law: The Case Of The American Indians In Seattle. Chadwick, Bruce A et al.

Constitutional Law—Unequal Protection For The American Indian Under The Major Crimes Act: United States Versus Antelope. Note.

Criminal Jurisdiction Over Indian Lands—A Journey Through A Jurisdictional Maze. Clinton, R N.

Discretionary Justice In Early Massachusetts. Lee, Carol F.

In Our Image: After Our Likeness—The Drive For The Assimilation Of Indian Court Systems. Kickingbird, K.

Indian Rights And The Constitutional Implications Of The Major Crimes Act. Martin, S L.

Looking Up The Indians: A Case Of Law Reform. Hagan, John.

Natives And The Law. Symposium.

Oliphant Versus Schlie: Recognition Of Tribal Criminal, Jurisdiction Over Non–Indians. Wasserman, R D.

Prison Reform And Indians. Keller, C.

The Victimization Of The American Indian. Dadrian, Vahakn N.

Tribal Courts, The Model Code And The Police Idea In American Indian Policy. Barsh, R L and Henderson, J Y.

Eskimos, Chicanos, Indians: Children Of Crisis, V4. Coles, Robert.

United States Indian Policy: A Critical Bibliography. Prucha, Francis P.

American Indians: The Reluctant Urbanites. Borman, L.

American Indian Courts And Tribal Self–Government. Collins, R B and Johnson, R W.

Bureau Of Indian Affairs Law Enforcement Division—Indian Police. Dijoseph, J.

Crime, Delinquency And The American Indian. Jensen, Gary and Stauss, Joseph and Harris, William.

Forced Conformity: Puritan Criminal Justice And Indians. Kawashima, Yasuhide.

Law Enforcement On Indian Reservations. Etheridge, D.

Suicide Epidemic On An Indian Reserve. Ward, J A and Fox, J.

The Sojourner In The American Indian Community: Methodological Issues And Concerns. Trimble, Joseph E.

Crime And The American Indian: A Survey Of The Literature. May, Phillip A.

Indians Before The Law: An Assessment Of Contravening Cultural/Legal Ideologies. French, Laurence.

American Indian Tribal Courts: The Costs Of Separate Justice. Brakel, Samuel J.

Bibliography On Racism: 1972–1975, V2. National Institute Of Mental Health.

Indian Treaties: Two Centuries Of Dishonor. Costo, Rupert and Henry, Jeanette.

Problem Areas In The Operation Of Tribal Police Programs. National Congress Of American Indians.

An Analysis Of Indian Violence. French, Laurence and Hornbuckle, J.

Criminal Justice And The American Indian. Randall, Archie and Randall, Betty.

Incarcerated Native. Lane, E B and Daniels, H W.

Indians And The Criminal Justice System. Starr, F M.

Legislation And Litigation Concerning American Indians. Deloria Jr, Vine.

The Economic Basis Of Indian Life. Sorkin, Allan.

The Indian Claims Commission. Lurie, Nancy.

Tribal Affiliation And Prevalence Of Alcohol Problems. Stratton, R and Zeiner, A and Paredes, A.

Indian Law: Oliphant v Suquamish Indian Tribe, 435 US 191 (1978). Berkey, C G.

American Indians And The Criminal Justice System. Benjamin, Roger and Choong Nam Kim.

From Indians To Chicanos: A Sociocultural History. Vigil, J D.

Savagism And Civility: Indians And Englishmen In Colonial Virginia. Sheehan, Bernard W.

The Inequality Of Justice: A Report On Crime And The Administration Of Justice In The Minority Coummunity. National Minority Advisory Council On Crim Just.

Sleeping It Off In Gallup, NM. Katel, Peter.

INDICTMENT

Indictment Under The 'Major Crimes Act'—An Exercise In Unfairness And Unconstitutionality. Dumars, T C.

INDIVIDUALISM

Individualism Reconsidered. Reisman, David.

INMATES *see* Prisoners

INSANITY

Post–War Trends In Employment, Crime, Insanity, And Heart Disease. Simpson, Ray Mars.

INSTITUTIONALIZATION, ADULT

Women's Prison: Sex And Social Structure. Ward, David A and Kassenbasum, Gene G.

Society Of Women: A Study Of A Women's Prison. Giallombardo, R.

The Prison And The Prisoner: 1967–1972. Tompkins, Dorothy Louise Culver.

An Examination Of Institutional Racism: Black People In California's Criminal Justice And Mental Health Systems. Ogleton, Betty and Crittendon, Stephanie and Seda, Cozetta.

Early Release From Incarceration: Race As A Factor In The Use Of Shock Probation. Peterson, David M and Friday, Paul.

Prisons: Instruments Of Law Enforcement Or Social Welfare? Jacobs, James B and Steele, Eric H.

Profile/Missouri. May, Edgar.

Race Factors In Responses To Interpersonal Stress Among Young Adult Offenders. Perry, A M and Kanson, H.

The Santa Fe Prison Riots: 'The Flower Of The Dragon'. Mandel, Jerry.

INSTITUTIONALIZATION, JUVENILE

Negro And White Male Institutionalized Delinquents. Axelrad, Sidney.

Negro Delinquents In Public Training. Buker, Gordon H and Adams, William T.

Seeman's 'Alienation And Social Learning In A Reformatory': Two Reactions. Coleman, James S et al.

Negro Boys In The Youth Development Centers Of Georgia. Smith, W C.

Suicide, And White Reformatory Girl's Preference For Negro Men. Hammer, M.

The Incarcerated Mexican–American Delinquent. Rudoff, Alvin.

A Comparison Of Mexican–American And Caucasian Male Juvenile Detainees. Hunter, Michael Nathan.

DAPs Of Black And Whites Juvenile Incarcerates. Baugh, B Duncan and Prytula, Robert E.

Violent Crime Indices Among Community–Retained Delinquents. Andrew, J M.

The Analysis Of Self–Concept And Self Actualization Manifestations By Incarcerated And Free Black Youth. Davis, Charles.

Who Gets Detained: An Empirical Analysis Of The Pre–Adjudicatory Detention Of Juveniles In Denver. Cohen, Lawrence E.

Runaways At The Training Institution In Central Ohio. Bartollas, C.

Norm Neutralization, Anomia And Self–Concept Among Institutionalized Female Delinquents. Lilly, J R and Ball, R A.

Investigating Ethnic Prejudice Among Boys In Residential Treatment. Schaeffer, C and Brown, S.

Poor Minority Juveniles Said More Likely To Be Locked Up. Anonymous.

Trends In State Correction; Juveniles And The Violent Young Offender. Vinter, Robert D.

INSULT

The Fire This Time: Effects Of Race Of Target, Insult, And Potential Retaliation On Black Aggression. Wilson, L and Rogers, R W.

INSURANCE

Recent Increase In Homicide. Metropolitan Life Insurance Company.

INTELLIGENCE

American White Criminal Intelligence. Murchison, Carl.

American White Criminal Intelligence. Murchison, Carl.

Types Of Crime And Intelligence Of Negro Criminals. Burfield, H.

Intelligence, Race, And Age As Selective Factors In Crime. Fox, Vernon.

Verbal Performance IQ Differences Of White And Negro Delinquents On The WISC And WAIS. Henning, John J and Levy, Russell H.

How Much Can We Boost IQ And Scholastic Achievement? Jensen, Arthur R.

The Mind Of The Negro, Orig Pub 1961. Thorpe, Earl E.

Race, Culture And Intelligence. Richardson, Ken (ed) and Spears, David (ed).

KANSAS

Long v Harris, 332 F Supp 262, (Kansas), US District Court D Kansas: October 6, 1971. Anonymous.

Native Americans And Discrimination In Kansas: Trials From Injustice. Bean, Jerry L.

Development Of A Comprehensive Personnel Plan For Non–Judicial Employees Of The Kansas Appellate Courts. Lawson, H O and Kuban, G B.

KANSAS CITY, MO

A New Concept In Police Recruiting. Perry, Jack.

KENTUCKY

The Legal Status Of The Negro. Magnum, Charles S.

Narrative Of The Sufferings Of Lewis And Milton Clarke: More Than Twenty Years Among The Slaveholders Of Kentucky. Clarke, Lewis and Clarke, Milton.

Legacy Of Violence: The Opera House Lynching. Elliot, Jeffrey M.

Jefferson's Nephews: A Frontier Tragedy. Merrill Jr, Boynton.

KING JR, REV MARTIN LUTHER

Stride Toward Freedom. King Jr, Martin Luther.

Letter From Birmingham City Jail. King Jr, Martin Luther.

Why We Can't Wait. King Jr, Martin Luther.

He Slew The Dreamer: My Search, With James Earl Ray, For The Truth About The Murder Of Martin Luther King. Huie, William Bradford.

An American Death: The True Story Of The Assassination Of Dr Martin Luther King, Jr, And The Greatest Manhunt Of Our Time. Frank, Gerold.

KU KLUX KLAN

The Challenge Of The Klan. Frost, Stanley.

The Klu Klux Klan. Mecklin, John M.

Bloody Williamson. Angle, Paul M.

White Terror: The Ku Klux Klan Conspiracy In Southern Reconstruction. Trelease, Alan.

The Klan. Sims, Patsy.

The True Story Of The Greensboro Massacre. Bermanzohn, Paul C and Bermanzohn, Sally A.

Did The FBI Kill Viola Liuzzo? Greene, Johnny.

The Violent Rebirth Of The Klan. King, Wayne.

LABELING

Race Labeling And The Press. Rudwick, Elliot M.

Race And The News Media. Fisher, Paul L (ed) and Lowenstein, Ralph L (ed).

Human Deviance, Social Problems, And Social Control. Lemert, Edwin M.

Hidden Deviance And The Labelling Approach: The Case For Drinking And Driving. Marshall, Harvey and Purdy, Ross.

Inequality In The Imposition Of A Criminal Label. Chiricos, Theodore G and Jackson, Phillip D and Waldo, Gordon P.

The 'Wetback' As Deviant: An Application Of Labeling Theory. Bustamante, Jorge A.

Police Race Attitudes And Labeling. Rafky, David M.

Status, Images, And Consequence: Once A Criminal Always A Criminal. Reed, John P and Reed, Robin S.

"The Labeling Approach To Deviance" in *Issues In The Classification Of Children*, Hobbs, Nicholas (ed), 88–100. Duster, Troy et al.

Imprisonment And The Expected Value Of Criminal Choice: A Specification And Test Of Aspects Of The Labeling Perspective. Harris, Anthony R.

Judicial Decision–Making In The Juvenile Court: An Empirical Test Of A Labelling/Conflict Proposition. Marshall, Ineke M.

LAFAYETTE, LA

Four Cities In Louisiana Defy US On Hiring More Blacks And Women. Anonymous.

LANDLORDS

The Poor Pay More. Caplovitz, David.

The Landlord–Tenant Relation In Low Income Areas. Vaugh, Ted.

Absentee Ownership And Management In The Black Ghetto: Social And Economic Consequences. Reiss Jr, Albert J and Aldrich, Howard.

The Integration Of Blacks In Suburban Neighborhoods: A Reexamination Of The Contact Hypothesis. Zeal, Carolyn and Humphrey, Craig.

LANGUAGE

Public Information Materials For Language Minorities. National Criminal Justice Reference Service.

Language As Obstacle And As Data In Sociological Research. Grimshaw, Allen.

Black English: Its History And Usage In The United States. Dillard, J L.

"Eliminating The Language Barrier" in *Police–Community Relationships*, Bopp, W (ed), 442–444. Ross, Donald J and Cobarruviaz, Louis.

Through The Veil Of Partial Comprehension: NY City's Hispanic Defendant And The Criminal Justice System. New York City Board Of Correction.

Handling The Needs Of Non–English–Speaking Persons. Blake, Frank.

California: Report To The Judicial Council On The Language Needs Of Non–English–Speaking Persons, Interim Phase 2 Report. U S Dept Of Justice, LEAA.

Tests Of The Language–Aggression Hypothesis. Boone, S L and Moutare, A.

No Comprendo: The Non–English–Speaking Defendant And The Criminal Process. Safford, Joan Bainbridge.

The Importance Of Spanish Language Training For Law Enforcement Officers. Tatum, William M.

Trying Non–English Conversant Defendants: The Use Of An Interpreter. Bergenfield, G.

"Bilingual Education And The Hispanic Challenge" in *1979 Annual Report Of The Carnegie Corporation Of New York.* Pifer, Alan.

LANSING, MI

Importance Of Police Contact In The Formulation Of Youths' Attitudes Toward Police. Rusinko, W T and Johnson, K W and Hornung, C A.

LATIN CULTURE see Hispanic Culture

LATINOS, LATINS see Hispanic

LAW, RESPECT FOR THE

Survey Of Negro Attitudes Toward Law. Zeitz, Leonard.

Poverty, Minorities, And Respect For Law. Wright, J Skelly.

Law, The American Value System, And The Black Community. Zangrando, Robert L and Schneider, Joanna.

LAW ENFORCEMENT see Police

LAW ENFORCEMENT ASSISTANCE ADMINISTRATION see Leaa

LAW LIBRARIES

Minorities Employed In Law Libraries. Brecht, A and Mills, R.

LAWMAKING

The Fugitive Slave Bill: Its History And Unconstitutionality. American Anti–Slavery Society.

Equality By Statute: The Revolution In Civil Rights. Berger, Monroe.

Virginia's Legislative Response To Riots And Their Underlying Causes. Wasson, Houston.

Legislative Inadequacies And Needs In The Prevention And Control Of Civil Disorders. Breckenridge, J B.

Society And The Legal Order. Schwartz, Richard D and Skolnick, Jerome M.

The Legislation Of Morality. Duster, Troy.

The Social Reality Of Crime. Quinney, Richard.

Law, Order And Power. Chambliss, William J and Seidman, Robert B.

How The Government Breaks The Law. Lieberman, Jethro K.

Comments On Anti–Crime Legislation: A Political And Sociological Analysis. Reid, Herbert O.

Racial And Ethnic Classifications: An Appraisal Of The Role Of Anthropology In The Lawmaking Process. Lundsgaarde, Henry P.

Racial, Economic And Political Factors In The Development Of America's First Drug Laws. Mark, Greg Yee.

The Discriminatory Application Of Penal Laws By State Judicial And Quasi–Judicial Officers. Weissman, Andrew B.

Alcohol Legalization And Native Americans: A Sociological Inquiry. May, Phillip A.

"Philosophical/Research Implications Of Definitions Of Crime" in *Crime And Its Impact On The Black Community*, Gary, L & Brown (eds), 51–55. Goodman, James A.

"Crime As A Concern Of Congress" in *Black Crime: A Police View*, Bryce, H J (ed), 21–28. Conyers, John R.

LAWYERS see Attorneys

LAYOFFS

City Layoffs—The Effect On Minorities And Women. New York City Commission On Human Rights.

LE FLORE, RON

Today: Ron LeFlore Only Steals Bases. Mitchell, Greg.

LEAA

Minority Recruitment In Corrections—New Federal Aid Requirements. American Bar Association.

LEAA

Report Of The LEAA Task Force On Women. U S Dept Of Justice, LEAA.

Civil Rights And Corrections—The Impact Of LEAA Compliance Requirements. Rice, H C.

A Review Of The Law Enforcement Assistance Administration's Relationship To The Black Community. National Urban League, Inc.

California: Report To The Judicial Council On The Language Needs Of Non–English–Speaking Persons, Interim Phase 2 Report. U S Dept Of Justice, LEAA.

Critical Equal Employment Issues In Criminal Justice. Jones, Clinton B.

LEAA's Research Solicitation: Police Use Of Deadly Force. Takagi, Paul.

The Law Enforcement Assistance Administration And Minority Communities. Salas, Luis P and Lewis, Ralph G.

The Inequality Of Justice: A Report On Crime And The Administration Of Justice In The Minority Coummunity. National Minority Advisory Council On Crim Just.

LEADERSHIP

Leadership By Women In Criminal Justice—There Is Room At The Top. Strosnider, C S.

LEGAL AID

Minority Lawyer: Link To The Ghetto. Clark, L D.

Indian Counsellor Project—Help For The Accused. Bennett, M C.

Black Lawyers Responsibility To Poor Communities. Banks, Sharon P.

Counsel For The Poor: Criminal Defense In Urban America. Hermann, Robert and Single, Eric and Boston, John.

LEGAL DEFENSE STRATEGY

A Comparison Of Defense Strategy And Race As Influences In Differential Sentencing. Kelly, Henry E.

LEGAL EDUCATION

Law Schools And The Negro. Gellhorn, E.

A Black Lawyers Study. Shuman, Jerome.

Teaching Corrections Law To Corrections Personnel. Statsky, William P.

Minority Opportunities In Law For Blacks, Puerto Ricans And Chicanos. Clark, C P (ed).

Step Toward Equal Justice—Programs To Increase Black Lawyers In The South, 1969–1973. Spearman, R W and Stevens, H.

Combatting Racism In American Law Schools. Ginger, Ann Fagan.

Preferential Law School Admissions And The Equal Protection Clause: An Analysis Of The Competing Arguments. Redish, M H.

Black And Minority Law Students: Stratum For Social Change. Bromall, Irvin.

Black Law Professors And The Integrity Of American Legal Education. Richardson, H J.

History And Role Of Black Law Schools. Washington, H R.

Legal Education Of Chicano Students: A Study In Mutual Accomodation And Cultural Conflict. Delgado, R and Romero, L M.

Careers In Law For Minorities: A Puerto Rican's Perspective On Recent Developments In Legal Education. Cabranes, C A.

Minority Candidate And The Bar Examination: A Symposium. Anonymous.

Minorities Employed In Law Libraries. Brecht, A and Mills, R.

LEGAL REPRESENTATION

Gideon's Trumpet. Lewis, Anthony.

A Criminal Justice System And The Indigent. Oaks, Dallin H and Lehman, Warren.

American Criminal Justice: The Defendant's Perspective. Casper, Jonathan D.

Counsel For The Poor: Criminal Defense In Urban America. Hermann, Robert and Single, Eric and Boston, John.

Criminal Justice Processing: The Determinants Of The Decision To Go To Trial. Sterling, Joyce S.

Justice And Reform: The Formative Years Of The American Legal Service Program. Johnson Jr, Earl.

Inadequate Defense Counsel—An Empirical Analysis Of Prisoners' Perceptions. Alpert, Geoffrey P.

Team Defense: The Holistic Approach: An Interview With Millard Farmer. Eisenberg, Howard.

LEGAL THEORY AND PRACTICE

Criminal Law In Colonial Virginia. Scott, Arthur P.

Law, Procedure And Punishment In Early Bureaucracies. Mac Leod, W C.

Let Me Live. Herndon, Angelo.

Navajo Common Law II: Navajo Law And Justice. Van Valkenburgh, R.

The Cheyenne Way: Conflict And Case Law In Primitive Jurisprudence. Llewellyn, K and Hoebel, E Adamson.

Slave Law And The Social Structure. Moore, Wilbert E.

Race Discrimination And The Law. Mc Williams, Carey.

The Origin Of The State. Lowie, R H.

The Law Of The Poor. Tenbroek, Jacobus (ed).

Anti–Miscegenation Laws And The Fourteenth Amendment: The Original Intent. Avins, A.

Negro And Indian: A Comparison Of Their Constitutional Rights. Kane, A.

Equality By Statute: The Revolution In Civil Rights. Berger, Monroe.

The Limits Of The Criminal Sanction. Packer, Herbert.

Crime And The Legal Process. Chambliss, William J.

Crime And Justice In Society. Quinney, Richard.

Criminality And Legal Order. Turk, Austin.

Race Distinctions In American Law, Org Pub 1910. Stephenson, Gilbert T.

Sociology Of Law. Aubert, V.

Cultural Bias In The American Legal System. Swett, Daniel.

Equality Under The Law. Hindelang, Michael J.

Red, White And Gray: Equal Protection And The American Indian. Mc Meekin, Daniel.

Society And The Legal Order. Schwartz, Richard D and Skolnick, Jerome M.

With Justice For Some: An Indictment Of The Law By Young Advocates. Wasserstein, Bruce (ed) and Green, Mark J (ed).

Can A Black Man Get A Fair Trial In This Country? Burns, Haywood.

"Legal Status Of The Slave In South Carolina, 1670–1740" in *Colonial American Essays In Political/Social Development*, Katz (ed), 404–415. Senese, Donald.

"Racism And American Law" in *Law Against The People*, Lefcourt, Robert (ed), 38–54. Burns, Haywood.

Law Against The People. Lefcourt, Robert (ed).

Law. Order And Power. Chambliss, William J and Seidman, Robert B

The Problem And Promise Of Black Men Of Law. Mc Gee Sr, Henry W.

"Racism In The Law" in *Race, Crime, And Justice*, Reasons, Charles E And Jack L Kuykendall (eds), 13–27. Crockett Jr, George W.

Black Faith In A Racist Land: Summary Review Of Racism In American Law. Bell Jr, Derrick A.

The New Racism: An Analysis Of The Use Of Racial And Ethnic Criteria In Decision–Making. Alexander, Elaine T and Alexander, Lawrence A.

The Prison As A Lawless Agency. Greenberg, David F and Stender, Fay.

United States Law On American Indians. Kleiner, J.

How The Government Breaks The Law. Lieberman, Jethro K.

Race, Racism And American Law. Bell Jr, Derrick A.

Black People And Tyranny Of American Law. Burns, Haywood.

Does Justice Have A Color: Law: Is It A Skin Game. Moore Jr, Howard.

Political Uses Of The Law. Burns, Haywood.

Racism And The Early American Legal Process, 1619–1896. Higginbotham Jr, A Leon.

Racism As Justice. Moore Jr, Howard.

Racism In American Courts: Cause For Black Disruption Or Despair? Bell Jr, Derrick A.

The Law Of Primitive Man. Hoebel, E Adamson.

Criminal Procedure In Slave Trials In The Antebellum South. Flanigan, Daniel J.

Fire And The Spirits—Cherokee Law From Clan To Court. Strickland, R.

Law And Control In Society. Akers, Ronald L and Hawkins, R.

American Indians And The Law. Rosen, Lawrence.

Whose Law: What Order? Chambliss, William J.

"The Subordination Of Coercive Law To Coercive Markets" in *Social Meaning Of Drugs*, Blum, K; S Feinglass And A Briggs (eds). Duster, Troy.

Criminology—Power, Crime And Criminal Law. Galliher, John F and Mc Cartney, James.

Public Law And Public Policy. Gardiner, John A (ed).

Judicial Protection Of Minorities. Sandalow, Terrance.

In The Matter Of Color. Higginbotham Jr, A Leon.

Commentary On The Philosophy Of Equality. Nagel, Thomas.

Equality, The Elusive Value. Dixon Jr, Robert G.

Symposium: The Quest For Equality. Anonymous.

The Philosophy Of Equality. Freund, Paul A.

The Quest For Equality. Handlin, Oscar.

The American Ideal Of Equality And Constitutional Change. Redenius, Charles M.

LIABILITY, CIVIL

City Liable Under Human Rights Act For Policeman's Racial Abuses. Anonymous.

LIBERATION

Liberation And Crime: The Invention Of The New Female Criminal. Weis, Joseph G.

LINEUPS

Do 'They All Look Alike' The Effects Of Race, Sex, Experience, And Attitudes On The Ability To Recognize Faces. Brigham, J C and Barkowitz, P.

LITERACY

English Literacy: Legal Sanction For Discrimination. Leibowitz, Arnold H.

LITIGATION

The Petitioners, The Story Of The Supreme Court Of The US And The Negro. Miller, Loren.

Cruel And Unusual: The Supreme Court And Capital Punishment. Meltsner, Michael.

Litigating Against The Death Penalty: The Strategy Behind *Furman.* Meltsner, Michael.

Background Paper On The Supreme Court's Death Penalty Decisions. American Civil Liberties Union.

The Uses Of Social Science In Trials With Political And Racial Overtones: The Trial Of Joan Little. Mc Conahay, John B and Mullin, Courtney J and Frederick, Jeffrey.

Suing The Police In Federal Court. Note.

Social Science Evidence In The Courts: Reaching Beyond The Adversary Process. Sperlich, Peter W.

LITTLE, JOANNE

Self–Defense Against Rape: The Joanne Little Case. Bond, Julian.

The Uses Of Social Science In Trials With Political And Racial Overtones: The Trial Of Joan Little. Mc Conahay, John B and Mullin, Courtney J and Frederick, Jeffrey.

The Innocence Of Joan Little. Reston Jr, James.

LIUZZO, VIOLA

Did The FBI Kill Viola Liuzzo? Greene, Johnny.

LIVINGSTON, KY

Jefferson's Nephews: A Frontier Tragedy. Merrill Jr, Boynton.

LOITERING

Street Corner Society. Whyte, William Foote.

Tally's Corner: A Study Of The Negro Streetcorner Men. Liebow, Elliot.

LOMBROSO, CESARE

Criminal Man According To The Classifications Of Cesare Lombroso. Ferrers, Gina Lombroso.

LOOTING

Patterns Of Looting And Property Norms: Conflict And Consensus In Community Emergencies. Dynes, R and Quarantelli, E.

The Detroit Riot: A Profile Of 500 Prisoners. U S Dept Of Labor, Manpower Administration.

Looting In Civil Disorders: An Index Of Social Change. Dynes, R and Quarantelli, E.

Shall We Shoot Looters? Clark, Ramsey.

"What Looting In Civil Disturbances Really Means" in *Law And Order: Modern Criminals,* Short Jr, James F (ed), 177–192. Dynes, R and Quarantelli, E.

The Blackout, in *1977 Annual Report Of The New York City Board Of Correction,* 17–24. New York City Board Of Correction.

A Report On The Blackout Looting: New York City, July 13, 1977. Curvin, Robert and Porter, Bruce.

LOS ANGELES

The Los Angeles Pinto: Background Papers And Advance Report Of The Chicano Pinto Project. Chicano Pinto Research Project, Inc.

The Zoot–Suit Riots. Mc Williams, Carey.

Crime And Punishment Among Minority Groups In Los Angeles County. Lemert, Edwin M and Rosberg, Judy.

The Adminstration Of Justice To Minority Groups In Los Angeles County. Lemert, Edwin M and Rosberg, Judy.

The Watts 'Manifesto' And The McCone Report. Rustin, Bayard.

Whitewash Over Watts. Blauner, Robert.

Los Angeles Riot Study, The Perception Of Police Brutality In South Central Los Angeles. Institute Of Government And Public Affairs.

The Development Of A Real Ideology Among Urban Negroes. Tomlinson, T M.

Black Attitudes Toward The Political System In The Aftermath Of The Watts Insurrection. Sears, David.

Interracial Social Contact And Middle Class White Reaction To The Watts Riot. Jeffries, Vincent and Ransford, H E.

Participation In The Los Angeles Riot. Sears, David and Mc Conahay, John.

Ideological Foundations For Negro Action: A Comparative Analysis Of Militant Views Of The Los Angeles Riots. Tomlinson, T M.

Racial Socialization, Comparison Levels, And The Watts Riot. Sears, David and Mc Conahay, John.

The Public Perception Of The Watts Riot As Social Protest. Jefferies, Vincent and Turner, R H and Morris, R T.

A Study Of Mexican–American Perceptions Of Law Enforcement Policies And Practices In East Los Angeles. Morales, Armando.

"The Watts–Los Angeles Riot" in *Rebellion And Retreat,* Palmer, S (ed), 248–272. Oberschall, Anthony.

Benefits From A Police Community Relations Program: What Can I Do, How Can I Help? Morton, Ted.

Black Ghetto Residents As Rioters. Moinat, Sheryl M et al.

The Dialectics Of Legal Repression: Black Rebels Before The American Criminal Courts. Balbus, Isaac D.

The Glass House Tapes: The Story Of An Agent–Provocateur And The New Police–Intelligence Complex. Tackwood, Louis E and Citizens Research And Investigation Committee.

"Police Deployment Theories And The Mexican–American Community" in *The Urban Policeman In Transition,* Snibbe, J (ed), 341–353. Morales, Armando.

The Black Community: Attitudes Toward Community Problems, Crime And The Police. Knowles, Lyle and Brewer, Jesse.

Community Organizing Of Gang Barrios. Pineda, Charles.

Los Angeles' Minority Policemen Express Their Concerns. Williford, Stanley O.

The Black Offender As Victim. Debro, Julius.

Criminal Victimization Surveys In The Nation's Five Largest Cities. U S Dept Of Justice, LEAA, NCJISS.

Personality Patterns Of White, Black, And Mexican American Patrolmen As Measured By The Sixteen Personality Factor Questionaire. Snibbe, H M and Fabricatore, Joseph and Azen, Stanley P.

Violence By Youth Gangs And Youth Groups In Major American Cities—Final Report. Miller, Walter B.

"Crimes Against The Elderly—Findings From Interviews With Blacks, Mex–Amer, And Whites" in *Justice And Older Americans,* Young, M (ed). Ragan, P K.

US Charges Los Angeles With Police Hiring Bias. Anonymous.

Homeboys: Gangs, Drugs, And Prison In The Barrios Of Los Angeles. Moore, Joan et al.

A Year With The Gangs Of East Los Angeles. Murphy, Suzanne.

Chicano Gangs In The East LA (Los Angeles, CA) Barrio. Torres, D M.

Estrangement, Machismo And Gang Violence. Erlanger, Howard S.

Joan W Moore, Et Al: Homeboys: Gangs, Drugs, And Prisons In The Barrios Of Los Angeles. Trujillo, Larry D.

East LA's Gang Project: Prevention Or Bribery? Bernstein, Dan.

LOUISIANA

see also Angola Prison, La; Clinton, La; Crowley, La; Danville, La; Lafayette, La; Westwego, La

Narrative Of The Barbarous Treatment Of Two Unfortunate Females, Natives Of Concordia LA By Joseph & Enoch, Runaway Slaves. Joseph and Enoch.

Trends In The Use Of Capital Punishment. Hartung, Frank E.

Effects Of Unemployment On White And Negro Prison Admissions In Louisiana. Dobbins, D A and Bass, Bernard M.

Report Of The Pennsylvania Joint Legislative Committee On Capital Punishment. Joint Legis Comm On Capital Punishment.

Differential Study Of Recidivism Among Negro And White Boys. Henton, Comradge L and Washington, Charles.

Southern Justice. Friedman, Leon (ed).

Die Nigger Die. Brown, H Rap.

Politics And Punishment: The History Of The Louisiana State Penal System. Carleton, Mark T.

LOUISIANA

A Structural Level Examination Of Forensic Hospitalization: Forensic Commitment Rates And Social Structural Features At Louisana Parishes. Bankston, William B.

Blacks And Women To Be Hired For Louisiana Police–Fire Jobs. Marro, Anthony.

Four Cities In Louisiana Defy US On Hiring More Blacks And Women. Anonymous.

Prison Plantation: The Story Of Angola. Vodicka, John.

LUMPENPROLETARIAT

Political And Lumpen Prisoners, The Question Of Compliance, And Socioliterary Investigation. Stratman, David V.

LYNCHING

see also Death Penalty

Does Lynching Thrive Under Democracy? Tyler, Ralph W.

Lynching, America's National Disgrace. Johnson, James Weldon.

Lynching And Political Areas. Young, Erle.

Lynchings And What They Mean. Southern Commision On The Study Of Lynching.

Lynching And The Law. Chadbourn, J H.

The Tragedy Of Lynching. Raper, Arthur.

A Sociological Study Of A Texas Lynching. Pruden, Durwood.

Judge Lynch, His First Hundred Years. Shay, Frank.

Ladies And Lynching. Nordyke, Lewis T.

"Chapter 4: The Lynching Mob" in *The Psychology Of Social Movements.* Cantril, Hadley.

The Changing Character Of Lynching. Ames, Jessie Daniel.

"Division X: Race Riots In The US, 1942–1946, Division XIII: Lynching" *Negro Year Book, 1947.* Guzman, Jessie Parkhurst (ed).

On Lynching. Barnett, Ida B Wells.

Legacy Of Violence: The Opera House Lynching. Elliot, Jeffrey M.

Revolt Against Chivalry: Jessie Daniel Ames And The Women's Campaign Against Lynching. Hall, Jacqueline Dowd.

M M P I

Inmate Personality Differences Related To Recidivism, Age And Race As Measured By The MMPI. Panton, J H.

The Validity Of The MMPI As A Discriminator Of Social Deviance Among Black Males. Elion, Victor H.

Validity Of The MMPI Pd Scale Among Black Males. Elion, Victor H and Megargee, Edwin I.

MMPI Differences Among Black Mexican–American And White Male Offenders. Mc Creary, C and Padilla, E.

MACHISMO

Social Character In A Mexican Village: A Sociopsychoanalytic Study. Fromm, Erich and Maccoby, Michael.

Estrangement, Machismo And Gang Violence. Erlanger, Howard S.

MAFIA

see also Crime, Organized

Mafia: The Prototypical Alien Conspiracy. Smith, Dwight C.

MAFIA, BLACK

Black Mafia: Ethnic Succession In Organized Crime. Ianni, Francis A J.

New Mafia: Black, Hispanic And Italian Styles. Ianni, Francis A J.

The Truth About The Black Mafia. Stewart, Ted.

MAFIA, MEXICAN *see* Mexican Mafia

MAGEE, RUCHELL

Ruchell Magee: Slave Rebel. Ruchell Magee Committee For Black Prisoners.

MAJOR CRIMES ACT

Constitutional Law—Unequal Protection For The American Indian Under The Major Crimes Act: United States Versus Antelope. Note.

Indian Rights And The Constitutional Implications Of The Major Crimes Act. Martin, S L.

MALCOLM X *see* X, Malcolm

MALES

A Case Of A 'Psychotic' Navaho Indian Male. Jewell, Donald P.

Negro And White Male Institutionalized Delinquents. Axelrad, Sidney.

A Comparison Of The Scores Of White And Negro Male Juvenile Delinquients On Three Projective Tests. Megargee, Edwin I.

Differences In Smoking, Drinking, And Social Behavior By Race And Delinquency Status In Adolescent Males. Schonfield, J.

The Performance Of Male Prisoners On The Marlowe–Crowne Social Desirability Scale: II, Differences As A Function Of Race And Crime. Fisher, Gary.

Aggressive Behavior Of Delinquent, Dependent, And 'Normal' White And Black Boys In Social Conflicts. Berger, Stephen E and Tedeschi, James T.

Alcohol Abuse: A Crucial Factor In The Social Problems Of Negro Men. King, Lucy J et al.

Father Absence And Antisocial Behavior In Negro And White Males. Mosher, L R.

Personality Factors In Delinquent Boys: Differences Between Blacks And Whites. Cross, Herbert J and Tracy, James J.

The Black Male Personality. Vontress, Clemmont E.

Delinquent Acting–Out And Task Of Sexual Identification In Black Male Adolescents—Replication Study. Mc Nabb, D P.

Resentment And Suspicion Among American Men. Blumenthal, M D.

Occupational Choice And Perception Of Attainment Blockage—Study Of Lower Class Delinquent And Nondelinquent Black Males. Picou, J S et al.

Race, Sex And Violence: A Laboratory Test Of The Sexual Threat Of The Black Male Hypothesis. Schulman, G I.

Self–Concept In Negro And White Pre–Adolescent Delinquent Boys. Wax, Douglas E.

The Validity Of The MMPI As A Discriminator Of Social Deviance Among Black Males. Elion, Victor H.

Pretreatment Criminality Of Male And Female Drug Abuse Patients In The United States. Ball, John C et al.

Validity Of The MMPI Pd Scale Among Black Males. Elion, Victor H and Megargee, Edwin I.

MMPI Differences Among Black Mexican–American And White Male Offenders. Mc Creary, C and Padilla, E.

A Comparative Analysis Of Male And Female Delinquency. Cernkovich, Stephen A and Giordano, Peggy C.

MALTHUS

The Legacy Of Malthus: The Social Costs Of The New Racism. Chase, Allan.

MANDATORY SENTENCES

see also Sentencing

The Effect Of Mandatory And Discretionary Death Sentences On Commutations And Executions In Pennsylvania. Riedel, Marc.

Discrimination In The Imposition Of Death Penalty: A Comparison Of The Characteristics Of Offenders Sentenced Pre–Furman And Post–Furman. Riede; Marc.

Felony Murder Rape, And The Mandatory Death Penalty. Bedau, Hugo Adam.

Mandatory Prison Sentences: Their Projected Effects On Crime And Prison Populations. Petersilia, Joan and Greenwood, Peter W.

Mandatory Prison Sentences: Their Projected Effects On Crime And Prison Populations. Petersilia, Joan and Greenwood, Peter W.

Preliminary Tabulations Reflecting Arbitrariness And Discrimination Under Post–'Furman' Capital Statutes. Bowers, William J and Pierce, Glenn L.

Arbitrariness And Discrimination Under Post–'Furman' Capital Statutes. Bowers, William J and Pierce, Glenn L.

MARIJUANA *see* Drugs

MARXISM

Introduction To Black Sociology. Staples, Robert.

Class, State And Crime. Quinney, Richard.

MARYLAND

see also Baltimore, Md

Equal Protection Of The Law And Fair Trials In Maryland. Mc Guinn, Henry J.

Report Of The Committee On Capital Punishment. Maryland Legislative Council.

The Administration Of Rape Cases In The City Of Baltimore And The State Of Maryland. Howard, Joseph C.

The Negro In Maryland, Orig Pub 1889. Brackett, Jeffrey R.

The Image Of The Negro In The Maryland Gazette, 1745–1774. Wax, Darold D.

The Origins Of Afro–American Society In Tidewater Maryland And Virginia, 1700 To 1790. Kulikoff, Allan.

MASCULINITY

see also Machismo

Violence And The Masculine Ideal. Toby, Jackson.'

MASCULINITY

The Black Male Personality. Vontress, Clemmont E.

The Effect Of Father Absence On Delinquent Males: Dependency And Hypermasculinity. Moran, Patricia Anne.

Compulsive Masculinity And Delinquency: An Empirical Investigation. Silverman, I J and Dinitz, Simon.

MASSACHUSETTS

see also Boston, Ma, Springield, Ma, Walpole Prison, Ma

In Constant Fear: The Brutal Story Of Life Within The Walls Of The Notorious Walpole State Prison, As Told To James B Shuman. Remick, Peter.

Discretionary Justice In Early Massachusetts. Lee, Carol F.

"Manpower Development—The Standards And Goals Process In Massachusetts" in *Criminal Justice Planning,* Scott, J E And S Dinitz (eds). Saltonstall, T L.

Prison And Plantation: Crime, Justice, And Authority In Massachusetts And South Carolina, 1767–1878. Hindus, Michael Stephen.

MATURITY

Psychological And Ethnic Correlates Of Interpersonal Maturity Among Delinquents. Werner, Eric.

MC KAY, HENRY

"Settling The Frontiers Of A Pioneer In American Criminology: Henry McKay"" in *Delinquency, Crime And Society,* Short Jr, James F (ed). Reiss Jr, Albert J.

MEDIA

Race Labeling And The Press. Rudwick, Elliot M.

The Press And The Oppressed. Jaffe, Carolyn.

Race And The News Media. Fisher, Paul L (ed) and Lowenstein, Ralph L (ed).

Tho Imago Of Tho Nogro In The Maryland Gazette, 1745–1774. Wax, Darold D.

The Mass Media And Racial Conflict. Hartman, Paul and Husband, Charles.

Mass Media And Racial Crisis: A Study Of The New Bethel Church Incident In Detroit. Warren, D I.

South Carolina Fugitives As Viewed Through Local Newspapers With Emphasis On Runaway Notices 1732–1800. Meaders, Daniel.

"Media, Crime And The Black Reality" in *Crime And Its Impact On The Black Community,* Gary, L E And L P Brown (eds), 97–108. Goodlett, Carlton B.

MEMPHIS, TN

Rescued From Evil: Origins Of The Juvenile Justice System In Memphis, Tennessee, 1900–1917. Shelden, Randall G.

MENLO PARK, CA

Changing Attitudes Of Black Youths. Cizanckas, Victor I and Purviance, Carlton W.

MENTAL HEALTH

The Psychology Of Murder. Palmer, S.

Drinking Patterns And Alcoholism Among American Negroes. Sterne, M.

Children Of The Detroit Riots: A Study Of Their Participation And Their Mental Health. Komisaruk, R and Pearson, Carol.

"Mental Illness And Criminal Intent" in *Changing Perspectives In Mental Illness,* Plog, S And R Edgerton (eds). Duster, Troy.

Black Rage. Grier, William H and Cobbs, Price M.

The Epidemiology Of Opiate Addiction In The United States. Ball, J C (ed) and Chambers, C D (ed).

The Mind Of The Negro, Orig Pub 1961. Thorpe, Earl E.

Black Psychology. Jones, Reginald L (ed).

"Race, Deprivation, And Drug Abuse In The USA" in *Proceedings Of The Anglo–American Conference On Drug Abuses,* 69–76. Holden Jr, Matthew.

Racism And Mental Health. Willie, Charles V et al (eds).

An Examination Of Institutional Racism: Black People In California's Criminal Justice And Mental Health Systems. Ogleton, Betty and Crittendon, Stephanie and Seda, Cozetta.

Men In Crisis: Human Breakdowns In Prison. Toch, Hans et al.

Special Report On Inequities In Mental Health Service Delivery. Fiman, Byron G.

Being Black Is Detrimental To One's Mental Health: Myth Or Reality? Cannon, Mildred S and Locke, Ben Z.

El Tecato: Cultural And Sociologic Factors Affecting Drug Use Among Chicanos. Casvantes, Edward J.

Division Of Special Mental Health Programs: Program Statement 1978–1979. National Institute Of Mental Health.

Mental Health: A Challenge To The Black Community. Gary, Lawrence E.

Institutional Racism In Mental Health And Criminal Justice. Morales, Armando.

Mental Health And Black Offenders. Owens, Charles E.

MERTON, ROBERT

Delinquency And Opportunity: A Theory Of Delinquent Gangs. Cloward, Richard A and Ohlin, Lloyd E.

MERTON, ROBERT K

Socioeconomic Status, Race, Level Of Aspiration And Juvenile Delinquency: A Limited Empirical Test Of Merton's Concept Of Deviation. Epps, Edgar G.

METHADONE

The Chicano Addict: An Analysis Of Factors Influencing Rehabilitation In A Treatment Program. Auman, Jon et al.

The Needle And The Boot: Heroin Maintenance. Cuskey, Walter R and Krasner, William.

Methadone: The Forlorn Hope. Epstein, Edward Jay.

Manny—A Criminal–Addict's Story. Retting, R P and Torres, M J and Garrett, G R.

National Directory Of Drug Abuse And Alcoholism Treatment Programs. National Institute On Alcohol Abuse And Alcoholism.

METHODOLOGY

"Interpretation Of Statistical Relations As A Research Operation" in *The Language Of Social Research,* Lazarsfeld And Rosenberg (eds). Lazarsfeld, Paul F.

Concepts And Methodology In The Field Of Juvenile Delinquency. Blue Jr, John T.

Delinquency Research: An Appraisal Of Analytic Methods. Hirschi, Travis and Selvin, Hanan C.

Say It With Figures. Zeisel, Hans.

"Test Factor Standardization As A Method Of Interpretation" in *Stages Of Social Research,* Forcese, Dennis P And Stephen Richer (eds). Rosenberg, Morris.

"Indian Drinking: Problems Of Data Collection And Interpretation" in *Proceedings Of The 1st Annual Alcohol Conf, NIAAA,* 217–236. Levy, Jerrold E and Kunitz, Stephen J.

"Prevalence: The Rare Datum In Delinquency Measurement" in *The Juvenile Justice System,* Klein, Malcolm (ed), 201–284. Gordon, Robert A.

Race, Achievement, And Delinquency—A Further Look At Delinquency In A Birth Cohort. Jensen, Gary F.

Determining Ethnic Origin In An Interview Survey: Problems And Recommendations. U S Dept Of H E W.

The Sojourner In The American Indian Community: Methodological Issues And Concerns. Trimble, Joseph E.

Race As A Determinant Of Criminal Sentences: A Methodological Critique And A Case Study. Gibson, James L.

MEXICAN-AMERICANS *see* Hispanic

MEXICAN MAFIA

America's Newest Crime Syndicate: The Mexican Mafia. Adams, Nathan M.

Inside The Mexican Mafia. Hammarley, John.

MEXICO

More Bars Against Mexicans. Taylor, Paul.

The Mexican In The United States. Bogardus, Emory S.

Mexico's Tres Marias Penal Colony. Jewell, Donald P.

A Demographic Profile Of The Mexican Immigration To The United States. Álvarez, José Hernández.

North From Mexico, Orig Pub 1949. Mc Williams, Carey.

Social Character In A Mexican Village: A Sociopsychoanalytic Study. Fromm, Erich and Maccoby, Michael.

Stranger In One's Land. Salazar, Ruben.

A Documentary History Of The Mexican Americans. Moquin, W E and Van Doren, C and Rivera, F.

American Attitudes Toward Mexican Immigration. Lipshultz, Robert J.

Los Mojados: The Wetback Story. Samora, Julian.

Mexican Immigration To The United States. Gamio, Manuel.

The Other Californians: Prejudice And Discrimination Under Spain, Mexico, And The United States To 1920. Heizer, Robert F and Almquist, Alan F.

Tree Of Hate: Propaganda And Prejudices Affecting United States Relations With The Hispanic World. Powell, Philip W.

MEXICO

Occupied America: The Chicano's Struggle Toward Liberation. Acuña, Rodolfo.

The Chicanos: A History Of Mexican Americans. Meier, Matt S and Rivera, Feliciano.

Political & Economic Aspects Of Mexican Immigration Into California And The US Since 1941. Williams, Dean L.

The Mexico–United States Border: Public Policy And Chicano Economic Welfare. Briggs Jr, Vernon M.

Unwanted Mexican Americans In The Great Depression—Tucson. Hoffman, Abraham.

A Descriptive Study Of The Control Of Illegal Mexican Migration In The Southwestern US. Toney, William T.

A History Of The Mexican American People. Samora, Julian and Simon, Patricia Vandel.

Anglo Over Bracero: A History Of The Mexican Worker In The United States From Roosevelt To Nixon. Kirstein, Peter N.

Desperate Mexican Children Swarm Over Border To Commit Crimes—Situation Seems Without Solution. Anonymous.

The Role Of Informal Policy Making In US–Mexico Border Cities. Sloan, J and West, J.

Mexican Migration To The United States: Causes, Consequences, And US Responses. Cornelius, Wayne A.

The Illegals. Halsell, Grace.

Views Across The Border: The United States And Mexico. Ross, Stanley R (ed).

Chicanos In A Changing Society: From Mexican Pueblos To American Barrios In Santa Barbara And Southern California, 1848–1930. Camarillo, Alberto.

Slave Trade Today: American Exploitation Of Illegal Aliens. Lewis, Sasha G.

Assignment In Mexico: The Experience Of United States Magistrates In The Mexican Prisoner Transfer Program. Peterson, R W.

Mexican Aliens Aren't A Problem: They're A Solution. Ehrlichman, John.

Mexican Nationals In US Prisons. Belsky, Michael.

MIAMI, FL

Vizzini. Vizzini, Sal.

Adams v Miami Police Benevolent Ass'n 454 F2d 1315, (Florida) US Court Of Appeals, Fifth Circuit February 2, 1972. Anonymous.

Manual For The Recruitment Of Minority And Females. Avello, J A and Mendoza, M G.

MICHIGAN

see also Detroit, MI; Jackson State Prison, MI; Lansing, MI; Ypsilanti, MI

Summaries Of Studies On The Recruitment And Retention Of Minority Correctional Employees. Beard, Eugene.

The Negro Offender In A Northern Industrial Area. Fox, Vernon and Volakalis, Joan.

Race, Social Status, And Criminal Arrest. Green, Edward.

A Comparison Of Blacks And Whites Committed For Evaluation Of Competency To Stand Trial On Criminal Charges. Cooke, Gerald and Pogany, Eric and Johnston, Norman G.

Judicial Selection And The Black Experience. Crockett Jr, George W.

Enforcement Workshop—Minority Quotas For Police Promotions: A Comment On Detroit Police Officers Association Versus Young. Sherman, Lawrence W.

MIGRATION

The Mexican In The United States. Bogardus, Emory S.

Puerto Ricans In New York. Mills, C Wright.

Up From Puerto Rico. Padilla, Elena.

The Newcomers: Negroes And Puerto Ricans In A Changing Metropolis. Handlin, Oscar.

La Vida: A Puerto Rican Family In The Culture Of Poverty—San Juan And New York. Lewis, Oscar.

Migration And Crime. Kinman, Judith L and Lee, Everett S.

Cubans In Exile: Disaffection And The Revolution. Fagen, R and Brody, R and O' Leary, T.

"European Migration And Crime" in *Crime And Culture: Essays In Honor Of Thorsten Sellin*, Wolfgang, Marvin E (ed), 189–220. Ferracuti, Franco.

American Attitudes Toward Mexican Immigration. Lipshultz, Robert J.

Los Mojados: The Wetback Story. Samora, Julian.

Mexican Immigration To The United States. Gamio, Manuel.

Puerto Rican Americans: The Meaning Of Migration To The Mainland. Fitzpatrick, Joseph P.

Migrant In The City: The Life Of A Puerto Rican Action Group. Rogler, Lloyd H.

Political & Economic Aspects Of Mexican Immigration Into California And The US Since 1941. Williams, Dean L.

Puerto Rico And The Puerto Ricans: A Study Of Puerto Rican History And Immigration To The United States. Hauberg, Clifford A.

The Mexico–United States Border: Public Policy And Chicano Economic Welfare. Briggs Jr, Vernon M.

For American Blacks: A New Identity—The Black Diaspora. Cannon, J Alfred.

A Descriptive Study Of The Control Of Illegal Mexican Migration In The Southwestern US. Toney, William T.

Anglo Over Bracero: A History Of The Mexican Worker In The United States From Roosevelt To Nixon. Kirstein, Peter N.

American Indians: The Reluctant Urbanites. Borman, L.

Mexican Migration To The United States: Causes, Consequences, And US Responses. Cornelius, Wayne A.

Going Home: The Puerto Ricans' New Migration. Stockton, William.

MILITARY CRIME

Racial Discrimination And The Military Judgment. Dembitz, Nanette.

The American Dilemma In Uniform: Race In The Armed Forces. Moskos, Charles.

Black–White Differences In Social Background And Military Drug Abuse Patterns. Nail, R L and Gunderson, E K E and Arthur, R J.

Racial Pattern Of Military Crimes In Vietnam. Kroll, J.

The Justice System And Sentencing: The Importance Of Race In The Military. Perry, Ronald W.

MILITARY MODEL

Riot Control Equipment. Brumgardt, J R.

The War Model In Criminal Justice: No Substitute For Victory. Christianson, Scott.

Police And Military In The Resolution Of Ethnic Conflict. Enloe, Cynthia.

MILWAUKEE, WI

Black And White Perceptions Of Justice In The City. Jacob, Herbert.

MIND CONTROL

Physical Manipulation Of The Brain. Swan, L Alex.

"What Is The Potential For Biological Violence Control" in *Biology And Crime*, Jeffrey, C Ray (ed). Moyer, Kenneth.

MINNEAPOLIS

An Analysis Of Negro Crime Statistics For Minneapolis For 1923, 1924, And 1925. Boie, Maurine.

MINNESOTA

see also Hennipin County, Mn; Ramsey County, Mn

Tribal Injustice—The Red Lake Court Of Indian Offenses. Lawrence, J W.

Violent Death And Alcohol Use Among The Chippewa In Minnesota. Westermeyer, Joseph and Brantner, John.

Indian Powerlessness In Minnesota. Westermeyer, Joseph.

Study Of Sentencing In Hennepin County And Ramsey County District Courts. Rhodes, W M.

American Indians And The Criminal Justice System. Benjamin, Roger and Choong Nam Kim.

MISSISSIPPI

see also Clarke County, Ms; Clarksdale, Ms; Jackson, Ms; Parchman Penitentiary, Ms

Summaries Of Studies On The Recruitment And Retention Of Minority Correctional Employees. Beard, Eugene.

Report Of The Pennsylvania Joint Legislative Committee On Capital Punishment. Joint Legis Comm On Capital Punishment.

Southern Justice. Friedman, Leon (ed).

Law And Order On The Mississippi Choctaw Reservation. Bobo, D.

Crosby Smith: Forgotten Witness To A Mississippi Nightmare. Shostak, David.

Mississippi Has Come A Long Way, But It Had A Long Way To Come. Gettinger, Steve.

MISSOURI

see also Kansas City, Mo; St Louis, Mo

Discrimination Against Negroes In The Adminstration Of Criminal Law In Missouri. Gerard, Jules B and Terry Jr, T Rankin.

Profile/Missouri. May, Edgar.

MOBILITY

Deprivation, Mobility, And Orientation Toward Protest Of The Urban Poor. Bowen, Donald Et Al.

Socioeconomic Mobility Among Three Generations Of Japanese Americans. Levine, Gene N and Montero, Darrel M.

MOLLS

Race, Sex And Gangs: The Molls. Miller, Walter B.

MONROE COUNTY, NY

Epidemiological Differences Between White And Nonwhite Suicide Attempters. Pederson, A M and Awad, G A and Kindler, A R.

MONTGOMERY, AL

Southern Justice. Friedman, Leon (ed).

MOOD

Profile Of Mood States: Racial Differences In A Delinquent Population. Fagan, T J and Lira, F T.

MOTLEY, CONSTANCE BAKER

Constance Baker Motley: Black Woman, Black Judge. Washington, Michelle.

MOTORISTS

Helping A Motorist In Distress: The Effects Of Sex, Race And Neighborhood. West, S G and Whitney, G and Schnedler, R.

MOYNIHAN, DANIEL PATRICK

The Moynihan Report And The Politics Of Controversy. Rainwater, Lee and Yancey, William L.

"The Moynihan Report: The Negro Family And Crime" in *The Sociology Of Crime And Delinquency*, Wolfgang, M et al (ed), 440–450. U S Dept Of Labor, Office Of Planning And Research.

A Black Perspective On Social Research: In Response To Merton. Johnson, Larry.

A Methodological Critique Of The Moynihan Report. Swan, L Alex.

Black Families And The Moynihan Report: A Research Evaluation. Berger, Alan S and Simon, William.

MUGGING *see* Robbery

MURDER *see* Homicide

MURTON, TOM

Accomplices To The Crime. Murton, Tom.

NAGEL, WILLIAM

Crime And Incarceration; A Reanalysis. Nagel, Jack H.

NARCOTICS *see* Drugs

NASSAU COUNTY, NY

Varieties Of Police Behavior: The Management Of Law And Order In Eight Communities. Wilson, James Q.

NAT ADV COMM ON CRIM JUST

Dynamics Of Courthouse Justice: A Critical Review Of The Literature. Neubauer, D W.

NAT ADV COMM ON CRIM JUSTICE

Corrections. National Advisory Commission On Crim Justice Standards & Goals.

Police. National Advisory Commission On Crim Justice Standards & Goals.

NAT COMMITTEE ON PRISON LABOR

Penal Servitude. Whitin, E Stagg.

NAT INSTITUTE OF CORRECTIONS

"The Minority Perspective And The 1980 NIC Program". Castro, Agenor L.

NATIONAL BAR ASSOCIATION

The National Bar Association—Not Just An Opinion. Ortique, Revius O.

NATIONAL GUARD

Actions Of Police And The Military In American Race Riots. Grimshaw, Allen.

The National Guard And Riot Control: The Need For Revision. Crum, L.

When Will The Troops Come Marching In: A Comment On The Historical Use Of Federal Troops To Quell Domestic Violence. Garland, R and Chikota, Richard.

NATIONAL LAWYERS GUILD

National Lawyers Guild As An All White Organization. Goodman, W.

Combatting Racism In American Law Schools. Ginger, Ann Fagan.

NATIONAL URBAN LEAGUE

Project LEMMP (Law Enforcement Minority Manpower Project)—Final Report. National Urban League, Inc.

State Of Black America, 1977. National Urban League, Inc.

Law Enforcement Minority Manpower Project—Final Report. Reynolds, L H.

NAVAJO

Navajo Common Law II: Navajo Law And Justice. Van Valkenburgh, R.

Notes On Navajo Suicide. Wyman, L and Thorne, B.

A Case Of A 'Psychotic' Navaho Indian Male. Jewell, Donald P.

Problems Of The Navajo Tribal Courts In Transition. Shepardson, Mary.

The Origins Of The Navajo Indian Police, 1872–1873. Jones Jr, Oakah L.

Navajo Drinking: Some Tentative Hypotheses. Ferguson, Francis N.

Navajo Criminal Homicide. Levy Jerrold E and Kunitz, Stephen J and Everett, Michael.

The Navajo Nation: An American Colony. U S Commission On Civil Rights.

Native American Justice—the Courts Of The Navajo Nation. Fahey, R P.

NEBRASKA

Clark et al v Wolff, 347 F Supp 887, (Nebraska), US District Court D Nebraska: May 24, 1972, 1972. Anonymous.

Conviction And Sentencing In The Fourth Judicial District Of Nebraska. Kulig, F H and Hawkinson, T.

NEBRASKA STATE PENITENTIARY

Erroneous Zone. Rice, David L.

NEGRO *see* Blacks

NEIGHBORHOOD

Anomie, In The Ghetto: A Study Of Neighborhood Type, Race And Anomie. Wilson, R A.

NEUTRALIZATION

Delinquency And Drift. Matza, David.

Norm Neutralization, Anomia And Self–Concept Among Institutionalized Female Delinquents. Lilly, J R and Ball, R A.

Control Theory Re–examined: Race And The Use Of Neutralizations Among Institutionalized Delinquents. Mannle, Henry W and Lewis, Peter W.

NEW ENGLAND

The Negro In Colonial New England. Greene, Lorenzo M.

The Significance Of The Captivity Narrative. Pearce, Roy H.

Wayward Puritans: A Study In The Sociology Of Deviance. Erikson, Kai T.

The Significance Of Disease In Extinction Of The New England Indians. Cook, Sherburne F.

The Invasion Of America: Indians, Colonialism, And The Cant Of Conquest. Jennings, Francis.

Forced Conformity: Puritan Criminal Justice And Indians. Kawashima, Yasuhide.

NEW HAVEN, CT

Interrogations In New Haven: The Impact Of *Miranda*. Wald, Michael et al.

NEW JERSEY

see also Hudson County, Nj, Newark, Nj, Rahway Prison, Nj

Abstract Of Analysis Of Jury Sentencing In Capital Cases. Wolf, Edwin D.

Death Sentences In New Jersey, 1907–1964. Bedau, Hugo Adam.

An Assessment Of Dogmatism Among Adult Inmates In A State Correctional Institution In New Jersey. Carden, Francis Xavier.

The Sixteenth Round. Carter, Rubin "Hurricane".

"Hispanics: The Anonymous Prisoners" in *New Jersey Correctional Master Plan*, V4. Lee, Robert Joe.

"Correctional Philosophy: A Special Issue: Race And Criminal Justice" in *New Jersey Correctional Master Plan*. New Jersey Dept Of Corrections.

A Profile Of Puerto Rican Prisoners In New Jersey And Its Implications For The Administration Of Justice. Lee, Robert Joe.

New Jersey Correctional Master Plan. New Jersey Dept Of Corrections.

Development Of A Plan For Bilingual Interpreters In The Criminal Courts Of New Jersey. Hippchen, L J.

Police Are Sued. Anonymous.

Police Recruit Minorities. Anonymous.

Descriptive Study Of Homicide In Hudson County (NJ), 1971–1977. Maguire, F J.

Sentencing Guidelines Project: Report To The Administrative Director Of The Courts On The Relationship Between Race And Sentencing. Sheflin, N.

NEW MEXICO

see also Gallup, Nm, Santa Fe Prison, Nm

Horace Mann's Letters On The Extension Of Slavery Into California And New Mexico. Mann, Horace.

The Spanish Americans Of New Mexico: A Distinctive Heritage. González, Nancie L.

Colonialism: The Case Of The Mexican–Americans. Moore, Joan W.

The Angry Chicano. Sunseri, Alvin R.

Court Administration In New Mexico. Colton, M L et al.

Crowded Prisons—A Review Of Psychological And Environmental Effects. Clements, C B.

Report Of The Attorney General On The February 2 And 3, 1980 Riot At The Penitentiary Of New Mexico: Part 2. New Mexico Attorney General.

Report Of The Attorney General On The February 2 And 3, 1980 Riot At The Penitentiary Of New Mexico: Part I. New Mexico Attorney General.

New Mexico: The Anatomy Of A Riot. Serrill, Michael S and Katel, Peter.

Prison Perspective (Santa Fe Prison Riot). Anonymous.

Sleeping It Off In Gallup, NM. Katel, Peter.

The Santa Fe Prison Riots: 'The Flower Of The Dragon'. Mandel, Jerry.

NEW YORK CITY

Proceedings Of The Conspiracy Formed By Some White People For Burning The City Of NY In America And Murdering The Inhabitants. Horsmanden, Daniel.

Puerto Ricans In New York. Mills, C Wright.

A Study Of The Administration Of Bail In New York City. Foote, Caleb.

Report From A Spanish Harlem 'fortress'. Hammer, Richard.

Walk Along The Worst Block: East 100th Street. Samuels, Gertrude.

Beyond The Melting Pot: The Negroes, Puerto Ricans, Jews, Italians, And Irish Of New York City. Glazer, Nathan and Moynihan, Daniel P.

Spanish Harlem. Sexton, Patricia Cayo.

Look For Me In The Whirlwind: The Collective Autobiography Of The New York 21. Balagon, Kuwasi et al.

Minority Recruiting In The New York City Police Department. Hunt Jr, Issac C and Cohen, Bernard.

Life In The Neighborhood: A Factor Analytic Study Of Puerto Rican Males In The New York City Area. Hoffman, Gerard and Fishman, Joshua A.

Levels Of Acculturation And Of Attitudes Toward Deviance, Criminal Behavior And Police Law Enforcement Practices Among Puerto Ricans In NYC. Cotton, W L.

Migrant In The City: The Life Of A Puerto Rican Action Group. Rogler, Lloyd H.

Police Power: A Study Of Provocation. Chevigny, Paul.

Through The Veil Of Partial Comprehension: NY City's Hispanic Defendant And The Criminal Justice System. New York City Board Of Correction.

Police Civil Service Selection Prodecures And New York City—Comparison Of Ethnic Groups. Chaiken, J M and Cohen, Bernard.

Police, Politics, And Pluralism In New York City: A Comparative Case Study. Viteritti, Joseph P.

The Briar Patch: The People Of The State Of New York V Lumumba Shakur Et Al. Kempton, Murray.

Minority Retention In The New York City Police Department. Cohen, Bernard.

An Analysis Of 248 Persons Killed By New York City Policemen. Jenkins, Betty and Faison, Adrienne.

Black–White Relations Among Police In The United States. Lynch, Gerald.

Black Police Attitudes In The New York City Police Department: An Exploratory Study. Wubnig, Michael.

Carlito's Way. Torres, Edwin.

Criminal Victimization Surveys In The Nation's Five Largest Cities. U S Dept Of Justice, LEAA, NCJIsS.

How The Criminal Justice System Fails The Spanish–Speaking Community Of New York City And What Should Be Done About It. Special Committee On Penal And Correctional Reform.

Puerto Ricans In New York City, Welfare Council Of New York City. Committee On Puerto Ricans.

A Preliminary Report On The Experience Of The Minority Judiciary In The City Of New York. Coalition Of Concerned Black Americans.

City Layoffs—The Effect On Minorities And Women. New York City Commission On Human Rights.

New York Cops Talk Back. Alex, Nicholas.

Violence By Youth Gangs And Youth Groups In Major American Cities—Final Report. Miller, Walter B.

Homicide And Robbery In New York City: An Economic Model. Mathieson, Donald and Passell, Peter.

Manny—A Criminal–Addict's Story. Retting, R P and Torres, M J and Garrett, G R.

"From Matron To Commanding Officer—Women's Changing Role In Law Enforcement" in Law Enforcement Bible, Scanlon, Robert A (ed). Acerra, L.

Blue Coats—Black Skin—The Black Experience In The New York City Police Department Since 1891. Alexander, J I.

Expectations Which Have Shaped Women's Role In Policing New York City. Sichel, J L.

Puerto Ricans And Health: Findings From New York City. Alers, Jose Oscar.

Shots Fired: An Examination Of New York City Police Firearms Discharges. Fyfe, James Joseph.

Wildcat Experiment—An Early Test Of Supported Work In Drug Abuse Rehabilitation. Friedman, L N.

Spanish Harlem. Shorris, Earl.

The Blackout, in 1977 Annual Report Of The New York City Board Of Correction, 17–24. New York City Board Of Correction.

The Regimentation Of Blacks On The Urban Frontier In Colonial Albany, New York City And Philadelphia. Williams, Oscar R.

A Report On The Blackout Looting: New York City, July 13, 1977. Curvin, Robert and Porter, Bruce.

Street Gangs—Profiles For Police. Collins, H C.

War On Narcotics—The State Of Hostilities In New York. Macguire, R J.

The Figgie Report On Fear Of Crime: America Afraid, Part 1, The General Public. A– T– O, Inc.

Matty Troy's Prison Diary. Klein, Joe (ed).

What Happened In Harlem: Analysis Of A Decline In Heroin Use Among A Generation Unit Of Urban Black Youth. Boyle, John M and Brunswick, Ann F.

NEW YORK STATE

see also Albany, Ny; Amsterdam, Ny; Attica Prison, Ny; Auburn Prison, Ny, Bedford Stuyvesant, Nyc; Brighton, Ny; Bronx, Ny; Brooklyn, Ny, Buffalo, Ny; Great Meadow Prison, Ny; Greenhaven Prison, Ny; Harlem, Nyc; Nassau County, Ny; New York City; Newburgh, Ny; Riker's Island Jail, Nyc; Sing Sing Prison, Ny, Syracuse, Ny

"New York State Dept Of Correctional Services Affirmative Action Proposal For 1980: A Historical Synopsis And General Commentary". Castro, Agenor L.

The Hispanic Experience In Criminal Justice. Sissons, Peter L.

Case For The Promotion Of Police Women In The City Of New York. Shpritzer, Felicia.

North Of Slavery. Litwack, Leon F.

The Slave Insurrection In New York In 1712. Scott, Kenneth.

Attica: My Story. Oswald, Russell G.

Attica: The Official Report Of The New York State Special Commission On Attica, [McKay Commission]. New York State Special Commission On Attica.

Black Bondage In The North. Mc Manus, Edgar J.

Crime And Law Enforcement In The Colony Of New York, 1691–1776. Greenberg, Douglas S.

Prison Without Walls: Report On New York Parole. Clark, Ramsey and Rudenstine, David.

Patterns Of Criminal Prosecution In Eighteenth–Century New York. Greenberg, Douglas S.

Greenhaven Diary. Conway, Edward.

Humanizing The System: Report Of Operations And Development For 1977. New York State, Dept Of Correctional Services.

Profile Of Puerto Rican Inmates Under Departmental Custody. Morgenbesser, Leonard.

A Prison And A Prisoner. Sheehan, Susan.

War On Narcotics—The State Of Hostilities In New York. Macguire, R J.

NEWARK, NJ

Rebellion In Newark. Hayden, Tom.

Howard Street. Heard, Nathan C.

The Puerto Ricans In Newark, New Jersey. Hidalgo, Hilda.

To Reach A Dream. Heard, Nathan C.

The Ecology Of Urban Unrest: The Case Of Arson In Newark, New Jersey. Georges, Daniel E.

NEWBURGH, NY
Varieties Of Police Behavior: The Management Of Law And Order In Eight Communities. Wilson, James Q.

NEWTON, HUEY
My Days In Solitary. Newton, Huey.

NEZ PERCES
Marital Instability And Juvenile Delinquency Among The Nez Percés. Ackerman, L A.

NIGHT RIDERS
Night Riders In Black Folk History. Fry, Gladys–Marie.

NONVIOLENCE
Nonviolence: A Christian Interpretation. Miller, William Robert.
"Political Crime And The Negro Revolution" in *Criminal Behavior Systems,* Clinard, Marshall B And Richard Quinney (eds). Moudelos, Joseph C.
CORE And The Strategy Of Non–Violence. Bell, Inge Powell.

NORFOLK PRISON, VA
Who Took The Weight: Black Voices From Norfolk Prison. Norfolk Prison Brothers.

NORMS
Crime As An American Way Of Life. Bell, Daniel.
Patterns Of Looting And Property Norms: Conflict And Consensus In Community Emergencies. Dynes, R and Quarantelli, E.
"Historical Patterns Of Violence In America" in *Violence In America,* Graham, Hugh D And T Gurr (eds), 45–83. Brown, Richard Maxwell.
Honor, Normative Ambiguity And Gang Violence. Horowitz, Ruth and Schwartz, Gary.

NORTH CAROLINA
see also Greensboro, N.
The County Court In North Carolina Before 1750. Mc Cain, Paul M.
The North Carolina Black Code. Browning, James B.
The Legal Status Of The Negro. Magnum, Charles S.
Research Note On Inter– And Intra–Racial Homicides. Garfinkel, Harold.
Selective Factors In Capital Punishment. Johnson, Elmer H.
The North Carolina Chain Gang: A Study Of County Convict Road Work, Orig Pub 1927. Steiner, Jesse F and Brown, Roy M.
Victim Characteristics And Helping Behavior In A Rural Southern Setting. Franklin, Billy J.
Waiting On Death Row: North Carolina. Lopez, Luisita.
Fatal Indian Violence In North Carolina. Kupferer, H J and Humphrey, J A.
Self–Defense Against Rape: The Joanne Little Case. Bond, Julian.
The Struggle Of Ben Chavis And The Wilmington 10. Davis, Angela Y.
Break De Chains Of Legalized Slavery. Anonymous.
Characteristics Of State Prisoners Who Demonstrate Severe Adjustment Problems. Adams, T C.
Violence And Victimization Within A State Prison System. Fuller, Dan A and Orsagh, Thomas.
The Innocence Of Joan Little. Reston Jr, James.
Slavery And Servitude In The Colony Of North Carolina. Bassett, John Spencer.

NORTH DAKOTA
United Tribes Of North Dakota Development Corportion: New Careers Program, Progress Report, April 1, 1973–April 30, 1973. United Tribes Of N Dakota Development Corp.

NORWALK, CT
Norwalk Police Battle In Court Over Racial Hiring Issues. Tomasson, Robert E.

OAKLAND, CA
Violent Men: An Inquiry Into The Psychology Of Violence. Toch, Hans.
"Black Offender And White Victim" in *Forcible Rape—The Crime, The Victim And The Offender,* Chappell, D; R Geis, And G Geis (eds). Agopian, Michael W.

OBEDIENCE
Interpersonal Dynamics In A Simulated Prison. Haney, Craig and Banks, Curtis and Zimbardo, Philip.

OCCUPATION
"Note On The Negroe's Relation To Work And Law Observation" in *Report On The Causes Of Crime,* V13. Reid, Ira De A.
Age, Occupation And Conviction Rates Of White And Negro Males: A Case Study. Forslund, Morris A.

OCCUPATIONAL CHOICE
Relative Occupational Anticipations And Aspirations Of Delinquents And Nondelinquents. Frederick, M A and Molnar, M.
Occupational Choice And Perception Of Attainment Blockage—Study Of Lower Class Delinquent And Nondelinquent Black Males. Picou, J S et al.
Careers In Law For Minorities: A Puerto Rican's Perspective On Recent Developments In Legal Education. Cabranes, C A.
A Profile Of Hispanics In The US Work Force. Newman, Morris.

OFFENDER-BASED STATISTICS
Offender–Based Transaction Statistics: New Directions In Data Collection And Reporting. Pope, Carl E.
The Influence Of Social And Legal Factors On Sentence Dispositions: A Preliminary Analysis Of Offender–Based Transaction Statistics. Pope, Carl E.

OFFENDER CLASSIFICATION
An Assessment Of Dogmatism Among Adult Inmates In A State Correctional Institution In New Jersey. Carden, Francis Xavier.
Analysis Of Classification Factors For Young Adult Offenders: Race Factors, V3. Wenk, E A and Halatyn, T V.
"Classifying Black Inmates: The Alabama Prison Classification Project" in *Blacks And Criminal Justice,* Owens And Bell (eds), 129–142. Owens, Charles E.
Hispanics In Corrections: The Statistical Dilemma In Finding Relevant Employee/Inmate Data. Castro, Agenor L.

OFFENDER TYPOLOGY
The Negro Armed Robber As A Criminal Type: The Construction And Application Of A Typology. Roebuck, Julian D and Cadwallader, Mervyn L.
The Negro Drug Addict As An Offender Type. Roebuck, Julian B.
The Offender: 1937–1963. Tompkins, Dorothy Louise Culver.
The Negro Numbers Man As A Criminal Type: The Construction And Application Of A Typology. Roebuck, Julian D.
Gang Member Delinquency: Its Extent, Sequence And Typology. Robin, Gerald D.
Criminal Typology. Roebuck, Julian B.
"Typology" in *Police–Community Relationships,* Bopp, W (ed). Brown, Lee P.
Offender Typologies—Two Decades Later. Gibbons, Don C.

OFFICIAL DATA
Uniform Crime Reports For The United States. U S Dept Of Justice, Federal Bureau Of Investigation.
Hidden Negro Criminality. Ramsey, D.
Crime Conditions In The United States As Reflected In Census Statistics Of Imprisoned Offenders. U S Dept Of Commerce, Bureau Of Census.
"Recent Statistics On Crime And The Foreign Born" in *Report On Crime And The Foreign Born,* V10. Bowler, Alida C.
Research Note On Inter– And Intra–Racial Homicides. Garfinkel, Harold.
The Extent And Characteristics Of Juvenile Delinquency Among Negroes In The United States. Douglas, Joseph H.
Measuring Delinquency: A Study Of Probation Department Referrals. Eaton, Joseph W.
Court Records, Undetected Delinquency And Decision–Making. Erickson, Maynard L and Empey La Mar, T.
Uniform Crime Reports: A Critical Appraisal. Wolfgang, Marvin E.
Statistics Concerning Race And Crime. Geis, Gilbert.
Age Composition And Patterns Of Change In Criminal Statistics. Sagi, P and Wellford, C.
On The Validity Of Official Statistics—A Comparative Study Of White, Black And Japanese High School Boys. Chambliss, William J and Nagasawa, Richard H.
Who Defines Delinquency: A Comparison Of Self–Reported And Officially–Reported Indices Of Delinquency For Three Racial Groups. Gould, Leroy C.
Standardization Of Negro Crime Rates For Negro–White Differences In Age And Status. Forslund, Morris A and Malry, L.
Persons Of Spanish Origin In The United States, November 1969. U S Dept Of Commerce, Bureau Of The Census.
The Stereotype Of The Criminal And The Social Consequences. Chapman, D.
Analysis Of Classification Factors For Young Adult Offenders: Race Factors, V3. Wenk, E A and Halatyn, T V.

OFFICIAL DATA

Sourcebook Of Criminal Justice Statistics: 1973. U S Dept Of Justice, LEAA, NCJISS.

Getting The Crime Rate Down: Political Pressure And Crime Reporting. Seidman, D and Couzens, M.

Criminal Victimization Surveys In The Nation's Five Largest Cities. U S Dept Of Justice, LEAA, NCJISS.

Homicide Trends In The United States, 1900–1974. Klebba, A Joan.

Offender–Based Transaction Statistics: New Directions In Data Collection And Reporting. Pope, Carl E.

Sourcebook Of Criminal Justice Statistics: 1974. U S Dept Of Justice, LEAA, NCJISS.

The Nations Jails: A Report On The Census Of Jails From The 1972 Survey Of Inmates Of Local Jails. U S Dept Of Justice, LEAA, NCJISS.

Analysis Of Arrest Rates For Trends In Criminality. Blumstein, Alfred and Nagin, Daniel S.

Criminal Victimization In Eight American Cities. Hindelang, Michael J.

Survey Of Inmates Of State Correctional Facilities, 1974. U S Dept Of Justice, LEAA, NCJISS.

Explaining Urban Crime Rates. Danziger, Sheldon.

Racial Disparities That Supposedly Do Not Exist: Some Pitfalls In Analysis Of Court Records. Nagel, Stuart and Neef, Marian.

The Influence Of Social And Legal Factors On Sentence Dispositions: A Preliminary Analysis Of Offender–Based Transaction Statistics. Pope, Carl E.

Capital Punishment 1976. U S Dept Of Justice, LEAA, NCJISS.

Census Of Prisoners In State Correctional Facilities 1973. U S Dept Of Justice, LEAA.

Criminal Victimization In The United States 1975. U S Dept Of Justice, LEAA, NCJISS.

Sourcebook Of Criminal Justice Statistics: 1976. U S Dept Of Justice, LEAA, NCJISS.

Sourcebook Of Criminal Justice: 1975. U S Dept Of Justice, LEAA, NCJIsS.

Ethnic/Racial Misidentification In Death: A Problem Which May Distort Suicide Statistics. Andress, V R.

"Law Enforcement Data Processing & Equal Employment Standards" in *2nd Annual Law Enforcement Data Processing Symposium.* Schandler, M L.

An Analysis Of The Evidence And Seriousness Of Self–Reported Delinquency And Crime. Tracy, Paul E.

Crime Rates, Crime Myths And Official Smokescreens. Chambliss, William J.

Criminal Victimization In The United States 1976. U S Dept Of Justice, LEAA, NCJISS.

Explaining Crime. Nettler, Gwynn.

Federal Sentencing Patterns: A Study Of Geographical Variations. U S Dept Of Justice, LEAA, NCJISS.

Prisoners In State And Federal Institutions On December 31, 1976. U S Dept Of Justice, LEAA, NCJISS.

Sourcebook Of Criminal Justice Statistics: 1977. U S Dept Of Justice, LEAA, NCJISS.

Capital Punishment, 1978. U S Dept Of Justice, LEAA, NCJISS.

Criminal Victimization In The United States 1977. U S Dept Of Justice, LEAA, NCJISS.

Prisoners In State And Federal Institutions On December 31, 1977. U S Dept Of Justice, LEAA, NCJISS.

Sourcebook Of Criminal Justice Statistics: 1978. U S Dept Of Justice, LEAA, NCJISS.

Crime—Some Popular Beliefs. Doleschal, Eugene.

Measuring Homicide By Police Officers. Sherman, Lawrence W and Langworthy, Robert H.

Criminal Victimization In The U S: Summary Findings Of 1978–1979 Changes In Crime And Of Trends Since 1973. U S Dept Of Justice, Bureau Of Justice Statistics.

Prisoners In State And Federal Institutions On December 31, 1978: National Prisoner Statistics Bulletin SD–NPS–PSF–6. U S Dept Of Justice, Bureau Of Justice Statistics.

Sourcebook Of Criminal Justice Statistics: 1979. U S Dept Of Justice, LEAA, NCJIS.

Execution Without Trial: Police Homicide And The Constitution. Sherman, Lawrence W.

OHIO

see also Cleveland, Oh, Columbus, Oh, Franklin County, Oh

Summaries Of Studies On The Recruitment And Retention Of Minority Correctional Employees. Beard, Eugene.

Capital Punishment, Staff Research Report No 46. Ohio Legislative Service Commission.

Ascertaining Police Bias In Arrests For Drunken Driving. Hyman, Merton M and Helrich, Alice R and Benson, Gwen.

Compulsive Masculinity And Delinquency: An Empirical Investigation. Silverman, I J and Dinitz, Simon.

Runaways At The Training Institution In Central Ohio. Bartollas, C.

Minority Recruitment Manual For Ohio Peace Officers Report, 1977. Snarr, R W and Mc Cauley, R P.

Effectiveness Of Volunteer Assistance To Parolees. Carlson, Eric W and Vito, Gennaro F and Parks, Evalyn C.

OKLAHOMA see Tulsa, Ok

Criminal's Image Of The City. Carter, R I and Hill, K Q.

OKTIBBEHA COUNTY, MS

Southern Justice. Friedman, Leon (ed).

OPPORTUNITY

Delinquency And Opportunity: A Theory Of Delinquent Gangs. Cloward, Richard A and Ohlin, Lloyd E.

Male Young Adult Criminality Deviant Values, And Differential Opportunities In Two Lower Class Negro Neighborhoods. Spergel, Irving.

Perceived Opportunities, Gang Membership, And Delinquency. Short Jr, James F and Rivera, Ramon and Tennyson, Ray.

"Illegitimate Opportunity Structures" in *Rebellion And Retreat*, Palmer, S (ed), 32–49. Cloward, Richard A and Ohlin, Lloyd E.

Aspiration Vs Opportunity: "Careers" In The Inner City. Bullock, Paul.

ORANGEBURG, SC

The Orangeburg Massacre. Nelson, Jack and Bass, Jack.

OREGON

Capital Punishment In Oregon 1903–1964. Bedau, Hugo Adam.

Race, Crime And Social Policy: The Chinese In Oregon, 1871–1885. Tracy, Charles A.

ORGANIZED CRIME see Crime, Organized

ORIENTALS see Asian–americans

OVERREACTION

Danger Of Police Overreaction. Sagalyn, Arnold.

OVERSEER see Slavery

OXNARD, CA

Chicanoizing Drug Abuse Programs. Aron, William S and Alger, Norman and Gonzales, Ricardo T.

PAPAGO

An Epidemiological Study Of Suicide And Attempted Suicide Among The Papago Indians. Conrad, R D and Kahn, M W.

PARANOIA

Paranoia And Racism In The United States. Biassey, E L.

PARCHMAN PENITENTIARY, MS

Mississippi Has Come A Long Way, But It Had A Long Way To Come. Gettinger, Steve.

PARDONS

Sourcebook On Probation, Parole And Pardons, 3rd Ed. Newman, Charles L.

PAROLE

Every Opportunity. Himes, Chester.

Personal Characteristics And Parole Outcome. Glaser, Daniel and O'Leary, Vincent.

Sourcebook On Probation, Parole And Pardons, 3rd Ed. Newman, Charles L.

Inequalities Of The Parole System In California. Bailey, D'Army.

The Decision To Parole: A Study Of The Parole Decision Process With Juveniles. Hussey, Frederick Alan.

"Understanding Probation And Parole" in *The Administration Of Criminal Justice: A View From Black America*, Brown, Lee P (ed), 48–61. Mc Connell, Leonard R.

Ethnic Self-Help Groups In Prison And On Parole. Burdman, Milton.

Prison Without Walls: Report On New York Parole. Clark, Ramsey and Rudenstine, David.

Reentry And The Black Parolee. Swan, L Alex.

California Prisoners 1976: Summary Statistics Of Felon Prisoners And Parolees. California Dept Of Corrections.

PAROLE

"Successful Passage Of Black Parolees From Prison To Prison" in *Crime And Its Impact On The Black Community*, Gary And Brown (eds), 177–194. Swan, L Alex.

Parolees' Perceptions Of The Justice System: Black–White Differences. Berman, John J.

Racial Bias In The Decision To Grant Parole. Carroll, Leo and Mondrick, Margaret E.

Impulsive And Premeditated Homicide: An Analysis Of Subsequent Parole Risk Of The Murderer. Heilbrun Jr, Alfred B and Heilbrun, Lynn C and Heilbrun, Kim L.

Race, Criminal Violence, And Length Of Parole. Heilbrun Jr, Alfred B.

Overcrowding In Texas Prisons, Special Legislative Report No 43. Texas House Of Representatives.

Racial Identity, Length Of Incarceration And Parole Decision Making. Elion, Victor H and Megargee, Edwin I.

Characteristics Of The Parole Population–1978. National Council On Crime And Delinquency.

Corrections: An Issues Approach. Schwartz, Martin D (ed) and Clear, Todd R (ed) and Travis I I I, Lawrence F (ed).

Women As Probation Parole, And Correctional Officers In The Criminal Justice Field—A Selected Bibliography. Martin, C A.

Effectiveness Of Volunteer Assistance To Parolees. Carlson, Eric W and Vito, Gennaro F and Parks, Evalyn C.

PATERNALISM

Chivalry And Paternalism—Disparities Of Treatment In The Criminal Justice System. Moulds, E F.

PATTERSON, HAYWOOD

Scottsboro Boy. Patterson, Haywood and Conrad, Earl.

PENAL SEVERITY

"Fluctuation Of Ethico–Juridicial Mentality In Criminal Law" in *Sociocultural Dynamics*, V3, 523–632. Sorokin, Pitirim A.

Crime And Punishment—1938. Ford, Nick and Hill, Mozell C.

An Essay On Crime And Punishments, Orig Pub 1763. Beccaria, Cesare Bonesana.

Changes In Penal Values. Christie, Nils.

Prejudice, Perception And Penal Judgements. Delk, J L.

Texas Sentencing Practices: A Statistical Study. Baab, George W and Ferguson, William R.

The Law: Rape, Race, Time And Death. Koeninger, R C.

Race, Crime And Sentence Length. Chiricos, Theodore G et al.

Latitude And Severity Of Sentencing Options, Race Of The Victim And Decisions Of Simulated Jurors. Kaplan, J.

The Dialectics Of Legal Repression: Black Rebels Before The American Criminal Courts. Balbus, Isaac D.

A Theory Of The Stability Of Punishment. Blumstein, Alfred and Cohen, Jacqueline.

The Use Of Discretion In Determining The Severity Of Punishment For Incarcerated Offenders. Scott, Joseph E.

Sentencing Of California Felony Offenders. Pope, Carl E.

Prison Reform In Social Perspective. Vogel, Richard.

Punishment And Social Organization: A Study Of Durkheim's Theory Of Penal Evolution. Spitzer, Steven.

Socioeconomic Status And Criminal Sentencing. Chiricos, Theodore G and Waldo, Gordon P.

Survey Of Inmates Of State Correctional Facilities, 1974. U S Dept Of Justice, LEAA, NCJISS.

The Dynamics Of A Homeostatic Punishment Process. Blumstein, Alfred and Cohen, Jacqueline and Nagin, Daniel S.

Census Of Prisoners In State Correctional Facilities 1973. U S Dept Of Justice, LEAA.

Mandatory Prison Sentences: Their Projected Effects On Crime And Prison Populations. Petersilia, Joan and Greenwood, Peter W.

Punishment And The Post–Industrial Society: A Study Of Unemployment, Crime And Imprisonment In The US. Jankovic, Ivan.

Prisoners In State And Federal Institutions On December 31, 1976. U S Dept Of Justice, LEAA, NCJIsS.

Crime Rates, Sanction Levels, And Constraints On Prison Population. Nagin, Daniel.

Inequality And The Legal Order: An Ecological Test Of The Conflict Model. Jacobs, David.

Mandatory Prison Sentences: Their Projected Effects On Crime And Prison Populations. Petersilia, Joan and Greenwood, Peter W.

Theory And Research On Variations In Penal Severity. Grabosky, P N.

Prisoners In State And Federal Institutions On December 31, 1977. U S Dept Of Justice, LEAA, NCJIsS.

Racial Identity, Length Of Incarceration And Parole Decision Making. Elion, Victor H and Megargee, Edwin I.

The Death Penalty: A Life And Death Issue. Lehtinen, Marlene W.

Prisoners In State And Federal Institutions On December 31, 1978: National Prisoner Statistics Bulletin SD–NPS–PSF–6. U S Dept Of Justice, Bureau Of Justice Statistics.

The Black Incarceration Rate In The United States: A Nationwide Problem. Christianson, Scott and Dehais, Richard.

PENNSYLVANIA

see also Philadelphia, Western Penitentiary Of Penn

The Negro In Pennsylvania: Slavery–Servitude–Freedom, 1639–1861. Turner, Edward Raymond.

Report Of The Pennsylvania Joint Legislative Committee On Capital Punishment. Joint Legis Comm On Capital Punishment.

The Effect Of Mandatory And Discretionary Death Sentences On Commutations And Executions In Pennsylvania. Riedel, Marc.

Demographically Disaggregated Projections Of Prison Populations. Blumstein, Alfred and Cohen, Jacqueline and Miller, Harold D.

Program For Women Offenders—How To Start, Fund, Maintain. Female Offenders Program Of Western Pennsylvania, Inc.

The Impact Of New Sentencing Laws On State Prison Populations In Pennsylvania; Final Report. Urban Systems Institute.

PEONAGE

see also Servitude

Peonage Or The New Negro Slavery. Chestnutt, Charles W.

Peonage—Its Origin And Growth. Malone, T H.

Peonage—The Five Year's Contract. Malone, T H.

Peonage—The Remedy. Malone, T H.

Peonage—Its Working And Features. Malone, T H.

Peonage Or Debt Slavery In The Land Of The Free. Huff, William Henry.

PEREMPTORY CHALLENGE

Peremptory Challenge: Systematic Exclusion Of Prospective Jurors On The Basis Of Race. Note.

Limiting The Peremptory Challenge: Representation Of Groups On Petit Juries. Comment.

Prosecutor's Exercise Of Peremptory Challenge To Exclude Non–White Jurors: A Common Law Privilege In Conflict With Equal Protection Clause. Comment.

Racial Discrimination In Jury Selection: *United States* V *Robinson.* Soja, Thomas.

PERSONALITY

Personality Differences Between Delinquent And Non–Delinquent Negro Boys. Daniel, Robert P.

Color, Class, Personality And Juvenile Delinquency. Clark, Kenneth B.

Inmate Personality Differences Related To Recidivism, Age And Race As Measured By The MMPI. Panton, J H.

Comparative Psychological Studies Of Negroes And Whites In The United States: 1959–1965. Dreger, Ralph M and Miller, Kent S.

"The Zoot Effect On Personality: A Race Riot Participant" in *Racial Violence In The United States*, Grimshaw, A (ed), 413–420. Clark, Kenneth and Barker, James.

Personality Characteristics Of White And Negro Adolescent Delinquents. Henning, John J.

Personality Factors In Delinquent Boys: Differences Between Blacks And Whites. Cross, Herbert J and Tracy, James J.

Rebels And Sambos: The Search For The Negro's Personality In Slavery. Stampp, Kenneth M.

The Black Male Personality. Vontress, Clemmont E.

"Prisoner Personality Development In Prison/On Becoming" in *prisons, Protest, And Politics*, Atkins, B (ed), 105–111. Cleaver, Eldridge.

Discrimination, Personality And Achievement—A Survey Of Northern Blacks. Crain, R L and Weisman, C S.

Prejudice, Punitiveness And Personality. Snortum, J and Ashear, V.

The Personality And Self Concept Characteristics Of Negro And White Delinquent And Non–Delinquent Boys. Zipper, Barry Oser.

The Impact Of Racism On Personality Development. Shannon, B E.

POLICE - CIVIL DISTURBANCES

The Police And Social Tension. Tyler, L G.

Police Riots: Collective Violence And Law Enforcement. Starls, R.

"The Police And The Community" in *Police–Community Relationships*, Bopp, W (ed), 133–143. National Advisory Commission On Civil Disorders.

American Black Ghetto Revolt: A New Perspective. Abudu, Margaret.

Riot Control Equipment. Brumgardt, J R.

Change In Crisis–Relevant Organizations: Police Departments And Civil Disturbances. Kreps, Gary A.

One Department's Confrontation Strategy. Thomas, H J.

The Reluctant Army: The Functioning Of Police Departments During Civil Disturbances. Wenger, D.

A Survey Of Support For Punitive Responses To Ghetto Disorders. Goldstein, Jay E.

Negro Demonstrations And The Law: Danville As A Test Case. Ely Jr, James W.

Police, Students, And Racial Hostilities. Ford, Robert et al.

POLICE - COMMUNITY RELATIONS

Police And Minority Groups: An Experiment. Kenny, Robert W.

Intergroup Relations For Police Officers. Epstein, Charlotte.

Race Tensions And The Police. Curry, Jesse E and King, G D and Eastman, G.

Police–Community Relations. Holden Jr, Matthew.

The Police Role In Racial Conflicts. Towler, Juby Earl.

Police Review Boards: An Historical And Critical Analysis. Brown, Lee P.

Minorities And The Police. Bayley, David H and Mendelsohn, Harold.

"Police In The Ghetto" in *Riot Commission, Supplemental Studies*, 103–114. Rossi, Peter et al.

Cops In The Ghetto: A Problem Of The Police System. Levy, Burton.

Handling Complaints Against The Police. Brown, Lee P.

Police–Community Relations. Yearwood, Homero.

Youth Patrols: An Experiment In Community Participation. Knopf, Terry Ann.

Cops And Blacks: Warring Minorities. Toch, Hans.

Evaluation Of Police–Community Relations Programs. Brown, Lee P.

Urban Law Enforcement: A Plea From The Ghetto. Byrn, Robert M.

Crime, Police, And Race Relations: A Study In Birmingham. Lambert, J R and Jenkinson, R F.

The Police And The Public. Reiss Jr, Albert J.

Police And Minority Groups: Toward A Theory Of Negative Contacts. Kuykendall, Jack L.

Police Control Of Juveniles. Black, Donald and Reiss Jr, Albert.

Police Perceptions Of A Hostile Ghetto: Realism Or Projection. Groves, Eugene and Rossi, Peter.

Police–Community Relations: A Need In Search Of Police Support. Mendelsohn, Robert A.

Police–Ghetto Relations: Some Findings And A Proposal For Structural Change. Mast, Robert.

Perceptions Of Police Relationships With Ghetto Citizens. Mathias, William J.

The Ghetto Resident's View Of Police Procedures And Their Constitutionality. Mathias, William J.

"Patterns Of Behavior In Police And Citizen Transactions" in *Race, Crime, And Justice*, Reasons, C E And J L Kuykendall (eds), 176–205. Black, Donald J and Reiss Jr, Albert J.

"Police And The Community" in *Race, Crime, And Justice*, Reasons, Charles E And Jack L Kuykendall (eds), 156–175. Kerner Commission.

"The Effects Of Prejudice On Minorities" in *Police–Community Relationships*, Bopp, W (ed), 86–90. Curry, Jesse E and King, Glen D.

"The Police And The Community" in *Police–Community Relationships*, Bopp, W (ed), 133–143. National Advisory Commission On Civil Disorders.

"The Police And The Urban Ghetto" in *Race, Crime, And Justice*, Reasons, Charles E And Jack L Kuykendall (eds), 236–258. Skolnick, Jerome M.

"The Role Of The Police" in *Police–Community Relationships*, Bopp, W (ed), 22–38. Terris, Bruce J.

Benefits From A Police Community Relations Program: What Can I Do, How Can I Help? Morton, Ted.

Establishing A Police–Community Relations Program. Brown, Lee P.

Police And Minority Groups: The Improvement Of Community Relations. Berleman, William C.

"The Police And Minority Groups" in *The Police And The Community*, 257–287. Radelet, Louis A.

Developing A Community And Computer Based Anti–Color–Code Strategy To Resist And Reduce Violent Crimes In Black Ghettoes. Haynes Jr, Andrew B.

"Police Deployment Theories And The Mexican–American Community" in *The Urban Policeman In Transition*, Snibbe, J (ed), 341–353. Morales, Armando.

Family Crisis Training: Upgrading The Police While Building A Bridge To The Minority Community. Katz, Myron.

Police Overperception Of Ghetto Hostility. Crawford, T J.

The Black Community: Attitudes Toward Community Problems, Crime And The Police. Knowles, Lyle and Brewer, Jesse.

The Police–Community Relations Movement: Conciliatory Responses To Violence. Kreps, Gary A and Weller, Jack M.

"Criminal Justice And The Minority Community" in *Urban Minority Groups In Houston: Problems, Progress And Prospects*, 205–248. Lede, Naomi W and Dixon, Hortense W.

Police And The Black Community. Wintersmith, Robert F.

The Community And The Police: Conflict Or Cooperation. Sealy, Lloyd G and Fink, Joseph.

A Personal Look At The Police And The Community. Coy, John T.

An Interaction Analysis Of Police–Black Relations. Cross, Stan and Renner, Edward.

Crime Prevention And The Protection Of Lives: A Mechanism To Change Police Behavior In The Community. Swan, L Alex.

Crime, Criminal Justice And The Black Community. Brown, Lee P.

The Politics Of Identification: A Perspective Of Police Accountability. Swan, L Alex.

American Minorities: The Justice Issue. Long, Elton et al.

Public Information And Law Enforcement. Mitchell, M C.

Minorities: A Wealth Of Resources. Pomerance, Rocky.

The Police And Black Separatism: A Problem For Public Policy. Lazin, F A.

"Bridges Over Troubled Waters" in *Black Perspectives On Crime And The Criminal Justice System*, Woodson, Robert L (ed), 79–106. Brown, Lee P.

"Community Relations Units In Police Departments" in *Black Crime: A Police View*, Bryce, H J (ed), 91–107. Holman, Ben.

"Improving Police Relations In The Black Community" in *Blacks And Criminal Justice*, Owens, Charles E And Jimmy Bell (eds), 114–127. Swan, L Alex.

"People And Police" in *Black Crime: A Police View*, Bryce, H J (ed), 109–128. Joyner, Irving and Scott, Elsie K.

The Class Nature Of The Urban Police During The Period Of Black Municipal Power. Green, Edward.

The Importance Of Spanish Language Training For Law Enforcement Officers. Tatum, William M.

Minority Police: Tramping Through A Racial Minefield. Cory, Bruce.

The Police, The Courts, And The Minority Community. Witt, James W.

The Police And The Ghetto. Cooper, John L.

POLICE - DEADLY FORCE

Violence And The Police. Westley, William A.

Racial Violence And Law Enforcement. Mc Millan, George.

Justifiable Homicide By Police Officers. Robin, Gerald D.

The Algiers Motel Incident. Hersey, John.

Arrests In Civil Disturbances: Reflections On The Use Of Deadly Force In Riots. Mc Ghee, Henry.

Shall We Shoot Looters? Clark, Ramsey.

Shootout In Cleveland: Black Militants And The Police (Violence Commission Report, Volume 5). Masotti, Louis and Corsi, Jerome.

The Death Of Fred Hampton. Calhoun, Lillian S.

The Orangeburg Massacre. Nelson, Jack and Bass, Jack.

Killings By Chicago Police, 1969–70: An Empirical Study. Harding, Richard and Fahey, Richard P.

An Analysis Of 248 Persons Killed By New York City Policemen. Jenkins, Betty and Faison, Adrienne.

Violence And The Police. Pinkney, Alphonso.

Figures (and Perhaps Some Facts) On Police Killing Of Civilians In The United States. Kobler, Arthur L.

Police Homicide In A Democracy. Kobler, Arthur L.

Minorities As Victims Of Police Shootings: Interpretation Of Racial Disproportionality And Police Use Of Deadly Force. Goldkamp, John S.

Peacekeeping—Police, Prisons And Violence. Toch, Hans.

Police Use Of Deadly Force. Milton, C H et al.

Police Violence As A Function Of Community Characteristics. Kania, Richard and Mackey, Wade C.

POLICE - DEADLY FORCE

The Effects Of Suspect Race And Situation Hazard On Police Officer Shooting Behavior. Inn, A and Wheeler, A C and Sparling, C L.

The Management Of Police Killings. Harring, Sid et al.

Issues In The Study Of Police Use Of Deadly Force. Takagi, Paul.

Shots Fired: An Examination Of New York City Police Firearms Discharges. Fyfe, James Joseph.

Living In Fear In Philadelphia. Walter, Greg.

To What Extent Was Enrique Soto The Creation Of Pedro Juan Soto? Kennedy, William.

Officer Race And Police Shooting. Fyfe, James J.

Race And Extreme Police–Citizen Violence. Fyfe, James J.

A Community Concern: Police Use Of Deadly Force. Brenner, Robert N (comp) and Kravitz, Marjorie (comp).

Dishonor In The Sun: The Violation Of Human Rights, Texas–Style. Lyon, Matthew.

LEAA's Research Solicitation: Police Use Of Deadly Force. Takagi, Paul.

Measuring Homicide By Police Officers. Sherman, Lawrence W and Langworthy, Robert H.

Execution Without Trial: Police Homicide And The Constitution. Sherman, Lawrence W.

Geographic Correlates Of Police Shooting: A Microanalysis. Fyfe, James J.

Police Use Of Deadly Force. Wilson, James Q.

POLICE - INVESTIGATION

Police Encounters With Juveniles. Piliavin, Irving and Briar, Scott.

Arrest: The Decision To Take A Suspect Into Custody. La Fave, Wayne, R.

Black Muslims And The Police. Brown, Lee P.

Interrogations In New Haven: The Impact Of *Miranda*. Wald, Michael et al.

Police Control Of Juveniles. Black, Donald and Reiss Jr, Albert.

Police Discretion And Discriminatory Enforcement. Tierger, Joseph H.

Police Power: A Study Of Provocation. Chevigny, Paul.

City Police. Rubinstein, Jonathan.

Origins Of Narcotic Control. Musto, David F.

The Briar Patch: The People Of The State Of New York V Lumumba Shakur Et Al. Kempton, Murray.

The Glass House Tapes: The Story Of An Agent–Provocateur And The New Police–Intelligence Complex. Tackwood, Louis E and Citizens Research And Investigation Committee.

Police Race Attitudes And Labeling. Rafky, David M.

Cointelpro: The FBI's Secret War On Political Freedom. Blackstone, Nelson.

Street Patrol: The Decision To Stop A Citizen. Bogomolny, Robert.

"Institutional Racism And Crime Clearance" in *Black Perspectives On Crime And The Criminal Justice System*, Woodson, Robert L (ed), 107–122. Peirson, Gwynne.

A Global Terrorist Coalition—Its Incipient Stage. Wolf, John B.

Othello. Volkman, Ernest.

POLICE - SUPPORT FOR

Police Encounters With Juveniles. Piliavin, Irving and Briar, Scott.

A Comment On The Police And The Kerner Report. Lehman, P.

Cops In The Ghetto: A Problem Of The Police System. Levy, Burton.

The Liberal Policeman: A Contradiction In Terms? Vega, W.

Home–Defense And The Police: Black And White Perspectives. Feagin, Joe R.

Police Perceptions Of A Hostile Ghetto: Realism Or Projection. Groves, Eugene and Rossi, Peter.

Police–Community Relations: A Need In Search Of Police Support. Mendelsohn, Robert A.

Support For Civil Liberties And Support For The Police. Block, Richard L.

Fear Of Crime And Fear Of The Police. Block, Richard L.

Ghetto Assessments Of Police Protection And Authority. Hahn, Harlan.

A Study Of Mexican–American Perceptions Of Law Enforcement Policies And Practices In East Los Angeles. Morales, Armando.

Levels Of Acculturation And Of Attitudes Toward Deviance, Criminal Behavior And Police Law Enforcement Practices Among Puerto Ricans In NYC. Cotton, W L.

America's New Anti–Police Sentiment. Odell, B N.

The Black Community: Attitudes Toward Community Problems, Crime And The Police. Knowles, Lyle and Brewer, Jesse.

Black–White Relations Among Police In The United States. Lynch, Gerald.

Why Notify The Police: The Victim's Decision To Notify The Police Of An Assault. Block, Richard L.

Evaluating The Police: A Comparison Of Black Street And Household Respondents. Boggs, Sara L and Galliher, John F.

Importance Of Police Contact In The Formulation Of Youths' Attitudes Toward Police. Rusinko, W T and Johnson, K W and Hornung, C A.

POLICE ABUSES

see also Police Brutality, Police Deadly Force

Racial Factors And Urban Law Enforcement. Kephart, William M.

Prejudice And Discrimination In Law Enforcement. Clowers, Norman L.

Prejudice And Discrimination In Law Enforcement. Clowers, Norman L.

Behind The Shield: Police In Urban Society. Niederhoffer, Arthur.

The Big Blue Line: Police Power Versus Human Rights. Cray, Ed.

The Police And The Public. Reiss Jr, Albert J.

The Self–Inflicted Wound. Graham, Fred P.

Socio–Legal Aspects Of Racially Motivated Police Misconduct. Comment.

The Ghetto Resident's View Of Police Procedures And Their Constitutionality. Mathias, William J.

Police Power: A Study Of Provocation. Chevigny, Paul.

Investigating The FBI. Watters, Pat (ed) and Gillers, Stephen (ed).

The Glass House Tapes: The Story Of An Agent–Provocateur And The New Police–Intelligence Complex. Tackwood, Louis E and Citizens Research And Investigation Committee.

Cointelpro: The FBI's Secret War On Political Freedom. Blackstone, Nelson.

City Liable Under Human Rights Act For Policeman's Racial Abuses. Anonymous.

Dishonor In The Sun: The Violation Of Human Rights, Texas–Style. Lyon, Matthew.

Suing The Police In Federal Court. Note.

Race And The Police: An Early Report On A Change Effort. Fyfe, James J.

Othello. Volkman, Ernest.

POLICE BRUTALITY

Violence And The Police. Westley, William A.

Los Angeles Riot Study, The Perception Of Police Brutality In South Central Los Angeles. Institute Of Government And Public Affairs.

The Big Blue Line: Police Power Versus Human Rights. Cray, Ed.

Police Brutality And Racial Prejudice: A First Close Look. Rinella, Vincent.

Violent Men: An Inquiry Into The Psychology Of Violence. Toch, Hans.

"Police Brutality: Answers To Key Questions" in *Law And Order: Police Encounters*, Lipsky, Michael (ed). Reiss Jr, Albert J.

The Police And The Public. Reiss Jr, Albert J.

Ando Sangrando (I Am Bleeding): A Study Of Mexican American - Police Conflict. Morales, Armando.

Violence And The Police. Pinkney, Alphonso.

Police Repression In America. Joyner, Irving.

Living In Fear In Philadelphia. Walter, Greg.

Mean Beats: Police Brutality In America. Rollins, Thomas M.

Race And Extreme Police–Citizen Violence. Fyfe, James J.

The Criminal Justice System: An Analysis Of Hispanic Issues. Baca, Salvador.

POLICE CORRUPTION

Sir Corner And Joe Smith: A Story Of Vice & Corruption In Chicago. Smith, Joseph.

The Big Blue Line: Police Power Versus Human Rights. Cray, Ed.

Varieties Of Police Behavior: The Management Of Law And Order In Eight Communities. Wilson, James Q.

The Cops Can't Find The Pusher. Christianson, K Scott.

City Police. Rubinstein, Jonathan.

Police Corruption: The System Is The Problem. Brown, William P.

POLICE HIRING AND PROMOTION

Case For The Promotion Of Police Women In The City Of New York. Shpritzer, Felicia.

Negro Police Employment In The Urban South. Rudwick, Elliot M.

A New Concept In Police Recruiting. Perry, Jack.

Minority Recruiting In The New York City Police Department. Hunt Jr, Issac C and Cohen, Bernard.

Minority Hiring And The Police. Margolis, R.

"Police Entry Testing And Minority Employment Implications" in *Police And Law Enforcement*, Curran, J (ed), 313–317. Vanagunas, Stanley.

Minorities In Corrections And Law Enforcement. Chicago State Univ Corrections Program.

POLICE HIRING AND PROMOTION

Police Civil Service Selection Prodecures And New York City—Comparison Of Ethnic Groups. Chaiken, J M and Cohen, Bernard.

Bridgeport Guardians, Inc v Members Of The Bridgeport Civil Service, 345 F Supp 779, US Dist Ct D Conn Jan 29, 1973. Anonymous.

Minority Retention In The New York City Police Department. Cohen, Bernard.

Police Recruitment: How Brown And Black Personnel View It. Gazell, James A.

Psychological View Of Women In Policing. Sherman, Lewis J.

Women In Law Enforcement. Crites, L.

"Minority Recruiting—Denver, Colorado" in *Police–Community Relations Series, V4: Case Studies In Minority Programs.* Platt, R (ed).

Analysis Of The Labor Market For Policemen, 2v. Wolitz, L B.

Project LEMMP (Law Enforcement Minority Manpower Project)—Final Report. National Urban League, Inc.

Women In Policing—A Manual. Abramowitz, A et al.

Alabama's State Police Leads In Black Percentage With 4:5%. Anonymous.

Bridgeport Guardians, Inc v Members Of Civil Service Com'n, 497 F 2d 113 (Conn), US Court Of Appeals, Second Circuit, June 3, 1974. Anonymous.

Los Angeles' Minority Policemen Express Their Concerns. Williford, Stanley O.

Minority Police: How Many Are There? Egerton, John.

The Attitudes Of Non–White Police Personnel Toward Retention. Gazell, James A.

Minority Recruitment Handbook, Revd, (Commission On Peace Officer Stand & Training). Williams, F E.

Minority Recruitment And Retention In The Des Moines Police Department: A Survey Of Opinions. Boettcher, W D.

Minority Recruitment And Retention In The Des Moines Police Department—A Survey Of Opinions. Boettcher, W D.

Police Selection And Career Assessment. Dunnette, M D and Motowidlo, S J.

Changing Status Of Women In Police Professions. Stuart, C G.

Equal Employment Opportunity And Affirmative Action In Law Enforcement Agencies. Jefferson, A M.

Law Enforcement And Affirmative Action. Williams, Samuel L.

Minority Recruiting: The Tucson Police Experience. Grant, R M and Milne, R and White, R.

Recruitment And Promotion Of A Minority Group Into An Established Institution—The Police. Regoli, R M and Jerome, D E.

Manual For The Recruitment Of Minority And Females. Avello, J A and Mendoza, M G.

Minority Recruitment Manual For Ohio Peace Officers Report, 1977. Snarr, R W and Mc Cauley, R P.

New York Cops Talk Back. Alex, Nicholas.

Study Of Problems And Methods Of Police Recruitment From Disadvantaged Minorities. Gazell, James A.

A View Of The Quota System In The San Francisco Police Department. Balzer, A.

Minority Employment In Police Services—A Management Analysis For Police Departments. Moore, L M and Schwartz, J A.

Profile Of A Good Police Officer. Barnabas, B.

Recruitment And Retention Of Minority Race Persons As Police Officers. Van Blaricon, D P.

Special Task Force—Positive Recruitment Of Qualified Minorities. Ronzan, J.

Ten Maxims: Minority Recruitment And Retention. Witt, James and Robinson, Eugene.

Police Personnel Selection Process. Territo, L and Swanson Jr, C R and Chamelin, N C.

Recruitment And Retention Of Females In Law Enforcement Occupations. Dutton, A and Britt, B.

"Women In Policing—Changing Perspectives On The Role" in *Criminal Justice Planning*, Scott, J E And S Dinitz (eds). Breece, C M and Garrett, G R.

Blacks And Women To Be Hired For Louisiana Police–Fire Jobs. Marro, Anthony.

Minorities' Constitutional Rights To Police Department Employment. Rothenberg, S and Barnes, M.

Norwalk Police Battle In Court Over Racial Hiring Issues. Tomasson, Robert E.

Police Are Sued. Anonymous.

Police Recruit Minorities. Anonymous.

St Paul—Police Department—Minority Recruitment Program. Rowan, Richard H and Griffin, James S.

US Charges Los Angeles With Police Hiring Bias. Anonymous.

Blue Coats—Black Skin—The Black Experience In The New York City Police Department Since 1891. Alexander, J I.

Houston: A Validity Study Of Police Officer Selection, Training And Promotion, V3. Jeannerett, P R and Dubin, J A.

Law Enforcement Minority Manpower Project—Final Report. Reynolds, L H.

Impact Of Racial Integration On The Police. Jacobs, James B and Cohen, Jay.

Police Careers For Women. Muro, D P.

Police Selection And Evaluation—Issues And Techniques. Spielberger, C D (ed).

The Impact Of Affirmative Action And Civil Service On American Police Personnel Systems. Locke, Hubert G.

Black Versus White In The Station House. Jones, Robert A.

Enforcement Workshop—Minority Quotas For Police Promotions: A Comment On Detroit Police Officers Association Versus Young. Sherman, Lawrence W.

Minority Police Hiring—Is Cooperation Possible? Saudler, D.

Psychological Examination In Police Selection. Crosby, A.

Race As An Employment Qualification To Meet Police Department Operational Needs. Comment.

Women Police: A Study Of Education, Attitudes, Problems. Martin, C A.

POLICE HISTORY

The Police Control Of The Slave In South Carolina. Henry, Howell M.

Policing The City: Boston, 1822–1885. Lane, Roger.

The Slave Catchers. Campbell, S W.

City Police. Rubinstein, Jonathan.

Indian Law Enforcement History. U S Dept Of Interior, Bureau Of Indian Affairs.

"From Matron To Commanding Officer—Women's Changing Role In Law Enforcement" in *Law Enforcement Bible*, Scanlon, Robert A (ed). Acerra, L.

"Century Of Women In Policing" in *Modern Police Administration*, Schultz, Donald O (ed). Price, B and Gavin, S.

POLICE INVESTIGATION

The Negro Offender: An Urban Research Project. Kephart, William M.

POLICE PATROLMEN

Study Of Role Conflict Among Policemen. Scott, James F.

Job Satisfaction In Policemen And Its Relation To Locus Of Control, Ego Strength And Performance. Munoz, Mona.

Police Recruitment: How Brown And Black Personnel View It. Gazell, James A.

Identifying Responsive Inner–City Policemen. Kelly, Rita Mae and Farber, Martin G.

Personality Patterns Of White, Black, And Mexican American Patrolmen As Measured By The Sixteen Personality Factor Questionaire. Snibbe, H M and Fabricatore, Joseph and Azen, Stanley P.

Race Differences In Police Patrolmen: A Failure To Replicate The Chicago Study. Snibbe, H M et al.

POLICE REVIEW BOARDS

Police Review Boards: An Historical And Critical Analysis. Brown, Lee P.

Handling Complaints Against The Police. Brown, Lee P.

POLICE TRAINING

Humanizing Law Enforcement: A Liberal Approach From A Conservative Stance. Maddocks, Lewis I.

Family Crisis Training: Upgrading The Police While Building A Bridge To The Minority Community. Katz, Myron.

Police Academy Training And Its Effects On Racial Prejudice. Reese, Charles D.

Police And The Behavioral Sciences. Steinberg, J L and Mc Evoy, D W.

POLICING OF MINORITIES

The Police And Minority Groups. Lohman, Joseph D.

Racial Factors And Urban Law Enforcement. Kephart, William M.

Catching The Criminal In Nineteenth–Century South Carolina. Williams, Jack Kenny.

POLICING OF MINORITIES

With His Pistol In His Hand: A Border Ballad And Its Hero. Paredes, Américo.

Police Work And The Negro. Rudwick, Elliot M.

Race Tensions And The Police. Curry, Jesse E and King, G D and Eastman, G.

I Don't Think The Cop Is My Friend. Samuels Gertrude.

The Negro, Prejudice And The Police. Cross, Granville J.

The Texas Rangers. Webb, Walter Prescott.

Cops Unsung Heroes In Racial Tragedy. Lahey, Edwin A.

Minorities And The Police. Bayley, David H and Mendelsohn, Harold.

"Police In The Ghetto" in *Riot Commission, Supplemental Studies*, 103–114. Rossi, Peter et al.

Police And Minority Groups: Toward A Theory Of Negative Contacts. Kuykendall, Jack L.

A Study Of Mexican-American Perceptions Of Law Enforcement Policies And Practices In East Los Angeles. Morales, Armando.

Police And Minority Groups: The Improvement Of Community Relations. Berleman, William C.

"The Police And Minority Groups" in *The Police And The Community*, 257–287. Radelet, Louis A.

"A Guide To Race Relations For Police Officers" in *The Urban Policeman In Transition*, Snibbe, J (ed), 302–340. Mc Entire, Davis and Powers, Robert B.

"Police Deployment Theories And The Mexican-American Community" in *The Urban Policeman In Transition*, Snibbe, J (ed), 341–353. Morales, Armando.

Police Academy Training And Its Effects On Racial Prejudice. Reese, Charles D.

Police Overperception Of Ghetto Hostility. Crawford, T J.

Police And The Black Community. Wintersmith, Robert F.

An Interaction Analysis Of Police–Black Relations. Cross, Stan and Renner, Edward.

Law And Order On The Reservation—A Look At The Indian Police. State Peace Officers Journal.

Los Angeles' Minority Policemen Express Their Concerns. Williford, Stanley O.

Policing A Divided Society. Banton, Michael.

Ghetto Cops. Henderson, Bruce.

Policing The Bronx. Bouza, Anthony.

The Police And Black Separatism: A Problem For Public Policy. Lazin, F A.

Police Operations. Peirson, Gwynne.

"New Directions In Law Enforcement" in *Crime And Its Impact On The Black Community*, Gary, L E And L P Brown (eds), 143–154. Brown, Lee P.

The Hispanic Tide—Some Implications Of Its Continuing Growth. Holman, Ben.

Black Crime: A Police View. Bryce, Harrington J (ed).

Policing In A Free Society. Goldstein, Herman.

"Bridges Over Troubled Waters" in *Black Perspectives On Crime And The Criminal Justice System*, Woodson, Robert L (ed), 79–106. Brown, Lee P.

Law Enforcement On Indian Reservations. Etheridge, D.

An Introductory Study Of Institutional Racism In Police Law Enforcement. Peirson, Gwynne W.

Problem Areas In The Operation Of Tribal Police Programs. National Congress Of American Indians.

Chinatown—No Longer A Cozy Assignment. Wilson, Rob.

The Enforcers. Johnson, Thomas A.

Gunpowder Justice: A Reassessment Of The Texas Rangers (Book Review). Trujillo, Larry D.

POLITICAL PRISONERS *see* Prisoners, Political

POLITICS

Political Justice: The Use Of Legal Procedure For Political Ends. Kirchheimer, Otto.

A Political History Of The Texas Penal System, 1829–1951. Crow, H.

Riot Commission Politics. Lipsky, Michael and Olson, David J.

The Political Economy Of Black Power. Franklin, Raymond.

"Politics, Public Order, And Pluralism" in *Politics Of Local Justice*, Klonski, James R And Robert I Mendelsohn (eds), 238–255. Holden Jr, Matthew.

The Politics Of Riot Commissions: A Collection Of Official Reports And Critical Essays. Platt, Anthony (ed).

Criminal Justice—Law And Politics. Cole, G F.

Justice Denied. Downie Jr, Leonard.

Ghetto Revolts: The Politics Of Violence In American Cities. Feagin, Joe R and Harlan, Alan.

"Black Political Consciousness In Northern State Prisons" in *Potential For Reform Of Criminal Justice*, Jacob, Herbert (ed). Morris, Frank L.

La Causa Politica: A Chicano Politics Reader. Garcia, F Chris.

Politics And Crime. Sylvester Jr, Sawyer F (ed) and Sagarin, Edward (ed).

"Crime And Social Policy: The Politics Of Race" in *Social Research And The Black Community*, Gary, Lawrence E (ed), 112–119. Swan, L Alex.

Race, Sex, And Gangs: Black Crusaders, The Rise And Fall Of Political Gangs. Helmreich, William B.

The Crime Society: Organized Crime And Corruption In America. Ianni, Francis A J and Reuss, Elizabeth.

The Politics Of Corrections: Town–Prison Relations As A Determinant Of Reform. Jacobs, James B.

Commission Politics: The Processing Of Racial Crisis In America. Lipsky, Michael and Olson, David J.

"Crime As A Concern Of Congress" in *Black Crime: A Police View*, Bryce, H J (ed), 21–28. Conyers, John R.

"Crime As A Concern Of City Hall" in *Black Crime: A Police View*, Bryce, H J (ed), 29–36. Jackson, Maynard H.

"Politics In A Biobehavioral Perspective" in *Biology And Crime*, Jeffrey, C R (ed). Kort, Fred and Maxson, Stephen C.

Hispanics In Local Government: A Growing Force. Pachon, Harry P.

POLLS

The Case For Limited Use Of Polls In The Jury Selection Process. Cannito, J A and Becker, K L.

POOR *see* Class

Poverty, Race And Violence. Fishman, J R.

Poverty, Minorities, And Respect For Law. Wright, J Skelly.

Discrimination In Supermarket, Prices And Location In Nashville. Steel, William F.

The Death Penalty: Continuing Threat To America's Poor. Hinds, Lennox S.

POWER

The Origin Of The State. Lowie, R H.

Race, Class, And Power. Mack, Raymond W (ed).

"Madness And Powerlessness" in *Power And Innocence: A Search For The Causes Of Violence*, 19–45. May, Rollo.

How The Government Breaks The Law. Lieberman, Jethro K.

Indian Powerlessness In Minnesota. Westermeyer, Joseph.

Social Problems And Public Policy, V1: Inequality And Justice, A Survey Of Inequalities Of Class, Status, Sex And P. Rainwater Lee (ed).

"Race And Three Forms Of Prisoner Power" in *Contemporary Corrections*, Huff, C (ed), 40–53. Carroll, Leo.

Criminology—Power, Crime And Criminal Law. Galliher, John F and Mc Cartney, James.

Genocide And State Power, 3rd Edition. Horowitz, Irving Louis.

PREDICTION

Predicting Juvenile Delinquency Among Negroes. Kramer, Samuel A.

"Identifying Juvenile Delinquents Among Negroes" in *Identification Of Predelinquents*, Glueck, S (ed), 22–35. Kramer, Samuel A.

"The Prediction Of Performance For Black And For White Police Patrolmen" in *The Urban Policeman In Transition*, Snibbe, J (ed), 66–82. Baehr, Melany E et al.

Impulsive And Premeditated Homicide: An Analysis Of Subsequent Parole Risk Of The Murderer. Heilbrun Jr, Alfred B and Heilbrun, Lynn C and Heilbrun, Kim L.

The Impact Of New Sentencing Laws On State Prison Populations In Pennsylvania; Final Report. Urban Systems Institute.

PREJUDICE

The Bases Of Race Prejudice. Park, Robert E.

Color And Human Nature. Warner, W Lloyd and Junker, Buford H and Adams, Walter A.

The Zoot-Suit Riots. Mc Williams, Carey.

The Nature Of Prejudice. Allport, Gordon W.

Slavery And The Genesis Of American Race Prejudice. Degler, Carl N.

Prejudice Toward Mexican And Negro Americans: A Comparison. Pinkney, Alphonso.

Prejudice And Discrimination In Law Enforcement. Clowers, Norman L.

Nigger: An Autobiography. Gregory, Dick and Lipsyte, Robert.

Prejudice And Discrimination In Law Enforcement. Clowers, Norman L.

The Negro, Prejudice And The Police. Cross, Granville J.

PREJUDICE

Racial And Cultural Minorities: An Analysis Of Prejudice And Discrimination. Simpson, George Eaton and Yinger, I Milton.

On Racial Violence. West, L J.

Effect Of Racial Characteristics Of Investigator On Self–Enumerated Responses To A Negro Prejudice Scale. Summers, G F and Hammonds, A D.

Prejudice, Perception And Penal Judgements. Delk, J L.

Protest And Prejudice. Marx, Gary T (ed).

Police Brutality And Racial Prejudice: A First Close Look. Rinella, Vincent.

The Origins Of Racism. Pinderhughes, C A.

The American Race Problem, Revd Ed By Jitsuichi Masuoka. Reuter, Edward Byron.

White Racism: Its History, Pathology And Practice. Schwartz, Barry N and Disch, Robert and Disch, Barry N.

"The Effects Of Prejudice On Minorities" in *Police–Community Relationships*, Bopp, W (ed), 86–90. Curry, Jesse E and King, Glen D.

Prejudice, Punitiveness And Personality. Snortum, J and Ashear, V.

Are Cops Prejudiced? Rafky, David M and Thibault, Edward and Lynch, Lawrence.

Physical Aggression As A Function Of Racial Prejudice And The Race Of The Target. Genthner, R W and Taylor, S P.

Police Academy Training And Its Effects On Racial Prejudice. Reese, Charles D.

Exploring Racial Prejudice On Voir Dire: Constitutional Requirements And Policy Considerations. Mormino, Susan C.

Antecedents Of Urban Indian Crime. Williams, L E.

Criminal Procedure—Voir Dire—The Right To Question Jurors On Racial Prejudice. Bryson, C B.

Investigating Ethnic Prejudice Among Boys In Residential Treatment. Schaeffer, C und Brown, S.

Personality And Situational Influences On Changes In Prejudice: A Replication Of Cook's Railroad Game In A Prison Setting. Foley, L A.

Voir Dire Of Jurors: Constitutional Limits To The Right Of Inquiry Into Prejudice. Gaba, J M.

The Case For Limited Use Of Polls In The Jury Selection Process. Cannito, J A and Becker, K L.

PRESIDENT'S CRIME COMMISSION

Race Of Victim And Of Offender For Rape, Robbery And Assault And Battery Offenses Known To The Police: Report To The Pres Crime Commission. Reiss Jr, Albert J.

"Riots And Crime—Historical Background" in *Task Force Report—Crime And Its Impact—An Assessment*, 116–122. President's Comm On Law Enforcement & Adm Of Justice.

Task Force Report: The Courts. President's Comm On Law Enforcement & Adm Of Justice.

Task Force Report: Drunkenness. President's Comm On Law Enforcement & Adm Of Justice.

Task Force Report: Juvenile Delinquency And Youth Crime. President's Comm On Law Enforcement & Adm Of Justice.

Task Force Report: Narcotics And Drugs. President's Comm On Law Enforcement & Adm Of Justice.

Task Force Report: Organized Crime. President's Comm On Law Enforcement & Adm Of Justice.

Task Force Report: The Police. President's Comm On Law Enforcement & Adm Of Justice.

Task Force Report: Corrections. President's Comm On Law Enforcement & Adm Of Justice.

Task Force Report: Crime And Its Impact—An Assessment. President's Comm On Law Enforcement & Adm Of Justice.

Task Force Report: Science And Technology. President's Comm On Law Enforcement & Adm Of Justice.

The Challenge Of Crime In A Free Society. President's Comm On Law Enforcement & Adm Of Justice.

PRIOR OFFENSE

Prior Offense As A Self–Fulfilling Prophecy. Farrell, Ronald A and Swigert, Victoria Lynn.

PRISON

see also Institutionalization

PRISON, ABOLITION OF

Break Down The Walls. Martin, John Bartlow.

Prison Reform: In Whose Interest? Jordan, Samuel.

"A View Of Prisons" in *The Administration Of Criminal Justice: A View From Black America*, Brown, Lee P (ed). Boone, John O.

Instead Of Prisons: A Handbook For Abolitionists. Knopp, Fay Honey et al.

PRISON, COPING IN

Human Behavior In A Concentration Camp. Cohen, Elie A.

The Society Of Captives: A Study Of A Maximum Security Prison. Sykes, Gresham M.

Inside The World's Toughest Prison. Ragen, Joseph and Finston, Charles.

Women's Prison: Sex And Social Structure. Ward, David A and Kassenbaum, Gene G.

Sexual Assaults In The Philadelphia Prison System And Sheriff's Vans. Davis, A J.

Soledad Brother: The Prison Letters Of George Jackson. Jackson, George.

"Prisoner Personality Development In Prison/On Becoming" in *prisons, Protest, And Politics*, Atkins, B (ed), 105–111. Cleaver, Eldridge.

Prison. Berry, Leonard J.

Jail House Blues: Studies Of Suicidal Behavior In Jail And Prison. Danto, Bruce L (ed).

An Assessment Of Dogmatism Among Adult Inmates In A State Correctional Institution In New Jersey. Carden, Francis Xavier.

Terror In The Prisons. Weiss, Carl and Friar, David James.

Impact Of Incarceration On The Black Inmate. Adair, A V et al.

In Prison: A Contagion Of Suicide. Christianson, Scott.

Erroneous Zone. Rice, David L.

In Constant Fear: The Brutal Story Of Life Within The Walls Of The Notorious Walpole State Prison, As Told To James B Shuman. Remick, Peter.

Men In Crisis: Human Breakdowns In Prison. Toch, Hans et al.

Short Eyes. Piñero, Miguel.

Bound And Free: The Poetry Of Warriors Behind Bars. Black Prisoners Of Florida State Prison, Starke.

My Rhythm Flows From A Different Beat. Lucas, Henry N.

"Race And Three Forms Of Prisoner Power" in *Contemporary Corrections*, Huff, C (ed), 40–53. Carroll, Leo.

Animal Factory. Bunker, Edward.

Culture And Crisis In Confinement. Johnson, Robert.

Greenhaven Diary. Conway, Edward.

Killing Time: Life In The Arkansas Penitentiary. Jackson, Bruce.

Living In Prison: The Ecology Of Survival. Toch, Hans.

Characteristics Of State Prisoners Who Demonstrate Severe Adjustment Problems. Adams, T C.

Humanitarian Reform And Biracial Sexual Assault In A Maximum Security Prison. Carroll, Leo.

A Prison And A Prisoner. Sheehan, Susan.

Dealing With Long–Term Confinement: Adaptive Strategies And Perspectives Among Long–Term Prisoners. Flanagan, Timothy J.

Prison Sexual Violence. Lockwood, Daniel.

PRISON - IMPACT OF

Human Behavior In A Concentration Camp. Cohen, Elie A.

The Social Functions Of A Prison. Galtung, Johan.

Mexico's Tres Marias Penal Colony. Jewell, Donald P.

Women Prisoners And Their Families. Zalba, S.

Solitudes Crowded With Loneliness. Kaufman, Bob.

An Exploratory Study Of The Effects Of Incarceration On The Families Of Negro Inmates Of A Medium–Security Prison. Schneller, Donald P.

Getting Busted: Personal Experiences Of Arrest, Trial And Prison. Firestone, Ross (ed).

Prisonization And Self Concept. Kennedy, Will Charles.

The Consequences Of Familial Separation For Chicano Inmates (School Of Ed). Gonzales, Josephine.

"Prisoner Personality Development In Prison/On Becoming" in *prisons, Protest, And Politics*, Atkins, B (ed), 105–111. Cleaver, Eldridge.

Explorations In Inmate–Family Relationships, Research Report No 46. Holt, Norman and Miller, Donald.

Maximum Security: Letters From California's Prisons. Pell, Eve (ed).

Prison. Berry, Leonard J.

The Black Family And The Prisons. Spain, Johnny.

"The Psychological Power And Pathology Of Imprisonment" in *Behavior Disorders: Perspectives And Trends*, Milton, O And R G Wahler (eds). Banks, W Curtis.

The Sexual Segregation Of American Prisoners. Note.

PRISON - IMPACT OF

Families And Friends Of Men In Prison: The Uncertain Relationship. Brodsky, Stanley L.

Impact Of Incarceration On The Black Inmate. Adair, A V et al.

The Dangerousness Of Imprisonment. Jones, David A.

Race And The Father–Son Connection: The Conditional Relevance Of Father Absence For The Orientations And Identities Of Adolescent Boys. Hunt, Larry L and Hunt, Janet G.

Some Social And Psychological Effects Of Incarceration On The Families Of Negro Prisoners. Schneller, Donald P.

The Prison Inmate As Victim. Drapkin, Israel.

Children Of Imprisoned Fathers. Sack, W H.

"Children Of Incarcerated Mothers" in *Child Development*, Green, R And T Yawkey (eds). La Point, Velma.

Crowded Prisons—A Review Of Psychological And Environmental Effects. Clements, C B.

Death Row. Jackson, Bruce and Christian, Diane.

PRISON CONSTRUCTION

The New Red Barn: A Critical Look At The Modern American Prison. Nagel, William G.

The System Propagates Crime. Jordan Jr, Vernon E.

Federal Prison Construction: Alternative Approaches. Congressional Budget Office.

New Jersey Correctional Master Plan. New Jersey Dept Of Corrections.

Prison Population And Policy Choices: V1 & 3. Rutherford, Andrew et al.

"Prison Construction Moratorium" in *Black Perspectives On Crime And The Criminal Justice System*, Woodson, Robert L (ed), 123–142. Boone, John O.

On Behalf Of A Moratorium On Prison Construction. Nagel, William G.

The Numbers Game. Miller, Marc.

Overcrowding In Texas Prisons, Special Legislative Report No 43. Texas House Of Representatives.

PRISON DISTURBANCES

see also Riots

Break Down The Walls. Martin, John Bartlow.

Behind The Prison Riots. Mac Cormick, Austin H.

Violence Behind Bars. Fox, Vernon.

A Social–Psychological Analysis Of Prison Riots: An Hypothesis. Hartung, Frank E and Floch, Maurice.

The Riot. Elli, Frank.

Causes, Preventive Measures And Methods Of Controlling Riots And Disturbances In Correctional Institutions. American Correctional Association.

Racism In Federal Prison. Wessner, Jim.

Using Racism At San Quentin. Minton Jr, Robert J and Rice, Stephen.

My Cure For Prison Riots: End Prison Racism. Moore, Winston E.

"Can We Avoid Riots In Prisons If We Fail To Eradicate Racism On The Outside" in *Proc Of 7th Annual Interagency Workshop*, 144–161. Higginbotham Jr, A Leon.

Attica Diary. Coons, William R.

Attica: My Story. Oswald, Russell G.

Attica: The Official Report Of The New York State Special Commission On Attica, [McKay Commission]. New York State Special Commission On Attica.

Racial Violence At San Quentin Prison/War Behind Walls. Bunker, Edward.

War Behind Walls. Bunker, Edward.

No Beast So Fierce. Bunker, Edward.

Peaceful Resolution Of Prison Conflict. National Council On Crime And Delinquency.

The Prosaic Sources Of Prison Violence. Mattick, Hans.

Terror In The Prisons. Weiss, Carl and Friar, David James.

In Prison: A Contagion Of Suicide. Christianson, Scott.

Men In Crisis: Human Breakdowns In Prison. Toch, Hans et al.

Stratification And Conflict Among Prison Inmates. Jacobs, James B.

Break De Chains Of Legalized Slavery. Anonymous.

"Dealing With Prison Violence" in *Prison Violence*, Cohen, Albert K; George F Cole, And Robert G Bailey (eds). Sumner, George W.

"The Organization Of Prison Violence" in *Prison Violence*, Cohen, Albert K; George F Cole, And Robert G Bailey (eds). Park, James W L.

Attica In 1976: The Lesson Not Learned. Christianson, Scott.

Culture And Crisis In Confinement. Johnson, Robert.

Peacekeeping—Police, Prisons And Violence. Toch, Hans.

Prison Homicide. Sylvester, Sawyer F and Reed, John P and Nelson, David P.

Stateville: The Penitentiary In Mass Society. Jacobs, James B.

Inside The Mexican Mafia. Hammarley, John.

Violence And Victimization Within A State Prison System. Fuller, Dan A and Orsagh, Thomas.

Riots And Acts Of Violence In The Penitentiaries: What Can We Learn? Chocla, M A.

Crowded Prisons—A Review Of Psychological And Environmental Effects. Clements, C B.

Prison Sexual Violence. Lockwood, Daniel.

Prisons In Turmoil. Irwin, John.

Report Of The Attorney General On The February 2 And 3, 1980 Riot At The Penitentiary Of New Mexico: Part 2. New Mexico Attorney General.

Report Of The Attorney General On The February 2 And 3, 1980 Riot At The Penitentiary Of New Mexico: Part 1. New Mexico Attorney General.

New Mexico: The Anatomy Of A Riot. Serrill, Michael S and Katel, Peter.

Prison Perspective (Santa Fe Prison Riot). Anonymous.

The Santa Fe Prison Riots: 'The Flower Of The Dragon'. Mandel, Jerry.

PRISON GUARDS

Projections On The Supply Of Minorities In Corrections–Related Occupations, 1975–1980. Beard, Eugene.

Summaries Of Studies On The Recruitment And Retention Of Minority Correctional Employees. Beard, Eugene.

The Society Of Captives: A Study Of A Maximum Security Prison. Sykes, Gresham M.

An Examination Of The Accuracy And Relevance Of Staff Perception Of The Inmate In The Correctional Institution. Hazelrigg, Lawrence E.

Staff Conceptions Of Inmate Characteristics: A Comparison Of Treatment And Custodial Staffs At Two Differing Institutions. Brown, Barry S et al.

Interpersonal Dynamics In A Simulated Prison. Haney, Craig and Banks, Curtis and Zimbardo, Philip.

Teaching Corrections Law To Corrections Personnel. Statsky, William P.

Hacks, Blacks And Cons: Race Relations In A Maximum Security Prison. Carroll, Leo.

Race Of Inmate, Race Of Officer, And Disciplinary Proceedings At A Federal Correctional Institution. Boyd, Jeffrey L.

Race Relations Training With Correctional Officers. Wittmer, J and Lanier, J E and Parker, M.

Stateville: The Penitentiary In Mass Society. Jacobs, James B.

Drop–Outs And Rejects: An Analysis Of The Prison Guard's Revolving Door. Grear, Mary P and Jacobs, James B.

Alabama Bound: Forty–Five Years Inside A Prison System. March, Ray A.

Balancing Inmates' Rights To Privacy With Equal Employment For Prison Guards. Reisner, S L.

Integrating The Keepers: A Comparison Of Black And White Prison Guards In Illinois. Jacobs, James B and Kraft, Larry J.

Women As Probation Parole, And Correctional Officers In The Criminal Justice Field—A Selected Bibliography. Martin, C A.

Should Women Guards Work In Prisons For Men? Potter, Joan.

PRISON INFRACTIONS

Pilot Study: Age, Race And Recidivism As Factors In Prison Infractions. Johnson, Elmer H.

Race Of Inmate, Race Of Officer, And Disciplinary Proceedings At A Federal Correctional Institution. Boyd, Jeffrey L.

Dealing With Long–Term Confinement: Adaptive Strategies And Perspectives Among Long–Term Prisoners. Flanagan, Timothy J.

PRISON LABOR

Penal Servitude. Whitin, E Stagg.

A History Of Penal Methods. Ives, George.

"Work And Law Observance In The Histories Of Men In Sing–Sing Prison" in *Report On The Causes Of Crime*, V1, 193–255,315–320. Kleeck, Mary V.

American Prisons: A Study In American Social History. Mc Kelvey, Blake.

A Political History Of The Texas Penal System, 1829–1951. Crow, H.

The Convict–Lease System In Florida, 1866–1923. Carper, Noel Gordon.

Report On The Penitentiaries Of The United States, Orig Pub 1835. Crawford, William.

PRISON LABOR

The Historical Background And Present Status Of The County Chain Gang In South Carolina. Brailsford, Daniel T.

Long Line Rider: The Story Of Cummins Prison Farm. Keith, K Wymand.

Politics And Punishment: The History Of The Louisiana State Penal System. Carleton, Mark T.

Wake Up Dead Man: Afro—American Worksongs From Texas Prisons. Jackson, Bruce (ed).

Kind And Usual Punishment: The Prison Business. Mitford, Jessica.

Organizing Behind Bars. Anonymous.

The Labor Law Problems Of The Prisoner. Clark, L and Parker, G.

Killing Time: Life In The Arkansas Penitentiary. Jackson, Bruce.

Prison Plantation: The Story Of Angola. Vodicka, John.

PRISON PROGRAM

Prisons: Instruments Of Law Enforcement Or Social Welfare? Jacobs, James B and Steele, Eric H.

PRISON PROGRAMS

"The Minority Perspective And The 1980 NIC Program". Castro, Agenor L.

Patterns Of Drug Abuse Epidemiology In Prisoners. Edmundson, Walter F et al.

Racial Issues In Corrections: Cultural Awareness—How To Achieve It. Fox, Vernon.

Rights Of Spanish Speaking Minorities. Nuñez, Luis.

Jail House Blues: Studies Of Suicidal Behavior In Jail And Prison. Danto, Bruce L (ed).

The New Red Barn: A Critical Look At The Modern American Prison. Nagel, William G.

Group Counseling For Offenders. Pew, Miriam L and Speer, David C and Williams, James.

Ethnic Self—Help Groups In Prison And On Parole. Burdman, Milton.

Health Care In Prisons. Pogue Jr, Frank.

"Ethical Issues In Research/Experimentation In Prison" in *House Judicary Comm Hearings On Prison Inmates In Medical Research.* Swan, L Alex.

Hispanic English Language Development In Prison. Bruno, N J and Orris Jr, J V and Gatje, C T.

A Close Look At The Hispanic Inmates And Methods Of Meeting Their Needs. Castro, Agenor L.

The Latino Prisoners In The US—Managing Effective Participation. Mc Collum, Sylvia.

The Muslims Are No Longer An Unknown Quantity. Butler, Keith.

Program For Women Offenders—How To Start, Fund, Maintain. Female Offenders Program Of Western Pennsylvania, Inc.

Bilingualism In Corrections: National Hispanic Conference On Law Enforcement And Criminal Justice. Castro, Agenor L.

Exploring The Re—Entry And Support Services For Hispanic Offenders, Natnl Hispanic Con L Enf, & CJ. Smith, Monica Herrera.

Mental Health And Black Offenders. Owens, Charles E.

PRISON REFORM

Accomplices To The Crime. Murton, Tom.

If They Come In The Morning: Voices Of Resistance. Davis, Angela Y et al.

Prison Reform: In Whose Interest? Jordan, Samuel.

The Prison: Voices From The Inside. Chang, Dae H (ed) and Armstrong, Warren B (ed).

Prison Reform In Social Perspective. Vogel, Richard.

Prisons: Instruments Of Law Enforcement Or Social Welfare? Jacobs, James B and Steele, Eric H.

Instead Of Prisons: A Handbook For Abolitionists. Knopp, Fay Honey et al.

Attica In 1976: The Lesson Not Learned. Christianson, Scott.

Prison Reform And Indians. Keller, C.

The Politics Of Corrections: Town—Prison Relations As A Determinant Of Reform. Jacobs, James B.

Report Of The Task Force Investigation Allegations Of Discriminatory Practices At The Joliet And Stateville Correctional Centers. Illinois Corrections Department.

Still Life: Inside Southern Prisons. Institute For Southern Studies.

Report Of The Attorney General On The February 2 And 3, 1980 Riot At The Penitentiary Of New Mexico: Part 2. New Mexico Attorney General.

PRISON SUBCULTURES

The Society Of Captives: A Study Of A Maximum Security Prison. Sykes, Gresham M.

The Vocabulary Of Race Relations In A Prison. Kantrowitz, N.

Hacks, Blacks And Cons: Race Relations In A Maximum Security Prison. Carroll, Leo.

Impact Of Incarceration On The Black Inmate. Adair, A V et al.

Street Gangs Behind Bars. Jacobs, James B.

Racial—Ethnic Identification In Prisons: 'Right On From The Inside'. Denfeld, D and Hopkins, Andrew.

Stratification And Conflict Among Prison Inmates. Jacobs, James B.

Prisoner Subcultures. Bowker, Lee H.

Stateville: The Penitentiary In Mass Society. Jacobs, James B.

"Race Relations And The Prisoner Subculture" in *Crime And Justice: An Annual Review Of Research,* Morris, N And M Tonry (eds). Jacobs, James B.

At Stateville, The Calm Is Tense. Krajick, Kevin.

PRISON WARDENS

Summaries Of Studies On The Recruitment And Retention Of Minority Correctional Employees. Beard, Eugene.

Inside The World's Toughest Prison. Ragen, Joseph and Finston, Charles.

PRISONERS, POLITICAL

The Crime Of Martin Sostre. Copeland, Vincent.

If They Come In The Morning: Voices Of Resistance. Davis, Angela Y et al.

A Black View Of Prison. Aswadu, Ahmad Ali.

Prison Or Slavery. Kasirika, Kaidi (Kenneth Divans) and Muntu, Maharibi (larry M West).

Prison Reform: In Whose Interest? Jordan, Samuel.

Who Is A Black Political Prisoner? Redenour, Ron.

Blood In My Eye. Jackson, George.

Ruchell Magee: Slave Rebel. Ruchell Magee Committee For Black Prisoners.

We Are All Prisoners Of War. Ahmad, Muhammad.

"Black Political Consciousness In Northern State Prisons" in *Potential For Reform Of Criminal Justice,* Jacob, Herbert (ed). Morris, Frank L.

Concepts Of Political Prisonerhood. Child, Richard.

Racism, Prisons, And Prisoners' Rights. Reasons, Charles E.

Rev Ben Chavis And The Wilmington Ten—A Fact Sheet. Anonymous.

The Political Prisoner Syndrome. Brody, Stuart A.

The War Model In Criminal Justice: No Substitute For Victory. Christianson, Scott.

The Morning Breaks: The Trial Of Angela Davis. Aptheker, Bettina.

Political And Lumpen Prisoners, The Question Of Compliance, And Socioliterary Investigation. Stratman, David V.

The Struggle Of Ben Chavis And The Wilmington 10. Davis, Angela Y.

Illusions Of Justice: Human Rights Violations In The United States. Hinds, Lennox S.

The Innocence Of Joan Little. Reston Jr, James.

"The San Quentin Six Case: Perspective And Analysis" in *Punishment And Penal Discipline,* Platt, Tony And Paul Takagi (eds), 165—175. Wald, Karen.

PRISONERS, WOMEN

Lady Sings The Blues, By Billie Holiday. Fagan, Eleanora and Dufty, William F.

Women Prisoners And Their Families. Zalba, S.

Women's Prison: Sex And Social Structure. Ward, David A and Kassenbasum, Gene G.

Society Of Women: A Study Of A Women's Prison. Giallombardo, R.

Women In Prison. Burkhart, Kathryn Watterson.

The Morning Breaks: The Trial Of Angela Davis. Aptheker, Bettina.

Break De Chains Of Legalized Slavery. Anonymous.

Female Offender Workshop Guide, Female Offender Resource Center. American Bar Association.

The Social System Of A Medium Security Women's Prison. Spencer, Elousie J.

Why Punish The Children: A Study Of Children Of Women Prisoners. Mc Gowan, Brenda G and Blumenthal, Karen L.

Women, Crime, And The Criminal Justice System. Bowker, Lee H and Chesney, Meda and Pollock, Joy.

Women's Jail—Pretrial And Post-Conviction Alternatives—A Report On Women Arrested In San Francisco. Bresler, L and Leonard, D.

"Children Of Incarcerated Mothers" in *Child Development,* Green, R And T Yawkey (eds). La Point, Velma.

"The Effect Of Race On Sentence" in *Theory And Research In Criminal Justice,* Conley, J A (ed). Foley, Linda and Rasch, Christine E.

PRISONERS, WOMEN

Program For Women Offenders—How To Start, Fund, Maintain. Female Offenders Program Of Western Pennsylvania, Inc.

The Innocence Of Joan Little. Reston Jr, James.

Women In The Criminal Justice System. Feinman, C.

Women, Crime, And Justice. Datesman, Susan K (ed) and Scarpitti, Frank R (ed).

PRISONERS OF WAR

We Are All Prisoners Of War. Ahmad, Muhammad.

Imprisoned In America: Prison Communications 1776 To Attica. Philip, Cynthia Owen (ed).

PRISONERS RIGHTS

Penal Servitude. Whitin, E Stagg.

Comment: Black Muslims In Prison—Of Muslim Rites And Constitutional Rights. Anonymous.

The Legal Challenge To Corrections: Implications For Manpower And Training. Cohen, Fred.

The Crime Of Martin Sostre. Copeland, Vincent.

Inside: Prison American Style. Minton Jr, Robert J (ed).

Establishing The Rule Of Law In Prisons: A Manual For Prisoners' Rights Litigation. Turner, William Bennett.

Fascism At Soledad. Rollins, Clifford (Jabali).

Prison Reform: In Whose Interest? Jordan, Samuel.

The Black Prisoner As Victim. Burns, Haywood.

A Bill Of No Rights: Attica And The American Prison System. Badillo, Herman and Haynes, Milton.

The Shame Of The Prisons. Bagdikian, Ben and Dash, Leon.

A Note On Sostre V McGinnis. Schwartz, Herman.

Long v Harris, 332 F Supp 262, (Kansas), US District Court D Kansas: October 6, 1971. Anonymous.

Rights Of Spanish Speaking Minorities. Nuñez, Luis.

The Prison As A Lawless Agency. Greenberg, David F and Stender, Fay.

After Conviction: A Review Of The American Correctional System. Goldfarb, Ronald L and Singer, Linda R.

The Brothers Of Attica. Clark, Richard X.

Clark et al v Wolff, 347 F Supp 887, (Nebraska), US District Court D Nebraska: May 24, 1972, 1972. Anonymous.

Enforcing The Constitutional Rights Of Prisoners. Singer, Linda R.

The Sexual Segregation Of American Prisoners. Note.

Kind And Usual Punishment: The Prison Business. Mitford, Jessica.

Ethnic Group Members And The Correctional System: A Question Of Human Rights. Dandurand, Yvon.

Racism, Prisons, And Prisoners' Rights. Reasons, Charles E.

Jails: The Ultimate Ghetto. Goldfarb, Ronald L.

The Dangerousness Of Imprisonment. Jones, David A.

Teterud v Gilliam, 385 F Supp 153, (Iowa), US District Court SD Iowa, CD November 20, 1974. Anonymous.

The Labor Law Problems Of The Prisoner. Clark, L and Parker, G.

Meeting The Special Needs Of Hispanic Inmates. Castro, Agenor L.

Reform Without Change: The Future Of Prisoners' Rights. Bronstein, Alvin J.

A Close Look At The Hispanic Inmates And Methods Of Meeting Their Needs. Castro, Agenor L.

Balancing Inmates' Rights To Privacy With Equal Employment For Prison Guards. Reisner, S L.

Corrections Law Developments: Prison Labor And Unionization—Legal Developments. Christianson, Scott.

Mississippi Has Come A Long Way, But It Had A Long Way To Come. Gettinger, Steve.

When Prisoners Sue: A Study Of Prisoner Section 1983 Suits In The Federal Courts. Turner, William Bennett.

Sex Discrimination In Prison Employment: The Bona Fide Occupational Qualification And Prisoners' Privacy Rights. Tharnish, D M.

PRISONERS UNIONS

Organizing Behind Bars. Anonymous.

Corrections Law Developments: Prison Labor And Unionization—Legal Developments. Christianson, Scott.

PRISONS, FEDERAL

The Negro Federal Offender. Debro, Julius.

Racism In Federal Prison. Wessner, Jim.

Caged. Bagdikian, Ben.

In Prison: Sometime Federal Prisoner 21669. O' Hare, Kate Richards.

Federal Prison Construction: Alternative Approaches. Congressional Budget Office.

Prisoners In State And Federal Institutions On December 31, 1976. U S Dept Of Justice, LEAA, NCJISS.

Prisoners In State And Federal Institutions On December 31, 1977. U S Dept Of Justice, LEAA, NCJISS.

Prisoners In State And Federal Institutions On December 31, 1978: National Prisoner Statistics Bulletin SD–NPS–PSF–6. U S Dept Of Justice, Bureau Of Justice Statistics.

PROBATION

Care Of The Negro Delinquent. Washington, Forrester B.

Negro Delinquent. Chivers, W R.

Measuring Delinquency: A Study Of Probation Department Referrals. Eaton, Joseph W.

Criteria For The Probation Officer's Recommendations To The Juvenile Court Judge. Cohn, Y.

Sourcebook On Probation, Parole And Pardons, 3rd Ed. Newman, Charles L.

Probation Supervision Of The Black Offender. Breer, William M.

"Understanding Probation And Parole" in *The Administration Of Criminal Justice: A View From Black America,* Brown, Lee P (ed), 48–61. Mc Connell, Leonard R.

Violent Crime Indices Among Community–Retained Delinquents. Andrew, J M.

Early Release From Incarceration: Race As A Factor In The Use Of Shock Probation. Peterson, David M and Friday, Paul.

Corrections: An Issues Approach. Schwartz, Martin D (ed) and Clear, Todd R (ed) and Travis I I I, Lawrence F (ed).

Women As Probation Parole, And Correctional Officers In The Criminal Justice Field—A Selected Bibliography. Martin, C A.

PROFESSIONALISM

Police Academy Training And Its Effects On Racial Prejudice. Reese, Charles D.

Teaching Corrections Law To Corrections Personnel. Statsky, William P.

The Police And Higher Education: The Challenge Of The Times. Brown, Lee P.

PROHIBITION

Prohibition And The Negro. Washington, Booker T.

PROPORTIONALITY

Eighth Amendment Proportionality. Clapp, Randy.

Disproportionality In Sentences Of Imprisonment. Anonymous.

Corrections Law Developments: Racial Discrimination And Prison Confinement—A Follow–Up. Christianson, Scott.

Corrections Law Developments: Legal Implications Of Racially Disproportionate Incarceration Rates. Christianson, Scott.

PROSECUTION

Conviction: The Determination Of Guilt Or Innocence Without Trial. Newman, Donald J.

Guidelines For Prosecuting Criminal Cases During Civil Disorders. National District Attorney's Association.

The Administration Of Rape Cases In The City Of Baltimore And The State Of Maryland. Howard, Joseph C.

Discrimination Against Negroes In The Adminstration Of Criminal Law In Missouri. Gerard, Jules B and Terry Jr, T Rankin.

Crime And Law Enforcement In The Colony Of New York, 1691–1776. Greenberg, Douglas S.

Justice And The American Indian, V5: Federal Prosecution Of Crimes Commited On Indian Reservations. Stewart Jr, L G.

Patterns Of Criminal Prosecution In Eighteenth–Century New York. Greenberg, Douglas S.

The 'Black Shift' Phenomenon In Criminal Justice. Adams, Stuart.

Alaska Felony Sentencing Patterns: A Multivariate Statistical Analysis (1974–1976), Preliminary Report. Alaska Judicial Council.

Judicial Council Findings Regarding Possible Racial Impact In Sentencing. Alaska Judicial Council.

Plea Bargaining—An Annotated Bibliography. Markowtiz, J.

Effects Of Race On Plea Bargaining Decisions. Horney, Julie.

PROSECUTORS

Memo For D A. Lake, Eleanor.

Conviction: The Determination Of Guilt Or Innocence Without Trial. Newman, Donald J.

Mob Violence And The Prosecuting Attorney. Karton, Robert.

PROSECUTORS

Black Judges, Police—But Few Prosecutors. Moore, A.

Black Justice Under White Law—Criminal Prosecutions Of Blacks In Antebellum South Carolina. Hindus, Michael Stephen.

Prosecutor's Exercise Of Peremptory Challenge To Exclude Non–White Jurors: A Common Law Privilege In Conflict With Equal Protection Clause. Comment.

Racial Discrimination In Jury Selection: *United States V Robinson*. Soja, Thomas.

PROSTITUTION

Sir Corner And Joe Smith: A Story Of Vice & Corruption In Chicago. Smith, Joseph.

Howard Street. Heard, Nathan C.

The Lively Commerce: Prostitution In The United States. Winick, Charles and Kinsie, Paul M.

PROTEST

Diary Of A Sit–In. Proudfoot, Merrill.

The Protest Movement And The Law. Marshall, Burke.

Protest And Prejudice. Marx, Gary T (ed).

Deprivation, Mobility, And Orientation Toward Protest Of The Urban Poor. Bowen, Donald Et Al.

Racial Disturbances As Collective Protest. Lang, Kurt and Lang, G.

The Public Perception Of Protest. Turner, Ralph.

The Puerto Ricans: Protest Or Submission. Maldonado– Denis, Manuel.

The Public Perception Of The Watts Riot As Social Protest. Jefferies, Vincent and Turner, R H and Morris, R T.

Symbolism In A 'Protest Psychosis'. Bromberg, Walter and Simon, Frank and Pasto, Tarmo A.

Negro Demonstrations And The Law: Danville As A Test Case. Ely Jr, James W.

PSYCHIATRIC HOSPITALIZATION

Some Effects Of A White Institution On Black Psychiatric Outpatients. Krebs, R L.

PSYCHIATRY

Racism And Psychiatry. Thomas, Alexander and Sillen, Samuel.

"The Future Of Psychiatric Criminology" in *Biology And Crime*, Jeffrey, C R (ed). Halleck, Seymour.

PSYCHOLOGICAL EXPERIMENTATION

Rosenzweig Picture—Frustration Study Results With Minority Group Juvenile Delinquents. Norman, Ralph D and Kleinfeld, Gerald J.

Variables In Interracial Aggression Anonymity, Expected Retaliation, And A Riot. Donnerstein, Edward et al.

PSYCHOLOGISTS

Institutional Racism And The American Psychological Association. Sawyer, Jack and Senn, David J.

The System–Maintenance Role Of The White Psychologist. Thomas, Charles W.

PSYCHOLOGY

Black Psychology. Jones, Reginald L (ed).

Notes On White And Black Psychology. Gordon, Thomas.

Criminal's Image Of The City. Carter, R I and Hill, K Q.

PSYCHOPATHOLOGY

Young Offenders: Psychopathology And Social Factors. London, N J and Myers, J K.

Life History Research In Psychopathology, V2. Roff, M (ed) and Robins, Lee N (ed) and Pollack, M (ed).

PSYCHOSIS

A Case Of A 'Psychotic' Navaho Indian Male. Jewell, Donald P.

Symbolism In A 'Protest Psychosis'. Bromberg, Walter and Simon, Frank and Pasto, Tarmo A.

PUBLIC OPINION

Los Angeles Riot Study, The Perception Of Police Brutality In South Central Los Angeles. Institute Of Government And Public Affairs.

Effects Of Racial Violence On Attitudes In The Negro Community. Justice, Blair.

The Fear Of Crime. Harris, Richard.

"Racial Attitudes In Fifteen American Cities" in *Riot Commission, Supplemental Studies*, 1–67. Campbell, A and Schuman, Howard.

Negro Opinions In Three Riot Cities. Mc Cord, William and Howard, John.

The Public Perception Of Protest. Turner, Ralph.

Home–Defense And The Police: Black And White Perspectives. Feagin, Joe R.

Support For Civil Liberties And Support For The Police. Block, Richard L.

'Law And Order' And The Criminal Justice System. Motley, Constance Baker.

Crime: A Common Concern. Joyner, Irving and Scott, Elsie K.

Public Opinion On Criminal And Legal Sanctions: An Examination Of Two Conceptual Models. Thomas, Charles and Cage, Robin J and Foster, Samuel C.

Public Saftey: Crime Is Up, But What About Punishment? Seidman, David.

Changing Attitudes Toward Capital Punishment. Rankin, J H.

The Case For Limited Use Of Polls In The Jury Selection Process. Cannito, J A and Becker, K L.

The Figgie Report On Fear Of Crime: America Afraid, Part 1, The General Public. A– T– O, Inc.

PUERTO RICANS *see* Hispanics

PUERTO RICO

Race Relations In Puerto Rico And The Virgin Islands. Williams, Eric.

The Morality Of Race Mixing In Puerto Rico. Rogler, C C.

Personal Crimes In Puerto Rico. Toro– Calder, Jaime.

Up From Puerto Rico. Padilla, Elena.

La Vida: A Puerto Rican Family In The Culture Of Poverty—San Juan And New York. Lewis, Oscar.

A Socio–Cultural And Socio–Legal Analysis Of Juvenile Delinquency In Puerto Rico. Kupperstein, Lenore R and Toro– Calder, Jaime.

The Puerto Ricans: Protest Or Submission. Maldonado– Denis, Manuel.

Puerto Rican Americans: The Meaning Of Migration To The Mainland. Fitzpatrick, Joseph P.

Puerto Rico And The Puerto Ricans: A Study Of Puerto Rican History And Immigration To The United States. Hauberg, Clifford A.

Puertoriquens In US—Impact Of Double–Discrimination. King, L M.

Delinquents And Nondelinquents In The Puerto Rican Slum Culture. Ferracuti, Franco and Dinitz, Simon and De Brenes, E Acosta.

Citizenship And The American Empire: Notes On The Legislative History Of The United States Citizenship Of Puerto Ricans. Cabranes, Jose A.

Going Home: The Puerto Ricans' New Migration. Stockton, William.

To What Extent Was Enrique Soto The Creation Of Pedro Juan Soto? Kennedy, William.

PUNISHMENT

A History Of Penal Methods. Ives, George.

Law, Procedure And Punishment In Early Bureaucracies. Mac Leod, W C.

American Prisons: A Study In American Social History. Mc Kelvey, Blake.

"Fluctuation Of Ethico–Juridicial Mentality In Criminal Law" in *Sociocultural Dynamics*, V3, 523–632. Sorokin, Pitirim A.

Police And Punishment Among Native Americans On The Plains. Mac Leod, W C.

Punishment And Social Structure. Rusche, Georg and Kirchheimer, Otto.

The Cheyenne Way: Conflict And Case Law In Primitive Jurisprudence. Llewellyn, K and Hoebel, E Adamson.

Crime And Punishment Among Minority Groups In Los Angeles County. Lemert, Edwin M and Roseberg, Judy.

Trends In The Use Of Capital Punishment. Hartung, Frank E.

A Study Of Minority Group Authoritarianism. Adelson, J A.

Criminology And Penology. Korn, Richard and Mc Corkle, Lloyd.

An Essay On Crime And Punishments, Orig Pub 1763. Beccaria, Cesare Bonesana.

Changes In Penal Values. Christie, Nils.

Moral Indignation And Middle Class Psychology: A Sociological Study, . Ranulf, Svend.

Prejudice, Perception And Penal Judgements. Delk, J L.

On Lynching. Barnett, Ida B Wells.

A Study Of The California Penalty Jury In First–Degree Murder Trials. Note.

Prejudice, Punitiveness And Personality. Snortum, J and Ashear, V.

Criminal Sentences: Law Without Order. Frankel, Marvin E.

Politics Of Punishment—A Critical Analysis Of Prisons In America. Wright, Erik Olin.

A Theory Of The Stability Of Punishment. Blumstein, Alfred and Cohen, Jacqueline.

Interpersonal Dynamics In A Simulated Prison. Haney, Craig and Banks, Curtis and Zimbardo, Philip.

RACE RELATIONS

Police Academy Training And Its Effects On Racial Prejudice. Reese, Charles D.

Police Overperception Of Ghetto Hostility. Crawford, T J.

Police Race Attitudes And Labeling. Rafky, David M.

White Conditioning Of Black Dependency. Mc Gee, D Phillip.

Hacks, Blacks And Cons: Race Relations In A Maximum Security Prison. Carroll, Leo.

Police And The Black Community. Wintersmith, Robert F.

The Unheavenly City Revisited: A Revision Of The Unheavenly City. Banfield, Edward C.

The White Man's Burden: Historical Origins Of Racism In The United States. Jordan, Winthrop D.

An Interaction Analysis Of Police–Black Relations. Cross, Stan and Renner, Edward.

Black–White Relations Among Police In The United States. Lynch, Gerald.

Identifying Responsive Inner–City Policemen. Kelly, Rita Mae and Farber, Martin G.

Los Angeles' Minority Policemen Express Their Concerns. Williford, Stanley O.

Minority Police: How Many Are There? Egerton, John.

"Toward A General Theory Of Racial And Ethnic Group Relations" in *Ethnicity: Theory And Experience*, Glazer, N And D Moynihan (eds). Gordon, M.

American Minorities: The Justice Issue. Long, Elton et al.

Race Relations In Corrections—An Annotated Bibliography. American Bar Association.

Minorities: A Wealth Of Resources. Pomerance, Rocky.

The Police And Black Separatism: A Problem For Public Policy. Lazin, F A.

From Plantation To Ghetto. Meier, August and Rudwick, Elliot.

United States—Comanche Relations. Hagan, W T.

Race Relations Training With Correctional Officers. Wittmer, J and Lanier, J E and Parker, M.

The Hispanic Tide—Some Implications Of Its Continuing Growth. Holman, Ben.

"Race And Three Forms Of Prisoner Power" in *Contemporary Corrections*, Huff, C (ed), 40–53. Carroll, Leo.

Black Crime: A Police View. Bryce, Harrington J (ed).

Black/Brown/White Relations: Race Relations In The 1970's. Willie, Charles V (ed).

Race And Races. Goldsby, Richard.

White Over Black: American Attitudes Toward The Negro, 1550–1812, Orig Pub 1968. Jordan, Winthrop D.

"Improving Police Relations In The Black Community" in *Blacks And Criminal Justice*, Owens, Charles E And Jimmy Bell (eds), 114–127. Swan, L Alex.

In The Matter Of Color. Higginbotham Jr, A Leon.

The Declining Significance Of Race. Wilson, William Julius.

Integrating The Keepers: A Comparison Of Black And White Prison Guards In Illinois. Jacobs, James B and Kraft, Larry J.

The Enforcers. Johnson, Thomas A.

"Race Relations And The Prisoner Subculture" in *Crime And Justice: An Annual Review Of Research*, Morris, N And M Tonry (eds). Jacobs, James B.

Race And Class In The Southwest: A Theory Of Racial Inequality. Barrera, Mario.

Black Versus White In The Station House. Jones, Robert A.

Minority Police: Tramping Through A Racial Minefield. Cory, Bruce.

The Police, The Courts, And The Minority Community. Witt, James W.

The Police And The Ghetto. Cooper, John L.

Hispanics Have To Work Closely With Blacks. Garcia, Robert.

Matty Troy's Prison Diary. Klein, Joe (ed).

RACE SUPREMACY

The Causes Of Race Superiority. Ross, Edward A.

The American Negro As A Dependent, Defective And Delinquent. Mc Cord, Charles H.

Pro–Slavery Thought In The Old South. Jenkins, William S.

The Leopard's Spots: Scientific Attitudes Toward Race In America, 1815–1859. Stanton, William.

Race And Reason: A Yankee View. Putnam, C.

Race: The History Of An Idea In America. Gossett, Thomas F.

White Separatists And Black Separatist: A Comparative Analysis. Feagin, Joe R.

The Eugenics Movement: Some Insight Into The Institutionalization Of Racism. Fong, Melanie and Johnson, Larry D.

Race And Races. Goldsby, Richard.

"Biology And Crime: The New Neo–Lombrosians" in *Biology And Crime*, Jeffrey, C Ray (ed). Jeffrey, C Ray.

The Violent Rebirth Of The Klan. King, Wayne.

Race Traits And Tendencies Of The American Negro. Hoffman, Frederick L.

RACIAL ATTITUDE INVENTORY

A Cluster Analytic Critique Of The Multifactor Racial Attitude Inventory. Gray, David B and Revelle, William.

RAHWAY PRISON, NJ

The Sixteenth Round. Carter, Rubin "Hurricane".

RAMSEY COUNTY, MN

Study Of Sentencing In Hennepin County And Ramsey County District Courts. Rhodes, W M.

RAPE

Violent Crime: Homicide, Assault, Rape And Robbery. National Commission On The Causes And Prevention Of Violence.

The Incidence Of The Death Penalty For Rape In Virginia. Partington, Donald H.

Race Of Victim And Of Offender For Rape, Robbery And Assault And Battery Offenses Known To The Police: Report To The Pres Crime Commission. Reiss Jr, Albert J.

Forcible Rape. Amir, Menachem.

Soul On Ice. Cleaver, Eldridge.

The Administration Of Rape Cases In The City Of Baltimore And The State Of Maryland. Howard, Joseph C.

Sexual Assaults In The Philadelphia Prison System And Sheriff's Vans. Davis, A J.

The Law: Rape, Race, Time And Death. Koeninger, R C.

Patterns In Forcible Rape. Amir, Menachem.

Patterns In Forcible Rape: A Review Essay. Mintz, Betty.

"Interracial Forcible Rape In A North American City" in *Victimology: A New Focus*, V1, Drapkin, Israel And Emilio Viano (eds), Chapter 9. Agopian, Michael W and Chappell, Duncan and Geis, Gilbert.

Toward A Cultural Interpretation Of Forcible Rape By American Blacks. Curtis, Lynn A.

Terror In The Prisons. Weiss, Carl and Friar, David James.

Rape, Race And The Death Penalty In Georgia. Wolfgang, Marvin E and Riedel, Marc.

Self–Defense Against Rape: The Joanne Little Case. Bond, Julian.

Sexual Assault: The Victim And The Rapist. Walker, Marcia J (ed) and Brodsky, Stanley L (ed).

Felony Murder Rape, And The Mandatory Death Penalty. Bedau, Hugo Adam.

Forcible Rape: The Crime, The Victim, And The Offender. Chappell, Duncan and Geis, Robley (ed) and Geis, Gilbert (ed).

"Black Offender And White Victim" in *Forcible Rape—The Crime, The Victim And The Offender*, Chappell, D; R Geis, And G Geis (eds). Agopian, Michael W.

"Race, Rape And The Death Penalty" in *Forcible Rape—The Crime, The Victim And The Offender*, Chappell, D; R Geis, And G Geis (eds). Wolfgang, Marvin E and Riedel, Marc.

"Rape, Race, And Research" in *Blacks And Criminal Justice*, Owens, Charles E And Jimmy Bell (eds). Evans, P.

Humanitarian Reform And Biracial Sexual Assault In A Maximum Security Prison. Carroll, Leo.

Criminal Violence, Criminal Justice. Silberman, Charles E.

Visible Man: A True Story Of Post–Racist America. Gilder, George.

Race And Involvement In Common Law Personal Crimes. Hindelang, Michael J.

Rape, Racism And The Capitalist Setting. Davis, Angela Y.

Aftermath Of Rape. Mc Cahill, T W and Meyer, L C and Fischman, A M.

The Innocence Of Joan Little. Reston Jr, James.

An Analysis Of Rape Patterns In White And Black Rapists. Heilbrun Jr, Alfred B and Cross, J M.

The Narrative & Confession Of Thomas Powers, A Negro, Who Was In The 10th Year Of His Age Was Executed For Committing A Rape. Powers, Thomas.

RAY, JAMES EARL

He Slew The Dreamer: My Search, With James Earl Ray, For The Truth About The Murder Of Martin Luther King. Huie, William Bradford.

An American Death: The True Story Of The Assassination Of Dr Martin Luther King, Jr, And The Greatest Manhunt Of Our Time. Frank, Gerold.

REBELLION

"Rebellious Youth" in *The Negro Family In The United States*, 268–280, Orig Pub 1949. Frazier, E Franklin.

RECIDIVISM

Inmate Personality Differences Related To Recidivism, Age And Race As Measured By The MMPI. Panton, J H.

Differential Study Of Recidivism Among Negro And White Boys. Henton, Comradge L and Washington, Charles.

Pilot Study: Age, Race And Recidivism As Factors In Prison Infractions. Johnson, Elmer H.

A Study Of Recidivism Among Female Juvenile Delinquents. Offord, D R and Aponte, J F and Frei, R J.

The Myth Of The Criminal Type. Sarbin, Theodore R.

Seriousness Of Delinquency, The Adjudicative Decision, And Recidivism—A Longitudinal Configuration Analysis. Meade, A.

Status, Images, And Consequence: Once A Criminal Always A Criminal. Reed, John P and Reed, Robin S.

An Analysis Of Proxemics And Self–Disclosing Behavior Of Recidivist And Non–Recidivist Adult Social Offenders. Braithwaite, Ronald L.

In Prison: Sometime Federal Prisoner 21669. O' Hare, Kate Richards.

"Successful Passage Of Black Parolees From Prison To Prison" in *Crime And Its Impact On The Black Community*, Gary And Brown (eds), 177–194. Swan, L Alex.

Recidivist Impacts Of Differential Sentencing Practices For Burglary Offenders. Burtell, Ted and Winfroo Jr, L Thomas.

The Search For Criminal Man. Rennie, Y.

Effectiveness Of Volunteer Assistance To Parolees. Carlson, Eric W and Vito, Gennaro F and Parks, Evalyn C.

RECONSTRUCTION

Penal Slavery And Southern Reconstruction. Mc Kelvey, Blake.

Been In The Storm So Long: The Aftermath Of Slavery. Litwack, Leon F.

REFORM

American Indian Policy In Crisis: Christian Reformers And The Indian: 1865–1900. Prucha, Francis P.

"Court Monitoring—A Necessity" in *Crime And Its Impact On The Black Community*, Gary, L E And L P Brown (eds), 165–175. Alexander, Harry T.

Reform Without Change: The Future Of Prisoners' Rights. Bronstein, Alvin J.

Justice And Reform: The Formative Years Of The American Legal Service Program. Johnson Jr, Earl.

REFORMATORY see Institutionalization, Juvenile

REGIMENTATION

The Regimentation Of Blacks On The Urban Frontier In Colonial Albany, New York City And Philadelphia. Williams, Oscar R.

REHABILITATION

The Chicano Addict: An Analysis Of Factors Influencing Rehabilitation In A Treatment Program. Auman, Jon et al.

Corrections: Problems Of Punishment And Rehabilitation. Sagarin, Edward (ed).

Do Prisons Rehabilitate? Chapman, Frank E.

Prisons: Instruments Of Law Enforcement Or Social Welfare? Jacobs, James B and Steele, Eric H.

Humanizing The System: Report Of Operations And Development For 1977. New York State, Dept Of Correctional Services.

Humanizing The System: Report Of Operations And Development For 1977. New York State, Dept Of Correctional Services.

Wildcat Experiment—An Early Test Of Supported Work In Drug Abuse Rehabilitation. Friedman, L N.

RELEASE DECISIONS

Sourcebook On Probation, Parole And Pardons, 3rd Ed. Newman, Charles L.

Delinquency Dispositions: Case Empirical Analysis Of Processing Decisions In Three Juvenile Courts. Cohen, Lawrence E.

Pre–Adjudicatory Detention In Three Juvenile Courts: An Empirical Analysis Of The Factors Related To Detention Decison Outcomes. Cohen, Lawrence E.

Post–Arrest Release Decisions: An Empirical Examination Of Social And Legal Criteria. Pope, Carl E.

"The Effect Of Race On Sentence" in *Theory And Research In Criminal Justice*, Conley, J A (ed). Foley, Linda and Rasch, Christine E.

Exploring The Re–Entry And Support Services For Hispanic Offenders, Natnl Hispanic Con L Enf, & CJ. Smith, Monica Herrera.

RELEASE ON RECOGNIZANCE *see* ROR

RELIGION

The Black Muslims In America. Lincoln, C Eric.

Assimilation In American Life: The Role Of Race, Religion, And National Origin. Gordon, Milton M.

Nonviolence: A Christian Interpretation. Miller, William Robert.

A Comparative Study Of Delinquents And Non–Delinquents: Family Affect, Religion, And Personal Income. Allen, Donald E and Sandhu, Harjit S.

Adolescence In The South: A Comparison Of White And Negro Attitudes About Home, School, Religion And Morality. Schab, F.

The Christian Doctrine Of Slavery, Org Pub 1857. Armstrong, George D.

Long v Harris, 332 F Supp 262, (Kansas), US District Court D Kansas: October 6, 1971. Anonymous.

Clark et al v Wolff, 347 F Supp 887, (Nebraska), US District Court D Nebraska: May 24, 1972, 1972. Anonymous.

Roll, Jordan, Roll: The World The Slaves Made. Genovese, Eugene D.

Violence As A Technique For Social Change For Black Americans. Wood, John Atkins.

American Indian Policy In Crisis: Christian Reformers And The Indian: 1865–1900. Prucha, Francis P.

REMEDY

Racial Remediation: An Historical Perspective On Current Conditions. Bell Jr, Derrick A.

Preferential Remedies And Affirmative Action In Employment In The Wake Of *Bakke*. Edwards, Harry T.

REPARATIONS

The Case For Black Reparations. Bittker, Boris.

RESEARCH

Research Note On Inter– And Intra–Racial Homicides. Garfinkel, Harold.

"Interpretation Of Statistical Relations As A Research Operation" in *The Language Of Social Research*, Lazarsfeld And Rosenberg (eds). Lazarsfeld, Paul F.

The Analysis Of Self–Descriptions By Members Of Delinquent Gangs. Strodtbeck, Fred L and Short Jr, James F and Kolegar, Ellen.

Effect Of Racial Characteristics Of Investigator On Self–Enumerated Responses To A Negro Prejudice Scale. Summers, G F and Hammonds, A D.

Pitfalls In Social Research: A Case Study. Voss, Harwin.

Delinquency Research: An Appraisal Of Analytic Methods. Hirschi, Travis and Selvin, Hanan C.

Task Force Report: Science And Technology. President's Comm On Law Enforcement & Adm Of Justice.

Ethical Problems In Studying A Politically Sensitive And Deviant Community. Rainwater, Lee and Pittman, D J.

Say It With Figures. Zeisel, Hans.

Language As Obstacle And As Data In Sociological Research. Grimshaw, Allen.

"Test Factor Standardization As A Method Of Interpretation" in *Stages Of Social Research*, Forcese, Dennis P And Stephen Richer (eds). Rosenberg, Morris.

Establishing Rapport With Deviant Groups. Beck, R A and Adams, J M.

Resistance To Community Surveys. Josephson, E.

Working Papers On Survey Research In Poverty Areas. Lansing, J and Withey, S B and Wolf, A C.

The Case Of The Racist Researcher. America, Richard F.

The Effects Of Black And White Interviewers On Black Responses In 1968. Schulman, H and Converse, J M.

Social Statistics. Blalock Jr, Hubert M.

Ethnic Minorities: Resistance To Being Researched. Sue, Derald W and Sue, Stanley.

Introduction To Symposium On White Researcher In Black Society. Clark, Cedric.

Notes From A White Researcher In Black Society. Couchman, I S B.

RESEARCH

Psychological Research And The Black Self-Concept: A Critical Review. Nobles, W W.

Social Constraints On Sociological Knowledge: Academics And Research Concerning Minorities. Moore, Joan W.

The Role Of White Researcher In Black Society. Clark, Cedric.

The Role Of The Researcher In Educational Settings: Perspectives On Research And Evaluation. Crockett, Stanley.

White Research In Black Communities: When Solutions Become A Part Of The Problem. Brazziel, William F.

Response Effects In Surveys: A Review And Synthesis. Sudman, S and Bradburn, N.

A Black Perspective On Social Research: In Response To Merton. Johnson, Larry.

Extra-Legal Attributes And Criminal Sentences: An Assessment Of A Sociological Viewpoint. Hagan, John.

The Culture Of Poverty Revisited: A Strategy For Research. Della Faxe, Richard L.

Ethnic Minority Family Research In An Urban Setting: A Process Of Exchange. Cromwell, R E and Vaughn, E C and Mindel, C H.

"Ethical Issues In Research/Experimentation In Prison" in *House Judicary Comm Hearings On Prison Inmates In Medical Research.* Swan, L Alex.

"Prevalence: The Rare Datum In Delinquency Measurement" in *The Juvenile Justice System,* Klein, Malcolm (ed), 201–284. Gordon, Robert A.

Racial Disparities That Supposedly Do Not Exist: Some Pitfalls In Analysis Of Court Records. Nagel, Stuart and Neef, Marian.

Determining Ethnic Origin In An Interview Survey: Problems And Recommendations. U S Dept Of H E W.

"Rape, Race, And Research" in *Blacks And Criminal Justice,* Owens, Charles E And Jimmy Bell (eds). Evans, P.

"Researching Black Justice: Description And Implications" in *Blacks And Criminal Justice,* Owens, Charles E And Jimmy Bell (eds), 25–33. Barnett, Samuel.

A Case Study Of Collaboration: The Chicano Pinto Research Project. Moore, Joan W.

Gathering Complete Response From Mexican-Americans By Personal Interview. Zusman, Marty E and Olson, Arnold O.

Merging Fieldwork And Survey Research In The Study Of A Minority Community. Tsukashima, Ronald T.

Relating Academic Research To Community Concerns: A Case Study In Collaborative Effort. Bengston, Vern L et al.

Research Among Racial And Cultural Minorities: An Overview. Montero, Darrel.

Respondent Militancy As A Control Variable For Interview Effect. Shosteck, Herschel.

Some Concluding Remarks: Research Among Racial And Cultural Minorities. Levine, Gene N.

Survey Methods For Minority Populations. Myers, Vincent.

Survey Researchers And Minority Communities. Weiss, Carol H.

The Difficulties Of A Minority Researcher In Minority Communities. Maykovich, Minako Kurokawa.

The Research Experience In A Chinese-American Community. Weiss, Melford S.

The Sojourner In The American Indian Community: Methodological Issues And Concerns. Trimble, Joseph E.

The Uses Of Social Science In Trials With Political And Racial Overtones: The Trial Of Joan Little. Mc Conahay, John B and Mullin, Courtney J and Frederick, Jeffrey.

"Urban Families And Assault: A Framework For Research Focused On Black Families" in *Colloquium On The Correlates Of Crime,* Otten, L (ed). Perry, L and Crowley, J E.

Explaining Crime. Nettler, Gwynn.

The Death Penalty: Social Philosophy And Social Science Research. Wolfgang, Marvin E.

Theory And Research In Criminal Justice: Current Perspectives. Conley, John A (ed).

Government Research Funding And Purchased Virtue: Some Examples From Criminology. Galliher, John F.

LEAA's Research Solicitation: Police Use Of Deadly Force. Takagi, Paul.

The Mexican American: A Critical Guide To Research Aids. Robinson, Barbara J (comp) and Robinson, J Cordell (comp).

"Race, Inferiority, Crime, And Research Taboos" in *Taboos In Criminology,* Sagarin, Edward (ed). Karmen, Andrew.

"Research On IQ, Race, And Delinquency: Taboo Or Not Taboo" in *Taboos In Criminology,* Sagarin, Edward (ed). Gordon, Robert A.

Social Science Evidence In The Courts: Reaching Beyond The Adversary Process. Sperlich, Peter W.

RESENTMENT AND SUSPICION

From Resentment To Confrontation: The Police, The Negroes, And The Outbreak Of The Nineteen-Sixties Riots. Fogelson, Robert.

Resentment And Suspicion Among American Men. Blumenthal, M D.

RESERVATION, INDIAN

Redman Reservations. Wissler, C.

Selected Social Problems Of Fort Hall Reservation. Minnis, Mhyra S.

Indian Policy After The Civil War: The Reservation Experience. Hagan, W T.

Law And Order On The Mississippi Choctaw Reservation. Bobo, D.

Contemporary Problems In Law Enforcement On American Indian Reservations. Kobetz, R W and Hamm, C W.

Indian Reservations, Anomic And Social Pathologies. Levy, Jerrold E and Kunitz, Stephen J.

Lawmen For The Reservation. Metareltis, G S.

Tribal Injustice—The Red Lake Court Of Indian Offenses. Lawrence, J W.

United States Law On American Indians. Kleiner, J.

Justice And The American Indian, V1. Johnson, R W.

Justice And The American Indian, V3: The Effect Of Having No Extradition Procedures For Indian Reservations. Steisel, M D.

Justice And The American Indian, V5: Federal Prosecution Of Crimes Commited On Indian Reservations. Stewart Jr, L G.

Adolescent Suicide On An Indian Reservation. Dizmang, Larry H Et Al.

Delinquency Among Wind River Indian Reservation Youth. Forslund, Morris A and Meyers, Ralph E.

The Navajo Nation: An American Colony. U S Commission On Civil Rights.

Indian Reservation Criminal Justice: Task Force Analysis, 1974–1975. U S Dept Of Interior, Bureau Of Indian Affairs.

Law Enforcement On Indian Reservations. Etheridge, D.

Suicide Epidemic On An Indian Reserve. Ward, J A and Fox, J.

Indian Law: Oliphant v Suquamish Indian Tribe, 435 US 191 (1978). Berkey, C G.

RESPONSIBILITY, CRIMINAL

Who Is The Criminal? Tappan, Paul W.

Crime As An American Way Of Life. Bell, Daniel.

Who Is The Victim? Quinney, Richard.

"The Offender As Victim" in *Victimology: A New Focus,* V3, Drapkin, Israel And Emilio Viano (eds), 113–120. Newman, Joseph.

Thinking About Crime. Wilson, James Q.

Imprisonment And The Expected Value Of Criminal Choice: A Specification And Test Of Aspects Of The Labeling Perspective. Harris, Anthony R.

No Excuse For Crime. Van Den Haag, Ernest.

RETALIATION

Variables In Interracial Aggression Anonymity, Expected Retaliation, And A Riot. Donnerstein, Edward et al.

The Fire This Time: Effects Of Race Of Target, Insult, And Potential Retaliation On Black Aggression. Wilson, L and Rogers, R W.

RETRIBUTION

Moral Indignation And Middle Class Psychology: A Sociological Study, . Ranulf, Svend.

REVOLUTION

Rebellion Or Revolution? Sanders, David.

"A Cause Of Some Great Revolutions And A Contained Rebellion" in *The History Of Violence In America,* Graham, Hugh D & T Gurr (eds), 690–730. Davies, James C.

Seize The Time. Seale, Bobby.

Soledad Brother: The Prison Letters Of George Jackson. Jackson, George.

Popular Uprisings And Civil Authority In Eighteenth-Century America. Maier, Pauline.

Separate But Equal: Revolution And Counter-Revolution In The American City. Horowitz, Irving L.

Chicano Manifesto. Rendon, Armando.

Radical Lawyers: Their Role In The Movement And In The Courts. Black, Jonathan (ed).

Blood In My Eye. Jackson, George.

To Die For The People. Newton, Huey P.

REVOLUTION

From Riot To Revolution. Pallas, John and Barber, Bob.
Canto Y Grito Mi Liberación. Sánchez, Ricardo.
The Problem Of Slavery In The Age Of Revolution, 1770–1823. Davis, David Brion.
Who Killed George Jackson: Fantasies, Paranoia And The Revolution. Durden–Smith, Jo.
Dark Smoke. Aguila, Pancho.
Black Bolshevik: Autobiography Of An Afro–American Communist. Haywood, H.

RIKER'S ISLAND JAIL, NYC

Matty Troy's Prison Diary. Klein, Joe (ed).

RIOT COMMISSION

Whitewash Over Watts. Blauner, Robert.
Riot Commission Politics. Lipsky, Michael and Olson, David J.

RIOT COMMISSIONS

The Watts 'Manifesto' And The McCone Report. Rustin, Bayard.
"Official Interpretations Of Racial Riots" in *Urban Riots: Violence And Social Change*, Connery, R H (ed), 151–163. Silver, Allan A.
Report Of The National Advisory Commission On Civil Disorders. Riot Commission.
"Between White And Blacks: The Faces Of American Institutions In The Ghetto" in *Riot Commission, Supplemental Studies*, 69–215. Rossi, Peter et al.
"Police In The Ghetto" in *Riot Commission, Supplemental Studies*, 103–114. Rossi, Peter et al.
"Racial Attitudes In Fifteen American Cities" in *Riot Commission, Supplemental Studies*, 1–67. Campbell, A and Schuman, Howard.
A Comment On The Police And The Kerner Report. Lehman, P.
Shootout In Cleveland: Black Militants And The Police (Violence Commission Report, Volume 5). Masotti, Louis and Corsi, Jerome.
The Politics Of Riot Commissions: A Collection Of Official Reports And Critical Essays. Platt, Anthony (ed).
The Effects Of The Findings Of The US National Advisory Commission On Civil Disorders: An Experimental Study Of Attitude Change. Davis, E E and Fine, M.
Commission Politics: The Processing Of Racial Crisis In America. Lipsky, Michael and Olson, David J.

RIOTS

The Chicago Race Riots. Sandburg, Carl.
The Eruption Of Tulsa. White, Walter.
American Slave Insurrections Before 1861. Wish, Harvey.
Slave Insurrections In The United States, 1800–1865. Carroll, Joseph Cephas.
Negro Slave Revolts In The United States, 1526–1860. Aptheker, Herbert.
Race Riot. Lee, Alfred McClung and Humphrey, Norman D.
Racial Conflict: Lessons Of The Detroit Riot. National Urban League, Inc.
What Caused The Detroit Riot? White, Walter and Marshall, Thurgood.
How To Prevent Race Riots. Rawshenbush, Winifred.
The Detroit Riots—And After. Norton, William J.
The Gestapo In Detroit. Marshall, Thurgood.
The Zoot–Suit Riots. Mc Williams, Carey.
War And Race Conflicts In The United States. Robinson, Bernard F.
Why Race Riots: Lessons From Detroit. Brown, Earl.
Race Riots Aren't Necessary. Lee, Alfred McClung.
Requiem On A Race Riot. Bingay, Malcolm W.
"Division X: Race Riots In The US, 1942–1946, Division XIII: Lynching" *Negro Year Book, 1947.* Guzman, Jessie Parkhurst (ed).
Behind The Prison Riots. Mac Cormick, Austin H.
Violence Behind Bars. Fox, Vernon.
A Social–Psychological Analysis Of Prison Riots: An Hypothesis. Hartung, Frank E and Floch, Maurice.
A Study In Social Violence: Urban Race Riot In The United States. Grimshaw, Allen.
An Account Of Some Of The Principal Slave Insurrections. Coffin, Joshua.
Actions Of Police And The Military In American Race Riots. Grimshaw, Allen.
Race Riots: New York, 1954. Shapiro, F C and Sullivan, J W.
Race Riot At East St Louis: July 2, 1917. Rudwick, Elliot M.
The Police Role In Racial Conflicts. Towler, Juby Earl.
Aftermath Of A Long, Hot Summer. Harper, Dean.

Changing Patterns Of Racial Violence In The United States. Grimshaw, Allen.
The Precipitants And Underlying Conditions Of Race Riots. Lieberson, Stanley and Silverman, Arnold.
The Role Of Police In Riotous Demonstrations. Leary, Howard.
The Wonder Is There Have Been So Few Riots. Clark, Kenneth B.
The Riot. Elli, Frank.
The Riot That Didn't Happen. Shellow, R and Roemer, D V.
The Watts 'Manifesto' And The McCone Report. Rustin, Bayard.
Whitewash Over Watts. Blauner, Robert.
"Riots And Crime—Historical Background" in *Task Force Report—Crime And Its Impact—An Assessment*, 116–122. President's Comm On Law Enforcement & Adm Of Justice.
Black Nationalism And Prospects For Violence In The Ghetto. Parker, G J.
Burn, Baby, Burn. Cohen, J and Murphy, W.
Community Relations And Riot Prevention. Momboisse, Raymond M.
Los Angeles Riot Study, The Perception Of Police Brutality In South Central Los Angeles. Institute Of Government And Public Affairs.
Rebellion In Newark. Hayden, Tom.
Rivers Of Blood, Years Of Darkness. Conot, Robert.
The Race War. Segal, R.
Breakdown Of Law And Order. Parmenter, Tom.
Notes On Instant Urban Renewal. Montgomery, Roger.
Open Letter On White Justice And The Riots. Rainwater, Lee.
"Crime And Vicious Environment" in *The Negro In Chicago: A Study Of Race Relations And A Race Riot In 1919*, Orig Pub 1919. Chicago Commission On Race Relations.
"Official Interpretations Of Racial Riots" in *Urban Riots: Violence And Social Change*, Connery, R H (ed), 151–163. Silver, Allan A.
"The Etiology Of The Race Riot" in *Violence In The Street*, Endelman, S (ed), 357–361. Endleman, S.
Effects Of Racial Violence On Attitudes In The Negro Community. Justice, Blair.
Guidelines For Prosecuting Criminal Cases During Civil Disorders. National District Attorney's Association.
Patterns Of Looting And Property Norms: Conflict And Consensus In Community Emergencies. Dynes, R and Quarantelli, E.
Preparation By Municipalities For Civil Disorders. Gill, Douglas.
Report Of The National Advisory Commission On Civil Disorders. Riot Commission.
Riots, Violence And Disorder: Civil Turbulence In Urban Communities. Masotti, Louis (ed).
The Algiers Motel Incident. Hersey, John.
The Anatomy Of A Riot. Lincoln, James H.
The Detroit Riot: A Profile Of 500 Prisoners. U S Dept Of Labor, Manpower Administration.
Urban Riots: Violence And Social Change. Connery, Robert H (ed).
"Who Riots: A Study Of Participation In The 1967 Riots" in *Riot Commission, Supplemental Studies*, 217–248. Fogelson, Robert and Hill, Robert.
An Urban Riot: A Juvenile Court Meets The Challenge. Walsh, James.
Arrests In Civil Disturbances: Reflections On The Use Of Deadly Force In Riots. Mc Ghee, Henry.
Bail And Civil Disorder. Calista, F P and Domonkas, Michael.
Black Rebellion And White Reaction. Wildavsky, Aaron.
Children Of The Detroit Riots: A Study Of Their Participation And Their Mental Health. Komisaruk, R and Pearson, Carol.
Contingency Planning For The Administration Of Justice During Civil Disorder And Mass Arrest. Friedman, H G.
Detroit 1967: Racial Violence Or Class Warfare. Corsi, Jerome.
Freedoms And The Politics Of Mass Participation: Perspective On The 1967 Detroit Riot. Smith, John and Smith, Lois.
From Resentment To Confrontation: The Police, The Negroes, And The Outbreak Of The Nineteen–Sixties Riots. Fogelson, Robert.
How The Police Abroad Handle Riots. Gillece, James et al.
Looting In Civil Disorders: An Index Of Social Change. Dynes, R and Quarantelli, E.
Mob Violence And The Prosecuting Attorney. Karton, Robert.
Negro Opinions In Three Riot Cities. Mc Cord, William and Howard, John.
New Answer To Riots: Keep White Police Away? Gillece, James et al.
Note, Riot Control: The Constitutional Limits Of Search, Arrest And Fair Trial Procedure. Anonymous.

RIOTS

On The Ecology Of Political Violence: 'The Long Hot Summer' As A Hypothesis. Schwartz, David.

Racial Disturbances As Collective Protest. Lang, Kurt and Lang, G.

Rebellion Or Revolution? Sanders, David.

Report Of The Special Committee On Criminal Law Problems In Civil Disorders. American Bar Association.

Riot Control And The Fourth Amendment. Note.

Shall We Shoot Looters? Clark, Ramsey.

The Development Of A Real Ideology Among Urban Negroes. Tomlinson, T M.

The Dynamics Of Recent Ghetto Riots. Hundly, James.

The Efficient Use Of Military Forces To Control Riots: Some Proposals For Congressional Action. Sultan, Allen and Howard, Richard.

The Form And Content Of Recent Riots. Mattick, Hans.

The Long Hot Summer: A Legal View. Gillece, James et al.

The National Guard And Riot Control: The Need For Revision. Crum, L.

The Study Of Urban Violence: Some Implications Of Laboratory Studies Of Frustration And Aggression. Berkowitz, Leonard.

Three Views Of Urban Violence: Civil Disturbance, Racial Revolt, Class Assault. Grimshaw, Allen.

Virginia's Legislative Response To Riots And Their Underlying Causes. Wasson, Houston.

When Will The Troops Come Marching In: A Comment On The Historical Use Of Federal Troops To Quell Domestic Violence. Garland, R and Chikota, Richard.

1967 Riots: A Test Of The Congruity Of Events. Wanderer, J J.

"The Zoot Effect On Personality: A Race Riot Participant" in *Racial Violence In The United States*, Grimshaw, A (ed), 413–420. Clark, Kenneth and Barker, James.

A Study Of Arrest Patterns In The 1960's Riots. Hill, Robert and Fogelson, Robert.

Civil Disorders: After–Action Reports, Professional Standards Division. International Association Of Chiefs Of Police.

Civil Disorder—Indicator Studies: Some Aspects Of Riot Susceptibility. Rae, R W.

Racial Violence In The US. Grimshaw, Allen (ed).

The Detroit Riot Of 1967. Locke, Hubert G.

The Harlem Riot Of 1935. Hill, Robert B.

"A Comparative Study Of Civil Strife" in *Violence In America*, Graham, Hugh D And T Gurr (eds), 572–626. Gurr, Ted.

An Index Of Riot Severity And Some Correlates. Wanderer, J J.

Black Attitudes Toward The Political System In The Aftermath Of The Watts Insurrection. Sears, David.

Danger Of Police Overreaction. Sagalyn, Arnold.

Internal Colonialism And Ghetto Revolt. Blauner, Robert.

Interracial Social Contact And Middle Class White Reaction To The Watts Riot. Jeffries, Vincent and Ransford, H E.

Legal Goals: The Curfew And Preventative Closings In Prevention And Control Of Civil Disorder. Runyan, Charles.

Neighborhood Structure And Riot Behavior In Detroit: Some Exploratory Findings. Warren, Donald.

Participation In The Los Angeles Riot. Sears, David and Mc Conahay, John.

Riot Commission Politics. Lipsky, Michael and Olson, David J.

The American City And Civil Disorders. Havlick, J R and Wade, Mary.

The Hunters Point Riot: Politics Of The Frustrated. Carmichael, Benjamin G.

The Response Of The Washington DC Community And Its Criminal Justice System To The April 1968 Riot. Cheminick, Paul W (ed).

The Response Of Police Agencies. Misner, Gordon.

The Revolt Of The Urban Ghettos, 1964–1967. Boskin, Joseph.

The Riot Curfew. Frese, Glenn.

The Woman Participant In Washington's Riots. Miller, Eugene.

White Institutions And Black Rage. Boesel, D et al.

Causes, Preventive Measures And Methods Of Controlling Riots And Disturbances In Correctional Institutions. American Correctional Association.

The Orangeburg Massacre. Nelson, Jack and Bass, Jack.

"What Looting In Civil Disturbances Really Means" in *Law And Order: Modern Criminals*, Short Jr, James F (ed), 177–192. Dynes, R and Quarantelli, E.

Civil Disturbances, Mass Processing And Misdemeanants: Rights, Remedies And Realities. Ginsberg, George and Starkman, Gary.

Cops And Rioters: Ghetto Perceptions Of Social Conflict And Control. Hahn, Harlan.

Ideological Foundations For Negro Action: A Comparative Analysis Of Militant Views Of The Los Angeles Riots. Tomlinson, T M.

Popular Uprisings And Civil Authority In Eighteenth–Century America. Maier, Pauline.

Racial Socialization, Comparison Levels, And The Watts Riot. Sears, David and Mc Conahay, John.

Riots: What Are The Options? Baker, Bruce.

The Phoenix Election Riot. Well, T H.

Toward Understanding Riots: Some Perspectives. Allen, V L.

Violence And Grievances: Reflections On The 1960's Riots. Fogelson, Robert.

My Cure For Prison Riots: End Prison Racism. Moore, Winston E.

The Causes Of Racial Disturbances: Tests Of An Explanation. Spilerman, S.

The Mass Media And Racial Conflict. Hartman, Paul and Husband, Charles.

The Public Perception Of The Watts Riot As Social Protest. Jefferies, Vincent and Turner, R H and Morris, R T.

"Can We Avoid Riots In Prisons If We Fail To Eradicate Racism On The Outside" in *Proc Of 7th Annual Interagency Workshop*, 144–161. Higginbotham Jr, A Leon.

Attica Diary. Coons, William R.

Police Riots: Collective Violence And Law Enforcement. Starls, R.

"The Watts–Los Angeles Riot" in *Rebellion And Retreat*, Palmer, S (ed), 248–272. Oberschall, Anthony.

American Black Ghetto Revolt: A New Perspective. Abudu, Margaret.

Angry Picketing. Ralph, C H.

Black Ghetto Residents As Rioters. Moinat, Sheryl M et al.

From Riot To Revolution. Pallas, John and Barbor, Bob.

Harlem And Detroit Riots Of 1943: A Comprehensive Analysis. Swan, L Alex.

Racial Violence At San Quentin Prison/War Behind Walls. Bunker, Edward.

Riot Control Equipment. Brumgardt, J R.

Ghetto Revolts: The Politics Of Violence In American Cities. Feagin, Joe R and Harlan, Alan.

Change In Crisis–Relevant Organizations: Police Departments And Civil Disturbances. Kreps, Gary A.

One Department's Confrontation Strategy. Thomas, H J.

Riot Regression: A Switch In Initiatives. Swan, L Alex.

The Causes Of Racial Disorders: A Grievance–Level Explanation. Morgan, W R and Clark, T N.

The Prosaic Sources Of Prison Violence. Mattick, Hans.

The Reluctant Army: The Functioning Of Police Departments During Civil Disturbances. Wenger, D.

When Whites Riot—The East St Louis Massacre. Swan, L Alex.

A Factor Analysis Of The Socio–Economic Structure Of Riot And Crime Prone Cities. Mc Nown, Robert F and Singell, Larry D.

Rumors, Race And Riots. Knopf, Terry Ann.

The Philadelphia Race Riot Of 1918. Franklin, Vincent P.

Continuities In Delinquency And Riot Patterns, In Black Residential Areas. Kapsis, Robert E.

Commission Politics: The Processing Of Racial Crisis In America. Lipsky, Michael and Olson, David J.

The Black Revolts: Racial Stratification In The USA. Scott, Joseph.

Riots And Acts Of Violence In The Penitentiaries: What Can We Learn? Chocla, M A.

The Blackout, in *1977 Annual Report Of The New York City Board Of Correction*, 17–24. New York City Board Of Correction.

A Report On The Blackout Looting: New York City, July 13, 1977. Curvin, Robert and Porter, Bruce.

Patterns Of Conflict Preceding The 1964 Riots: Harlem And Bedford—Stuyvesant. Monti, D J.

Prisons In Turmoil. Irwin, John.

Report Of The Attorney General On The February 2 And 3, 1980 Riot At The Penitentiary Of New Mexico: Part I. New Mexico Attorney General.

Report Of The Attorney General On The February 2 And 3, 1980 Riot At The Penitentiary Of New Mexico: Part 2. New Mexico Attorney General.

New Mexico: The Anatomy Of A Riot. Serrill, Michael S and Katel, Peter.

Prison Perspective (Santa Fe Prison Riot). Anonymous.

RIOTS

The Santa Fe Prison Riots: 'The Flower Of The Dragon'. Mandel, Jerry.

RIOTS, PREVENTION

How To Prevent Race Riots. Rawshenbush, Winifred.

RIVERA, JOSE

Real West Side Story, Life Of Jose Rivera. Morgan, T B.

ROBBERY

Violent Crime: Homicide, Assault, Rape And Robbery. National Commission On The Causes And Prevention Of Violence.

The Negro Armed Robber As A Criminal Type: The Construction And Application Of A Typology. Roebuck, Julian D and Cadwallader, Mervyn L.

Race Of Victim And Of Offender For Rape, Robbery And Assault And Battery Offenses Known To The Police: Report To The Pres Crime Commission. Reiss Jr, Albert J.

Outside The Law: A Thief's Primer. Jackson, Bruce.

Robbery And The Criminal Justice System. Conklin, John E.

The Mugging. Hunt, Morton.

Violence And Robbery: A Case Study. Normandeau, Andre.

Armed Robbery. Mac Donald, John M.

Thinking About Crime. Wilson, James Q.

An Empirical Examination Of Conflict Theory: Race And Sentence Length. Dison, Jack E.

Homicide And Robbery In New York City: An Economic Model. Mathieson, Donald and Passell, Peter.

Race And Involvement In Common Law Personal Crimes. Hindelang, Michael J.

Criminal's Image Of The City. Carter, R I and Hill, K Q.

Robbery And Burglary—A Study Of The Characteristics Of The Persons Arrested And The Handling Of Their Cases In Court. Williams, K M and Luclanovic, J.

ROCHESTER, NY

Twenty–Two Years A Slave And Forty Years A Freeman. Stewart, Austin.

ROLE PLAYING

Role Playing And Group Experience To Facilitate Attitude And Value Changes Among Black And White Police Officers. Teahan, John E.

ROUGHNECKS

Race, Sex And Gangs: The Saints And The Roughnecks. Chambliss, William J.

RUMOR

Race And Rumors Of Race. Odum, Howard W.

Where Rumor Raged. Rosenthal, Marilynn.

Rumors, Race And Riots. Knopf, Terry Ann.

RUNAWAYS

Runaways At The Training Institution In Central Ohio. Bartollas, C.

Differential Treatment Between Runaway Boys And Girls In Juvenile Court. Mann, Coramae R.

SAFETY

Public Saftey: Crime Is Up, But What About Punishment? Seidman, David.

Community Safety And Criminal Activity In Black Suburbs. Nichols Jr, Woodrow W.

SAINTS

Race, Sex And Gangs: The Saints And The Roughnecks. Chambliss, William J.

SAMBOS

Slavery: A Problem In American Institutional & Intellectual Life. Elkins, Stanley M.

Rebels And Sambos: The Search For The Negro's Personality In Slavery. Stampp, Kenneth M.

SAN DIEGO, CA

Police Recruitment: How Brown And Black Personnel View It. Gazell, James A.

The Attitudes Of Non–White Police Personnel Toward Retention. Gazell, James A.

SAN FRANCISCO, CA

Chinatown: Its History, Its People, Its Importance. Jue, George K.

Delinquent, Neglected And Dependent Chinese Boys And Girls Of The San Francisco Bay Region. Lee, R H.

Report On Crime And The Foreign Born, Orig Pub 1931. Abbott, Edith.

Juvenile Delinquency In San Francisco's Chinese–American Community: 1961–1966. Abbott, Kenneth A and Abbott, Elizabeth Lee.

Inter–Ethnic Conflict. Glazer, Nathan.

The Black Offender As Victim. Debro, Julius.

Violence By Youth Gangs And Youth Groups In Major American Cities—Final Report. Miller, Walter B.

A View Of The Quota System In The San Francisco Police Department. Balzer, A.

Women's Jail—Pretrial And Post–Conviction Alternatives—A Report On Women Arrested In San Francisco. Bresler, L and Leonard, D.

Chinatown—No Longer A Cozy Assignment. Wilson, Rob.

Black Versus White In The Station House. Jones, Robert A.

Lights And Shadows Of Chinatown. Bode, William.

SAN JOSE, CA

"Eliminating The Language Barrier" in Police–Community Relationships, Bopp, W (ed), 442–444. Ross, Donald J and Cobarruviaz, Louis.

SAN JUAN, PR

La Vida: A Puerto Rican Family In The Culture Of Poverty—San Juan And New York. Lewis, Oscar.

SAN QUENTIN PRISON, CA

Using Racism At San Quentin. Minton Jr, Robert J and Rice, Stephen.

George Jackson Radicalized The Brothers In Soledad And San Quentin. Szulc, Tad.

Racial Violence At San Quentin Prison/War Behind Walls. Bunker, Edward.

No Beast So Fierce. Bunker, Edward.

Chicano Prisoners: The Key To San Quentin. Davidson, R Theodore.

SAN QUENTIN SIX

The San Quentin Six: A Case Of Vengeance. Jordan, Fania Davis.

"The San Quentin Six Case: Perspective And Analysis" in Punishment And Penal Discipline, Platt, Tony And Paul Takagi (eds), 165–175. Wald, Karen.

SANTA BARBARA, CA

Chicanos In A Changing Society: From Mexican Pueblos To American Barrios In Santa Barbara And Southern California, 1848–1930. Camarillo, Alberto.

SANTA CLARA COUNTY, CA

Ascertaining Police Bias In Arrests For Drunken Driving. Hyman, Merton M and Helrich, Alice R and Benson, Gwen.

SANTA FE PRISON, NM

Report Of The Attorney General On The February 2 And 3, 1980 Riot At The Penitentiary Of New Mexico: Part 2. New Mexico Attorney General.

Report Of The Attorney General On The February 2 And 3, 1980 Riot At The Penitentiary Of New Mexico: Part 1. New Mexico Attorney General.

New Mexico: The Anatomy Of A Riot. Serrill, Michael S and Katel, Peter.

Prison Perspective (Santa Fe Prison Riot). Anonymous.

The Santa Fe Prison Riots: 'The Flower Of The Dragon'. Mandel, Jerry.

SATISFACTION WITH COUNSEL

Prisoners' Attitudes Toward Components Of The Legal And Judicial System. Hicks, Donald A and Alpert, Geoffrey P.

Inadequate Defense Counsel—An Empirical Analysis Of Prisoners' Perceptions. Alpert, Geoffrey P.

SCHOOLS

The Role Of School In Juvenile Delinquency Prevention. Hipps, Irene.

Crisis In Black And White. Silberman, Charles E.

Schools And Delinquency. Polk, Kenneth and Schafer, Walter E.

"Crime And The Public Schools" in Crime And Its Impact On The Black Community, Gary, L E And L P Brown (eds), 59–68. Banks, Samuel L.

SCOTTSBORO BOYS

Scottsboro Boy. Patterson, Haywood and Conrad, Earl.

SEALE, BOBBY

The Trial Of Bobby Seale. Seale, Bobby.

SEASON

Aftermath Of A Long, Hot Summer. Harper, Dean.

On The Ecology Of Political Violence: 'The Long Hot Summer' As A Hypothesis. Schwartz, David.

The Long Hot Summer: A Legal View. Gillece, James et al.

Crime And Environment. Harries, Keith D.

SEATTLE, WA

The Response Of Adults To Delinquency Prevention Programs: The Race Factor. Hackler, J C and Linden, E.

SEATTLE, WA

The Assimilation Of American Indians Into Urban Society: The Seattle Case. Chadwick, Bruce A and Stauss, Joseph H.

Antecedents Of Urban Indian Crime. Williams, L E.

Confrontation With The Law: The Case Of The American Indians In Seattle. Chadwick, Bruce A et al.

SECONDARY GROUPS

Racial Assimilation In Secondary Groups With Particular Reference To The Negro. Park, Robert E.

SEGREGATION, RACIAL

Fifty—Eight Lonely Men. Peltason, J W.

Patterns Of Segregation And Discrimination: Contributing Factors To Crime Among Negroes. Vontress, Clemmont E.

A Minority Group In American Society. Yinger, J Milton.

SELF-CONCEPT

Degeneration And Crime: The Twin Evils Of Discrimination And Oppression. Newsom, John T C.

Cats, Kicks, And Color. Finestone, Harold.

A Memorandum On Identity And Negro Youth. Erikson, Eric H.

Prisonization And Self Concept. Kennedy, Will Charles.

Racial Group Membership Role Orientation And Police Conduct Among Urban Policemen. Scott, James F.

"Prisoner Personality Development In Prison/On Becoming" in *prisons, Protest, And Politics*, Atkins, B (ed), 105—111. Cleaver, Eldridge.

Delinquency And Adolescent Self—Conceptions: A Study Of The Personal Relevance Of Infraction. Jensen, Gary F.

Job Satisfaction In Policemen And Its Relation To Locus Of Control, Ego Strength And Performance. Munoz, Mona.

The Personality And Self Concept Characteristics Of Negro And White Delinquent And Non—Delinquent Boys. Zipper, Barry Osei.

Black Policemen: A Study Of Self—Images. Bannon, James D and Wilt, G Marie.

Delinquent Acting—Out And Task Of Sexual Identification In Black Male Adolescents—Replication Study. Mc Nabb, D P.

Psychological Research And The Black Self—Concept: A Critical Review. Nobles, W W.

The Impact Of Racism On Personality Development. Shannon, B E.

"Black Political Consciousness In Northern State Prisons" in *Potential For Reform Of Criminal Justice*, Jacob, Herbert (ed). Morris, Frank L.

A Comparison Of Negro, Anglo And Spanish—American Adolescents' Self—Concepts. Healey, G W and Deblassie, R R.

Self—Concept In Negro And White Pre—Adolescent Delinquent Boys. Wax, Douglas E.

Success Values: Are They Universal Or Class Differentiated? Della Faxe, Richard L.

The Adjudication Process And Self—Conception. Thorsell, Bernard A and Chambers, Robert.

The Analysis Of Self—Concept And Self Actualization Manifestations By Incarcerated And Free Black Youth. Davis, Charles.

The Effects Of Racial Milieu And Parental Racial Attitudes And Rearing Practices On Black Children's Racial Identity/Self—Esteem/Behavior. Smith, Willie D.

Race And The Father—Son Connection: The Conditional Relevance Of Father Absence For The Orientations And Identities Of Adolescent Boys. Hunt, Larry L and Hunt, Janet G.

Race, Deprivation And Adolescent Self—Images. Hulbary, W E.

Racial—Ethnic Identification In Prisons: 'Right On From The Inside'. Denfeld, D and Hopkins, Andrew.

"Black Self—Identity And Crime" in *Crime And Its Impact On The Black Community*, Gary, L E And L P Brown (eds), 109—120. Gullattee, Alyce C.

Race, Achievement, And Delinquency—A Further Look At Delinquency In A Birth Cohort. Jensen, Gary F.

Race, Commitment To Deviance, And Spoiled Identity. Harris, Anthony R.

Internal Colonialism: White, Black And Chicano Self Conceptions. Hurstfield, Jennifer.

Self—Esteem And Achievement Of Black And White Adolescents. Simmons, R G et al.

Hispanics In The US: Ethnic 'Sleeping Giant' Awakens, Part 4. Godsell, Geoffrey.

Hispanics In The US: Ethnic 'Sleeping Giant' Awakens, Part 5. Godsell, Geoffrey.

Hispanics In The US: Ethnic 'Sleeping Giant' Awakens, Part 2. Godsell, Geoffrey.

Hispanics In The US: Ethnic 'Sleeping Giant' Awakens, Part 3. Godsell, Geoffrey.

Hispanics In The US: Ethnic 'Sleeping Giant' Awakens, Part 1. Godsell, Geoffrey.

SELF-CONTROL

Internal—External Control And Black Militancy. Forward, J R and Williams, J R.

Level Of Aspiration And Locus Of Control In Disadvantaged Children. Milgram, N A et al.

Tests Of The Language—Aggression Hypothesis. Boone, S L and Moutare, A.

The Black Minority Criminal And Violent Crime: The Role Of Self Control. Heilbrun Jr, Alfred B and Heilbun, Kirk S.

SELF-DEFENSE

Self—Defense Against Rape: The Joanne Little Case. Bond, Julian.

SELF-FULFILLING PROPHECY

Prior Offense As A Self—Fulfilling Prophecy. Farrell, Ronald A and Swigert, Victoria Lynn.

SELF-REPORT STUDIES

A Self—Report Comparison Of Indian And Anglo Delinquency In Wyoming. Forslund, Morris A and Cranston, Virginia A.

The Analysis Of Self—Descriptions By Members Of Delinquent Gangs. Strodtbeck, Fred L and Short Jr, James F and Kolegar, Ellen.

Who Defines Delinquency: A Comparison Of Self—Reported And Officially—Reported Indices Of Delinquency For Three Racial Groups. Gould, Leroy C.

Changing Patterns Of Delinquent Behavior Among Americans 13 16 Years Old, 1967-1972: Report # 1 Of The National Survey Of Youth, 1972. Gold, Martin and Reimer, David J.

An Analysis Of The Evidence And Seriousness Of Self—Reported Delinquency And Crime. Tracy, Paul E.

Perceived Risk Of Punishment And Self—Reported Delinquency. Jensen, Gary F and Erickson, Maynard L and Gibbs, Jack P.

Race And Involvement In Common Law Personal Crimes. Hindelang, Michael J.

Race And Involvement In Common Law Personal Crime: A Response To Hindelang. Mc Neely, Roger and Pope, Carl.

Correlates Of Delinquency: The Illusion Of Discrepancy Between Self—Report And Offical Measures. Hindelang, Michael J and Hirschi, Travis and Weis, Joseph G.

Reconciling Race And Class Differences In Self—Reported And Official Estimates Of Delinquency. Elliot, D S.

SELF CONTROL

Impulsive And Premeditated Homicide: An Analysis Of Subsequent Parole Risk Of The Murderer. Heilbrun Jr, Alfred B and Heilbrun, Lynn C and Heilbrun, Kim L.

SELLIN, THORSTEN

Book Review—Slavery And The Penal System. Christianson, Scott.

SENIORITY

Equal Opportunity And Seniority—Trends And Manpower Implications. Craft, J A.

Seniority Is Healthy. Fischer, B.

Affirmative Action Versus Seniority—Is Conflict Inevitable? Cebulski, B G.

SENSITIVITY TRAINING

Intergroup Relations For Police Officers. Epstein, Charlotte.

Humanizing Law Enforcement: A Liberal Approach From A Conservative Stance. Maddocks, Lewis I.

"A Guide To Race Relations For Police Officers" in *The Urban Policeman In Transition*, Snibbe, J (ed), 302—340. Mc Entire, Davis and Powers, Robert B.

Race Relations Training With Correctional Officers. Wittmer, J and Lanier, J E and Parker, M.

SENTENCING

The Offender And The Court: A Statistical Analysis Of Sentencing Of Delinquents. Frankel, Emil.

The Effect Of The Depression On Prison Commitments And Sentences. Stern, Leon Thomas.

Selective Factors In Capital Punishment. Johnson, Elmer H.

Judicial Attitudes Toward Sentencing. Green, Edward.

SERIOUSNESS

Seriousness Of Delinquency, The Adjudicative Decision, And Recidivism—A Longitudinal Configuration Analysis. Meade, A.

An Analysis Of The Evidence And Seriousness Of Self-Reported Delinquency And Crime. Tracy, Paul E.

SERVITUDE

The History Of Negro Servitude In Illinois And Of The Slavery Agitation In That State 1719–1864. Harris, N Dwight.

Peonage Or The New Negro Slavery. Chestnutt, Charles W.

The Negro In Pennsylvania: Slavery—Servitude—Freedom, 1639–1861. Turner, Edward Raymond.

Servant Into Slave: The Evolution Of The Legal Status Of The Negro Laborer In Colonial Virginia. Palmer, Paul C.

Servitude And Slavery In Colonial South Carolina, 1670–1776. Duncan, John Donald.

In The Matter Of Color. Higginbotham Jr, A Leon.

Slavery And Servitude In The Colony Of North Carolina. Bassett, John Spencer.

SEWARD, WILLIAM

Mr Seward For The Defense. Conrad, Earl.

SEX OFFENSES see Crime, Sex; Rape

see also Rape

SHAW, NATE

All God's Dangers: The Life Of Nate Shaw. Rosegarten, Theodore.

SHERIFFS

The Changing Role Of The County Sheriff. Brown, Lee P.

SHOPLIFTING

Observer's Reporting Of Shoplifting As A Function Of Thief's Race And Sex. Dertke, M C and Penner, L A and Ulrich, K.

SILBERMAN, CHARLES E

Books Of The Times. Wilkins, Roger.

Criminal Violence: An Exchange. Anonymous.

Silberman—Back To Root Causes. Anonymous.

The Politics Of Explaining Crime. Kelman, Mark G.

SIN

The Problem Of Slavery In Western Culture. Davis, David Brion.

The Crime Of Reform. Davis, David Brion.

SING SING PRISON, NY

"Work And Law Observance In The Histories Of Men In Sing–Sing Prison" in Report On The Causes Of Crime, V1, 193–255,315–320. Kleeck, Mary V.

The Negro Goes To Sing Sing. Reid, Ira De A.

On The Penitentiary System In The United States And Its Application In France, Francis Lieber (trans), Orig Pub 1833. Beaumont, Gustave De and Tocqueville, Alexis De.

SLAVE FAMILY

American Slavery As It Is: Testimony Of A Thousand Witnesses. American Anti– Slavery Society.

The Slave Community: Plantation Life In The Antebellum South. Blassingame, John W.

A Slave Family In The Ante–bellum South. Schweninger, Loren.

Slave Testimony: Two Centuries Of Letters, Speeches, Interviews, And Autobiographies. Blassingame, John W (ed).

SLAVE NARRATIVES

Twenty–Two Years A Slave And Forty Years A Freeman. Stewart, Austin.

The Confessions Of Nat Turner, The Leader Of The Late Insurrection In Southampton, Va. Turner, Nat.

American Slavery As It Is: Testimony Of A Thousand Witnesses. American Anti– Slavery Society.

The Autobiography Of A Fugitive Negro. Ward, Samuel Ringgold.

David Walker's Appeal To The Coloured Citizens Of The World 1829. Walker, David.

Many Thousand Gone: The Ex–Slaves' Account Of Their Bondage And Freedom. Nichols, Charles H.

My Bondage And My Freedom. Douglass, Frederick.

Once A Slave: The Slaves' View Of Slavery. Feldstein, Stanley.

Black Men In Chains: Narrative By Escaped Slaves. Nichols, Charles H.

The Slave Community: Plantation Life In The Antebellum South. Blassingame, John W.

Where I'm Bound: Patterns Of Slavery And Freedom In Black American Autobiography. Smith, Sidonie.

Slave Testimony: Two Centuries Of Letters, Speeches, Interviews, And Autobiographies. Blassingame, John W (ed).

The Victim As Criminal And Artist: Literature From The American Prison. Franklin, H Bruce.

Underground Rail Road Record. Still, William.

SLAVE TRADE

Slave Ships And Slaving. Dow, George Francis (ed).

Black Mother: The Years Of The African Slave Trade. Davidson, Basil.

Suppression Of The African Slave Trade To The United States, 1638–1870.(orig pub 1898). Du Bois W E B (ed).

Sins Of The Fathers: A Study Of The Atlantic Slave Traders, 1441–1807. Pope– Hennessy, James.

They Came In Chains: Americans From Africa. Redding, J Saunders.

Preferences For Slaves In Colonial America. Wax, Darold D.

SLAVERY

Twenty–Two Years A Slave And Forty Years A Freeman. Stewart, Austin.

The History Of Negro Servitude In Illinois And Of The Slavery Agitation In That State 1719–1864. Harris, N Dwight.

Peonage Or The New Negro Slavery. Chestnutt, Charles W.

The Negro In Pennsylvania: Slavery—Servitude—Freedom, 1639–1861. Turner, Edward Raymond.

The Police Control Of The Slave In South Carolina. Henry, Howell M.

American Negro Slavery: A Survey Of The Supply, Employment And Control Of Negro Labor As Determined By The Plantation Régime. Phillips, Ulrich Bonnell.

Pro–Slavery Thought In The Old South. Jenkins, William S.

American Slavery As It Is: Testimony Of A Thousand Witnesses. American Anti– Slavery Society.

The Negro In Colonial New England. Greene, Lorenzo M.

Capitalism And Slavery. Williams, Eric.

New Charter On Slavery. Huff, William Henry.

Trial And Imprisonment Of Jonathan Walker, At Pensacola, For Aiding Slaves To Escape From Bondage. Walker, Jonathan.

Horace Mann's Letters On The Extension Of Slavery Into California And New Mexico. Mann, Horace.

The Fugitive Slave Bill: Its History And Unconstitutionality. American Anti– Slavery Society.

The Peculiar Institution: Slavery In The Ante–Bellum South. Stampp, Kenneth M.

The Martyrs & The Fugitive, Or A Narrative Of The Captivity, Sufferings & Death Of An African Family & The Escape Of Their Son. Platt, Reverend S H.

Slavery And The Genesis Of American Race Prejudice. Degler, Carl N.

North Of Slavery. Litwack, Leon F.

Chattel Slavery And Concentration Camps. Thorpe, Earl E.

The Legal Status Of The Slave In South Carolina, 1670–1740. Sirmans, M Eugene.

Slavery In The Cities: The South, 1820–1860. Wade, Richard.

The Economics Of Slavery And Other Studies In Econometric History. Conrad, Alfred H and Meyer, John R.

The Problem Of Slavery In Western Culture. Davis, David Brion.

Servant Into Slave: The Evolution Of The Legal Status Of The Negro Laborer In Colonial Virginia. Palmer, Paul C.

Rebelliousness And Docility In The Negro Slave: A Critique Of The Elkins Thesis. Genovese, Eugene D.

Resistance To Slavery. Frederickson, George M and Lasch, Christopher.

From Slavery To Freedom. Franklin, John Hope.

Judicial Cases Concerning American Slavery And The Negro, 5v. Catterall, Helen H (ed).

My Bondage And My Freedom. Douglass, Frederick.

The Christian Doctrine Of Slavery, Org Pub 1857. Armstrong, George D.

The Negro In Maryland, Orig Pub 1889. Brackett, Jeffrey R.

Black Man, Red Man, And White American: The Constitutional Approach To Genocide. Willhelm, Sidney M.

Our Racist History. Van Woodward, C Vann.

The Image Of The Negro In The Maryland Gazette, 1745–1774. Wax, Darold D.

The Slave Catchers. Campbell, S W.

"Legal Status Of The Slave In South Carolina, 1670–1740" in Colonial American Essays In Political/Social Development, Katz (ed), 404–415. Senese, Donald.

The Black Image In The White Mind: The Debate On Afro–American Character And Destiny, 1817–1914. Frederickson, George M.

SLAVERY

Prison Or Slavery. Kasirika, Kaidi (Kenneth Divans) and Muntu, Maharibi (larry M West).

History Of The Rise And Fall Of The Slave Power In America, 3v. Wilson, Henry.

Servitude And Slavery In Colonial South Carolina, 1670–1776. Duncan, John Donald.

The Slave Community: Plantation Life In The Antebellum South. Blassingame, John W.

Black Bondage In The North. Mc Manus, Edgar J.

Historians And The Origins Of British North American Slavery. Starr, Raymond.

Racism And The Early American Legal Process, 1619–1896. Higginbotham Jr, A Leon.

Black Majority: Negroes In Colonial South Carolina From 1670 Through The Stone Rebellion. Wood, Peter H.

Roll, Jordan, Roll: The World The Slaves Made. Genovese, Eugene D.

The White Man's Burden: Historical Origins Of Racism In The United States. Jordan, Winthrop D.

Criminal Procedure In Slave Trials In The Antebellum South. Flanigan, Daniel J.

The Problem Of Slavery In The Age Of Revolution, 1770–1823. Davis, David Brion.

New Evidence Of Black Unrest In Colonial Brooklyn. Skemer, Don C.

Jefferson's Nephews: A Frontier Tragedy. Merrill Jr, Boynton.

Roots. Haley, Alex.

Slavery And The Penal System. Sellin, Thorsten.

White Over Black: American Attitudes Toward The Negro, 1550–1812, Orig Pub 1968. Jordan, Winthrop D.

Book Review—Slavery And The Penal System. Christianson, Scott.

In The Matter Of Color. Higginbotham Jr, A Leon.

The Historical Development Of Imprisonment Of Blacks In The US. Christianson, Scott.

Ancient Slavery And Modern Ideology. Finley, Moses I.

Prison And Plantation: Crime, Justice, And Authority In Massachusetts And South Carolina, 1767–1878. Hindus, Michael Stephen.

The Crime Of Reform. Davis, David Brion.

Fugitive Slaves 1619–1865. Mc Dougall, Marion Gleason.

Slavery And Servitude In The Colony Of North Carolina. Bassett, John Spencer.

SLAVERY, PENAL

Penal Servitude. Whitin, E Stagg.

Penal Slavery And Southern Reconstruction. Mc Kelvey, Blake.

American Prisons: A Study In American Social History. Mc Kelvey, Blake.

An Essay On Crime And Punishments, Orig Pub 1763. Beccaria, Cesare Bonesana.

On The Penitentiary System In The United States And Its Application In France, Francis Lieber (trans), Orig Pub 1833. Beaumont, Gustave De and Tocqueville, Alexis De.

Break De Chains Of Legalized Slavery. Anonymous.

Slavery And The Penal System. Sellin, Thorsten.

The Historical Development Of Imprisonment Of Blacks In The US. Christianson, Scott.

Prison And Plantation: Crime, Justice, And Authority In Massachusetts And South Carolina, 1767–1878. Hindus, Michael Stephen.

The Crime Of Reform. Davis, David Brion.

SLAVERY - BLACK DRIVER

The Man In The Middle, The Black Slave Driver. Miller, Randall M.

SLAVERY - EMANCIPATION

Twenty–Two Years A Slave And Forty Years A Freeman. Stewart, Austin.

The Negro In Pennsylvania: Slavery–Servitude–Freedom, 1639–1861. Turner, Edward Raymond.

The Negro In Colonial New England. Greene, Lorenzo M.

North Of Slavery. Litwack, Leon F.

The African Colonization Movement, 1816–1865. Staudenraus, P J.

The Freedmen Of South Carolina. Nordhoff, Charles.

The Free Negro And The South Carolina Courts, 1790–1860. Senese, Donald.

From Slavery To Freedom. Franklin, John Hope.

Many Thousand Gone: The Ex–Slaves' Account Of Their Bondage And Freedom. Nichols, Charles H.

The Negro In Maryland, Orig Pub 1889. Brackett, Jeffrey R.

Neither Slave Nor Free: The Freedman Of African Descent In The Slave Societies Of The New World. Cohen, David M (ed) and Greene, Jack P (ed).

Black Bondage In The North. Mc Manus, Edgar J.

Where I'm Bound: Patterns Of Slavery And Freedom In Black American Autobiography. Smith, Sidonie.

Philanthropy Of Bargain Prices: Notes On The Economics Of Gradual Emancipation. Fogel, Robert William and Engerman, Stanley L.

Been In The Storm So Long: The Aftermath Of Slavery. Litwack, Leon F.

SLAVERY - OVERSEER

American Negro Slavery: A Survey Of The Supply, Employment And Control Of Negro Labor As Determined By The Plantation Régime. Phillips, Ulrich Bonnell.

The Southern Planatation Overseer: As Revealed In His Letters. Bassett, John Spencer.

The Slave Community: Plantation Life In The Antebellum South. Blassingame, John W.

The Man In The Middle, The Black Slave Driver. Miller, Randall M.

SLAVERY - SLAVE IDENTITY

Slave Names In Colonial South Carolina. Cohen, Hennig.

Slavery: A Problem In American Institutional & Intellectual Life. Elkins, Stanley M.

Rebels And Sambos: The Search For The Negro's Personality In Slavery. Stampp, Kenneth M.

Roll, Jordan, Roll: The World The Slaves Made. Genovese, Eugene D.

Slave Testimony: Two Centuries Of Letters, Speeches, Interviews, And Autobiographies. Blassingame, John W (ed).

SLAVERY REBELLION & RESISTANCE

An Account Of The Late Intended Insurrection Among A Portion Of The Blacks Of This City. Hamilton Jr, James.

The Confessions Of Nat Turner, The Leader Of The Late Insurrection In Southampton, Va. Turner, Nat.

American Slave Insurrections Before 1861. Wish, Harvey.

Slave Insurrections In The United States, 1800–1865. Carroll, Joseph Cephas.

Negro Slave Revolts In The United States, 1526–1860. Aptheker, Herbert.

A History Of The Amistad Captives. Barber, John Warner.

Narrative Of The Barbarous Treatment Of Two Unfortunate Females, Natives Of Concordia LA By Joseph & Enoch, Runaway Slaves. Joseph and Enoch.

Day To Day Resistance To Slavery. Bauer, Raymond A and Bauer, Alice H.

Proceedings Of The Conspiracy Formed By Some White People For Burning The City Of NY In America And Murdering The Inhabitants. Horsmanden, Daniel.

Narrative Of The Sufferings Of Lewis And Milton Clarke: More Than Twenty Years Among The Slaveholders Of Kentucky. Clarke, Lewis and Clarke, Milton.

American Slave Discontent In Records Of The High Courts. Russell, Marion J.

Slavery: A Problem In American Institutional & Intellectual Life. Elkins, Stanley M.

An Account Of Some Of The Principal Slave Insurrections. Coffin, Joshua.

The Slave Insurrection In New York In 1712. Scott, Kenneth.

The Vesey Plot: A Reconsideration. Wade, Richard.

Towards Freedom: An Analysis Of Slave Revolts In The United States. Kilson, Marion D De B.

David Walker's Appeal To The Coloured Citizens Of The World 1829. Walker, David.

Rebelliousness And Docility In The Negro Slave: A Critique Of The Elkins Thesis. Genovese, Eugene D.

Resistance To Slavery. Fredickson, George M and Lasch, Christopher.

Black Resistance Before The Civil War. Cheek, William F (ed).

The Slave Catchers. Campbell, S W.

"Slave Resistance In The US" in *Key Issues In The Afro–American Experience*, Huggins, N; M Kilson And D M Fox (eds). Aptheker, Herbert.

Black Resistance/White Law: A History Of Constitutional Racism In America. Berry, Mary F.

Black Men In Chains: Narrative By Escaped Slaves. Nichols, Charles H.

Denmark Vesey: The Slave Conspiracy Of 1822. Starobin, Robert (ed).

SUBCULTURES

Street Corner Society. Whyte, William Foote.

Growing Up And Its Price In Three Puerto Rican Subcultures. Wolf, K L.

Group Process And Gang Delinquency. Gordon, Robert A et al.

The Subculture Of Violence: Towards An Integrated Theory In Criminology. Wolfgang, Marvin E and Ferracuti, Franco.

Comment On Lerman's 'Gangs, Networks, And Subcultural Delinquency'. Short Jr, James F.

Violence By Blacks And Low–Income Whites: Some New Evidence On The Subculture Of Violence Thesis. Erlanger, Howard S.

The Empirical Status Of The Subculture Of Violence Thesis. Erlanger, Howard S.

The 'Low–Riders': Portrait Of An Urban Youth Subculture. Holtz, Janice Marie Allard.

Criminal Violence, Criminal Justice. Silberman, Charles E.

Subculture Of Violence: Youth Offender Value Systems. Poland, James M.

The Santa Fe Prison Riots: 'The Flower Of The Dragon'. Mandel, Jerry.

SUBORDINATION

Occupational Benefits To Whites From The Subordination Of Negroes. Glenn, Norval.

Negro Subordination And White Gains. Cutright, Phillip.

White Gains From Negro Subordination. Glenn, Norval.

White Gains From Black Subordination In 1960 And 1970. Dowdall, George.

Subordinating The Poor. Feagin, Joe R.

SUBURBS

Community Safety And Criminal Activity In Black Suburbs. Nichols Jr, Woodrow W.

SUCCESS

Success Values: Are They Universal Or Class Differentiated? Dolla Faxe, Richard L.

SUICIDE

Notes On Navajo Suicide. Wyman, L and Thorne, B.

African Homicide And Suicide. Bohannon, P (ed).

Suicide And Homicide: A Comparative Analysis By Race And Occupaltional Levels. Lalli, Michael and Turner, Stanley.

Suicide, And White Reformatory Girl's Preference For Negro Men. Hammer, M.

Suicides And Homicides Among Indians. Ogden, Michael and Spector, M I and Hill Jr, C A.

Jail House Blues: Studies Of Suicidal Behavior In Jail And Prison. Danto, Bruce L (ed).

Suicide, Homicide, And Alcoholism Among American Indians—Guidelines For Help. Frederick, C J.

Epidemiological Differences Between White And Nonwhite Suicide Attempters. Pederson, A M and Awad, G A and Kindler, A R.

Adolescent Suicide On An Indian Reservation. Dizmang, Larry H Et Al.

An Epidemiological Study Of Suicide And Attempted Suicide Among The Papago Indians. Conrad, R D and Kahn, M W.

In Prison: A Contagion Of Suicide. Christianson, Scott.

Notes Toward An Epidemiology Of Urban Suicide. Morris, Jeffrey B Et Al.

Suicide And Culture In Fairbanks: A Comparison Of Three Cultural Groups In A Small City Of Interior Alaska. Parkin, M.

Men In Crisis: Human Breakdowns In Prison. Toch, Hans et al.

American Indian Suicide—Fact And Fantasy. Shore, James H.

Culture And Crisis In Confinement. Johnson, Robert.

Ethnic/Racial Misidentification In Death: A Problem Which May Distort Suicide Statistics. Andress, V R.

Suicide Among Blacks. Jedlicka, D et al.

Suicide Epidemic On An Indian Reserve. Ward, J A and Fox, J.

Violent Death In The City: Suicide, Accident, And Murder In Nineteenth–Century Philadelphia. Lane, Roger.

"Black Female Suicides: Is The Excitement Justified" in *The Black Woman*, Rodgers–Rose, La Frances (ed). Aldridge, Delores P.

SUPREME COURT, U S

Fifty Years Of Negro Citizenship As Qualified By The United States Supreme Court. Woodson, Carter G.

A Nation Within A Nation, The Negro And The Supreme Court. Konvitz, Milton R.

The Upgrading Of The Negro's Status By Supreme Court Decisions. Alexander, Raymond Pace.

The Supreme Court On Racial Discrimination. Tussman, Joseph (ed).

Negro In The Supreme Court, 1963. Gill, Robert L.

Negro In The Supreme Court. Gill, Robert L.

Gideon's Trumpet. Lewis, Anthony.

Current Racial Legal Developments. Donegan, Charles E and Hunter, Jerry.

The Petitioners, The Story Of The Supreme Court Of The US And The Negro. Miller, Loren.

Judicial Cases Concerning American Slavery And The Negro, 5v. Catterall, Helen H (ed).

The Self–Inflicted Wound. Graham, Fred P.

El Chicano And The Constitution: The Legacy Of Hernandez Versus Texas. Comment.

Blacks, Due Process And Efficiency In The Clash Of Values As The Supreme Court Moves To The Right. Mc Gee Jr, Henry W.

The Viability And Reliability Of The US Supreme Court As An Institution For Social Change And Progress Beneficial To Blacks. Tollett, Kenneth S.

"Police Entry Testing And Minority Employment Implications" in *Police And Law Enforcement*, Curran, J (ed), 313–317. Vanagunas, Stanley.

Cruel And Unusual: The Supreme Court And Capital Punishment. Meltsner, Michael.

Litigating Against The Death Penalty: The Strategy Behind *Furman*. Meltsner, Michael.

The Erosion Of The Fourth Amendment Exclusionary Rule. Quintana, Marsha A.

Background Paper On The Supreme Court's Death Penalty Decisions. American Civil Liberties Union.

Constitutional Law—Unequal Protection For The American Indian Under The Major Crimes Act: United States Versus Antelope. Note.

The Death Penalty: Social Philosophy And Social Science Research. Wolfgang, Marvin E.

The Death Penalty And The Current State Of The Law. Davis, Peggy C.

The American Ideal Of Equality And Constitutional Change. Redenius, Charles M.

SUQUAMISH TRIBE

Indian Law: Oliphant v Suquamish Indian Tribe, 435 US 191 (1978). Berkey, C G.

SUTHERLAND, EDWIN H

Changing Criminals: The Application Of The Theory Of Differential Association. Cressey, Donald R.

Delinquency And Opportunity: A Theory Of Delinquent Gangs. Cloward, Richard A and Ohlin, Lloyd E.

Thinking About Crime. Wilson, James Q.

SYRACUSE, NY

Varieties Of Police Behavior: The Management Of Law And Order In Eight Communities. Wilson, James Q.

TATE, WILLIE

"An Interview With Willie Tate" in *Punishment And Penal Discipline*, Platt, Tony And Paul Takagi (eds), 176–183. Begel, Debby.

TEAM DEFENSE

Team Defense: The Holistic Approach: An Interview With Millard Farmer. Eisenberg, Howard.

TEAM POLICING

Neighborhood Team Policing And Management. Brown, Lee P.

Neighborhood Team Policing: A Viable Concept In Multanomah County. Brown, Lee P and Martin, E E.

TENNESSEE *see* Memphis, Tn

The Legal Status Of The Negro. Magnum, Charles S.

The Dangerousness Of Imprisonment. Jones, David A.

TERRORISM

Sniping—A New Pattern Of Violence? Knopf, Terry Ann.

A Global Terrorist Coalition—Its Incipient Stage. Wolf, John B.

Terrorism And Criminal Justice: An International Perspective. Crelinsten, Ronald (ed).

To What Extent Was Enrique Soto The Creation Of Pedro Juan Soto? Kennedy, William.

TEST, TAPPING

Delinquents And The Tapping Test. Andrew, J M.

TESTING, EMPLOYMENT

Testing And Equal Opportunity—Getting A Fair Chance. White, W P.

TESTING, INTELLIGENCE

Cultural And Racial Variations In Patterns Of Intellect, Peformance Of Negro And White Children On The Bellevue Adult Intelligence Scale. Machover, Solomon.

Discriminative Value And Patterns Of The Wechsler—Bellevue Scales In The Examination Of Delinquent Negro Boys. Franklin, J C.

Verbal Performance IQ Differences Of White And Negro Delinquents On The WISC And WAIS. Henning, John J and Levy, Russell H.

IQ Tests And Their Educational Supporters. Jorgensen, Carl C.

IQ: Heritability And Inequality, Part I. Block, N J and Dworkin, G.

Race Differences In Intelligence. Loehlin, John C and Lindzey, Gardner and Spuhler, J N.

IQ: Heritability And Inequality, Part II. Block, N J and Dworkin, G.

The Cyril Burt Question: New Findings. Dorfman, D D.

TESTING, PSYCHOLOGICAL

A Psychological And Educational Survey Of 1916 Prisoners In The Western Penitentiary Of Pennsylvania. Root Jr, William T.

The Effect Of The Ethnic Grouping Of The Experimenter Upon Children's Responses To Tests Of An Ethnic Nature. Vaughn, G M.

The Performance Of Male Prisoners On The Marlowe—Crowne Social Desirability Scale: II, Differences As A Function Of Race And Crime. Fisher, Gary.

Juvenile Delinquents: Relationships Between Wisc Scores, Offenses, Race, Chronological Age, And Residence. Mc Conochie, W A.

Bender—Gestalt Protocols Of Adult Negro Male Offenders: Normative Data. Matranga, James T and Jensen, Diane E and Prandoni, Jaques R.

Screening For Emotional And Psychological Fitness In Correctional Officer Hiring. Goldstein, B.

Factorial Dimensions Of Jesness Inventory With Black Delinquents. Woodbury, Roger and Shurling, James.

Personality Patterns Of White, Black, And Mexican American Patrolmen As Measured By The Sixteen Personality Factor Questionaire. Snibbe, H M and Fabricatore, Joseph and Azen, Stanley P.

Psychological Examination In Police Selection. Crosby, A.

Psychological Testing Of Incarcerated Hispanics, Natl Hispanic Con L Enf & CJ. Torre, Marcella De La.

TEXAS

see also Dallas, Tx, El Paso, Tx, Houston, Tx

A Sociological Study Of A Texas Lynching. Pruden, Durwood.

The Legal Status Of The Negro. Magnum, Charles S.

With His Pistol In His Hand: A Border Ballad And Its Hero. Paredes, Américo.

African Homicide And Suicide. Bohannon, P (ed).

Significance Of The Racial Factor In The Length Of Prison Sentences. Bullock, Henry Allen.

A Political History Of The Texas Penal System, 1829–1951. Crow, H.

Texas Sentencing Practices: A Statistical Study. Baab, George W and Ferguson, William R.

Outside The Law: A Thief's Primer. Jackson, Bruce.

The Negro Law Enforcement Officer In Texas. Cole, D A et al.

Capital Punishment In Texas, 1924–1968. Koeninger, R C.

Colonialism: The Case Of The Mexican—Americans. Moore, Joan W.

The Texas Supreme Court And The Trial Rights Of Blacks. Nash, A E Keir.

A Synopsis Of Offenders Receiving The Death Sentence In Texas. Texas Dept Of Corrections, Div Of Research.

Wake Up Dead Man: Afro—American Worksongs From Texas Prisons. Jackson, Bruce (ed).

Chicano Revolt In A Texas Town. Shockley, John Staples.

Equal Employment And The Texas Criminal Justice System. Texas Office Of The Governor.

Prison Reform In Social Perspective. Vogel, Richard.

An Empirical Examination Of Conflict Theory: Race And Sentence Length. Dison, Jack E.

Equal Employment Opportunity For Minorities In Municipal Government. Hall, G and Saltzstein, A.

Overcrowding In Texas Prisons, Special Legislative Report No 43. Texas House Of Representatives.

Spouse Abuse In Texas—A Special Report. Stachura, S and Teske Jr, R H C.

Dishonor In The Sun: The Violation Of Human Rights, Texas—Style. Lyon, Matthew.

Inadequate Defense Counsel—An Empirical Analysis Of Prisoners' Perceptions. Alpert, Geoffrey P.

TEXAS RANGERS

The Texas Rangers. Webb, Walter Prescott.

Gunpowder Justice: A Reassessment Of The Texas Rangers. Samora, Julian and Bernal, Joe and Pena, Albert.

Gunpowder Justice: A Reassessment Of The Texas Rangers (Book Review). Trujillo, Larry D.

THEFT, MOTOR VEHICLE

Auto Theft: Offender And Offense Characteristics. Mc Caghy, Charles H and Giordano, Peggy C and Henson, Trudy Knicely.

TONG WARS

New Style Highbinder Fights Tong Wars Today. Manion, Jack.

Tong War. Gong, Eng Ying and Grant, Bruce.

The Hatchet Men. Dillon, Richard H.

TRAINING SCHOOLS see Institutionalization, Juvenile

TREATMENT, CLINICAL

Some Effects Of A White Institution On Black Psychiatric Outpatients. Krebs, R L.

Black Psychology. Jones, Reginald L (ed).

Racism And Psychiatry. Thomas, Alexander and Sillen, Samuel.

"Behavior Therapy And The Black Delinquent" in *Behavior Therapy With Delinquents*, Stumphauzer, J (ed), 49–53. Kimbles, Samuel L.

A Look At The Effect Of Racism On Clinical Work. Cooper, S.

The Effect Of Client Race And Social Class On Clinical Judgements. Fischer, J and Miller, H.

The Needle And The Boot: Heroin Maintenance. Cuskey, Walter R and Krasner, William.

The System—Maintenance Role Of The White Psychologist. Thomas, Charles W.

A Brief Review Of The Effects Of Race In Clinical Service Interactions. Siegel, J M.

The Validity Of The MMPI As A Discriminator Of Social Deviance Among Black Males. Elion, Victor H.

Pretreatment Criminality Of Male And Female Drug Abuse Patients In The United States. Ball, John C et al.

Ecologic—Biochemical Approaches To The Treatment Of Delinquents And Criminals. Hippchen, Leonard J (ed).

The Effects Of Ethnicity, Age And Sex Upon Processing Through And Emergency Alcohol Health Care Delivery System. Westie, K S and Mc Bride, D C.

TREATMENT, NON-CLINICAL

Staff Conceptions Of Inmate Characteristics: A Comparison Of Treatment And Custodial Staffs At Two Differing Institutions. Brown, Barry S et al.

Some Evidence Of Race Bias In The Diagnosis And Treatment Of The Juvenile Offender. Lewis, Dorothy O and Balla, David A and Shanok, Shelley S.

TRES MARIAS PENAL COL, MEXICO

Mexico's Tres Marias Penal Colony. Jewell, Donald P.

TRIAL

Mr Seward For The Defense. Conrad, Earl.

One Man's Freedom. Williams, Edward B.

A Study Of The California Penalty Jury In First—Degree Murder Trials. Note.

Fairness And Formalism In The Trials Of Blacks In The State Supreme Courts Of The Old South. Nash, A E Keir.

Native Americans And Discrimination In Kansas: Trials From Injustice. Bean, Jerry L.

Criminal Procedure In Slave Trials In The Antebellum South. Flanigan, Daniel J.

Criminal Justice Processing: The Determinants Of The Decision To Go To Trial. Sterling, Joyce S.

Race, Recruitment And Representation: Background Differences In Black And White Trial Judges. Uhlman, Thomas M.

The Psychology Of Eyewitness Testimony. Yarmey, A Daniel.

TRIALS, POLITICAL

Scottsboro Boy. Patterson, Haywood and Conrad, Earl.

The Trial Of Bobby Seale. Seale, Bobby.

Look For Me In The Whirlwind: The Collective Autobiography Of The New York 21. Balagon, Kuwasi et al.

TRIALS, POLITICAL

Latitude And Severity Of Sentencing Options, Race Of The Victim And Decisions Of Simulated Jurors. Kaplan, J.

The Briar Patch: The People Of The State Of New York V Lumumba Shakur Et Al. Kempton, Murray.

The Dialectics Of Legal Repression: Black Rebels Before The American Criminal Courts. Balbus, Isaac D.

The Morning Breaks: The Trial Of Angela Davis. Aptheker, Bettina.

The Uses Of Social Science In Trials With Political And Racial Overtones: The Trial Of Joan Little. Mc Conahay, John B and Mullin, Courtney J and Frederick, Jeffrey.

Illusions Of Justice: Human Rights Violations In The United States. Hinds, Lennox S.

TRIBAL COURTS *see* Courts, Tribal

TRUANCY

Are Educational Norms And Goals Conforming, Truant And Delinquent Adolescent Influenced By Group Position In American Society? Reiss Jr, Albert J and Rhodes, Albert Louis.

TUCSON, AZ

Minority Recruiting: The Tucson Police Experience. Grant, R and Milne, R and White, R.

TULSA, OK

The Eruption Of Tulsa. White, Walter.

TURNER, NAT

The Confessions Of Nat Turner, The Leader Of The Late Insurrection In Southampton, Va. Turner, Nat.

The Southampton Slave Revolt Of 1831. Tragle, Henry Irving.

UNEMPLOYMENT

Social Aspects Of The Business Cycle. Davies, George R.

Unemployment And Prison Commitments. Simpson, Ray Mars.

Post—War Trends In Employment, Crime, Insanity, And Heart Disease. Simpson, Ray Mars.

Research Memorandum On Crime In The Depression. Sellin, Thorsten.

The Effect Of The Depression On Prison Commitments And Sentences. Stern, Leon Thomas.

Effects Of Unemployment On White And Negro Prison Admissions In Louisiana. Dobbins, D A and Bass, Bernard M.

Economic Deprivation And Extremism: A Study Of Unemployed Negroes. Street, D and Leggett, J C.

Black Metropolis: A Study Of Negro Life In A Northern City, Rev'd Ed Orig Pub 1945. Cayton, Horace R and Drake, St Clair.

The Prison Of Unemployment. Taggert, R.

Theories Of Poverty And Unemployment. Gordon, David M.

Race And Economics. Sowell, Thomas.

Unemployment And Prison Population Trends In Georgia: 1967–1974. Cox, George H and Carr, Timothy S.

"Employment And Discrimination" in *Crime And Its Impact On The Black Community*, Gary, L E And L P Brown (eds), 69–76. Padgett, Squire.

Inequality, Unemployment And Crime: A Cross–National Analysis. Krohn, M D.

Iowa Prison Crisis: Economic Problem. Bruner, Charles.

Punishment And The Post–Industrial Society: A Study Of Unemployment, Crime And Imprisonment In The US. Jankovic, Ivan.

Labor Market And Imprisonment. Jankovic, Ivan.

Crime And Employment Issues: A Collection Of Policy Relevant Monographs. American University Law School.

Crime—Unemployment Cycle. Becnel, B.

UNIVERSITY OF WASHINGTON

DeFunis Versus Odegaard And The University Of Washington, 3v. Ginger, Ann Fagan (ed).

URBANIZATION

The Urbanization Of Negroes In The United States. Farley, Reynolds.

The Urban Crisis And Crime. Krantz, Sheldon and Kramer, William D.

UTAH

Utah—Manpower And Training. Utah Council On Criminal Justice Adminstration.

VALUES

The Lower–Class Value Stretch. Rodman, Hyman.

Values And Gang Delinquency: A Study Of Street–Corner Groups. Gordon, Robert A et al.

Soul Side: Inquires Into Ghetto Culture And Community. Hannerz, Ulf.

Subculture Of Violence: Youth Offender Value Systems. Poland, James M.

Psychological World Of The Juvenile Delinquent. Offer, D.

VANDALISM

Caste, Class And Vandalism. Bates, William.

Graffiti And Crime: A Transcultural Study Of Narcissistic Rage. Lomas, H D and Singer, R D.

VENGEANCE

Deadline, Vengeance, And Tribute: A Prescription For Black Juvenile Delinquency. Echols, Alvin E.

VERDICTS

Socioeconomic Factors Influencing Jury Verdict. Adler, Freda.

VESEY, DENMARK

An Account Of The Late Intended Insurrection Among A Portion Of The Blacks Of This City. Hamilton Jr, James.

The Vesey Plot: A Reconsideration. Wade, Richard.

Denmark Vesey: The Slave Conspiracy Of 1822. Starobin, Robert (ed).

VICE CRIME *see* Specific Offense

The Ethnic Vice Industry. Light, I.

VICE LORDS

The Vice Lords: Warriors Of The Streets. Keiser, R Lincoln.

VICTIM ASSISTANCE

Blaming The Victim. Ryan, William.

VICTIMIZATION

The Criminal And His Victim. Von Hentig, Hans.

Patterns In Criminal Homicide. Wolfgang, Marvin E.

Race Of Victim And Of Offender For Rape, Robbery And Assault And Battery Offenses Known To The Police: Report To The Pres Crime Commission. Reiss Jr, Albert J.

The Poor Pay More. Caplovitz, David.

Sexual Assaults In The Philadelphia Prison System And Sheriff's Vans. Davis, A J.

Blaming The Victim. Ryan, William.

Patterns In Forcible Rape. Amir, Menachem.

The Black Prisoner As Victim. Burns, Haywood.

New Perspectives On Urban Crime. American Bar Association.

The Mugging. Hunt, Morton.

Biracial Aggression: I, Effect Of Verbal Attack And Sex Of Victim. Gentry, W D.

Who Is The Victim? Quinney, Richard.

Mortality Trends For Homicide By Age, Color, And Sex: United States, 1960–1972. Klebba, A Joan.

Victimization And Perception Of Crime In A Ghetto Community. Kleinman, Paula H and David, Deborah S.

Who Called The Cops: Decisions To Report Criminal Victimization. Hawkins, R O.

"Victim Precipitated Criminal Homicide" in *Crime And Criminal Justice*, Patterson, D (ed), 80–90. Wolfgang, Marvin E.

"Victims, Harm And Justice" in *Victimology: A New Focus*, V1, Drapkin, Israel And Emilio Viano (eds), 77–87. Reiman, Jeffrey.

Terror In The Prisons. Weiss, Carl and Friar, David James.

Victimology: A New Focus, V1. Drapkin, Israel (ed) and Viano, Emilio (ed).

The Black Offender As Victim. Debro, Julius.

Victim Characteristics And Helping Behavior In A Rural Southern Setting. Franklin, Billy J.

Why Notify The Police: The Victim's Decision To Notify The Police Of An Assault. Block, Richard L.

"The Offender As Victim" in *Victimology: A New Focus*, V3, Drapkin, Israel And Emilio Viano (eds), 113–120. Newman, Joseph.

Criminal Victimization Surveys In The Nation's Five Largest Cities. U S Dept Of Justice, LEAA, NCJIsS.

In Constant Fear: The Brutal Story Of Life Within The Walls Of The Notorious Walpole State Prison, As Told To James B Shuman. Remick, Peter.

Evaluating The Police: A Comparison Of Black Street And Household Respondents. Boggs, Sara L and Galliher, John F.

Crime & Its Impact On The Black Community. Gary, Lawrence E (ed) and Brown, Lee P (ed).

Crime In The Minority Community. Joyner, Irving and Scott, Elsie K.

Criminal Victimization In Eight American Cities. Hindelang, Michael J.

"Dealing With Prison Violence" in *Prison Violence*, Cohen, Albert K; George F Cole, And Robert G Bailey (eds). Sumner, George W.

VICTIMIZATION

"The Organization Of Prison Violence" in *Prison Violence*, Cohen, Albert K; George F Cole, And Robert G Bailey (eds). Park, James W L.

Book Review On Frank G Carrington's *The Victims*. Wilson, Jerry V.

Crime Prevention For Older Americans: Multanomah County's Victimization Study. Brown, Lee P and Ritai, Marlene A Young.

Crime Victims And Public Social Policy. Hudson, Joe and Galaway, Burt.

Minorities As Victims Of Police Shootings: Interpretation Of Racial Disproportionality And Police Use Of Deadly Force. Goldkamp, John S.

The Prison Inmate As Victim. Drapkin, Israel.

The Victimization Of The American Indian. Dadrian, Vahakn N.

Criminal Victimization In The United States 1975. U S Dept Of Justice, LEAA, NCJISS.

Forcible Rape: The Crime, The Victim, And The Offender. Chappell, Duncan and Geis, Robley (ed) and Geis, Gilbert (ed).

Victims, Crime And Social Control. Liegenhagen, Edward A.

"Black Offender And White Victim" in *Forcible Rape—The Crime, The Victim And The Offender*, Chappell, D; R Geis, And G Geis (eds). Agopian, Michael W.

Humanitarian Reform And Biracial Sexual Assault In A Maximum Security Prison. Carroll, Leo.

Some Social Characteristics Of Young Gunshot Fatalities. Klein, D et al.

Violence And Victimization Within A State Prison System. Fuller, Dan A and Orsagh, Thomas.

Criminal Victimization Of American Minorities: A Course Outline. Austin, Roy L.

Criminal Victimization In The United States 1976. U S Dept Of Justice, LEAA, NCJISS.

Victims Of Personal Crime: An Empirical Foundation For A Theory Of Victimization. Hindelang, Michael J and Gottfredson, Michael and Garofalo, James.

"Crime And Criminal Justice: Their Impact Upon Asian American Communities" in *National Minority Advisory Council Report.* Takagi, Paul.

Race And Involvement In Common Law Personal Crime: A Response To Hindelang. Mc Neely, Roger and Pope, Carl.

The Victims. Renshaw, Benjamin H and Lehnen, Robert.

Violent Crime Perpetrated Against The Elderly In The City Of Dallas, October 1974–September 1975. Georges, Daniel E and Kirksey, Kirk.

Aftermath Of Rape. Mc Cahill, T W and Meyer, L C and Fischman, A M.

Criminal Victimization In The United States 1977. U S Dept Of Justice, LEAA, NCJISS.

Black On Black Crime—The Cause, The Consequences, The Cures. Johnson, J H (ed).

Criminal Victimization In The U S: Summary Findings Of 1978–1979 Changes In Crime And Of Trends Since 1973. U S Dept Of Justice, Bureau Of Justice Statistics.

Prison Sexual Violence. Lockwood, Daniel.

The Hispanic Victim: National Crime Survey Report SD–NCS–N–16A, NCJ–67706. U S Dept Of Justice, Bureau Of Justice Statistics.

Urban Structure And Victimization. Decker, David L and Shicor, David and O' Brien, Robert M.

VIETNAM

The Politics Of Heroin In Southeast Asia. Mc Coy, Albert.

Racial Pattern Of Military Crimes In Vietnam. Kroll, J.

VIOLENCE

"The Pattern Of Violence" in *Culture In The South*, Couch, W T (ed), 678–692. Brearly, H C.

"Historical Patterns Of Violence In America" in *Violence In America*, Graham, Hugh D And T Gurr (eds), 45–83. Brown, Richard Maxwell.

Violence And Robbery: A Case Study. Normandeau, Andre.

Limitations For The Prevention Of Violence: The Latin American Reality And Its Criminological Theory. Del Olmo, Rosa.

Social Control, Violence And Radicalization: Behavioral Data. Adamek, R J and Lewis, J M.

VIOLENCE, COLLECTIVE

Does Lynching Thrive Under Democracy? Tyler, Ralph W.

Lynching, America's National Disgrace. Johnson, James Weldon.

Lynching And The Law. Chadbourn, J H.

The Tragedy Of Lynching. Raper, Arthur.

Ladies And Lynching. Nordyke, Lewis T.

"Chapter 4: The Lynching Mob" in *The Psychology Of Social Movements.* Cantril, Hadley.

Behind The Prison Riots. Mac Cormick, Austin H.

The Precipitants And Underlying Conditions Of Race Riots. Lieberson, Stanley and Silverman, Arnold.

The Riot. Elli, Frank.

Rebellion In Newark. Hayden, Tom.

Rivers Of Blood, Years Of Darkness. Conot, Robert.

Report Of The National Advisory Commission On Civil Disorders. Riot Commission.

Urban Riots: Violence And Social Change. Connery, Robert H (ed).

Contingency Planning For The Administration Of Justice During Civil Disorder And Mass Arrest. Friedman, H G.

Detroit 1967: Racial Violence Or Class Warfare. Corsi, Jerome.

Mob Violence And The Prosecuting Attorney. Karton, Robert.

Negro Opinions In Three Riot Cities. Mc Cord, William and Howard, John.

On The Ecology Of Political Violence: 'The Long Hot Summer' As A Hypothesis. Schwartz, David.

Racial Disturbances As Collective Protest. Lang, Kurt and Lang, G.

Report Of The Special Committee On Criminal Law Problems In Civil Disorders. American Bar Association.

The Development Of A Real Ideology Among Urban Negroes. Tomlinson, T M.

The Study Of Urban Violence: Some Implications Of Laboratory Studies Of Frustration And Aggression. Berkowitz, Leonard.

Three Views Of Urban Violence: Civil Disturbance, Racial Revolt, Class Assault. Grimshaw, Allen.

"A Cause Of Some Great Revolutions And A Contained Rebellion" in *The History Of Violence In America*, Graham, Hugh D & T Gurr (eds), 690–730. Davies, James C.

"International War And Domestic Turmoil" in *Violence In America*, Graham, Hugh D And T Gurr (eds), 550–569. Tanter, Raymond.

"Patterns Of Collective Racial Violence" in *The History Of Violence In America*, Graham, Hugh D And T Gurr (eds), 412–444. Janowitz, Morris.

An Index Of Riot Severity And Some Correlates. Wanderer, J J.

The Revolt Of The Urban Ghettos, 1964–1967. Boskin, Joseph.

The Violent Gang. Yablonsky, Lewis.

Violence And Grievances: Reflections On The 1960's Riots. Fogelson, Robert.

The Public Perception Of The Watts Riot As Social Protest. Jefferies, Vincent and Turner, R H and Morris, R T.

Police Riots: Collective Violence And Law Enforcement. Starls, R.

Harlem And Detroit Riots Of 1943: A Comprehensive Analysis. Swan, L Alex.

Inter–Ethnic Conflict. Glazer, Nathan.

Ghetto Revolts: The Politics Of Violence In American Cities. Feagin, Joe R and Harlan, Alan.

The Causes Of Racial Disorders: A Grievance–Level Explanation. Morgan, W R and Clark, T N.

The Prosaic Sources Of Prison Violence. Mattick, Hans.

Honor, Normative Ambiguity And Gang Violence. Horowitz, Ruth and Schwartz, Gary.

Rumors, Race And Riots. Knopf, Terry Ann.

Violence By Youth Gangs And Youth Groups In Major American Cities—Final Report. Miller, Walter B.

Peacekeeping—Police, Prisons And Violence. Toch, Hans.

The Black Revolts: Racial Stratification In The USA. Scott, Joseph.

Gunfights In The Cocaine Coral. Schorr, Mark.

Riots And Acts Of Violence In The Penitentiaries: What Can We Learn? Chocla, M A.

Understanding Violence. Newman, Graeme R.

Estrangement, Machismo And Gang Violence. Erlanger, Howard S.

The True Story Of The Greensboro Massacre. Bermanzohn, Paul C and Bermanzohn, Sally A.

Prison Perspective (Santa Fe Prison Riot). Anonymous.

The Santa Fe Prison Riots: 'The Flower Of The Dragon'. Mandel, Jerry.

VIOLENCE, FUNCTIONS OF

The Functions Of Social Conflict. Coser, Lewis A.

Some Social Functions Of Violence. Coser, Lewis A.

The Functions Of Racial Conflict. Hines, Joseph.

VIOLENCE, FUNCTIONS OF

"Political Crime And The Negro Revolution" in *Criminal Behavior Systems*, Clinard, Marshall B And Richard Quinney (eds). Moudelos, Joseph C.

Violence And The American Character Structure. Holden Jr, Matthew.

Social Sources Of Support For Violence And Non–Violence In A Negro Ghetto. Feagin, Joe R.

"Black Violence In The 20th Century" in *Violence In America*, Graham, Hugh D And T Gurr (eds). Meier, August and Rudwick, Elliott.

On Theories Of Urban Violence. Lupsha, Peter.

Violence And The Negro Struggle For Equality In The USA. Barnett, I.

Violence And The Struggle For Existence. Daniels, D N (ed) and Gilula, M F (ed) and Ochberg, F M (ed).

Popular Uprisings And Civil Authority In Eighteenth–Century America. Maier, Pauline.

Using Racism At San Quentin. Minton Jr, Robert J and Rice, Stephen.

The Police And Social Tension. Tyler, L G.

"Violence And The Social Structure" in *Rebellion And Retreat*, Palmer, S (ed), 83–94. Coser, Lewis A.

Violence As A Technique For Social Change For Black Americans. Wood, John Atkins.

"The Organization Of Prison Violence" in *Prison Violence*, Cohen, Albert K; George F Cole, And Robert G Bailey (eds). Park, James W L.

Understanding Violence. Newman, Graeme R.

VIOLENCE, INDIVIDUAL

The Negro And Homicide. Brearley, H C.

Homicide In The United States. Brearley, H C.

Native Son. Wright, Richard.

Notes On Navajo Suicide. Wyman, L and Thorne, B.

Research Note On Inter– And Intra–Racial Homicides. Garfinkel, Harold.

African Homicide And Suicide. Bohannon, P (ed).

Ecological Pattern Of Negro Homicide. Pettigrew, Thomas F and Spier, Rosalind B.

The Wretched Of The Earth. Fanon, Frantz.

Violence And The Masculine Ideal. Toby, Jackson.

Violence In Ghetto Children. Coles, R.

Suicide And Homicide: A Comparative Analysis By Race And Occupational Levels. Lalli, Michael and Turner, Stanley.

Violent Men: An Inquiry Into The Psychology Of Violence. Toch, Hans.

Poverty, Race And Violence. Fishman, J R.

Suicides And Homicides Among Indians. Ogden, Michael and Spector, M I and Hill Jr, C A.

Violence Against Children. Gil, D G.

"Madness And Powerlessness" in *Power And Innocence: A Search For The Causes Of Violence*, 19–45. May, Rollo.

Violence And Robbery: A Case Study. Normandeau, Andre.

Suicide, Homicide, And Alcoholism Among American Indians—Guidelines For Help. Frederick, C J.

Child Abuse As Psychopathology: A Sociological Critique And Reformulation. Gelles, R J.

Epidemiological Differences Between White And Nonwhite Suicide Attempters. Pederson, A M and Awad, G A and Kindler, A R.

"A Psychiatric Study Of Parents Who Abuse Infants And Small Children" in *The Battered Child*, Helter, R E And C H Kempe (eds). Steele, B F and Pollock, C B.

Adolescent Suicide On An Indian Reservation. Dizmang, Larry H Et Al.

An Epidemiological Study Of Suicide And Attempted Suicide Among The Papago Indians. Conrad, R D and Kahn, M W.

Notes Toward An Epidemiology Of Urban Suicide. Morris, Jeffrey B Et Al.

Suicide And Culture In Fairbanks: A Comparison Of Three Cultural Groups In A Small City Of Interior Alaska. Parkin, M.

American Indian Suicide—Fact And Fantasy. Shore, James H.

Fatal Indian Violence In North Carolina. Kupferer, H J and Humphrey, J A.

Pathologies Among Homicide Offenders: Some Cultural Profiles. Landau, S F.

Some Social Characteristics Of Young Gunshot Fatalities. Klein, D et al.

Suicide Among Blacks. Jedlicka, D et al.

Suicide Epidemic On An Indian Reserve. Ward, J A and Fox, J.

The Black Minority Criminal And Violent Crime: The Role Of Self Control. Heilbrun Jr, Alfred B and Heilbun, Kirk S.

Black Violence. Button, James W.

Impulsive And Premeditated Homicide: An Analysis Of Subsequent Parole Risk Of The Murderer. Heilbrun Jr, Alfred B and Heilbrun, Lynn C and Heilbrun, Kim L.

Race, Criminal Violence, And Length Of Parole. Heilbrun Jr, Alfred B.

Officer Race And Police Shooting. Fyfe, James J.

Understanding Violence. Newman, Graeme R.

"The Violent Brain: Is It Everyone's Brain" in *Biology And Crime*, Jeffrey, C R (ed). Ginsburg, Benson E.

VIOLENCE, OFFICIAL

Police Violence As A Function Of Community Characteristics. Kania, Richard and Mackey, Wade C.

VIOLENCE, POLITICAL

On The Ecology Of Political Violence: 'The Long Hot Summer' As A Hypothesis. Schwartz, David.

Three Views Of Urban Violence: Civil Disturbance, Racial Revolt, Class Assault. Grimshaw, Allen.

Violence And Black America: The Political Implications. Staples, Robert.

American Minorities: The Justice Issue. Long, Elton et al.

Malcolm X: An Untold Story? Anonymous.

VIOLENCE, RACIAL

The Chicago Race Riots. Sandburg, Carl.

Lynching And Political Areas. Young, Erle.

"The Negro And Racial Conflict" in *Our Racial And National Minorities*, Brown, F J And J S Roucek (eds), 549–560. Johnson, James Weldon.

Race Riot. Lee, Alfred McClung and Humphrey, Norman D.

Racial Conflict: Lessons Of The Detroit Riot. National Urban League, Inc.

What Caused The Detroit Riot? White, Walter and Marshall, Thurgood.

Why Race Riots: Lessons From Detroit. Brown, Earl.

A Study In Social Violence: Urban Race Riot In The United States. Grimshaw, Allen.

Racial Violence And Law Enforcement. Mc Millan, George.

Race Riots: New York, 1954. Shapiro, F C and Sullivan, J W.

Race Riot At East St Louis: July 2, 1917. Rudwick, Elliot M.

The Police Role In Racial Conflicts. Towler, Juby Earl.

"Riots And Crime—Historical Background" in *Task Force Report—Crime And Its Impact—An Assessment*, 116–122. President's Comm On Law Enforcement & Adm Of Justice.

Black Nationalism And Prospects For Violence In The Ghetto. Parker, G J.

"The Etiology Of The Race Riot" in *Violence In The Street*, Endelman, S (ed), 357–361. Endleman, S.

Effects Of Racial Violence On Attitudes In The Negro Community. Justice, Blair.

"The Zoot Effect On Personality: A Race Riot Participant" in *Racial Violence In The United States*, Grimshaw, A (ed), 413–420. Clark, Kenneth and Barker, James.

Racial Violence In The US. Grimshaw, Allen (ed).

The Harlem Riot Of 1935. Hill, Robert B.

"Black Violence In The 20th Century" in *Violence In America*, Graham, Hugh D And T Gurr (eds). Meier, August and Rudwick, Elliott.

"Patterns Of Collective Racial Violence" in *The History Of Violence In America*, Graham, Hugh D And T Gurr (eds), 412–444. Janowitz, Morris.

"The Dynamics Of Black And White Violence" in *The History Of Violence In America*, Graham, Hugh D And T Gurr (eds), 444–464. Comer, James P.

Correlates Of Civil Rights Activity And Negro Intra–Racial Violence. Mc Donald, Thomas D.

City Characteristics And Racial Violence. Jiobu, R M.

Rumors, Race And Riots. Knopf, Terry Ann.

Violence, Race And Culture. Curtis, Lynn A.

The Black Revolts: Racial Stratification In The USA. Scott, Joseph.

VIOLENCE COMMISSION

Crimes Of Violence (Violence Commission Report, Volume 11). Mulvihill, D J et al.

A Comment On The Police And The Kerner Report. Lehman, P.

VIRGIN ISLANDS

Race Relations In Puerto Rico And The Virgin Islands. Williams, Eric.

The Virgin Islands And Its Judicial System. Moore, Herman E.

VIRGINIA

see also Norfolk Prison, Va

Criminal Law In Colonial Virginia. Scott, Arthur P.

The Jails Of Virginia: A Study Of The Local Penal System. Hoffer, Frank William and Mann, Delbert Martin and House, Floyd Nelson.

The Negroes And Crime In Virginia. Chamberlain, B P.

The Legal Status Of The Negro. Magnum, Charles S.

Trends In The Use Of Capital Punishment. Hartung, Frank E.

WHITE, VIRGIL

Requiem For Virgil White. Hunt, Ridgely.

WHITES

American White Criminal Intelligence. Murchison, Carl.

American White Criminal Intelligence. Murchison, Carl.

Cultural And Racial Variations In Patterns Of Intellect, Peformance Of Negro And White Children On The Bellevue Adult Intelligence Scale. Machover, Solomon.

The Zoot–Suit Riots. Mc Williams, Carey.

The First Generation And A Half: Notes On The Delinquency Of Native Whites Of Mixed Parentage. Von Hentig, Hans.

Differentials In Crime Rates Between Negroes And Whites, Based On Comparisons Of Four Socio–Economically Equated Areas. Moses, Earl R.

Negro And White Male Institutionalized Delinquents. Axelrad, Sidney.

The Negro Offender In A Northern Industrial Area. Fox, Vernon and Volakalis, Joan.

A Self–Report Comparison Of Indian And Anglo Delinquency In Wyoming. Forslund, Morris A and Cranston, Virginia A.

Effects Of Unemployment On White And Negro Prison Admissions In Louisiana. Dobbins, D A and Bass, Bernard M.

Lawlessness And Violence In America And Their Special Manifestations In Changing Negro–White Relations. Grimshaw, Allen.

Differential Study Of Recidivism Among Negro And White Boys. Henton, Comradge L and Washington, Charles.

Occupational Benefits To Whites From The Subordination Of Negroes. Glenn, Norval.

"Negro And White Sex Crime Rates" in *Sexual Behavior And The Law*, Slovenko, Ralph (ed), 210–220. Savitz, Leonard D and Lief, H I.

Negro Subordination And White Gains. Cutright, Phillin

A Comparison Of The Scores Of White And Negro Male Juvenile Delinquients On Three Projective Tests. Megargee, Edwin I.

Racial Perspectives And Attitudes Among Negro And White Delinquent Boys: An Empirical Examination. Segal, Bernard E.

White Gains From Negro Subordination. Glenn, Norval.

Verbal Performance IQ Differences Of White And Negro Delinquents On The WISC And WAIS. Henning, John J and Levy, Russell H.

Adolescence In The South: A Comparison Of White And Negro Attitudes About Home, School, Religion And Morality. Schab, F.

Black Rebellion And White Reaction. Wildavsky, Aaron.

Comparative Psychological Studies Of Negroes And Whites In The United States: 1959–1965. Dreger, Ralph M and Miller, Kent S.

Negro–White Differentials And Delinquency. Stephenson, Richard M and Scarpitti, Frank R.

Delinquency In Three Cultures. Rosenquist, Carl M and Megargee, Edwin I.

Psychometric And Demographic Comparisons Of Negro And White Delinquents. Levine, B L.

"The Dynamics Of Black And White Violence" in *The History Of Violence In America*, Graham, Hugh D And T Gurr (eds), 444–464. Comer, James P.

Aggressive Behavior Of Delinquent, Dependent, And 'Normal' White And Black Boys In Social Conflicts. Berger, Stephen E and Tedeschi, James T.

Black Man, Red Man, And White American: The Constitutional Approach To Genocide. Willhelm, Sidney M.

Father Absence And Antisocial Behavior In Negro And White Males. Mosher, L R.

On The Validity Of Official Statistics—A Comparative Study Of White, Black And Japanese High School Boys. Chambliss, William J and Nagasawa, Richard H.

Suicide, And White Reformatory Girl's Preference For Negro Men. Hammer, M.

"Negro And White Crime Rates," in *The Sociology Of Crime And Delinquency*, 2nd Ed, Wolfgang, M et al (ed), 430–439. Moses, Earl R.

A Comparison Of Negro And White Crime Rates. Forslund, Morris A.

Age, Occupation And Conviction Rates Of White And Negro Males: A Case Study. Forslund, Morris A.

Home–Defense And The Police: Black And White Perspectives. Feagin, Joe R.

Personality Characteristics Of White And Negro Adolescent Delinquents. Henning, John J.

Black And White Perceptions Of Justice In The City. Jacob, Herbert.

Imitation Of Self–Reward Standards By Black And White Female Delinquents. Thelan, Mark H and Fryrear, Jerry L.

Personality Factors In Delinquent Boys: Differences Between Blacks And Whites. Cross, Herbert J and Tracy, James J.

Some Effects Of A White Institution On Black Psychiatric Outpatients. Krebs, R L.

The Effects Of Black And White Interviewers On Black Responses In 1968. Schulman, H and Converse, J M.

White Separatists And Black Separatist: A Comparative Analysis. Feagin, Joe R.

"A Comparison Of White–Black Offender Groups" in *Sexual Behaviors*, Resnick, H L And Marvin E Wolfgang (eds). Gebhard, Paul H.

The Attitudes Of Black And White High School Seniors Toward Integration. Mastroianni, M and Khatena, J.

Characteristics Of The Population By Ethnic Origin: March 1972 And 1971. U S Dept Of Commerce, Bureau Of The Census.

The Personality And Self Concept Characteristics Of Negro And White Delinquent And Non–Delinquent Boys. Zipper, Barry Oser.

"The Prediction Of Performance For Black And For White Police Patrolmen" in *The Urban Policeman In Transition*, Snibbe, J (ed), 66–82. Baehr, Melany E et al.

National Lawyers Guild As An All White Organization. Goodman, W.

When Whites Riot—The East St Louis Massacre. Swan, L Alex.

A Comparison Of Mexican–American And Caucasian Male Juvenile Detainees. Hunter, Michael Nathan.

A Comparison Of Blacks And Whites Committed For Evaluation Of Competency To Stand Trial On Criminal Charges. Cooke, Gerald and Pogany, Eric and Johnston, Norman G.

A Comparison Of Negro, Anglo And Spanish–American Adolescents' Self–Concepts. Healey, G W and Deblassie, R R.

Black–White Relations Among Police In The United States. Lynch, Gerald.

Black–White Differences In Social Background And Military Drug Abuse Patterns. Nail, R L and Gunderson, E K E and Arthur, R J.

DAPs Of Black And Whites Juvenile Incarcerates. Baugh, B Duncan and Prytula, Robert E.

Self–Concept In Negro And White Pre–Adolescent Delinquent Boys. Wax, Douglas E.

An Analysis Of Proxemics And Self–Disclosing Behavior Of Recidivist And Non–Recidivist Adult Social Offenders. Braithwaite, Ronald L.

A Longitudinal Study Of Attitude Shifts Among Black And White Police Officers. Teahan, John E.

Differential Effects Of Group Counseling With Black And White Female Delinquents One Year Later. Redferin, D L.

Inequality In The Types Of Sentences Received By Native Americans And Whites. Hall, Edwin L and Simkus, Albert A.

Personality Patterns Of White, Black, And Mexican American Patrolmen As Measured By The Sixteen Personality Factor Questionaire. Snibbe, H M and Fabricatore, Joseph and Azen, Stanley P.

Role Playing And Group Experience To Facilitate Attitude And Value Changes Among Black And White Police Officers. Teahan, John E.

The Sex Offenses Of Blacks And Whites. Kirk, Stuart A.

Parolees' Perceptions Of The Justice System: Black–White Differences. Berman, John J.

Racial Discrimination And White Gain. Szymanski, Albert.

"Crimes Against The Elderly—Findings From Interviews With Blacks, Mex–Amer, And Whites" in *Justice And Older Americans*, Young, M (ed). Ragan, P K.

MMPI Differences Among Black Mexican–American And White Male Offenders. Mc Creary, C and Padilla, E.

Integrating The Keepers: A Comparison Of Black And White Prison Guards In Illinois. Jacobs, James B and Kraft, Larry J.

Internal Colonialism: White, Black And Chicano Self Conceptions. Hurstfield, Jennifer.

Self–Esteem And Achievement Of Black And White Adolescents. Simmons, R G et al.

An Analysis Of Rape Patterns In White And Black Rapists. Heilbrun Jr, Alfred B and Cross, J M.

Black Versus White In The Station House. Jones, Robert A.

Effectiveness Of Volunteer Assistance To Parolees. Carlson, Eric W and Vito, Gennaro F and Parks, Evalyn C.

WICHITA, KS

Profile Of A Good Police Officer. Barnabas, B.

WILMINGTON 10

Rev Ben Chavis And The Wilmington Ten—A Fact Sheet. Anonymous.

The Struggle Of Ben Chavis And The Wilmington 10. Davis, Angela Y.

WIND RIVER, WY

A Self—Report Comparison Of Indian And Anglo Delinquency In Wyoming. Forslund, Morris A and Cranston, Virginia A.

Delinquency Among Wind River Indian Reservation Youth. Forslund, Morris A and Meyers, Ralph E.

WINDOW ROCK, AZ

Navajo Criminal Homicide. Levy Jerrold E and Kunitz, Stephen J and Everett, Michael.

WISCONSIN

see also Milwaukee, WI

The Criminal Physique: A Preliminary Report On The Physical Examination Of 1521 Prisoners At Wisconsin State Prison. Sleyster, Rock.

Wisconsin Council On Criminal Justice: Equal Opportunity/Affirmative Action Program For 1978. Robinson, N E.

Wisconsin Criminal Justice Information: Crime And Arrests 1979. Wisconsin Dept Justice, Div Law Enf Serv.

WOLFGANG, MARVIN E

Correlates Of Civil Rights Activity And Negro Intra—Racial Violence. Mc Donald, Thomas D.

Violence By Blacks And Low—Income Whites: Some New Evidence On The Subculture Of Violence Thesis. Erlanger, Howard S.

The Empirical Status Of The Subculture Of Violence Thesis. Erlanger, Howard S.

WOMEN *see Females*

Psychological View Of Women In Policing. Sherman, Lewis J.

Women In Law Enforcement. Crites, L.

Changing Status Of Women In Police Professions. Stuart, C G.

Women In Policing. Triplett, Peggy E.

Blacks And Women To Be Hired For Louisiana Police—Fire Jobs. Marro, Anthony.

Four Cities In Louisiana Defy US On Hiring More Blacks And Women. Anonymous.

Women Police: A Study Of Education, Attitudes, Problems. Martin, C A.

WOMEN'S LIBERATION

Sisterhood Is Powerful: An Anthology Of Writings From The Women's Liberation Movement. Morgan, Robin (ed).

WYOMING

A Self—Report Comparison Of Indian And Anglo Delinquency In Wyoming. Forslund, Morris A and Cranston, Virginia A.

Delinquency Among Wind River Indian Reservation Youth. Forslund, Morris A and Meyers, Ralph E.

X, MALCOLM

The Autobiography Of Malcolm X: With The Assistance Of Alex Haley. X, Malcolm.

The Last Year Of Malcolm X: The Evolution Of A Revolutionary. Breitman, George.

Where I'm Bound: Patterns Of Slavery And Freedom In Black American Autobiography. Smith, Sidonie.

Malcolm X Speaks, Orig Pub 1965. X, Malcolm.

Malcolm X: An Untold Story? Anonymous.

XYY CHROMOSOME

YY Syndrome In An American Negro. Telfer, M A and Baker, D and Longtin, L.

An XYY Survey In A Negro Prison Population. Fattig, W Donald.

The XYY Offender: A Modern Myth? Fox, Richard G.

YOUNG LORDS

House Of Lords. Anonymous.

Right On With The Young Lords. Yglesias, Jose.

The Young Lords And The Spanish Congregation. Kelley, Dean M.

Palante: Young Lords Party. Young Lords and Abramson, Michael.

YOUTH PATROLS

Youth Patrols: An Experiment In Community Participation. Knopf, Terry Ann.

YOUTHFUL OFFENDERS

The Youthful Male Offender In Alabama: A Study In Delinquency Causation. Caldwell, Morris G.

The Youthful Offender: A Descriptive Analysis. Sumpter, Roy G.

Race As A Factor In The Intra—Prison Outcomes Of Youthful First Offenders. Brown, Shirley Ann Vinsing.

YPSILANTI, MI

Race, Social Status, And Criminal Arrest. Green, Edward.

Guidance on the Use of the Author Index with Abstracts

Author's Name

This section is arranged alphabetically, by author's (or co-author's, editor's, or compiler's) last name. Articles by multiple authors or editors are listed under each author's or editor's name, except when the number is greater than three persons, in which case the listing includes only the first author's name followed by ET AL. Names preceded by the articles DE, LA, LE, etc., or by the prepositions DA, DE, VAN, VON, etc. are treated as if the article or preposition were a part of the last name.

Some popular periodicals do not list the author's name, in which case the author listed in the *Index* is ANONYMOUS. The tradition in the field of law is for articles which have been written by members of the law review to be unsigned. In these instances, the listed author is NOTE. Moreover, some law journal articles are listed as COMMENT. Some confusion has lately arisen in the field, as some law journals have begun to allow students to sign their articles at the end of their article. In these instances, the Editor has sought to list the author's name, rather than the traditional NOTE.

Order of Bibliographical Information

Each entry in this section begins with the author's name, followed by the full title of the publication or unpublished work, the volume (followed by the number in parentheses), pagination, and date. This information is sometimes followed by a brief abstract, which attempts to summarize the contents in less than 250 words.

Abstracts

Most abstracts have been written by the *Index* staff. Those which are followed by the sign * were adapted from the National Criminal Justice Reference Service, U.S. Department of Justice. In the future, the Editor intends to rely primarily upon the authors themselves, by requesting them to furnish brief abstracts of their work. Any author wishing to receive a form and instructions for preparing such an abstract should contact the Editor in response to the notice at the end of this *Index*.

Obtaining Copies of the Documents

Copies of the works referenced in the *Index* can often be obtained by writing directly to the publisher. Please consult the lists of periodicals and book publishers listed in the front of the *Index*. Documents followed by the sign * are available—in limited quantities and on a first-come, first-served basis—from NCJRS. To receive an order form, write to: SNI/NCJRS, National Criminal Justice Reference Service, Box 6000, Rockville, MD 20850.

Usefulness of this Section

One of the advantages of this section is that it is designed to enable the user to identify an author's various works, regardless of whether he or she was listed as the first, second, or third author. The organization also enables the user to identify an author's publishing associations and range of interests within the range covered by this *Index*.

A- T- O, Inc. *The Figgie Report On Fear Of Crime: America Afraid, Part 1, The General Public.* Willoughby Ohio A–T–O 1980.

ABBOTT, Edith. *Report On Crime And The Foreign Born*, Orig Pub 1931. Montclair NJ Patterson Smith 1968.

The evolution of public opinion concerning immigrants and crime is traced through the various periods of American history—colonial, Revolutionary, Civil War, and up to the time of the first federal immigration act (1882). The attitudes and developments of the "modern period" (1882 to 1931) are described, including actions taken to reduce (or eliminate) the entry of convicts from other countries. Public opinion is then compared for different historical periods. Statistics are presented relating nationality to crime rate, type of crime, and number of arrests in cities of varying sizes. Violations of federal prohibition laws by foreign–born persons are also tabulated, as well as petty offenses, commitments to reformatories, and offenses committed by native–born children of immigrant parents. Factors which could bring foreigners into conflict with the law, but which would not affect natives, (e.g., language, foreign law, and custom) are analyzed. A large section of the report is devoted to the problem of criminal justice and Mexicans in the US, specifically in Texas, Illinois, and several California cities.*

ABBOTT, Elizabeth Lee and Abbott, Kenneth A. Juvenile Delinquency In San Francisco's Chinese–American Community: 1961–1966. *Nat Taiwan U J Soc* 4,45–56 1968.

ABBOTT, Kenneth A and Abbott, Elizabeth Lee. Juvenile Delinquency In San Francisco's Chinese–American Community: 1961–1966. *Nat Taiwan U J Soc* 4,45–56 1968.

ABELES, R P. Relative Deprivation, Rising Expectations And Black Militancy. *J Soc Issues* 32(2),119–137 1976.

ABERLE, S and Brophy, W. *The Indian: America's Unfinished Business.* Norman Univ Oklahoma Pr 1966.

ABRAHAMSON, M J and Burgess, R L and Hamblin, R L. "Diagnosing Delinquency" in *Law And Order: Modern Criminals*, Short Jr, James F (ed), 19–31. Chicago Aldine 1970.

ABRAMOWITZ, A et al. *Women In Policing—A Manual.* Washington DC Police Foundation 1974.

A survey and guide to police agencies and municipal governments in the successful recruitment, training, and utilization of female police officers, with emphasis on obstacles faced by policewomen. Case studies of the experiences of several police forces in employing female police officers are first provided. An outline for a six–month recruitment campaign, and suggestions on monitoring the recruitment effort are also given.*

ABRAMOWITZ, S I and Nassi, A J. From Phrenology To Psychosurgery And Back Again: Biological Studies In Criminality. *Am J Orthopsych* 46,591–607 O 1976.

ABRAMSON, Michael and Young Lords. *Palante: Young Lords Party.* NY McGraw–Hill 1971.

ABUDU, Margaret. American Black Ghetto Revolt: A New Perspective. *Police J* 45,13–23 1972.

ACERRA, L. "From Matron To Commanding Officer—Women's Changing Role In Law Enforcement" in *Law Enforcement Bible*, Scanlon, Robert A (ed). South Hackensack NJ Stoeger 1978.

The changing role of women in law enforcement, from the first police matrons hired in 1891 to the present, is reviewed. Emphasis is on female police in NYC. During the early 1970s, experiments in NYC and Washington, D. C. demonstrated that women could peform a wide range of patrol duties as well as their male counterparts. In NYC, height requirements were abolished and women participated in the same training as men. Increasing career development opportunities for female officers should result in an increase in female applicants. What is now needed is that police departments, and the male officers project a positive attitude toward women's drive for equality. A system of controls must be built into the system that will ensure true equality of assignment and policy formulations should incorporate the female officer's point of view, particularly in those areas directly relevant to her role.*

ACKERMAN, L A. Marital Instability And Juvenile Delinquency Among The Nez Perćes. *Am Anthrop* 73,593–603 1971.

ACUÑA, Rodolfo. "Freedom In A Cage" in *Reinterpretation Of American History And Culture*, Cartwright, William H And Robert L Watson, Jr (eds). Washington DC NC Social Stud 1973.

This chapter, a précis of Acũna's *Occupied America: The Chicano Struggle for Liberation*, offers an overview of the Mexican American's quest for self–determination and cultural pluralism in America. Mexico became independent in 1821 and the republic that emerged included much of what is now the US' Southwest. However, through conquest and colonization over half of Mexico became part of the US. From Texas to California a master–servant relationship evolved, aided by Anglo–American technology, law enforcement officials, and the overwhelming number of Anglo–Americans who entered the region. Primarily due to better economic opportunities over one–eighth of Mexico's population migrated to the US between 1910 and 1930. A new identity began to emerge which, in 1968, became symbolized by the term "Chicano." The label "Mexican–American" was rejected because for many it meant assimilation into Anglo society, while "Chicano" represented many youths' commitment to the poor Mexican. Victories in Texas in 1969 by La Raza Unida Party, a Chicano political party, were seen by many as the first step by Chicanos to recapture political and economic control of their destinies.

ACUÑA, Rodolfo. *Occupied America: The Chicano's Struggle Toward Liberation.* San Francisco Canfield Pr 1972.

ADAIR, A V et al. Impact Of Incarceration On The Black Inmate. *J Afro–Am I* 2(2),167–178 1974.

Prison, which represents an institutionalized component of the criminal justice system, is examined as a subsystem which interacts with the larger social system, and racism is seen as playing a major role in that interaction process. The article focuses upon ecological aspects of imprisonment; that is, both the internal and external forces that impinge upon the prison inmate. These forces include the abuse of scientific experimentation on captive populations, the depersonalizing process which denies prisoners the opportunity to express values learned in the larger society, and the separation of prisoners from their families. A strategy for change is offered to encourage the gradual abandonment of the tradition punitive prison.

ADAMEK, R J and Lewis, J M. Social Control, Violence And Radicalization: Behavioral Data. *Social Prob* 22,663–674 Je 1975.

ADAMS, J M and Beck, R A. Establishing Rapport With Deviant Groups. *Social Prob* 18,102–117 1970.

ADAMS, Nathan M. America's Newest Crime Syndicate: The Mexican Mafia. *Read Digest* 111,97–102 N 1977.

ADAMS, Stuart. The 'Black Shift' Phenomenon In Criminal Justice. *Just Syst J* 2(2),185–194 Wint 1976.

A study of women offenders in the District of Columbia revealed that the deeper the penetration the system, the blacker the offender cohort. White women were apparently filtered out at higher rates at each step of the process. In order to investigate possible explanations of this phenomenon, data dealing with offense type and commitment history were examined. Offense differences were not sufficient to adequately explain the variation in final outcomes. Past studies have shown that police, as a result of prejudice or perhaps easy accessibility, arrest a disproportionate number of minorities. The plea–bargaining process, and especially the prosecutor's tendency to over–indict, might result in discrimination against minorities at the prosecutorial stage. Inadequate representation by public defenders at the trial stage, especially the tendency for public defenders to suggest that defendants plead guilty, may further discriminate against minorities. Although data presented are somewhat inconclusive, they do suggest that minorities may be victims of inferior justice.

ADAMS, T C. Characteristics Of State Prisoners Who Demonstrate Severe Adjustment Problems. *J Clin Psyc* 33(4),1100–1103 O 1977.

A comparative study of characteristics of state prison inmates who demonstrate good adjustment and those who demonstrate severe maladjustment in prison is described. Subjects ranged from 18 to 59 years old and were assigned to the North Carolina Div. of Prisons. The infraction group (INF) consisted of prisoners who had committed 2 or more serious infractions during an 18–month period of imprisonment. 9 infractions, ranging from threatening personnel and assault to arson and murder, were included. Noninfraction group (NINF) subjects had no serious infractions during their current or any previous prison term. Background factors assessed included race, education, training school record, marital status, alcohol and drug use, crime classification and conduct at time of crime, and military service and work record. Chi square analysis of data found no significant differences between the two groups on race, alcohol/drug use, marital status, crime classification, or conduct at the time of crime. Findings support the hypothesis that prison maladjustment is associated with prior social adjustment.

ADAMS, Walter A and Warner, W Lloyd and Junker, Buford H. *Color And Human Nature.* Washington DC Am Coun On Educ 1941.

ADAMS, William T and Baker, Gordon H. Negro Delinquents In Public Training. *J Negro Ed* 32,294–300 1963.

ADELSON, J A. A Study Of Minority Group Authoritarianism. *J Abnor & Soc Psychol* 48,477–485 1953.

ADLER, F S. *The Female Offender In Philadelphia.* Unpub PhD Diss Univ of Penn 1972.

ADLER, Freda. Empathy As A Factor In Determining Jury Verdicts. *Criminology* 12(1),127–128 My 1974.

ADLER, Freda. Socioeconomic Factors Influencing Jury Verdict. *NYU Rev L & S C* 3,1–10 1973.

ADLER, N and Goleman, D. Gambling And Alcoholism: Symptom Substitution And Functional Equivalents. *Q J Stud Alc* 30(3),733–736 1969.

Similar psychodynamics (e.g., orality and suicidal behavior) have been proposed for both gambling and alcoholism. Gambling as a form of symptom substitution for alcoholism has been observed in Jews (Jews in California prisons frequently cited gambling, not alcoholism, as the precipitating factor in their criminal career), and Balinese, Amerinds (prior to the European's arrival) and American Chinese. The Amerinds have now shifted from a gambling to a drinking pattern. It was hypothesized that cultures in which gambling is prevalent will show little drinking, and vice versa. Of the 117 cultures represented in the Yale University Human Relations Area Files, 17 had neither drinking nor gambling, 58 had drinking but not gambling, 21 had both and 33 had gambling but not drinking (the hypothesized mutual exclusion is significant, p .0005). The concept of functional equivalence, or "equipotentiality," could be relevant to the psychosocial study of alcoholism, according to the authors.

AGOPIAN, Michael W. "Black Offender And White Victim" in *Forcible Rape—The Crime, The Victim And The Offender*, Chappell, D; R Geis, And G Geis (eds). NY Columbia Univ Pr 1977.

The study sample consisted of 66 instances of interracial forcible rape reported during 1971 in Oakland, California. Analysis concentrated on 63 instances of black male–white female offenses. Two–thirds of the rapists chose a victim in the same 10–year age bracket or younger. The data confirmed that warm weather months are peak season for rape. A relationship was also seen between age of the offender and season of the year, which indicates that school vacations and seasonal employment might be related. 40% of the offenses took place in nonresidential settings not including automobiles, which accounted for an additional 22% of the cases. Multiple offender rapes were considerably rare in Oakland and prior relationship between the offender and the victim proved to be slight, findings strikingly different from other studies of interracial rape. The variations among findings in interracial rape studies may be explained by differences in police reporting and recording, police–community relations, demographic factors, and race relations.*

AGOPIAN, Michael W and Chappell, Duncan and Geis, Gilbert. "Interracial Forcible Rape In A North American City" in *Victimology: A New Focus*, V1, Drapkin, Israel And Emilio Viano (eds), Chapter 9. Lexington MA Lexington 1974.

AGUILA, Pancho. *Dark Smoke.* San Francisco Second Coming Pr 1977. Poems by a Chicano revolutionary in California's Folsom prison.

AHLGREN, R D. Ayuda. *Leg Aid Brief* 29,2 1970.

AHMAD, Muhammad. We Are All Prisoners Of War. *Black Scholar* 4(2),3–5 O 1972.

AKERS, Ronald L and Hawkins, R. *Law And Control In Society.* Englewood Cliffs NJ Prentice–Hall 1975.

AKERS, Ronald L. Socio–Economic Status And Delinquent Behavior: A Retest. *J Res Crim Del* 5(1),38–46 1968.

ALASKA JUDICIAL COUNCIL. *Alaska Felony Sentencing Patterns: A Multivariate Statistical Analysis (1974–1976), Preliminary Report.* Anchorage Judicial Council 1977.

ALASKA JUDICIAL COUNCIL. *Judicial Council Findings Regarding Possible Racial Impact In Sentencing.* Anchorage Judicial Council 1978.

ALDRICH, Howard and Reiss Jr, Albert J. Absentee Ownership And Management In The Black Ghetto: Social And Economic Consequences. *Social Prob* 18,319–338 Wint 1971.

This paper seeks to examine the extent of absentee ownership of small businesses in the black ghettoes of three large American cities and to derive quantitative estimates of the impact that absentee ownership and management have on social and economic conditions in such areas. Non–ghetto businesses are compared with ghetto businesses to separate the effects of common business conditions from the fact of location in a particular area. Data are from a survey of 659 small businesses in Chicago, Boston, and Washington, D. C. The findings support the contention of critics that absentee owned or managed businesses dominate the economy of the black ghetto. However, the same condition also applies to non–ghetto, low–income white areas. The paper concludes with estimates of the degree to which absentee owned or managed businesses control the flow of important resources in the areas studied.

ALDRIDGE, Delores P. "Black Female Suicides: Is The Excitement Justified" in *The Black Woman*, Rodgers–Rose, La Frances (ed). Beverly Hills CA Sage 1980.

ALERS, Jose Oscar. *Puerto Ricans And Health: Findings From New York City.* Bronx NY Fordham Hisp R Cen 1978.

ALEX, Nicholas. *Black In Blue.* NY App–Cent–Croft 1969.

ALEX, Nicholas. *New York Cops Talk Back.* NY Wiley 1976.

Contains chapter exploring the "resentments of white policemen," in which the author suggests that NYC policemen's anti–integration attitudes are often expressed indirectly by code words such as "decline in standards." Complaints about "decline in physical requirements" are also mentioned, since, according to the author, they sometimes refer to admission of Puerto Rican men or women. Likewise, "decline in written test standards" often refers to minority candidates, who tend not to perform as well as whites on standardized written exams.

ALEXANDER, Elaine T and Alexander, Lawrence A. The New Racism: An Analysis Of The Use Of Racial And Ethnic Criteria In Decision–Making. *San Diego L Rev* 9,190–263 F 1972.

ALEXANDER, Gordon G. Role Of The Police And The Courts In The Survival Of Black Youth. *J Afro–Am I* 4(2),235–240 Spr 1976.

ALEXANDER, Harry T. "Court Monitoring—A Necessity" in *Crime And Its Impact On The Black Community*, Gary, L E And L P Brown (eds), 165–175. Washington DC Howard Univ 1976.

ALEXANDER, Harry T. "The Black Judge As A Change Agent" in *The Administration Of Criminal Justice: A View From Black America*, Brown, Lee P (ed), 23–27. Washington DC Howard U 1974.

ALEXANDER, Harry T and Washington, M. Black Judges In White America. *Black L J* 1(3),245+ Wint 1971.

ALEXANDER, J I. *Blue Coats—Black Skin—The Black Experience In The New York City Police Department Since 1891.* Hicksville NY Exposition Pr 1978.

ALEXANDER, Lawrence A and Alexander, Elaine T. The New Racism: An Analysis Of The Use Of Racial And Ethnic Criteria In Decision–Making. *San Diego L Rev* 9,190–263 F 1972.

ALEXANDER, Raymond Pace. Blacks And The Law. *NYS Bar J* 43(1),15–23 Ja 1971.

Alexander, a distinguished Philadelphia lawyer and graduate of Harvard Law School, presents an autobiographical account of the obstacles he has faced as a black person in the legal profession. He describes being denied membership in honor clubs and law clubs despite an excellent academic record. He describes being turned away from a Philadelphia law firm despite recommendations from the Dean of Harvard Law School. He describes difficulties which he confronted after being admitted to the bar in southern states and the experience of being compelled, as a lawyer, to sit in the segregated "colored" section of a southern court. These and other discriminatory experiences led to a strong determination on his part to be "successful" as well as to help fight racist practices so that others will not face such obstacles. He concludes his account on an optimistic note, citing much improvement and tremendous change in the social and legal fields in the past fifteen years.

ALEXANDER, Raymond Pace. Judicial Temper. *Opport* 14,263–66+ 1936.

ALEXANDER, Raymond Pace. The Upgrading Of The Negro's Status By Supreme Court Decisions. *J Negro History* 30(2),117–149 1945.

ALGER, Norman and Gonzales, Ricardo T and Aron, William S. Chicanoizing Drug Abuse Programs. *Human Org* 33(4),388–390 Wint 1974.

The problem of drug addiction and its antecedent conditions in the

Chicano population of the La Colonia community in Oxnard, California are discussed. The residents of La Colonia are described as being caught in a cycle of poverty, lack of education, and discrimination. Such conditions lead to the creation in the population of a negative self–image, which results in the use of illicit drugs as a means of escape. Several therapeutic interventions suggested by these conditions are described and it is shown how they might be incorporated into a drug abuse treatment program designed to meet the needs of the Chicano drug addicts.

ALKER, Howard L and Hoslicka, Carl and Mitchell, Michael. Jury Selection As A Biased Social Process. *Law & Soc Rev* 11(1),9–41 1976.

ALLEN, Donald E and Sandhu, Harjit S. A Comparative Study Of Delinquents And Non–Delinquents: Family Affect, Religion, And Personal Income. *Soc Forces* 46(2),263–268 1967.

ALLEN, Harry E and Dynes, Patrick S and Carlson, Eric W. "Aggressive And Simple Sociopaths: Ten Years Later" in *Biology And Crime*, Jeffrey, C R (ed). Beverly Hills CA Sage 1979.

ALLEN, John. *Assault With A Deadly Weapon: The Autobiography Of A Street Criminal.* NY Pantheon 1977.
Autobiography of a black street hustler in the slums of Washington D. C. His career in crime is recounted in graphic detail and ends with his paralysis after a shoot–out with police. Includes chapters on family background, first conviction, gangs, robbery, prison life, heroin addiction.

ALLEN, R L. *Black Awakening In Capitalist America.* Garden City NY Anchor 1970.

ALLEN, V L. Toward Understanding Riots: Some Perspectives. *J Soc Issues* 26(1),1–18 1970.

ALLPORT, Gordon W. *The Nature Of Prejudice.* NY Doubleday 1958.

ALMAGUER, Tomás. Historical Notes On Chicano Oppression: The Dialectics Of Racial And Class Domination In North America. *Aztlan* 5(1–2),27 47 1974.

ALMQUIST, Alan F and Heizer, Robert F. *The Other Californians: Prejudice And Discrimination Under Spain, Mexico, And The United States To 1920.* Berkeley CA U CA Pr 1971.

ALPERT, Geoffrey P and Hicks, Donald A. Prisoners' Attitudes Toward Components Of The Legal And Judicial System. *Criminology* 14(4),461–482 F 1977.
Results of a 1974 study of the attitudes of 241 male prisoners in the Washington State prison system toward the police, lawyers, law and the judicial system are presented. Attitudes toward police were largely negative, attitudes toward the more abstract aspects of the law and the judicial system were equivocal and attitudes toward lawyers were generally positive. Prisoners who had retained private counsel were generally more positive in their attitudes in all three areas. Where violent offenses were involved, prisoners showed considerable negativeness toward police and lawyers. Race of the prisoners was related to the extent of negativeness of attitude in all areas, but much less so in the case of lawyers than of police, the law and judicial system. Married prisoners are more likely to report positive attitudes and previous criminal convictions are associated with negative attitudes. Educational status had a relatively weak influence upon attitudes toward police and lawyers, but appears to be of greater influence in the law and judicial system area. Those who were employed prior to arrest appear to be slightly less negative in all areas.

ALPERT, Geoffrey P. Inadequate Defense Counsel—An Empirical Analysis Of Prisoners' Perceptions. *Am J Crim L* 7(1),1–21 Mr 1979.
A cohort of 186 male prisoners and a group of 81 female prisoners admitted to the Texas Department of Corrections during the fall of 1976 were questioned about their perceptions of their defense counsel. Each prisoner was asked for background information and questioned on three sets of items relating to the duties delineated in the Decoster case. Analysis was conducted of attitudes towards counsel's competence and variables affecting perception of whether defense counsel discussed defense strategies and focus of defense, prisoner's perceptions of having been advised of rights, and prisoner's satisfaction with counsel investigation and preparation of case. Results show that classification of prisoners into correct groups on questions dealing with attorney investigative competence was affected significantly by length of sentence, total years spent in prison, bail achievement, type of attorney, race, and age. Overall, most prisoners feel that private counsels are usually better prepared than public–supported counsels. A model for ensuring comprehensive 'effective defense' is provided.*

ALTER, Julius. *Crimes Of Puerto Ricans In Brooklyn.* Unpub MA Thesis Brooklyn College 1958.

ÁLVAREZ, José Hernández. A Demographic Profile Of The Mexican Immigration To The United States. *J I–A S* 8(3),471–496 1966.

ALVIREZ, D and Bean, F. "The Mexican American Family" in *Ethnic Families In America*, Mindel, C And R Habenstein (eds). NY Elsevier 1976.

AMERICA, Richard F. The Case Of The Racist Researcher. *Black L J* 1(1),77–85 Spr 1971.

AMERICAN ANTI- SLAVERY SOCIETY. *American Slavery As It Is: Testimony Of A Thousand Witnesses.* NY AASS 1839.

AMERICAN ANTI- SLAVERY SOCIETY. *The Fugitive Slave Bill: Its History And Unconstitutionality.* NY Wm Harned 1850.

AMERICAN BAR ASSOCIATION. *Female Offender Workshop Guide*, Female Offender Resource Center. Washington DC ABA 1977.

AMERICAN BAR ASSOCIATION. *Minority Recruitment In Corrections—New Federal Aid Requirements.* Washington DC ABA 1973.
Amplification of two Equal Employment Opportunity requirements applicable to grantees of LEAA, with special emphasis on their significance to correctional systems. The first of these requirements deals with affirmative action by LEAA grantees to remedy deficiencies in the number of minority group persons, including women, employed in their work force and the elimination of discriminatory minimum height standards (height standards not covered in this pamphlet). The second requirement concerns the problem of site selection of correctional facilities where the location may have an adverse impact on minority employment.*

AMERICAN BAR ASSOCIATION. *New Perspectives On Urban Crime.* Washington DC ABA 1972.

AMERICAN BAR ASSOCIATION. *Race Relations In Corrections—An Annotated Bibliography.* Washington DC ABA 1975.
Listing of 42 books, articles, studies, and government publications on race relations problems within the correctional system, covering 1968 to 1975, plus 20 court decisions in this area dating back to 1961. The general bibliography is categorized by the following subject headings: general discrimination and racism, legal analyses and standards, state prison studies, minority staff recruitment, affirmative action models and training materials, and racial problems as seen by inmates. The court decisions listed deal with the required desegregation of correctional facilities, first amendment rights, job discrimination, recruitment of minorities in corrections, and parole.*

AMERICAN BAR ASSOCIATION. Report Of The Special Committee On Criminal Law Problems In Civil Disorders. *Am Crim L Q* 6,58–65 1968.

AMERICAN CIVIL LIBERTIES UNION OF FLORIDA. *Rape: Selective Electrocution Based On Race.* Miami FL ACLU 1964.
This study is based on figures obtained from the Federal *National Prisoner Statistics*, and uncited information concerning certain case histories in Florida (two counties excluded because of insufficient data). The study first breaks down all executions for rape in the US 1930–1963 by race, and compares these figures with a similar breakdown of executions for murder during the same period. The number of death sentences between 1940 and 1964 is given, and broken down by race and by the ultimate disposition of the sentence. Case histories are given for six (out of 54) persons receiving death sentences for rape during this period who were white. All of them were said to have raped white victims; four of the six, and the only one executed, raped white children. The study then breaks the total number of death sentenced and executed rapists in the sample down by race of the defendant and the race of the victim. The study concludes that race seems to be a factor both in sentencing and commuting in rape cases in Florida.

AMERICAN CIVIL LIBERTIES UNION. *Background Paper On The Supreme Court's Death Penalty Decisions.* NY ACLU 1976.

AMERICAN CORRECTIONAL ASSOCIATION. *Causes, Preventive Measures And Methods Of Controlling Riots And Disturbances In Correctional Institutions.* Washington DC ACA 1970.

AMERICAN ENTERPRISE INSTITUTE FOR PUBLIC POLICY RESEARCH. *Affirmative Action—The Answer To Discrimination?* Washington DC Am Ent Inst PPR 1976.
Lawyers, academicians, and journalists discuss the legal and moral consequences of affirmative action, a federal program for combating discrimination. The transcript of the panel discussion is presented without

editorial comment. The debate centers around these broad questions: how far should the government intrude into the private sector in dictating goals to eliminate discrimination? Should performance capabilities be the sole criterion in hiring? Do affirmative action programs entail preferential treatment? If so, is preferential treatment constitutional? Is there a distinction between goals and quotas? Has the Department of Health, Education, and Welfare been successful in its enforcement of affirmative action guidlines? The panel, moderated by Ralph K. Winter, Jr., of Yale Law School, includes Owen Fiss, professor of law at Yale Law School; Richard Posner, professor of law at the University of Chicago Law School; Vera Glaser, syndicated columnist for Knight Newspapers and WTOP radio commentator; William Raspberry, columnist for the Washington Post; and Paul Seabury, professor of political science at the University of California at Berkeley.

AMERICAN FRIENDS SERVICE COMMITTEE. *Struggle For Justice.* NY Hill & Wang 1971.

AMERICAN MANAGEMENT ASSOCIATION. *How To Eliminate Discriminatory Practices––A Guide To EEO (Equal Employment Opportunity).* NY Am Man Assoc 1975.

AMERICAN UNIVERSITY LAW SCHOOL. *Crime And Employment Issues: A Collection Of Policy Relevant Monographs.* Washington DC US Dept Labor 1978.

Issue papers and a selected bibliography on the relationship between crime and employment/unemployment focus on the employment–related needs of youthful offenders and institutions that provide support.*

AMES, Jessie Daniel. *The Changing Character Of Lynching.* Atlanta Comm Interrac Coop 1942.

AMIR, Menachem. *Patterns In Forcible Rape.* Chicago Univ Chicago Pr 1971.

Modified version of a Ph. D. dissertation completed at the University of Pennsylvania in 1965, this study reports the patterns of 646 cases of forcible rape in Philadelphia in 1958 and 1960. Amir's findings, which contradicted many earlier studies of rape, included the conclusion that there was a significant association between forcible rape and the race of both victims and offenders, in absolute numbers and in terms of their proportion in the general population. Black women were found to be victimized at a rate 12 times higher than white women; and black offenders were rapists at a rate 12 times greater than whites. However, rape was found to be an intraracial event.

AMIR, Menachem. Forcible Rape. *Fed Prob* 31,51–58 Mr 1967.

ANDERSON JR, Charles W. The South's Challenge To The Negro Lawyer. *Nat Bar J* 3(1),29–42 1945.

ANDRESS, V R. Ethnic/Racial Misidentification In Death: A Problem Which May Distort Suicide Statistics. *Forensic Sci* 9(3),179–183 1977.

This paper discusses how two salient features of a decedent (surname and residence location) can distort the ethnic/racial classification of the suicide victim. Because many Southern California Indians have Spanish surnames and most do not reside on an Indian reservation it is shown that the suicide statistics may represent an over–estimation of actual Mexican–American suicidal deaths while simultaneously representing an under–estimation of the suicides among American Indians of the region.

ANDREW, J M. Delinquents And The Tapping Test. *J Clin Psyc* 33(3),786–791 1977.

ANDREW, J M. Violent Crime Indices Among Community–Retained Delinquents. *Crim Just B* 1(2),123–130 1974.

This field study was performed in the course of clinical and consultative work within the California Subsidy Program (the state of California pays each county probation department per offender for sending fewer offenders to penal institutions), as an effort toward program evaluation. One need to accomplish program evaluation was a method to evaluate the extent and degree of violent crime within the subject population, making it possible to chart trends over time, and to identify results of differential treatment methods or placements. As hypothesized, sex differences emerged on the Violence Scale but the male/female gap seems to be closing. However, hypothesized ethnic differences (Anglo–Caucasians and non–Anglos) failed to emerge. An unexpected time–period difference was also seen. Although the sex/time interaction was not significant, Caucasian females appeared to show a greater increase than other groups in the Study I (January 1971–March 1973) Study II (April 1973–November 1973) comparison.

ANGLE, Paul M. *Bloody Williamson.* NY Knopf 1952.

This book contains an account of the Ku Klux Klan in Southern Illinois.

ANONYMOUS. *Break De Chains Of Legalized Slavery.* Durham NC NC Prison Project 1976.

Ten women convicts who participated in the 1975 rebellion at the North Carolina Women's Prison in Raleigh contributed these sketches.

ANONYMOUS. *Captive Voices: An Anthology From Folsom Prison.* Paradise CA Dustbooks 1975.

ANONYMOUS. *Poetry Of Prison: Poems By Black Prisoners.* Chicago Du Sable Museum 1972.

ANONYMOUS. Adams v Miami Police Benevolent Ass'n 454 F2d 1315, (Florida) US Court Of Appeals, Fifth Circuit February 2, 1972. *Civil Rts Ct Dig* 5(6),2 1972.

The Court of Appeals for Florida upheld a trial court order that all black police officers in good standing on the Miami Police Force be admitted to membership in the Miami Police Benevolent Association, despite the fact that there is an association comprised solely of black officers which performs the same or similar function and has similar benefits. The appellate court concluded that the district court correctly decided that appellees were excluded from the appellant organization solely because of their color.

ANONYMOUS. Alabama's State Police Leads In Black Percentage With 4:5%. *NYT* ,22 D 10 1974.

This article reports the results of a national survey conducted by the Race Relations Information Center. The survey disclosed that blacks still constituted a tiny minority of state police forces in contrast with the uniformed forces of major cities. Although Alabama has a larger percentage of blacks among uniformed state policemen than any other state police agency in the nation (4.5% of 28 troopers—all added since a Federal Court order was issued 3 years ago), it still remains below the court–ordered hiring ration of one black for every white until the state force becomes 25% black, the percentage of blacks in Alabama. The survey also noted that every Southern state now has blacks on its state police force, with Mississippi's six being the lowest number.

ANONYMOUS. Blacks And The US Criminal Justice System. *J Afro–Am I* 2(2),87–178 1974.

ANONYMOUS. Bridgeport Guardians, Inc v Members Of Civil Service Com'n, 497 F 2d 113 (Conn), US Court Of Appeals, Second Circuit, June 3, 1974. *Civil Rts Ct Dig* 7(12),3 1974.

In Bridgeport Guardians, Inc v. Members of Civ. Serv. Com'n., the US Court of Appeals of Connecticut held that the evidence that 35 Puerto Ricans and blacks had passed required examinations and were eligible for appointment to the police force, and that 271 Puerto Ricans and blacks applying for examination demonstrated that the absence of minority group representation in supervisory ranks did not undercut the recruitment of minority members and did not require affirmative action to increase minority representation in supervisory ranks. The Court also ruled that the reduction of the life of the eligibility list for the rank of sergeant from its normal 2 year span to 1 year after appointment of the fifteenth minority patrolman was appropriate remedy to insure proper minority representation in supervisory ranks of the police department.

ANONYMOUS. Bridgeport Guardians, Inc v Members Of The Bridgeport Civil Service, 345 F Supp 779, US Dist Ct D Conn Jan 29, 1973. *Civil Rts Ct Dig* 6(7),3 1973.

A Civil Rights Act suit, challenging the constitutionality of the hiring and promotion procedures of the Bridgeport, Connecticut Police Department, brought by black and Puerto Rican members of the force who failed the patrolman's examination, is discussed in Bridgeport Guardians, Inc. v. Members of the Bridgeport Civil Service. The District Court of Connecticut ruled that the patrolman's examination is discriminatory in its effect where, as used, it classifies applicants by race and national origin without sufficient evidence of job relatedness to justify such a result.

ANONYMOUS. Can You Photograph *Suspicious–Looking Blacks* Who Enter The Premises? *Prot Man* 2175,1 Ap 1 1978.

ANONYMOUS. Castro v Beecher, 459 F 2d 725 (Mass), US Court Of Appeals, First Circuit, May 24, 1972. *Civil Rts Ct Dig* 5(11),2 1972.

An action by black and Spanish–surnamed police job applicants against the city authorities charging discrimination in recruiting policies for policemen is reported. The court issued guidelines for the hiring of minority policemen, indicating that preferential status in a priority pool was a more feasible method than instituting a quota or percentage representation system.

ANONYMOUS. City Liable Under Human Rights Act For Policeman's Racial Abuses. *Crim L Rep* 18(21),2453–2454 F 25 1976.

ANONYMOUS. Clark et al v Wolff, 347 F Supp 887, (Nebraska), US District Court D Nebraska: May 24, 1972, 1972. *Eccles Court Dig* 11(6),6 1973.

In Clark et al v. Wolff, the District Court for Nebraska dismissed an action by inmates of a state correctional complex claiming alleged deprivation of freedom of exercise of religion. Grounds for the action were: 1) denial of respect of certain religious books and periodicals; 2) denial of visitation by a black Muslim minister; and 3) deprival of dietary accomodations. In dismissing the action, the Court found no evidence that requests for certain publications had been made nor that the minister's visit had been requested. The dietary request was rejected on grounds that it was self–imposed and not commanded by any religious stricture. Sanitation restrictions were cited as additional reasons for not allowing two gallons of milk supplied to each plaintiff to accumulate for consumption only between the hours of 4:00 and 6:00 p.m.

ANONYMOUS. Collins v State, 494 P 2d 956 (Nev) Sup Ct Of Nev, March 14, 1972. *Civil Rts Dig* 5(6),5 1972.

The Supreme Court of Nevada affirmed conviction for robbery over defendant's appeals that his request for a jury composed of 6 black persons and 6 white persons had been improperly denied. The ruling was based on absence of evidence that members of the appellant's race were systematically excluded from jury service.

ANONYMOUS. Comment: Black Muslims In Prison—Of Muslim Rites And Constitutional Rights. *Colum L Rev* 62,1488–1504 1961.

ANONYMOUS. Criminal Violence: An Exchange. *NY Rev Bks* 26(3),45–46 Mr 8 1979.

ANONYMOUS. Davis v Washington, 348 F Supp 15 (Dist Of Col) US Dist Ct DC July 21, 1972. *Civil Rts Ct Dig* 6(4),5 1973

The US District Court for the District of Columbia upheld the testing procedure for applicants for employment as police officer which tested verbal ability, vocabulary, reading and comprehension. The court found the testing to be reasonably and directly related to the requirements of the police recruit training program and not designed or administered to discriminate against black applicants who are otherwise qualified.

ANONYMOUS. Desperate Mexican Children Swarm Over Border To Commit Crimes—Situation Seems Without Solution. *Juv Just Dig* 5(8),7 Ap 22 1977.

ANONYMOUS. End Of The Rope: Seeking Justice In Houston. *Time* 111(16),20–21 Ap 17 1978.

ANONYMOUS. Exclusion Of Blacks From Juries Voids Fifteen–Year–Old Conviction. *Crim L Bull* 14(3),265 My–Je 1978.

ANONYMOUS. Four Cities In Louisiana Defy US On Hiring More Blacks And Women. *NYT* ,6 Jl 2 1977.

The Louisiana cities of Lafayette, Abbeville, Crowley and Westwego have decided that they would rather risk a federal suit than meet government guidelines on hiring more women and blacks in their police and fire departments. The Justice Department has said that it would sue to cut off Federal grants.

ANONYMOUS. Hispano En Presidios Eu Buscan Logar Mejor Trato: Barrera Del Idioma Es Obstáculo. *El Mundo* ,1+ D 31 1978.

ANONYMOUS. Hodnett v Slayton, 343 F Supp 1142 (Va) US Dist Ct WD Va, May 16, 1972. *Civil Rts Ct Dig* 6(9),4 1973.

A habeas corpus petitioner, who was convicted of armed robbery and sentenced to 20 years, questions the method of selection of the petit and grand juries. The Court dismissed the petition stating in part that to obtain relief petitioner must show purposeful racial discrimination. The Court held that there were no positive indications of discrimination nor does the opportunity for discrimination appear from the record.

ANONYMOUS. House Of Lords. *Time* 95(2),33 Ja 12 1970.

ANONYMOUS. Long v Harris, 332 F Supp 262, (Kansas), US District Court D Kansas: October 6, 1971. *Eccles Court Dig* 10(6),5 1972.

The US District Court (Kansas) in Long v. Harris denied application for relief in a habeas corpus proceeding by black Muslim federal prisoners contending improper segregated confinement. Denial was based on the fact that the segregated confinement was not based on an arbitrary decision but rather because the black Muslim prisoners were engaged in a power struggle within their religion and thereby posed a threat to themselves and others and to the safety and security of the prison.

ANONYMOUS. Malcolm X: An Untold Story? *Al–Qalam* 1,whole Issue Jl 1980.

ANONYMOUS. Minority Candidate And The Bar Examination: A Symposium. *Black L J* 5,129–201 1976.

ANONYMOUS. Disproportionality In Sentences Of Imprisonment. *Colum L Rev* 79,1119–1167 O 1979.

ANONYMOUS. Note. Riot Control: The Constitutional Limits Of Search, Arrest And Fair Trial Procedure. *Colum L Rev* 68,85–115 1968.

ANONYMOUS. Organizing Behind Bars. *Time* 103,93–94 My 13 1974.

ANONYMOUS. Police Are Sued. *NYT* ,71 My 10 1977.

This brief article reports on the suits against seven New Jersey police departments brought by the State Division on Civil Rights. The division joined a complaint, filed by the Hispanic Law Enforcement Society of Essex County, which alleged discrimination against Hispanic–surnamed applicants who had qualified for jobs in seven named cities. The article also points out that while these cities have substantial numbers of Spanish–speaking persons, there are virtually no bilingual police officers in their police departments. For example, Union City, with a 70% Hispanic population, has but four or five Hispanic police officers.

ANONYMOUS. Police Recruit Minorities. *NYT* ,49 Je 19 1977.

This article notes the successful efforts of the New Jersey State Police to increase minority group representation in its ranks. The force, before these efforts, consisted of 39 blacks, Hispanics, and women out of a total of 1750 officers. It is expected that, at the completion of the next state police training course, 90 blacks, Hispanics, or women will be added to the force.

ANONYMOUS. Poor Minority Juveniles Said More Likely To Be Locked Up. *Crim Cont Dig* 11(7),10 F 21 1977.

ANONYMOUS. Prison Perspective (Santa Fe Prison Riot). *Albuq J* Spec Sect, Mr 30 1980.

ANONYMOUS. Race–Discrimination Picture Is Confusing. *Am Bar A J* 64,309,311 Mr 1978.

ANONYMOUS. Rev Ben Chavis And The Wilmington Ten—A Fact Sheet. *Freedomways* 14(2),104–105 1974.

ANONYMOUS. Silberman—Back To Root Causes. *Police Mag* 2(2),34–37 1979.

In the interview, Silberman points out fallacies in the economic theory of crime, notes the extent to which the police are dependent on citizens for informaton leading to arrests, and advocates improved police–community mediators. Silberman rejects the notion that the crime problem is one of social class rather than of race, pointing out that although NYC Puerto Ricans are poorer, less educated, and have lived in the city a shorter time than blacks, blacks are arrested for violent crimes four times as often as Puerto Ricans. Silberman also cites ways in which data on sentencing discrimination can be misleading. Reflecting on the comment in his book that the cultural devices that once kept black violence under control have broken down and have not been replaced by new cultural controls, Silberman observes that these new controls must come from within the black community.*

ANONYMOUS. Southern State Hit With Alien Juvenile Crime Wave. *Juv Just Dig* 4(6),4–5 Mr 26 1976.

ANONYMOUS. Symposium: The Quest For Equality. *Wash U L Q* 1979(1),1–208 Wint 1979.

ANONYMOUS. Teterud v Gilliam, 385 F Supp 153, (Iowa), US District Court SD Iowa, CD November 20, 1974. *Mental Health Court Digest* 19(2),1 1975.

In Teterud versus Gillman, a US District Court in Iowa upheld an American–Indian inmate of the State Penitentiary challenging enforcement of the prison's hair regulation against him and other Indian inmates. Plaintiff claimed and established that hair played a central role in his religion and that he was sincere in his belief. A psychiatrist supported plaintiff's position and testified that plaintiff was his patient, and that he first came for treatment for a passive–aggressive personality based in part upon childhood rejection, including feelings of being "unworthy as an Indian." The psychiatrist advised the plaintiff that his low opinion of himself could change and that he should take pride in being an Indian. The psychiatrist also testified that the compelled cutting of plaintiff's hair would generally be counterproductive to rehabilitation.

ANONYMOUS. The Anguish Of Blacks In Blue. *Time* 96(21),13–14 N 23 1970.

This article reports on the activities of black police associations in the US. Their complaints and efforts to change the practices of law enforcement in their communities are discussed. A major aim of these groups—increasing the numbers of black cops on duty in the ghetto—rests on the argument that black cops perform better, more fairly and more intelligently than whites in black community law enforcement. The proportions of blacks on major city police departments are also given.

ANONYMOUS. The Black Cops. *Newsweek* 74,54 Ag 4, 1969.

In this article, spokesmen for various black police associations describe the "new" black cops as black men who are part of a larger movement. It is the black officer's new assertiveness, according to the article, that "could alter not only the image of the cop in the slums but the character of police justice." This article also reports on tensions rising in departments between white and black policemen. For example, in NY and Washington black cops have physically prevented white cops from beating up black prisoners; and in Detroit and Chicago, black and white cops have pulled guns on each other. The article asserts that the black policeman's new pride is not likely to disappear, but rather, as recruitment programs bring more blacks into police work, it can only grow stronger.

ANONYMOUS. The Negro Crime Rate: A Failure In Integration. *Time* 71,16 Ap 21 1958.

ANONYMOUS. US Charges Los Angeles With Police Hiring Bias. *NYT* ,10 Je 3 1977.

The Justice Department charged the Los Angeles Police Department with discrimination against women, blacks and persons with Spanish surnames in its hiring practices. The suit charged the police department with "traditionally following a practice of failing or refusing" to recruit women and minority-group members on an equal basis with white males.

ANONYMOUS. United States v McDaniels, 379 F Supp 1243, (Louisiana) US District Court E D Louisiana, May 22 1974. *Civil Rts Ct Dig* 8(2),3 1975.

In United States v. McDaniels, the Court granted motion for a new trial following conviction, on the defendant's challenge to the fairness of the selection of the jury. The Court ruled that the defendant failed to show that there was a systematic exclusion of blacks from jury duty in the district. However, the Court held that the prosecutor's pattern of systematic exclusion of black jurymen from the venire must be considered. It was concluded that the jury was so unrepresentative as to render the trial unfair.

ANSON, R. Hispanics In The United States: Yesterday, Today And Tomorrow. *Futurist* 14,25–27+ Ag 1980.

APONTE, J F and Frei, R J and Offord, D R. A Study Of Recidivism Among Female Juvenile Delinquents. *Corr Psychi J Soc Ther* 14(3),160–174 1968.

APTHEKER, Bettina. *The Morning Breaks: The Trial Of Angela Davis.* NY International Pub 1975.

APTHEKER, Herbert (ed). *A Documentary History Of The Negro People In The United States.* NY International Pub 1951.

APTHEKER, Herbert. "Slave Resistance In The US" in *Key Issues In The Afro–American Experience*, Huggins, N; M Kilson And D M Fox (eds). NY Harcourt Brace 1971.

APTHEKER, Herbert. *Negro Slave Revolts In The United States, 1526–1860.* NY International Pub 1939.

ARAUJO, M U and Chang, W B C. Interpreters For The Defense: Due Process For The Non–English–Speaking Defendant. *Cal L Rev* 63(3),801–823 1975.

ARIZONA COMMITTEE TO THE U S COMMISSION ON CIVIL RIGHTS. *Justice In Flagstaff: Are These Rights Inalienable?* Washington DC USCCR 1977.

ARMBRISTER, Trevor. The Lonely Struggle Of The Black Cop. *Read Digest* ,123–126 Mr 1971.

This paper is based upon dozens of informed interviews with law enforcement personnel in twelve cities across the US. The black policeman is an asset to any police department because of his effectiveness in relating to the black community. However, black policemen still encounter covert and overt discrimination in recruiting, assignment and promotions. Because of this, blacks remain under–represented on police forces and few are in high ranking positions. Official discrimination is often mirrored in the anti–black attitudes of white officers. Black policemen not only face opposition in the force, but are often scorned by black militants in their own

neighborhood as well. Blacks, who in the past have been passive and ignored discriminatory practices and abuse in black neighborhoods, are now beginning to challenge departmental policies. The "new breed" of black policemen is insisting that they are "black men first, policemen second." New black organizations have been formed to fight discrimination, reform police practices and establish new links to the black community.

ARMISTEAD, Henry M. Racial Exclusion In Jury Trials. *Ark Bar Assoc Rep* ,99–115 1933.

ARMSTRONG, George D. *The Christian Doctrine Of Slavery*, Org Pub 1857. NY Negro Univ Pr 1969.

ARMSTRONG, Warren B (ed) and Chang, Dae H (ed). *The Prison: Voices From The Inside.* Cambridge MA Schenkman Pub 1972.

ARNOLD, William R. Race And Ethnicity Relative To Other Factors In Juvenile Court Dispositions. *Am J Soc* 77(2),211–227 1971.

Research up to this point has been inconclusive about whether the overrepresentation of minority–group members in official correctional statistics is mostly a function of artifacts of data collection, the nature and volume of crimes committed or bias in the correctional process. This paper examines data from the records of a juvenile court in Lake City, Florida. The likelihood that the probation officers will submit more cases from minority groups than from Anglos for formal court hearings is reduced below statistical significance when appropriate factors are considered—except for those for whom extensive handling seems most logical. The likelihood that the judge will send more minority–group members than Anglos to the Youth Authority, however, persists for most categories of offenders even when these considerations are taken into account. The biases appear to consist largely of letting Anglos "get off easy" rather than of requiring uncalled–for "treatment" for minority–group members. Findings suggest that about two–thirds of the differential handling is not explained by appropriate considerations.*

ARON, William S and Alger, Norman and Gonzales, Ricardo T. Chicanoizing Drug Abuse Programs. *Human Org* 33(4),388–390 Wint 1974.

The problem of drug addiction and its antecedent conditions in the Chicano population of the La Colonia community in Oxnard, California are discussed. The residents of La Colonia are described as being caught in a cycle of poverty, lack of education, and discrimination. Such conditions lead to the creation in the population of a negative self–image, which results in the use of illicit drugs as a means of escape. Several therapeutic interventions suggested by these conditions are described and it is shown how they might be incorporated into a drug abuse treatment program designed to meet the needs of the Chicano drug addicts.

ARTHUR. *The Life And Dying Speech Of Arthur, A Negro Man.* Boston A Broadside 1768.

ARTHUR, R J and Nail, R L and Gunderson, E K E. Black–White Differences In Social Background And Military Drug Abuse Patterns. *Am J Psychiatry* 131(10),1097–1102 1974.

ASHEAR, V and Snortum, J. Prejudice, Punitiveness And Personality. *J Pers Assess* 36,291–301 1972.

ASHMAN, Allan and Wilder, Curtis. The Black Judge In America: A Statistical Profile. *Judicature* 57(1),18–21 Je–Jl 1973.

The findings of a national survey of black judges, taken by the American Judicature Society in 1971–1972, are presented. A 5–page questionnaire was sent to 286 black judges. Responses were received from 167. The survey focused primarily on a number of background characteristics and the geographical distribution of black judges. An underrepresentation of black judges was found both in Federal Courts, where 7% of the judges were black, and State and City Courts, where only 1% of the judges were black. Underrepresentation was most severe in the South. Although 75 of the respondents were born in the South, only 18 held judgeships there. Almost two–thirds of the black judges were appointed rather than elected to their judgeship. Eighty–six percent of the judges sat in either trial courts or courts of limited jurisdiction. Only two black judges were found on the bench of State Supreme Courts and seven held judgeships in intermediate State Courts of Appeal. In conclusion it was emphasized that appointing bodies must be made aware of and responsive to the need for more black judges in higher judicial positions.

ASWADU, Ahmad Ali. A Black View Of Prison. *Black Scholar* 2(8,9),28–31 Ap–My 1971.

ATKINS, B and Pogrebin, M. *The Invisible Justice System Discretion And The Law.* Cincinnati Anderson 1978.

AUBERT, V. *Sociology Of Law.* Baltimore Penguin Books 1969.

AUERBACH, Jerold S. *Unequal Justice: Lawyers And Social Change In Modern America.* NY Oxford Univ Pr 1976.

AUMAN, Jon et al. *The Chicano Addict: An Analysis Of Factors Influencing Rehabilitation In A Treatment Program.* Bethesda MD NIMH 1972.

AUSTIN, Roy L. *Criminal Victimization Of American Minorities: A Course Outline.* Albany SUNYA C J 1978.

This is an undergraduate course outline prepared in conjunction with an LEAA–sponsored project on Minority Education in Criminal Justice. Austin, a black sociologist, examines the nature and scope of minority victimization in the US. Following an introductory lecture describing the meaning of crime and criminalization and the various senses in which the term criminal victimization applies to the experiences of minorities, the course proceeds to discuss minorities in America's social structures, the involvement of minorities in crime, legislation of victimization (e.g., the "criminalization" of minority group members via the creation of laws effecting minorities only is here considered a legitimate concern of victimology), lynching, illegal business practices in the ghetto, maladministration of justice, ingroup victimization and, finally, assignment of blame and its implications. An excellent annotated bibliography is included for each section. Copies are available from School of Criminal Justice, SUNYA, 135 Western Ave., Albany, NY 12222.

AUSTIN, Roy L. Race, Father–Absence And Female Delinquency. *Criminology* 15(4),487–504 F 1978.

Discussions of the influence of father–absence on delinquency often show special concern for the relatively high rate of father–absence among black Americans. However, for the four delinquent offenses studied, father–absence had detrimental effects only on whites, especially girls. The only significant effect among black girls was favorable to the father–absent girls. Further, contrary to Datesman and Scarpitti (1975), parental control has similar effects on delinquency and on the relationship between father–absence and delinquency for blacks and whites. It appears that policies which reduce the stigma of father–absence for white girls are more likely to succeed in reducing delinquency due to father–absence than policies of economic improvement.

AUTUNES, G et al. Ethnicity, Socioeconomic Status And The Etiology Of Psychological Distress. *Sociol Soc Res* 58(4),361–368 1974.

To identify the mechanisms for the inverse association between social class and psychological distress, the authors used a research design created by Dohrenwend and Dohrenwend contrasting the distress levels of Anglos, blacks and Mexican–Americans for two levels of socioeconomic status. Their data support a social selection rather than a social stress explanation of this relationship.

AVELLO, J A and Mendoza, M G. *Manual For The Recruitment Of Minority And Females.* Washington DC USGPO 1976.

Specific techniques are recommended to help the Miami, Fla., Police Department minority candidates with the potential to become successful police officers. Each strategy is spelled out in detail and illustrated.*

AVINS, A. Anti–Miscegenation Laws And The Fourteenth Amendment: The Original Intent. *Va L Rev* 52,1224-1255 1966.

AWAD, G A and Kindler, A R and Pederson, A M. Epidemiological Differences Between White And Nonwhite Suicide Attempters. *Am J Psychiatry* 130(10),1071–1076 1973.

Using the Monroe County (NY) Psychiatric Case Register, the authors attempted to determine differences between white and non–white suicide attempters, to identify the factors that are associated with self–destructive behavior in both groups, and to determine the subsequent mortality rate among suicide attempters. They found a number of differences between whites and non–whites and concluded that the motivation for suicide, the techniques used to treat attempts, and the degree of risk of further psychiatric difficulty may be different for the two groups.

AXELRAD, Sidney. Negro And White Male Institutionalized Delinquents. *Am J Soc* 57,569–574 1952.

The case records of 300 institutionalized delinquents—179 Negro, 121 white—were analyzed to determine whether the courts were committing Negro and white children on the same basis and whether the two groups differed in family constellations. The study discloses that Negro children are committed younger, for less serious offenses, with fewer previous court appearances, and with less prior institutionalization. Negro children came from "unstable" homes and from homes with a different kind of family pathology than the white delinquents.

AZEN, Stanley P and Snibbe, H M and Fabricatore, Joseph. Personality Patterns Of White, Black, And Mexican American Patrolmen As Measured By The Sixteen Personality Factor Questionaire. *Am J Comm Psy* 3(3),221–227 1975.

The Sixteen Personality Factor Questionnaire was administered to 491 white, black, and Chicano patrolmen of the Los Angeles Sheriff's Department to obtain a normative police profile. Multi–variate analysis revealed that the average patrolman appeared brighter, more reserved, dominant and tough–minded than the average male. Comparisons were made for 29 black, 33 Mexican–American and 399 white officers. Mexican American officers emerged as more conservative and relaxed than whites, while black officers appeared more experimental, analytical and group–oriented. A comparison with an independent police sample revealed common traits of self–assurance and conservatism. Results were compared with a social worker's profile and discussed in relation to the police officer's actual job activities and community needs.

BAAB, George W and Ferguson, William R. Texas Sentencing Practices: A Statistical Study. *Tex L Rev* 14(3),471–503 1967.

BACA, Salvador. *The Criminal Justice System: An Analysis Of Hispanic Issues.* Unpub MA Thesis Calif St Univ LA 1980.

BADILLO, Herman and Haynes, Milton. *A Bill Of No Rights: Attica And The American Prison System.* NY Outerbridge Lazard 1972.

BAEHR, Melany E et al. "The Prediction Of Performance For Black And For White Police Patrolmen" in *The Urban Policeman In Transition*, Snibbe, J (ed), 66–82. Springfield IL Chas C Thomas 1973.

In a followup to research by the Chicago Police Department, a predictive study was conducted on performance of black and white patrolmen. Four steps are crucial to validate a test battery in a multiracial population: 1) determining whether or not the groups show different results on any predictor (test) variables; 2) determining if the groups show different results on criterion (job performance) variables; 3) determining if any differences could lead to discrimination against either group; and 4) determining what statistical technique will provide the most accurate representation of the relationship between predictor and criterion variables for each group. The groups were more often similar on the predictor variables than they were different, although they scored differently on all areas of the test battery. Ambiguous differences were found in criterion variables, and separate validations defining racially distinct prediction equations are needed to insure lack of discrimination between groups essential attributes to successful performance were determined via multiple regression.

BAGDIKIAN, Ben. *Caged.* NY Harper & Row 1976.

BAGDIKIAN, Ben and Dash, Leon. *The Shame Of The Prisons.* NY Pocket Books 1972.

BAHER, M E. *Practitioner's View Of EEOC Requirements With Special Reference To Job Analysis.* Chicago U Chicago Ind R C 1976.

One of the trends evident in civil rights legislation since the Civil Rights Act of 1964 has been the extension of technical requirements for validation of employment practices. This paper deals with validation of employment procedures and specifically with the first step in the total validation process—the job analysis.*

BAHR, Howard (ed) and Chadwick, Bruce (ed) and Day, Robert (ed). *Native Americans Today: Sociological Perspectives.* NY Harper & Row 1972.

BAILEY, D'Army. Inequalities Of The Parole System In California. *Howard L J* 17,797–804 1973.

BAILEY, Ronald. Black Studies In Historical Perspective. *J Soc Issues* 29(1),97–108 1973.

BAKER, Bruce. Riots: What Are The Options? *Police J* 43,361–366 1970.

BAKER, D and Longtin, L and Telfer, M A. YY Syndrome In An American Negro. *Lancet* 1(13),95 1968.

BAKER, Gordon H and Adams, William T. Negro Delinquents In Public Training. *J Negro Ed* 32,294–300 1963.

BAKER, J L. Indians, Alcohol And Homicide. *J Soc Ther* 5,270–275 1959.

The cases of 36 American Indians incarcerated at Leavenworth on manslaughter and murder charges are discussed; use of alcohol, behavior patterns, age, and psychiatric characteristics are emphasized.*

BAKER, S C. Negro Criminality. *N Car L J* 1,27+ My 1900.

BAKER, Timothy and Mann, Fredrica and Friedman, C Jack. Selectivity In The Criminal Justice System. *Prison J* 55(1),23–34 1975.

BALAGON, Kuwasi et al. *Look For Me In The Whirlwind: The Collective Autobiography Of The New York 21.* NY Random House 1971.

BALBUS, Isaac D. *The Dialectics Of Legal Repression: Black Rebels Before The American Criminal Courts.* New Brunswick NJ Transaction Books 1973.

BALDWIN, James. *The Fire Next Time.* NY Delta 1964.

BALL, J C (ed) and Chambers, C D (ed). *The Epidemiology Of Opiate Addiction In The United States.* Springfield IL Chas C Thomas 1970.

Presents research findings on female, Negro, Chinese–American, Puerto Rican, and Mexican–American addicts, the phenomenon of onset of drug use, concurrent barbiturate addiction, historical diffusion of the intravenous method of hypodermic infections, nativity of US addicts—their parentage and geographic mobility, and the medical and life history aspects of drug addiction.

BALL, J C and Lau, M. The Chinese Narcotic Addict In The United States. *Soc Forces* 45,68–72 S 1966.

BALL, John C et al. Pretreatment Criminality Of Male And Female Drug Abuse Patients In The United States. *Addict Dis* 1,481–489 1975.

Data from the Drug Abuse Reporting Program for 1969–73 containing information on 42,293 drug abuse patients is reported. The patient population is described by race, sex, age, prior arrests, prior criminal convictions, and length of prior incarcerations.

BALL, R A and Lilly, J R. Norm Neutralization, Anomia And Self–Concept Among Institutionalized Female Delinquents. Tucson A S C 1976.

BALLA, David A and Shanok, Shelley S and Lewis, Dorothy O. Some Evidence Of Race Bias In The Diagnosis And Treatment Of The Juvenile Offender. *Am J Orthopsych* 49(1),53–61 1979.

BALZER, A. A View Of The Quota System In The San Francisco Police Department. *J Polic Sci Adm* 4(2),124–133 1976.

BANFIELD, Edward C. *The Unheavenly City Revisited: A Revision Of The Unheavenly City.* Boston Little, Brown 1974.

BANFIELD, Edward C. *The Unheavenly City: The Nature And The Future Of Our Urban Crisis.* Boston Little, Brown 1968.

BANKS, Curtis and Zimbardo, Philip and Haney, Craig. Interpersonal Dynamics In A Simulated Prison. *Int J Crimin Pen* 1(1),69–97 1973.

BANKS, Samuel L. "Crime And The Public Schools" in *Crime And Its Impact On The Black Community*, Gary, L E And L P Brown (eds), 59–68. Washington DC Howard U 1976.

Basic causes of disorder in schools are discussed. Particular emphasis is given to those factors relevant to the situation of black youths in this country. The extent and nature of the problem is also discussed as are what the author calls "strategies for improvement."

BANKS, Sharon P. Black Lawyers Responsibility To Poor Communities. *J Afro-Am I* 2(2),129–138 1974.

BANKS, Taunya L. "Discretionary Justice And The Black Offender" in *Blacks And Criminal Justice*, Owens, Charles E And Jimmy Bell (eds), 37–46. Lexington MA Heath 1977.

BANKS, Taunya L. Discretionary Decision–Making In The Criminal Justice System And The Black Offender: Some Alternatives. *Black L J* 5(1),20–29 1975.

BANKS, W Curtis. "The Psychological Power And Pathology Of Imprisonment" in *Behavior Disorders: Perspectives And Trends*, Milton, O And R G Wahler (eds). Philadelphia Lippincott 1973.

BANKSTON, William B. *A Structural Level Examination Of Forensic Hospitalization: Forensic Commitment Rates And Social Structural Features At Louisana Parishes.* Unpub PhD Diss Univ of Tennessee 1976.

BANNON, James D and Wilt, G Marie. Black Policemen: A Study Of Self–Images. *J Polic Sci Adm* 1(1),21–29 Mr 1973.

This article reports the results of a study of black officers in the Detroit Police Department conducted from the Fall 1970 to Spring 1971. The purpose was to investigate the role of the black policeman within two social contexts: a societally and institutionally defined bureaucratic functional setting—the police department; and within a dually defined and enacted role of public servant and figure of authority. There appeared to be an ambivalence on the part of black policemen over integration. The men favored the hiring of more blacks, but expressed a concern that standards not be reduced to facilitate this goal. Many officers believed tht complete equality of opportunity had not yet been achieved and that discrimination still existed. The majority felt that black policemen have greater rapport and provide better service than white policemen. The black officer seems to feel he has more insight, is more sympathetic and understanding of a black citizen's situation and that these attributes are conveyed to the black citizenry, result in the black citizenry feeling more trusting and accepting of the black policeman than of his white counterpart.

BANTON, Michael. Policing A Divided Society. *Police J* 47,304–321 1974.

BANTON, Michael. Race And Public Order In An American City. *Police J* 45,198–213 1972.

BARBER, Bob and Pallas, John. From Riot To Revolution. *Issues Crim* 7(2),1–19 Fall 1972.

BARBER, John Warner. *A History Of The Amistad Captives.* New Haven The Author 1840.

BARKER, James and Clark, Kenneth. "The Zoot Effect On Personality: A Race Riot Participant" in *Racial Violence In The United States*, Grimshaw, A (ed), 413–420. Chicago Aldine 1969.

The authors present and analyze the details of a rioter's account of his involvement in the Harlem Riot. The participant is seen as displaying the personality of a person "socially isolated, rejected, discriminated against, and chronically humiliated."

BARKOWITZ, P and Brigham, J C. Do 'They All Look Alike' The Effects Of Race, Sex, Experience, And Attitudes On The Ability To Recognize Faces. *J App So P* 8(4),306–318 1978.

Results of an experiment conducted at Florida State University with black and white college students demonstrated that subjects were significantly more accurate in identifying pictures showing faces belonging to their own race. Contrary to assumptions made by many legal authorities and criminal justice personnel, neither racial attitude nor reported amount of quality of interracial experience was related to their ability to recognize pictures. The authors also discuss implications for police lineups and eyewitness identification.

BARNABAS, B. Profile Of A Good Police Officer. *Law & Order* 24 (5),32+ May 1976.

A test was developed for police applicants in Wichita (KS) to predict successful training and performance in compliance with equal employment opportunity and affirmative action laws. The test measures personality parameters, adjustment under stress, vocational interests as well as the standard intelligence, vocabulary, oral comprehension, and clerical efficiency tests. The test was found to be highly efficient in predicting applicant success.*

BARNES, Harry Elmer and Teeters, Negley K. *New Horizons In Criminology.* Englewood Cliffs Prentice–Hall 1959.

Chapter VII examines "Nationality, Race and Crime," with sections on Mexican–American delinquency, minority races and criminality, Negro crime, and Oriental and Native American crime. The authors reject theories of racial inferiority or superiority. If the Negro's criminality is high, they conclude, it is due largely to the black's socio–economic handicaps and to conditions flowing from his longstanding conflict with the white man.

BARNES, M and Rothenberg, S. Minorities' Constitutional Rights To Police Department Employment. *Police L Q* 6(2),23–31 1977.

Brief review of statutory background against discriminatory employment practices in the public sector, focusing on police, and discussion of the concept of disproportionate racial impact. This concept, enunciated by the Supreme Court in Griggs v. Duke Power Company (1971) holds that if an employment test can be shown to have a disproportionate result on certain protected groups, the employer must demonstrate that the test is valid and relates to the job requirements. Federal court litigation concerning the Chicago Police Department is used as an example of this doctrine. Additionally, the author discusses judicially imposed employment quotas and preferential affirmative action hiring practices as remedies for discrimination. The article concludes by citing a report showing that women can perform competently as police officers.*

BARNETT, A. On Urban Homicide. *J Crim Jus* 3(2),85–110 1975.

BARNETT, Ida B Wells. *On Lynching.* NY Arno Pr 1969.

BARNETT, I. Violence And The Negro Struggle For Equality In The USA. *Int J Off Ther* 13(2),76–81 1969.

BARNETT, Samuel. "Researching Black Justice: Description And Implications" in *Blacks And Criminal Justice*, Owens, Charles E And Jimmy Bell (eds), 25–33. Lexington MA Heath 1977.

Studies indicate that the black citizen has suffered from a repressive criminal justice system. Social and economic conditions of the black man and the system are discussed.*

BARNHART, Edward N and Matson, Floyd M and Tenbroek, Jacobus. "The Attack On Japanese Americans During World War II" in *Conspiracy*, Curry, Richard O And Thomas M Brown (eds). NY Holt Rinehart Wins 1972.

BARNHART, Kenneth E. Negro Homicides In The United States. *Opport* 10,212–214,225 Jl 1932.

BARRERA, Mario. *Race And Class In The Southwest: A Theory Of Racial Inequality*. Notre Dame U Notre Dame Pr 1979.

BARRON, Milton L (ed). *Minorities In A Changing World*. NY Knopf 1967.

BARSH, R L and Henderson, J Y. Tribal Courts, The Model Code And The Police Idea In American Indian Policy. *Law & Contemp Prob* 40(1),25–60 Wint 1976.

BARTELL, Ted and Winfree Jr, L Thomas. Recidivist Impacts Of Differential Sentencing Practices For Burglary Offenders. *Criminology* 15(3),387–396 N 1977.

BARTOLLAS, C. Runaways At The Training Institution In Central Ohio. *Can J Crim & Corr* 17(3),221–235 1975.

BASS, Bernard M and Dobbins, D A. Effects Of Unemployment On White And Negro Prison Admissions In Louisiana. *J Crim L Crimin & Pol Sci* 48(15),522–525 Ja–F 1958.

This study of admissions to the Louisiana State Penitentiary during 1941–54 reinforces the hypothesis that unemployment is an important factor influencing prison commitments. A lower association was found between unemployment and Negro prison admissions than for unemployment and white prison admissions. The authors suggest that this may be due to the tendency of Negroes to commit relatively more crimes against the person than whites, while whites were more often committed for property offenses.

BASS, Jack and Nelson, Jack. *The Orangeburg Massacre*. NY Ballantine 1970.

BASSETT, John Spencer. *Slavery And Servitude In The Colony Of North Carolina*. Baltimore MD Johns Hopkins Pr 1896.

BASSETT, John Spencer. *The Southern Planatation Overseer: As Revealed In His Letters*. NY Negro Univ Pr 1925.

A sympathetic portrait of the 19th–century plantation overseer.

BATES, William. Caste, Class And Vandalism. *Social Prob* 9(4),349–353 1962.

In an attempt to test notions suggested by Albert Cohen, in *Delinquent Boys* (Glencoe, Illinois: Free Press, 1955), and Bernard Lander, in *Towards an Understanding of Juvenile Delinquency* (New York: Columbia University Press, 1954), this study examined hypotheses that the correlation between social rank and vandalism is higher than the correlation between social rank and delinquency in general; that a higher correlation between percent non–white and total delinquency than between social rank and total delinquency would be found; that a higher correlation of vandalism with percent non–white than of total delinquency with percent non–white would be found; and that, on partial correlation, the relationship between vandalism and percent non–white controlling on social rank would remain meaningfully high, and the relationship between vandalism and social rank, controlling on percent non–white, would drop close to insignificance. All hypotheses but the first were supported, leading the author to infer that the relationship between vandalism and percent non–white is a "real" relationship.

BATTA, I D and Mc Culloch, J W and Smith, N J. A Study Of Juvenile Delinquency Amongst Asians And Half–Asians: A Comparative Study In A Northern Town Based On Official Statistics. *Br J Crimin* 15(1),32–42 Ja 1975.

BAUER, Alice H and Bauer, Raymond A. Day To Day Resistance To Slavery. *J Negro Hist* 27,388–419 O 1942.

BAUER, Raymond A and Bauer, Alice H. Day To Day Resistance To Slavery. *J Negro Hist* 27,388–419 O 1942.

BAUGH, B Duncan and Prytula, Robert E. DAPs Of Black And Whites Juvenile Incarcerates. *J Abnor Ch Psychol* 2(3),229–238 1974.

Two groups of male juvenile incarcerates were separated on the basis of race, matched in terms of age, recidivism, and intelligence test scores, and given the Draw–A–Person Test (DAP). Figures drawn were male and female. The drawings were scored on 14 emotional indicators. The results of the present study offer little consistent or conclusive support for the hypothesis that differences influenced by race can be found in the projective drawings of black and white subjects. The commonly held impressions that there are more incidences of neurotic or psychotic features in the projective tests of black subjects and that the projective drawings of black subjects are generally inferior to the projective drawings of white subjects were not supported by the present study.

BAYLEY, David H and Mendelsohn, Harold. *Minorities And The Police*. NY Macmillan 1968.

BEACH, W G. *Oriental Crime In California: A Study Of Offenses Committed By Orientals In That State, 1900–1927*. Stanford CA Stanford Univ Pr 1932.

BEAN, F and Alvirez, D. "The Mexican American Family" in *Ethnic Families In America*, Mindel, C And R Habenstein (eds). NY Elsevier 1976.

BEAN, Jerry L. Native Americans And Discrimination In Kansas: Trials From Injustice. *U Kan L Rev* 20(3),468–485 1972.

Discrimination in public accomodations concerning American Indians in Kansas is discussed. The Kansas Commission on Civil Rights, working with the Kansas Act Against Discrimination has had a paucity of complaints from Indians, but this discrimination is not rare. The Act is one tool for assuring equal protection for American Indians and other minorities but has been only partially successful, owing to enforcement difficulties. There is a tremendous gap between what Indians and other minority groups believe to be discrimination and what has been proscribed as such by the Kansas legislature and courts. Still, complaints under the Act and the Kansas penal civil rights statute, and law suits based on the 1964 Federal Civil Rights Acts can work, within the framework of the legislative and judicial systems, to assuage injustice. There seems to be little reason not to broaden the term public accomodations by statutory amendment or construction to include schools, hospitals, and police departments. Further, elimination of discrimination in Kansas would be more readily attained if the Attorney General would prosecute civil rights complaints.

BEARD, Eugene. *Projections On The Supply Of Minorities In Corrections–Related Occupations, 1975–1980*. Washington DC Howard U n.d.

Minorities constitute approximately 16.8% of the US population and make up about 49% of the inmates of federal and state prisons. Only about 8% of correctional employees are minority group members, and minorities are absent or under–represented in the middle and top level administrative, professional, and supervisory ranks of correctional personnel. The situation is significantly better only in nursing, social work, and teaching. Supporting data are provided. Recommendations are made that efforts be made to make students in specialized occupations more aware of career opportunities in corrections; universities be helped to increase or develop corrections–related courses or subspecialties; and scholarship or fellowship assistance tied to postgraduate work in corrections be provided.*

BEARD, Eugene. *Study Of The Attitudes And Perceptions Of Black Correctional Employees As A Basis For Designing Recruitment And Retention Strategies*. Washington DC Howard U n.d.

This study interviewed 304 black custodial officers, 117 other black correctional personnel, 128 black inmates, 52 wardens, superintendents, and assistants, and 35 ex–correctional employees to develop a profile of the black correctional worker, identify problems faced by these workers, and suggest procedures and techniques for recruiting and retaining black correctional employees. Black employees reported the same problems—administrators seemed more interested in the advancement of whites, evaluations were seen as more favorable to whites, and there seemed little hope of job improvement. Custodial personnel expressed dissatisfaction with shifts and working hours, the noncustodial with variety in job assignments and chances for increased pay. Inmates felt that there should be an ethnic mix of custodial personnel. Black inmates felt black personnel had a greater understanding of their problems and did a better job of preparing them for reentry into society. It is recommended that more blacks be recruited for training leading to supervisory positions.*

BEARD, Eugene. *Summaries Of Studies On The Recruitment And Retention Of Minority Correctional Employees.* Washington DC Howard U n.d.

The methods, findings, and recommendations of three studies concerned with the recruitment and retention of minority correctional employees are summarized. The first study examined minority recruitment, screening, selection, promotion, and retention policies and practices of state prisons in California, Michigan, Mississippi, and Ohio. The findings indicate that national standards and goals for minority recruitment are not being met, and that there is little hope of major improvement in the near future. The second study employs data from California, Louisiana, Mississippi, New Jersey, Michigan, and Ohio to determine the number of minorities in corrections–related occupations. Minority groups are found to be underrepresented in such occupations in 1975, and the underrepresentation is predicted to continue through 1980. Efforts to make minority students in specialized areas (e.g., medicine, law, social work) aware of career opportunities in corrections are urged. A study of the attitudes and perceptions of black correctional employees led to survey findings which provide the basis for recommendations pertaining to recruitment, selection, and retention principles.*

BEARD, Eugene and Brown, Lee P and Gary, Lawrence E. *Attitudes And Perceptions Of Black Police Officers Of The District Of Columbia Metropolitan Police Department.* Washington DC Howard U 1976.

This study reports data on the recruitment, job assignments, promotion, interpersonal relations, retention, and attrition of black officers in the Metropolitan Police Department (MPD). Other topics covered include: background and personal characteristics; interpersonal relations among police officers and their perceptions of the community's attitudes towards the MPD; attitudes of black officers towards MPD supervisors and officials and the issue of discrimination in department policies and regulation; job satisfaction and promotion opportunities; and significant problems confronting the police department, police profession, and police officers.*

BEARD, Eugene. The Black Police In Washington DC. *J Polic Sci Adm* 5(1),48–52 1977.

A study was undertaken of the entire population of black officers in the Metropolitan Police Department of Washington D. C. to collect data on attitudes of black policemen. Most black officers were well–educated, became interested in police work by the age of 14 and joined the department to make the black community a better place in which to live. One–third of the parents or spouses did not approve of the officer's decision to become a police officer. Nearly 84% held the lowest rank. More than 65% reported they trusted few or no white officers. Black officers rarely socialized with white officers. More than 80% believed blacks were discriminated against in hiring, job assignments, enforcements of rules and regulations and job performance ratings. Nearly half of the black officers expressed the opinion that white citizens are more cooperative than blacks. Fifty–two percent of the black officers lived outside the District of Columbia. Eighty–four percent of the black officers were satisfied with police work. Only 25% thought their chances for promotion were better than average. Just over half of the black officers intended to make police work their career.

BEAUMONT, Gustave De and Tocqueville, Alexis De. *On The Penitentiary System In The United States And Its Application In France,* Francis Lieber (trans), Orig Pub 1833. Carbondale S Illinois Univ Pr 1964.

"The freed person commits more crimes than the slave...because, becoming emancipated, he has to provide for himself, which, during his bondage, he was not obliged to do.... His actions, involuntary when he was a slave, become now disorderly: judgment cannot guide him, for he has not exercised it: he is improvident, because he never has learned to think of futurity. His passions, not progressively developed, assail him with violence. He is the prey of wants, which he does not know how to provide for, and thus obliged to steal, or to die. Hence so many free Negroes in the prisons, and hence their greater mortality than that of slaves. Only it seems to us necessary to acknowledge, that the transition from slavery to liberty, produces a state more fatal than favorable to the freed generation...."

BECCARIA, Cesare Bonesana. *An Essay On Crime And Punishments,* Orig Pub 1763. Indianapolis Bobbs–Merrill 1963.

BECK, R A and Adams, J M. Establishing Rapport With Deviant Groups. *Social Prob* 18,102–117 1970.

BECKER, A M. Women In Corrections—A Process Of Change. *Resol Corr Prob & I* 1(4),19–21 Sum 1975.

A description of the California Department of Corrections personnel program undertaken to provide equal employment opportunities to female correctional workers by gradual and controlled increases in women employees. The basic intent of the California Corrections effort is to employ women in numbers that are reflective of the surrounding community. The assumption is that female employees can perform in correctional work situations equally as well as males. in 1974, an affirmative action program of logical and progressive expansion in the use of female employees was implemented; this plan would allow facilities to expand the number of offices at different rates because of different traditions and physical plants. This program has resulted in the employment of about 100 female officers in such jobs as safety coordinator, chief of inmate appeals, parole agents, and counselors. All California institutions now employ female officers, and some have opened all posts to females—including posts which require direct contact with inmates.*

BECKER, K L and Cannito, J A. The Case For Limited Use Of Polls In The Jury Selection Process. *Rutgers J Computers* 7(1),111–134 1979.

The development of survey research techniques in litigation is discussed with emphasis on the factors affecting the accuracy of polls and the use of survey findings to assess public prejudices. Where community attitudes must be weighed before a trial, survey research presents the most scientific method of assessing public understanding. Because a well–conducted survey is the most accurate and often most practical method of ascertaining public opinion, surveys are useful litigation tools to complement the existing judicial process. By the 1950's it was well–settled that surveys would be admitted as evidence in order to establish whether a particular trade symbol had sufficient recognition. However, proponents of surveys met with little success when introducing them to support a change of venue motion. Indications of local prejudice against a defendant or of racial bias in the community must be proven by the defendant. The courts are generally suspicious of the accuracy of surveys financed by one side in litigation, when the usual voir dire procedures are deemed sufficient to prevent jury bias. However, careful use of research may allow attorneys to develop profiles of 'ideal' jurors in particular cases.*

BECKHAM, A S. Juvenile Delinquency And The Negro. *Opport* 9,300–302 1931.

BECKMAN, Eric. Criminal Justice And Politics In America From The Sedition Act To Watergate And Beyond. *J Polic Sci Adm* 5(3),285–289 1977.

BECNEL, B. Crime—Unemployment Cycle. *Afl–Cio Am F* 85(11),9–14 N 78.

Studies showing the destructive aspects of unemployment, particularly as it stimulates the development of criminal survival patterns, are discussed. Increases in prison population, homicides, and property crimes correlate with the rise and fall of periods of high unemployment. Age and race are closely related to both crime and unemployment. Young, black males are disproportionately represented in the offender population. This is also the group disproportionately represented in the ranks of the unemployed. Increasing the costs of crime through harsher sentences is futile in the face of economic deprivation. The most effective means for reducing crime, particularly among urban, black youth, is to provide viable, legitimate survival alternatives to crime, which essentially requires providing jobs at a living wage. A program instituted by the AFL–CIO Human Resources Development Institute places ex–offenders in jobs with companies having unions, thus guaranteeing job security and relatively high wages. The program has representatives in more than 50 cities. This project has been shown to reduce the recidivism rate for ex–offenders by about 25 percent.*

BEDAU, Hugo Adam (ed). *The Death Penalty In America.* NY Anchor 1967.

BEDAU, Hugo Adam (ed) and Pierce, Chester M (ed). *Capital Punishment In The United States.* NY AMS Pr 1976.

BEDAU, Hugo Adam. Capital Punishment In Oregon 1903–1964. *Ore L Rev* 23,1–39 1965.

This study was based on information obtained from prison records, public records of communications, questionnaires sent to various court clerks and district attorneys, and from the federal *National Prisoner Statistics.* The non–white percentage of the total number of persons executed between 1930 and 1964, is given for the US, eleven western states, and

Washington, Oregon and Idaho. Also given is this percentage for Oregon for the years 1903–1964. The author compares the percentage of non–whites sentenced to death or executed in Oregon to the percentage of non–whites in the state as a whole. A distribution of whites by nativity was made; and combined with the racial distribution, figures are given for five–year periods 1903–1964. The author drew no firm conclusions regarding racial prejudice in death sentencing in Oregon. However, he concluded that "an inference of bias in the use of commutation authority...is not supportable in Oregon on the basis of the data."

BEDAU, Hugo Adam. Death Sentences In New Jersey, 1907–1964. *Rutgers L Rev* 19,1–49 1964.

Data were obtained from admission, execution and classification records of the NJ State Prison, briefs in that state's Supreme Court, memoranda provided by the NJ Bureau of Social Research and newspapers. The author broke down the sample (all persons convicted of first–degree murder and sentenced to death between 1907 and 1960) by race and ultimate disposition of sentence. Although a much higher proportion of non–whites than whites who were sentenced to death were executed, the samples were not sufficiently large to permit significance to be determined. The sample was broken down by type of conviction (felony– or non–felony murder), race and disposition. No significant correlations were found, except between felony murder and execution for whites. A distribution was made of racial and nativity characteristics of persons sentenced to death under mandatory and under discretionary sentencing policies. A significant correlation between type of sentencing procedure and racial and nativity characteristics of the group sentenced was found. A greater proportion of non–whites were sentenced under discretionary scheme. The author attributes this, however, to population changes.

BEDAU, Hugo Adam. Felony Murder Rape, And The Mandatory Death Penalty. *Suffolk U L Rev* 10,493–520 Spr 1976.

BEGEL, Debby. "An Interview With Willie Tate" in *Punishment And Penal Discipline*, Platt, Tony And Paul Takagi (eds), 176–183. Berkeley CA Crime & Soc Just 1980.

This interview with a prisoner recently acquitted of charges of murder, assault and conspiracy in the San Quentin 6 trial, describes Tate's early years and commitment to prison as a young man. He recalls his prison relationship with George Jackson, his views on prison, and his political philosophy.

BELDEN, Bauman L. Capital Punishment In 1740. *Mag Am Hist* 25,85–86 Ja 1891.

BELL JR, Derrick A. *Race, Racism And American Law*. Boston Little, Brown 1973.

This casebook, by a professor of law at Harvard University, contains cases and relevant article and book excerpts, relating to the development of racism in American law; the rights of citizenship; right to education; rights to housing; rights of employment; and right to justice. Bell explains that his casebook, the first devoted specifically to a study of racism in law, is based on the belief that racial cases warrant special attention by students of law.

BELL JR, Derrick A. Black Faith In A Racist Land: Summary Review Of Racism In American Law. *Howard L J* 17,299–318 1972.

BELL JR, Derrick A. Racial Remediation: An Historical Perspective On Current Conditions. *Notre Dame Law* 52,5–29 1976.

BELL JR, Derrick A. Racism In American Courts: Cause For Black Disruption Or Despair? *Cal L Rev* 61,165–204 Ja 1973.

Bell discusses the impact of racism at all stages of trial and sentencing. The response to verbal attacks on racism in the courts often consists of avoidance mechanisms or structural reforms that fail to attack the root issue of racism in the courts. When faced with the more serious racial problems, Bell contends, courts tend to seek solutions that guarantee maximum protection to vested majority interests and which provide only that protection to the black victims necessary to substitute calm for disruption. Judicial preference for deciding issues on procedural rather than substantive grounds, he argues, has permitted courts to endorse the democratic ideal while leaving all but the most odious practices virtually intact. Bell contends that black defendants refrain from disruptive courtroom behavior, not because they lack provocation, but because nothing in their experience provides them with any hope for justice. The persistence of blatant racism in the courts, he argues, leaves most black defendants feeling that it is impossible for a black person to get a fair trial in America, since even such simple matters as dress, speech, and manner may be misinterpreted.

BELL, Daniel. Crime As An American Way Of Life. *Ant Rev* 13,131–154 Je 1953.

BELL, Edward F. The Black Lawyer, An American Hero. *Howard L J* 17,319–325 1972.

BELL, Inge Powell. *CORE And The Strategy Of Non–Violence*. NY Random House 1968.

The author's study stems from her experience as a participant–observer in the Congress of Racial Equality (CORE) in 1961–64. Her history of CORE's origins and development in the civil rights movement of the early 1960's is enthusiastically endorsed by CORE leaders. Powell explains the nonviolent ideology of the organization and outlines its strategy for change. She also cites its weaknesses, which became more pronounced during the late 1960's, with the emergence of the Black Power Movement, Black Separatism, and violent anti–war protests.

BELL, Jimmy (ed) and Owens, Charles E (ed). *Blacks And Criminal Justice*. Lexington MA Heath 1977.

Readings by various authors cover aspects of the criminal justice system, including racial discrimination, black female offenders, recruitment of blacks into the professional ranks, and judicial decision–making. An index is included.

BELL, Jimmy. "Higher Education: Roles In Criminal Justice" in *Blacks And Criminal Justice*, Owens, Charles E And Jimmy Bell (eds), 113–117. Lexington MA Heath 1977.

Since crime has reached excessive proportions in black communities, society must ask itself how the criminal justice system can reduce those crime rates. Higher education can make invaluable contributions in this endeavor. Research can provide insight into black crime, confinement, and rehabilitation. Research in criminal justice, however, is often "agency determined," and serves political or institutional interests. Higher education, which is not subordinate to agency mandate, can retain the objectivity necessary for scholarly research. Since blacks have been underrepresented in the criminal justice professions, postsecondary institutions need to actively recruit blacks in their criminal justice, correctional psychology, and law programs. In addition, postsecondary educational opportunities should be made available to inmates. Finally, higher education could become involved with criminal justice affairs in the community, contributing to programs such as prerelease, work release, parole, diversification, therapy, and special services.*

BELL, Jimmy and Joyner, Irving. "Crime In The Black Community" in *Blacks And Criminal Justice*, Owens, Charles E And Jimmy Bell (eds), 69–74. Lexington MA Heath 1977.

Causal factors leading to crime and its alarming increase in the black community are examined, and programs to aid in crime reduction are presented. Studies indicate that the economically deprived individual may opt for crime as a means of access to the mainstream of American society, or may view crime as a necessary evil to counteract years of economic oppression. Moreover, complaints about inequities in law enforcement, unresponsiveness, and even abuse have contributed to the black community's general mistrust of police. Unemployment, which is higher among blacks, is viewed as a possible cause of the high crime rate among blacks. Evidence suggests that the typical offender is a young black male, a local resident, and undereducated. A comprehensive approach to alleviate crime in the black community is suggested. This includes community–based action programs, education programs, victim–oriented programs, and economic improvement programs; it calls for a more sensitive and responsible criminal justice system and improved community relations.*

BELSKY, Michael. Mexican Nationals In US Prisons. *Agenda* 19(3),20–21 My–Je 1980.

BENGSTON, Vern L et al. Relating Academic Research To Community Concerns: A Case Study In Collaborative Effort. *J Soc Issues* 33(4),75–92 1977.

BENJAMIN, Roger and Choong Nam Kim. *American Indians And The Criminal Justice System*. Minneapolis U Minn CU & RA 1980.

The first of two reports to study the relationship of American Indians and the criminal justice system in Minnesota, this monograph compares the treatment of Native Americans, blacks, and whites from arrest through incarceration.

BENNETT, M C. Indian Counsellor Project—Help For The Accused. *Can J Crim & Corr* 15(1),1–6 Ja 1973.

BENOKRAITIC, Nijoye Vaicartis. *Institutional Racism: A Empirical Study Of Blacks And The Jury Selection Process In Ten Southern States.* Unpub PhD Diss Univ Texas Austin 1975.

BENSING, Robert C and Schroeder, Oliver. *Homicide In An Urban Community.* Springfield IL Chas C Thomas 1960.

BENSON, Gwen and Hyman, Merton M and Helrich, Alice R. Ascertaining Police Bias In Arrests For Drunken Driving. *Q J Stud Alc* 33(1),148–159 1972.

Of the 640 men aged 25 to 54 arrested for driving while intoxicated in Santa Clara County (Calif.) and the 383 in Franklin County (Columbus, Ohio, metropolitan area) during the first 6 months of 1962, about one–third had been involved in automobile accidents. The arrest–vulnerability ratios by ethnicity, were more than twice as high among the socially disadvantaged sectors in both counties: 1.90 vs. 0.89 for the Spanish (Mexican) vs. non–Spanish whites in Santa Clara, 1.98 vs. 0.86 for the Negroes vs. whites in Franklin. Potential police bias against the disadvantaged groups was measured by comparing (1) the percentages of ADWI involved in accidents and (2) their blood alcohol concentrations (BAC) according to ethnicity and the 4 social and economic census–tract variables. It is concluded that the high ADWI rate among the minority and disadvantaged groups probably reflects accurately a greater frequency of drunken driving among them rather than a police bias in arrests.

BERGENFIELD, G. Trying Non–English Conversant Defendants: The Use Of An Interpreter. *Ore L Rev* 57(4),549–565 1978.

BERGER, Alan S and Simon, William. Black Families And The Moynihan Report: A Research Evaluation. *Social Prob* 22(2),145–161 1974.

Employing a random sample of the 14–18–year–old population of Illinois, the authors seek to test Daniel Patrick Moynihan's controversial thesis that black families socialize children very differently from the way white families socialize children. This study found few such differences. Even in lower–class families there was no indication that black families were dramatically different from white families.

BERGER, B. "Black Culture Or Lower Class Culture" in *Soul*, Rainwater, Lee (ed). Chicago Aldine 1970.

BERGER, C J. Law, Justice And The Poor. *Acad Pol Sci Pro* 29,52–59 1968.

BERGER, Monroe. *Equality By Statute: The Revolution In Civil Rights.* Garden City NY Anchor 1968.

BERGER, Stephen E and Tedeschi, James T. Aggressive Behavior Of Delinquent, Dependent, And 'Normal' White And Black Boys In Social Conflicts. *J Exp Soc Psych* 5(3),352–370 1969.

BERKEY, C G. Indian Law: Oliphant v Suquamish Indian Tribe, 435 US 191 (1978). *Cath U L Rev* 28,663–687 Spr 1979.

The controversy culminating in Oliphant began in 1973 when the Suquamish Tribe in Washington enacted a code that extended criminal jurisdiction over non–Indians.tribal police officers then arrested two non–Indian residents of the reservation for assault and for recklessly endangering another person. The Supreme Court reversed the decision of the Court of Appeals and found that the tribal court possessed no inherent power to try and punish non–Indian violators of tribal criminal laws. Jurisdiction over non–Indians could not be assumed without specific Congressional authorization. Historically, American courts have consistently recognized the inherent and residual sovereignty of Indian tribes over their people and territory. Nevertheless, the court's holding place severe legal restriction on Indian sovereignty and raised the possibility of further judicial erision of Indian rights. In Oliphant, the Court largely ignored this body of case law. oliphant does not preclude the exercise of sovereign power by Indian tribes over their own members and the exercise of civil jurisdiction over reservation territory.

BERKOWITZ, Leonard. The Study Of Urban Violence: Some Implications Of Laboratory Studies Of Frustration And Aggression. *Am Behav Sci* 2,14–17 Mr–Ap 1968.

Berkowitz applies the "frustration–aggression" hypothesis to the urban riots of the 1960's. In particular, he discusses the effect of police acting as an aggressive eliciting stimulus to frustrated, angry ghetto residents. In such a situation a rather innocuous police action against a minority member can become a precipitating event for a riot. Different police responses to this phenomena are discussed as well as their possible effects on the riot situation.

BERKSON, Larry C and Crockett Jr, George W and De Bow, Russell R. *National Roster Of Black Judicial Officers, 1980.* Chicago IL Am Judicature Soc 1980.

BERLEMAN, William C. Police And Minority Groups: The Improvement Of Community Relations. *Crim Delinq* 18(2),160–167 1972.

Two options for reconciling the polarity of police and poor nonwhites are discussed: (1) placing between police and the disaffected community an intervening governmental agency such as a community relations unit, a civilian review board, or an ombudsman; and (2) educating police and community leaders so that they may better understand each other, thereby modifying antagonisms and procedures. Neither option can be effective by itself, nor are the options discussed here to be considered exhaustive. A mix of available options is needed, as well as further constructive innovation.

BERMAN, John J. Parolees' Perceptions Of The Justice System: Black–White Differences. *Criminology* 13(4),507–520 1976.

This paper presents the attitudes of 87 Illinois parolees towards the criminal justice system. It was found that parolees held rather negative views toward the police, but were reluctant to label their own contacts with police as harassment. The parolees experienced a considerable amount of pluralistic ignorance about the extent of harassment of ex–offenders. They also held very negative views of courts and lawyers. On the other hand, respondents were somewhat positive towards the parole system and held very positive views of their own parole agents. This could be attributable either to the counselor orientation of parole officers or to their tendency to let minor parole violations slide. Racial differences were found in the area of court and police harassment, with blacks being more negative. Nevertheless, no black–white differences were found in the area of personal experiences, lawyers or the parole system. In the area of police and courts, results were consistent with past studies showing black–white differences in community attitudes.

BERMAN, S. Affirmative Action Position. *Labor Law J* 27(8),490–497 Ag 1976.

Focusing on the affirmative action position *vis–a–vis* use of the seniority system in layoffs, this article notes the pros and cons of the debate and suggests several alternatives to gutting the seniority system. The economic recession in the mid–1970's put into sharp focus the conflict between seniority provisions in labor–management contracts and national labor policy contained in Title vII of the 1964 Civil Rights Act. Specifically, organizations representing minorities and women claim that layoffs under last–hired, first–fired seniority provisions negated gains made under Title VII in the late 1960's when employment was expanding. Seniority layoff provisions have come under attack because under certain circumstances layoffs reflect original discriminatory hiring. It should be noted, however, that the affirmative action provision does not advocate abolishment of the seniority system as a layoff determinant. Rather, awarding of constructive seniority is implied (i.e., wronged groups would be placed in their rightful place in the seniority hierarchy).*

BERMANZOHN, Paul C and Bermanzohn, Sally A. *The True Story Of The Greensboro Massacre.* NY Cesar Cauce 1980.

BERMANZOHN, Sally A and Bermanzohn, Paul C. *The True Story Of The Greensboro Massacre.* NY Cesar Cauce 1980.

BERNAL, Joe and Pena, Albert and Samora, Julian. *Gunpowder Justice: A Reassessment Of The Texas Rangers.* Notre Dame U Notre Dame Pr 1979.

BERNSTEIN, Dan. East LA's Gang Project: Prevention Or Bribery? Correct Mag 6(3),36–42 Je 80.

BERRERA, M and Munos, C and Ornelasin, C. "The Barrio As An Internal Colony," in *Urban Affairs Annual Review*, V6, Hahn, Harlan (ed), 465–498. Beverly Hills CA Sage 1972.

BERRY, Brian J and Dahmann, Donald C. Population Redistribution In The US In The 1970's. *Pop & Dev Rev* 4,443–471 1977.

BERRY, Leonard J. *Prison.* NY Grossman Pub 1972.

A journalist's on–site interviews of inmates and staff in several prisons around the country examines racial attitudes and conflict.

BERRY, Mary F. *Black Resistance/White Law: A History Of Constitutional Racism In America.* NY App–Cent–Croft 1971.

BETHELL, Tom. Against Bilingual Education: Why Johnny Can't Speak English. *Harper's Mag* 258,30–33 F 1979.

Bilingual education program began in 1968 with the passage of Title VII. It was designed to develop pilot projects aimed at helping "poor children who were educationally disadvantaged because of their inability to speak English." Aided by support of HEW's Office for Civil Rights, and a favorable Supreme Court decision, Congressional appropriations for the program increased from 7.5 million to 85 million dollars by 1975. Originally intended as a transition process leading students into conventional classes, bilingual education became increasingly viewed as bicultural education, maintaining students in the classes much longer than necessary. Although instruction is given in about 70 languages, Spanish accounts for about 80% of the program, leading to the conclusion that bilingual education is the Hispanic equivalent of affirmative action. The program is expected to continue its growth largely because it is not politically expedient to oppose it. A study commissioned by HEW concluded that children in bilingual classes performed no better than children from similar backgrounds in regular English classes. It is time to return to the melting pot and work on a program to improve English literacy.

BIASSEY, E L. Paranoia And Racism In The United States. *Nat Med Assoc J* 64,353–358 1972.

Much of the prejudice and racism in America is paranoid in origin and developed by the self-serving, defensive maneuvers of the majority. Prejudice and racist views are necessary to the white man in order to maintain the status quo in which the black man is dominated and subjugated, so that the spoils of labor belong only to the white man and the crumbs are left to the black. Racism is one of the American ideas that is localized in American society today. In America today, the Negro, the Puerto Rican, and the American Indian are being subverted. The news media, the mass television media, the radio, the magazines and all manner of communication channels contribute to the image of what a specific people can be or are. There are some completely fair, unbiased presentations; but in many others, there is editorializing and a considerable amount of unfairness. There are many who are irresponsible enough to stir up the people and create suspicions to gain their own ends. It is concluded that in America today we start out with a false assumption about a person or a group of people, accept that false assumption, and act toward that person as if it were true.

BILLINGSLEY, Andrew. *Black Families In White America*. Englewood Cliffs NJ Prentice-Hall 1968.

BINGAY, Malcolm W. Requiem On A Race Riot. *Negro Dig* 4,59–63 Ag 1946.

BITTKER, Boris. *The Case For Black Reparations*. NY Random House 1973.

Bittker discusses whether there is a legal basis for seeking compensation for injuries due to racist misconduct by public officials.

BITTNER, Egon (ed) and Messinger, Sheldon L (ed). *Criminology Review Yearbook*, V1. Beverly Hills CA Sage 1979.

BLACK PRISONERS OF FLORIDA STATE PRISON, Starke. *Bound And Free: The Poetry Of Warriors Behind Bars*. Washington DC King Publications 1976.

Collection of poems and other writings by black prisoners in the Florida State Prison at Starke.

BLACK, Charles L. *Capital Punishment: The Inevitability Of Caprice And Mistake*. NY Norton 1974.

BLACK, Donald J and Reiss Jr, Albert J. "Patterns Of Behavior In Police And Citizen Transactions" in *Race, Crime, And Justice*, Reasons, C E And J L Kuykendall (eds), 176–205. Pacific Palisades CA Goodyear 1972.

BLACK, Donald and Reiss Jr, Albert. Police Control Of Juveniles. *Am Sociol Rev* 35,63–77 1970.

BLACK, Jonathan (ed). *Radical Lawyers: Their Role In The Movement And In The Courts*. NY Avon 1971.

BLACKBURN, Sara (ed). *White Justice*. NY Harper Colophon 1971.

BLACKHORSE, F D. Prison And Native People. *Indian Hist* 8,54–56 1975.

BLACKSTONE, Nelson. *Cointelpro: The FBI's Secret War On Political Freedom*. NY Vintage 1976.

An investigation of counterintelligence activities during the late 1960's and early 1970's, including documents relating to the Federal Bureau of Investigation's efforts to discredit the Black Panthers.

BLACKWELL, James E. *The Black Community: Diversity And Unity*. NY Harper & Row 1975.

BLAKE, Frank. Handling The Needs Of Non-English-Speaking Persons. *Pol Chief* 42(1),18–26 1975.

BLAKE, Herman. Black Nationalism. *Ann Am Poli* 382,16–25 Mr 1969.

BLALOCK JR, Hubert M. *Social Statistics*. NY McGraw-Hill 1972.

BLALOCK, Hubert M. *Toward A Theory Of Minority-group Relations*. NY Wiley 1967.

BLANCHARD, E B and Unikel, I P. Psychopathy, Race, And Delay Of Gratification By Adolescent Delinquents. *J Nerv Ment Dis* 156,57–60 1973.

BLASSINGAME, John W (ed). *Slave Testimony: Two Centuries Of Letters, Speeches, Interviews, And Autobiographies*. Baton Rouge LA LSU Pr 1977.

This anthology of slave testimony represents a much-needed effort to systematically describe slavery from the words of the slaves themselves instead of relying on descriptions from masters, abolitionists, and journalists. Using letters, interviews, autobiographies and other sources exhumed from various manuscript collections, scrapbooks, periodicals, archives, etc., Blassingame presents a rich assortment of original, first-hand accounts, which the author says, "reveal the mind of the slave, his private world, the accommodations he worked out with his master, how he survived from day to day, and the configuration of his culture and family life." Accounts of slave punishments, crimes by masters and slaves, and experiences of runaways, are included.

BLASSINGAME, John W. *The Slave Community: Plantation Life In The Antebellum South*. NY Oxford Univ Pr 1972.

BLAUNER, Robert. *Racial Oppression In America*. NY Harper & Row 1972.

BLAUNER, Robert. "Black Culture: Lower Class Result Or Ethnic Creation" in *Soul*, Rainwater, Lee (ed), 129–166. Chicago Aldine 1970.

BLAUNER, Robert. Internal Colonialism And Ghetto Revolt. *Social Prob* 16,393–408 Spr 1969.

Blauner's seminal attempt to relate the concept of "colonialism" as developed by Stokley Carmichael and Eldridge Cleaver to sociological analysis notes the modifications he thinks are necessary before the concept can be meaningfully applied to the American scene.

BLAUNER, Robert. Whitewash Over Watts. *Trans-Act* 3(3),3–9 Mr–Ap 1966.

Blauner, a sociologist who served as a consultant to the McCone Commission investigating the causes of the Watts riots of 1965, charges that the commission's work amounted to a political whitewash. Blauner offers his own analysis of the deeper meaning of the outbreak and suggests several reasons why the panel failed to confront the community's legitimate grievances.

BLEDA, S E and Petersen, D M and Schwirian, K P. The Drug Arrest: Empirical Observations On The Age, Sex And Race Of Drug Law Offenders In A Midwestern City. *Drug Forum* 6(4),371–386 1977–78.

BLOCH, Herbert A and Geis, Gilbert. *Man, Crime, And Society*, Rev'd Ed. NY Random House 1970.

BLOCH, Herbert A. The Juvenile Gang: A Cultural Reflex. *Ann Am Poli* 347,20–29 1963.

Since the 1950's American sociologists studying delinquency have become increasingly concerned with the effects of class differences on youthful deviance. Class research stems in part from a research interest developed during the Depression, yet sociologists have not always been accurate in depicting class differences and in claiming identification of exclusive criteria of differences between class groups. Some of the results have been a failure to comprehend realistically the full dimensions of the changing class structure in the US and a readiness to attribute forms of youthful deviance, including delinquency, to reactive compensations of working-class youths toward middle-class values and limitations of egress from a restrictive background. In what tends to become a relatively simple and unencumbered view there has been a conspicuous avoidance of reference to pervasive behavioral practices of various types which characterize the culture as a whole. Unlike scholars elsewhere, for reasons which may reflect the current American culture mentality, sociologists in the US appear to be minimizing significant facts of intergenerational struggle.

BLOCK, N J and Dworkin, G. IQ: Heritability And Inequality, Part I. *Philos Pub Aff* 3(4),331–409 1974.

Part 1 of this article is organized around three questions: (1) can we reasonably ask whether I. Q. tests measure intelligence? (Sections I and II);

(2) assuming we can, how good are the arguments that I. Q. tests do measure intelligence? (Sections II–VI); (3) if I. Q. tests do not measure intelligence, what do they measure? (Sections VII and VIII). Part 2 considers heritability estimates; race, research, and responsibility.

BLOCK, N J and Dworkin, G. IQ: Heritability And Inequality, Part II. *Philos Pub Aff* 4(1),40–99 1975.

BLOCK, Richard L. Community, Environment And Violent Crime. *Criminology* 17(1),46–57 My 1979.

BLOCK, Richard L. Fear Of Crime And Fear Of The Police. *Social Prob* 19(1),91–101 Sum 1971.

Based on a nationwide random sample survey, Block concludes that fear of crime is only weakly related to either support for the police or protection from them. Blacks were found to be more fearful of the police and less supportive of the police. The data collected by the National Opinion Research Center (NORC) in the summer of 1966 found victims of crime less likely to support the police and more likely to support increased protection of civil liberties than non–victims.

BLOCK, Richard L. Support For Civil Liberties And Support For The Police. *Am Behav Sci* 13,781–796 1970.

BLOCK, Richard L. Why Notify The Police: The Victim's Decision To Notify The Police Of An Assault. *Criminology* 11(4),555–569 F 1974.

BLOCK, Richard. Homicide In Chicago: A Nine–Year Study (1965–1973). *J Crim L & Crimin* 66(4),496–510 D 1975.

BLOOMFIELD, Neil J and Stahl, David and Sussman, Frederick B. *The Community And Racial Crisis.* NY Practising L Ins 1966.

BLUE JR, John T. Concepts And Methodology In The Field Of Juvenile Delinquency. *J Hum Relat* 7,473–482 1959.

BLUE JR, John T. The Relationship Of Juvenile Delinquency, Race And Economic Status. *J Negro Ed* 17,469–477 1948.

In his study of juvenile delinquency in Detroit, Blue considered two causal factors and their relationship to delinquency: race and economic status. The hypothesis for his work was that economic status is more closely related to juvenile delinquency than is race or, stated another way: "if racial differences could be held constant, the delinquency rates for non–white persons would vary with their economic status in the same manner and degree as the delinquency rates for white persons vary with their economic status." He concludes that the evidence resulting from the computation and analysis of zero order and partial correlation coefficients for delinquency, race, and economic status using respectively as indices—delinquency rates, percent of dwellings occupied by non–white persons, and average rents—support the hypothesis that economic status is more closely related, than race, to juvenile delinquency.

BLUMENTHAL, Karen L and Mc Gowan, Brenda G. *Why Punish The Children: A Study Of Children Of Women Prisoners.* Hackensack NJ NCCD 1978.

BLUMENTHAL, M D. Resentment And Suspicion Among American Men. *Am J Psychiatry* 130(8),876–880 1973.

When a representative national sample of men between the ages of 16 and 64 were interviewed with respect to their levels of resentment and suspicion and their attitudes toward violence, resentment and suspicion appeared to be related both to race and to social class. However, they were not related to attitudes toward the use of violence for gaining social control.

BLUMSTEIN, Alfred and Cohen, Jacqueline. A Theory Of The Stability Of Punishment. *J Crim L & Crim* 64,198–207 1973.

BLUMSTEIN, Alfred and Cohen, Jacqueline and Miller, Harold D. *Demographically Disaggregated Projections Of Prison Populations.* Pittsburgh Carnegie–M USI 1978.

This monograph on the impact of new sentencing laws on state prison populations in Pa. confirms the widespread expectation that mandatory minimum prison sentences for particular classes of felonies are likely to result in a substantial increase in the prisoner population. The authors predict that the new laws will have a greater effect on blacks than whites, thereby increasing the proportion of black prisoners.

BLUMSTEIN, Alfred and Cohen, Jacqueline and Nagin, Daniel S. The Dynamics Of A Homeostatic Punishment Process. *J Crim L & Crimin* 67(4),317–334 1976.

BLUMSTEIN, Alfred and Nagin, Daniel S. Analysis Of Arrest Rates For Trends In Criminality. *Socio–Econ Plan Sci* 9,221–227 1975.

BOBO, D. *Law And Order On The Mississippi Choctaw Reservation.* Washington DC NILECJ 1970.

BODE, William. *Lights And Shadows Of Chinatown.* San Francisco H S Crocker 1896.

BOESEL, D et al. White Institutions And Black Rage. *Trans–Act* 6,10–19 1969.

BOETTCHER, W D. *Minority Recruitment And Retention In The Des Moines Police Department: A Survey Of Opinions.* Des Moines IA Chamb of Commerce 1975.

Findings of a study to assess the effectiveness of the Des Moines Police Department Juvenile Liasion Project in increasing minority recruitment and identifying deterrents to minority recruitment and retention. Incidence data regarding minority applications were obtained from the personnel department. Data regarding deterring factors were obtained through interviews with past and present minority officers, minority community leaders and citizens, and school personnel. Incidence data indicate that the number of minority officers has consistently remained low. Interview responses suggest that further intensification of recruitment efforts is needed within the community and within the high schools with special efforts to involve counselors. Respondents suggested the need for a concentrated educational program, at all grade levels within the schools to further the understanding of law enforcement and to acquaint students with the advantages of law enforcement careers.*

BOETTCHER, W D. *Minority Recruitment And Retention In The Des Moines Police Department—A Survey Of Opinions.* Des Moines IA Chamb Of Commerce 1975.

BOGARDUS, Emory S. *The Mexican In The United States.* Los Angeles Univ S CA Pr 1934.

BOGARDUS, Emory S. Gangs Of Mexican–American Youth. *Sociol Soc Res* 28,55–56 1943.

BOGGS, Sara L and Galliher, John F. Evaluating The Police: A Comparison Of Black Street And Household Respondents. *Social Prob* 22,393–406 1975.

BOGOMOLNY, Robert. Street Patrol: The Decision To Stop A Citizen. *Crim L Bull* 12(5),544–582 1976.

BOHANNON, P (ed). *African Homicide And Suicide.* Princeton Princeton Univ Pr 1960.

Seventy–one percent of 41 African tribal groups studied had lower homicide rates than whites of South Carolina and Texas in 1949–1951. This indicates that it is cultural and not biological factors which are responsible for the high homicide rate among Negro Americans.

BOIE, Maurine. An Analysis Of Negro Crime Statistics For Minneapolis For 1923, 1924, And 1925. *Opport* 6,171–173 Je 1928.

BOND, Julian. Civil Rights Movement––To The Courtroom. *Trial* 13(3),40–42 Mr 1977.

BOND, Julian. Self–Defense Against Rape: The Joanne Little Case. *Black Scholar* 6(6),29–31 1975.

A plea is made for public support of Joanne Little, a black woman charged with killing a jail guard who tried to rape her. Circumstances surrounding the trial and her indictment for first degree murder are reviewed, and the question whether the defendant can be ensured a fair trial in North Carolina is considered. Important issues relating to her trial include: 1) the right of a woman to defend herself against sexual attack; 2) the sexual control of male guards and trustees over women prisoners; and 3) the discriminatory use of the death penalty against poor people and blacks.

BONGER, Willem Adriaen. *Criminality And Economic Conditions.* (orig pub 1916). Bloomington Indiana Univ Pr 1969.

BONGER, Willem Adriaen. *Race And Crime*, Margaret Mathews Hordyk (trans). NY Columbia Univ Pr 1943.

Bonger, a Dutch criminologist, completed this book shortly before the Nazi invasion of Holland and much of what he has to say is directed at Nazi racist ideas and policies against Jews. A chapter devoted to Negro criminality concludes that blacks are disproportionately represented in crime in the US; however Bonger rejects the suggestion that this is due to purported lower intelligence or other so–called inherent inferiority.

BOOKER, Simeon. J Edgar Hoover—The Negro And The FBI. *Ebony* 17,29–34 1962.

BOONE, John O. "A View Of Prisons" in *The Administration Of Criminal Justice: A View From Black America*, Brown, Lee P (ed). Washington DC Howard U 1974.

BOONE, John O. "Prison Construction Moratorium" in *Black Perspectives On Crime And The Criminal Justice System*, Woodson, Robert L (ed), 123–142. Boston G K Hall 1977.

Boone, who is black and a former commissioner of corrections for the State of Mass., favors a national moratorium on prison construction as a crime prevention tactic.

BOONE, S L and Moutare, A. Tests Of The Language–Aggression Hypothesis. *Psychol Rep* 39(3),851–857 1976.

This study tested the hypothesis that language is related to aggression in two ways: that relatively low levels of proficiency in the use of language should be associated with relatively high levels of observable aggression and that high levels of language proficiency should be associated with low levels of aggression. The vocabulary subset of the Wechsler Intelligence Scale for Children, the Metropolitan Achievement Test in Reading, the total number of words spoken durng a free speech session, and the number of different words used during that session constituted the language measures. Aggression of 132 subjects, ranging in age from 9 to 13 years, was measured using an adaptation of the physical and verbal aggression categories used by Walters, Pearce, and Dahms. The results supported both predictions for the comparisons between black subjects and Puerto Rican subjects but not for the white subjects.

BORMAN, L. American Indians: The Reluctant Urbanites. *Center Mag* 10,44–45 Mr 1977.

BOSKIN, Joseph. The Revolt Of The Urban Ghettos, 1964–1967. *Ann Am Poli* 382,1–14 1969.

BOSTON, John and Hermann, Robert and Single, Eric. *Counsel For The Poor: Criminal Defense In Urban America*. Lexington MA Lexington 1977.

BOTTOMS, A E. Delinquency Amongst Immigrants. *Race* 8,357–383 1967.

BOUZA, Anthony. Policing The Bronx. *J Polic Sci Adm* 3(1),55–58 1975.

BOWEN, Donald Et Al. Deprivation, Mobility, And Orientation Toward Protest Of The Urban Poor. *Am Behav Sci* 2,20–24 Mr–Ap 1968.

BOWERS, R A (ed) and Lange, A G (ed). *Fraud And Abuse In Government Benefit Programs*. Washington DC NILECJ 1979.

A study of fraud and abuse control issues in 15 government benefit programs is documented. The study involved interviews with 134 federal, state, and local programs administrators, fraud investigators, prosecutors, quality control officials, and others charged with responsibility for benefit program operations, integrity, and control, plus questionnaire surveys of state attorneys general and 123 other state officials. The following programs are included in the study: food stamps, summer food service program for children, rural housing, Medicare, Medicaid, aid to families with dependent children, vocational education, rehabilitation housing loans, federal disaster assistance, unemployment insurance, comprehensive employment and training program, minority business development, physical disaster loan assistance, veterans educational assistance, and veterans home loan guaranty program.*

BOWERS, William J. *Discrimination In Capital Punishment: Characteristics Of The Condemned(Stearns Research Center)*. Boston Northeastern U 1972.

The data for this study are drawn from *National Prisoner Statistics*, and N. Teeters and C. Zibulka, *Executions Under State Authority* (1968). The figures are flawed by the fact that certain (notably southern) states still carried on executions under local authority during the sampled periods, and that some states (notably PA, NV, and CA) did not provide full information on race. The basic figures for this study consist of a distribution of the sample by race, age, offense and level of appeal. Even more extensive distributions of these data are made showing mean age at execution for those having appeals by race and offense; percentage having appeals by age at execution by race by offense; mean age at execution for those sentenced for murder by geographic region (south, non–south) by appeal by race; the percentage having appeals before execution for murder by region by race; and by year (before 1930, 1930–1940, after 1940) by age (above or below 30). Bowers directs his discussion to the limitations of appeals for non–whites, which he suggests might relate to the fact that non–whites are executed younger.

BOWERS, William J and Carr, Andrea and Pierce, Glenn L. *Executions In America*. Lexington MA Heath 1974.

Presents extensive data about the characteristics of persons executed in the US. Regional differences and racial disproportionality are examined in detail.

BOWERS, William J and Pierce, Glenn L. Capital Punishment As A Case Study In The Incremental Evaluation Of Guided Discretion. Philadelphia A S C 1979.

BOWERS, William J and Pierce, Glenn L. *Preliminary Tabulations Reflecting Arbitrariness And Discrimination Under Post–'Furman' Capital Statutes*. Boston NE Univ Cen ASR 1979.

BOWERS, William J and Pierce, Glenn L. Arbitrariness And Discrimination Under Post–'Furman' Capital Statutes. *Crim Delinq* 26(4),563–635 O 1980.

BOWKER, Lee H. *Prisoner Subcultures*. Lexington MA Heath 1977.

BOWKER, Lee H and Chesney, Meda and Pollock, Joy. *Women, Crime, And The Criminal Justice System*. Lexington MA Lexington 1978.

BOWKER, Lee Harrington and Pollock, Joy. *Prisons And Prisoners: A Bibliographic Guide*. San Francisco R & E Research 1978.

Theoretical approaches to prisons and prisoners and such specialized topics as prison violence and minority and family relations are referenced in this bibliography on prisoner subcultures.*

BOWLER, Alida C. "Recent Statistics On Crime And The Foreign Born" in *Report On Crime And The Foreign Born*, V10. Washington DC NCLOE 1931.

BOYD, Jeffrey L. Race Of Inmate, Race Of Officer, And Disciplinary Proceedings At A Federal Correctional Institution. *FCI Res Rep* 8(1),1–35 1976.

Racial bias has been alleged to exist at correctional institutions because they represent a closed society in which a disproportionate share of inmates are black and most staff are white. The present study examined two aspects of the relationship between inmate race and disciplinary proceedings: (1) the rates at which white and black inmates received conduct reports (shots) and the nature of the infractions, and (2) differences in how black and white correctional officers, matched for length of employment, handled disciplinary matters. Ten black officers and 20 white officers were in the sample. Inmate population totaled 846 whites and 475 blacks. Results showed that black and white inmates were treated essentially the same. Black and white officers did not differ in the average number of shots submitted, but did differ in kinds of offenses reported. In addition, black officers submitted a disproportionate number of shots on black inmates. Differences in correctional officer behavior indicate that black and white officers face differing professional problems. Results are applicable only to the institution studied.*

BOYLE, John M and Brunswick, Ann F. What Happened In Harlem: Analysis Of A Decline In Heroin Use Among A Generation Unit Of Urban Black Youth. *J Drug Issues* 10(1),109–130 Wint 1980.

Heroin among a cross–section of black adolescents in Harlem dropped from 8% in 1970–71 to less than 30.5% in 1975–76, reflecting in part the sharp decline in heroin initiation among younger birth cohorts. The authors' research, which was supported by the National Institute on Druge Abuse, indicates that among black youths born in 1950, 22% had initiated heroin use by age 18. Among those born in 1957, however, the figure was 3%.

BRACKETT, Jeffrey R. The Negro In Maryland, Orig Pub 1889. Freeport NY Books Libraries Pr 1969.

BRADBURN, N and Sudman, S. *Response Effects In Surveys: A Review And Synthesis*. Chicago IL Aldine 1974.

BRAILSFORD, Daniel T. The Historical Background And Present Status Of The County Chain Gang In South Carolina. *S Car L Rev* 21,53–69 1969.

BRAITHWAITE, John. *Inequality, Crime And Public Policy*. Boston Routledge & Kegan 1979.

BRAITHWAITE, Ronald L. *An Analysis Of Proxemics And Self–Disclosing Behavior Of Recidivist And Non–Recidivist Adult Social Offenders*. Unpub PhD Diss Michigan St Univ 1975.

Self–reported differences in self–disclosure (SD) and proxemic distance parameters of black (B), white (W) and Chicano (C) prison inmates were studied, along with differences between recidivist (R) and nonrecidivist (NR) inmates from each of these ethnic groups. Subjects were tested on the Jourard Self–Disclosure Questionnaire, behavioral measures of proxemic distance and area need, and the Paranoia subscale of the Minnesota Multiphasic Personality Inventory (MMPI). Hypotheses predicted significant differences among the three race groups and between NR–R groups. Repeated measures analysis of SD for targets crossed with race indicated significant differences which were graphically displayed to further depict the SD patterns. A hypothesized significant negative correlation between total SD and Paranoia subscale score was not supported. Significant differences among races also occurred in the proxemic area, mainly attributable to the Chicano and white groups. A hypothesized negative correlation between total SD score and proxemic area for races was supported only for the white group.

BRAKEL, S J. American Indian Tribal Courts—Separate: 'Yes' Equal: 'Probably Not'. *Am Bar A J* 62,1002–1006 Ag 1976.

BRAKEL, Samuel J. *American Indian Tribal Courts: The Costs Of Separate Justice.* Chicago IL Am Bar Found 1978.

Assesses functioning of six separate tribal courts with comparative reference to experience of seven tribes under regular state jurisdiction. Argues that tribal courts are essentially white American creations not uniquely beneficial for most reservation residents and that integration with regular courts is likely to take place in the long run. Suggests measures to improve functioning of tribal courts where separate systems continue.

BRANDEIS UNIV: LEMBERG CENTER FOR THE STUDY OF VIOLENCE. *Sniping Incidents: A New Pattern Of Violence?* Waltham MA Brandeis, Lemberg 1969.

BRANTNER, John and Westermeyer, Joseph. Violent Death And Alcohol Use Among The Chippewa In Minnesota. *Minn Med* 55(8),749–752 1972.

Violent death occurs five times more often among Indian people in Minnesota (most of whom are Chippewa) than among the general population. It is the most common cause of death for Indians in Minnesota, during recent years. In Minneapolis, violent deaths among Indians are significantly more often associated with alcohol use than in the general population. In general, Chippewa victims of violent death resemble such victims in the general population with regard to sex, age, and blood alcohol level. A notable exception to this is homicide, which occurs at an earlier age among Chippewa than it does among other American Indians, whereas, unlike other Indian groups, suicide is less frequent.

BRAZZIEL, William F. White Research In Black Communities: When Solutions Become A Part Of The Problem. *J Soc Issues* 29(1),41–44 1973.

BREARLEY, H C. *Homicide In The United States.* Chapel Hill Univ N Car Pr 1932.

BREARLEY, H C. The Negro And Homicide. *Soc Forces* 9,247–253 1930.

BREARLY, H C. "The Pattern Of Violence" in *Culture In The South*, Couch, W T (ed), 678–692. Chapel Hill Univ N Car Pr 1934.

BRECHT, A and Mills, R. Minorities Employed In Law Libraries. *Law Lib J* 71,283–288 1978.

BRECKENRIDGE, J B. Legislative Inadequacies And Needs In The Prevention And Control Of Civil Disorders. *Pol Chief* 36(11),48–53 N 1969.

BREECE, C M and Garrett, G R. "Women In Policing—Changing Perspectives On The Role" in *Criminal Justice Planning*, Scott, J E And S Dinitz (eds). NY Praeger 1977.

Literature on legal, social, and other influences on the role of women in police work is reviewed, and their status is assessed. The involvement of women in police work has been linked with the stereotyping of personality characteristics and of female roles. Together with the paramilitary image of police agencies, stereotyped views have reduced the probabilities of women entering police work and have confined career mobility for policewomen to such areas as juvenile work, meter patrol, and administrative duties. Social reactions to the use of women in police agencies and on patrol vary according to population group, although studies indicate that the public generally is not opposed to women in policing. The greatest resistance to the use of policewomen, particularly on patrol duty, comes from male officers. Improved public image, less violence in police–citizen encounters, overall reduction of police violence, and better handling of rape and sex crime victims are among advantages associated with the use of female patrol officers in pilot programs. Major disadvantages include adverse effects on the morale of male officers and the tendency of male officers to be overly protective of their female colleagues.*

BREER, William M. Probation Supervision Of The Black Offender. *Fed Prob* 36(2),31–36 1972.

Some ways in which a white probation officer might strive to work more effectively with the black probationer are explored. It is essential that the caseworker be aware that black America, especially in the ghetto, is in many ways culturally different from the mainstream of national society. Aspects of the black subculture most relevant to the probation officer are discussed.

BREITER, Tony (ed). Hispanics And The US Criminal Justice System. *Agenda* 10(3),2 My–Je 1980.

BREITMAN, George. *The Last Year Of Malcolm X: The Evolution Of A Revolutionary.* NY Schocken 1968.

BRENNER, Robert N (comp) and Kravitz, Marjorie (comp). *A Community Concern: Police Use Of Deadly Force.* Washington DC NCJRS 1979.

BRENNER, Robert N (comp) and Kravitz, Marjorie (comp) and Ray, M W (comp). *Firearm Use In Violent Crime: A Selected Bibliography.* Rockville MD NCJRS 1978.

This bibliography with abstracts concerns firearm use in violent crime and is directed at researchers, criminal justice practitioners, and other interested persons. Books, journal articles, and reports are included.*

BRESLER, L and Leonard, D. *Women's Jail—Pretrial And Post–Conviction Alternatives—A Report On Women Arrested In San Francisco.* San Francisco Unitarian U S C 1978.

A year–long study was conducted by the Women's Jail Project of the Unitarian Universalist Service Committee in San Francisco, to determine the kinds of pretrial and post–conviction alternatives for female arrestees in the city. Results of the study suggested that (1) the women arrested differed from the general population in ethnicity; (2) cash or surety bail continued to be the most common form of pretrial release; (3) women diverted were usually younger than those sentenced to jail; (4) women diverted were charged with less serious misdemeanors than their sentenced counterparts; and (5) the ethnicity ratio of women sentenced was significantly different from the general population of women in the city and the population booked. The majority of women were charged with "prostitution" and other victimless crimes. Recommendations, a glossary, a bibliography, and description of methodology is included.

BREWER, B and Wales, E. Graffiti In The 1970's. *J Soc Psychol* 99,115–123 1976.

BREWER, Jesse and Knowles, Lyle. The Black Community: Attitudes Toward Community Problems, Crime And The Police. *Pol Chief* 40(8),48–51 1973.

Knowles and Brewer present the results of a survey of blacks in a Los Angeles community. Those surveyed viewed unemployment and crimes as the most serious problems facing the community. Nearly half of the residents who had an opinion on police service in the community rated it as good or very good, one–fourth rated it "fair" and the rest "poor." Of the two–thirds of the respondents who reported having had previous contact with police, 72% had been pleased with the conduct of the officers while the remaining 28% had been displeased. Suggestions offered by respondents on how improved relations between police and the community might be accomplished included heavy support for police involvement in youth programs (mentioned by a majority of respondents) and footbeats (mentioned by nearly one–third of respondents). The need for person–to–person contact with citizens is evidenced by the vast majority of citizens who responded negatively to the assignment of only black officers to the black community.

BRIAR, Scott and Piliavin, Irving. Police Encounters With Juveniles. *Am J Soc* 70,206–214 S 1964.

BRIGGS JR, Vernon M. *The Mexico–United States Border: Public Policy And Chicano Economic Welfare.* Austin Univ Tex Cen S H R 1974.

BRIGHAM, J C and Barkowitz, P. Do 'They All Look Alike' The Effects Of Race, Sex, Experience, And Attitudes On The Ability To Recognize Faces. *J App So P* 8(4),306–318 1978.

Results of an experiment conducted at Florida State University with black and white college students demonstrated that subjects were significantly more accurate in identifying pictures showing faces belonging to their own race. Contrary to assumptions made by many legal authorities and criminal justice personnel, neither racial attitude nor reported amount of quality of interracial experience was related to their ability to recognize pictures. The authors also discuss implications for police lineups and eyewitness identification.

BRINTON, Hugh P. Negroes Who Run Afoul Of The Law. *Soc Forces* 11(1),96–101 O 1932.

BRITO, Silvester John. *The Development And Change Of The Peyote Ceremony Through Time And Space.* Unpub PhD Diss Indiana Univ 1976. The manner in which and reasons why the ritual of the peyote religion developed into a more complex phenomenon than in its early prototype when first introduced to Indians north of the Rio Grande was examined. Topics include the sociocultural religious atmosphere for the setting of a new religion, an description of a typical Plains peyote ceremony and its current major variants, ethnohistorical viewpoints of major leaders within the Native American Church regarding changes in the religion, and major developmental states of current ritual. It is demonstrated that not only has change taken place within the ritual process, but also that communicants are both covertly and overtly aware of these changes and the manner in which they have occurred. The ceremony is seen as serving two functins: 1) strengthening of the peyote tradition by endowing it with greater prestige through incorporation of nativistic beliefs which are reinforced in turn by Christian syncretic elements; and 2) promotion of intertribal brotherhood (Pan-Indian nationalism) through the behavioral interactions of communicants.

BRITT, B and Dutton, A. *Recruitment And Retention Of Females In Law Enforcement Occupations.* NY Nat Urb League 1977.
Interview techniques and affirmative action programs for women in law enforcement occupations are discussed as part of the National Urban League's Law Enforcement Minority Manpower Project for Minority Recruitment. Some of the suggested techniques for interviewing female applicants are as follows: (1) make the female applicant feel comfortable and on an equal footing with other candidates; (2) advise the woman that the agency is interested in candidates of both sexes; (3) introduce the potential employee to senior women in the organization; never ask a female candidate questions regarding marital status, marriage plans, or child care requirements unless the same questions are asked male applicants; and (5) allow the candidate to describe nontraditional work experience such as volunteer or civic work, bearing in mind that a woman may be anxious to prove herself in nontraditional functions even though her work history involved secretarial or volunteer employment. Procedures for establishing and administering an affirmative action plan involve providing an honest picture of the extent of utilization of females.*

BRODSKY, Stanley L (ed) and Walker, Marcia J (ed). *Sexual Assault: The Victim And The Rapist.* Lexington MA Lexington 1976.

BRODSKY, Stanley L. *Families And Friends Of Men In Prison: The Uncertain Relationship.* Lexington MA Lexington 1974.

BRODY, R and O' Leary, T and Fagen, R. *Cubans In Exile: Disaffection And The Revolution.* Stanford CA Stanford Univ Pr 1968.

BRODY, Stuart A. The Political Prisoner Syndrome. *Crim Delinq* 20,97–106 1974.

BROMALL, Irvin. Black And Minority Law Students: Stratum For Social Change. *J Nonwh Con Per Guid* 3,114–120 1975.

BROMBERG, Walter and Simon, Frank and Pasto, Tarmo A. Symbolism In A 'Protest Psychosis'. *Israel Ann Psychi Rel Disc* 10(2),164–179 1972.
A special type of reactive psychosis among Negro prisoners charged with aggressive crimes is described along with case material. Because the clinical picture, usually diagnosed as schizophrenia, contained distinct elements of African ideology, Muslim religious doctrine and distinct anti-Caucasian hostility with reflections on centuries-old white domination of non white peoples, it was labeled protest psychosis. The illness was short-lived, and started abruptly after either arraignment or indictment for an aggressive crime. While the prisoners were in confinement they demonstrated mutism, destructive wild behavior, incoherence, hallucinations of auditory or visual type, bizarre utterances and mannerisms. Included in the discussion are a series of drawings made by one patient which demonstrate the underlying dynamics of the protest reaction. It is noted that the patient was unaware, on recovery several months later, that he had produced such artistic material while psychotic.

BROMBERG, Walter. Delinquency Among Minorities: Afro-Americans. *Corr Psychi J Soc Ther* 14(4),209–212 1968.
Bromberg, a psychiatrist with 35 years of experience in dealing with child, adolescent and adult Negro criminals, comments that basic cultural and neuromuscular differences contribute to greater black involvement in "aggressive crime."

BRONSTEIN, Alvin J. Reform Without Change: The Future Of Prisoners' Rights. *Civil Lib Rev* 4,27–45 S–O 1977.

BROPHY, W and Aberle, S. *The Indian: America's Unfinished Business.* Norman Univ Oklahoma Pr 1966.

BROTZ, H (ed). *Negro Social And Political Thought, 1850–1920.* NY Basic Books 1966.

BROWN JR, William H. Racial Discrimination In The Legal Profession. *Judicature* 15,461–473 1930.

BROWN, B and Thompson, F J. Commitment To The Disadvantaged Among Urban Administrators—The Case Of Minority Hiring. *Urb Aff Q* 13(3),355–378 Mr 1978.
Potential correlates of attitudinal commitment for minority hiring among urban personnel officers are examined in this research paper. Sociopolitical beliefs concerning equality would be powerful predictors of attitudes toward recruiting nonwhites.*

BROWN, Barry S et al. Staff Conceptions Of Inmate Characteristics: A Comparison Of Treatment And Custodial Staffs At Two Differing Institutions. *Criminology* 9(2,3),316–329 Ag–N 1971.

BROWN, Claude. *Manchild In The Promised Land.* NY Macmillan 1965.
Fictionalized autobiographical account of a black delinquent.

BROWN, Claude. *The Children Of Ham.* NY Stein & Day 1976.

BROWN, Earl. *Why Race Riots: Lessons From Detroit.* NY Public Aff Comm 1944.

BROWN, F J and Roucek, J S. *On Racial And National Minorities.* NY Prentice–Hall 1937.

BROWN, H Rap. *Die Nigger Die.* NY Dial Pr 1969.

BROWN, Lee P (ed). *The Administration Of Criminal Justice: A View From Black America.* Washington DC Howard U 1974.

BROWN, Lee P (ed) and Gary, Lawrence E (ed). *Crime & Its Impact On The Black Community.* Washington DC Howard U 1976.
The following topics are explored in Part 1: (1) Historical Overview of Crime and Blacks since 1876 (2) Black Attitudes Toward Crime and Crime Prevention (3) Black Business and the Crime of Uneconomic Communities (4) Lessons in Crime from the All–Black Town and (5) Philosophical and Research Implications of Definitions of Crime. Part 2 focuses on factors influencing crime in the black community including: (1) Crime and the Public Schools: A Critical Appraisal (2) Employment and Discrimination: Variables in Crime (3) The Impact of Alcohol on Crime (4) Race and Family Violence: The Internal Colonialism Perspective and (5) Media, Crime and the Black Community. Part 3 discusses ways of addressing the crime problem and includes: (1) Black Self–Identity and Crime (2) Citizen Action as a Deterrent to Crime (3) The Criminal Justice System: Innovations, Failures and Alternatives (4) New Directions in Law Enforcement (5) Police Authority and the Low–Income Family Research (6) Court Monitoring—A Necessity (7) New Directions in Corrections and (8) Successful Passage of Black Parolees: From Prison to Prison.

BROWN, Lee P. "Bridges Over Troubled Waters" in *Black Perspectives On Crime And The Criminal Justice System*, Woodson, Robert L (ed), 79–106. Boston G K Hall 1977.

BROWN, Lee P. "Causes Of Crime" in *Black Crime: A Police View*, Bryce, H J (ed), 37–66. Washington DC Jt Ctr Polit Stud 1977.
The extent of crime among blacks and its economic and social costs to the black community are discussed. Several studies of the causes of black crime are cited which support the author's opinion that crime in the black community is due in large part to the relative deprivation of blacks in America. This deprivation is, however, related to race. Brown, a black law enforcement professional, contends that in order to deal effectively with crime in the black community, "we must first address the crimes society visits on the black community. Unemployment, underemployment, sub–standard housing, infant mortality, disease, poverty, inadequate education, racism, discrimination, inadequate health care, physical deterioration, overcrowding, drugs, and other social and economic ills are at the heart of the crime problem." The author suggests some policies to deal with these causative or contributing factors.

BROWN, Lee P. "Impact Of Crime/Criminal Justice System On The Black Community" in *Social Research And The Black Community*, Gary, Lawrence E (ed), 88–98. Washington DC Howard U 1974.

BROWN, Lee P. "New Directions In Law Enforcement" in *Crime And Its Impact On The Black Community*, Gary, L E And L P Brown (eds), 143–154. Washington DC Howard U 1976.

BROWN, Lee P. "Typology" in *Police–Community Relationships*, Bopp, W (ed). Springfield IL Chas C Thomas 1972.

BROWN, Lee P and Gary, Lawrence E and Beard, Eugene. *Attitudes And Perceptions Of Black Police Officers Of The District Of Columbia Metropolitan Police Department.* Washington DC Howard U 1976.

This study reports data on the recruitment, job assignments, promotion, interpersonal relations, retention, and attrition of black officers in the Metropolitan Police Department (MPD). Other topics covered include: background and personal characteristics; interpersonal relations among police officers and their perceptions of the community's attitudes towards the MPD; attitudes of black officers towards MPD supervisors and officials and the issue of discrimination in department policies and regulation; job satisfaction and promotion opportunities; and significant problems confronting the police department, police profession, and police officers.*

BROWN, Lee P and Martin, E E. Neighborhood Team Policing: A Viable Concept In Multanomah County. *Pol Chief* 43(5),84–87 1976.

BROWN, Lee P and Ritai, Marlene A Young. Crime Prevention For Older Americans: Multanomah County's Victimization Study. *Pol Chief* 43(9),385–389 1976.

BROWN, Lee P. Black Muslims And The Police. *J Crim L Crimin & Pol Sci* 56,119–126 Mr 1965.

BROWN, Lee P. Crime, Criminal Justice And The Black Community. *J Afro–Am I* 2(2),87–100 1974.

BROWN, Lee P. Establishing A Police–Community Relations Program. *Police* 16(8),57–65 1972.

BROWN, Lee P. Evaluation Of Police–Community Relations Programs. *Police* 14(2),27–31 1969.

BROWN, Lee P. Handling Complaints Against The Police. *Police* 12(5),74–81 1968.

BROWN, Lee P. Neighborhood Team Policing And Management. *Pol Chief* 43(11),72–76 1976.

BROWN, Lee P. Police Review Boards: An Historical And Critical Analysis. *Police* 10,19–29 Jl–Ag 1966.

BROWN, Lee P. The Changing Role Of The County Sheriff. *Pol Chief* 43(3),50–52 1976.

BROWN, Lee P. The Police And Higher Education: The Challenge Of The Times. *Criminology* 12(1),114–124 My 1974.

BROWN, Lee P. The Victimizers. *Nat Cities* 16(9),16–18 S 1978.

BROWN, Richard Maxwell. "Historical Patterns Of Violence In America" in *Violence In America*, Graham, Hugh D And T Gurr (eds), 45–83. NY Bantam 1969.

BROWN, Richard Maxwell. Southern Violence—Regional Problem Or National Nemesis—Legal Attitudes Toward Southern Homicide In Historical Perspective. *Vand L Rev* 32(1),225–250 1979.

BROWN, Roy M and Steiner, Jesse F. *The North Carolina Chain Gang: A Study Of County Convict Road Work*, Orig Pub 1927. Montclair NJ Patterson Smith 1969.

This history of the chain gang in North Carolina contends there is no doubt that the underlying motive for the use of prisoners in county chain gangs was economic. The authors insist that the early development of the Southern prison system in the two decades immediately following the Civil War was primarily aimed at "dealing with the Negro prisoner." Blacks were strongly overrepresented in both county and state prisons throughout the South after slavery was abolished. The chain gangs performed many jobs, the most important of which was road construction.

BROWN, S and Schaeffer, C. Investigating Ethnic Prejudice Among Boys In Residential Treatment. *J Soc Psychol* 100(2),317–318 1976.

BROWN, Shirley Ann Vinsing. *Race As A Factor In The Intra–Prison Outcomes Of Youthful First Offenders.* Unpub PhD Diss Univ of Michigan 1975.

The study sample consisted of 547 inmates drawn from the total population of male first offenders 23 years of age and under who had been admitted to, and paroled or discharged from, one large midwestern state prison system between 1969 and 1972. The population was divided into white and non–white, and a simple random sample of equal proportions was taken using the table of random numbers. A comparison of black and white first offenders revealed no significant differences on institutional adjustment. However, all things being equal, blacks were generally better adjusted than whites in prison. Weak tendencies in the data also revealed inter–institutional differences – inmates at medium custody institutions were rated well adjusted more often than those at minimum and maximum custody institutions and blacks were rated better adjusted than whites at the minimum and maximum custody institutions. Race was found to be most important in relation to release decisions. Study results revealed that fewer blacks than whites were recommended for parole and that more blacks than whites were denied parole. These relations were strongest at the more custodial institutions.*

BROWN, Waln K. Black Female Gangs In Philadelphia. *Int J Off Ther Comp Crim* 21(3),221–228 S 1977.

BROWN, Waln K. Black Gangs As Family Extensions. *Int J Off Ther Comp Crim* 22(1),39–45 1978.

Lower–class black family life is explored as a contributing factor to black gang delinquency. The author examines the gang as a training vehicle in survival techniques, asserting that young members learn to build large personal networks for mutual aid and support, and that this experience helps them to function safely and efficiently in the ghetto.

BROWN, William P. Police Corruption: The System Is The Problem. *Nation* ,456–459 Ap 9 1973.

BROWNFIELD, Allan C and Parker, J A. *What The Negro Can Do About Crime.* NY Arlington House 1974.

Portrays rootlessness, permissiveness, moral relativism, the media's concentration on violence, narcotics, and welfare's nourishment of dependency as causes of inner city crime and suggests approaches for bringing change.*

BROWNING, James B. The North Carolina Black Code. *J Negro Hist* 15,461–473 1930.

BRUMGARDT, J R. Riot Control Equipment. *Mil Pol J* 21(6),11–12 1972.

BRUNER, Charles. Iowa Prison Crisis: Economic Problem. *Des Moines Trib* , My 17 1976.

BRUNO, N J and Orris Jr, J V and Gatje, C T. Hispanic English Language Development In Prison. Stormville NY Greenhaven Prison 1976.

BRUNSWICK, Ann F and Boyle, John M. What Happened In Harlem: Analysis Of A Decline In Heroin Use Among A Generation Unit Of Urban Black Youth. *J Drug Issues* 10(1),109–130 Wint 1980.

Heroin among a cross–section of black adolescents in Harlem dropped from 8% in 1970–71 to less than 30.5% in 1975–76, reflecting in part the sharp decline in heroin initiation among younger birth cohorts. The authors' research, which was supported by the National Institute on Druge Abuse, indicates that among black youths born in 1950, 22% had initiated heroin use by age 18. Among those born in 1957, however, the figure was 3%.

BRYCE, Harrington J (ed). *Black Crime: A Police View.* Washington DC Jt Ctr Polit Stud 1977.

Papers collected in this text explore ways to reduce crime in the black community, particularly black–on–black crime. The papers were presented at a 1976 conference sponsored by LEAA, the Police Foundation, and the Joint Center for Political Studies. It drew the nation's highest ranking black law enforcement officials and resulted in the creation of National Organization of Black Law Enforcement Executives (NOBLE). After a statistical background on black crime and black law enforcement personnel, chapters cover such topics as: crime as the concern of elected officials; crime in the black community (causes of crime and the role of police in reducing crime) and police–community relations. A chapter also deals with policies to increase the number of black police executives and the dilemma of black police executives. The list of recommendations made at each workshop session center on four major areas: how to alleviate causes of crime, how to control crime, how to improve police–community relations, and the role of the black police executive.*

BRYMER, Richard and Farris, Buford. A Five–Year Encounter With A Mexican–American Conflict Gang: Its Implications For Delinquency Theory. *Pro Sw Soc Assoc* 15,49–55 1965.

BRYSON, C B. Criminal Procedure—Voir Dire—The Right To Question Jurors On Racial Prejudice. *Ohio S L J* 37(2),412–430 1976.

BULL, R and Clifford, B R. *Psychology Of Person Identification.* London Routledge & Kegan 1978.

Presents psychological research pertaining to personal identification and its bearing upon the reliability of eyewitness testimony. Information on racial factors in police lineups is included.

BULLINGTON, Bruce. *Heroin Use In The Barrio.* Lexington MA Heath 1977.

BULLOCK, Clifton. *Baby Chocolate And Other Stories.* NY William Frederick 1976.

Fiction by black convict in Lorton, Va.

BULLOCK, Henry Allen. Significance Of The Racial Factor In The Length Of Prison Sentences. *J Crim L Crimin & Pol Sci* 52,411–417 1961.

In an attempt to test the validity of the charge that Negroes are treated differently by juries and that they receive longer sentences than whites for certain crimes, Bullock collected data on 3,644 inmates in a Texas state prison (Huntsville), in 1958. The survey was conducted by R. C. Koeninger and covered white and Negro prisoners who had been committed for burglary, rape and murder. Some evidence of racial discrimination was found; Bullock concluded it was apparently motivated more by the desire to protect the white community than to effect the reformation of the offender.

BULLOCK, Paul. *Aspiration Vs Opportunity: "Careers" In The Inner City.* Ann Arbor Univ Mich–Wayne S 1973.

BUNDY, Mary Lee (ed) and Gilchrist, Irvin (ed). *The National Civil Rights Directory: An Organized Directory.* College Park MD Urban Info Interpr 1979.

BUNDY, Mary Lee (ed) and Harmon, Kenneth R (ed). *The National Prison Directory.* College Park MD Urban Info Interpr 1975.

BUNKER, Edward. *Animal Factory.* NY Viking Pr 1977.

BUNKER, Edward. *No Beast So Fierce.* NY Norton 1973.

BUNKER, Edward. Racial Violence At San Quentin Prison/War Behind Walls. *Court Rev* 11(5),4–12 1972.

Racial violence in San Quentin prison in California is discussed. From a convict's viewpoint there is so much racial paranoia within San Quentin prison that provocation is unnecessary to incite to violence. Even in the prison yard the races segregate themselves. Rumors of racial conflict often spawn confrontations between individuals and groups of prisoners. Black militant rhetoric appears to have increased racial polarization in prison beyond conciliation. An almost religious doctrine of hate sees murder as martyrdom for the killer. Recent experiences in prisoner violence indicate to the convict at least that in California prisons it is too late for rapprochement between races.

BUNKER, Edward. War Behind Walls. *Harper's Mag* 244,39–47 F 1972.

BURDMAN, Milton. Ethnic Self–Help Groups In Prison And On Parole. *Crim Delinq* 20,107–118 Ap 1974.

BURFIELD, H. Types Of Crime And Intelligence Of Negro Criminals. *Pedagog Sem* 35,239–247 1925.

BURGESS, Ernest W and Mc Kenzie, Roderick D and Park, Robert E. *The City.* Chicago Univ Chicago Pr 1925.

BURGESS, R L and Hamblin, R L and Abrahamson, M J. "Diagnosing Delinquency" in *Law And Order: Modern Criminals*, Short Jr, James F (ed), 19–31. Chicago Aldine 1970.

BURKE, P and Turk, A. Factors Affecting Post Arrest Dispositions: A Model For Analysis. *Social Prob* 22,313–332 1975.

BURKHART, Kathryn Watterson. *Women In Prison.* NY Popular Lib 1973.

BURNHAM, David. El Barrio's Worst Block Is Not All Bad. *NYT Mag*, Ja 5 1969.

BURNS, Haywood. "Racism And American Law" in *Law Against The People*, Lefcourt, Robert (ed), 38–54. NY Vintage 1971.

BURNS, Haywood. Black People And Tyranny Of American Law. *Ann Am Poli* 407,156–166 1973.

In this historical analysis of racism in the American legal system, Burns contends that the dominant experience for blacks in America "has been one in which the law acted as the vehicle by which the generalized racism in the society was made particular and converted into standards and policies of subjugation and social control." Outlining the role played by the law in the oppression of blacks in America, Burns points to the heavy reliance of the American slave system on the legal system. Even after the Civil War, the black codes were used to regulate the activity of the blacks. Apartheid remained the law of the land until the Supreme Court decision in *Brown v. Board of Education* in 1954 and the Civil Rights Act of 1955 (the first Federal Civil Rights legislation since congress had passed the Civil Rights Act of 1876). Today, Burns contends, racism continues to permeate an overwhelming white justice system. Blacks continue to be systematically excluded from juries – though no longer through express construction of

jury statutes, but through unfair procedures for compiling lists of prospective jurors and racist use of the preemptory challenge by prosecutors.

BURNS, Haywood. Can A Black Man Get A Fair Trial In This Country? *NYT Mag*, Jl 12 1970.

BURNS, Haywood. Political Uses Of The Law. *Howard L J* 17,760–774 1973.

BURNS, Haywood. The Black Prisoner As Victim. *Black L J* 1(2),120–124 Sum 1971.

A graduate of Harvard University, Cambridge and Yale Law School contends that any quest for justice is incomplete that does not consider the black prisoner as a victim of a criminal society.

BURRELL, Berkeley G. "Black Business And The Crime Of Uneconomic Communities" in *Crime And Its Impact On The Black Community*, Gary, L E & L P Brown (eds), 31–38. Washington DC Howard U 1976.

Discusses the plight of black business in white society. Data are presented as to the locations, extent of, types and survival rates of black owned businesses in the US. A realistic implementation of free enterprise in black communities is impossible without a full–scale assault that addresses the larger issue of community economic development in these communities. The minority businessman must assume the essential leadership role in this movement toward economic independence, according to the author.

BURSTEIN, P. Equal Employment Opportunity Legislation And The Income Of Women And Nonwhites. *Am Sociol Rev* 44(3),367–391 Je 1979.

BUSTAMANTE, Jorge A. "The So–Called Crime Of Being A Wetback" in *Chicanos, Life/Struggles Of The Mexican Minority In The US*, Lopez Y Rivas, G (ed). NY Monthly Rev Pr 1973.

BUSTAMANTE, Jorge A. The 'Wetback' As Deviant: An Application Of Labeling Theory. *Am J Soc* 77(4),706–718 1972.

This paper deals with some of the questions that arise from the deviant character of those who cross the US–Mexico border without inspection, and the process of interaction through which the label "wetback" is "created" and used. The historical context of immigration to the United States as related to cheap labor demands is described, and the emergence of the label "wetback" is discussed. The roles of the persons involved in the violation of the immigration law and some of the socioeconomic implications of those roles are analyzed through labeling theory. The process of interaction in which those roles become visible is discussed in terms of the interests, power, and consequences of each role with respect to those of the other roles in the process. The concept of "antilaw enterpreneur" is introduced, and its explanatory potential is indicated.

BUTCHER, P. *The Minority Presence In American Literature, 1600–1900*, 2v. Washington DC Howard U 1977.

BUTLER, Keith. Simon Evans: A Preacher's Son Discovers Islam. *Correct Mag* 4(2),58–59 1978.

BUTLER, Keith. The Muslims Are No Longer An Unknown Quantity. *Correct Mag* 4(2),55–63 1978.

BUTTON, James W. *Black Violence.* Princeton NJ Princeton Univ Pr 1978.

BYRN, Robert M. Urban Law Enforcement: A Plea From The Ghetto. *Crim L Bull* 5,125–136 1969.

CABOT, Philippe Sidney DeQ. *Juvenile Delinquency: A Critical Annotated Bibliography.* Westport CT Greenwood Pr 1971.

CABRANES, C A. Careers In Law For Minorities: A Puerto Rican's Perspective On Recent Developments In Legal Education. *Revista Cen Abogados P R* 37,727–738 1976.

CABRANES, Jose A. Citizenship And The American Empire: Notes On The Legislative History Of The United States Citizenship Of Puerto Ricans. *Univ Penn L Rev* 127(2),391–493 D 1978.

CADWALLADER, Mervyn L and Roebuck, Julian D. The Negro Armed Robber As A Criminal Type: The Construction And Application Of A Typology. *Pac Soc Rev* 4,21–25 1961.

The authors contrast the backgrounds of 32 black males with patterns of arrests for armed robbery, with those of 368 other black males also studied and categorized in a typology of 13 criminal patterns. The empirical data demonstrates that the armed robbers differ in kind and degree from other criminal types in terms of theoretically relevant social and psychological factors. Armed robbers were a group of "hardened, anti–social recidivists, the products of disorganized homes and slum neighbors where they came in contact with criminal norms and activities at an early age." Case histories showed a pattern of unadjustment at home, school, and in the community. As adults they sought out criminal companions of a similar type, and took real pride in their criminal style—the taking of property by force. Most had developed some skills and a *modus operandi* in their criminal activities. These offenders comprised a more homogeneous category personality–wise than did any other criminal–pattern group, with the possible exception of the drug offenders.

CAGE, Robin J and Foster, Samuel C and Thomas, Charles. Public Opinion On Criminal And Legal Sanctions: An Examination Of Two Conceptual Models. *J Crim L & Crimin* 67(1),110–116 1976.

Public evaluation of appropriate legal sanctions are examined in order to see whether they reflect the level of agreement implied by the consensus model. Private citizens were asked to evaluate the relative seriousness of a variety of acts and suggest what type of sanctions they feel are appropriate for those who engage in the acts. In regard to the first dimension, remarkable similarity was found in the offense rankings from those above and below the median sample income, occupational prestige, and educational level. A very high degree of similarity was found on the lengths of sentences assigned to the set of possible offenses. The basic expectation of the consensus model, i.e., that there would be consensus on these two dimensions across social groupings, was supported. Findings were not supportive of a conflict model which would predict variations between different categories of the population.

CAGE, Robin and Thomas, Charles. The Effect Of Social Characteristics In Juvenile Court Dispositions. *Sociol Q* 18,237–252 Spr 1977.

CAHALAN, Margaret. Trends In Incarceration In The United States Since 1880: A Summary Of Reported Rates And Distribution Of Offenses. *Crim Delinq* 25(1),9–41 Ja 1979.

Based on an examination of government reports on federal, state, and local penal facilities for adults and juveniles published since 1880, the author concludes that the rate of incarceration has increased over time. During the 19th century, blacks and foreign–born as well as members of other nonwhite racial groups and other non–English–speaking persons, constituted a large percentage of those incarcerated. In this century, decline in the number of foreign–born prisoners has been replaced by rising overrepresentation of blacks and Hispanics.

CAHN, Edmund N. *The Sense Of Injustice: An Anthropocentric View Of Law.* NY New York Univ Pr 1949.

CALDWELL, Loretta and Greene, Helen E Taylor. "Implementing A Black Perspective In Criminal Justice" in *Improving Management In Criminal Justice*, Cohn, Alvin W And Benjamin Ward (eds). Beverly Hills CA Sage 1980.

CALDWELL, Morris G. The Youthful Male Offender In Alabama: A Study In Delinquency Causation. *Sociol Soc Res* 37,236–243 1953.

CALHOUN, J B. Population Density And Social Pathology. *Sci Am* 206,139–148 1962.

CALHOUN, Lillian S. The Death Of Fred Hampton. *Chicago Journ Rev* 2(12),13+ D 1969.

CALIFORNIA DEPT OF CORRECTIONS. *California Prisoners 1976: Summary Statistics Of Felon Prisoners And Parolees.* Sacramento Dept Corrections 1976.

CALIFORNIA DEPT OF CORRECTIONS. *California Prisoners 1977 And 1978: Summary Of Statistics Of Felony Prisoers And Parolees.* Sacramento Dept Corrections 1979.

CALIFORNIA DEPT OF THE YOUTH AUTHORITY. *California: Affirmative Action Statistics, Report No 3.* Sacramento Youth Authority 1975.

This report shows the extent to which the California Youth Authority had met its employment goals for ethnic minorities and women through March 31, 1975, and provides pertinent breakdowns of these personnel statistics. The ethnic group and employment goals, and sex distribution and employment goals are reviewed. Statistics are provided on the sex and ethnic group personnel distribution by facility, and the sex and, ethnic group personnel distribution by parole zone. Personnel distributions by occupatinal categories are also reported. In addition to the personnel statistics, comparative data are presented which show the ethnic and sex distributions of the Youth Authority ward population for the current reporting period. It is noted that as of March 1975, 29.5% of Youth Authority personnel were from minority groups and 37.1% were women. These figures are both 1.1% below the projected affirmative action goals for these groups.*

CALIFORNIA RURAL LEGAL ASSISTANCE. "A Study Of Grand Jury Service" in *Race, Crime, And Justice*, Reasons, Charles E And Jack L Kuykendall (eds), 324–339. Pacific Palisades CA Goodyear 1972.

CALISTA, F P and Domonkas, Michael. Bail And Civil Disorder. *J Urban L* 45,815–839 1968.

CALLANAN, Thomas J. "The Ex–Offender As Paraprofessional" in *Corrections*, Sagarin, E (ed), 145–152. NY Praeger 1973.

In a paper presented at the Second Interamerican Congress of Criminology held in November 1972 in Caracas, the use of the exoffender paraprofessional as an agent of direct service in a correctional setting was examined. Although more than 40 states have prohibitions against the employment of probationers or parolees, the exoffender is able to act as a bridge of communication between the largely white middle–class professional and the predominantly black, Puerto Rican, Mexican–American, Indian or other deprived client group. Many of the exoffenders are able to bring the unique qualities of empathy, folk wisdom and communication with their peers to their jobs. The personal ego building aspects of helping others is also important to the helpers who enjoy being important to others. Problems include professional jealousy, overidentification with the agency, client suspicion and unwarranted feelings of expertise on the part of the exoffender. The use of the exoffender should be investigated for possible contributions to future changes in the correctional system.

CALVERT, R J R. *Affirmative Action—A Comprehensive Recruitment Manual.* Garrett Park MD Garrett Park Pr 1979.

A manual for employers wanting to develop an equal opportunity employment program, this volume presents data on the status of minority employment, recruiting sources, campaigning, interviewing, and hiring minorities. The text opens with a detailed analysis of minority groups––Asians, American Indians and Alaskan Natives, blacks, Hispanics––and their employment status nationwide, through history, and in various types of professions and skills. A checklist of errors generally made by personnel officers or supervisors to the detriment of minority applicants is provided along with a list of training and employment standards and job classification requirements. Recruitment of minorities through colleges and universities is considered in a section which contains a state–by–state listing of colleges along with their concentrations of minority enrollments; and information on, and a directory of, predominantly black colleges and universities and those with a large enrollment of other minorities are included. State–by–state information also is presented on minority media, useful in recruiting minorities, along with a bibliography of minority publications and radio and television stations with large minority appeal.*

CAMARILLO, Alberto. *Chicanos In A Changing Society: From Mexican Pueblos To American Barrios In Santa Barbara And Southern California, 1848–1930.* Cambridge MA Harvard Univ Pr 1979.

CAMPBELL, A and Schuman, Howard. "Racial Attitudes In Fifteen American Cities" in *Riot Commission, Supplemental Studies*, 1–67. Washington DC USGPO 1968.

CAMPBELL, S W. *The Slave Catchers.* Chapel Hill Univ N Car Pr 1970.

CAMPBELL, Valencia. Double Marginality Of Black Policemen : A Reassessment. *Criminology* 17(4),477–484 F 1980.

The extent to which black policemen are victims of "double marginality," as minority group members and as police officers is examined. It is found to account for little of the variation in either black officers' perception of public involvement in police affairs or their perception of police authority. The applicability of the marginality concept in explaining black officers' perceptions today is questioned.

CAMPOS, Leonel. The Employment Of Hispanics In Corrections. Dallas N I C 1979.

CANADY, Herman B. "The Negro In Crime" in *Encyclopedia Of Criminology*, Branham, V C And S B Kutask (eds). NY Philosophical Lib 1949.

CANNITO, J A and Becker, K L. The Case For Limited Use Of Polls In The Jury Selection Process. *Rutgers J Computers* 7(1),111–134 1979.

The development of survey research techniques in litigation is discussed with emphasis on the factors affecting the accuracy of polls and the use of survey findings to assess public prejudices. Where community attitudes must be weighed before a trial, survey research presents the most scientific method of assessing public understanding. Because a well–conducted survey is the most accurate and often most practical method of ascertaining public opinion, surveys are useful litigation tools to complement the existing judicial process. By the 1950's it was well—settled that surveys would be admitted as evidence in order to establish whether a particular trade symbol had sufficient recognition. However, proponents of surveys met with little success when introducing them to support a change of venue motion. Indications of local prejudice against a defendant or of racial bias in the community must be proven by the defendant. The courts are generally suspicious of the accuracy of surveys financed by one side in litigation, when the usual voir dire procedures are deemed sufficient to prevent jury bias. However, careful use of research may allow attorneys to develop profiles of 'ideal' jurors in particular cases.*

CANNON, J Alfred. For American Blacks: A New Identity—The Black Diaspora. *Urb Health* 4(1),34–35,48 1975.

Juvenile mental distress is approached from the context that there is a general and deep identity crisis among American blacks, and that the juvenile is acting out this distress. The suspected inverse relationship between black militancy and fighting gang proliferation is cited as a prime example of the need for more emphasis on cause determination than programs of symptom suppression. It is felt that the black juvenile is a victim of a general community depression and anger. The identity of the American as a black "diasporan" who is still related to his ancestral African homeland is discussed. It is felt that the concept of a black diaspora presents the black American with the necessary grand identity and enables him to integrate his multiple aspirations and drives into a more holistic mission. An intense educational effort to create and clarify the black diasporan identity is advocated, in order to allow the black juvenile to contribute positively to this country.

CANNON, Mildred S and Locke, Ben Z. *Being Black Is Detrimental To One's Mental Health: Myth Or Reality?* Atlanta Atlanta Univ Pr 1976.

CANTOR, Milton. The Image Of The Negro In Colonial Literature. *New Eng Q* 36,452–477 D 1963.

Examines the origin and development of racist stereotypes in American colonial literature.

CANTOR, Nathaniel. Crime And The Negro. *J Negro Hist* 16,61–66 1931.

CANTRIL, Hadley. "Chapter 4: The Lynching Mob" in *The Psychology Of Social Movements*. NY Wiley 1941.

CAPLOVITZ, David. *The Poor Pay More.* NY Free Pr 1967.

CARDEN, Francis Xavier. *An Assessment Of Dogmatism Among Adult Inmates In A State Correctional Institution In New Jersey.* Unpub PhD Diss Fordham Univ 1974.

Dogmatism was investigated in a group of incarcerated criminals, a group popularly considered to be closeminded. Levels of criminality were hypothesized to be inversely related to levels of dogmatism scores. Subjects were 113 male criminals and 43 male noncriminal controls. No significant differences were obtained in dogmatism scores between criminal and control subjects. The only hypothesis fully supported found a positive relationship between religious fundamentalism and dogmatism in both racial groups. Dogmatism (D–Scale) validity was not supported when socially significant behavior was used as a criterion. The following racial differences were reported: 1) no relationship between dogmatism and anxiety was found for black subjects; and 2) among white subjects a correlation was found between conflict with authority and dogmatism scores.

CARLETON, Mark T. *Politics And Punishment: The History Of The Louisiana State Penal System.* Baton Rouge LA LSU Pr 1971.

CARLSON, Eric W and Allen, Harry E and Dynes, Patrick S. "Aggressive And Simple Sociopaths: Ten Years Later" in *Biology And Crime*, Jeffrey, C R (ed). Beverly Hills CA Sage 1979.

CARLSON, Eric W and Vito, Gennaro F and Parks, Evalyn C. Effectiveness Of Volunteer Assistance To Parolees. *Evaluation Review* 4(3),323–338 Je 1980.

This study of recidivism was conducted in Ohio comparing the postprogram recidivism of 107 program participants with a group of offenders eligible for the program but not matched with a volunteer—helper, and with a randomly selected group of offenders. The results indicate that the postprogram recidivism of the experimental group differed along racial lines, with the black members experiencing increased recidivism whereas the whites' recidivism was reduced.

CARLSTON, K S. *Social Theory And African Tribal Organization: The Development Of Socio—Legal Theory.* Urbana Univ Illinois Pr 1968.

CARMICHAEL, Benjamin G. "Urban Street Crime—Hustling" in *Black Perspectives On Crime And The Criminal Justice System*, Woodson, Robert L (ed), 23–36. Boston G K Hall 1977.

CARMICHAEL, Benjamin G. The Hunters Point Riot: Politics Of The Frustrated. *Issues Crim* 4(2),123–132 Fall 1969.

CARMICHAEL, Benjamin G. Youth Crime In Urban Communities: A Descriptive Analysis Of Street Hustlers And Their Crimes. *Crim Delinq* 21,139–148 1975.

CARPER, Noel Gordon. *The Convict—Lease System In Florida, 1866–1923.* Unpub PhD Diss Florida State Univ 1964.

CARR, A L and Johanson, S M. Extent Of Washington Criminal Jurisdiction Over Indians. *Wash L Rev* 33,289–302 Fall 1958.

A 1956 decision of the Washington Supreme Court demonstrated that there are approximately 15,000 Indians living on reservations who are not amenable to criminal prosecution under state law in certain situations; in many instances, they are not amenable to either state or federal prosecution. It is recommended that the State of Washington use the means made available by Congress to remedy the situation and amend the state constitutions for the purpose of assuming jurisdiction over all Indians of the state.*

CARR, Andrea and Pierce, Glenn L and Bowers, William J. *Executions In America.* Lexington MA Heath 1974.

Presents extensive data about the characteristics of persons executed in the US. Regional differences and racial disproportionality are examined in detail.

CARR, James. *Bad: An Autobiography.* NY Herman Graf 1975.
Autobiography of Black Panther leader.

CARR, Timothy S and Cox, George H. *Unemployment And Prison Population Trends In Georgia: 1967–1974.* Atlanta GA Dept Corrections 1975.

CARRINGTON, Frank G. *Neither Cruel Nor Unusual.* NY Arlington House 1978.

CARRO, John. Hispanics Underrepresented As Criminal Justice Professionals. *Just Assist News* 1(7),2,7 S 1980.

CARROLL, Joseph Cephas. *Slave Insurrections In The United States, 1800–1865.* Boston Chapman & Crimes 1938.

CARROLL, Leo. "Race And Three Forms Of Prisoner Power" in *Contemporary Corrections*, Huff, C (ed), 40–53. Beverly Hills CA Sage 1977.

CARROLL, Leo. *Hacks, Blacks And Cons: Race Relations In A Maximum Security Prison.* Lexington MA Lexington 1974.

A description and analysis of the structure of race relations in one maximum security prison are presented. The system is depicted as existing in a precarious state of equilibrium. Among the more important conditions maintaining the structure were: humanitarian reforms, a policy of managed racial integration, racial prejudice and black revolutionary ideology imported into the prison, the size and relative solidarity of groups in contact, and interests shared as a result of common deprivations. It is indicated that race relations in the custodial prison will assume the form of a protracted conflict with the level and type of conflict dependent upon custodial repression and size of black prisoner population. It is noted, however, that therapeutic communities contain the potential for reducing racial conflict as a byproduct of the treatment process through the introduction of superordinate goals and opportunities for equal status contact.

CARROLL, Leo and Mondrick, Margaret E. Racial Bias In The Decision To Grant Parole. *Law & Soc Rev* 11(1),93–107 1976.

Virtually all past research in the area of racial discrimination has focused on the police courts. Less visible decisions where unfettered discretion makes discrimination even more likely have not been adequately studied. The present study looked at proportions of black and white prisoners paroled and also at the criteria by which each prisoner was evaluated. Data clearly suggest the operation of racial bias. Black prisoners were evaluated according to different criteria than whites. Specifically, the requirement of participation in institutional treatment programs was imposed on black prisoners and not on whites. Consequently, most black prisoners who were paroled (77%) served significantly longer proportions of their sentences than did similar white prisoners. Data is consistent with the interpretation that the bias of the parole board was not racial per se but a bias against perceived militancy. Participation in treatment programs was much more likely to be required for those blacks perceived as militant (the younger black prisoners convicted of drug and violent offenses) than for the older black property offenders.

CARROLL, Leo. Humanitarian Reform And Biracial Sexual Assault In A Maximum Security Prison. *Urb Life* 5,417–437 1977.

CARSTAIRS, George M. "Overcrowding And Human Aggression" in *The History Of Violence In America*, Graham, Hugh D And T Gurr (eds), 751–764. NY Praeger 1969.

CARTE, Gene E. Police Representation And The Dilemma Of Recruitment. *Issues Crim* 6(1),85–95 Wint 1971.

Carte identifies the primary failure of recruitment of minorities for police work as the refusal of police and political leaders to recognize the political content of police work. When token representation threatens to become active representation, charges of reverse discrimination and favoritism are used to prevent real changes from occurring. Carte also contends that established recruitment procedures have tended to favor a certain type of recruit; black men must be willing to give up certain political rights and accept service as a passive representative. Cartre concludes by reiterating what he sees as the primary problem in recruitment: adherence to a predetermined model of what a policeman should be like and what functions he should perform. The single most important criterion for all police recruitment is a local residency requirement. If active representation is to be the goal of the recruitment process, then the content of policing should be determined by the community that is served. A policeman with a stake in the community he serves is much more likely to respond to what that community really values.

CARTER, Michael. Crime In Harlem. *Crisis* 46(12),366–377 1939.

CARTER, R I and Hill, K Q. *Criminal's Image Of The City.* NY Pergamon Pr 1979.

The study sample was based on known property offenders currently residing in three of Oklahoma's correctional institutions who had been convicted of burglary, robbery, or larceny. A stratified sampling procedure was used to collect a matching noncriminal sample. Gestalt, Field, and Personal Construct theories were used as a basis for measuring individual area perceptions, and the semantic differential was adopted as a perception measurement tool. Findings indicate that criminals' area images are shaped by their vocational interests so that they perceive more crime activity, police protection, and greater difficulty of committing crime in the city than do noncriminals. Criminals, particularly blacks, are likely to choose a crime target in a familiar area. Whites are more concerned with the risk and difficulty of committing the offense that an area presents. Both groups tended to avoid high status neighborhoods. Statistical analyses indicate that the patterning of crime is systematically related to area images held by criminals, that these images are themselves differentiable, and that certain image components are more powerful than others in influencing criminal behavior.*

CARTER, R L. The Black Lawyer. *Humanist* 29(5),13–14 S–O 1969.

CARTER, Robert M and Smith, A La Mont. The Death Penalty In California: A Statistical And Composite Portrait. *Crim Delinq* 15,62–76 1969.

The data for this descriptive study came mostly from the files of the California Department of Corrections. The study includes a breakdown by race of the 187 men executed in California between 1938 and 1963; the number of these men grouped by age (five–year intervals) and race; the same data by race and place of birth. The sample is also broken down by claimed educational achievement, and by Intelligence Quotient.

CARTER, Rubin "Hurricane". The Sixteenth Round. NY Warner 1975.
The author was the Number 1 contender for the middleweight boxing championship when, in 1967, he and another man were sentenced to life imprisonment in New Jersey for the murder of three whites in a barroom. Carter insists he is innocent and offers his personal history.

CASPER, Jonathan D. American Criminal Justice: The Defendant's Perspective. Englewood Cliffs NJ Prentice–Hall 1972.

CASPER, Jonathan D. Criminal Justice: The Consumer Perspective. Washington DC NILECJ 1972.

CASPER, Jonathan D. Having Their Day In Court—Defendant Evaluations Of The Fairness Of Their Treatment. *Law & Soc Rev* 12(2),237–251 Wint 1978.
To examine correlates of defendants' evaluations of fairness of their treatment by the court, interviews were conducted with 628 alleged felons following their arrest and upon completion of their case. Alienation, race,

and prior criminal history were all found to affect evaluations of fairness with the highly alienated, black, and previously convicted tending to view their treatment as less fair. However, prior record and being black were also related to dispositions, although the relationship between race and fairness perceptions remains even when sentence is controlled.*

CASTRO, Agenor L. "New York State Dept Of Correctional Services Affirmative Action Proposal For 1980: A Historical Synopsis And General Commentary". Albany NY Dept Corrections n.d.

CASTRO, Agenor L. "The Hispanic Inmate In Our Nation's Prisons Today". Albany NY Dept Corrections n.d.

CASTRO, Agenor L. "The Minority Perspective And The 1980 NIC Program". Albany NY Dept Corrections n.d.

CASTRO, Agenor L. Bilingualism In Corrections: National Hispanic Conference On Law Enforcement And Criminal Justice. Washington DC US Dept Justice 1980.

CASTRO, Agenor L. Hispanics In Corrections: The Statistical Dilemma In Finding Relevant Employee/Inmate Data. Dallas N I C 1979.

CASTRO, Agenor L. A Close Look At The Hispanic Inmates And Methods Of Meeting Their Needs. *Am J Correct* 40(1),15–18 Mr–Ap 1978.
The author, special advisor on intergroup relations to the New York State Department of Correctional Services, explores the unique problems of Hispanic inmates in the continental US. These include many barriers resulting from their inability to speak English and the correction system's inability to provide bilingual services. Formation of the National Hispanic Correctional Association is discussed.

CASTRO, Agenor L. Hispanics In The System—Trying To Count The Numbers. *Agenda* 10(3),14–19 My–Je 1980.

CASTRO, Agenor L. Meeting The Special Needs Of Hispanic Inmates. *Agenda* 1(5),37–40 S–O 1977.
The author, special advisor on Hispanics for the NY Dept. of Corrections, contends that a dramatic increase in the number of Hispanic prisoners in state and local correctional facilities has bolstered the need for more special programs for Puerto Rican and Chicano inmates. Bilingual programs, recruitment of additional Hispanic staff, and creation of more recreational and entertainment activities in Spanish, are sought. Anglo staff should also be given sensitivity training to reduce tensions in prison.

CASTRO, Agenor L. Profiling The Hispanic Inmate: A Correctional Dilemma. *NY J Crim Just* ,8–9 Ja 1–15 1975.

CASAVANTES, Edward J. El Tecato: Cultural And Sociologic Factors Affecting Drug Use Among Chicanos. Washington DC Nat Coal Span Spea 1976.

CATTERALL, Helen H (ed). Judicial Cases Concerning American Slavery And The Negro, 5v. NY Octagon Bks 1968.

CATTON, Chick Hong. Apparent Minority Ethnocentricity And Majority Antipathy. *Am Sociol Rev* 27,178–191 1962.

CAVAN, Ruth S. Negro Family Disorganization And Juvenile Delinquency. *J Negro Ed* 28(3),230–239 1959.
Cavan begins her article by stating: "The development of delinquent attitudes and behavior is closely linked to the social groups in which the boy or girl is reared. The family is the key group, the first cultural matrix to leave its impress on the personality and the group that maintains a more or less continuous contact until late adolescence." The following three aspects of family life, in personality formation related to delinquency, are discussed: (1) family transmission of lower class culture; (2) interpersonal relationships that are associated with delinquency; and (3) family influence in the development of the child's concept of himself as delinquent or non–delinquent. Cavan concludes, after much discussion, that it appears that while Negro delinquents originate in the same types of families as white delinquents, these unfavorable conditions are much more frequently found in the families of Negro delinquents.

CAYTON, Horace R and Drake, St Clair. *Black Metropolis: A Study Of Negro Life In A Northern City*, Rev'd Ed Orig Pub 1945. NY Harper & Row 1962.

CEBULSKI, B G. *Affirmative Action Versus Seniority—Is Conflict Inevitable?* Berkeley CA U CA Inst Ind Rel 1977.
The conflict between traditional seniority systems, and effective affirmative action programs is examined, with a view to providing public sector employers and employee organizations with alternatives to conflict. The focus of this monograph, the second in a series on public employee relations issues in California, is the problem that arises when layoffs by

seniority cut into employment gains made by minorities and women under affirmative action.*

CEDENO, C and Reckless, Walter and Toro– Calder, Jaime. A Comparative Study Of Puerto Rican Attitudes Toward The Legal System Dealing With Crime. *J Crim L Crimin Pol Sci* 59(4),536–541 1968.

CERNKOVICH, Stephen A and Giordano, Peggy C. A Comparative Analysis Of Male And Female Delinquency. *Sociol Q* 20,131–145 1979.
It is generally assumed that males are much more likely than females to commit delinquent acts, and that when females deviate their misconduct is significantly less serious than that of males. This paper examines the recent contention that the delinquent behavior of males and females is more similar than assumed. Self–report questionnaires were administered in 1977 to a sample of 822 male and female adolescents selected from two urban high schools in a large midwestern state. Following Hindelang (1971), the authors concentrate on the types of delinquent acts most frequently reported, as well as the extent of involvement in these acts. While males tend to commit most offenses more frequently than females, the pattern of delinquency is virtually identical for the two groups. This uniformity holds for race–sex subgroups, although there are more similarities in delinquency within racial groups than within sex groups.

CHADBOURN, J H. *Lynching And The Law.* Chapel Hill Univ N Car Pr 1933.

CHADWICK, Bruce (ed) and Day, Robert (ed) and Bahr, Howard (ed). *Native Americans Today: Sociological Perspectives.* NY Harper & Row 1972.

CHADWICK, Bruce A et al. Confrontation With The Law: The Case Of The American Indians In Seattle. *Phylon* 37(2),163–171 1976.

CHADWICK, Bruce A and Stauss, Joseph H. The Assimilation Of American Indians Into Urban Society: The Seattle Case. *Human Org* 34(4),359–369 1975.
The level of assimilation of American–Indians living in Seattle,Washington, was assessed using a seven stage model of assimilation developed by Gordon. In addition, two hypotheses concerning the antecedents of assimilation were tested. Results reveal that on only two of the seven stages did Indians in Seattle evidence a significant level of assimilation. The overall level of assimilation of urban Indians was fairly low, especially in the area of political participation and conflict with the dominant power structure. Tests of the first hypothesis, which predicted that other stages leading to total assimilation would inevitably follow from structural assimilation, reveal that the degree of structural assimilation was not related to the other stages. Results also fail to support the second hypothesis, which concerned the relationship between length of time lived in the city and assimilation.

CHAIKEN, J M and Cohen, Bernard. *Police Civil Service Selection Prodecures And New York City—Comparison Of Ethnic Groups.* NY Rand Instit 1973.
The attorneys for both sides in a lawsuit retained the NYC–Rand Institute to conduct an independent, impartial analysis of the civil service examination scores of white and minority–group applicants for the position of patrolman in the NYC Police Department and the effect of the written examination, as compared to other parts of the appointment process, on the number of men appointed from each ethnic group. The plaintiffs in this case, the Guardians Association and the Hispanic Society, have alleged that the written entry–level civil service examination and other parts of the appointment process discriminate unlawfully against blacks and Hispanics. The defendants are the NYC Civil Service Commission, the Department of Personnel, and the Police Department. The Institute collected data about the subjects from several sources. Statistical tests showed that the scores of blacks were not significantly different from those for Hispanics, while the differences in scores between whites and minority–group members were highly significant the analysis therefore confirmed the plaintifs' allegations.*

CHAMBERLAIN, B P. *The Negroes And Crime In Virginia.* Charlottesville Univ of Virginia 1936.

CHAMBERS, C D (ed) and Ball, J C (ed). *The Epidemiology Of Opiate Addiction In The United States.* Springfield IL Chas C Thomas 1970.
Presents research findings on female, Negro, Chinese–American, Puerto Rican, and Mexican–American addicts, the phenomenon of onset of drug use, concurrent barbiturate addiction, historical diffusion of the intravenous method of hypodermic infections, nativity of US addicts—their parentage

and geographic mobility, and the medical and life history aspects of drug addiction.

CHAMBERS, C D and Cuskey, W R and Moffett, A D. Demographic Factors In Opiate Addiction Among Mexican Americans. *Pub Health Rep* 85(6),523–531 1970.

CHAMBERS, Carl D and Cuskey, Walter R and Moffett, Arthur D. "Mexican American Opiate Addicts" in *The Epidemiology Of Opiate Addiction In The United States*, Ball, John C (ed). Springfield IL Chas C Thomas 1970.

CHAMBERS, Robert and Thorsell, Bernard A. The Adjudication Process And Self–Conception. *Per Soc Psyc Bull* 1(1),327–329 1974.

CHAMBLISS, William J. *Crime And The Legal Process.* NY McGraw–Hill 1969.

CHAMBLISS, William J. *Crime Rates, Crime Myths And Official Smokescreens.* Stockholm Sweden Univ of Stockholm 1978.

CHAMBLISS, William J. *Whose Law: What Order?* NY Wiley 1976.

CHAMBLISS, William J and Nagasawa, Richard H. On The Validity Of Official Statistics—A Comparative Study Of White, Black And Japanese High School Boys. *J Res Crim Del* 6(1),71–77 1969.
Analysis of official and unofficial self–report delinquency rates of black, white, and Japanese youths in a large metropolitan area produced the conclusion that official statistics are so misleading that they are virtually useless as indicators of actual deviance in the population. It is suggested that the visibility of the offenses, the bias of the policing agencies, and the demeanor of the youth account for the rate and distribution of delinquency among the three groups and that official rates are a complete distortion of the actual incidence. Self–report rates did not differ significantly for the three groups.

CHAMBLISS, William J and Seidman, Robert B. *Law, Order And Power.* Menlo Park CA Addison–Wesley 1971.

CHAMBLISS, William J. Race, Sex And Gangs: The Saints And The Roughnecks. *Society* 11(1),24–31 1974.

CHAMELIN, N C and Territo, L and Swanson Jr, C R. *Police Personnel Selection Process.* Indianapolis Bobbs–Merrill 1977.
Intended for adminstrators and supervisors involved in designing and implementing a personnel selection process. This book analyzes the selection process from the entrance examination through probationary employment.*

CHAN, Janet and Waller, Irvin. Prison Use: A Canadian And International Comparison. *Crim L Q* 17,47–71 D 1974.

CHANG, Dae H (ed) and Armstrong, Warren B (ed). *The Prison: Voices From The Inside.* Cambridge MA Schenkman Pub 1972.

CHANG, W B C and Araujo, M U. Interpreters For The Defense: Due Process For The Non–English–Speaking Defendant. *Cal L Rev* 63(3),801–823 1975.

CHAPMAN, D. The Stereotype Of The Criminal And The Social Consequences. *Int J Crimin Pen* 1(1),15–30 1973.

CHAPMAN, Frank E. Do Prisons Rehabilitate? *Freedomways* 15(2),96–100 1975.

CHAPMAN, Frank E. Pages From The Life Of A Black Prisoner. *Freedomways* 11,332–345 1971.

CHAPPELL, Duncan and Geis, Gilbert and Agopian, Michael W. "Interracial Forcible Rape In A North American City" in *Victimology: A New Focus*, V1, Drapkin, Israel And Emilio Viano (eds), Chapter 9. Lexington MA Lexington 1974.

CHAPPELL, Duncan and Geis, Robley (ed) and Geis, Gilbert (ed). *Forcible Rape: The Crime, The Victim, And The Offender.* NY Columbia Univ Pr 1977.

CHASE, Allan. *The Legacy Of Malthus: The Social Costs Of The New Racism.* NY Knopf 1977.
Philosophical analysis of scientific racism, as it has developed since the works of the Scotish economist.

CHASE, Stanley Harvey. A Study Of Drug Addiction And Conformity Behavior: A Biosocial Approach To The Understanding Of A Form Of Social Deviance. Unpub PhD Diss Long Island Univ 1975.
Drug addiction and conformity behavior in black addict inmates of a correctional institution were studied using a biosocial approach to the understanding of this form of deviance. The black subjects were studied under three majority group conditions: with all black addict inmate

confederates or peer condition (BMG); with white addict inmates (WPM); and with white middle–class members (WMC). Subjects were administered the Asch test to measure conformity under each condition, and they completed a questionnaire assessing attitudes toward the majority group. It was hypothesized that the black addict subjects would show significantly more conformity to the peer group than to the white middle–class group, and results confirm this prediction. Implications of the results for treatment of drug addicts are discussed. Moreover, suggestions for future research on conformity behavior of other deviant subcultural groups is proposed, and a refinement in experimental design is suggested.

CHAVES, F J. Counseling Offenders Of Spanish Heritage. *Fed Prob* 40(1),29–33 1976.

CHEEK, William F (ed). *Black Resistance Before The Civil War.* NY Glencoe Pr 1970.

CHEMINICK, Paul W (ed). The Response Of The Washington DC Community And Its Criminal Justice System To The April 1968 Riot. *George Wash L Rev* 37,862–1012 1969.

CHESNEY, Meda and Pollock, Joy and Bowker, Lee H. *Women, Crime, And The Criminal Justice System.* Lexington MA Lexington 1978.

CHESTNUTT, Charles W. Peonage Or The New Negro Slavery. *Voice Negro* 1(9),394–397 1904.

CHEVIGNY, Paul. *Police Power: A Study Of Provocation.* NY Pantheon 1972.

The events leading up to the trial, the court proceedings, and the aftermath of the trial of three Black Panthers in the New Dunston Hotel conspiracy case are presented. The home life of the Cain brothers, the magistrate's court in Brooklyn, the activities of the Black Panthers in Brooklyn and the infiltration of Wilbert Thomas into the Black Panthers are discussed. The arrest and the relationship of the jury and the lawyers are also included. A history of political provocation includes events from both Europe and the US. Remedies and failures concerning the law are presented.

CHEVIGNY, Paul. Toward Equal Protection In The Administration Of Law: A Racially Integrated Courtroom. *Law In Tran Q* 3,1–12 1966.

CHICAGO COMMISSION ON RACE RELATIONS. "Crime And Vicious Environment" in *The Negro In Chicago: A Study Of Race Relations And A Race Riot In 1919*, Orig Pub 1919. NY Arno Pr 1968.

The general crime situation in Chicago, the limitations of official statistics on black crime, the black experience in courts and prisons, and the effect of environmental influences on black crime are discussed. The effects of substandard housing and recreational facilities are mentioned, as are the psychological effects of ostracism, exploitation and insults. The influence of an "infective" environment and the proximity of vice districts to areas of high black concentration are also discussed. A lengthy section is devoted to views of various authorities on such topics as the infrequency of professional and group crime among blacks, sex crime among blacks, "offenses against morals," lying and stealing, types of black crime, mentally defective criminals, change in character of crime or increase in crime due to migration, liability of blacks to arrest, discrimination in the courts, legal representation for black defendants, identification, probation, and parole, vice in black residence areas and economic and industrial aspects of black crime.

CHICAGO STATE UNIV CORRECTIONS PROGRAM. *Minorities In Corrections And Law Enforcement.* Chicago Chicago State Univ 1973. Proceedings from a conference on "Minorities in Corrections and Law Enforcement" are presented. The three primary goals of the conference were to: (1) increase awareness for the acute need for recruitment and training of minority group members in corrections and law enforcement; (2) assist agency administrators and policy planners in undertaking more sophisticated and successful minority recruitment programs; and (3) increase the skills of participants in the proper and full utilization of minority group workers in corrections and law enforcement.

CHICANO PINTO RESEARCH PROJECT, Inc. *A Model For Chicano Drug Use And For Effective Utilization Of Employment And Training Resources By Barrio Addicts And Ex–Offenders.* Los Angeles Chicano Pinto Proj 1979.

CHICANO PINTO RESEARCH PROJECT, Inc. *The Los Angeles Pinto: Background Papers And Advance Report Of The Chicano Pinto Project.* Los Angeles Chicano Pinto Proj n.d.

"Pinto" is a term used by Mexican–Americans to refer to inmates or ex–inmates who have served sentences in "la pinta"—the penitentiary. This project is staffed in large measures by "Pintos." Its report examines

gang neighborhoods of Mexican–Americans in Los Angeles, the extent to which the Mexican–American prison experience is different from other ethnic groups, the handicaps the Pinto faces after release from prison, and the extent of resistance on the part of resident Mexican–Americans in dealing with the problems of gangs, drugs, and ex–convicts.

CHIKOTA, Richard and Garland, R. When Will The Troops Come Marching In: A Comment On The Historical Use Of Federal Troops To Quell Domestic Violence. *J Urban L* 45,881–901 1968.

CHILD, Richard. Concepts Of Political Prisonerhood. *New Eng J Prison L* 1(1),1–33 Spr 1974.

CHIRICOS, Theodore G et al. Race, Crime And Sentence Length. New Orleans A S A 1972.

CHIRICOS, Theodore G and Jackson, Phillip D and Waldo, Gordon P. Inequality In The Imposition Of A Criminal Label. *Social Prob* 19(4),553–572 Spr 1972.

CHIRICOS, Theodore G and Waldo, Gordon P. Socioeconomic Status And Criminal Sentencing. *Am Sociol Rev* 40,753–772 D 1975.

CHIVERS, W R. Negro Delinquent. *Nat Prob Assn Yearbk* ,46–59 1942.

CHOCLA, M A. Riots And Acts Of Violence In The Penitentiaries: What Can We Learn? *Queens L J* 4,162–178 Sum 1978.

CHOWENHILL, R C and Street, P B and Wood, R C. *Alcohol Use Among Native Americans: A Selective Annotated Bibliography.* Berkeley CA Social Res Group 1976.

CHRISMAN, Robert. Black Prisoners, White Law. *Black Scholar* 2(8,9),44–46 Ap–My 1971.

CHRISTIAN, Diane and Jackson, Bruce. *Death Row.* Boston Beacon Pr 1980.

CHRISTIANSEN, K O and Mednick, S. *Biosocial Bases Of Criminal Behavior.* NY Gardner 1977.

CHRISTIANSON, K Scott. The Cops Can't Find The Pusher. *Nation* 213(18),462–464 N 29 1971.

CHRISTIANSON, Scott. The Historical Development Of Imprisonment Of Blacks In The US. San Francisco A S C 1980.

A nationwide survey conducted in 1979 revealed a pattern of vastly disproportionate incarceration rates for blacks, and comparisons with earlier surveys indicates that the problem of black overrepresentation in prison has grown worse, not better, as more attention purportedly has been paid to affirmative action, alternatives to incarceration and community–based corrections. However, blacks have been overrepresented in prison since prisons began; for American blacks, incarceration has represented the modern equivalent of the system of chattel slavery it replaced. The author contends that the political, social, economic and legal impact of imprisonment upon blacks has been seriously neglected. The time has come to challenge this policy.

CHRISTIANSON, Scott and Dehais, Richard. *The Black Incarceration Rate In The United States: A Nationwide Problem.* Albany SUNYA C J 1980.

The clearest trend in corrections in the US during the 1970s was the massive increase in the number of persons imprisoned in state correctional facilities. Through the computation of incarceration rates it is shown that black Americans, in particular, black males, are heavily overrepresented among this growing prison population. The authors provide rates for the 50 states and D. C. for 1973, 1978 and 1979. Surprisingly, this racial disproportionality is not limited geographically, but depicts a problem nationwide in scope. Preliminary analysis of the most recent data indicates increasing disparity between black and white incarceration rates. More research is needed in this area. The relationship between crime rates and incarceration rates should be explored, and by statistically controlling for race, discrimination in the criminal justice process could be examined. In addition, there is a need for detailed study of the factors contributing to the heightened black incarceration rate, its effects on the black family, and strategies for reducing the overrepresentation of black males in prisons throughout the nation.

CHRISTIANSON, Scott. Attica In 1976: The Lesson Not Learned. *Nation* , D 4 1976.

CHRISTIANSON, Scott. Book Review—Slavery And The Penal System. *Crim L Bull* 13(2),168–170 Mr–Ap 1977.

CHRISTIANSON, Scott. Corrections Law Developments: Legal Implications Of Racially Disproportionate Incarceration Rates. *Crim L Bull* 16(1),59–63 Ja–F 1980.

Numerous studies have noted a glaring difference in the extent to which blacks have been imprisoned relative to whites. Official statistics show that this differential treatment exists nationwide. Moreover, recent evidence indicates that this overrepresentation of blacks among prison populations has increased, even though greater attention has purportedly been paid to civil rights. Unfortunately, nowhere near as much serious scholarly attention has been directed to this problem, as to the similar question of racial disproportionality in the imposition of capital punishment. Nevertheless, comparable statistical information is available for both forms of punishment. Given that prison data are of sufficient reliability and recentness, it would seem that many of the constitutional issues raised for the death penalty can be applied to incarceration as well. The author urges social scientists and members of the bar to work together to address this problem.

CHRISTIANSON, Scott. Corrections Law Developments: Prison Labor And Unionization—Legal Developments. *Crim L Bull* 14(3),243–247 My–Je 1978.

CHRISTIANSON, Scott. Corrections Law Developments: Racial Discrimination And Prison Confinement—A Follow–Up. *Crim L Bull* 16(6),616–621 N–D 1980.

CHRISTIANSON, Scott. In Prison: A Contagion Of Suicide. *Nation* 219(8),243–244 S 21 1974.

CHRISTIANSON, Scott. The War Model In Criminal Justice: No Substitute For Victory. *Crim Just B* 1(3),247–276 S 1974.

The criminal justice system operates on a war model. War mentality pervades the entire criminal justice process, determining to an important extent how we treat criminal "enemies." The war model is characterized by identification of enemies and heroes, estimate of the enemy's strengths and weaknesses, development of strategy, development of military weapons and resources, utilization of dishonest language, and establishment of goals and objectives which are designed to produce "victory." The author argues that we must eliminate the system's distasteful emphasis on force, physical courage, weapons, and the twin concepts of enemies and heroes. Society can no longer afford to wage war in the trenches or in the streets.

CHRISTIE, Nils. *Changes In Penal Values.* London Tavistock 1963.

CICOUREL, Aaron V. *The Social Organization Of Juvenile Justice.* NY Wiley 1968.

CIZANCKAS, Victor I and Purviance, Carlton W. Changing Attitudes Of Black Youths. *Pol Chief* 40(3),42–45 1973.

The relationship of the attitudes toward police among minority group youths was studied, and a systematic procedure employed to modify those attitudes is described. A viable ride along program was established by the Menlo Park Police Department for black youths who had formerly declined to participate. The central hypothesis of the study was that the ride along experience would produce a significantly favorable change in attitude toward police officers among those youths who particpated. The experimental group consisted of 50 subjects, the control group of 86. The instrument used was the Attitude Toward Police Scale (ATP). Findings indicate that the police ride along program produced a highly significant and favorable shift in attitudes toward police among those minority youths who participated in the program.

CLAGHORN, Kate M. *The Immigrant's Day In Court.* NY Harper & Bros 1923.

CLAPP, Randy. Eighth Amendment Proportionality. *Am J Crim L* 7,253–276 Jl 1979.

CLARK, C P (ed). *Minority Opportunities In Law For Blacks, Puerto Ricans And Chicanos.* NY Law Journal Pr 1974.

CLARK, Cedric. Introduction To Symposium On White Researcher In Black Society. *J Soc Issues* 29(1),1–10 1973.

CLARK, Cedric. The Role Of White Researcher In Black Society. *J Soc Issues* 29(1),109–118 1973.

CLARK, Kenneth B. *Dark Ghetto.* NY Harper & Row 1965.

CLARK, Kenneth B. Color, Class, Personality And Juvenile Delinquency. *J Negro Ed* 28(3),240–250 1959.

This paper examined recent data on the incidence of juvenile delinquency in a Northern urban community in order to determine the degree to which the factors of color, class and caste influence the amount and type of delinquency among Negro youth. The findings are interpreted in terms of the theory and data on the effects of minority status on personality patterns. Clark contends that "any contemporary theory which seeks to

understand the problem of the disproportionate amount of delinquency in Negro youth must take into account our present knowledge of the complex relationship between personality and minority status."

CLARK, Kenneth B. The Role Of Race. *NYT Mag* ,25–26,28,30,33 O 5 1980.

CLARK, Kenneth B. The Wonder Is There Have Been So Few Riots. *NYT Mag* , S 5 1965.

Clark contends that racism is ignored until it explodes in Watts or Harlem. "The wonder is that there have been so few riots, that Negroes generally are law–abiding in a world where the law itself has seemed the enemy." Noting that during the LA riot of 1965 it was the Negro ghetto which the Negro burned, not the white community, Clark suggests that "a desire for self–destruction" may have been a "subconscious factor." It is misguided to expect individuals who have been systematically excluded from the privileges of middle–class life to behave according to middle–class values. Inmates of the ghetto do not respect property because they lack property. The riots have occurred in precisely those communities where whites have prided themselves on their liberal racial policies. Much of the new civil rights legislation, however, has focused on the plight of Southern Negroes without adequately addressing the plight of those in the North. Meaningful change, he asserts, must address the problems which Negroes face everyday: inferior schools, bad housing, infant mortality and disease, delinquency, and drug addiction. The ghetto must be destroyed rationally, by plan, not by random self–destructing forces.

CLARK, Kenneth and Barker, James. "The Zoot Effect On Personality: A Race Riot Participant" in *Racial Violence In The United States*, Grimshaw, A (ed), 413–420. Chicago Aldine 1969.

The authors present and analyze the details of a rioter's account of his involvement in the Harlem Riot. The participant is seen as displaying the personality of a person "socially isolated, rejected, discriminated against, and chronically humiliated."

CLARK, L D. Minority Lawyer: Link To The Ghetto. *Am Bar A J* 55,61+ Ja 1969.

CLARK, L and Parker, G. The Labor Law Problems Of The Prisoner. *Rutgers L Rev* 28(4),840–860 Spr 1975.

CLARK, Ramsey. *Crime In America.* NY Simon & Schuster 1970.

Popular liberal treatise on crime in the US, written by a former Attorney General.

CLARK, Ramsey and Rudenstine, David. *Prison Without Walls: Report On New York Parole.* NY Praeger 1975.

CLARK, Ramsey. Shall We Shoot Looters? *Pop Govt* 35,5–8 S 1968.

CLARK, Richard X. *The Brothers Of Attica.* NY Links Books 1973.

Clark, a black Muslim militant who was in NY's Attica state prison at the time of the 1971 uprising, offers his views on the institution and the rebellion.

CLARK, T N and Morgan, W R. The Causes Of Racial Disorders: A Grievance–Level Explanation. *Am Sociol Rev* 38(5),611–624 1973.

CLARKE, Lewis and Clarke, Milton. *Narrative Of The Sufferings Of Lewis And Milton Clarke: More Than Twenty Years Among The Slaveholders Of Kentucky.* Boston Bela Marsh 1846.

CLARKE, Milton and Clarke, Lewis. *Narrative Of The Sufferings Of Lewis And Milton Clarke: More Than Twenty Years Among The Slaveholders Of Kentucky.* Boston Bela Marsh 1846.

CLARKE, Stevens H and Koch, Gary. The Influence Of Income And Other Factors On Whether Criminal Defendants Go To Prison. *Law & Soc Rev* 11(1),57–92 1976.

CLEAR, Todd R (ed) and Travis I I I, Lawrence F (ed) and Schwartz, Martin D (ed). *Corrections: An Issues Approach.* Cincinnati Anderson 1980.

CLEAVER, Eldridge. "Prisoner Personality Development In Prison/On Becoming" in *prisons, Protest, And Politics*, Atkins, B (ed), 105–111. Englewood Cliffs NJ Prentice–Hall 1972.

The effect of two prison sentences, served at Soledad Prison in California, is described. Negro prisoners feel that they are being abused, that their imprisonment is simply another form of the oppression which they have known all their lives, rather than being payment of a debt to society. This feeling is at the root of radical consciousness among black prisoners.

CLEAVER, Eldridge. *Soul On Ice.* NY McGraw–Hill 1968.

Autobiography of a former pimp and rapist turned Black Panther. Best–seller.

CLEMENTS, C B and Wool, R. Adolescent Verbal Behavior—Investigation Of Noncontent Styles As Related To Race And Delinquency Status. *J Abnor Ch Psychol* 3(3),245–254 1975.

CLEMENTS, C B. Crowded Prisons—A Review Of Psychological And Environmental Effects. *Law Human Beh* 3(3),217–225 1979.
Psychological and environmental effects of prison crowding are examined, based on evaluation of the New Mexico State Penitentiary action suits claiming oppressive conditions. The article is based in part on testimony given at an October 1978 hearing on overcrowded conditions at the New Mexico State Penitentiary. The resulting inability of inmates to control privacy and social space can induce stress. Reactions to stress may include aggressiveness, vigilance, guardedness, aloofness, physical disease, and withdrawal. In a crowded prison, both physical and verbal aggression will increase. Prison crowding both produces exaggerated ways of coping and undermines treatment efforts. Insufficient jobs or programs lower both self–esteem and skills. Organizing into protective groups, aggressive behavior, and attempts to be transferred to single cells are additional responses to crowding. Crowding directly heightens frequency of interpersonal friction and resulting violence. The percentage of prisoners in protective custody indicates the extent to which prisoners live in fear. Overcrowding has multiple negative effects on prisoner adjustment. These effects may occur without crowding but are magnified by it.

CLIFFORD, B R and Bull, R. *Psychology Of Person Identification*. London Routledge & Kegan 1978.
Presents psychological research pertaining to personal identification and its bearing upon the reliability of eyewitness testimony. Information on racial factors in police lineups is included.

CLINTON, R N. Criminal Jurisdiction Over Indian Lands—A Journey Through A Jurisdictional Maze. *Ariz L Rev* 18(3),503–585 1976.

CLINTON, R N. Development Of Criminal Jurisdiction Over Indian Lands—The Historical Perspective. *Ariz L Rev* 17(4),951–991 1975.

CLOWARD, Richard A and Ohlin, Lloyd E. *Delinquency And Opportunity: A Theory Of Delinquent Gangs*. Glencoe IL Free Pr 1960.
Attempts to link the structural theories of Durkheim and Merton with the differential association theory of Sutherland and the cultural transmission theory of Shaw and McKay. The authors consider differential opportunity structures to be important in their analysis of American delinquency; the criminal subculture is seen as offering lower–class youths another (often illegal) opportunity structure. They predicted that delinquency would become increasingly violent as a result of disintegration of the slum and recommended reorganization of slum communities as a means of delinquency prevention.

CLOWARD, Richard A and Ohlin, Lloyd E. "Illegitimate Opportunity Structures" in *Rebellion And Retreat*, Palmer, S (ed), 32–49. Columbus Chas Merrill 1972.
Alternative opportunity structures generated by successful integrative relationships across age levels and between criminal and conventional elements in low–income neighborhoods are discussed. The pressure generated by restrictions on legitimate access to success goals are drained off. Social controls over the conduct of the young are effectively exercised, limiting expressive behavior and constraining the discontented to adopt instrumental, albeit criminalistic, styles of life.

CLOWERS, Norman L. Prejudice And Discrimination In Law Enforcement. *Police* 9,42–45 F 1964.

CLOWERS, Norman L. Prejudice And Discrimination In Law Enforcement. *Police* 8,50–54 N–D 1963.

CLUM, W. *Apache Agent: The Story Of John P Clum*. Boston Houghton Mifflin 1936.

COALITION OF CONCERNED BLACK AMERICANS. A Preliminary Report On The Experience Of The Minority Judiciary In The City Of New York. *Howard L J* 18,495–541 1975.
The findings of a unique study, focusing on inequities in the administration of justice as perceived by minority judiciary themselves is presented. Based on questionnaires and in–depth interviews with black and Hispanic judges in NYC, 24 of 39 judges responded. All respondents agreed that more black and Puerto Rican judges are needed. They also noted that there is an extremely limited number of black lawyers in NYC from which judges could be drawn. The data collected showed that an elective system to select judges may be preferred by minority judges. Many comments made by judges indicated that "there seems to be realization on the part of black and Hispanic judges that race discrimination and class discrimination are

integral parts of our present–day judicial system." Both plea–bargaining and the money–bail system were criticized. Overall, their comments "clearly do not project a very positive future for black and Hispanic people within the system of justice." Recommendations by the judges primarily focused on the need for a greater distribution of information in regard to the inequities associated with the court system and the general public.

COBARRUVIAZ, Louis and Ross, Donald J. "Eliminating The Language Barrier" in *Police–Community Relationships*, Bopp, W (ed), 442–444. Springfield IL Chas C Thomas 1972.
Efforts by the San Jose, California, police department to enhance communication with their large population of non–English–speaking citizens are briefly reported. Aimed mainly at the Mexican–American population, a local radio station was used to indoctrinate the citizens regarding police procedures and functions during the course of short weekend broadcasts in Spanish. The basic format was designed so as to cover every aspect of the police department's responsibility, with emphasis on the patrol function.

COBB, Charles E. 'Behavior Modification' In The Prison System. *Black Scholar* 5(8),41–44 My 1974.

COBBS, Price M and Grier, William H. *Black Rage*. NY Bantam 1969.

COBDEN, Lynn. The Grand Jury—Its Use And Misuse. *Crim Delinq* 22(2),149–165 Ap 1976.

COCHRANE, Hortense S. The Delinquent Negro Child. *Phylon* 10,252–253 1949.

COFFIN, Joshua. *An Account Of Some Of The Principal Slave Insurrections*. NY A AS Pr 1860.

COHAN, M. *Iowa - Department Of Public Safety - Equal Employment Opportunity Coordinator - Preliminary Evaluation*. Des Moines IA Dept Pub Safety 1976.
The performance of a full–time coordinator hired to promote female and minority recruitment, to develop hiring procedures, and to oversee equal employment opportunities is evaluated. The goal of the coordinator position is to enable the Iowa Department of Public Safety to implement affirmative action and equal opportunity programs in its highway patrol, criminal investigation, vice, narcotics, and research and administrative units. The coordinator's performance during her first year with the department is evaluated in terms of progress toward 11 objectives. The coordinator's efforts resulted in interviews with 13 women and 30 minority persons. Of those interviewed, 5 women and 4 minority persons joined the department. The coordinator contacted college placement offices and attended career day sessions at colleges and universities in order to promote public safety career opportunities for women and minorities. These and other activities led to the conclusion that the coordinator has performed satisfactorily. Continuation of the grant supporting her employment is recommended. The guide used in an evaluative interview with the coordinator is included.*

COHEN, Bernard and Chaiken, J M. *Police Civil Service Selection Prodecures And New York City—Comparison Of Ethnic Groups*. NY Rand Instit 1973.
The attorneys for both sides in a lawsuit retained the NYC–Rand Institute to conduct an independent, impartial analysis of the civil service examination scores of white and minority–group applicants for the position of patrolman in the NYC Police Department and the effect of the written examination, as compared to other parts of the appointment process, on the number of men appointed from each ethnic group. The plaintiffs in this case, the Guardians Association and the Hispanic Society, have alleged that the written entry–level civil service examination and other parts of the appointment process discriminate unlawfully against blacks and Hispanics. The defendants are the NYC Civil Service Commission, the Department of Personnel, and the Police Department. The Institute collected data about the subjects from several sources. Statistical tests showed that the scores of blacks were not significantly different from those for Hispanics, while the differences in scores between whites and minority–group members were highly significant the analysis therefore confirmed the plaintifs' allegations.*

COHEN, Bernard and Hunt Jr, Issac C. *Minority Recruiting In The New York City Police Department*. NY Rand Instit 1971.

COHEN, Bernard and Wolfgang, Marvin E. *Crime And Race: Conceptions And Misconceptions*. NY Inst Hum Rel Pr 1970.
Definitions of race and crime are examined and crime rates of blacks and other ethnic groups are discussed. The authors reject any interpretation of higher crime rates among blacks which would suggest that blacks as a race

are more prone to crime. Rather, such figures simply demonstrate the greater likelihood that black citizens will be exposed to conditions that result in arrest, conviction and imprisonment. An analysis of victim–offender relationships reveal that most assaultive crimes are predominantly intragroup, intraracial acts. Chapters on police and courts attribute disproportionate arrest and incarceration rates of blacks to bias in the adminstration of justice. In a chapter entitled "Seeking An Explanation" genetic theories of crime are rejected in favor of approaches premised on an argument that criminal behavior is learned and that environmental influences are paramount.

COHEN, Bernard. Minority Retention In The New York City Police Department. *Criminology* 11(3),287–306 N 1973.

According to Cohen, the purpose of the study was to analyze the various phases of the recruitment process required of candidates who successfully pass the written examination. He sought to identify the major points of applicant attrition, the attrition probabilities at each phase, and some of the factors that operate to unfairly reduce the number of successful applicants. Blacks and Puerto Ricans comprise about 30% of the city's population, but only 18% of all police appointees. Blacks were subject to greater attrition than other ethnic groups. Most candidate attrition seemed to be a result of the individual's apparent lack of motivation to act during the recruitment process rather than outright rejection by either the Police Department of Personnel or the Police Department. Cohen states that one reason for this might be the 17–month span between the time a candidate takes the written exam and his final appointment as a probationary patrolman. Cohen also reports that the personal character investigation did not appear to discriminate against particular groups.

COHEN, Carl. Race And The Equal Protection Of The Laws. *Lincoln L Rev* 10,117–157 1977.

COHEN, David M (ed) and Greene, Jack P (ed). *Neither Slave Nor Free: The Freedman Of African Descent In The Slave Societies Of The New World*. Baltimore MD Johns Hopkins Pr 1972.

COHEN, Elie A. *Human Behavior In A Concentration Camp*. NY Norton 1953.

COHEN, Fred. *The Legal Challenge To Corrections: Implications For Manpower And Training*. Washington DC Jt Comm Corr Man T 1969.

COHEN, Hennig. Slave Names In Colonial South Carolina. *Am Speech* 28,102–107 My 1952.

COHEN, Jacqueline and Blumstein, Alfred. A Theory Of The Stability Of Punishment. *J Crim L & Crim* 64,198–207 1973.

COHEN, Jacqueline and Miller, Harold D and Blumstein, Alfred. *Demographically Disaggregated Projections Of Prison Populations*. Pittsburgh Carnegie–M USI 1978.

This monograph on the impact of new sentencing laws on state prison populations in Pa. confirms the widespread expectation that mandatory minimum prison sentences for particular classes of felonies are likely to result in a substantial increase in the prisoner population. The authors predict that the new laws will have a greater effect on blacks than whites, thereby increasing the proportion of black prisoners.

COHEN, Jacqueline and Nagin, Daniel S and Blumstein, Alfred. The Dynamics Of A Homeostatic Punishment Process. *J Crim L & Crimin* 67(4),317–334 1976.

COHEN, J and Murphy, W. *Burn, Baby, Burn*. NY Avon 1967.

COHEN, Jay and Jacobs, James B. Impact Of Racial Integration On The Police. *J Polic Sci Adm* 6(2),168–183 1978.

A literature search is described which shows that ghetto residents are much more hostile toward all police, black and white, than are nonghetto residents. Race relations within police departments are generally tense. A NY study indicated that black ghetto residents felt that black policemen had "sold out" to the white establishment. Black police have responded in two ways—by being more lenient with black offenders or by being particularly diligent in the prosecution of offenders which they see as threatening to black communities. Police departments were reluctant to integrate. A series of Supreme Court decisions were required to break this pattern. By 1977 a new type of black police officer had emerged. More militant than other recruits, these officers have often banded together with others in Afro–American police leagues, such as those found in NY and Chicago. These groups are demanding equal opportunity in hiring and promotion. A white backlash appears to be developing, but its form is not yet clear. The tension of this racial situation is threatening the traditional feeling of sociality among American police forces.*

COHEN, Lawrence E. *Delinquency Dispositions: Case Empirical Analysis Of Processing Decisions In Three Juvenile Courts*. Washington DC LEAA 1975.

COHEN, Lawrence E. *Pre–Adjudicatory Detention In Three Juvenile Courts: An Empirical Analysis Of The Factors Related To Detention Decison Outcomes*. Washington DC LEAA 1975.

COHEN, Lawrence E. *Who Gets Detained: An Empirical Analysis Of The Pre–Adjudicatory Detention Of Juveniles In Denver*. Washington DC LEAA 1975.

COHEN, Lawrence E and Kluegel, James R. Determinants Of Juvenile Court Disposition Ascriptive And Achieved Factors In Two Metropolitan Courts. *Am Sociol Rev* 43(2),163–176 Ap 1978.

COHEN, Warren H and Mause, Phillip I. The Indian: The Forgotten American. *Harv L Rev* 81,1818–1858 1968.

COHN, Alvin W (ed) and Ward, Benjamin (ed). *Improving Management In Criminal Justice*. Beverly Hills CA Sage 1980.

COHN, Y. Criteria For The Probation Officer's Recommendations To The Juvenile Court Judge. *Crim Delinq* 9(3),262–275 1963.

COLE, D A et al. *The Negro Law Enforcement Officer In Texas*. Huntsville TX Sam Houston ICC 1969.

COLE, G F. *Criminal Justice—Law And Politics*. Belmont CA Wadsworth Pub Co 1972.

COLEMAN, James S et al. Seeman's 'Alienation And Social Learning In A Reformatory': Two Reactions. *Am J Soc* 70(1),76–84 1964.

COLES, Robert. *Eskimos, Chicanos, Indians: Children Of Crisis*, V4. Boston A Little Brown 1977.

COLES, Robert. Race And Crime Control. *Ky L J* 53(3),451–460 1965.

COLES, Robert. The Question Of Negro Crime. *Harper's Mag* 228,134–139 Ap 1964.

COLES, R. Violence In Ghetto Children. *Child* 14(3),101–104 1967.

A noted child psychiatrist looks at the home, school and street experiences of ghetto children. Irrelevant education, uninterested teachers, welfare workers who often appear to be nothing but the handmaidens of the police, and the conditions of life in the streets, serve to produce anger, frustration, and violence in children from close–knit, highly moral families which have, if anything, *better* prepared them for life than have the families of their middle–class counterparts.

COLIN, Howard. What Colour Is The 'Reasonable Man'? *Crim L Rev* 44,558–567 Spr 1959.

COLLINS, H C. *Street Gangs—Profiles For Police*. NY NYC Police Dept 1979.

These 30 brief profiles instruct law enforcement officials in street–gang behavior, depicting the general problems gangs present, their antisocial and criminal value system, and their lifestyle. The profiles describe the constellation of factors and variables that have influenced and precipitated the occurrences of an 8–year gang history that began in the Borough of the Bronx, in 1971. The NY gang of the 1970's no longer restricts its violence to enemy gangs, but now strikes out at the community. With names like the Savage Skulls, Black Assassins, Black Spades, Turbans, Reapers, and Bachelors, the gangs have increased in membership and have become embroiled in disorder, violence, and crime. The typical member is 16–23 years old, black or Hispanic, male, and from a low socioeconomic, crowded area. However, female auxiliaries often exist within gangs, with these members acting as sex partners, intelligence gatherers, and weapon carriers for the male members. Of total gang membership, 10 to 15% are hardcore. Street gangs are more antipolice and antiestablishment than the gangs of the 1950's; better armed, more violent, with gang rapes and homicides becoming common and more directed at profitmaking.*

COLLINS, R B and Johnson, R W. American Indian Courts And Tribal Self–Government. *Am Bar A J* 63,808–815 Je 1977.

COLTON, M L et al. *Court Administration In New Mexico*. Williamsburg VA Nat Cen State Cts 1975.

Studies were undertaken to examine the operation of the Administrative Office of the Courts (AOC) in New Mexico in order to identify problem areas and recommend methods for their amelioration. To this end, a team of analysts visited every judicial district court, a representative sampling of magistrate court operations was made, and interviews were conducted with all AOC employees. Among the findings were effective employee grievance procedures and affirmative action plans to ensure more equitable employment practices are lacking.*

COMER, James P. "The Dynamics Of Black And White Violence" in *The History Of Violence In America*, Graham, Hugh D And T Gurr (eds), 444–464. NY Praeger 1969.

COMMENT. Citado A Comparecer—Language Barriers And Due Process—Is Mailed Notice In English Constitutionally Sufficient? Cal L Rev 61,1395–1421 1973.

COMMENT. Civil Petitioner's Right To Representative Grand Juries And Statistical Method Of Showing Discrimination In Jury Selection Cases Generally. *UCLA L Rev* 20,581+ 1973.

COMMENT. Constitutional Law: The Right Of An Accused To Question Prospective Jurors Concerning A Specific Prejudice At Voir Dire. *Howard L J* 20,527–536 1977.

COMMENT. Conviction Records As Barriers To Employment—Racial Discrimination Under Title 7: Green Versus Missouri Pacific Railroad. *Wash U L Q* 1976(1),122–134 1976.

This decision held that statistical evidence supports a finding that a blanket rule against hiring ex–offenders is, prima facie, racially discriminatory, and cannot be justified by business necessity. This case comment analyzes this decision along with other pertinent case law dealing with racially discriminatory business personnel policies under Title VII of the Civil Rights Act of 1964.*

COMMENT. Developments In The Law—Section 1981. *Harvard C R–C L Rev* 15(1),29–277 Spr 1980.

COMMENT. Discriminatory Jury Selection: Reversible Error Regardless Of Defendant's Own Race. *U Miami L Rev* 27,238–242 1972.

COMMENT. El Chicano And The Constitution: The Legacy Of Hernandez Versus Texas. *U San Fran L Rev* 6,129+ 1971.

COMMENT. Jury Selection, Equal Protection, Deliberate Inclusion Of Negroes On Grand Jury Held Constitutional. *NYU L Rev* 42,364–370 1967.

COMMENT. Limiting The Peremptory Challenge: Representation Of Groups On Petit Juries. *Yale L J* 86(8),1715–1741 1977.

COMMENT. Negro Lawyers In Virginia: A Survey. *Va L Rev* 51,521+ 1965.

COMMENT. Prosecutor's Exercise Of Peremptory Challenge To Exclude Non–White Jurors: A Common Law Privilege In Conflict With Equal Protection Clause. *U Cinc L Rev* 46,554–571 1977.

COMMENT. Race As An Employment Qualification To Meet Police Department Operational Needs. *NYU L Rev* 54(2),413–445 My 1979.

COMMENT. Socio–Legal Aspects Of Racially Motivated Police Misconduct. *Duke L J* 4,751–783 1971.

Analyzes apparent psychological–sociological cases of racially motivated police misconduct, including police brutality against blacks. Examines available federal remedies, their history and development.

COMMENT. Voir Dire—The Due Process Clause Of The Fourteenth Amendment [And Jurors' Racial Prejudice]. *Am J Crim L* 4,180–193 1975–76.

COMMITTEE ON PUERTO RICANS. *Puerto Ricans In New York City*, Welfare Council Of New York City. NY Arno Pr 1975.

COMMONS, John R. *Races And Immigrants In America*. NY Macmillan 1915.

COMMUNITY SERVICE SOCIETY. *Statement In Opposition To Capital Punishment*. NY CSS 1977.

CONDIT, J E and Lewandowski, D G and Saccuzzo, D P. Efficiency Of Peabody Picture Vocabulary In Estimating WISC Scores For Delinquents. *Psychol Rep* 38(2),359–362 1976.

i. Q.s on the Peabody Picture Vocabulary Test for 106 lower–class males 13 to 16 years were related to WISC I. Q.s (assessed by student examiners) in three different ranges (80–89, 70–79, below 70) as a function of race. Both group and individual results were consistent with previous data showing the Peabody scale generally overestimates the I. Q.s of retarded subjects. The results also indicate that the Peabody tended to underestimate the I. Q.s of 34 "dull normal" subjects. The utility of the Peabody in estimating the Wechsler I. Q. of juvenile offenders is of doubtful value, according to the authors.

CONGRESSIONAL BUDGET OFFICE. *Federal Prison Construction: Alternative Approaches*. Washington DC US Congress 1977.

CONKLIN, John E. *Robbery And The Criminal Justice System*. Philadelphia Lippincott 1972.

CONLEY, John A (ed). *Theory And Research In Criminal Justice: Current Perspectives*. Cincinnati Anderson 1979.

CONNERY, Robert H (ed). *Urban Riots: Violence And Social Change*. NY Vintage 1968.

CONOT, Robert. *Rivers Of Blood, Years Of Darkness*. NY Bantam 1967. Conot, a special consultant to the National Advisory Commission on Civil Disorders, presents a highly evocative journalisitic account of the Watts riot of 1965. "The Los Angeles riot," he contends, "brought into focus the massive pattern of segregation in urban areas—a segregation so vast it dwarfs that of the South." Conot describes life in the ghetto in rich detail and uses eyewitness accounts of the riot which he compiled from a variety of sources. In addition to conducting interviews with nearly 1,000 persons, he obtained documents and other assistance from Los Angeles District Attorney's office, the California National Guard, the California Attorney General, the Los Angeles police and fire departments, the LA County Probation Dept., and the County Human Relations Commission, to name a few.

CONRAD, Alfred H and Meyer, John R. *The Economics Of Slavery And Other Studies In Econometric History*. Chicago IL Aldine 1964.

CONRAD, Earl. *Mr Seward For The Defense*. NY Rinehart 1956.

This popular case study recreates a famous murder trial of 1846, in which William H. Seward (former governor of NY and later Lincoln's Secretary of State) defended a black convict named William Freeman on the plea of insanity. The trial was held in Auburn, NY.

CONRAD, Earl and Patterson, Haywood. *Scottsboro Boy*. NY Doubleday 1950.

CONRAD, R D and Kahn, M W. An Epidemiological Study Of Suicide And Attempted Suicide Among The Papago Indians *Am J Psychiatry* 131(1),69–72 1974.

CONVERSE, J M and Schulman, H. The Effects Of Black And White Interviewers On Black Responses In 1968. *Public Opin Q* 35,44–68 1971.

CONWAY, Edward. *Greenhaven Diary*. NY Zebra/Scorpio 1977.

The diary of a convict in NY's Greenhaven, a maximum–security prison.

CONYERS, John R. "Crime As A Concern Of Congress" in *Black Crime: A Police View*, Bryce, H J (ed), 21–28. Washington DC Jt Ctr Polit Stud 1977.

COOK, Sherburne F. The Significance Of Disease In Extinction Of The New England Indians. *Human Biol* 45,485–508 1973.

COOKE, Gerald and Pogany, Eric and Johnston, Norman G. A Comparison Of Blacks And Whites Committed For Evaluation Of Competency To Stand Trial On Criminal Charges. *J Psychi L* 2(3),319–337 1974.

Blacks and whites committed for evaluation of competency to stand trial were compared. All males referred to the Michigan Center for Forensic Psychiatry for competency evaluation in 1969 were grouped according to race, and differences on demographic variables. Criminal charges, diagnosis, competency finding, and disposition were studied. A subsample of 70 blacks and 70 whites was analyzed for characteristics associated with MMPI administration and for differences in MMPI profile. The results are consistent with previous literature and indicate a tendency to clinically overestimate psychopathology in blacks, though there is no supporting evidence for a difference in level of pathology in terms of the more objective MMPI measure. The profound effects of this overestimation on disposition are discussed, and a number of solutions are proposed.

COONS, William R. *Attica Diary*. NY Stein & Day 1972.

Diary of a convict who observed the 1971 Attica prison rebellion.

COOPER, John L. *The Police And The Ghetto*. Port Washington NY Kennikat Pr 1980.

COOPER, Paulette. *Growing Up Puerto Rican*. NY Mentor Books 1973.

COOPER, S. A Look At The Effect Of Racism On Clinical Work. *Soc Casework* 54(2),76–84 1973.

COOT, Beverly Blair. Black Representation In The Third Branch. *Black L J* 1(3),260–279 Wint 1971.

This study seeks to explain variations in the degree of black representation in the legal profession in different states. Blair stresses the need for "descriptive representation" where "one person represents another by being sufficiently like him." 37 states were studied. Blair presents data to support her hypothesis that in the most racist states with the highest percentage of blacks in the population, underrepresentation in the judiciary will be the most extreme. Blair also found that the lack of black lawyers correlates with the lack of black judges. However, the scarcity of black lawyers does not account for the total absence of black appellate judges (in the South) or the small number of black judges in major courts. This study looks at differences in the number of black jurists in northern and southern state–level courts in metropolitan areas, as well as in federal courts. Blair concludes that having black judges at the trial level may be more important than at the appellate level.

COPELAND, Vincent. *The Crime Of Martin Sostre.* NY McGraw–Hill 1970.

Martin Sostre, a prisoner of black and Puerto Rican background, was one of the key figures of the prisoners' rights movement of the late 1960's and early '70s. The subject of several landmark court decisions, he claimed to have been framed by the Buffalo police. This book offers a sympathetic biography and raises questions about the case against him.

CORNELIUS, Wayne A. *Mexican Migration To The United States: Causes, Consequences, And US Responses.* Cambridge MA MIT Pr 1978.

CORSI, Jerome and Masotti, Louis. *Shootout In Cleveland: Black Militants And The Police (Violence Commission Report, Volume 5).* Washington DC USGPO 1969.

A detailed narrative of the events of July 23, 1968 when seven persons were killed and fifteen wounded in a Cleveland shootout between the police and black radicals. The short book organizes the details to facilitate analysis, raises questions where they are warranted, and mirrors the shootout in Cleveland against the events that led up to it and those it precipitated.

CORSI, Jerome. Detroit 1967: Racial Violence Or Class Warfare. *J Urban L* 45,641–671 1968.

CORTÉS, C E. *Harvard Encyclopedia Of American Ethnic Groups.* Cambridge MA Harvard Univ Pr 1980.

CORTES, Juan B and Gatti, Florence M. *Delinquency And Crime: A Biopsychosocial Approach.* NY Seminar Pr 1972.

Higher rates of crime among blacks than among whites are explained by postulating both higher mesomorphy and more disruption in the family environment among blacks than among whites. Data is presented which shows a higher incidence of mesomorphic physique among delinquents than among non–delinquents.

CORY, Bruce. Minority Police: Tramping Through A Racial Minefield. *Police Mag* 2(2),4–14 1979.

This overview of the status of minorities in policing includes profiles of the police departments in Detroit and Dallas. The numbers of minorities on police forces have increased, attitudes of and toward minority police have improved, and minority police organizations have become increasingly vocal. However, old attitudes linger and minority officers at times experience both scorn from the community and lack of respect from their white counterparts. In Detroit, the city's policy of promoting equal numbers of white and black officers to vacancies at the rank of sergeant has brought law suits charging reverse discrimination. In 1972, the Dallas Police chief set an ambitious minority–hiring goal as part of an ill–fated 5–year plan to reform his department. Some link Dallas' problem in recruiting minorities to the department's requirement of college training for recruits. But police and city administrators deny such a link, and the department's black officers support the requirement.*

COSER, Lewis A. *The Functions Of Social Conflict.* Glencoe IL Free Pr 1956.

COSER, Lewis A. "Violence And The Social Structure" in *Rebellion And Retreat*, Palmer, S (ed), 83–94. Columbus Chas Merrill 1972.

Major forms of conflict that give rise to outward directed physical violence, such as homicide, are examined, focusing on sociocultural situations where individuals do not have access to the institutionalized means for attaining cultural goals. Ways in which the socialization process, through the use of punishment, generates violent tendencies in those who pass through it, are also discussed. Differential homicide rates exist in related notions of frustration and relative deprivation, with members of lower socioeconomic status turning more often to violent aggression to deal with these conditions. External enforcement of conformity in the lower classes makes them susceptible to acting out aggression. This is further supported by the fact that this class is disproportionately involved in mob actions and in acts of violence during revolutions. In these cases, the prevailing social and political situations cause women and youth to be transformed from absolute deprivation into relative deprivation, which accounts for their high rate of participation along with the lower classes.

COSER, Lewis A. Some Social Functions Of Violence. *Ann Am Poli* 364,8–18 1966.

American social science has traditionally been somewhat remiss in examining social conflict and social violence because of its excessive commitment to models of social harmony; this has resulted in a tame view of social structures. This paper proposes to redress the balance somewhat by discussing three social functions of violence: violence as a form of achievement (for blacks and others so located in the social structure that they are barred from legitimate access to the ladder of achievement), violence as a danger signal (under the assumption that human beings will resort to violent action only under extremely frustrating, ego–damaging and anxiety–producing conditions, incidents such as the urban riots of the 1960's may be seen as a means of forcibly bringing to the attention of white public opinion and the white power structure the critical need for social change), and violence as a catalyst (one of the latent functions of the violent response of southern policemen to the non–violent tactics of civil rights protesters was to arouse a previously lethargic community to a sense of indignation and revulsion). A plea is made that the study of social violence be given greater emphasis in further research.

COSTO, Rupert and Henry, Jeanette. *Indian Treaties: Two Centuries Of Dishonor.* San Francisco Indian Historia Pr 1978.

COTTON, W L. *Levels Of Acculturation And Of Attitudes Toward Deviance, Criminal Behavior And Police Law Enforcement Practices Among Puerto Ricans In NYC.* Unpub PhD Diss New York Univ 1972.

This research study, based on attitudes and opinion questionnaires and interviews in East Harlem, indicates that the degree of acculturation significantly affects attitudes toward criminal behavior, the law, and police. Length of residence in the US, English proficiency, non–Puerto Rican associations, and ethnic identification (American or Puerto Rican) were major determinants of degree of acculturation. The more acculturated respondents were more likely to agree with middle class white attitudes toward crime causes and prevention, favoring increased police power and stronger laws. Less acculturated respondents stressed poverty, living conditions, discrimination, and drug use as crime causes, and amelioration of these conditions was given priority for crime prevention. Most felt the police to be ineffective and brutal toward Puerto Ricans, although some of the least acculturated seemed to have retained some respect for them. The author concludes that there is a need to make the law and its representatives more relevant to the needs of the Puerto Rican community.*

COUCHMAN, I S B. Notes From A White Researcher In Black Society. *J Soc Issues* 29(1),45–52 1973.

COUNCIL ON MUNICIPAL PERFORMANCE. City Crime: Theories About Crime And Its Control. *Crim L Bull* 9(7),563–604 1973.

COUZENS, M and Seidman, D. Getting The Crime Rate Down: Political Pressure And Crime Reporting. *Law & Soc Rev* 8,457–493 1974.

COX, George H and Carr, Timothy S. *Unemployment And Prison Population Trends In Georgia: 1967–1974.* Atlanta GA Dept Corrections 1975.

COX, Oliver Cromwell. *Caste, Class And Race.* NY Doubleday 1948.

COY, John T. A Personal Look At The Police And The Community. *Pol Chief* 41(3),57–59 1974.

A black policeman's view of police–community relations is presented. Bad press, lack of confidence, racism, and callousness are prominent in poor police–community relations. It is contended that most police function to the best of their abilities but are the victims of public misperceptions. Police need good public relations, based on reality and not on an image.

CRAFT, J A. Equal Opportunity And Seniority—Trends And Manpower Implications. *Labor Law J* 26(12),750–758 D 1975.

CRAIN, R L and Weisman, C S. *Discrimination, Personality And Achievement—A Survey Of Northern Blacks.* NY Seminar Pr 1972.

CRANSTON, Virginia A and Forslund, Morris A. A Self–Report Comparison Of Indian And Anglo Delinquency In Wyoming. *Criminology* 13(2),193–198 Ag 1975.

Delinquency among Native American (Indian) and white adolescents in the Wind River Indian Reservation area of Wyoming was compared, based on a self–report questionnaire survey. The results demonstrate little overall difference in the delinquent behavior of Indian and Anglo males, with the exception of a greater involvement of Indian males in delinquent activities centering around the school. The Indian female appeared to be considerably more involved than the white female in running away from home and in a variety of offenses centering around the school, theft, vandalism, and assault. When social class was controlled, there was a substantial reduction in the number of offenses for which there were significant differences between the two races.

CRAWFORD, T J. Police Overperception Of Ghetto Hostility. *J Polic Sci Adm* 1(2),168–174 Jl 1973.

CRAWFORD, William. *Report On The Penitentiaries Of The United States*, Orig Pub 1835. Montclair NJ Patterson Smith 1969.

William Crawford (1788–1847), a London merchant and philanthropist who was prominent in penal reform and the abolition of the slave trade, was commissioned by the Home Office in 1831 to investigate the US prison system. He toured 14 penitentiaries, and numerous local jails, often interviewing the prisoners in their cells, out of the earshot of officials. His extensive report offers the most comprehensive and the most detailed investigation into American prison conditions during the early 19th century. The appendix contains detailed statistics on racial composition and offense characteristics of the prison populations.

CRAY, Ed. *The Big Blue Line: Police Power Versus Human Rights.* NY Coward McCann 1967.

CRELINSTEN, Ronald (ed). *Terrorism And Criminal Justice: An International Perspective.* Lexington MA Lexington 1978.

CRESSEY, Donald R (ed) and Ward, David A (ed). *Delinquency, Crime, And Social Process.* NY Harper 1969.

CRESSEY, Donald R. "Crime" in *Contemporary Social Problems*, Merton, R K And R A Nisbet (eds). NY Harcourt Brace 1961.

The author, a prominent sociologist, states: "Not all Negroes, working–class persons, etc., become criminals because some are presented with an excess of anti–criminal behavior patterns, but the *chances* of being presented with an excess of criminal behavior patterns are better if one is a Negro, a member of the working class, a young male, an urban dweller, and a native American than they are if one is white, middle–class, old, a rural resident or an immigrant."

CRESSEY, Donald R and Sutherland, Edwin H. *Principles Of Criminology*, Orig Pub 1924. NY Lippincott 1970.

CRESSEY, Donald R. Changing Criminals: The Application Of The Theory Of Differential Association. *Am J Soc* 61,116–120 1955.

CRITES, L (ed) and Hepperle, W L (ed). *Women In The Courts.* Williamsburg VA Nat Cen State Cts 1978.

This anthology examines the extent of commitment on the part of the judiciary to liberating women from their inferior status in American society.*

CRITES, L. Women In Law Enforcement. *Man Info Serv Rep* 5s 1973.

Basic misconceptions about women's emotional instability and lack of self confidence are examined in the context that they have impeded the employment of women in patrol work. The author presents a list of cities and counties which are known to be utilizing women on patrol. He indicates that there are benefits to the police department which makes such use of policewomen. Some of the benefits mentioned are fewer citizen complaints for such charges as police brutality, increased attention to the service nature of police work, and improved capability in a surveillance situation where the policewoman can be inconspicuous. The author discusses the planning of such programs in the areas of recruitment, testing, screening, training, and selection of uniforms. He advocates caution in the use of such guides as the officer's arrest record and attitude surveys to evaluate the policewoman's performance.*

CRITTENDON, Stephanie and Seda, Cozetta and Ogleton, Betty. *An Examination Of Institutional Racism: Black People In California's Criminal Justice And Mental Health Systems.* Boulder CO W I C H E 1974.

The data indicate that there are racial differences in the treatment of people within, and between, the mental health and criminal justice systems. Blacks are greatly overrepresented in prisons and are slightly overrepresented in mental hospitals. While the proportion of blacks in the general population in California rose from 4.4% to 7.3% from 1950 to 1970, the proportion of blacks in prisons rose from 23% to 35%. The proportion of blacks in mental hospitals increased only from 8% to 10%. In 1970 if a person were black and institutionalized, chances were about 3 to 1 that he went to a prison rather than a mental hospital, while if a person were white, the chances were about 3 to 1 that he went to a mental hospital. These figures contrast sharply with those 1950 figures which indicate that both blacks and whites were more likely to go to mental hospitals. The decreased use of institutionalization has resulted in a reduced white population in prisons and mental hospitals from 1950 to 1970, while the black population in these institutions practically doubled.

CROCKETT JR, George W. "Challenge For The Judicial System: Economic And Racial Equality" in *Blacks And Criminal Justice*, Owens, Charles E And Jimmy Bell (eds). Lexington MA Heath 1977.

CROCKETT JR, George W. "Race And The Courts" in *The Administration Of Criminal Justice: A View From Black America*, Brown, Lee P (ed), 12–22. Washington DC Howard U 1974.

Judge Crockett discusses the role of judicial discretion in the perpetration of racial injustice through the courts. Noting that roughly two–thirds of American law is discretionary, he suggests two alternative means to combat the failure of judges to apply the same standard in all cases. The first of these, the enactment of laws mandating specific consequences for certain factual situations, is rejected because of the potential for prosecutors not to prosecute and for judges and juries not to convict when the penalty is deemed inappropriate. As a second and more viable alternative, Crockett makes a call for more black judges. Noting the paucity of blacks presently serving as judges in America, he argues that the existence of more black judges would reduce the incidence of judicial discretion having a racially discriminatory effect since black judges "usually can be depended on to use (their) judicial discretion to advance the only end of the law, namely to achieve justice and equality for everyone." He adds a caveat, however, hinting that a recent rise in the number of black jurists may explain statements by the ABA and other "legal luminaries" advocating a changeover from elected to apppointed judges.

CROCKETT JR, George W. "Racism In The Law" in *Race, Crime, And Justice*, Reasons, Charles E And Jack L Kuykendall (eds), 13–27. Pacific Palisades CA Goodyear 1972.

Crockett traces a tradition of legally countenanced racial discrimination from the slave trade sanctioned by the Constitution, through the attempts of an abolitionist–minded Congress to legislate civil rights and the success of the Supreme Court in flouting these attempts, to the situation of "camouflaged" racism (in which slogans, such as "law and order" and "crime in the streets" are used to mask anti–black sentiment) during the Kennedy–Johnson era. Racism has persisted, he argues, due to the economic interests of the propertied class. A "national psychosis" has been created by segregation and inferiorization, both *de facto* and *de jure.* "It has taken the Supreme Court 100 years to come around to a repudiation of (its post civil–war stance) to an acceptance of those principals of equality proclaimed in the 1875 Civil Rights Act." But even now, he continues, the law in regard to civil rights remains unclear.

CROCKETT JR, George W. A Black Judge Speaks. *Judicature* 53(9),360–372 1970.

CROCKETT JR, George W and De Bow, Russell R and Berkson, Larry C. *National Roster Of Black Judicial Officers, 1980.* Chicago IL Am Judicature Soc 1980.

CROCKETT JR, George W. Commentary: Black Judges And The Black Judicial Experience. *Wayne L Rev* 19,61–71 1972.

Crockett emphasizes the problem of racial segregation in our court system and law enforcement agencies. He also cites the critical need for "minority representation," i.e., the need for more blacks in positions of judicial decision–making to represent the interests of their group. He notes the paradox that black litigants, jurists and judges have made great strides in breaking down racism in some areas, but not in their own area—the courts. He points out that although one out of eight Americans is black only one of 60 judges is black, and uneven geographical distribution distorts the representation even further. Few of today's black judges have been on the bench ten years or more and most are on the magistrate or municipal court level.

CROCKETT JR, George W. Judicial Selection And The Black Experience. *Judicature* 58(8),438–442 1975.

The Michigan experience and controversy over the suggested change from an elective to an appointive system of judicial selection and its implications for black judges are discussed. Michigan has had a popularly–elected judiciary ever since its first constitution in 1835. The change to an appointive system is vigorously advocated by the leadership of the Detroit Bar Association, the State Bar of Michigan, the Michigan League of Women Voters, and the major Detroit press. The change is just as determinedly opposed by the Wolverine (black) Bar Association, the leadership of the State Federation of Labor, the Michigan Judges Association, and by most judges and attorneys located outside the metropolitan areas. It is noted that of the 700 Federal judges only 20 are black and these came from geographic areas where the black voting potential is crucial.

CROCKETT JR, George W. Justice, The Courts, And Change. *J App Beh Sci* 10(3),361–366 1974.

Changes in the judicial system were examined. When changes occur, they impinge first on those areas of the court facing greatest tension and pressure; one such area in the last decade has been the urban court system. Present day black presence in the courtroom, arising from the political importance and presence of blacks in the cities, has led to momentous progress in the entire system of justice. This includes the increased presence of blacks on the bench, as members of the juries, and changes generated in the bail system. The New Bethel case in Detroit provides a classic example of the inbred and self–perpetuating "arrangement" for the handling of poor and black arrestees, and arrangement including arrests without evidence, detentions without the right to counsel, abusive practices by police and jailers, and unreasonably high bail.

CROCKETT JR, George W. Racism In The Courts. *J Pub L* 20,385–389 1971.

Crockett points out that, in the war against racism, the battleground today is the lowest trial courts, where "legally approved racism–classism flourishes in its most virulent form. In this battle, "the chief artillery has to be the trial judge himself. He is the one in absolute command; he is the sole repository of that tremendous force for good or evil which we'll call 'judicial' discretion." He stresses the importance of increasing the number of black trial judges: "A black judge (i.e., one who is 'psychologically' as distinguished from 'physically' black) will necessarily be more effective in eradicating racism from the judicial process in his court because he will be able to recognize it when he sees it."

CROCKETT JR, George W. The Role Of The Black Judge. *J Pub L* 20,391–400 1971.

Judge Crockett, of the Detroit Recorder Court, emphasizes the role of lawyers and judges, whom he refers to as "architects of the legal system," in promoting a more just and equitable criminal process. Crockett illustrates ways in which blacks and other poor people have not received equal justice. He mentions the police practice of arresting black men after court hours, the setting of high bail, the differences in quality of counsel, and the acute pressure on blacks and other poor people to plead guilty rather than exercise their right to stand trial. He feels that the legal profession bears the major responsibility for ridding the system of racism. Crockett believes that a black judge must be a reformist. He stresses the fact that the law is not clear and unambiguous, so a judge can adapt the common law to meet the needs which he perceives. Crockett gives an example of one way he copes with the problem of police brutality. He has refused to send a convicted defendant, who had been severely beaten by police, to prison.

CROCKETT, Stanley. The Role Of The Researcher In Educational Settings: Perspectives On Research And Evaluation. *J Soc Issues* 29(1),81–85 1973.

CROMWELL, R E and Vaughn, E C and Mindel, C H. Ethnic Minority Family Research In An Urban Setting: A Process Of Exchange. *Am Sociologist* 10,141–150 1975.

CRONHEIM, A J and Schwartz, A H. Non–English–Speaking Persons In The Criminal Justice System: Current State Of The Law. *Cornell L Rev* 61(2),289–311 1976.

CROSBY, A. Psychological Examination In Police Selection. *J Polic Sci Adm* 7(2),215–229 1979.

CROSS, Granville J. The Negro, Prejudice And The Police. *J Crim L Crimin & Pol Sci* 55,405–411 1964.

CROSS, Herbert J and Tracy, James J. Personality Factors In Delinquent Boys: Differences Between Blacks And Whites. *J Res Crim Del* 8(1),10–22 Ja 1971.

CROSS, J M and Heilbrun Jr, Alfred B. An Analysis Of Rape Patterns In White And Black Rapists. *J Soc Psychol* 108(1),83–87 1979.

CROSS, Malcolm. Colonialism And Ethnicity: A Theory And Comparative Case Study. *Ethn & Racial S* 1(1),37–59 Ja 1978.

CROSS, Stan and Renner, Edward. An Interaction Analysis Of Police–Black Relations. *J Polic Sci Adm* 2(1),54–61 1974.

An interaction analysis of police–black relations is made. The components of interaction affecting behavior at an interactional level of analysis include: role definition conflict, evaluative conflict, mutual role relationship, and threat. Through an interactional analysis, understanding can be established which would help both police and blacks behave in a way in which fulfills the expectations of the other. Such communication at a behavioral level should open the way for further mutual accommodation at the level of social roles and at the level of factors which support individual emotional reactions and attitudes. The model outlined indicates what steps may be taken to improve interactions and what aspects are outside the realm of the approach. It permits an empirical approach, subject to evaluation and refinement, which can specify the degree of differentiation necessary to adequately conceptualize the reference groups of blacks or police.

CROW, H. A Political History Of The Texas Penal System, 1829–1951. Unpub PhD Diss Univ Texas Austin 1964.

CROWLEY, J E and Perry, L. "Urban Families And Assault: A Framework For Research Focused On Black Families" in *Colloquium On The Correlates Of Crime*, Otten, L (ed). Bedford MA Mitre Corp 1978.

Focusing on urban black families, this paper presents a conceptual framework for the comprehensive study of assaultive behavior in the family. Among the assumptions: (1) a wide range of assaultive behaviors must be examined; (2) both factors which provoke assault and factors which inhibit it must be considered, along with the interactions between these factors; (3) the family must be studied in the context of the community in which it resides; (4) the family is viewed as a conflict management system, which means that the study of assaultive behavior must focus on the role of such behavior in response to internal and external change and conflict; (5) any research design must allow for multiple comparisons to be made within and between racial and neighborhood stress groups; and (6) multiple health outcomes should also be included in the research. Several specific areas are reviewed: family structure, sex–role performance and expectations, family resources, and child–rearing practices. Variations in these dimensions are hypothesized to be related to the presence of assaultive behavior, and coping processes are suggested as possible mediators of the effect.*

CRUM, L. The National Guard And Riot Control: The Need For Revision. *J Urban L* 45,863–880 1968.

CRUSE, H. The Crisis Of The Negro Intellectual: From Its Origins To The Present. NY Morrow 1967.

CULVER, Dorothy Campbell (comp). Bibliography Of Crime And Criminal Justice, 1927–1931, Orig Pub 1934. Montclair NJ Patterson Smith 1969.

CURRY, Jesse E and King, G D and Eastman, G. Race Tensions And The Police. Springfield IL Chas C Thomas 1962.

CURRY, Jesse E and King, Glen D. "The Effects Of Prejudice On Minorities" in *Police–Community Relationships*, Bopp, W (ed), 86–90. Springfield IL Chas C Thomas 1972.

The effect of prejudice on minority groups' relations with society in general, and with the police in particular, is briefly examined. Prevailing attitudes regarding the "inferiority" of blacks and other minority groups and their frustrations at being denied social and economic justice and opportunity have led to conditions of alienation and lawlessness. When these groups are uncooperative and antagonistic toward the police the officers respond in the same manner. Under conditions of mutual antagonism, it is nearly impossible for the police to enforce law and order fairly. A primary goal in the area of race relations, therefore, is to insure that each officer's conduct with members of a minority group is above reproach so as to gradually establish an attitude of confidence and cooperation on both sides.

CURTIS, Lynn A. Toward A Cultural Interpretation Of Forcible Rape By American Blacks. Toronto World Soc Cong 1974.

The author contends that, within a broad interpretive framework of economic–racial determinism and poverty subcultural adaptation, a central impulse mechanism in the development of violent contracultural patterns among some poor young black males is the redirection and exaggeration of certain expressions of manliness. He further maintains that role modeling is a central transmission mechanism within the ghetto–slum. This general model is applied to a specific criminal behavior form, forcible rape. The analysis examines how acceptance of contracultural patterns can help facilitate rape in specified contexts. The following additional variables are among those important in understanding reported rape by blacks on blacks: reinforcement from white males, the male's verbal skill and ability to isolate a female, the female's ability to control the situation, and the social distance between subsequent offender and victim. Reported rape by blacks on whites is assessed through black politicalization and social integration perspectives. Concluding observations deal with cross–cultural comparison and the difficulty in distinguishing between "pathology" and "normalcy" in cultural criminology.*

CURTIS, Lynn A. *Violence, Race And Culture.* Lexington MA Heath 1975.

The author states his objective is to determine just how useful a cultural interpretation of violence is in understanding criminal homicide, aggravated assault, forcible rape, and robbery committed by blacks in the contemporary US...." Chapters 2, 3, 4, and 5 build a general interpretative framework in which culture is viewed as a variable intervening between more basic structural determinants of poor black behaviors and violent criminal outcomes. A "multidimensional value space" model is conceived in which some poor blacks simultaneously accept dominant cultural, black poverty subcultural, and violent contracultural values, behaviors and meanings. Chapters 6, 7, and 8 apply this model to homicide, assault, rape and robbery by poor blacks, asking how an adherence to violent contraculture can facilitate these behaviors, yet arguing that many other variables are essential for a complete understanding of the phenomenon. Chapter 9 proposes research that might logically follow; Chapter 10 draws certain policy implications; and Chapter 11 concludes on a more philosophical note with comparisons to labeling theory and speculations on the meaning of normalcy.

CURTIS, Lynn A and Wolfgang, Marvin E. Criminal Violence: Patterns And Policy In Urban America. *Int Rev Crim Pol* 30,7–11 1972.

CURVIN, Robert and Porter, Bruce. *A Report On The Blackout Looting: New York City, July 13, 1977.* NY Gardner 1979.

Not only the results but also the root causes of the large scale looting during the 1977 NYC blackout are examined and compared with events during the 1965 NY blackout. Looters were mainly blacks and Hispanics, unemployed, male, between the ages of 16 and 25, and not particularly poor. Furniture and household appliances accounted for the largest part of looted goods. The looting, which manifested drastic shifts in the result of a variety of forces and attitudes, including declining legitimacy, criminality, and material aspirations, as well as poverty recently inhabited by the city's poor. It signals a change in the inner city: a corps of hardened, street–type urban dwellers has developed which operates in a shadow economy of hustle and crime and is made up of castoffs of the traditional economic system, mostly persons associalized in youth homes and prisons.*

CUSKEY, W R and Moffett, A D and Chambers, C D. Demographic Factors In Opiate Addiction Among Mexican Americans. *Pub Health Rep* 85(6),523–531 1970.

CUSKEY, Walter R and Krasner, William. The Needle And The Boot: Heroin Maintenance. *Society* 10(4),45–52 1973.

Ethical and practical problems which arise in heroin and methadone maintenance programs are discussed. Programs offered at traditional facilities such as Federal hospitals at Lexington and Fort Worth, are outlined, along with newer more controversial approaches such as the drug free therapeutic communities, which rely on faith, exhortation, and rebirth of the inner self. Clinical resistance to heroin maintenance on moral grounds is examined; the complaint of black leaders is voiced that maintenance is a colonialist policy intended to keep black people in a docile, stupefied state.

CUSKEY, Walter R and Moffett, Arthur D and Chambers, Carl D. "Mexican American Opiate Addicts" in *The Epidemiology Of Opiate Addiction In The United States*, Ball, John C (ed). Springfield IL Chas C Thomas 1970.

CUTRIGHT, Phillip. Inequality: A Cross–Sectional Analysis. *Am Sociol Rev* 32,562–578 Ag 1967.

CUTRIGHT, Phillip. Negro Subordination And White Gains. *Am Sociol Rev* 30(1),110–112 1965.

CZAJKOSKI, Eugene H. Comment: Involving The Humanities In Doctoral Education In Criminology And Criminal Justice. *J Crim Jus* 6,195–197 1978.

DADRIAN, Vahakn N. The Victimization Of The American Indian. *Victimol* 1(4),517–537 Wint 1976.

Dadrian examines the theme of the victimization of the American Indian at the hand of white settlers. Using a sociological perspective, he postulates that the diversity of Indian victimization is a function of two basic determinants: interactional and structural. Dadrian applies his expertise on genocide to the American Indian experience.

DAHMANN, Donald C and Berry, Brian J. Population Redistribution In The US In The 1970's. *Pop & Dev Rev* 4,443–471 1977.

DAHRENDORF, Ralf. *Class And Class Conflict In Industrial Society.* Palo Alto CA Stanford Univ Pr 1959.

DALDIO, Maria Gomez. Hispanic Women Offenders And Ex–Offenders. Dallas N I C 1979.

DALE, Le Afrique. A Day's Work. *Black Scholar* 2(8,9),47–49 Ap–My 1971.

DANDURAND, Yvon. Ethnic Group Members And The Correctional System: A Question Of Human Rights. *Can J Crim & Corr* 16(1),35–52 1974.

DANIEL, Robert P. Personality Differences Between Delinquent And Non–Delinquent Negro Boys. *J Negro Ed* 1,318–387 1932.

The author states that three special conclusions stand out from his study: (1) delinquents differ from non–delinquents in the things they do and the way they feel, chiefly in degree rather than in kind; (2) the results indicate a value in the use of objective personality and character measures in the discovery of personality symptoms of delinquency tendencies which would be the bases of an attendant individual diagnosis and adjustment procedure by a trained psychologist; and (3) in addition to evaluating the concomitancy of various personality factors with Negro male juvenile delinquency, the study has indicated the applicability of certain personality tests in measuring Negro delinquents as compared with Negro non–delinquents and at the same time has raised the question of the probable inapplicability of the norms of these tests to Negro subjects.

DANIEL, Walter G. The Role Of Youth Character–Building Organizations In Juvenile Delinquency Prevention. *J Negro Ed* 28(3),310–317 1959.

DANIELS, D N (ed) and Gilula, M F (ed) and Ochberg, F M (ed). *Violence And The Struggle For Existence.* Boston Little, Brown 1970.

DANIELS, H W and Lane, E B. Incarcerated Native. *Can J Crim* 20(3),308–316 Jl 1978.

DANTO, Bruce L (ed). *Jail House Blues: Studies Of Suicidal Behavior In Jail And Prison.* Orchard Lake MI Epic Publications 1973.

DANZIGER, Sheldon. Explaining Urban Crime Rates. *Criminology* 14(2),291–296 Ag 1976.

DARITY, William A and Turner, Castellano. Fears Of Genocide Among Black Americans As Related To Age, Sex, And Region. *Am J Public Health* 63(12),1029–1034 D 1973.

DARROW, Clarence. *Crime: Its Causes And Treatment.* NY Thos Y Crowell 1922.

DASH, Leon and Bagdikian, Ben. *The Shame Of The Prisons.* NY Pocket Books 1972.

DASHWOOD, Alan. Juries In A Multi–Racial Society. *Crim L Rev* 57,85–94 F 1972.

DATESMAN, Susan K (ed) and Scarpitti, Frank R (ed). *Women, Crime, And Justice.* NY Oxford Univ Pr 1980.

The relations among women, crime, and justice are explored in this collection of articles, which focuses on the etiology and patterns of female crime, women in the criminal justice system, and crime and emancipation. The readings are intended to enhance criminology study, delinquency and criminal justice courses, courses in sex roles, and women's studies. The etiology of female crime is viewed from the perspectives of existing literature, with attention to sociological and psychological causative factors. The justice system's discriminatory practices are addressed in terms of the sexist attitudes, chivalry, and paternalism that result in sentencing disparities and misguided, inadequate detention programs. Discrimination against both juvenile and adult female offenders is considered; legal solutions are weighed and arguments cited in support of the Equal Rights Amendment. A special article addresses the dilemma of mothers behind bars and the parental rights of incarcerated women. Final remarks analyze the relationship of women's crime and women's emancipation, concluding that despite the increase in female crimes, the Equal Rights Movement has not had a causative effect.*

DATESMAN, Susan K and Scarpitti, Frank R. "Unequal Protection For Males And Females In The Juvenile Courts" in *Juvenile Delinquency*, Ferdinand, Theodore N (ed), 59–77. Beverly Hills CA Sage 1977.

DAVID, Deborah S and Kleinman, Paula H. Visibility And Contact With Others: Mediating Factors In The Neighborhood Crime Complex. Jerusalem Int Symp Victimol 1973.

The authors sampled residents in the Bedford–Stuyvesant/Fort Greene area to discover patterns of victimization, and the relationships of victimization and social characteristics to perception of crime. The sample, located in an area high in narcotic addiction and crime, found that the respondents of each of four race–ethnic groups report roughly the same rates of victimization, and the proportions are similar who perceive that crime in the area is high.

DAVID, Deborah S and Kleinman, Paula H. Victimization And Perception Of Crime In A Ghetto Community. *Criminology* 11(3),307–343 N 1973.
This paper presents results of a study which explored the relationship between victimization and perception of crime with relevant demographic factors. A sample of residents were interviewed in the Bedford–Stuyvesant/Fort Greene area of New York, an area high in narcotic addiction and crime. Four ethnic groups in the area, blacks, Puerto Ricans, British West Indians and whites, were compared. Data shows that respondents of the four groups report roughly the same rates of victimization and similar proportions of the groups perceive crime as high. Those of high socio–economic status have higher victimization rates and larger proportion of high SES people perceive crime as being high (except among West Indians). No differences were found in victimization or perception of crime between males and females. The impact of age differs for each race/ethnic group. A high degree of visibility to and contact with others was found to be positively related to victimization. The relationship between visibility/contact and perceptions was less clear since it varied between groups and indicators were inconsistent.

DAVID, Pedro R. The World Of The Burglar: Five Criminal Lives. Albuquerque Univ N Mex Pr 1974.
Five interviews with petty criminals are reported which were part of a project directed by law enforcement agencies to reduce property crime in Albuquerque. The people interviewed, a white, a black, and three Chicanos, one of whom is a woman, are intended to be paradigmatic examples of certain types of criminals. Two theoretical appendices are included.

DAVIDSON, Basil. Black Mother: The Years Of The African Slave Trade. Boston Little, Brown 1961.

DAVIDSON, R Theodore. Chicano Prisoners: The Key To San Quentin. NY Holt Rinehart Wins 1974.
The author, an anthropologist, was invited by prison officials to study the effect of subcultural factors in the high incidence of violence and reluctance to participate in "rehabilitation" programs as manifested by Chicano prisoners at San Quentin State Prison in California. Davidson spent 20 months (to Feb. 1968) as a participant observer in the institution. He states that Chicano prisoners see themselves as representative of the Chicano community. Their sense of machismo governs their behavior and contributes to Chicano solidarity. The convict code among Chicanos is strong and this works against inmate cooperation with prison authorities. Staff members, who are predominantly Anglo, have little understanding of Chicano values or concerns, and many carry negative stereotypes about Mexican–American people.

DAVIE, Maurice R. Negroes In American Society. NY McGraw–Hill 1949.

DAVIES, Arthur J. Anguish Of A Dead Man. *Black Scholar* 2(8,9),34–41 Ap–My 1971.

DAVIES, George R. Social Aspects Of The Business Cycle. *Q J* 12(2),107–121 Ja 1922.

DAVIES, James C. "A Cause Of Some Great Revolutions And A Contained Rebellion" in *The History Of Violence In America*, Graham, Hugh D & T Gurr (eds), 690–730. NY Praeger 1969.

DAVIS, A J. Sexual Assaults In The Philadelphia Prison System And Sheriff's Vans. *Trans–Act* 6,8–16 D 1968.

DAVIS, Angela Y et al. If They Come In The Morning: Voices Of Resistance. NY Signet 1971.

DAVIS, Angela Y. Rape, Racism And The Capitalist Setting. *Black Scholar* 9(7),24–30 Ap 1978.

DAVIS, Angela Y. The Struggle Of Ben Chavis And The Wilmington 10. *Black Scholar* 6(7),26–31 1975.
The case before the North Carolina federal court system of the Rev. Ben Chavis and the Wilmington Ten is described. It is argued that black militants are persecuted by the powerful racist whites in that state. It is contended that the black defendants killed a white person during racial strife while trying to defend themselves after the police refused to step in and protect the blacks.

DAVIS, Bruce L (comp). Criminological Bibliographies. Westport CT Greenwood Pr 1973.

DAVIS, Charles. The Analysis Of Self–Concept And Self Actualization Manifestations By Incarcerated And Free Black Youth. Unpub PhD Diss Univ of Pitts 1975.
Factors which may organize behavior integration in incarcerated and free male black youth were investigated, emphasizing self–concept and self–actualization as seen in the theories of existential phenomenology of Frederick C. Thorne. Incarcerated black and white subjects were first tested on two scales devised by Dr. Thorne, and a matched group of high school students was then tested on the same instruments. Results indicate that: (1) the self–concept of black male incarcerated youth is slightly more positive than that of free black male youth; (2) the free black males were more self–actualized than incarcerated black males; (3) the self–concept of free black males was slightly more positive than that of white free males; and (4) free black males felt less self–actualized than free white males. Other relevant data obtained through administration of the two scales are also discussed.

DAVIS, David Brion. The Problem Of Slavery In The Age Of Revolution, 1770–1823. Ithaca NY Cornell Univ Pr 1975.

DAVIS, David Brion. The Problem Of Slavery In Western Culture. Ithaca Cornell Univ Pr 1966.

DAVIS, David Brion. The Crime Of Reform. *NY Rev Bks* 27,14,16,17 Je 26 1980.
Davis, a Pulitzer Prize–winning historian specializing in slavery, considers black slavery as a penal institution, and suggests that some penal systems have acquired many of the characteristics of chattel slavery. While original sin supplied much of the justification for slavery, imprisonment for blacks is justified on the basis that they committed a crime.

DAVIS, E E and Fine, M. The Effects Of The Findings Of The US National Advisory Commission On Civil Disorders: An Experimental Study Of Attitude Change. *Human Rel* 28(3),209–227 1975.

DAVIS, E R. The Delinquent Girl In Chicago: I—A Comprison Of Four National And Racial Groups. *Smith Coll Stud Soc Wk* 3,249–259 1933.

DAVIS, J P (ed). The American Negro Reference Book. Englewood Cliffs Prentice Hall 1966.

DAVIS, John A. Blacks, Crime And American Culture. *Ann Am Poli* 423,89–98 Ja 1976.
The thesis that cultural domination was more damaging than economic domination to black self–esteem is explored. It is contended that attacks on blacks and black culture, justified by legal interpretations, destroyed the blacks' faith in society's justice. Data which indicate that social inequalities have been perpetuated under the law and that blacks were aware of this are presented. Economic oppression under the law created the condition in which the connection between crime and punishment lost the power to constrain antisocial acts. Blacks often admired resistance while whites developed extreme paranoia that blacks were out to take their lives and property. The records show that blacks victimize blacks. The predominant crime pattern among blacks is against property, and the rate is not significantly higher than for whites. In crime against persons, black rates are higher than white rates.

DAVIS, John A. Justification For No Obligation: Views Of Black Males Toward Crime And The Criminal Law. *Issues Crim* 9(2),69–87 Fall 1974.
The study method was primarily participant observation. 150 black males, from 18 to 30 years of age were interviewed. An attempt was also made to contact persons who reasonably approximated the class like variations among blacks. Subjects were asked to identify any factors which they believed would account for the higher criminal law violation rates among blacks. The factors most often mentioned included the incompatibility of black–white interests, the this unequal access, , the injustice of unequal access to institutional participation, and the weight of history of unjust treatment. Also mentioned were the initial involuntary servitude of blacks, the lack of rights and privileges for blacks under the law, and the statement that black people are a conquered people. Several conditions which may affect the emergence of criminality among blacks were indicated. These conditions are the awareness of grievances concerning unjust conditions leading to lower repsect for law enforcement among blacks and the awareness, acceptance of and willingness to engage in illegal activity as a solution to grievances resulting from feelings of injustice.

DAVIS, Kenneth Culp. *Discretionary Justice: A Preliminary Inquiry.* Baton Rouge LA LSU Pr 1969.

DAVIS, Lenwood G. *Crime In The Black Community—An Exploratory Bibliography.* Monticello IL Coun Plan Librar 1975.

Approximately 300 complete bibliographic citations are presented for reports, studies, theses, books, and articles dealing with crime in the black community. While most of the citations are fairly recent (1967 on), there are entries from each decade of the twentieth century. Entries are arranged alphabetically by type of publication.*

DAVIS, Lenwood G. *The Administration Of Criminal Justice: An Exploratory Bibliography.* Monticello IL Coun Plan Librar 1975.

DAVIS, Lenwood G. "Historical Overview Of Crime And Blacks Since 1876" in *Crime And Its Impact On The Black Community,* Gary, L E And L P Brown (eds), 3–11. Washington DC Howard U 1976.

Davis contends that historically the black community has not only been concerned about crime but has consistently, though often without recognition from the white majority, attempted to address this. White society has used a double standard of justice when applying the judicial process to blacks and that information relating to black criminality has often been distorted and manipulated by white statisticians to give faulty impressions and erroneous information to the society at large. Davis concludes with the call to black social scientists to re-examine previous and neglected statistical data on crime so as to provide the black community with "new information in which we can insubstantiate the many myths about blacks and crime."

DAVIS, Peggy C. The Death Penalty And The Current State Of The Law. *Crim L Bull* 14(1),7–17 Ja–F 1978.

DAWES, H L. "The Indians And Law" in *Americanizing The American Indians,* Prucha, Francis P (ed). Cambridge MA Harvard Univ Pr 1973.

DAWIDOWICZ, Lucy S. *The War Against The Jews, 1933–1945.* NY Holt Rinehart Wins 1975.

DAWKINS, M P and Harper, Frederick D. Alcohol Abuse In The Black Community. *Black Scholar* 8(6),23–31 1977.

DAWSON, Robert O. *Sentencing: The Decision As To Type, Length, And Conditions Of Sentence.* Boston Little, Brown 1969.

DAY, B. *Sexual Life Between Blacks And Whites: The Roots Of Racism.* NY World 1972.

DAY, Robert (ed) and Bahr, Howard (ed) and Chadwick, Bruce (ed). *Native Americans Today: Sociological Perspectives.* NY Harper & Row 1972.

DE BOW, Russell R and Berkson, Larry C and Crockett Jr, George W. *National Roster Of Black Judicial Officers, 1980.* Chicago IL Am Judicature Soc 1980.

DE BRENES, E Acosta and Ferracuti, Franco and Dinitz, Simon. *Delinquents And Nondelinquents In The Puerto Rican Slum Culture.* Columbus Ohio St Univ Pr 1975.

DE CANI, John L. Statistical Evidence In Jury Discrimination Cases. *J Crim L & Crimin* 65(2),234–238 1974.

DE COSTA, Frank A. Disparity And Inequality Of Criminal Sentences: Constitutional And Legislative Remedies. *Howard L J* 14,29–59 1968.

DE LORIA JR, Vine. *Behind The Trail Of Broken Treaties.* NY Bantam 1974.

DE VEREAUX, G and Loeb, E M. Some Notes On Apache Criminality. *J Crim Psychop* 4,424–430 1943.

DEBLASSIE, R R and Healey, G W. A Comparison Of Negro, Anglo And Spanish–American Adolescents' Self–Concepts. *Adoles* 9(33),15–24 1974.

The purposes of this study were to determine if differences existed in the self–concept among Negro–, Anglo–, and Spanish–American adolescents and the extent to which these differences were influenced by ethnic group membership, socioeconomic position, or sex, or the interaction among these variables. Of the fourteen measures of self–concept assessed in this study, four scores were affected by the ethnic variable, Self Criticism, Defensive–Positive, Self–Satisfaction, and Moral–Ethical Self. The Total Positive Score (the overall general measure of self–concept– did not differ significantly among the three ethnic groups. Socioeconomic position was found to influence two of the fourteen scales utilized in this study, Social Self and Self Satisfaction. However, once again, the Total Positive Score did not differ significantly among the four socioeconomic class positions. The Total Positive Score was not significantly affected by sex differences.

However, Physical Self, a specific measure of the total self–cOncept, was significantly affected by sex differences. No significant interaction effects were found.

DEBRO, Julius. *Institutional Racism In Federal Sentencing.* Unpub D Crim Just Diss Univ of Calif 1976.

DEBRO, Julius. *The Negro Federal Offender.* Unpub MA Thesis San Jose St Col 1968.

DEBRO, Julius. "Institutional Racism" in *Black Perspectives On Crime And The Criminal Justice System,* Woodson, Robert L (ed). 143–160. Boston G K Hall 1977.

DEBRO, Julius. "Perspectives Of Blacks" in *Social Research And The Black Community,* Gary, Lawrence E (ed), 105–111. Washington DC Howard U 1974.

DEBRO, Julius and Taylor, Helen. *Study On The Status Of Black Criminology In The United States.* College Park Univ MD ICJ & C 1978.
A search of the criminological literature produced by black American scholars. Includes recommendations for future study and evaluations of black criminology, with bibliography on black criminology.

DEBRO, Julius. The Black Offender As Victim. *J Afro–Am I* 2(2),149–165 1974.

This paper presents and examines various theories that have attempted to explain black criminality. Noting that most studies which cite differential treatment as accounting for the statistical disparity between races and classes in criminal behavior have drawn their data from state agencies, Debro then reports findings from a study he conducted in San Francisco and Los Angeles by which he attempts to answer "the broader question of whether discrimination exists within the criminal justice system at the federal level." His findings suggest that while discrimination does exist in sentencing within federal districts, it is much more subtle and covert than that which exists at the state or local level. The present system, which takes into account such legitimate factors as seriousness of the offense, prior record, educational background at the time of sentencing, works to the disadvantage of the minority offender. Debro also points out that no matter how objective the court process appears to be, the black offender will continue to perceive himself as a victim as long as the bureaucracy of that process remains as white as it is.

DECKER, David L and Shicor, David and O' Brien, Robert M. *Urban Structure And Victimization.* Lexington MA Lexington 1980.

DEGHER, Douglas William. *Native Americans In The Justice System: An Analysis Of Two Rural Washington Counties.* Unpub PhD Diss Washington St Univ 1975.

The relationship between American–Indians and the American justice system was examined in Indian and non–Indian offenders from two rural Washington counties. Arrest court records were first examined to obtain evidence relating the treatment of the two groups in the courts through five stages of justice administration: cited and released data, bail information, use of court facilities, disposition, and sentencing patterns. A survey questionnaire was also used to obtain perceptions of law enforcement personnel and the quality of the job that they do. Arrest and court data show much less discrimination toward Indians than assumed. Only upon entry into the system (cited and released and bail sections) are Indians at a disadvantage. The survey data, however, show that Indians are much more negative than non–Indians in perceptions of law enforcement personnel and feel that they are treated unjustly within the law and justice system. The survey data were concerned more with interpersonal contacts between citizens and enforcement personnel than with arrest and court data. Perhaps on–the–street contacts between Indians and police are where definitions of discrimination develop.

DEGLER, Carl N. Slavery And The Genesis Of American Race Prejudice. *Comp Stud Hist & Soc* 2,49–65 O 1959.

DEHAIS, Richard and Christianson, Scott. *The Black Incarceration Rate In The United States: A Nationwide Problem.* Albany SUNYA C J 1980.
The clearest trend in corrections in the US during the 1970s was the massive increase in the number of persons imprisoned in state correctional facilities. Through the computation of incarceration rates it is shown that black Americans, in particular, black males, are heavily overrepresented among this growing prison population. The authors provide rates for the 50 states and D. C. for 1973, 1978 and 1979. Surprisingly, this racial disproportionality is not limited geographically, but depicts a problem nationwide in scope. Preliminary analysis of the most recent data indicates increasing disparity between black and white incarceration rates. More

research is needed in this area. The relationship between crime rates and incarceration rates should be explored, and by statistically controlling for race, discrimination in the criminal justice process could be examined. In addition, there is a need for detailed study of the factors contributing to the heightened black incarceration rate, its effects on the black family, and strategies for reducing the overrepresentation of black males in prisons throughout the nation.

DEL CASTILLO, Adelaida (ed) and Mora, Magdalena. *Mexican Women In The United States: Struggles Past And Present.* Los Angeles U CA Chicano Stud 1980.

DEL OLMO, Rosa. Limitations For The Prevention Of Violence: The Latin American Reality And Its Criminological Theory. *Crim & Soc Just* 3,21–29 Spr–Sum 1975.

DEL PINAL, Jorge H. "The Penal Population Of California" in *Voices: Readings From El Grito*, Octavio Ignacio Romano (ed). Berkeley Quinto Sol Pubs 1973.

DELGADO, R and Romero, L M. Legal Education Of Chicano Students: A Study In Mutual Accomodation And Cultural Conflict. *New Mex L Rev* 5,177–231 1975.

DELK, J L. *Prejudice, Perception And Penal Judgements.* Unpub PhD Diss Louisiana St Univ 1967.

DELLA FAXE, Richard L. Success Values: Are They Universal Or Class Differentiated? *Am J Soc* 80,153–169 1974.

DELLA FAXE, Richard L. The Culture Of Poverty Revisited: A Strategy For Research. *Social Prob* 21(3),609–621 1974.

DELORIA JR, Vine. Legislation And Litigation Concerning American Indians. *Ann Am Poli* 436,86–96 Mr 1978.

DELORIA, Vine. *Custer Died For Your Sins.* NY Avon 1969.

DEMBITZ, Nanette. Racial Discrimination And The Military Judgment. *Colum L Rev* 46,175–239 Mr 1945.
Considers the internment of Japanese–Americans during World War 2.

DEMBO, R et al. A Framework For Developing Drug Abuse Prevention Strategies For Young People In Ghetto Areas. *J Drug Educ* 6(4),313–325 1976.

DENFELD, D and Hopkins, Andrew. Racial–Ethnic Identification In Prisons: 'Right On From The Inside'. *Int J Crimin Pen* 3(4),355–366 N 1975.

DERTKE, M C and Penner, L A and Ulrich, K. Observer's Reporting Of Shoplifting As A Function Of Thief's Race And Sex. *J Soc Psychol* 94,213–221 1974.

DETROIT BUREAU OF GOVERNMENTAL RESEARCH, Inc. Report Of The Mayor's Committee On Race Relations. *Public Busi* 4,7–8 Mr 10 1927.

DEWOLF, L H. *Crime And Justice In America—A Paradox Of Conscience.* NY Harper & Row 1975.

DICKENS, Al. *Uncle Yah Yah.* Detroit Harlo 1976.
Narratives by a black convict.

DIGGS, Mary H. The Problems And Needs Of Negro Youth As Revealed By Delinquency And Crime Statistics. *J Negro Ed* 9,311–320 1940.

DIJOSEPH, J. Bureau Of Indian Affairs Law Enforcement Division—Indian Police. *Trooper* 2(7),102–103,105 Wint 1977.

DILLARD, J L. *Black English: Its History And Usage In The United States.* NY Random House 1972.

DILLINGHAM, Gerald. A Survey: Black Attitudes Toward Police And The Courts. *Black World* 24(2),4–13 1974.

DILLON, Richard H. *The Hatchet Men.* NY Coward McCann 1962.

DINITZ, Simon and De Brenes, E Acosta and Ferracuti, Franco. *Delinquents And Nondelinquents In The Puerto Rican Slum Culture.* Columbus Ohio St Univ Pr 1975.

DINITZ, Simon and Silverman, I J. Compulsive Masculinity And Delinquency: An Empirical Investigation. *Criminology* 11(4),498–515 F 1974.
The sample was drawn from a representative cross–section of the population at the Fairfield School for Boys, a facility operated by the Ohio Youth Commission. Each subject was administered a questionnaire which included a Compulsive Masculinity Index, the Lykken Scale, and the Zuckerman Scale. The Compulsive Masculinity Index was used to measure the boys' self–identification with tough behavior and sexual athleticism. The Lykken Scale was included to measure impulsiveness and proneness to activities that are high risk in nature and excitement oriented. It also

measures general hostility. The Zuckerman Scale was included to measure field dependency–tendency to be effected by environmental influences including peer pressures. Each respondent was asked to rate himself and all the other boys in his cottage according to how manly he considered himself and each other boy to be. This study suggests that delinquent boys from female–based households were more hyper–masculine than delinquents from other types of households. It was also shown that black delinquents as a group define themsleves as being more manly and tough than white delinquents in the same training school.

DISCH, Barry N and Schwartz, Barry N and Disch, Robert. *White Racism: Its History, Pathology And Practice.* NY Dell 1970.

DISCH, Robert and Disch, Barry N and Schwartz, Barry N. *White Racism: Its History, Pathology And Practice.* NY Dell 1970.

DISON, Jack E. *An Empirical Examination Of Conflict Theory: Race And Sentence Length.* Unpub PhD Diss N Texas St Univ 1976.
The author based his research on a study of the persons incarcerated in the Texas Department of Corrections for robbery. Members of minorities were alleged to represent the powerless. Measures of association and selected control variables were used dealing with characteristics of the victim. Circumstances of the crime, and circumstances of legal disposition. The study found a weak relationship between race of the offender and sentence length, even considering proportional reduction in error. These findings tend not to support the conflict perspective of societal reaction to crime.

DIXON JR, Robert G. Equality, The Elusive Value. *Wash U L Q* 1979(1),5–10 Wint 1979.

DIXON, Hortense W and Lede, Naomi W. "Criminal Justice And The Minority Community" in *Urban Minority Groups In Houston: Problems, Progress And Prospects*, 205–248. Houston TX Southern Univ 1974.

DIZMANG, Larry H Et Al. Adolescent Suicide On An Indian Reservation *Am J Orthopsych* 44(1),43–49 1974.
The backgrounds of 10 American Indians who committed suicide before the age of 25 are compared statistically with a matched control group from the same tribe. The contrast is significant in at least six variables that point to the greater individual, familial, and cultural disruption experienced by the suicidal youths. Suggestions for treatment and prevention based on the experience of this tribe are offered.

DOBBINS, D A and Bass, Bernard M. Effects Of Unemployment On White And Negro Prison Admissions In Louisiana. *J Crim L Crimin & Pol Sci* 48(15),522–525 Ja–F 1958.
This study of admissions to the Louisiana State Penitentiary during 1941–54 reinforces the hypothesis that unemployment is an important factor influencing prison commitments. A lower association was found between unemployment and Negro prison admissions than for unemployment and white prison admissions. The authors suggest that this may be due to the tendency of Negroes to commit relatively more crimes against the person than whites, while whites were more often committed for property offenses.

DOLAN, Thomas J. The Case For Double Jeopardy: Black And Poor. *Int J Crimin Pen* 1(2),129–150 1973.
The historical perspective and the current case for double jeopardy (black and poor) are presented. It is suggested that a full appreciation of current inequities within the court correctional process demands a consideration of the economic and social background which leads to and complements such inequities. Changes cannot be affected without first determining the cause of the situation. A brief review of statistics is given. The historical perspective is discussed in terms of paternalism and competition. The current situation is discussed in the areas of: arrest, bail, charging and sentencing, legal counsel, and juries.

DOLESCHAL, Eugene and Klapmuts, Nora. Toward A New Criminology. *Crim Delin Lit* 5(4),607–626 1973.

DOLESCHAL, Eugene. Crime—Some Popular Beliefs. *Crim Delinq* 25(1),1–8 Ja 1979.
The popular beliefs that the crime rate is increasing, that US courts are lenient with criminals, that poor blacks commit a disproportionate number of crimes, and that crime undermines society are examined. Based upon a 1972 University of Michigan national study of juvenile delinquency, it is shown that crime is evenly distributed across all socioeconomic groups. It is further revealed from studies of financial losses suffered due to various types of crime that crimes committed by the affluent involve about eleven times the amount of money compared to crimes committed by poor minority

offenders. While most Americans believe that crime undermines the positive fabric of society, it is argued that stable levels of crime and the expression of deviancy serve to reinforce group values and stimulate needed socioeconomic change.*

DOLESCHAL, Eugene. Rate And Length Of Imprisonment. *Crim Delinq* 23(1),51–56 Ja 1977.

DOLLARD, John. *Caste And Class In A Southern Town.* New Haven CT Yale Univ Pr 1937.

DOMONKAS, Michael and Calista, F P. Bail And Civil Disorder. *J Urban L* 45,815–839 1968.

DONEGAN, Charles E and Hunter, Jerry. Current Racial Legal Developments. *Howard L J* 12(2),299 1966.

DONNERSTEIN, Edward et al. Variables In Interracial Aggression Anonymity, Expected Retaliation, And A Riot. *J Pers Soc Psychol* 22(2),236–245 1972.

Two experiments employing white subjects examined the effects of anonymity, expected retaliation, race of target, and a campus racial disturbance on delivered and anticipated aggression (electric shock). Prior to statistical treatment, the data were subjected to principal components analyses, with three aggression components being identified: general direct aggression, extremes in direct aggression, and indirect aggression. In Experiment I, it was found that less direct and more indirect forms of aggression were delivered to black than to white targets when there was opportunity for the target to retaliate. When retaliation was unlikely, the subjects delivered more direct forms of aggression to black than to white targets. Following a campus racial disturbance, there were increases in direct forms of aggression toward black targets, with such aggression now being less dependent on the opportunity for retaliation (Experiment II). In both experiments more direct aggression was anticipated from black than from white targets. The results support the conclusion that white persons have learned to fear black retaliation, and hence avoid direct forms of aggression in certain defined situations.

DOO, L W. Dispute Settlement In Chinese American Communities. *Am J Comp L* 21,627–663 Fall 1973.

DOOB, C B. Family Background And Peer Group Deviance In A Puerto Rican District. *Sociol Q* 11,523–532 Fall 1970.

DORFMAN, D D. The Cyril Burt Question: New Findings. *Sci* 2s 29 1978.

DORSEN, Norman and Emerson, Thomas I and Haber, David. *Political And Civil Rights In The United States.* Boston Little, Brown 1967.

DOUGLAS, Joseph H. The Extent And Characteristics Of Juvenile Delinquency Among Negroes In The United States. *J Negro Ed* 28(3),214–229 1959.

Douglas wants his article "to add further testimony to the observation that until now adequate data simply are not available by which to make valid comparisons between the Negro group and other groups in the nation as to either the extent or characteristics of juvenile delinquency among them." From information that is now available (for example, data on arrests, referrals to courts, and commitments to state or federal institutions), it is revealed, Douglas says, that on the overall basis Negroes manifest a highly disproportionate share of criminal and other anti–social behavior as related to their proportion in the total population and when compared to that of other minority groups Douglas expresses agreement with the view that sees delinquency as symptomatic of a wide range and variety of social disorders and feels that "until these causative aspects of the phenomenon are successfully removed, or otherwise brought under control, society doubtless will continue to manifest this and other forms of maladjustment."

DOUGLASS, Frederick. *My Bondage And My Freedom.* NY Dover 1969.

Born and brought up in slavery, Frederick Douglass (1817?–1895) achieved worldwide fame as an abolitionist lecturer, editor, and organizer. This is his most detailed autobiography, offering graphic descriptions of slavery, his violent resistance, and his escape to the North. Extensive attention is devoted to the black family under slavery.

DOVIDIO, J F and Gaertner, S L. The Subtlety Of White Racism, Arousal, And Helping Behavior. *J Pers Soc Psychol* 35(10),691–707 1977.

Two hypotheses were tested: (a) white bystanders are more likely to discriminate against black victims in situations in which failure to intervene could be attributable to factors other than the victim's race; (b) there is a causal relationship between arousal induced by witnessing an emergency and bystander responsiveness, as proposed by Piliavin, Rodin, and Piliavin. Consistent with the first hypothesis, Study 1 found that black victims were

discriminated against when the subject had the opportunity to diffuse responsibility; however, blacks and whites were helped equally when the subject was the only bystander. Study 2 failed to demonstrate a predicted interaction between the victim's race and the ambiguity of the emergency.

DOW, George Francis (ed). *Slave Ships And Slaving.* Salem MA Marine Res Society 1927.

DOWDALL, George. White Gains From Black Subordination In 1960 And 1970. *Social Prob* 22(2),162–183 1974.

DOWNIE JR, Leonard. *Justice Denied.* Baltimore Penguin Books 1972.

DRAKE, St Clair and Cayton, Horace R. *Black Metropolis: A Study Of Negro Life In A Northern City*, Rev'd Ed Orig Pub 1945. NY Harper & Row 1962.

DRAKE, St Clair. The Social And Economic States Of The Negro In The United States. *Daedalus* 94,771–814 1965.

DRAPKIN, Israel (ed) and Viano, Emilio (ed). *Victimology: A New Focus, V1.* Lexington MA Lexington 1974.

DRAPKIN, Israel. The Prison Inmate As Victim. *Victimol* 1(1),98–106 Spr 1976.

DREGER, Ralph M and Miller, Kent S. Comparative Psychological Studies Of Negroes And Whites In The United States: 1959–1965. *Psychol Bull* 70,1–58 1968.

DREW, James. Judicial Discretion And The Sentencing Process. *Howard L J* 17,859–864 1973.

DREYFUSS, Joel. Are Hispanics The 'minority For The 1980's'? *Des Moines Reg* ,9a Jl 5 1979.

DU BOIS, W E B (ed). *Some Notes On Negro Crime, Particularly In Georgia*, Orig Pub 1904. NY Octagon Books 1968.

DU BOIS, W E B (ed). *Suppression Of The African Slave Trade To The United States, 1638–1870*(orig pub 1898), NY Russell & Russell 1965.

DU BOIS, W E B (ed). *The Souls Of Black Folk*, Orig Pub 1904. Greenwich CT Fawcett Pub 1965.

DU BOIS, W E B. "Pauperism And Alcoholism" in *The Philadelphia Negro*, Orig Pub 1899, 269–286. NY Schocken 1967.

DU BOIS, W E B. "The Negro Criminal" in *The Philadelphia Negro*, Chapter 13, Orig Pub 1899. NY Schocken 1967.

DuBois traces the history of Negro crime in Philadelphia. When the enslaved Negro people arrived in the Colonies, they faced oppressive social surroundings. Any act that led to a disturbance was subject to sanctions, the most common being public whippings. From 1830 to 1850, Negroes comprised less than one–fourteenth of the population, yet they were responsible for almost one–third of serious crimes. Discrimination against the Negro was common. He was arrested on less cause, given longer sentences, frequently held without being brought to trial, and pardoned far less often than white criminals. He presents statistics on the percentage of Negroes among those arrested in Philadelphia from 1864–96, and a graph of the proportion of Negro convicts received at the Eastern Penitentiary from 1829–95. After 1880, Negroes began large scale migration to the cities, and rapid increases in their crime rate were associated with this movement. Although much Negro crime can be accounted for by ignorance and susceptibility to the temptations of city life, the bulk of serious crime should be attributed to a distinct class of habitual criminals.

DU BOIS, W E B. The Negro And Crime. *Ind Mag* ,1355–1357 My 18 1899.

DU PONT, R L and Nurco, D N. Preliminary Report On Crime And Addiction Within A Community—Wide Population Of Narcotic Addicts. *Drug Alcoh Dep* 2(2),109–121 1977.

Criminality incidence in 252 black and white male addicts identified as narcotics abusers by the Baltimore, MD., Police Department, 1952–1971, is examined for racial differences before and after first regular drug use. Findings generally support previous studies concerning the increase of criminal activity after the onset of narcotic addiction. Black addicts tend to commit more crimes and more serious crimes, than white addicts before first use of narcotics and after the onset of addiction.*

DUBIN, J A and Jeannerett, P R. *Houston: A Validity Study Of Police Officer Selection, Training And Promotion, V3.* Washington DC NCJRS 1978.

Using the chi–square statistic for analysis, the Houston Police Department employment practices are evaluated for adverse impact on minority groups including females, blacks, and Hispanics.*

DUFTY, William F and Fagan, Eleanora. *Lady Sings The Blues, By Billie Holiday*. NY Doubleday 1956.

The biography of Billie Holiday, the black blues singer, covering her problems with drugs and experience in jail.

DUMARS, T C. Indictment Under The 'Major Crimes Act'—An Exercise In Unfairness And Unconstitutionality. *Ariz L Rev* 10,691–705 1968.

Daniel Hosay and two other Apache Indians were indicted in the US District Court for the District of Arizona. They were charged with violating 18 US Code Section 1153, "aiding and abetting an assault with a dangerous and deadly weapon," as defined in Arizona statutes. Since the defendants were Apache Indians, a normally routine judicial process was changed into a jurisdictional maze.*

DUNBAUGH, Frank M. *United States Incarceration Rates By State And Race, 1979*. Annapolis MD Dunbaugh n.d.

This booklet reports the results of the author's nationwide survey of prisoners in custody during mid–1979. Statistics are listed for blacks, Native Americans, Hispanics and whites.

DUNBAUGH, Frank M. Racially Disproportionate Rates Of Incarceration In The United States. *Prison L Mon* 1(9),1–4 1979.

Reports data from 1973 showing rates of incarceration per 100,000 for the 50 states and the District of Columbia. Blacks are strongly overrepresented compared to whites, and there are indications that this disproportionality may be increasing.

DUNBAUGH, Frank and Harris, Kay. Premise For A Sensible Sentencing Debate. *Hofstra L Rev* 7(2),417–456 Wint 1979.

DUNCAN, B L. Differential Social Perception And Attribution Of Intergroup Violence: Testing The Lower Limits Of Stereotyping Of Blacks. *J Pers Soc Psychol* 34(4),590–598 1976.

DUNCAN, John Donald. *Servitude And Slavery In Colonial South Carolina, 1670–1776*. Unpub PhD Diss Emory Univ 1972.

South Carolina imported more than 100,000 black slaves, more than any other American colony. Servitude of whites and Indians also played an important role in this colony's development. Among the topics the author discusses are crime and offenses of the various bondsmen, especially escape, sex crimes, arson, poisoning and suicide.

DUNNETTE, M D and Motowidlo, S J. *Police Selection And Career Assessment*. Minneapolis Personnel Decision 1975.

The major objective of this research program was to develop new methods for evaluating persons who apply for positions in police work and for assessing the potential of present police officers being considered for promotion. In order to accomplish this, critical features of four different police jobs were determined. These jobs were general patrol officer, investigator/detective, patrol sergeant, and intermediate command. The means by which these critical features and other information such as job performance ratings were utilized to develop and validate two personnel evaluation instruments are described in detail.*

DURAN, P H. *The Chicana: A Comprehensive Bibliographic Study*. Los Angeles Univ of Calif n.d.

DURDEN-SMITH, Jo. *Who Killed George Jackson: Fantasies, Paranoia And The Revolution*. NY Knopf 1976.

DURKHEIM, Emile. "The Normal And The Pathological" in *Social Deviance*, Farrell, Ronald And Victoria Swigert (eds). Philadelphia Lippincott 1975.

DUSTER, Troy et al. "The Labeling Approach To Deviance" in *Issues In The Classification Of Children*, Hobbs, Nicholas (ed), 88–100. San Francisco CA Jossey–Bass 1975.

DUSTER, Troy. "Drugs And Drug Control" in *Crime And Justice In American Society*, Douglas, J (ed). Indianapolis Bobbs–Merrill 1971.

DUSTER, Troy. "Mental Illness And Criminal Intent" in *Changing Perspectives In Mental Illness*, Plog, S And R Edgerton (eds). NY Holt Rinehart Wins 1969.

DUSTER, Troy. "The Subordination Of Coercive Law To Coercive Markets" in *Social Meaning Of Drugs*, Blum, K; S Feinglass And A Briggs (eds). NY Basic Books 1977.

DUSTER, Troy. *The Legislation Of Morality*. NY Free Pr 1970.

DUSTER, Troy. Patterns Of Deviant Reaction: Some Theoretical Issues. *Social Psychi* 3(1),1–7 1968.

DUTTON, A and Britt, B. *Recruitment And Retention Of Females In Law Enforcement Occupations*. NY Nat Urb League 1977.

Interview techniques and affirmative action programs for women in law enforcement occupations are discussed as part of the National Urban League's Law Enforcement Minority Manpower Project for Minority Recruitment. Some of the suggested techniques for interviewing female applicants are as follows: (1) make the female applicant feel comfortable and on an equal footing with other candidates; (2) advise the woman that the agency is interested in candidates of both sexes; (3) introduce the potential employee to senior women in the organization; never ask a female candidate questions regarding marital status, marriage plans, or child care requirements unless the same questions are asked male applicants; and (5) allow the candidate to describe nontraditional work experience such as volunteer or civic work, bearing in mind that a woman may be anxious to prove herself in nontraditional functions even though her work history involved secretarial or volunteer employment. Procedures for establishing and administering an affirmative action plan involve providing an honest picture of the extent of utilization of females.*

DWORKIN, G and Block, N J. IQ: Heritability And Inequality, Part I. *Philos Pub Aff* 3(4),331–409 1974.

Part 1 of this article is organized around three questions: (1) can we reasonably ask whether I. Q. tests measure intelligence? (Sections I and II); (2) assuming we can, how good are the arguments that I. Q. tests do measure intelligence? (Sections II–VI); (3) if I. Q. tests do not measure intelligence, what do they measure? (Sections VII and VIII). Part 2 considers heritability estimates; race, research, and responsibility.

DWORKIN, G and Block, N J. IQ: Heritability And Inequality, Part II. *Philos Pub Aff* 4(1),40–99 1975.

DYKE, J V. Grand Jury—Representative Or Elite. *Hastings L J* 28(1),37–71 S 1976.

DYNES, Patrick S and Carlson, Eric W and Allen, Harry E. "Aggressive And Simple Sociopaths: Ten Years Later" in *Biology And Crime*, Jeffrey, C R (ed). Beverly Hills CA Sage 1979.

DYNES, R and Quarantelli, E. *Patterns Of Looting And Property Norms: Conflict And Consensus In Community Emergencies*. Columbus OH Ohio State Univ 1968.

DYNES, R and Quarantelli, E. "What Looting In Civil Disturbances Really Means" in *Law And Order: Modern Criminals*, Short Jr, James F (ed), 177–192. Chicago Aldine 1970.

DYNES, R and Quarantelli, E. Looting In Civil Disorders: An Index Of Social Change. *Am Behav Sci* 2,7–10 Mr–Ap 1968.

Authors view the distinct looting patterns occurring during the ghetto revolts as violent "collective bargaining," whereby the existing "property rights" in the black community which were previously accepted are not being directly challenged by a significant proportion of the black community. In short, the looting is an index of social change where previous definitions of property rights are being redefined.

EASTMAN, G and Curry, Jesse E and King, G D. *Race Tensions And The Police*. Springfield IL Chas C Thomas 1962.

EATON, Joseph W. *Measuring Delinquency: A Study Of Probation Department Referrals*. Pittsburgh Univ Pittsburgh Pr 1961.

ECHOLS, Alvin E. Deadline, Vengeance, And Tribute: A Prescription For Black Juvenile Delinquency. *Crim Delinq* 16(4),357–362 1970.

ECKERMAN, William et al. *Drug Usage And Arrest Charges: A Study Of Drug Usage And Arrest Charges Among Arrestees In Six Metropolitan Areas Of The United States*. Washington DC US Dept Justice 1971.

ECKLAND, Bruce K. Genetics And Sociology: A Reconsideration. *Am Sociol Rev* 32,193–194 1967.

EDITORIAL. Death Penalty's Comeback. *Nation* 223(19),586–588 N 9 1974.

EDMUNDSON, Walter F et al. Patterns Of Drug Abuse Epidemiology In Prisoners. *Indus Med Surg* 41(1),15–19 1972.

A health survey of two thirds (470) of the population (92% male) of a county jail revealed that a larger proportion of the whites (58%) than the Negroes (43%) were regular users of illicit drugs.

EDWARDS, Harry T. A New Role For The Black Law Graduate—A Reality Or An Illusion. *Mich L Rev* 69,1407–1442 Ag 1971.

Edwards goes beyond a discussion of the shortage of black lawyers to look at its societal impact. He also discusses the steps which must be taken in order to increase the number of black lawyers and change their position within the legal profession so that they may become a significant and influential force in the fight for social justice. His main point is that black lawyers, at the present time, tend to be nudged into "neighborhood practices" or "legal service" programs to provide legal services to the poor. A survey conducted at the University of Michigan Law school in 1971 indicated that 85% of the black students felt they did not have equal opportunity with whites in securing placement services. These unfavorable responses were corroborated by the fact that no graduating blacks were being placed into corporate practice, judicial clerkships, etc., even though the University of Michigan Placement Service is overwhelmingly oriented toward this area of career opportunity.

EDWARDS, Harry T. Preferential Remedies And Affirmative Action In Employment In The Wake Of *Bakke*. *Wash U L Q* 1979(1),113–136 Wint 1979.

EGAN, Frank J and Lee, Yuk. The Geography Of Urban Crime: The Spatial Pattern Of Serious Crime In The City Of Renuer. *Proc Assoc Am Geog* 4,59–64 1972.

EGERTON, John. Minority Police: How Many Are There? Race Rel Rep ,19–21 N 1974.

EHRLICHMAN, John. Mexican Aliens Aren't A Problem: They're A Solution. *Esquire* 92(8),54–64 Ag 1979.

EISENBERG, Howard. Team Defense: The Holistic Approach: An Interview With Millard Farmer. *NLADA Brief* 36,16–18,27–29 Mr 1979.
Millard Farmer is the nation's most successful specialist in defending capital defendants at trial. In this interview he describes his philosophy and methods of operation.

EISNER, V. Effect Of Parents In The Home On Juvenile Delinquency. *Public Health Rep* 81(10),905–910 1966.

ELION, Victor H and Megargee, Edwin I. Racial Identity, Length Of Incarceration And Parole Decision Making. *J Res Crim Del* 16(2),232–245 1979.
Focusing on the amount of time served and the frequency of parole in a sample of 958 youthful offenders from a cohort of 1,345 consecutive admissions to a federal correctional institution, the authors investigated racial differences in black–white sentence patterns at the parole stage. No significant differences were found in the actual amount of time served, but a significantly higher number of whites than blacks were granted parole. Discriminant function analysis did not show race to be significantly associated with decision to grant parole; instead, the authors indentified the primary factor as entry sentence.

ELION, Victor H and Megargee, Edwin I. Validity Of The MMPI Pd Scale Among Black Males. *J Consult Clin Psyc* 43(2),166–172 1975.
The validity of the MMPI Psychopathic Deviate (Pd) and Pd + .4K scales to discriminate levels of social deviance among young black men was investigated. Black inmates at a federal correctional institution had significantly higher scores on both scales than culturally deprived black university students. Recidivists had significantly higher scores than first offenders. The two scales validly differentiate levels of social deviance, but the norms for the scales appear to show racial bias.

ELION, Victor H. The Validity Of The MMPI As A Discriminator Of Social Deviance Among Black Males. *FCI Res Rep* 6(3),1–15 1974.
Because of the large percentage of black clients served by the criminal justice system and the fact that the Minnesota Multiphasic Personality Inventory (MMPI) appears to be the most widely used personality assessment device in penal and correctional institutions, research has been conducted to determine how valid the MMPI is for assessing social deviancy among blacks. The validity of the MMPI Pd and Pd + AK scales in detecting antisocial behavior among young black men is demonstrated to equal or exceed their validity among whites as reported in the literature. The study also shows that these scales can discriminate black criminals from black noncriminals: the magnitude and the statistical significance of the mean differences were similar to those reported in studies contrasting white criminals and noncriminals. The study shows that both scales can differentiate recidivists from nonrecidivists within a black prison sample, and the differentiation is better for blacks than for whites. Scale 4 can discriminate among black university students; no similar study among white students is known.

ELKINS, Stanley M. *Slavery: A Problem In American Institutional & Intellectual Life*. Chicago Univ Chicago Pr 1959.
Elkins compares chattel slavery in the American South with that in the West Indies and Brazil, and concludes that the American institution was very different in some important respects. He examines the character of the American Negro slave and questions the white stereotype of the Southern slave as being childlike, irresponsible, incapable of thought or foresight,

lazy, ignorant, and dependent. Drawing on the literature on Nazi concentration camps to explore the psychological consequences of being totally powerless for a long period of time, he finds many striking parallels to slavery. In the third part he discusses abolitionists as moralistic, fanatical, uncompromising and vituperative.

ELLI, Frank. *The Riot*. NY Coward McCann 1966.
An account of a prison riot.

ELLIOT, D S. Reconciling Race And Class Differences In Self–Reported And Official Estimates Of Delinquency. *Am Sociol Rev* 45(1),95–110 F 1980.
Unlike self–report data, official arrest data have shown differences in delinquent behavior by race and class. Self–reporting has been criticized for being unreliable. The instrument used in the present study addressed common criticisms of self–report measures by representing the full range of delinquent acts, providing better discrimination at the high end of the frequency continuum, providing a moderate recall period, capturing seasonal variations, and permitting direct comparison with other self–report and official measures. The study used a national probability sample of 1,726 youths aged 11 to 17. Results showed (1) significant race differences for total delinquency and for crimes against property, (2) blacks reported significantly higher frequencies than whites on both measures, (3) class differentials appeared for total delinquency and for predatory crimes against the person and (4) youth from lower socioeconomic backgrounds had higher scores than did working–class or middle–class groups. Results suggest a relatively high involvement of lower class black youth in serious offenses against persons. Also, the findings imply that criticism of many self–report measures is well founded.*

ELLIOT, Jeffrey M. Legacy Of Violence: The Opera House Lynching. *Negro Hist Bull* 37,303 O–N 1974.
The author presents a short description of a lynching in a Kentucky opera house and an NAACP resolution on lynching.

ELLIOT, Mabel A. Delinquent Behavior Of Peoples. *Phylon* 10,242–251 1949.

ELY JR, James W. Negro Demonstrations And The Law: Danville As A Test Case. *Vand L Rev* 27(5),927–968 1974.
Racial disturbances in Danville, Virginia in the 1960's have raised a series of important legal questions such as how the law, both state and federal, responded to the outbreak of racial demonstrations, what role the courts and the Kennedy administration played in handling the Negro protest movement, what the Danville imbroglio suggested about the feasibility of the resort to direct action tactics. It is concluded that the Danville experience suggests the limitations of mass demonstrations as a tactic to encourage social change and shows the ease with which the South could maintain racial segregation without federal intervention.

EMERSON, Robert M. *Judging Delinquents: Context And Process In The Juvenile Court*. Chicago IL Aldine 1969.

EMERSON, Thomas I and Haber, David and Dorsen, Norman. *Political And Civil Rights In The United States*. Boston Little, Brown 1967.

EMPEY LA MAR, T and Erickson, Maynard L. Court Records, Undetected Delinquency And Decision–Making. *J Crim L Crimin & Pol Sci* 54,456–469 My–Je 1963.

ENDLEMAN, S. "The Etiology Of The Race Riot" in *Violence In The Street*, Endelman, S (ed), 357–361. Chicago Quadrangle Books 1968.

ENGERMAN, Stanley L and Fogel, Robert William. Philanthropy Of Bargain Prices: Notes On The Economics Of Gradual Emancipation. *J Leg Stud* 3(2),377–402 Je 1974.
These historians argue that the primary economic burden of gradual emancipation of the slaves in eight northeastern states during the late 18th and early 19th century was purposefully shifted to the slaves themselves; legislation served to prevent the burden from falling on the slaveowners or the general taxpayers. In their econometric approach, they neglect to mention how imprisonment and other mechanisms of social control were developed to replace chattel slavery as a means of containing emancipated slaves.

ENGLAND, Ralph W and Taft, Donald R. *Criminology*. NY Macmillan 1964.

ENLOE, Cynthia. Police And Military In The Resolution Of Ethnic Conflict. *Ann Am Poli* 433,137–149 S 1977.

ENOCH and **JOSEPH.** *Narrative Of The Barbarous Treatment Of Two Unfortunate Females, Natives Of Concordia LA By Joseph & Enoch, Runaway Slaves.* NY Authors 1842.

ENRIQUES, Evangelina and Mirandé, Alfredo. *La Chicana: The Mexican American Woman.* Chicago Univ Chicago Pr 1979.

EPPS, Edgar G. Socioeconomic Status, Race, Level Of Aspiration And Juvenile Delinquency: A Limited Empirical Test Of Merton's Concept Of Deviation. *Phylon* 28(1),16—27 Spr 1967.

EPSTEIN, Charlotte. *Intergroup Relations For Police Officers.* Baltimore Williams & Wilkins 1962.

EPSTEIN, Edward Jay. Methadone: The Forlorn Hope. *Pub Interest* 36,3—24 Sum 1974.

ERICKSON, Maynard L and Empey La Mar, T. Court Records, Undetected Delinquency And Decision—Making. *J Crim L Crimin & Pol Sci* 54,456—469 My—Je 1963.

ERICKSON, Maynard L and Gibbs, Jack P and Jensen, Gary F. Perceived Risk Of Punishment And Self—Reported Delinquency. *Soc Forces* 57,57—78 1978.

To examine the relationship between perceived risk of punishment and self—reported delinquency, the authors sampled students in six Arizona high schools. Personal risk was found to be inversely related to delinquency even when social condemnation of delinquent offenses, attachment to conventional persons, and several status characteristics of the students were taken into account.

ERIKSON, Eric H. A Memorandum On Identity And Negro Youth. *J Soc Issues* 20,29—42 1964.

ERIKSON, Kai T. *Wayward Puritans: A Study In The Sociology Of Deviance.* NY Wiley 1966.

ERLANGER, Howard S. *Violence By Blacks And low—Income Whites: Some New Evidence On The Subculture Of Violence Thesis.* Madison Univ Wisconsin Pr 1974.

ERLANGER, Howard S. Estrangement, Machismo And Gang Violence. *Social Sci Q* 60(2),235—248 S 1979.

Factors considered in this study of Chicano "barrios" in East Los Angeles include the importance of machismo, political conditions of the community, and the relationship of estrangement to political action and violent behavior. Interpretations are based on more than 35 interviews, two—thirds with Chicano males aged 15 to 30 who came from many different gangs. Remaining respondents included police and probation officers and program directors. The only time when there was a viable opportunity to express courage and dignity outside the gang setting was during the movement period of late 1967 through early 1972. During this time, identity with the broader community became primary and a sense of power to influence the institutions affecting the community emerged. Gang—related violence decreased markedly. As a sense of estrangement from a community identity returned, gang violence increased. These interpretations suggest that violence may not flow from values that directly encourage it, but may instead occur when structural circumstances prevent achievement of related values; theories of deviance should be linked to theories of power and its distribution.

ERLANGER, Howard S. The Empirical Status Of The Subculture Of Violence Thesis. *Social Prob* 22(2),280—291 1974.

ESSIEN- UDOM, E U. *Black Nationalism: A Search For Identity In America.* Chicago Univ Chicago Pr 1962.

ETHERIDGE, D. Law Enforcement On Indian Reservations. *Pol Chief* 44(4),74—77 Ap 1977.

EVANS, P. "Rape, Race, And Research" in *Blacks And Criminal Justice,* Owens, Charles E And Jimmy Bell (eds). Lexington MA Heath 1977.

The typical rapist, it was found, was a young "ordinary guy," with one exception of being more prone to violence. More than half of the assaults were premeditated, and rapists often acted in groups. Rapists arrested fell within the low socioeconomic level; blacks were disproportionately represented. Records of black—white rape have been tainted by racial prejudice and economic and cultural biases, which makes it difficult to shed light on the subject of interracial rape. Attempts to explain black—on—white rape through ghetto male sexuality describe the great masculine prestige attached to intercourse and the number of females one attracts. Some explanations locate the cause in the new black awareness and the desire of blacks to attack the source of their frustration—whites; other causes are seen in the increased social interaction of white women with black men.

Available evidence does indicate, however, that interracial rape acts are exceptionally few in number. Reported rape is mostly a intraracial phenomenon, and can be explained by elements of sexual and aggressive urges. There is a need to conduct more extensive research on the black rapist.*

EVERETT, Michael and Levy Jerrold E and Kunitz, Stephen J. Navajo Criminal Homicide. *Sw J Anthrop* 25(2),124—152 1969.

Theories of homicide among the Navajo and its relation to alcohol consumption and cultural factors are examined. Common theories on the Navajo have assumed that their homicide rate would be proportionally higher than that for the rest of the population because of increased alcohol use, the instability of Navajo marriage, and the stresses placed on males as they abandon traditional roles and enter a wage economy. From the files of the Navajo Olice in Window Rock, Ariz., 43 cases of criminal homicide committed between 1956 and 1965 were extracted for study, which involved Navajos on or near the reservation. These cases were compared with a study of homicide in Philadelphia between 1948 and 1952. Navajo homicide rates were stable and comparable with those of the general population. No relationship was discovered between homicide and alcohol. These findings contrasted with those of the Philadelphia project in which use of alcohol was positively associated with violence. The Navajo offender was typically a married male between 35 and 39 years old who had killed his wife as as result of sexual jealousy or a domestic quarrel. A very high proportion committed suicide after the act of homicide.*

EVERTS, P and Schwirian, K. Metropolitan Crime Rates And Relative Deprivation. *Criminologica* 5,43—52 1968.

EWING, J A and Rouse, B A and Pellizzari, E D. Alcoholic Sensitivity And Ethnic Background. *Am J Psychiatry* 131(2),206—210 1974.

FABRICATORE, Joseph and Azen, Stanley P and Snibbe, H M. Personality Patterns Of White, Black, And Mexican American Patrolmen As Measured By The Sixteen Personality Factor Questionaire. *Am J Comm Psy* 3(3),221—227 1975.

The Sixteen Personality Factor Questionaire was administered to 491 white, black, and Chicano patrolmen of the Los Angeles Sheriff's Department to obtain a normative police profile. Multi—variate analysis revealed that the average patrolman appeared brighter, more reserved, dominant and tough—minded than the overage male. Comparisons were made for 29 black, 33 Mexican-American and 399 white officers. Mexican American officers emerged as more conservative and relaxed than whites, while black officers appeared more experimental, analytical and group—oriented. A comparison with an independent police sample revealed common traits of self—assurance and conservatism. Results were compared with a social worker's profile and discussed in relation to the police officer's actual job activities and community needs.

FAGAN, Eleanora and Dufty, William F. *Lady Sings The Blues, By Billie Holiday.* NY Doubleday 1956.

The biography of Billie Holiday, the black blues singer, covering her problems with drugs and experience in jail.

FAGAN, T J and Lira, F T. Profile Of Mood States: Racial Differences In A Delinquent Population. *Psychol Rep* 43(2),348—350 1978.

FAGEN, R and Brody, R and O' Leary, T. *Cubans In Exile: Disaffection And The Revolution.* Stanford CA Stanford Univ Pr 1968.

FAHEY, R P. Native American Justice——the Courts Of The Navajo Nation. *Judicature* 59(1),10—17 Je—Jl 1975.

FAHEY, Richard P and Harding, Richard. Killings By Chicago Police, 1969—70: An Empirical Study. *S Cal L Rev* 46(2),284—315 Mr 1973.

FAISON, Adrienne and Jenkins, Betty. *An Analysis Of 248 Persons Killed By New York City Policemen.* NY Metrop App Res Cen 1974.

FAITH, Karlene (ed). *Soledad Prison: University Of The Poor.* Palo Alto CA Sci & Behav Bks 1975.

Poetry and other writings by prisoners in California's maximum—security Soledad prison.

FALKNER, Roland P. Crime And The Census. *Ann Am Poli* 9,42—69 Ja 1897.

Examining census figures from 1850—1890, it is determined that if the amount of crime means the ratio between the offenses committed in a given year and the population at that time, a correct idea of crime is not presented. By reporting the number of prisoners at a particular time, rather than the number of individuals committed during a year, census figures do not take account of differences in sentence length. This presents a distorted picture: (1) it furnishes no basis for a calculation of the increase of crime (2) in depicting the geographical distribution of crime, it favors one locality at the expense of another; (3) it exaggerates the number of the male sex in the aggregate of crime; (4) it assigns to the Negro, a larger, and to the foreign—born white a smaller, share in the total of crime than belongs to each; (5) it distorts the picture of the relative frequency of different classes of crimes.

FANON, Frantz. *The Wretched Of The Earth.* NY Grove Pr 1963.

Fanon, a black psychiatrist writing in Algeria, presents a challenging inquiry into the dehumanizing nature of colonial oppression, and draws up an inventory of the possibilities of eventual freedom for the world's subject peoples. Fanon conducts for the first time since Engels and Sorel, an examination of the role of violence as the most efficient mid—wife of historical change. He demonstrates how violence in the colonized countries of today's cold—war world reflects the violent relations between capitalism and socialism, and shows how violence affords a colonized people its first sense of community outlining the complex play of polarized "Manichean" relations which both unite and divide European colonists and native populations, he shows the limits of spontaneous individual action, and points out the necessity and dangers of organized action. He traces, in short, the historical dialectic that leads from slavery to statehood—from a period of chauvinism, racism, tribalism, criminality and religious rivalries, through the armed struggle for liberation, to full nationhood.

FARBER, Martin G and Kelly, Rita Mae. Identifying Responsive Inner—City Policemen. *J Appl Psyc* 59(3),259–263 1974.

This study sought to develop an operational definition of "responsiveness" and is based on a sample of subjects classified as extreme on the basis of their performance on four "Fear of Citizens Scales." The subjects were drawn from the District of Columbia Metropolitan Police Department. Twelve of the original 509 subjects were classified, either in the positive (responsiveness) or negative (non—responsiveness) group. The two most important variables correlated with responsiveness were race and place of residence. While race seems quite significant in determining the extent to which policemen develop negative perceptions of inner—city residents, it does not seem as strongly associated with those who possess a positive view. Only 17% of the most negative officers lived in the city, whereas 53% of the most positive ones were city residents. They state that the effect of race on the place of residence can be seen by the fact that of the 17 most positive respondents living in Washington, D. C., 13 (77%) were black; of the 15 most positive respondents living outside the city, 14 (93%) were white.

FARLEY, Frank H and Sewell, Trevor. Attribution And Achievement Motivation Differences Between Delinquent And Non—Delinquent Black Adolescents. *Adoles* 10(34),391–397 Fall 1975.

To examine, with black subjects, the assumption that delinquents are less achievement motivated than nondelinquents, a 2 x 2 factorial design with two dependent measures (locus of control and achievement motivation) was used with delinquents versus nondelinquents and male versus females. Subjects were black fulltime sophomore students at an inner—city high school in a midwestern city. Results fail to support the hypothesis that delinquents would be more external in perceived locus of control than nondelinquents, at least for black adolescents. This lack of attribution difference between the delinquent and nondelinquent subjects is felt to be of great significance in the discussion of black adolescents' personality and world view, and of particular interest in the analysis of delinquency. it is suggested that feelings of helplessness against the system and attendant frustration are not involved in black juvenile delinquency.

FARLEY, Frank H and Sewell, Trevor. Test Of An Arousal Theory Of Delinquency—Stimulation—Seeking In Delinquent And Nondelinquent Black Adolescents. *Crim Just B* 3(4),315–320 1976.

FARLEY, Reynolds. *Growth Of The Black Population: A Study Of Demographic Trends.* Chicago Markham Pub 1970.

FARLEY, Reynolds. The Urbanization Of Negroes In The United States. *J Soc Hist* 1,241–258 Spr 1968.

FARRELL, Ronald A and Swigert, Victoria Lynn. *Murder, Inequality, And The Law.* Lexington MA Heath 1976.

Examines the differential treatment of minorities in murder cases. Covers all aspects of the mechanics of law, including the assignment of attorneys, award of bail, selection of trial format, jury selection, etc.

FARRELL, Ronald A and Swigert, Victoria Lynn. Prior Offense As A Self—Fulfilling Prophecy. *Law & Soc Rev* 12(3),437–454 Spr 1978.

Explorations of differential justice suggest that apparent relationships between class, race, and legal treatment may be explained by the more extensive conviction histories found among lower class and minority populations. But these findings have emerged without adequate exploration of the antecedents of a defendant's criminal record. This study views the conviction awarded a defendant as the first stage in the construction of a prior offense record. Path analytic techniques are applied to data drawn from a sample of persons arrested for murder in order to examine the nature of relationships among the demographic characteristics of defendants, their prior offense records, access to legal resources, and ultmate dispositions. Patterns evident from the analysis suggest that the operation of the criminal record in the legal system constitutes a continual cycle in the confirmation of criminality. Prior record, itself partly a product of discretionary treatment, becomes a salient factor in the accumulation of additional convictions not only through its direct effect but also through its influence on access to private counsel and bail.*

FARRIS, Buford and Brymer, Richard. A Five—Year Encounter With A Mexican—American Conflict Gang: Its Implications For Delinquency Theory. *Pro Sw Soc Assoc* 15,49–55 1965.

FATTIG, W Donald. An XYY Survey In A Negro Prison Population. *J Hered* 61,10 1970.

This study of 100 black male prisoners over six feet tall failed to discover any XYY individuals.

FEAGIN, Joe R. *Subordinating The Poor.* Englewood Cliffs NJ Prentice—Hall 1975.

FEAGIN, Joe R and Harlan, Alan. *Ghetto Revolts: The Politics Of Violence In American Cities.* NY Macmillan 1973.

FEAGIN, Joe R. Home—Defense And The Police: Black And White Perspectives. *Am Behav Sci* 13,791–814 1970.

FEAGIN, Joe R. Social Sources Of Support For Violence And Non—Violence In A Negro Ghetto. *Social Prob* 15,432–441 1968.

FEAGIN, Joe R. White Separatists And Black Separatist: A Comparative Analysis. *Social Prob* 19,162–166 Fall 1971.

FEINMAN, C. *Women In The Criminal Justice System.* NY Praeger 1980.

The author examines the "Madonna/Whore" stereotype which has governed the history of women in the criminal justice system. She also argues that the employment gains women have achieved within the criminal justice system have been exaggerated, noting that, as of 1978, women still accounted for only 10% of all correction officers, 3% of law enforcment officers, 9% of lawyers, 4% of judges, and about 1% of the administrators in these fields.

FELDSTEIN, Stanley. *Once A Slave: The Slaves' View Of Slavery.* NY Morrow 1971.

FEMALE OFFENDERS PROGRAM OF WESTERN PENNSYLVANIA, Inc. *Program For Women Offenders—How To Start, Fund, Maintain.* Pittsburgh Fem Off Prog W Pa 1979.

The typical woman offender is described as black, approximately 26 years old, unskilled, undereducated, unmotivated, lonely, subject to excessive drug or alcohol abuse, and having a low income. Her most frequent prison ofense is disorderly conduct; her second most frequent, prostitution. Arrest histories most often reveal a combination of disorderly conduct, drunkenness, vagrancy, larceny, drug abuse, prostitution, and occasionally, forgery or burglary. Crimes females most often commit, not necessarily resulting in imprisonment, include fraudulent use of credit cards, retail theft and bad checks, drug— and alcohol—related crimes, prostitution, and homicide (usually involving an abusive spouse or paramour). Women offenders show strong dependency needs and are often actual or potential child abusers. This handbook tells how to begin and fund a program for women offenders; select an office, staff, and board of directors; work with women offenders in intake, job placement, and prerelease counseling, and select volunteers. Appendices describe a woman offender's project and timetable, sample budget, program forms, including an employment training questionnaire, volunteer programs, and job development programs.*

FERDINAND, Theodore W and Luchterhand, Elmer G. Inner—City Youth, The Police, The Juvenile Court And Justice. *Social Prob* 17,510–527 1970.

FERDINAND, Theodore. The Criminal Patterns Of Boston Since 1849. *Am J Soc* 73,84–99 Jl 1967.

FERGUSON, Francis N. Navajo Drinking: Some Tentative Hypotheses. *Human Org* 27,159–167 1968.

FERGUSON, R F. Policemen: Agents Of Change—A Crime Prevention Report. *Crim Prev Rev* 2(3),1–13 1975.

FERGUSON, William R and Baab, George W. Texas Sentencing Practices: A Statistical Study. *Tex L Rev* 14(3),471–503 1967.

FERRACUTI, Franco. "European Migration And Crime" in *Crime And Culture: Essays In Honor Of Thorsten Sellin*, Wolfgang, Marvin E (ed), 189–220. NY Wiley 1968.

FERRACUTI, Franco and Dinitz, Simon and De Brenes, E Acosta. *Delinquents And Nondelinquents In The Puerto Rican Slum Culture*. Columbus Ohio St Univ Pr 1975.

FERRACUTI, Franco and Wolfgang, Marvin E. *The Subculture Of Violence: Towards An Integrated Theory In Criminology*. London Tavistock 1967.

Drawing upon information gathered from psychological and sociological studies of violence, the authors posit a theory which holds that there exists a subculture of violence in large urban communities. The overt expression of violence, they contend, is part of a normative subcultural group's ethos. The development of favorable attitudes toward, and use of violence in this subculture involve learned behavior and a process of differential learning, association, or identification. Because the use of violence in such a subculture is not necessarily viewed as illicit conduct, the users do not have to deal with feelings of guilt about their aggression. Widely considered as a pioneering attempt to develop an interdisciplinary approach in criminology, this book identifies inner–city Negroes as the most violent group in American society; however the authors reject biological or genetic explanations in favor of environmental factors.

FERRERS, Gina Lombroso. *Criminal Man According To The Classifications Of Cesare Lombroso.* NY Putnam 1911.

FEY, H E and Mc Nickle, D. *Indians And Other Americans*. NY Harper 1959.

FIELD, H S and Holley, W H. Equal Employment Opportunity And Its Implications For Personnel Practices. *Labor Law J* 27(5),278–286 My 1976.

FIGLIO, Robert M and Sellin, Thorsten and Wolfgang, Marvin E. *Delinquency In A Birth Cohort.* Chicago Univ Chicago Pr 1972.

In this study of a cohort of all males born in 1945 who resided in the City of Philadelphia at least from their tenth until their eighteenth birthday (n = 9,945), 50 percent of non–whites had a recorded police contact between the ages of seven and eighteen while only 29 percent of whites had such contact. Race was found to be strongly related to delinquency regardless of socioeconomic status. Indeed, no other variable emerged quite so clearly as did race as a determinant of contrast. This holds true for nearly every offense, but the racial difference was most pronounced for serious crime. IQ was found to differentiate between races, between social classes and between delinquents and nondelinquents with each race and class. Lower SES and nonwhite delinquents were more likely to use weapons in commissin of crime, though gun use was relatively infrequent. Nonwhites were more likely to be repeat offenders, and of repeaters, nonwhites were much more likely to become chronic offenders.

FIMAN, Byron G. *Special Report On Inequities In Mental Health Service Delivery.* Rockville MD NIMH 1975.

FINE, M and Davis, E E. The Effects Of The Findings Of The US National Advisory Commission On Civil Disorders: An Experimental Study Of Attitude Change. *Human Rel* 28(3),209–227 1975.

FINESTONE, Harold. Cats, Kicks, And Color. *Social Prob* 5,3–13 Jl 1957.

The author utilizes Herbert Blumer's concept of expressive social movements and Johan Huizinga's description of the play element in culture in this analysis of black adolescent and young adult heroin addicts as a social type. Being a "cat," he writes, is "an expression of one possible type of adaptation to...blocking and frustration (of opportunities to achieve or to identify with status positions in the larger society), in which a segment of the population turns in upon itself and attempts to develop within itself criteria for the achievement of social status and the rudiments of a satisfactory social life." Adopting Huizinga's model of play, it is argued that the generic characteristics of the social type of the cat are those of play. Thus, the activities of the cat are voluntary in that he is free to give his allegiance to new forms of activity; they are a form of escape; and they are limited and esoteric in character, giving the cat the feeling of belonging to an elite.

FINK, Arthur E. *Causes Of Crime: Biological Theories In The United States, 1800–1915.* Philadelphia Univ of Penn Pr 1938.

Well–documented historical survey of 19th– and early 20th–century biological theories to explain the "causes" of crime.

FINK, Joseph and Sealy, Lloyd G. *The Community And The Police: Conflict Or Cooperation.* Somerset Wiley 1974.

FINKELSTEIN, Michael. Application Of Statistical Decision Theory To The Jury Discrimination Cases. *Harv L Rev* 80,338–376 1966.

FINLEY, Moses I. *Ancient Slavery And Modern Ideology.* London Chatto & Windus 1980.

FINSTON, Charles and Ragen, Joseph. *Inside The World's Toughest Prison.* Springfield IL Chas C Thomas 1962.

FIRESTONE, Ross (ed). *Getting Busted: Personal Experiences Of Arrest, Trial And Prison.* NY Douglas Book Corp 1970.

Anthology of accounts by persons who describe their own arrest, trial and imprisonment. Minorities included are Malcolm X, Billie Holiday, Eldridge Cleaver, H. Rap Brown, Dick Gregory, Piero Heliczer, Piri Thomas, and Etheridge Knight.

FISCHER, B. Seniority Is Healthy. *Labor Law J* 27(8),497–503 Ag 1976.

FISCHER, J and Miller, H. The Effect Of Client Race And Social Class On Clinical Judgements. *Clin S Work J* 1(2),100–109 1973.

FISCHMAN, A M and Mc Cahill, T W and Meyer, L C. *Aftermath Of Rape.* Lexington MA Heath 1979.

This book is based on the Philadelphia Sexual Assault Survey of 1,401 women of all ages who reported a rape or sexual assault to Philadelphia authorities between April 1, 1973, and June 30, 1974. Attempted and statutory rape cases were included in this study designed for rape victims and their counselors, includng social workers, rape crisis center staff, and psychiatrists. Female social workers conducted initial and followup interviews with 790 women, and psychiatrists conducted interviews with 331 women or 41.9% of the sample. Other data were drawn from police files, eyewitness accounts of 25 rape cases, and a comparison of the study's findings with those of national studies and other research in the area of sexual assault. Among the findings were that age, marriage, employment, victim history, and kind of rape affected postrape adjustment; that police support was influenced by the presence of a policewoman, victim–offender relationship, victim history and appearance, and race; and that case outcome was related to victim history, race of judge and victim, kind of trial and rape, and type of reporting.*

FISH, P G. Evaluating The Black Judicial Applicant. *Judicature* 62(10),495–501 1979.

Focusing on the Carter Administration's new circuit judge nominating commission, this study argues that blacks can only achieve a fair share of judgeships if screening obstacles that affect blacks more than whites are overcome. Detailed recommendations for bringing this about are advanced.

FISHEL JR, Leslie and Quarles, Benjamin. *The Negro American: A Documentary History.* Glenview IL Scott Foresman 1967.

FISHER, Gary. The Performance Of Male Prisonsers On The Marlowe–Crowne Social Desirability Scale: II, Differences As A Function Of Race And Crime. *J Clin Psyc* 23(4),473–475 1967.

FISHER, Paul L (ed) and Lowenstein, Ralph L (ed). *Race And The News Media.* NY Praeger 1967.

Critical assessments of the performance of the news media in covering race riots, sit–ins, and conventional street crime, written by professional journalists.

FISHMAN, J R. Poverty, Race And Violence. *Am J Psychother* 23(4),599–607 1969.

FISHMAN, Joshua A and Hoffman, Gerard. Life In The Neighborhood: A Factor Analytic Study Of Puerto Rican Males In The New York City Area. *Int J Comp Soc* 12,85–100 1971.

FITZPATRICK, Joseph J. "Cultural Differences, Not Criminal Offenses" in *Politics And Crime*, Sylvester Jr, Sawyer F And Edward Sagarin (eds), 119–126. NY Praeger 1974.

The problems involved in a cultural definition of criminal behavior and its implications are explored. The problems of the legitimization of criminal behavior, faced by specific segments of the population, are focused upon. Courts are faced with inflexibility in the enforcement of the laws, especially when directed towards those whose cultural background does not identify criminal behavior as such. Future adjustments that can alleviate the problem are the use of an ombudsman or mediator, a growing awareness within the court, and alternatives to the inflexible court system.

FITZPATRICK, Joseph P. *Puerto Rican Americans: The Meaning Of Migration To The Mainland.* Englewood Cliffs NJ Prentice–Hall 1971.

FITZPATRICK, Joseph. "The Puerto Rican Family" in *Ethnic Families In America*, Mindel, C And R Habenstein (eds). NY Elsevier 1976.

FLANAGAN, Timothy J. Dealing With Long–Term Confinement: Adaptive Strategies And Perspectives Among Long–Term Prisoners. Philadelphia A S C 1979.

FLANIGAN, Daniel J. Criminal Procedure In Slave Trials In The Antebellum South. *J Southern Hist* 40,537–564 1974.

FLICKINGER, S J. The American Indian. *Fed B J* 10,212–216 Wint 1960.

FLOCH, Maurice and Hartung, Frank E. A Social–Psychological Analysis Of Prison Riots: An Hypothesis. *J Crim L Crimin & Pol Sci* 47(1),51–57 My–Je 1956.

FOGEL, Robert William and Engerman, Stanley L. Philanthropy Of Bargain Prices: Notes On The Economics Of Gradual Emancipation. *J Leg Stud* 3(2),377–402 Je 1974.

These historians argue that the primary economic burden of gradual emancipation of the slaves in eight northeastern states during the late 18th and early 19th century was purposefully shifted to the slaves themselves; legislation served to prevent the burden from falling on the slaveowners or the general taxpayers. In their econometric approach, they neglect to mention how imprisonment and other mechanisms of social control were developed to replace chattel slavery as a means of containing emancipated slaves.

FOGELSON, Robert and Hill, Robert. *A Study Of Arrest Patterns In The 1960's Riots.* NY Bur App Soc Res 1969.

FOGELSON, Robert and Hill, Robert. "Who Riots: A Study Of Participation In The 1967 Riots" in *Riot Commission, Supplemental Studies*, 217–248. Washington DC USGPO 1968.

FOGELSON, Robert. From Resentment To Confrontation: The Police, The Negroes, And The Outbreak Of The Nineteen–Sixties Riots. *Poli Sci Q* 83,217–247 Je 1968.

Fogelson presents a rounded discussion of the major sources of Negro hostility towards the police: brutality; harassment; inadequate law enforcement in ghetto areas; ineffective police complaint procedures, as well as presenting the police perspective to these issues. The benefits and liabilities of some possible solutions to these problems are also discussed.

FOGELSON, Robert. Violence And Grievances: Reflections On The 1960's Riots. *J Soc Issues* 26(1),141–164 1970.

FOLEY, L A. Personality And Situational Influences On Changes In Prejudice: A Replication Of Cook's Railroad Game In A Prison Setting. *J Pers Soc Psychol* 34(5),846–856 1976.

FOLEY, Linda and Rasch, Christine E. "The Effect Of Race On Sentence" in *Theory And Research In Criminal Justice*, Conley, J A (ed). Cincinnati Anderson 1979.

FONER, Philip (ed). *The Black Panthers Speak.* Philadelphia Lippincott 1970.

FONG, Melanie and Johnson, Larry D. The Eugenics Movement: Some Insight Into The Institutionalization Of Racism. *Issues Crim* 9(2),89–115 Fall 1974.

FOOTE, Caleb. A Study Of The Administration Of Bail In New York City. *Univ Penn L Rev* 106,685–730 1958.

FORBES, Gordon B and Mitchell, Shirley. Attribution Of Blame, Anger, & Aggression In [Poor] Female Negro Adults. *J Soc Psychol* 83,73–78 1971.

Attribution of blame, feelings of anger, and direction of anger in response to interracial frustration were investigated in 31 adult female Negroes. It was found that Negroes attributed more blame to the frustrators when a white frustrated a Negro than when a Negro frustrated a white. Feelings of anger and direction of anger were not related to race of frustrator.

FORD, Nick and Hill, Mozell C. Crime And Punishment—1938. *Opport* 16(9),270–272 1938.

FORD, Robert et al. Police, Students, And Racial Hostilities. *J Polic Sci Adm* 3(1),9–14 1975.

FORSLUND, Morris A. *Race And Crime.* Unpub PhD Diss Yale Univ 1967.

FORSLUND, Morris A. A Comparison Of Negro And White Crime Rates. *J Crim L Crimin & Pol Sci* 61,214–217 Je 1970.

According to Forslund, what is lacking in the literature that focuses on the relationship between race and crime in the US is "a series of rates on the same population ranging from arrest rates to rates of institutionalization that would make it possible to ascertain the influence of the type of rate computed on the extent to which the recorded Negro crime rate exceeds the white crime rate." Utilizing data on rates of arrest, offense, conviction, and institutionalization obtained from Stamford, Conn. for the period 1959 through 1961, Forslund has attempted to fill this gap in the literature. His findings indicate that regardless of the type of rate considered, Negro rates were substantially higher than those for whites. In all instances, Negro female rates were several times higher than those of white females and, with exceptions of institutional sentence and actual institutionalization rates, were only slightly lower than white male rates. The Negro female rate for institutional sentences was found to be substantially higher than the white male rate, and the Negro female rate for actual institutionalizations was found to be substantially lower than that for white males.

FORSLUND, Morris A. Age, Occupation And Conviction Rates Of White And Negro Males: A Case Study. *Rocky Mt J Soc Sci* 7,141–146 1970.

FORSLUND, Morris A and Cranston, Virginia A. A Self–Report Comparison Of Indian And Anglo Delinquency In Wyoming. *Criminology* 13(2),193–198 Ag 1975.

Delinquency among Native American (Indian) and white adolescents in the Wind River Indian Reservation area of Wyoming was compared, based on a self–report questionnaire survey. The results demonstrate little overall difference in the delinquent behavior of Indian and Anglo males, with the exception of a greater involvement of Indian males in delinquent activities centering around the school. The Indian female appeared to be considerably more involved than the white female in running away from home and in a variety of offenses centering around the school, theft, vandalism, and assault. When social class was controlled, there was a substantial reduction in the number of offenses for which there were significant differences between the two races.

FORSLUND, Morris A and Malry, L. Standardization Of Negro Crime Rates For Negro–White Differences In Age And Status. *Rocky Mt J Soc Sci* 7,151–160 1970.

Obtaining data from the local police department, a sample was taken of all persons arrested in Stamford, Conn., from 1959 to 1961 (3,717 arrests). Subjects were 16 years of age or older and were charged with offenses other than motor vehicle law violation. Using occupation as an indicator of socioeconomic status, crime rates were computed for males and females separately for each age and occupational category. Negro rates were then standardized to those expected if the Negro age and occupational structures were the same as those of whites, under the assumption of constant Negro rates for each age and occupational category. Despite their limitation, the findings of the study show that the disproportionate concentration of Negroes in the lower socioeconomic strata and in the younger age categories of the US account for a substantial proportion of the excess of the Negro over the white crime rate. However, standardization of offense rates for specific offenses by occupation, and especially by age, does not result in equal reductions in rates for all offenses. Further studies should be conducted, taking into account age and occupation variables of crime rate comparisons.*

FORSLUND, Morris A and Meyers, Ralph E. Delinquency Among Wind River Indian Reservation Youth. *Criminology* 12(1),97–106 My 1974.

This study investigates the magnitude and dimensions of the delinquency problem among Indian youths from the Wind River Reservation in Wyoming by examining official records from 1967–1971. The Reservation rates were found to be nearly five times the national average. It also appears that the proportion of court appearances of Reservation youth for serious offenses is much lower than in the nation as a whole, while the proportion of court appearances involving minor offenses are much higher (a higher percentage of charges were for alcohol–related offenses). These findings were consistent with the findings of previous studies. A cohort analysis which looked at all individuals who turned 18 years of age sometime during fiscal year 1971 showed that a large number of cases were disposed of by the juvenile officer and not even referred to court. In addition, many youths were arrested off the reservation and never came before Indian Court. These findings indicate that the delinquency involvement of Reservation youths is much greater than that revealed by court records alone.

FORWARD, J R and Williams, J R. Internal–External Control And Black Militancy. *J Soc Issues* 26(1),75–92 1970.

FOSTER, Samuel C and Thomas, Charles and Cage, Robin J. Public Opinion On Criminal And Legal Sanctions: An Examination Of Two Conceptual Models. *J Crim L & Crimin* 67(1),110–116 1976.

Public evaluation of appropriate legal sanctions are examined in order to see whether they reflect the level of agreement implied by the consensus model. Private citizens were asked to evaluate the relative seriousness of a variety of acts and suggest what type of sanctions they feel are appropriate for those who engage in the acts. In regard to the first dimension, remarkable similarity was found in the offense rankings from those above and below the median sample income, occupational prestige, and educational level. A very high degree of similarity was found on the lengths of sentences assigned to the set of possible offenses. The basic expectation of the consensus model, i.e., that there would be consensus on these two dimensions across social groupings, was supported. Findings were not supportive of a conflict model which would predict variations between different categories of the population.

FOX, Daniel M and Huggins, Nathan and Kilson, Martin. *Key Issues In The Afro–American Experience*. NY Harcourt Brace 1971.

FOX, J and Ward, J A. Suicide Epidemic On An Indian Reserve. *Can Psychi Assoc J* 22,8 D 1977.

FOX, Richard G. The XYY Offender: A Modern Myth? J Crim L Crimin & Pol Sci 62(1),59–73 1971.

FOX, Vernon. *Violence Behind Bars*. Westport CN Greenwood Pr 1956.

FOX, Vernon and Volakalis, Joan. The Negro Offender In A Northern Industrial Area. *J Crim L Crimin & Pol Sci* 46,641–647 1956.

This study of social, psychological and occupational differences between black and white inmates of a Michigan State Prison found that blacks were more likely to be committed for assaultive crimes, more likely to be migrants from the South (although there was a trend toward reduction below statistical significance of the difference in proportion of native born whites and blacks), younger, less likely to be formally married, of lower occupational status, and of lower I. Q. (96.6 for whites and 83.4 for blacks) than whites. Culture conflict and social disorganization are suggested to be significant factors in black crime.

FOX, Vernon. Intelligence, Race, And Age As Selective Factors In Crime. *J Crim L Crimin & Pol Sci* 37,141–152 1946.

FOX, Vernon. Racial Issues In Corrections: Cultural Awareness—How To Achieve It. *Am J Correct* 34(6),12–17 1972.

FRANGIER, Charles and Henretta, Juan C and Urnever, James D. Racial Differences In Criminal Sentencing. Boston A S A 1979.

FRANK, Gerold. *An American Death: The True Story Of The Assassination Of Dr Martin Luther King, Jr, And The Greatest Manhunt Of Our Time.* Garden City NY Doubleday 1972.

FRANK, J B. Can The Courts Erase The Color Line? Buffalo L Rev 2,28–44 1952.

FRANK, Jerome. *Courts On Trial: Myth And Reality In American Justice.* Princeton Princeton Univ Pr 1973.

FRANK, Susan and Quinlan, Donald M. Ego Development And Female Delinquency: A Cognitive–Developmental Approach. *J Abnorm Psychol* 85(5),505–510 O 1976.

FRANKEL, Emil. The Offender And The Court: A Statistical Analysis Of Sentencing Of Delinquents. *J Am Inst Cr L Crim* 31,448–456 D 1940.

FRANKEL, Marvin E. *Criminal Sentences: Law Without Order.* NY Hill & Wang 1973.

FRANKLIN, Billy J. Victim Characteristics And Helping Behavior In A Rural Southern Setting. *J Soc Psychol* 93,93–100 1974.

Victim characteristics and helping behavior in a rural southern setting were investigated. It was hypothesized that the race, sex, and community identification of a victim influence the likelihood that he will receive help from rural white Southerners. Data from a field experiment conducted in the rural mountain region of western North Carolina reveal the predicted race difference, but sex and community identification variation was insignificant. When data were compared with previously reported results from a study in NYC, the predicted difference in overall helping rates was observed. However, the proportion of blacks who received help is identical to the proportion receiving help in the NYC sample.

FRANKLIN, H Bruce. *The Victim As Criminal And Artist: Literature From The American Prison.* NY Oxford Univ Pr 1978.

Franklin, a Professor of English and American Studies, examines American prisoner writings as a literary genre and important historical and sociological resource. His analysis concludes that convict narratives, like slave narratives, constitute a large and socially significant body of literature. A very extensive annotated bibliography is included.

FRANKLIN, J C. Discriminative Value And Patterns Of The Wechsler–Bellevue Scales In The Examination Of Delinquent Negro Boys. *Ed & Psychol M* 5,71–85 1945.

FRANKLIN, John Hope. *From Slavery To Freedom.* NY Knopf 1968.

FRANKLIN, Raymond. The Political Economy Of Black Power. *Social Prob* 16,286–301 Wint 1969.

FRANKLIN, Vincent P. The Philadelphia Race Riot Of 1918. *Penn Mag Hist Biog* 99,336–350 Jl 1975.

This case study of an urban "race riot" in Philadelphia is one of several similar studies of disturbances in American cities during World War I. The author attributes as one cause of the Philadelphia riot the massive migration of blacks into the city as workers in the war effort, contending that the influx exceeded the boundaries of the black ghetto and thus threatened white residents. Most riot incidents consisted of attacks by white mobs against black newcomers, against which the white police provided little protection. In some cases, the policemen themselves committed unjustified violent acts, resulting in at least one fatality. The four–day disturbances resulted in four deaths, several hundred injuries, and extensive property damage to black residents. Franklin observes that the Philadelphia riot is unlike most Northern urban riots in that it occurred in an "ecologically contested area" rather than in the "Negro slum." He credits the riot as having several beneficial effects. It mobilized the black community, successfully challenged police brutality, and began to challenge the dominant white establishment.

FRASER, C Gerald. Black Policemen Denounce Racism. *NYT* ,13 Je 11 1971.

Fraser reports on a conference attended by black policemen and white officials of police fraternal organizations. The conference was held in Philadelphia and dealt with the issue of racial polarity in police departments. Black policemen won assurance from the representative of New York City's PBA that that association would go on record never to tolerate any racism or to defend it in the NYC Police Department. The two groups (black policemen and white officials) were at odds, however, on the question of representation. Blacks contended that the predominantly white police organization did not represent the interests of the black policemen, while the whites said the organizations represented all police officers, arguing that "we only see blue."

FRAZIER, E Franklin. "Crime And Delinquency" in *The Negro In The United States*, 638–653, Orig Pub 1949. NY Macmillan 1965.

Frazier discusses early studies of black crime after emancipation and before mass migrations to the North, studies of black crime between the World Wars, a study of crime in Harlem, Johnson's study of the administration of justice to blacks, World War II era studies of black crime, and studies of juvenile delinquency among blacks. He concludes that crime and juvenile delinquency among blacks is the product of a complex of economic and social forces characteristic of areas of social disorganization. Where stable families with economic security are concentrated, crime rates are low. Thus, rates of crime and juvenile delinquency among blacks are not higher than among whites when studied in relation to the social disorganization of the areas in which blacks are concentrated in cities.

FRAZIER, E Franklin. "Juvenile Delinquency" in *The Negro Family In Chicago.* Chicago Univ Chicago Pr 1932.

FRAZIER, E Franklin. "Rebellious Youth" in *The Negro Family In The United States*, 268–280, Orig Pub 1949. Chicago Univ Chicago Pr 1973.

High rates of juvenile delinquency among blacks are attributed to the disorganization of black family life in the urban environment. Several studies are cited in support of the argument that criminal influences in the neighborhood and lack of parental control due to broken homes and working mothers contribute to high rates of delinquency in black ghettoes.

FRAZIER, E Franklin. *Black Bourgeoisie.* NY Collier Books 1962.

FRAZIER, E Franklin. *The Negro Family In The United States*, Orig Pub 1949. Chicago Univ Chicago Pr 1966.

FREDERICK, C J. *Suicide, Homicide, And Alcoholism Among American Indians—Guidelines For Help.* Rockville MD US Dept HEW 1973.

FREDERICK, Jeffrey and Mc Conahay, John B and Mullin, Courtney J. The Uses Of Social Science In Trials With Political And Racial Overtones: The Trial Of Joan Little. *Law & Contemp Prob* 41(1),205–229 Wint 1977.

FREDERICK, M A and Molnar, M. Relative Occupational Anticipations And Aspirations Of Delinquents And Nondelinquents. *J Res Crim Del* 6(1),1–7 1969.

FREDERICKSON, George M. *The Black Image In The White Mind: The Debate On Afro–American Character And Destiny, 1817–1914.* NY Harper & Row 1971.

FREDERICKSON, George M and Lasch, Christopher. Resistance To Slavery. *Civil War Hist* 13,315–329 1967.

FREE, L A and Watts, W. *Aspirations And Social Concerns—Crime, Blacks, Inequality And Women.* Washington DC Potomac Associates 1976.

The survey research analysis was based on a national sampling of 1,071 Americans. Public concerns reflected a desire for a better standing of living, good personal health, and a happy family life. Inflation, threat of war and social decay were the areas about which fear was expressed. A hope for peace was found systematically throughout the cross–section of the population. Americans were also found to be very disturbed about crime, violence, and related issues of drugs and drug abuse. Efforts to combat these problems are not well viewed and increased federal government spending is thought to be a solution. The survey revealed a noticeable hardening of the public's attitude toward criminals. In comparison to other major problems facing the nation, the condition and problems of blacks did not rank especially high. Most americans assign a high priority to government spending to allieviate the problem. The lower- to middle–income urban whites are most adamant about government economic assistance to blacks.*

FREI, R J and Offord, D R and Aponte, J F. A Study Of Recidivism Among Female Juvenile Delinquents. *Corr Psychi J Soc Ther* 14(3),160–174 1968.

FRENCH, Laurence. Indians Before The Law: An Assessment Of Contravening Cultural/Legal Ideologies. New Orleans A C J S 1978.

FRENCH, Laurence. An Assessment Of The Black Female Prisoners In The South. *Signs* 3(2),483–488 Wint 1978.

FRENCH, Laurence and Hornbuckle, J. An Analysis Of Indian Violence. *Am Indian Q* 3(4),335–356 Wint 1978.

FRENCH, Laurence. The Incarcerated Black Female: The Case Of Social Double Jeopardy. *J Black St* 8(3),321–335 1978.

FRENCH, Laurence. The Minority Perspective On Violence. *Int J Comp App Crim Just* 3(1),43–49 Spr 1979.

Members of the visible minority groups (e.g., blacks, Hispanics, and Native Americans) have long been overrepresented as both offenders and victims of violent crime. These same groups are underrepresented as members of the formal legal control system (e.g., law enforcement, the judiciary, corrections departments and legislative bodies). Few attempts have been made to analyze this phenomenon from a minority perspective and many of the existing interpretations suffer from ethnocentrism. The author (a white college professor from Nebraska) attempts to examine criminal violence from "the cultural perspective."

FRESE, Glenn. The Riot Curfew. *Cal L Rev* 57,450–489 1969.

FREUDENBERGER, Herbert J. The Dynamics And Treatment Of The Young Drug Abuser In An Hispanic Therapeutic Community. *J Psyched Drug* 7(3),273–280 Jl–S 1975.

FREUND, Paul A. The Philosophy Of Equality. *Wash U L Q* 1979(1),11–24 Wint 1979.

FRIAR, David James and Weiss, Carl. *Terror In The Prisons.* Indianapolis Bobbs–Merrill 1974.

FRIDAY, Paul and Peterson, David M. Early Release From Incarceration: Race As A Factor In The Use Of Shock Probation. *J Crim L & Crimin* 66,79–97 Mr 1975.

Legal and nonlegal variables that differentiate between those prisoners who are released on probation by the courts after a period of short–term incarceration and those who remain imprisoned are considered. Data to determine the variables which differentiated between those felons who received early releases and those who remained in the institution were collected at a medium security prison for male offenders between the ages of sixteen and thirty. The sample design included all persons granted early release from prison. The following nonlegal variables were found to be associated with early release—race, education, father's education and legal residence, and the legal variables found were probation department recommendation, offense, prior record, number of bills of indictment and plea.*

FRIEDMAN, C Jack and Baker, Timothy and Mann, Fredrica. Selectivity In The Criminal Justice System. *Prison J* 55(1),23–34 1975.

FRIEDMAN, H G. Contingency Planning For The Administration Of Justice During Civil Disorder And Mass Arrest. *Am U L Rev* 18,77–97 1968.

FRIEDMAN, L N. *Wildcat Experiment—An Early Test Of Supported Work In Drug Abuse Rehabilitation.* Washington DC US Dept HEW 1978.

This monograph evaluates a NYC–supported work program that hired groups formerly considered unemployable such as heroin addicts and criminal offenders. Participants were placed largely in city jobs such as construction and maintenance. Wildcat applicants were randomly assigned to sample groups of 194 experimentals and 297 controls, unemployables not in supported work programs and studied for 3 years. About 90% of each group were male, 60% were black, 30% were Hispanic, and 10% were white. Typical members were 31 years old, had 8 arrests and 4 convictions, had an 11–year heroin addiction, and had been enrolled in a drug treatment program for 1 year. Most were on welfare and had not worked for at least 6 months. The Wildcat significantly increased employment stability and earning capacity of its employees reduced dependency on welfare, and experimentals were less likely to be arrested during the first year than were controls. Wildcat did not have a significant impact on drug or alcohol use. Experimentals were more likely to marry and support other people. The report found that, using a cost–benefit calculation, the taxpayer received one dollar and 12 cents for every dollar invested in Wildcat.*

FRIEDMAN, Leon (ed). *Southern Justice.* NY Meridian Books 1967.
Nineteen lawyers with first–hand experience in handling civil rights cases in the South describe the operation of the legal system there during the 1960's. Local police and sheriffs, prosecuting attorneys, trial courts, juries, state and federal appeals courts, and the FBI are covered.

FROMM, Erich and Maccoby, Michael. *Social Character In A Mexican Village: A Sociopsychoanalytic Study.* Englewood Cliffs NJ Prentice–Hall 1970.

FROST, Stanley. *The Challenge Of The Klan.* Indianapolis Bobbs–Merrill 1924.

FRY, Gladys–Marie. *Night Riders In Black Folk History.* Knoxville Univ of Tenn Pr 1977.

FRY, John. *Fire And Blackstone.* Philadelphia Lippincott 1969.
The Blackstone Rangers, or Black P Stone Nation, originated in Chicago's South Side during the 1960's as a gang and later was transformed into a political organization.

FRYREAR, Jerry L and Thelan, Mark H. Imitation Of Self–Reward Standards By Black And White Female Delinquents. *Psychol Rep* 29(2),667–671 1971.

FUJIMOTO, Tetsuya. Social Class And Crime: The Case Of The Japanese–Americans. *Issues Crim* 10(1),73–93 Spr 1975.
An historical review of the Japanese immigrant movement and the occupational patterns of Japanese–Americans is provided, and discussed in relation to the low crime rate among Japanese–American citizens.*

FULLER, Dan A and Orsagh, Thomas. Violence And Victimization Within A State Prison System. *Crim Just Rev* 2(2),35–55 1977.
A comprehensive quantitative profile of victimization in prisons in North Carolina was conducted to determine the rate of assault among prisoners, the causes, victim characteristics, and possible preventive measures. Three data bases were used: (1) a sample of records of disciplinary hearings in ten prison institutions in North Carolina during the last quarter of 1975—126 assaultive events in all; (2) interviews with prison supervisors in each of the institutions; and (3) a stratified sample of approximately 400 inmates from six of the institutions. Inmate victimization rates are considerably lower than the public, and even informed observers, suppose them to be. The victimization rates vary markedly by race, age, and institution. White victimization rates are higher than black victimization rates because blacks are more likely to victimize across racial lines. Increasing the quantity and efficiency of supervision is a direct and obvious means for reducing assault and victimization. A more refined classification of the inmate population by their propensity to commit assault would increase the efficiency of supervision.

FYFE, James J. Officer Race And Police Shooting. Philadelphia A S C 1979.

FYFE, James J. Race And Extreme Police–Citizen Violence. Cincinnati A C J S 1979.

FYFE, James J. Race And The Police: An Early Report On A Change Effort. San Francisco A S C 1980.

FYFE, James J. Geographic Correlates Of Police Shooting: A Microanalysis. *J Res Crim Del* 17(1),101–113 Ja 1980.

FYFE, James Joseph. *Shots Fired: An Examination Of New York City Police Firearms Discharges.* Unpub PhD Diss SUNY Albany 1978.

GABA, J M. Voir Dire Of Jurors: Constitutional Limits To The Right Of Inquiry Into Prejudice. *U Colo L Rev* 48,525–545 1977.

GAERTNER, S L and Dovidio, J F. The Subtlety Of White Racism, Arousal, And Helping Behavior. *J Pers Soc Psychol* 35(10),691–707 1977.

Two hypotheses were tested: (a) white bystanders are more likely to discriminate against black victims in situations in which failure to intervene could be attributable to factors other than the victim's race; (b) there is a causal relationship between arousal induced by witnessing an emergency and bystander responsiveness, as proposed by Piliavin, Rodin, and Piliavin. Consistent with the first hypothesis, Study 1 found that black victims were discriminated against when the subject had the opportunity to diffuse responsibility; however, blacks and whites were helped equally when the subject was the only bystander. Study 2 failed to demonstrate a predicted interaction between the victim's race and the ambiguity of the emergency.

GAERTNER, S L. The Role Of Racial Attitudes In Helping Behavior. *J Soc Psychol* 97,95–101 1975.

Although a number of studies have demonstrated that the victim's race affects the probability that a bystander will intervene and help during an emergency, the process by which attitudes affect helping behavior is unclear. This study suggests that attitudes toward the victim may affect helping behavior by influencing the bystander's interpretation of the degree to which help is needed. The results indicate that when a bystander was the only witness, black victims were helped as frequently as white victims. However, bystanders together with other passive witnesses were more likely to help the white victim than the black victim.

GALARZA, Ernest and Gallegos, Herman and Samora, Julian. *Mexican Americans In The Southwest.* Santa Barbara CA McNally & Loftin 1969.

GALAWAY, Burt and Hudson, Joe. Crime Victims And Public Social Policy. *J Sociol & Soc Wel* 3(6),629–635 Jl 1976.

GALLEGOS, Herman and Samora, Julian and Galarza, Ernest J. *Mexican Americans In The Southwest.* Santa Barbara CA McNally & Loftin 1969.

GALLIHER, John F and Boggs, Sara L. Evaluating The Police: A Comparison Of Black Street And Household Respondents. *Social Prob* 22,393–406 1975.

GALLIHER, John F and Mc Cartney, James. *Criminology—Power, Crime And Criminal Law.* Homewood IL Dorsey Pr 1977.

GALLIHER, John F. Government Research Funding And Purchased Virtue: Some Examples From Criminology. *Crim & Soc Just* 11,44–50 Spr–Sum 1979.

GALTUNG, Johan. The Social Functions Of A Prison. *Social Prob* 6,127–140 Fall 1958.

GAMIO, Manuel. *Mexican Immigration To The United States.* NY Dover 1971.

GANS, Herbert J. *The Urban Villagers.* NY Free Pr 1962.

GARCIA, F Chris. *La Causa Politica: A Chicano Politics Reader.* Notre Dame U Notre Dame Pr 1974.

GARCIA, Robert. Hispanics Have To Work Closely With Blacks. *NYT*, n 30 1980.

GARDINER, John A (ed). *Public Law And Public Policy.* NY Praeger 1977.

GARFINKEL, Harold. Research Note On Inter– And Intra–Racial Homicides. *Soc Forces* 27,369–381 1949.

Data are presented regarding the treatment afforded white and black offenders involved in inter– and intraracial homicides, and a hypothesis is offered based on race of offender and victim to account for some peculiarities that were found such as: types of trials, indictments, convictions, and sentences. Data cover an 11 year period beginning in 1930, from 10 North Caroina counties. Generally speaking, the men and women of both races killed their own kind, but intrasex murders were

significantly higher among blacks. Analysis of the types of trials conducted, indictments, convictions, and sentencing shows a vivid clash between formal judicial values and the informal values of the prevailing white power structure. Informal social controls were used with extreme consistency to maximize penalties for major crimes of first and second degree murder when the offender was a Negro and the victim was white, while the fact that a Negro had been victimized was an inconsequential factor in outcome.

GARLAND, R and Chikota, Richard. When Will The Troops Come Marching In: A Comment On The Historical Use Of Federal Troops To Quell Domestic Violence. *J Urban L* 45,881–901 1968.

GAROFALO, James. Social Structure And Rates Of Imprisonment: A Research Note. Cincinnati A C J S 1979.

In this study, Garofalo, a criminologist, found a correlation between racial composition and rate of imprisonment that was too strong to be accounted for by indirect relationships through violent and property crimes.

GAROFALO, James and Hindelang, Michael J and Gottfredson, Michael. *Victims Of Personal Crime: An Empirical Foundation For A Theory Of Victimization.* Cambridge MA Ballinger 1978.

GARRETT, G R and Breece, C M. "Women In Policing––Changing Perspectives On The Role" in *Criminal Justice Planning*, Scott, J E And S Dinitz (eds). NY Praeger 1977.

Literature on legal, social, and other influences on the role of women in police work is reviewed, and their status is assessed. The involvement of women in police work has been linked with the stereotyping of personality characteristics and of female roles. Together with the paramilitary image of police agencies, stereotyped views have reduced the probabilities of women entering police work and have confined career mobility for policewomen to such areas as juvenile work, meter patrol, and administrative duties. Social reactions to the use of women in police agencies and on patrol vary according to population group, although studies indicate that the public generally is not opposed to women in policing. The greatest resistance to the use of policewomen, particularly on patrol duty, comes from male officers. Improved public image, less violence in police–citizen encounters, overall reduction of police violence, and better handling of rape and sex crime victims are among advantages associated with the use of female patrol officers in pilot programs. Major disadvantages include adverse effects on the morale of male officers and the tendency of male officers to be overly protective of their female colleagues.*

GARRETT, G R and Retting, R P and Torres, M J. *Manny––A Criminal–Addict's Story.* Boston Houghton Mifflin 1977.

A convicted drug user provides a firsthand account of an addict's day–to–day existence, both in prison and on the streets. Intended for an academic audience interested in deviance, crime, corrections, and criminal justice, this first–person narrative traces the life of Manny Torres, a young Puerto Rican heroin addict born in New York city. Manny provides a view of a variegated criminal career that accepted social science techniques ordinarily could not have rendered. Written in the frank and straightforward language of street people, dope addicts, and prison convicts, it provides a link between reality and social theory, and includes chapters on drug–related street crime, prison life, and Manny's experiences at Synanon, a drug detoxification institute. Selected references are included at the end of each chapter. The narrative is followed by a brief outline of the structuralist position and an integrated theoretical perspective designed to expose students to a social world that few experience.*

GARVEY, Marcus. *Philosophy And Opinions Of Marcus Garvey,* Amy Jacques–Garvey (ed). NY Atheneum 1970.

Marcus Garvey's prison messages of 1925 are included in this collection.

GARY, Lawrence E (ed) and Brown, Lee P (ed). *Crime & Its Impact On The Black Community.* Washington DC Howard U 1976.

The following topics are explored in Part 1: (1) Historical Overview of Crime and Blacks since 1876 (2) Black Attitudes Toward Crime and Crime Prevention (3) Black Business and the Crime of Uneconomic Communities (4) Lessons in Crime from the All–Black Town and (5) Philosophical and Research Implications of Definitions of Crime. Part 2 focuses on factors influencing crime in the black community including: (1) Crime and the Public Schools: A Critical Appraisal (2) Employment and Discrimination: Variables in Crime (3) The Impact of Alcohol on Crime (4) Race and Family Violence: The Internal Colonialism Perspective and (5) Media, Crime and the Black

Community. Part 3 discusses ways of addressing the crime problem and includes: (1) Black Self–Identity and Crime (2) Citizen Action as a Deterrent to Crime (3) The Criminal Justice System: Innovations, Failures and Alternatives (4) New Directions in Law Enforcement (5) Police Authority and the Low–Income Family Research (6) Court Monitoring—A Necessity (7) New Directions in Corrections and (8) Successful Passage of Black Parolees: From Prison to Prison.

GARY, Lawrence E. *Mental Health: A Challenge To The Black Community*. Philadelphia Dorrance & Co 1978.

GARY, Lawrence E and Beard, Eugene and Brown, Lee P. *Attitudes And Perceptions Of Black Police Officers Of The District Of Columbia Metropolitan Police Department*. Washington DC Howard U 1976.
This study reports data on the recruitment, job assignments, promotion, interpersonal relations, retention, and attrition of black officers in the Metropolitan Police Department (MPD). Other topics covered include: background and personal characteristics; interpersonal relations among police officers and their perceptions of the community's attitudes towards the MPD; attitudes of black officers towards MPD supervisors and officials and the issue of discrimination in department policies and regulation; job satisfaction and promotion opportunities; and significant problems confronting the police department, police profession, and police officers.*

GARZA, H. Administration Of Justice: Chicanos In Monterey County. *Aztlan* 4,137–146 Spr 1973.

GATJE, C T and Bruno, N J and Orris Jr, J V. Hispanic English Language Development In Prison. Stormville NY Greenhaven Prison 1976.

GATTI, Florence M and Cortes, Juan B. *Delinquency And Crime: A Biopsychosocial Approach*. NY Seminar Pr 1972.
Higher rates of crime among blacks than among whites are explained by postulating both higher mesomorphy and more disruption in the family environment among blacks than among whites. Data is presented which shows a higher incidence of mesomorphic physique among delinquents than among non–delinquents.

GAVIN, S and Price, B. "Century Of Women In Policing" in *Modern Police Administration*, Schultz, Donald O (ed). Houston Gulf 1979.
The history and status of women in policing is discussed, and barriers to full acceptance of female police officers are identified.*

GAYLIN, Willard. *Partial Justice: A Study Of Bias In Sentencing*. NY Knopf 1974.

GAZELL, James A. *Study Of Problems And Methods Of Police Recruitment From Disadvantaged Minorities*. NY Nat Urb League 1976.
This study analyzes the occupational expectations and motives of minority group policemen and examines their perceptions toward the San Diego Police Department's recruitment and retention policies and practices. A 1970 survey questionnaire revealed that minority persons were motivated to join a police department because of the nature of the job itself, rather than for economic benefit, although only the brown officers felt that they had some special value to the department. Generally, police respondents felt that the department's recruitment and intake system was 'fair' toward minority–group persons, although they were somewhat critical of the oral interview, probation evaluation, and, to a lesser extent, the written exam. Nearly half of the police respondents said that their job had not turned out according to their expectations, with racism cited as the unexpected factor. In general, minority persons were more critical of the police department than of the fire department, and blacks were more critical of their department than browns.*

GAZELL, James A. Police Recruitment: How Brown And Black Personnel View It. *Police L Q* 2(4),19–29 1973.
Attitudes of brown and black sworn personnel toward the recruitment system used by the City of San Diego Police Department are examined. Conclusions from interviews fall into two classes: motives for seeking police work, and beliefs about organizational motives for hiring nonwhites. Officers interviewed preferred the police to the fire department for professional rather than economic reasons, and sought entrance into the profession through encouragement of relatives and friends. According to Mexican–American and Negro officers, the Police Department primarily wanted them to improve its effectiveness, applied fair standards to all candidates, and ascribed the paucity of brown and black policemen in the organization to lack of interest in such work.

GAZELL, James A. The Attitudes Of Non–White Police Personnel Toward Retention. *Police L Q* 3(3),12–21 1974.
The attitudes of Mexican–American and black police officers toward their

jobs with the City of San Diego Police Department (SDPD) are examined. Through interviews it was revealed that officers stayed with the job mainly because of professional satisfaction, not because of its economic benefits. They ascribed job success to the possession of professional, interpersonal, conforming, and sapiental traits. It was reported that the job had turned out according to their expectations. However, by race, they differed sharply over the circumstances under which they would leave their jobs. Beliefs about departmental motives for retaining them were also explored. It was felt that continued retention was attributed to competent job performance and that the promotions system is generally fair. However, by race, they disagreed over the existence of departmentally created obstacles to advancement.

GEBHARD, Paul H. "A Comparison Of White–Black Offender Groups" in *Sexual Behaviors*, Resnick, H L And Marvin E Wolfgang (eds). Boston Little, Brown 1972.

GEHLKER, Gretchen and Mc Farland, Anita and Willick, Daniel H. Social Class As A Factor Affecting Judicial Disposition. *Criminology* 13(1),57–77 My 1975.

GEIS, Gilbert (ed) and Chappell, Duncan and Geis, Robley (ed). *Forcible Rape: The Crime, The Victim, And The Offender*. NY Columbia Univ Pr 1977.

GEIS, Gilbert and Agopian, Michael W and Chappell, Duncan. "Interracial Forcible Rape In A North American City" in *Victimology: A New Focus*, V1, Drapkin, Israel And Emilio Viano (eds), Chapter 9. Lexington MA Lexington 1974.

GEIS, Gilbert and Bloch, Herbert A. *Man, Crime, And Society*, Rev'd Ed. NY Random House 1970.

GEIS, Gilbert. Statistics Concerning Race And Crime. *Crim Delinq* 11,142–150 1965.
Statistics purporting to show the amount of crime in a society possess serious shortcomings as accurate indicators of the item they are measuring. The breakdown of such figures into racial and ethnic categories not only compounds the statistical errors, but also introduces elements of general social concern. Such breakdowns should be eliminated in official reports since they contain, besides their inaccuracy, elements which are socially disruptive and disadvantageous.

GEIS, Robley (ed) and Geis, Gilbert (ed) and Chappell, Duncan. *Forcible Rape: The Crime, The Victim, And The Offender*. NY Columbia Univ Pr 1977.

GELLES, R J. Child Abuse As Psychopathology: A Sociological Critique And Reformulation. *Am J Orthopsych* 43,611–621 Jl 1973.

GELLHORN, E. Law Schools And The Negro. *Duke L J* 1,1069+ 1968.

GENERAL SERVICES ADMINISTRATION. Employee Selection Procedures—Adoption Of Question And Answers To Clarify And Provide A Common Interpretation Of The Uniform Guidelines. *Fed Reg* 44(43),11996–12009 Mr 2 1979.
Answers to questions about the federal government's Uniform Guidelines on Nondiscrimination in Employee Selection Policies and Practices are presented. The uniform guidelines were issued in September 1978 by agencies with primary responsibility for enforcing federal equal employment opportunity laws, the purpose being to establish a single federal positin on prohibition of discrimination in employment practices. The basic principle of the guidelines is that selection procedures which have an adverse impact on the employment opportunities of any race, religion, sex, or ethnic group are unlawful unless the validity (i.e., job–relatedness) of the procedures is established. The guidelines provide direction for employers in determining whether adverse impact exists, in validating selection procedures, and in documenting these efforts.*

GENOVESE, Eugene D. *From Rebellion To Revolution: Afro–American Slave Revolts In The Making Of The Modern World*. Baton Rouge LA LSU Pr 1980.

GENOVESE, Eugene D. *Roll, Jordan, Roll: The World The Slaves Made*. NY Pantheon 1974.
Genovese's landmark study of life under Southern chattel slavery reassesses many longstanding myths—the genial mammy, the emasculated black male, the all–powerful overseer and master, the obsequious black preacher, and the accommodating "house nigger." He argues that the slaves created a collective identity of spirit and pride which enabled them to survive one of the greatest crimes in history—the crime of slavery.

GENOVESE, Eugene D. Rebelliousness And Docility In The Negro Slave: A Critique Of The Elkins Thesis. *Civil War Hist* 13,293–314 1967.

GENTHNER, R W and Taylor, S P. Physical Aggression As A Function Of Racial Prejudice And The Race Of The Target. *J Pers Soc Psychol* 27(2),207–210 1973.

GENTRY, W D. Biracial Aggression: I, Effect Of Verbal Attack And Sex Of Victim. *J Soc Psychol* 88,75–82 1972.

GEORGES- ABEYIE, Daniel E. *The Criminal Justice System And Minority Crime.* Albany SUNYA C J 1980.

As the first in a series of monographs on minorities and criminal justice, this work provides a brief overview of selected topics and issues dealing with minority crime, victimization and the criminal justice process. Its purpose is to stimulate informed debate by seeking to dispel some misguided perspectives, and to expose some perceived injustices regarding the criminal justice system. The writings of many authors are discussed to present the reader with a variety of viewpoints which any serious student of criminal justice must consider. The author, a black urban geographer, focuses on blacks and crime.

GEORGES, Daniel E. *The Geography Of Crime And Violence: A Spatial And Ecological Perspective.* Washington DC Assoc Am Geog 1978.

This bibliography by a black urban geographer contains listings on crime analysis from a spatial perspective. The parts include: (1) the crime problem: seriousness and extent; (2) geography of crime: a geographic or social ecological approach?; (3) ecological principles and concepts applied to the patial analysis of crime; (4) crime data sources and general ground rules for studying the geography of crime; (5) conclusion; (6) census tract exercise, including an introduction to regression and correlation analysis.

GEORGES, Daniel E and Kirksey, Kirk. Violent Crime Perpetrated Against The Elderly In The City Of Dallas, October 1974–September 1975. *J Environ Syst* 7(2),149–197 1977–78.

GEORGES, Daniel E. The Ecology Of Urban Unrest: The Case Of Arson In Newark, New Jersey. *J Environ Syst* 5(3),203–228 1975.

GERARD, Jules B and Terry Jr, T Rankin. Discrimination Against Negroes In The Adminstration Of Criminal Law In Missouri. *Wash U L Q* 1970,415–438 1970.

GERLACH, Don R. Black Arson In Albany, NY: November 1793. *J Black St* 3,301–312 1977.

The fire which ravaged Albany, NY in November 1793 was attributed to black slaves before there was any evidence to that effect. City officials immediately imposed a strict curfew and two women and a man (all slaves) were arrested and charged with arson. The women pleaded guilty but the male slave was convicted after a trial. All three were sentenced to be executed. The women were hanged and after the man confessed his guilt, he too was hanged.

GERMANN, A C. Changing The Police: The Impossible Dream? *Police J* 44,197–206 Jl–S 1971.

GERSHENOVITZ, A and Willie, Charles V. Juvenile Delinquency In Racially Mixed Areas. *Am Sociol Rev* 29(5),740–744 O 1964.

GERSHMAN, Carl. A Matter Of Class. *NYT Mag* ,o 5 1980.

GETTINGER, Steve. Mississippi Has Come A Long Way, But It Had A Long Way To Come. *Correct Mag* 5(2),4–13 Je 1979.

The Parchman facility, which eventually grew to incorporate several labor camps and a brutal maximum security containment spread across 22,000 acres of a former cotton plantation, was founded after Sherman's troops burned Mississippi's only prison during the Civil War. At first, prisoners were shipped to Parchman, only to be rented out to local cotton farmers who starved, brutalized, and often murdered the largely black inmates put in their charge. After much public outcry the state stopped the practice, turning the labor instead to growing cotton and soybeans on Parchman's own vast acreage. However, brutal conditions prevailed. It was not until 1972, when a New York civil rights lawyer filed suit on behalf of inmate Nazareth Gates and others, that the conditions at Parchman were publicly aired and ordered relieved. Since that landmark federal ruling mandating swift, comprehensive reform at Parchman, has served as a model to the nation in terms of its deliberate and speedy efforts to upgrade state facilities by reducing prison overcrowding, redesigning minimum and maximum security facilities, and eliminating forced prison farm labor.*

GHALI, Sonia. Culture Sensitivity And The Puerto Rican Client. *Soc Casework* 58,459–474 1977.

GIALLOMBARDO, R. *Society Of Women: A Study Of A Women's Prison.* NY Wiley 1966.

GIBBONS, Don C. Offender Typologies—Two Decades Later. *Br J Crimin* 15,140–156 Ap 1975.

GIBBS, I L. Institutional Racism In Social Welfare. *Child Wel* 50(10),582–587 1971.

GIBBS, Jack P and Jensen, Gary F and Erickson, Maynard L. Perceived Risk Of Punishment And Self–Reported Delinquency. *Soc Forces* 57,57–78 1978.

To examine the relationship between perceived risk of punishment and self–reported delinquency, the authors sampled students in six Arizona high schools. Personal risk was found to be inversely related to delinquency even when social condemnation of delinquent offenses, attachment to conventional persons, and several status characteristics of the students were taken into account.

GIBSON, James L. Race As A Determinant Of Criminal Sentences: A Methodological Critique And A Case Study. *Law & Soc Rev* 12(3),455–478 Spr 1978.

The author contends that several conceptual methodological deficiencies have plagued research on racial discrimination in criminal courts. Discrimination is usually conceptualized as a function of societal or institutional forces rather than as an attribute of individual decision makers, producing research designs that analyze decisions of courts rather than decisions of individual judges. However, a finding of no discrimination in aggregate court data does not preclude the possibility that individual judges discriminate against or in favor of minorities. In addition, research has largely been concerned with description rather than explanation, and has therefore failed to illuminate the decisional processes that produce discrimination. Each of these criticisms is substantiated by data from the Fulton County (Georgia) Superior Court relating to the period from 1968 through 1970. The findings suggest three patterns of sentencing among judges: problack, antiblack, and nondiscriminatory. Discrimination seems to flow from both the attitudinal predispositions of the judges and the process they employ to make decisions.

GIL, D G. Violence Against Children. *J Marriag Fam* 33,637–648 N 1971.

GILCHRIST, Irvin (ed) and Bundy, Mary Lee (ed). *The National Civil Rights Directory: An Organized Directory.* College Park MD Urban Info Interpr 1979.

GILDER, George. *Visible Man: A True Story Of Post–Racist America.* NY Basic Books 1978.

A recreation of the case of a young black man in Albany, NY who is accused of raping a white woman.

GILL, Douglas. *Preparation By Municipalities For Civil Disorders.* Chapel Hill Univ N Car Pr 1968.

GILL, Robert L. Negro In The Supreme Court. *Negro Ed Rev* 14,101–125 1963.

GILL, Robert L. Negro In The Supreme Court, 1963. *Negro Ed Rev* 15,19–39 1963.

GILL, Robert L. Shaping Of Race Relations By The Federal Judiciary. *Negro Ed Rev* 11,15–23 1960.

GILLECE, James et al. How The Police Abroad Handle Riots. *US News* 65(1),30–31 Jl 1 1968.

A brief outline of the methods used by the police in other countries in handling demonstrations and riots.

GILLECE, James et al. New Answer To Riots: Keep White Police Away? *US News* 65(6),30–31 Ag 5 1968.

Brief description of the violent 1968 Cleveland riot and a unique attempt at handling it which entailed removing all white police and National Guardsmen from the area while allowing black civilian representatives to "cool down" the riot area.

GILLECE, James et al. The Long Hot Summer: A Legal View. *Notre Dame Law* 43,913–1016 1968.

GILLERS, Stephen (ed) and Watters, Pat (ed). *Investigating The FBI.* NY Ballantine 1973.

GILLIN, John. Ethos Components In Modern Latin American Culture. *Am Anthrop* 57,488–500 1955.

GILULA, M F (ed) and Ochberg, F M (ed) and Daniels, D N (ed). *Violence And The Struggle For Existence.* Boston Little, Brown 1970.

GINGER, Ann Fagan (ed). *DeFunis Versus Odegaard And The University Of Washington,* 3v. Dobbs Ferry NY Oceana Pubs 1974.

GINGER, Ann Fagan (ed). *Minimizing Racism In Jury Trials.* Berkeley CA Nat Lawy Guild 1968.

GINGER, Ann Fagan. Combatting Racism In American Law Schools. *Guild Pract* 31,701–706 1974.

GINSBERG, George and Starkman, Gary. Civil Disturbances, Mass Processing And Misdemeanants: Rights, Remedies And Realities. *J Crim L Crimin & Pol Sci* 61,39–50 1970.

GINSBURG, Benson E. "The Violent Brain: Is It Everyone's Brain" in *Biology And Crime*, Jeffrey, C R (ed). Beverly Hills CA Sage 1979.

GINZBERG, Eli. Black Power And Student Unrest: Reflections On Columbia University And Harlem. *George Wash L Rev* 37,835–847 1969.

GIORDANO, Peggy C and Cernkovich, Stephen A. A Comparative Analysis Of Male And Female Delinquency. *Sociol Q* 20,131–145 1979.

It is generally assumed that males are much more likely than females to commit delinquent acts, and that when females deviate their misconduct is significantly less serious than that of males. This paper examines the recent contention that the delinquent behavior of males and females is more similar than assumed. Self–report questionnaires were administered in 1977 to a sample of 822 male and female adolescents selected from two urban high schools in a large midwestern state. Following Hindelang (1971), the authors concentrate on the types of delinquent acts most frequently reported, as well as the extent of involvement in these acts. While males tend to commit most offenses more frequently than females, the pattern of delinquency is virtually identical for the two groups. This uniformity holds for race–sex subgroups, although there are more similarities in delinquency within racial groups than within sex groups.

GIORDANO, Peggy C and Henson, Trudy Knicely and Mc Caghy, Charles H. Auto Theft: Offender And Offense Characteristics. *Criminology* 15(3),367–385 N 1977.

GLASER, Daniel (ed). *Crime In The City.* NY Harper & Row 1970.

GLASER, Daniel and O' Leary, Vincent. *Personal Characteristics And Parole Outcome.* Washington DC US Dept HEW 1966.

This study of parole for the National Parole Institute is concerned with the relationship of parole outcome to personal characteristics. The characteristics examined included sex, race, age, offense, prior criminal record, intelligence, and body dimensions. The authors found little marked or consistent difference in the parole violation rates of blacks and whites, and concluded that this fact might have reflected more careful selection of blacks for parole than whites, or more frequent institutionalization of unadvanced offenders among blacks than among whites. In the Southwest, Mexican–Americans were found to have about the same parole violation rate as whites and blacks, and Native Americans were found to have an average or somewhat higher rate of parole violation. They concluded: "In general, the evidence on race and nationality as a factor in the evaluation of parolees suggests that it is not of much predictive validity in itself."

GLASER, Daniel. The Compatibility Of Free Will And Determinism In Criminology: Comments On An Alleged Problem. *J Crim L & Crimin* 67(4),486–490 1976.

GLAZER, Nathan (ed) and Moynihan, Daniel Patrick (ed). *Ethnicity: Theory And Experience.* Cambridge MA Harvard Univ Pr 1975.

GLAZER, Nathan. *Affirmative Discrimination: Ethnic Inequality And Public Policy.* NY Basic Books 1975.

GLAZER, Nathan and Moynihan, Daniel P. *Beyond The Melting Pot: The Negroes, Puerto Ricans, Jews, Italians, And Irish Of New York City.* Cambridge MA MIT Pr 1963.

GLAZER, Nathan. Blacks And Ethnic Groups: The Difference, And The Political Differences It Makes. *Social Prob* 18,444–461 Spr 1971.

GLAZER, Nathan. Inter–Ethnic Conflict. *Social Wk* 17(3),3–9 1972.

Interethnic conflict, or primarily the conflicts among white ethnic groups in the US, is discussed. Interethnic conflict, however, is closely tied to interracial conflict: the rise of ethnic consciousness has been inspired by black history movements; the tactics of the civil rights movement have been adopted by the ethnics; the two groups share an unclear ethnic status in the many groups now involved; and there is a similarity of issues, particularly in political representation, between interethnic and interracial groups. Thus it makes little sense to distinguish between interethnic and interracial conflict in the US in the 1970's. Two examples of this conflict interplay are seen in the situation of the Chinese in San Francisco and the Jews in NYC. These suggest that the lines of conflict have emerged over ethnic succession, contrasting cultures, and the role of the federal government. Current

interethnic conflicts inevitably involve the federal government, thus becoming more public and more serious. As the government becomes more committed to the establishment of equality among groups, the likelihood of interethnic conflict becomes even greater.

GLEASON, J (ed). *American Indian In The Criminal Justice System: A Selected Bibliography.* Champaign IL Nat Clear Crim Jus n.d.

GLENN, Norval. Occupational Benefits To Whites From The Subordination Of Negroes. *Am Sociol Rev* 28(3),443–448 Je 1963.

GLENN, Norval. White Gains From Negro Subordination. *Social Prob* 14,159–178 Fall 1966.

Author examines the extent of occupational and economic benefits that whites in the US derive from the subordination of Negroes. He found that many whites in southern urbanized areas benefit from a large disavantaged Negro population but concluded there was inadequate basis on which to draw a similar conclusion concerning the total white population.

GLUECK, Eleanor and Glueck, Sheldon. *Physique And Delinquency.* NY Harper & Bros 1956.

GLUECK, Sheldon and Glueck, Eleanor. *Physique And Delinquency.* NY Harper & Bros 1956.

GLYNN, Clement. Carmical v Craven: De Facto Racial Segregation In Jury Selection. *Hastings L J* 23(4),1291–1308 1972.

The application of a neutral intelligence test to screen potential jurors, ruled a denial of equal protection by the Ninth Circuit Court, thus representing de facto discrimination in the case of Carmical v. Craven is discussed. This decision was made when it was established that the test was not reasonably related to the selection of competent jurors and that a disproportionate number of blacks had been excluded from jury service. The fact that the test had been devised and administered in good faith by county officials was held to be no defense to the constitutional infirmity. Possible ramifications which may now develop are discussed in terms of jury selection procedures that may now be developed to achieve racially balanced juries in order to minimize the risk of postconviction attack on equal protection grounds.

GODSELL, Geoffrey. Hispanics In The US: Ethnic 'Sleeping Giant' Awakens, Part 3. *Christ Sci Mon* ,11–13 Ap 30 1980.

GODSELL, Geoffrey. Hispanics In The US: Ethnic 'Sleeping Giant' Awakens, Part 2. *Christ Sci Mon* ,11–13 Ap 29 1980.

GODSELL, Geoffrey. Hispanics In The US: Ethnic 'Sleeping Giant' Awakens, Part 4. *Christ Sci Mon* ,11–13 My 1 1980.

GODSELL, Geoffrey. Hispanics In The US: Ethnic 'Sleeping Giant' Awakens, Part 5. *Christ Sci Mon* ,12–13 My 2 1980.

GODSELL, Geoffrey. Hispanics In The US: Ethnic 'Sleeping Giant' Awakens, Part 1. *Christ Sci Mon* ,3 Ap 28 1980.

GOFF, R W. An Approach To Minority Recruitment. *FBI L Enf Bull* 47(7),16–21 Jl 1978.

Considerations in designing and implementing a successful minority recruitment program in police agencies are examined within the context of an Indiana State Police program. The program should be written in a direct manner so it can be followed and understood, and should include a recorded breakdown of the ultimate departmental goal in measurable units for later evaluation. Analysis of geographic and demographic data, past programs by similar organizations, and management commitment provide a necessary foundation for a successful recruitment program. Efforts must be made to ensure that all units have full knowledge of the program. In minority recruitment, emphasis on community service, security, prestige, and pay can help overcome alienation and negative attitudes of potential minority applicants. Recruitment techniques may include direct recruiter contact with minority group members, soliciting referrals from minority community leaders, and contact with potential minority applicants by onduty officers. Paid or public service media campaigns and posters and recruitment literature may also be effective.*

GOLD, Martin. *Delinquent Behavior In An American City.* Belmont CA Brooks/Cole 1970.

GOLD, Martin and Reimer, David J. *Changing Patterns Of Delinquent Behavior Among Americans 13-16 Years Old, 1967-1972: Report # 1 Of The National Survey Of Youth, 1972.* Ann Arbor MI Inst Soc Res 1974.

Findings of the National Survey of Youth, derived from samples of 847 and 661 youths drawn in 1967 and 1972, include data on delinquent behavior, self–esteem and anxiety that was constructed from self–reports.

Appendices include tables examining self-reported delinquent behavior by race, age, sex, socio-economic status and residence.

GOLD, Martin and Reimer, David. Changing Patterns Of Delinquent Behavior Among Americans 13 Through 16 Years Old: 1967–1972. *Crim Delin Lit* 7(4),483—517 D 1975.

GOLD, Martin and Williams, Jay R. From Delinquent Behavior To Official Delinquency. *Social Prob* 19,209–228 Fall 1972.

GOLDFARB, Ronald L. *Jails: The Ultimate Ghetto.* Garden City NY Doubleday 1975.

GOLDFARB, Ronald L. *Ransom: A Critique Of The American Bail System.* NY Harper & Row 1965.

GOLDFARB, Ronald L and Singer, Linda R. *After Conviction: A Review Of The American Correctional System.* NY Simon & Schuster 1973.

Two attorneys provide a legalistic, in-depth description of the American correctional system. Major cases in the area of prisoners' rights are noted and explained in this comprehensive and massively documented critique.

GOLDKAMP, John S. Minorities As Victims Of Police Shootings: Interpretation Of Racial Disproportionality And Police Use Of Deadly Force. *Just Syst J* 2(2),169–183 Wint 1976.

GOLDMAN, Nathan. *The Differential Selection Of Juvenile Offenders For Court Appearance.* NY NCCD 1963.

GOLDMAN, S. Should There Be Affirmative Action For The Judiciary? *Judicature* 62(10),488–494 1979.

Objections to the Carter Administration's affirmative action policy of placing women and ethnic minorities on the federal bench are rejoined.*

GOLDSBY, Richard. *Race And Races.* NY Macmillan 1977.

GOLDSCHMID, M L (ed). *Black Americans And White Racism.* NY Holt Rinehart Wins 1970.

GOLDSTEIN, B. *Screening For Emotional And Psychological Fitness In Correctional Officer Hiring.* Washington DC ABA 1975.

This monograph summarizes the results of a national questionnaire survey of screening techniques used for selection of line correctional officers in institutions. A response of 45 states and the District of Columbia assures a comprehensive national picture of steps taken to assess the crucial qualities of psychological and emotional fitness in new line officers. The survey indicates that the four main screening devices employed are oral interviews, background information and investigations, regular use of testing, and medical examinations. Variations in the nature and extent of the foregoing devices as techniques of psychological screening are considerable in each of the categories. The monograph includes other data and analysis such as rejection rates, the fact that most responding states (65%) consider their current procedures effective, the particular types of personality tests used to determine psychological fitness, screening problems raised by civil rights and equal employment opportunity laws and criteria, and the posture of current reform thinking and standards on line officer fitness and qualifications.*

GOLDSTEIN, Herman. *Policing A Free Society.* Cambridge MA Ballinger 1977.

GOLDSTEIN, Jay E. *A Survey Of Support For Punitive Responses To Ghetto Disorders.* Unpub PhD Diss Washington Univ 1974.

GOLEMAN, D and Adler, N. Gambling And Alcoholism: Symptom Substitution And Functional Equivalents. *Q J Stud Alc* 30(3),733–736 1969.

Similar psychodynamics (e.g., orality and suicidal behavior) have been proposed for both gambling and alcoholism. Gambling as a form of symptom substitution for alcoholism has been observed in Jews (Jews in California prisons frequently cited gambling, not alcoholism, as the precipitating factor in their criminal career), and Balinese, Amerinds (prior to the European's arrival) and American Chinese. The Amerinds have now shifted from a gambling to a drinking pattern. It was hypothesized that cultures in which gambling is prevalent will show little drinking, and vice versa. Of the 117 cultures represented in the Yale University Human Relations Area Files, 17 had neither drinking nor gambling, 58 had drinking but not gambling, 21 had both and 33 had gambling but not drinking (the hypopthesized mutual exclusion is significant, p .0005). The concept of functional equivalence, or "equipotentiality," could be relevant to the psychosocial study of alcoholism, according to the authors.

GOMBERG, P. IQ And Race: A Discussion Of Some Confusions. *Ethics* 85(3),258–266 1975.

GÓMEZ- QUIÑONES, Juan. Toward A Perspective On Chicano History. *Aztlan* 2,1–49 1971.

GONG, Eng Ying and Grant, Bruce. *Tong War.* NY N L Brown 1930.

GONZALES, Josephine. The Consequences Of Familial Separation For Chicano Inmates (School Of Ed). Berkeley Univ of Calif 1971.

GONZALES, Ricardo T and Aron, William S and Alger, Norman. Chicanoizing Drug Abuse Programs. *Human Org* 33(4),388–390 Wint 1974.

The problem of drug addiction and its antecedent conditions in the Chicano population of the La Colonia community in Oxnard, California are discussed. The residents of La Colonia are described as being caught in a cycle of poverty, lack of education, and discrimination. Such conditions lead to the creation in the population of a negative self-image, which results in the use of illicit drugs as a means of escape. Several therapeutic interventions suggested by these conditions are described and it is shown how they might be incorporated into a drug abuse treatment program designed to meet the needs of the Chicano drug addicts.

GONZÁLEZ, Nancie L. *The Spanish Americans Of New Mexico: A Distinctive Heritage.* Los Angeles U CA Mex Am S P 1967.

GOODLETT, Carlton B. "Media, Crime And The Black Reality" in *Crime And Its Impact On The Black Community,* Gary, L E And L P Brown (eds), 97–108. Washington DC Howard U 1976.

Goodlett begins his article by reviewing the controversy which rages in this country concerning the relationship between the media and crime. He contends that although they do not actively encourage crime, "the mass media of our nation may very well be moving toward a state in which our keen sense of outrage and compassion is dulled. We may find we not only can tolerate brutality but also we crave it as an essential element in our daily diet." Goodlett also contends that "the media is an instrument utilized by a racist society to reinforce its myth of racial superiority." He concludes that mass communication media among blacks are for all intents and purposes nonexistent.

GOODMAN, James A. "Philosophical/Research Implications Of Definitions Of Crime" in *Crime And Its Impact On The Black Community,* Gary, L & Brown (eds), 51–55. Washington DC Howard U 1976.

The author says "crime as a construct has been defined in terms that rarely have any relationship to the factors that are paramount in the lives of black people." The accepted theories in the literature on criminology, he says, tend to reflect a monolithic view of the black community. Such a perception, thus, "does not allow for the differentiation necessary to the process of research to properly be applied to the issue of crime in the black community." Goodman points out that those theories that are applied to black people are generated by people who reject the sanctity of black life and are not consonant with the reality of black life in America. Goodman concludes his article by stating that the black researcher should not play the "value free" game but rather must raise questions and seek answers that are meaningful. "It is mandatory for the black community to redefine itself, in operational terms, in order to develop a more humane and viable approach to the concept of crime in the black context.

GOODMAN, M E. *Race Awareness In Young Children.* Reading MA Addison–Wesley 1952.

GOODMAN, W. National Lawyers Guild As An All White Organization. *Guild Pract* 30,74–86 1973.

GORDON, David M. *Problems In Political Economy: An Urban Perspective.* Lexington MA Heath 1977.

GORDON, David M. *Theories Of Poverty And Unemployment.* Lexington MA Heath 1972.

GORDON, David M. Capitalism, Class And Crime In America. *Crim Delinq* 19(2),163–186 Ap 1973.

The author, a white economist, observes that most crimes in the US share a single important similarity—"they represent rational responses to the competitiveness and inequality of life in capitalist societies...." Many crimes can usefully be explained by the structure of class institutions and the duality of the public system of the enforcement and administration of justice. That duality, in turn, can fruitfully be explained by the dynamic view of the class–biased role of public institutions and the vested interests which evolve out of the State's activities. It seems unlikely that we can change the patterns of crime and punishment, for the kinds of changes we would need would appear substantially to threaten the stability of the capitalist system. If we managed somehow to eliminate ghetto crime, for instance, the competitiveness, inequalities, and racism of our institutions would tend to reproduce it. Gordon concluded that we must somehow change the entire structure of institutions in order to eliminate the causes of crime.

GORDON, David M. Class And The Economics Of Crime. *Rev Rad Poli Econ* 3,51–75 1971.

GORDON, G and Meers, D R. Aggression And Ghetto–Reared American Negro Children. *Psych Q* 41,585–607 1972.

GORDON, M. "Toward A General Theory Of Racial And Ethnic Group Relations" in *Ethnicity: Theory And Experience*, Glazer, N And D Moynihan (eds). Cambridge MA Harvard Univ Pr 1975.

GORDON, Milton M. *Assimilation In American Life: The Role Of Race, Religion, And National Origin.* NY Oxford Univ Pr 1964.

GORDON, Robert A et al. *Group Process And Gang Delinquency.* Chicago Univ Chicago Pr 1965.

GORDON, Robert A et al. Values And Gang Delinquency: A Study Of Street–Corner Groups. *Am J Soc* 69(2),109–128 1963.

Contrary to expectation, the data indicated no differences between gang, lower–class, and middle–class boys, both Negro and white, in their evaluation and legitimation of behaviors representing middle–class prescriptive norms. These middle–class behaviors were also rated higher than deviant behaviors governed by middle–class proscriptive norms. The samples differed most in their attitude toward the deviant behaviors, with gang boys most tolerant, middle–class boys least tolerant. Blacks were found to evaluate semantic differential images of "someone who makes easy money by pimping and other illegal hustles," "someone who makes out with every girl he wants" and "myself as I usually am" significantly higher than whites within each of the three social levels. This suggests to the authors the existence of a narcissistic syndrome among black adolescent males. However, contrary to expectation, blacks at each social level did *not* evaluate a toughness image higher than their white counterparts. This finding led the authors to infer a degree of independence between attitudes toward the sexual and the aggressive expression of masculinity.

GORDON, Robert A. "Prevalence: The Rare Datum In Delinquency Measurement" in *The Juvenile Justice System*, Klein, Malcolm (ed), 201–284. Beverly Hills CA Sage 1976.

GORDON, Robert A. Crime And Cognition: An Evolutionary Perspective, Second International Symposium On Criminology. Sao Paulo Brazil Bio Med–For Crim 1975.

The author cites his own earlier studies which found that the "prevalence" (proportion of an age–cohort that become delinquent by age 18) of official delinquency among blacks is three to four times as large as among whites, and he presents a theory which relates race to delinquency by way of IQ, which is argued to be genetically determined. Expanding on the work of Arthur Jensen, the author argues that "delinquents come disproportionately from populations that are quite adequate in Level I (associative or role learning) ability, but which are low, by the standards of modern industrial societies, in Level II (IQ) ability." Whites and blacks, and middle–class and lower–class populations, are claimed to differ less on measures of Level I than of Level II ability, which is argued to be in large measure genetically determined. Level I ability is claimed to represent an earlier stage of evolutionary development, and hence is genetically fixed to a greater degree in the species.

GORDON, Robert A. "Research On IQ, Race, And Delinquency: Taboo Or Not Taboo" in *Taboos In Criminology*, Sagarin, Edward (ed). Beverly Hills CA Sage 1980.

GORDON, Thomas. Notes On White And Black Psychology. *J Soc Issues* 29(1),87–95 1973.

GOSSETT, Thomas F. *Race: The History Of An Idea In America.* Dallas TX SMU Pr 1963.

This Ford–funded study explores how ideas of race have affected currents of thought in the US, with primary emphasis on 19th and 20th century writings. Chapters include: Early Race Theories; England's American Colonies and Race Theories; Eighteenth–Century Anthropology; Nineteenth–Century Anthropology; The Teutonic Origins Theory; The Study of Language and Literature; Race and Social Darwinism; The Social Gospel and Race; Literary Naturalism and Race; The Indian in the Nineteenth Century; The Status of the Negro: 1865–1915; Anti–Immigration Agitation: 1865–1915; Imperialism and the Anglo Saxon; World War I and Racism; Racism in the 1920's; The Scientific Revolt Against Racism; The Battle Against Prejudice. While little attention is devoted directly to the role of race in theories of criminality, some analysis is performed on the works of Charles H. Cooley, Richard Dugdale, Charles Loring Brace, Auguste Comte, Charles Darwin, Francis Galton, Francis Lieber, and various other theorists whose works have been important in the development of criminology.

GOSSETT, W T. Bar Must Encourage More Negro Lawyers. *Trial* 4,22+– 1968.

GOTTFREDSON, Michael and Garofalo, James and Hindelang, Michael J. *Victims Of Personal Crime: An Empirical Foundation For A Theory Of Victimization.* Cambridge MA Ballinger 1978.

GOULD, Leroy C. Who Defines Delinquency: A Comparison Of Self–Reported And Officially–Reported Indices Of Delinquency For Three Racial Groups. *Social Prob* 16,325–336 1969.

Because of the limitations inherent in "official" delinquency statistics, many criminologists have turned to self–report delinquency measures. In doing this, however, they have failed to examine the relationship (both empirical and theoretical) between these two measures of delinquency. This article reports such an examination involving three racial groups: Negroes, Caucasians, and Orientals. The study finds: (1) that the traditional relationship between race and delinquency does not hold when self–report delinquency measures are used and (2) that officially reported and self–reported delinquency are related only among Caucasians. The paper discusses the implications of these findings for criminological theory and argues that criminologists should recognize at least three distinct concepts of delinquency: delinquent acts, official delinquency, and self–perceived delinquency.

GRABOSKY, P N. Theory And Research On Variations In Penal Severity. *Br J L Soc* 5,103–114 Sum 1978.

GRAHAM, Fred P. *The Self–Inflicted Wound.* NY Macmillan 1970.
A nationally known journalist and attorney covers the Warren years of the US Supreme Court in the context of the turbulent 1960's.

GRAHAM, Fred P. Black Crime: The Lawless Image. *Harper's Mag* 241,64–65,68–71 S 1970.

GRANT, Bruce and Gong, Eng Ying. *Tong War.* NY N L Brown 1930.

GRANT, Edwin. Scum From The Melting Pot. *Am J Soc* 30,641–651 My 1925.

GRANT, J B. *Indian Justice Planning Project (Arizona State Justice Planning).* Phoenix Ariz Just Plan 1971.

GRANT, R and Milne, R and White, R. Minority Recruiting: The Tucson Police Experience. *J Polic Sci Adm* 3(2),197–202 1975.

The attempts of the Tucson Police Department to recruit qualified minorities (blacks and Mexican–Americans) into police work are examined in this article. In November 1971 a black officer was assigned to the personnel section as a minority recruiter. In less than 18 months the black complement of the agency rose from 3 to 11, or 2.83% of commissioned strength and Mexican–American representation rose from 35 to 42 or 10.7% of all police officer positions. The technique employed by the recruiter was one which emphasized personal contact and discussion of police work. The following steps were taken by the department: elimination of the Otis Employment Test, permanent assignment of a minority recruiting officer, termination of minimum height and weight requirements, adoption of a validated Police Officer Entrance Examination, reclassification of "policeman/policewoman" to "police officer," an end to separate assignments based on sex, modification of physical agility requirements and the adoption of a selective Certification Program for minorities. The program initiated by this department has been highly successful, and has been extended to attract other groups including Native–Americans and women.

GRAY, David B and Revelle, William. A Cluster Analytic Critique Of The Multifactor Racial Attitude Inventory. *Psycholog Rec* 22(1),103–112 1972.

The Multifactor Racial Attitude Inventory (MRAI), a major 10 factor measurement of whites' attitudes toward blacks, was reanalyzed by using a new hierarchical cluster technique to locate factors with greater unidimensionality. Four clusters emerged (public, private, black superiority, and gradualism) with reliabilities between .90 and .66. The mean intercorrelation between the four new clusters was .23, contrasted to .54 for the 10 MRAI factors. All four of the new clusters met a 39% or less overlap criterion, whereas only three of the original 10 factors met this criterion. The four scale solution produced subscales with markedly greater independence than existed for the subscales in the 10 factor solution.

GREAR, Mary P and Jacobs, James B. *Drop—Outs And Rejects: An Analysis Of The Prison Guard's Revolving Door. Crim Just Rev* 2(2),57—70 1977.

Results of a sample survey of 55 former prison guards indicate that the most significant factor accounting for high employee turnover among guards is race. Young urban blacks have trouble relating to fellow guards and young rural whites have difficulty relating with black inner—city prisoners.

GREBLER, Leo and Moore, Joan W and Guzman, Ralph C. *The Mexican—American People: The Nation's Second Largest Minority.* NY Free Pr 1970.

GREEN, Charles Bernard. *Rel Bet Selected Personal Char Of Confined Narcotic Off And The Amn't Of Time Serv'd Prior To Their Official Referral Consideration.* Unpub PhD Diss US Internat Univ 1972.

The possible relationships between selected personality characteristics of confined narcotic offenders and the amount of time served (number of weeks criterion) prior to their official referral for release to outpatient status were investigated. Subjects were assigned to three groups based on ethnic classification. There was no significant relationship between the actual number of weeks and the predicted number of weeks served by each group separately and combined. No score on the Tennessee Self—Concept Scale was significantly related to the number of weeks criterion for any group. There was no correlation between selected personality characteristics and the factor and the number of weeks criterion. The three groups were not different statistically in terms of the number of weeks served prior to referral for release to outpatient status. Given the age, ethnic classification, and the subscales of the two instruments used, it is possible to predict the number of weeks criterion. The Mexican—American residents spend significantly more time to referral to outpatient status than whites.

GREEN, Edward. *Judicial Attitudes Toward Sentencing.* NY Macmillan 1961.

GREEN, Edward. *Inter— And Intra—Racial Crime Relative To Sentencing. J Crim L Crimin & Pol Sci* 55,348—358 1964.

GREEN, Edward. *Race, Social Status, And Criminal Arrest. Am Sociol Rev* 35,476—490 1970.

To examine the relationship between race and crime, the black/white arrest rate differential for selected years between 1942 and 1965 in Ypsilanti, Mich., were analyzed on the basis of demographic variables. Data indicate disproportionately high arrest rates for both black and white males, youths 17 to 24 years old, semiskilled and unskilled occupational classes, unemployed individuals, and non—Michigan (predominately southern) natives. The racial variation does not reflect age or sex variations between the two races since these are approximately equivalent. The races do, however, significantly differ in the distribution of occupational and natal (place of birth) characteristics. When these differences are controlled, the arrest rates for the two races tend toward parity, with slightly higher arrest rates for whites in several instances. Even for serious crimes of violence, migrant whites incur substantially higher arrest rates than native—born (i.e., in Michigan) blacks at every occupational level. Moreover, although the incidence of black crime has greatly increased between 1942 and 1965 owing to the increase in black population, the rate of black crime has decreased.*

GREEN, Edward. *The Class Nature Of The Urban Police During The Period Of Black Municipal Power. Crim & Soc Just* 9,49—62 Spr—Sum 1978.

GREEN, Mark J (ed) and Wasserstein, Bruce (ed). *With Justice For Some: An Indictment Of The Law By Young Advocates.* Boston Beacon Pr 1970.

GREENBERG, David F and Stender, Fay. *The Prison As A Lawless Agency. Buffalo L Rev* 21(3),799—838 Spr 1972.

"The genius of the American criminal justice system has been the extent to which it has accomodated itself to the heterogeneity of the American population. It might be very difficult to sustain lawlessness in prisons or in court if all of us were exposed to it." But most Americans are never processed by the police, courts, and prisons. "With few exceptions, this unenviable experience is reserved for those with dark skin, little money, for cultural deviants, and those with threatening ideas." The reason, they contend, is not that these groups are the most criminal in our society; the explanation lies in the systemic biases and discriminatory institutional practices which characterize the law and its enforcement.

GREENBERG, Douglas S. *Crime And Law Enforcement In The Colony Of New York, 1691—1776.* Ithaca NY Cornell Univ Pr 1974.

GREENBERG, Douglas S. *Patterns Of Criminal Prosecution In Eighteenth—Century New York. NY Hist* 56(2),132—153 Ap 1975.

GREENBERG, Jack. *Race Relations And American Law.* NY Columbia Univ Pr 1959.

GREENE, Helen E Taylor (comp). *A Comprehensive Bibliography Of Criminology And Criminal Justice Literature By Black Authors From 1895 To 1978.* Hyattsville MD Ummah 1979.

This bibliography is intended as a research tool for indentifying criminal justice and criminology literature by black authors. While race and crime is a prominent theme in criminology, the black perspective on this issue has been neglected. This bibliography is intended to bring black perspectives and insights to the mainstream of criminology literature. The bibliography was compiled in a literature search of the Library of Congress, the Howard University Moorland Spingarn Research Center, and the University of Maryland. Though several authors whose race could not be determined were omitted, the present compilation represents the majority of writings by black authors. Covering periodical literatue, literature in edited volumes, and chapters from books, the first section contains 253 entries, while the section on books has 39 entries. The special reports category contains 31 listings, and the final section on theses and dissertations presents 26 publications. Most of the material dates from the 1970's but there are publications included that date from 1907. The bibliography is not annotated. Author and subject indexes are provided.*

GREENE, Helen E Taylor and Caldwell, Loretta. "Implementing A Black Perspective In Criminal Justice" in *Improving Management In Criminal Justice*, Cohn, Alvin W And Benjamin Ward (eds). Beverly Hills CA Sage 1980.

GREENE, Jack P (ed) and Cohen, David M (ed). *Neither Slave Nor Free: The Freedman Of African Descent In The Slave Societies Of The New World.* Baltimore MD Johns Hopkins Pr 1972.

GREENE, Johnny. *Did The FBI Kill Viola Liuzzo?* Playboy ,101+ O 1980.

GREENE, Lorenzo M. *The Negro In Colonial New England.* NY Columbia Univ Pr 1942.

GREENWOOD, Peter W and Petersilia, Joan. *Mandatory Prison Sentences: Their Projected Effects On Crime And Prison Populations.* Santa Monica CA Rand Corp 1977.

GREENWOOD, Peter W and Petersilia, Joan. *Mandatory Prison Sentences: Their Projected Effects On Crime And Prison Populations. J Crim L & Crimin* 69(4),604—615 Wint 1978.

GREGORY, Dick and Lipsyte, Robert. *Nigger: An Autobiography.* NY E P Dutton 1964.

GRIER, William H and Cobbs, Price M. *Black Rage.* NY Bantam 1969.

GRIFFIN, James S and Rowan, Richard H. *St Paul——Police Department——Minority Recruitment Program. Pol Chief* 44(1),18,20 Ja 1977.

The recruitment effort reported in this article was begun in 1970 after a federal court decision was rendered against St. Paul, Minnesota. At the time of this suit, seven members (1.4%) of the 525 police officers in St. Paul were black, while blacks comprised 3.5% of the city's population. The total minority population of St. Paul was 6%. James Griffin, co—author of this article, was placed in charge of minority recruitment for the St. Paul Police Department——the goal of the department was set at hiring 60 black male applicants. The following programs were used to attain this goal: oral—interview tutorial sessions stressing the typical questions asked of persons during that phase of the application process, physical training and preparation for the physical agility test, written exam tutorials with discussion and practice test—taking, media support and coverage of the recruitment effort along with community—disseminated brochures and fliers, and meetings with interested groups including schools and colleges. The authors report that the results of this program have been good. Of the 94 minority persons who took the exam for police work, 53 passed.

GRIGGS, E A et al. *Conducting Civil Rights Compliance Reviews——A Manual Draft.* Washington DC Univ Research Corp 1978.

A standardized format for selecting LEAA grant and fund recipient agencies for civil rights compliance reviews and for conducting these reviews is presented in this manual by the Office for Civil Rights Compliance (OCRC). The manual begins with background material on the purpose of the civil rights compliance review (to ensure that no person is discriminated against regarding participation in, employment with, or receiving benefits from programs or activities funded by the Crime Control or Juvenile Justice Acts).

Then the four elements of the review process are described, i.e., selection of an agency for review, notification of the agency of its selection, site visits to the agency, and conveyance of findings or recommendations. The full text of statutory provisions under which OCRC conducts compliance reviews is furnished as well as an easy–to–understand summary of the LEAA subpart d and e regulations regarding compliance reviews.*

GRIGGS, E and Sayer, K. *Equal Employment Opportunity Plan Development Participant's Reference Handbook.* Washington DC Univ Research Corp 1976.

Training materials are presented from a workshop on equal employment opportunity and affirmative action compliance program development for recipients of LEAA assistance. The materials were part of a 2–day workshop in Colorado that focused on LEAA equal employment opportunity laws, rules, and regulations; the purpose and philosophy of affirmative recruitment; and techniques and skills required for undertaking affirmative action programs and developing equal employment opportunity plans at the agency level. The handbook also includes US Department of Justice rules and regulations on nondiscrimination in federally assisted crime control and juvenile delinquency programs (and related questions and answers); LEAA guidelines for complying with the rules and regulations; uniform guidelines on employee selection procedures proposed in December 1977 by four federal agencies; the US Civil Service Commission's guidelines for evaluating state and local government personnel operations; guidelines on eliminating sexist language from writing; and a glossary of affirmative action terminology.*

GRIMSHAW, Allen (ed). *Racial Violence In The US.* Chicago IL Aldine 1969.

GRIMSHAW, Allen. *A Study In Social Violence: Urban Race Riot In The United States.* Unpub PhD Diss Univ of Penn 1959.

GRIMSHAW, Allen. Actions Of Police And The Military In American Race Riots. *Phylon* 24,271–289 1963.

Reviewing some of the major outbreaks of interracial violence occuring in the US during this century, the author posits that the actions or inactions of external forces of control, i.e., police and military, play a pivotal role in the occurrence or non–occurrence of racial violence. The tactical goals of police anti–riot procedures are examined as to their effectiveness and applicability.

GRIMSHAW, Allen. Changing Patterns Of Racial Violence In The United States. *Notre Dame Law* 40,534–548 1965.

Grimshaw outlines several major periods in US history where Negro–white race relations have been characterized by a significant amount of violence. The most intense conflicts have arisen when the subordinate minority groups have attempted to disrupt the social status quo, or when the dominant white majority has perceived such an attempt. Unlike the earlier civil rights activities which focused largely on the goals of the black middle class, American ghetto riots seen as expressions of protest from the black underclass who have not shared in these black gains. The ghetto disturbances have focused on more mundane concerns such as economic subsistence and everyday relations with the police. Viewing the modern riots as uprisings of a minority in a minority, the author posits they will become more class oriented rather than race oriented uprisings.

GRIMSHAW, Allen. Language As Obstacle And As Data In Sociological Research. *Items* 23,17–21 1969.

GRIMSHAW, Allen. Lawlessness And Violence In America And Their Special Manifestations In Changing Negro–White Relations. *J Negro Hist* 44(1),52–72 Ja 1959.

GRIMSHAW, Allen. Three Views Of Urban Violence: Civil Disturbance, Racial Revolt, Class Assault. *Am Behav Sci* 2,2–7 Mr–Ap 1968.

In contrast to earlier racial riots, the events of the 1960's have a complexity of motivation and of relations to the larger social structure which eludes any easy interpretation. The author identifies three main sets of interpretations, the principal proponents of each perspective, and then relates the various explanations to the locations of their proponents within the social structure.

GRISWOLD, David B. Police Discrimination: An Elusive Question. *J Polic Sci Adm* 6(1),61–66 Mr 1978.

GRISWOLD, Erwin N. The *Bakke* Problem—Allocation Of Scarce Resources In Education And Other Areas. *Wash U L Q* 1979(1),55–80 Wint 1979.

GROSS, B R. *Discrimination In Reverse—Is Turnabout Fair Play?* NY New York Univ Pr 1978.

Along with a catalog and analysis of every argument offered in favor of reverse discrimination, the concept of reverse discrimination and its consequences are discussed philosophically. According to this analysis, arguments in favor of reverse discrimination should be opposed by showing that (1) they are unsound, (2) some of their premises and conclusions violate the principles which make possible a liberal and democratic society, and (3) the substantive outcome reverse discrimination is supposed to yield is unlikely to occur. It is a necessary condition of reverse discrimination, according to the text, that it be directed to groups, thus distinguishing it from preferential treatment, which is not so directed. Major questions raised concerning these arguments are listed, and arguments against reverse discrimination are presented. No argument for or against reverse discrimination is by itself decisive. However, the balance of argument is heavily against reverse discrimination and preferential treatment both for moral and for practical reasons. Finally, comments on the justice of reverse discrimination and its administration are noted.*

GROSSACK, M. Group Belongingness Among Negroes. *J Soc Psychol* 43,167–180 1956.

GROVES, Eugene and Rossi, Peter. Police Perceptions Of A Hostile Ghetto: Realism Or Projection. *Am Behav Sci* 13,727–744 1970.

GRUBER, Murray. The Nonculture Of Poverty Among Black Youths. *Social Wk* 17(3),50–58 1972.

In his study of the aspirations, expectations, and attitudes toward protest of Negro youths in Cleveland, Gruber found the culture of poverty theory to be both theoretically and empirically inadequate. Gruber states that most of the youths interviewed subscribed to the great American dream of getting on. They were not part of a stagnant cultural backwater; if anything, he states, they tended to overestimate what they would be able to achieve educationally and occupationally. Gruber also found that no unilinear relationship existed between the hardships experienced by a group and the development of protest movement. Of the various ways of conceptualizing deprivation, however, he found only two measures linked to protest: expected deprivation and relative deprivation. According to Gruber, these measures suggest that men protest when they envision their future rewards as few, regardless of how low their current status is or how immobile they may appear to be. Gruber concludes by recommending a shift in emphasis from a policy of socialization and resocialization as implied in the culture of poverty theory.

GRUPP, Stanley E. Multiple Drug Use In A Sample Of Experienced Marijuana Smokers. *Int J Addic* 7(3),481–491 1972.

A selected sample of 90 experienced marijuana smokers, composed of 30 college students, 30 prison inmates, and 30 ghetto blacks were interviewed via a 27–page questionnaire to determine the pattern of use of drugs other than marijuana. Persons who had used heroin, regardless of the extent of their experience, were not included in the sample. The data indicated that 81% had some experience with at least one other drug besides marijuana. Barbiturates were mentioned by 50%; amphetamines by 40%; some type of hallucinogen by 33%. In terms of the frequency of drugs mentioned, college students reported using an average of 3.4, prison inmates an average of 2.7, and ghetto blacks an average of 1.4. College students were least, and ghetto blacks most apt to be intensive drug users. The results of the study indicate that marijuana users are not a homogeneous group, are not all oriented to marijuana in the same way, are not of similar character, and show varying patterns in the use of drugs other than marijuana.

GUBLER, B H. *Constitutional Analysis Of The Criminal Jurisdiction And Procedural Guarantees Of The American Indian.* Palo Alto CA R & E Research 1963.

GULLATTEE, Alyce C. "Black Self–Identity And Crime" in *Crime And Its Impact On The Black Community*, Gary, L E And L P Brown (eds), 109–120. Washington DC Howard U 1976.

GUNDERSON, E K E and Arthur, R J and Nail, R L. Black–White Differences In Social Background And Military Drug Abuse Patterns. *Am J Psychiatry* 131(10),1097–1102 1974.

GURR, Ted. "A Comparative Study Of Civil Strife" in *Violence In America*, Graham, Hugh D And T Gurr (eds), 572–626. NY Bantam 1969.

GUTIERREZ, G G. The Undocumented Immigrant: The Limits Of Cost–Benefit Analysis. *Pub Man* 62(9),8–11 O 1980.

The extent of administrative and fiscal burdens attributable to the presence of undocumented immigrants in American cities cannot be easily assessed. A complete cost–benefit analysis must consider that some costs may be offset by contributions to local revenues. The assumption that scarce resources are being absorbed by other than deserving citizens simply has not been substantiated. The problem of illegal immigration over the Mexican–American border is more suitably addressed through international relations. Factors to be considered are more likely within the province of federal agencies, not local city management.

GUZMAN, Jessie Parkhurst (ed). "Division X: Race Riots In The US, 1942–1946, Division XIII: Lynching" *Negro Year Book, 1947.* Tuskegee AL Tuskegee Institute 1947.

GUZMAN, Ralph C and Grebler, Leo and Moore, Joan W. *The Mexican–American People: The Nation's Second Largest Minority.* NY Free Pr 1970.

HABENSTEIN, R (ed) and Mindel, C H (ed). *Ethnic Families In America.* NY Elsevier 1976.

HABER, David and Dorsen, Norman and Emerson, Thomas I. *Political And Civil Rights In The United States.* Boston Little, Brown 1967.

HACKER, Andrew. The Violent Black Minority. *NYT Mag* , My 10 1970.

HACKER, Ervin. Criminality And Immigration. *J Am Inst Cr L Crim* 20,429–438 1929.

HACKLER, J C and Linden, E. The Response Of Adults To Delinquency Prevention Programs: The Race Factor. *J Res Crim Del* 7(1),31–45 1970. Delinquency prevention programs usually attempt to modify a select number of boys who either share individual characteristics or live in a specific area. Rarely is it asked if such programs have an impact on parents or other adults who come into conract with these boys. The Opportunities for Youth Project in Seattle seemed to have little impact on boys who participated in terms of traditional instruments used to evaluate such experiments. However, the positive attitudes of the boys toward the project caused suspicion that the program did make an impact on the residents. This paper questions the assumption that people living in lower class areas are apathetic and unresponsive to experimental programs. The data suggest that Negro residents and parents were more supportive of the youth employment program than white residents. These differences might be explained by "differential perceived mobility"; that is, Negroes may see themselves as upwardly mobile (at least in terms of opportunities for their children) while whites in central areas may view themselves as downwardly mobile.

HAGAN, John. Criminal Justice In Rural And Urban Communities: A Study Of The Bureaucratization Of Justice. *Soc Forces* 55,597–612 Mr 1977.

HAGAN, John. Extra–Legal Attributes And Criminal Sentences: An Assessment Of A Sociological Viewpoint. *Law & Soc Rev* 8,357–383 Spr 1974.

HAGAN, John. Looking Up The Indians: A Case Of Law Reform. *Can F* 55,16–18 1976.

HAGAN, W T. Indian Policy After The Civil War: The Reservation Experience. Indian Hist Soc Lectures 1970.

HAGAN, W T. *Indian Police And Judges.* New Haven CT Yale Univ Pr 1966.

HAGAN, W T. *United States—Comanche Relations.* New Haven CT Yale Univ Pr 1976.

HAHN, Harlan. Cops And Rioters: Ghetto Perceptions Of Social Conflict And Control. *Am Behav Sci* 13,761–780 1970.

HAHN, Harlan. Ghetto Assessments Of Police Protection And Authority. *Law & Soc Rev* 6(1),183–194 1971.

HALATYN, T V and Wenk, E A. *Analysis Of Classification Factors For Young Adult Offenders: Race Factors,* V3. San Francisco NCCD 1974. This California–based project was undertaken to organize the results of an extensive data collection on the youthful offender and to provide a resource for the correctional theorist working with this most important offender group. Background data, personality and other test results, academic and vocational skills and attitudes, and psychiatric factors, as well as offense related information and the ratings and recommendations of institutional staffs were obtained on 4,146 male California Youth Authority parolees. This effort was envisioned as a prerequisite to the development of typological descriptions of youthful offenders that may ultimately influence their treatment and rehabilitation. After providing a brief background on the entire study and a review of the literature on the

relationship of race and delinquency, this volume presents comparative data on black, Mexican–American, and white Youth Authority parolees. Controlling for race, the study presents information on academic, intelligence, vocational, personality, psychiatric, and offense–related factors. The relationship of these variables to parole success is also analyzed.*

HALEY, Alex. *Roots.* NY Dell 1976.

HALIKAS, J A et al. The Black Addict: I Methodology, Chronology Of Addiction, And Overview Of The Population. *Am J Drug Al Ab* 3,529–543 1976.

HALL, Edwin L and Simkus, Albert A. Inequality In The Types Of Sentences Received By Native Americans And Whites. *Criminology* 13(2),199–222 Ag 1975.

A comparison of the distribution of the types of sentences imposed on Native American offenders and white offenders by the district courts of a western state reveals that the Native American offenders are more likely to receive sentences involving incarceration in the state prison and are less likely to receive sentences which would allow them partially to escape stigmatization as convicted felons. The introduction of a number of test factors revealed that these ethnic differences in the sentence received would only slightly be explained by ethnic differences in the kinds of offenses involved or in other differences in the legal and personal background characteristics of the offenders. A number of possible explanations of the discrepancies in the sentencing of Native Americans and whites are discussed. It is suggested that these discrepancies in themselves may contribute to an increased probability that the Native American offenders will engage in future criminal activity and that these offenders will continue to receive harsher sentences than white offenders.

HALL, G and Saltzstein, A. Equal Employment Opportunity For Minorities In Municipal Government. *Social Sci Q* 57,864–872 Mr 1977.

This study examines the differences in employment patterns for black and Mexican Americans in municipal governments and delineates some of the conditions underlying racial employment patterns. The study utilized newly available data on 26 Texas cities with a population of over 50,000. Employment data contained in Equal Employment Opportunity–3 forms were aggregated by city to create two dependent varibles for both black and Spanish–surnamed employees: (1) percentage of professionals in city government who belong to each group, (2) use index for each group which considers both a mnority group's representation in an organization and its distribution across salary levels. Despite the small sample size and its restriction to Texas cities, the findings suggested that unexpected complexities in urban minority employment could affect the success of personnel policies. Policies stressing education and training were found more effective with Spanish–surnamed population than with black employees. It was found that federal strategies to enhance the employment status of minorities in municipal governments must take into consideration the specific group requiring assistance.*

HALL, Jacqueline Dowd. *Revolt Against Chivalry: Jessie Daniel Ames And The Women's Campaign Against Lynching.* NY Columbia Univ Pr 1979.

HALL, N E and Waldo, Gordon P. Delinquency Potential And Attitudes Toward The Criminal Justice System. *Soc Forces* 49(2),291–298 1970.

HALLECK, Seymour. "The Future Of Psychiatric Criminology" in *Biology And Crime*, Jeffrey, C R (ed). Beverly Hills CA Sage 1979.

HALLIDAY, A P. Thirty Delinquent Negro Children. *Smith Coll Stud Soc Wk* 1,238–259 1931.

HALSELL, Grace. *The Illegals.* NY Stein & Day 1978.
An inquiry into the plight of "illegal aliens" along the US–Mexican border, and the system designed to prevent their entry.

HAMBLIN, R L and Abrahamson, M J and Burgess, R L. "Diagnosing Delinquency" in *Law And Order: Modern Criminals*, Short Jr, James F (ed), 19–31. Chicago Aldine 1970.

HAMILTON JR, James. *An Account Of The Late Intended Insurrection Among A Portion Of The Blacks Of This City.* Charleston n. p. 1822.

HAMM, C W and Kobetz, R W. Contemporary Problems In Law Enforcement On American Indian Reservations. *Pol Chief* 37(7),58–61 Jl 1970.

HAMMARLEY, John. Inside The Mexican Mafia. *New West* 2,67–71 D 19 1977.

HAMMER, M. Suicide, And White Reformatory Girl's Preference For Negro Men. *Corr Psychi J Soc Ther* 15(3),99–102 1969.

HAMMER, Richard. Report From A Spanish Harlem 'fortress'. *NYT Mag*, Ja 5 1962.

HAMMOND, Phillip and Palmore, E B. Interacting Factors In Juvenile Delinquency. *Am Sociol Rev* 29,848–854 1964.

HAMMONDS, A D and Summers, G F. Effect Of Racial Characteristics Of Investigator On Self–Enumerated Responses To A Negro Prejudice Scale. *Soc Forces* 44,515–518 1966.

HANDLIN, Oscar. *The Newcomers· Negroes And Puerto Ricans In A Changing Metropolis.* NY Doubleday 1959.

It seems possible to conclude...that the division of...[black and Puerto Ricans] and the wider deviations of the Negroes, are due to the forces that weaken their sense of purpose in life—to the shock of migration with its attendant disruptions of family authority, to low economic conditions and slum life, and to the feebleness of internal communal institutions which deprive these groups of control and disciplines.

HANDLIN, Oscar. The Quest For Equality. *Wash U L Q* 1979(1),35–50 Wint 1979.

HANDMAN, L R. Underrepresentation Of Economic Groups On Federal Juries. *Boston U L Rev* 57(1),198–224 Ja 1977.

HANEY, Craig and Banks, Curtis and Zimbardo, Philip. Interpersonal Dynamics In A Simulated Prison. *Int J Crimin Pen* 1(1),69–97 1973.

HANNERZ, Ulf. *Soul Side: Inquires Into Ghetto Culture And Community.* NY Columbia Univ Pr 1969.

HARDING, Richard and Fahey, Richard P. Killings By Chicago Police, 1969–70: An Empirical Study. *S Cal L Rev* 46(2),284–315 Mr 1973.

HARLAN, Alan and Feagin, Joe R. *Ghetto Revolts: The Politics Of Violence In American Cities.* NY Macmillan 1973.

HARMON, Kenneth R (ed) and Bundy, Mary Lee (ed). *The National Prison Directory.* College Park MD Urban Info Interpr 1975.

HARPER, Dean. Aftermath Of A Long, Hot Summer. *Trans–Act* 2,7–11 Jl–Ag 1965.

HARPER, Frederick D (ed). *Alcohol Abuse And Black America.* Alexandria VA Douglass Pub 1976.

HARPER, Frederick D. "The Impact Of Alcohol On Crime In The Black Community" in *Crime And Its Impact On The Black Community*, Gary, L P & L E Brown (eds), 77–84. Washington DC Howard U 1976.

The author notes that although it has been found through national surveys that there is no significant difference between the proportion of blacks who drink and whites who drink, when it comes to heavy drinking blacks tend to drink more heavily than their white counterparts, especially on weekends. Among women, while a larger proportion of black women do not drink, of those black women who do drink, a large proportion are heavy drinkers. The author presents and discusses some historical, sociological and psychological hypotheses with which to explain these facts. He then notes the extent of offenses committed or suffered under the influence of alcohol and considers the question, "what are conditions in the black community that interact with alcohol abuse to influence criminal offenses or the acting out in ways which are legally and socially unacceptable?"

HARPER, Frederick D and Dawkins, M P. Alcohol Abuse In The Black Community. *Black Scholar* 8(6),23–31 1977.

HARRIES, Keith D. *Crime And Environment.* Springfield IL Chas C Thomas 1980.

This study focuses on the relationship between human and physical environments and criminal behavior. The first human environment considered is the macroenvironment, which is urban, regional and national in scope. Emphasis is placed on the characteristics of urbanization, city size, and population density as they relate to crime. A generalized interurban ecological model of variations in crime rates among american cities is also analyzed, using such variables as physical context, minority status, socioeconomic status, and resources allocated to law enforcement. The second level of human environment is the microenvironment, or local environment. Discussions of burglary, rape, assault, and robbery refer to distribution of the crime in space and time, characteristics of victims, and socioeconomic variables. Density and crowding should be distinguished in future studies, since overcrowding seems to have a positive relationship to crime while density does not. The relationship of crime and climate is treated seasonally and in terms of weather influences.*

HARRIES, Keith D. *The Geography Of Crime And Justice.* NY McGraw–Hill 1974.

No geographical study can explain why crime occurs or exactly how to control it, but an understanding of spatial interrelationships may assist in both endeavors. Crime and justice vary significantly from place to place and the descriptive and analytical tools of the geographer are therefore useful additions to the social science effort to gain a better understanding of the nature and causes of crime. Chapter 1 concentrates on preliminary concepts and definitions. Subsequent chapters treat spatial variations in detail. Chapters 2–4 approach geographical variations in crime at progressively smaller scales of area resolution––the state, intermetropolitan, and intrametropolitan levels. Chapter 5 looks descriptively at geographical variations in selected elements of the criminal justice system: variations in law; law enforcement standards; sentencing patterns; capital punishment; judicial selection process; jury selection procedures and jail facilities. Chapter 6 discusses some of the possible contributions of geographical analyses of crime and justice.

HARRIES, Keith D. Recent Literature On The Geography Of Crime: Review And Comment. *Pa Geographer* 13(3),3–9 1975.

HARRIES, Keith D. Rejoinder To Richard Peet 'The Geography Of Crime; A Political Critique'. *Prof Geog* 27(3),280–282 1975.

HARRING, Sid et al. The Management Of Police Killings. *Crim & Soc Just* 8,34–43 Fall–Wint 1977.

HARRIS, Anthony R. Imprisonment And The Expected Value Of Criminal Choice: A Specification And Test Of Aspects Of The Labeling Perspective. *Am Sociol Rev* 40(1),71–87 F 1975.

HARRIS, Anthony R. Race, Commitment To Deviance, And Spoiled Identity. *Am Sociol Rev* 41,432–442 1976.

Data generated by 234 young black and white inmates in 1971 challenge the assumption, widely held within the labelling perspective, that "spoiled identity" is a necessary, socially invariant outcome of deviant commitment and self–definition. The findings reveal that while for whites "criminal" self–typing is significantly related to the spoiling of identity, as operationalized by a series of measures of psychological well–being, for blacks the relationship between such typing and identity spoilation is not significant. Even stronger cross–race interaction is observed on a related aspect of identity: while for whites instrumental commitment to criminal choice is also associated with heightened identity spoilation, for blacks higher levels of criminal commitment are associated with lessened spoilation (i.e., higher levels of psychological well–being). An argument is developed which attempts to interpret these findings in the more general theoretical context of caste, social membership, and ascribed versus attained status.

HARRIS, Kay and Dunbaugh, Frank. Premise For A Sensible Sentencing Debate. *Hofstra L Rev* 7(2),417–456 Wint 1979.

HARRIS, N Dwight. *The History Of Negro Servitude In Illinois And Of The Slavery Agitation In That State 1719–1864.* Chicago A A McClurg 1904.

HARRIS, Richard E. *A Study Of Teen–age Behavior Among Negroes, Mexicans, Puerto Ricans, Japanese, Chinese, Filipino And American Indians.* Los Angeles Wetzel Pub Co 1954.

HARRIS, Richard. *The Fear Of Crime.* NY Praeger 1968.

HARRIS, William and Jensen, Gary and Stauss, Joseph. Crime, Delinquency And The American Indian. *Human Org* 36(3),252–257 Fall 1977.

HARSHA, W J. "Law For The Indians" in *Americanizing The American Indians*, Prucha, Francis P (ed). Cambridge MA Harvard Univ Pr 1973.

HART, L G. *Working For You––A Guide To Employing Women In Non–Traditional Jobs.* Washington DC Wider Opp Women 1977.

HART, Philip A. Swindling And Knavery, Inc. *Playboy*, 155–162 Ag 1972.

HARTMAN, Paul and Husband, Charles. The Mass Media And Racial Conflict. *Race* 12,267–282 Ja 1971.

The news media play a crucial role in maintaining an informed state of public opinion and a functioning democracy by providing information, defining issues and interpreting events. The authors identify a number of factors pertaining to the news media which operate to structure the news coverage of race related matters in a way that causes people to see the situation primarily as one of actual or potential conflict. The result is that real conflict is amplified and potential for conflict created.

HARTUNG, Frank E and Floch, Maurice. A Social–Psychological Analysis Of Prison Riots: An Hypothesis. *J Crim L Crimin & Pol Sci* 47(1),51–57 My–Je 1956.

HARTUNG, Frank E. Trends In The Use Of Capital Punishment. *Ann Am Poli* 284,8–19 1952.

This study was primarily based on data from the North Carolina Board of Charities on commitments for capital crimes, and *National Prisoner Statistics* on executions. The 200 condemned persons admitted to North Carolina prisons between 1910 and 1928 are broken down by race, sex, literacy, and race and sex by type of offense. It then distributes *National Prisoner Statistics* data on executions for the entire US 1930–1950 by race; and figures for the same source for the period 1937–1940 by race and by sex. Using similar data for 1940–1946, persons executed who were under twenty years old were distributed by race. The study then gives data (no source given) on rape convictions and executions in Virginia (1909–1950) and Louisiana (1900–1950) by race. The author concludes that "(t)he death penalty is in this country predominantly and disproportionately imposed upon Negroes, the poor and the less educated, and men."

HASSON, Robert C. *The Socio Cultural Context Of Deviance.* Boulder CO U CO TriEthn R P 1963.

HAUBERG, Clifford A. *Puerto Rico And The Puerto Ricans: A Study Of Puerto Rican History And Immigration To The United States.* NY Twayne 1974.

HAVLICK, J R and Wade, Mary. The American City And Civil Disorders. *Urb Data Serv* 1,1–32 1969.

HAWKINS, R O. Who Called The Cops: Decisions To Report Criminal Victimization. *Law & Soc Rev* 7,427–444 1973.

HAWKINS, R and Akers, Ronald L. *Law And Control In Society.* Englewood Cliffs NJ Prentice–Hall 1975.

HAWKINSON, T and Kulig, F H. Conviction And Sentencing In The Fourth Judicial District Of Nebraska. *Creighton L Rev* 8,923–978 1975.

This selection presents two articles which investigate the effects of pretrial release, prior arrests, and plea negotiations on convictions and sentencing of felonies in Douglas County, Nebraska. Both the studies analyzed the felony filings in Douglas County District Court in the years 1970, 1971, and 1972, which were terminated by October 1973 as a result of dismissal by the court or prosecutor, a guilty plea, or an adjudication. The first study found that pretrial release and prior arrest apparently do not have an effect on one's chances of getting convicted, as demonstrated by the conviction rates in Douglas County. However, it was shown that pretrial release and race have a significant effect on the sentence imposed. Also, prior arrest record of the defendant was found to have a similar effect on the sentence imposed, but this influence was not as clearly shown by the data. The results of the second study indicated that there is a distinct advantage derived from pleading guilty as opposed to pleading not guilty and ultimately receiving a conviction sentence. The effect of such factors as race, pretrial disposition, age, and sentencing judge on sentencing outcomes is also discussed.*

HAYDEN, Tom. *Rebellion In Newark.* NY Random House 1967.

HAYNER, Norman S. Social Factors In Oriental Crime. *Am J Soc* 44,980–918 1938.

HAYNER, Norman S. Variability In The Criminal Behavior Of American Indians. *Am J Soc* 47,602–613 Ja 1942.

HAYNES JR, Andrew B. *Developing A Community And Computer Based Anti–Color–Code Strategy To Resist And Reduce Violent Crimes In Black Ghettoes.* Unpub PhD Diss Syracuse Univ 1973.

The project consisted of integrating the following components into an effective operating procedure: formal and informal inputs from the black and law enforcement communities; the Bayesian statistics technique for decision–making; authoritative documentation of key concepts from the literature; evaluation of group personality traits and reaction patterns; leadership personality models; individual and role personality models to demonstrate the effects of multirole responsibilities on leadership and decision–making; computer based information systems to match events and solution clues; color code considerations encountered and coped with in the project; contributions to it from the civil rights and black power movements; past and potential effects of black policemen and the quest for black unity; potential opposition from the criminal revolutionary liberal coalition; effects on the housing–jobs–education triangle; effects of the image of corruption in local law enforcement; contribution of court congestion; effect of black demands for community control; influence on local and national education policies; and the potential of computer based information systems.

HAYNES, Milton and Badillo, Herman. *A Bill Of No Rights: Attica And The American Prison System.* NY Outerbridge Lazard 1972.

HAYWOOD, H. *Black Bolshevik: Autobiography Of An Afro–American Communist.* Chicago Liberator Pr 1978.

HAZELRIGG, Lawrence E. An Examination Of The Accuracy And Relevance Of Staff Perception Of The Inmate In The Correctional Institution. *J Crim L Crimin & Pol Sci* 58,204–210 1967.

HEALEY, G W and Deblassie, R R. A Comparison Of Negro, Anglo And Spanish–American Adolescents' Self–Concepts. *Adoles* 9(33),15–24 1974.

The purposes of this study were to determine if differences existed in the self–concept among Negro–, Anglo–, and Spanish–American adolescents and the extent to which these differences were influenced by ethnic group membership, socioeconomic position, or sex, or the interaction among these variables. Of the fourteen measures of self–concept assessed in this study, four scores were affected by the ethnic variable, Self Criticism, Defensive–Positive, Self–Satisfaction, and Moral–Ethical Self. The Total Positive Score (the overall general measure of self–concept– did not differ significantly among the three ethnic groups. Socioeconomic position was found to influence two of the fourteen scales utilized in this study, Social Self and Self Satisfaction. However, once again, the Total Positive Score did not differ significantly among the four socioeconomic class positions. The Total Positive Score was not significantly affected by sex differences. However, Physical Self, a specific measure of the total self–cOncept, was significantly affected by sex differences. No significant interaction effects were found.

HEARD, Nathan C. *Howard Street.* NY Dial Pr 1968.
This novel about the lives of black prostitutes and pimps in Newark, nJ, was written by a prisoner serving time for armed robbery.

HEARD, Nathan C. *To Reach A Dream.* NY Dial Pr 1972.
Novel about a black street hustler in Newark, NJ.

HEATH, G L. *Off The Pigs: The History And Literature Of The Black Panther Party.* NY Scarecrow Pr 1976.

HEILBRUN JR, Alfred B and Cross, J M. An Analysis Of Rape Patterns In White And Black Rapists. *J Soc Psychol* 108(1),83–87 1979.

HEILBRUN JR, Alfred B and Heilbrun, Lynn C and Heilbrun, Kim L. Impulsive And Premeditated Homicide: An Analysis Of Subsequent Parole Risk Of The Murderer. *J Crim L & Crimin* 69(1),108–114 Mr 1978.

The sample included 58 whites and 106 blacks representing all paroled murderers under the Georgia prison system between 1973 and 1976. the impulsivity and premeditation variable was rated from data gathered at the time of the crime. The success rate was 44 percent, with the mean age for successful parolees 45.81 years and for unsuccesful parolees, 40.78 years. Analysis indicates (1) unsuccessful parolees tend to have committed more impulsive murders than successful parolees; (2) the tendency for impulsive murderers to fail on parole is more evident than the tendency for premeditated murderers to succeed; (3) blacks and whites do not differ in impulsivity nor in their rates of success on parole; (4) violent crime recidivism is higher among black parole faiilures than among whites parole failures; (5) both racial groups have relatively high violation rates for drinking related problems, but blacks are significantly more in violation for possession of firearms; and (6) violent crime recidivists had engaged in more premeditated acts of homicide than had parolees who failed parole for nonviolent crime or a technical violation.*

HEILBRUN JR, Alfred B and Heilbrun Kirk S. The Black Minority Criminal And Violent Crime: The Role Of Self Control. *Br J Crimin* 17(4),270–277 O 1977.

This investigation shows that black criminals who have committed violent crimes are characterized by poorer impulse control than white criminals who have committed violent crimes. Subjects included 72 white and 54 black male felons evaluated for parole at the Georgia Diagnostic and Classification Center at Jackson. In addition, data from a 1976 investigation involving 100 white prisoners and 100 black prisoners were reanalyzed. Three measurement approaches involving widely varying characteristics were employed to assess that aspect of self–control that involves the ability to delay a motivated or habitual inclination to act given the presence of a deterrent to such action. The specific hypothesis tested stated that poorer self–control is characteristic of black violent offenders relative to white violent offenders but that black nonviolent criminals do not differ in self—control from white nonviolent criminals. Both aspects of this hypothesis were supported, and the findings could prove useful in predicting parole outcome.*

HEILBRUN JR, Alfred B. Race, Criminal Violence, And Length Of Parole. *Br J Crimin* 18(1),53–61 1978.

The relationship between race of the criminal, violence of the crime, and length of the parole period on the success or failure of the parole is studied from files of the Georgia Board of Pardons and Paroles. Records of 1509 male felons were drawn. Parole periods for these randomly selected persons ranged from 3 months to over 2 years; 63% had committed nonviolent crimes, 58% were black, and 53% had successful paroles. Black violent offenders outnumbered white violent offenders two to one. It was found that violent offenders had greater parole success for shorter periods of time, but as the tracking period extended they were no better risks than nonviolent offenders. Interestingly, murderers had a 16% success rate, compared to a 42% success rate for those convicted of robbery, 65% for those convicted of manslaughter, 68% for sexual offenders, and 70% for assault offenders. Highest success rates were more 80% for drug offenses, arson, and driving under the influence. Race was insignificant in determining parole outcome, except for the impulsive behavior noted for the black violent offender.*

HEILBRUN, Kim L and Heilbrun Jr, Alfred B and Heilbrun, Lynn C. Impulsive And Premeditated Homicide: An Analysis Of Subsequent Parole Risk Of The Murderer. *J Crim L & Crimin* 69(1),108–114 Mr 1978.

The sample included 58 whites and 106 blacks representing all paroled murderers under the Georgia prison system between 1973 and 1976. the impulsivity and premeditation variable was rated from data gathered at the time of the crime. The success rate was 44 percent, with the mean age for successful parolees 45.81 years and for unsuccessful parolees, 40.78 years. Analysis indicates (1) unsuccessful parolees tend to have committed more impulsive murders than successful parolees; (2) the tendency for impulsive murderers to fail on parole is more evident than the tendency for premeditated murderers to succeed; (3) blacks and whites do not differ in impulsivity nor in their rates of success on parole; (4) violent crime recidivism is higher among black parole failures than among whites parole failures; (5) both racial groups have relatively high violation rates for drinking related problems, but blacks are significantly more in violation for possession of firearms; and (6) violent crime recidivists had engaged in more premeditated acts of homicide than had parolees who failed parole for nonviolent crime or a technical violation.*

HEILBRUN, Lynn C and Heilbrun, Kim L and Heilbrun Jr, Alfred B. Impulsive And Premeditated Homicide: An Analysis Of Subsequent Parole Risk Of The Murderer. *J Crim L & Crimin* 69(1),108–114 Mr 1978.

The sample included 58 whites and 106 blacks representing all paroled murderers under the Georgia prison system between 1973 and 1976. the impulsivity and premeditation variable was rated from data gathered at the time of the crime. The success rate was 44 percent, with the mean age for successful parolees 45.81 years and for unsuccesful parolees, 40.78 years. Analysis indicates (1) unsuccessful parolees tend to have committed more impulsive murders than successful parolees; (2) the tendency for impulsive murderers to fail on parole is more evident than the tendency for premeditated murderers to succeed; (3) blacks and whites do not differ in impulsivity nor in their rates of success on parole; (4) violent crime recidivism is higher among black parole failures than among whites parole failures; (5) both racial groups have relatively high violation rates for drinking related problems, but blacks are significantly more in violation for possession of firearms; and (6) violent crime recidivists had engaged in more premeditated acts of homicide than had parolees who failed parole for nonviolent crime or a technical violation.*

HEILBRUN, Kirk S and Heilbrun Jr, Alfred B. The Black Minority Criminal And Violent Crime: The Role Of Self Control. *Br J Crimin* 17(4),270–277 O 1977.

This investigation shows that black criminals who have committed violent crimes are characterized by poorer impulse control than white criminals who have committed violent crimes. Subjects included 72 white and 54 black male felons evaluated for parole at the Georgia Diagnostic and Classification Center at Jackson. In addition, data from a 1976 investigation involving 100 white prisoners and 100 black prisoners were reanalyzed. Three measurement approaches involving widely varying characteristics were employed to assess that aspect of self—control that involves the ability to delay a motivated or habitual inclination to act given

the presence of a deterrent to such action. The specific hypothesis tested stated that poorer self—control is characteristic of black violent offenders relative to white violent offenders but that black nonviolent criminals do not differ in self—control from white nonviolent criminals. Both aspects of this hypothesis were supported, and the findings could prove useful in predicting parole outcome.*

HEILIGMAN, A C. Racism In United States: Drug Legislation And The Trade—Off Behind It. *Drug Forum* 7(1),19–26 1978–79.

HEIZER, Robert F and Almquist, Alan F. *The Other Californians. Prejudice And Discrimination Under Spain, Mexico, And The United States To 1920.* Berkeley CA U CA Pr 1971.

HELD, Barbara S and Levine, David and Swartz, Virginia D. Interpersonal Aspects Of Dangerousness. *Crim Just B* 6,49–58 Mr 1979.

HELLER, Celia S. *Mexican—American Youth: Forgotten Youth At The Crossroads.* NY Random House 1966.

HELMER, John. *Drugs And Minority Oppression.* NY Seabury Pr 1975.

The author attempts to show a relationship between drug crackdowns against blacks, Chinese and Mexican Americans and fear of economic competition.

HELMREICH, William B. Race, Sex, And Gangs: Black Crusaders, The Rise And Fall Of Political Gangs. *Society* 11(4),44–450 1974.

A report on an organization of militant young ghetto dwellers who were determined to influence and improve both their own political and economic situation and that of the residents of their community is presented. They attempted to establish an economic base for blacks, to ease racial tensions, to establish a black guard to protect the community, to persuade young blacks not to use drugs, urge blacks not to join the armed forces, and to raise the general level of consciousness of the older residents in the ghetto. The antidrug program was considered one of their most significant accomplishments. The organization disbanded after 5 months due to political and police opposition, negative image produced by the media, and lack of unity even in the community.

HELRICH, Alice R and Benson, Gwen and Hyman, Merton M. Ascertaining Police Bias In Arrests For Drunken Driving. *Q J Stud Alc* 33(1),148–159 1972.

Of the 640 men aged 25 to 54 arrested for driving while intoxicated in Santa Clara County (Calif.) and the 383 in Franklin County (Columbus, Ohio, metropolitan area) during the first 6 months of 1962, about one—third had been involved in automobile accidents. The arrest—vulnerability ratios by ethnicity, were more than twice as high among the socially disadvantaged sectors in both counties: 1.90 vs. 0.89 for the Spanish (Mexican) vs. non—Spanish whites in Santa Clara, 1.98 vs. 0.86 for the Negroes vs. whites in Franklin. Potential police bias against the disadvantaged groups was measured by comparing (1) the percentages of ADWI involved in accidents and (2) their blood alcohol concentrations (BAC) according to ethnicity and the 4 social and economic census—tract variables. It is concluded that the high ADWI rate among the minority and disadvantaged groups probably reflects accurately a greater frequency of drunken driving among them rather than a police bias in arrests.

HENDERSON, Bruce. *Ghetto Cops.* Chatsworth CA Major Books 1975.

HENDERSON, J Y and Barsh, R L. Tribal Courts, The Model Code And The Police Idea In American Indian Policy. *Law & Contemp Prob* 40(1),25–60 Wint 1976.

HENNING, John J and Levy, Russell H. Verbal Performance IQ Differences Of White And Negro Delinquents On The WISC And WAIS. *J Clin Psyc* 23(2),164–168 1967.

This study tests the generality of verbal inferiority of 2,361 black and white male delinquents committed to the Illinois Youth Commission in 1963 and 1964. The Verbal minus Performance I. Q. difference was examined separately at 15 age levels, for white and Negro subjects, some tested with the WISC [Weschler Intelligence Scale for Children] and others tested with the WAIS [Weschler Adult Intelligence Scale]. The whites produced higher Performance I. Q.'s in relation to Verbal I. Q.'s than did the Negroes. When the pattern of subtest rankings from this study was compared with the subtest pattern of delinquent poor readers and non—delinquent poor readers from two studies reported in the literature, the [white] samples showed consistently significant correlations with both poor reader patterns, while the [black] groups lacked this relationship. This was interpreted by the authors as support for the idea that a reading disability pattern rather than sociopathic personality as such is what is being seen in the intrasubtest Weschler pattern of white, male delinquents.

HENNING, John J. Personality Characteristics Of White And Negro Adolescent Delinquents. *Correct Psy* 4,12–14 1970.

HENRETTA, Juan C and Urnever, James D and Frangier, Charles. Racial Differences In Criminal Sentencing. Boston A S A 1979.

HENRY, Howell M. *The Police Control Of The Slave In South Carolina.* Emory VA Emory & Henry 1914.

HENRY, Jeanette and Costo, Rupert. *Indian Treaties: Two Centuries Of Dishonor.* San Francisco Indian Historia Pr 1978.

HENSON, Trudy Knicely and Mc Caghy, Charles H and Giordano, Peggy C. Auto Theft: Offender And Offense Characteristics. *Criminology* 15(3),367–385 N 1977.

HENTON, Comradge L and Washington, Charles. Differential Study Of Recidivism Among Negro And White Boys. *J Genet Psyc* 98,247–253 1961.

This study of eight black and eight white boys, three– and four–time recidivists serving sentences in Louisiana State Training Schools for Boys, compares the ages, socio–economic status, marital status of parents, religion, disposition of parents in the home, intellectual factors, emotional factors, offenses and main reasons for recidivism of the boys in the two groups. Generally similar patterns emerged for both groups.

HEPBURN, John R and Voss, H L. Patterns Of Criminal Homicide: A Comparison Of Chicago And Philadelphia. *Criminology* 8(1),21–45 My 1970.

HEPBURN, John R. Race And The Decision To Arrest: An Analysis Of Warrants Issued. *J Res Crim Del* 15(1),54–73 Ja 1978.

All adult arrests (n=28,235) in a large midwestern city in 1974 were analyzed to assess the relationship, if any, between race and subsequent issuance of a warrant by the prosecutor. After controls for offense type, age, sex, and racial composition of neighborhood were introduced, nonwhites continued to have a large proportion of arrests that were not upheld by a warrant. The author discusses the results in terms of conflict and labeling theory.

HEPPERLE, W L (ed) and Crites, L (ed). *Women In The Courts.* Williamsburg VA Nat Cen State Cts 1978.

This anthology examines the extent of commitment on the part of the judiciary to liberating women from their inferior status in American society.*

HERJANIC, B L and Robins, Lee N and West, P A. Arrests And Delinquency In Two Generations: A Study Of Black Urban Families And Their Children. *J Child Psyc & Psychi* 16(2),125–140 1975.

HERMANN, Robert and Single, Eric and Boston, John. *Counsel For The Poor: Criminal Defense In Urban America.* Lexington MA Lexington 1977.

HERNANDEZ, Conrado. Comunidades Latinas Deben Cooperar Con Prisones. *El Diario–La Prensa* ,4 Ja 21 1979.

HERNDON, Angelo. *Let Me Live.* NY Random House 1937.

This personal account was written by a black organizer who was sentenced to prison under an old Georgia law prohibiting slave insurrections.

HERNTON, C C. *Sex And Racism In America.* NY Grove Pr 1965.

HERRERA, Chris L. "Minority Recruiting: Denver Colorado" in *Community Relations: Studies In Minority Programs*, V4, Platt, R (ed), 52–55. Kennedale TX Criminal Just Pr 1974.

This article presents an address by Captain Chris L Herrera of the Denver Police Department presented at the Fifth Annual Convention of the National Association of Police–Community Relations. The author explains the successful programs undertaken in Denver to recruit minority persons into police work. The recruiting process is outlined and recommendations are put forth. As Captain Herrera reported: "The Denver metropolitan area population is about 2–1/2 million with about 15% minorities. The Denver police department has at the present time 11% minorities. The last 2 police classes were made up of equal numbers of minority and majority recruits and it appears that in the near future the 'proper' representation will be reached."

HERSEY, John. *The Algiers Motel Incident.* NY Knopf 1968.

An award–winning author's powerful account of the Detroit race riot of 1967, focusing on the police use of deadly force.

HERSKOVITS, Melville J. *The Myth Of The Negro Past.* NY Harpers 1941.

HESSLINK, G K. *Black Neighbors: Negroes In A Northern Rural Community.* NY Bobbs–Merrill 1974.

HEWITT, J and Miller, M. Conviction Of A Defendant As A Function Of Juror–Victim Racial Similarity. *J Soc Psychol* 105(1),156–160 1978.

HICKS, Donald A and Alpert, Geoffrey P. Prisoners' Attitudes Toward Components Of The Legal And Judicial System. *Criminology* 14(4),461–482 F 1977.

Results of a 1974 study of the attitudes of 241 male prisoners in the Washington State prison system toward the police, lawyers, law and the judicial system are presented. Attitudes toward police were largely negative, attitudes toward the more abstract aspects of the law and the judicial system were equivocal and attitudes toward lawyers were generally positive. Prisoners who had retained private counsel were generally more positive in their attitudes in all three areas. Where violent offenses were involved, prisoners showed considerable negativeness toward police and lawyers. Race of the prisoners was related to the extent of negativeness of attitude in all areas, but much less so in the case of lawyers than of police, the law and judicial system. Married prisoners are more likely to report positive attitudes and previous criminal convictions are associated with negative attitudes. Educational status had a relatively weak influence upon attitudes toward police and lawyers, but appears to be of greater influence in the law and judicial system area. Those who were employed prior to arrest appear to be slightly less negative in all areas.

HIDALGO, Hilda. *The Puerto Ricans In Newark, New Jersey.* Newark Aspira 1971.

HIGGINBOTHAM JR, A Leon. "Can We Avoid Riots In Prisons If We Fail To Eradicate Racism On The Outside" in *Proc Of 7th Annual Interagency Workshop*, 144–161. Huntsville TX Sam Houston ICC 1972.

Racial violence in the prisons today is seen as a reflection of continuing racism on the outside, and until society comes to grips with the problem, the prison systems will continue to display tension and polarization. Quotations and case histories are used to show the development and continuation of racial discrimnation in society and in the law courts and prisons. Blacks are seen as having been Americans as long or longer than many whites, but they have been categorically denied many rights. The hope of civilization lies with correction of the internal injustices in society.

HIGGINBOTHAM JR, A Leon. *In The Matter Of Color.* NY Oxford Univ Pr 1978.

HIGGINBOTHAM JR, A Leon. Eradication Of Racism And Poverty As A Means Of Stopping Escalation Of Crime And Violence: A Dream Deferred. *Crim Delinq* 18(1),30–34 1972.

An essay on the criminal justice system contends that the escalation of crime and violence cannot be stopped unless a civic commitment is made to the immediate eradication of racism and poverty. If the dreams of the black and poor are deferred much longer, serious racial and criminal justice problems will emerge in the cities. It is felt that priorities must be reordered to include all Americans. American institutions and government must take notice of the gross inequities in the country, and respond to these by working for massive change.

HIGGINBOTHAM JR, A Leon. Racism And The Early American Legal Process, 1619–1896. *Ann Am Poli* 407,1–17 1973.

HIGHAM, John. *Strangers In The Lands: Patterns Of American Nativism, 1860–1925.* NY Atheneum 1963.

HILL JR, C A and Ogden, Michael and Spector, M I. Suicides And Homicides Among Indians. *Public Health Rep* 85(1),75–80 1970.

HILL, H. Affirmative Action And The Quest For Job Equality. *Rev Black Pol Econ* 6,263–278 Spr 1976.

Discrimination in employment is not the result of random acts of bigotry, but is the consequence of systematic institutionalized patterns that are established in society. Thus, sweeping measures are necessary if racial employment patterns are to be fundamentally changed. Affirmative action programs based on numerical goals and timetables are an essential component in achieving this change. Affirmative action programs and racial quotas have been charged with creating "reverse discrimination." A major source of organized opposition to affirmative acton developed in litigation under the Civil Rights Act, Title VII. Lawsuits which base their cause of action on the exploitation of white ethnic workers ought not to forget that the black population has been the most systematically exploited group in American society. The federal courts have recognized that employment discrimination is class discrimination, that relief must go to the class, and that numerical quotas are the most effective means of relief. The

US Supreme Court has held that mathematical racial ratios could be used as the starting place for remedies.*

HILL, Joseph T. Negro And Crime. *Southern Workman* 65,345–351 1936.

HILL, K Q and Carter, R I. *Criminal's Image Of The City*. NY Pergamon Pr 1979.

The study sample was based on known property offenders currently residing in three of Oklahoma's correctional institutions who had been convicted of burglary, robbery, or larceny. A stratified sampling procedure was used to collect a matching noncriminal sample. Gestalt, Field, and Personal Construct theories were used as a basis for measuring individual area perceptions, and the semantic differential was adopted as a perception measurement tool. Findings indicate that criminals' area images are shaped by their vocational interests so that they perceive more crime activity, police protection, and greater difficulty of committing crime in the city than do noncriminals. Criminals, particularly blacks, are likely to choose a crime target in a familiar area. Whites are more concerned with the risk and difficulty of committing the offense that an area presents. Both groups tended to avoid high status neighborhoods. Statistical analyses indicate that the patterning of crime is systematically related to area images held by criminals, that these images are themselves differentiable, and that certain image components are more powerful than others in influencing criminal behavior.*

HILL, Mozell C and Ford, Nick. Crime And Punishment—1938. *Opport* 16(9),270–272 1938.

HILL, Mozell. The Metropolis And Juvenile Delinquency Among Negroes. *J Negro Ed* 28(3),277–285 1959.

This discussion attempts to view juvenile delinquency as a way of life in urban living. Its main emphasis is on the deviant behavior of minority youth, particularly Negroes, living in segregated communities in heterogeneous, multi–group metropolitan areas of the US. The primary purpose of such an approach is to disclose the nature and peculiar cultural components of the social relationship between individuals and groups in racial and cultural minority (segregated) communities of standard metropolitan areas. Negroes who live in blighted areas suffer from discrimination, rejection and lack of integration into the society. Juvenile delinquency is generated by this lack of integration rather than by processes of social disorganization.

HILL, Robert B. *The Harlem Riot Of 1935*. NY Arno Pr 1969.

HILL, Robert and Fogelson, Robert. *A Study Of Arrest Patterns In The 1960's Riots*. NY Bur App Soc Res 1969.

HILL, Robert and Fogelson, Robert. "Who Riots: A Study Of Participation In The 1967 Riots" in *Riot Commission, Supplemental Studies*, 217–248. Washington DC USGPO 1968.

HIMES, Chester. *Lonely Crusade*. NY Knopf 1947.

HIMES, Chester. *My Life Of Absurdity*. Garden City NY Doubleday 1976.

HIMES, Chester. *The Quality Of Hurt*. Garden City NY Doubleday 1972.

HIMES, Chester. Every Opportunity. *Esquire* 7(5),99,129–130 My 1937. A short story about a black parolee in the 1930's.

HINDELANG, Michael J. *Criminal Victimization In Eight American Cities*. Cambridge MA Ballinger 1976.

HINDELANG, Michael J and Gottfredson, Michael and Garofalo, James. *Victims Of Personal Crime: An Empirical Foundation For A Theory Of Victimization*. Cambridge MA Ballinger 1978.

HINDELANG, Michael J and Hirschi, Travis. Intelligence And Delinquency: A Revisionist Review. *Am Sociol Rev* 42(4),571–587 Ag 1977.

Recent research on intelligence and delinquency suggests that the relation is at least as strong as the relation of either class or race to official delinquency; however, the relation is stronger than the relation of either class or race to self–reported delinquency. In their analysis the authors trace the developments leading to the current conclusion that IQ is not an important factor in delinquency. The recent position, they conclude, had its roots in (1) a medical to sociological paradigm shift in the 20th century; (2) the failure of recent research to substantiate the early exorbitant claims that low IQ was a necessary and sufficient condition for illegal behavior; (3) the research of Sutherland and other prominent scholars, who rejected the IQ–delinquency hypothesis; (4) reservations about the validity of the measurement of both IQ and delinquency; (5) erroneous interpretations of

research findings; (6) speculation about factors which might account for the relation. The authors content that iQ has an effect on delinquency independent of class and race, arguing that this effect is mediated through a host of school variables.

HINDELANG, Michael J and Hirschi, Travis and Weis, Joseph G. Correlates Of Delinquency: The Illusion Of Discrepancy Between Self–Report And Offical Measures. *Am Sociol Rev* 44,995–1014 D 1979.

The notion that official and self–report methods produce discrepant results with respect to sex, race, and class is largely illusory. When the domain limitations of self–reports are recognized, the conclusion of general consistency between self–reports and official correlates for sex, race, and class emerges. This consistency and other evidence from victimization surveys, studies of the reliability and validity of self–reports, and studies of biases in criminal justice processing, suggest that both official data and self–reports provide valid indicators of the demographic characteristics of offenders, *within the domain of behavior effectively tapped by each method*. Data is presented in support of the contention that "blacks and whites differ in *serious* delinquent behavior," and that "slef–reports fail to find racial differences in large part because self–report instruments generally do not pick up the most serious kinds of street crime," which are most likely to result in detection and apprehension and in which blacks are disproportionately involved.

HINDELANG, Michael J. Equality Under The Law. *J Crim L Crimin & Pol Sci* 60,306–313 S 1969.

HINDELANG, Michael J. Race And Involvement In Common Law Personal Crimes. *Am Sociol Rev* 43(1),93–109 F 1978.

Most contemporary sociological theories of crime predict that blacks will be overrepresented among arrestees in common–law personal crimes. These theories differ, however, in the extent to which this overrepresentation is attributed to disproportionate involvement in criminal offenses versus criminal justice system selection biases. Studies that have relied upon official data have generally supported the differential involvement hypothesis, whereas studies relying on self–report techniques generally have supported the differential selection hypothesis. National victimization survey data on victims' reports of offenders' racial characteristics are introduced as a third measurement technique in order to shed additional light on this controversy. These data for rape, robbery, and assault are generally consistent with official data on arrestees and support the differential involvement hypothesis. Some evidence of differential selection for criminal justice processing is found; however, most of the racial disproportionality in arrest data is shown by victimization survey data to be attributable to the substantially greater involvement of blacks in the common–law personal crimes of rape, robbery, and assault.

HINDS, Lennox S. *Illusions Of Justice: Human Rights Violations In The United States*. Iowa City Univ Iowa Soc Wk 1978.

HINDS, Lennox S. National Legal Network: Organizing For Change; Black Lawyers And The Criminal Justice System. *Black L J* 3(1),96–102 Spr 1973.

HINDS, Lennox S. The Death Penalty: Continuing Threat To America's Poor. *Freedomways* 18(1),39–43 1978.

HINDUS, Michael Stephen. *Prison And Plantation: Crime, Justice, And Authority In Massachusetts And South Carolina, 1767–1878*. Chapel Hill Univ N Car Pr 1980.

This comparative study of crime, justice and authority contrasts Mass., an industrial–urban state, and S. Car., a rural–slaveholding state, during the 19th century. Using a wide array of primary sources, the author suggests that criminal justice evolved differently in the two states for three reasons: tradition, economic and social development, and slavery. Despite their obvious structural differences, each state treated its most marginal population harshly because that class—whether slaves or the so–called "criminal class"—was perceived as the greatest threat to the social and economic system.

HINDUS, Michael Stephen. Black Justice Under White Law—Criminal Prosecutions Of Blacks In Antebellum South Carolina. *J Am Hist* 63(3),575–599 1976.

HIMES, Joseph S. Crime In Negro Columbus. *Opport* 16(9),302–305 1938.

HIMES, Joseph S. Notes On Negro Crime. *J Crim L Crimin & Pol Sci* 30,280–281 1939.

HIMES, Joseph S. Social Class And Delinquent Etiology. *J Hum Relat* 6(4),89–93 1958.

HIMES, Joseph. The Functions Of Racial Confict. *Soc Forces* 45,1–10 S 1966.

HIPPCHEN, L J. Development Of A Plan For Bilingual Interpreters In The Criminal Courts Of New Jersey. *Just Syst J* 2(3),258–269 1977.

HIPPCHEN, Leonard J (ed). *Ecologic—Biochemical Approaches To The Treatment Of Delinquents And Criminals.* NY Van Nostrand 1979.

HIPPS, Irene. The Role Of School In Juvenile Delinquency Prevention. *J Negro Ed* 28(3),318–328 1959.

HIRSCHI, Travis and Hindelang, Michael J. Intelligence And Delinquency: A Revisionist Review. *Am Sociol Rev* 42(4),571–587 Ag 1977.

Recent research on intelligence and delinquency suggests that the relation is at least as strong as the relation of either class or race to official delinquency; however, the relation is stronger than the relation of either class or race to self-reported delinquency. In their analysis the authors trace the developments leading to the current conclusion that IQ is not an important factor in delinquency. The recent position, they conclude, had its roots in (1) a medical to sociological paradigm shift in the 20th century; (2) the failure of recent research to substantiate the early exorbitant claims that low IQ was a necessary and sufficient condition for illegal behavior; (3) the research of Sutherland and other prominent scholars, who rejected the IQ–delinquency hypothesis; (4) reservations about the validity of the measurement of both IQ and delinquency; (5) erroneous interpretations of research findings; (6) speculation about factors which might account for the relation. The authors content that iQ has an effect on delinquency independent of class and race, arguing that this effect is mediated through a host of school variables.

HIRSCHI, Travis. *Causes Of Delinquency.* Berkeley CA U CA Pr 1969.

In presenting a "Control Theory" of delinquency, Hirschi argues that the causes of crime among blacks are no different from those among whites. Data indicate that when verbal achievement scores are held constant, the relation between race and official delinquency is reduced, leading the author to infer that "differences in academic achievement go a long way toward explaining Negro–white differences in delinquent activity." Although most of the data analysis is restricted to whites due to the greater unreliability of data on blacks in the sample, the assumption that the causes of delinquency are the same for both races permits determination of the causes of delinquency among blacks without actually studying them. Data is presented which questions the assumption that blacks are disproportionately involved in delinquency. Hirschi believes that delinquency is explained by a weak bond between the individual and society. Delinquents in his sample were less likely than non–delinquents to exhibit strong attachment to parents, peers and school. They were less committed to conventional lines of action, less involved in conventional activities and believed less strongly that the rules of society were binding upon them.

HIRSCHI, Travis and Rudisill, David. The Great American Search: Causes Of Crime, 1876–1976. *Ann Am Poli* 423,14–22 Ja 1976.

HIRSCHI, Travis and Selvin, Hanan C. *Delinquency Research: An Appraisal Of Analytic Methods.* NY Free Pr 1967.

HIRSCHI, Travis and Weis, Joseph G and Hindelang, Michael J. Correlates Of Delinquency: The Illusion Of Discrepancy Between Self–Report And Offical Measures. *Am Sociol Rev* 44,995–1014 D 1979.

The notion that official and self–report methods produce discrepant results with respect to sex, race, and class is largely illusory. When the domain limitations of self–reports are recognized, the conclusion of general consistency between self–reports and official correlates for sex, race, and class emerges. This consistency and other evidence from victimization surveys, studies of the reliability and validity of self–reports, and studies of biases in criminal justice processing, suggest that both official data and self–reports provide valid indicators of the demographic characteristics of offenders, *within the domain of behavior effectively tapped by each method.* Data is presented in support of the contention that "blacks and whites differ in *serious* delinquent behavior," and that "slef–reports fail to find racial differences in large part because self–report instruments generally do not pick up the most serious kinds of street crime," which are most likely to result in detection and apprehension and in which blacks are disproportionately involved.

HODGDON, J and Wallman, K K. Race And Ethnic Standards For Federal Statistics And Administrative Reporting. *Stat Reptr* 77(10),450–454 1977.

HOEBEL, E Adamson. *The Law Of Primitive Man.* NY Atheneum 1974.

HOEBEL, E Adamson and Llewellyn, K. *The Cheyenne Way: Conflict And Case Law In Primitive Jurisprudence.* Norman Univ Oklahoma Pr 1941.

HOFFER, Frank William and Mann, Delbert Martin and House, Floyd Nelson. *The Jails Of Virginia: A Study Of The Local Penal System.* NY D Appleton & Co 1933.

HOFFMAN, Abraham. *Unwanted Mexican Americans In The Great Depression—Tucson.* Tucson Univ Ariz Pr 1974.

HOFFMAN, Frederick L. *Race Traits And Tendencies Of The American Negro.* NY Macmillan 1896.

Prison statistics are presented in support of the author's contention that the criminality of blacks exceeds that of any other race of any numerical importance in the US. It is argued that the excess of black criminality cannot be entirely explained as a result of the "conditions of life" since other nationalities live in conditions which are just as bad, or worse, yet their crime rates are lower. Among other points, it is noted that crime was almost non–existent among black slaves, that, "owing to his characteristic negligence the Negro when guilty of capital crimes is more easily apprehended than the white criminal." "Until the Negro learns to respect life, property, and chastity, until he learns to believe in the value of a personal morality operating in his everyday life, the criminal tendencies...will increase, and by so much the social and economic efficiency of the race will be decreased."

HOFFMAN, Gerard and Fishman, Joshua A. Life In The Neighborhood: A Factor Analytic Study Of Puerto Rican Males In The New York City Area. *Int J Comp Soc* 12,85–100 1971.

HOGAN, B. Blacks Versus Women—When Victims Collide. *Bus & Soc Rev* ,71–77 Sum 1974.

When minorities and women compete for employment gains, a coalition can enlarge the benefits for both. A seminar strategy which cuts through stereotypes and helps minorities and women work together is described. Equal Opportunity Employment (EOE) programs were first aimed at black males, then were expanded to include other minorities, and finally women were accepted into the EOE program. The hostilities among these groups often reach explosive proportions.*

HOGARTH, John. *Sentencing As A Human Process.* Toronto Univ Toronto Pr 1971.

HOLDEN JR, Matthew. "Politics, Public Order, And Pluralism" in *Politics Of Local Justice*, Klonski, James R And Robert I Mendelsohn (eds), 238–255. Boston Little, Brown 1970.

HOLDEN JR, Matthew. "Race, Deprivation, And Drug Abuse In The USA" in *Proceedings Of The Anglo–American Conference On Drug Abuses*, 69–76. London Royal Soc Medicine 1973.

HOLDEN JR, Matthew. Police–Community Relations. *Ment Hyg* 46,107–115 1962.

HOLDEN JR, Matthew. The Modernization Of Urban Law And Order. *Urb Aff Q* 1,92–101 1966.

HOLDEN JR, Matthew. Violence And The American Character Structure. *Med Opin & Rev* 3,100–109 1967.

HOLLEY, W H and Field, H S. Equal Employment Opportunity And Its Implications For Personnel Practices. *Labor Law J* 27(5),278–286 My 1976.

HOLMAN, Ben. "Community Relations Units In Police Departments" in *Black Crime: A Police View*, Bryce, H J (ed), 91–107. Washington DC Jt Ctr Polit Stud 1977.

HOLMAN, Ben. The Hispanic Tide—Some Implications Of Its Continuing Growth. *Pol Chief* 43(11),54–55 1976.

HOLT, Norman and Miller, Donald. *Explorations In Inmate–Family Relationships, Research Report No 46.* Sacramento Dept Corrections 1972.

HOLTZ, Janice Marie Allard. The 'Low-Riders': Portrait Of An Urban Youth Subculture. *Youth & Society* 6(4),495–508 1975.

A description is given of the low riders, an urban youth subculture of Mexican Americans in East Los Angeles. The identity of a low rider is constituted by the possession of a certain type of automobile which has been modifed according to subcultural group standards. Activities of the group, such as cruising the boulevard, are described in detail. The predominant form of formal social organization among low riders is car clubs. Functions and purposes served and prescribed by the subculture are discussed.

HOLZMAN, Harold R. "Learning Disabilities And Juvenile Delinquency: Biological And Sociological Theories" in *Biology And Crime*, Jeffrey, C R (ed). Beverly Hills CA Sage 1979.

HOOTON, Earnest Albert. *Crime And The Man*. Cambridge MA Harvard Univ Pr 1939.

HOPKINS, Andrew and Denfeld, D. Racial—Ethnic Identification In Prisons: 'Right On From The Inside'. *Int J Crimin Pen* 3(4),355–366 N 1975.

HORNBUCKLE, J and French, Laurence. An Analysis Of Indian Violence. *Am Indian Q* 3(4),335–356 Wint 1978.

HORNEY, Julie. Effects Of Race On Plea Bargaining Decisions. San Francisco A S C 1980.

HORNUNG, C A and Rusinko, W T and Johnson, K W. Importance Of Police Contact In The Formulation Of Youths' Attitudes Toward Police. *J Crim Jus* 6(1),53–67 Spr 1978.

The significance of positive and negative contacts between police and juveniles as determinants of juveniles' attitudes toward police is examined in a study of 1,200 pupils in the ninth grade in Lansing, Mich. The survey instrument, which was administered in the late 1960's, measured the nature and extent of experiences with police, self—reported delinquent behavior and defiance of parental authority, and attitudes toward police. Positive contacts are predictive of positive attitudes, particularly for youths who have had a negative encounter with police, for those who report frequent involvement in deviance, and for those who report defying their parents. Negative contacts are predictive of negative attitudes, particularly for white youths, for youths who report infrequent deviant behavior, and for youths who have had little or no positive contact with police. Positive contacts can neutralize the effects of negative contacts; and positive contacts do not diminish the tendency for black youths to be negative in their opinions of police. Police management must explore ways to improve the attitudes of black youth toward the police.*

HOROWITZ, Irving Louis. *Genocide And State Power*, 3rd Edition. New Brunswick NJ Transaction Books 1979.

Chapters include: life, Death and Sociology/Defining Genocide/Functional and Existential/Visions of Genocide/Genocide and a New Definition of Social Systems/Individualism and State Power/Collectivism and State Power/Democracy and Terrorism/Human Rights and Foreign Policy/Personal Life and Social Structure.

HOROWITZ, Irving L. Separate But Equal: Revolution And Counter—Revolution In The American City. *Social Prob* 17,294–312 Wint 1970.

HOROWITZ, Ruth and Schwartz, Gary. Honor, Normative Ambiguity And Gang Violence. *Am Sociol Rev* 39(2),238–251 1974.

HORSMANDEN, Daniel. *Proceedings Of The Conspiracy Formed By Some White People For Burning The City Of NY In America And Murdering The Inhabitants*. NY James Parker 1744.

HORVATH, Ronald J. A Definition Of Colonialism. *Curr Anthr* 13,45–51 1972.

HOSLICKA, Carl and Mitchell, Michael and Alker, Howard L. Jury Selection As A Biased Social Process. *Law & Soc Rev* 11(1),9–41 1976.

HOUSE, Floyd Nelson and Hoffer, Frank William and Mann, Delbert Martin. *The Jails Of Virginia: A Study Of The Local Penal System*. NY D Appleton & Co 1933.

HOUSTON, Charles M. Commonwealth Versus William Brown. *Opport* 11,109–111 1933.

HOWARD, John R (ed). *Awakening Minorities: American Indians, Mexican Americans, Puerto Ricans*. New Brunswick NJ Transaction Books 1972.

HOWARD, John and Mc Cord, William. Negro Opinions In Three Riot Cities. *Am Behav Sci* 2,24–27 Mr–Ap 1968.

HOWARD, Joseph C. *The Administration Of Rape Cases In The City Of Baltimore And The State Of Maryland*. Baltimore Monument Bar Assn 1968.

HOWARD, Joseph C. Racial Discrimination In Sentencing. *Judicature* 59(3),120–125 1975.

This examination of factors in the sentencing of black defendants attempts to explain how attitudes brought to the bench affect judges' perceptions of defendants and, hence, their disposition of sentences. Racism in sentencing is often discounted by the majority because it is generally a subconscious reaction to history and social climate. Judges tend to empathize and sympathize more easily with individuals sharing their color, philosophy and life style. They relate to the victims; hence, interracial and intergender crimes are dealt with more severely than intra—racial and intra—gender crimes. The "less than human concept" permits harsher sentencing (e.g., death penalty) to be used against those perceived as different and therefore deserving of less. Disparate treatment is more readily utilized against members of groups conceived as not "belonging" to the larger society due to perceived social or cultural defects. Finally, a penchant for punishing people regarded as threats to the system (e.g., militants and political activists) is noted, such that judges may accord "special treatment" when they are dealing with unpopular cases.

HOWARD, Kenneth I and Short Jr, James F and Tennyson, Ray A. Behavior Dimensions Of Gang Delinquency. *Am Sociol Rev* 28(3),411–429 Je 1963.

HOWARD, Richard and Sultan, Allen. The Efficient Use Of Military Forces To Control Riots: Some Proposals For Congressional Action. *J Urban L* 45,849–862 1968.

HOYER, W J and Wise, V L. "Minority Elderly" in *Police And The Elderly*, Goldstein, A P et al (eds). Elmsford NY Pergamon Pr 1979.

A review of the problem of crime against the elderly as it affects the black and Spanish, and its implications for police—community relations and police training are provided. Two areas that are especially troublesome for the minority aged are fear of crime and fear of police. Crime rates against minorities are higher and are increasing at a faster rate than against whites. Minority elderly are more likely to live in poverty and to be concentrated in central city ghettos or rural pockets of poverty. Minority elderly are also more fearful of police as a result of having lived during an era when police brutality, racial oppression, and discrimination were more common. Police work in minority communities is especially difficult because of lack of understanding and cooperation between police and minorities, especially the elderly. Understanding the ways in which minorities have been oppressed and denied equal opportunity is helpful to effective police work. The shift from crime—centered law enforcement to full—service policing emphasizing police—community relations must gather momentum to strengthen cooperation between the police and minorities.*

HUANG, K and Pilisok, M. At The Threshold Of The Golden Gate: Special Problems Of A Neglected Minority. *Am J Orthopsych* 47(4),701–713 1977.

HUDSON, Joe and Galaway, Burt. Crime Victims And Public Social Policy. *J Sociol & Soc Wel* 3(6),629–635 Jl 1976.

HUFF, William Henry. New Charter On Slavery. *Nat Bar J* 2,65–69 1944.

HUFF, William Henry. Peonage Or Debt Slavery In The Land Of The Free. *Nat Bar J* 3(1),43–49 1945.

HUGGINS, Nathan and Kilson, Martin and Fox, Daniel M. *Key Issues In The Afro—American Experience*. NY Harcourt Brace 1971.

HUGHES, Graham. American Terror. *NY Rev Bks* 25,3 Ja 25 1979.

HUIE, William Bradford. *He Slew The Dreamer: My Search, With James Earl Ray, For The Truth About The Murder Of Martin Luther King*. NY Delacorte Pr 1970.

HULBARY, W E. Race, Deprivation And Adolescent Self—Images. *Social Sci Q* 56(1),105–114 1975.

HUMPHREY, Craig and Zeal, Carolyn. The Integration Of Blacks In Suburban Neighborhoods: A Reexamination Of The Contact Hypothesis. *Social Prob* 18,462–474 Spr 1971.

HUMPHREY, J A and Kupferer, H J. Fatal Indian Violence In North Carolina. *Anthrop Q* 48(4),236–244 O 1975.

HUMPHREY, Norman D and Lee, Alfred McClung. *Race Riot*. NY Dryden Pr 1943.

HUMPHREY, Norman D. Police And Tribal Welfare In Plains Indian Cultures. *J Crim L & Crimin* 33,147 1942.

HUNDLY, James. The Dynamics Of Recent Ghetto Riots. *J Urban L* 45,627–639 1968.

Underlying causes are (1) the perception of a crisis in achieving aspirations; (2) perception that legitimate channels for change are blocked; (3) ghettoites' hope that rioting will bring changes; (4) the possibility that many people can interact under conditions of reduced social control; and (5) breakdown of accepted social control mechanisms. The main factors responsible for producing a riot are (1) the presence of rumors of a riot; (2) an event which typifies grievances; (3) the physical convergence of people;

and (4) the arousal of a sense of indignation and emergence of suggested courses of action. The process by which a riot develops involves (1) keynoting, or formation of consensus around suggestions for action; (2) hostile, deviant acts which go unpunished; and (3) emergence of focused hostility and norms for the types of deviant activities the crowd will sanction. Rioting crowds develop definite group structure, which suggests the possibility of predictable methods for controlling such crowds.

HUNT JR, Issac C and Cohen, Bernard. *Minority Recruiting In The New York City Police Department.* NY Rand Instit 1971.

HUNT, Janet G and Hunt, Larry L. Race And The Father–Son Connection: The Conditional Relevance Of Father Absence For The Orientations And Identities Of Adolescent Boys. *Social Prob* 23(1),35–52 1975.

HUNT, Larry L and Hunt, Janet G. Race And The Father–Son Connection: The Conditional Relevance Of Father Absence For The Orientations And Identities Of Adolescent Boys. *Social Prob* 23(1),35–52 1975.

HUNT, Morton. *The Mugging.* NY Atheneum 1972.

HUNT, Ridgely. Requiem For Virgil White. *Chicago Trib Mag* ,33–48 Ja 23 1972.
Hunt discusses the effect of gangs in a black community in Chicago and the death of one youth forced to become a gang member for self–protection.

HUNTER, Deairich. Ducks Versus Hard Rocks. *Newsweek* 96,14–15 Ag 18 1980.
A 15–year–old black high school student describes Brooklin street life. The "ducks" (or "suckers") are the minority of kids, who go to school every day and hope to attend college. They are frequently being robbed and beaten up by the "hard rocks," who spend their time using drugs, drinking, skipping school.

HUNTER, Jerry and Donegan, Charles E. Current Racial Legal Developments. *Howard L J* 12(2),299 1966.

HUNTER, Michael Nathan. *A Comparison Of Mexican–American And Caucasian Male Juvenile Detainees.* Unpub PhD Diss Univ of Utah 1974.
The family history, self–concept, and sports interest of two atypical ethnic populations of male youth comprised of Mexican–Americans and Caucasians who were institutionalized because of delinquent behavior were examined. No great differences in the self–concept of Mexican–American and Caucasian detainees was observed. Sports participation and sports interest appeared not to occupy a prominent role in the life of the detainees. Sports interest and sports participation involving their sons was not deemed very important by parents of the detainees. The family history of the detainees reflected several inadequacies in most areas examined for subjects from both ethnic groups. Delinquency tended to begin at an early age for all detainees, and multiple offenses were common. Both Mexican–American detainees and Caucasian detainees were weak in the Measured characteristics of self–concept.

HURON, C B and Lipshutz, R J. Achieving A More Representative Federal Judiciary. *Judicature* 62(10),483–485 1979.
The Carter administration's combination of merit selection and affirmative action to improve the quality of the federal bench and make it more representative of the populace is described by counsel to the President.*

HURST, Charles E. *The Anatomy Of Social Inequality.* St Louis C V Mosby 1979.

HURSTFIELD, Jennifer. Internal Colonialism: White, Black And Chicano Self Conceptions. *Ethn & Racial S* 1(1),60–77 Ja 1978.

HUSBAND, Charles and Hartman, Paul. The Mass Media And Racial Conflict. *Race* 12,267–282 Ja 1971.
The news media play a crucial role in maintaining an informed state of public opinion and a functioning democracy by providing information, defining issues and interpreting events. The authors identify a number of factors pertaining to the news media which operate to structure the news coverage of race related matters in a way that causes people to see the situation primarily as one of actual or potential conflict. The result is that real conflict is amplified and potential for conflict created.

HUSSEY, Frederick Alan. *The Decision To Parole: A Study Of The Parole Decision Process With Juveniles.* Unpub PhD Diss Brandeis Univ 1974.
The release decision in the area of juvenile parole was examined to determine what variables contribute to the decision, to examine the interaction of these variables and to determine whether particular policies or trends inhere in the decisions made by the parole board. Data from the

case records of 424 juvenile males released from one institution in a one–year period indicate that: (1) in the case of whites, the variables associated with the release decision are congruent with traditional juvenile justice philosophy and yet are different from those predictive for blacks and Mexican–Americans; (2) the constellation of variables predicitve of Mexican–American release indicates that these incarcerated youth find themselves in a situation where they neither understand the situational demands nor are they themselves understood; and (3) consistent with other criminal justice research, it appears that blacks are treated in a racially discriminatory and prejudiced manner. The most critical policy issues raised involves the unequal dispensation of justice and treatment.

HYMAN, Merton M and Helrich, Alice R and Benson, Gwen. Ascertaining Police Bias In Arrests For Drunken Driving. *Q J Stud Alc* 33(1),148–159 1972.
Of the 640 men aged 25 to 54 arrested for driving while intoxicated in Santa Clara County (Calif.) and the 383 in Franklin County (Columbus, Ohio, metropolitan area) during the first 6 months of 1962, about one–third had been involved in automobile accidents. The arrest–vulnerability ratios by ethnicity, were more than twice as high among the socially disadvantaged sectors in both counties: 1.90 vs. 0.89 for the Spanish (Mexican) vs. non–Spanish whites in Santa Clara, 1.98 vs. 0.86 for the Negroes vs. whites in Franklin. Potential police bias against the disadvantaged groups was measured by comparing (1) the percentages of ADWI involved in accidents and (2) their blood alcohol concentrations (BAC) according to ethnicity and the 4 social and economic census–tract variables. It is concluded that the high ADWI rate among the minority and disadvantaged groups probably reflects accurately a greater frequency of drunken driving among them rather than a police bias in arrests.

IANNI, Francis A J. *Black Mafia: Ethnic Succession In Organized Crime.* NY Simon & Schuster 1974.
Black Mafia is about the emergence of a new kind of black power—the takeover of crime operations by black and Puerto Rican crime organizations that are systematically replacing the Italian families whose syndicates once stretched unchallenged throughout the US. Through the use of participant observation and paid informants, the author has gained a first hand observation of this ethnic succession taking place. The first section of the book describes black crime organizations in the Central Harlem area of NYC—a pimp and his prostitutes, a band of thieves which steals goods "downtown" and then sells them in Harlem, and a ring of dope pushers. The author next describes the historical and cultural background of organized crime in the US. Special cases uncovered in the research are presented in the third section and include a Spanish–speaking network in which a number of different criminal activities operating out of three areas are held together by the bonds of kinship and childhood friendship. The final section offers conclusions that lead to a different definition of organized crime in American society and to some recommendations about what can be done to control it.*

IANNI, Francis A J. *Ethnic Succession In Organized Crime: A Summary Report.* Washington DC NILECJ 1973.
"Ethnic succession" in organized crime, is the process by which successive urban immigrant groups use organized criminal activity as a means to attain wealth and power before gaining a foothold in legitimate business. This has been known to social scientists for some time but has only recently been systematically studied. This report examines the process and develops a model of how new member groups organize themselves to achieve their goals and how these groups develop and enforce rules to maximize their criminal efforts. The reseach strategy used was to gather data through participant observation in the NYC area. Models of organized crime groups among blacks and Puerto Ricans were generated through the technique of network analysis, an anthropligical tool used to chart social interactions. Organized crime is then analyzed from three aspects—the social behavioral field, person–to–person contacts, and patterned social relations. Analysis of the observations showed organized crime networks operating predominantly within youthful groups, through inmate alliances continued after release from prison, and in criminal businesses.*

IANNI, Francis A J and Reuss, Elizabeth. *The Crime Society: Organized Crime And Corruption In America.* NY New Am Lib 1976.

IANNI, Francis A J. New Mafia: Black, Hispanic And Italian Styles. *Society* 11(3),26–39 1974.
The author examines the networks of criminal operation in order to determine the types of relationships which bring people together, foster

some kind of criminal partnership, then lead to the formation of organized criminal networks. Two types of linkages exist: causal relationships, which serve to introduce individuals to each other and into joint criminal ventures; and criminal relationships, which are based on a common core of activity in crime. The author found two forms of associational networks in his field experience: the childhood gang and the prison court. The second type of behavioral organization is the entrepreneurial network. This seems to be a more advanced form among blacks and Puerto Ricans than the associational types. It is the model of the small businessman, the individual entrepreneur, whose legal activities are carried out through a network of individuals related to him in that activity.

IIYAMA, P and Nishi, S M and Johnson, B B. *Drug Use And Abuse Among US Minorities: An Annotated Bibliography*. NY Praeger 1976.

This annotated bibliography of studies addressing the issue of drug use, primarily narcotics use, among blacks, Mexican–Americans, Puerto Ricans, Asian–Americans, and native Americans, contains 245 annotated citations and an introductory essay.*

ILLINOIS CORRECTIONS DEPARTMENT. *Report Of The Task Force Investigation Allegations Of Discriminatory Practices At The Joliet And Stateville Correctional Centers*. Springfield ICD 1978.

INN, A and Wheeler, A C and Sparling, C L. The Effects Of Suspect Race And Situation Hazard On Police Officer Shooting Behavior. *J App So P* 7(1),27–37 1977.

Results of this study suggest that racial bias is not a factor in police shooting decisions.

INSTITUTE FOR SOUTHERN STUDIES. Still Life: Inside Southern Prisons. *S Exposure* 6(4),entire Issue Wint 1978.

INSTITUTE OF GOVERNMENT AND PUBLIC AFFAIRS. *Los Angeles Riot Study, The Perception Of Police Brutality In South Central Los Angeles*. Berkeley CA U CA Inst G & PA 1967.

INTERNATIONAL ASSOCIATION OF CHIEFS OF POLICE. *Civil Disorders: After–Action Reports*, Professional Standards Division. Washington DC IACP 1969.

IRELAN, L M and Moles, O C and O' Shea, R M. Ethnicity, Poverty And Selected Attitudes: A Test Of The Culture Of Poverty Hypothesis. *Soc Forces* 47,405–413 1969.

IRWIN, John. *Prisons In Turmoil*. Boston Little, Brown 1980.

A prominent sociologist and ex–convict examines the turbulent state of American prisons. Chapters are devoted to the black prisoner movement and racial violence in prison, as well as to racial divisions between prisoners and between prisoners and staff.

IRWIN, John. *The Felon*. Englewood Cliffs NJ Prentice–Hall 1970.

IRWIN, Will. *Pictures Of Old Chinatown*. NY Moffat, Yard 1908.

IVES, George. *A History Of Penal Methods*. London Stanley Paul 1914.

IVIE, S D. Discrimination In Selection And Promotion Of Minorities And Women In Municipal Employment. *Urb Lawyer* 7(3),540–555 Sum 1975.

Litigation cases are noted to serve as guidelines for city attorneys to advise clients about their duties as equal opportunity employers of minorities and women.*

JACKSON, Bruce (ed). *Wake Up Dead Man: Afro–American Worksongs From Texas Prisons*. NY Harvard Univ Pr 1972.

JACKSON, Bruce. *Get Your Ass In The Water And Swim Like Me: Narrative Poetry From Black Oral Tradition*. Cambridge MA Harvard Univ Pr 1974.

JACKSON, Bruce. *In The Life: Versions Of The Criminal Experience*. NY Macmillan 1972.

JACKSON, Bruce. *Killing Time: Life In The Arkansas Penitentiary*. Ithaca NY Cornell Univ Pr 1977.

Professor Jackson, director of the Center for Studies in American Culture, depicts life inside the Cummins Prison Farm in Arkansas through vivid words and photographs. A memoir by a long–run inmate, describing brutal conditions of earlier years, is included, as are extracts from Jackson's interviews with prisoners, guards, and administrators.

JACKSON, Bruce. *Outside The Law: A Thief's Primer*. NY Macmillan 1969.

Autobiography of a professional thief, as told in a Texas state prison over a period of years. The author claims to have verified most of his statements through interviews with fellow thieves, wardens, lawyers, and a police chief.

JACKSON, Bruce and Christian, Diane. *Death Row*. Boston Beacon Pr 1980.

JACKSON, George. *Blood In My Eye*. NY Bantam 1972.

Published after Jackson's death in 1971, these prison papers and letters expressed the author's revolutionary creed and call for violence.

JACKSON, George. *Soledad Brother: The Prison Letters Of George Jackson*. NY Bantam 1970.

When he was 18, Jackson was sentenced to one year to life for robbing 70 dollars from a California gas station. During his confinement, he underwent many changes and became interested in writing and radical politics. Much of his imprisonment was spent in solitary confinement and at age 28 he was charged with the murder of a guard in Soledad Prison. Jackson's prison letters are among the most powerful documents in all of prison literature and they made him an internationally famous figure. A year after their publication he was shot to death inside San Quentin Prison in one of the most controversial cases in American prison history. The book offers a shattering account of one black man's efforts to survive in a hostile and degrading society.

JACKSON, Ida Joyce. Do Negroes Constitute A Race Of Criminals? Color Am Mag 12,252–255 1907.

JACKSON, Maynard H. "Crime As A Concern Of City Hall" in *Black Crime: A Police View*, Bryce, H J (ed), 29–36. Washington DC Jt Ctr Polit Stud 1977.

JACKSON, Maynard H. The Black American And The Legal Profession: A Study Of Commitment. *J Pub L* 20,377–380 1971.

Jackson discusses the contributions made by black lawyers as well as the obstacles they have had to face. He gives a brief historical sketch of the first black persons in various positions in the legal profession, and concludes that "when considered in light of the impediments and shackles born of a system of racism, the gains of the black lawyer are nothing short of phenomenal."

JACKSON, Phillip D and Waldo, Gordon P and Chiricos, Theodore G. Inequality In The Imposition Of A Criminal Label. *Social Prob* 19(4),553–572 Spr 1972.

JACOB, Herbert. Black And White Perceptions Of Justice In The City. *Law & Soc Rev* 6(1),68–89 1971.

In this study of three neighborhoods (one black ghetto and two white areas—one working class, one middle–class) in Milwaukee, Jacob examined perceptions of the police, judges, and courts, satisfaction with contacts with law enforcement agencies and the effects of such contacts upon a general sense of justice or injustice. Black respondents were more likely to perceive the police in a less favorable way than either group of whites. Jacob also notes that blacks more frequently reported dissatisfaction with their contacts with the police. However, significant differences were observed, within neighborhoods, such that some blacks were more favorable to police than some whites, leading Jacob to conclude that a prediction cannot be made on the basis of race alone as to how favorable or unfavorable a person's perception of the police will be.

JACOBS, David. Inequality And The Legal Order: An Ecological Test Of The Conflict Model. *Soc Prob* 25(5),515–525 1978.

The author hypothesizes that imprisonment would likely be used more in political systems where unequally distributed resources favor the affluent, and that this economic inequality would result in high imprisonment ratios for burglary and larceny. He examined this hypothesis with a cross–sectional analysis of American states using data collected in 1960. Economic inequality was measured with a gini index computed on the distribution of personal incomes in 1959. Imprisonments for specific index crimes in 1960 were divided by the mean of crimes known to the police in 1959 and 1960. Jacobs' prediction and that of the conflict theorists was supported, providing additional support for the conflict view. Inequality was related to imprisonment for property crimes only when higher income groups were more likely to be victimized.

JACOBS, James B. "Race Relations And The Prisoner Subculture" in *Crime And Justice: An Annual Review Of Research*, Morris, N And M Tonry (eds). Chicago Univ Chicago Pr 1979.

JACOBS, James B. *Stateville: The Penitentiary In Mass Society*. Chicago Univ Chicago Pr 1977.

The author, a sociologist and legal scholar, presents what he claims is the first historical examination of a total prison organization—administrators, guards, prisoners and special interest groups. The subject is Stateville maximum–security prison in Illinois. Jacobs devotes special attention to the administration's attempts to deal with prisoner gangs, employee unions, proliferating interest groups, and interventionist courts.

JACOBS, James B and Cohen, Jay. Impact Of Racial Integration On The Police. *J Polic Sci Adm* 6(2), 168–183 1978.

A literature search is described which shows that ghetto residents are much more hostile toward all police, black and white, than are nonghetto residents. Race relations within police departments are generally tense. A NY study indicated that black ghetto residents felt that black policemen had "sold out" to the white establishment. Black police have responded in two ways—by being more lenient with black offenders or by being particularly diligent in the prosecution of offenders which they see as threatening to black communities. Police departments were reluctant to integrate. A series of Supreme Court decisions were required to break this pattern. By 1977 a new type of black police officer had emerged. More militant than other recruits, these officers have often banded together with others in Afro–American police leagues, such as those found in NY and Chicago. These groups are demanding equal opportunity in hiring and promotion. A white backlash appears to be developing, but its form is not yet clear. The tension of this racial situation is threatening the traditional feeling of sociality among American police forces.*

JACOBS, James B and Grear, Mary P. Drop–Outs And Rejects: An Analysis Of The Prison Guard's Revolving Door. *Crim Just Rev* 2(2), 57–70 1977.

Results of a sample survey of 55 former prison guards indicate that the most significant factor accounting for high employee turnover among guards is race. Young urban blacks have trouble relating to fellow guards and young rural whites have difficulty relating with black inner–city prisoners.

JACOBS, James B and Kraft, Larry J. Integrating The Keepers: A Comparison Of Black And White Prison Guards In Illinois. *Social Prob* 25, 304–318 F 1978.

The assumption that replacing white rural prison guards with young black urban guards will lessen significantly tension and conflict in the prison community is tested. An attitude questionnaire was given to 165 white and 66 black guards working at Stateville and Joliet maximum security prisons in Illinois. About 75% of the prison population is black and 10% Latino, with the majority from the Chicago metropolitan area. Even though the black correction officers were younger, more urban, better educated, and more liberal than the white, there were no consistent differences in their attitudes toward prisoners, staff, correctional goals, or occupation. Contrary to expectation, black guards were as suspicious of inmates as white guards, and black guards did not relate more effectively to black inmates. The most significant finding was that black guards were more likely to be embarrassed to tell others what they did for a living. It is concluded that hiring more black guards is not a panacea for prison unrest.*

JACOBS, James B and Steele, Eric H. Prisons: Instruments Of Law Enforcement Or Social Welfare? *Crim Delinq* 21(4), 348–355 O 1975.

JACOBS, James B. Stratification And Conflict Among Prison Inmates. *J Crim L & Crimin* 66(4), 476–482 D 1975.

JACOBS, James B. Street Gangs Behind Bars. *Social Prob* 21(3), 395–409 1974.

JACOBS, James B. The Politics Of Corrections: Town–Prison Relations As A Determinant Of Reform. *Social Service Review* 50(4), 623–631 D 1976.

JACOBSEN, Alvin. Crime Trends In Southern And Non–Southern Cities: A Twenty–Year Perspective. *Soc Forces* 54, 226–241 1975.

JAFFE, Carolyn. The Press And The Oppressed. *J Crim L Crimin & Pol Sic* 56(1), 1–17 1965.

JANKOVIC, Ivan. *Punishment And The Post–Industrial Society: A Study Of Unemployment, Crime And Imprisonment In The US.* Unpub PhD Diss U Calif Sant Barb 1977.

JANKOVIC, Ivan. Labor Market And Imprisonment. *Crim & Soc Just* 8, 17–31 Fall–Wint 1977.

JANKOVIC, Ivan. Social Class And Criminal Sentencing. *Crim & Soc Just* 10, 9–16 Fall–Wint 1978.

JANOWITZ, Morris. "Patterns Of Collective Racial Violence" in *The History Of Violence In America*, Graham, Hugh D And T Gurr (eds), 412–444. NY Praeger 1969.

JASPOVICE, Martin L and Sperlich, Peter W. Grand Juries, Grand Jurors And The Constitution: Statistical Decision Theory And The Selection Of Grand Jurors. *Hastings Const L Q* 1, 63–95 1974.

JASPOVICE, Martin L and Sperlich, Peter W. Methods For The Analysis Of Jury Panel Selection: Testing For Discrimination In A Series Of Panels. *Hastings Const L Q* 6, 787–852 1979.

JAYEWARDENE, C H S. Violence Among The Eskimos. *Can J Crim* 17(4), 307–314 1975.

JEANNERETT, P R and Dubin, J A. *Houston: A Validity Study Of Police Officer Selection, Training And Promotion, V3.* Washington DC NCJRS 1978.

Using the chi–square statistic for analysis, the Houston Police Department employment practices are evaluated for adverse impact on minority groups including females, blacks, and Hispanics.*

JEDLICKA, D et al. Suicide Among Blacks. *Phylon* 38(4), 448–455 D 1977.

JEDLICKA, Davor and Lee, Everett and Shin, Yongsock. Homicide Among Blacks. *Phylon* 38(4), 398–407 D 1977.

JEFFERIES, Vincent and Turner, R H and Morris, R T. The Public Perception Of The Watts Riot As Social Protest. *Am Sociol Rev* 36(3), 443–451 1971.

JEFFERSON, A M. Equal Employment Opportunity And Affirmative Action In Law Enforcement Agencies. *Resol Corr Prob & I* 1(4), 15–18 Sum 1975. An examination of the federal legislation and US Supreme Court decisions relating to equal employment opportunity is followed by an analysis of specific law enforcement practices found to be discriminatory. Three pieces of federal law have been the basis of most challenges to the employment practices of employers, both public and private: Section 1981 of the Civil Rights Act of 1866, Title VII of the Civil Rights Act of 1964, and the Fourteenth Amendment of the United States Constitution. There are other provisions of federal statutory law that may be used as a basis for an attack on racially and sexually discriminatory employment patterns, but these three sources are fundamental.*

JEFFERSON, Burtell. "Policies For Increasing The Number Of Black Police Executives" in *Black Crime: A Police View*, Bryce, H J (ed), 131–139. Washington DC Jt Ctr Polit Stud 1977.

JEFFREY, C Ray (ed). *Biology And Crime.* Beverly Hills CA Sage 1979.

JEFFREY, C Ray. "Biology And Crime: The New Neo–Lombrosians" in *Biology And Crime*, Jeffrey, C Ray (ed). Beverly Hills CA Sage 1979.

The editor introduces a series of papers presented at the 1978 annual meeting of the American Society of Criminology with some comments on the role of biology in the interdisciplinary field of criminology. Jeffrey contends that although significant advances have been made in recent years, biology in context with crime still brings to mind the outdated ideas of Lombroso. The implications of genetics have been relatively ignored in comparison with those of behaviorism and social determinism. In addition, the rejuvenation of the classical school notions of free will and deterrence have reduced consideration of the biological sciences. Jeffrey calls for a biosocial interdisciplinary approach to criminology arguing that behavior can be understood and that "crime can be prevented rather than treated or punished." Man's social systems must be examined in relation to his biological ones.

JEFFREY, C Ray. "Punishment And Deterrence: A Psychobiological Statement" in *Biology And Crime*, Jeffrey, C Ray (ed). Beverly Hills CA Sage 1979.

JEFFRIES, Vincent and Ransford, H E. Interracial Social Contact And Middle Class White Reaction To The Watts Riot. *Social Prob* 16, 312–324 Wint 1969.

JENCKS, Christopher. *Inequality: A Reassessment Of The Effect Of Family And Schooling In America.* NY Harper & Row 1972.

JENKINS, Betty and Faison, Adrienne. *An Analysis Of 248 Persons Killed By New York City Policemen.* NY Metrop App Res Cen 1974.

JENKINS, Sam and Newton, Charles H and Shelden, Randall. The Homogenization Process Within The Juvenile Justice System. *Int J Crimin Pen* 3(3), 213–227 1975.

JENKINS, William S. *Pro–Slavery Thought In The Old South.* Chapel Hill Univ N Car Pr 1935.

JENKINSON, R F and Lambert, J R. *Crime, Police, And Race Relations: A Study In Birmingham.* NY Oxford Univ Pr 1970.

JENNINGS, Francis. *The Invasion Of America: Indians, Colonialism, And The Cant Of Conquest.* NY Norton 1975.

JENSEN, Arthur R. How Much Can We Boost IQ And Scholastic Achievement? *Harv Educ Rev* , 95 Wint 1969.

JENSEN, Diane E and Prandoni, Jaques R and Matranga, James T. Bender—Gestalt Protocols Of Adult Negro Male Offenders: Normative Data. *Perc Mot Sk* 35(1),101—102 Ag 1972.

JENSEN, Gary F and Erickson, Maynard L and Gibbs, Jack P. Perceived Risk Of Punishment And Self—Reported Delinquency. *Soc Forces* 57,57—78 1978.

To examine the relationship between perceived risk of punishment and self—reported delinquency, the authors sampled students in six Arizona high schools. Personal risk was found to be inversely related to delinquency even when social condemnation of delinquent offenses, attachment to conventional persons, and several status characteristics of the students were taken into account.

JENSEN, Gary F. Delinquency And Adolescent Self—Conceptions: A Study Of The Personal Relevance Of Infraction. *Social Prob* 20(1),84—102 1972.

The personal relevance of infraction in variable sociocultural contexts is studied by examining the association between delinquency and adolescent self—conceptions among junior and senior high school students differentiated on the basis of race and status. Using questionnaire data and official police records, official delinquent evaluations and personal delinquent evaluations were found to be positively related. However, the strength of the relationship was found to vary between blacks and whites, by status among whites, and by attachment to the law among both blacks and whites. Moreover, while delinquents tend to be lower in self—esteem than nondelinquents, this relationship was found to vary as well. Delinquents and nondelinquents differ most among middle to upper status blacks and least among low status blacks. Finally, attachment to parents conditioned the relationship at each status level. Self—conceptions and delinquent action patterns are interdependent. But, at the same time, the sociocultural context seems to shape that interdependency.

JENSEN, Gary F. Race, Achievement, And Delinquency—A Further Look At Delinquency In A Birth Cohort. *Am J Soc* 82(2),379—387 1976.

This paper outlines the consequences of "an inadequate and cursory use of tabular analysis" in Wolfgang, Figlio, and Sellin's *Delinquency in a Birth Cohort*. Through a reconstruction and reanalysis of some of the data presented, the author claims to have found that the verbal model proposed in that work concerning the interrelationships and relative importance of several variables was in error. An alternative model fits the data much better and supports conclusions in marked contrast to those stated. Contrary to the model suggested in *Delinquency in a Birth Cohort*, the relation between achievement level and delinquency is not a spurious one due to a common association with race. Moreover, achievement appears to be at least as strongly related to delinquency status as are race and social class.

JENSEN, Gary and Stauss, Joseph and Harris, William. Crime, Delinquency And The American Indian. *Human Org* 36(3),252—257 Fall 1977.

JEROME, D E and Regoli, R M. Recruitment And Promotion Of A Minority Group Into An Established Institution—The Police. *J Polic Sci Adm* 3(4),410—416 D 1975.

The policies and practices of police departments in major US cities are examined to determine trends in the hiring and promotion of black police officers. Reasons for the underrepresentation of blacks on police forces are first examined. These include discriminatory hiring practices, the inability of blacks to pass white—oriented written entrance examinations, and reluctance of blacks to join police forces. The need for special efforts in recruiting blacks is discussed, and examples of several recruiting programs are provided. Among these are the training of blacks through community service officer or police cadet programs, and advertising campaigns designed to encourage blacks to join the police. Patterns of black promotion and black representation on police forces are considered in the final section. The data indicate that blacks are underrepresented on police forces throughout the US and that once they are hired they are not promoted as easily as whites.*

JESSOR, Lee. Cultural Factors And Socialization Into Deviance. Boulder CO U CO TriEthn R P 1963.

JESSOR, Richard. Theory And Method In The Study Of Deviance In A Tri—Ethnic Community. Boulder CO U CO TriEthn R P 1963.

JEWELL, Donald P. A Case Of A 'Psychotic' Navaho Indian Male. *Human Org* 11(1),32—36 1952.

JEWELL, Donald P. Mexico's Tres Marias Penal Colony. *J Crim L Crimin & Pol Sci* 48,410—413 1959.

JIOBU, R M. City Characteristics And Racial Violence. *Social Sci Q* 55(1),52—64 1974.

JOHANSON, S M and Carr, A L. Extent Of Washington Criminal Jurisdiction Over Indians. *Wash L Rev* 33,289—302 Fall 1958.

A 1956 decision of the Washington Supreme Court demonstrated that there are approximately 15,000 Indians living on reservations who are not amenable to criminal prosecution under state law in certain situations; in many instances, they are not amenable to either state or federal prosecution. It is recommended that the State of Washington use the means made available by Congress to remedy the situation and amend the state constitutions for the purpose of assuming jurisdiction over all Indians of the state.*

JOHNSON JR, Earl. *Justice And Reform: The Formative Years Of The American Legal Service Program.* New Brunswick NJ Transaction Books 1978.

JOHNSON, Audrey L. "The Legitimation Of Violence: Political Socialization And New Gangs" in *Poltics And Crime*, Sylvester Jr, Sawyer F And Edward Sagarin (eds). NY Praeger 1974.

JOHNSON, B B and Iiyama, P and Nishi, S M. *Drug Use And Abuse Among US Minorities: An Annotated Bibliography.* NY Praeger 1976.

This annotated bibliography of studies addressing the issue of drug use, primarily narcotics use, among blacks, Mexican—Americans, Puerto Ricans, Asian—Americans, and native Americans, contains 245 annotated citations and an introductory essay.*

JOHNSON, C S and Weatherford, Willis D. "Chapter 22" in *Race Relations*. Boston Heath 1934.

JOHNSON, Charles S. *The Negro In American Civilization: A Study Of Negro Life And Relations In The Light Of Social Research.* NY Henry Holt 1930.

In Chapter XXII, "Law Observance and Administration," numerous studies of the nature and extent of black crime are discussed. All sources point to a higher crime rate among blacks than among whites but it is noted that poor recordkeeping and biased law enforcement undermine the dependability of statistics on black crime. Illiteracy, unfavorable environment, age distributions and unfamiliarity with urban life are cited as factors requiring further serious study in relation to black crime. Chapter XXIII, "Juvenile Delinquency" recounts several studies and concludes that "In general there is a higher percentage of Negro than white delinquents; the contributing causes...are largely environmental (low wages, making it necessary for both parents to work away from home leaving the children unsupervised; broken homes; migration; proximity to houses of prostitution and "bootlegging joints" and crowded housing conditions).

JOHNSON, E A. Medico—Legal Jurisprudence. *Color Am Mag* 12(2),104—110 1907.

JOHNSON, Elmer H. *Crime, Correction And Society.* Homewood Dorsey Pr 1964.

JOHNSON, Elmer H. Pilot Study: Age, Race And Recidivism As Factors In Prison Infractions. *Can J Corr* 8,268—283 1966.

JOHNSON, Elmer H. Selective Factors In Capital Punishment. *Soc Forces* 36,165—169 1957.

This study was based on data obtained from the Prison Department of North Carolina. The author compares mean years of education of males, fifteen years and over in the state as a whole with the comparable figures for: prison admittees; death row admittees; death row admittees who were not executed; and death row admittees who were executed; all for the period 1940—1954. He compared occupational distribution for the state, for prison admittees and for death row admittees for this same period. A distribution was also made of the capital offenders committed to prison in North Carolina between 1909—1954 by offense and race, and figures were given for the percent of admittees executed in each racial group during the periods 1909—1933 and 1934—1954. The data indicated to the author that "capital punishment operates differentially on the basis of the type of crime and type of offender."

JOHNSON, Guy B. "Patterns Of Race Conflict" in *Race Relations And The Race Problem*, Thompson, Edgar T (ed), 125—151. Durham NC Duke Univ Pr 1939.

JOHNSON, Guy B. The Negro And Crime. *Ann Am Poli* 271,93–104 1941.

Black crime is discussed in the context of the caste position of blacks in American society. The author agrees that black crime rates are considerably higher than white crime rates, but this is attributed to a history of slavery and a persistent status of subordination which have dehumanized blacks. Insofar as poverty and social disorganization contribute to crime, discrimination is emphasized and segregated housing patterns have caused blacks to suffer from these conditions more than whites. The administration of justice itself is considered an aspect of the caste relationship, contributing to both real and reported rates of black crime.

JOHNSON, J H (ed). Black On Black Crime––The Cause, The Consequences, The Cures. *Ebony* 34,1–162 Ag 1979.

"Black on black crime" has reached a critical level. Although the black community is not responsible for the external conditions that create breeding grounds for crime, the community has the responsibility of doing what it can to attack the problem from within. This response is needed because such crime creates mistrust, uncertainty, fear, and anxiety in the community. Such crime has driven businesses and jobs from the community. Most important the young have been profoundly affected by crime as they are most often the perpetrators and the victims. Such underlying causes of crime as racism and oppression manifest themselves in high unemployment rates, drug addiction, the breakdown of the urban family, and an unjust criminal justice system. In addition, the prison system serves as training for further crime and the media may contribute to the crime problem by its portrayals of violence. Responses to the problem include the Push for Excellence Program, community involvement programs, reform of the criminal justice system, alleviating the economic ills of the ghetto, and the reaffirmation of religious values.*

JOHNSON, James Weldon. "The Negro And Racial Conflict" in *Our Racial And National Minorities*, Brown, F J And J S Roucek (eds), 549–560. NY Prentice–Hall 1937.

JOHNSON, James Weldon. Lynching, America's National Disgrace. *Curr Hist* 19,596–601 Ja 1924.

JOHNSON, James Weldon. More Than Murder: Administration Of Justice. *Crisis* 78,135 1971.

JOHNSON, K W and Hornung, C A and Rusinko, W T. Importance Of Police Contact In The Formulation Of Youths' Attitudes Toward Police. *J Crim Jus* 6(1),53–67 Spr 1978.

The significance of positive and negative contacts between police and juveniles as determinants of juveniles' attitudes toward police is examined in a study of 1,200 pupils in the ninth grade in Lansing, Mich. The survey instrument, which was administered in the late 1960's, measured the nature and extent of experiences with police, self–reported delinquent behavior and defiance of parental authority, and attitudes toward police. Positive contacts are predictive of positive attitudes, particularly for youths who have had a negative encounter with police, for those who report frequent involvement in deviance, and for those who report defying their parents. Negative contacts are predictive of negative attitudes, particularly for white youths, for youths who report infrequent deviant behavior, and for youths who have had little or no positive contact with police. Positive contacts can neutralize the effects of negative contacts; and positive contacts do not diminish the tendency for black youths to be negative in their opinions of police. Police management must explore ways to improve the attitudes of black youth toward the police.*

JOHNSON, Larry D and Fong, Melanie. The Eugenics Movement: Some Insight Into The Institutionalization Of Racism. *Issues Crim* 9(2),89–115 Fall 1974.

JOHNSON, Larry. A Black Perspective On Social Research: In Response To Merton. *Issues Crim* 9(1),55–70 1974.

The theory of "social structure and anomie" of Robert K. Merton, which has had such an effect upon the study of criminology that it has defined the parameters of most contemporary research into crime and delinquency, is explained and refuted. Merton's functionalist school has cast Third World and poor people as villains rather than victims. The bias generally is in favor of the status quo, especially with respect to the extant social structure. Far too many white scholars, including Merton, seem to feel that substantively there is an isomorphism between scholarship and their values. Opportunist white scholars such as Merton, Daniel Moynihan and Elliot Liebow are attacked for their claim to have learned insight into the black experience. The insider–outsider doctrine is debated, in relation to whether white scholars should, or could understand black community sociology.

JOHNSON, R C and Roebuck, Julian D. The 'Short Con' Man. *Crim Delinq* 10(3),235–248 1964.

JOHNSON, R C. Political Economy Of Criminal Oppression. *Black Scholar* 8(6),14–22 1977.

JOHNSON, R W. Justice And The American Indian, V1. Washington DC LEAA 1974.

JOHNSON, R W and Collins, R B. American Indian Courts And Tribal Self–Government. *Am Bar A J* 63,808–815 Je 1977.

JOHNSON, R and Roebuck, Julian B. The Negro Drinker And Assaulter As A Criminal Type. *Crim Delinq* 8,21–33 1962.

JOHNSON, Robert. Culture And Crisis In Confinement. Lexington, MA Heath 1977.

Examines the relationship between ethnic and cultural background and suicidal crises among Latin, black, and white inmates.

JOHNSON, Thomas A. The Enforcers. *Nation's Cities* 16(9),26–28 S 1978.

JOHNSTON, Norman (ed) and Wolfgang, Marvin E (ed) and Savitz, Leonard D (ed). *The Sociology Of Crime And Delinquency*. NY Wiley 1970.

JOHNSTON, Norman G and Cooke, Gerald and Pogany, Eric. A Comparison Of Blacks And Whites Committed For Evaluation Of Competency To Stand Trial On Criminal Charges. *J Psychi L* 2(3),319–337 1974.

Blacks and whites committed for evaluation of competency to stand trial were compared. All males referred to the Michigan Center for Forensic Psychiatry for competency evaluation in 1969 were grouped according to race, and differences on demographic variables. Criminal charges, diagnosis, competency finding, and disposition were studied. A subsample of 70 blacks and 70 whites was analyzed for characteristics associated with MMPI administration and for differences in MMPI profile. The results are consistent with previous literature and indicate a tendency to clinically overestimate psychopathology in blacks, though there is no supporting evidence for a difference in level of pathology in terms of the more objective MMPI measure. The profound effects of this overestimation on disposition are discussed, and a number of solutions are proposed.

JOHNSTONE, Abraham. The Address Of Abraham Johnstone, A Black Man, Who Was Hanged In New Jersey. Philadelphia For The Purchasers 1797.

JOINT LEGIS COMM ON CAPITAL PUNISHMENT. *Report Of The Pennsylvania Joint Legislative Committee On Capital Punishment.* Harrisburg PA State Of PA 1961.

The Committee's data relative to discrimination in the application of capital punishment are taken from *National Prisoner Statistics*. Data for the United States as a whole are given for executions for rape in the period 1930–1960 by race. Rape executions in Florida, Louisiana, Mississippi and Alabama are also given by race (all black) as are burglary executions for the period in the only two jurisdictions which have capital punishment for burglary (North Carolina and Alabama). The Committee concluded that it was evident that "white persons who committed such crimes (as burglary and rape) benefited from more favorable decisions by juries and pardon authorities." The *Report* also notes, but does not comment on the fact that, during the studied period, nationwide, less than one percent of persons executed were women.

JONES JR, Oakah L. The Origins Of The Navajo Indian Police, 1872–1873. *Ariz & West* 8,225–238 Aut 1966.

JONES, Clinton B. "Criminal Justice/Racial Justice Nexus" in *Critical Issues In Criminal Justice*, Iacovetta, R G And D H Chang (eds). Chapel Hill NC Univ N Car Pr 1979.

The relationship between racial and criminal justice issues is discussed in a historical framework beginning with the days of slavery in America through to the present.*

JONES, Clinton B. Critical Equal Employment Issues In Criminal Justice. *J Polic Sci Adm* 7(2),129–137 1979.

The interrelationships between Equal Employment Opportunity (EEO) and the criminal justice system are explored. Because of inadequate staff and administrative organization, EEO delegates enforcement responsibilities to other federal agencies, including the Law Enforcement Assistance Administration (LEAA). LEAA's own civil rights stance, however, discriminates against minorities and women with its workforce statistically underrepresented by these groups. Therefore, aggressive enforcement of EEO policies will become a top priority issue only when minorities and women become more effective influencers of the subordinate sociopolitical system.*

JONES, David A. *The Dangerousness Of Imprisonment.* Unpub PhD Diss SUNY Albany 1975.

A methodology for comparing the health of adult male state prisoners with the health of adult male parolees and probationers from a Tennessee penitentiary was developed and tested. Health indicators, including mortality trends, incidence of acute morbidity conditions, prevalence of selected chronic digestive conditions, selected psychological distress symptoms, and symptoms of mental illness such as self—destructive sequelae and short—term/long—term disability, were studied and validated. Prisoners reported most varieties of morbidity conditions at much higher rates than probationers or parolees. Age, race, and length of imprisonment were influencing factors, as was marital status and education. Psychological distress was a negative inverse indicator of acute physical morbidity in black prisoners and in prisoners of both races when controlled by marital status. Mortality among black prisoners under 25 years old was exorbitantly high and caused by homicide. Overall findings indicate that, despite greater access to medical treatment by prisoners, incarceration was more dangerous to the physical and mental health than life outside prison.

JONES, E Terrence. Crime Change Patterns In American Cities. *J Crim Jus* 4(4),333—340 Wint 1976.

JONES, Mark E. Racism In Special Courts. *J Pub L* 20,401—406 1971. Judge Jones, of the Chicago Circuit Court, discusses special courts in terms of a two—class structure. From Class I come the rule and lawmakers such as judges and legislators. This class is predominantly white and adheres to traditional middle—class values, and in turn finds it easy to conform to the decrees of the lawmakers. Class II consists of the poor, the illiterate, the unconventional, the defiers of authority. They find it very difficult to conform to the decrees of the lawmakers. 90% of the non—white population falls into this category. We can look at the disproportionate number of non—white people who came before our special courts as evidence of racism in the law. He cites courts which handle gambling cases as a manifestation of this racism. One does not see Class I members arrested for such gambling activities as playing the stock market, wagering at the race track and playing cards at country clubs. One sees instead a preponderance of Class II members arrested for throwing dice or playing cards in more observable places where they are easier to arrest. Jones claims that the Court System is run to the disadvantage of Class II members.

JONES, Martin C and Jones, Martin H. Counselor, Community And The Black Prisoner. *Black Scholar* 4(2),46—55 O 1972.

JONES, Martin H and Jones, Martin C. Counselor, Community And The Black Prisoner. *Black Scholar* 4(2),46—55 O 1972.

JONES, Reginald L (ed). *Black Psychology.* NY Harper & Row 1972.

JONES, Robert A. Black Versus White In The Station House. *Nation* ,368—370 O 13 1979.

Jones reports on the growth and activities of the black police association in San Francisco, the Officers for Justice. While fighting racism within the department was cited by this group as a major concern, the O. F. J. also wants to promote a police depatment that is honest, professional and compassionate. The size of its membership is a problem for the group.

JONES, T. Blacks In The American Criminal Justice System: A Study Of Sanctioned Deviance. *J Sociol & Soc Wel* 5(3),356—373 1978.

The professional involvement of black Americans in a criminal justice system that many have labeled as inimical to the development of blacks in America is addressed. The integration of blacks into the public employment sector often creates or perpetuates class conflict, where middle—class blacks are against lower—class blacks. The difficulty black workers in the criminal justice system have in formulating a clear position with regard to what their attitudes and behavior should be is related to the reward—punishment mechanism, the acculturation process, and the status of their position. In addition to this difficulty, black social workers have traditionally been viewed with suspicion, indifference, and even hostility. A framework for analyzing functions of blacks in the criminal justice system is presented that encompasses the extent of black involvement in the system. It takes into account who has authority, how authority is used in relation to blacks, and outcomes of the use of authority.*

JONGEWARD, D and Scott, D. *Affirmative Action For Women—A Practical Guide For Women And Management.* Reading MA Addison—Wesley 1977.

JORDAN JR, Vernon E. The System Propagates Crime. *Crim Delinq* 20(3),233—240 1974.

The author, executive director of the National Urban League, urges a moratorium on the use of crime as an issue by politicians. He argues that the root cause of crime is economic and thus that effective anticrime measures must seek economic solutions such as equal employment The criminal justice system is viewed as contributing to crime rather than as an apparatus for reducing it. Jordan favors decriminalization of victimless offenses, equal justice for blacks and the poor instead of discrimination, and gradual abolition of imprisonment.

JORDAN, Fania Davis. The San Quentin Six: A Case Of Vengeance. *Black Scholar* 5(6),44—50 Mr 1974.

JORDAN, Samuel. Prison Reform: In Whose Interest? *Crim L Bull* 7(9),779—787 N 1971.

The author, an inmate of the Pennsylvania state prison system, provides an analysis of imprisonment and prison reform. Black prisoners, he writes, are unavoidably aware of the power configurations that exist in a racist, capitalist society, which is why they have led the way in struggling against the system. Jordan rejects the reformer's goal of improving the prison, in favor of an abolitionist position.

JORDAN, Winthrop D. *The White Man's Burden: Historical Origins Of Racism In The United States.* NY Oxford Univ Pr 1974.

JORDAN, Winthrop D. *White Over Black: American Attitudes Toward The Negro, 1550—1812*, Orig Pub 1968. NY Norton 1977.

This is the classic historical study of the origins of racism toward blacks in the US. It contains perceptive analysis of racism in criminal justice as well as slavery.

JORGENSEN, Carl C. IQ Tests And Their Educational Supporters. *J Soc Issues* 29(1),33—40 1973.

JOSEPH AND ENOCH. *Narrative Of The Barbarous Treatment Of Two Unfortunate Females, Natives Of Concordia LA By Joseph & Enoch, Runaway Slaves.* NY Authors 1842.

JOSEPHSON, E. Resistance To Community Surveys. *Social Prob* 18,117—129 1970.

JOSEPHY JR, A M. Toward Freedom: The American Indian In The Twentieth Century. Indian Hist Soc Lectures 1970.

JOYNER, Irving and Bell, Jimmy. "Crime In The Black Community" in *Blacks And Criminal Justice*, Owens, Charles E And Jimmy Bell (eds), 69—74. Lexington MA Heath 1977.

Causal factors leading to crime and its alarming increase in the black community are examined, and programs to aid in crime reduction are presented. Studies indicate that the economically deprived individual may opt for crime as a means of access to the mainstream of American society, or may view crime as a necessary evil to counteract years of economic oppression. Moreover, complaints about inequities in law enforcement, unresponsiveness, and even abuse have contributed to the black community's general mistrust of police. Unemployment, which is higher among blacks, is viewed as a possible cause of the high crime rate among blacks. Evidence suggests that the typical offender is a young black male, a local resident, and undereducated. A comprehensive approach to alleviate crime in the black community is suggested. This includes community—based action programs, education programs, victim—oriented programs, and economic improvement programs; it calls for a more sensitive and responsible criminal justice system and improved community relations.*

JOYNER, Irving and Scott, Elsie K. *Crime In The Minority Community.* NY Comm Racial Just 1976.

JOYNER, Irving and Scott, Elsie K. "People And Police" in *Black Crime: A Police View*, Bryce, H J (ed), 109—128. Washington DC Jt Ctr Polit Stud 1977.

JOYNER, Irving and Scott, Elsie K. Crime: A Common Concern. *Crim Just Iss* 2, 1975.

JOYNER, Irving. Police Repression In America. *J Poli Repr* 1(1),41—46 1975.

JUE, George K. *Chinatown: Its History, Its People, Its Importance.* San Francisco Chamb Of Commerce 1951.

JUNKER, Buford H and Adams, Walter A and Warner, W Lloyd. *Color And Human Nature.* Washington DC Am Coun On Educ 1941.

JUST, Bernice. Bail And Pre–Trial Detention In The District Of Columbia: An Empirical Analysis. *Howard L J* 17,844–857 1973.

JUSTICE, Blair. *Effects Of Racial Violence On Attitudes In The Negro Community.* Houston Rice Univ 1968.

JUSTICE, Blair. *Violence In The City.* Fort Worth TX Tex Christian U Pr 1969.

KAHN, M W and Conrad, R D. An Epidemiological Study Of Suicide And Attempted Suicide Among The Papago Indians. *Am J Psychiatry* 131(1),69–72 1974.

KANIA, Richard and Mackey, Wade C. Police Violence As A Function Of Community Characteristics. *Criminology* 15(1),22–48 My 1977.

KANDEL, D B. Race, Maternal Authority And Adolescent Aspiration. *Am J Soc* 76(6),999–1020 1971.

KANE, A. Negro And Indian: A Comparison Of Their Constitutional Rights. *Ariz L Rev* 7,244–251 1966.

KANSON, H and Perry, A M. Race Factors In Responses To Interpersonal Stress Among Young Adult Offenders. *Crim Just B* 4(1),45–61 Mr 1977.
Previous research has shown that young adult prison inmates display an anxious, acquiescent, depressive–like reaction pattern under conditions of interpersonal stress. The present study evaluated racial factors in this area and found that, relative to white prisoners, black inmates manifest more frequent acquiescence, fewer reports of anger, and generally higher autonomic reactivity. The results are discussed in terms of offender rehabilitation and special problems faced by black prisoners.*

KANTROWITZ, N. The Vocabulary Of Race Relations In A Prison. *Pub Am Dialect* 51,23–34 1969.

KAPLAN, J. Latitude And Severity Of Sentencing Options, Race Of The Victim And Decisions Of Simulated Jurors. *Law & Soc Rev* 7(1),87–98 Fall 1972.

KAPSIS, Robert E. Black Ghetto Diversity And Anomie: A Sociopolitical View. *Am J Soc* 83,1132–1153 1978.
On the basis of responses to two anomie scales across different black neighborhoods, this study reports findings compatible with the viewpoint that the American black urban ghettoes harbor a rich variety of subculturally distinct residential areas. More specifically, it suggests that sociopolitical variables which highlight the relationship between neighborhoods and the structures of power in the city are a more important source of subcultural differences between black residential areas than are variables derived from census data such as rate of racial turnover.

KAPSIS, Robert E. Continuities In Delinquency And Riot Patterns, In Black Residential Areas. *Social Prob* 23(5),567–580 1976.
This study suggests that riots represent a direct continuity rather than a sharp discontinuity with pre–existing social conditions. Evidence is presented that patterns of neighborhood involvement during a 1968 disturbance resembled prior neighborhood delinquency patterns. In two racially changing neighborhoods, the incidence of pre–riot delinquency was higher than in a more racially stable one, while during the course of the riot, the incidence of riot–related violence escalated in the former and dramatically declined in the latter. The adequacy of a social control model to explain similarities between delinquency and riot–related action is empirically tested and the strength of friendship and institutional ties in the low delinquency area is explored. Results are consistent with a growing body of evidence indicating that the "irrational" or "bizarre" features of collective behavior episodes have been unduly exaggerated.

KAPSIS, Robert E. Residential Succession And Delinquency: A Test Of Shaw And McKay's Theory Of Cultural Transmission. *Criminology* 15(2),459–486 F 1978.

KARMEN, Andrew. "Race, Inferiority, Crime, And Research Taboos" in *Taboos In Criminology*, Sagarin, Edward (ed). Beverly Hills CA Sage 1980.

KARSON, Michael and Lerner, Richard M. Racial Stereotypes Of Early Adolescent White Children. *Psychol Rep* 32(2),381–382 1973.
The current status of a group (n=406) of whites' racial attitudes was examined by comparing the relative favorableness–unfavorableness of white early adolescents' social stereotypes toward white and black people. Subjects were asked to attribute each of 48 items from a verbal checklist to a picture of either a white or a black male. The results

indicated that subjects held a predominantly unfavorable view of the black figure and a predominantly positive view of the white figure.

KARTON, Robert. Mob Violence And The Prosecuting Attorney. *J Crim L Crimin & Pol Sci* 59,167–170 1968.

KASIRIKA, Kaidi (Kenneth Divans) and Muntu, Maharibi (larry M West). Prison Or Slavery. *Black Scholar* 3(2),6–12 O 1971.

KASSENBASUM, Gene G and Ward, David A. *Women's Prison: Sex And Social Structure.* Chicago IL Aldine 1965.

KATEL, Peter and Serrill, Michael S. New Mexico: The Anatomy Of A Riot. *Correct Mag* 6(2),6–24 Ap 1980.

KATEL, Peter. Sleeping It Off In Gallup, NM. *Correct Mag* 6(4),16–21 Ag 1980.
Response of the Gallup, New Mexico Police Department to the weekend influx of Navajo Indians from the nearby reservation, with descriptions of the policy toward public intoxication.

KATZ, Michael. Patterns Of Arrest And The Dangers Of Public Visibility. *Crim L Bull* 9(4),311–324 1973.

KATZ, Myron. Family Crisis Training: Upgrading The Police While Building A Bridge To The Minority Community. *J Polic Sci Adm* 1(1),30–35 Mr 1973.
Family crisis training for policemen is discussed as a means of building better community relations, especially with the minority community. Law enforcement personnel need special training programs to function as mental health paraprofessionals in coping with the difficult problem of familiy crisis intervention. Such training should include: interviewing skills; basic knowledge of human behavior with emphasis on problem areas such as alcoholism, depression and suicide; knowledge of available social service agencies; self–insight and tactics to ensure the physical safety of patrolmen and disputants. Training should be intensive with a high degree of learner participation. Role–playing, the use of professional actors, videotape feedback and group discussions are valuable aids; a day In a social agency and a followup training period are recommended.

KAUFMAN, Bob. *Solitudes Crowded With Loneliness.* NY New Directions 1965.
The jail poems of a San Francisco early "beat poet."

KAWASHIMA, Yasuhide. Forced Conformity: Puritan Criminal Justice And Indians. *U Kan L Rev* 25(3),361–373 1977.

KEIL, Charles. *Urban Blues.* Chicago Univ Chicago Pr 1966.

KEISER, R Lincoln. *The Vice Lords: Warriors Of The Streets.* NY Holt Rinehart Wins 1969.

KEITH, K Wymand. *Long Line Rider: The Story Of Cummins Prison Farm.* NY McGraw–Hill 1971.

KELLER, C. Prison Reform And Indians. *Indian Hist* 9(1),34–38 Wint 1976.

KELLEY, Dean M. The Young Lords And The Spanish Congregation. *Christ Cen* 87(7),208–211 F 18 1970.

KELLOR, Frances A. The Criminal Negro. *Arena* 25,419–428 Ap 1901.

KELLOR, Frances A. The Criminal Negro. *Arena* 25,190–197· F 1901.

KELLOR, Frances A. The Criminal Negro. *Arena* 25,308–316 Mr 1901.

KELLOR, Frances A. The Criminal Negro. *Arena* 25,510–520 My 1901.

KELLOR, Frances A. The Criminal Negro. *Arena* 25,59–68 Ja 1901.

KELLY, Arlene and Nolde, Hans C and Wolfgang, Marvin E. Comparison Of The Executed And Commuted Among Admissions To Death Row. *J Crim L Crimin & Pol Sci* 53,301–311 S 1962.
This study of commutation rates was based on case records of 439 persons sentenced to death and received on death row in Pennsylvania between 1914 and 1958. The percentages of whites and of Negroes were compared, and it was found that a significantly smaller proportion of Negroes than whites received commutations. With the type of crime held constant, it was found that a significantly lower percentage of Negro felony–murderers than white felony–murderers received commutations; with the sample limited to Negroes and native–born whites committed for felony–murder, the difference was even more pronounced. The study concluded that "[t]he one factor that links each of the others together is race; for while more offenders convicted of felony murder and offenders with court–appointed counsel are executed than offenders convicted of non–felony murder and offenders with private counsel, respectively, these

differences are produced by the fact that significantly more Negroes than whites are executed."

KELLY, Henry E. "Biosociology And Crime" in *Biology And Crime*, Jeffrey, C R (ed). Beverly Hills CA Sage 1979.

KELLY, Henry E. A Comparison Of Defense Strategy And Race As Influences In Differential Sentencing. *Criminology* 14(2),241–249 Ag 1976.

KELLY, R S and Thorkelson, M M. Equal Employment Opportunity—Affirmative Action Programs For Federal Government Contractors. *Bus Lawyer* 31(3),1509–1515 Ap 1976.

Problems faced by federal contractors in developing realistic and acceptable affirmative action programs are discussed. Contractors are advised to take the following steps: (1) develop better data on availability of minorities and females, proper recruiting areas, and necessary job skills, in order to establish realistic goals and timetables and to withstand unreasonable demands from compliance agencies; (2) resist the proposed affected class rule on grounds of unclear authority for its enforcement; (3) observe disclosure developments with a view to protecting affirmative action plan documents from discovery or Freedom of Information Act requests; and (4) prepare to challenge compliance agency attempts to undertake enforcement actions without hearings required by due process.*

KELLY, Rita Mae and Farber, Martin G. Identifying Responsive Inner–City Policemen. *J Appl Psyc* 59(3),259–263 1974.

This study sought to develop an operational definition of "responsiveness" and is based on a sample of subjects classified as extreme on the basis of their performance on four "Fear of Citizens Scales." The subjects were drawn from the District of Columbia Metropolitan Police Department. Twelve of the original 509 subjects were classified, either in the positive (responsiveness) or negative (non–responsiveness) group. The two most important variables correlated with responsiveness were race and place of residence. While race seems quite significant in determining the extent to which policemen develop negative perceptions of inner–city residents, it does not seem as strongly associated with those who possess a positive view. Only 17% of the most negative officers lived in the city, whereas 53% of the most positive ones were city residents. They state that the effect of race on the place of residence can be seen by the fact that of the 17 most positive respondents living in Washington, D. C., 13 (77%) were black; of the 15 most positive respondents living outside the city, 14 (93%) were white.

KELMAN, Mark G. The Politics Of Explaining Crime. *Stanford L Rev* 31(3),527–539 F 1979.

KEMPTON, Murray. *The Briar Patch: The People Of The State Of New York V Lumumba Shakur Et Al.* NY Delta 1973.

This award–winning book investigates the highly publicized case in 1969 in which NYC Police detectives raided the residences of 19 Black Panthers and arrested them on a variety of charges. Kempton recreates their controversial trial before State Supreme Court Justice John M. Murtagh.

KENNEDY, D B. *The Dysfunctional Alliance: Emotion And Reason In Justice Administration.* Cincinnati Anderson 1978.

KENNEDY, Robert F. Crime In The Cities: Improving The Administration Of Criminal Justice. *J Crim L Crimin & Pol Sci* 58,142–154 1967.

KENNEDY, Will Charles. *Prisonization And Self Concept.* Unpub PhD Diss UCLA 1970.

KENNEDY, William. To What Extent Was Enrique Soto The Creation Of Pedro Juan Soto? San Juan Star Mag ,1–5 Ag 20 1978.

Writer William Kennedy, a close friend of Pedro Juan Soto, one of Puerto Rico's leading novelists, conducted his own inquiry into the shooting death of Soto's teen–age son. Carlos Enrique "Quico" Soto was gunned down by police who said they were thwarting an alleged terrorist attempt.

KENNY, Robert W. *Police And Minority Groups: An Experiment.* Sacramento Calif Atty Gen 1946.

KEPHART, William M. *Racial Factors And Urban Law Enforcement.* Philadelphia Univ of Penn Pr 1957.

KEPHART, William M. Racial Factors And Urban Law Enforcement. *Br J Delinq* 5(2),144–145 O 1954.

KEPHART, William M. The Negro Offender: An Urban Research Project. *Am J Soc* 60,46–50 Jl 1954.

Part of a larger survey dealing with racial factors and law enforcement, this study examines the interaction between the white policemen and Negro offenders in Philadelphia. Printed questionnaires were distributed to all white patrolmen assigned to district duty. The response rate was 51.5% of the 2,101 questionnaires. The respondents generally believed that Negro criminality is explainable neither in terms of low economic status nor on the basis of differential treatment by the police or by the courts, but is attributable to the prevalence of low moral standards and a looseness in community organization. This view is reflected in the comments of police commanders: "The Negro is a menace to this city," and so on. A majority (65.4%) of the white patrolmen replied that they would have an objection to riding with a Negro patrolman; and a majority (51.8%) stated they were more strict with negro than with white offenders.

KERNER COMMISSION. "Police And The Community" in *Race, Crime, And Justice*, Reasons, Charles E And Jack L Kuykendall (eds), 156–175. Pacific Palisades CA Goodyear 1972.

KHATENA, J and Mastroianni, M. The Attitudes Of Black And White High School Seniors Toward Integration. *Sociol Soc Res* 56(2),221–227 1972. 142 high school seniors (blacks: 12 boys and 16 girls; whites: 51 boys and 63 girls) from an integrated school and an all white school were administered a questionnaire on interracial attitudes. Black subjects showed a significant trend towards integration whereas white subjects appeared to be generally undecided about integration on such issues as marriage, schooling and equal job opportunity; they were also segretationists on matters like close friends, neighborhood and club memberships. Perceptions of black and white subjects were significantly different regarding matters of leadership, job satisfaction and opportunity, government effectiveness in handling racial problems, the justification of breaking the law, and whether the US is a better place to live in.

KICKINGBIRD, K. In Our Image: After Our Likeness—The Drive For The Assimilation Of Indian Court Systems. *Am Crim L Rev* 13(4),675–700 Spr 1976.

KILLIAN, Lewis. *The Impossible Revolution: Black Power And The American Dream.* NY Random House 1968.

KILSON, Marion D De B. Towards Freedom: An Analysis Of Slave Revolts In The United States. *Phylon* 25(1),175–187 Spr 1964.

KILSON, Martin and Fox, Daniel M and Huggins, Nathan. *Key Issues In The Afro–American Experience.* NY Harcourt Brace 1971.

KIMBALL, Bruce A. An Historical Perspective On The Constitutional Debate Over Affirmative Action Admissions. *J Law & Ed* 7(1),31–49 Ja 1978.

KIMBLES, Samuel L. "Behavior Therapy And The Black Delinquent" in *Behavior Therapy With Delinquents*, Stumphauzer, J (ed), 49–53. Springfield IL Chas C Thomas 1973.

Use of behavior therapy with black delinquents is critically viewed. Consideration is given to implicit goals of control and manipulation which run counter to the lifestyle of the black individual and create harm in terms of estrangement, lessening the number of behavioral choices, and removing traits which are adaptive devices developed in response to the environment.

KINDLER, A R and Pederson, A M and Awad, G A. Epidemiological Differences Between White And Nonwhite Suicide Attempters. *Am J Psychiatry* 130(10),1071–1076 1973.

Using the Monroe County (NY) Psychiatric Case Register, the authors attempted to determine differences between white and non–white suicide attempters, to identify the factors that are associated with self–destructive behavior in both groups, and to determine the subsequent mortality rate among suicide attempters. They found a number of differences between whites and non–whites and concluded that the motivation for suicide, the techniques used to treat attempts, and the degree of risk of further psychiatric difficulty may be different for the two groups.

KING JR, Martin Luther. *Letter From Birmingham City Jail.* Valley Forge PA Am Baptist Conv 1963.

KING JR, Martin Luther. *Stride Toward Freedom.* NY Harper & Bros 1958.

KING JR, Martin Luther. *Why We Can't Wait.* NY Harper & Row 1963.

KING, G D and Eastman, G and Curry, Jesse E. *Race Tensions And The Police.* Springfield IL Chas C Thomas 1962.

KING, Glen D and Curry, Jesse E. "The Effects Of Prejudice On Minorities" in *Police–Community Relationships*, Bopp, W (ed), 86–90. Springfield IL Chas C Thomas 1972.

The effect of prejudice on minority groups' relations with society in general, and with the police in particular, is briefly examined. Prevailing attitudes regarding the "inferiority" of blacks and other minority groups and their frustrations at being denied social and economic justice and opportunity have led to conditions of alienation and lawlessness. When these groups are uncooperative and antagonistic toward the police the officers respond in the same manner. Under conditions of mutual antagonism, it is nearly impossible for the police to enforce law and order fairly. A primary goal in the area of race relations, therefore, is to insure that each officer's conduct with members of a minority group is above reproach so as to gradually establish an attitude of confidence and cooperation on both sides.

KING, L M. Puertoriquens In US—Impact Of Double–Discrimination. *Civil Rts Dig* 6,20–27 Spr 1974.

KING, Lucy J et al. Alcohol Abuse: A Crucial Factor In The Social Problems Of Negro Men. *Am J Psychiatry* 125(12),1682–1690 1969.

KING, W M (ed) and Vance, M (ed). *Blacks, Crime & Criminal Justice: An Introductory Bibliography.* Monticello IL Coun Plan Librar 1974.
Alphabetical listing (by author) of over 200 books, articles, government publications, dissertations and theses. A separate list of the journals cited is included at the beginning of the bibliography.*

KING, Wayne. The Violent Rebirth Of The Klan. *NYT Mag* ,150+ D 7 1980.

KINMAN, Judith L and Lee, Everett S. Migration And Crime. *Int Migration Dig* 3,7–14 Spr 1966.

KINSIE, Paul M and Winick, Charles. *The Lively Commerce: Prostitution In The United States.* NY New Am Lib 1971.

KIRCHHEIMER, Otto. *Political Justice: The Use Of Legal Procedure For Political Ends.* Princeton Princeton Univ Pr 1961.

KIRCHHEIMER, Otto and Rusche, Georg. *Punishment And Social Structure.* NY Columbia Univ Pr 1939.
This classic historical work on punishment and social structure suggests that every system of production tends to develop punishments which correspond to its productive relationships. The authors contend that it is thus "necessary to investigate the origin and fate of penal systems, the use or avoidance of specific punishments, and the intensity of penal practices as they are determined by social forces, above all by economic and then fiscal forces." One of their hypotheses is that punishments become more severe in periods of poor economic conditions. Some analysis of the relationship between slavery and imprisonment is included.

KIRK, Stuart A. The Sex Offenses Of Blacks And Whites. *Arch Sex Beh* 4(3),295–302 1975.
Comparative data is presented on 47 black and 47 white sex offenders in terms of the nature of the offense and victim characteristics. It was found that black offenders were more likely than white offenders to engage in vaginal intercourse with their victims, showed a trend to use force in their offenses, and were more likely to select adult female victims. These differences, however, appear to be due primarily to class rather than racial differences. Limitations of these data are discussed.

KIRKSEY, Kirk and Georges, Daniel E. Violent Crime Perpetrated Against The Elderly In The City Of Dallas, October 1974–September 1975. *J Environ Syst* 17(2),149–197 1977–78.

KIRSTEIN, Peter N. *Anglo Over Bracero: A History Of The Mexican Worker In The United States From Roosevelt To Nixon.* Saratoga CA R & E Research 1977.

KLAPMUTS, Nora and Doleschal, Eugene. Toward A New Criminology. *Crim Delin Lit* 5(4),607–626 1973.

KLEBBA, A Joan. *Homicide Trends In The United States, 1900–1974.* Rockville MD Nat Cen Heal Stat 1975.

KLEBBA, A Joan. *Mortality Trends For Homicide By Age, Color, And Sex: United States, 1960–1972.* Rockville MD Nat Cen Heal Stat 1973.

KLEECK, Mary V. "Work And Law Observance In The Histories Of Men In Sing–Sing Prison" in *Report On The Causes Of Crime*, V1, 193–255,315–320. Washington DC NCLOE 1931.
This analysis of 300 inmates of Sing–Sing prison in NY for the period 1830–1927 found that approximately 59% of the Negro prisoners were not gainfully employed at the time the offense was committed, compared to only 38% of the whites.

KLEIN, D et al. Some Social Characteristics Of Young Gunshot Fatalities. *Accident Anal Prev* 9,171–182 1977.

KLEIN, Joe (ed). Matty Troy's Prison Diary. NY 13,55–56+ D 8 1980.
Just five years ago, Matthew Troy was one of the most powerful politicians in New York. But now convicted on charges of tax fraud for the second time, he is sentenced to serve 26 weekends in jail at Riker's Island. Excerpts from a diary he kept present an "outsider's" view of life in prison from a protective custody cell. Brief daily entries describe in anecdotal fashion topics including "crazy" inmates in solitary confinement, importation of contraband, Hispanic prisoners, race relations, homosexuality and violence.

KLEIN, Malcolm. *Street Gangs And Street Workers.* Englewood Cliffs NJ Prentice–Hall 1971.

KLEINER, J. United States Law On American Indians. *Case & Comment* 77(4),3–7 Jl–Ag 1972.

KLEINFELD, Gerald J and Norman, Ralph D. Rosenzweig Picture––Frustration Study Results With Minority Group Juvenile Delinquents. *J Genet Psyc* 92,61–67 1958.
Contrast was made on the Rosenzweig Picture–Frustration Study between 20 juvenile delinquents and 44 controls, all Spanish–American males ranging (age) from 15 to 18 and members of the same minority group. Correlations were also determined for relationship between amount of overt aggression as ascertained from ratings of behavior by a competent judge and the test. However, comparison of the study group with Rosenzweig's normative group revealed considerable difference in Picture–Frustration Study response patterns. This variation in Picture–Frustration Study response would seem to be in part culturally determined and further normative study appears warranted.

KLEINMAN, Paula H and David, Deborah S. Visibility And Contact With Others: Mediating Factors In The Neighborhood Crime Complex. Jerusalem Int Symp Victimol 1973.
The authors sampled residents in the Bedford–Stuyvesant/Fort Greene area to discover patterns of victimization, and the relationships of victimization and social characteristics to perception of crime. The sample, located in an area high in narcotic addiction and crime, found that the respondents of each of four race–ethnic groups report roughly the same rates of victimization, and the proportions are similar who perceive that crime in the area is high.

KLEINMAN, Paula H and David, Deborah S. Victimization And Perception Of Crime In A Ghetto Community. *Criminology* 11(3),307–343 N 1973.
This paper presents results of a study which explored the relationship between victimization and perception of crime with relevant demographic factors. A sample of residents were interviewed in the Bedford–Stuyvesant/Fort Greene area of New York, an area high in narcotic addiction and crime. Four ethnic groups in the area, blacks, Puerto Ricans, British West Indians and whites, were compared. Data shows that respondents of the four groups report roughly the same rates of victimization and similar proportions of the groups perceive crime as high. Those of high socio–economic status have higher victimization rates and larger proportion of high SES people perceive crime as being high (except among West Indians). No differences were found in victimization or perception of crime between males and females. The impact of age differs for each race/ethnic group. A high degree of visibility to and contact with others was found to be positively related to victimization. The relationship between visibility/contact and perceptions was less clear since it varied between groups and indicators were inconsistent.

KLINEBERG, Otto (ed). *Characteristics Of The American Negro.* NY Harper & Bros 1944.

KLINGBERG, Frank J. *An Appraisal Of The Negro In Colonial South Carolina: A Study Of Americanization.* Washington DC Associated Pub 1941.

KLUEGEL, James R and Cohen, Lawrence E. Determinants Of Juvenile Court Disposition Ascriptive And Achieved Factors In Two Metropolitan Courts. *Am Sociol Rev* 43(2),163–176 Ap 1978.

KLUEGEL, James R. The Causes And Cost Of Racial Exclusion From Job Authority. *Am Sociol Rev* 43(3),285–301 Je 1978.

KLUGER, Richard. *Simple Justice.* NY Knopf 1975.

KNIGHT, Etheridge (ed). *Black Voices From Prison.* NY Pathfinder Pr 1970.
Knight, a former prisoner, wrote these poems and essays while serving an 8–year sentence at Indiana State Prison from 1960–68. Some short

stories, autobiographical sketches, and other writings by fellow convicts are included.

KNIGHT, Etheridge. *Poems From Prison*. Detroit Broadside Pr 1968.

KNOPF, Terry Ann. *Rumors, Race And Riots*. New Brunswick NJ Transaction Books 1975.

Knopf examines and critiques three major models of rumor formation: the psychological approach, emphasizing the emotional needs and drives of the individual; the functional approach which views as a form of "improvised news"; and the conspiratorial approach which considers rumors as deliberately planted rather than spontaneous. Rumors are viewed as merely one of a series of determinants that lead to collective violence. Among the others are (1) conditions of stress, (2) a rigid social structure supported by racist ideology, (3) and a hostile belief system held separately by different groups. The role of rumors in racial disturbances that occurred between 1967 and 1970 is examined in detail and compared to their role in earlier periods of unrest. The function and performance of rumor control centers are also evaluated.

KNOPF, Terry Ann. *Youth Patrols: An Experiment In Community Participation*. Cambridge MA Brandeis Univ 1969.

KNOPF, Terry Ann. Sniping—A New Pattern Of Violence? Trans—Act 6(9),22—29 1969.

KNOPP, Fay Honey et al. *Instead Of Prisons: A Handbook For Abolitionists*. Syracuse NY Safer Society Pr 1976.

The authors advocate that prisons be abolished in favor of a variety of alternatives. Imprisonment is examined in relation to slavery. Creative programs in community empowerment and alternatives to incarceration are described.

KNOWLES, Louis L (ed) and Prewitt, Kenneth (ed). *Institutional Racism In America*. Englewood Cliffs NJ Prentice—Hall 1969.

KNOWLES, Lyle and Brewer, Jesse. The Black Community: Attitudes Toward Community Problems, Crime And The Police. *Pol Chief* 40(8),48—51 1973.

Knowles and Brewer present the results of a survey of blacks in a Los Angeles community. Those surveyed viewed unemployment and crimes as the most serious problems facing the community. Nearly half of the residents who had an opinion on police service in the community rated it as good or very good, one—fourth rated it "fair" and the rest "poor." Of the two—thirds of the respondents who reported having had previous contact with police, 72% had been pleased with the conduct of the officers while the remaining 28% had been displeased. Suggestions offered by respondents on how improved relations between police and the community might be accomplished included heavy support for police involvement in youth programs (mentioned by a majority of respondents) and footbeats (mentioned by nearly one—third of respondents). The need for person—to—person contact with citizens is evidenced by the vast majority of citizens who responded negatively to the assignment of only black officers to the black community.

KNOWLTON, Clark S. Analysis Of Selected Social And Cultural Characteristics Involving Juvenile Delinquency In Mexican—American Slums Of South El Paso. *Pro Sw Soc Assoc* 16,62—65 1966.

KOBETZ, R W and Hamm, C W. Contemporary Problems In Law Enforcement On American Indian Reservations. *Pol Chief* 37(7),58—61 Jl 1970.

KOBLER, Arthur L. Figures (and Perhaps Some Facts) On Police Killing Of Civilians In The United States. *J Soc Issues* 31(1),185—191 1975.

KOBLER, Arthur L. Police Homicide In A Democracy. *J Soc Issues* 31(1),163—181 1975.

KOCH, Gary and Clarke, Stevens H. The Influence Of Income And Other Factors On Whether Criminal Defendants Go To Prison. *Law & Soc Rev* 11(1),57—92 1976.

KOCHMAN, T (ed). *Rappin' And Stylin' Out*. Urbana Univ Illinois Pr 1972.

KOENINGER, R C. Capital Punishment In Texas, 1924—1968. *Crim Delinq* 15,132—141 1969.

The data for this study are taken from reports of the Texas Department of Health, and the Texas Department of Corrections, and primarily concern 460 persons sentenced to death in that state between 1924 and 1968 whose sentences were either carried out or disposed of some other way. The sample was first broken down by race (Negro, white, and Latin) and offense (murder, rape, or robbery). A full description of the race and sex of

the victims of each group is given, and in discussing the problem of racial bias the figures 3.5:1 and 1:3.5 are given as the ratios of death to term sentences for Negroes, and for whites and Latins, respectively. Finally, the distribution by race and offense of the 360 persons who were actually executed in the study period were given, as is such a distribution for those who had their sentence commuted. The author concludes from the examined data that "(a)pplication of the death penalty is unequal; most of those executed were poor, young, and ignorant."

KOENINGER, R C. The Law: Rape, Race, Time And Death. *Pro Sw Soc Assoc* 19,192—196 1969.

KOLEGAR, Ellen and Strodtbeck, Fred L and Short Jr, James F. The Analysis Of Self—Descriptions By Members Of Delinquent Gangs. *Sociol Q* 3(4),331—356 1962.

KOMISARUK, R and Pearson, Carol. Children Of The Detroit Riots: A Study Of Their Participation And Their Mental Health. *J Urban L* 45,599—626 1968.

KONVITZ, Milton R. A Nation Within A Nation, The Negro And The Supreme Court. *Am Scholar* 11,69—78 Wint 1941—42.

KORN, Richard and Mc Corkle, Lloyd. *Criminology And Penology*. NY Holt Rinehart Wins 1959 .

KORT, Fred and Maxson, Stephen C. "Politics In A Biobehavioral Perspective" in *Biology And Crime*, Jeffrey, C R (ed). Beverly Hills CA Sage 1979.

KOZOL, Jonathan. *Death At An Early Age: The Destruction Of The Hearts And Minds Of Negro Children In The Boston Schools*. Boston Houghton Mifflin 1967.

KRAFT, Larry J and Jacobs, James B. Integrating The Keepers: A Comparison Of Black And White Prison Guards In Illinois. *Social Prob* 25,304—318 F 1978.

The assumption that replacing white rural prison guards with young black urban guards will lessen significantly tension and conflict in the prison community is tested. An attitude questionnaire was given to 165 white and 66 black guards working at Stateville and Joliet maximum security prisons in Illinois. About 75% of the prison population is black and 10% Latino, with the majority from the Chicago metropolitan area. Even though the black correction officers were younger, more urban, better educated, and more liberal than the white, there were no consistent differences in their attitudes toward prisoners, staff, correctional goals, or occupation. Contrary to expectation, black guards were as suspicious of inmates as white guards, and black guards did not relate more effectively to black inmates. The most significant finding was that black guards were more likely to be embarrassed to tell others what they did for a living. It is concluded that hiring more black guards is not a panacea for prison unrest.*

KRAJICK, Kevin. At Stateville, The Calm Is Tense. *Correct Mag* 6(3),6—19 Je 1980.

KRAMER, Samuel A. "Identifying Juvenile Delinquents Among Negroes" in *Identification Of Predelinquents*, Glueck, S (ed), 22—35. NY Intercont Medical 1972.

The retrospective application of the Glueck Prediction Table on a population of lower—class Negro boys is presented. The five family items in the Glueck scale were used in a questionnaire presented to severely delinquent, mildly delinquent, and nondelinquent Negro boys. Differences among the three groups are significant. Family seems to be the only institution for effective social control and external strength in adverse environmental conditions. A great gap in the family situations were observed between the nondelinquent and delinquent groups. Although the Glueck scale is viewed as a useful tool in the investigation, subsequent investigations should be concerned with Negroes in middle—class situations for further validation. The questionnaire, its guidelines, and the scores for the three groups are provided.

KRAMER, Samuel A. Predicting Juvenile Delinquency Among Negroes. *Sociol Soc Res* 48(4),478—489 Jl 1964.

KRAMER, William D and Krantz, Sheldon. The Urban Crisis And Crime. *Boston U L Rev* 50,343—359 1970.

KRANTZ, Sheldon and Kramer, William D. The Urban Crisis And Crime. *Boston U L Rev* 50,343—359 1970.

KRASNER, William and Cuskey, Walter R. The Needle And The Boot: Heroin Maintenance. *Society* 10(4),45—52 1973.

Ethical and practical problems which arise in heroin and methadone maintenance programs are discussed. Programs offered at traditional facilities such as Federal hospitals at Lexington and Fort Worth, are outlined, along with newer more controversial approaches such as the drug free therapeutic communities, which rely on faith, exhortation, and rebirth of the inner self. Clinical resistance to heroin maintenance on moral grounds is examined; the complaint of black leaders is voiced that maintenance is a colonialist policy intended to keep black people in a docile, stupefied state.

KRAVITZ, Marjorie (comp) and Brenner, Robert N (comp). *A Community Concern: Police Use Of Deadly Force*. Washington DC NCJRS 1979.

KRAVITZ, Marjorie (comp) and Ray, M W (comp) and Brenner, Robert N (comp). *Firearm Use In Violent Crime: A Selected Bibliography*. Rockville MD NCJRS 1978.

This bibliography with abstracts concerns firearm use in violent crime and is directed at researchers, criminal justice practitioners, and other interested persons. Books, journal articles, and reports are included.*

KREBS, R L. Some Effects Of A White Institution On Black Psychiatric Outpatients. *Am J Orthopsych* 41(4),589–596 1971.

KREPS, Gary A and Weller, Jack M. The Police–Community Relations Movement: Conciliatory Responses To Violence. *Am Behav Sci* 16(3),402–412 1973.

A study made by Michigan State University concluded that the primary objective of community relations programs was race relations. Police community relations programs have already survived the conditions which impelled their adoption and expansion from 1965 through 1970. The threat of escalating, costly violence activated a tolerance for ideas which were once too sensitive to be considered.

KREPS, Gary A. Change In Crisis–Relevant Organizations: Police Departments And Civil Disturbances. *Am Behav Sci* 16(3),356–367 1973.

KRISBERG, Barry. *Crime And Privilege. Toward A New Criminology*. Englewood Cliffs NJ Prentice–Hall 1975.

KRISBERG, Barry. Gang Youth And Hustling: The Psychology Of Survival. *Issues Crim* 9(1),115–131 1974.

KROHN, M D. Inequality, Unemployment And Crime: A Cross–National Analysis. *Sociol Q* 17,303–313 Sum 1976.

KROLL, J. Racial Pattern Of Military Crimes In Vietnam. *Psychi* 39(1),51–64 1976.

Every military prisoner sentenced to the US Disciplinary Barracks in 1968–1969 for offenses committed in Vietnam was studied. Significant racial differences were found in the types of crimes committed. The sample population consisted of 293 prisoners. Twice as many white soldiers (41) as black (17) were incarcerated for away without leave (AWOL). However, 40 black soldiers versus 19 white soldiers refused field combat. Twice as many black soldiers as white were convicted for violent crimes against other US soldiers (43 versus 26), while 36 white soldiers versus 6 black soldiers were incarcerated for crimes against Vietnamese. The incidence of incarceratins per 100,000 soliders was much higher for blacks for every category of crime except violence against a Vietnamese natinal. Indepth study of the prisoners found that the white soldiers carried a racial mindset into the Vietnamese war and often extended racial hostility toward the Vietnamese. Black soldiers, coming from the civil rights movements and racial tension of the 1960's, tended to see the Vietnamese in a more sympathetic light.*

KROLL, Michael A. Prisoners Of Race. Washington DC N C B L 1978.

KUBAN, G B and Lawson, H O. *Development Of A Comprehensive Personnel Plan For Non–Judicial Employees Of The Kansas Appellate Courts*. Washington DC Am UL Inst ASJ 1977.

Position descriptions, affirmative action practices, and pay, promotion, raise, and leave policies for nonjudicial personnel of the Kansas Supreme Court and Court of Appeals are evaluated, and a pay plan is proposed.*

KULIG, F H and Hawkinson, T. Conviction And Sentencing In The Fourth Judicial District Of Nebraska. *Creighton L Rev* 8,923–978 1975.

This selection presents two articles which investigate the effects of pretrial release, prior arrests, and plea negotiations on convictions and sentencing of felonies in Douglas County, Nebraska. Both the studies analyzed the felony filings in Douglas County District Court in the years 1970, 1971, and 1972, which were terminated by October 1973 as a result of dismissal by the court or prosecutor, a guilty plea, or an adjudication. The first study found that pretrial release and prior arrest apparently do not have an effect on one's chances of getting convicted, as demonstrated by the conviction rates in Douglas County. However, it was shown that pretrial

release and race have a significant effect on the sentence imposed. Also, prior arrest record of the defendant was found to have a similar effect on the sentence imposed, but this influence was not as clearly shown by the data. The results of the second study indicated that there is a distinct advantage derived from pleading guilty as opposed to pleading not guilty and ultimately receiving a conviction sentence. The effect of such factors as race, pretrial disposition, age, and sentencing judge on sentencing outcomes is also discussed.*

KULIKOFF, Allan. The Origins Of Afro–American Society In Tidewater Maryland And Virginia, 1700 To 1790. *Wm & Mary Q* 35(2),226–259 Ap 1978.

KUNITZ, Stephen J and Everett, Michael and Levy Jerrold E. Navajo Criminal Homicide. *Sw J Anthrop* 25(2),124–152 1969.

Theories of homicide among the Navajo and its relation to alcohol consumption and cultural factors are examined. Common theories on the Navajo have assumed that their homicide rate would be proportionately higher than that for the rest of the population because of increased alcohol use, the instability of Navajo marriage, and the stresses placed on males as they abandon traditional roles and enter a wage economy. From the files of the Navajo Olice in Window Rock, Ariz., 43 cases of criminal homicide committed between 1956 and 1965 were extracted for study, which involved Navajos on or near the reservation. These cases were compared with a study of homicide in Philadelphia between 1948 and 1952. Navajo homicide rates were stable and comparable with those of the general population. No relationship was discovered between homicide and alcohol. These findings contrasted with those of the Philadelphia project in which use of alcohol was positively associated with violence. The Navajo offender was typically a married male between 35 and 39 years old who had killed his wife as as result of sexual jealousy or a domestic quarrel. A very high proportion committed suicide after the act of homicide.*

KUNITZ, Stephen J and Levy, Jerrold F. "Indian Drinking: Problems Of Data Collection And Interpretation" in *Proceedings Of The 1st Annual Alcohol Conf, NIAAA*, 217–236. Rockville MD NIAAA 1973.

The problems of data collection and interpretation of data concerning American Indian drinking habits are explored. It is suggested that uniform methods of investigation, explicit definitions and a multidisciplinary approach be used. It is clear that Indian drinking differs from drinking in the rest of society but it is not clear whether there is a unified pathology that can be called alcoholism. Clinically oriented researchers should observe and measure the causative agents of alcoholism among Indians directly, if possible. Some of the factors to be investigated include: whether alcoholism is determined by sociocultural factors; whether there is a physiological addiction present; and whether a psychological predisposition to drink can be determined.

KUNITZ, Stephen J and Levy, Jerrold E. Indian Reservations, Anomic And Social Pathologies. *Sw J Anthrop* 27,97–128 1971.

KUNITZ, Stephen J and Levy, Jerrold E. Notes On Some White Mountain Apache Social Pathologies. *Plateau* 42,22–19 1969.

KUPFERER, H J and Humphrey, J A. Fatal Indian Violence In North Carolina. *Anthrop Q* 48(4),236–244 O 1975.

KUPPERSTEIN, Lenore R and Toro– Calder, Jaime. *A Socio–Cultural And Socio–Legal Analysis Of Juvenile Delinquency In Puerto Rico*. Rio Piedras Univ Puerto Rico 1969.

KUYKENDALL, Jack L (ed) and Reasons, Charles E. *Race, Crime And Justice*. Pacific Palisades CA Goodyear 1972.

This anthology includes articles by authoritative figures concerned with the patterns of unjust treatment of minorities dealing with the following subjects: (1) racism in the administration of justice (2) crime rates and causes, (3) the convergence of race and crime, (4) Negro and white crime rates, (5) minority–police groups and negative contacts, (6) police and the ghetto, (7) negro treatment in the courts of justice, (8) segregated justice for Native Americans, etc. Major recommendations are concerned with development of police–community relations and changes in non–democratic racist patterns of thought embedded in administration of justice systems.*

KUYKENDALL, Jack L. Police And Minority Groups: Toward A Theory Of Negative Contacts. *Police* 15(1),47–55 1970.

L E A A, Office Of Civil Rights Compliance. *Civil Rights Enforcement Under The Jordan Amendment: Progress, 1976–1978*. Washington DC US Dept Justice 1978.

LEAA's office of civil rights compliance was established to ensure that recipients of grant funds comply with the nondiscrimination provisions. This report highlights the activities of the office since the 1977 Jordan Amendment. The Jordan Amendment to the Omnibus Crime Control Act eliminated agency discretion in initiating the cutoff of funding and provided for 'triggers' that would automatically begin administrative procedures for the cutoff of funding to grant recipients not complying with civil rights provisions of the act.*

LA FAVE, Wayne, R. *Arrest: The Decision To Take A Suspect Into Custody.* Boston Little, Brown 1965.

LA POINT, Velma. "Children Of Incarcerated Mothers" in *Child Development*, Green, R And T Yawkey (eds). Lexington MA Heath 1979.

LA VIOLETTE, Forrestt and Silvert, K H. A Theory Of Stereotypes. *Soc Forces* 29,257–262 1951.

LAHEY, Edwin A. Cops Unsung Heroes In Racial Tragedy. *J Crim L Crimin & Pol Sci* 56(2),246 1965.

LAKE, Eleanor. Memo For D A. *Survey Midm* 84,107–108 Ap 1948.

LALLI, Michael and Savitz, Leonard D. *Delinquency And City Life.* Washington DC NILECJ 1972.

This interim report on the causes of delinquency among black boys in Philadelphia seeks to explain why some but not all boys in the most depressed urban areas, in the same social and economic circumstances, become delinquent. The findings of 532 interviews with black boys and their mothers are presented. The attitudes concerning family, education, aspirations, fear of crime, behavior changes, and self were measured. Dropping out of school was found to be a consequence of delinquency and not a cause. Both delinquent and nondelinquent boys agreed with middle class values. Delinquents were found to be more fearful of victimization and were more apt to take some precautions. The source of income rather than low socio–economic status itself leads to low self–esteem.*

LALLI, Michael and Turner, Stanley. Suicide And Homicide: A Comparative Analysis By Race And Occupaltional Levels. *J Crim L Crimin & Pol Sci* 59,191–200 1968.

LAMBERT, J R and Jenkinson, R F. *Crime, Police, And Race Relations: A Study In Birmingham.* NY Oxford Univ Pr 1970.

LANDAU, S F. Pathologies Among Homicide Offenders: Some Cultural Profiles. *Br J Crimin* 15,157–166 Ap 1975.

LANDER, Bernard. *Towards An Understanding Of Juvenile Delinquency.* NY Columbia Univ Pr 1954.

LANE, E B and Daniels, H W. Incarcerated Native. *Can J Crim* 20(3),308–316 Jl 1978.

LANE, Roger. *Policing The City: Boston, 1822–1885.* Cambridge MA Harvard Univ Pr 1967.

LANE, Roger. *Violent Death In The City: Suicide, Accident, And Murder In Nineteenth–Century Philadelphia.* Cambridge MA Harvard Univ Pr 1979.

LANG, G and Lang, Kurt. Racial Disturbances As Collective Protest. *Am Behav Sci* 2,11–13 Mr–Ap 1968.

LANG, Kurt and Lang, G. Racial Disturbances As Collective Protest. *Am Behav Sci* 2,11–13 Mr–Ap 1968.

LANGE, A G (ed) and Bowers, R A (ed). *Fraud And Abuse In Government Benefit Programs.* Washington DC NILECJ 1979.

A study of fraud and abuse control issues in 15 government benefit programs is documented. The study involved interviews with 134 federal, state, and local programs administrators, fraud investigators, prosecutors, quality control officials, and others charged with responsibility for benefit program operations, integrity, and control, plus questionnaire surveys of state attorneys general and 123 other state officials. The following programs are included in the study: food stamps, summer food service program for children, rural housing, Medicare, Medicaid, aid to families with dependent children, vocational education, rehabilitation housing loans, federal disaster assistance, unemployment insurance, comprehensive employment and training program, minority business development, physical disaster loan assistance, veterans educational assistance, and veterans home loan guaranty program.*

LANGLEY, J A. Garveyism And African Nationalism. *Race* 11,157–172 O 1969.

The impact of Marcus Garvey's Pan–Negro Movement on Negro freedom movements in the United States and Africa is examined in light of Negro demands during the 1960's.

LANGWORTHY, Robert H and Sherman, Lawrence W. Measuring Homicide By Police Officers. *J Crim L & Crimin* 70(4),546–560 Wint 1979.

LANIER, J E and Parker, M and Wittmer, J. Race Relations Training With Correctional Officers. *Pers & Guid J* ,302–306 F 1976.

A four–day Florida workshop in race relations for correctional officers is described, in which empathy and open and honest communication are stressed. Emphasis is first upon developing good communication and understanding between black and white workshop participants. They are then encouraged to relate their new understanding of racial communication barriers to the prison setting. The workshop methods rely heavily upon the active participation of the workshop attendees. While no data has yet been analyzed in order to evaluate this workshop program, such a project is said to be underway. It is said that within two years of the writing of this report, over one–half of Florida's correctional officers will have attended the workshop.

LANSING, J and Withey, S B and Wolf, A C. *Working Papers On Survey Research In Poverty Areas.* Ann Arbor MI Inst Soc Res 1971.

LASCH, Christopher and Frederickson, George M. Resistance To Slavery. *Civil War Hist* 13,315–329 1967.

LAU, M and Ball, J C. The Chinese Narcotic Addict In The United States. *Soc Forces* 45,68–72 S 1966.

LAWRENCE, J W. Tribal Injustice––The Red Lake Court Of Indian Offenses. *N Dak L Rev* 48(4),639–659 1972.

The history of the Minnesota Red Lake Court of Indian Offenses is reviewed; the court is criticized for failure to provide justice according to Indian tradition or federal requirements.

LAWSON, H O and Kuban, G B. *Development Of A Comprehensive Personnel Plan For Non–Judicial Employees Of The Kansas Appellate Courts.* Washington DC Am UL Inst ASJ 1977.

Position descriptions, affirmative action practices, and pay, promotion, raise, and leave policies for nonjudicial personnel of the Kansas Supreme Court and Court of Appeals are evaluated, and a pay plan is proposed.*

LAWYER, David. The Dilemma Of The Black Badge. *Pol Chief* 35,22–25 1968.

LAZARSFELD, Paul F. "Interpretation Of Statistical Relations As A Research Operation" in *The Language Of Social Research*, Lazarsfeld And Rosenberg (eds). NY Free Pr 1955.

LAZIN, F A. The Police And Black Separatism: A Problem For Public Policy. *J Polic Sci Adm* 3(1),1–8 1975.

LEA, H C. Increase Of Crime And Positive Criminology. *Forum* 17,666–675 Ag 1894.

LEARY, Howard. The Role Of Police In Riotous Demonstrations. *Notre Dame Law* 40,499–507 1965.

LEDE, Naomi W and Dixon, Hortense W. "Criminal Justice And The Minority Community" in *Urban Minority Groups In Houston: Problems, Progress And Prospects*, 205–248. Houston TX Southern Univ 1974.

LEE, Alfred McClung. *Race Riots Aren't Necessary.* NY Public Aff Comm 1945.

LEE, Alfred McClung and Humphrey, Norman D. *Race Riot.* NY Dryden Pr 1943.

LEE, Carol F. Discretionary Justice In Early Massachusetts. *Essex Inst Hist Coll* 112,120–139 Ap 1976.

LEE, Everett S and Kinman, Judith L. Migration And Crime. *Int Migration Dig* 3,7–14 Spr 1966.

LEE, Everett and Shin, Yongsock and Jedlicka, Davor. Homicide Among Blacks. *Phylon* 38(4),398–407 D 1977.

LEE, R H. Delinquent, Neglected And Dependent Chinese Boys And Girls Of The San Francisco Bay Region. *J Soc Psychol* 36,15–34 1952.

LEE, Robert Joe. "Hispanics: The Anonymous Prisoners" in *New Jersey Correctional Master Plan*, V4. Trenton NJ Dept Corrections 1976.

Hispanics account for 8.5% of all prisoners in New Jersey. Most staff members working with Hispanic prisoners are Cuban or Anglo–American, while almost all Hispanic prisoners are Puerto Rican. Hispanic inmates are less educated than other inmates: 13% cannot read English and 10% cannot read Spanish. Most Latin prisoners report good employment histories. Criminal behavior is a post–migration phenomenon; 44% have not been convicted before. Hispanic offenders feel they are in prison because of injustice, happenstance, drugs, pride, economic need, and aimlessness. Heroin addiction is related to the offenses for 79% of the addicts; 36% of all prisoners were addicts. The author regards the language barrier as a complex problem. Most Latins (80%) prefer to speak Spanish. A few (8%) cannot speak English at all.

LEE, Robert Joe. *A Profile Of Puerto Rican Prisoners In New Jersey And Its Implications For The Administration Of Justice.* Unpub MA Thesis Rutgers Univ 1977.

Eighty–three Puerto Rican prisoners at four penal institutions in New Jersey—a state adult facility, a state youth facility, a county correctional institution, and another for county detention—were interviewed with a questionnaire containing 287 variables. Analysis of the results consisted of frequency distributions and cross–tabulations. A copy of the questionnaire is included in the appendix.

LEE, Rose Hum. *The Chinese In The United States.* London Oxford Univ Pr 1960.

LEE, Yuk. A Rejoinder To 'The Geography Of Crime: A Political Critique'. *Prof Geog* 27(3),284–285 1975.

LEE, Yuk and Egan, Frank J. The Geography Of Urban Crime: The Spatial Pattern Of Serious Crime In The City Of Renuer. *Proc Assoc Am Geog* 4,59–64 1972.

LEFCOURT, Robert (ed). *Law Against The People.* NY Vintage 1971.

LEGGETT, J C and Street, D. Economic Deprivation And Extremism: A Study Of Unemployed Negroes. *Am J Soc* 67(1),53–57 1961.

LEHMAN, P. A Comment On The Police And The Kerner Report. *Issues Crim* 4(1),61–65 1968.

LEHMAN, Warren and Oaks, Dallin H. *A Criminal Justice System And The Indigent.* Chicago Univ Chicago Pr 1968.

LEHNEN, Robert and Renshaw, Benjamin H. The Victims. *Nat Cities* 16(9),13–15 S 1978.

LEHTINEN, Marlene W. The Death Penalty: A Life And Death Issue. *USA Today* 107(2404),32–36 1979.

LEHTINEN, Marlene W. The Value Of Life: An Argument For The Death Penalty. *Crim Deling* 23(3),237 252 1977

LEIBOWITZ, Arnold H. English Literacy: Legal Sanction For Discrimination. *Notre Dame Law* 45(1),7–67 Fall 1969.

LEM, K. Asian American Employment—From Outright Exclusion To Modern Discrimination. *Civil Rts Dig* 9,12–21 Fall 1976.

Employment problems faced by the three largest subgroups of Asian Americans—the Japanese, Chinese, and Filipinos—are reported.*

LEMERT, Edwin M. *Human Deviance, Social Problems, And Social Control.* Englewood Cliffs NJ Prentice–Hall 1972.

LEMERT, Edwin M and Rosberg, Judy. The Adminstration Of Justice To Minority Groups In Los Angeles County. Berkeley CA U Ca Pr 1948.

LEMERT, Edwin M and Roseberg, Judy. Crime And Punishment Among Minority Groups In Los Angeles County. *Pro Pac Coa Soc Soci* ,133–145 1946.

LEONARD, D and Bresler, L. *Women's Jail—Pretrial And Post–Conviction Alternatives—A Report On Women Arrested In San Francisco.* San Francisco Unitarian U S C 1978.

A year–long study was conducted by the Women's Jail Project of the Unitarian Universalist Service Committee in San Francisco, to determine the kinds of pretrial and post–conviction alternatives for female arrestees in the city. Results of the study suggested that (1) the women arrested differed from the general population in ethnicity; (2) cash or surety bail continued to be the most common form of pretrial release; (3) women diverted were usually younger than those sentenced to jail; (4) women diverted were charged with less serious misdemeanors than their sentenced counterparts; and (5) the ethnicity ratio of women sentenced was significantly different from the general population of women in the city and the population booked. The majority of women were charged with "prostitution" and other victimless crimes. Recommendations, a glossary, a bibliography, and description of methodology is included.

LERNER, Richard M and Karson, Michael. Racial Stereotypes Of Early Adolescent White Children. *Psychol Rep* 32(2),381–382 1973.

The current status of a group (n = 406) of whites' racial attitudes was examined by comparing the relative favorableness–unfavorableness of white early adolescents' social stereotypes toward white and black people. Subjects were asked to attribute each of 48 items from a verbal checklist to a picture of either a white or a black male. The results indicated that subjects held a predominantly unfavorable view of the black figure and a predominantly positive view of the white figure.

LESTER, Anthony. *Justice In The American South.* London England Amnesty Intn 1965.

LESTER, David and Perdue, William C. Racial Differences In The Personality Of Murderers. *Perc Mot Sk* 38(3),726 Je 1974.

LETCHER, Maxine. "Black Women And Homicide" in *Lethal Aspects Of Urban Violence*, Rose, Harold M (ed), 83–90. Lexington MA Heath 1979.

LEVINE, B L. *Psychometric And Demographic Comparisons Of Negro And White Delinquents.* Unpub PhD Diss IL Inst Techn 1969.

LEVINE, David and Swartz, Virginia D and Held, Barbara S. Interpersonal Aspects Of Dangerousness. *Crim Just B* 6,49–58 Mr 1979.

LEVINE, Gene N and Montero, Darrel M. Socioeconomic Mobility Among Three Generations Of Japanese Americans. *J Soc Issues* 29(2),33–48 1973.

LEVINE, Gene N. Some Concluding Remarks: Research Among Racial And Cultural Minorities. *J Soc Issues* 33(4),175–178 1977.

LEVINE, M J. Meeting Compliance Review Standards—The Problem Of Federal Contractors. *Labor Law J* 28(10),632–640 O 1977.

Steps in a compliance review conducted by the Office of Federal Contract Compliance (OFCC) and measures employers can take to conform to the procedural requirements are detailed.*

LEVY, Burton. Cops In The Ghetto: A Problem Of The Police System. *Am Behav Sci* 2,31–34 Mr–Ap 1968.

LEVY, Jerrold E and Kunitz, Stephen J. "Indian Drinking: Problems Of Data Collection And Interpretation" in *Proceedings Of The 1st Annual Alcohol Conf, NIAAA*, 217–236. Rockville MD NIAAA 1973.

The problems of data collection and interpretation of data concerning American Indian drinking habits are explored. It is suggested that uniform methods of investigation, explicit definitions and a multidisciplinary approach be used. It is clear that Indian drinking differs from drinking in the rest of society but it is not clear whether there is a unified pathology that can be called alcoholism. Clinically oriented researchers should observe and measure the causutive agents of alcoholism among Indians directly, if possible. Some of the factors to be investigated include: whether alcoholism is determined by sociocultural factors; whether there is a physiological addiction present; and whether a psychological predisposition to drink can be determined.

LEVY, Jerrold E and Kunitz, Stephen J. Indian Reservations, Anomic And Social Pathologies. *Sw J Anthrop* 27,97–128 1971.

LEVY, Jerrold E and Kunitz, Stephen J. Notes On Some White Mountain Apache Social Pathologies. *Plateau* 42,22–19 1969.

LEVY, Russell H and Henning, John J. Verbal Performance IQ Differences Of White And Negro Delinquents On The WISC And WAIS. *J Clin Psyc* 23(2),164–168 1967.

This study tests the generality of verbal inferiority of 2,361 black and white male delinquents committed to the Illinois Youth Commission in 1963 and 1964. The Verbal minus Performance I. Q. difference was examined separately at 15 age levels, for white and Negro subjects, some tested with the WISC [Weschler Intelligence Scale for Children] and others tested with the WAIS [Weschler Adult Intelligence Scale]. The whites produced higher Performance I. Q.'s in relation to Verbal I. Q.'s than did the Negroes. When the pattern of subtest rankings from this study was compared with the subtest pattern of delinquent poor readers and non–delinquent poor readers from two studies reported in the literature, the [white] samples showed consistently significant correlations with both poor reader patterns, while the [black] groups lacked this relationship. This was interpreted by the authors as support for the idea that a reading disability pattern rather than sociopathic personality as such is what is being seen in the intrasubtest Weschler pattern of white, male delinquents.

LEWANDOWSKI, D G and Saccuzzo, D P and Condit, J E. Efficiency Of Peabody Picture Vocabulary In Estimating WISC Scores For Delinquents. *Psychol Rep* 38(2),359–362 1976.

I. Q.s on the Peabody Picture Vocabulary Test for 106 lower–class males 13 to 16 years were related to WISC I. Q.s (assessed by student examiners) in three different ranges (80–89, 70–79, below 70) as a function of race. Both group and individual results were consistent with previous data showing the Peabody scale generally overestimates the I. Q.s of retarded subjects. The results also indicate that the Peabody tended to underestimate the I. Q.s of 34 "dull normal" subjects. The utility of the Peabody in estimating the Wechsler I. Q. of juvenile offenders is of doubtful value, according to the authors.

LEWIS, Anthony. *Gideon's Trumpet.* NY Random House 1964.

LEWIS, Dorothy O and Balla, David A and Shanok, Shelley S. Some Evidence Of Race Bias In The Diagnosis And Treatment Of The Juvenile Offender. *Am J Orthopsych* 49(1),53–61 1979.

LEWIS, H. Juvenile Delinquency Among Negroes: A Critical Summary. *J Negro Ed* 28,371–387 1959.

LEWIS, J M and Adamek, R J. Social Control, Violence And Radicalization: Behavioral Data. *Social Prob* 22,663–674 Je 1975.

LEWIS, Oscar. La Vida: A Puerto Rican Family In The Culture Of Poverty—San Juan And New York. NY Random House 1965.

LEWIS, Oscar. The Children Of Sanchez. NY Random House 1961.

LEWIS, Peter W and Mannle, Henry W. Control Theory Re–examined: Race And The Use Of Neutralizations Among Institutionalized Delinquents. *Criminology* 17(1),58–74 My 1979.

When tests designed to measure socialization (intensity of prosocial commitments) and neutralization (acceptance of justifications for antisocial behavior) were administered to 148 black and 166 white incarcerated delinquents (males and females, average age 15.3 years), the hypothesis that blacks would score higher than whites on both dimensions was borne out, as was the expectation that socialization and neutralization would be negatively correlated for both groups. Although the negative correlation was weaker for blacks than for whites the difference was not of the magnitude expected. That blacks were more socialized is interpreted as a reflection of their having been exposed to less norm–destroying deviance than their white counterparts before being incarcerated, which in turn reflects the tendency of the juvenile system to incarcerate blacks more readily than whites. The negative correlation between socialization and neutralization is an indication that youths with weaker bonds to the social order are more inclined to seek rationalization of their antisocial behavior, attempting to bolster self–esteem.*

LEWIS, Peter W and Peoples, Kenneth D. Constitutional Rights Of The Accused—Cases And Comments. Philadelphia W B Saunders 1979.

LEWIS, Peter W. Killing The Killers: A Post–*Furman* Profile Of Florida's Condemned. *Crim Delinq* 25(2),200–218 Ap 1979.

LEWIS, Ralph G and Salas, Luis P. The Law Enforcement Assistance Administration And Minority Communities. *J Polic Sci Adm* 7(4),379–399 D 1979.

LEWIS, Sasha G. Slave Trade Today: American Exploitation Of Illegal Aliens. Boston Beacon Pr 1979.

LIEBERMAN, Jethro K. How The Government Breaks The Law. Baltimore Penguin Books 1973.

LIEBERSON, Stanley and Silverman, Arnold. The Precipitants And Underlying Conditions Of Race Riots. *Am Sociol Rev* 30,887–898 D 1965.

The immediate precipitants and underlying conditions of 76 race riots in the US between 1913 and 1963 are examined, using journalistic accounts and census data. The precipitants tend to be highly charged violations of one racial group by the other—rape, murder, assault, and police brutaltiy. Since many of these precipitants are normally dealt with by established community institutions and because the response is not restricted to the alleged aggressor, various underlying conditions must be present. Hypotheses derived from earlier case studies and texts on collective behavior are examined to determine why riots occur where they do rather than in other cities of comparable size and location. Occupational and municipal government characteristics influence the occurrence of riots; demographic and housing characteristics do not. Riots seem most likely to occur in communitites where institutional malfunctioning, cross–pressures, or other inadequacies are such that the city is unable to resolve racial problems.

LIEBOW, Elliot. Tally's Corner: A Study Of The Negro Streetcorner Men. Boston Little, Brown 1967.

LIEF, H I and Savitz, Leonard D. "Negro And White Sex Crime Rates" in *Sexual Behavior And The Law*, Slovenko, Ralph (ed), 210–220. Springfield IL Chas C Thomas 1965.

LIEGENHAGEN, Edward A. Victims, Crime And Social Control. NY Praeger 1977.

LIGHT, I. The Ethnic Vice Industry. *Am Sociol Rev* 42(3),464–479 1977. A comparison of blacks and Chinese in the vice industry, 1880–1940, confirms the guiding role of American society which rewarded ethnics' participation in prostitution but restricted legal earning opportunities. Nonetheless, divergent demographic and cultural characteristics of

Chinese and blacks differentailly affected the internal organizations of each group's vice industry as well as the process of industrial succession.

LIGHTFOOT JR, R M. Negro Crime In A Small Urban Community. Charlottesville Univ of Virginia 1934.

LILLY, J R and Ball, R A. Norm Neutralization, Anomia And Self–Concept Among Institutionalized Female Delinquents. Tucson A S C 1976.

LINCOLN, C Eric. The Black Muslims In America. Boston Beacon Pr 1961.

LINCOLN, James H. The Anatomy Of A Riot. NY McGraw–Hill 1968.

LIND, Andrew W. Some Ecological Patterns Of Community Disorganization In Honolulu. *Am J Soc* 36(2),206–220 S 1930.

LIND, Andrew W. The Ghetto And The Slum. *Soc Forces* 9(2),206–215 D 1930.

LINDEN, E and Hackler, J C. The Response Of Adults To Delinquency Prevention Programs: The Race Factor. *J Res Crim Del* 7(1),31–45 1970. Delinquency prevention programs usually attempt to modify a select number of boys who either share individual characteristics or live in a specific area. Rarely is it asked if such programs have an impact on parents or other adults who come into conract with these boys. The Opportunities for Youth Project in Seattle seemed to have little impact on boys who participated in terms of traditional instruments used to evaluate such experiments. However, the positive attitudes of the boys toward the project caused suspicion that the program did make an impact on the residents. This paper questions the assumption that people living in lower class areas are apathetic and unresponsive to experimental programs. The data suggest that Negro residents and parents were more supportive of the youth employment program than white residents. These differences might be explained by "differential perceived mobility"; that is, Negroes may see themselves as upwardly mobile (at least in terms of opportunities for their children) while whites in central areas may view themselves as downwardly mobile.

LINDESMITH, Alfred R. The Addict And The Law. Bloomington Indiana Univ Pr 1965.

LINDZEY, Gardner and Spuhler, J N and Loehlin, John C. Race Differences In Intelligence. San Francisco CA W H Freeman 1975.

LIPSHULTZ, Robert J. American Attitudes Toward Mexican Immigration. San Francisco R & E Research 1971.

LIPSHUTZ, R J and Huron, C B. Achieving A More Representative Federal Judiciary. *Judicature* 62(10),483–485 1979.

The Carter administration's combination of merit selection and affirmative action to improve the quality of the federal bench and make it more representative of the populace is described by counsel to the President.*

LIPSKY, D B (ed). Evaluating The -impact Of Affirmative Action—A Look At The Federal Contract Compliance Program—A Symposium. *Indust Lab Rel Rev* 29(4),485–584 Jl 1976.

The impact of the Affirmative Action Program (AAP) is evaluated in terms of the effectiveness of the Federal Contract Compliance Program (FCCP) through five papers presented at the Ithaca, NY, Evaluation Conference.*

LIPSKY, Michael and Olson, David J. Commission Politics: The Processing Of Racial Crisis In America. New Brunswick NJ Transaction Books 1977.

LIPSKY, Michael and Olson, David J. Riot Commission Politics. *Trans–Act* 6(9),9–21 1969.

LIPSYTE, Robert and Gregory, Dick. Nigger: An Autobiography. NY E P Dutton 1964.

LIRA, F T and Fagan, T J. Profile Of Mood States: Racial Differences In A Delinquent Population. *Psychol Rep* 43(2),348–350 1978.

LISKA, Allen E and Tausig, Mark. Theoretical Interpretations Of Social Class And Racial Differentials In Legal Decision Making For Juveniles. *Sociol Q* 20,197–208 1979.

LITWACK, Leon F. Been In The Storm So Long: The Aftermath Of Slavery. NY Knopf 1980.

This is a rich scholarly account, based largely on primary sources, describing the immediate aftermath of the emancipation of black slaves in the American South. Litwack examines the transition from bondage to freedom of 4 million black slaves. About the double standard of justice that existed during Reconstruction, the author provides numerous examples in court practices. "The double standard of white justice was nowhere clearer," he writes, "than in the disparate punishments meted out to whites and blacks convicted of similar crimes" (pp. 285–6). Discrimination in jury selection, selective enforcement, inequitable punishment, efforts to create biracial police forces, and official use of deadly force are among the criminal justice issues considered. However the Thirteenth Amendment is barely examined.

LITWACK, Leon F. *North Of Slavery.* Chicago Univ Chicago Pr 1961.

LIVERMORE, Jean. Identification Of Teen–Age Girls With Mexican–American Minority. *Am J Orthopsych* 30,630–636 1960.

LIZOTTE, Alan J. Extra–Legal Factors In Chicago's Criminal Courts: Testing The Conflict Model Of Criminal Justice. *Social Prob* 25(5),564–580 1978.

LLEWELLYN, K and Hoebel, E Adamson. *The Cheyenne Way: Conflict And Case Law In Primitive Jurisprudence.* Norman Univ Oklahoma Pr 1941.

LLOYD, R G. Juvenile Delinquency In A Period Of Tension. *Negro Ed Rev* 1,10–16 1950.

LOCKE, Ben Z and Cannon, Mildred S. *Being Black Is Detrimental To One's Mental Health: Myth Or Reality?* Atlanta Atlanta Univ Pr 1976.

LOCKE, Hubert G. *The Detroit Riot Of 1967.* Detroit Wayne St Univ 1969.

LOCKE, Hubert G. *The Impact Of Affirmative Action And Civil Service On American Police Personnel Systems.* Washington DC NILECJ 1979.

The impact of civil service and affirmative action programs on minority employment in the law enforcement setting is addressed in this monograph. Whether due to enlightened police leadership, community pressures, political circumstances, civil service intervention, or a combination of all these factors, the racial characteristics of American policing have begun to change substantially over the past decade. Ten years ago, approximately 4% of the sworn police personnel in the nation were racial minorities; today, that figure has risen to 10%. Findings of the public service administration show that one of the most important factors in changing the nature and quality of policing is the courage and commitment of police leadership. Increasing minority and female participation in the ranks of sworn police officers is a crucial part of this change process, but such efforts are not enhanced by a reliance on the regulatory role of civil service. Several suggestions for institutionalizing this change process are noted.*

LOCKWOOD, Daniel. *Prison Sexual Violence.* NY Elsevier 1980.

LOEB, E M and De Vereaux, G. Some Notes On Apache Criminality. *J Crim Psychop* 4,424–430 1943.

LOEHLIN, John C and Lindzey, Gardner and Spuhler, J N. *Race Differences In Intelligence.* San Francisco CA W H Freeman 1975.

LOHMAN, Joseph D. *The Police And Minority Groups.* Chicago Chicago Park Dist 1947.

LOHMAN, Joseph D and Reitzes, Dietrich C. Note On Race Relations In Mass Society. *Am J Soc* 58,240–246 N 1952.

LOHMAN, Joseph D. Juvenile Delinquency: A Social Dimension. *J Negro Ed* 28(3),286–299 1959.

Lohman contends that in order to assess the true magnitude of the juvenile delinquency problem, we must examine more basic population and community conditions with which this problem is highly correlated. Accordingly, Lohman focuses his attention on those institutions—the family and school, police and courts—which have had to adapt to that "combination of change population and growing urbanism, unsettling and disturbing local community life, that constitutes the core of the juvenile delinquency problem." Popular myths surrounding delinquency and delinquents are also discussed.

LOMAS, H D and Singer, R D. *Graffiti And Crime: A Transcultural Study Of Narcissistic Rage.* Rockville MD NCJRS 1979.

Graffiti and criminal aggression are studied in terms of archaic narcissism, i.e., the phenomenon of narcissistic rage, with attention given to cultural and psychological influences on crime. Chicanos and other persons of Latin descent have a propensity to produce graffiti. Understanding certain aspects of the Chicano personality, particularly those aspects related to feelings of exclusion, resentment, and desire for revenge, can be helpful in bridging the gap between majority cultures and institutions and Chicanos. To the extent graffiti are linked to specific personality disturbances that lend themselves to criminal behavior, the study of developmental, cultural, and psychological determinants represents a study of the correlates of crime. A study is proposed to compare the production of graffiti by Chicanos and Anglos.*

LOMBROSO, Cesare. "Neue Verbrecher–Studien" (1907) in *Race And Crime*, Bonger, Adriaan, Trans Margaret Mathews Hordyk, Reprint Of 1943 Edition, 48–49. Montclair NJ Patterson Smith 1969.

"Even if he (the Negro) is dressed in the European way and has accepted the customs of modern culture, all too often there remains in him the lack of respect for the life of his fellow men, the disregard for life which all wild people have in common." Bonger claims that blacks regard murder as an ordinary occurrence, "even a glorious occurrence when it is inspired by feelings of vengeance. This mentality is furthered in the Negro by his scorn of his white fellow–citizens, and by bestial sexual impulses."

LONDON, N J and Myers, J K. Young Offenders: Psychopathology And Social Factors. *Arch Gen Psychiatry* 4(3),274–282 1961.

LONG, Elton et al. *American Minorities: The Justice Issue.* Englewood Cliffs NJ Prentice–Hall 1975.

The history of racial injustice, prejudice and discrimination in America is traced in historical progression and the acts of "private and official violence" exhibited both by minorities and by members of the white middle–class establishment are considered. The history of each dominant minority group in America is summarized. Primary focus is on black Americans: civil rights struggles, violent confrontations of blacks, and whites, political trials, and discrimination in the correctional system. Antidiscrimination standards are outlined for police and correctional personnel, and a way to better police–community relations is suggested.

LONGERS JR, J F. Racism And Its Effects On Puerto Rican Continentals. *Soc Casework* 55,2+ 1974.

LONGTIN, L and Telfer, M A and Baker, D. YY Syndrome In An American Negro. *Lancet* 1(13),95 1968.

LOOK, L W. The Greenbrier Incident. *Cal Youth Author Q* 22(1),5–8 1969.

LOPEZ, Luisita. Waiting On Death Row; North Carolina. *Progressive* 38(5),38–39 My 1974.

LOWENSTEIN, Ralph L (ed) and Fisher, Paul L (ed). *Race And The News Media.* NY Praeger 1967.

Critical assessments of the performance of the news media in covering race riots, sit–ins, and conventional street crime, written by professional journalists.

LOWENSTEIN, Ralph and Skoler, Daniel L. *Non Discrimination, Equal Opportunity And Legal Issues On Minorities In Corrections.* Washington DC ABA 1973.

LOWENSTEIN, Ralph and Skoler, Daniel. Minorities In Correction—Nondiscrimination, Equal Opportunity And Legal Issues. *Crim Delinq* 20(4),339–346 1974.

Examines new policies and trends in the employment of minorities in the field of corrections. One of the most striking manpower problems in our correctional systems is the vast disparity in racial composition between inmate populations and correctional staffs. This imbalance has stimulated a move to increased minority hiring in correction. In the past two or three years, developments on three levels—rhetoric, judicial decisions, and administrative regulations—offer hope that the goal of increased minority hiring will be realized.

LOWIE, R H. *The Origin Of The State.* NY Russell & Russell 1962.

LUCAS, Henry N. *My Rhythm Flows From A Different Beat.* Washington DC King Publications 1976.

LUCHTERHAND, Elmer G and Ferdinand, Theodore W. Inner–City Youth, The Police, The Juvenile Court And Justice. *Social Prob* 17,510–527 1970.

LUCIANOVIC, J and Williams, K M. *Robbery And Burglary—A Study Of The Characteristics Of The Persons Arrested And The Handling Of Their Cases In Court.* Washington DC Inst Law & Soc Res 1979.

LUCTERHAND, Elmer and Weller, Leonard. Effects Of Class, Race, Sex And Educational Status On Patterns Of Aggression Of Lower Class Youth. *J Youth Ado* 5(1),59–71 Mr 1976.

The influence of class, race, sex and educational status on ways of handling aggression and temper control were studied by means of responses to open– and closed–ended questions. The sample consisted of 1,844 inner–city youth in two northern cities. Race was found to be the only important discriminator: blacks were less aggressive and exhibited more temper control than whites, but once aggression occurred blacks were more likely than whites to assault others. Results are interpreted in terms of self—identity and blacks' fears of the consequences of aggressive responses.

LUDLOW, H T. First Come, First Served, And Some Other Problems Of Manpower Policy—Making. *Conf Bd Rec* 12,50–55 Ag 1975.

LUNDSGAARDE, Henry P. Racial And Ethnic Classifications: An Appraisal Of The Role Of Anthropology In The Lawmaking Process. *Houston L Rev* 10(3),641–654 Mr 1973.

LUPSHA, Peter. On Theories Of Urban Violence. *Urb Aff Q* 4,273–296 1969.

LURIE, Nancy Oestreich. Indian Drinking Patterns. *Am J Orthopsych* 42(4),554 1972.

In a letter to the editor it is stated that the folk taxonomy of drinking patterns employed widely by Indian people is a reliable and useful categorization to distinguish between behavior sets followed by Indians under different sociocultural circumstances. In a recent article Westermeyer provided an independent and specific test of the hypothesis that Indian drinking is a means of validating Indian identity. Indian drinking is a functionally adaptive cultural pattern that, along with others, serves to express resistance to the threat posed by white society to the continuation of Indian sociocultural distinctiveness. Indian people can and do choose to alternate between patterns of Indian drinking and white drinking according to their own assessment of behavior appropriate to a given social setting. There are differences among total abstainers, some of whom are marginal to the Indian community; not only do they not drink but they do not participate much or at all in any Indian community activities and see abstinence as a "ticket" to acceptance as white.

LURIE, Nancy. The Indian Claims Commission. *Ann Am Poli* 436,97–110 Mr 1978.

LYLES, Barbara. "The Criminal Justice System" in *Crime And Its Impact On The Black Community*, Gary, L E And L P Brown (eds), 48–61. Washington DC Howard U 1976.

LYMAN, Stanford M. *Chinese Americans.* NY Random House 1974.

LYNCH, Gerald. Black—White Relations Among Police In The United States. *Police J* 47,56–64 1974.

The relationships between black and white policemen and their development over time in the US are examined in relation to possible hiring policies of non—white policemen in the United Kingdom. Two alternative hiring approaches are evaluated with references to US experiences in these areas. The hiring issue is discussed from four points of view: (a) the police administration, (b) the white policeman, (c) the black policeman, and (d) the public—black and white. Attitudes of the public are stressed as the most influential factor in the realization that blacks as well as whites have the job of policing society. nYC's police department is studied from the administrative aspect, and comparisons of its experiences with Irish policemen entering the force in the 1860's and 1870's to the present day black situation are drawn.

LYNCH, Hollis R. *The Black Urban Condition.* NY Thos Y Crowell 1973.

LYNCH, Lawrence and Rafky, David M and Thibault, Edward. Are Cops Prejudiced? *Pol Chief* 40(3),60–62 1973.

LYON, F Emory. Race, Betterment And The Crime Doctors. *J Am Inst Cr L Crim* 5,887–891 1915.

LYON, Matthew. Dishonor In The Sun: The Violation Of Human Rights, Texas—Style. *Vill Voice* 24(18),24–27 My 7 1979.

MAC CORMICK, Austin H. Behind The Prison Riots. *Ann Am Poli* 239,17–27 My 1954.

MAC DONALD JR, A P. Black Power. *J Negro Ed* 44(4),547–554 1975.
The Black Power movement and its implications for the black community are discussed. It is suggested that participants in the initial riots were externals whose rioting was expressive behavior stemming from frustration brought about by increased awareness of relative deprivation. The responsive reaction of society caused internally oriented blacks to reinterpret the expressive behavior as instrumental and shifted external blacks to more internal orientations. The behaviors of those with an internal locus of control differ from those of externals as level of discontent is increased. Rioting or violent protest, though traditionally thought of as expressive behavior, came to be seen as instrumental behavior because it worked. The passage of time, a history of failure of the blacks to work through the system, and effective communication of relative deprivation acted collectively to trigger explosive expressive behavior of the black external. Internals also turned to violent protest as an instrumental act when they observed the effectiveness of violent protest over working through the system.

MAC DONALD, John M. *Armed Robbery.* Springfield IL Chas C Thomas 1975.

MAC LEOD, W C. Law, Procedure And Punishment In Early Bureaucracies. *J Am Inst Cr L Crim* 25, 1934.

MAC LEOD, W C. Police And Punishment Among Native Americans On The Plains. *J Am Inst Cr L Crim* 28,181–201 1937.
The internal police systems of Indian tribes, systems with powers to enforce orders and inflict punishment for disobedience, have been a neglected aspect of Indian studies. However, review of early literature makes reference to police organization and practices in descriptions of customs of the Ojibway, Cree, Osage, Pawnee, Menominee, Oglala, Blackfoot, and other tribes. Tribal variations were numerous, but, basically, the policing function was performed by a fraternity of warriors with ceremonial and social responsibilities assigned by the tribal chiefs. Aside from their police duty, members of the police organizations did not work. Their varied functions included policing hunts and marches, enforcing attendance at religious ceremonies, supervising public works, acting as guards and sentinels, protecting property, arbitrating quarrels, and curbing personal violence in order to prevent murder. Severe flogging and destruction of the offender's property were the usual forms of punishment meted out by the police.*

MACCOBY, Michael and Fromm, Erich. *Social Character In A Mexican Village: A Sociopsychoanalytic Study.* Englewood Cliffs NJ Prentice—Hall 1970.

MACGUIRE, R J. War On Narcotics—The State Of Hostilities In New York. *Drug Enf* 6(3),6–9 1979.
Progress in fighting drug traffic, and suggested innovations for future police activities are discussed by the police commissioner of NYC. Although blacks and Hispanics compose 36% of NYC's population, these groups represent 67% of the addict population. The total cost of drug treatment in NY State is 94 million dollars less than the total cost of retaining addicts in correctional institutions. New strategies are suggested for combatting organized drug traffic. Coordinated intelligence activities should be upgraded, with condition—oriented rather than target—oriented efforts designed to expose and attack the illegal criminal drug enterprise. Undercover agents might have to remain undercover for years. Court—authorized eavesdropping must be designed to expose the character of the illegal business and not merely establish evidence of an ad hoc crime. Plea—bargaining policies ought to reflect a commitment to the broad intelligence objectives of this new approach. Finally, the financial ramifications of these criminal enterprises should be seriously studied.*

MACHOVER, Solomon. *Cultural And Racial Variations In Patterns Of Intellect, Peformance Of Negro And White Children On The Bellevue Adult Intelligence Scale.* NY Columbia Teach Col 1943.

MACK, Raymond W (ed). *Race, Class, And Power.* NY Am Book Co 1963.

MACKEY, Wade C and Kan ia, Richard. Police Violence As A Function Of Community Characteristics. *Criminology* 15(1),22–48 My 1977.

MADDOCKS, Lewis I. Humanizing Law Enforcement: A Liberal Approach From A Conservative Stance. *Soc Act* 38(8),8–19 1972.

MAGNUM, Charles S. *The Legal Status Of The Negro.* Chapel Hill Univ N Car Pr 1940.
This book—length study of racial inequalities before the law contains a listing (compiled from State Prison Departments and Departments of Public Welfare) of comparative proportions of death sentences to executions for blacks and whites in Florida, Kentucky, Tennessee and Virginia for the period 1928–1938; Texas, 1924–1928; South Carolina, 1912–1938; North Carolina, 1909–1928 and 1927–1938. The author concludes from this that "a greater percentage of condemned colored felons are actually executed than whites."

MAGUIRE, F J. *Descriptive Study Of Homicide In Hudson County (NJ), 1971–1977.* Unpub MA Thesis Rutgers Univ 1978.
This analysis of 418 cases of criminal homicide that occurred in Hudson County, NJ, from January 1971 through December 1977 encompasses race, sex, and age of victim and offender, and time and method of commission. Data for the study were gathered from the files of the county prosecutor's office. Males predominated as both victims (74.6%) and offenders (88.4%). Constituting 10.03% of the county's population, blacks were responsible for 45.8% of all homicides. Homicide was

predominantly an intraracial crime. The greatest deviation from this generality was in the number of Hispanics killing blacks.*

MAIER, Pauline. Popular Uprisings And Civil Authority In Eighteenth—Century America. *Wm & Mary Q* 27,3–35 1970.

MALDONADA - DENIS, Manuel. The Puerto Ricans: Protest Or Submission. *Ann Am Poli* 382,26–31 Mr 1969.

The situation of Puerto Ricans in the US cannot be seen as abstracted from that of those living in Puerto Rico. Puerto Rico has been a colony of the US since 1898, and the most pervasive characteristic of its population—both in the Island and in the Mainland—is its colonialist mentality or world view: hence, the attitude of submission and acquiescence characteristic of the Puerto Ricans. The only forces in Puerto Rico that represent Puerto Rican protest against the perpetuation of colonialism in Puerto Rico are the proindependence groups. In this respect, their goal is similar to that of the Black Power advocates in the US, because both groups are faced with a similar situation. Only when Puerto Ricans have achieved decolonization, both psychologically and politically, will they be able to come of age as a true protest movement. Otherwise they run the risk of a total destruction of Puerto Rican nationality, and cultural assimilation by the US.

MALINOVICH, M M. Second Thoughts On Crime And Sympathy. *Humanist* 38(5),24–27 1978.

Young blacks react to their joblessness by becoming involved in drugs and crime. This reaction has been condoned as only natural by those who forward the notion of minority offenders as social victims, and has been promoted by the criminal justice system's willingness to bargain with offenders rather than punish them. Acceptance of crime as a natural response for ghetto youth has served as a self—fulfilling prophecy and has encouraged the channeling of a potentially strong political force into a dead—end diversion that helps to maintain an outdated economic and social status quo. It seems reasonable to believe that well intentioned sympathy for criminals helps both to keep crime rates high and to prevent the very changes that represent the best long—range solution to crime. There is little hope of eradicating unemployment, housing, education, and health problems in the ghetto as long as ghetto youths are engaged in crime rather than in political activity.*

MALLORY, Mae. The Framing Of Ahmad Evans. *Black Scholar* 2(8–9),19–23 1971.

MALON J V. *The PAS Study Of Delinquency And Race.* Unpub PhD Diss Univ of Missouri 1971.

MALONE, T H. Peonage—Its Origin And Growth. *Voice Negro* 3(1),27–29 1906.

MALONE, T H. Peonage—Its Working And Features. *Voice Negro* 3(2),114–116 1906.

MALONE, T H. Peonage—The Five Year's Contract. *Voice Negro* 3(4),263–265 1906.

MALONE, T H. Peonage—The Remedy. *Voice Negro* 3(6),443–444 1906.

MALRY, L and Forslund, Morris A. Standardization Of Negro Crime Rates For Negro—White Differences In Age And Status. *Rocky Mt J Soc Sci* 7,151–160 1970.

Obtaining data from the local police department, a sample was taken of all persons arrested in Stamford, Conn., from 1959 to 1961 (3,717 arrests). Subjects were 16 years of age or older and were charged with offenses other than motor vehicle law violation. Using occupation as an indicator of socioeconomic status, crime rates were computed for males and females separately for each age and occupational category. Negro rates were then standardized to those expected if the Negro age and occupational structures were the same as those of whites, under the assumption of constant Negro rates for each age and occupational category. Despite their limitation, the findings of the study show that the disproportionate concentration of Negroes in the lower socioeconomic strata and in the younger age categories of the US account for a substantial proportion of the excess of the Negro over the white crime rate. However, standardization of offense rates for specific offenses by occupation, and especially by age, does not result in equal reductions in rates for all offenses. Further studies should be conducted, taking into account age and occupation variables of crime rate comparisons.*

MANDEL, Jerry. Hispanics In The Criminal Justice System: The 'Non—Existent Problem. *Agenda* 9(3),16–20 My–Je 1979.

MANDEL, Jerry. The Santa Fe Prison Riots: 'The Flower Of The Dragon'. *Agenda* 10(3),4–10 My–Je 1980.

MANDELL, Betty R (ed). *Welfare In America: Controlling The "Dangerous Classes".* Englewood Cliffs NJ Prentice—Hall 1975.

MANGOLD, Margaret M. *La Causa Chicana: The Movement For Justice.* NY Family Serv Assoc 1972.

A variety of the concerns of the Chicano and his relationships to major contemporary American institutions and to the racism inherent in them, are discussed. Numerous issues, including historical distortions, racism, the effects of mass media, psychological testing, the family and its role in the social system, and the role of social work in the community, are examined. It is noted that change must occur if the self—worth and the rich heritage of the Chicano is to be preserved.

MANION, Jack. New Style Highbinder Fights Tong Wars Today. *NYT* ,4 O 19 1924.

MANN, Coramae R. *The Juvenile Female In The Judicial Process.* Unpub PhD Diss Univ of Illinois 1976.

MANN, Coramae R. Differential Treatment Between Runaway Boys And Girls In Juvenile Court. *Juv & Fam Ct J* 30(2),37–48 1979.

Differential treatment of female status offenders in one of the largest juvenile court jurisdictions in the country is assessed in an analysis of dispositions in cases involving 50 female and 50 male runaways. The study subjects constituted a quota sample drawn from runaway cases appearing in the Minors—in=Need—of—Supervision (MINS) court of a Midwestern city. Female runaways received the most severe court sanction more often than male runaways, were more often held in custody at the time of their MINS hearing, and were more often held in custody than females charged with criminal offenses. Only 6% of all cases involved court—ordered physical examinations, but all of these cases involved females. Sexual misbehavior appeared to be presumed by the court as justification for medical scrutiny. Uniform crime reports indicated that white runaways were arrested eight times as frequently as blacks, but the majority of runaways handled by this court were black. Both black females and white females were punished more severely than black males; black males were placed under supervision (the least sentence) 72% of the time.*

MANN, Delbert Martin and House, Floyd Nelson and Hoffer, Frank William. *The Jails Of Virginia: A Study Of The Local Penal System.* NY D Appleton & Co 1933.

MANN, Fredrica and Friedman, C Jack and Baker, Timothy. Selectivity In The Criminal Justice System. *Prison J* 55(1),23–34 1975.

MANN, Horace. *Horace Mann's Letters On The Extension Of Slavery Into California And New Mexico.* Washington DC Brunner/Mazel 1850.

MANNLE, Henry W and Lewis, Peter W. Control Theory Re—examined: Race And The Use Of Neutralizations Among Institutionalized Delinquents. *Criminology* 17(1),58–74 My 1979.

When tests designed to measure socialization (intensity of prosocial commitments) and neutralization (acceptance of justifications for antisocial behavior) were administered to 148 black and 166 white incarcerated delinquents (males and females, average age 15.3 years), the hypothesis that blacks would score higher than whites on both dimensions was borne out, as was the expectation that socialization and neutralization would be negatively correlated for both groups. Although the negative correlation was weaker for blacks than for whites the difference was not of the magnitude expected. That blacks were more socialized is interpreted as a reflection of their having been exposed to less norm—destroying deviance than their white counterparts before being incarcerated, which in turn reflects the tendency of the juvenile system to incarcerate blacks more readily than whites. The negative correlation between socialization and neutralization is an indication that youths with weaker bonds to the social order are more inclined to seek rationalization of their antisocial behavior, attempting to bolster self—esteem.*

MARCH, Ray A. *Alabama Bound: Forty—Five Years Inside A Prison System.* University AL Univ AL Pr 1978.

MARDEN, Charles F and Meyer, Gladys. *Minorities In American Society.* NY Am Book Co 1962.

MARGOLIS, R. Minority Hiring And The Police. *New L* 54(16),13–16 Ag 9 1971.

MARK, Greg Yee. Racial, Economic And Political Factors In The Development Of America's First Drug Laws. *Issues Crim* 10(1),49–72 Spr 1975.

MARKOWTIZ, J. *Plea Bargaining—An Annotated Bibliography.* Chicago IL Am Judicature Soc 1978.

Over 350 books and articles ranging in publication date from 1927 through 1978 are listed in a comprehensive, annotated bibliography on plea bargaining.*

MAROULES, Nicholas and White, Teresa and Rubinstein, Michael L. *Statistical Analysis Of Misdemeanor Sentences In Anchorage And Fairbanks: 1974–1976.* Anchorage Judicial Council 1979.

MARQUETTE UNIVERSITY, Center For Criminal Justice Agency Organization . *Marquette University—Center For Criminal Justice Agency Organization And Minority Employment Opportunities—Final Report.* Milwaukee WI Marquette Univ 1975.

Compendium of the activities of a center designed to accumulate and disseminate knowledge to promote equal opportunities for minorities in the various criminal justice fields.*

MARRO, Anthony. Blacks And Women To Be Hired For Louisiana Police–Fire Jobs. *NYT*,14 Je 30 1977.

This article reports on a consent decree obtained by the US Justice Department in Federal Court that will require most of the large cities in Louisiana, with the exception of New Orleans, to hire significant numbers of women and blacks for their police and fire departments. This decree is the result of a class action suit brought by the Justice Department's Civil Rights Division. That suit charged a number of cities and parishes with violations of the Civil Rights Act of 1964, the L. E. A. A. Funding Act of 1968, and the Revenue Sharing Act of 1972 by discriminating against blacks and women in the staffing of police and fire departments. The consent decree was signed by 23 of the 45 defendants. This agreement will require these cities and parishes to fill half of all vacancies for police and fire–fighting jobs with qualified blacks until the percentage of blacks in the police and fire departments equals the percentage of blacks in the local work force. In like manner, 25% of police vacancies and 15% of all fire department vacancies are to be filled with women to reach their percentage in the job force.

MARSHALL, Burke. The Protest Movement And The Law. *Va L Rev* 51,785–803 1965.

MARSHALL, Harvey and Purdy, Ross. Hidden Deviance And The Labelling Approach: The Case For Drinking And Driving. *Social Prob* 19(4),541–553 Spr 1972.

MARSHALL, Harvey and Short Jr, James F and Rivera, Ramon. Adult–Adolescent Relations And Gang Delinquency. *Pac Soc Rev* 7(2),59–65 Fall 1964.

MARSHALL, Ineke M. *Judicial Decision–Making In The Juvenile Court: An Empirical Test Of A Labelling/Conflict Proposition.* Unpub PhD Diss Bowling Green St U 1978.

MARSHALL, Thurgood and White, Walter. *What Caused The Detroit Riot?* NY NAACP 1943.

MARSHALL, Thurgood. The Gestapo In Detroit. *Crisis* 50,232–234 1943.

MARTIN, C A. *Capable Cops—Women Behind The Shield—A Selected Bibliography On Women Police Officers.* Monticello IL Vance Bibliog 1979.

This selected bibliography on woman police officers contains 148 citations with publications arranged alphabetically by author.*

MARTIN, C A. *Women As Probation Parole, And Correctional Officers In The Criminal Justice Field—A Selected Bibliography.* Monticello IL Vance Bibliog 1980.

This annotated bibliography presents citations of 140 publications on the subject of women as probation, parole, and correctional officers in the criminal justice field.*

MARTIN, C A. Women Police: A Study Of Education, Attitudes, Problems. *J Stud Tech Careers* 1(3),220–227 1979.

A reported survey of 554 policewomen reveals that women in law enforcement would like to see substantial changes in training methods as well as in departmental policies and attitudes. Questionnaires returned from 320 police departments indicate that women police play a major role in crime prevention. Only 2% of the nation's sworn officers are women, despite indications of the advantages of women in many aspects of police work.*

MARTIN, E E and Brown, Lee P. Neighborhood Team Policing: A Viable Concept In Multanomah County. *Pol Chief* 43(5),84–87 1976.

MARTIN, George. *Judicial Administration And Racial Discrimination: Fifteen Years Of Literature.* Chicago IL Am Judicature Soc 1976.

MARTIN, George. Judicial Administration And Racial Discrimination: Fifteen Years Of Literature. *Judicature* 53(9),395–400 1970.

MARTIN, J David and Mc Connell, Jon P. Black Militant Ideology And The Law: Some Indications From A Questionnaire Study. *Criminology* 10(1),111–116 My 1972.

MARTIN, John Bartlow. Break Down The Walls. NY Ballantine 1954.

MARTIN, S E. Breaking And Entering—Policewomen In The Police World. Unpub PhD Diss American Univ 1977.

MARTIN, S L. Indian Rights And The Constitutional Implications Of The Major Crimes Act. *Notre Dame Law* 52,109–135 1976.

MARTINEZ, Douglas. The 1980 Census: Making Sure We Count. *Nuestro* 3(11),18–20 1979.

MARX, Gary T (ed). *Protest And Prejudice.* NY Harper & Row 1967.

MARYLAND LEGISLATIVE COUNCIL. *Report Of The Committee On Capital Punishment.* Baltimore MD Legis Council 1962.

This study is based on data in the records of the Maryland State Penitentiary. It distributes the total number of prisoners received there between 1936–61 under sentence of death according to race by age (5–year intervals) by offense by ultimate disposition of sentence. The Committee concluded that "the Negro has had a greater chance of execution upon sentence of death than the... white offender...." This study also contains data supplied by the Baltimore Criminal Justice Commission, concerning homicides in that city in 1960. Data are given for, *inter alia*: place of occurrence by race and sex of defendant; presence of alcohol by race and sex of victim; hour and place of occurence by race and sex of victim; method and weapon by race and sex of defendant; violence by race and sex of defendant by presence of alcohol; type of defendant–victim relationship by race and sex of victim and place of violence; disposition of trial by race and sex of defendant; degree of criminal homicide convicted by race and sex of defendant; minimum sentence by degree of homicide convicted and race.

MASOTTI, Louis (ed). *Riots, Violence And Disorder: Civil Turbulence In Urban Communities.* Beverly Hills CA Sage 1968.

MASOTTI, Louis and Corsi, Jerome. *Shootout In Cleveland: Black Militants And The Police (Violence Commission Report, Volume 5).* Washington DC USGPO 1969.

A detailed narrative of the events of July 23, 1968 when seven persons were killed and fifteen wounded in a Cleveland shootout between the police and black radicals. The short book organizes the details to facilitate analysis, raises questions where they are warranted, and mirrors the shootout in Cleveland against the events that led up to it and those it precipitated.

MAST, Robert. Police–Ghetto Relations: Some Findings And A Proposal For Structural Change. *Race* 11,447–462 Ap 1970.

Author contends that the traditional approaches to improved police–ghetto relations (police professionalization, increased black recruitment, training programs) are futile efforts due to strong normative structures within police systems and the implicit role of the police as the protectors of the status quo. Existing structures in the police–ghetto relationship must be reorganized and the author posits the idea of an indigenous police force as a possible solution.

MASTROIANNI, M and Khatena, J. The Attitudes Of Black And White High School Seniors Toward Integration. *Sociol Soc Res* 56(2),221–227 1972.

142 high school seniors (blacks: 12 boys and 16 girls; whites: 51 boys and 63 girls) from an integrated school and an all white school were administered a questionnaire on interracial attitudes. Black subjects showed a significant trend towards integration whereas white subjects appeared to be generally undecided about integration on such issues as marriage, schooling and equal job opportunity; they were also segretationists on matters like close friends, neighborhood and club memberships. Perceptions of black and white subjects were significantly different regarding matters of leadership, job satisfaction and opportunity, government effectiveness in handling racial problems, the justification of breaking the law, and whether the US is a better place to live in.

MATHIAS, William J. Perceptions Of Police Relationships With Ghetto Citizens. *Pol Chief* 38(4),78–83 Ap 1971.

Mathias reports some of the findings from his survey done of 160 respondents in two census tracts, one black and one white, in Atlanta, Georgia. Questions attempted to measure citizen perception of the amount of crime in Atlanta and of conditions in their own neighborhoods. The study notes the following: 58.3% of the respondents felt crime was rising. (A rise in crime was reported in the Uniform Crime Reports.) Citizens over–estimated the average number of murders per month in Atlanta (at 34 compared to an actual average of 12). Males were generally more satisfied than females, suggesting that males had less fear of being victimized. Blacks generally gave more unfavorable responses concerning neighborhood conditions and were more likely than whites to report observed crimes to the police. Although the Model Neighborhoods area where the survey is done is a high crime area, only 11.9% of the respondents saw it as less than safe, and 3.3% viewed it as the worst area in the city. This might be attributed to lack of mobility within the city.

MATHIAS, William J. The Ghetto Resident's View Of Police Procedures And Their Constitutionality. *Pol Chief* 38(5),64–67 1971.

A survey was conducted of residents in black and white census tracts in Atlanta, Georgia to determine whether or not people believed that the police had the right to stop citizens and the extent to which questioning should be allowed. Respondents were evenly divided between responding "yes," "no" and "it depends" on the question of whether police had the right to stop and ask citizens for identification. As to whether police had the right to ask for information beyond identification, half felt "it depends" and one–third answered "no." In responses to a third question, four out of ten respondents gave a qualified answer ("it depends") on whether police could search citizens and a small number felt police did not have the right to search on a stop. Blacks were more likely to say "no" to all three questions. Race was found to be a significant factor in the responses given.

MATHIESON, Donald and Passell, Peter. Homicide And Robbery In New York City: An Economic Model. *J Leg Stud* 5(1),83–98 Ja 1976.

MATRANGA, James T and Jensen, Diano E and Prandoni, Jaques R. Bender–Gestalt Protocols Of Adult Negro Male Offenders: Normative Data. *Perc Mot Sk* 35(1),101–102 Ag 1972.

MATSON, Floyd M and Tenbroek, Jacobus and Barnhart, Edward N. "The Attack On Japanese Americans During World War II" in *Conspiracy*, Curry, Richard O And Thomas M Brown (eds). NY Holt Rinehart Wins 1972.

MATTICK, Hans. The Form And Content Of Recent Riots. *U Chi L Rev* 35,660–685 1968.

MATTICK, Hans. The Prosaic Sources Of Prison Violence. *Public Wel* 31(4),54–60 1973.

The prosaic sources of prison violence are discussed. Some historical examples of prison violence are cited which point out the changing racial composition of prison inmates, regional differences, and changes in sentencing practices. These are external factors which must be understood as contributory elements. Viewed internally the prisons are unisexual, age graded, total institutions of social control. They are closed communities where keepers and kept go through their daily routine. It is in these mundane routines that the sources of prison violence are found. The prisoners and their keepers strike a complex bargain, which is ambiguous as to its precise limits and levels, and variable as to time, place, circumstance, and personalities. In the prison situation the white minority now feel the mounting pressure of the darker majorities, and guards and administrators are unable to bargain in the traditional way with inmates. Evidence that the prison problem is being faced is discussed.

MATZA, David. *Delinquency And Drift.* NY Wiley 1964.

MAUSE, Phillip I and Cohen, Warren H. The Indian: The Forgotten American. *Harv L Rev* 81,1818–1858 1968.

MAXSON, Stephen C and Kort, Fred. "Politics In A Biobehavioral Perspective" in *Biology And Crime*, Jeffrey, C R (ed). Beverly Hills CA Sage 1979.

MAY, Edgar. Profile/Missouri. *Correct Mag* 2(3),51–62 Mr 1976.

MAY, Phillip A. Crime And The American Indian: A Survey Of The Literature. Dallas A S C 1978.

MAY, Phillip A. *Alcohol Legalization And Native Americans: A Sociological Inquiry.* Unpub PhD Diss Univ of Montana 1976.

MAY, Rollo. "Madness And Powerlessness" in *Power And Innocence: A Search For The Causes Of Violence*, 19–45. NY Norton 1972.

Definitions of power and powerlessness as the author uses them, are given and are followed by an explanation of violence in terms of the efforts to deny or overcome powerlessness. Power is defined according to its Latin

etymology, "to be able," and encompasses effective ways of influencing others and of achieving the feeling of personal significance. Powerlessness is defined as weakness or helplessness. Violence is explained as the end product of constant conflict between the two traits. The author's explanation of several well–known theories of violence are expounded upon and case histories are included to support his viewpoint. The hypothesis that aggression is normal and that total suppresion of all aggressiveness is harmful is presented.

MAYKOVICH, Minako Kurokawa. The Difficulties Of A Minority Researcher In Minority Communities. *J Soc Issues* 33(4),108–119 1977.

MAYS, Benjamin E. The Role Of The Negro Community In Delinquency Prevention Among Negro Youth. *J Negro Ed* 28,366–370 1959.

MC BRIDE, D C and Westie, K S. The Effects Of Ethnicity, Age And Sex Upon Processing Through And Emergency Alcohol Health Care Delivery System. *Br J Addict* 74(1),21–29 1979.

This study provides a basic demographic profile of an emergency room alcohol patient population, and examines the relationships of age, ethnicity and sex to type of complaint at admission, likelihood of referral for further aid, type of psychiatric diagnosis given, and ultimate disposition of the case.

MC CAFFERTY, James A. "The Death Sentence" in *The Death Penalty In America*, Bedau, Hugo Adam (ed), 90–103. NY Anchor 1967.

This descriptive study, based on data obtained from the US Bureau of Prisons, contains a distribution of all prisoners executed in the US in 1960 by age (five–year, 19–45, groups), race (white,non–white), and elapsed time from sentence to execution. Also included is a similar distribution of prisoners under sentence of death whose cases were disposed of in that year (not including executions); of prisoners received in prisons that year under sentence of death (also distributed by defense and by month); and to similar distribution of prisoners under sentence of death as of January 1 and December 31 of that year.

MC CAGHY, Charles H and Giordano, Peggy C and Henson, Trudy Knicely. Auto Theft: Offender And Offense Characteristics. *Criminology* 15(3),367–385 N 1977.

MC CAHILL, T W and Meyer, L C and Fischman, A M. *Aftermath Of Rape.* Lexington MA Heath 1979.

This book is based on the Philadelphia Sexual Assault Survey of 1,401 women of all ages who reported a rape or sexual assault to Philadelphia authorities between April 1, 1973, and June 30, 1974. Attempted and statutory rape cases were included in this study designed for rape victims and their counselors, includng social workers, rape crisis center staff, and psychiatrists. Female social workers conducted initial and followup interviews with 790 women, and psychiatrists conducted interviews with 331 women or 41.9% of the sample. Other data were drawn from police files, eyewitness accounts of 25 rape cases, and a comparison of the study's findings with those of national studies and other research in the area of sexual assault. Among the findings were that age, marriage, employment, victim history, and kind of rape affected postrape adjustment; that police support was influenced by the presence of a policewoman, victim–offender relationship, victim history and appearance, and race; and that case outcome was related to victim history, race of judge and victim, kind of trial and rape, and type of reporting.*

MC CAIN, Paul M. The County Court In North Carolina Before 1750. *Hist Pap Trinity Coll Hist So* 12, 1916.

MC CANDLESS, Boyd R and Person, Scott and Roberts, Albert. Perceived Opportunity, Delinquency, Race, And Body Build Among Delinquent Youth. *J Consult Clin Psyc* 38,281–287 1972.

The subjects were delinquent, institutionalized black or white 15– to 17–year old boys from impoverished backgrounds. Variables investigated were perception of legitimate and illegitimate opportunity, admitted and committed delinquency, race and age of investigator and S, urbanization of residence, type of body build, physical attractiveness, and I. Q. Modest support was obtained for the hypothesis that perception of little legitimate opportunity is accompanied by high admitted delinquency, particularly for white boys (the white boys were found to perceive less opportunity and to admit more delinquency than the black boys). Perception of opportunity was not correlated with committed delinquency, and the relation between admitted and committed delinquency was low. Age and race of investigator entered into no significant relationships with any of the variables studied for either black or white boys.

MC CARTNEY, James and Galliher, John F. *Criminology—Power, Crime And Criminal Law.* Homewood IL Dorsey Pr 1977.

MC CAULEY, R P and Snarr, R W. *Minority Recruitment Manual For Ohio Peace Officers Report, 1977.* London OH Ohio PO Tr Acad 1976.

Guidelines pertaining to minority recruitment of Ohio peace officers are presented. Covered are the bases for antidiscrimination policies, discrimination in law enforcement, and remediation of discriminatory practices. The manual is designed to assist local law enforcement agencies in their efforts to increase representation of ethnic minorities and women as sworn peace officers. It is emphasized that minority recruitment does not refer to preferential hiring practices; rather, the goal is to attract the most qualified minority group members. In a democratic society, all persons should be permitted to participate in governmental processes. The rights of minority and women applicants are supported by the 14th amendment of the constitution, the Civil Rights Act and the Equal Employment Opportunity Act, IEAA, the Ohio Civil Rights Commission, and the courts. The organizational philosophy and commitment, policies and procedures, needs and goals, and requisite resources of the law enforcement personnel system are discussed within the context of discrimination issues and answers.*

MC CLORY, R. *The Man Who Beat Clout City.* Chicago Swallow Pr 1977.

The story of a black police officer's struggle to end Chicago's long history of departmental racism is recounted. Soon after Renault Robinson, an intelligent and highly motivated young black man, joined the Chicago Police force, he encountered a pervasive and deep-seated racial bigotry which eventually drove him and a handful of black officers to organize the Afro-American Patrolmen's League, in order to focus attention on the internal operations of the Chicago Police Department. Specifically, the league was organized to improve the relationship between the black community and the department, to improve the relationships between black and white police officers, and to bring about police reform. However, Robinson and other league members, as well as the entire Chicago Police Department, were soon involved in a racial controversy that resulted in Robinson's suspension, departmental plots to link the League with criminal conspiracies, and eventually, to Robinson's reinstatement and court decision that would affect police departments across the country.*

MC COLLUM, Sylvia. The Latino Prisoners In The US—Managing Effective Participation. *Q J Corr* 2(2),42–45 1978.

A US Bureau of Prisoners internship, in 1973, yielded information including: demographic data on Spanish-speaking inmates in the federal prison system, the effects of utilizing inmate translators, the distribution in prisons of bilingual staff members, and educational provisions made for the Latino prisoner. Policy recommendations based on this data were presented. The impact of this information on the Bureau of Prisons treatment programming for this minority, which comprises almost one-fifth of the federal inmate population, was discussed.

MC CONAHAY, John B and Mullin, Courtney J and Frederick, Jeffrey. The Uses Of Social Science In Trials With Political And Racial Overtones: The Trial Of Joan Little. *Law & Contemp Prob* 41(1),205–229 Wint 1977.

MC CONAHAY, John and Sears, David. Participation In The Los Angeles Riot. *Social Prob* 17,3–19 Sum 1969.

MC CONAHAY, John and Sears, David. Racial Socialization, Comparison Levels, And The Watts Riot. *J Soc Issues* 26(1),121–140 1970.

MC CONNELL, Jon P and Martin, J David. Black Militant Ideology And The Law: Some Indications From A Questionnaire Study. *Criminology* 10(1),111–116 My 1972.

MC CONNELL, Leonard R. "Understanding Probation And Parole" in *The Administration Of Criminal Justice: A View From Black America*, Brown, Lee P (ed), 48–61. Washington DC Howard U 1974.

MC CONOCHIE, W A. Juvenile Delinquents: Relationships Between Wisc Scores, Offenses, Race, Chronological Age, And Residence. *Correct Psy* 4(3),103–110 1970.

MC CORD, Charles H. *The American Negro As A Dependent, Defective And Delinquent.* Nashville Pr Of Benson 1914.

"The average Negro is a child in every essential element of character, exhibiting those characteristics that indicate a tendency to lawless impulse and weak inhibition."

MC CORD, William and Howard, John. Negro Opinions In Three Riot Cities. *Am Behav Sci* 2,24–27 Mr–Ap 1968.

MC CORKLE, Lloyd and Korn, Richard. *Criminology And Penology.* NY Holt Rinehart Wins 1959.

MC COY, Albert. *The Politics Of Heroin In Southeast Asia.* NY Harper & Row 1972.

MC CREARY, C and Padilla, E. MMPI Differences Among Black Mexican–American And White Male Offenders. *J Clin Psyc* 33,171–177 1977.

MC CULLOCH, J W and Smith, N J and Batta, I D. A Study Of Juvenile Delinquency Amongst Asians And Half–Asians: A Comparative Study In A Northern Town Based On Official Statistics. *Br J Crimin* 15(1),32–42 Ja 1975.

MC DONALD, Thomas D. *Correlates Of Civil Rights Activity And Negro Intra–Racial Violence.* Unpub PhD Diss S Illinois Univ 1972.

The relationship between Negro intraracial violence and civil rights activity was studied. Issue is taken with Wolfgang's rejection of the frustration–aggression hypothesis and his characterization of the dominant culture as nonviolent. A lead was also taken from the research of Solomon (1965) who presented data revealing an apparent decrease in Negro intraracial aggravated assault during two years of sustained peaceful civil rights activity. Data were gathered on homicide from the cities of St. Louis and Boston, while that on homicide and aggravated assault were gathered from Atlanta. No significant relationship was found between Negro intraracial homicide and civil rights activity in any of these cities. In Atlanta a trend was found for a relationship between aggravated assault and civil rights activity. Solomon's proposition that such activity alleviates frustration in the Negro community and thereby reduces Negro intraracial violent crime in rejected, and an alternative interpretation suggested that civil rights activity may aggravate frustration, or at least the expression of aggression.

MC DOUGALL, Marion Gleason. *Fugitive Slaves 1619–1865.* Boston Ginn & Co 1891.

MC ENTIRE, Davis and Powers, Robert B. "A Guide To Race Relations For Police Officers" in *The Urban Policeman In Transition*, Snibbe, J (ed), 302–340. Springfield IL Chas C Thomas 1973.

A race relations guide for police officers is presented, stressing developments, particularly in the 1940's, that contributed to tensions between minority groups and law enforcement authorities. Topics include desired official attitude of police toward minorities, complications caused by racial prejudices, group distinctions that lead people to mistakenly believe they are inferior; behavior traits of these groups and reasons for their mistrust and antagonism toward the police, particularly on the part of blacks and Mexican–Americans; and practical police methods in race relations, stressing the recommendations of the Interim Report of the Peace Officers Committee on Civil Disturbance (1945) regarding preventive measures.

MC EVOY, D W and Steinberg, J L. *Police And The Behavioral Sciences.* Springfield IL Chas C Thomas 1974.

MC FARLAND, Anita and Willick, Daniel H and Gehlker, Gretchen. Social Class As A Factor Affecting Judicial Disposition. *Criminology* 13(1),57–77 My 1975.

MC GEE JR, Henry W. Blacks, Due Process And Efficiency In The Clash Of Values As The Supreme Court Moves To The Right. *Black L J* 2(3),220–231 Wint 1972.

MC GEE SR, Henry W. The Problem And Promise Of Black Men Of Law. *Black L J* 1(1),28–37 Spr 1971.

This article focuses primarily on the social implications of the expected large scale increase in the number of attorneys from racial minority groups. McGee posits that it is possible that an increase in the number of black lawyers could help decrease anti–black prejudice and have a salutatory effect on race relations. Larger numbers of black lawyers demonstrating their ability to accomplish essential legal tasks could also have a positive effect on the black self–esteem and black pride, in additon to helping to overcome the inadequate image people hold of black attorneys.

MC GEE, D Phillip. White Conditioning Of Black Dependency. *J Soc Issues* 29(1),53–56 1973.

MC GHEE, Henry. Arrests In Civil Disturbances: Reflections On The Use Of Deadly Force In Riots. *Rutgers L Rev* 22,716–732 1968.

MC GOWAN, Brenda G and Blumenthal, Karen L. *Why Punish The Children: A Study Of Children Of Women Prisoners.* Hackensack NJ NCCD 1978.

MC GUINN, Henry J. Equal Protection Of The Law And Fair Trials In Maryland. *J Negro Hist* 24,143–166 1939.

MC KAY, Henry and Shaw, Clifford. *Juvenile Delinquency And Urban Areas*. Chicago Univ Chicago Pr 1942.

MC KELVEY, Blake. *American Prisons: A Study In American Social History*. Chicago Univ Chicago Pr 1936.

MC KELVEY, Blake. Penal Slavery And Southern Reconstruction. *J Negro Hist* 20(1),153–179 1935.

MC KENZIE, Roderick D and Park, Robert E and Burgess, Ernest W. *The City*. Chicago Univ Chicago Pr 1925.

MC KEOWN, James Edward. Poverty, Race And Crime. *J Crim L Crimin & Pol Sci* 39,480–484 1948.

This survey of American cities with populations over 100,000 shows direct relationships between poverty and "crimes of the proletariat" (murder, robbery, assault, burglary, and larceny) and between inadequate housing conditions and these crimes. All coefficients were positive for black populations, lending support to the conclusion that disproportionate criminality exists among blacks, at least as far as these five types of crimes are concerned. McKeown correlated the rates for murder, robbery, assault and larceny in 96 cities in 1940, with fifteen 1939–1948 indices of socio–economic conditions. Results supported conclusions previously made by criminologists that poverty and slum conditions are positively associated with crime that the foreign born and their children are less prone to criminality than native born, and that blacks are more involved in non–white collar crime than their white counterparts. An inverse relationship was found between community economic prosperity and crime. This is in contrast to a finding reported by Ogburn in 1935 of a low positive relationship between 1929 wage level and 1939 crime rates.

MC LAUGHLIN, John B. *Gypsy Lifestyles*. Lexington MA Lexington 1980.

MC LEMORE, L B and Mitchell, G T. Police Conduct And The Black Community—The Case Of Jackson, Mississippi. *J Poli Repr* 1(1),97–110 1975.

MC MANUS, Edgar J. *Black Bondage In The North*. Syracuse NY Syracuse Univ Pr 1973.

Historical study of slavery in the Northern states, especially NY.

MC MEEKIN, Daniel. Red, White And Gray: Equal Protection And The American Indian. *Stanford L Rev* 21,1236–1248 My 1969.

MC MILLAN, George. *Racial Violence And Law Enforcement*. Atlanta S Regional Council 1960.

MC MILLAN, George. Racial Violence And Law Enforcement. *New South* 15,1–32 N 1960.

MC NABB, D P. Delinquent Acting–Out And Task Of Sexual Identification In Black Male Adolescents—Replication Study. *Smith Coll Stud Soc Wk* 44,23+ 1973.

MC NEELY, Roger L and Pope, Carl E. Racial Issues In The Measurement Of Criminal Involvement. New Orleans A C J S 1978.

MC NEELY, Roger and Pope, Carl. Race And Involvement In Common Law Personal Crime: A Response To Hindelang. *Rev Black Pol Econ* 8,405–410 Sum 1978.

This critique evaluates an article written by Hindelang that uses victim survey data to study the representation of blacks in criminal events and the extent to which selection bias influences overrepresentation. The analysis begins by comparing findings generated from official data sources and self–report research to findings obtained from National Victimization Surveys. Victimization surveys suffer from some of the same methodological problems associated with the self–report technique. The degree to which victim respondents accurately remember events is unclear. More importantly, there is no definitive body of knowledge about the accuracy of a victim's perception regarding characteristics of incidents or offenders. Simply put, victim, offender, and official perceptions of crime and delinquency are not congruent. Studies dealing with the representation of blacks in criminal activities are cited, although these studies are far from conclusive concerning the degree to which selection bias operates within the criminal justice system.*

MC NICKLE, D and Fey, H E. *Indians And Other Americans*. NY Harper 1959.

MC NICKLE, Roma (ed). *Differences That Make The Difference*. Washington DC Jt Comm Corr Man T 1967.

MC NOWN, Robert F and Singell, Larry D. A Factor Analysis Of The Socio–Economic Structure Of Riot And Crime Prone Cities. *Ann Reg Sci* 8(1),1–13 1974.

MC WILLIAMS, Carey. *North From Mexico*, Orig Pub 1949. Westport CT Greenwood Pr 1968.

MC WILLIAMS, Carey. Race Discrimination And The Law. *Sci & Society* 9(1),1–22 Wint 1945.

MC WILLIAMS, Carey. The Zoot–Suit Riots. *New R* 108(25),818–820 Je 21 1943.

Article describes the circumstances surrounding the so–called "Zoot–Suit Riots" of 1943 on Los @angeles where Mexican–Americans and blacks were attacked by angry white males stirred up into a frenzy by a prejudicial press campaign and poor law enforcement practices.

MEADE, A. Seriousness Of Delinquency, The Adjudicative Decision, And Recidivism—A Longitudinal Configuration Analysis. *J Crim L & Crimin* 64(4),478–485 1973.

MEADERS, Daniel. South Carolina Fugitives As Viewed Through Local Newspapers With Emphasis On Runaway Notices 1732–1800. *J Negro Hist* 60(2),288–319 Ap 1975.

MECKLIN, John M. *The Klu Klux Klan*. NY Harcourt Brace 1924.

MEDNICK, S and Christiansen, K O. *Biosocial Bases Of Criminal Behavior*. NY Gardner 1977.

MEERS, D R and Gordon, G . Aggression And Ghetto–Reared American Negro Children. *Psych Q* 41,585–607 1972.

MEGARGEE, Edwin I. A Comparison Of The Scores Of White And Negro Male Juvenile Delinquients On Three Projective Tests. *J Proj Tech Pers Assess* 30(6),530–535 1966.

MEGARGEE, Edwin I and Elion, Victor H. Racial Identity, Length Of Incarceration And Parole Decision Making. *J Res Crim Del* 16(2),232–245 1979.

Focusing on the amount of time served and the frequency of parole in a sample of 958 youthful offenders from a cohort of 1,345 consecutive admissions to a federal correctional institution, the authors investigated racial differences in black–white sentence patterns at the parole stage. No significant differences were found in the actual amount of time served, but a significantly higher number of whites than blacks were granted parole. Discriminant function analysis did not show race to be significantly associated with decision to grant parole; instead, the authors indentified the primary factor as entry sentence.

MEGARGEE, Edwin I and Elion, Victor H. Validity Of The MMPI Pd Scale Among Black Males. *J Consult Clin Psyc* 43(2),166–172 1975.

The validity of the MMPI Psychopathic Deviate (Pd) and Pd + .4K scales to discriminate levels of social deviance among young black men was investigated. Black inmates at a federal correctional institution had significantly higher scores on both scales than culturally deprived black university students. Recidivists had significantly higher scores than first offenders. The two scales validly differentiate levels of social deviance, but the norms for the scales appear to show racial bias.

MEGARGEE, Edwin I and Rosenquist, Carl M. *Delinquency In Three Cultures*. Austin Univ Texas Pr 1969.

MEIER, August. *Negro Thought In America, 1880–1915*. Ann Arbor Univ Michigan Pr 1963.

MEIER, August and Rudwick, Elliot. *From Plantation To Ghetto*. NY Hill & Wang 1976.

MEIER, August and Rudwick, Elliott. "Black Violence In The 20th Century" in *Violence In America*, Graham, Hugh D And T Gurr (eds). NY Bantam 1969.

MEIER, Matt S and Rivera, Feliciano. *The Chicanos: A History Of Mexican Americans*. NY Am Century Series 1972.

MELTSNER, Michael. *Cruel And Unusual: The Supreme Court And Capital Punishment*. NY Random House 1973.

MELTSNER, Michael. Litigating Against The Death Penalty: The Strategy Behind *Furman*. *Yale L J* 82(6),1111–1139 My 1973.

MEMMI, A. *The Colonizer And The Colonized*. Boston Beacon Pr 1967.

MENDELSOHN, Harold and Bayley, David H. *Minorities And The Police*. NY Macmillan 1968.

MENDELSOHN, Robert A. Police–Community Relations: A Need In Search Of Police Support. *Am Behav Sci* 13,745–760 1970.

MENDOZA, M G and Avello, J A. *Manual For The Recruitment Of Minority And Females*. Washington DC USGPO 1976.

Specific techniques are recommended to help the Miami, Fla., Police Department minority candidates with the potential to become successful police officers. Each strategy is spelled out in detail and illustrated.*

MENDOZA, Ruben. Tapping The Talents Of A New Generation. *Pub Man* 62(9),5–7 O 1980.

With 85% of the Hispanic population living in urban areas, the role of the American city manager for the new generation of Hispanics is of particular importance. A Hispanic in the role of city manager can add a sensitivity to the needs of minorities that can be vital in handling future problems and crises. The International City Management Association is working with universities and administrators on the training, placement and development of such individuals. As the composition of city councils changes, the greater Hispanic representation will influence employment opportunities for minorities. Gradually, the entire range of positions will open up to Hispanics and their interaction with other races will likely be a positive step toward improving the quality of city life for all.

MERRILL JR, Boynton. *Jefferson's Nephews: A Frontier Tragedy*. Princeton Princeton Univ Pr 1976.

This historical case study of the murder of a young slave in Livingston, Ky. in 1811 provides a rare in–depth exploration of violent crimes against slaves. The murderers were white descendants of Thomas Jefferson. A substantial bibliography, footnotes and an index are included.

MERTON, Robert K. Social Structure And Anomie. *Am Sociol Rev* 3,672–682 O 1938.

MESSINGER, Sheldon L (ed) and Bittner, Egon (ed). *Criminology Review Yearbook*, V1. Beverly Hills CA Sage 1979.

MESSOLONGHITES, Louisa. *Multicultural Perspectives On Drug Abuse And Its Prevention: A Resource Book*. Rockville MD US Dept HEW 1979.

METARELTIS, G S. Lawmen For The Reservation. *FBI L Enf Bull* 40(7),16–20,30–31 Jl 1971.

METROPOLITAN LIFE INSURANCE COMPANY. Recent Increase In Homicide. *Stat Bull* 27,9–10 Ap 1946.

MEYER, Gladys and Marden, Charles F. *Minorities In American Society*. NY Am Book Co 1962.

MEYER, John R and Conrad, Alfred H. *The Economics Of Slavery And Other Studies In Econometric History*. Chicago IL Aldine 1964.

MEYER, L C and Fischman, A M and Mc Cahill, T W. *Aftermath Of Rape*. Lexington MA Heath 1979.

This book is based on the Philadelphia Sexual Assault Survey of 1,401 women of all ages who reported a rape or sexual assault to Philadelphia authorities between April 1, 1973, and June 30, 1974. Attempted and statutory rape cases were included in this study designed for rape victims and their counselors, includng social workers, rape crisis center staff, and psychiatrists. Female social workers conducted initial and followup interviews with 790 women, and psychiatrists conducted interviews with 331 women or 41.9% of the sample. Other data were drawn from police files, eyewitness accounts of 25 rape cases, and a comparison of the study's findings with those of national studies and other research in the area of sexual assault. Among the findings were that age, marriage, employment, victim history, and kind of rape affected postrape adjustment; that police support was influenced by the presence of a policewoman, victim–offender relationship, victim history and appearance, and race; and that case outcome was related to victim history, race of judge and victim, kind of trial and rape, and type of reporting.*

MEYERS, Ralph E and Forslund, Morris A. Delinquency Among Wind River Indian Reservation Youth. *Criminology* 12(1),97–106 My 1974.

This study investigates the magnitude and dimensions of the delinquency problem among Indian youths from the Wind River Reservation in Wyoming by examining official records from 1967–1971. The Reservation rates were found to be nearly five times the national average. It also appears that the proportion of court appearances of Reservation youth for serious offenses is much lower than in the nation as a whole, while the proportion of court appearances involving minor offenses are much higher (a higher percentage of charges were for alcohol–related offenses). These findings were consistent with the findings of previous studies. A cohort analysis which looked at all individuals who turned 18 years of age sometime during fiscal year 1971 showed that a large number of cases were disposed of by the juvenile officer and not even referred to court. In addition, many youths were arrested off the reservation and never came before Indian Court.

These findings indicate that the delinquency involvement of Reservation youths is much greater than that revealed by court records alone.

MIDDLETON, A B. Characteristics Of Criminals. *St Louis Med Era* 8,230–232 Mr 1899.

MILGRAM, N A et al. Level Of Aspiration And Locus Of Control In Disadvantaged Children. *Psychol Rep* 27(2),343–350 1970.

MILLER, Carroll L. Educational Level And Juvenile Delinquency Among Negroes. *J Negro Ed* 28(3),268–276 1959.

MILLER, D R. *The Crime Classes—Causes And Cures*. Dayton OH United Brethren 1903.

MILLER, Donald and Holt, Norman. *Explorations In Inmate–Family Relationships, Research Report No 46*. Sacramento Dept Corrections 1972.

MILLER, Eugene. The Woman Participant In Washington's Riots. *Fed Prob* 33(2),30–34 1969.

MILLER, H and Fischer, J. The Effect Of Client Race And Social Class On Clinical Judgements. *Clin S Work J* 1(2),100–109 1973.

MILLER, Harold D and Blumstein, Alfred and Cohen, Jacqueline. *Demographically Disaggregated Projections Of Prison Populations*. Pittsburgh Carnegie–M USI 1978.

This monograph on the impact of new sentencing laws on state prison populations in Pa. confirms the widespread expectation that mandatory minimum prison sentences for particular classes of felonies are likely to result in a substantial increase in the prisoner population. The authors predict that the new laws will have a greater effect on blacks than whites, thereby increasing the proportion of black prisoners.

MILLER, Herbert A and Park, Robert E. *Old World Traits Transplanted*. NY Harper & Row 1921.

MILLER, Kent S and Dreger, Ralph M. Comparative Psychological Studies Of Negroes And Whites In The United States: 1959–1965. *Psychol Bull* 70,1–58 1968.

MILLER, Loren. "Race, Poverty And The Law" in *The Law Of The Poor*, Tenbroek, Jacobus (ed), 62–82. San Francisco CA Chandler 1966.

MILLER, Loren. *The Petitioners, The Story Of The Supreme Court Of The US And The Negro*. Cleveland Meridian Books 1967.

MILLER, M and Hewitt, J. Conviction Of A Defendant As A Function Of Juror–Victim Racial Similarity. *J Soc Psychol* 105(1),156–160 1978.

MILLER, Marc. The Numbers Game. *S Exposure* 6(4),25–29 Wint 1978.

MILLER, Randall M. The Man In The Middle, The Black Slave Driver. *Am Herit* ,40–49 O–N 1979.

Black slave drivers in the ante–bellum South are examined as "policemen of the fields and the quarters." The author contends that the drivers stood between masters and slaves and that as a result they sought to curry favor with both. He views the drivers' experience as another example of the complexity of slavery, and suggests that whites and blacks "depended on the man in the middle."

MILLER, Walter B. *Violence By Youth Gangs And Youth Groups In Major American Cities—Final Report*. Cambridge MA Harv L Sch Cen C J 1976.

While three major reports prepared by federal–level commissions found that youth gangs are not a problem of major concern, this report indicates that youth gang violence in the mid–1970's is a serious crime problem. The minimum number of gangs is estimated to be 760 for the 6 cities reporting serious gang problems (NY, Chicago, Los Angeles, Philadelphia, Detroit, and San Francisco), and the number of gang members for those 6 cities is estimated to be 28,500. A higher but still conservative estimate for those same cities is 2,700 gangs and 81,500 gang members. Gang members, predominantly male, range in age from 10 to 21, originate in low–income communities, are predominantly black or Hispanic (although Asian–origin gangs are appearing), and use firearms and other weapons to kill or intimidate other gang members and the general public. Violence perpetrated by members of youth gangs is probably more lethal today than at any other time. Also unique to the present period is the degree to which gang activities are conducted within public schools at all levels (elementary, junior, and senior high).*

MILLER, Walter B. "Youth Gangs In The Urban Crisis Era" in *Delinquency, Crime And Society*, Short Jr, James F (ed), 91–128. Chicago Univ Chicago Pr 1976.

MILLER, Walter B. Ideology And Criminal Justice Policy. *J Crim L & Crimin* 64(2),455–473 1973.

MILLER, Walter B. Lower Class Culture As A Generating Milieu Of Gang Delinquency. *J Soc Issues* 14,5–19 1958.

MILLER, Walter B. Race, Sex And Gangs: The Molls. *Society* 11(1),32–35 1974.

MILLER, William Robert. *Nonviolence: A Christian Interpretation*. NY Schocken 1966.

MILLS, C Wright. *Puerto Ricans In New York*. NY Harper & Row 1950.

MILLS, Charles K. The Brain Of A Negro Murderer. *Pro Path Soc Phila* 11,215–216 1881–1883.

MILLS, R and Brecht, A. Minorities Employed In Law Libraries. *Law Lib J* 71,283–288 1978.

MILNE, R and White, R and Grant, R. Minority Recruiting: The Tucson Police Experience. *J Polic Sci Adm* 3(2),197–202 1975.

The attempts of the Tucson Police Department to recruit qualified minorities (blacks and Mexican–Americans) into police work are examined in this article. In November 1971 a black officer was assigned to the personnel section as a minority recruiter. In less than 18 months the black complement of the agency rose from 3 to 11, or 2.83% of commissioned strength and Mexican–American representation rose from 35 to 42 or 10.7% of all police officer positions. The technique employed by the recruiter was one which emphasized personal contact and discussion of police work. The following steps were taken by the department: elimination of the Otis Employment Test, permanent assignment of a minority recruiting officer, termination of minimum height and weight requirements, adoption of a validated Police Officer Entrance Examination, reclassification of "policeman/policewoman" to "police officer," an end to separate assignments based on sex, modification of physical agility requirements and the adoption of a selective Certification Program for minorities. The program initiated by this department has been highly successful, and has been extended to attract other groups including Native–Americans and women.

MILTON, C H et al. *Police Use Of Deadly Force*. Washington DC Police Foundation 1977.

MINDEL, C H (ed) and Habenstein, R (ed). *Ethnic Families In America*. NY Elsevier 1976.

MINDEL, C H and Cromwell, R E and Vaughn, E C. Ethnic Minority Family Research In An Urban Setting: A Process Of Exchange. *Am Sociologist* 10,141–150 1975.

MINGLE, James R. *Black And Hispanic Enrollment In Higher Education, 1978: Trends In The Nation And The South*. Atlanta S Regional Ed Bd 1980.

MINNIS, Mhyra S. Juvenile Delinquency: Clique Interaction Among Three Ethnic Groups. *Pro Sw Soc Assoc* 19,187–191 1968.

MINNIS, Mhyra S. Selected Social Problems Of Fort Hall Reservation. *Sociol Soc Res* 46(4),436–445 Jl 1962.

MINNIS, Mhyra S. The Juvenile Delinquent's Home–Differentiated Attitudinal And Behavioral Patterns Among Three Ethnic Groups. *Pro SW Soc Assoc* 18,157–162 Mr 1967.

MINNIS, Mhyra S. The Relationship Of The Social Structure Of An Indian Community To Adult And Juvenile Delinquency. *Soc Forces* 41(4),395–402 My 1963.

MINTON JR, Robert J (ed). *Inside: Prison American Style*. NY Random House 1971.

MINTON JR, Robert J and Rice, Stephen. Using Racism At San Quentin. *Ramparts* 8,18–24 Ja 1970.

MINTZ, Betty. Patterns In Forcible Rape: A Review Essay. *Crim L Bull* 9(8),703–710 1973.

A review of an influential book dealing with rape is presented. The conclusion that rape is phenomenally high among blacks and that there is something in the black subculture which supports violence generally, and rape in particular, is contended. The reviewer propounds an alternative thesis to Amir's *Patterns of Forcible Rape*.

MIRANDÉ, Alfredo and Enriques, Evangelina. *La Chicana: The Mexican American Woman*. Chicago Univ Chicago Pr 1979.

MISNER, Gordon. The Response Of Police Agencies. *Ann Am Poli* 382,109–119 Mr 1969.

MITCHELL, Charles L. The Black Philadelphia Lawyer. *Villanova L Rev* 20(2–3),371–402 1975.

The problems facing black attorneys in Philadelphia are discussed in order to highlight racial discrimination within the legal profession. The black attorneys were questioned about their prelegal experience, legal training and admission to the bar, and characteristics of their professional life. An analysis of their experience shows that racial prejudice combined with the continuing lack of education and resources limits the number of blacks who join the legal profession. Today the future for black attorneys is promising as employment openings increase. Nevertheless the day of the individual practitioner is over and black attorneys will have to abandon the traditional practices and seek more group involvement in firms, politics, and professional organizations.

MITCHELL, Clifford C. When Prisoners Run Amuck. *Abbott's Wkly* ,4 Ja 6 1934.

MITCHELL, Clifford C. When Prisoners Run Amuck. *Abbott's Wkly* ,4,13 D 23 1933.

MITCHELL, G T and Mc Lemore, L B. Police Conduct And The Black Community—The Case Of Jackson, Mississippi. *J Poli Repr* 1(1),97–110 1975.

MITCHELL, Greg. Today: Ron LeFlore Only Steals Bases. *Correct Mag* 6(5),39–41 O 1980.

MITCHELL, Lonnie E. Aspiration Levels Of Negro Delinquent, Dependent, And Public School Boys. *J Negro Ed* 26,80–85 1957.

MITCHELL, M C. *Public Information And Law Enforcement*. Santa Cruz CA Davis Pub Co 1975.

MITCHELL, Michael and Alker, Howard L and Hoslicka, Carl. Jury Selection As A Biased Social Process. *Law & Soc Rev* 11(1),9–41 1976.

MITCHELL, Shirley and Forbes, Gordon B. Attribution Of Blame, Anger, & Aggression In [Poor] Female Negro Adults. *J Soc Psychol* 83,73–78 1971.

Attribution of blame, feelings of anger, and direction of anger in response to interracial frustration were investigated in 31 adult female Negroes. It was found that Negroes attributed more blame to the frustrators when a white frustrated a Negro than when a Negro frustrated a white. Feelings of anger and direction of anger were not related to race of frustrator.

MITFORD, Jessica. *Kind And Usual Punishment: The Prison Business*. NY Knopf 1974.

MOFFETT, A D and Chambers, C D and Cuskey, W R. Demographic Factors In Opiate Addiction Among Mexican Americans. *Pub Health Rep* 85(6),523–531 1970.

MOFFETT, Arthur D and Chambers, Carl D and Cuskey, Walter R. "Mexican American Opiate Addicts" in *The Epidemiology Of Opiate Addiction In The United States*, Ball, John C (ed). Springfield IL Chas C Thomas 1970.

MOINAT, Sheryl M et al. Black Ghetto Residents As Rioters. *J Soc Issues* 28(4),45–62 1972.

Los Angeles riot participants, both actual and psychological, were compared with nonparticipants to see if participation could be predicted, using stepwise multiple linear regression analysis and a second form of linear regression analysis (Wood's algorithm). Data were from 586 interviews of black residents, representing a random sample of the riot curfew area. Neither active nor psychological riot participation could be predicted when age and sex were not controlled, but significant prediction was possible when the population was divided into four groups by age and sex. The usefulness of the regression in characterizing rioters versus nonrioters is limited because a large number of independent variables is needed. Results support the theory that rioting is a community phenomenon.

MOLES, O C and O' Shea, R M and Irelan, L M. Ethnicity, Poverty And Selected Attitudes: A Test Of The Culture Of Poverty Hypothesis. *Soc Forces* 47,405–413 1969.

MOLINA, Mauricio. Less Spanish, Please. *NYT* ,op–ed Page Mr 12 1980.

MOLNAR, M and Frederick, M A. Relative Occupational Anticipations And Aspirations Of Delinquents And Nondelinquents. *J Res Crim Del* 6(1),1–7 1969.

MOMBOISSE, Raymond M. *Community Relations And Riot Prevention*. Springfield IL Chas C Thomas 1967.

MONAHAN, Thomas P. Family Status And The Delinquent Child: A Reappraisal And Some New Findings. *Soc Forces* 35(3),250–258 Mr 1957.

MONAHAN, Thomas P. On The Trend In Delinquency. *Soc Forces* 40,158–168 1961.

MONDRICK, Margaret E and Carroll, Leo. Racial Bias In The Decision To Grant Parole. *Law & Soc Rev* 11(1),93–107 1976.

Virtually all past research in the area of racial discrimination has focused on the police courts. Less visible decisions where unfettered discretion makes discrimination even more likely have not been adequately studied. The present study looked at proportions of black and white prisoners paroled and also at the criteria by which each prisoner was evaluated. Data clearly suggest the operation of racial bias. Black prisoners were evaluated according to different criteria than whites. Specifically, the requirement of participation in institutional treatment programs was imposed on black prisoners and not on whites. Consequently, most black prisoners who were paroled (77%) served significantly longer proportions of their sentences than did similar white prisoners. Data is consistent with the interpretation that the bias of the parole board was not racial per se but a bias against perceived militancy. Participation in treatment programs was much more likely to be required for those blacks perceived as militant (the younger black prisoners convicted of drug and violent offenses) than for the older black property offenders.

MONTAGU, Ashley. Man's Most Dangerous Myth: The Fallacy Of Race. NY World 1942.

MONTEIL, Miguel. The Chicano Family: A Review Of Research. *Social Wk* 18(2),22–31 Mr 1973.

MONTERO, Darrel M and Levine, Gene N. Socioeconomic Mobility Among Three Generations Of Japanese Americans. *J Soc Issues* 29(2),33–48 1973.

MONTERO, Darrel. Research Among Racial And Cultural Minorities: An Overview. *J Soc Issues* 33(4),1–10 1977.

This introduction to research among racial and cultural minorities has three objectives: (a) to briefly review the status of research among minorities, (b) to present an overview of the volume's papers, and (c) to discuss recurring themes in the articles. Social scientists have become increasingly self-conscious concerning their research and teaching in the field of race and ethnic relations. A growing literature has reported problems and pitfalls of conducting social research among minorities. Montero points out that contributors are themselves group members and identifies the following themes in the articles. (1) In order to study a minority community, it is fruitful and necessary to gain their acceptance. (2) Researchers should seek to formulate theoretical propositions regarding minority populations. (3) Field research methods can be extremely helpful in studying minority groups. (4) Surveys, including interviews, can be useful; however, researchers must be aware of potential problems of reliability and validity. (5) Ethical, political, and ideological concerns frequently create problems.

MONTGOMERY, Roger. Notes On Instant Urban Renewal. *Trans–Act* 4,9–13 S 1967.

MONTI, D J. Patterns Of Conflict Preceding The 1964 Riots: Harlem And Bedford—Stuyvesant. *J Conflic Res* 23(1),41–69 1979.

MOORE JR, Howard. Does Justice Have A Color: Law: Is It A Skin Game. *N Car Cent L J* 5,2–14 Fall 1973.

MOORE JR, Howard. Racism As Justice. *Black L J* 3(1),54–66 Spr 1973.

MOORE JR, William. The Vertical Ghetto: Everyday Life In An Urban Project. NY Random House 1969.

MOORE, A. Black Judges, Police—But Few Prosecutors. *Phila Inquirer* , Jl 21 1974.

MOORE, Herman E. The Virgin Islands And Its Judicial System. *Nat Bar J* 3(4),349–360 1945.

MOORE, Joan et al. Homeboys: Gangs, Drugs, And Prison In The Barrios Of Los Angeles. Philadelphia Temple Univ Pr 1978.

Gang activity in Los Angeles barrios is considered in the context of the Chicano experience in California. The historical development and operation of Chicano gangs, with particular reference to three gangs, is discussed in relation to the tripartite economic structure (primary labor market, welfare economy, and illegal economy) of the urban barrio and to the impact of Anglo institutions on barrio life. Particular attention is paid to the intricate association between gangs and narcotics. The Chicano experience in prison is discussed in some depth. Perceptions of crime and attitudes toward crime in the barrio are discussed in a chapter which contrasts "square" and "deviant" attitudes. Finally, a "policy for the barrios" is suggested, which takes cognizance of three major factors

responsible for continuities of life in the barrios: barrio ethnic cohesiveness, traditions and emphases; institutional experiences at the barrio societal levels; and the tripartite economy and opportunity structure.

MOORE, Joan W. Mexican Americans, With Alfredo Cuellar. Englewood Cliffs NJ Prentice—Hall 1970.

MOORE, Joan W. Mexican Americans: Problems And Prospects. Madison Univ Wisc Inst RP 1966.

MOORE, Joan W. A Case Study Of Collaboration: The Chicano Pinto Research Project. *J Soc Issues* 33(4),144–158 1977,

MOORE, Joan W and Guzman, Ralph C and Grebler, Leo. *The Mexican—American People: The Nation's Second Largest Minority*. NY Free Pr 1970.

MOORE, Joan W. Colonialism: The Case Of The Mexican—Americans. *Social Prob* 17,463–472 1970.

"Colonialism" has been increasingly used by minority ideologies to account for their situation in the US. Adapting the concept for social sciences involves serious conceptual analysis. This is an attempt to specify the concept in the case of Mexican Americans, with political particpation on the elite and on the mass level illustrating the varieties of internal colonialism to which this population has been subjected. Three "culture areas" are delineated: New Mexico, with "classic colonialism"; Texas, with "conflict colonialism"; and California with "economic colonialism." Ecology of settlement; historical discontinuities; and proportions of voluntary—immigrant as compared with charter—member descendants in the minority are among the factors distinguishing the three types. The Chicano militant ideology incorporates symbols which attempt to transcend these regional differences.

MOORE, Joan W. LUCHA In Agencyland: A Chicano Self—Help Organization Meets The Establishment. *Growth Chan* 3,43–50 1972.

MOORE, Joan W. Social Constraints On Sociological Knowledge: Academics And Research Concerning Minorities. *Social Prob* 21,65–77 1973.

MOORE, L M and Schwartz, J A. Minority Employment In Police Services—A Management Analysis For Police Departments. *Western City* ,13–14 N 1976.

Minority recruitment, selection, retention, and promotion problems are discussed, along with the legal issues involved. Management recommendations are offered in dealing with the situation. Historical discrimination, lack of adequate information, limited resources, and massive and sometimes confusing laws are cited as problems with which the administrator must deal in seeking to increase minority employment. Recommendations for management action are as follows: give priority rating to minority employment; assign the police department rather than the city personnel department to the responsibility of minority employment; conduct a thorough assessment of the problem which should lead to specific short—term and long—term plans; provide training for administrative personnel and line officers which will facilitate their support and leadership in minority employment; and police personnel policies and practices regarding hiring and promotion should be made more flexible.*

MOORE, Loring B. Due Process Of Law In Race Cases. *Nat Bar J* 2(3),240–262 1944.

MOORE, Wilbert E. Slave Law And The Social Structure. *J Negro Hist* 26,171–202 Ap 1941.

MOORE, Winston E. My Cure For Prison Riots: End Prison Racism. *Ebony* 27,86+ D 1971.

MOQUIN, W E and Van Doren, C and Rivera, F. *A Documentary History Of The Mexican Americans*. NY Bantam 1971.

MORA, Magdalena and Del Castillo, Adelaida (ed). *Mexican Women In The United States: Struggles Past And Present*. Los Angeles U CA Chicano Stud 1980.

MORALES, Armando. *A Study Of Mexican—American Perceptions Of Law Enforcement Policies And Practices In East Los Angeles*. Unpub DSW Diss Univ of S Calif 1972.

A study was made of Mexican—American perceptions of selected law enforcement policies and practices in East Los Angeles, which witnessed eight riots during 1970–71. Interviews were conducted by college students having bilingual and bicultural capabilities regarding residents' experience of or knowledge of conflict with law enforcement agencies in the East Los Angeles area. It was found that: (1) over half of the Mexican—American respondents believed that the various unpopular forms of law enforcement practices were happening in their area, had observed them, or had known someone to whom they happened; (2) slightly less than 45% had actually experienced these practices. The findings are interpreted as a general complaint of the community against law enforcement practices. The critical perceptions of this behavior were related to the general lack of explicit, precise, official departmental written policies and guidelines. This had the effect of granting the officer in the field the responsibility of applying a general rule of thumb approach in his community work. Further explorations are recommended to determine other dynamics that contribute to these tensions.

MORALES, Armando. *Ando Sangrando (I Am Bleeding): A Study Of Mexican American - Police Conflict.* La Puente CA Perspective Pubs 1972.

MORALES, Armando. *Criminal Injustice From The Chicano Point Of View.* Fairlawn R E Burdick 1972.
A series of cases of police brutality are presented from the Chicano point of view as a basis for an analysis of criminal injustice. The core of the monograph is the idea that police force comes from outside minority communities and thus subjugates rather than protects the victims of a society that remains unequal in terms of economic and political powers. Anti–Chicano brutality and exploitation are traced from 1853 to shatter the stereotype of the Chicano who does not try to protect either himself or his legal rights. Allport's five–point scale of prejudice is used to highlight the suffering of Chicanos under the penal system in the US Riots in Los Angeles in 1970 and throughout the Southwest are examined (with 46 photographs) as a reasonable response to the system.

MORALES, Armando. "Police Deployment Theories And The Mexican–American Community" in *The Urban Policeman In Transition*, Snibbe, J (ed), 341–353. Springfield IL Chas C Thomas 1973.
Literature regarding theories of police patrol development, with emphasis on ethnic minority communities, is reviewed. A case involving a Mexican–American community within the jurisdiction of the Los Angeles Police Department is discussed. Police deployment is heaviest in minority sections based on the belief that racial minority groups commit more crime. Deployment is based on the number of officers needed to perform three types of tasks: incidents requiring police action reported by a victim or witness, inspectional services, and routine preventive patrol. Even though there is a higher incidence of crime in the middle–class Anglo–Saxon community, as revealed by statistics from one Los Angeles community, there are more policemen deployed in the poorer minority communities. It also appears that larger numbers of arrests in these communities for such violations as drunkeness are due to the greater over representation of police in the area, rather than the fact that there are actually more occurrences than in more affluent communities. More comprehensive planning on the part of police administrators is required regarding deployment.

MORALES, Armando. Institutional Racism In Mental Health And Criminal Justice. *Soc Casework* 59(7),387–395 1978.

MORAN, Patricia Anne. *The Effect Of Father Absence On Delinquent Males: Dependency And Hypermasculinity.* Unpub PhD Diss St Louis Univ 1972.
The effects of father–absence on the delinquent adolescent was studied through the hypothesis that such subjects would have a greater covert feminine identification, and that their overt masculine interest patterns would exceed a father–present group. Further hypotheses were: 1) father–absent delinquents would be more field–dependent and would equal or exceed the father–present group on measures of overt masculinity; 2) Negro delinquents would be more field–dependent than white delinquents. 40 delinquent subjects were divided into four groups based on father–presence or father–absence and race. Statistical analysis of the results showed father–absent delinquents being more field–dependent than the father–present group, and the father–absent subjects expressing overtly more masculine interest patterns. Unlike the findings of the previous research, the Negro delinquents were not significantly more field–dependent than whites. Discussion of the findings centers upon the overcompensating hypermasculinity developed among delinquents, possibly as a result of a basic feminine identification.

MORGAN JR, Charles. "Segregated Justice" in *Race, Crime, And Justice*, Reasons, Charles E And Jack Kuykendall (eds), 277–283. Pacific Palisades CA Goodyear 1972.

MORGAN, Robin (ed). *Sisterhood Is Powerful: An Anthology Of Writings From The Women's Liberation Movement.* NY Random House 1970.

MORGAN, T B. Real West Side Story, Life Of Jose Rivera. *Look* F 6 1960 F 15 1960.

MORGAN, W R and Clark, T N. The Causes Of Racial Disorders: A Grievance–Level Explanation. *Am Sociol Rev* 38(5),611–624 1973.

MORGENBESSER, Leonard. *Profile Of Puerto Rican Inmates Under Departmental Custody.* Albany NY Dept Corrections 1977.

MORMINO, Susan C. Exploring Racial Prejudice On Voir Dire: Constitutional Requirements And Policy Considerations. *Boston U L Rev* 54(2),394–424 1974.

MORRIS, Frank L. "Black Political Consciousness In Northern State Prisons" in *Potential For Reform Of Criminal Justice*, Jacob, Herbert (ed). Beverly Hills CA Sage 1974.

MORRIS, Jeffrey B Et Al. Notes Toward An Epidemiology Of Urban Suicide. *Compreh Psychi* 15(6),537–547 1974.
An investigation designed to apply epidemiological tools and concepts to illuminate factors involved in the pathogenesis of suicide, and to provide clues for its prevention is discussed. A series of clinical psychological variables including reports of interpersonal stress, depression, alcoholism, addiction, and a behavioral measure of suicidal intent are analyzed, including information regarding traditional epidemiological factors. Findings indicate that young black males, as well as divorced persons of both sexes, represent established high–risk population subgroups. In contrast to reports of high suicide rates among the elderly, no evidence is found of a direct linear increase in suicide risk with increasing age. It is suggested that an overall increase in suicide by drug overdose, and in particular the use of prescription drugs, suggests the need for public health legislation to require the inclusion of an emetic or some other agent as a deterrent to overdose in the widely prescribed psychotherapeutic drugs.

MORRIS, Norval (ed) and Tonry, Michael (ed). *Crime And Justice: An Annual Review Of Research*, V1. Chicago Univ Chicago Pr 1979.

MORRIS, R T and Jefferies, Vincent and Turner, R H. The Public Perception Of The Watts Riot As Social Protest. *Am Sociol Rev* 36(3),443–451 1971.

MORRIS, Terrence. *The Criminal Area.* London Routledge & Kegan 1958.

MORTON, Carol. Black Cops: Black And Blue Ain't White. *Ramparts* 10,21–25 My 1972.
Morton reports on the new breed of black cops that has emerged over the past few years. While they don't fit into the convenient categories of "militant" or "leftist," Morton asserts they have become acutely aware of their blackness, are no longer straddling the fence, and are firmly aligning themselves with the interests of the black community. Discrepancies between population and police force representation remain, however, and Morton asserts that such discrepancies are "clear evidence of what we already know—on historic exclusion of blacks, unequal hiring procedures, half–hearted recruitment attempts in minority neighborhoods, and the traditional disenchantment of the black community with city police departments. In other words, racism and its consequences."

MORTON, Ted. Benefits From A Police Community Relations Program: What Can I Do, How Can I Help? *Pol Chief* 39(7),36–37 1972.
A police community relations program established in a Los Angeles ghetto is described. The neighborhood is composed of a black majority and a Spanish–speaking minority. Businesses were encouraged to remain in the neighborhood through the establishment of an association which offered tax deductibility for contributions. These funds were used to develop programs to induce more favorable attitudes toward policemen. These included athletic leagues, summer cinema program, school programs, Spanish language programs, model airplane building, grooming, and employment preparation. The success of the program can be seen in the changed attitudes of both the residents and the police and the greater cooperation between the two.

MOSBY, Thomas Speed. *Causes And Cures Of Crime.* St Louis C V Mosby 1913.

MOSCOW, Alvin. *Merchants Of Heroin.* NY Dial Pr 1968.

MOSES, Earl R. "Negro And White Crime Rates," in *The Sociology Of Crime And Delinquency*, 2nd Ed, Wolfgang, M et al (ed), 430–439. NY Wiley 1970.

MOSES, Earl R. Community Factors In Negro Delinquency. *J Negro Ed* 5(2),220–227 1936.
Moses notes that "it seems safe to assume that the problem of delinquency among Negroes in Chicago is not a problem of race but is more intimately

bound up with settlement in areas of deterioration where delinquent patterns prevail, and the deteriorated character of areas to which Negroes are primarily restricted."

MOSES, Earl R. Delinquency In The Negro Community. *Opport* 2,304–307 1933.

MOSES, Earl R. Differentials In Crime Rates Between Negroes And Whites, Based On Comparisons Of Four Socio–Economically Equated Areas. *Am Sociol Rev* 12,411–420 1947.

Moses attempts to correct what he considers a major problem in most studies comparing black and white crime rates. Past studies have failed to take into account socioeconomic positions of the groups compared. Moses compares crime rates for four contiguous, socio–economically equated areas, two black and two white, in Baltimore. Moses found that wide differentials in crime rate exist even when contiguous areas are equated socio–economically, i.e., black rates tend to be much higher. Types of offenses committed were also influenced by the racial factor, i.e., blacks were more prone to offenses against the person than were their white counterparts. All murder and manslaughter offenses in these contiguous areas were committed by blacks. Data on conviction rates revealed no reason to expect that blacks were more readily convicted than whites, thus ruling out an element of policy which could have influenced crime rates. Moses suggests certain social conditions in black areas out of which arise elements conducive to greater criminality.

MOSHER, L R. Father Absence And Antisocial Behavior In Negro And White Males. *Act Paedops* 36(6–7),186–202 1969.

MOSKOS, Charles. The American Dilemma In Uniform: Race In The Armed Forces. *Ann Am Poli* 406,44–106 1973.

MOTLEY, Constance Baker. "The Legal Status Of The Negro In The United States" in *The American Negro Reference Book*, Davis, John P (ed), 404–521. Englewood Cliffs NJ Prentice–Hall 1966.

MOTLEY, Constance Baker. 'Law And Order' And The Criminal Justice System. *J Crim L & Crim* 64,259–269 1973.

MOTOWIDLO, S J and Dunnette, M D. *Police Selection And Career Assessment.* Minneapolis Personnel Decision 1975.

The major objective of this research program was to develop new methods for evaluating persons who apply for positions in police work and for assessing the potential of present police officers being considered for promotion. In order to accomplish this, critical features of four different police jobs were determined. These jobs were general patrol officer, investigator/detective, patrol sergeant, and intermediate command. The means by which these critical features and other information such as job performance ratings were utilized to develop and validate two personnel evaluation instruments are described in detail.*

MOUDELOS, Joseph C. "Political Crime And The Negro Revolution" in *Criminal Behavior Systems*, Clinard, Marshall B And Richard Quinney (eds). NY Holt Rinehart Wins 1967.

Mouledous considers political crime as having two dimensions: (1) actions directed against the state, and (2) conduct derived from unlawful state power. He views nonviolent civil disobedience against unlawful Southern policies as a legitimate activity.

MOULDS, E F. Chivalry And Paternalism—Disparities Of Treatment In The Criminal Justice System. *West Pol Q* 31(3),415–430 S 1978.

The two groups most depicted in the literature on equality of treatment by law as victims of potential and actual discriminatory treatment have been racial minorities and the poor. The explanation generally offered for the preferential treatment of women is that it is a result of chivalry. It is hypothesized that less harsh handling of female defendants, as opposed to male defendants, does take place and that this differential treatment can be described accurately as a form of paternalism. Two particular areas, however, in the treatment of females appear to deviate from the norm of gentleness. The first area is that of special indeterminate sentencing statutes for women in states that sentence men to determinate and shorter sentences for the same crime. The second area involves stricter supervision by the system of young women than of young men. The findings of an empirical analysis of disparate treatment show that women receive more gentle treatment, and such treatment is not related to race, type of crime, or prior record. What the data from the empirical analysis do not show is why differential treatment exists.*

MOUTARE, A and Boone, S L. Tests Of The Language–Aggression Hypothesis. *Psychol Rep* 39(3),851–857 1976.

This study tested the hypothesis that language is related to aggression in

two ways: that relatively low levels of proficiency in the use of language should be associated with relatively high levels of observable aggression and that high levels of language proficiency should be associated with low levels of aggression. The vocabulary subset of the Wechsler Intelligence Scale for Children, the Metropolitan Achievement Test in Reading, the total number of words spoken durng a free speech session, and the number of different words used during that session constituted the language measures. Aggression of 132 subjects, ranging in age from 9 to 13 years, was measured using an adaptation of the physical and verbal aggression categories used by Walters, Pearce, and Dahms. The results supported both predictions for the comparisons between black subjects and Puerto Rican subjects but not for the white subjects.

MOYER, Kenneth. "What Is The Potential For Biological Violence Control" in *Biology And Crime*, Jeffrey, C Ray (ed). Beverly Hills CA Sage 1979.

MOYNIHAN, Daniel P and Glazer, Nathan. *Beyond The Melting Pot: The Negroes, Puerto Ricans, Jews, Italians, And Irish Of New York City*. Cambridge MA MIT Pr 1963.

MOYNIHAN, Daniel Patrick (ed) and Glazer, Nathan (ed). *Ethnicity: Theory And Experience*. Cambridge MA Harvard Univ Pr 1975.

MOYNIHAN, Daniel Patrick. *The Negro Family: The Case For National Action*. Washington DC US Dept Labor 1965.

Disproportionate rates of crime and delinquency among black Americans are attributed to the matriarchal structure into which the black community in the US has essentially been forced by centuries of mistreatment. This matriarchal structure, "because it is so out of line with the rest of the American society, seriously retards the progress of the group as a whole, and imposes a crushing burden on the Negro male and, in consequence, on a great many Negro women as well." He adds: "The combined impact of poverty, failure, and isolation among Negro youth has had the predictable outcome in a disasterous delinquency and crime rate."

MULLIN, Courtney J and Frederick, Jeffrey and Mc Conahay, John B. The Uses Of Social Science In Trials With Political And Racial Overtones: The Trial Of Joan Little. *Law & Contemp Prob* 41(1),205–229 Wint 1977.

MULLIN, Gerald W. *Flight And Rebellion: Slave Resistance In Eighteenth Century Virginia*. NY Oxford Univ Pr 1972.

MULVIHILL, D J et al. *Crimes Of Violence (Violence Commission Report, Volume 11)*. Washington DC USGPO 1968.

MUNOS, C and Ornelasin, C and Berrera, M. "The Barrio As An Internal Colony," in *Urban Affairs Annual Review*, V6, Hahn, Harlan (ed), 465–498. Beverly Hills CA Sage 1972.

MUNOZ, Mona. *Job Satisfaction In Policemen And Its Relation To Locus Of Control, Ego Strength And Performance*. Unpub PhD Diss City Univ of NY 1973.

Job satisfaction in policemen and its relation to locus of control, ego strength, and performance was investigated, testing four hypotheses predicting a positive relationship between: (1) work satisfaction and internal locus of control; (2) work satisfaction and ego strength; (3) internal locus of control and ego strength; and (4) work satisfaction and indices of performance. Subjects were Negro, white, and Puerto Rican patrolmen from the NY Housing Authority, and instruments included the Job Description Index, the Internal–External Locus of Control Scale, the Barron Ego Scale, and a background questionnaire. Patrolmen were very dissatisfied with their work when compared with a stratified sample of workers, possibly because of societal ambivalence concerning exercise of control over citizens, inadequate training in complex interpersonal crisis management, and dislike of service functions. Hypotheses one, two, and part of hypothesis four were supported.

MUNTU, Maharibi (Larry M West) and Kasirika, Kaidi (Kenneth Divans). Prison Or Slavery. *Black Scholar* 3(2),6–12 O 1971.

MURCHISON, Carl. American White Criminal Intelligence. *J Am Inst Cr L Crim* 15(3),435–494 1924.

MURCHISON, Carl. American White Criminal Intelligence. *J Am Inst Cr L Crim* 15(2),239–316 1924.

MURILLO, Nathan. "Mexican–American Family" in *Chicanos: Social And Psychological Perspectives*. St Louis C V Mosby 1976.

MURO, D P. *Police Careers For Women*. NY Simon & Schuster 1979.

This volume introduces law enforcement as a viable career choice for women, providing illustrations of police work and generalizations about the role of police in society.*

MURPHY, Suzanne. A Year With The Gangs Of East Los Angeles. *Ms* ,56–60 Jl 1978.

MURPHY, W and Cohen, J. *Burn, Baby, Burn*. NY Avon 1967.

MURTON, Tom. *Accomplices To The Crime*. NY Grove Pr 1969.

MUSTO, David F. *Origins Of Narcotic Control*. New Haven CT Yale Univ Pr 1973.

MYERS JR, S L. "Incidence Or Justice" in *Costs Of Crime*, Gray, C M (ed). Beverly Hills CA Sage 1979.

Blacks are overrepresented among the arrested, convicted, incarcerated, and those labeled criminals. Accounting for only one–tenth of the 1967 US population, they accounted for almost three–quarters of all arrests. Three types of explanations for this disparity have been advanced. Some economists argue that disparities in legitimate opportunities explain higher crime rates among blacks. A second explanation is based on alleged disparities in the criminal justice system. Although racial discrimination may exist, this discrimination does not explain why blacks have higher crime rates. The third class of explanations for disparity asserts simply that blacks have different tastes or preferences from the rest of the population. Although these explanations are not mutually exclusive or exhaustive, they are not empirically refutable. The disagreement over whether blacks bear an excessive burden of offender costs of crime depends ultimately on whether the distribution of costs is fair. Moreover, the differing incidence of justice arising from alternative notions of fairness can have significant implications for the economic efficiency of the criminal justice system.*

MYERS, J K and London, N J. Young Offenders: Psychopathology And Social Factors. *Arch Gen Psychiatry* 4(3),274–282 1961.

MYERS, Vincent. Survey Methods For Minority Populations. *J Soc Issues* 33(4),11–19 1977.

MYRDAL, Gunnar. "Crime" in *An American Dilemma: The Negro Problem And Modern Democracy*, 966–979. NY Harper & Row 1944.

Statistics on black crime have not only all the weaknesses of crime statistics generally...but also special weaknesses due to the caste situation and to certain characteristics of the Negro population. Thus, black crime rates are artificially inflated by the disproportionate representation of blacks in the types of crimes which more frequently result in apprehension and punishment and in age and nativity groups more often involved in crime. Unequal justice reduces the comparability of white and black crime rates. Poverty and ignorance of legal rights reduce the chances for blacks to influence the outcome of legal troubles. A final group of causes of black crime is connected with the slavery tradition and the caste situation. Expectations that blacks will supplement their wages by petty pilfering, desire for revenge for discriminatory and insulting treatment and hostility toward the law as a result of being excluded from white society and its lawmaking processes serve to encourage high rates of black crime.

NAGASAWA, Richard H and Chambliss, William J. On The Validity Of Official Statistics—A Comparative Study Of White, Black And Japanese High School Boys. *J Res Crim Del* 6(1),71–77 1969.

Analysis of official and unofficial self–report delinquency rates of black, white, and Japanese youths in a large metropolitan area produced the conclusion that official statistics are so misleading that they are virtually useless as indicators of actual deviance in the population. It is suggested that the visibility of the offenses, the bias of the policing agencies, and the demeanor of the youth account for the rate and distribution of delinquency among the three groups and that official rates are a complete distortion of the actual incidence. Self–report rates did not differ significantly for the three groups.

NAGEL, Jack H. *Crime And Incarceration; A Reanalysis*. Philadelphia U of Penn P & U P 1977.

A methodological critique and reanalysis of William G Nagel's data "On Behalf of a Moratorium on Prison Construction" is presented in this study by his son. This analysis indicate that: heavy reliance incarceration fails to reduce crime; high unemployment but not poverty per se tends to result in higher crime rates; urbanized states are likely to have more crime than rural states; prison construction and utilization are unaffected cross states by relative crime rates; and percentage black population does not affect crime rates but does affect incarceration rates. Preliminary least–squares regression indicates that the causal pattern for property crimes may differ from that for violent crimes (urbanization and unemployment rate affect violent crime less than property crime) and that states with large black populations have more violent crime but not more property crime. Results

suggest that reducing unemployment might be an effective means for reducing crime.*

NAGEL, Stuart. "The Tipped Scales Of American Justice" in *Law And Order: The Scales Of Justice*, Blumberg, Abraham S (ed), 47–66. NY Aldine 1970.

NAGEL, Stuart and Neef, Marian. Racial Disparities That Supposedly Do Not Exist: Some Pitfalls In Analysis Of Court Records. *Notre Dame Law* 52,87–94 1976.

NAGEL, Stuart and Weitzman, Leonard J. Double Standard Of American Justice. *Society* 9(5),18–25 1972.

NAGEL, Stuart. Bringing The Values Of Jurors In Line With The Law. *Judicature* 63(10),189–195 1979.

Results of a jury decisionmaking study suggest that an individual juror's propensity to convict is greater than the propensity to acquit, particularly when the case involves harm to the victim. Interviews with 300 subjects provided data for analysis of juror propensity to convict or acquit and of the differences in those propensities across types of jurors are willing to convict when they perceive defendant's probability of guilt to be only .55.*

NAGEL, Stuart. Disparities In Criminal Procedures. *UCLA L Rev* 14(5),1272–1305 1967.

NAGEL, Thomas. Commentary On The Philosophy Of Equality. *Wash U L Q* 1979(1),25–32 Wint 1979.

NAGEL, William G. *The New Red Barn: A Critical Look At The Modern American Prison*. NY Walker & Co 1973.

NAGEL, William G. On Behalf Of A Moratorium On Prison Construction. *Crim Delinq* 23(2),154–172 Ap 1977.

The author (a former prison administrator), compared crime rates from the 15 states that built the most new prison cells from 1955 to 1975 with those in the 15 states that did the least prison construction over the same period. He found that crime rose 167 percent in the high–construction states and 145 percent in low–construction states. While this analysis is rather elementary, it nonetheless stands as a rebuttal of the assumption that prison construction deters crime. The greater part of Nagel's paper consisted of a cross–sectional analysis of all 50 states using a large number of variables; a number of methodological weaknesses are apparent. These include: (1) the use of graphical scatterplots of states' ranking on two variables, which is open to subjective interpretation and gives ordinal measures weaker than the original data from which they were derived; (2) bivariate analysis, which may provide misleading associations as a result of effects of unincluded variables; and (3) an indirect rather than direct relationship between crime and incarceration rates. His analysis ignored two causal relationships—higher crime rates result in more people being jailed but imprisoning more criminals prevents crime.*

NAGIN, Daniel S and Blumstein, Alfred. Analysis Of Arrest Rates For Trends In Criminality. *Socio– Econ Plan Sci* 9,221–227 1975.

NAGIN, Daniel S and Blumstein, Alfred and Cohen, Jacqueline. The Dynamics Of A Homeostatic Punishment Process. *J Crim L & Crimin* 67(4),317–334 1976.

NAGIN, Daniel. Crime Rates, Sanction Levels, And Constraints On Prison Population. *Law & Soc Rev* 12,341–366 Spr 1978.

NAIL, R L and Gunderson, E K E and Arthur, R J. Black–White Differences In Social Background And Military Drug Abuse Patterns. *Am J Psychiatry* 131(10),1097–1102 1974.

NAPPER, George. "Perception Of Crime" in *Black Perspectives On Crime And The Criminal Justice System*, Woodson, Robert L (ed), 5–22. Boston G K Hall 1977.

NASH, A E Keir. A More Equitable Past: Southern Supreme Courts And The Protection Of The Ante–Bellum Negro. *No Car L Rev* 48,197–242 1970.

NASH, A E Keir. Fairness And Formalism In The Trials Of Blacks In The State Supreme Courts Of The Old South. *Va L Rev* 56(1),64–101 F 1970.

NASH, A E Keir. The Texas Supreme Court And The Trial Rights Of Blacks. *J Am Hist* 58,622–642 1971.

NASH, Gary B. The Image Of The Indian In The Southern Colonial Mind. *Wm & Mary Q* 29,197–230 1972.

NASSI, A J and Abramowitz, S I. From Phrenology To Psychosurgery And Back Again: Biological Studies In Criminality. *Am J Orthopsych* 46,591–607 O 1976.

NATIONAL ADVISORY COMMISSION ON CIVIL DISORDERS. "The Police And The Community" in *Police–Community Relationships*, Bopp, W (ed), 133–143. Springfield IL Chas C Thomas 1972.

Findings of the National Advisory Commission on Civil Disorders regarding hostile relations between the police and the community, particularly in the urban black ghetto, are briefly reported. Five basic problem areas are cited: (1) the need for change in police operations in the ghetto to ensure proper individual conduct and to eliminate abrasive and discriminative practices; (2) the need for more adequate police protection of minority residents so as to eliminate their high sense of insecurity; (3) the need for effective mechanisms through which the citizen can have his grievances handled; (4) the need for policy guidelines to assist police in areas where police conduct can create tension; and (5) the need to develop community support for law enforcement. Recommendations are made for specific action in each of these areas.

NATIONAL ADVISORY COMMISSION ON CRIM JUSTICE STANDARDS & GOALS. *Corrections.* Washington DC US Dept Justice 1973.

NATIONAL ADVISORY COMMISSION ON CRIM JUSTICE STANDARDS & GOALS. *Police.* Washington DC US Dept Justice 1973.

Suggestions for overall improvement in delivery of police services for greater protection against crime. Suggestions for more effective utilization of manpower include continued consolidation, stricter personnel requirements, increased employee benefits, and the employment of more women, minorities, and civilians in police work.*

NATIONAL AMERICAN INDIAN COURT JUDGES ASSOC. *Criminal Court Procedures Manual: A Guide For American Indian Court Judges.* Washington DC NILECJ n.d.

NATIONAL AMERICAN INDIAN COURT JUDGES ASSOC. *Justice And The American Indian, V2.* Washington DC LEAA 1974.

NATIONAL CIVIL SERVICE LEAGUE. *Institutes On Affirmative Action Leadership Development In Correctional Institutions: Final Report.* Washington DC N I X 1977.

Examines the attempts that have been made by administrators in the state prisons to employ affirmative action guidelines. The study helped to provide information to correctional adminstrators about the relevant law and regulations on affirmative action, and to help them understand LEAA's affirmative action guidelines. It also was designed to enhance managers' abilities to plan, implement, measure, and direct affirmative action, as well as to monitor changes in systems with respect to racial balance in work forces and nondiscrimination within the service population. In terms of results, the study found that no adult state system had attained the goal of having an ethnic distribution of its correctional work force stand in a 70 percent ratio to the ethnic distribution of the inmate population, and that most had a long way to go.*

NATIONAL COMMISSION ON THE CAUSES AND PREVENTION OF VIOLENCE. *Violent Crime: Homicide, Assault, Rape And Robbery.* NY Braziller 1969.

NATIONAL CONFERENCE OF CHRISTIANS AND JEWS. *Justice System Interpreter Certification: Task Force Report.* NY Nat Con Chr & Jews n.d.

NATIONAL CONGRESS OF AMERICAN INDIANS. *Problem Areas In The Operation Of Tribal Police Programs.* Washington DC NCJRS 1978.

This study by the National Congress of American Indians, surveys salaries, training, duties, political problems arising from the peculiar status of the American Indian reservations, and problems arising from relationships with community police off the reservation. Several professional recommendations are made, including better salaries, better fringe benefits, better training and more training opportunities, and councils and boards to handle community and tribal relations. Adminstrative/personnel recommendations are made. These include job qualifications and standards, grievance procedures, hiring practices, and public relations. A chart gives a wage/education level/job description profile for police officers on the eight reservations visited. Other charts summarize education and specialized training offered, community attitudes, and police morale. A detailed explanation of the status of American Indian reservations under United States law is given. Appendices give organizations and agencies contacted, a list of state planning agencies, and studies from the Bureau of Indian Affairs.*

NATIONAL COUNCIL ON CRIME AND DELINQUENCY. *Characteristics Of The Parole Population–1978.* Hackensack NJ NCCD 1980.

Part of the Uniform Parole Reports series, this report contains discussion and statistics on the characteristics of the adult parole population in the United States as of December 1978. The report is divided into five sections. The first four sections cover parolees who entered parole supervision in 1977 in terms of the following variables: (1) national profile according to sex, age, race/ethnicity, education, time served in prison, commitment offense, known prior prison commitments, type of admissions, etc.; (2) time served in prison according to sex, age, race/ethnicity, commitment offense, and known prior prison commitments; (3) 1–year parole status according to sex, age, race/ethnicity, commitment offense, known prior prison commitments, type of admission, and time served in prison; and (4) new convictions according to commitment offense. The fifth section is devoted to longer–term trends in parole status and covers persons entering parole supervision in 1975, 1976, and 1977. Data sources and tables are presented in the appendixes.*

NATIONAL COUNCIL ON CRIME AND DELINQUENCY. *Peaceful Resolution Of Prison Conflict.* Hackensack NJ NCCD 1973.

NATIONAL COUNCIL ON CRIME AND DELINQUENCY. Women In Criminal Justice—A Policy Statement. *Crim Delinq* 22(1),1–2 1976.

Prescriptions for the more effective utilization of women in every branch of the criminal justice system are presented by the Board of Directors of the National Council on Crime and Delinquency (NCCD).*

NATIONAL CRIMINAL JUSTICE REFERENCE SERVICE. *General Recruitment Strategies For Criminal Justice Agencies.* Washington DC USGPO 1979.

Federal equal employment opportunity guidelines are noted, and suggestions to effectively bring women and minorities into the criminal justice system are discussed in this pamphlet. Eight federal laws and executive orders requiring equal employment opportunity in criminal justice agencies are summarized. Agencies are encouraged to remove artificial barriers to women and minority job applicants and to implement job analysis, redefine job specifications, and flexible, innovative work scheduling to broaden the range of potential employees.*

NATIONAL CRIMINAL JUSTICE REFERENCE SERVICE. *Public Information Materials For Language Minorities.* Washington DC USGPO n.d.

NATIONAL DISTRICT ATTORNEY'S ASSOCIATION. *Guidelines For Prosecuting Criminal Cases During Civil Disorders.* Chicago Nat Dis Attys A 1968.

NATIONAL INSTITUTE OF MENTAL HEALTH. *Bibliography On Racism: 1972–1975, V2.* Washington DC US Dept HEW 1978.

NATIONAL INSTITUTE OF MENTAL HEALTH. *Division Of Special Mental Health Programs: Program Statement 1978–1979.* Washington DC USGPo 1978.

NATIONAL INSTITUTE ON ALCOHOL ABUSE AND ALCOHOLISM. *National Directory Of Drug Abuse And Alcoholism Treatment Programs.* Washington DC US Dept HEW 1979.

NATIONAL MINORITY ADVISORY COUNCIL ON CRIM JUST. *The Inequality Of Justice: A Report On Crime And The Administration Of Justice In The Minority Coummunity.* Washington DC US Dept Justice 1980.

NATIONAL URBAN LEAGUE, Inc. *A Review Of The Law Enforcement Assistance Administration's Relationship To The Black Community.* NY Nat Urb League 1976.

This report charges that LEAA's hiring policy is discriminatory toward blacks, and that LEAA has not involved blacks in cutting crime. This review is based on testimony by the National Urban League at a Congressional subcommittee hearing in March 1976. It mentions the high crime rate in the black community to indicate that innocent blacks are often the victims of black crime. However, the report claims, police agencies and the LEAA have often been unmindful of this. Not only has the LEAA been lax in creating crime prevention programs that involve the black community, but, the report says, LEAA has not promoted blacks to upper management and policy–making positions. The urban league asserts that if funding for law enforcement programs is not to be seen as anti–black in character, LEAA will have to take a more affirmative effort to involve blacks.*

NATIONAL URBAN LEAGUE, Inc. *Project LEMMP (Law Enforcement Minority Manpower Project)—Final Report.* NY Nat Urb League 1974. Final report on a project to stimulate the hiring of minority employees by law enforcement agencies in Sacramento (CA), Little Rock (AK), and Springfield (mA). The project involved screening a film on the LEMMP project to interested agencies and preparing candidates to take the entrance examination through tutoring. Reports from the three cities indicate that 3,665 minority men and women were successfully interviewed. Of these, 87 were placed with police departments, 141 with law enforcement related agencies, and 119 with unrelated agencies.*

NATIONAL URBAN LEAGUE, Inc. *Racial Conflict: Lessons Of The Detroit Riot.* NY Nat Urb League 1943.

NATIONAL URBAN LEAGUE, Inc. *State Of Black America, 1977.* NY Nat Urb League 1977.

The status of black Americans is assessed, with reference to a survey conducted by the National Urban League among its 107 affiliates. The survey questionnaire asked the executive directors of the affiliates to rank the major problems facing black communities and to comment on the mood of these communities. In order of priority, the major concerns cited were employment, housing, education, health and social welfare, politics and community planning, and public safety and crime. Many respondents called for crime prevention and control efforts, particularly in areas of drug abuse and crimes committed by blacks against blacks. The need for better police protection in black communities and for speedier trials was cited. Concern was expressed that many law enforcement officials were anti-black. Other crime-related problems cited included the disproportionate number of blacks in prisons and unequal treatment in the court system. The report summarizes the survey findings and then discusses the status of black Americans with regard to the problem areas identified in the survey. Recommendations are presented relative to the economy, employment, education, housing, health, social welfare, and crime.*

NATIONAL URBAN LEAGUE, Inc. *Strategies For Controlling Crime—A Position Paper.* NY Nat Urb League 1978.

To make any meaningful reduction in crime rates, the federal government must work toward reducing the social and economic conditions underlying this crime. It must deviate from its traditional reliance solely on the criminal justice system as a means of crime control. Areas which should be attacked include: (1) making all levels of the federal government aware of the impact of federal policies on crime-related social conditions; (2) reducing unemployment, which is strongly correlated with crime rates; (3) providing adequate and decent housing, thus reducing population density which is associated with crime; (4) revitalizing the cities; (5) promoting black economic development; (6) improving health care; (7) providing adequate drug treatment and enforcement; (8) instituting handgun control to eliminate accidental as well as intentional shootings; (9) reducing television violence; (10) improving education; (11) increasing apprehension of white-collar criminals whose frauds and unlawful business practices take an especially heavy toll among the poor; (12) enforcing civil rights; (13) promoting affirmative action programs. These problems are called contributing, if not causal factors of crime among blacks.*

NATIONAL URBAN LEAGUE, Inc. *The Who, What, When, Where, Why And How Of Minority Recruiting For Criminal Justice Careers.* NY Nat Urb League n.d.

A manual written specifically for law enforcement personnel describes six methods pertinent to successful minority recruitment. The manual was written under the National Urban League's Law Enforcement Minority Manpower Project (LEMMP). This project, funded under a grant from LEAA, is an outgrowth of the League's successful 3-year recruiting activities in 10 cities. During this period, LEMMP recruited, screened, and interviewed over 16,000 minority candidates. Five thousand of these were placed in law enforcement agencies across the country. The report is in six sections based on queries pertinent to successful minority recruitment: Why recruit minority personnel? Where do you start recruiting? How do you get your message across? What supportive techniques are needed? With what groups do you link? When is your campaign successful? Positions in related law enforcement work are described. The manual is illustrated with photographs.*

NEEF, Marian and Nagel, Stuart. Racial Disparities That Supposedly Do Not Exist: Some Pitfalls In Analysis Of Court Records. *Notre Dame Law* 52,87–94 1976.

NELLI, Humbert S. Italians And Crime In Chicago: The Formative Years, 1890–1920. *Am J Soc* 74(4),373–391 1969.

NELSON, David P and Sylvester, Sawyer F and Reed, John P. *Prison Homicide.* NY Spectrum Pub 1977.

NELSON, Jack and Bass, Jack. *The Orangeburg Massacre.* NY Ballantine 1970.

NEMETH, C and Sosis, R H. A Simulated Jury Study: Characteristics Of The Defendant And The Jurors. *J Soc Psychol* 90,221–229 1973.

NETO, Virginia and Palmer, Ted. *Patterns Of Conflict Among Higher Maturity Urban Negro Delinquents (Community Treatment Project).* Sacramento Youth Authority 1969.

NETTLER, Gwynn. *Explaining Crime.* NY McGraw-Hill 1978.

NEUBAUER, D W. Dynamics Of Courthouse Justice: A Critical Review Of The Literature. *Just Syst J* 5(1),70–78 1979.

Reform movements focusing on the extent of discretion have failed to consider the dynamics of the courts. Rather than concentrating on case characteristics of charge, age of suspect, and race, the scholars ought to measure the perceptual techniques and shorthands which guide judges and attorneys in their work. Reformers and the National Advisory Commission on Criminal Justice Standards should be sensitive to the conflicts over the courts' goals.*

NEW JERSEY DEPT OF CORRECTIONS. "Correctional Philosophy: A Special Issue: Race And Criminal Justice" in *New Jersey Correctional Master Plan.* Trenton NJ Dept Corrections 1977.

NEW JERSEY DEPT OF CORRECTIONS. *New Jersey Correctional Master Plan.* Trenton NJ Dept Corrections 1977.

NEW MEXICO ATTORNEY GENERAL. *Report Of The Attorney General On The February 2 And 3, 1980 Riot At The Penitentiary Of New Mexico: Part I.* Santa Fe Office Atty Gen 1980.

NEW MEXICO ATTORNEY GENERAL. *Report Of The Attorney General On The February 2 And 3, 1980 Riot At The Penitentiary Of New Mexico: Part 2.* Santa Fe Office Atty Gen 1980.

NEW YORK CITY BOARD OF CORRECTION. Through The Veil Of Partial Comprehension: NY City's Hispanic Defendant And The Criminal Justice System. NYC NYC Bd Correct 1973.

NEW YORK CITY BOARD OF CORRECTION. The Blackout, in *1977 Annual Report Of The New York City Board Of Correction,* 17–24. NY NYC Bd Correct 1978.

The Board sought to determine whether there was adequate planning for a blackout emergency, whether the Department of Corrections responded appropriately and whether such consequences as occurred could be avoided in the future. The majority of those arrested in conjunction with the blackout were confined in overcrowded, unsanitary conditions. Pre-arraignment court detention pens were not designed for prolonged periods of incarceration, yet this was the function they came to serve as a result of an extensive backlog of cases and courtroom delays. Among the deficiencies noted were: unbearable heat, insufficient bedding, poor food service, inadequate sanitary facilities and not enough medical attention (especially for drug addicts). The difficulties presented for the criminal justice system by this massive intake of offenders do not justify inhumane conditions. The Board criticizes the City for neglecting to implement a plan prepared in 1969 by the Vera Institute of Justice, an updated version of which could have resulted in a more orderly, efficient and humane operation.

NEW YORK CITY COMMISSION ON HUMAN RIGHTS. *City Layoffs—The Effect On Minorities And Women.* NY NYC Human Rights 1976.

From 1974 to 1975, New York City budget cuts reduced the municipal workforce by 46,436 workers (28.2 percent). The disproportionately high number of Hispanics, blacks, and women laid off has offset equal opportunity quotas. Whites represented 67 percent of the workforce but accounted for only 52 percent of the separations, while minorities represented 32 percent of the workforce but 43 percent of the separations.*

NEW YORK STATE SPECIAL COMMISSION ON ATTICA. *Attica: The Official Report Of The New York State Special Commission On Attica,* [McKay Commission]. NY Bantam 1972.

Based on extensive investigation and interviewing, this report was designed to inform the public about events that transpired at the Attica Correctional Facility between September 9th and 13th, 1971, that resulted in the deaths of 32 inmates and 11 correctional employees. Racism is a recurring theme throughout the report. It is implicated in everything from the daily inmate–inmate interactions to those involving staff, and from the tensions leading to the uprising through the activities of police and staff upon retaking control of the facility. The prisoner population at Attica (2,243 persons) was comprised of 54% blacks, 37% whites and 8.7% Spanish–speaking inmates. Most were poor black city dwellers, convinced there was a double standard of justice based on judicial discrimination by race. In contrast, a group of white rural residents performed the custodial functions of correction officers. Increasingly, the new younger inmates were becoming less tolerant of the racism and humiliation that characterized prison life. Simultaneously, there was a growth of militant organizations within the institution seeking change.

NEW YORK STATE, Dept Of Correctional Services. *Humanizing The System: Report Of Operations And Development For 1977.* Albany NY Dept Corrections 1977.

NEWMAN, Charles L. *Sourcebook On Probation, Parole And Pardons,* 3rd Ed. Springfield IL Chas C Thomas 1968.

NEWMAN, Donald J. *Conviction: The Determination Of Guilt Or Innocence Without Trial.* Boston Little, Brown 1966.

NEWMAN, Donald J. *Introduction To Criminal Justice,* 2nd Ed. Philadelphia Lippincott 1978.

NEWMAN, Graeme R. *Understanding Violence.* NY Harper & Row 1979.

NEWMAN, Joseph. "The Offender As Victim" in *Victimology: A New Focus,* V3, Drapkin, Israel And Emilio Viano (eds), 113–120. Lexington MA Lexington 1975.

Sixteen questions were asked of offenders, most of whom were serving sentences of over two years. Fifty percent claimed to be the victim before or after the offending act.

NEWMAN, Joseph. *Crime In America: Causes And Cures.* Washington DC US News Books 1972.

NEWMAN, Morris. A Profile Of Hispanics In The US Work Force. *Monthly Lab Rev* ,3–13 D 1978.

NEWMAN, William. *American Pluralism.* NY Harper & Row 1973.

NEWSOM, John T C. Degeneration And Crime: The Twin Evils Of Discrimination And Oppression. *Voice Negro* 3(6),495–497 1906.

NEWTON, Charles H and Shelden, Randall and Jenkins, Sam. The Homogenization Process Within The Juvenile Justice System. *Int J Crimin Pen* 3(3),213–227 1975.

NEWTON, Huey P. *To Die For The People.* NY Random House 1972.

NEWTON, Huey. My Days In Solitary. *Ramparts* 11,30–34+ My 1973.

NICHOLS JR, Woodrow W. Community Safety And Criminal Activity In Black Suburbs. *J Black St* 9(3),311–334 Mr 1979.

Four hypotheses are tested: (1) black residential areas not located within central cities are relatively crime–free; (2) crime occurring in black suburban communities is more property–oriented than people–oriented; (3) crime in "colonizing" black suburban areas (with populations less than 10,000, located far from the central city) has increased at a slower pace than crime in "ghettoizing" black suburbs (with populations greater than 10,000, located near the central–city ghetto); and (4) the increase in suburban crime seems to be directly related to nonblack, urban–suburban migration. In 1966, blacks were arrested for only 16% of suburban crimes, but in 1972, they accounted for 23%. Much of this increase seems to be related to the increase of blacks in the ghettoizing portions of suburban rings. The SES of blacks in suburbia leads to the tentative conclusion that black suburban communities have not contributed to the upsurge of suburban crime; most crime committed in the suburbs is property–oriented (particularly burglary); and ghettoizing areas appear to have the highest crime rates, probably due to their proximity to the central cities.*

NICHOLS, Charles H. *Black Men In Chains: Narrative By Escaped Slaves.* NY Lawrence Hill 1972.

NICHOLS, Charles H. *Many Thousand Gone: The Ex–Slaves' Account Of Their Bondage And Freedom.* Bloomington Indiana Univ Pr 1969.

This history of slavery consists of slave narratives which recount the capture of Africans, the African slave trade, enslavement in America, life under slavery, slave punishments and coping devices, and experiences of fugitive blacks. An extensive bibliography, footnotes, and an introduction are included.

NIEDERHOFFER, Arthur. *Behind The Shield: Police In Urban Society.* NY Doubleday 1967.

NISHI, S M and Johnson, B B and Iiyama, P. *Drug Use And Abuse Among US Minorities: An Annotated Bibliography.* NY Praeger 1976.

This annotated bibliography of studies addressing the issue of drug use, primarily narcotics use, among blacks, Mexican–Americans, Puerto Ricans, Asian–Americans, and native Americans, contains 245 annotated citations and an introductory essay.*

NOBLES, W W. Psychological Research And The Black Self–Concept: A Critical Review. *J Soc Issues* 29(1),11–31 1973.

NOLDE, Hans C and Wolfgang, Marvin E and Kelly, Arlene. Comparison Of The Executed And Commuted Among Admissions To Death Row. *J Crim L Crimin & Pol Sci* 53,301–311 S 1962.

This study of commutation rates was based on case records of 439 persons sentenced to death and received on death row in Pennsylvania between 1914 and 1958. The percentages of whites and of Negroes were compared, and it was found that a significantly smaller proportion of Negroes than whites received commutations. With the type of crime held constant, it was found that a significantly lower percentage of Negro felony–murderers than white felony–murderers received commutations; with the sample limited to Negroes and native–born whites committed for felony–murder, the difference was even more pronounced. The study concluded that "[t]he one factor that links each of the others together is race; for while more offenders convicted of felony murder and offenders with court–appointed counsel are executed than offenders convicted of non–felony murder and offenders with private counsel, respectively, these differences are produced by the fact that significantly more Negroes than whites are executed."

NORDHOFF, Charles. *The Freedmen Of South Carolina.* NY Chas L Evans 1963.

NORDYKE, Lewis T. Ladies And Lynching. *Survey Gr* 28,683–686 N 1939.

NORFOLK PRISON BROTHERS. *Who Took The Weight: Black Voices From Norfolk Prison.* Boston Little, Brown 1972.

NORMAN, Ralph D and Kleinfeld, Gerald J. Rosenzweig Picture––Frustration Study Results With Minority Group Juvenile Delinquents. *J Genet Psyc* 92,61–67 1958.

Contrast was made on the Rosenzweig Picture–Frustration Study between 20 juvenile delinquents and 44 controls, all Spanish–American males ranging (age) from 15 to 18 and members of the same minority group. Correlations were also determined for relationship between amount of overt aggression as ascertained from ratings of behavior by a competent judge and the test. However, comparison of the study group with Rosenzweig's normative group revealed considerable difference in Picture–Frustration Study response patterns. This variation in Picture–Frustration Study response would seem to be in part culturally determined and further normative study appears warranted.

NORMANDEAU, Andre. Violence And Robbery: A Case Study. *Act Criminologica* 5(1),11–106 1972.

A study of violence and robbery is presented. It was found that the Negro patterns of robbery should approximate the white pattern in the future for all variables studied: degree of seriousness and injury; incidence of detection; sex; age; means of attack; temporal, spatial and ecological characteristics of the robberies; the presence of alcohol; previous record; incidence of conviction; and type of adjudication. Results also indicate that there is a clear difference between robbery and other crimes of violence (homicide, rape, and aggravated assault) in the characteristics of the victims, offenders, and methods of operation of the offenses. It is suggested that further studies on crime against property (burglary, larceny, and auto theft) be done to test the hypothesis that robbery is primarily a crime against property.

NORTON, William J. The Detroit Riots––And After. *Survey Gr* 32,317–318 Ag 1943.

NOTE. A Study Of The California Penalty Jury In First–Degree Murder Trials. *Stanford L Rev* 21,1297–1391 F 1969.

The data for this extensive analysis of sentencing in single–jury trials were obtained for all 238 first–degree murder convictions cases tried by such juries in California between 1958–1966. Questionnaires were filled out by students taking information from Department or Corrections and the State Medical Facility's files, and by prosecutors, judges and defense attorneys involved in each of the cases. A list of some hundred variables was used in evaluating and comparing each case. The effect of racial factors was considered for whites, blacks, and Mexican–Americans. The study concludes that "the juries administered the system extremely satisfactorily in the race area"; but that "our results strongly suggest that a blue–collar background was by itself an aggravation and clearly indicate that a white collar background was by itself a significant mitigation."

NOTE. Constitutional Law—Juror Selection—Equal Protection Denied When Master Grand Jury Lists Significantly Underrepresents Defendant's Race. *Miss L J* 46,539–548 1975.

NOTE. Constitutional Law—Unequal Protection For The American Indian Under The Major Crimes Act: United States Versus Antelope. *Temple L Q* 50,109–123 1976.

NOTE. Developing An Equal Protection Standard For Gender Discrimination Cases—Where's The Rub? *Rutgers Camden L J* 11(2),293–325 Wint 1980.

NOTE. La Opinion Serves Notice To The Spanish Speaking Community? *S West Univ L Rev* 3,143 1971.

NOTE. Peremptory Challenge: Systematic Exclusion Of Prospective Jurors On The Basis Of Race. *Miss L J* 39,157–165 1967.

NOTE. Pretrial Diversion From The Criminal Process. *Yale L J* 83,827–854 1974.

NOTE. Riot Control And The Fourth Amendment. *Harv L Rev* 81,625–637 1968.

NOTE. Suing The Police In Federal Court. *Yale L J* 88(4),781–824 1979.

NOTE. The Equal Protection Clause And Imprisonment Of The Indigent For Non–Payment Of Fines. *Mich L Rev* 64(5),938–947 Mr 1966.

NOTE. The Right To An Interpreter. *Rutgers L Rev* 27,245–274 1974.

NOTE. The Sexual Segregation Of American Prisoners. *Yale L J* 82(6),1229–1273 My 1973.

This note explores the differences in treatment accorded male and female prisoners in this country, and examines these differences and assesses their constitutionality in light of the 14th Amendment. Female inmates are seen as more disadvantaged largely due to two factors—scale considerations and societal stereotyping. Because there are fewer female inmates, fewer prisons are in existence. This is seen adding to remoteness of facilities, heterogeneity of the prison population and the level of institutional services. Other treatment disadvantages arise from the application of society stereotypes that influence the type of physical environment, the kind of and number of recreational and educational facilities and the type of institutional staff allowed in female institutions. In light of the 14th Amendment equal protection clause, much of the differential treatment of males and females seems permissible. However, there is hope that the adoption of an intermediate standard of the 14th Amendment review might render some of the differentials in treatment unconstitutional. But, the ratification of the proposed Equal Rights Amendment is seen as holding out the most promise for "equality."

NOTE. The Thirteenth Amendment And Private Affirmative Action. *Yale L J* 89(2),399–420 D 1979.

NOYES, William B. The Criminal Type. *J Soc Sci* 24,31–42 Ap 1888.

NUÑEZ, Luis. Rights Of Spanish Speaking Minorities. *Am J Correct* 34(6),24–26 1972.

NURCO, D N and Du Pont, R L. Preliminary Report On Crime And Addiction Within A Community—Wide Population Of Narcotic Addicts. *Drug Alcoh Dep* 2(2),109–121 1977.

Criminality incidence in 252 black and white male addicts identified as narcotics abusers by the Baltimore, MD., Police Department, 1952–1971, is examined for racial differences before and after first regular drug use. Findings generally support previous studies concerning the increase of criminal activity after the onset of narcotic addiction. Black addicts tend to commit more crimes and more serious crimes, than white addicts before first use of narcotics and after the onset of addiction.*

NYE, F Ivan and Short Jr, James F and Olson, Virgil J. Socio–Economic Status And Delinquent Behavior. *Am J Soc* 63,381–389 1958.

O' BRIEN, Robert M and Decker, David L and Shicor, David. *Urban Structure And Victimization*. Lexington MA Lexington 1980.

O' BRYANT, Tilman B. "The Role Of Black Police Officers" in *The Administration Of Criminal Justice: A View From Black America*, Brown, Lee P (ed), 8–11. Washington DC Howard U 1974.

O'Bryant reiterates the statements made by Ward (in "The Need for Black Officers," 1974). He stresses both the need for black involvement in the

criminal justice system and the roles blacks can play in order to have an impact on its administration. The article reads like an impromptu response to Ward's prepared statement with somewhat more emphasis placed on the quality and kind of service law enforcement officials must render their communities today. Again, the plea is to "get involved." O'Bryant argues that "to stand on the outside and to fight the system is like fighting a duel, only the system has a fencing sword and you have a straight pin. It isn't likely that you're going to win."

O' HARE, Kate Richards. *In Prison: Sometime Federal Prisoner* 21669. Seattle Univ Washington Pr 1976.

O' LEARY, T and Fagen, R and Brody, R. *Cubans In Exile: Disaffection And The Revolution*. Stanford CA Stanford Univ Pr 1968.

O' LEARY, Vincent and Glaser, Daniel. *Personal Characteristics And Parole Outcome*. Washington DC US Dept HEW 1966.

This study of parole for the National Parole Institute is concerned with the relationship of parole outcome to personal characteristics. The characteristics examined included sex, race, age, offense, prior criminal record, intelligence, and body dimensions. The authors found little marked or consistent difference in the parole violation rates of blacks and whites, and concluded that this fact might have reflected more careful selection of blacks for parole than whites, or more frequent institutionalization of unadvanced offenders among blacks than among whites. In the Southwest, Mexican–Americans were found to have about the same parole violation rate as whites and blacks, and Native Americans were found to have an average or somewhat higher rate of parole violation. They concluded: "In general, the evidence on race and nationality as a factor in the evaluation of parolees suggests that it is not of much predictive validity in itself."

O' SHEA, R M and Irelan, L M and Moles, O C. Ethnicity, Poverty And Selected Attitudes: A Test Of The Culture Of Poverty Hypothesis. *Soc Forces* 47,405–413 1969.

OAKS, Dallin H and Lehman, Warren. *A Criminal Justice System And The Indigent*. Chicago Univ Chicago Pr 1968.

OBERSCHALL, Anthony. "The Watts–Los Angeles Riot" in *Rebellion And Retreat*, Palmer, S (ed), 248–272. Columbus Chas Merrill 1972.

The events leading up to the 1965 race riots in the Watts area of Los Angeles are traced, stressing the conflict between a cross–section of the lower–class black community with the white power structure. The underlying antagonism caused by the conflict and poor police–community relations led to the rebellion. No evidence was found of conspiracy or organized leadership. The rioters were angry, frustrated people, acting in similarly rebellious ways at the same time and place. There was much intentional destruction of stores and businesses that took advantage of blacks. The incident illustrates that when conflict is high and opportunity structures are inaccessible, social controls break down and violence results. The collective significance of the events is that the civil rights gains made by the Negro movement that have benefited the southern blacks and middle–class Negroes have not removed the fundamental sources of grievances of a large portion of the black population.

OCHBERG, F M (ed) and Daniels, D N (ed) and Gilula, M F (ed). *Violence And The Struggle For Existence*. Boston Little, Brown 1970.

ODELL, B N. America's New Anti–Police Sentiment. *Pol Chief* 40(3),52–55 1973.

ODUM, Howard W. *Race And Rumors Of Race*. Chapel Hill Univ N Car Pr 1943.

OFARI, E. *The Myth Of Black Capitalism*. NY Monthly Rev Pr 1970.

OFFER, D. *Psychological World Of The Juvenile Delinquent*. NY Basic Books 1979.

The methods, findings, and treatment implications of a long–term, indepth study of 55 juvenile delinquents admitted to the Illinois State Psychiatric Institute from 1969 through 1974 are reported. The study used a combination of clinical observation and behavioral science methods to identify psychological variables important in elucidating delinquent behavior. The study subjects included representatives of different socioeconomic classes, races, and sexes. The study report includes detailed discussion of such dimensions as impulsivity, cognition, family communication, self–image, psychopathology, and value systems.*

OFFORD, D R and Aponte, J F and Frei, R J. A Study Of Recidivism Among Female Juvenile Delinquents. *Corr Psychi J Soc Ther* 14(3),160–174 1968.

OGDEN, Michael and Spector, M I and Hill Jr, C A. Suicides And Homicides Among Indians. *Public Health Rep* 85(1),75–80 1970.

OGLETON, Betty and Crittendon, Stephanie and Seda, Cozetta. *An Examination Of Institutional Racism: Black People In California's Criminal Justice And Mental Health Systems.* Boulder CO W I C H E 1974.

The data indicate that there are racial differences in the treatment of people within, and between, the mental health and criminal justice systems. Blacks are greatly overrepresented in prisons and are slightly overrepresented in mental hospitals. While the proportion of blacks in the general population in California rose from 4.4% to 7.3% from 1950 to 1970, the proportion of blacks in prisons rose from 23% to 35%. The proportion of blacks in mental hospitals increased only from 8% to 10%. In 1970 if a person were black and institutionalized, chances were about 3 to 1 that he went to a prison rather than a mental hospital, while if a person were white, the chances were about 3 to 1 that he went to a mental hospital. These figures contrast sharply with those 1950 figures which indicate that both blacks and whites were more likely to go to mental hospitals. The decreased use of institutionalization has resulted in a reduced white population in prisons and mental hospitals from 1950 to 1970, while the black population in these institutions practically doubled.

OHIO LEGISLATIVE SERVICE COMMISSION. *Capital Punishment,* Staff Research Report No 46. Columbus OH Legis Serv Comm 1962.

The data for the part of this study relevant to discrimination were gathered from Ohio judicial reports, Department of Corrections records, Ohio Pardon and Parole Commission records and various clerks of courts. A distribution was first made of persons charged with, persons convicted of, and persons sentenced for, first–degree murder, by sex between 1955 and 1958. A racial distribution was then given for the state as a whole (as of 1950), the prison population on a particular day in 1960, and of murderers in prison, by sentence (life–death). Economic status of death sentenced persons was also examined: by comparing the number of them represented by private counsel with the number of court–appointed counsel; and by grouping a sample of 67 prisoners by occupation, and comparing the distribution therein with the prison– and state populations'. Educational achievement was also distributed and compared to the state and prison figures. The study concluded, at least with reference to racial inequities, that although "Ohio statistics do not indicate that Negroes are more likely than whites to be sentenced to death, a greater percentage of whites than Negroes sentenced to death received commutations."

OHLIN, Lloyd E and Cloward, Richard A. *Delinquency And Opportunity: A Theory Of Delinquent Gangs.* Glencoe IL Free Pr 1960.

Attempts to link the structural theories of Durkheim and Merton with the differential association theory of Sutherland and the cultural transmission theory of Shaw and McKay. The authors consider differential opportunity structures to be important in their analysis of American delinquency; the criminal subculture is seen as offering lower–class youths another (often illegal) opportunity structure. They predicted that delinquency would become increasingly violent as a result of disintegration of the slum and recommended reorganization of slum communities as a means of delinquency prevention.

OHLIN, Lloyd E and Cloward, Richard A. "Illegitimate Opportunity Structures" in *Rebellion And Retreat,* Palmer, S (ed), 32–49. Columbus Chas Merrill 1972.

Alternative opportunity structures generated by successful integrative relationships across age levels and between criminal and conventional elements in low–income neighborhoods are discussed. The pressure generated by restrictions on legitimate access to success goals are drained off. Social controls over the conduct of the young are effectively exercised, limiting expressive behavior and constraining the discontented to adopt instrumental, albeit criminalistic, styles of life.

OLMSTED, Sophia A and Probst, Nathan. The Rising Puerto Rican Problem. *Bar Bull* 9, Mr 1952.

OLSON, Arnold O and Zusman, Marty E. Gathering Complete Response From Mexican–Americans By Personal Interview. *J Soc Issues* 33(4),46–55 1977.

OLSON, David J and Lipsky, Michael. *Commission Politics: The Processing Of Racial Crisis In America.* New Brunswick NJ Transaction Books 1977.

OLSON, David J and Lipsky, Michael. Riot Commission Politics. *Trans–Act* 6(9),9–21 1969.

OLSON, Virgil J and Nye, F Ivan and Short Jr, James F. Socio–Economic Status And Delinquent Behavior. *Am J Soc* 63,381–389 1958.

OPPORTUNITY SYSTEMS, Inc. *Analytic Report On The Civil Rights Compliance Survey,* 3v. Washington DC Opport Systems 1977.

This three–volume report presents a survey of correctional agencies funded by LEAA to determine compliance with civil rights legislation barring discrimination on the basis of race and sex. Federally funded state and local correctional agencies are characterized with regard to their treatment of minority and female clientele. Data address the issue of rehabilitation through the use of training programs aimed at the preparation of clientele for re–entry into the society outside of the agency or institution. The report is organized in the following manner: a description of the agencies which responded to the survey with usable data and some of the characteristics of these agencies; a description of the population of the agencies, including comparisons between the minority and nonminority populations; and an assessment of the types of educational, vocational, general maintenance, and prison industry programs in specific agencies, as well as an indication of the regions and state showing large numbers of agencies with low rates of participation of minorities in each type of program.*

ORDAHL, George W and Singer, H Douglas. A Study Of Prisoners At The Joliet Penitentiary. *Inst Q* 6,19–24 S 30 1915.

OREBAUGH, David A. *Crime, Delinquency, And Immigration.* Boston Gorham Pr 1929.

ORNELASIN, C and Berrera, M and Munos, C. "The Barrio As An Internal Colony," in *Urban Affairs Annual Review,* V6, Hahn, Harlan (ed), 465–498. Beverly Hills CA Sage 1972.

ORRIS JR, J V and Gatje, C T and Bruno, N J. Hispanic English Language Development In Prison. Stormville NY Greenhaven Prison 1976.

ORROCK, R. The Advocates. *Cal Youth Author Q* 24(2),38–40 1971.

ORSAGH, Thomas and Fuller, Dan A. Violence And Victimization Within A State Prison System. *Crim Just Rev* 2(2),35–55 1977.

A comprehensive quantitative profile of victimization in prisons in North Carolina was conducted to determine the rate of assault among prisoners, the causes, victim characteristics, and possible preventive measures. Three data bases were used: (1) a sample of records of disciplinary hearings in ten prison institutions in North Carolina during the last quarter of 1975—126 assaultive events in all; (2) interviews with prison supervisors in each of the institutions; and (3) a stratified sample of approximately 400 inmates from six of the institutions. Inmate victimization rates are considerably lower than the public, and even informed observers, suppose them to be. The victimization rates vary markedly by race, age, and institution. White victimization rates are higher than black victimization rates because blacks are more likely to victimize across racial lines. Increasing the quantity and efficiency of supervision is a direct and obvious means for reducing assault and victimization. A more refined classification of the inmate population by their propensity to commit assault would increase the efficiency of supervision.

ORTIQUE, Revius O. The National Bar Association—Not Just An Opinion. *Judicature* 53(9),390–394 1970.

OSOFSKY, Gilbert (ed). *The Burden Of Race: A Documentary History Of Negro–White Relations In America.* NY Harper Torchbook 1968.

OSWALD, Russell G. *Attica: My Story.* Garden City NY Doubleday 1972.

Autobiography and memoir of the 1971 Attica uprising, by the commissioner of the NY State Dept of Corrections. Oswald attributes much of the blame for the revolt to black militants and their supporters.

OTTEN, Laura (ed). *Colloquium On The Correlates Of Crime And The Determinants Of Criminal Behavior.* Bedford MA Mitre Corp 1978.

OVERBY, Andrew. "Discrimination In The Administration Of Justice" in *Race, Crime, And Justice,* Reasons, Charles E And Jack L Kuykendall (eds), 264–276. Pacific Palisades CA Goodyear 1972.

OWENS, Charles E (ed) and Bell, Jimmy (ed). *Blacks And Criminal Justice.* Lexington MA Heath 1977.

Readings by various authors cover aspects of the criminal justice system, including racial discrimination, black female offenders, recruitment of blacks into the professional ranks, and judicial decision–making. An index is included.

OWENS, Charles E. *Blacks And The Criminal Justice System: Proceedings Form The Conference Held February 24–27, 1974 At The University Of Alabama.* Washington DC NCJRS 1974.

The five papers presented are but a small representation of the many papers presented during the conference. The papers included deal with broad and specific concerns of blacks in the criminal justice system. One paper highlights the relationship of the 'system' to blacks. Another focuses on legal and legislative issues and their impact on blacks. A third reviews and evaluates research conducted on blacks in the criminal justice system and provides direction for future research. A critical look at the black community, the relationships of the police to this population, and a model for community control of the police is presented in a fourth paper. The final essay discusses recruitment and retention problems of black employees and some of the internal conflicts black correctional workers experience. A tentative constitution and goals for the National Association of Blacks in Criminal Justice are included. The objectives involve minority representation and participation in criminal justice policy making, the recruitment of blacks and minorities into all areas of criminal justice, and to serve as a vehicle for input into legislation and social policy formulation.*

OWENS, Charles E. *Mental Health And Black Offenders.* Lexington MA Lexington 1980.

Because most black offenders come from inner–city environments, they can be discussed as a group for mental–health–treatment purposes. Owens looks at black crime, black mental illness, and black expectations of mental–health programs. The author investigates the appropriateness of current testing methods, reviews therapeutic models used in prisons, and devises strategies for mental–health professionals to use in altering the criminal–justice system. The book is designed for mental health professionals working in corrections.

OWENS, Charles E. "Classifying Black Inmates: The Alabama Prison Classification Project" in *Blacks And Criminal Justice*, Owens And Bell (eds), 129–142. Lexington MA Heath 1977.

OWENS, Charles E. "Looking Back Black" in *Blacks And Criminal Justice*, Owens, Charles E And Jimmy Bell (eds), 7–15. Lexington MA Heath 1977.

OWENS, Charles E. "Now Directions In Corrections" in *Crime And Its Impact On The Black Community*, Gary, L E And L P Brown (eds), 177–194. Washington DC Howard U 1976.

OWENS, Charles E. "What Price Justice: An Introduction" in *Blacks And Criminal Justice*, Owens, Charles E And Jimmy Bell (eds), 3–6. Lexington MA Heath 1977.

OWENS, Holloway O and Wyrick, Saunders. "Black Women: Income And Incarceration" in *Blacks And Criminal Justice*, Owens, Charles E And Jimmy Bell (eds), 85–92. Lexington MA Heath 1977.

The relationship between income and incarceration for black women and programs to help ex–offenders gain meaningful employment in society are discussed. Although black males are the most disproportionately imprisoned, statistics also indicate that the black female remains overrepresented. Pronounced parallels exist between the black female labor market and the low economic profile of black female offenders. The black female offender not only is statistically poor, but also young, undereducated, and often single. She is also likely to have dependent children, which makes her low or no income status even more alarming. Black unemployment continues to be high, with a particularly high rate for black teenagers. It is not surprising, then, that the crimes for which black females are most frequently incarcerated are economically related. The next most common convictions are related to drug offenses. Since there is no difference between the economic needs of the black female offender before and after her incarceration, it is easy to predict her reversion to crime; this trend toward recidivism can also be observed with drug offenders.*

PACHON, Harry P. Hispanics In Local Government: A Growing Force. *Pub Man* 62(9),2–4 O 1980.

Hispanics are becoming an increasingly important force in American life. Numbering 18.5 million, they are expected to be this country's largest minority in the near future. Composed of Mexican, Puerto Rican, Latin and Cuban Americans, the differences in national origin and accompanying diversity distinguish Hispanics from other minority groups. This diversity is one limiting factor on the political power of the Hispanic community. Nevertheless, voting power has resulted in greater representation at all levels of government, but especially at the local level. Here, increasing responsibility to serve a growing Hispanic population will likely result in the recruitment of Hispanic professionals and more bilingual and bicultural policies. Perhaps most important is the public contact level where minority police officers, caseworkers, etc. are more likely to communicate with, and understand minority group members.

PACKER, Herbert. *The Limits Of The Criminal Sanction.* Stanford CA Stanford Univ Pr 1968.

PADGETT, Squire. "Employment And Discrimination" in *Crime And Its Impact On The Black Community*, Gary, L E And L P Brown (eds), 69–76. Washington DC Howard U 1976.

The impact of unemployment and the "last hired, first fired" syndrome on the black community and the crime problem is discussed. Some history is presented, with special emphasis given the period immediately preceeding and following the passage of Title VII of the Civil Rights Act of 1964. Relevant court cases are cited and discussed.

PADILLA, E and Mc Creary, C. MMPI Differences Among Black Mexican–American And White Male Offenders. *J Clin Psyc* 33,171–177 1977.

PADILLA, Elena. *Up From Puerto Rico.* NY Columbia Univ Pr 1958.

PALLAS, John and Barber, Bob. From Riot To Revolution. *Issues Crim* 7(2),1–19 Fall 1972.

PALMER, Albert. *Orientals In American Life.* NY Friendship Pr 1934.

PALMER, Edward. Black Police In America. *Black Scholar* 5(2),19–27 O 1973.

Palmer, a black policeman and co–founder of Afro–American Patrolman's league in Chicago, discusses the problems of the black policeman from the time he is a police candidate, through the recruit–training stage, to the time he goes on the beat. In order to be eligible for the job, the person must first avoid a police record and obtain a high–school diploma. Other ruses may be used to eliminate the black candidate, however the "master eliminator," is the interviewer, laden with white values, ready to exclude anyone who deviates from them. Once at the recruit stage there is the danger that the black recruit will succumb to informal peer group pressure and become "a cop" rather than "a black cop." During training, he will be taught from the white point of view and chances are further increased that the black recruit will also lose his black identity and be isolated from his roots. Once on the beat, the black patrolman will patrol black communities. He concludes that if properly organized, black policemen could be a strong force in stopping the brutality, harassment, intimidation and murder of black people by the police.

PALMER, Paul C. Servant Into Slave: The Evolution Of The Legal Status Of The Negro Laborer In Colonial Virginia. *Southern Atlantic Q* 65,355–379 1966.

PALMER, S. *The Psychology Of Murder.* NY Thos Y Crowell 1962.

PALMER, Ted and Neto, Virginia. *Patterns Of Conflict Among Higher Maturity Urban Negro Delinquents (Community Treatment Project).* Sacramento Youth Authority 1969.

PALMORE, E B and Hammond, Phillip. Interacting Factors In Juvenile Delinquency. *Am Sociol Rev* 29,848–854 1964.

PALYS, T S. An Assessment Of Legal And Cultural Stigma Regarding Unskilled Workers. *Can J Crim & Corr* 18(3),247–257 1976.

PANCOAST, H S. "The Indian Before The Law" in *Americanizing The American Indians*, Prucha, Francis P (ed). Cambridge MA Harvard Univ Pr 1973.

PANTON, J H. Inmate Personality Differences Related To Recidivism, Age And Race As Measured By The MMPI. *J Correct Psych* 4,28–35 1959.

PAREDES, A and Stratton, R and Zeiner, A. Tribal Affiliation And Prevalence Of Alcohol Problems. *Q J Stud Alc* 39(7),1166–1177 1978.

PAREDES, Américo. *With His Pistol In His Hand: A Border Ballad And Its Hero.* Austin Univ Texas Pr 1958.

PARK, James W L. "The Organization Of Prison Violence" in *Prison Violence*, Cohen, Albert K; George F Cole, And Robert G Bailey (eds). Lexington MA Lexington 1976.

PARK, Robert E. "Race Prejudice And Japanese American Relations" in *Race And Culture*, Hughes, Everett C et al (eds). Glencoe IL Free Pr 1950.

PARK, Robert E and Burgess, Ernest W and Mc Kenzie, Roderick D. *The City.* Chicago Univ Chicago Pr 1925.

PARK, Robert E and Miller, Herbert A. *Old World Traits Transplanted.* NY Harper & Row 1921.

PARK, Robert E. Negro Race Consciousness As Reflected In Race Literature. *Am Rev* 1,505–517 S 1923.

PARK, Robert E. Racial Assimilation In Secondary Groups With Particular Reference To The Negro. *Am J Soc* 19,606–623 Mr 1914.

PARK, Robert E. The Bases Of Race Prejudice. *Ann Am Poli* 140,11–20 N 1928.

PARK, Robert E. The Concept Of Social Distance: As Applied To The Study Of Racial Attitudes And Racial Relations. *J App Soc* 8,339–344 Jl 1924.

PARKER, G J. *Black Nationalism And Prospects For Violence In The Ghetto.* Santa Monica Rand Corp 1967.

PARKER, G and Clark, L. The Labor Law Problems Of The Prisoner. *Rutgers L Rev* 28(4),840–860 Spr 1975.

PARKER, J A and Brownfield, Allan C. *What The Negro Can Do About Crime.* NY Arlington House 1974.

Portrays rootlessness, permissiveness, moral relativism, the media's concentration on violence, narcotics, and welfare's nourishment of dependency as causes of inner city crime and suggests approaches for bringing change.*

PARKER, M and Wittmer, J and Lanier, J E. Race Relations Training With Correctional Officers. *Pers & Guid J* ,302–306 F 1976.

A four–day Florida workshop in race relations for correctional officers is described, in which empathy and open and honest communication are stressed. Emphasis is first upon developing good communication and understanding between black and white workshop participants. They are then encouraged to relate their new understanding of racial communication barriers to the prison setting. The workshop methods rely heavily upon the active participation of the workshop attendees. While no data has yet been analyzed in order to evaluate this workshop program, such a project is said to be underway. It is said that within two years of the writing of this report, over one–half of Florida's correctional officers will have attended the workshop.

PARKIN, M. Suicide And Culture In Fairbanks: A Comparison Of Three Cultural Groups In A Small City Of Interior Alaska. *Psychi* 37(1),60–67 1974.

PARKS, Evalyn C and Carlson, Eric W and Vito, Gennaro F. Effectiveness Of Volunteer Assistance To Parolees. *Evaluation Review* 4(3),323–338 Je 1980.

This study of recidivism was conducted in Ohio comparing the postprogram recidivism of 107 program participants with a group of offenders eligible for the program but not matched with a volunteer–helper, and with a randomly selected group of offenders. The results indicate that the postprogram recidivism of the experimental group differed along racial lines, with the black members experiencing increased recidivism whereas the whites' recidivism was reduced.

PARMENTER, Tom. Breakdown Of Law And Order. *Trans–Act* 4,13–21 S 1967.

A first–hand account of the 1967 Detroit riots are presented from the perspective of ghetto dwellers who participated in it.

PARTINGTON, Donald H. The Incidence Of The Death Penalty For Rape In Virginia. *Wash & Lee L Rev* 22,43–75 1965.

The data for the part of this study relevant to racial discrimination were obtained from *National Prisoner Statistics* and the Virginia Bureau of Records. Total numbers of executions for rape for each of the United States are given, for the period 1930–1966, by race. Figures are also given for the total number of persons convicted of and sentenced to death for "rape crimes" (rape, statutory rape, attempted rape) in Virginia from 1908 to 1963, in six–year periods, by race.

PASSELL, Peter and Mathieson, Donald. Homicide And Robbery In New York City: An Economic Model. *J Leg Stud* 5(1),83–98 Ja 1976.

PASTO, Tarmo A and Bromberg, Walter and Simon, Frank. Symbolism In A 'Protest Psychosis'. *Israel Ann Psychi Rel Disc* 10(2),164–179 1972.

A special type of reactive psychosis among Negro prisoners charged with aggressive crimes is described along with case material. Because the clinical picture, usually diagnosed as schizophrenia, contained distinct elements of African ideology, Muslim religious doctrine and distinct anti–Caucasian hostility with reflections on centuries–old white domination of non white peoples, it was labeled protest psychosis. The illness was short–lived, and started abruptly after either arraignment or indictment for an aggressive crime. While the prisoners were in confinement they demonstrated mutism, destructive wild behavior, incoherence, hallucinations of auditory or visual type, bizarre utterances and mannerisms. Included in the discussion are a series of drawings made by one patient which demonstrate the underlying dynamics of the protest

reaction. It is noted that the patient was unaware, on recovery several months later, that he had produced such artistic material while psychotic.

PATI, G and Reilly, C W. Reversing Discrimination—A Perspective. *Hum Res Man* 16,25–31 Wint 1977.

PATTERSON, Haywood and Conrad, Earl. *Scottsboro Boy.* NY Doubleday 1950.

PAUST, J J. Unconstitutional Detention Of Mexican And Canadian Prisoners By The United States Government. *Vand J Trans L* 12,67–72 Wint 1979.

PAYNE, Ethel L. "Citizens Action As A Deterrent To Crime" in *Crime And Its Impact On The Black Community*, Gary, L E And L P Brown (eds), 122–126. Washington DC Howard U 1976.

PEARCE, Roy H. The Significance Of The Captivity Narrative. *Am Lit* 19,1–20 1947.

PEARSON, Carol and Komisaruk, R. Children Of The Detroit Riots: A Study Of Their Participation And Their Mental Health. *J Urban L* 45,599–626 1968.

PEATTIE, Lisa R. *The View From The Barrio.* Ann Arbor Univ Michigan Pr 1968.

PEDERSON, A M and Awad, G A and Kindler, A R. Epidemiological Differences Between White And Nonwhite Suicide Attempters. *Am J Psychiatry* 130(10),1071–1076 1973.

Using the Monroe County (NY) Psychiatric Case Register, the authors attempted to determine differences between white and non–white suicide attempters, to identify the factors that are associated with self–destructive behavior in both groups, and to determine the subsequent mortality rate among suicide attempters. They found a number of differences between whites and non–whites and concluded that the motivation for suicide, the techniques used to treat attempts, and the degree of risk of further psychiatric difficulty may be different for the two groups.

PEET, Richard. The Geography Of Crime: A Political Critique. *Prof Geog* 27(3),277–280 1975.

PELL, Eve (ed). *Maximum Security: Letters From California's Prisons.* NY E P Dutton 1972.

PELLIZZARI, E D and Ewing, J A and Rouse, B A. Alcoholic Sensitivity And Ethnic Background. *Am J Psychiatry* 131(2),206–210 1974.

PELTASON, J W. *Fifty–Eight Lonely Men.* NY Harcourt 1961.

PEÑA, Albert and Samora, Julian and Bernal, Joe. *Gunpowder Justice: A Reassessment Of The Texas Rangers.* Notre Dame U Notre Dame Pr 1979.

PENALOSA, F. Recent Changes Among Chicanos. *Sociol Soc Res* 55,47–52 O 1970.

PENNER, L A and Ulrich, K and Dertke, M C. Observer's Reporting Of Shoplifting As A Function Of Thief's Race And Sex. *J Soc Psychol* 94,213–221 1974.

PEOPLES, Kenneth D and Lewis, Peter W. *Constitutional Rights Of The Accused—Cases And Comments.* Philadelphia W B Saunders 1979.

PERDUE, William C and Lester, David. Racial Differences In The Personality Of Murderers. *Perc Mot Sk* 38(3),726 Je 1974.

PERRY, A M and Kanson, H. Race Factors In Responses To Interpersonal Stress Among Young Adult Offenders. *Crim Just B* 4(1),45–61 Mr 1977.

Previous research has shown that young adult prison inmates display an anxious, acquiescent, depressive–like reaction pattern under conditions of interpersonal stress. The present study evaluated racial factors in this area and found that, relative to white prisoners, black inmates manifest more frequent acquiescence, fewer reports of anger, and generally higher autonomic reactivity. The results are discussed in terms of offender rehabilitation and special problems faced by black prisoners.*

PERRY, Jack. A New Concept In Police Recruiting. *Pol Chief* 36(6),42 1969.

Perry describes a technique of recruiting adopted by the Kansas City Police Department. A recruiting team of two young officers, one black and one white, was utilized. Their assignments were to 1) help improve the image of the police department 2) increase the number of black officers. This was accomplished by waging a major publicity campaign making use of all kinds of media. The team developed the concept that in the police department all men were brothers under the skin. Much personal contact with community agencies and citizens and advertising in colleges and military installations was carried out by the team. Cash incentives were offered to any police employee who recruited a new officer. At the end of six months, 114 new officers had been appointed from 600 applicants. Blacks made up 15% of the new officer class. The department currently averages five or six new applicants each day.

PERRY, L and Crowley, J E. "Urban Families And Assault: A Framework For Research Focused On Black Families" in *Colloquium On The Correlates Of Crime*, Otten, L (ed). Bedford MA Mitre Corp 1978.

Focusing on urban black families, this paper presents a conceptual framework for the comprehensive study of assaultive behavior in the family. Among the assumptions: (1) a wide range of assaultive behaviors must be examined; (2) both factors which provoke assault and factors which inhibit it must be considered, along with the interactions between these factors; (3) the family must be studied in the context of the community in which it resides; (4) the family is viewed as a conflict management system, which means that the study of assaultive behavior must focus on the role of such behavior in response to internal and external change and conflict; (5) any research design must allow for multiple comparisons to be made within and between racial and neighborhood stress groups; and (6) multiple health outcomes should also be included in the research. Several specific areas are reviewed: family structure, sex-role performance and expectations, family resources, and child-rearing practices. Variations in these dimensions are hypothesized to be related to the presence of assaultive behavior, and coping processes are suggested as possible mediators of the effect.*

PERRY, Robert L. The Black Matriarchy Controversy And Black Male Delinquency. *J Afro-Am I* 4,363-373 1976.

PERRY, Ronald W. The Justice System And Sentencing: The Importance Of Race In The Military. *Criminology* 15(2),225-234 Ag 1977.

The relationship between race and sentence severity is examined in a study of data on incarcerated Navy and Marine Corps personnel. The analysis is concerned with the argument that much of the variation in sentences for whites and blacks is due not only to characteristics of the offenders, but also to characteristics of the sentencing process. Because the standardized sentencing process in the military eliminates many of the uncontrolled influences characteristic of civilian studies, a clearer assessment of the importance of race in sentencing determination should be possible. Data on the demographic and social characteristics, military status, and offenses of all enlisted-grade prisoners serving a sentence in Naval and Marine Corps confinement institutions during the last quarter of 1972 are analyzed. No significant differences in sentence length between blacks and whites are found. Where small differences do exist, whites usually receive longer sentences that blacks. The largest difference is in the major military offense category, in which whites' sentences average approximately 4 months longer than blacks'.

PERSON, Scott and Roberts, Albert and Mc Candless, Boyd R. Perceived Opportunity, Delinquency, Race, And Body Build Among Delinquent Youth. *J Consult Clin Psyc* 38,281-287 1972.

The subjects were delinquent, institutionalized black or white 15- to 17-year old boys from impoverished backgrounds. Variables investigated were perception of legitimate and illegitimate opportunity, admitted and committed delinquency, race and age of investigator and S, urbanization of residence, type of body build, physical attractiveness, and I. Q. Modest support was obtained for the hypothesis that perception of little legitimate opportunity is accompanied by high admitted delinquency, particularly for white boys (the white boys were found to perceive less opportunity and to admit more delinquency than the black boys). Perception of opportunity was not correlated with committed delinquency, and the relation between admitted and committed delinquency was low. Age and race of investigator entered into no significant relationships with any of the variables studied for either black or white boys.

PETERSEN, D M and Schwirian, K P and Bleda, S E. The Drug Arrest: Empirical Observations On The Age, Sex And Race Of Drug Law Offenders In A Midwestern City. *Drug Forum* 6(4),371-386 1977-78.

PETERSILIA, Joan and Greenwood, Peter W. *Mandatory Prison Sentences: Their Projected Effects On Crime And Prison Populations.* Santa Monica CA Rand Corp 1977.

PETERSILIA, Joan and Greenwood, Peter W. Mandatory Prison Sentences: Their Projected Effects On Crime And Prison Populations. *J Crim L & Crimin* 69(4),604-615 Wint 1978.

PETERSON, David M and Friday, Paul. Early Release From Incarceration: Race As A Factor In The Use Of Shock Probation. *J Crim L & Crimin* 66,79-97 Mr 1975.

Legal and nonlegal variables that differentiate between those prisoners who are released on probation by the courts after a period of short-term incarceration and those who remain imprisoned are considered. Data to determine the variables which differentiated between those felons who received early releases and those who remained in the institution were collected at a medium security prison for male offenders between the ages of sixteen and thirty. The sample design included all persons granted early release from prison. The following nonlegal variables were found to be associated with early release—race, education, father's education and legal residence, and the legal variables found were probation department recommendation, offense, prior record, number of bills of indictment and plea.*

PETERSON, R W. Assignment In Mexico: The Experience Of United States Magistrates In The Mexican Prisoner Transfer Program. *Fed Prob* 43,665-713 1979.

PETERSON, William. Success Story: Japanese-American Style. *NYT Mag* ,40 Ja 9 1966.

PETTIGREW, Thomas F (ed). *Racial Discrimination In The United States.* NY Harper & Row 1975.

PETTIGREW, Thomas F. "Negro American Crime" in *A Profile Of The Negro American*, 136-156. Princeton Van Nostrand 1964.

Negro American crime rates are high, particularly for crimes involving aggression, such as aggravated assault and homicide, and for escapist crimes, such as gambling, drug addiction, and drunkenness. Although racial discrimination still exists throughout much of the US at each stage of the judicial process, this discrimination alone cannot account for all of the discrepancy; there are considerable data which indicate that a multiplicity of social factors produce these criminal patterns among Negroes. One broad set of factors is socioeconomic: compared with white Americans, Negroes are concentrated in those social sectors which exhibit high crime rates regardless of race. Negroes are more often lower class and poor, slum residents of the nation's largest metropolitan areas, victims of severe family disorganization, Southern in origin, young, and unemployed. "The salient feature of Negro Americans is that they have accepted and internalized American culture, but are generally denied the chief rewards and privileges of that culture. High crime rates are but one consequence of this situation."

PETTIGREW, Thomas F and Spier, Rosalind B. Ecological Pattern Of Negro Homicide. *Am J Soc* 67(6),621-629 My 1962.

PETTIGREW, Thomas. *A Profile Of The Negro American.* Princeton NJ Van Nostrand 1964.

PEW, Miriam L and Speer, David C and Williams, James. Group Counseling For Offenders. *Social Wk* 18(1),74-79 1973.

The results of a community-based group counseling program for offenders in St. Paul, Minn., are discussed. The program has been successful both in rehabilitation and crime prevention, attracting wide and favorable attention in the city's legal circles and among residents of its inner city. This project has provided promising evidence that offenders will make significant voluntary use of community-based group counseling and intensive individual services. There are also indications that such group and individual services contribute to a decrease in the number of subsequent offenses committed.

PFOHL, Stephen J. Book Review: Criminal Violence And The Poor Black Male. *J Res Crim Del* 13(1),96-101 Ja 1976.

PHILIP, Cynthia Owen (ed). *Imprisoned In America: Prison Communications 1776 To Attica.* NY Harper & Row 1973.

A collection of US prison communications from the Revolutionary War era to Attica is compiled, focusing on the common criminal but also including nontraditional prisoner roles such as suffragists, war demonstrators, American Indians, and Japanese internees. It is noted that prisoners are an integral part and expression of the American way of life. Forms of communication included combine writing with prison artwork, songs, handicrafts, graffiti, diary excerpts, and letters. Historically interesting and culturally significant conclusions are reached.

PHILLIBER, W W. Patterns Of Alienation In Inner City Ghettos. *Human Rel* 30(4),303-310 1977.

PHILLIPS, Phillip D. Radical Theory, Relevance, And The Geography Of Crime. *Prof Geog* 27(3),283-284 1975.

PHILLIPS, Ulrich Bonnell. *American Negro Slavery: A Survey Of The Supply, Employment And Control Of Negro Labor As Determined By The Plantation Régime.* NY D Appleton & Co 1918.

PICOU, J S et al. Occupational Choice And Perception Of Attainment Blockage—Study Of Lower Class Delinquent And Nondelinquent Black Males. *Adoles* 9(34),289+ 1974.

PIERCE, Chester M (ed) and Bedau, Hugo Adam (ed). *Capital Punishment In The United States.* NY AMS Pr 1976.

PIERCE, Glenn L and Bowers, William J. Capital Punishment As A Case Study In The Incremental Evaluation Of Guided Discretion. Philadelphia A S C 1979.

PIERCE, Glenn L and Bowers, William J. *Preliminary Tabulations Reflecting Arbitrariness And Discrimination Under Post–'Furman' Capital Statutes.* Boston NE Univ Cen ASR 1979.

PIERCE, Glenn L and Bowers, William J and Carr, Andrea. *Executions In America.* Lexington MA Heath 1974.

Presents extensive data about the characteristics of persons executed in the US. Regional differences and racial disproportionality are examined in detail.

PIERCE, Glenn L and Bowers, William J. Arbitrariness And Discrimination Under Post–'Furman' Capital Statutes. *Crim Delinq* 26(4),563–635 O 1980.

PEIRSON, Gwynne W. *An Introductory Study Of Institutional Racism In Police Law Enforcement.* Unpub PhD Diss Univ of Calif 1978.

PEIRSON, Gwynne. *Police Operations.* Chicago Nelson–Hall 1976.

PEIRSON, Gwynne. "Institutional Racism And Crime Clearance" in *Black Perspectives On Crime And The Criminal Justice System*, Woodson, Robert L (ed), 107–122. Boston G K Hall 1977.

PEIRSON, Gwynne. "The Role Of Police In Reducing Crime" in *Black Crime: A Police View*, Bryce, H J (ed), 67–88. Washington DC Jt Ctr Polit Stud 1977.

PIFER, Alan. "Bilingual Education And The Hispanic Challenge" in *1979 Annual Report Of The Carnegie Corporation Of New York.* NY Carnegie Corp NY 1979.

PILEGGI, Nicholas. A Juvenile Time Bomb. NY 13,25–28 N 3 1980.

The case of Juan Nuñez is reported to illustrate the failures of our juvenile justice system to either meet the needs of youngsters, or to insure protection for society. Like many other offenders, Juan had a history of encounters with authorities beginning at age 11. Despite a violent purse snatching, injuring an 85–year–old woman, and an arrest for gang involvement including weapons and drug possession, he was not convicted. Instead, this now 15–year–old boy with recognized psychological problems and a clinical assessment of dangerousness, was allowed to walk. He committed murder within two months time. Although this boy was in obvious need of professional attention, no suitable facility could be found to accept him. So, he was left in the custody of his parents, whose control over Juan was demonstrably ineffective. Even after his arrest for homicide, while his competency to stand trial was being determined, Juan spent 17 months in several facilities without receiving any significant psychiatric care. Assuming the trend continues, he will likely be out in less than ten years to once again put the public's welfare in jeopardy.

PILIAVIN, Irving and Briar, Scott. Police Encounters With Juveniles. *Am J Soc* 70,206–214 S 1964.

PILIAVIN, Irving and Werthman, Carl. "Gang Members And The Police" in *The Police: Six Sociological Essays*, Bordua, David J (ed), 58–98. NY Wiley 1967.

PILISOK, M and Huang, K. At The Threshold Of The Golden Gate: Special Problems Of A Neglected Minority. *Am J Orthopsych* 47(4),701–713 1977.

PINDERHUGHES, C A. The Origins Of Racism. *Int J Psychi* 8,934–941 1969.

PINEDA, Charles. Community Organizing Of Gang Barrios. *Cal Youth Author Q* 27(3),36–38 1974.

Some special techniques for parole agents and social caseworkers to use when working with the gang barrios in the East Los Angeles, California community are presented. One example is given to show how this knowledge protects the parole agent or caseworker. It is noted that a strong point to remember when working with the Chicano community, or other minority type of gang, is that, to be effective in an ethnic community, community organization operations must take into account both the instinctive subculture of gangs and the ethnic subculture of the community which the gangs share.

PIÑERO, Miguel. *Short Eyes.* NY Hill & Wang 1975.

PINKNEY, Alphonso. *Violence And The Police.* Englewood Cliffs NJ Prentice–Hall 1975.

PINKNEY, Alphonso. Crime And Justice: VI: Race And Crime. *Law Enf News* 18(3),11–13 Mr 1978.

PINKNEY, Alphonso. Prejudice Toward Mexican And Negro Americans: A Comparison. *Phylon* 24,353–359 1963.

PITTMAN, D J and Rainwater, Lee. Ethical Problems In Studying A Politically Sensitive And Deviant Community. *Social Prob* 14,4–10 1967.

PLATT, Anthony (ed). *The Politics Of Riot Commissions: A Collection Of Official Reports And Critical Essays.* NY Collier Books 1971.

Riot commissions must be examined and understood within the political environment in which they are formed. Four critical areas in the politics of riot commissions are examined: (1) the origins and mandates of riot commissions, (2) their internal organization and staff relationships, (3) their conceptions and theories of riots, (4) the nature and effectiveness of their recommendations. The author argues that riot commissions have traditionally failed because of a combination of structural and organizational conditions which precludes fundamental research and investigation and hence, their recommendations are merely symbolic efforts at alleviating the basic causes of the riots.

PLATT, Anthony. 'Street' Crime—A View From The Left. *Crim & Soc Just* 9,26–34 Spr–Sum 1978.

According to this Marxist–Leninist interpretation: "The problem of 'street' crime should be approached not only as a product of the unequal distribution of wealth and chaotic labor market practices, but also as an important aspect of the demoralizing social relations and individualistic ideology that characterize the capitalist mode of production at its highest stage of development."

PLATT, Anthony and Takagi, Paul. Intellectuals For Law And Order: A Critique Of The New "Realists". *Crim & Soc Just* 8,1–31 Fall–Wint 1977.

PLATT, R (ed). "Minority Recruiting––Denver, Colorado" in *Police–Community Relations Series, V4: Case Studies In Minority Programs.* Kennedale TX Criminal Just Pr 1974.

PLATT, Reverend S H. *The Martyrs & The Fugitive, Or A Narrative Of The Captivity, Sufferings & Death Of An African Family & The Escape Of Their Son.* NY Daniel Fanshaw 1859.

PLATT, Tony and Takagi, Paul. Behind The Gilded Ghetto: An Analysis Of Race, Class And Crime In Chinatown. *Crim & Soc Just* 9,2–25 Spr–Sum 1978.

POGANY, Eric and Johnston, Norman G and Cooke, Gerald. A Comparison Of Blacks And Whites Committed For Evaluation Of Competency To Stand Trial On Criminal Charges. *J Psychi L* 2(3),319–337 1974.

Blacks and whites committed for evaluation of competency to stand trial were compared. All males referred to the Michigan Center for Forensic Psychiatry for competency evaluation in 1969 were grouped according to race, and differences on demographic variables. Criminal charges, diagnosis, competency finding, and disposition were studied. A subsample of 70 blacks and 70 whites was analyzed for characteristics associated with MMPI administration and for differences in MMPI profile. The results are consistent with previous literature and indicate a tendency to clinically overestimate psychopathology in blacks, though there is no supporting evidence for a difference in level of pathology in terms of the more objective MMPI measure. The profound effects of this overestimation on disposition are discussed, and a number of solutions are proposed.

POGREBIN, M and Atkins, B. *The Invisible Justice System Discretion And The Law.* Cincinnati Anderson 1978.

POGUE JR, Frank. Health Care In Prisons. *J Afro–Am I* 2(1),73–77 1974.

POGUE JR, Frank. The Truth About Negro Crime. *Negro Dig/Blk Wor* 15,16–26 1966.

POINSETT, Alex. The Dilemma Of The Black Policeman. *Ebony* 27,123–132 My 1971.

In recent years, police forces have been characterized by rising hostility and tension between black and white officers due to conservative, often racist, attitudes of white policemen, discriminatory practices against black officers in the areas of promotions and patrol assignments, and various forms of police abuse and brutality aimed at members of the black community. The black officer on the force often becomes caught between demands of police norms and white colleagues and his loyalties to the black community. An increasing number of black police organizations have been set up to help officers deal with the contradictions they face and yet retain their black identity and protect the rights of black citizens and officers alike.

POLAND, James M. Subculture Of Violence: Youth Offender Value Systems. *Crim Just B* 5(2),159–164 Je 1978.

POLIKOFF, Alexander. *Housing The Poor: A Case For Heroism.* Cambridge MA Ballinger 1978.

POLK, Kenneth and Schafer, Walter E. *Schools And Delinquency.* Englewood Cliffs NJ Prentice-Hall 1972.

POLLACK, M (ed) and Roff, M (ed) and Robins, Lee N (ed). *Life History Research In Psychopathology*, V2. Minneapolis Univ Minnesota Pr 1972.

POLLAK, Otto. *The Criminality Of Women.* Philadelphia Univ of Penn Pr 1950.

POLLOCK, C B and Steele, B F. "A Psychiatric Study Of Parents Who Abuse Infants And Small Children" in *The Battered Child*, Helfer, R E And C H Kempe (eds). Chicago Univ Chicago Pr 1974.

POLLOCK, Joy and Bowker, Lee H and Chesney, Meda. *Women, Crime, And The Criminal Justice System.* Lexington MA Lexington 1978.

POLLOCK, Joy and Bowker, Lee Harrington. *Prisons And Prisoners: A Bibliographic Guide.* San Francisco R & E Research 1978.

Theoretical approaches to prisons and prisoners and such specialized topics as prison violence and minority and family relations are referenced in this bibliography on prisoner subcultures.*

POMERANCE, Rocky. Minorities: A Wealth Of Resources. *Pol Chief* 42(1),8 1975.

POPE- HENNESSY, James. *Sins Of The Fathers: A Study Of The Atlantic Slave Traders, 1441–1807.* NY Knopf 1968.

POPE, Carl E. *Offender–Based Transaction Statistics: New Directions In Data Collection And Reporting.* Washington DC LEAA 1975.

POPE, Carl E. *Sentencing Of California Felony Offenders.* Washington DC LEAA 1975.

POPE, Carl E and Mc Neely, Roger L. Racial Issues In The Measurement Of Criminal Involvement. New Orleans A C J S 1978.

POPE, Carl E. Post–Arrest Release Decisions: An Empirical Examination Of Social And Legal Criteria. *J Res Crim Del* 15(1),35–53 Ja 1978.

This article examines the influence of social and legal factors on decisions by police to drop charges against burglary arrestees before trial. The data were derived from a crime–specific burglary program sponsored by the California Council on Criminal Justice between April 1972 and May 1973. Characteristics of apprehended burglary suspects include such demographic information as age, race, sex, number of crime partners involved in the incident, and distance from the offender's residence to place of occurrence. Legal factors focus on an offender's previous criminal hisotry, including prior burglary record, prior drug record, and the like. Applying the technique of predictive attribute analysis, the research focuses on the importance of the above characteristics with regard to postarrest dispositions. One–fifth of all the apprehended burglary offenders were released by the police and thus not held for prosecution. Those most likely to be released after arrest included offenders aged 17 or under, females, and whites. The variable "prior record" accounts for most of the initial variation in postarrest release decisions.

POPE, Carl E. Race And Crime Revisited. *Crim Delinq* 25(3),347–357 Jl 1979.

The author, a white criminologist, examines the relationship between race and crime as reflected in the literature and evaluates explanations based upon these findings. Pope contends that much of the debate about the extent of black involvement in crime is reducible to a methodological issue. Studies using official data sources consistently show that blacks are overrepresented in arrest, conviction, and prison statistics. While victim survey results support these findings, self–report research fails to demonstrate a relationship between race and crime. Further, the disproportionate amount of black involvement in officially measured crime and delinquency is frequently explained by selection bias based on racial characteristics. Such explanations, however, are not consistently supported by research findings. The paper concludes by outlining two promising perspectives for future research.

POPE, Carl E. The Influence Of Social And Legal Factors On Sentence Dispositions: A Preliminary Analysis Of Offender–Based Transaction Statistics. *J Crim Jus* 4,203–221 1976.

POPE, Carl and Mc Neely, Roger. Race And Involvement In Common Law Personal Crime: A Response To Hindelang. *Rev Black Pol Econ* 8,405–410 Sum 1978.

This critique evaluates an article written by Hindelang that uses victim survey data to study the representation of blacks in criminal events and the extent to which selection bias influences overrepresentation. The analysis begins by comparing findings generated from official data sources and self–report research to findings obtained from National Victimization Surveys. Victimization surveys suffer from some of the same methodological problems associated with the self–report technique. The degree to which victim respondents accurately remember events is unclear. More importantly, there is no definitive body of knowledge about the accuracy of a victim's perception regarding characteristics of incidents or offenders. Simply put, victim, offender, and official perceptions of crime and delinquency are not congruent. Studies dealing with the representation of blacks in criminal activities are cited, although these studies are far from conclusive concerning the degree to which selection bias operates within the criminal justice system.*

PORTER, Bruce and Curvin, Robert. *A Report On The Blackout Looting: New York City, July 13, 1977.* NY Gardner 1979.

Not only the results but also the root causes of the large scale looting during the 1977 NYC blackout are examined and compared with events during the 1965 NY blackout. Looters were mainly blacks and Hispanics, unemployed, male, between the ages of 16 and 25, and not particularly poor. Furniture and household appliances accounted for the largest part of looted goods. The looting, which manifested drastic shifts in the result of a variety of forces and attitudes, including declining legitimacy, criminality, and material aspirations, as well as poverty recently inhabited by the city's poor. It signals a change in the inner city: a corps of hardened, street–type urban dwellers has developed which operates in a shadow economy of hustle and crime and is made up of castoffs of the traditional economic system, mostly persons associalized in youth homes and prisons.*

POTASH, D. Mandatory Inclusion Of Racial Minorities On Jury Panels. *Black L J* 3(1),80–95 Spr 1973.

POTTER, Joan. Should Women Guards Work In Prisons For Men? *Correct Mag* 6(5),30–38 O 1980.

POUSSAINT, A. *Why Blacks Kill Blacks.* NY Emerson Hall 1972.

POVEDA, Tony G. The Image Of The Criminal: A Critique Of Crime And Delinquency Theories. *Issues Crim* 5(1),59–83 Wint 1970.

POWELL, Philip W. *Tree Of Hate: Propaganda And Prejudices Affecting United States Relations With The Hispanic World.* NY Basic Books 1971.

POWERS, Robert B and Mc Entire, Davis. "A Guide To Race Relations For Police Officers" in *The Urban Policeman In Transition*, Snibbe, J (ed), 302–340. Springfield IL Chas C Thomas 1973.

A race relations guide for police officers is presented, stressing developments, particularly in the 1940's, that contributed to tensions between minority groups and law enforcement authorities. Topics include desired official attitude of police toward minorities, complications caused by racial prejudices, group distinctions that lead people to mistakenly believe they are inferior; behavior traits of these groups and reasons for their mistrust and antagonism toward the police, particularly on the part of blacks and Mexican–Americans; and practical police methods in race relations, stressing the recommendations of the Interim Report of the Peace Officers Committee on Civil Disturbance (1945) regarding preventive measures.

POWERS, Thomas. *The Narrative & Confession Of Thomas Powers, A Negro, Who Was In The 10th Year Of His Age Was Executed For Committing A Rape.* Norwich CT n. p. 1796.

POWLEDGE, Fred. *Black Power, White Resistance: Notes On The New Civil War.* NY World 1967.

PRANDONI, Jaques R and Matranga, James T and Jensen, Diane E. Bender–Gestalt Protocols Of Adult Negro Male Offenders: Normative Data. *Perc Mot Sk* 35(1),101–102 Ag 1972.

PRESIDENT'S COMM ON LAW ENFORCEMENT & ADM OF JUSTICE. "Riots And Crime—Historical Background" in *Task Force Report—Crime And Its Impact—An Assessment*, 116–122. Washington DC USGPO 1967.

This paper summarized 19th and 20th–century race riots in New York City, St Louis, Chicago, Detroit, and Los Angeles. Two major patterns in race riots emerge. The 1863 Draft Riots in New York, the 1916 St Louis Riot, and the 1943 Detroit Riot are examples of the first pattern. Violence resulted from white resistance to social and economic progress by negroes, and negro response to resistance. Their basic design was the infliction of personal injury by whites on negroes and by negroes on whites. People and homes were the important targets. This pattern of rioting is contrasted to the disturbances in Harlem during 1935 and 1943 and in the Watts section of Los Angeles during 1965. Each of these riots was precipitated by a police incident, and furious mob hostility was vented against police. Mob violence was particularly directed against white business establishments, and extensive property damage resulted.*

PRESIDENT'S COMM ON LAW ENFORCEMENT & ADM OF JUSTICE. *Task Force Report: Drunkenness.* Washington DC USGPO 1967.

PRESIDENT'S COMM ON LAW ENFORCEMENT & ADM OF JUSTICE. *Task Force Report: The Courts.* Washington DC USGPO 1967.

PRESIDENT'S COMM ON LAW ENFORCEMENT & ADM OF JUSTICE. *Task Force Report: Juvenile Delinquency And Youth Crime.* Washington DC USGPO 1967.

PRESIDENT'S COMM ON LAW ENFORCEMENT & ADM OF JUSTICE. *Task Force Report: Narcotics And Drugs.* Washington DC USGPO 1967.

PRESIDENT'S COMM ON LAW ENFORCEMENT & ADM OF JUSTICE. *Task Force Report: Organized Crime.* Washington DC USGPO 1967.

PRESIDENT'S COMM ON LAW ENFORCEMENT & ADM OF JUSTICE. *Task Force Report: Crime And Its Impact—An Assessment.* Washington DC USGPO 1967.

PRESIDENT'S COMM ON LAW ENFORCEMENT & ADM OF JUSTICE. *Task Force Report: Corrections.* Washington DC USGPO 1967.

PRESIDENT'S COMM ON LAW ENFORCEMENT & ADM OF JUSTICE. *Task Force Report: The Police.* Washington DC USGPO 1967.

PRESIDENT'S COMM ON LAW ENFORCEMENT & ADM OF JUSTICE. *Task Force Report: Science And Technology.* Washington DC USGPO 1967.

PRESIDENT'S COMM ON LAW ENFORCEMENT & ADM OF JUSTICE. *The Challenge Of Crime In A Free Society.* Washington DC USGPO 1967.

PREWITT, Kenneth (ed) and Knowles, Louis L (ed). *Institutional Racism In America.* Englewood Cliffs NJ Prentice–Hall 1969.

PRICE- WILLIAMS, D R and Ramirez, M. *Ethnic Differences In Delay Of Gratification. J Soc Psychol* 93,23–30 1974.

Questions related to the problem of accepting a small reward immediately or waiting for a bigger reward were given to 180 fourth grade children composed of three ethnic groups sampled from a relatively poor socioeconomic region of a South–Western area in the US. In addition questions related to the factor of trust in the promises of investigators to deliver the bigger reward were undertaken. The sample consisted of 60 Anglos, blacks, and Mexican Americans, respectively; each ethnic group divided in turn into an equal number of boys and girls. Results showed that at the fourth–grade level black and Mexican–American children were more prone than Anglo children to accept the immediate gratification rather than choose the later and bigger reward. No sex differences within each ethnic group were found, with the exception of the Mexican–American group for one out of the three conditions tested. The factor of mistrust in the promises of the investigators was noticeable in the black children, despite the fact that they were tested by black investigators.

PRICE, A G. *White Settlers And Native Peoples.* Cambridge MA Cambridge Univ Pr 1950.

PRICE, B and Gavin, S. "Century Of Women In Policing" in *Modern Police Administration*, Schultz, Donald O (ed). Houston Gulf 1979.

The history and status of women in policing is discussed, and barriers to full acceptance of female police officers are identified.*

PROBST, Nathan and Olmsted, Sophia A. *The Rising Puerto Rican Problem. Bar Bull* 9, Mr 1952.

PROUDFOOT, Merrill. *Diary Of A Sit–In.* Chapel Hill Univ N Car Pr 1962.

PRUCHA, Francis P. *The Image Of The Indian In Pre–Civil War America.* Indian Hist Soc Lectures 1970.

PRUCHA, Francis P. *American Indian Policy In Crisis: Christian Reformers And The Indian: 1865–1900.* Norman Univ Oklahoma Pr 1976.

PRUCHA, Francis P. *Americanizing The American Indians.* Cambridge MA Harvard Univ Pr 1973.

PRUCHA, Francis P. *United States Indian Policy: A Critical Bibliography.* Bloomington Indiana Univ Pr 1977.

PRUDEN, Durwood. *A Sociological Study Of A Texas Lynching.* Dallas TX SMU Stud Soc 1937.

PRYTULA, Robert E and Baugh, B Duncan. *DAPs Of Black And Whites Juvenile Incarcerates. J Abnor Ch Psychol* 2(3),229–238 1974.

Two groups of male juvenile incarcerates were separated on the basis of race, matched in terms of age, recidivism, and intelligence test scores, and given the Draw–A–Person Test (DAP). Figures drawn were male and female. The drawings were scored on 14 emotional indicators. The results of the present study offer little consistent or conclusive support for the hypothesis that differences influenced by race can be found in the projective drawings of black and white subjects. The commonly held impressions that there are more incidences of neurotic or psychotic features in the projective tests of black subjects and that the projective drawings of black subjects are generally inferior to the projective drawings of white subjects were not supported by the present study.

PUGH JR, M. *Social Disorganization And Crime. J Hum Relat* 9,411–420 1961.

PURDY, Ross and Marshall, Harvey. *Hidden Deviance And The Labelling Approach: The Case For Drinking And Driving. Social Prob* 19(4),541–553 Spr 1972.

PURVIANCE, Carlton W and Cizanckas, Victor I. *Changing Attitudes Of Black Youths. Pol Chief* 40(3),42–45 1973.

The relationship of the attitudes toward police among minority group youths was studied, and a systematic procedure employed to modify those attitudes is described. A viable ride along program was established by the Menlo Park Police Department for black youths who had formerly declined to participate. The central hypothesis of the study was that the ride along experience would produce a significantly favorable change in attitude toward police officers among those youths who particpated. The experimental group consisted of 50 subjects, the control group of 86. The instrument used was the Attitude Toward Police Scale (ATP). Findings indicate that the police ride along program produced a highly significant and favorable shift in attitudes toward police among those minority youths who participated in the program.

PUTNAM, C. *Race And Reason: A Yankee View.* Washington DC Pub Aff Pr 1961.

QUARANTELLI, E and Dynes, R. *Patterns Of Looting And Property Norms: Conflict And Consensus In Community Emergencies.* Columbus OH Ohio State Univ 1968.

QUARANTELLI, E and Dynes, R. "What Looting In Civil Disturbances Really Means" in *Law And Order: Modern Criminals*, Short Jr, James F (ed), 177–192. Chicago Aldine 1970.

QUARANTELLI, E and Dynes, R. *Looting In Civil Disorders: An Index Of Social Change. Am Behav Sci* 2,7–10 Mr–Ap 1968.

Authors view the distinct looting patterns occurring during the ghetto revolts as violent "collective bargaining," whereby the existing "property rights" in the black community which were previously accepted are not being directly challenged by a significant proportion of the black community. In short, the looting is an index of social change where previous definitions of property rights are being redefined.

QUARLES, Benjamin and Fishel Jr, Leslie. *The Negro American: A Documentary History.* Glenview IL Scott Foresman 1967.

QUINLAN, Donald M and Frank, Susan. *Ego Development And Female Delinquency: A Cognitive–Developmental Approach. J Abnorm Psychol* 85(5),505–510 O 1976.

QUINNEY, Richard (ed). *Criminal Justice In America.* Boston Little, Brown 1974.

QUINNEY, Richard. *Class, State And Crime.* NY David McKay 1977.

QUINNEY, Richard. *Crime And Justice In Society.* Boston Little, Brown 1969.

QUINNEY, Richard. *Criminology: Analysis And Critique Of Crime In America.* Boston Little, Brown 1975.

QUINNEY, Richard. *Critique Of Legal Order: Crime Control In Capitalist Society.* Boston Little, Brown 1974.

QUINNEY, Richard. *The Social Reality Of Crime.* Boston Little, Brown 1970.

Quinney suggests that how criminal definitions are formulated and applied is a very important, and neglected, part of the social reality of crime. Criminal definitions are formulated by authorized agents in a politically organized society, and applied by the segments in society that have the power to shape the enforcement and administration of the criminal law. Crime—makers are as worthy of study as crime—breakers. The more that legal agents evaluate behaviors and persons as worthy of criminal definition, the greater the probability that criminal definitions will be applied. Illustrations involving race are provided.

QUINNEY, Richard. Crime, Delinquency, And Social Areas. *J Res Crim Del* 1(2),149–154 Jl 1964.

Social area analysis was employed in an ecological study of crime and delinquency in a metropolitan area. It was found that crime rates were negatively correlated with economic status and positively correlated with racial status. Delinquency rates were negatively correlated with economic status and family status and positively correlated with racial status. The proportion of delinquency to crime was positively correlated with economic status and negatively correlated with family status and racial status. Further analysis according to the grouping of census tracts into social areas and racial areas revealed qualifications of the correlations.

QUINNEY, Richard. Who Is The Victim? Criminology 10(2),314–323 Ag 1972.

Shifts focus of victimization to include victims of police force, the victims of war, the victims of the correctional system, the victims of state violence, the victims of oppression of any sort.

QUINTANA, Marsha A. The Erosion Of The Fourth Amendment Exclusionary Rule. *Howard LJ* 17,805–822 1973.

RADELET, Louis A. "The Police And Minority Groups" in *The Police And The Community,* 257–287. Beverly Hills CA Glencoe Pr 1973.

Practical, psychological, and sociological considerations of police—Community relations presented in the book "The Police and the Community" are expanded upon. The scope of the field, including police perceptions of their role, of community relations, and their use of discretion in actual situations, is examined. Psychological considerations, including the structure of the community, prejudice, and rumor, are discussed. A theoretical model (personality and social structure analysis) of police morale is given. The sociological considerations of the black and Mexican—American populations, countercultural conflict, black teenage culture, and the Black Panther phenomenon are considered. A model for handling citizen complaints is given. The police relationship with the criminal justice system, police—media relations, and police—political relationships are examined. The proceedings of a symposium on the assessment of Attica are given, as well as 16 special programs on improving police—community relations.

RAE, R W. *Civil Disorder—Indicator Studies: Some Aspects Of Riot Susceptibility.* McLean VA Research Anal Corp 1969.

RAFKY, David M and Thibault, Edward and Lynch, Lawrence. Are Cops Prejudiced? Pol Chief 40(3),60–62 1973.

RAFKY, David M. Police Race Attitudes And Labeling. *J Polic Sci Adm* 1(1),65–86 Jl 1973.

RAFKY, David M. Racial Discrimination In Urban Police Departments. *Crim Delinq* 21(3),233–242 Jl 1975.

A model of intentional and unintentional, interpersonal and interorganizational factors in racial discrimination in police recruitment is presented together with results of a study of role divestment in white urban police. Underlying the frequently heard charges of inadequate minority group representation and unsatisfactory efforts to increase minority participation is the assumption that law enforcement agencies are guilty of racial discrimination. Discrimination, as frequently used implies a systematic and intentional exclusion of blacks, and tends to ignore unintentional and fortuitous factors which may act as barriers to black employment in police departments. Such barriers may be intentional or unintentional and may be in the individual, in the organization, or in the society.

RAGAN, P K. "Crimes Against The Elderly—Findings From Interviews With Blacks, Mex—Amer, And Whites" in *Justice And Older Americans,* Young, M (ed). Lexington MA Heath 1977.

Data from a 1974 survey of 1,269 blacks, Mexican—Americans, and whites in Los Angeles, and from other sources are examined in a study of crimes against the elderly. The study explores three stereotypes concerning the elderly: that crime is one of the serious problems faced by older people; that crime affects the elderly much more than other groups; and that the typical victim is an elderly white woman. The findings suggest that most older people do not perceive crime as one of their most serious problems. Overall, blacks reported greater problems with crime than did Mexcian—Americans and whites. However, among older respondents, differences by race are not as great. Overall, older women do not bear as disproportionate a share of the problems of crime as is imagined. However, differences between older men and women are much more striking among blacks and Mexican—Americans, with women reporting crime problems much more often. Lower SES is not consistently related to perception of crime as a problem. A brief review of national statistics on victimization suggests that, in general, the elderly are not disproportionately victimized by crime.*

RAGEN, Joseph and Finston, Charles. *Inside The World's Toughest Prison.* Springfield IL Chas C Thomas 1962.

RAINWATER LEE (ED). *Social Problems And Public Policy,* V1: Inequality And Justice, A Survey Of Inequalities Of Class, Status, Sex And P. Chicago IL Aldine 1974.

This reader is concerned with justice and equity in the distribution of resources to individuals and groups. After a survey of philosophical and social equality, the book deals with the relationship of people to economic institutions, with status inequalities (especially racial, ethnic and sexual), and with inequalities of power. One section is devoted to inequalities among nations. The book concludes with a discussion of the effect of these inequalities.

RAINWATER, Lee. *Behind Ghetto Walls: Black Families In A Federal Slum.* Chicago IL Aldine 1970.

This book is about the family lives of some 10,000 children and adults who live in an all—Negro housing project in St Louis. The infamous Pruitt—Igoe complex has since been abandoned.

RAINWATER, Lee and Pittman, D J. Ethical Problems In Studying A Politically Sensitive And Deviant Community. *Social Prob* 14,4–10 1967.

RAINWATER, Lee and Yancey, William L. *The Moynihan Report And The Politics Of Controversy.* Cambridge MA MIT Pr 1967.

RAINWATER, Lee. Open Letter On White Justice And The Riots. *Trans—Act* 4,22–32 S 1967.

Rainwater maintains that the root cause of the urban race riots lies in a caste system deeply imbedded in American society which has created a situation in which a very large proportion of blacks are denied the opportunity to achieve an average American standard of living. The riots provide a type of "opportunity structure" for different types of ghetto dwellers to pursue highly varied goals.

RALPH, C H. Angry Picketing. *Police Rev* 80,107 1972.

RAMIREZ, M and Price— Williams, D R. Ethnic Differences In Delay Of Gratification. *J Soc Psychol* 93,23–30 1974.

Questions related to the problem of accepting a small reward immediately or waiting for a bigger reward were given to 180 fourth grade children composed of three ethnic groups sampled from a relatively poor socioeconomic region of a South—Western area in the US. In addition questions related to the factor of trust in the promises of investigators to deliver the bigger reward were undertaken. The sample consisted of 60 Anglos, blacks, and Mexican Americans, respectively; each ethnic group divided in turn into an equal number of boys and girls. Results showed that at the fourth—grade level black and Mexican—American children were more prone than Anglo children to accept the immediate gratification rather than choose the later and bigger reward. No sex differences within each ethnic group were found, with the exception of the Mexican—American group for one out of the three conditions tested. The factor of mistrust in the promises of the investigators was noticeable in the black children, despite the fact that they were tested by black investigators.

RAMSEY, D. *Hidden Negro Criminality.* Charlottesville VA Univ of Virginia 1915.

RANDALL, Archie and Randall, Betty. Criminal Justice And The American Indian. *Indian Hist* 11,42–48 1978.

RANDALL, Betty and Randall, Archie. Criminal Justice And The American Indian. *Indian Hist* 11,42–48 1978.

RANGE, Peter R. Will He Be The First? NYT Mag ,29,72,74,76,78,80 Mr 11 1979.

RANKIN, J H. Changing Attitudes Toward Capital Punishment. *Soc Forces* 58(1),194–211 S 1979.

RANSFORD, H E and Jeffries, Vincent. Interracial Social Contact And Middle Class White Reaction To The Watts Riot. *Social Prob* 16,312–324 Wint 1969.

RANSFORD, H E. Skin Color, Life Chances, And Anti–White Attitudes. *Social Prob* 18,164–178 1970.

Among 312 Negro males interviewed shortly after the Watts riot, dark Negroes were found to be in lower occupational and income positions than light Negroes, even with education (as a measure of skill) held constant. Thus, skin color per se appears to structure opportunity, irrespective of educational investment (college graduates are an exception to this statement). Further, dark Negroes expressed more "anti–white system" feelings than light Negroes with higher proportions willing to use violence, expressing hostility towards whites, and opposed to integration as a goal. However, color is only a strong predictor of "anti–white system" feelings among working– and lower–class persons, among those with no social contact with whites, and among those who feel powerless to exert control through institutional channels.

RANULF, Svend. Moral Indignation And Middle Class Psychology: A Sociological Study,. NY Schocken 1964.

RAPER, Arthur. The Tragedy Of Lynching. Chapel Hill Univ N Car Pr 1933.

RASCH, Christine E and Foley, Linda. "The Effect Of Race On Sentence" in *Theory And Research In Criminal Justice*, Conley, J A (ed). Cincinnati Anderson 1979.

RAU, Richard M. Sentencing In The Federal District Courts. Washington DC LEAA 1972.

RAWSHENBUSH, Winifred. How To Prevent Race Riots. *Am Mercury* 57,302–309 S 1943.

RAY, M W (comp) and Brenner, Robert N (comp) and Kravitz, Marjorie (comp). *Firearm Use In Violent Crime: A Selected Bibliography.* Rockville MD NCJRS 1978.

This bibliography with abstracts concerns firearm use in violent crime and is directed at researchers, criminal justice practitioners, and other interested persons. Books, journal articles, and reports are included.*

READ, J C. Equal Employment Opportunity Under Federal Contracts. *Labor Law J* 28(1),3–12 Ja 1977.

REASONS, Charles E. "Crime And The American Indian" in *Native Americans Today: Sociological Perspectives*, Bahr, Howard; Bruce Chadwick, And Robert Day (eds). NY Harper & Row 1972.

REASONS, Charles E. "Race, Crime And The Criminologist" in *The Criminologist: Crime And The Criminal*, 89–97. Santa Monica CA Goodyear 1974.

The influence of the social milieu of the criminologist is discussed as it relates to criminological theorizing, particularly in regard to race. Political aspects of crime and crime control are highlighted and it is anticipated that although the racial variable will remain one of the focal concerns of criminologists, the traditional, antiseptic "kinds of environment" approach will yield to a more politically oriented conflict approach in keeping with the contemporary milieu. Includes an extensive bibliography.

REASONS, Charles E and Kuykendall, Jack L (ed). *Race, Crime And Justice*. Pacific Palisades CA Goodyear 1972.

This anthology includes articles by authoritative figures concerned with the patterns of unjust treatment of minorities dealing with the following subjects: (1) racism in the administration of justice (2) crime rates and causes, (3) the convergence of race and crime, (4) Negro and white crime rates, (5) minority–police groups and negative contacts, (6) police and the ghetto, (7) negro treatment in the courts of justice, (8) segregated justice for Native Americans, etc. Major recommendations are concerned with development of police–community relations and changes in non–democratic racist patterns of thought embedded in administration of justice systems.*

REASONS, Charles E. Racism, Prisons, And Prisoners' Rights. *Issues Crim* 9(2),3–20 Fall 1974.

REASONS, Charles E. The Politicizing Of Crime, The Criminal And The Criminologist. *J Crim L & Crimin* 64(4),471–477 1973.

Criminology has become politicized by conflict surrounding definitions of crime and justice. The making of laws and their administration are now considered relevant to criminologists.

REASONS, Charles E. The Politics Of Drugs: An Inquiry In The Sociology Of Social Problems. *Sociol Q* 15(3),381–404 1974.

RECKLESS, Walter C. The Crime Problem, Orig Pub 1950. NY App–Cen–Crof 1967.

RECKLESS, Walter C and Smith, Mapheus. *Juvenile Delinquency*. NY McGraw–Hill 1932.

RECKLESS, Walter and Toro– Calder, Jaime and Cedeno, C. A Comparative Study Of Puerto Rican Attitudes Toward The Legal System Dealing With Crime. *J Crim L Crimin Pol Sci* 59(4),536–541 1968.

REDDING, J Saunders. They Came In Chains: Americans From Africa. Philadelphia Lippincott 1973.

REDENIUS, Charles M. The American Ideal Of Equality And Constitutional Change. Port Washington NY Kennikat Pr 1981.

REDENOUR, Ron. Who Is A Black Political Prisoner? Black L J 1(1),16–26 Spr 1971.

REDFERIN, D L. Differential Effects Of Group Counseling With Black And White Female Delinquents One Year Later. *J Negro Ed* 44(4),530–537 1975.

REDISH, M H. Preferential Law School Admissions And The Equal Protection Clause: An Analysis Of The Competing Arguments. *UCLA* 22,343–400 1974.

REED, John P and Nelson, David P and Sylvester, Sawyer F. *Prison Homicide*. NY Spectrum Pub 1977.

REED, John P and Reed, Robin S. Status, Images, And Consequence: Once A Criminal Always A Criminal. *Sociol Soc Res* 57,460–472 1973.

REED, Robin S and Reed, John P. Status, Images, And Consequence: Once A Criminal Always A Criminal. *Sociol Soc Res* 57,460–472 1973.

REESE, Charles D. Police Academy Training And Its Effects On Racial Prejudice. *J Polic Sci Adm* 1(3),257–268 1973.

REGOLI, R M and Jerome, D E. Recruitment And Promotion Of A Minority Group Into An Established Institution––The Police. *J Polic Sci Adm* 3(4),410–416 D 1975.

The policies and practices of police departments in major US cities are examined to determine trends in the hiring and promotion of black police officers. Reasons for the underrepresentation of blacks on police forces are first examined. These include discriminatory hiring practices, the inability of blacks to pass white–oriented written entrance examinations, and reluctance of blacks to join police forces. The need for special efforts in recruiting blacks is discussed, and examples of several recruiting programs are provided. Among these are the training of blacks through community service officer or police cadet programs, and advertising campaigns designed to encourage blacks to join the police. Patterns of black promotion and black representation on police forces are considered in the final section. The data indicate that blacks are underrpresented on police forces throughout the US and that once they are hired they are not promoted as easily as whites.*

REID, Herbert O. Comments On Anti–Crime Legislation: A Political And Sociological Analysis. *Howard L J* 17,865–866 1973.

REID, Herbert O. The Administration Of Criminal Justice In The Minority Communities. *Howard L J* 17,275–295 1972.

REID, Ira De A. "Note On The Negroe's Relation To Work And Law Observation" in *Report On The Causes Of Crime*, V13. Washington DC NCLOE 1931.

REID, Ira De A. A Study Of 200 Negroes In The Western Penitentiary Of Pennsylvania. *Opport* 3,168–169 1925.

REID, Ira De A. Race And Crime. *Friend J* 3,772–774 1957.

REID, Ira De A. The Negro Goes To Sing Sing. *Opport* 10(2),215–217 1932.

REILLY, C W and Pati, G. Reversing Discrimination––A Perspective. *Hum Res Man* 16,25–31 Wint 1977.

REIMAN, Jeffrey H. The Rich Get Richer And The Poor Get Prison. NY Wiley 1979.

A radical criminologist examines the ideology and economic bias inherent in the US Criminal justice system. Specific attention is devoted to the role of race, but the author's primary contention is that class factors are most important. This book is widely used as an undergraduate introductory text.

REIMAN, Jeffrey. "Victims, Harm And Justice" in *Victimology: A New Focus*, V1, Drapkin, Israel And Emilio Viano (eds), 77–87. Lexington MA Lexington 1974.

REIMER, David J and Gold, Martin. *Changing Patterns Of Delinquent Behavior Among Americans 13-16 Years Old, 1967-1972: Report # 1 Of The National Survey Of Youth, 1972.* Ann Arbor MI Inst Soc Res 1974.

Findings of the National Survey of Youth, derived from samples of 847 and 661 youths drawn in 1967 and 1972, include data on delinquent behavior, self-esteem and anxiety that was constructed from self-reports. Appendices include tables examining self-reported delinquent behavior by race, age, sex, socio-economic status and residence.

REIMER, David and Gold, Martin. Changing Patterns Of Delinquent Behavior Among Americans 13 Through 16 Years Old: 1967–1972. *Crim Delin Lit* 7(4),483—517 D 1975.

REISMAN, David. *Individualism Reconsidered.* Glencoe IL Free Pr 1954.

REISNER, S L. Balancing Inmates' Rights To Privacy With Equal Employment For Prison Guards. *Women's Rts L Reptr* 4(4),243–251 Sum 1978.

Constitutional reasons for inmates' right to privacy and attempts to synthesize this right with equal opportunity for prison guards are examined in this law journal note. In Dothard v. Robinson (1977) the US Supreme Court ruled that Alabama was not required to hire women as guards in its maximum security male penitentiaries. The decision was based on the bona fide occupational qualification (BFOQ) exception to Title VII's ban on sex discrimination in employment. However, that decision ignored the issue of an inmate's right to be free from observation by guards of the opposite sex while undressing, using toilet facilities, or being searched. The article discusses this right to privacy and examines the court cases (both of the lower federal courts and of the US Supreme Court) in which there was court recognition of the right to privacy.*

REISS JR, Albert J. "Police Brutality: Answers To Key Questions" in *Law And Order: Police Encounters*, Lipsky, Michael (ed). New Brunswick NJ Transaction Books 1970.

REISS JR, Albert J. *Race Of Victim And Of Offender For Rape, Robbery And Assault And Battery Offenses Known To The Police: Report To The Pres Crime Commission.* Washington DC USGPO 1966.

REISS JR, Albert J. *The Police And The Public.* New Haven CT Yale Univ Pr 1970.

REISS JR, Albert J. "Settling The Frontiers Of A Pioneer In American Criminology: Henry McKay" in *Delinquency, Crime And Society*, Short Jr, James F (ed). Chicago Univ Chicago Pr 1976.

REISS JR, Albert J and Aldrich, Howard. Absentee Ownership And Management In The Black Ghetto: Social And Economic Consequences. *Social Prob* 18,319–338 Wint 1971.

This paper seeks to examine the extent of absentee ownership of small businesses in the black ghettoes of three large American cities and to derive quantitative estimates of the impact that absentee ownership and management have on social and economic conditions in such areas. Non-ghetto businesses are compared with ghetto businesses to separate the effects of common business conditions from the fact of location in a particular area. Data are from a survey of 659 small businesses in Chicago, Boston, and Washington, D. C. The findings support the contention of critics that absentee owned or managed businesses dominate the economy of the black ghetto. However, the same condition also applies to non-ghetto, low-income white areas. The paper concludes with estimates of the degree to which absentee owned or managed businesses control the flow of important resources in the areas studied.

REISS JR, Albert J and Black, Donald J. "Patterns Of Behavior In Police And Citizen Transactions" in *Race, Crime, And Justice*, Reasons, C E And J L Kuykendall (eds), 176–205. Pacific Palisades CA Goodyear 1972.

REISS JR, Albert J and Rhodes, Albert Louis. Are Educational Norms And Goals Conforming, Truant And Delinquent Adolescent Influenced By Group Position In American Society? *J Negro Ed* 28(3),252–267 1959.
Describes the educational achievement goals and the value placed on schooling by an adolescent population, considers their aspirations in relation to these goals and examines the differences among conforming, truant and delinquent adolescents in relation to these goals. The question examined in this paper is: Are these relationships independent of the adolescent's group position in society as represented by his race, sex, I. Q., socio-economic status and age? The authors find low academic achievement, retardation, absenteeism, and overageness in significantly greater proportions among delinquents than non-delinquents, and that

these characteristics differentiate the educational activities and attainments of Negroes and whites. Several hypotheses are suggested and discussed in light of these findings.

REISS JR, Albert J. Discretionary Justice In The United States. *Int J Crimin Pen* 2(2),181–205 1974.

REISS JR, Albert and Black, Donald. Police Control Of Juveniles. *Am Sociol Rev* 35,63–77 1970.

REITZES, Dietrich C and Lohman, Joseph D. Note On Race Relations In Mass Society. *Am J Soc* 58,240–246 N 1952.

REMICK, Peter. *In Constant Fear: The Brutal Story Of Life Within The Walls Of The Notorious Walpole State Prison*, As Told To James B Shuman. NY Reader's Dig Pr 1975.

Sexual assaults and other violence in the Walpole State Prison in Massachusetts are recounted by a prisoner.

RENDON, Armando. *Chicano Manifesto.* NY Collier Books 1971.

RENNER, Edward and Cross, Stan. An Interaction Analysis Of Police–Black Relations. *J Polic Sci Adm* 2(1),54–61 1974.

An interaction analysis of police–black relations is made. The components of interaction affecting behavior at an interactional level of analysis include: role definition conflict, evaluative conflict, mutual role relationship, and threat. Through an interactional analysis, understanding can be established which would help both police and blacks behave in a way in which fulfills the expectations of the other. Such communication at a behavioral level should open the way for further mutual accommodation at the level of social roles and at the level of factors which support individual emotional reactions and attitudes. The model outlined indicates what steps may be taken to improve interactions and what aspects are outside the realm of the approach. It permits an empirical approach, subject to evaluation and refinement, which can specify the degree of differentiation necessary to adequately conceptualize the reference groups of blacks or police.

RENNIE, Y. *The Search For Criminal Man.* Lexington MA Heath 1978.

RENSHAW, Benjamin et al. Blacks And Crime—Can America Break The Chain Of Failure. *Nat Cities* 16(9),11–18,23–30 S 1978.

This symposium on blacks, crime, and the criminal justice system purports to dispel myths that have built up around blacks and their neighborhoods by citing research data on victims, offenders, and criminal justice personnel. It is common belief that black persons are more likely than whites to be victims and victimizers and to live in dangerous neighborhoods in the central city that are hotbeds of crime. Statistics reported in LEAA's Annual Crime Victimization Surveys, however, provide another picture of urban crime and crime victims: race is not a major factor in victimization, but, instead, factors such as residence, age, and sex are important. Young men residing in central cities are most vulnerable to crime, and blacks do not suffer more from crime than whites. It is true, however, that black communities experience a higher crime rate, but the crime loss is not usually major. Crime and the fear of crime in deprived neighborhoods in the central city (usually black neighborhoods) leads to social isolation, withdrawal, and aggressiveness. Persons living in such neighborhoods suffer from discrimination and rejection, and juvenile delinquency flourishes under such conditions.

RENSHAW, Benjamin H and Lehnen, Robert. The Victims. *Nat Cities* 16(9),13–15 S 1978.

RESTON JR, James. *The Innocence Of Joan Little.* NY Bantam 1979.

RETTING, R P and Torres, M J and Garrett, G R. *Manny––A Criminal–Addict's Story.* Boston Houghton Mifflin 1977.

A convicted drug user provides a firsthand account of an addict's day–to–day existence, both in prison and on the streets. Intended for an academic audience interested in deviance, crime, corrections, and criminal justice, this first–person narrative traces the life of Manny Torres, a young Puerto Rican heroin addict born in New York city. Manny provides a view of a variegated criminal career that accepted social science techniques ordinarily could not have rendered. Written in the frank and straightforward language of street people, dope addicts, and prison convicts, it provides a link between reality and social theory, and includes chapters on drug–related street crime, prison life, and Manny's experiences at Synanon, a drug detoxification institute. Selected references are included at the end of each chapter. The narrative is followed by a brief outline of the structuralist position and an integrated theoretical perspective designed to expose students to a social world that few experience.*

REUSS, Elizabeth and Ianni, Francis A J. *The Crime Society: Organized Crime And Corruption In America*. NY New Am Lib 1976.

REUTER, Edward Byron. *The American Race Problem*, Revd Ed By Jitsuichi Masuoka. NY Thos Y Crowell 1970.

REVELLE, William and Gray, David B. A Cluster Analytic Critique Of The Multifactor Racial Attitude Inventory. *Psycholog Rec* 22(1),103–112 1972.

The Multifactor Racial Attitude Inventory (MRAI), a major 10 factor measurement of whites' attitudes toward blacks, was reanalyzed by using a new hierarchical cluster technique to locate factors with greater unidimensionality. Four clusters emerged (public, private, black superiority, and gradualism) with reliabilities between .90 and .66. The mean intercorrelation between the four new clusters was .23, contrasted to .54 for the 10 MRAI factors. All four of the new clusters met a 39% or less overlap criterion, whereas only three of the original 10 factors met this criterion. The four scale solution produced subscales with markedly greater independence than existed for the subscales in the 10 factor solution.

REX, John. *Race Relations And Sociological Theory*. London Weidenfel & Nich 1971.

REYNOLDS, L H. *Candidate Preparation And Retention*. NY Nat Urb League 1977.

REYNOLDS, L H. *Eliminators*. NY Nat Urb League 1977.

Barriers to police recruitment of minorities are discussed as part of a series of training aids prepared by the Urban League's Law Enforcement Minority Manpower Project (LEMMP). Some of the prohibitions against successful minority recruitment include the use of visual acuity tests which bar appointment to the force without 20/20 vision in some areas, height standards which are currently under attack if they are not job related, residency requirements, and the prefiling of applications which eliminates candidates who hear of the test after the termination date. Solutions to these barriers are proposed, including allowing applicants to have corrected vision to 20/30, disallowing height standards, requiring candidates to fulfill the residency requirement within 30 days, and integrating the date for the prefiling of applications into the test date.*

REYNOLDS, L H. *How To Utilize Community Resources*. NY Nat Urb League 1977.

Methods for preparing a police candidate for all examinations are discussed as part of a series of training aids prepared by the Urban League's Law Enforcement Minority Manpower Project (LEMMP). Minority candidates for police jobs often need more help and encouragement to pass screening examinations than their white male counterparts. This guide suggests that LEMMP personnel arrange meetings for groups of minority candidates to practice examination techniques by taking sample exams. This practice should reduce their fears and maintain their interest. Candidates can be prepared for oral interviews in counseling sessions designed to teach them how to avoid improper posture, sullen attitudes, incoherent responses to questions, and breaking eye contact with the interviewer. The recruitment specialist should provide the candidate with suggested answers to commonly asked questions.*

REYNOLDS, L H. *Law Enforcement Minority Manpower Project—Final Report*. NY Nat Urb League 1978.

The work of Phase 4 of the National Urban League's Law Enforcement Minority Manpower Project, initiated to increase the number of minority men and women in the criminal justice system, is reviewed and evaluated.*

REYNOLDS, L H. *Oral Interview Standards*. NY Nat Urb League 1977.

The uniform oral interview standards discussed in this manual were developed as a part of the National Urban League's Law Enforcement Minority Manpower Project for successful minority recruitment. All interviewers should accept three specific kinds of uniform standards: (1) standards regarding the type of information obtainable from a short interview that would be most helpful in judging suitability for hiring as firefighters or police officers; (2) standards of interviewing techniques to obtain useful information efficiently without improper or unproductive questions; and (3) standards of grading applied uniformly and impartially. All interviewers should ask candidates to discuss their educational and work background to search for evidence regarding character motivation, attitudes and work habits. Other important questions that may be asked during the interview process are included in the interview rater's worksheet that is appended to this document.*

REYNOLDS, L H. *Potential Candidates And Using Community Resources For Recruiting*. NY Nat Urb League 1977.

Employing community resources to locate potential candidates is discussed in this report, developed as a part of the National Urban League's Law Enforcement Minority Manpower Project for minority recruitment. Among community resources to be contacted in any effort to recruit minority candidates are the local Veterans' Administration office, plants with layoff lists, community college and universities, social service agencies, civic social groups, barber shops, sports programs, recreation spots, high schools, and churches. Employment and placement counselors and personnel officers should be contacted when approaching veterans affairs offices, industrial plants, high school, and colleges.*

REYNOLDS, Reid and Robey, Bryant and Russell, Cheryl. Demographics Of The 1980's. *Am Demog* ,11–19 Ja 80.

RHODES, Albert Louis and Reiss Jr, Albert J. Are Educational Norms And Goals Conforming, Truant And Delinquent Adolescent Influenced By Group Position In American Society? *J Negro Ed* 28(3),252–267 1959.

Describes the educational achievement goals and the value placed on schooling by an adolescent population, considers their aspirations in relation to these goals and examines the differences among conforming, truant and delinquent adolescents in relation to these goals. The question examined in this paper is: Are these relationships independent of the adolescent's group position in society as represented by his race, sex, I. Q., socio–economic status and age? The authors find low academic achievement, retardation, absenteeism, and overageness in significantly greater proportions among delinquents than non–delinquents, and that these characteristics differentiate the educational activities and attainments of Negroes and whites. Several hypotheses are suggested and discussed in light of these findings.

RHODES, W M. Study Of Sentencing In Hennepin County And Ramsey County District Courts. *J Leg Stud* 6(2),333–353 Je 1977.

To examine the relative impact on sentencing of legal, organizational, and extralegal variables, an analysis of four types of felony cases in the Hennepin and Ramsey County, Minnesota, district courts was performed. Legal factors analyzed included crime committed, past criminal record, and mitigating circumstances. Organizational factors which affect sentencing decisions include plea bargaining, personal attitudes of judges, legal representation, and pretrial status. Race, sex, age and SES may also affect sentencing. Sentencing was compared in the two counties for narcotics possession, burglary/unlawful entry, larceny, and forgery. Cases included all those in the four categories which were closed during 1970. Since defendant information on past criminal record, mitigating circumstances, legal representation, and SES were unavailable, these were not included in the statistical analyses. Results indicate a number of differences between the two counties. Male sex and minority group membership were both associated with a greater likelihood of prison sentencing. Finally, there is no evidence that differential sentencing is a consequence of the difference in judges within the court system.*

RICE, Berkeley. The New Gangs Of Chinatown. *Psych Tod* 10(12),60–69 My 1977.

RICE, Charles E. The Negro Crime Rate: Its Causes And Cure. *Mod Age* 10,343–358 1966.

RICE, David L. *Erroneous Zone*. Washington DC King Publications 1975.
Poetry by a black convict in Nebraska State Penitentiary.

RICE, H C. Civil Rights And Corrections—The Impact Of LEAA Compliance Requirements. *Resol Corr Prob & I* 1(4),4–6 Sum 1975.

A detailed overview of the impact of LEAA's Equal Employment Opportunity regulations on correctional personnel policies, programs, and procedures. Civil rights compliance operations chart their formal beginnings from the issuance by LEAA of Equal Employment Opportunity regulations. These regulations prohibit discrimination in the employment practices of the recipients of LEAA funds. In March 1972, the Equal Employment Opportunity Commission was given concurrent jurisdiction with LEAA in assuring that Equal Employment Opportunity standards are met by recipients of LEAA funds. This article first defines "employment practices" and the specific minority groups protected by these regulations. Specific LEAA guidelines and sections of the regulations are explained with respect to affirmative action programs, construction of new facilities, legislative changes, equal employment compliance reports, and procedural requirements in cases of noncompliance. Emphasis in this article is generally directed towards the impact of these regulations on corrections.*

RICE, John Andrew. Inside The South. *Common Gr* 1,26–34 Spr 1941.

RICE, Stephen and Minton Jr, Robert J. Using Racism At San Quentin. *Ramparts* 8,18–24 Ja 1970.

RICHARDSON, H J. Black Law Professors And The Integrity Of American Legal Education. *Black L J* 4,495–505 1975.

RICHARDSON, Ken (ed) and Spears, David (ed). *Race, Culture And Intelligence.* Harmondsworth England Penguin Books 1972.

RIEDEL, Marc. Discrimination In The Imposition Of Death Penalty: A Comparison Of The Characteristics Of Offenders Sentenced Pre–Furman And Post–Furman. *Temple L Q* 49,261–287 Wint 1976.
The 1972 landmark decision of the US Supreme Court in Furman v. Georgia proposed mandatory sentencing and guided jury discretion as means of reducing racial discrimination in the imposition of capital punishment. Riedel argues on the basis of statistical analysis that such methods do not reduce racial discrimination, and in fact, that they may make it worse.

RIEDEL, Marc. *The Effect Of Mandatory And Discretionary Death Sentences On Commutations And Executions In Pennsylvania.* Harrisburg PA Governor's Comm 1973.

RIEDEL, Marc and Wolfgang, Marvin E. "Race, Rape And The Death Penalty" in *Forcible Rape—The Crime, The Victim And The Offender*, Chappell, D; R Geis, And G Geis (eds). NY Columbia Univ Pr 1977.
Research was begun in 1965 to examine the relationship between race and sentencing for rape in 11 states in which rape was a statutory capital offense. A sample of counties was chosen representing the urban–rural and black–white demographic distribution of each state; every case of conviction for rape between 1945 and 1965 was recorded. Variables included offender and victim characteristics of offense, nature of relations between victim and offender, circumstances of offense, and of the trial. If a variable was shown to have a significant relationship with type of sentence, it was then cross–tabulated with race of the defendant, and a chi–square test was performed to determine statistical significance. Over two dozen aggravating variables that might have accounted for the higher proportion of blacks sentenced to death were analyzed. None withstood the test of significance. The only statistically meaningful variable was race. The authors advocate that the Supreme Court declare the death penalty unconstitutional and urge further research into discrimination at all stages in the administration of justice.*

RIEDEL, Marc and Wolfgang, Marvin E. Race, Judicial Discretion And The Death Penalty. *Ann Am Poli* 407,119–133 1973.
Wolfgang and Riedel discuss the holding by the Supreme Court in *Furman v. Georgia* that the death penalty, by virtue of its infrequent and arbitrary application constitutes cruel and unusual punishment in violation of the 8th and 14th Amendments to the Constitution. Using as their point of departure the opinions in that case of Justices William O. Douglas and Thurgood Marshall, both of which suggest the possibility of discriminatory application of the death penalty, Wolfgang and Riedel focus on previously unpublished studies of rape and the death penalty to support their conclusion that "racial variables are systematically and consistently related to the imposition of the death penalty." Noting that blacks who victimized whites were sentenced to death approximately eighteen times more frequently than defendants in any other racial combination of defendant and victim (they present evidence from their analysis of rape in seven states) they demonstrate that it is the racial factor of the relationship between defendant and victim, rather than the non–racial factor of a contemporaneous offense, that results in the disproportionate imposition of the death penalty against black defendants.

RIEDEL, Marc and Wolfgang, Marvin E. Rape, Race And The Death Penalty In Georgia. *Am J Orthopsych* 45(4),658–668 1975.
Following the 1972 US Supreme Court decision on capital punishment, the Georgia legislature enacted a death penalty statute that attempts to avoid constitutional objections by establishing discretionary standards for judge and jury sentencing. This paper analyzes discretionary death sentencing for 361 rape cases in Georgia, comparing legal and nonlegal variables. Results indicate that blacks convicted of raping whites were disproportionately sentenced to death.

RIFFENBURGH, Arthur S. Cultural Influences And Crime Among Indian–Americans Of The Southwest. *Fed Prob* 28(3),38–46 1964.

RIMMER, J et al. Alcoholism, Sex, Socioeconomic Status And Race In Two Hospitalized Samples. *Q J Stud Alc* 32(4),942–952 1971.

RINELLA, Vincent. Police Brutality And Racial Prejudice: A First Close Look. *J Urban L* 45,773–804 1968.

RIOT COMMISSION. *Report Of The National Advisory Commission On Civil Disorders.* NY Bantam 1968.
The Commission was directed to deal with three basic questions concerning the outbreak of urban violence during the 1960's: (1) What happened? (2) Why did it happen? (3) What can be done to prevent it from happening again? (1) The Commission found "no evidence that all or any of the disorders... were planned or directed by any organization or group...." While the Report indicates there was no "typical" riot, several common features were identified. (2) The Commission concluded that the basic underlying cause of the racial disorders was "white racism" and the actions and conditions created by white Americans. (3) After recounting the historical roots of the basic causes, the Commission recommended: special housing, education, employment and welfare programs; more responsive grievance mechanisms; expansion of decision–making opportunities for ghetto areas and improved police practices to avoid indiscriminate and excessive use of force.

RITAI, Marlene A Young and Brown, Lee P. Crime Prevention For Older Americans: Multanomah County's Victimization Study. *Pol Chief* 43(9),385–389 1976.

RIVERA, F and Moquin, W E and Van Doren, C. *A Documentary History Of The Mexican Americans.* NY Bantam 1971.

RIVERA, Feliciano and Meier, Matt S. *The Chicanos: A History Of Mexican Americans.* NY Am Century Series 1972.

RIVERA, J. Justice, Deprivation And The Chicano. *Aztlan* 6,123–136 Spr 1973.

RIVERA, Ramon and Marshall, Harvey and Short Jr, James F. Adult–Adolescent Relations And Gang Delinquency. *Pac Soc Rev* 7(2),59–65 Fall 1964.

RIVERA, Ramon and Tennyson, Ray and Short Jr, James F. Perceived Opportunities, Gang Membership, And Delinquency. *Am Sociol Rev* 30(1),56–67 1965.

ROBERTS, Albert and Mc Candless, Boyd R and Person, Scott. Perceived Opportunity, Delinquency, Race, And Body Build Among Delinquent Youth. *J Consult Clin Psyc* 38,281–287 1972.
The subjects were delinquent, institutionalized black or white 15– to 17–year old boys from impoverished backgrounds. Variables investigated were perception of legitimate and illegitimate opportunity, admitted and committed delinquency, race and age of investigator and S, urbanization of residence, type of body build, physical attractiveness, and I. Q. Modest support was obtained for the hypothesis that perception of little legitimate opportunity is accompanied by high admitted delinquency, particularly for white boys (the white boys were found to perceive less opportunity and to admit more delinquency than the black boys). Perception of opportunity was not correlated with committed delinquency, and the relation between admitted and committed delinquency was low. Age and race of investigator entered into no significant relationships with any of the variables studied for either black or white boys.

ROBEY, Bryant and Russell, Cheryl and Reynolds, Reid. Demographics Of The 1980's. *Am Demog* ,11–19 Ja 80.

ROBIN, Gerald D. Gang Member Delinquency: Its Extent, Sequence And Typology. *J Crim L Crimin & Pol Sci* 55(1),59–69 Mr 1964.

ROBIN, Gerald D. Justifiable Homicide By Police Officers. *J Crim L Crimin & Pol Sci* 54,225–231 My–Je 1963.

ROBINS, Lee N (ed) and Pollack, M (ed) and Roff, M (ed). *Life History Research In Psychopathology*, V2. Minneapolis Univ Minnesota Pr 1972.

ROBINS, Lee N. "Actuarial Evaluation Of The Causes/Consequences Of Deviant Behavior In Young Black Men" in *Life History Research*, Roff, M et al (eds). Minneapolis Univ Minnesota Pr 1972.

ROBINS, Lee N and West, P A and Herjanic, B L. Arrests And Delinquency In Two Generations: A Study Of Black Urban Families And Their Children. *J Child Psyc & Psychi* 16(2),125–140 1975.

ROBINS, Lee N and Wish, Eric. Childhood Deviance As A Developmental Process: A Study Of 223 Urban Black Men From Birth To 18. *Soc Forces* 56,448–473 1977.
Is deviance a developmental process in which one type of deviant act leads to another? This paper proposes a number of criteria that would need to be met for such a process to exist, and it applies them to data from records and retrospective interviews about the ages at which 13 kinds of

childhood behaviors began. Results appear consistent with both a quantitative developmental process, i.e., one in which the probability of committing a new type of deviance is in part a function of the variety of acts previously committed, and a qualitative one, i.e., one in which having committed one particular type of deviant act makes it more probable for the subject to act out another subsequent type of deviance.

ROBINSON JR, W Stitt. The Legal Status Of The Indian In Colonial Virginia. *Va Mag Hist Biog* 61,249–259 1953.

ROBINSON, Barbara J (comp) and Robinson, J Cordell (comp). *The Mexican American: A Critical Guide To Research Aids.* Greenwich CT JAI Pr 1980.

ROBINSON, Bernard F. Ethnic Factors In Crime. *Corr Psychi J Soc Ther* 10(4),191–201 1964.

ROBINSON, Bernard F. War And Race Conflicts In The United States. *Phylon* 4,311–327 1943.

ROBINSON, Billy "Hands". Love: A Hard Legged Triangle. *Black Scholar* 3(1),29–48 S 1971.

ROBINSON, Eugene and Witt, James. Ten Maxims: Minority Recruitment And Retention. *Pol Chief* 43(9),57–59 1976.

The US Justice Department established the Center for Criminal Justice Agency Organization and Minority Employment Opportunities within the Marquette University Law School in 1971. The purpose of the Center is to promote, through research, reflection and technical assistance, equal opportunities for minorities in the various Criminal Justice fields. According to the authors, this article represents a compendium of observations made by the Center's staff during the course of some 100 technical assistance visits to various law enforcement and correctional agencies throughout the nation.

ROBINSON, J Cordell (comp) and Robinson, Barbara J (comp). *The Mexican American: A Critical Guide To Research Aids.* Greenwich CT JAI Pr 1980.

ROBINSON, L O. Women In The Criminal Justice System. *Crim Def* 3(3),11–16 My 1976.

This article describes the increase of women in the criminal justice field. Increasingly, women are being employed at all levels and in all segments of the criminal justice system—corrections, law enforcement, the judiciary, probation and parole, and as prosecutors, public defenders, and private criminal defense lawyers. However, the criminal justice system must begin an accelerated game of "catch–up" to insure that it does not continue to ignore the largely untapped resource of women as employees. Particularly with the increasing numbers of adult and juvenile female offenders, and the increasing attention being paid to female victims of crime, additional women employees, the article asserts, are a must.*

ROBINSON, N E. *Wisconsin Council On Criminal Justice: Equal Opportunity/Affirmative Action Program For 1978.* Madison Council On CJ 1977.

The agency responsible for administering federal criminal justice assistance in Wisconsin reports its progress in meeting goals related to equal emloyment opportunity, affirmative action, and equality in service provision.*

ROBINSON, Sophia. How Effective Are Current Delinquent Preventive Measures? J Negro Ed 28(3),351–365 1959.

RODMAN, Hyman. The Lower–Class Value Stretch. *Soc Forces* 42,205–215 1963.

RODRIGUEZ, R. The Bakke Debate: A Mexican–American Protests That Affirmative Action Is Unfair To Minorities. *Politicks & O Hu Int* 1(4),13–14 1977.

RODRIQUEZ, J. Alienation Of A New Generation Of Chicanos. *Aztlan* 6,147–154 Spr 1973.

ROEBUCK, Julian B. Criminal Typology. Springfield IL Chas C Thomas 1967.

ROEBUCK, Julian B and Johnson, R. The Negro Drinker And Assaulter As A Criminal Type. *Crim Delinq* 8,21–33 1962.

ROEBUCK, Julian B and Weeber, S C. *Political Crime In The United States—Analyzing Crime By And Against Government.* NY Praeger 1978.

A typology of political crime—offenses by and against government—in the United States from 1960 to 1978 is constructed in a text for students of criminology, social problem, deviance, and related subjects. The typology is based primarily on the action patterns of offenses committed by persons or groups during the normal course of their activities as employees or

members of formal organizations. Thus, the focus is on criminal organization patterns.*

ROEBUCK, Julian B. The Negro Drug Addict As An Offender Type. *J Crim L Crimin & Pol Sci* 53(1),36–43 Mr 1962.

ROEBUCK, Julian D and Cadwallader, Mervyn L. The Negro Armed Robber As A Criminal Type: The Construction And Application Of A Typology. *Pac Soc Rev* 4,21–25 1961.

The authors contrast the backgrounds of 32 black males with patterns of arrests for armed robbery, with those of 368 other black males also studied and categorized in a typology of 13 criminal patterns. The empirical data demonstrates that the armed robbers differ in kind and degree from other criminal types in terms of theoretically relevant social and psychological factors. Armed robbers were a group of "hardened, anti–social recidivists, the products of disorganized homes and slum neighbors where they came in contact with criminal norms and activities at an early age." Case histories showed a pattern of unadjustment at home, school, and in the community. As adults they sought out criminal companions of a similar type, and took real pride in their criminal style—the taking of property by force. Most had developed some skills and a *modus operandi* in their criminal activities. These offenders comprised a more homogeneous category personality–wise than did any other criminal–pattern group, with the possible exception of the drug offenders.

ROEBUCK, Julian D and Johnson, R C. The 'Short Con' Man. *Crim Delinq* 10(3),235–248 1964.

ROEBUCK, Julian D. The Negro Numbers Man As A Criminal Type: The Construction And Application Of A Typology. *J Crim L Crimin & Pol Sci* 54,48–60 Mr 1963.

Roebuck developed a typology of 13 "criminal types," by means of analysis of arrest histories of 1,155 blacks entering the D. C. Reformatory of Corton, Virginia from 1954–1955. The typology makes explicit use of legal terms and gives special emphasis to the criminal career. After development of the typology, 33 characteristics of the school and personal background factors of an offender were compared for the different criminal types. This particular study compares a group of black offenders who had a high frequency of charges as numbers game operators to the remainder of the sample (384 black offenders). Results showed that numbers offenders did differ markedly from other categories of ofenders, lending credence to the utility of the typology. Among other things, numbers men were older, more intelligent, more literate and came from stable homes relatively free of emotional conflict, economic deprivation and physical violence. Roebuck believes that knowledge of characteristics is helpful in formulating explanations of what disposed these men to this type of crime and determining treatment prospects.

ROEMER, D V and Shellow, R. The Riot That Didn't Happen. *Social Prob* 14,221–233 1966.

ROFF, M (ed) and Robins, Lee N (ed) and Pollack, M (ed). *Life History Research In Psychopathology*, V2. Minneapolis Univ Minnesota Pr 1972.

ROGERS, R W and Wilson, L. The Fire This Time: Effects Of Race Of Target, Insult, And Potential Retaliation On Black Aggression. *J Pers Soc Psychol* 32(5),857–864 1975.

ROGLER, C C. The Morality Of Race Mixing In Puerto Rico. *Soc Forces* 25(2),77–81 1947.

ROGLER, Lloyd H. *Migrant In The City: The Life Of A Puerto Rican Action Group.* NY Basic Books 1972.

ROLLINS, Clifford (Jabali). Fascism At Soledad. *Black Scholar* 2(8,9),24–27 Ap–My 1971.

ROLLINS, Thomas M. Mean Beats: Police Brutality In America. *Pol Today* 5(6),49–53 N–D 1978.

ROMANO, Octavio Ignacio (ed). *Voices: Readings From El Grito, A Journal Of Contemporary Mexican American Thought, 1967–1973.* Berkeley CA Quinto Sol Pubs 1973.

ROMERO, L M and Delgado, R. Legal Education Of Chicano Students: A Study In Mutual Accomodation And Cultural Conflict. *New Mex L Rev* 5,177–231 1975.

RONZAN, J. Special Task Force—Positive Recruitment Of Qualified Minorities. *Pol Chief* 43(7),50–52 1976.

ROOT JR, William T. *A Psychological And Educational Survey Of 1916 Prisoners In The Western Penitentiary Of Pennsylvania.* Pittsburgh Bd Trust W Penit 1927.

"The Negro criminal... is a victim of a vicious circle of social, biological and economic causes; lack of education, no trade training commensurate with the intelligence he has; a set of moral, social and leisure habits adjusted to a rural Southern community; victim of caste, forced to live in discarded houses of the dominant race; restricted in employment and social opportunity, the Negro is forced daily to feel inferiority and humiliation in a thousand ways. All this must be given consideration if judging his status in the criminal world."

ROSALDO, R et al. *Chicano*. NY Morrow 1974.

ROSBERG, Judy and Lemert, Edwin M. The Adminstration Of Justice To Minority Groups In Los Angeles County. Berkeley CA U Ca Pr 1948.

ROSE, Harold M. *The Geography Of Despair. Ann Am Geog* 68(4),453–464 1978.

ROSBERG, Judy and Lemert, Edwin M. Crime And Punishment Among Minority Groups In Los Angeles County. *Pro Pac Coa Soc Soci* ,133–145 1946.

ROSEGARTEN, Theodore. *All God's Dangers: The Life Of Nate Shaw.* NY Knopf 1974.
Biography of an Alabama sharecropper, told in his own words through interviews. During his 88 years, his experience with racism and poverty produces many revelations.

ROSEN, Lawrence. *American Indians And The Law.* New Brunswick NJ Transaction Books 1976.

ROSEN, Lawrence. Matriarchy And Lower Class Negro Male Delinquency. *Social Prob* 17,175–189 Sum 1969.
This seeks to be an empirical study of the issue of matriarchy and delinquency among lower–class Negro males. The factors of absent father, sex of main wage earner, main decision–making and most influential adult were investigated for the households of 921 Negro males, ages 13–15, who resided in a lower–class Negro high–delinquent area. Even though some significant differences were found for the total sample, not a single variable proved to be a major factor. The suggestion is made that the factor of matriarchy may be only one of numerous "original causes" which "push" a lower–class Negro male into delinquency.

ROSENBERG, Morris. "Test Factor Standardization As A Method Of Interpretation" in *Stages Of Social Research*, Forcese, Dennis P And Stephen Richer (eds). Englewood Cliffs NJ Prentice–Hall 1970.

ROSENBLOOM, D H. *Federal Equal Employment Opportunity—Politics And Public Personnel Administration.* NY Praeger 1977.
This analysis of Equal Employment Opportunity (EEO) in the federal bureaucracy focuses on the contest between those seeking to maintain the traditional merit system and those seeking a more representative federal service. The analysis concludes that representation—the belief that all segments of the population should be represented in the federal work force—will occupy a key position in public personnel adminstration in the future.*

ROSENQUIST, Carl M and Megargee, Edwin I. *Delinquency In Three Cultures.* Austin Univ Texas Pr 1969.

ROSENTHAL, Marilynn. Where Rumor Raged. *Trans–Act* 8,34–43 F 1971.

ROSS, Donald J and Cobarruviaz, Louis. "Eliminating The Language Barrier" in *Police–Community Relationships*, Bopp, W (ed), 442–444. Springfield IL Chas C Thomas 1972.
Efforts by the San Jose, California, police department to enhance communication with their large population of non–English–speaking citizens are briefly reported. Aimed mainly at the Mexican–American population, a local radio station was used to indoctrinate the citizens regarding police procedures and functions during the course of short weekend broadcasts in Spanish. The basic format was designed so as to cover every aspect of the police department's responsibility, with emphasis on the patrol function.

ROSS, Edward A. The Causes Of Race Superiority. *Ann Am Poli* 18,67–89 Jl 1901.

ROSS, Stanley R (ed). *Views Across The Border: The United States And Mexico.* Albuquerque Univ N Mex Pr 1978.

ROSSI, Peter et al. "Between White And Blacks: The Faces Of American Institutions In The Ghetto" in *Riot Commission, Supplemental Studies*, 69–215. Washington DC USGPO 1968.

ROSSI, Peter et al. "Police In The Ghetto" in *Riot Commission, Supplemental Studies*, 103–114. Washington DC USGPO 1968.

ROSSI, Peter and Groves, Eugene. Police Perceptions Of A Hostile Ghetto: Realism Or Projection. *Am Behav Sci* 13,727–744 1970.

ROSTOW, Eugene V. The Japanese American Cases—A Disaster. *Yale L J* 54,488–533 Je 1945.

ROTHENBERG, S and Barnes, M. Minorities' Constitutional Rights To Police Department Employment. *Police L Q* 6(2),23–31 1977.
Brief review of statutory background against discriminatory employment practices in the public sector, focusing on police, and discussion of the concept of disproportionate racial impact. This concept, enunciated by the Supreme Court in Griggs v. Duke Power Company (1971) holds that if an employment test can be shown to have a disproportionate result on certain protected groups, the employer must demonstrate that the test is valid and relates to the job requirements. Federal court litigation concerning the Chicago Police Department is used as an example of this doctrine. Additionally, the author discusses judicially imposed employment quotas and preferential affirmative action hiring practices as remedies for discrimination. The article concludes by citing a report showing that women can perform competently as police officers.*

ROTTENBERG, Simon (ed). *The Economics Of Crime And Punishment.* Washington DC Am Ent Inst PPR 1973.

ROUCEK, J S and Brown, F J. *On Racial And National Minorities.* NY Prentice–Hall 1937.

ROUSE, B A and Pellizzari, E D and Ewing, J A. Alcoholic Sensitivity And Ethnic Background. *Am J Psychiatry* 131(2),206–210 1974.

ROWAN, Richard H and Griffin, James S. St Paul—Police Department—Minority Recruitment Program. *Pol Chief* 44(1),18,20 Ja 1977.
The recruitment effort reported in this article was begun in 1970 after a federal court decision was rendered against St. Paul, Minnesota. At the time of this suit, seven members (1.4%) of the 525 police officers in St. Paul were black, while blacks comprised 3.5% of the city's population. The total minority population of St. Paul was 6%. James Griffin, co–author of this article, was placed in charge of minority recruitment for the St. Paul Police Department—the goal of the department was set at hiring 60 black male applicants. The following programs were used to attain this goal: oral–interview tutorial sessions stressing the typical questions asked of persons during that phase of the application process, physical training and preparation for the physical agility test, written exam tutorials with discussion and practice test–taking, media support and coverage of the recruitment effort along with community–disseminated brochures and fliers, and meetings with interested groups including schools and colleges. The authors report that the results of this program have been good. Of the 94 minority persons who took the exam for police work, 53 passed.

RUBIN, L. The Racist Liberals—An Episode In A County Jail. *Trans–Act* 5(9),39–44 1968.

RUBINSTEIN, Jonathan. *City Police.* NY Farrar Straus Gir 1973.

RUBINSTEIN, Michael L and Maroules, Nicholas and White, Teresa. *Statistical Analysis Of Misdemeanor Sentences In Anchorage And Fairbanks: 1974–1976.* Anchorage Judicial Council 1979.

RUCHELL MAGEE COMMITTEE FOR BLACK PRISONERS. Ruchell Magee: Slave Rebel. *Black Scholar* 4(2),41–45 O 1972.

RUDENSTINE, David and Clark, Ramsey. *Prison Without Walls: Report On New York Parole.* NY Praeger 1975.

RUDISILL, David and Hirschi, Travis. The Great American Search: Causes Of Crime, 1876–1976. *Ann Am Poli* 423,14–22 Ja 1976.

RUDOFF, Alvin. The Incarcerated Mexican–American Delinquent. *J Crim L Crimin & Pol Sci* 62,224–238 1971.

RUDWICK, Elliot M. *Race Riot At East St Louis: July 2, 1917.* Carbondale S Illinois Univ Pr 1964.

RUDWICK, Elliot M. Negro Police Employment In The Urban South. *J Negro Ed* 30,102–108 Mr 1961.

RUDWICK, Elliot M. Police Work And The Negro. *J Crim L Crimin & Pol Sci* 50(5),596–599 1960.

RUDWICK, Elliot M. Race Labeling And The Press. *J Negro Ed* 31,177–181 1962.
This article examines the practice and policy of indicating the race of non–white suspects and offenders in newspapers. The justifications for and arguments against such a practice are noted.

RUDWICK, Elliot M. The Southern Negro Policeman And The White Offender. *J Negro Ed* 30,426–431 Fall 1961.

RUDWICK, Elliot and Meier, August. *From Plantation To Ghetto*. NY Hill & Wang 1976.

RUDWICK, Elliott and Meier, August. "Black Violence In The 20th Century" in *Violence In America*, Graham, Hugh D And T Gurr (eds). NY Bantam 1969.

RUNYAN, Charles. Legal Goals: The Curfew And Preventative Closings In Prevention And Control Of Civil Disorder. *Pol Chief* 36(11),54–58 N 1969.

RUSCHE, Georg and Kirchheimer, Otto. *Punishment And Social Structure*. NY Columbia Univ Pr 1939.

This classic historical work on punishment and social structure suggests that every system of production tends to develop punishments which correspond to its productive relationships. The authors contend that it is thus "necessary to investigate the origin and fate of penal systems, the use or avoidance of specific punishments, and the intensity of penal practices as they are determined by social forces, above all by economic and then fiscal forces." One of their hypotheses is that punishments become more severe in periods of poor economic conditions. Some analysis of the relationship between slavery and imprisonment is included.

RUSHFORD, Norman B et al. Violent Deaths In A Metropolitan County: Changing Patterns In Homicide, 1958–1974. *N Eng J Med* 297(10),531–538 1977.

RUSINKO, W T and Johnson, K W and Hornung, C A. Importance Of Police Contact In The Formulation Of Youths' Attitudes Toward Police. *J Crim Jus* 6(1),53–67 Spr 1978.

The significance of positive and negative contacts between police and juveniles as determinants of juveniles' attitudes toward police is examined in a study of 1,200 pupils in the ninth grade in Lansing, Mich. The survey instrument, which was administered in the late 1960's, measured the nature and extent of experiences with police, self–reported delinquent behavior and defiance of parental authority, and attitudes toward police. Positive contacts are predictive of positive attitudes, particularly for youths who have had a negative encounter with police, for those who report frequent involvement in deviance, and for those who report defying their parents. Negative contacts are predictive of negative attitudes, particularly for white youths, for youths who report infrequent deviant behavior, and for youths who have had little or no positive contact with police. Positive contacts can neutralize the effects of negative contacts; and positive contacts do not diminish the tendency for black youths to be negative in their opinions of police. Police management must explore ways to improve the attitudes of black youth toward the police.*

RUSK, Marian T. *A Study Of Delinquency Among Urban Mexican–American Youth*. Unpub PhD Diss Univ of S Calif 1969.

RUSSELL, Cheryl and Reynolds, Reid and Robey, Bryant. Demographics Of The 1980's. *Am Demog* ,11–19 Ja 80.

RUSSELL, Marion J. American Slave Discontent In Records Of The High Courts. *J Negro Hist* 31(4),411–434 1946.

RUSTIN, Bayard. The Watts 'Manifesto' And The McCone Report. *Commentary* 41,29–35 Mr 1966.

Author describes the conditions in the Watts ghetto which caused the residents to rise up in violent protest: unemployment; inadequate schools; dilapidated housing and police brutality. He then compares these to the official findings of the McCone Report which was commissioned to investigate the causes of the riots and prescribe remedies against any such future outbreaks. The McCone Report, the author argues, misses the point of the Watts riots and their causes which makes its remedies and recommendations virtually meaningless.

RUTHERFORD, Andrew et al. *Prison Population And Policy Choices: V1 & 3*. Washington DC NILECJ 1977.

RYAN, William. *Blaming The Victim*. NY Vintage 1971.

SACCUZZO, D P and Condit, J E and Lewandowski, D G. Efficiency Of Peabody Picture Vocabulary In Estimating WISC Scores For Delinquents. *Psychol Rep* 38(2),359–362 1976.

i. Q.s on the Peabody Picture Vocabulary Test for 106 lower–class males 13 to 16 years were related to WISC I. Q.s (assessed by student examiners) in three different ranges (80–89, 70–79, below 70) as a function of race. Both group and individual results were consistent with previous data showing the Peabody scale generally overestimates the I. Q.s of retarded subjects. The results also indicate that the Peabody tended to underestimate the I. Q.s of 34 "dull normal" subjects. The utility of the

Peabody in estimating the Wechsler I. Q. of juvenile offenders is of doubtful value, according to the authors.

SACK, W H. Children Of Imprisoned Fathers. *Psychi* 40(2),163–174 1977.

SAFFORD, Joan Bainbridge. No Comprendo: The Non–English–Speaking Defendant And The Criminal Process. *J Crim L & Crimin* 68(1),15–30 1977.

SAGALYN, Arnold. Danger Of Police Overreaction. *J Crim L Crimin & Pol Sci* 60,517–519 S 1969.

SAGARIN, Edward (ed). *Corrections: Problems Of Punishment And Rehabilitation*. NY Praeger 1973.

SAGARIN, Edward (ed). *Taboos In Criminology*. Beverly Hills CA Sage 1980.

SAGARIN, Edward (ed) and Sylvester Jr, Sawyer F (ed). *Politics And Crime*. NY Praeger 1974.

SAGARIN, Edward. Race And Crime: A Revisit To An Old Concept. *Am J Orthopsych* 37(2),363–364 1967.

SAGI, P and Wellford, C. Age Composition And Patterns Of Change In Criminal Statistics. *J Crim L Crimin & Pol Sci* 59,29–36 1968.

SALAS, Luis P and Lewis, Ralph G. The Law Enforcement Assistance Administration And Minority Communities. *J Polic Sci Adm* 7(4),379–399 D 1979.

SALAS, Luis P and Schneider, Ronald. Evaluating The Dade County Citizen Dispute, Settlement Program. *Judicature* 63(10),174–183 1979.

SALAZAR, Ruben. *Stranger In One's Land*. Washington DC USCCR 1970.

SALINAS, Raul R. *Viaje/Trip*. Providence RI Hellcoal Pr 1973.

SALOMON, Frederic et al. Civil Rights Activity And Reduction Of Crime Among Negroes. *Arch Gen Psychiatry* 12,227–236 1965.

SALTONSTALL, T L. "Manpower Development—The Standards And Goals Process In Massachusetts" in *Criminal Justice Planning*, Scott, J E And S Dinitz (eds). NY Praeger 1977.

Massachusetts' efforts to rectify prison and parole manpower problems through the establishment of realistic standards and goals for minority representation, staff development, and education and training are discussed. Civil service laws and procedures, coupled with a lack of incentive for educational development of inservice correctional personnel, have contributed to the low average level of education of Massachusetts' state correction officers. There is virtually no educational requirement for veterans who wish to become corrections officers. Approximately 84 percent of all state corrections officers in Massachusetts are veterans. There are few incentives or resources available to permit inservice officers to pursue educational opportunities. Although there are 21 higher education programs in law enforcement in the state, only 4 such programs are available in corrections. Another manpower problem relates to the racial imbalance between corrections personnel and inmates. Historically, corrections and criminal justice in general have failed to generate the resources needed to fulfill their public mandates.*

SALTZSTEIN, A and Hall, G. Equal Employment Opportunity For Minorities In Municipal Government. *Social Sci Q* 57,864–872 Mr 1977.

This study examines the differences in employment patterns for black and Mexican Americans in municipal governments and delineates some of the conditions underlying racial employment patterns. The study utilized newly available data on 26 Texas cities with a population of over 50,000. Employment data contained in Equal Employment Opportunity–3 forms were aggregated by city to create two dependent varibles for both black and Spanish–surnamed employees: (1) percentage of professionals in city government who belong to each group, (2) use index for each group which considers both a mnority group's representation in an organization and its distribution across salary levels. Despite the small sample size and its restriction to Texas cities, the findings suggested that unexpected complexities in urban minority employment could affect the success of personnel policies. Policies stressing education and training were found more effective with Spanish–surnamed population than with black employees. It was found that federal strategies to enhance the employment status of minorities in municipal governments must take into consideration the specific group requiring assistance.*

SAMORA, Julian. *Los Mojados: The Wetback Story*. Notre Dame U Notre Dame Pr 1971.

SAMORA, Julian and Bernal, Joe and Pena, Albert. *Gunpowder Justice: A Reassessment Of The Texas Rangers*. Notre Dame U Notre Dame Pr 1979.

SAMORA, Julian and Galarza, Ernest0 and Gallegos, Herman. *Mexican Americans In The Southwest*. Santa Barbara CA McNally & Loftin 1969.

SAMORA, Julian and Simon, Patricia Vandel. *A History Of The Mexican American People*. Notre Dame U Notre Dame Pr 1977.

SAMUELS GERTRUDE. I Don't Think The Cop Is My Friend. *NYT Mag*, Mr 20 1962.

SAMUELS, Gertrude. Walk Along The Worst Block: East 100th Street. *NYT Mag*, S 30 1962.

SANBORN, Frank B. "Negro Crime" in *Notes On Negro Crime, Particularly In Georgia*, Du Bois, W E D (ed). Atlanta Atlanta Univ 1904.

SÁNCHEZ, Ricardo. *Canto Y Grito Mi Liberación*. Garden City NY Doubleday 1973.

SANDALOW, Terrance. Judicial Protection Of Minorities. *Mich L Rev* 75,1162–1195 Ap–My 1977.

SANDBURG, Carl. *The Chicago Race Riots*. NY Harcourt Brace 1919.

SANDERS, David. Rebellion Or Revolution? New Pol 6,24–29 1968.

SANDHU, Harjit S and Allen, Donald E. A Comparative Study Of Delinquents And Non–Delinquents: Family Affect, Religion, And Personal Income. *Soc Forces* 46(2),263–268 1967.

SARBIN, Theodore R. *The Myth Of The Criminal Type*. Middletown CN Wesleyan U C Adv S 1969.

SASSOWER, D L. Women Judges. *Trial* 12(1),25,31,34–35 Ja 1976.
Barriers to equality for women presented by laws and judicial decisions are discussed, and the need for more women judges and lawyers is stressed. The author contends that the best system of judicial selection is one that is used in many other countries: a nonpolitical professional judiciary chosen on the basis of competitive qualifying examinations and promoted on the basis of experience and proven ability. Such a method is said to offer equal opportunities on the bench to all segments of society. The increase in the number of women attending law school and the advent of feminist law firms are noted.*

SAUDLER, D. Minority Police Hiring—Is Cooperation Possible? Trooper 4(3),69–75 Ag 1979.
This overview of minority hiring practices in law enforcement states that black power, the woman's movement, and enforcement of minority hiring quotas has improved the minority hiring situation. However, whatever gains minorities have made in penetrating predominantly white police forces are more likely the result of financial pressures than of a changing attitude. In Chicago, it was only after a judge ruled on racial and sexual quotas for hiring and promotion of minorities within the Police Department that 28.4 million in federal revenue sharing was released to the city. Many police departments have abolished height requirements that are discriminatory to Hispanics and women. Surveys on the effectiveness of women police officers have been encouraging, and there are signs of a steady increase of minorities in US police forces. Blacks and Hispanics, however, continue to complain of undue harassment from white police. Disutes over the use of deadly force by police when dealing with minorities is a major cause of problems in police minority relations.*

SAVITZ, Leonard D (ed) and Johnston, Norman (ed) and Wolfgang, Marvin E (ed). *The Sociology Of Crime And Delinquency*. NY Wiley 1970.

SAVITZ, Leonard D. "Black Crime" in *Comparative Studies Of Blacks And Whites In The US*, Miller, K S And R M Dreger (eds), 467–516. NY Seminar Pr 1973.
Savitz reviews and critiques research on differential delinquency rates, adult crime, criminal victimization, inter– and intra–racial crimes, law enforcement and administration of justice in the black community, black representation on juries, and psychological and sociological modes of explanation of black crime. Data consistently reveal that blacks, particularly in urban settings, are disproportionately involved in juvenile delinquency and adult crime when measured by official statistics, racial differences are considerably less when self–reports are used. Discrimination in the administration of justice probably cannot account for racial differences in official crime rates since excessive severity with regard to black–white offenses is more than offset by systematic indifference to the far more numerous black–on–black crimes.

SAVITZ, Leonard D. *Crime And The American Negro*. NY Free Pr 1968.

SAVITZ, Leonard D and Lalli, Michael. *Delinquency And City Life*. Washington DC NILECJ 1972.
This interim report on the causes of delinquency among black boys in Philadelphia seeks to explain why some but not all boys in the most depressed urban areas, in the same social and economic circumstances, become delinquent. The findings of 532 interviews with black boys and their mothers are presented. The attitudes concerning family, education, aspirations, fear of crime, behavior changes, and self were measured. Dropping out of school was found to be a consequence of delinquency and not a cause. Both delinquent and nondelinquent boys agreed with middle class values. Delinquents were found to be more fearful of victimization and were more apt to take some precautions. The source of income rather than low socio–economic status itself leads to low self–esteem.*

SAVITZ, Leonard D and Lief, H I. "Negro And White Sex Crime Rates" in *Sexual Behavior And The Law*, Slovenko, Ralph (ed), 210–220. Springfield IL Chas C Thomas 1965.

SAWICKI, Donna M. *A Comparison Of Ethnic And Criminal Groups On Three Aspects Of Alienation*. Unpub PhD Diss St Louis Univ 1974.
The relationship between various indexes of alienation and criminal and racial subgrouping, was examined in imprisoned blacks, whites and Mexican–Americans. Three types of offenders in each group (people, property and neutral) were studied within the framework of Merton's work and social learning theory. Instruments included Rotter's I–E Scale, the Srole Anomia Scale, and need values, expectancies and disparities were measured for two need areas, recognition and affiliation. A correlation was predicted with the other alienation indexes. As predicted, the I–E differentiated between ethnic groups, while the Srole did not, although, as predicted, a trend toward significance was found. No differences occurred between groups on affiliation and recognition values or on social contact measures, while a significant difference occurred between groups for recognition disparity scores opposite to the predicted direction. Contrary to hypotheses, no significant differences occurred between people and property offenders, but were found between high people offenders and affiliation need values in the opposite direction. This finding is discussed in the context of frustration–aggression theory.

SAWYER, Jack and Senn, David J. Institutional Racism And The American Psychological Association. *J Soc Issues* 29(1),67–79 1973.

SAX, Richard M. Why It Hurts To Be Black And Blue. *Issues Crim* 4(1),1–11 1968.
Sax examines why blacks have decided not to wear blue. In so doing he examines recruitment within the context of the 1960's racial riots. He believes that integration within police departments was a possibility before the riots; that such integration after their occurrence has become all but impossible. He believes that the market is no longer there—the game now being played by blacks is the white man's game but on black terms. Sax claims that the black community has seen that the white community will respond to violence and confrontation. The attack, in the form of increased violence, is directed specifically at the police. Thus, any black person who would presently dare accept employment as a police officer places his future in social isolation from the rest of the black community. He notes that being black and wearing blue is impossible today. He concludes his article by advocating the establishment of an area police department recruited from and trained by the black community and responsible to a structure established by the local churches.

SAYER, K and Griggs, E. *Equal Employment Opportunity Plan Development Participant's Reference Handbook*. Washington DC Univ Research Corp 1976.
Training materials are presented from a workshop on equal employment opportunity and affirmative action compliance program development for recipients of LEAA assistance. The materials were part of a 2–day workshop in Colorado that focused on LEAA equal employment opportunity laws, rules, and regulations; the purpose and philosophy of affirmative recruitment; and techniques and skills required for undertaking affirmative action programs and developing equal employment opportunity plans at the agency level. The handbook also includes US Department of Justice rules and regulations on nondiscrimination in federally assisted crime control and juvenile delinquency programs (and related questions and answers); LEAA guidelines for complying with the rules and regulations;

uniform guidelines on employee selection procedures proposed in December 1977 by four federal agencies; the US Civil Service Commission's guidelines for evaluating state and local government personnel operations; guidelines on eliminating sexist language from writing; and a glossary of affirmative action terminology.*

SCARBOROUGH, W S. The Negro Criminal Class—How Best Reached—Part I. *Voice Negro* 2(11),803–804 1905.

SCARBOROUGH, W S. The Negro Criminal Class—How Best Reached—Part II. *Voice Negro* 2(12),867–869 1905.

SCARPITTI, Frank R (ed) and Datesman, Susan K (ed). *Women, Crime, And Justice.* NY Oxford Univ Pr 1980.

The relations among women, crime, and justice are explored in this collection of articles, which focuses on the etiology and patterns of female crime, women in the criminal justice system, and crime and emancipation. The readings are intended to enhance criminology study, delinquency and criminal justice courses, courses in sex roles, and women's studies. The etiology of female crime is viewed from the perspectives of existing literature, with attention to sociological and psychological causative factors. The justice system's discriminatory practices are addressed in terms of the sexist attitudes, chivalry, and paternalism that result in sentencing disparities and misguided, inadequate detention programs. Discrimination against both juvenile and adult female offenders is considered; legal solutions are weighed and arguments cited in support of the Equal Rights Amendment. A special article addresses the dilemma of mothers behind bars and the parental rights of incarcerated women. Final remarks analyze the relationship of women's crime and women's emancipation, concluding that despite the increase in female crimes, the Equal Rights Movement has not had a causative effect.*

SCARPITTI, Frank R and Datesman, Susan K. "Unequal Protection For Males And Females In The Juvenile Courts" in *Juvenile Delinquency*, Ferdinand, Theodore N (ed), 59–77. Beverly Hills CA Sage 1977.

SCARPITTI, Frank R and Stephenson, Richard M. Juvenile Court Dispositions: Factors In The Decision Making Process. *Crim Delinq* 17,142–151 1971.

SCARPITTI, Frank R and Stephenson, Richard M. Negro–White Differentials And Delinquency. *J Res Crim Del* 5(1),122–133 1968.

Analysis of 1193 sixteen– and seventeen–year–old male delinquents, who had no prior institutionalization but were assigned by the juvenile court to one of four correctional programs, revealed that the Negro youths were disproportionately represented, had a higher Delinquency History Score, and were more likely to be in–program failures and recidivists. Consideration of racial, social, and economic differences did not adequately account for the delinquency differentials, nor was there evidence of discriminative treatment in the limited data available for analysis.

SCHAB, F. Adolescence In The South: A Comparison Of White And Negro Attitudes About Home, School, Religion And Morality. *Adoles* 3(9),33–38 1968.

SCHAEFFER, C and Brown, S. Investigating Ethnic Prejudice Among Boys In Residential Treatment. *J Soc Psychol* 100(2),317–318 1976.

SCHAFER, Stephen. *The Political Criminal: The Problem Of Morality And Crime.* NY Free Pr 1974.

SCHAFER, Stephen. "Anomie, Culture Conflict, And Crime" in *Crime And Culture: Essays In Honor Of Thorsten Sellin*, Wolfgang, Marvin E (ed), 83–92. NY Wiley 1968.

SCHAFER, Walter E and Polk, Kenneth. *Schools And Delinquency.* Englewood Cliffs NJ Prentice–Hall 1972.

SCHANDLER, M L. "Law Enforcement Data Processing & Equal Employment Standards" in *2nd Annual Law Enforcement Data Processing Symposium.* Washington DC NCJRS 1978.

SCHERMERHORN, R A. *Comparative Ethnic Relations.* NY Random House 1970.

SCHILLER, Barry M. Racial Conflict And Delinquency: A Theoretical Approach. *Phylon* 30(3),261–271 Fall 1969.

Contemporary sociologists' approach to race is confounded by their biases and tradition. A more macro approach might seriously question basic assumptions about American social structure, might see Negroes, as well as other minority groups, as playing a subordinate, exploited role in the society.

SCHNEDLER, R and West, S G and Whitney, G. Helping A Motorist In Distress: The Effects Of Sex, Race And Neighborhood. *J Pers Soc Psychol* 31(4),691–698 1975.

SCHNEIDER, Joanna and Zangrando, Robert L. Law, The American Value System, And The Black Community. *Rutgers Camden L J* 3,32–44 Spr 1971.

SCHNEIDER, Ronald and Salas, Luis P. Evaluating The Dade County Citizen Dispute, Settlement Program. *Judicature* 63(10),174–183 1979.

SCHNELLER, Donald P. *An Exploratory Study Of The Effects Of Incarceration On The Families Of Negro Inmates Of A Medium–Security Prison.* Unpub PhD Diss Catholic Univ 1966.

SCHNELLER, Donald P. Some Social And Psychological Effects Of Incarceration On The Families Of Negro Prisoners. *Am J Correct* 37(1),29–33 Ja–F 1975.

This article reports the author's study of the effects of imprisonment on the families of medium–security prison inmates. The author measures three components of change that occurred in 93 families after the incarceration of the male head of household. These components deal with changes in social acceptance, economic status, and sexual and emotional needs. The results indicate that emotional and financial problems are the most problematic, especially for happily married couples. However, social acceptance was not found to be a serious problem for the families in this study. All of the prisoners were black, due to the very heavy representation of blacks in the total population from which the sample was taken.

SCHOENFELD, W N. Notes On A Bit Of Psychological Nonsense: Race Differences In Intelligence. *Psycholog Rec* 24(1),17–32 1974.

SCHONFIELD, J. Differences In Smoking, Drinking, And Social Behavior By Race And Delinquency Status In Adolescent Males. *Adoles* 1,367–380 1966.

SCHORR, Mark. Gunfights In The Cocaine Coral. *N Y* 11,48–57 S 25 1978.

SCHRAG, Clarence. *Crime And Justice: American Style.* Washington DC USGPO 1971.

SCHRIEKE, B. *Alien Americans.* NY Viking Pr 1936.

SCHROEDER, Oliver and Bensing, Robert C. *Homicide In An Urban Community.* Springfield IL Chas C Thomas 1960.

SCHULMAN, G I. Race, Sex And Violence: A Laboratory Test Of The Sexual Threat Of The Black Male Hypothesis. *Am J Soc* 79(5),1260–1277 1974.

SCHULMAN, H and Converse, J M. The Effects Of Black And White Interviewers On Black Responses In 1968. *Public Opin Q* 35,44–68 1971.

SCHULTZ, D. *Coming Up Black: Patterns Of Ghetto Socialization.* Englewood Cliffs NJ Prentice–Hall 1969.

SCHULTZ, Leroy G. Why The Negro Carries Weapons. *J Crim L Crimin & Pol Sci* 53(4),476–483 1962.

Schultz begins by noting that little has been written on the Negro as a weapons carrier and that which has been done is questionable in terms of validity and usefulness. While Schultz attempts to give more insight into the characteristics and motivations of Negroes arrested and convicted for possession of weapons, he recognizes that his conclusions, based on only 50 cases in the City of St. Louis, are far from generalizable. The motivation for carrying a weapon in 70% of the 50 cases interviewed was found to be derived from a need for protection. This group, according to Schultz, "voiced a chronic concern about being attacked and the need for self–defense and assumed automatically that others in their environment were also carrying weapons, or if not actually carrying weapons, acted as if they were." It is Schultz's contention, inferred from his own data and that of previous literature, that the offense of weapons carrying is reflective of "the major stress and tensions of the social life in the sub–culture of the lower class Negro." Alternatives, in terms of corrections and law enforcement, are discussed.

SCHUMAN, Howard and Campbell, A. "Racial Attitudes In Fifteen American Cities" in *Riot Commission, Supplemental Studies*, 1–67. Washington DC USGPO 1968.

SCHUSKY, E L. Indian Dilemma. *Int J Comp Soc* 11,58–66 Mr 1970.

SCHWARTZ, A H and Cronheim, A J. Non–English–Speaking Persons In The Criminal Justice System: Current State Of The Law. *Cornell L Rev* 61(2),289–311 1976.

SCHWARTZ, Barry N and Disch, Robert and Disch, Barry N. *White Racism: Its History, Pathology And Practice.* NY Dell 1970.

SCHWARTZ, David. On The Ecology Of Political Violence: 'The Long Hot Summer' As A Hypothesis. *Am Behav Sci* 11,24–28 1968.

SCHWARTZ, Gary and Horowitz, Ruth. Honor, Normative Ambiguity And Gang Violence. *Am Sociol Rev* 39(2),238–251 1974.

SCHWARTZ, Herman. A Note On Sostre V McGinnis. *Buffalo L Rev* 21(3), Spr 1972.

SCHWARTZ, J A and Moore, L M. Minority Employment In Police Services—A Management Analysis For Police Departments. *Western City* ,13–14 N 1976.

Minority recruitment, selection, retention, and promotion problems are discussed, along with the legal issues involved. Management recommendations are offered in dealing with the situation. Historical discrimination, lack of adequate information, limited resources, and massive and sometimes confusing laws are cited as problems with which the administrator must deal in seeking to increase minority employment. Recommendations for management action are as follows: give priority rating to minority employment; assign the police department rather than the city personnel department to the responsibility of minority employment; conduct a thorough assessment of the problem which should lead to specific short–term and long–term plans; provide training for administrative personnel and line officers which will facilitate their support and leadership in minority employment; and police personnel policies and practices regarding hiring and promotion should be made more flexible.*

SCHWARTZ, Martin D (ed) and Clear, Todd R (ed) and Travis I I I, Lawrence F (ed). *Corrections: An Issues Approach.* Cincinnati Anderson 1980.

SCHWARTZ, Richard D and Skolnick, Jerome M. *Society And The Legal Order.* NY Basic Books 1970.

SCHWENINGER, Loren. A Slave Family In The Ante–bellum South. *J Negro Hist* 60,29–44 Ja 1975.

SCHWIRIAN, K P and Bleda, S E and Petersen, D M. The Drug Arrest: Empirical Observations On The Age, Sex And Race Of Drug Law Offenders In A Midwestern City. *Drug Forum* 6(4),371–386 1977–78.

SCHWIRIAN, K and Everts, P. Metropolitan Crime Rates And Relative Deprivation. *Criminologica* 5,43–52 1968.

SCOTT, Arthur P. *Criminal Law In Colonial Virginia.* Chicago Univ Chicago Pr 1930.

SCOTT, D and Jongeward, D. *Affirmative Action For Women—A Practical Guide For Women And Management.* Reading MA Addison–Wesley 1977.

SCOTT, Elsie K. "Black Attitudes Toward Crime And Crime Prevention" in *Crime And Its Impact On The Black Community*, Gary, L E And L P Brown (eds), 13–30. Washington DC Howard U 1976.

This article presents the findings of an attitudinal survey conducted during the early part of 1975. The sample used was a cluster sample consisting of persons attending three conferences on crime and the black community in New York City. Attitudes towrd crime victimization, crime in the black community and police and citizen crime prevention efforts are explored. The problems surrounding research in this area are highlighted as are implications and suggestions for future research.

SCOTT, Elsie K and Joyner, Irving. *Crime In The Minority Community.* NY Comm Racial Just 1976.

SCOTT, Elsie K and Joyner, Irving. "People And Police" in *Black Crime: A Police View*, Bryce, H J (ed), 109–128. Washington DC Jt Ctr Polit Stud 1977.

SCOTT, Elsie K and Joyner, Irving. Crime: A Common Concern. *Crim Just Iss* 2, 1975.

SCOTT, James F. *Study Of Role Conflict Among Policemen.* Unpub PhD Diss Indiana Univ 1968.

This dissertation assesses the influence of racial identity on the occurrence of conflicts in the official behavior of Negro policemen. The study dealt with Negro and white policemen in a midwestern urban police force. To determine the effects of racial background in relation to other factors comparisons were made between samples of Negro and white policemen in terms of such social characteristics as duty assignment, educational background, and rank on the police force. Methods employed in gathering data and the techniques applied to its analysis are discussed.*

SCOTT, James F. Racial Group Membership Role Orientation And Police Conduct Among Urban Policemen. *Phylon* 31(1),5–15 1970.

This paper attempts an analysis of whether racial group membership of white and black policemen influences their professional performance. Data is presented to describe one important dimension of police role performance; i.e., universalistic vs. particularistic standards by which policemen deal with other people. Responses were analyzed in regard to questions asked about the degree of familiarity policemen would permit with certain groups of people, how policemen and others felt about the exclusionary rule, and whether they felt police courtesy would promote conformity in others. White and black officers were found to differ in four of the eight instances. Thus, although neither of the factors were found to exert a uniform influence on the police role in either a universalistic or particularistic direction, race did seem to have a slightly stronger influence on particularism in police role, and duty assignment a slightly stronger influence on universalistic role performance.

SCOTT, Joseph E. The Use Of Discretion In Determining The Severity Of Punishment For Incarcerated Offenders. *J Crim L & Crimin* 65(2),214–224 1974.

SCOTT, Joseph. *The Black Revolts: Racial Stratification In The USA.* New Brunswick NJ Transaction Books 1977.

SCOTT, Kenneth. The Slave Insurrection In New York In 1712. *NYHSQ* 45,43–74 Ja 1961.

SEALE, Bobby. *Seize The Time.* NY Vintage 1970.

SEALE, Bobby. *The Trial Of Bobby Seale.* NY Arbor House 1970.

SEALY, Lloyd G. "The Dilemma Of Black Police Executives" in *Black Crime: A Police View*, Bryce, H J (ed), 141–156. Washington DC Jt Ctr Polit Stud 1977.

SEALY, Lloyd G and Fink, Joseph. *The Community And The Police: Conflict Or Cooperation.* Somerset Wiley 1974.

SEARS, David and Mc Conahay, John. Participation In The Los Angeles Riot. *Social Prob* 17,3–19 Sum 1969.

SEARS, David and Mc Conahay, John. Racial Socialization, Comparison Levels, And The Watts Riot. *J Soc Issues* 26(1),121–140 1970.

SEARS, David. Black Attitudes Toward The Political System In The Aftermath Of The Watts Insurrection. *Midw J Pol Sci* 13,515–544 N 1969.

SEDA, Cozetta and Ogleton, Betty and Crittendon, Stephanie. *An Examination Of Institutional Racism: Black People In California's Criminal Justice And Mental Health Systems.* Boulder CO W I C H E 1974.

The data indicate that there are racial differences in the treatment of people within, and between, the mental health and criminal justice systems. Blacks are greatly overrepresented in prisons and are slightly overrepresented in mental hospitals. While the proportion of blacks in the general population in California rose from 4.4% to 7.3% from 1950 to 1970, the proportion of blacks in prisons rose from 23% to 35%. The proportion of blacks in mental hospitals increased only from 8% to 10%. In 1970 if a person were black and institutionalized, chances were about 3 to 1 that he went to a prison rather than a mental hospital, while if a person were white, the chances were about 3 to 1 that he went to a mental hospital. These figures contrast sharply with those 1950 figures which indicate that both blacks and whites were more likely to go to mental hospitals. The decreased use of institutionalization has resulted in a reduced white population in prisons and mental hospitals from 1950 to 1970, while the black population in these institutions practically doubled.

SEGAL, Bernard E. Racial Group Membership And Juvenile Delinquency. *Soc Forces* 43(1),70–81 O 1964.

SEGAL, Bernard E. Racial Perspectives And Attitudes Among Negro And White Delinquent Boys: An Empirical Examination. *Phylon* 27(4),27–39 1966.

A standardized interview and a "projective stimulus" interview, consisting of a set of photos of blacks and whites interacting in a variety of different settings, were administered to lower and working–class, black and white delinquent boys in a state training school. The black boys were found to have a significantly higher mean racial awareness score than the white boys. The black boys were far more likely than the white boys to think that blacks lack chances to "get ahead in the world" equivalent to those of whites. They were also more likely than the white boys to be critical of their own racial group although the degree of group self–hatred was much higher among those committed for technical offenses (these boys were more concerned with satisfying their mobility aspirations and therefore rejected certain aspects of black lifestyle believed to give it a lower–class character). Relative deprivation and the frustration produced by the status of blacks as marginal to the mainstream of American culture are concluded to be important factors in delinquency among blacks and among others who are in many ways similar to them.

SEGAL, R. *The Race War.* NY Viking Pr 1967.

SEIDMAN, D and Couzens, M. Getting The Crime Rate Down: Political Pressure And Crime Reporting. *Law & Soc Rev* 8,457–493 1974.

SEIDMAN, David. Public Saftey: Crime Is Up, But What About Punishment? Ann Am Poli 435,248–267 Ja 1978.

Social Indicators, 1976 contains a chapter entitled "Public safety," which is found to be both insufficiently informative and inappropriately precise. An assessment is made of how well this chapter answers a minimum set of questions regarding crimes: what is happening? what is doing it? to whom is it happening? with what response? and why? It is concluded that these questions are not well answered, primarily as a result of limitations in the available data base. The sensitivity of the link between race and crime may account for the fact that no equivalent of the *SI '73* chart showing arrest rates by race is included in *SI '76.* Blacks have higher arrest rates. Differential police treatment of blacks and whites may account for some of the differences, but not all; blacks have higher victimization rates as well. Differences between blacks and whites in age distribution, income, and so forth could account for the rest, but the data do not exist to test the hypothesis.

SEIDMAN, Robert B and Chambliss, William J. *Law, Order And Power.* Menlo Park CA Addison–Wesley 1971.

SELLIN, Thorsten (ed). *The Death Penalty.* NY Harper & Row 1967.

SELLIN, Thorsten. "The Negro And The Problem Of Law Observance And Administration" in *The Negro In American Civilization,* Johnson, C S (ed). NY Henry Holt 1930.

It appears that the Negro comes more frequently into contact with criminal justice than the white, but whether he is more criminal is impossible to say with any degree of certainty. The data permit only one conclusion: that the Negro appears to be *arrested, convicted,* and *committed to penal institutions* more frequently than the white. Any other conclusion would be based on the assumption that the proportionate number of arrests, convictions or commitments to the total number of offenses actually committed is the same in both groups. This assumption is untenable, for there are factors, which seriously distort the arrest, conviction and commitment rates for Negroes without affecting these rates for whites. (Racial attitudes of the dominant white group are reflected in statistics on arrests, convictions and prison commitments of blacks and the rates which have been used as a crime index are deficient in other respects—for instance, the high proportion of young men in the black population will bear a direct relation to black crime rates since crime is most frequent among young men.)

SELLIN, Thorsten. *Culture Conflict And Crime.* NY Social Sci Res C 1938.

SELLIN, Thorsten. *Research Memorandum On Crime In The Depression.* NY Social Sci Res C 1937.

SELLIN, Thorsten. *Slavery And The Penal System.* NY Elsevier 1976.

SELLIN, Thorsten. *The Penalty Of Death.* Beverly Hills CA Sage 1980.

SELLIN, Thorsten. A Note On Capital Executions In The United States. *Br J Delinq* 11,6–14 1960.

This fairly general survey includes information taken from the Bureau of the Census Division of Criminal Statistics. Executions in the United States were distributed by race (white, Negro, American Indian, Oriental) for each year 1930–1947, and by race by offense (murder, rape, other [not including espionage]) for each year 1936–1947. The proportion of persons executed who were Negroes was found to be very high (greater than 60%) for each offense, and was found to increase with time.

SELLIN, Thorsten and Wolfgang, Marvin E and Figlio, Robert M. *Delinquency In A Birth Cohort.* Chicago Univ Chicago Pr 1972.

In this study of a cohort of all males born in 1945 who resided in the City of Philadelphia at least from their tenth until their eighteenth birthday (n = 9,945), 50 percent of non–whites had a recorded police contact between the ages of seven and eighteen while only 29 percent of whites had such contact. Race was found to be strongly related to delinquency regardless of socioeconomic status. Indeed, no other variable emerged quite so clearly as did race as a determinant of contrast. This holds true for nearly

every offense, but the racial difference was most pronounced for serious crime. IQ was found to differentiate between races, between social classes and between delinquents and nondelinquents with each race and class. Lower SES and nonwhite delinquents were more likely to use weapons in commissin of crime, though gun use was relatively infrequent. Nonwhites were more likely to be repeat offenders, and of repeaters, nonwhites were much more likely to become chronic offenders.

SELLIN, Thorsten. Race Prejudice In The Administration Of Justice. *Am J Soc* 41,212–217 S 1935.

SELLIN, Thorsten. The Negro Criminal: A Statistical Note. *Ann Am Poli* 140,52–64 N 1928.

Various measures of black crime are examined. The stated purpose of the article is "to indicate some of the ways by which the differential treatment to which the Negro is subjected by our agencies of criminal justice artificially increases his *apparent* criminality, while that of the white is, by virtue of the same treatment, so reduced that comparisons between the two become exceedingly hazardous unless this situation is properly evaluated and the rates corrected in light of the findings. While it is not argued that *real* criminality among blacks is as low or lower than it is among whites, the responsibility for any difference "lies where power, authority, and discrimination has its source, the dominant white group."

SELVIN, Hanan C and Hirschi, Travis. *Delinquency Research: An Appraisal Of Analytic Methods.* NY Free Pr 1967.

SENESE, Donald. "Legal Status Of The Slave In South Carolina, 1670–1740" in *Colonial American Essays In Political/Social Development,* Katz (ed), 404–415. Boston Little, Brown 1971.

SENESE, Donald. The Free Negro And The South Carolina Courts, 1790–1860. *S Car H M* 68,140–153 1967.

SENGSTACK, Mary. The Corporation And The Ghetto. *J Urban L* 45,673–703 1968.

SENN, David J and Sawyer, Jack. Institutional Racism And The American Psychological Association. *J Soc Issues* 29(1),67–79 1973.

SERRILL, Michael S and Katel, Peter. New Mexico: The Anatomy Of A Riot. *Correct Mag* 6(2),6–24 Ap 1980.

SERVÍN, Manuel. *An Awakening Minority: The Mexican Americans,* 2nd Ed. Beverly Hills Glencoe Pr 1974.

SEWELL, Trevor and Farley, Frank H. Attribution And Achievement Motivation Differences Between Delinquent And Non–Delinquent Black Adolescents. *Adoles* 10(34),391–397 Fall 1975.

To examine, with black subjects, the assumption that delinquents are less achievement motivated than nondelinquents, a 2 x 2 factorial design with two dependent measures (locus of control and achievement motivation) was used with delinquents versus nondelinquents and male versus females. Subjects were black fulltime sophomore students at an inner–city high school in a midwestern city. Results fail to support the hypothesis that delinquents would be more external in perceived locus of control than nondelinquents, at least for black adolescents. This lack of attribution difference between the delinquent and nondelinquent subjects is felt to be of great significance in the discussion of black adolescents' personality and world view, and of particular interest in the analysis of delinquency. it is suggested that feelings of helplessness against the system and attendant frustration are not involved in black juvenile delinquency.

SEWELL, Trevor and Farley, Frank H. Test Of An Arousal Theory Of Delinquency—Stimulation–Seeking In Delinquent And Nondelinquent Black Adolescents. *Crim Just B* 3(4),315–320 1976.

SEXTON, Patricia Coyo. *Spanish Harlem.* NY Harper & Row 1965.

SHANNON, B E. Implications Of White Racism For Social Work Practice. *Soc Casework* 51(5),270–276 1970.

SHANNON, B E. The Impact Of Racism On Personality Development. *Soc Casework* 54(9),519–525 1973.

SHANOK, Shelley S and Lewis, Dorothy O and Balla, David A. Some Evidence Of Race Bias In The Diagnosis And Treatment Of The Juvenile Offender. *Am J Orthopsych* 49(1),53–61 1979.

SHAPIRO, F C and Sullivan, J W. *Race Riots: New York, 1954.* NY Thos Y Crowell 1964.

SHAPIRO, Fred C. *Whitmore.* NY Pyramid 1970.

SHAW, Clifford et al. *Delinquency Areas.* Chicago Univ Chicago Pr 1929.

SHAW, Clifford and Mc Kay, Henry. *Juvenile Delinquency And Urban Areas.* Chicago Univ Chicago Pr 1942.

SHAY, Frank. *Judge Lynch, His First Hundred Years.* NY Ives Washburn 1938.

SHEEHAN, Bernard W. *Savagism And Civility: Indians And Englishmen In Colonial Virginia.* Cambridge MA Cambridge Univ Pr 1980.

SHEEHAN, Susan. *A Prison And A Prisoner.* Boston Houghton Mifflin 1978.

An in-depth account of life inside New York's Greenhaven State Correctional Facility, a maximum-security prison. The author, a freelance journalist, presents excerpts from extensive interviews with prisoners and staff. The prison routine is described in unusual detail. Sheehan writes that about 20 percent of the black and Puerto Rican prisoners had common-law marriages before they entered. She also mentions department efforts to hire more blacks and Hispanics as guards after the Attica prison uprising of 1971. In October 1976, she reports, there were 75 black and 20 Hispanic officers at Greenhaven.

SHEFLIN, N. *Sentencing Guidelines Project: Report To The Administrative Director Of The Courts On The Relationship Between Race And Sentencing.* Trenton NJ Admin Off Cts 1979.

The project's data base contains over 800 items of information from each of the 15,130 cases recorded in New Jersey from October 1976, to September 1977. Although about equal numbers of whites and blacks were convicted of crimes during the year, blacks received more prison sentences and longer terms. However, when the category of crime is considered, the disparities are reduced. For example, blacks receive almost 70% of the robbery convictions, which have an overall incarceration rate of 80%. To further test the relationship between race and sentencing, a model was constructed which examined each case in terms of variables, using multiple regression, t-tests, and chow tests. The report concludes that racially different but otherwise similar offenders sentenced for like offenses receive corresponding sentences. However, individuals are justifiably concerned about the disproportionate involvement of minority offenders in the criminal justice process.*

SHELDEN, Randall G. *Rescued From Evil: Origins Of The Juvenile Justice System In Memphis, Tennessee, 1900–1917.* Unpub PhD Diss S Illinois Univ 1976.

SHELDEN, Randall and Jenkins, Sam and Newton, Charles H. The Homogenization Process Within The Juvenile Justice System. *Int J Crimin Pen* 3(3),213–227 1975.

SHELDON, W H. *The Varieties Of Human Physique*, With Collaboration Of S S Stevens And W B Tucker. NY Harper 1940.

SHELLOW, R and Roemer, D V. The Riot That Didn't Happen. *Social Prob* 14,221–233 1966.

SHEPARDSON, Mary. Problems Of The Navajo Tribal Courts In Transition. *Human Org* 23(1),250–253 S 1964.

SHERMAN, Lawrence W and Langworthy, Robert H. Measuring Homicide By Police Officers. *J Crim L & Crimin* 70(4),546–560 Wint 1979.

SHERMAN, Lawrence W. Enforcement Workshop—Minority Quotas For Police Promotions: A Comment On Detroit Police Officers Association Versus Young. *Crim L Bull* 15(1),79–84 1979.

This commentary deals with a case involving the Detroit Police Officers Association in Michigan and a white police officer named Young who charged the Association with discriminatory practices in promotion. The judge held that the Detroit Police Department's policy since 1974 of promoting one black officer to sergeant for every white officer promoted unlawfully discriminates against white officers, primarily because there was no proof of past discrimination in the department and because employers may not voluntarily adopt a quota type of relief. Other factors influencing the judge's decision were that operational needs of the department did not justify the affirmative action plan, since there was no evidence that the increased number of minorities in supervisory ranks had improved the overall effectiveness of the department, and that the appropriate geographical area for defining the labor force from which police officers are drawn is the 1970 Census definition of the Detroit Standard Metropolitan Statistical Area. The author argues that there are unique concerns in law enforcement that may justify different laws governing employment practices.*

SHERMAN, Lawrence W. Execution Without Trial: Police Homicide And The Constitution. *Vand L Rev* 33,71–100 1980.

SHERMAN, Lewis J. Psychological View Of Women In Policing. *J Polic Sci Adm* 1(4),383–394 1973.

This study presents evidence showing that women can perform most police functions as effectively as men and occupy police jobs usually filled by men. Several examples of effective police work by policewomen in Indianapolis, Miami, Peoria, and Washington, D. C. are cited.*

SHICOR, David and O' Brien, Robert M and Decker, David L. *Urban Structure And Victimization.* Lexington MA Lexington 1980.

SHIN, Yongsock and Jedlicka, Davor and Lee, Everett. Homicide Among Blacks. *Phylon* 38(4),398–407 D 1977.

SHOCKLEY, John Staples. *Chicano Revolt In A Texas Town.* Notre Dame U Notre Dame Pr 1974.

SHOCKLEY, W. A Try Simplest Cases Approach To The Heredity—Poverty—Crime Problem. *Proc Nat Acad Sci* 57,1767–1774 Je 1967.

SHOHAM, S. Race And Crime. *Criminologist* 4(4),109–113 N 1969.

SHORE, James H. American Indian Suicide—Fact And Fantasy. *Psychi* 38(1),86–91 1975.

An epidemiology report on American Indian suicide patterns in the Pacific Northwest is presented. Fourteen males and six females committed suicide in the 3 years studied, the average age being 27 years. Eight males chose hanging and six chose shooting, whereas three females hung themselves, two had large drug overdoses, and one stepped in front of a car. Eleven of the 20 suicides occurred on the only Northwest reservation in the intermountain West. There were 82, 77, and 118 suicide attempts in the years 1969 to 1971, respectively, including 89 males and 162 females. The profile of the completed suicide subject is that of an Indian male, single or separated, with the suicide occurring in the home or jail. Alcohol abuse or solvent sniffing was involved in 75% of the cases. Results clarify previous misconceptions about the "American Indian suicide phenomenon."

SHORES, Arthur D. The Negro At The Bar: The South. *Nat Bar J* 2(3),266–272 1944.

SHORRIS, Earl. Spanish Harlem. *Harper's Mag* 257(1537),63–74 Je 1978.

The history of race riots in the US has gone through three stages of development. In the 19th and early 20th centuries, race riots were one-sided affairs in which whites assaulted Negroes without fear of retaliation. The riots of WWI and WWII years, on the other hand, were two-sided battles in which Negroes attacked white mobs, defended themselves and fought back. The riots of the 1960's represent a third type of racial conflict in which Negroes frustrated by ghetto life, clashed with policemen who had become symbols of oppression.

SHORT JR, James F. "Gang Delinquency And Anomie" in *Anomie And Deviant Behavior: A Discussion And Critique*, Clinard, Marshall B (ed), 98–127. NY Free Pr 1964.

SHORT JR, James F and Kolegar, Ellen and Strodtbeck, Fred L. The Analysis Of Self-Descriptions By Members Of Delinquent Gangs. *Sociol Q* 3(4),331–356 1962.

SHORT JR, James F and Olson, Virgil J and Nye, F Ivan. Socio-Economic Status And Delinquent Behavior. *Am J Soc* 63,381–389 1958.

SHORT JR, James F and Rivera, Ramon and Marshall, Harvey. Adult-Adolescent Relations And Gang Delinquency. *Pac Soc Rev* 7(2),59–65 Fall 1964.

SHORT JR, James F and Rivera, Ramon and Tennyson, Ray. Perceived Opportunities, Gang Membership, And Delinquency. *Am Sociol Rev* 30(1),56–67 1965.

SHORT JR, James F and Tennyson, Ray A and Howard, Kenneth I. Behavior Dimensions Of Gang Delinquency. *Am Sociol Rev* 28(3),411–429 Je 1963.

SHORT JR, James F. Comment On Lerman's 'Gangs, Networks, And Subcultural Delinquency'. *Am J Soc* 73(4),515–517 Ja 1968.

SHORT JR, James F. Street Corner Groups And Patterns Of Delinquency: A Progress Report. *Am Cath Sociol R* 24,13–32 Spr 1963.

SHOSTAK, David. Crosby Smith: Forgotten Witness To A Mississippi Nightmare. *Negro Hist Bull* 38(1),320–325 D-Ja 1974–75.

SHOSTECK, Herschel. Respondent Militancy As A Control Variable For Interview Effect. *J Soc Issues* 33(4),36–45 1977.

SHPRITZER, Felicia. Case For The Promotion Of Police Women In The City Of New York. *J Crim L Crimin & Pol Sci* 50(4),415–419 1959.

A history of the employment of policewomen in the city of NY is traced, and the lack of promotional opportunities as of 1959 is discussed.*

SHULMAN, Harry Manuel. "Ethnicity, Crime And Delinquency" in *Readings In Criminology And Penology*, Dressler, D (ed), 261–266. NY Columbia Univ Pr 1964.

Shulman critiques some of the major approaches to the study of criminality and ethnicity. Significant and often contradictory findings of these studies are reported. Shulman concludes that "wherever there are minority peoples in the United States who have made no great progress up the socioeconomic ladder and who have at the same time given up a certain amount of their ethnic solidarity and separateness, there is excessive juvenile delinquency." He notes, however, that there is evidence that marked differences in rate obtain among different ethnic groups, different nativity groups, and different socioeconomic levels in given ethnic groups. Along these lines Shulman concludes his article by asking whether the basic element in the excessive delinquency of certain stages of immigrant adjustment lies in "culture conflict or in frustrations in the struggle for equality in status and recognition, in which the element of culture difference may be only one factor among many in the competitive social order."

SHUMAN, Jerome. A Black Lawyers Study. *Howard L J* 16(2),225–313 1971.

SHURLING, James and Woodbury, Roger. Factorial Dimensions Of Jesness Inventory With Black Delinquents. *Ed & Psychol M* 35(4),979–981 1975.

The personality dimensions in the Jesness Inventory (JI) were identified among black male delinquents. A random sample of 250 black male delinquents was administered the JI. A principal components factor analysis with a varimax rotation identified three factors: 1) self-estrangement, 2) social isolation, and 3) immaturity. The proportions of total common factor variance accounted for by the three factors were .511, .286, and .203, respectively. These results suggest that the factors might be a part of a large alienation construct in black delinquents.

SICHEL, J L. *Expectations Which Have Shaped Women's Role In Policing New York City*. Washington DC NCJRS 1978.

SIEGAL, Bernard J. "Defensive Cultural Adaptation" in *The History Of Violence In America*, Graham, Hugh D And T Gurr (eds), 764–787. NY Praeger 1969.

SIEGEL, J M. A Brief Review Of The Effects Of Race In Clinical Service Interactions. *Am J Orthopsych* 44(4),555–562 1974.

SIEVERDES, Christopher M and Thomas, Charles W. Juvenile Court Intake: An Analysis Of Discretionary Decision–Making. *Criminology* 12(4),413–432 F 1975.

SIKES, M P. *Administration Of Injustice*. NY Harper & Row 1975.

SILBERMAN, Charles E. *Criminal Violence, Criminal Justice*. NY Random House 1978.

Charles E Silberman's book on violence has attracted considerable attention, as did his earlier books on race problems (*Crisis in Black and White*) and education (*Crisis in the Classroom*). Silberman contends that crime is essentially a race problem and that, until the root causes of crime are eliminated, law enforcement strategies can have little impact. Among his more controversial assertions are that most criminals eventually get caught and punished, that plea bargaining should not be abolished, that few serious criminals escape punishment because of lenient judges, and that police have not been hampered by such US Supreme Court holdings as the Miranda decision and the exclusionary rule.*

SILBERMAN, Charles E. *Crisis In Black And White*. NY Random House 1964.

SILLEN, Samuel and Thomas, Alexander. *Racism And Psychiatry*. NY Brunner/Mazel 1972.

SILVER, Allan A. "Official Interpretations Of Racial Riots" in *Urban Riots: Violence And Social Change*, Connery, R H (ed), 151–163. NY Vintage 1968.

SILVER, Isidore (ed). *The Crime Establishment*. Englewood Cliffs NJ Prentice–Hall 1974.

SILVERMAN, Arnold and Lieberson, Stanley. The Precipitants And Underlying Conditions Of Race Riots. *Am Sociol Rev* 30,887–898 D 1965.

The immediate precipitants and underlying conditions of 76 race riots in the US between 1913 and 1963 are examined, using journalistic accounts and census data. The precipitants tend to be highly charged violations of one racial group by the other—rape, murder, assault, and police brutaltiy. Since many of these precipitants are normally dealt with by established community institutions and because the response is not restricted to the alleged aggressor, various underlying conditions must be present. Hypotheses derived from earlier case studies and texts on collective behavior are examined to determine why riots occur where they do rather than in other cities of comparable size and location. Occupational and municipal government characteristics influence the occurrence of riots; demographic and housing characteristics do not. Riots seem most likely to occur in communitites where institutional malfunctioning, cross–pressures, or other inadequacies are such that the city is unable to resolve racial problems.

SILVERMAN, I J and Dinitz, Simon. Compulsive Masculinity And Delinquency: An Empirical Investigation. *Criminology* 11(4),498–515 F 1974.

The sample was drawn from a representative cross–section of the population at the Fairfield School for Boys, a facility operated by the Ohio Youth Commission. Each subject was administered a questionnaire which included a Compulsive Masculinity Index, the Lykken Scale, and the Zuckerman Scale. The Compulsive Masculinity Index was used to measure the boys' self–identification with tough behavior and sexual athleticism. The Lykken Scale was included to measure impulsiveness and proneness to activities that are high risk in nature and excitement oriented. It also measures general hostility. The Zuckerman Scale was included to measure field dependency–tendency to be effected by environmental influences including peer pressures. Each respondent was asked to rate himself and all the other boys in his cottage according to how manly he considered himself and each other boy to be. This study suggests that delinquent boys from female–based households were more hyper–masculine than delinquents from other types of households. It was also shown that black delinquents as a group define themsleves as being more manly and tough than white delinquents in the same training school.

SILVERSTEIN, Lee. *Defense Of The Poor: The National Report*, 3v. Chicago IL ABA 1965.

SILVERT, K H and La Violette, Forrestt. A Theory Of Stereotypes. *Soc Forces* 29,257–262 1951.

SIMKUS, Albert A and Hall, Edwin L. Inequality In The Types Of Sentences Received By Native Americans And Whites. *Criminology* 13(2),199–222 Ag 1975.

A comparison of the distribution of the types of sentences imposed on Native American offenders and white offenders by the district courts of a western state reveals that the Native American offenders are more likely to receive sentences involving incarceration in the state prison and are less likely to receive sentences which would allow them partially to escape stigmatization as convicted felons. The introduction of a number of test factors revealed that these ethnic differences in the sentence received would only slightly be explained by ethnic differences in the kinds of offenses involved or in other differences in the legal and personal background characteristics of the offenders. A number of possible explanations of the discrepancies in the sentencing of Native Americans and whites are discussed. It is suggested that these discrepancies in themselves may contribute to an increased probability that the Native American offenders will engage in future criminal activity and that these offenders will continue to receive harsher sentences than white offenders.

SIMMEN, Edward (ed). *The Chicano: From Caricature To Self–Portrait*. NY Mentor Books 1971.

SIMMONS, R G et al. Self–Esteem And Achievement Of Black And White Adolescents. *Social Prob* 26(1),86–96 1978.

SIMON, Frank and Pasto, Tarmo A and Bromberg, Walter. Symbolism In A 'Protest Psychosis'. *Israel Ann Psychi Rel Disc* 10(2),164–179 1972.

A special type of reactive psychosis among Negro prisoners charged with aggressive crimes is described along with case material. Because the clinical picture, usually diagnosed as schizophrenia, contained distinct elements of African ideology, Muslim religious doctrine and distinct anti–Caucasian hostility with reflections on centuries–old white domination of non white peoples, it was labeled protest psychosis. The illness was short–lived, and started abruptly after either arraignment or indictment for an aggressive crime. While the prisoners were in confinement they demonstrated mutism, destructive wild behavior, incoherence, hallucinations of auditory or visual type, bizarre utterances and mannerisms. Included in the discussion are a series of drawings made by one patient which demonstrate the underlying dynamics of the protest reaction. It is noted that the patient was unaware, on recovery several months later, that he had produced such artistic material while psychotic.

SIMON, Patricia Vandel and Samora, Julian. *A History Of The Mexican American People*. Notre Dame U Notre Dame Pr 1977.

SIMON, William and Berger, Alan S. Black Families And The Moynihan Report: A Research Evaluation. *Social Prob* 22(2),145–161 1974.

Employing a random sample of the 14–18–year–old population of Illinois, the authors seek to test Daniel Patrick Moynihan's controversial thesis that black families socialize children very differently from the way white families socialize children. This study found few such differences. Even in lower–class families there was no indication that black families were dramatically different from white families.

SIMPSON, George Eaton and Yinger, J Milton. *Racial And Cultural Minorities: An Analysis Of Prejudice And Discrimination*. NY Harper & Row 1965.

SIMPSON, Ray Mars. Post–War Trends In Employment, Crime, Insanity, And Heart Disease. *J Soc Psychol* 6(1),125–129 F 1935.

SIMPSON, Ray Mars. Unemployment And Prison Commitments. *J Am Inst Cr L Crim* 23,404–414 1932.

SIMS, Patsy. *The Klan*. Briarcliff Manor NY Stein & Day 1978.

SINGELL, Larry D and Mc Nown, Robert F. A Factor Analysis Of The Socio–Economic Structure Of Riot And Crime Prone Cities. *Ann Reg Sci* 8(1),1–13 1974.

SINGER, H Douglas and Ordahl, George W. A Study Of Prisoners At The Joliet Penitentiary. *Inst Q* 6,19–24 S 30 1915.

SINGER, Linda R and Goldfarb, Ronald L. *After Conviction: A Review Of The American Correctional System*. NY Simon & Schuster 1973.

Two attorneys provide a legalistic, in–depth description of the American correctional system. Major cases in the area of prisoners' rights are noted and explained in this comprehensive and massively documented critique.

SINGER, Linda R. Enforcing The Constitutional Rights Of Prisoners. *Howard L J* 17,823–832 1973.

SINGER, R D and Lomas, H D. *Graffiti And Crime: A Transcultural Study Of Narcissistic Rage*. Rockville MD NCJRS 1979.

Graffiti and criminal aggression are studied in terms of archaic narcissism, i.e., the phenomenon of narcissistic rage, with attention given to cultural and psychological influences on crime. Chicanos and other persons of Latin descent have a propensity to produce graffiti. Understanding certain aspects of the Chicano personality, particularly those aspects related to feelings of exclusion, resentment, and desire for revenge, can be helpful in bridging the gap between majority cultures and institutions and Chicanos. To the extent graffiti are linked to specific personality disturbances that lend themselves to criminal behavior, the study of developmental, cultural, and psychological determinants represents a study of the correlates of crime. A study is proposed to compare the production of graffiti by Chicanos and Anglos.*

SINGLE, Eric and Boston, John and Hermann, Robert. *Counsel For The Poor: Criminal Defense In Urban America*. Lexington MA Lexington 1977.

SIRMANS, M Eugene. The Legal Status Of The Slave In South Carolina, 1670–1740. *Southern Hist* 28,462–473 N 1962.

SISSONS, Peter L. *The Hispanic Experience In Criminal Justice*. Bronx NY Fordham Hisp R Cen n.d.

SKEMER, Don C. New Evidence Of Black Unrest In Colonial Brooklyn. *J Long Is Hist* 12,46–49 Fall 1975.

SKOLER, Daniel L and Lowenstein, Ralph. *Non Discrimination, Equal Opportunity And Legal Issues On Minorities In Corrections*. Washington DC ABA 1973.

SKOLER, Daniel and Lowenstein, Ralph. Minorities In Correction—Nondiscrimination, Equal Opportunity And Legal Issues. *Crim Deling* 20(4),339–346 1974.

Examines new policies and trends in the employment of minorities in the field of corrections. One of the most striking manpower problems in our correctional systems is the vast disparity in racial composition between inmate populations and correctional staffs. This imbalance has stimulated a move to increased minority hiring in correction. In the past two or three years, developments on three levels—rhetoric, judicial decisions, and administrative regulations—offer hope that the goal of increased minority hiring will be realized.

SKOLNICK, Jerome M. "The Police And The Urban Ghetto" in *Race, Crime, And Justice*, Reasons, Charles E And Jack L Kuykendall (eds), 236–258. Pacific Palisades CA Goodyear 1972.

SKOLNICK, Jerome M and Schwartz, Richard D. *Society And The Legal Order*. NY Basic Books 1970.

SLEYSTER, Rock. Physical Basis Of Crime As Observed By A Prison Physican. *Bull Am Acad Med* 14,396–407 D 1913.

SLEYSTER, Rock. The Criminal Physique: A Preliminary Report On The Physical Examination Of 1521 Prisoners At Wisconsin State Prison. *J Am Med Assoc* 60,1351–1353 My 3 1913.

SLOAN, J and West, J. The Role Of Informal Policy Making In US–Mexico Border Cities. *Social Sci Q* 58(2),270–282 1977.

SLOTKIN, Richard. Narratives Of Negro Crime In New England, 1775–1880. *Am Q* 25,3–31 Mr 1973.

SMITH JR, Griffin. The Mexican Americans: A People On The Move. *Nat Geogr* 157(6),780–808 Je 1980.

Richly photographed profile of Mexican–American people and lifestyles. Chicanos "tend to share a sense of being controlled by external forces, of being on the margin of society as a powerless class...a symbolic bond of brotherhood forged by suffering and a perception of injustice," according to one Mexican–American educator.

SMITH, A La Mont and Carter, Robert M. The Death Penalty In California: A Statistical And Composite Portrait. *Crim Deling* 15,62–76 1969.

The data for this descriptive study came mostly from the files of the California Department of Corrections. The study includes a breakdown by race of the 187 men executed in California between 1938 and 1963; the number of these men grouped by age (five–year intervals) and race; the same data by race and place of birth. The sample is also broken down by claimed educational achievement, and by Intelligence Quotient.

SMITH, A R. Black Perspective On Pretrial Diversion. *Urb League Rev* 1(2),25–28 Fall 1975.

SMITH, D D et al. *Delinquency 1975—United States Estimates Of Cases Processed By Courts With Juvenile Jurisdiction.* Pittsburgh Nat Cen Juv Just 1979.

First in a series, this annual report on delinquency presents 1975 national estimates of youthful law violators and data on how they are processed by the juveniles justice system. Information in this report will aid decisionmakers, planners, and researchers to chart future course of juvenile justice in the United States. During 1975, there were 66,240,000 young people below the age of 18 involved in some way with juvenile court. Based on the child population at risk, an estimated 1,406,100 of juvenile cases were disposed of by the courts with youth jurisdiction. The rate of cases to individuals, a general measure of both court activity and delinquent activity is 45.8 cases per 1,000 youth population at risk. Data indicates that males are three times more likely to be processed by the courts than females and that cases involving members of racial minorities are proportionately more likely to be handled by the courts. An estimated 63,942,100 of these young people can be defined as low risk (0 to 9 years) or relatively high risk (10 and older). This latter group, referred to as the child population at risk, numbered 30,720,490 during 1975.*

SMITH, Dwight C. Mafia: The Prototypical Alien Conspiracy. *Ann Am Poli* 423,75–88 Ja 1976.

SMITH, Gerald W. The Value Of Life, Arguments Against The Death Penalty: A Reply To Professor Lehtinen. *Crim Deling* 23(3),253–259 1977.

SMITH, John and Smith, Lois. Freedoms And The Politics Of Mass Participation: Perspective On The 1967 Detroit Riot. *J Urban L* 45,503–562 1968.

SMITH, Joseph. *Sir Corner And Joe Smith: A Story Of Vice & Corruption In Chicago*. NY Exposition Pr 1963.

SMITH, Lois and Smith, John. Freedoms And The Politics Of Mass Participation: Perspective On The 1967 Detroit Riot. *J Urban L* 45,503–562 1968.

SMITH, Mapheus and Reckless, Walter C. *Juvenile Delinquency*. NY McGraw–Hill 1932.

SMITH, Monica Herrera. Exploring The Re–Entry And Support Services For Hispanic Offenders, Natnl Hispanic Con L Enf, & CJ. Washington DC US Dept Justice 1980.

SMITH, N J and Batta, I D and Mc Culloch, J W. A Study Of Juvenile Delinquency Amongst Asians And Half–Asians: A Comparative Study In A Northern Town Based On Official Statistics. *Br J Crimin* 15(1),32–42 Ja 1975.

SMITH, Reginald H. *Justice And The Poor*. NY Scribner's 1919.

SMITH, Sidonie. *Where I'm Bound: Patterns Of Slavery And Freedom In Black American Autobiography.* Westport CT Greenwood Pr 1974.

The life stories of seven twentieth century black Americans (Richard Wright, Langston Hughes, Malcolm X, Eldridge Cleaver, Maya Angelou, Horace Cayton, and Claude Brown) form the basis for an examination of the psychology and social psychology of the problematic quest for self, the most salient dimension of the black American experience. The class slave narrative, which recounts the break from an oppressive and self–destroying society and the correlative flight to a new place (geographical and social) that promised self–realization, provides the model.

SMITH, W C. Negro Boys In The Youth Development Centers Of Georgia. *J Negro Ed* 38,69–73 1969.

SMITH, Willie D. *The Effects Of Racial Milieu And Parental Racial Attitudes And Rearing Practices On Black Children's Racial Identity/Self–Esteem/Behavior.* Unpub PhD Diss Stanford Univ 1975.
The holistic notion of self–concept was examined reducing its generality to the single dimension of self–esteem and identity. Specifically, the self–concepts and behaviors of 4–year old black children living and attending preschools in two racially different environments (black versus white milieu) were examined, along with the effect of parental racial attitudes toward whites and interaction of rearing patterns and environmental variables. Racial identity and self–esteem varied distinctly in the two groups. In the white milieu, parents with high anti–white attitudes had children with lower self–esteem than those with low anti–white attitudes, but racial identity showed no significant differences based on these attitudes. In the black milieu, parents with high anti–white attitudes had children with higher racial identity, but self–esteem did not differ. Results suggest that the racial milieu has a significant main effect on identity and self–esteem, and aggression for black children. In both milieus, however, low self–esteem children were more aggressive

SMYTH, J A. Negro Criminality. *Southern Workman* 29,625+ N 1911.

SNARR, R W and Mc Cauley, R P. *Minority Recruitment Manual For Ohio Peace Officers Report, 1977.* London OH Ohio PO Tr Acad 1976.
Guidelines pertaining to minority recruitment of Ohio peace officers are presented. Covered are the bases for antidiscrimination policies, discrimination in law enforcement, and remediation of discriminatory practices. The manual is designed to assist local law enforcement agencies in their efforts to increase representation of ethnic minorities and women as sworn peace officers. It is emphasized that minority recruitment does not refer to preferential hiring practices; rather, the goal is to attract the most qualified minority group members. In a democratic society, all persons should be permitted to participate in governmental processes. The rights of minority and women applicants are supported by the 14th amendment of the constitution, the Civil Rights Act and the Equal Employment Opportunity Act, IEAA, the Ohio Civil Rights Commission, and the courts. The organizational philosophy and commitment, policies and procedures, needs and goals, and requisite resources of the law enforcement personnel system are discussed within the context of discrimination issues and answers.*

SNIBBE, H M et al. Race Differences In Police Patrolmen: A Failure To Replicate The Chicago Study. *Am J Comm Psy* 4(2),155–160 1976.

SNIBBE, H M and Fabricatore, Joseph and Azen, Stanley P. Personality Patterns Of White, Black, And Mexican American Patrolmen As Measured By The Sixteen Personality Factor Questionaire. *Am J Comm Psy* 3(3),221–227 1975.
The Sixteen Personality Factor Questionnaire was administered to 491 white, black, and Chicano patrolmen of the Los Angeles Sheriff's Department to obtain a normative police profile. Multi–variate analysis revealed that the average patrolman appeared brighter, more reserved, dominant and tough–minded than the average male. Comparisons were made for 29 black, 33 Mexican–American and 399 white officers. Mexican American officers emerged as more conservative and relaxed than whites, while black officers appeared more experimental, analytical and group–oriented. A comparison with an independent police sample revealed common traits of self–assurance and conservatism. Results were compared with a social worker's profile and discussed in relation to the police officer's actual job activities and community needs.

SNORTUM, J and Ashear, V. Prejudice, Punitiveness And Personality. *J Pers Assess* 36,291–301 1972.

SOJA, Thomas. Racial Discrimination In Jury Selection: *United States V Robinson. Albany L Rev* 41,623–638 1977.

SOLLENBERGER, Richard T. Chinese–American Child–Rearing Practices And Juvenile Delinquency. *J Soc Psychol* 74(1),13–23 1968.

SOLOMON, Frederic et al. *Civil Rights Activity And Reduction In Crime Among Negroes.* Washington DC Howard U Cen Y C S 1964.

SOMERVILLE, B. Double Standards In Law Enforcement With Regard To Minority Status. *Issues Crim* 4(1),35–43 1968.

SORKIN, Allan. The Economic Basis Of Indian Life. *Ann Am Poli* 436,13–26 Mr 1978.

SOROKIN, Pitirim A. "Fluctuation Of Ethico–Juridicial Mentality In Criminal Law" in *Sociocultural Dynamics,* V3, 523–632. NY Am Book Co 1937.

SOSIS, R H and Nemeth, C. A Simulated Jury Study: Characteristics Of The Defendant And The Jurors. *J Soc Psychol* 90,221–229 1973.

SOUTHERN COMMISION ON THE STUDY OF LYNCHING. *Lynchings And What They Mean.* Atlanta S C S Lynching 1931.

SOUTHERN REGIONAL COUNCIL. Negro Police In Southern Cities. *New South* 2,1–5,7 O 1947.
Survey reports 279 Negro police employed in 54 cities in 11 Southern states.

SOUTHERN REGIONAL COUNCIL. Negro Police In Southern Cities. *New South* 3,7–8 S 1948.
Survey reports 279 Negro police employed in 54 cities in 11 Southern states.

SOWELL, Thomas. *Race And Economics.* NY David McKay 1975.

SPAIN, Johnny. The Black Family And The Prisons. *Black Scholar* 4(2),18–31 O 1972.

SPARLING, C L and Inn, A and Wheeler, A C. The Effects Of Suspect Race And Situation Hazard On Police Officer Shooting Behavior. *J App So P* 7(1),27–37 1977.
Results of this study suggest that racial bias is not a factor in police shooting decisions.

SPEAR, Allan. *Black Chicago: The Making Of A Negro Ghetto, 1890–1920.* Chicago Univ Chicago Pr 1967.

SPEAR, Allan. The Changing Nature Of Racial Violence. *New Pol* 5,115–122 Mr 1967.

SPEARMAN, R W and Stevens, H. *Step Toward Equal Justice—Programs To Increase Black Lawyers In The South, 1969–1973.* NY Carnegie Corp NY 1974.
Results of an extensive evaluation of a number of grant programs designed to increase the number of black lawyers in the South between 1969 and 1973 are presented. Grants from private foundations, corporations, and individuals provided support for programs of the Earl Warren Legal Training Program, Inc., the National Association for the advancement of Colored People Legal Defense and Educational Fund (LDF), and the Law Students Civil Rights Research Council (LSCRRC). The series of grants constituted a broad systems approach to the needs of blacks in 11 states. Results of the evaluation indicate that since 1969 the number of black first–year law students has increased from 22 to 171 in 17 Southern law schools, 375 black students were enrolled in these schools in 1973, and a majority of these black students intended to practice law in the South.*

SPEARS, David (ed) and Richardson, Ken (ed). *Race, Culture And Intelligence.* Harmondsworth England Penguin Books 1972.

SPECIAL COMMITTEE ON PENAL AND CORRECTIONAL REFORM. *How The Criminal Justice System Fails The Spanish–Speaking Community Of New York City And What Should Be Done About It.* NY NY County L Assn 1975.

SPECTOR, M I and Hill Jr, C A and Ogden, Michael. Suicides And Homicides Among Indians. *Public Health Rep* 85(1),75–80 1970.

SPEER, David C and Williams, James and Pew, Miriam L. Group Counseling For Offenders. *Social Wk* 18(1),74–79 1973.
The results of a community–based group counseling program for offenders in St. Paul, Minn., are discussed. The program has been successful both in rehabilitation and crime prevention, attracting wide and favorable attention in the city's legal circles and among residents of its inner city. This project has provided promising evidence that offenders will make significant voluntary use of community–based group counseling and intensive individual services. There are also indications that such group and individual services contribute to a decrease in the number of subsequent offenses committed.

SPENCER, Elousie J. *The Social System Of A Medium Security Women's Prison.* Unpub PhD Diss Univ of Kansas 1978.

SPERGEL, Irving. Male Young Adult Criminality Deviant Values, And Differential Opportunities In Two Lower Class Negro Neighborhoods. *Social Prob* 10(3),237–250 Wint 1963.

SPERLICH, Peter W and Jaspovice, Martin L. Grand Juries, Grand Jurors And The Constitution: Statistical Decision Theory And The Selection Of Grand Jurors. *Hastings Const L Q* 1,63–95 1974.

SPERLICH, Peter W and Jaspovice, Martin L. Methods For The Analysis Of Jury Panel Selection: Testing For Discrimination In A Series Of Panels. *Hastings Const L Q* 6,787–852 1979.

SPERLICH, Peter W. Social Science Evidence In The Courts: Reaching Beyond The Adversary Process. *Judicature* 63(6),280–289 1980.

SPIELBERGER, C D (ed). *Police Selection And Evaluation—Issues And Techniques.* NY Praeger 1979.
The state of knowledge regarding police selection is reviewed and evaluated: methodological and practical problems encountered in the development and use of selection procedures are identified.*

SPIER, Rosalind B and Pettigrew, Thomas F. Ecological Pattern Of Negro Homicide. *Am J Soc* 67(6),621–629 My 1962.

SPILERMAN, S. The Causes Of Racial Disturbances: Tests Of An Explanation. *Am Sociol Rev* 36(3),427–442 1971.

SPIRER, Jess. *Negro Crime.* Baltimore MD Johns Hopkins Pr 1940.

SPITZER, Steven. Punishment And Social Organization: A Study Of Durkheim's Theory Of Penal Evolution. *Law & Soc Rev* 9(4),613–635 1975.

SPUHLER, J N and Loehlin, John C and Lindzey, Gardner. *Race Differences In Intelligence.* San Francisco CA W H Freeman 1975.

SQUIRES, G D. *Affirmative Action—A Guide For The Perplexed.* East Lansing MI Mich SI U I C D 1977.
Major legislation, court decisions, executive orders, and implementing regulations related to civil rights enforcement in employment, education, housing, voting rights, and federally–assisted programs are summarized. The major federal civil rights legislation, orders, and regulations enacted in the past two decades show the most extensive changes in employment, where the concept of affirmative action is being applied. This handbook explains the rationale behind affirmative action: what it means, what it requires, of whom it is required, and the consequences of noncompliance. The basic steps in developing, implementing, and evaluating an affirmative action program are reviewed, and a list of sources that can assist in mounting such a program is provided. A directory of the major federal civil rights agencies that can offer asistance and information is included, together with a bibliography containing publications that explain what civil rights law requires, how and where to file complaints, recommendations for action, and evaluations of current enforcement efforts.*

ST LOUIS HUMAN DEVELOPMENT PLANNING PROJECT. *The Sources Of Delinquency: A Diagnostic Study.* St Louis Hum Dev Plan Proj 1963.

STACHURA, S and Teske Jr, R H C. *Spouse Abuse In Texas—A Special Report.* Huntsville TX Sam Houston CJC 1979.

STAHL, David and Sussman, Frederick B and Bloomfield, Neil J. *The Community And Racial Crisis.* NY Practising L Ins 1966.

STAMPP, Kenneth M. *The Civil Rights Record: Black Americans The The Law.* NY Thos Y Crowell 1970.

STAMPP, Kenneth M. *The Peculiar Institution: Slavery In The Ante–Bellum South.* NY Knopf 1956.

STAMPP, Kenneth M. Rebels And Sambos: The Search For The Negro's Personality In Slavery. *J Southern Hist* 37,367–392 Ag 1971.

STANTON, William. *The Leopard's Spots: Scientific Attitudes Toward Race In America, 1815–1859.* Chicago Univ Chicago Pr 1960.

STAPLES, Robert. "Black Crime And Delinquency" in *Introduction To Black Sociology*, 212–247. NY McGraw–Hill 1976.
This document uses the colonial model to explain the relationship between black oppression and the disproportionate amount of crime found in its environs. In a colonial setting the subject group is set apart geographically from the dominant group, which exposes it to a different set of cultural standards that have no legitimacy in the colonizer's society. The native has a status which is never equal to that of the white settler. Because their own cultural values have not legitimacy in the settler's world, natives must conform to standards that are alien to them and which they possess no

resources to meet. This kind of vicious cycle determines the form of black crime in the United States, and the political and economic inequalities inherent in a colonial setting inevitably influence the Afro–American's chances for equal justice under the law. Achieving justice for blacks under the legal system is difficult because the laws reflect the racial inequality in this country. The legalization of the colonial order is best represented by the US Constitution, which contains three provisions legally establishing the subjugated colonized status of blacks. Ways to reduce some of the inequities are discussed.*

STAPLES, Robert. "Towards A Sociology Of The Black Family" in *Afro–Americans: A Social Science Perspective*, Dennis, Rutledge M And Charles Jarmon (eds). Washington DC Univ Pr America 1976.
This paper is a summary and analysis of research and theory on black families in the past decade. In the macro–sociological section the theories on black family life are critically analyzed for their theoretical and methodological validity. The second section presents micro–sociological research findings on black family life and is more of a summary of the research literature on this subject. These research findings are presented according to the typical family stage sequences of black family life, from dating behavior to parental roles and socialization processes. In his overall assessment of works on the black family the author concludes that the imposition of ethnocentric values on the analysis of black family life preclude the application of much of the current research and theory to the development of a viable sociology of the black family.

STAPLES, Robert. *Introduction To Black Sociology.* NY McGraw–Hill 1976.

STAPLES, Robert. "Race And Family Violence" in *Crime And Its Impact On The Black Community*, Gary, L E And L P Brown (eds), 85–96. Washington DC Howard U 1976.
Black family violence and the machinations of internal colonialism are inextricably linked. The crucial variable in maintaining the practice of intra–family violence among blacks has been their status as a colonized people. There is no reason to believe that the lower–class or blacks are any more prone to violence than the middle class or white population. Yet they are so over–represented in the official statistics on crimes of family violence as to preclude any explanation other than racial and economic forces as being responsible. With the attendant fragility of marriages, female–headed households and parent–child tensions, violence continues to be a primary source of conflict resolution in the family. It is a violence that was introduced to Afro–Americans in the period of slavery that has persisted. While a greater emphasis on family solidarity, respect for women, and value of children can do much to reduce violence within the black family, only by eliminating the cause of, and cultural support for, violence in the larger society, can we expect a lasting solution.

STAPLES, Robert. The Myth Of The Black Matriarchy. *Black Scholar* 1(3–4),8–16 1970.
Characterizing the myth of the black matriarchy as a "cruel hoax," Staples begins his article by stating that this myth adds insult to injury to black liberation. "For the black female," he states, "her objective reality is a society where she is economically exploited because she is both female and black; she must face the inevitable situation of a shortage of black males because they have been taken out of circulation by America's neo–colonialist wars, railroaded into prisons, or killed off early by the effects of ghetto living conditions. To label her a matriarch is a classical example of what Malcolm X called making the victim the criminal." Staples attempts to explode this myth by examining the historical role of the black woman and the development of that role as it was influenced by the political and economic organization of American society.

STAPLES, Robert. To Be Young, Black And Oppressed. *Black Scholar* 7(4),2–9 1975.
White colonialist interests are served vis–a–vis young blacks by providing irrelevant ineffective educational programs to blacks, which precipitate dropping out of school, the development of low self–esteem, and an inability to compete with whites in the job market. A proportionately high rate of poorly educated young blacks who cannot find employment in the job market fuels the ranks of the "volunteer" military services, which are in turn dominated by white colonialists. Many young blacks turn to crime and the subculture of gangs in order to survive economically and socially. Black females turn to motherhood to find an identity, and in the absence of an income–earning male in the family, become increasingly dependent on the meagre welfare income provided by the white colonialists. Young, black males who turn to crime and even those who do not are harrassed by the

police and disproportionately imprisoned in comparison to the treatment of white offenders. The effective alienation of young blacks from white colonialist society increases control over blacks, debilitating consequences to the black community and creates a potential for revolution.*

STAPLES, Robert. Violence And Black America: The Political Implications. *Black World* 23(7),16–34 1974.

Using concepts derived from Fanon's *The Wretched of the Earth,* it is argued that "the common belief that black violence is a threat to civilized society actually derives from the power of a colonial society to define what is legitimate or illegitimate violence." Black violence is seen as an exaggerated form of the normative pattern of violence which is institutionalized in America's social structure. Several theories of black violence (e.g., relative deprivation and the "matriarchy myth") are refuted and a model of internal colonialism, is advanced. This model proposed that "Black violence is a reflection of colonial relationships—a social order in which race defines life chances, opportunities for subsistence and social rewards, and access to social position." It is argued that the dynamics force disproportionally more blacks into the lowest class of society. Due to this and to the dehumanizing effects of racism, violence must be explained in the context of colonial rather than class relationships.

STAPLES, Robert. White Racism, Black Crime And American Justice: An Application Of The Colonial Model To Explain Crime And Race. *Phylon* 36,14–22 Mr 1975.

The colonial model is applied to explain the relationship between race and crime, and empirical evidence is presented in support of the theory. The law itself is formulated by white men to protect white interests, and is oppressive of black people. In order that policemen enforce the white man's rule, they are primarily members of the colonizer's group, and also represent the more authoritarian and racist members of the sector. Studies have revealed anti–black attitudes on the part of the police and it has been shown that a disproportionate number of police killings involve black victims. Blacks complain that police are more tolerant of illegal activities in black communities and treat calls for help from black areas as much less urgent. Many times these crimes are committed against other blacks. High homicide rates among blacks are explained by Fanon as an expression by the natives of aggression felt toward the colonizers but directed against their own people. Thus, while blacks are generally given longer prison terms than whites for the same crime, they get shorter sentences for murder.

STARKMAN, Gary and Ginsberg, George. Civil Disturbances, Mass Processing And Misdemeanants: Rights, Remedies And Realities. *J Crim L Crimin & Pol Sci* 61,39–50 1970.

STARLS, R. *Police Riots: Collective Violence And Law Enforcement.* Belmont CA Wadsworth Pub Co 1972.

STAROBIN, Robert (ed). *Denmark Vesey: The Slave Conspiracy Of 1822.* Englewood Cliffs NJ Prentice–Hall 1972.

STARR, F M. Indians And The Criminal Justice System. *Can J Crim* 20(3),317–323 Jl 1978.

STARR, Raymond. Historians And The Origins Of British North American Slavery. *Historian* 36,1–18 N 1973.

STATE OF COLORADO. *Helping Understand Delinquent Behavior In An Urban Setting.* Denver CO Denver Juvenile Ct 1971.

The present volume of readings was conceived as a method of exposing staff in the Denver Juvenile Court to current writings about the nature and extent of social forces which in one way or another are impinging on the Court's present and projected clientele groups. The book is divided into four sections. Section I contains articles of relevance to deviancy, identity, and role identification. Section II covers the structural–institutional side of socialization, considering institutions both inside and outside the juvenile justice system. Section III portrays the different subcultures and subworlds in which adolescents are socialized, emphasizing blacks and Chicanos but also covering what is known as the counterculture and drug culture. It is noted that the material on Mexican–American life may fail in either quality or quantity mainly because of a paucity of work done on this group. It is also noted that work on the influence of peer groups is absent because of defects in those articles available on the subject. Section IV examines the role of power in the juvenile courts system.

STATE PEACE OFFICERS JOURNAL. Law And Order On The Reservation––A Look At The Indian Police. *State Peace Off J* 12(23),46–48,50 Mr–Ap 1974.

STATSKY, William P. Teaching Corrections Law To Corrections Personnel. *Fed Prob* 37,42–45 Je 1973.

STAUDENRAUS, P J. *The African Colonization Movement, 1816–1865.* NY Columbia Univ Pr 1961.

STAUSS, Joseph H and Chadwick, Bruce A. The Assimilation Of American Indians Into Urban Society: The Seattle Case. *Human Org* 34(4),359–369 1975.

The level of assimilation of American–Indians living in Seattle, Washington, was assessed using a seven stage model of assimilation developed by Gordon. In addition, two hypotheses concerning the antecedents of assimilation were tested. Results reveal that on only two of the seven stages did Indians in Seattle evidence a significant level of assimilation. The overall level of assimilation of urban Indians was fairly low, especially in the area of political participation and conflict with the dominant power structure. Tests of the first hypothesis, which predicted that other stages leading to total assimilation would inevitably follow from structural assimilation, reveal that the degree of structural assimilation was not related to the other stages. Results also fail to support the second hypothesis, which concerned the relationship between length of time lived in the city and assimilation.

STAUSS, Joseph and Harris, William and Jensen, Gary. Crime, Delinquency And The American Indian. *Human Org* 36(3),252–257 Fall 1977.

STEEL, William F. Discrimination In Supermarket, Prices And Location In Nashville. *Rev Black Poli Econ* 4, 1930-33 Wint 1974.

STEELE, B F and Pollock, C B. "A Psychiatric Study Of Parents Who Abuse Infants And Small Children" in *The Battered Child*, Helter, R E And C H Kempe (eds). Chicago Univ Chicago Pr 1974.

STEELE, Eric H and Jacobs, James B. Prisons: Instruments Of Law Enforcement Or Social Welfare? *Crim Delinq* 21(4),348–355 O 1975.

STEINBERG, J L and Mc Evoy, D W. *Police And The Behavioral Sciences.* Springfield IL Chas C Thomas 1974.

STEINER, Jesse F and Brown, Roy M. *The North Carolina Chain Gang: A Study Of County Convict Road Work*, Orig Pub 1927. Montclair NJ Patterson Smith 1969.

This history of the chain gang in North Carolina contends there is no doubt that the underlying motive for the use of prisoners in county chain gangs was economic. The authors insist that the early development of the Southern prison system in the two decades immediately following the Civil War was primarily aimed at "dealing with the Negro prisoner." Blacks were strongly overrepresented in both county and state prisons throughout the South after slavery was abolished. The chain gangs performed many jobs, the most important of which was road construction.

STEISEL, M D. *Justice And The American Indian, V3: The Effect Of Having No Extradition Procedures For Indian Reservations.* Washington DC LEAA 1974.

STENCEL, S. Reverse Discrimination. *Edit Res Rep* 11(4),563–580 Ag 6 1976.

STENDER, Fay and Greenberg, David F. The Prison As A Lawless Agency. *Buffalo L Rev* 21(3),799–838 Spr 1972.

"The genius of the American criminal justice system has been the extent to which it has accomodated itself to the heterogeneity of the American population. It might be very difficult to sustain lawlessness in prisons or in court if all of us were exposed to it." But most Americans are never processed by the police, courts, and prisons. "With few exceptions, this unenviable experience is reserved for those with dark skin, little money, for cultural deviants, and those with threatening ideas." The reason, they contend, is not that these groups are the most criminal in our society; the explanation lies in the systemic biases and discriminatory institutional practices which characterize the law and its enforcement.

STEPHENSON, G T. Education And Crime Among Negroes. *Southern Atlantic Q* 15,14–20 1917.

STEPHENSON, Gilbert T. *Race Distinctions In American Law*, Org Pub 1910. NY Negro Univ Pr 1969.

STEPHENSON, Richard M and Scarpitti, Frank R. Juvenile Court Dispositions: Factors In The Decision Making Process. *Crim Delinq* 17,142–151 1971.

STEPHENSON, Richard M and Scarpitti, Frank R. Negro–White Differentials And Delinquency. *J Res Crim Del* 5(1),122–133 1968.

Analysis of 1193 sixteen– and seventeen–year–old male delinquents, who had no prior institutionalization but were assigned by the juvenile court to one of four correctional programs, revealed that the Negro youths were disproportionately represented, had a higher Delinquency History Score, and were more likely to be in–program failures and recidivists. Consideration of racial, social, and economic differences did not adequately account for the delinquency differentials, nor was there evidence of discriminative treatment in the limited data available for analysis.

STERLING, Joyce S. *Criminal Justice Processing: The Determinants Of The Decision To Go To Trial.* Unpub PhD Diss Univ of Denver 1977.

STERN, Leon Thomas. The Effect Of The Depression On Prison Commitments And Sentences. *J Am Inst Cr L Crim* 31,696–711 Mr–Ap 1941.

STERNE, M. *Drinking Patterns And Alcoholism Among American Negroes.* St Louis Wash Univ S S Inst 1966.

STEVENS, H and Spearman, R W. *Step Toward Equal Justice—Programs To Increase Black Lawyers In The South, 1969–1973.* NY Carnegie Corp NY 1974.

Results of an extensive evaluation of a number of grant programs designed to increase the number of black lawyers in the South between 1969 and 1973 are presented. Grants from private foundations, corporations, and individuals provided support for programs of the Earl Warren Legal Training Program, Inc., the National Association for the advancement of Colored People Legal Defense and Educational Fund (LDF), and the Law Students Civil Rights Research Council (LSCRRC). The series of grants constituted a broad systems approach to the needs of blacks in 11 states. Results of the evaluation indicate that since 1969 the number of black first–year law students has increased from 22 to 171 in 17 Southern law schools, 375 black students were enrolled in these schools in 1973, and a majority of these black students intended to practice law in the South.*

STEVENS, William K. Black Policemen Bring Reform. *NYT* ,1 Ag 11 1974.

Stevens reports on the "new kind of black policeman" and the changes he has brought to the major cities of this country. Stevens sees such changes as part of the reformist thrust these officers are bringing into the departments they serve. The primary goal of the black officer is the arrest of criminals who prey on the black community. Black officers also see merit in making themselves as much a part of the community as possible so that the large law–abiding majority becomes the policeman's ally. Stevens reports that in cities where blacks have become a significant portion of the police force, there is evidence that their mere presence has worked some changes. These changes include the reduction of prejudice on the part of their white colleagues in dealings with the black population and the effect this has to have on that population. Stevens does note, however, that such changes will be short–lived without the full commitment of police departments and the promotion of more blacks into command positions.

STEWART JR, L G. *Justice And The American Indian, V5: Federal Prosecution Of Crimes Commited On Indian Reservations.* Washington DC LEAA 1974.

STEWART, Austin. *Twenty–Two Years A Slave And Forty Years A Freeman.* Rochester NY Wm Alling 1857.

STEWART, Omer. Questions Regarding American Indian Criminality. *Human Org* 23(1),61–66 S 1964.

In 1960, for the nation as a whole, the rate of Indian criminality per 100,000 population was 7 times that of the national average, while the Indian rate for all arrests was nearly 3 times that of blacks and 8 times that of whites. Drunkenness accounted for 71% of all Indian arrests during that year, while the number of Indian arrests for all alcohol–related crimes was 12 times greater than the national average and over 5 times that of blacks. The rate of arrests for all suspected crimes for the nation was 4 times higher for urban centers than for rural areas, but for Indians the urban rate was 24 times that of the rural. The Indian rate for alcohol–related offenses in urban areas was about 37 times the white rate and 15 times the black rate.*

STEWART, Ted. The Truth About The Black Mafia. *Sepia* 23(8),18–22 Ag 1974.

STILL, William. *Underground Rail Road Record.* Philadelphia People's Pub Co 1879.

STOCKTON, William. Going Home: The Puerto Ricans' New Migration. *NYT Mag* ,20–22,88–93 N 12 1978.

STONE, D. On The Question Of Repression: An Analysis Of Repression And The Response Of The Black Community. *J Poli Repr* 1(1),71–78 1975.

STRATMAN, David V. Political And Lumpen Prisoners, The Question Of Compliance, And Socioliterary Investigation. *Stanford L Rev* 27,1629–1641 Jl 1975.

STRATTON, J. Cops And Drunks—Police Attitudes And Actions In Dealing With Drunks. *Int J Addic* 8(4),613–621 1973.

STRATTON, R and Zeiner, A and Paredes, A. Tribal Affiliation And Prevalence Of Alcohol Problems. *Q J Stud Alc* 39(7),1166–1177 1978.

STRAYER, R. A Study Of The Negro Alcoholic. *Q J Stud Alc* 22(1),111–123 1961.

STREET, D and Leggett, J C. Economic Deprivation And Extremism: A Study Of Unemployed Negroes. *Am J Soc* 67(1),53–57 1961.

STREET, Lloyd. "Lessons In Crime From The All–Black Town" in *Crime And Its Impact On The Black Community*, Gary, L E And L P Brown (eds). Washington DC Howard U 1976.

The author, a black sociologist, argues that blacks need to study crime and develop theories from a black point of view; and blacks must determine the extent to whch law and the criminal justice system contribute to crime among blacks.

STREET, P B and Wood, R C and Chowenhill, R C. *Alcohol Use Among Native Americans: A Selective Annotated Bibliography.* Berkeley CA Social Res Group 1976.

STRICKLAND, R. *Fire And The Spirits—Cherokee Law From Clan To Court.* Norman Univ Oklahoma Pr 1975.

STRODTBECK, Fred L and Short Jr, James F and Kolegar, Ellen. The Analysis Of Self–Descriptions By Members Of Delinquent Gangs. *Sociol Q* 3(4),331–356 1962.

STROSNIDER, C S. *Leadership By Women In Criminal Justice—There Is Room At The Top.* Unpub PhD Diss S Houston St Univ 1978.

This dissertation explores the opportunities for women in criminal justice professions and offers suggestions for increasing the number of women in these jobs.

STUART, C G. Changing Status Of Women In Police Professions. *Pol Chief* 42(4),61–62,81 1975.

Although the status of women in police professions has improved considerably since 1971, some of the changes in sexually discrimnatory attitudes and hiring practices have been superficial.*

STUDLER, D T. Social Context And Attitudes Toward Coloured Immigrants. *Br J Sociol* 28(2),168–184 1977.

STYLES, Fitzhugh Lee. *Negroes And The Law.* Boston Christopher Pub 1937.

SUDMAN, S and Bradburn, N. *Response Effects In Surveys: A Review And Synthesis.* Chicago IL Aldine 1974.

SUE, Derald W and Sue, Stanley. Ethnic Minorities: Resistance To Being Researched. *Prof Psy* 3(1),11–17 1972.

The research psychologist is meeting increasing resistance from ethnic minorities to being researched. Much prejudice and discrimination has been directed toward ethnic minorities and feelings of mistrust and fear of exploitation pervade the relations of psychologists and minority members. Ethnic minorities see psychology as a study determined to maintain the power of the Establishment, and they resent the feelings of some pathologists that the injustices which have been dealt them are due to their own psychological maladjustment rather than to the failures of society. The ethnic researcher must take several steps in order to improve relations with minorities for future research, including the attraction of minorities into professions of the social sciences, and making research on minorities a community endeavor.

SUE, Stanley and Sue, Derald W. Ethnic Minorities: Resistance To Being Researched. *Prof Psy* 3(1),11–17 1972.

The research psychologist is meeting increasing resistance from ethnic minorities to being researched. Much prejudice and discrimination has been directed toward ethnic minorities and feelings of mistrust and fear of exploitation pervade the relations of psychologists and minority members. Ethnic minorities see psychology as a study determined to maintain the power of the Establishment, and they resent the feelings of some pathologists that the injustices which have been dealt them are due to their own psychological maladjustment rather than to the failures of society. The ethnic researcher must take several steps in order to improve relations with minorities for future research, including the attraction of minorities into professions of the social sciences, and making research on minorities a community endeavor.

SULLIVAN, J W and Shapiro, F C. *Race Riots: New York, 1954*. NY Thos Y Crowell 1964.

SULLIVAN, T T. Importance Given Selected Job Characteristics By Individuals Who Possess A Criminal Justice Degree. *Crim Just Rev* 2(2),93–100 1977.

The importance given selected job characteristics by 758 persons who had received criminal justice degrees were examined. It was found tht job expectations varied significantly by race and by sex within race. The study population consisted of 717 males (49 of whom were black) and 47 females (of whom 7 were black). Median age was 25 years with a range of 18 to 63 years. Blacks consistently ranked as very important the variables of income, colleague compatibility, geographic location, and opportunity for advancement. Whites tended to rate these variables as moderately important. Blacks felt dissatisfied with their jobs more so than whites and felt that their education had little or no effect on their performance. Whites were more satisfied and stressed that education had a definite effect on their performance. Both groups gave opportunity for advancement and prestige high rankings. Differences between racial groups by sex reflected racial differences as a whole. However, white females felt their education had little effect on salary and promotion, while black females felt education had a definite effect.*

SULTAN, Allen and Howard, Richard. The Efficient Use Of Military Forces To Control Riots: Some Proposals For Congressional Action. *J Urban L* 45,849–862 1968.

SUMMERS, G F and Hammonds, A D. Effect Of Racial Characteristics Of Investigator On Self–Enumerated Responses To A Negro Prejudice Scale. *Soc Forces* 44,515–518 1966.

SUMNER, George W. "Dealing With Prison Violence" in *Prison Violence*, Cohon, Albert K, George F Cole, And Robert G Bailey (eds). Lexington MA Lexington 1976.

SUMPTER, Roy G. The Youthful Offender: A Descriptive Analysis. *Can J Crim & Corr* 14(3),282–296 1972.

SUNG, Betty Lee. *The Story Of The Chinese In America*. NY Collier Books 1967.

SUNSERI, Alvin R. The Angry Chicano. *Ethn & Min Stud* 1(1),2–5 1973.

The historical background of Chicanos in New Mexico and the reasons for present day anger related to discrimination are examined. Chicanos believe they must establish a cultural identity that enables them to respect themselves, must learn about their history and they demand programs dealing with La Raza and the Mexican–American heritage. Chicanos feel that the Anglo–American must end the attitude of contempt and disdain that has characterized Anglo–American treatment of the Mexican–American since the first confrontation between the two groups. It is concluded that the Chicano is angry, and it is not beyond possibility that he might resort to violence.

SUSSMAN, Frederick B and Bloomfield, Neil J and Stahl, David. *The Community And Racial Crisis*. NY Practising L Ins 1966.

SUTHERLAND, Edwin H. *Principles In Criminology*. Philadelphia Lippincott 1924.

SUTHERLAND, Edwin H and Cressey, Donald R. *Principles Of Criminology*, Orig Pub 1924. NY Lippincott 1970.

SUTTLES, Gerald. *The Social Order Of The Slum*. Chicago Univ Chicago Pr 1971.

SUTTON, L Paul. *Federal Criminal Sentencing: Perspectives Of Analysis And A Design For Research*. Washington DC LEAA 1978.

SUTTON, Lester P. *Criminal Sentencing: An Empirical Analysis Of Variations On Sentences Imposed In Federal District Courts*. Unpub PhD Diss SUNY Albany 1975.

SUVAK, Daniel (comp). *Memoirs Of American Prisoners: An Annotated Bibliography*. Metuchen NJ Scarecrow Pr 1979.

Comprehensive bibliography of American prison memoirs divided into 3 sections: civil prisoners, voluntary prisoners, and military prisoners. Items entered under name of prisoner whose story is the subject of the book. Annotation describes purpose of book; some have critical evaluation of book. A list of all prisons discussed in the book, with their addresses, is given after each entry. Also includes indexes by author/title and prison.

SWAN, L Alex. "Ethical Issues In Research/Experimentation In Prison" in *House Judicary Comm Hearings On Prison Inmates In Medical Research*. Washington DC USGPO 1976.

SWAN, L Alex. "Crime And Social Policy: The Politics Of Race" in *Social Research And The Black Community*, Gary, Lawrence E (ed), 112–119. Washington DC Howard U 1974.

SWAN, L Alex. "Improving Police Relations In The Black Community" in *Blacks And Criminal Justice*, Owens, Charles E And Jimmy Bell (eds), 114–127. Lexington MA Heath 1977.

SWAN, L Alex. "Juvenile Delinquency, Justice & Black Youth" in *Black Perspectives On Crime And The Criminal Justice System*, Woodson, Robert L (ed), 55–78. Boston G K Hall 1977.

SWAN, L Alex. "Successful Passage Of Black Parolees From Prison To Prison" in *Crime And Its Impact On The Black Community*, Gary And Brown (eds), 177–194. Washington DC Howard U 1976.

SWAN, L Alex. A Methodological Critique Of The Moynihan Report. *Black Scholar* 5(9),18–24 Je 1974.

SWAN, L Alex. Crime Prevention And The Protection Of Lives: A Mechanism To Change Police Behavior In The Community. *J Afro–Am I* 2(2),119–128 1974.

SWAN, L Alex. Harlem And Detroit Riots Of 1943: A Comprehensive Analysis. *Berkeley J Soc* 16,75–93 1971–72.

SWAN, L Alex. Notes On Blacks And The Penal System. *Forum* 10(3),4 1974.

SWAN, L Alex. Physical Manipulation Of The Brain. *Social Policy* 8(1),52–54 1977.

SWAN, L Alex. Reentry And The Black Parolee. *J Soc Behav Sci* 21(2/3),104–116 1975.

SWAN, L Alex. Riot Regression: A Switch In Initiatives. *J Soc Behav Sci* 19(3/4),52–64 1973.

SWAN, L Alex. The Politics Of Identification: A Perspective Of Police Accountability. *Crim Delinq* 20,119–128 Ap 1974.

SWAN, L Alex. When Whites Riot—The East St Louis Massacre. *Int Socialist Rev* 34(9),12–24 1973.

SWANSON JR, C R and Chamelin, N C and Territo, L. *Police Personnel Selection Process*. Indianapolis Bobbs–Merrill 1977.

Intended for adminstrators and supervisors involved in designing and implementing a personnel selection process. This book analyzes the selection process from the entrance examination through probationary employment.*

SWARTZ, Virginia D and Held, Barbara S and Levine, David. Interpersonal Aspects Of Dangerousness. *Crim Just B* 6,49–58 Mr 1979.

SWETT, Daniel. Cultural Bias In The American Legal System. *Law & Soc Rev* 5,79–110 Ag 1969.

SWIGERT, Victoria Lynn and Farrell, Ronald A. *Murder, Inequality, And The Law*. Lexington MA Heath 1976.

Examines the differential treatment of minorities in murder cases. Covers all aspects of the mechanics of law, including the assignment of attorneys, award of bail, selection of trial format, jury selection, etc.

SWIGERT, Victoria Lynn and Farrell, Ronald A. Prior Offense As A Self–Fulfilling Prophecy. *Law & Soc Rev* 12(3),437–454 Spr 1978.

Explorations of differential justice suggest that apparent relationships between class, race, and legal treatment may be explained by the more extensive conviction histories found among lower class and minority populations. But these findings have emerged without adequate exploration of the antecedents of a defendant's criminal record. This study views the conviction awarded a defendant as the first stage in the construction of a prior offense record. Path analytic techniques are applied to data drawn from a sample of persons arrested for murder in order to examine the nature of relationships among the demographic characteristics of defendants, their prior offense records, access to legal resources, and ultmate dispositions. Patterns evident from the analysis suggest that the operation of the criminal record in the legal system constitutes a continual cycle in the confirmation of criminality. Prior record, itself partly a product of discretionary treatment, becomes a salient factor in the accumulation of additional convictions not only through its direct effect but also through its influence on access to private counsel and bail.*

SYDNOR, Charles S. The Southerner And The Laws. *J Southern Hist* 6,3–23 1940.

Although the South is not a political entity with clearly defined boundaries, nevertheless, certain unifying characteristics and principles of southern history can still be identified. Just prior to the Civil War, southern attitudes toward Federal law and Divine law were remarkably similar. Both the

Constitution and the Bible were respected and regarded as supreme documents, whose validity and original literal meaning remained unchanged over time. This perspective, which contrasted sharply with the northern one, developed largely out of conflict with the North on the issue of slavery. Meanwhile, several factors were operating in the Old South to reduce the extent to which statutory law influenced the life of the Southerner. Ruralness, slavery, the plantation system and most importantly, an unwritten code governing the social order served to restrict the segment of life controlled by state law.

SYKES, Gresham M. *The Society Of Captives: A Study Of A Maximum Security Prison.* Princeton Princeton Univ Pr 1958.

SYLVESTER JR, Sawyer F (ed) and Sagarin, Edward (ed). *Politics And Crime.* NY Praeger 1974.

SYLVESTER, Sawyer F and Reed, John P and Nelson, David P. *Prison Homicide.* NY Spectrum Pub 1977.

SYMPOSIUM. Capital Punishment Symposium. *J Behav Econ* 6(1–2),1–397 Sum–Wint 1977.

SYMPOSIUM. Natives And The Law. *Discussion* 4(4),whole Issue D 1976.

SZULC, Tad. George Jackson Radicalized The Brothers In Soledad And San Quentin. *NYT Mag* ,10–11,16–23 Ag 1 1972.

SZYMANSKI, Albert. Racial Discrimination And White Gain. *Am Sociol Rev* 41,403–414 Je 1976.

TABB, W K. Race Relations, Models And Social Change. *Social Prob* 18,431–443 Spr 1971.

TABB, William. *The Political Economy Of The Black Ghetto.* NY Norton 1970.

TACKWOOD, Louis E and Citizens Research And Investigation Committee. *The Glass House Tapes: The Story Of An Agent–Provocateur And The New Police–Intelligence Complex.* NY Avon 1973.

The author, a black former undercover agent for the "Red Squad" of the Los Angeles Police Dept, later revealed his experiences to a radical political group, which published this detailed expose of police anti–subversive activities.

TAFT, Donald R and England, Ralph W. *Criminology.* NY Macmillan 1964.

TAFT, Donald R. Nationality And Crime. *Am Sociol Rev* 1,724–736 1936.

TAGGERT, R. *The Prison Of Unemployment.* Baltimore MD Johns Hopkins Pr 1972.

TAKAGI, Paul. Issues In The Study Of Police Use Of Deadly Force. Rockville MD NCJRS 1978.

Studies suggest there is close relationship between poverty, number of blacks in the population, homicide, and police use of deadly force. Relationships between race and police use of force are examined. After quoting studies which show that blacks have significantly higher homicide rates than whites and that a significantly higher proportion of blacks are killed by police, possible explanations are examined. The paucity of data is described. The FBI will not release data on police use of force, and police chiefs are also reluctant. A compounding problem is the fact that persons shot in the back are lumped together with the figures for bank robbers, shooting it out with the police. Studies are needed to compare blacks and whites of similar socioeconomic backgrounds to determine whether it is the race or the poverty level which is significant. To determine the role of race and racism, it is also necessary to codify the circumstances of each police–caused death, similar to Knoohuizen's study of Chicago Police killings. It is suggested that the relationships uncovered combine both racism and the stress as caused by poverty and long–term unemployment or underemployment.*

TAKAGI, Paul. "Crime And Criminal Justice: Their Impact Upon Asian American Communities" in *National Minority Advisory Council Report.* Washington DC LEAA Min Ad Com 1978.

TAKAGI, Paul and Platt, Anthony. Intellectuals For Law And Order: A Critique Of The New "Realists". *Crim & Soc Just* 8,1–31 Fall–Wint 1977.

TAKAGI, Paul and Platt, Tony. Behind The Gilded Ghetto: An Analysis Of Race, Class And Crime In Chinatown. *Crim & Soc Just* 9,2–25 Spr–Sum 1978.

TAKAGI, Paul. LEAA's Research Solicitation: Police Use Of Deadly Force. *Crim & Soc Just* 11,51–61 Spr–Sum 1979.

TAKAGI, Paul. The Correctional System. *Crim & Soc Just* 2,82–89 Fall–Wint 1974.

TANTER, Raymond. "International War And Domestic Turmoil" in *Violence In America*, Graham, Hugh D And T Gurr (eds), 550–569. NY Bantam 1969.

TAPPAN, Paul W. Who Is The Criminal? *Am Sociol Rev* 12,96–102 F 1947.

TATUM, William M. The Importance Of Spanish Language Training For Law Enforcement Officers. *Pol Chief* 45(3),44–45 Mr 1978.

TAUSIG, Mark and Liska, Allen E. Theoretical Interpretations Of Social Class And Racial Differentials In Legal Decision Making For Juveniles. *Sociol Q* 20,197–208 1979.

TAYLOR, Helen and Debro, Julius. *Study On The Status Of Black Criminology In The United States.* College Park Univ MD ICJ & C 1978. A search of the criminological literature produced by black American scholars. Includes recommendations for future study and evaluations of black criminology, with bibliography on black criminology.

TAYLOR, Paul. "The Mexican Immigrant And The Problem Of Crime And Criminal Justice" in *Report On Crime And The Foreign Born.* Washington DC NCLOE 1931.

TAYLOR, Paul. More Bars Against Mexicans. *Survey Gr* 19, Ap 1930.

TAYLOR, S P and Genthner, R W. Physical Aggression As A Function Of Racial Prejudice And The Race Of The Target. *J Pers Soc Psychol* 27(2),207–210 1973.

TAYLOR, Victor E. Heroin And The Black Community. *Am Scholar* 40(4),691–694 1971.

TEAHAN, John E. A Longitudinal Study Of Attitude Shifts Among Black And White Police Officers. *J Soc Issues* 31(1),47–56 1975.

TEAHAN, John E. Role Playing And Group Experience To Facilitate Attitude And Value Changes Among Black And White Police Officers. *J Soc Issues* 31(1),35–46 1975.

TEDESCHI, James T und Berger, Stephen E. Aggressive Behavior Of Delinquent, Dependent, And 'Normal' White And Black Boys In Social Conflicts. *J Exp Soc Psych* 5(3),352–370 1969.

TEDWELL, D. Indian Career Officer. *Pol Chief* 36(11),30–31 N 1969.

TEETERS, Negley K and Barnes, Harry Elmer. *New Horizons In Criminology.* Englewood Cliffs Prentice–Hall 1959.

Chapter VII examines "Nationality, Race and Crime," with sections on Mexican–American delinquency, minority races and criminality, Negro crime, and Oriental and Native American crime. The authors reject theories of racial inferiority or superiority. If the Negro's criminality is high, they conclude, it is due largely to the black's socio–economic handicaps and to conditions flowing from his longstanding conflict with the white man.

TELFER, M A and Baker, D and Longtin, L. YY Syndrome In An American Negro. *Lancet* 1(13),95 1968.

TELLER, H M. "Courts Of Indian Offenses" in *Americanizing The American Indians*, Prucha, Francis P (ed). Cambridge MA Harvard Univ Pr 1973.

Forty black and forty white female delinquents observed a black or white male model who employed liberal or stringent standards of self–reward. Even when given explicit normative information, S's imitated the self–reward standards of the model. There were no differences in imitation as a function of S's race or model's race. Comparison with a comparable recent study showed that the black male delinquents imitated the white liberal model more than the black female delinquents.

TENBROEK, Jacobus (ed). *The Law Of The Poor.* San Francisco Cesar Cauce 1966.

TENBROEK, Jacobus and Barnhart, Edward N and Matson, Floyd M. "The Attack On Japanese Americans During World War II" in *Conspiracy*, Curry, Richard O And Thomas M Brown (eds). NY Holt Rinehart Wins 1972.

TENNYSON, Ray A and Howard, Kenneth I and Short Jr, James F. Behavior Dimensions Of Gang Delinquency. *Am Sociol Rev* 28(3),411–429 Je 1963.

TENNYSON, Ray and Short Jr, James F and Rivera, Ramon. Perceived Opportunities, Gang Membership, And Delinquency. *Am Sociol Rev* 30(1),56–67 1965.

TERRELL, Mary Church. Service Which Must Be Rendered In The South. *Voice Negro* 2(3),182–186 1905.

TERRIS, Bruce J. "The Role Of The Police" in *Police–Community Relationships*, Bopp, W (ed), 22–38. Springfield IL Chas C Thomas 1972. Problems facing the modern police department as a result of the rapid increases in violent crime, particularly in urban areas, are discussed, stressing that difficulties in police–community relations are actually problems in police–minority group relations. Relations with militant, disadvantaged, and alienated ghetto citizens, such as blacks, Puerto Ricans, and Mexican–Americans, will not be lessened by conventional police professionalism which includes higher education, human relations training, and minority recruitment. Instead, persons skilled in interpersonal relations, including teachers, recreation workers, and social workers, should be encouraged to seek police careers, and the concept of lateral entry should be expanded so that these professionals will not have to begin at the bottom of the organizational structure.

TERRITO, L and Swanson Jr, C R and Chamelin, N C. *Police Personnel Selection Process*. Indianapolis Bobbs–Merrill 1977.

Intended for adminstrators and supervisors involved in designing and implementing a personnel selection process. This book analyzes the selection process from the entrance examination through probationary employment.*

TERRY JR, T Rankin and Gerard, Jules B. Discrimination Against Negroes In The Adminstration Of Criminal Law In Missouri. *Wash U L Q* 1970,415–438 1970.

TERRY, Robert M. Discrimination In The Handling Of Juvenile Offenders By Social Control Agencies. *J Res Crim Del* 4(2),218–230 Jl 1967.

TERRY, Robert M. The Screening Of Juvenile Offenders. *J Crim L Crimin & Pol Sci* 58,173–181 1967.

TESKE JR, R H C and Stachura, S. *Spouse Abuse In Texas—A Special Report*. Huntsville TX Sam Houston CJC 1979.

TEXAS DEPT OF CORRECTIONS, Div Of Research. *A Synopsis Of Offenders Receiving The Death Sentence In Texas*. Austin TX Dept Corrections 1972.

The source of the data used in this descriptive study are not given, but are presumably Texas Department of Corrections records, as the study covers only that period (1924–1971) during which executions were carried out under state, rather than county, authority in Texas. The death row population in Texas (29 persons) is broken down by race, by offense, by offense by race, and race by offense. Various groups within the total study population (all prisoners remanded to the Texas department of Corrections under sentence of death since (1924) were also broken down by various characteristics. Figures are given for the number and percent of persons received under sentence of death by offense and by race (Caucasian, Negro, Mexican, American Indian). The total number of persons who had death setences commuted during the study period is also broken down; by offense, by race, and by offense by race. No conclusions were drawn from any of these data.

TEXAS HOUSE OF REPRESENTATIVES. *Overcrowding In Texas Prisons*, Special Legislative Report No 43. Austin TX House Of Rep 1979.

TEXAS OFFICE OF THE GOVERNOR. *Equal Employment And The Texas Criminal Justice System*. Austin TX Governor's Office 1975.

This manual, both a background and program document, is designed to give Texas agencies an understanding of Equal Opportunity Law and its principles as they relate to attracting qualified minority and women applicants.*

THARNISH, D M. Sex Discrimination In Prison Employment: The Bona Fide Occupational Qualification And Prisoners' Privacy Rights. *Iowa L Rev* 65(2),428–445 Ja 1980.

The balancing tests used by the courts in resolving cases on sex discrimination in prison employment are analyzed, with emphasis on the court's approach in Gunther v. Iowa State Men's Reformatory.*

THAYER, J. "A People Without Law" in *Americanizing The American Indians*, Prucha, Francis P (ed). Cambridge MA Harvard Univ Pr 1973.

THELAN, Mark H and Fryrear, Jerry L. Imitation Of Self–Reward Standards By Black And White Female Delinquents. *Psychol Rep* 29(2),667–671 1971.

THIBAULT, Edward Allen. *An Exploratory Study Of Police Alienation With Emphasis On Attitudes Toward Minority Groups*. Unpub PhD Diss Syracuse Univ 1972.

Police alienation in the Syracuse, NY Police Department was investigated with emphasis on attitudes toward minority groups. Several dimensions of police culture were analyzed: the social isolation of the police, the police perception of danger and violence, the semimilitary nature of police organizations, the cult of secrecy, the status of police in the local and national community, the sense of community developed by the police as a subculture, the history of police work and the traditional organization and traditional purposes of police work. Alienation was examined as a dependent, independent and intervening variable. Generally alienation was seen to increase along with negative attitudes toward the public, the media, the courts and the law, and race. The Middleton Alienation Scale was seen to have a close relationship with the Bogardus Social Distance Scale in relation to blacks and with what labels police use for black people. Anomie was seen as a reinforcer of negative values toward race when such structural values as time on the force, time in rank, rank itself and duties are related to attitudes towards prointegration.

THIBAULT, Edward and Lynch, Lawrence and Rafky, David M. Are Cops Prejudiced? Pol Chief 40(3),60–62 1973.

THOMAS, Alexander and Sillen, Samuel. *Racism And Psychiatry*. NY Brunner/Mazel 1972.

THOMAS, Charles W and Sieverdes, Christopher M. Juvenile Court Intake: An Analysis Of Discretionary Decision–Making. *Criminology* 12(4),413–432 F 1975.

THOMAS, Charles W. The System–Maintenance Role Of The White Psychologist. *J Soc Issues* 29(1),57–65 1973.

THOMAS, Charles and Cage, Robin J and Foster, Samuel C. Public Opinion On Criminal And Legal Sanctions: An Examination Of Two Conceptual Models. *J Crim L & Crimin* 67(1),110–116 1976.

Public evaluation of appropriate legal sanctions are examined in order to see whether they reflect the level of agreement implied by the consensus model. Private citizens were asked to evaluate the relative seriousness of a variety of acts and suggest what type of sanctions they feel are appropriate for those who engage in the acts. In regard to the first dimension, remarkable similarity was found in the offense rankings from those above and below the median sample income, occupational prestige, and educational level. A very high degree of similarity was found on the lengths of sentences assigned to the set of possible offenses. The basic expectation of the consensus model, i.e., that there would be consensus on these two dimensions across social groupings, was supported. Findings were not supportive of a conflict model which would predict variations between different categories of the population.

THOMAS, Charles and Cage, Robin. The Effect Of Social Characteristics In Juvenile Court Dispositions. *Sociol Q* 18,237–252 Spr 1977.

THOMAS, H J. One Department's Confrontation Strategy. *FBI L Enf Bull* 42,2–8 1973.

THOMAS, Piri. *Down These Mean Streets*. NY Knopf 1967.

THOMAS, Piri. *Savior, Savior, Hold My Hand*. NY Doubleday 1972.

THOMAS, Piri. *Seven Long Times*. NY Praeger 1974.

Piri Thomas was born in NY's Spanish Harlem in 1928 and as a young man was sentenced to from 5 to 15 years in prison for armed robbery. In this book, he describes his odyssey from the streets to prison, where he spent seven years in Great Meadow, a maximum–security institution. A glossary, containing Hispanic prison lingo, is included.

THOMPSON, Anna J–. A Survey Of Crime Among Negroes In Philadelphia. *Opport* 4,217–219 Jl–S 1926.

THOMPSON, F J and Brown, B. Commitment To The Disadvantaged Among Urban Administrators—The Case Of Minority Hiring. *Urb Aff Q* 13(3),355–378 Mr 1978.

Potential correlates of attitudinal commitment for minority hiring among urban personnel officers are examined in this research paper. Sociopolitical beliefs concerning equality would be powerful predictors of attitudes toward recruiting nonwhites.*

THOMPSON, Roger M. American Language Loyalty And The Validity Of The 1970 Census. *Int J Soc Lang* 2,7–18 1974.

THORKELSON, M M and Kelly, R S. Equal Employment Opportunity—Affirmative Action Programs For Federal Government Contractors. *Bus Lawyer* 31(3),1509–1515 Ap 1976.

Problems faced by federal contractors in developing realistic and acceptable affirmative action programs are discussed. Contractors are advised to take the following steps: (1) develop better data on availability of minorities and females, proper recruiting areas, and necessary job skills, in order to establish realistic goals and timetables and to withstand unreasonable demands from compliance agencies; (2) resist the proposed affected class rule on grounds of unclear authority for its enforcement; (3) observe disclosure developments with a view to protecting affirmative action plan documents from discovery or Freedom of Information Act requests; and (4) prepare to challenge compliance agency attempts to undertake enforcement actions without hearings required by due process.*

THORNBERRY, Terence P. Race, Socioeconomic Status And Sentencing In The Juvenile Justice System. *J Crim L Crimin & Pol Sci* 64(1),90–98 1973.

This study of a birth cohort of male born in Philadelphia and living there between the ages of 10 and 17 attempts to determine whether blacks and members of low socio–economic status (SES) receive more severe dispositions than whites and members of high SES. Thornberry cites several studies to demonstrate the weakness of the assumptions of Lemert, Clinard and others to argue that blacks and low–SES subjects are more likely than their white and high–SES counterparts to be treated more severely in the juvenile system. He then draws comparisons to note the difference in disposition for blacks and whites at the level of police, intake and juvenile court. His findings, conflicting with previous research, indicate that blacks and low–SES subjects are more likely than whites and high–SES subjects to receive a more severe disposition at each of the three stages, even when the legal variables of seriousness and previous offenses are held constant. Thus, seriousness of the offense and number of previous offenses cannot be used to explain differential dispositions by race and socio–economic status.

THORNBROUGH, Emma Lou. *The Negro In Indiana; A Study Of A Minority.* Indianapolis Indian Histor Bur 1957.

THORNE, B and Wyman, L. Notes On Navajo Suicide. *Am Anthrop* 47,278–288 1945.

THORPE, Earl E. *The Mind Of The Negro*, Orig Pub 1961. Westport CT Greenwood Pr 1970.

THORPE, Earl E. Chattel Slavery And Concentration Camps. *Negro Hist Bull* 25,171–176 My 1962.

THORSELL, Bernard A and Chambers, Robert. The Adjudication Process And Self–Conception. *Per Soc Psyc Bull* 1(1),327–329 1974.

THRASHER, Frederick M. "Race And Nationality In The Gang" in *The Gang: A Study Of 1,313 Gangs In Chicago*, Orig Pub 1927, 130–154. Chicago Univ Chicago Pr 1963.

"The gang... is one manifestation of the disorganization incident to cultural conflict among diverse nations and races gathered together in one place and themselves in contact with a civilization foreign and largely inimical to them."

TIERGER, Joseph H. Police Discretion And Discriminatory Enforcement. *Duke L J* 4,717–743 1971.

TISDALE, Celes (ed). *Betcha Ain't: Poems From Attica.* Detroit Broadside Pr 1974.

TOBY, Jackson. "Hoodlum Or Business Man: An American Dilemma" in *The Jews: Social Patterns Of An American Group*, Sklare, Marshall (ed). NY Free Pr 1958.

TOBY, Jackson. The Differential Impact Of Family Disorganization. *Am Sociol Rev* 22,505–512 1957.

TOBY, Jackson. The New Criminology Is The Old Sentimentality. *Criminology* 16(4),516–526 F 1979.

TOBY, Jackson. Violence And The Masculine Ideal. *Ann Am Poli* 364,19–27 1966.

Given the family structure common in urban industrial societies, it is harder for boys to grow up confident in their fundamental masculinity than for boys in the extended families of preliterate societies. One response to doubts about masculinity is compulsive masculinity: an exaggerated insistence on characteristics differentiating males from females. Superior strength and a readiness to exhibit it obviously fill the specifications. This analysis explains why violence, though punishable by law and condemned by custom, nevertheless remains a clandestine masculine ideal in Western culture. the assumptions of this ideal are most explicitly formulated in certain subcultures —and especially among those segments of the population unable to wield symbolic power (i.e., adolescents, and minority groups). Excerpts from a tape–recorded interview with an imprisoned armed robber illustrate these assumptions.

TOCH, Hans et al. *Men In Crisis: Human Breakdowns In Prison.* Chicago IL Aldine 1975.

TOCH, Hans. *Living In Prison: The Ecology Of Survival.* NY Free Pr 1977.

TOCH, Hans. *Peacekeeping—Police, Prisons And Violence.* Lexington MA Heath 1977.

Professor Toch, a white psychologist, examines the violence encountered by the police and prisons as well as the violence these criminal justice agencies generate as they perform their perceived responsibilities. The author highlights the occupational practices and the socialization processes of the police which contribute to police–community hostility which sometimes leads to an escalation of violence.

TOCH, Hans. *Violent Men: An Inquiry Into The Psychology Of Violence.* Chicago IL Aldine 1969.

TOCH, Hans. Cops And Blacks: Warring Minorities. *Nation* 208(16),491–493 Ap 21 1969.

TOCQUEVILLE, Alexis De and Beaumont, Gustave De. *On The Penitentiary System In The United States And Its Application In France*, Francis Lieber (trans), Orig Pub 1833. Carbondale S Illinois Univ Pr 1964.

"The freed person commits more crimes than the slave...because, becoming emancipated, he has to provide for himself, which, during his bondage, he was not obliged to do.... His actions, involuntary when he was a slave, become now disorderly: judgment cannot guide him, for he has not exercised it: he is improvident, because he never has learned to think of futurity. His passions, not progressively developed, assail him with violence. He is the prey of wants, which he does not know how to provide for, and thus obliged to steal, or to die. Hence so many free Negroes in the prisons, and hence their greater mortality than that of slaves. Only it seems to us necessary to acknowledge, that the transition from slavery to liberty, produces a state more fatal than favorable to the freed generation...."

TOLCHIN, S. Exclusion Of Women From The Judicial Process. *Signs* 2(4),877–887 Sum 1977.

Equity in judicial representation with respect to women, in both federal and state court systems, is considered.*

TOLIVER, Lawrence. Sentencing In South Carolina. *J Afro–Am I* 2(2),139–148 1974.

TOLLETT, Kenneth S. The Viability And Reliability Of The US Supreme Court As An Institution For Social Change And Progress Beneficial To Blacks. *Black L J* 2(3),197–219 Wint 1972.

TOLLETT, Kenneth. Bugs In The Driving Dream: The Technocratic War Against Poverty. *Howard L J* 17,775–797 1973.

TOMASSON, Robert E. Norwalk Police Battle In Court Over Racial Hiring Issues. *NYT* ,36 N 1977.

This article reports on the suit brought by the Norwalk (Conn.) Guardian Association et al. against the city of Norwalk. The suit, brought under a Federal civil rights statute, contends that the plaintiff, minority applicants to the Norwalk Police Department, were victims of discriminatory hiring practices. Tomasson notes that, while Norwalk has a population that is 15% black and Hispanic, it currently has only 1 Hispanic and 10 blacks on its 145–member police force. An affirmative action program agreed upon while the case was pending was later voided by the judge involved.– while blacks have asserted that the departmental writtentest may be culturally biased, whites in the department have begun to allege reverse discrimination with any attempts to modify the hiring practice. White applicants rejected the contention that blacks could work more effectively than whites in the black community. They also defended the written exam as providing a valid assessment of a person's ability to perform police work.

TOMLINSON, T M. Ideological Foundations For Negro Action: A Comparative Analysis Of Militant Views Of The Los Angeles Riots. *J Soc Issues* 26(1),93–120 1970.

TOMLINSON, T M. The Development Of A Real Ideology Among Urban Negroes. *Am Behav Sci* 2,27–31 Mr–Ap 1968.

Analyzing the data obtained from the Los Angeles Riot Study (L. A. R. S.), the author found widespread support and justification for the riots as a form of protest among blacks which has created a riot ideology within black communities across the nation. He dismisses the recommendations of Riot Commissions due to their political considerations and then proposes his own recommendations.

TOMPKINS, Dorothy Louise Culver. *The Offender: 1937–1963.* Berkeley CA U CA Inst G Stud 1963.

TOMPKINS, Dorothy Louise Culver. *The Prison And The Prisoner: 1967–1972.* Berkeley CA U CA Inst G Stud 1972.

TONEY, William T. *A Descriptive Study Of The Control Of Illegal Mexican Migration In The Southwestern US.* San Francisco R & E Research 1977.

TONRY, Michael (ed) and Morris, Norval (ed). *Crime And Justice: An Annual Review Of Research*, V1. Chicago Univ Chicago Pr 1979.

TORO- CALDER, Jaime. *Personal Crimes In Puerto Rico.* Unpub MA Thesis Univ of Wisconsin 1950.

TORO- CALDER, Jaime and Cedeno, C and Reckless, Walter. A Comparative Study Of Puerto Rican Attitudes Toward The Legal System Dealing With Crime. *J Crim L Crimin Pol Sci* 59(4),536–541 1968.

TORO- CALDER, Jaime and Kupperstein, Lenore R. *A Socio–Cultural And Socio–Legal Analysis Of Juvenile Delinquency In Puerto Rico.* Rio Piedras Univ Puerto Rico 1969.

TORRE, Marcella De La. Psychological Testing Of Incarcerated Hispanics, Natl Hispanic Con L Enf & CJ. Washington DC US Dept Justice 1980.

TORRES, D M. Chicano Gangs In The East LA (Los Angeles, CA) Barrio. *Cal Youth Author Q* 32(3),5–13 Fall 1979.

A distinctive feature of East LA is the presence of numerous youth gangs or barrios which feud over territories. The relation of the barrios to the community and its formal organizations has traditionally been one of alienation. When the Youth Authority's Gang Violence Reduction Project began its work, the project found that service agencies in the community generally did not work with hardcore gang members. However, since 1978 more agencies include gang members among their clients. The project has opened many community facilities, such as parks and other residential centers, to gang members. Generally, however, gangs' relations with law enforcement are negative. Gangs form a subsociety of their own which seems to exist just beneath that of the dominant society. Substancee abuse is widespread in the barrios as is crime. Feuding among gangs is constant and attacks can include use of knives and guns; fights usually occur when individuals are under the influence of alcohol or other drugs. As long as barrios feel surounded by a hostile environment, the gang tradition and violence will continue.*

TORRES, Edwin. *Carlito's Way.* NY E P Dutton 1975.

TORRES, M J and Garrett, G R and Retting, R P. *Manny––A Criminal–Addict's Story.* Boston Houghton Mifflin 1977.

A convicted drug user provides a firsthand account of an addict's day–to–day existence, both in prison and on the streets. Intended for an academic audience interested in deviance, crime, corrections, and criminal justice, this first–person narrative traces the life of Manny Torres, a young Puerto Rican heroin addict born in New York city. Manny provides a view of a variegated criminal career that accepted social science techniques ordinarily could not have rendered. Written in the frank and straightforward language of street people, dope addicts, and prison convicts, it provides a link between reality and social theory, and includes chapters on drug–related street crime, prison life, and Manny's experiences at Synanon, a drug detoxification institute. Selected references are included at the end of each chapter. The narrative is followed by a brief outline of the structuralist position and an integrated theoretical perspective designed to expose students to a social world that few experience.*

TOWLER, Juby Earl. *The Police Role In Racial Conflicts.* Springfield IL Chas C Thomas 1964.

TRACY, Charles A. Race, Crime And Social Policy: The Chinese In Oregon, 1871–1885. *Crim & Soc Just* 14,11–26 Wint 1980.

TRACY, James J and Cross, Herbert J. Personality Factors In Delinquent Boys: Differences Between Blacks And Whites. *J Res Crim Del* 8(1),10–22 Ja 1971.

TRACY, Paul E. *An Analysis Of The Evidence And Seriousness Of Self–Reported Delinquency And Crime.* Unpub PhD Diss Univ of Penn 1978.

TRAGLE, Henry Irving. *The Southampton Slave Revolt Of 1831.* NY Vintage 1973.

TRAVIS I I I, Lawrence F (ed) and Schwartz, Martin D (ed) and Clear, Todd R (ed). *Corrections: An Issues Approach.* Cincinnati Anderson 1980.

TREIMAN, B R et al. *Alcohol Use Among The Spanish Speaking: A Selective Annotated Bibliography.* Berkeley CA Social Res Group 1976.

This bibliography lists reference material dealing with the drinking patterns, behavior, problems, treatment, and related issues concerning Mexican–Americans and Puerto Ricans, with an emphasis on the more contemporary research; each citation is accompanied by a detailed abstract. The bibliography includes primarily those published items that contribute in some measure to the totality of information in the specific subjective areas of alcohol, drinking patterns and behavior drinking problems and the treatment of alcoholism.

TRELEASE, Alan. *White Terror: The Ku Klux Klan Conspiracy In Southern Reconstruction.* NY Harper & Row 1971.

TRICHE, C W. *Capital Punishment Dilemma, 1950–1977: A Subject Bibliography.* Troy NY Whitston Pub Co 1979.

This partially annotated bibliography on capital punishment includes international literature published between 1950 and 1977 organized by author and by nearly 170 subject headings.*

TRIMBLE, Joseph E. The Sojourner In The American Indian Community: Methodological Issues And Concerns. *J Soc Issues* 33(4),150–174 1977.

TRIPLETT, Peggy E. Women In Policing. *Pol Chief* 43(12),46–49 D 1976.

Developments in knowledge concerning white and black female police officers as reported at the 1974 and 1975 workshops on women in policing of the National Black Police Association Convention are discussed. Among the areas examined were patrol effectiveness, job assignments, uniforms, male/female partners and other topics. The workshops served to illustrate that the most controversial topic on women in policing is whether or not the female can adequately perform patrol functions. Several studies are currently underway to resolve this question.*

TRUJILLO, Larry D. Gunpowder Justice: A Reassessment Of The Texas Rangers (Book Review). *Crim & Soc Just* 13,61–64 Sum 1980.

TRUJILLO, Larry D. Joan W Moore, Et Al: Homeboys: Gangs, Drugs, And Prisons In The Barrios Of Los Angeles. *Crim & Soc Just* 12,69–77 Wint 1979.

TRUJILLO, Larry D. La Evolucion Del 'Bandido' Al 'Pachuco': A Critical Examination And Evaluation Of Criminological Literature On Chicanos. *Issues Crim* 9(2),43–67 Fall 1974.

One group that has suffered at the hands of traditional criminological theory construction and its subsequent practice is the Chicano. Criminological research has provided information and techniques for manipulating, controlling, and repressing Chicanos. In addition, criminological literature has helped to create myths, stereotypes, and negative images of Chicanos as "innately criminal," "natural thieves," "prone to lawlessness," etc. Trujillo's purpose is to critically examine and evaluate traditional criminological literature on Chicanos. The analysis traces the origins of the distorted image of the Chicano in the context of crime and criminality, and suggests the need for new analytical paradigms for the examination of criminological phenomena among Chicanos. Attention (is) focused on the period between 1848 when the Treaty of Guadalupe Hidalgo was signed, and 1943, the beginning of the era of the "pachuco." A plea is made for a new, more sensitive perspective toward Chicanos.

TSUKASHIMA, Ronald T. Merging Fieldwork And Survey Research In The Study Of A Minority Community. *J Soc Issues* 33(4),133–143 1977.

TUCKER, Sterling. "The Ghetto, The Ghettoized And Crime" in *Police–Community Relationships*, Bopp, W (ed), 144–155. Springfield IL Chas C Thomas 1972.

The relationship between conditions in the urban ghetto and incidence of crime is examined, stressing the self–defeating and often purposeless life of inner–city residents that has historically led to a higher crime rate. Social and economic deprivation, lack of space and privacy, and the poor physical conditions of ghetto housing have led to disillusionment and alienation toward a governmental structure that apparently does nothing to improve the situation. This frustration is highest for the black slum dweller who also is fighting generations of racial discrimination. Recent developments, however, indicate a trend toward self–help in many ghetto communities. This self–help includes aid in drug rehabilitation as well as movement toward establishing black–owned profitmaking inner–city businesses. A variety of community services are also being offered to families and young people in need of help.

TUCKER, Sterling. Racial Discrimination In Jury Selection In Virginia. *Va L Rev* 52,736–750 1966.

TURBOW, D. Washington V Davis: Reassessing The Bars To Employment Discrimination. *Brooklyn L Rev* 43(3),747–772 1977.

TURK, A and Burke, P. Factors Affecting Post Arrest Dispositions: A Model For Analysis. *Social Prob* 22,313–332 1975.

TURK, Austin. *Criminality And Legal Order.* Chicago Rand McNally 1969.

TURK, Austin. Conflict And Criminality. *Am Sociol Rev* 31,338–352 Je 1966.

TURNER, C B and Wilson, W J. Dimensions Of Racial Ideology: A Study Of Urban Black Attitudes. *J Soc Issues* 32(2),139–152 1976.

TURNER, Castellano and Darity, William A. Fears Of Genocide Among Black Americans As Related To Age, Sex, And Region. *Am J Public Health* 63(12),1029–1034 D 1973.

TURNER, Edward Raymond. *The Negro In Pennsylvania: Slavery–Servitude–Freedom, 1639–1861.* Washington DC AHA 1911.

TURNER, Nat. *The Confessions Of Nat Turner, The Leader Of The Late Insurrection In Southampton, Va.* Richmond VA Thos R Gray 1832.

TURNER, R H and Morris, R T and Jefferies, Vincent. The Public Perception Of The Watts Riot As Social Protest. *Am Sociol Rev* 36(3),443–451 1971.

TURNER, Ralph. The Public Perception Of Protest. *Am Sociol Rev* 34,815–830 D 1969.

TURNER, Stanley and Lalli, Michael. Suicide And Homicide: A Comparative Analysis By Race And Occupaltional Levels. *J Crim L Crimin & Pol Sci* 59,191–200 1968.

TURNER, William Bennett. Establishing The Rule Of Law In Prisons: A Manual For Prisoners' Rights Litigation. *Stanford L Rev* 23,473–518 1971.

TURNER, William Bennett. When Prisoners Sue: A Study Of Prisoner Section 1983 Suits In The Federal Courts. *Harv L Rev* 92(3),610–663 Ja 1979.

The author examines the rapid proliferation of suits by prisoners in the federal courts under 42 USC Sect. 1983 and presents the results of an empirical study of the litigation from 1976–78. The percentage of claims identified as involving "racial discrimination" ranged from 0% in D. Vt. and 0.8 in D. Mass., to 4.3 in E. D. Va., 4.9 in E. D. Calif. and 9.7 in N. D. Col.

TUSSMAN, Joseph (ed). *The Supreme Court On Racial Discrimination.* NY Oxford Univ Pr 1963.

TYLER, L G. The Police And Social Tension. *Police J* 44,175–178 Ap–Je 1971.

TYLER, Ralph W. Does Lynching Thrive Under Democracy? Color Am Mag 14(8),477–479 1908.

U S CIVIL SERVICE COMMISSION. *Equal Employment Opportunity Statistics—Federal Civilian Workforce Statistics.* Washington DC USCSC 1977.

This second edition of a semiannual report on equal employment opportunity statistics provides data on full–time, white–collar employment for designated minorities in the federal civilian workforce.*

U S CIVIL SERVICE COMMISSION. *Guidelines For Agency Internal Evaluation Of Equal Employment Opportunity Programs.* Washington DC USCSC 1974.

U S COMMISSION ON CIVIL RIGHTS. *Mexican Americans And The Administration Of Justice In The Southwest.* Washington DC USGPO 1970.

U S COMMISSION ON CIVIL RIGHTS. *Puerto Ricans In The Continental United States: An Uncertain Future.* Washington DC USGPO 1976.

U S COMMISSION ON CIVIL RIGHTS. *The Federal Civil Rights Enforcement Effort––1974: Volume VI, To Extend Federal Financial Assistance.* Washington DC USGPO 1974.

U S COMMISSION ON CIVIL RIGHTS. *The Navajo Nation: An American Colony.* Washington DC USGPO 1975.

U S COMMISSION ON CIVIL RIGHTS. *The Southwest Indian Report.* Washington DC USGPO 1973.

U S COMMISSION ON CIVIL RIGHTS. *Toward An Understanding Of Bakke.* Washington DC USGPO 1979.

This publication purports to increase understanding of affirmative action by presenting the complete text of the Bakke decision and the Equal Opportunity Commission's voluntary affirmative action guidelines.*

U S COMMISSION ON CIVIL RIGHTS. *Unfinished Business—Twenty Years Later—A Report Submitted To The USCCR By 51 State Advisory Committees.* Washington DC USCCR 1977.

State–by–state reports of the 51 advisory committees to the US Commission on Civil Rights provide an overview of national progress, both achievements and failures, and present challenge for the future. State reports focus on women's issues ranging from equal credit and employment opportunity to domestic violence. A second major area of research has

been civil rights in the criminal justice system, particularly in prisons and in police–community relations. Recommendations for minority staffing of correctional institutions reflect awareness of the need for equal employment opportunities and for ethnic and cultural sensitivity between prisoners and their keepers. At the same time, shifting composition of the cities requires local police forces to be sensitive to the ever–changing cultural characteristics of their communities. Increased recruitment of indigenous police officers and locally initiated training are recommended.*

U S COMPTROLLER GENERAL. *Federal Employment Examinations—Do They Achieve Equal Opportunity And Merit Principle Goals?* Washington DC US Comp Gen 1979.

To determine whether examining procedures for civil service positions are achieving equal opportunity and merit principle goals, this report examines four federal employment examinations. Analyses of the Professional and Administrative Career Examination (PACE) and the Junior Federal Assistant (JFA) test found that black applicants passed the written tests at a substantially lower rate than whites and other racial minorities, and that few blacks who passed scored high enough to have a realistic chance of employment consideration.*

U S DEPT OF COMMERCE, Bureau Of Census. *Crime Conditions In The United States As Reflected In Census Statistics Of Imprisoned Offenders.* Washington DC USGPO 1926.

U S DEPT OF COMMERCE, Bureau Of The Census. *Characteristics Of The Population By Ethnic Origin: March 1972 And 1971.* Washington DC USGPO 1973.

U S DEPT OF COMMERCE, Bureau Of The Census. *Negro Population: 1790–1915.* Washington DC USGPO 1918.

U S DEPT OF COMMERCE, Bureau Of The Census. *Persons Of Spanish Origin In The United States, November 1969.* Washington DC USGPO 1971.

U S DEPT OF COMMERCE, Bureau Of The Census. *Persons Of Spanish Origin In The United States: March 1974.* Washington DC USGPO 1974.

U S DEPT OF COMMERCE, Bureau Of The Census. *Persons Of Spanish Origin In The United States: March 1973.* Washington DC USGPO 1974.

U S DEPT OF COMMERCE, Bureau Of The Census. *Persons Of Spanish Origin In The United States: March 1972 And 1971.* Washington DC USGPO 1973.

U S DEPT OF COMMERCE, Bureau Of The Census. *Persons Of Spanish Origin In The United States: March 1975.* Washington DC USGPO 1975.

U S DEPT OF COMMERCE, Bureau Of The Census. *Persons Of Spanish Origin In The United States: March 1978.* Washington DC USGPO 1979.

U S DEPT OF COMMERCE, Bureau Of The Census. *The Social And Economic Status Of The Black Population In The United States, 1974.* Washington DC USGPO 1975.

U S DEPT OF H E W. *Determining Ethnic Origin In An Interview Survey: Problems And Recommendations.* Washington DC USGPO 1977.

U S DEPT OF INTERIOR, Bureau Of Indian Affairs. *Indian Law Enforcement History.* Washington DC USGPO 1975.

U S DEPT OF INTERIOR, Bureau Of Indian Affairs. *Indian Reservation Criminal Justice: Task Force Analysis, 1974–1975.* Washington DC USGPO 1976.

U S DEPT OF JUSTICE, Bureau Of Justice Statistics. *Criminal Victimization In The U S: Summary Findings Of 1978–1979 Changes In Crime And Of Trends Since 1973.* Washington DC US Dept Justice 1980.

U S DEPT OF JUSTICE, Bureau Of Justice Statistics. *Prisoners In State And Federal Institutions On December 31, 1978: National Prisoner Statistics Bulletin SD–NPS–PSF–6.* Washington DC USGPO 1980.

U S DEPT OF JUSTICE, Bureau Of Justice Statistics. *Profile Of Inmates Of Local Jails: Sociodemographic Findings From The 1978 Survey Of Inmates Of Local Jails.* Washington DC USGPO 1980.

An estimated 158,000 persons were being held in the country's 3,500 jails at the time of a nationwide survey conducted in February 1978 by the Bureau of the Census for the Bureau of Justice Statistics. Not only convicted criminals, but a sizable minority charged but not convicted were represented in this total, a 12% increase in that recorded by a comparable survey taken in 1972. Blacks and young persons continued to be represented disproportionately; in fact, the jail population in 1978 was more youthful than in 1972. People experiencing economic hardships contributed disproportionately to the jail population. Predetention employment rates and incomes were far lower than those in the general population, and many inmates had been financially dependent on public welfare benefits. Black female inmates were the most likely of the four largest race–sex groups to have been living in poverty. Drug and alcohol abuse had played a significant role in the lives of many inmates.*

U S DEPT OF JUSTICE, Bureau Of Justice Statistics. *The Hispanic Victim: National Crime Survey Report SD–NCS–N–16A, NCJ–67706.* Washington DC US Dept Justice 1980.

U S DEPT OF JUSTICE, Bureau Of Prisons, Education Branch. *Population Breakdown Of Spanish–Speaking Residents.* Washington DC US Bureau Prisons 1973.

U S DEPT OF JUSTICE, Federal Bureau Of Investigation. *Uniform Crime Reports For The United States.* Washington DC USGPO Ann.

U S DEPT OF JUSTICE, LEAA. *California: Report To The Judicial Council On The Language Needs Of Non–English–Speaking Persons, Interim Phase 2 Report.* San Francisco Calif Judic Coun 1976.

U S DEPT OF JUSTICE, LEAA. *Census Of Prisoners In State Correctional Facilities 1973.* Washington DC USGPO 1977.

U S DEPT OF JUSTICE, LEAA. *Report Of The LEAA Task Force On Women.* Washington DC NCJRS 1975.

This task force report discusses issues and makes recommendations concerning women as recipients in the LEAA system, women in criminal justice administration, and women as offenders, victims, and personnel. The task force reviewed LEAA–funded programs intended to provide equal services on an equal basis to persons in the criminal justice system. Current LEAA funding patterns and ongoing programs most directly related to the needs of women were also analyzed. In particular, issues and LEAA policies were examined for women as offenders, female juvenile offenders, girls and women as victims, women as employees and volunteers, and women as grant, loan, and contract recipients. The status of women as employees in LEAA is also reviewed. The task force found a general lack of attention to women's needs in most programs and this inattention was found to stem partly from a lack of awareness of the special needs of women. Partly it was thought to be due to the precedence given to other priorities. Most of the programs considered to be significant for women lacked adequate representation of women in policy making and supervisory positions.*

U S DEPT OF JUSTICE, LEAA, NCJISS. *Capital Punishment 1976.* Washington DC USGPO 1977.

On December 31, 1976, there were 444 inmates under sentence of death in state and federal institutions in the United State, compared with 473 a year earlier. The year–end count of black prisoners under death sentences dropped below the number of whites for the first time since 1966. On December 31, 1975, 28 states had prisoners under sentence of death, whereas 22 states and the District of Columbia had none. A year later the number of states holding at least 1 death row inmate declined to 23. Among individual states, Florida, with 81 persons on death row, had the largest number of prisoners awaiting executions. California and ohio ranked second and third. Collectively, these 3 states accounted for one–half the total death–row population.

U S DEPT OF JUSTICE, LEAA, NCJISS. *Capital Punishment, 1978.* Washington DC USGPO 1979.

This report, one in a series published under the National Prisoners Statistics Program, provides information on prisoners under sentence of death in the US in 1978 and on trends regarding capital punishment. The trends are traced from 1976 to 1978, and recent developments in the death penalty laws of the states are highlighted. Inmates under sentence of death are distributed by region and state and are differentiated by age, sex, race, hispanic origin, marital status at the time of imprisonment, and level of education.

U S DEPT OF JUSTICE, LEAA, NCJISS. *Criminal Victimization In The United States 1975.* Washington DC USGPO 1977.

U S DEPT OF JUSTICE, LEAA, NCJISS. *Criminal Victimization In The United States 1977.* Washington DC USGPO 1979.

The fifth in a series of annual reports dealing with findings from the national crime survey, this publication presents data on selected crimes of violence and theft for calendar year 1977. The data include events that were reported to the police and those that were not. The following crimes were investigated: (1) personal crimes, including rape, robbery, assault, and personal larceny; (2) property crimes, including burglary, household larceny, and motor vehicle theft. Selected findings are covered in a special section, which also makes reference to consistencies in the patterns of victimization since 1973. Information concerning rates of victimization for the Hispanic population, not covered in previous annual reports, is presented.*

U S DEPT OF JUSTICE, LEAA, NCJISS. *Criminal Victimization In The United States 1976.* Washington DC USGPO 1978.

U S DEPT OF JUSTICE, LEAA, NCJISS. *Criminal Victimization Surveys In The Nation's Five Largest Cities.* Washington DC USGPO 1975.

U S DEPT OF JUSTICE, LEAA, NCJISS. *Federal Sentencing Patterns: A Study Of Geographical Variations.* Washington DC USGPO 1978.

U S DEPT OF JUSTICE, LEAA, NCJISS. *Prisoners In State And Federal Institutions On December 31, 1977.* Washington DC USGPO 1979.

U S DEPT OF JUSTICE, LEAA, NCJISS. *Prisoners In State And Federal Institutions On December 31, 1976.* Washington DC USGPO 1978.

U S DEPT OF JUSTICE, LEAA, NCJISS. *Sourcebook Of Criminal Justice Statistics: 1974.* Washington DC USGPO 1975.

U S DEPT OF JUSTICE, LEAA, NCJISS. *Sourcebook Of Criminal Justice Statistics: 1973.* Washington DC USGPO 1974.

U S DEPT OF JUSTICE, LEAA, NCJISS. *Sourcebook Of Criminal Justice Statistics: 1976.* Washington DC USGPO 1977.

U S DEPT OF JUSTICE, LEAA, NCJISS. *Sourcebook Of Criminal Justice Statistics: 1979.* Washington DC USGPO 1980.

This Sourcebook presents a broad spectrum of criminal justice data (588 tables and 88 figures) in an easy–to–use, comprehensive reference document. Statistics from 120 sources are compiled in 6 groupings. characteristics of the criminal justice system, public attitudes toward crime and criminal–justice–related topics, nature and distribution of known offenses, characteristics and distribution of persons arrested, judicial processing of defendants, and persons under correctional supervision. Tables and figures for 1979 are cross–referenced with their 1978 edition counterparts, and a subject index is furnished. The appendices present definitions and methodology for easier comparison between sources. An annotated bibliography of sources also is included, along with a list of source publishers and their addresses.*

U S DEPT OF JUSTICE, LEAA, NCJISS. *Sourcebook Of Criminal Justice Statistics: 1977.* Washington DC USGPO 1978.

U S DEPT OF JUSTICE, LEAA, NCJISS. *Sourcebook Of Criminal Justice Statistics: 1978.* Washington DC USGPO 1979.

U S DEPT OF JUSTICE, LEAA, NCJISS. *Sourcebook Of Criminal Justice: 1975.* Washington DC USGPO 1977.

U S DEPT OF JUSTICE, LEAA, NCJISS. *Survey Of Inmates Of State Correctional Facilities, 1974.* Washington DC USGPO 1976.

U S DEPT OF JUSTICE, LEAA, NCJISS. *The Nations Jails: A Report On The Census Of Jails From The 1972 Survey Of Inmates Of Local Jails.* Washington DC USGPO 1975.

U S DEPT OF JUSTICE, National Criminal Justice Reference Service. *Affirmative Action In Criminal Justice.* Washington DC NCJRS 1979.

The relationship of equal opportunity employment laws to the criminal justice system is discussed, including affirmative action programs, barriers to change, and establishment of goals and grievance procedures.*

U S DEPT OF JUSTICE, National Institute Of Justice. *Affirmative Action Equal Employment Opportunity In The Criminal Justice System: A Selected Bibliography.* Washington DC NCJRS 1980.

U S DEPT OF JUSTICE. Justice For Hispanics Often Falls Short. *Justice Assistance News* 1(7),1,3 S 1980.

U S DEPT OF LABOR, Manpower Administration. *The Detroit Riot: A Profile Of 500 Prisoners.* Washington DC USGPO 1968.

Eleven days after the outbreak of the Detroit, Mich. riot of July 23, 1967, the US Labor Department contracted with the Behavior Research institute of Detroit to introduce into an ongoing survey of arrested riot–participants, questions designed to shed additional light on their employment status and indebtedness. Information was collected on the characteristics of the prisoners; the nature of their job and weekly earnings; their home situation; their views as to the causes of the riot; the degree to which they knew what was taking place; and their ranking of Negro leaders. Limited information on employment and indebtedness was obtained on 496 prisoners; more extensive information was collected in 157 of those interviewed. The survey was not based on a scientific sample.

U S DEPT OF LABOR, Office Of Planning And Research. "The Moynihan Report: The Negro Family And Crime" in *The Sociology Of Crime And Delinquency*, Wolfgang, M et al (ed), 440–450. NY Wiley 1970.

U S GENERAL ACCOUNTING OFFICE. *Female Offenders: Who Are They And What Are The Problems Confronting Them?* Washington DC USGAO 1979.

This study provides a better understanding of the needs and problems of female offenders and suggests better ways for the criminal justice system to deal with these women. Female offenders have traditionally been forgotten and their problems ignored by criminologists, lawyers, penologists, and social scientists. To further understanding of their concerns, information was gathered through literature reviews, visits to correctional facilities, and interviews with inmates and corrections officials. Findings indicate that most female offenders come from racial or ethnic minorities: black, hispanic, or american indian. They are, for the most part, younger than the general population––under 30––and have less education. Many have had troubled or abused childhoods.*

U S SENATE COMMITTEE ON THE JUDICIARY. *Juvenile Delinquency (Indians).* Washington DC USGPO 1955.

U S SENATE COMMITTEE ON THE JUDICIARY. *Juvenile Delinquency (Indians).* Washington DC USGPO 1954.

U S SENATE COMMITTEE ON THE JUDICIARY. *Juvenile Delinquency Among The Indians.* Washington DC USGPO 1955.

U S SENATE COMMITTEE ON THE JUDICIARY. *Juvenile Delinquency Among The Indians.* Washington DC USGPO 1956.

UHLMAN, Thomas M. *Racial Justice: Black Judges And Defendants In An Urban Trial Court.* Lexington MA Lexington 1979.

The sentencing behavior of black judges and the treatment of black defendants in an urban trial court were studied to explore the relationship between courts and race. To understand the politics of race in courts. Information used to analyze the sentencing behavior of black judges and the treatment of black defendants was obtained from judicial autobiographies, case histories of felony defendants, and personal interviews. Background data on 16 black and 79 white judges were derived. Data on defendants include felony cases docketed and disposed of between July 1968 and June 1974. In evaluating defedant treatment, 43,602 cases disposed of via bench trials, jury trials, or guilty pleas were examined, along with sentences meted out to 32,731 black and white defendants found guilty in these deliberations. Findings revealed that race–related background differences were minimal on the city's courts. Black judges tended to convict and sentence black defendants more often and more harshly than white defendants.*

UHLMAN, Thomas M. Race, Recruitment And Representation: Background Differences In Black And White Trial Judges. *West Pol Q* ,457–470 D 1977.

ULRICH, K and Dertke, M C and Penner, L A. Observer's Reporting Of Shoplifting As A Function Of Thief's Race And Sex. *J Soc Psychol* 94,213–221 1974.

UNIKEL, I P and Blanchard, E B. Psychopathy, Race, And Delay Of Gratification By Adolescent Delinquents. *J Nerv Ment Dis* 156,57–60 1973.

UNITED TRIBES OF N DAKOTA DEVELOPMENT CORP. *United Tribes Of North Dakota Development Corportion: New Careers Program, Progress Report, April 1, 1973–April 30, 1973.* Washington DC NCJRS 1973.

Problems of the Bureau of Indian Affairs "New Careers Program," designed to train Indians for positions in the criminal justice system. Participants are trained for such jobs as probation officer, alcoholic offender counselor, and associate judge. A bureau freeze on further new careers hiring has resulted in some problems with trainee turnover and discipline, according to this corporation report, primarily because trainees know that user agencies will do anything to avoid losing trainees, thereby losing job slots. Because the trainee outlook is uncertain, the New Careers staff is considering alternative routes of employment for program graduates. This report includes the program's funding status and a trainee roster broken down by reservation, job slot, and individual turnover.

UNIVERSITY OF NEBRASKA. *Indian Justice––A Research Bibliography.* Washington DC Nat Cen Prosec Man 1975.

URBAN SYSTEMS INSTITUTE. *The Impact Of New Sentencing Laws On State Prison Populations In Pennsylvania; Final Report.* Pittsburgh Carnegie–M USI 1979.

UNNEVER, James D and Frangier, Charles and Henretta, Juan C. Racial Differences In Criminal Sentencing. Boston A S A 1979.

UTAH COUNCIL ON CRIMINAL JUSTICE ADMINSTRATION. *Utah—Manpower And Training.* Salt Lake City Utah C Cr J Admin 1977.

VAN BLARICON, D P. Recruitment And Retention Of Minority Race Persons As Police Officers. *Pol Chief* 43(9),60–64 1976.

A recruiting and testing system to achieve minority representation in a police department, developed by the Bellevue, Washington, Police Department, is described. The process involved the use of culturally non–biased aptitude tests, ranking of composite test scores within minority group classifications, and psychological and physical testing.*

VAN DEN BERGHE, Pierre L. *Intergroup Relations: Sociological Perspectives.* NY Basic Books 1972.

This book contains a collection of reprints from the *American Sociological Review* representative of American sociology throughout the more than three decades of the *Review*. The book is divided into the following sections: (1) theory, (2) the ethnography of race and ethnic relations, (3) the African Diaspora and cultural survivals: the Frazier–Herskovits Debate, (4) endogamy and exogamy, (5) race and ethnic attitudes, (6) the demography and ecology of racism, (7) responses to oppression, (8) the culture of racism.

VAN DEN BERGHE, Pierre L. *Race And Racism: A Comparative Perspective.* NY Wiley 1967.

VAN DEN HAAG, Ernest. In Defense Of The Death Penalty: A Legal–Practical–Moral Analysis. *Crim L Bull* 14(1),51–68 Ja–F 1978.

VAN DEN HAAG, Ernest. No Excuse For Crime. *Ann Am Poli* 423,133–141 Ja 1976.

Some criminologists regard offenders as victims of conditions beyond their control which produce a "cause and effect" relationship that spawns criminal behavior. The theory that labels such offenders as "political prisoners" is considered flawed, because the author defines a political criminal as one who breaks the law in attempts to change the sociopolitical system. Socioeconomic conditions do not have the characterized direct influence upon behavior as suggested by certain theorists. The idea that the poor should be excused for deviant behavior because of their deprived living conditions while the wealthy and powerful should be punished lacks scientific consistency. The view that capitalism is the cause and socialism the cure for crime ignores the basic patterns of social behavior and government by law that provide the background for crime in any society, regardless of its sociopolitical structure. The differences between black and white crime rates may well be explained by environmental circumstances; however, the existence of divergent behavior in individuals who live apparently under the same conditions is believed to reveal a much more complex interaction between a person and his or her environment.*

VAN DOREN, C and Rivera, F and Moquin, W E. *A Documentary History Of The Mexican Americans.* NY Bantam 1971.

VAN VALKENBURGH, R. *Navajo Common Law II: Navajo Law And Justice. Museum N Ariz Note* 9(10),51–54 1937.

VAN VECHTEN, C C. "The Criminality Of The Foreign Born" in *Readings In Criminology And Penology*, Dressler, D (ed), 253–260. NY Columbia Univ Pr 1964.

VAN WOODWARD, C Vann. Our Racist History. *NY Rev Bks* 12,5–11 F 27 1969.

VANAGUNAS, Stanley. "Police Entry Testing And Minority Employment Implications" in *Police And Law Enforcement*, Curran, J (ed), 313–317. NY AMS Pr 1973.

The 1971 Supreme Court decision in Griggs v Duke Power Company is analyzed in terms of its impact on the use of intelligence or other tests as a screening procedure for employment in law enforcement of minority group individuals. In Griggs, the Court held that while discriminatory intent is a factor in considering employment intelligence tests, the Civil Rights Act is mainly concerned with the consequences of using such tests. If Griggs is sweepingly applied to the police profession, a period of anarchy can be readily foreseen in the recruit selection standards of police departments not prepared to offer hard facts on the relationship between test instruments and the officer's job. Doubt is being voiced as to the success of general intelligence tests to predict police job performance. The Griggs decision has the potential of adding to the discord between the Courts and the police community.

VANCE, M (ed) and King, W M (ed). *Blacks, Crime & Criminal Justice: An Introductory Bibliography.* Monticello IL Coun Plan Librar 1974.

Alphabetical listing (by author) of over 200 books, articles, government publications, dissertations and theses. A separate list of the journals cited is included at the beginning of the bibliography.*

VANDER ZANDEN, J. *American Minority Relations.* NY Ronald Pr 1972.

VANDIVER, Richard. *A Selected Bibliography Of Paperback Books On Crime.* Carbondale S II CSC & Del 1970.

List of book materials only. Divided into six content areas: general criminology, special types of criminality, juvenile delinquency, the criminal justice system, biography—case history, and of special interest to Black Americans. Includes list of publishers and addresses.

VAUGH, Ted. The Landlord—Tenant Relation In Low Income Areas. *Social Prob* 16,208–218 Fall 1968.

VAUGHN, E C and Mindel, C H and Cromwell, R E. Ethnic Minority Family Research In An Urban Setting: A Process Of Exchange. *Am Sociologist* 10,141–150 1975.

VAUGHN, G M. The Effect Of The Ethnic Grouping Of The Experimenter Upon Children's Responses To Tests Of An Ethnic Nature. *Br J Soc Cl Psy* 2,66–70 1963.

VAUGHN, R G. Preferences In Public Employment. *Am U L Rev* 25(3),659–715 1976.

VAZ, Edmund W. Exploration In The Institutionalization Of Juvenile Delinquency. *J Crim L Crimin & Pol Sci* 62,396–405 1971.

VEGA, W. The Liberal Policeman: A Contradiction In Terms? *Issues Crim* 4(1),15–33 1968.

VIANO, Emilio (ed) and Drapkin, Israel (ed). *Victimology: A New Focus, V1.* Lexington MA Lexington 1974.

VIGIL, J D. *From Indians To Chicanos: A Sociocultural History.* St Louis C V Mosby 1980.

VINTER, Robert D. Trends In State Correction; Juveniles And The Violent Young Offender. *Crim Delinq* 25(2),145–161 Ap 1979.

VIRGINIA CORRECTIONS DEPARTMENT. *Annual Statistical Report Of Felons & Misdemeanants Committed To The VA State Correctional System During The Year Ended June 30, 1977.* Richmond VA Corrections Dept 1978.

VITERITTI, Joseph P. *Police, Politics, And Pluralism In New York City: A Comparative Case Study.* Beverly Hills CA Sage 1973.

VITO, Gennaro F and Parks, Evalyn C and Carlson, Eric W. Effectiveness Of Volunteer Assistance To Parolees. *Evaluation Review* 4(3),323–338 Je 1980.

This study of recidivism was conducted in Ohio comparing the postprogram recidivism of 107 program participants with a group of offenders eligible for the program but not matched with a volunteer—helper, and with a randomly selected group of offenders. The results indicate that the postprogram recidivism of the experimental group differed along racial lines, with the black members experiencing increased recidivism whereas the whites' recidivism was reduced.

VIZZINI, Sal. *Vizzini.* NY Arbor House 1972.

Cuban drug smuggling in the Miami area is described in this book.

VODICKA, John. Prison Plantation: The Story Of Angola. *S Exposure* 6(4),32–38 Wint 1978.

VOGEL, Richard. Prison Reform In Social Perspective. *Tex Observ* ,3–5 Ja 31 1975.

VOLAKALIS, Joan and Fox, Vernon. The Negro Offender In A Northern Industrial Area. *J Crim L Crimin & Pol Sci* 46,641–647 1956.

This study of social, psychological and occupational differences between black and white inmates of a Michigan State Prison found that blacks were more likely to be committed for assaultive crimes, more likely to be migrants from the South (although there was a trend toward reduction below statistical significance of the difference in proportion of native born whites and blacks), younger, less likely to be formally married, of lower occupational status, and of lower I. Q. (96.6 for whites and 83.4 for blacks) than whites. Culture conflict and social disorganization are suggested to be significant factors in black crime.

VOLKMAN, Ernest. Othello. *Penthouse* ,69+ Ap 1980.

VOLLMAN, T. Criminal Jurisdiction In Indian Country: Tribal Sovereignty And Defendant's Rights In Conflict. *U Kan L Rev* 22(3),387–412 1974.

VON HENTIG, Hans. *The Criminal And His Victim.* New Haven CT Yale Univ Pr 1949.

VON HENTIG, Hans. Criminality Of The Negro. *J Am Inst Cr L Crim* 30,662–680 1940.

VON HENTIG, Hans. The Criminality Of The Colored Woman, Series C. *U Colo Stud* I,231–260 My 1942.

VON HENTIG, Hans. The Delinquency Of The American Indian. *J Crim L Crimin & Pol Sci* 36,75–84 Jl–Ag 1945.

The types and causes of crimes committed by American Indians were analyzed in a 1945 study based on Uniform Crime Reports and census information. During the period 1935 to 1944 arrests of Indians increased, and arrests and prison admissions were proportionately higher for Indians than for whites. Indians in the US in 1945 were subject to three jurisdictions—federal, state, and Indian courts—but most cases were decided by Indian courts. Many Indians identified by the census were not full-blooded, and the definition of how much Indian blood legally constituted an Indian varied considerably. Although the superintendents of Indian reservations exercised some discretionary power over the Indian courts, this privilege had no legal basis. A 1929 survey of Indians showed that drunkenness accounted for over half of all Indian offenses. Other offenses, such as sex, game law, and certain property offenses were not offenses by traditional Indian law. While the Indian courts punished with jail sentences, the regular courts relied on fines because of prison overcrowding and the belief that jail was often more comfortable than the Indians' homes.*

VON HENTIG, Hans. The First Generation And A Half: Notes On The Delinquency Of Native Whites Of Mixed Parentage. *Am Sociol Rev* 10,792–798 D 1945.

VONTRESS, Clemmont E. Patterns Of Segregation And Discrimination: Contributing Factors To Crime Among Negroes. *J Negro Ed* 31,108–116 1962.

The patterns of segregation and discrimination are directly or indirectly contributory to crime among Negroes in the US. The characteristics of the ghettoed Negro population include poverty, ignorance of the law, lack of influential connections, Southern patterns of illegality, and the use of weapons in fights. Concentration in cities and in young adult ages in the North operate to make Negro crime rate higher than crime by whites.

VONTRESS, Clemmont E. The Black Male Personality. *Black Scholar* 2(10),10–16 1971.

VOSS, H L and Hepburn, John R. Patterns Of Criminal Homicide: A Comparison Of Chicago And Philadelphia. *Criminology* 8(1),21–45 My 1970.

VOSS, Harwin. Ethnic Differentials In Delinquency In Honolulu. *J Crim L Crimin & Pol Sci* 54,322–327 My–Je 1963.

VOSS, Harwin. Pitfalls In Social Research: A Case Study. *Am Sociologist* 3,66–70 1966.

WACHETEL, Paul. Change And Resistance: A Psychotherapeutic View Of Race Relations. *Colum Forum* 11,18–21 1968.

WADE, Mary and Havlick, J R. The American City And Civil Disorders. *Urb Data Serv* 1,1–32 1969.

WADE, Richard. *Slavery In The Cities: The South, 1820–1860.* nY Oxford Univ Pr 1964.

WADE, Richard. The Vesey Plot: A Reconsideration. *J Southern Hist* 30,143–161 1964.

WAKEFIELD, Dan. *Island In The City.* Boston Houghton Mifflin 1959.

WALD, Karen. "The San Quentin Six Case: Perspective And Analysis" in *Punishment And Penal Discipline*, Platt, Tony And Paul Takagi (eds), 165–175. Berkeley CA Crime & Soc Just 1980.

WALD, Michael et al. Interrogations In New Haven: The Impact Of *Miranda. Yale L J* 76,1519–1648 1967.

WALDO, Gordon P and Chiricos, Theodore G and Jackson, Phillip D. Inequality In The Imposition Of A Criminal Label. *Social Prob* 19(4),553–572 Spr 1972.

WALDO, Gordon P and Chiricos, Theodore G. Socioeconomic Status And Criminal Sentencing. *Am Sociol Rev* 40,753–772 D 1975.

WALDO, Gordon P and Hall, N E. Delinquency Potential And Attitudes Toward The Criminal Justice System. *Soc Forces* 49(2),291–298 1970.

WALES, E and Brewer, B. Graffiti In The 1970's. *J Soc Psychol* 99,115–123 1976.

WALKER, David. *David Walker's Appeal To The Coloured Citizens Of The World 1829.* NY Hill & Wang 1965.

WALKER, D. Citizen Contact And Legal System Support. *Social Sci Q* 58(1),3–14 1977.

To examine the relationship between public support for four legal institutions and policy outputs and outcomes, interviews were conducted with a stratified probability sample of 1,146 adults in North Carolina. The four institutions were the police, the state courts, the state correctional institutions, and the US Supreme Court. both diffuse and specific support was given to the police, the state courts, state prisons, and the Supreme Court, in that order, by majority of the respondents. In terms of specific support, only the police received positive specific support. Assessment of the relationships between race, age, education, and income indicated that no socioeconomic or racial variable is significantly related to support for all four institutions.*

WALKER, Jonathan. *Trial And Imprisonment Of Jonathan Walker, At Pensacola, For Aiding Slaves To Escape From Bondage.* Boston Anti–Slav Office 1845.

WALKER, Lynn. The Legal Eye—The Black Death Penalty. *Essence* 3,28 Mr 1973.

WALKER, Marcia J (ed) and Brodsky, Stanley L (ed). *Sexual Assault: The Victim And The Rapist.* Lexington MA Lexington 1976.

WALLER, Irvin and Chan, Janet. Prison Use: A Canadian And International Comparison. *Crim L Q* 17,47–71 D 1974.

WALLMAN, K K and Hodgdon, J. Race And Ethnic Standards For Federal Statistics And Administrative Reporting. *Stat Reptr* 77(10),450–454 1977.

WALSH, James. An Urban Riot: A Juvenile Court Meets The Challenge. *Crim Delinq* 14,306–314 1968.

WALTER, Greg. Living In Fear In Philadelphia. *Penthouse* 9,52–58,82 My 1978.

WANDERER, J J. An Index Of Riot Severity And Some Correlates. *Am J Soc* 74(5),500–505 1969.

WANDERER, J J. 1967 Riots: A Test Of The Congruity Of Events. *Social Prob* 16,193–197 Fall 1968.

WARD, Benjamin (ed) and Cohn, Alvin W (ed). *Improving Management In Criminal Justice.* Beverly Hills CA Sage 1980.

WARD, Benjamin. "The Need For Black Police Officers" in *The Administration Of Criminal Justice: A View From Black America,* Brown, Lee P (ed), 3–7. Washington DC Howard U 1974.

Ward makes a plea for increased interest and involvement by blacks in the criminal justice system. The country is in a panic, he says—a panic whose code words are "law and order" and "more cops." Because of this panic, national priorities are being dislocated and blacks are being faced with the loss of hard won goals. It is therefore necessary, Ward states, for blacks to enter the criminal justice system to move it from within. Police power must be emphasized over political power. Blacks must start thinking about attaining power proportionate to their numbers in the major cities of this country. That power is the real power in the community.

WARD, David A (ed) and Cressey, Donald R (ed). *Delinquency, Crime, And Social Process.* NY Harper 1969.

WARD, David A and Kassenbaum, Gene G. *Women's Prison: Sex And Social Structure.* Chicago IL Aldine 1965.

WARD, J A and Fox, J. Suicide Epidemic On An Indian Reserve. *Can Psychi Assoc J* 22,8 D 1977.

WARD, Samuel Ringgold. *The Autobiography Of A Fugitive Negro.* London John Snow 1855.

WARE, Gilbert (ed). *From The Black Bar.* NY G P Putnam's 1976.

WARE, Gilbert. Black Judges, White Justice. *NY L J* 156(31),1,4 Ag 13 1971.

WARING, J H N. "Some Causes Of Criminality Among Colored Persons" in *The Negro In The Cities Of The North.* NY Charity Organ Soc 1905.

WARNER, W Lloyd and Junker, Buford H and Adams, Walter A. *Color And Human Nature.* Washington DC Am Coun On Educ 1941.

WARNHEIS, Paul L. "Crime And Criminal Justice Among The Mexicans Of Illinois" in *Report On Crime And The Foreign Born,* V11. Washington DC NCLOE 1931.

WARREN, D I. Mass Media And Racial Crisis: A Study Of The New Bethel Church Incident In Detroit. *J Soc Issues* 28(1),111–131 1972.

WARREN, Donald. Neighborhood Structure And Riot Behavior In Detroit: Some Exploratory Findings. *Social Prob* 16,464–484 Spr 1969.

WASHBURN, W E. *The American Indian And The United States: A Documentary History.* NY Random House 1973.

WASHBURN, W. *The Indian In America.* NY Harper & Row 1975.

WASHINGTON, Booker T. Negro Crime And **Strong Drink.** *J Am Inst Cr L Crim* 3(3) 384–392 1912.

WASHINGTON, Booker T. Prohibition And The Negro. *Color Am Mag* 14(5),266–269 1908.

WASHINGTON, Charles and Henton, Comradge L. Differential Study Of Recidivism Among Negro And White Boys. *J Genet Psyc* 98,247–253 1961.

This study of eight black and eight white boys, three— and four—time recidivists serving sentences in Louisiana State Training Schools for Boys, compares the ages, socio—economic status, marital status of parents, religion, disposition of parents in the home, intellectual factors, emotional factors, offenses and main reasons for recidivism of the boys in the two groups. Generally similar patterns emerged for both groups.

WASHINGTON, Forrester B. Care Of The Negro Delinquent. *Nat Prob Assn Yearbk* ,218–228 1932–33.

WASHINGTON, H R. History And Role Of Black Law Schools. *Howard L J* 18,385–422 1975.

WASHINGTON, Josephine T. Child Saving In Alabama. *Color Am Mag* 14(1),48–51 1908.

WASHINGTON, M and Alexander, Harry T. Black Judges In White America. *Black L J* 1(3),245+ Wint 1971.

WASHINGTON, Michelle. Constance Baker Motley: Black Woman, Black Judge. *Black L J* 1(2),173–179 Sum 1971.

WASKOW, Arthur I. *From Race Riot To Sit–In.* NY Doubleday 1965.

WASSERMAN, R D. Oliphant Versus Schlie: Recognition Of Tribal Criminal, Jurisdiction Over Non–Indians. *Utah L Rev* 1976(3),631–645 1976.

WASSERSTEIN, Bruce (ed) and Green, Mark J (ed). *With Justice For Some: An Indictment Of The Law By Young Advocates.* Boston Beacon Pr 1970.

WASSON, Houston. Virginia's Legislative Response To Riots And Their Underlying Causes. *Va L Rev* 54,1031–1063 1968.

WATSON, Wilbur. *Stress And Old Age.* New Brunswick NJ Transaction Books 1979.

By focusing on signs of postrelocation mortality, psychosocial distress, and coping behavior in two groups of inner—city elderly black people, *Stress and Old Age* provides new insight and helps fill the information void created by the lack of research on relocation effects among the minority elderly. Watson provides new insight to distinctions between survivors and nonsurvivors by focusing on various sociological factors not previously examined or given only scant attention. He develops policy implications for training direct care workers and managers of long—term care institutions who face the prospect of relocating large numbers of racially homogeneous and mixed resident populations, but who have not yet come to grips with the many ramifications associated with the relocation of elderly, infirm, poor people.

WATTENBERG, W W. Factors Linked To Race Among Boys In Trouble With Detroit Police 1948. *J Negro Ed* 23,186–189 1954.

WATTERS, Pat (ed) and Gillers, Stephen (ed). *Investigating The FBI.* NY Ballantine 1973.

WATTS, Frederick P. A Comparative Clinical Study Of Delinquent And Nondelinquent Boys. *J Negro Ed* 19(2),190–207 1941.

WATTS, W and Free, L A. *Aspirations And Social Concerns—Crime, Blacks, Inequality And Women.* Washington DC Potomac Associates 1976.

The survey research analysis was based on a national sampling of 1,071 Americans. Public concerns reflected a desire for a better standing of living, good personal health, and a happy family life. Inflation, threat of war and social decay were the areas about which fear was expressed. A hope for peace was found systematically throughout the cross—section of the population. Americans were also found to be very disturbed about crime, violence, and related issues of drugs and drug abuse. Efforts to combat these problems are not well viewed and increased federal government spending is thought to be a solution. The survey revealed a noticeable hardening of the public's attitude toward criminals. In comparison to other major problems facing the nation, the condition and problems of blacks did not rank especially high. Most americans assign a high priority to government spending to allieviate the problem. The lower- to middle-income urban whites are most adamant about government economic assistance to blacks.*

WAX, Darold D. Preferences For Slaves In Colonial America. *J Negro Hist* 58(4),371–401 O 1973.

Although the number of slaves transported to the English continental colonies represented only a small percentage of the Africans carried across the Atlantic during the slave trade—probably less than 5%, with the majority going to the West Indies—the slave trade was important to the American colonies. The author challenges old assumptions that "seasoned slaves" (slaves who had spent some time in the West Indies before being sent on to America) were preferred over slaves sent directly from Africa. On the contrary, he cites evidence that so-called "seasoned" slaves were often regarded as "refuse," in part because many colonial merchants thought that slaves sold from the West Indies were usually disposed of because they had been belligerent, refractory, or exhibited "criminal" tendencies that made them unattractive. Wax points to statutes in several American colonies which sought to restrict the importation of malefactors and troublemakers. This was one reason, he suggests, why the vast majority of slaves sent to America came directly from Africa.

WAX, Darold D. The Image Of The Negro In The Maryland Gazette, 1745–1774. *Journ Q* 45(1),73–80 Spr 1969.

WAX, Douglas E. Self-Concept In Negro And White Pre-Adolescent Delinquent Boys. *Br J Crimin* 14(2),165–171 Ap 1974.

Fifty-five Negro and white pre-adolescent delinquent boys were administered a version of the Osgood Semantic Differential Technique designed as an exploratory measure of self-concept. Of the concepts tested, only one attained a significant level of difference between the two groups. "Boys who get into trouble" was perceived by the Negro group as generally a more positive concept. The black group was also found to show a less favorable perception of itself in the future and a lower aspiration level than the white group. It is suggested that such results might offer confirmation for the notion of blocked access to means and goals within the social system. The author contends that the Negro pre-adolescent delinquent identity may be "an aspect of self-perception, shaped by opportunities within the society and the perception of the adult sex role. For the similar group of white delinquents, the criminal role remains ego-alien, that is, in conflict with the concept of self."

WEATHERFORD, Willis D and Johnson, C S. "Chapter 22" in *Race Relations*. Boston Heath 1934.

WEBB, Walter Prescott. *The Texas Rangers*. Dallas Univ Texas Pr 1965.

WEEBER, S C and Roebuck, Julian B. *Political Crime In The United States—Analyzing Crime By And Against Government*. NY Praeger 1978.

A typology of political crime—offenses by and against government—in the United States from 1960 to 1978 is constructed in a text for students of criminology, social problem, deviance, and related subjects. The typology is based primarily on the action patterns of offenses committed by persons or groups during the normal course of their activities as employees or members of formal organizations. Thus, the focus is on criminal organization patterns.*

WEGLYN, Michi. *Years Of Infamy*. NY Morrow 1976.

WEINER, Normal L and Willie, Charles V. Decisions By Juvenile Officers. *Am J Soc* 77(2),199–210 1971.

WEIS, Joseph G and Hindelang, Michael J and Hirschi, Travis. Correlates Of Delinquency: The Illusion Of Discrepancy Between Self-Report And Offical Measures. *Am Sociol Rev* 44,995–1014 D 1979.

The notion that official and self-report methods produce discrepant results with respect to sex, race, and class is largely illusory. When the domain limitations of self-reports are recognized, the conclusion of general consistency between self-reports and official correlates for sex, race, and class emerges. This consistency and other evidence from victimization surveys, studies of the reliability and validity of self-reports, and studies of biases in criminal justice processing, suggest that both official data and self-reports provide valid indicators of the demographic characteristics of offenders, *within the domain of behavior effectively tapped by each*

method. Data is presented in support of the contention that "blacks and whites differ in *serious* delinquent behavior," and that "slef-reports fail to find racial differences in large part because self-report instruments generally do not pick up the most serious kinds of street crime," which are most likely to result in detection and apprehension and in which blacks are disproportionately involved.

WEIS, Joseph G. Liberation And Crime: The Invention Of The New Female Criminal. *Crim & Soc Just* 6,17–27 Fall–Wint 1976.

WEISBOND, R G. *Genocide: Birth Control And The Black American*. Westport CY Greenwood Pr 1975.

WEISMAN, C S and Crain, R L. *Discrimination, Personality And Achievement—A Survey Of Northern Blacks*. NY Seminar Pr 1972.

WEISS, Carl and Friar, David James. *Terror In The Prisons*. Indianapolis Bobbs–Merrill 1974.

WEISS, Carol H. Survey Researchers And Minority Communities. *J Soc Issues* 33(4),20–35 1977.

WEISS, Melford S. The Research Experience In A Chinese–American Community. *J Soc Issues* 33(4),120–132 1977.

WEISSMAN, Andrew B. The Discriminatory Application Of Penal Laws By State Judicial And Quasi–Judicial Officers. *Northw Univ L Rev* 69(4),489–554 1975.

WEITZMAN, Leonard J and Nagel, Stuart. Double Standard Of American Justice. *Society* 9(5),18–25 1972.

WELFORD, Harrison. *Sowing The Wind*, . NY Grossman Pub 1972.

WELL, T H. The Phoenix Election Riot. *Phylon* 31(1),58–69 1970.

WELLER, Jack M and Kreps, Gary A. The Police–Community Relations Movement: Conciliatory Responses To Violence. *Am Behav Sci* 16(3),402–412 1973.

A study made by Michigan State University concluded that the primary objective of community relations programs was race relations. Police community relations programs have already survived the conditions which impelled their adoption and expansion from 1965 through 1970. The threat of escalating, costly violence activated a tolerance for ideas which were once too sensitive to be considered.

WELLER, Leonard and Lucterhand, Elmer. Effects Of Class, Race, Sex And Educational Status On Patterns Of Aggression Of Lower Class Youth. *J Youth Ado* 5(1),59–71 Mr 1976.

The influence of class, race, sex and educational status on ways of handling aggression and temper control were studied by means of responses to open- and closed-ended questions. The sample consisted of 1,844 inner–city youth in two northern cities. Race was found to be the only important discriminator: blacks were less aggressive and exhibited more temper control than whites, but once aggression occurred blacks were more likely than whites to assault others. Results are interpreted in terms of self–identity and blacks' fears of the consequences of aggressive responses.

WELLFORD, C and Sagi, P. Age Composition And Patterns Of Change In Criminal Statistics. *J Crim L Crimin & Pol Sci* 59,29–36 1968.

WENGER, D. The Reluctant Army: The Functioning Of Police Departments During Civil Disturbances. *Am Behav Sci* 16(3),326–342 1973.

WENK, E A and Halatyn, T V. *Analysis Of Classification Factors For Young Adult Offenders: Race Factors*, V3. San Francisco NCCD 1974.

This California–based project was undertaken to organize the results of an extensive data collection on the youthful offender and to provide a resource for the correctional theorist working with this most important offender group. Background data, personality and other test results, academic and vocational skills and attitudes, and psychiatric factors, as well as offense related information and the ratings and recommendations of institutional staffs were obtained on 4,146 male California Youth Authority parolees. This effort was envisioned as a prerequisite to the development of typological descriptions of youthful offenders that may ultimately influence their treatment and rehabilitation. After providing a brief background on the entire study and a review of the literature on the relationship of race and delinquency, this volume presents comparative data on black, Mexican–American, and white Youth Authority parolees. Controlling for race, the study presents information on academic, intelligence, vocational, personality, psychiatric, and offense–related factors. The relationship of these variables to parole success is also analyzed.*

WERNER, Eric. Psychological And Ethnic Correlates Of Interpersonal Maturity Among Delinquents. *Br J Crimin* 15(1),51–68 Ja 1975.

This investigation evaluated the relationship of Warren's interpersonal maturity (I–level) system of developmental stages to a statistical typology of 934 delinquents which was derived from configurational characteristics of cluster scores on three oblique dimensions of the California Psychological Inventory. CPI cluster analysis and the evaluation of the I–level/CPI typology relationship were both carried out separately for white and non–white sub–samples. The significant I–level/CPI typology relationship found, though consistent with theoretical expectations, was small. As expected, no differences were found between whites and non–whites in terms of the correlates of maturity diagnosis. The relationship of I–level to non–verbal intelligence was also evaluated and some general implications of this association for both the construct of interpersonal maturity and the issue of ethnic group differences in I–level distribution were considered.

WERTHMAN, Carl and Piliavin, Irving. "Gang Members And The Police" in *The Police: Six Sociological Essays*, Bordua, David J (ed), 58–98. NY Wiley 1967.

WESLEY, C H. *Negro Labor In The United States, 1850–1925.* NY Vanguard Pr 1927.

WESSNER, Jim. Racism In Federal Prison. *Peacemaker* 23(6),1–2 My 2 1970.

A draft resister who spent 19 months in federal prisons during the Vietnam war offers examples of how racism in prison functions to the advantage of staff and the disadvantage of inmates. At Ashland Federal Youth Center, all of the guards were white, and according to Wessner, "they were also from the most openly and proudly racist segment of Americn society...." Nearly one–quarter of the prisoners were black and all were young, which put them in conflict with the guards. The author describes an incident following an inmate attack on a correction officer, which resulted in violent reprisals. He also describes harassment of Black Muslim inmates.

WEST, J and Sloan, J. The Role Of Informal Policy Making In US–Mexico Border Cities. *Social Sci Q* 58(2),270–282 1977.

WEST, John S. Negroes On Juries. *Car Selden Soc Yearbk* 9,53–62 1947.

WEST, L J. On Racial Violence. *Northwest Med* 64(9),679–682 1965.

WEST, P A and Herjanic, B L and Robins, Lee N. Arrests And Delinquency In Two Generations: A Study Of Black Urban Families And Their Children. *J Child Psyc & Psychi* 16(2),125–140 1975.

WEST, S G and Whitney, G and Schnedler, R. Helping A Motorist In Distress: The Effects Of Sex, Race And Neighborhood. *J Pers Soc Psychol* 31(4),691–698 1975.

WESTERMEYER, Joseph and Brantner, John. Violent Death And Alcohol Use Among The Chippewa In Minnesota. *Minn Med* 55(8),749–752 1972.

Violent death occurs five times more often among Indian people in Minnesota (most of whom are Chippewa) than among the general population. It is the most common cause of death for Indians in Minnesota, during recent years. In Minneapolis, violent deaths among Indians are significantly more often associated with alcohol use than in the general population. In general, Chippewa victims of violent death resemble such victims in the general population with regard to sex, age, and blood alcohol level. A notable exception to this is homicide, which occurs at an earlier age among Chippewa than it does among other American Indians, whereas, unlike other Indian groups, suicide is less frequent.

WESTERMEYER, Joseph. Indian Powerlessness In Minnesota. *Society* 10(3),45–47,50–52 1973.

WESTIE, K S and Mc Bride, D C. The Effects Of Ethnicity, Age And Sex Upon Processing Through And Emergency Alcohol Health Care Delivery System. *Br J Addict* 74(1),21–29 1979.

This study provides a basic demographic profile of an emergency room alcohol patient population, and examines the relationships of age, ethnicity and sex to type of complaint at admission, likelihood of referral for further aid, type of psychiatric diagnosis given, and ultimate disposition of the case.

WESTLEY, William A. Violence And The Police. *Am J Soc* 59,34–41 Jl 1953.

WEYL, Nathaniel. Race, Nationality And Crime. *Mankind Q* 14,41 1973.

WEYL, Nathaniel. The Geography Of Stupidity In The USA. *Mankind Q* 15(2),117–123 1974.

Regional and racial differences in intelligence in the US are discussed, based on data obtained from the Armed Forces Qualification Test (AFQT) administered in 1968 to both whites (non–blacks) and blacks. Excluding Alaska, Hawaii, Guam, and Puerto Rico, 6.3% of the non–blacks and 35.5% of the blacks nationally failed the AFQT. The zones of greatest white stupidity as revealed by the AFQT failures are the Appalachians and the deep South, in that order. This is attributed to regional distribution of deported felons and indentured laborers in the American colonies, a high rate of inbreeding, the emigration of the more able elements, and a climate not conducive to mental alertness. The regions of greatest intelligence among white draftees are the northern states from the Pacific to the Great Lakes and Rhode Island. probable causes include a homogenous stock of Nordic elements, absence of descendants of deported persons, absence of cities with large populations of delinquents and chronic welfare clients, and a bracing climate.

WHEELER, A C and Sparling, C L and Inn, A. The Effects Of Suspect Race And Situation Hazard On Police Officer Shooting Behavior. *J App So P* 7(1),27–37 1977.

Results of this study suggest that racial bias is not a factor in police shooting decisions.

WHEELER, William Henry III. Blackness Is My Mental Health: A Mind Set For Black Drug Abuse Prevention And Treatment Programs. *J Nonwh Con Per Guid* 4(2),64–70 1976.

WHITE, J. *Justice And The American Indian, V4: Examination Of The Basis Of Tribal Law And Order Authority.* Washington DC LEAA 1974.

WHITE, R and Grant, R and Milne, R. Minority Recruiting: The Tucson Police Experience. *J Polic Sci Adm* 3(2),197–202 1975.

The attempts of the Tucson Police Department to recruit qualified minorities (blacks and Mexican–Americans) into police work are examined in this article. In November 1971 a black officer was assigned to the personnel section as a minority recruiter. In less than 18 months the black complement of the agency rose from 3 to 11, or 2.83% of commissioned strength and Mexican–American representation rose from 35 to 42 or 10.7% of all police officer positions. The technique employed by the recruiter was one which emphasized personal contact and discussion of police work. The following steps were taken by the department: elimination of the Otis Employment Test, permanent assignment of a minority recruiting officer, termination of minimum height and weight requirements, adoption of a validated Police Officer Entrance Examination, reclassification of "policeman/policewoman" to "police officer," an end to separate assignments based on sex, modification of physical agility requirements and the adoption of a selective Certification Program for minorities. The program initiated by this department has been highly successful, and has been extended to attract other groups including Native–Americans and women.

WHITE, Teresa and Rubinstein, Michael L and Maroules, Nicholas. *Statistical Analysis Of Misdemeanor Sentences In Anchorage And Fairbanks: 1974–1976.* Anchorage Judicial Council 1979.

WHITE, W P. Testing And Equal Opportunity—Getting A Fair Chance. *Civil Rts Dig* 7,42–51 Spr 1975.

WHITE, Walter and Marshall, Thurgood. *What Caused The Detroit Riot?* NY NAACP 1943.

WHITE, Walter. The Eruption Of Tulsa. *Nation* 112,909–910 Je 29 1921.

WHITIN, E Stagg. *Penal Servitude.* NY Nat Comm Priso Lab 1912.

Leader of the National Committee on Prison Labor's fight against the contract labor system in American prisons, the author identifies penal servitude as the last surviving vestige of the old slave system. He urges repeal of that clause of the 13th Amendment which approves slavery and involuntary servitude as a punishment for crime.

WHITNEY, G and Schnedler, R and West, S G. Helping A Motorist In Distress: The Effects Of Sex, Race And Neighborhood. *J Pers Soc Psychol* 31(4),691–698 1975.

WHYTE, William Foote. *Street Corner Society.* Chicago Univ Chicago Pr 1942.

WILCOX, Preston. Book Review On *Black Voices From Prison*, By Etheridge Knight. *Black Scholar* 2(8,9),54,55 Ap–My 1971.

WILLCOX, Walter R. *Negro Criminality: An Address Delivered Before The American Social Science Association At Saratoga, September 6, 1899.* Boston G H Ellis 1899.

WILDAVSKY, Aaron. Black Rebellion And White Reaction. *Pub Interest* 30,3–16 Spr 1968.

WILDER, Curtis and Ashman, Allan. The Black Judge In America: A Statistical Profile. *Judicature* 57(1),18–21 Je–Jl 1973.

The findings of a national survey of black judges, taken by the American Judicature Society in 1971–1972, are presented. A 5–page questionnaire was sent to 286 black judges. Responses were received from 167. The survey focused primarily on a number of background characteristics and the geographical distribution of black judges. An underrepresentation of black judges was found both in Federal Courts, where 7% of the judges were black, and State and City Courts, where only 1% of the judges were black. Underrepresentation was most severe in the South. Although 75 of the respondents were born in the South, only 18 held judgeships there. Almost two–thirds of the black judges were appointed rather than elected to their judgeship. Eighty–six percent of the judges sat in either trial courts or courts of limited jurisdiction. Only two black judges were found on the bench of State Supreme Courts and seven held judgeships in intermediate State Courts of Appeal. In conclusion it was emphasized that appointing bodies must be made aware of and responsive to the need for more black judges in higher judicial positions.

WILKINS, Leslie T. The Concept Of Cause In Criminology. *Issues Crim* 3(2),149–165 1968.

WILKINS, Roger. Books Of The Times. *NYT*, Mr 8 1979.

WILKINS, Thurman. *Cherokee Tragedy.* NY Macmillan 1971.

WILLCOX, Walter F. *Negro Criminality: An Address Delivered Before The American Social Sciences Association At Saratoga, September 6, 1899.* Boston G H Ellis 1899.

WILLHELM, Sidney M. Black Man, Red Man, And White American: The Constitutional Approach To Genocide. *Catalyst*,1–62 Spr 1969.

WILLIAM, George C. *The Negro Offender.* NY Russell Sage Found 1922.

WILLIAMS, Dean L. *Political & Economic Aspects Of Mexican Immigration Into California And The US Since 1941.* Saratoga CA R & E Research 1973.

WILLIAMS, Edward B. *One Man's Freedom.* NY Atheneum 1962.

WILLIAMS, Eric. *Capitalism And Slavery.* Chapel Hill Univ N Car Pr 1944.

This seminal economic study of slavery contends that the origins of Negro slavery were economic, not racial. The author, then Prime Minister of Trinidad and Tobago, seeks to trace the important role that the slave trade and slavery played in the early Anglo–American capitalist system.

WILLIAMS, Eric. Race Relations In Puerto Rico And The Virgin Islands. *For Affairs* 23,308–317 Ja 1945.

WILLIAMS, F E. *Minority Recruitment Handbook, Revd, (Commission On Peace Officer Stand & Training).* Sacramento Commission 1975.

Minority recruitment may be one of the greatest challenges confronting law enforcement agencies today. There exists a hostility on the part of certain segments of the community toward the police, and the simultaneous demand by many of these same people for a greater inclusion of minorities into law enforcement ranks. The overall goal of California's Project MORE (Minority Officer Recruitment Effort) is to contribute toward the increase of minority personnel in California law enforcement. This publication, developed by the staff of Project MORE, is designed to be utilized in a systematic approach to minority recruitment. Several features which must be provided in a minority recruitment effort are outlined. These include a commitment to minority recruitment from management, the community, and education institutions; the proper organizational placement, selection and training of recruiters; and the development of community resources and community involvement in the recruiting effort. A minority recruitment plan for police is then outlined.*

WILLIAMS, Franklin H. The Death Penalty And The Negroes. *Crisis* 67(8),501–512 1960.

This survey utilizes data from *National Prisoner Statistics.* It gives the total number of executions in the US from 1930–1959, by race; the same figures for seventeen southern states; the same figures for those states for rape. It then gives the number of executions in the year 1959 for each state by race and offense, and the number of executions for each state for each year

1930–1959. The author concludes from examining these statistics that "the shockingly disproportionate number of Negro executions for rape and murder is convincing proof that the death penalty is being used in some areas as a discriminatory weapon."

WILLIAMS, Hubert. The System. *Nat Cities* 16(9),23–25 S 1978.

WILLIAMS, J R and Forward, J R. Internal–External Control And Black Militancy. *J Soc Issues* 26(1),75–92 1970.

WILLIAMS, Jack Kenny. Catching The Criminal In Nineteenth–Century South Carolina. *J Crim L Crimin & Pol Sci* 46,264–271 1955.

WILLIAMS, James and Pew, Miriam L and Speer, David C. Group Counseling For Offenders. *Social Wk* 18(1),74–79 1973.

The results of a community–based group counseling program for offenders in St. Paul, Minn., are discussed. The program has been successful both in rehabilitation and crime prevention, attracting wide and favorable attention in the city's legal circles and among residents of its inner city. This project has provided promising evidence that offenders will make significant voluntary use of community–based group counseling and intensive individual services. There are also indications that such group and individual services contribute to a decrease in the number of subsequent offenses committed.

WILLIAMS, Jay R and Gold, Martin. From Delinquent Behavior To Official Delinquency. *Social Prob* 19,209–228 Fall 1972.

WILLIAMS, K M and Lucianovic, J. *Robbery And Burglary—A Study Of The Characteristics Of The Persons Arrested And The Handling Of Their Cases In Court.* Washington DC Inst Law & Soc Res 1979.

WILLIAMS, L E. *Antecedents Of Urban Indian Crime.* Unpub PhD Diss Brigham Young Univ 1976.

Data for this study were obtained from questionnaires administered to 122 Indians and 303 white adults in Seattle, Wash. The Seattle Police Department, computer record of all arrests, convictions, and sentencing was obtained for 1971. Analysis of Police records revealed that 32,000 arrests were made during the year, of which more than 3,800 involved Indians. The Indian arrest rate is 10 times higher than the white arrest rate and over twice that of blacks. No Indian was released by the court in the year studied, and 26% of all defendants sentenced to serve time were Indians, although they represented only 12% of the arrests. No Indian was given probation or warnings, or was committed to a state hospital. Multiple regression analysis was used with a dependent variable of self–reported arrest. Most of the psychological and cultural indicators had little impact, contrasting with previous studies' findings. Thus, urban Indian crime does not appear to stem from the Indians' social class or cultural distinctiveness, but rather from subjection to prejudice in the administration of justice.*

WILLIAMS, Oscar R. The Regimentation Of Blacks On The Urban Frontier In Colonial Albany, New York City And Philadelphia. *J Negro Hist* 63(4),329–338 1978.

The greatest concentration of blacks in the Middle Colonies was in Albany, NYC and Philadelphia, according to the author. Authority over blacks was more rigid in rural areas because of greater physical isolation and social distance. In urban areas the greatest racial control problem was posed by the blurred distinctions between free blacks and slaves. "Slave codes," some of which applied to all Negroes, were viewed as a deterrent to crime. Williams suggests that the level of legal repression depended upon the proportion of slaves in the population.

WILLIAMS, Robert F. *Negroes With Guns.* NY Marzani & Munsell 1962.

WILLIAMS, Robert L. Scientific Racism And IQ: The Silent Mugging Of The Black Community. *Psych Tod* 7(12),32+ 1974.

The use of intelligence tests as instruments of scientific racism is discussed. The results of these tests place a disproportionate number of blacks in classes for mentally retarded, special education classes or lower education tracks. The concept of Ebonics, distinguished from black English, is presented, based on linguistic and paralinguistic features that represent the communicative competence of West African, Caribbean and US slave descendants of African ancestors. Such a concept reinforces the need for a culture specific test that would more fairly evaluate intelligence. Other areas of racist research are discussed including a trend toward genocide. Recommendations for future testing, laws, and public awareness are presented.

WILLIAMS, Samuel L. Law Enforcement And Affirmative Action. *Pol Chief* 42(2),72–75 F 1975.

Williams characterizes court–ordered quotas as nothing short of legal dynamite placed at the doors of institutions closed to minorities. He also feels that quotas are unfortunate because they represent a confession of serious failure on the part of the institution involved. The entrance of minorities into a department under a judge–fashioned statistical umbrella can only lead to an organization that will be divided for the foreseeable future. Within the police context those programs conventionally grouped under the rubric of affirmative action must reflect the nature and spirit of what Williams understands to be the essense of affirmative action—a basic, unqualified commitment by the police administrator to seek to reshape those elements of the current police experience which function to make the police environment hostile or inhospitable to the minority group individual.

WILLIAMSON, Henry (pseudonym). *Hustler: The Autobiography Of A Thief*, R Lincoln Keiser (ed). NY Doubleday 1965.

WILLICK, Daniel H and Gehlker, Gretchen and Mc Farland, Anita. Social Class As A Factor Affecting Judicial Disposition. *Criminology* 13(1),57–77 My 1975.

WILLIE, Charles V (ed). *Black/Brown/White Relations: Race Relations In The 1970's.* New Brunswick NJ Transaction Books 1977.

The civil–rights revolution of the 1950s and 1960s created new forms of interaction among the races, including a variety of responses such as cooperation, withdrawal, and aggressiveness, and it identified adaptations sanctioned and supported by social institutions. This collection presents analysis of the effects of institutional racism upon all races, explains the variety of adjustment that racial minorities make to their conditions, and indicates the strategies most likely to be successful for minority groups.

WILLIE, Charles V et al (eds). *Racism And Mental Health.* Pittsburgh Univ Pittsburgh Pr 1973.

WILLIE, Charles V et al. Race And Delinquency. *Phylon* 26,240–246 1965.

WILLIE, Charles V and Gershenovitz, A. Juvenile Delinquency In Racially Mixed Areas. *Am Sociol Rev* 29(5),740–744 O 1964.

WILLIE, Charles V and Weiner, Normal L. Decisions By Juvenile Officers. *Am J Soc* 77(2),199–210 1971.

WILLIFORD, Stanley O. Los Angeles' Minority Policemen Express Their Concerns. *Race Rel Rep* ,1,4–5 O 28 1974.

This article reports the results of an attitude survey of Los Angeles' 7200 man police force in 1973. The position of three minority police organizations (black, Latin and Asian) is also discussed. Of particular concern to the black organization was the "alarming increase in internal investigations involving black officers and the disproportionate degree of disciplinary actions resulting." The feeling that blacks have not benefitted significantly from recruitment efforts was also expressed. This feeling is supported by the fact that black membership on the Los Angeles Police Department is about 5% of the total force and has remained such over the past ten years. The Latin Police organization expressed many of the same concerns as the black organization but, according to the survey, not to the same degree. Not only did Latins see less to gripe about but many also felt that black officers received more favorable treatment. The Asian organization expressed concern with the lack of Asian representation on the police force (Asians make up 4% of the population but only .04% of the department) and also the lack of promotions for its members.

WILSON, Henry. *History Of The Rise And Fall Of The Slave Power In America*, 3v. Boston J R Osgood 1872–77.

WILSON, James Q. *Thinking About Crime.* NY Random House 1975.
Wilson, a professor of government at Harvard Univ, says he is as concerned with how to think about crime as he is with crime itself. His work is limited to predatory crimes for profit, however, and barely addresses violent acts of homicide, aggravated assault, or white–collar and victimless crimes. Substantial attention is devoted to racial characteristics of offenders. However Wilson opts for a class analysis of crime.

WILSON, James Q. *Varieties Of Police Behavior: The Management Of Law And Order In Eight Communities.* Cambridge MA Harvard Univ Pr 1968.

WILSON, James Q. Police Use Of Deadly Force. *FBI L Enf Bull* 49,16–21 Ag 1980.

WILSON, Jerry V. Book Review On Frank G Carrington's *The Victims.* *Victimol* 1(2),345–353 Sum 1976.

WILSON, L and Rogers, R W. The Fire This Time: Effects Of Race Of Target, Insult, And Potential Retaliation On Black Aggression. *J Pers Soc Psychol* 32(5),857–864 1975.

WILSON, R A. Anomie, In The Ghetto: A Study Of Neighborhood Type, Race And Anomie. *Am J Soc* 77(1),66–88 1971.

WILSON, Rob. Chinatown—No Longer A Cozy Assignment. *Police Mag* 1(3),19+ 1978.

Rivalry among youth gangs of Chinese–Americans showing elements of an organized crime involvement, coupled with the reserve of noncriminal Chinese–American residents presents problems for the San Francisco police. The killing of 5 persons and the wounding of 11 others in the Golden Dragon Restaurant has brought the number of gang–related murders to 37 since 1969. Only eight suspects have been convicted in these cases, and police are blaming the investigative impasse on a subculture of fear in the Chinatown community and noncooperation from community residents. Chinese–Americans counter with assertions of police neglect and racism. The explosion of youth violence is forcing police departments and insular Chinese–American communities together in a tense confrontation posing unique community relations and investigative problems. San Francisco, NYC, and Los Angeles are each trying different approaches to these problems, but in none has the youth gang problem been resolved.*

WILSON, T R. *The Black Codes Of The South.* University AL Univ AL Pr 1965.

WILSON, W J and Turner, C B. Dimensions Of Racial Ideology: A Study Of Urban Black Attitudes. *J Soc Issues* 32(2),139–152 1976.

WILSON, William Julius. *The Declining Significance Of Race.* Chicago Univ Chicago Pr 1978.

WILT, G Marie and Bannon, James D. Black Policemen. A Study Of Self–Images. *J Polic Sci Adm* 1(1),21–29 Mr 1973.

This article reports the results of a study of black officers in the Detroit Police Department conducted from the Fall 1970 to Spring 1971. The purpose was to investigate the role of the black policeman within two social contexts: a societally and institutionally defined bureaucratic functional setting—the police department; and within a dually defined and enacted role of public servant and figure of authority. There appeared to be an ambivalence on the part of black policemen over integration. The men favored the hiring of more blacks, but expressed a concern that standards not be reduced to facilitate this goal. Many officers believed tht complete equality of opportunity had not yet been achieved and that discrimination still existed. The majority felt that black policemen have greater rapport and provide better service than white policemen. The black officer seems to feel he has more insight, is more sympathetic and understanding of a black citizen's situation and that these attributes are conveyed to the black citizenry, result in the black citizenry feeling more trusting and accepting of the black policeman than of his white counterpart.

WINFREE JR, L Thomas and Bartell, Ted. Recidivist Impacts Of Differential Sentencing Practices For Burglary Offenders. *Criminology* 15(3),387–396 N 1977.

WINICK, Charles and Kinsie, Paul M. *The Lively Commerce: Prostitution In The United States.* NY New Am Lib 1971.

WINSLOW, R W. *Emergence Of Deviant Minorities—Social Problems And Social Change.* San Ramon CA Consensus Pub 1972.

Discussion of societal reactions to youth, the poor, homosexuals, alcoholics, prostitutes, pornography supporters, and those convicted to crime. Selections include excerpts from the Kerner Report on Civil Disorders, the Moynihan Report on the Negro Family, and the President's Commission Report on Law Enforcement and Administration of Justice. The author devotes a separate section to each group defined as a deviant minority. By his definition, the author has in mind people whose morality or way of life is in conflict with the law and values of society and who are coming out in the open to assert the validity of their value systems. The final chapters present a description of treatment of deviant minorities in San Francisco, with a tolerant approach which has led to the breakdown of stereotypes and reduction in crime and aggression on the part of the deviants.*

WINTERSMITH, Robert F. *Police And The Black Community.* Lexington MA Lexington 1974.

WIRTH, Louis. Culture Conflict And Misconduct. *Soc Forces* 9(4),484–492 My 1931.

WISCONSIN DEPT JUSTICE, Div Law Enf Serv. *Wisconsin Criminal Justice Information: Crime And Arrests 1979.* Madison Crime Info Bureau 1980.

WISE, V L and Hoyer, W J. "Minority Elderly" in *Police And The Elderly,* Goldstein, A P et al (eds). Elmsford NY Pergamon Pr 1979.

A review of the problem of crime against the elderly as it affects the black and Spanish, and its implications for police–community relations and police training are provided. Two areas that are especially troublesome for the minority aged are fear of crime and fear of police. Crime rates against minorities are higher and are increasing at a faster rate than against whites. Minority elderly are more likely to live in poverty and to be concentrated in central city ghettos or rural pockets of poverty. Minority elderly are also more fearful of police as a result of having lived during an era when police brutality, racial oppression, and discrimination were more common. Police work in minority communities is especially difficult because of lack of understanding and cooperation between police and minorities, especially the elderly. Understanding the ways in which minorities have been oppressed and denied equal opportunity is helpful to effective police work. The shift from crime–centered law enforcement to full–service policing emphasizing police–community relations must gather momentum to strengthen cooperation between the police and minorities.*

WISH, Eric and Robins, Lee N. Childhood Deviance As A Developmental Process: A Study Of 223 Urban Black Men From Birth To 18. *Soc Forces* 56,448–473 1977.

Is deviance a developmental process in which one type of deviant act leads to another? This paper proposes a number of criteria that would need to be met for such a process to exist, and it applies them to data from records and retrospective interviews about the ages at which 13 kinds of childhood behaviors began. Results appear consistent with both a quantitative developmental process, i.e., one in which the probability of committing a new type of deviance is in part a function of the variety of acts previously committed, and a qualitative one, i.e., one in which having committed one particular type of deviant act makes it more probable for the subject to act out another subsequent type of deviance.

WISH, Harvey. American Slave Insurrections Before 1861. *J Negro Hist* 22(3),299–320 Jl 1937.

WISSLER, C. *Redman Reservations.* NY Collier Books 1938.

WITHEY, S B and Wolf, A C and Lansing, J. *Working Papers On Survey Research In Poverty Areas.* Ann Arbor MI Inst Soc Res 1971.

WITT, James and Robinson, Eugene. Ten Maxims: Minority Recruitment And Retention. *Pol Chief* 43(9),57–59 1976.

The US Justice Department established the Center for Criminal Justice Agency Organization and Minority Employment Opportunities within the Marquette University Law School in 1971. The purpose of the Center is to promote, through research, reflection and technical assistance, equal opportunities for minorities in the various Criminal Justice fields. According to the authors, this article represents a compendium of observations made by the Center's staff during the course of some 100 technical assistance visits to various law enforcement and correctional agencies throughout the nation.

WITTMER, J and Lanier, J E and Parker, M. Race Relations Training With Correctional Officers. *Pers & Guid J* ,302–306 F 1976.

A four–day Florida workshop in race relations for correctional officers is described, in which empathy and open and honest communication are stressed. Emphasis is first upon developing good communication and understanding between black and white workshop participants. They are then encouraged to relate their new understanding of racial communication barriers to the prison setting. The workshop methods rely heavily upon the active participation of the workshop attendees. While no data has yet been analyzed in order to evaluate this workshop program, such a project is said to be underway. It is said that within two years of the writing of this report, over one–half of Florida's correctional officers will have attended the workshop.

WOLF, A C and Lansing, J and Withey, S B. *Working Papers On Survey Research In Poverty Areas.* Ann Arbor MI Inst Soc Res 1971.

WOLF, Edwin D. Abstract Of Analysis Of Jury Sentencing In Capital Cases. *Rutgers L Rev* 19,56–64 1964.

The number of persons sentenced to death in New Jersey in five–year periods 1937–1961 was first given, by race. These figures were compared to racial proportions in the four Census 1930–1960, and to increases in Negro commitments for felonies, and it was observed that neither of these factors could adequately explain the increase in the proportion of Negro death sentences. To determine whether the high proportion of death sentence given Negroes was due to a higher proportion of murders committed by Negroes being felony–murders, the type of crime was considered as a function of race; again a meaningful correlation was found. Sentence was considered as a function of type of crime by race, and it was found that there was a significant relationship between the type of crime and sentence for Negroes, but not for whites; sentence was also distributed as a function of race by type of crime, and no correlation between race and sentence was found for a given type of crime.

WOLF, John B. A Global Terrorist Coalition—Its Incipient Stage. *Police J* 50(4),328–339 Ja 12 1977.

WOLF, K L. Growing Up And Its Price In Three Puerto Rican Subcultures. *Psychi* 15(4),401–433 N 1952.

WOLFGANG, Marvin E (ed) and Savitz, Leonard D (ed) and Johnston, Norman (ed). *The Sociology Of Crime And Delinquency.* NY Wiley 1970.

WOLFGANG, Marvin E. "Race And Crime" in *Changing Concepts Of Crime And Its Treatment,* Klare, H J (ed). Oxford Pergamon Pr 1966.

WOLFGANG, Marvin E. "Victim Precipitated Criminal Homicide" in *Crime And Criminal Justice,* Patterson, D (ed), 80–90. NY MSS Inform 1974.

Empirical data from the files of the Philadelphia Police Department were used to analyze characteristics of victim precipitated (VP) homicides. Information is based on 588 cases of criminal homicide, of which 150 were designated VP. Comparison of the VP group with non VP cases reveals significantly higher proportions of the following characteristics among VP homicides: Negro victims; Negro offenders; male victims; female offenders; stabbings; victim offender relationship involving male victims of female offenders; mate slayings; husbands who are victims in mate slayings; alcohol in the homicide situation; alcohol in the victim; and victims with a previous arrest record and a previous record of assault.

WOLFGANG, Marvin E. *Patterns In Criminal Homicide.* NY Wiley 1958.

WOLFGANG, Marvin E. "Sociological Factors In Homicide" in *Rebellion And Retreat,* Palmer, S (ed), 95–108. Columbus Chas Merrill 1972.

The sociological characteristics of offender and victims in 588 Philadelphia homicides were studied. These persons are poor, oppressed, and locked from achieving the stated goals of society. A subculture of violence therefore develops in which such persons become involved. Findings indicate that homicide is a crime of passion that is not generally premeditated and is not a psychotic manifestation. It usually develops out of conflict between the prevailing middle class values of society and the values of a subsocial or subcultural group. The greater the degree of integration of the individual into this subculture, the more likely is violent behavior. Highest rates of rape, aggravated assault, and recidivism among these groups are additional confirmation of the existence of this subculture. The race factor in criminal homicide is alarming and should alert both white and black leaders of the need for integrating deviant blacks and members of other minority groups into the community.

WOLFGANG, Marvin E and Cohen, Bernard. *Crime And Race: Conceptions And Misconceptions.* NY Inst Hum Rel Pr 1970.

Definitions of race and crime are examined and crime rates of blacks and other ethnic groups are discussed. The authors reject any interpretation of higher crime rates among blacks which would suggest that blacks as a race are more prone to crime. Rather, such figures simply demonstrate the greater likelihood that black citizens will be exposed to conditions that result in arrest, conviction and imprisonment. An analysis of victim–offender relationships reveal that most assaultive crimes are predominantly intragroup, intraracial acts. Chapters on police and courts attribute disproportionate arrest and incarceration rates of blacks to bias in the adminstration of justice. In a chapter entitled "Seeking An Explanation" genetic theories of crime are rejected in favor of approaches premised on an argument that criminal behavior is learned and that environmental influences are paramount.

WOLFGANG, Marvin E and Curtis, Lynn A. Criminal Violence: Patterns And Policy In Urban America. *Int Rev Crim Pol* 30,7–11 1972.

WOLFGANG, Marvin E and Ferracuti, Franco. *The Subculture Of Violence: Towards An Integrated Theory In Criminology*. London Tavistock 1967.

Drawing upon information gathered from psychological and sociological studies of violence, the authors posit a theory which holds that there exists a subculture of violence in large urban communities. The overt expression of violence, they contend, is part of a normative subcultural group's ethos. The development of favorable attitudes toward, and use of violence in this subculture involve learned behavior and a process of differential learning, association, or identification. Because the use of violence in such a subculture is not necessarily viewed as illicit conduct, the users do not have to deal with feelings of guilt about their aggression. Widely considered as a pioneering attempt to develop an interdisciplinary approach in criminology, this book identifies inner–city Negroes as the most violent group in American society; however the authors reject biological or genetic explanations in favor of environmental factors.

WOLFGANG, Marvin E and Figlio, Robert M and Sellin, Thorsten. *Delinquency In A Birth Cohort*. Chicago Univ Chicago Pr 1972.

In this study of a cohort of all males born in 1945 who resided in the City of Philadelphia at least from their tenth until their eighteenth birthday (n = 9,945), 50 percent of non–whites had a recorded police contact between the ages of seven and eighteen while only 29 percent of whites had such contact. Race was found to be strongly related to delinquency regardless of socioeconomic status. Indeed, no other variable emerged quite so clearly as did race as a determinant of contrast. This holds true for nearly every offense, but the racial difference was most pronounced for serious crime. IQ was found to differentiate between races, between social classes and between delinquents and nondelinquents with each race and class. Lower SES and nonwhite delinquents were more likely to use weapons in commission of crime, though gun use was relatively infrequent. Nonwhites were more likely to be repeat offenders, and of repeaters, nonwhites were much more likely to become chronic offenders.

WOLFGANG, Marvin E and Kelly, Arlene and Nolde, Hans C. Comparison Of The Executed And Commuted Among Admissions To Death Row. *J Crim L Crimin & Pol Sci* 53,301–311 S 1962.

This study of commutation rates was based on case records of 439 persons sentenced to death and received on death row in Pennsylvania between 1914 and 1958. The percentages of whites and of Negroes were compared, and it was found that a significantly smaller proportion of Negroes than whites received commutations. With the type of crime held constant, it was found that a significantly lower percentage of Negro felony–murderers than white felony–murderers received commutations; with the sample limited to Negroes and native–born whites committed for felony–murder, the difference was even more pronounced. The study concluded that "[t]he one factor that links each of the others together is race; for while more offenders convicted of felony murder and offenders with court–appointed counsel are executed than offenders convicted of non–felony murder and offenders with private counsel, respectively, these differences are produced by the fact that significantly more Negroes than whites are executed."

WOLFGANG, Marvin E and Riedel, Marc. "Race, Rape And The Death Penalty" in *Forcible Rape—The Crime, The Victim And The Offender*, Chappell, D; R Geis, And G Geis (eds). NY Columbia Univ Pr 1977.

Research was begun in 1965 to examine the relationship between race and sentencing for rape in 11 states in which rape was a statutory capital offense. A sample of counties was chosen representing the urban–rural and black–white demographic distribution of each state; every case of conviction for rape between 1945 and 1965 was recorded. Variables included offender and victim characteristics of offense, nature of relations between victim and offender, circumstances of offense, and of the trial. If a variable was shown to have a significant relationship with type of sentence, it was then cross–tabulated with race of the defendant, and a chi–square test was performed to determine statistical significance. Over two dozen aggravating variables that might have accounted for the higher proportion of blacks sentenced to death were analyzed. None withstood the test of significance. The only statistically meaningful variable was race. The authors advocate that the Supreme Court declare the death penalty unconstitutional and urge further research into discrimination at all stages in the administration of justice.*

WOLFGANG, Marvin E and Riedel, Marc. Race, Judicial Discretion And The Death Penalty. *Ann Am Poli* 407,119–133 1973.

Wolfgang and Riedel discuss the holding by the Supreme Court in *Furman v. Georgia* that the death penalty, by virtue of its infrequent and arbitrary application constitutes cruel and unusual punishment in violation of the 8th and 14th Amendments to the Constitution. Using as their point of departure the opinions in that case of Justices William O. Douglas and Thurgood Marshall, both of which suggest the possibility of discriminatory application of the death penalty, Wolfgang and Riedel focus on previously unpublished studies of rape and the death penalty to support their conclusion that "racial variables are systematically and consistently related to the imposition of the death penalty." Noting that blacks who victimized whites were sentenced to death approximately eighteen times more frequently than defendants in any other racial combination of defendant and victim (they present evidence from their analysis of rape in seven states) they demonstrate that it is the racial factor of the relationship between defendant and victim, rather than the non–racial factor of a contemporaneous offense, that results in the disproportionate imposition of the death penalty against black defendants.

WOLFGANG, Marvin E and Riedel, Marc. Rape, Race And The Death Penalty In Georgia. *Am J Orthopsych* 45(4),658–668 1975.

Following the 1972 US Supreme Court decision on capital punishment, the Georgia legislature enacted a death penalty statute that attempts to avoid constitutional objections by establishing discretionary standards for judge and jury sentencing. This paper analyzes discretionary death sentencing for 361 rape cases in Georgia, comparing legal and nonlegal variables. Results indicate that blacks convicted of raping whites were disproportionately sentenced to death.

WOLFGANG, Marvin E. The Death Penalty: Social Philosophy And Social Science Research. *Crim L Bull* 14(1),18–33 Ja–F 1978.

WOLFGANG, Marvin E. Uniform Crime Reports: A Critical Appraisal. *Univ Penn L Rev* 111,708–738 1963.

WOLITZ, L B. *Analysis Of The Labor Market For Policemen, 2v.* Unpub PhD Diss Univ of Calif 1974.

This project examines shortages of police manpower and analyzes the economic content of police hiring standards. A single–buyer multiple–seller market model to explain shortages is rejected in favor of a dynamic shortage model and a more rigorous model stressing the interaction of wages, hiring standards, authorized employment levels, vacancy rates. Through multiple regression techniques, the characteristics sought by the Oakland (California) Police Department testing process between 1965 and 1971 are defined. The probability of success is greatly increased, and is also raised by previous police experience and high previous wages. It is decreased by minority group status and local residence. Recent changes are reviewed, such as aggressive minority recruiting and affirmative action programs, which have greatly increased minority representation on the force.*

WOOD, A L. Minority Group Criminality And Cultural Integration. *J Crim L Crimin & Pol Sci* 37,498–510 1947.

WOOD, John Atkins. *Violence As A Technique For Social Change For Black Americans*. Unpub PhD Diss Baylor Univ 1975.

Contemporary views regarding the use of violence by blacks as a technique for social change were studied. The issue is first placed within the larger context of current conflicting social strategies and power redistribution. Views of several black spokesmen are examined, and an ambivalence towards violence was observed, since they see it as not necessary but possibly inevitable if racial justice is to be secured. The relationship of the issue to the criteria of the Just War theory is then analyzed using a widely accepted model for social change to determine if planned racial violence meets the criteria. It was found that the current black community is far too uncertain and disorganized to use violence successfully, but could accomplish widespread destruction. Study of Biblical materials indicated that the ambivalence also prevents both proponents and opponents from building a clear case in support of their arguments. Six limitations which stem from the Christian tradition are identified, and it is predicted that any resort to violence by blacks will likely be directed toward specific goals and will be short lived. Much depends on the outcome of current nonviolent, political and direct action tactics.

WOOD, Peter H. *Black Majority: Negroes In Colonial South Carolina From 1670 Through The Stone Rebellion*. NY Knopf 1974.

WOOD, R C and Chowenhill, R C and Street, P B. *Alcohol Use Among Native Americans: A Selective Annotated Bibliography.* Berkeley CA Social Res Group 1976.

WOODBURY, Roger and Shurling, James. Factorial Dimensions Of Jesness Inventory With Black Delinquents. *Ed & Psychol M* 35(4),979–981 1975.

The personality dimensions in the Jesness Inventory (JI) were identified among black male delinquents. A random sample of 250 black male delinquents was administered the JI. A principal components factor analysis with a varimax rotation identified three factors: 1) self-estrangement, 2) social isolation, and 3) immaturity. The proportions of total common factor variance accounted for by the three factors were .511, .286, and .203, respectively. These results suggest that the factors might be a part of a large alienation construct in black delinquents.

WOODLEY, Richard. *Dealer: Portrait Of A Cocaine Merchant.* NY Holt Rinehart Wins 1971.

Journalistic account of a New York City drug dealer, his lifestyle and business.

WOODSON, Carter G. Fifty Years Of Negro Citizenship As Qualified By The United States Supreme Court. *J Negro Hist* 6,1–53 1921.

WOODSON, Robert L (ed). *Black Perspectives On Crime And The Criminal Justice System.* Boston G K Hall 1977.

Papers are presented from a symposium of black criminologists, criminal justice experts, community organizers, and ex-criminals to discuss alternatives for the black community in crime prevention programs. Problem areas considered in the papers include: the perceptions of crime by residents of the black community; urban street crime, including prostitution, robbery, and small-time drug trafficking; and juvenile delinquency, particularly with regard to black youths. The problems involved in policing the black community and police-community relations are considered. Institutional racism at all levels of the criminal justice system, in particular among police officers and in the prisons, and its effect on the attitudes of the black community are analyzed. The effect of prison conditions on black inmates and the relationship of a moratorium on prison construction to crime prevention are considered.*

WOODWARD, C Vann. *The Strange Career Of Jim Crow.* NY Oxford Univ Pr 1966.

WOOL, R and Clements, C B. Adolescent Verbal Behavior—Investigation Of Noncontent Styles As Related To Race And Delinquency Status. *J Abnor Ch Psychol* 3(3),245–254 1975.

WORK, Monroe N. Negro Criminality In The South. *Ann Am Poli* 49,74–80 1913.

WRIGHT, Bruce Mc M. Bangs And Whimpers: Black Youths In The Courts. *Freedomways* 15(3),178–187 1975.

WRIGHT, Bruce McM. A Black Brood On Black Judges. *Judicature* 57(1),21–22 Je–Jl 1973.

Judge Wright of the NYC Criminal Court severely criticizes black judges for their predominantly "mute and bland conduct" and their unwillingness to "rock the boat." He feels that few black judges are "ferociously devoted to humanism in the law" and that most black judges have become "pillars of the black bourgeoise." One exception noted is Judge George W. Crockett of the Detroit Recorders' Court. Wright also discusses the selection process of black judges. He feels that in heavily black areas, the elective process helps to assure the election of a black judge. He points to NYC, the city which has more black judges than any other, where few judges are appointed. In the courts (e.g., Court of Claims or Court of Appeals) where judges are appointed there is a smaller proportion of black judges.

WRIGHT, Erik Olin. *Politics Of Punishment—A Critical Analysis Of Prisons In America.* NY Harper & Row 1973.

WRIGHT, J Skelly. Judicial Review And The Equal Protection Clause. *Harvard C R–C L Rev* 15(1),1–28 Spr 1980.

WRIGHT, J Skelly. Poverty, Minorities, And Respect For Law. *Duke L J* 3(3),425–451 1970.

WRIGHT, Richard. *Native Son.* NY Harper & Row 1940.

WUBNIG, Michael. *Black Police Attitudes In The New York City Police Department: An Exploratory Study.* Unpub PhD Diss City Univ of NY 1975.

Attitudes, perceptions and problems of black NYC police during the period April 1972 to June 1973 were studied via analysis of responses to questionnaires concentrating on possible sources of status strain for the black policeman between his ascribed status of race and his achieved status of occupation. It was found that the single strong basis for possible status strain was seen to develop in lack of acceptance by white supervisors and the belief that blacks and other minorities were excluded as a matter of policy from positions of power in the department. However, the impact of these evaluations in creating status strain was seen as being weakened both by the internal development of a black police group identity through solidarity and politicization. The effect of these developments was interpreted as creating a black police solidarity expressing itself in the nature of internally generated instrumental behavior, and this was hypothesized as contrasting with an earlier type of black police behavior in which the primary mechanisms of adjustment were individual.

WYATT, D W. Racial Handicaps In The Negro Delinquent. *Probation* 21,112–115 1943.

WYLIE, Max. *400 Miles From Harlem: Courts, Crime And Corrections.* NY Macmillan 1972.

WYMAN, L and Thorne, B. Notes On Navajo Suicide. *Am Anthrop* 47,278–288 1945.

WYRICK, Saunders and Owens, Holloway O. "Black Women: Income And Incarceration" in *Blacks And Criminal Justice*, Owens, Charles E And Jimmy Bell (eds), 85–92. Lexington MA Heath 1977.

The relationship between income and incarceration for black women and programs to help ex-offenders gain meaningful employment in society are discussed. Although black males are the most disproportionately imprisoned, statistics also indicate that the black female remains overrepresented. Pronounced parallels exist between the black female labor market and the low economic profile of black female offenders. The black female offender not only is statistically poor, but also young, undereducated, and often single. She is also likely to have dependent children, which makes her low or no income status even more alarming. Black unemployment continues to be high, with a particularly high rate for black teenagers. It is not surprising, then, that the crimes for which black females are most frequently incarcerated are economically related. The next most common convictions are related to drug offenses. Since there is no difference between the economic needs of the black female offender before and after her incarceration, it is easy to predict her reversion to crime; this trend toward recidivism can also be observed with drug offenders.*

X, Malcolm. *Malcolm X Speaks*, Orig Pub 1965. NY Pathfinder Pr 1976.

X, Malcolm. *The Autobiography Of Malcolm X: With The Assistance Of Alex Haley.* NY Grove Pr 1964.

This is the autobiography of the black man who rose from hoodlum, thief, dope peddler and pimp, to become one of the most influential figures of the Black Power revolution of the 1960's. Malcolm X describes his childhood, his early criminal career, his imprisonment and politicization as a Black Muslim minister and exponent of black separatism, and his philosophy. Shortly after the book appeared, he was assassinated by a team of gunmen in a NYC ballroom.

YABLONSKY, Lewis. *The Violent Gang.* Baltimore Penguin Books 1970.

YANCEY, William L and Rainwater, Lee. *The Moynihan Report And The Politics Of Controversy.* Cambridge MA MIT Pr 1967.

YARMEY, A Daniel. *The Psychology Of Eyewitness Testimony.* NY Free Pr 1979.

YEARWOOD, Homero. Police–Community Relations. *Issues Crim* 4(1),45–57 1968.

YEE, Ming S. *The Melancholy History Of Soledad Prison.* NY Harpers Mag Pr 1973.

YGLESIAS, Jose. Right On With The Young Lords. *NYT Mag* ,32–33 Je 7 1970.

YINGER, J Milton. *A Minority Group In American Society.* NY McGraw–Hill 1965.

YINGER, J Milton and Simpson, George Eaton. *Racial And Cultural Minorities: An Analysis Of Prejudice And Discrimination.* NY Harper & Row 1965.

YOST, James Alvin. *The Relative Function Of Kin: A Comparative Study Of Middle And Lower Class Black Families.* Unpub PhD Diss Univ of Colorado 1973.

In–depth focused interviews were held to obtain more reliable data regarding the relative function of kin in middle and lower–class black families. In addition to standard socioeconomic data, time series information was collected on family structure, intensity of familial relationships, conflicts and decision–making, community involvement, and real and ideal methods of obtaining information, meeting daily needs, and dealing with crises. The results confirm the hypotheses, but also reveal that it is often misleading to think only in terms of discrete categories, such as classes. To do so frequently obscures the dynamics of upward mobility and changes in behavior. The results also tend to support Valentine's contention that social classes represent adaptation to differing circumstances, not differing socialization processes.

YOUNG, Erle. Lynching And Political Areas. *Sociol Soc Res* 12,348–353 Mr–Ap 1928.

YOUNG, Marlene A (ed). *Justice And Older Americans.* Lexington MA Heath 1977.

YOUNG, Vernetta D. Women, Race And Crime. *Criminology* 18(1),26–34 My 1980.

This paper examines the relationship between women, race, and crime as presented by Freda Adler from two perspectives. First, the explanatory mechanisms based on assumptions about the historical impact of slavery on the black family are assessed using literature from the field of Afro–American studies. Second, the empirical assertions concerning the pattern of crime for black and white males and females are examined using victim survey data.

YOUNG, Virginia Heyer. A Black American Socialization Pattern. *Am Ethnol* 1(2),405–413 1974.

The socialization patterns of black Americans are discussed. It is felt that the teaching of behavioral conventions is not as effective a socialization technique in American Negro societies as in stable and integrated societies. An alternative type of socialization in an urban group is presented: the teaching of techniques of judging and adjusting to persons in authority while preserving a commitment to one's own goals. This behavior complex provides a new perspective for the analysis of the bicultural position of the group and for the description of a loosely structured culture.

ZALBA, S. *Women Prisoners And Their Families.* Los Angeles Delmar 1964.

ZANGRANDO, Robert L and Schneider, Joanna. Law, The American Value System, And The Black Community. *Rutgers Camden L J* 3,32–44 Spr 1971.

ZEAL, Carolyn and Humphrey, Craig. The Integration Of Blacks In Suburban Neighborhoods: A Reexamination Of The Contact Hypothesis. *Social Prob* 18,462–474 Spr 1971.

ZEINER, A and Paredes, A and Stratton, R. Tribal Affiliation And Prevalence Of Alcohol Problems. *Q J Stud Alc* 39(7),1166–1177 1978.

ZEISEL, Hans. *Say It With Figures.* NY Harper & Row 1968.

ZEITZ, Leonard. Survey Of Negro Attitudes Toward Law. *Rutgers L Rev* 19,288–316 1965 .

ZIMBARDO, Philip and Haney, Craig and Banks, Curtis. Interpersonal Dynamics In A Simulated Prison. *Int J Crimin Pen* 1(1),69–97 1973.

ZIPPER, Barry Oser. *The Personality And Self Concept Characteristics Of Negro And White Delinquent And Non–Delinquent Boys.* Unpub PhD Diss Univ of N Car 1973.

The social psychological significance of aggressive antisocial behavior in lower–class black and white males was investigated. The controversy regarding differences in social opportunities as related to delinquency in blacks was also considered by studying personality differences between black nondelinquents and delinquents and between corresponding white groups. Instruments included the MMPI, the Tennessee Concept Scale, and the Harris–Lingoes subscales. The most important results were those of of the test of interaction. Those using Harris–Lingoes and TSCS variables yielded significant differences, while those using the MMPI did not. For whites, the greater the pathology of delinquents suggested operation of effective sanctions against delinquent behavior and/or the existence of nondelinquent alternatives. Personality findings for blacks indicated that these social inhibitors of delinquent behavior choice characterize the black culture less, suggesting that situational factors play a larger role in delinquent behavior choice among blacks.

ZUSMAN, Marty E and Olson, Arnold O. Gathering Complete Response From Mexican–Americans By Personal Interview. *J Soc Issues* 33(4),46–55 1977.

Guidance on the Use of the Index to Judicial Cases Involving American Minorities

Judicial cases involving American minorities are grouped by subject heading and listed chronologically. Appearance under a subject heading does not necessarily indicate that this was the primary issue decided by the court—only that it was addressed in one opinion or more. Nor does the appearance of a case citation necessarily mean that the decision still stands, for in some instances these cases may have been overturned on appeal, or superceded by another decision.

In the future, this feature of the *Index* will be expanded and improved. Although this listing is by no means completely comprehensive, the Editor hopes that it will be of some use to those who are engaged in legal work involving American minorities. All of the cases cited are discussed in Articles, Notes and Comments referenced in the Subject Index.

INDEX TO JUDICIAL CASES INVOLVING AMERICAN MINORITIES

SUBSTANTIAL UNDERREPRESENTATION

Carmical v. Craven, 457 F.2d 582 (9th Cir. 1971), *cert. denied*, 409 U.S. 929 (1972).

United States v. Whitley, 491 F.2d 1248 (8th Cir.), *cert. denied*, 416 U.S. 990 (1974).

Quadra v. Superior Court of San Francisco, 403 F.Supp. 486 (N.D. Cal. 1975).

United States v. Goff, 509 F.2d 825 (5th Cir.), *cert. denied*, 423 U.S. 827 (1975).

United States v. Jenkins, 496 F.2d 57 (2d Cir. 1974), *cert. denied*, 420 U.S. 925 (1975).

United States v. Test, 550 F.2d 577 (10th Cir. 1976).

Castaneda v. Partida, 430 U.S. 482 (1972).

United States v. Kleifgen, 557 F.2d 1293 (95th Cir. 1977).

TESTING FOR POLICE APPLICANTS

Davis v. Washington, 348 F.Supp. 15 (Dist. of Col.), U.S. Dist. Ct., D.C. July 2l, 1972.

THREE-PRONG TEST

Gomillion v. Lightfoot, 364 U.S. 339 (1960).

VISITS FOR PRISONERS

Clark *et al.* v. Wolff, 347 F.Supp. 887 (Neb.), U.S. Dist. Ct., Neb., May 24, 1972.

WRITTEN TESTS FOR EMPLOYMENT (police)

Davis v. Washington, 348 F.Supp. 15 (Dist of Col.), U.S. Dist. Ct., D.C., July 21, 1972.

Bridgeport Guardians, Inc. v. Members of the Bridgeport Civil Service, 345 F. Supp. 779, U.S. Dist. Ct. D. Conn., Jan. 29, 1973.

Bridgeport Guardians, Inc., v. Members of Civ. Serv. Com'n., 497 F.2d 1113 (Conn.) U.S. Ct. of Appeals, 2d Cir., June 3, 1974.

ABOUT THE CENTER ON MINORITIES AND CRIMINAL JUSTICE

The Center on Minorities and Criminal Justice was created in 1980 as an outgrowth of efforts by the School of Criminal Justice, State University of New York at Albany, to foster better awareness of minority perspective, problems, and concerns in the area of crime and punishment. Its major activities include the following:

1. The recruitment and support of Minority Graduate Fellows in Criminal Justice;

2. The production and dissemination of the *Index to Minorities & Criminal Justice*, which monitors and reports on the developing literature relating to American minorities and criminal justice;

3. The formation of a national Documentation Center for use in the study of minority-focused issues; and

4. The pursuit of significant research with and about minority persons and criminal justice.

Other publications from the Center include:

Document Number	Author	Title & Date
000999	Daniel E. Georges-Abeyie, Ph.D.	The Criminal Justice System and Minority Crime (1980)
		Description: An Abstract of this document appears in this edition.
000506	Scott Christianson and Richard Dehais	The Black Incarceration Rate in the United States: A Nationwide Problem (1980)
		Description: An abstract of this document appears in this edition.
0004000	Scott Christianson and Barry DeFoe (comps.)	Minorities and the Criminal Justice Process: A Selected Bibliography (1980)
		Description: 241 sources on the processing of minority persons by the American criminal justice system.

Center on Minorities and Criminal Justice
School of Criminal Justice
State University of New York at Albany
135 Western Avenue
Draper Hall
Albany, NY 12222
(Tel. 518-455-6183)

Logo design by Bruce Jennings, Prisoners Accelerated Creative Exposure (PACE)

Minority Fellowships in Criminal Justice

The Graduate School of Criminal Justice

State University of New York at Albany

PROGRAMS OF STUDY. The School of Criminal Justice, founded in 1967, is regarded as the nation's leading graduate school of criminal justice. Offering a rigorous, interdisciplinary program of study and research culminating in the M.A. and Ph.D. degrees, it seeks to cultivate intelligent and innovative thinking about the nature of crime and the problems of crime control in a democratic society. Major areas of study include criminology, law and social control, the criminal justice process, and strategies of individual, organizational, and social change.

RESEARCH FACILITIES. Field research is a central thrust of this program. Students are trained in advanced research techniques and receive valuable field experience in policy analysis, planning, and theory construction. Faculty are selected for their distinguished achievements in teaching and research and their service in noteworthy organizations in the field.

Studies begin in late August, or with a six-week introductory session in late June. Admission is highly competitive.

For Further Information, please contact:

**Center on Minorities & Criminal Justice
School of Criminal Justice
SUNYA
135 Western Avenue
Albany, NY 12222**

(518)455-6278

FINANCIAL AID IS AVAILABLE. Applications, academic transcripts, and GRE or LSAT scores should be submitted by May 1.